Greek
Islands

Korina Miller,
Alexis Averbuck, Anna Kaminski, Craig McLachlan, Zora O'Neill,
Leonid Ragozin, Andrea Schulte-Peevers, Helena Smith, Greg Ward,
Richard Waters

Contents

GREEK CUISINE P43

Contents

Contents

ON THE ROAD

PATMOS P390

IVAN MATEEV/GETTY IMAGES ©

Contents

ZAKYNTHOS P526

Welcome to the Greek Islands

The Greek Islands ignite the imagination and satisfy the soul with a history laced in mythical tales and told through ancient, sun-bleached ruins.

Experience Island Life

Sink your toes deep into the sand and listen to the warm Aegean lap the shore like you have nowhere else to be. This is island life. Soak up the majestic beauty of Santorini or indulge in the pulsing nightlife of Mykonos. Wander through lush wildflowers in spring or laze on isolated sandy coves in summer. Become acquainted with the melancholy throb of *rembetika* (blues songs) and the tang of homemade tzatziki. The days melt from one to the next, filled with miles of aquamarine coastline blessed with some of Europe's cleanest beaches. Many travellers simply settle down and never go home.

Satisfy Your Appetite

On the islands, you'll often be fed like long-lost family from traditional dishes heaped with pride. Island hopping is a culinary adventure and a tour of regional cuisine. Each island's local cheese is unique, and its wild greens and honey distinct. Head to a harbour to watch the daily catch tumble from the fishermen's nets, and look for people collecting wild produce on the hillsides. On many islands, you'll encounter the Italian legacy of pasta with a Greek slant, like rich sauces with mussels steamed in ouzo. On others, the Ottoman past surfaces in spiced sweets and pastries.

Time Travel

Surround yourself with the ancient ruins of Delos or wander through the reconstructed Minoan palace of Knossos and you can almost sense the ancient Greeks moving alongside you. The spellbinding city of Akrotiri, dug out from beneath the ash of Santorini's massive volcanic eruption, and the medieval walled city of Rhodes let you step through a window into times past. Beyond these celebrated sites are the quieter ruins scattered on nearly every island, filled with mystery and often overgrown with wildflowers – from the enormous marble statues of Naxos to the colourful 2nd-century mosaics on Kos. Greek ruins are as impressive as they are numerous.

Get Active

The islands sit like floating magnets for anyone who enjoys the great outdoors. Wander along cobbled Byzantine footpaths, hike into volcanoes, kayak with dolphins, watch for sea turtles and cycle through lush forests. The Greek islands are also an excellent place to try new pursuits, with some of the world's top kitesurfing, diving and rock climbing locations. With wide, open skies and a vast and varied landscape that begs to be conquered, it's easy to understand how so many myths of gods and giants originated here.

Why I Love the Greek Islands

By Korina Miller, Writer

I was marooned on Tilos – a speck of an island adrift in the Aegean. My ferry had been cancelled and warm rain fell in torrential sheets, drenching me to the bone. This was not my island dream. I made my way to a beachside pub, housed in a turn-of-the-century stone building. Inside I was welcomed unceremoniously into the old boys' club with a shot of ouzo that slid down my throat like liquid sunshine. Someone picked out a tune on a guitar as singing filled the room. Island life comes in many guises but the warmth and the welcome are universal.

For more about our writers, see p608

Above: Karpathos (p345), Dodecanese

Greek Islands

Adriatic
Sea

**MACEDONIA
(FYROM)**

Promahonas

Exohi

TIRANA ✪

Evzoni

Doïrani

Dram

Kilkis

Serres

Niki

Florina

Edessa

Giannitsa

MACEDONIA

ALBANIA

Kotas

Naoussa

Thessaloniki

Kristallopigi

Veria

Alexandria

Kalamaria

Kastoria

Ptolemaida

Halkidiki

Kozani

Katerini

*Gulf of
Kassandra*

Mertziani

*Lake
Aliakmonas*

Litohoro

**Kassandra
Peninsula**

ITALY

Konitsa

Mt Olympus ▲

Metsovo

Tirnavos

Corfu
Byzantine, Venetian, French
and British influences (p493)

Corfu

**Corfu Town
(Kerkyra)** ◉

Sagiada

Ioannina ◉

Kalambaka

Larissa ◉

**Pelion
Peninsula**

EPIROS

Trikala

THESSALY Volos

Igoumenitsa

Karditsa

Alonnis

Parga

Arta

GREECE

Skiathos

**Skopelo:
Sporades**

*Ionian
Sea*

Preveza

*Lake
Kremasta*

Karpenisi

Lamia ◉

Agios
Konstantinos

Lefkada Town

**STEREA
ELLADA**

Mytikas

Mt Iti ▲

Lefkada

Agrinio

Nafpaktos

Mt Parnassos ▲

Evia

Assos

Ithaki

Messolongi

Delphi

Thiva
(Thebes)

Marathon

Sami

Patra ◉

*Gulf of
Corinth*

Mt Parintha ▲

Argostoli

Kefallonia

Diakofto

Perahora

ATHENS ★

IONIAN ISLANDS

Agios Nikolaos

Kyllini

Loutraki

Piraeus

Raf

Zakynthos Town

Amaliada

Corinth

Lav

Zakynthos

Pyrgos

Olympia

Mycenae

Epidavros

Aegina

*Saron
Gulf*

ATTIC

Megalopoli

⊚Tripoli

Nafplio

Poros

Kyparissia

PELOPONNESE

Spetses

Hydra

Kalamata

Sparta

Pylos

Mystras

Geraki

Gythio

Monemvasia

Areopoli

*Lakonian
Gulf*

Neapoli

*Myrtoön
Sea*

Crete
Unique culture, cuisine
and customs (p266)

*MEDITERRANEAN
SEA*

Kythira

Antikythir

Samaria Gorge
Magnificent canyon rich in
wildflowers and wildlife (p310)

Kissamos

Paleohora

BULGARIA

Ormenio
Kastanies
Edirne
Orestiada

Didymotiho

THRACE

Xanthi
⊚Komotini

İstanbul

Kipi

Sea of Marmara

⊚Kavala
Alexandroupoli

Thasos

Thracian Sea

The Dardanelles

Gallipoli Peninsula

Samothraki

Imvros (Gökçeada)

TURKEY

Myrina
Limnos

NORTHEASTERN AEGEAN ISLANDS

Lesvos
Rolling olive groves and cool pine forests (p435)

Agios Efstratios

Lesvos
Mytilini Town

Skyros

Psara
Chios

Aegean Sea
Chios Town
Çeşme

İzmir

Santorini
Spectacular clifftop sunsets (p226)

lea Styra

Karystos

Kuşadası

Gavrio
Andros

Kea
Tinos

Ikaria
Samos

Rhodes' Old Town
Magical, walled medieval town (p328)

Syros
Mykonos

Fourni Islands

Kythnos
Delos
Patmos

Milas

CYCLADES
Hora (Naxos)

Leros

⊚Bodrum

Serifos
Antiparos

Donousa
Kalymnos

Sifnos
Paros
Naxos

Kos Town
Kos

Datça Peninsula

⊚Marmaris

Kimolos
Little Cyclades

Amorgos
Datça

Sikinos
Ios

Astypalea

Symi

Milos
Folegandros

Nisyros

Rhodes Town

Kastellorizo (Megisti)

Anafi
Tilos

Rhodes

MEDITERRANEAN SEA

Karpathian Sea
Santorini (Thira)

Aegean Sea
Halki

Lindos

Kattavia

Preveli Beach
Palm-fringed sands overlooked by a monastery (p296)

DODECANESE

Saria

Olympos

Sea of Crete

Karpathos

Pigadia

Kasos

Knossos
Restored Minoan palace (p278)

lania
Crete

Rethymno
Iraklio

Plakias
Moni Arkadiou
Knossos
Sitia

Agia Galini
Agios Nikolaos
Ierapetra

Gavdos
Matala

ELEVATION

4000m
3000m
2000m
1000m
500m
0

0 — 100 km
0 — 50 miles

Greeks Islands'
Top 16

1

Island Hopping in the Cyclades

1 From the spirited nightlife and celebrity hideaways of Mykonos and Ios, to the isolated sandy coasts of tiny, far-flung specks such as Anafi, hopping through the Cyclades (p159) is a Greek experience not to be missed. Peppered with ancient ruins (try Delos), mystical castles (head to Naxos), lush scenery and dramatic coastlines (visit Milos), the islands are spread like Greek jewels across the sea. Speed over the Aegean on catamarans and sway on old-fashioned ferry boats. You won't regret a single saltwater-splashed second of it. Paros (p191), Cyclades

Santorini Sunsets

2 There's more to Santorini (p226) than sunsets, but this remarkable island, shaped by the fire of prehistoric eruptions, has made the celebratory sunset its own. On summer evenings, the clifftop towns of Fira and Oia (pictured below) are packed with visitors awed by the vast blood-red canvas of the cliff face as the sun struts its stuff. You can catch the sunset without the crowds from almost anywhere along the cliff edge. And if you miss sundown, you can always face east at first light for some fairly stunning sunrises.

ADRIENNE PITTS/LONELY PLANET ©

BALATE DORIN/SHUTTERSTOCK ©

SISOJE/GETTY IMAGES ©

Easter Festivities on Patmos

3 The Greek calendar is chock-full of festivals and holidays, but the biggest event of the Greek Orthodox church is Easter. And the best place to experience it is on Patmos (p390) in the Dodecanese. The island comes to life with fireworks, dancing in the streets, huge outdoor lamb roasts and plenty of ouzo shots. Begin by witnessing the moving, candlelit processions of flower-filled biers through the capital on Good Friday. By Saturday night you'll be shouting 'Hristos Anesti' (Christ is Risen) and cracking vibrant red-dyed eggs.

Rhodes' Old Town

4 Getting lost in Rhodes' Old Town (p329) is a must. Away from the crowds, you'll find yourself meandering down twisting cobbled alleyways with soaring archways and lively squares. In these hidden corners, your imagination will take off with flights of medieval fancy. Explore the ancient Knights' Quarter, the old Jewish neighbourhood or the Turkish Quarter. Hear traditional live music in tiny tavernas or dine on fresh seafood at atmospheric outdoor restaurants. Wander along the top of the city's walls, with the sea on one side and a bird's-eye view into this living museum.

Samaria Gorge

5 The dramatic gorge of Samaria (p310) is the most-trodden canyon in Crete – and with good reason. Starting at Omalos and running down through an ancient riverbed to the Libyan Sea, it's home to varied wildlife, soaring birds of prey and a dazzling array of wildflowers in spring. It's a full day's walk (about six hours down) but the jaw-dropping views make it worth every step. To get more solitude, try lesser-known gorges such as Imbros Gorge, which runs roughly parallel to Samaria.

Cretan Cuisine

6 Waistlines be damned: Crete (p266) is the perfect place to indulge. The island's Mediterranean diet is known for its health benefits but the farm-fresh produce; aromatic herbs; straight-from-the-ocean seafood; soft, tangy cheese and world-class virgin olive oil make it legendary. Whether it's a bowl of snails, fresh artichokes, mussels or figs, the essence of this rustic cuisine is a balance of flavours. It's hard to beat traditional hand-spun filo, a salad of *horta* (wild greens) picked from a backyard garden and red mullet just hauled in. Seafood bruschetta

Experiencing the Acropolis

7 Regal on its Athens hilltop, the elegant Acropolis (p67) remains the quintessential landmark of Western civilisation. Explore it early in the morning or soak up the view from a dinnertime terrace; no matter how you experience the Acropolis, you will be mesmerised by its beauty, history and sheer size. Beyond the Parthenon, you can find quieter spots such as the exquisite Temple of Athena Nike and the Theatre of Dionysos. Nearby, the Acropolis Museum showcases the surviving treasures of the Acropolis.

6

7

Hydra

8 Everyone approaches Hydra (p149) by sea. There is no airport, there are no cars. The white-gold houses of the tiny island's stunningly preserved stone village fill a natural cove and hug the edges of the surrounding mountains. Below, sailboats, caïques (little boats) and mega-yachts fill Hydra's quays, while locals and vacationers fill the harbourside cafes. Here, a mere hour and a half from Athens, you'll find a great cappuccino, rich naval and architectural history, and the raw sea coast beckoning you for a swim.

Knossos

9 Rub shoulders with the ghosts of the mighty Minoans. Knossos (p278) was their Bronze Age capital over 4000 years ago, from which they ruled vast parts of the Aegean. After their sophisticated civilisation mysteriously disappeared less than a thousand years later, an extraordinary wealth of frescoes, sculptures, jewellery and structures lay buried under the Cretan soil until the site's excavation in the early 20th century. Despite a controversial partial reconstruction, Knossos remains one of the most important archaeological sites in the Mediterranean. Palace of Knossos (p278)

Cutting-Edge Capital

10 Life in Athens (p60) is a magnificent mash-up of the ancient and the contemporary. Beneath the majestic facades of the many venerable landmarks, the city is teeming with life and creativity. Galleries and clubs hold the exhibitions, performances and installations of the city's booming arts scene. Fashionable restaurants and humble tavernas rustle up plate after plate of satisfying fare. Soulful *rembetica* (blues songs) serenade the cobbled streets, while discos and bars abound and swing deep into the night.

Preveli Beach

11 Crete's Preveli Beach (p296) is one of Greece's most iconic. Bisected by a freshwater river and flanked by cliffs concealing sea caves, Preveli is a thick ribbon of soft sand on the Libyan Sea, with clear pools of water along its palm-lined riverbank that are perfect for cool dips. The beach lies under the sacred gaze of a magnificent monastery perched high above. Once the centre of anti-Ottoman resistance and later a shelter for Allied soldiers, this tranquil building offers magnificent views.

Hania

12 Getting lost in the cobbled lanes of Hania (p297) is like wandering back in time. This former Venetian port town is a warren of history and beauty, with stunning Venetian and Turkish architecture. The pastel-hued buildings along the crescent harbour (pictured below) seem to shimmer with the reflection of the sea. Delve into the pedestrianised shopping streets for local crafts; dine on some of Crete's top dishes in pavement tavernas; and relax with a sunset walk out to the lighthouse: Hania's offerings excel in all of these pursuits.

Corfu

13 The story of Corfu (p493) is written across the handsome facades of its main town's buildings. This is a place that crams a remarkable mix of architecture into its small area. Stroll past Byzantine fortresses, neoclassical 19th-century British buildings, Orthodox church towers and the Venetian Old Town. Beyond the town, Corfu offers lush green mountains, rolling countryside and dramatic coastlines. And if the architecture and scenery aren't enough, come to enjoy the Italian-influenced food.

JOHN CAZ/500PX ©

KLIKKIPETRA/SHUTTERSTOCK ©

Skyros

14 Soak up the artistic vibe in the vibrant island community of Skyros (p485). The potters here are among the most accomplished in Greece, and their wares among the most beautiful. The island's ceramics date back to the days when passing pirates traded pottery and other pilfered treasures for local goods, spurring Skyrians on to begin their own pottery tradition. Skyros Town, Magazia and Atsitsa have open studios where visitors can check out this legacy of larceny. If visiting in spring, witness further artistry in the carved goat masks and the spirited dancing of the island's wild Carnival.

Lesvos

15 Bulky and imposing, Lesvos (p435) does its size justice with tremendously varied landscape. Rolling olive groves and cool pine forests stretch into grassy plains, where one of the world's few petrified forests stands. The island's coast is lined with beaches, many hardly touched by tourism. Lesvos' capital, Mytilini, is energised by a large student population and a busy cafe and bar scene aided by fine local ouzo and wine. Some exploration will reveal a medieval castle town and two exquisite Byzantine churches. The only thing you may be short of here is time.

Olymbos

16 On Karpathos, secluded mountaintop villages have developed unique cultures. Olymbos (p349) looks precarious at best, perched high above the plunging rocky shoreline. Once the daytrippers leave, the village exudes a certain quietness. Along narrow cobbled alleyways, women bake bread in communal ovens and men whittle on doorsteps. They're dressed the way they've dressed for centuries and speak a language nearly lost. In a shrinking world, there aren't many places like Olymbos left. Soak up some of the magic while it still survives.

Need to Know

For more information, see Survival Guide (p573)

Currency
Euro (€)

Language
Greek

Visas
Generally not required for stays of up to 90 days; however, travellers from some nations may require a visa, so double-check with the Greek embassy.

Money
In cities, debit and credit cards are accepted but in out-of-the-way locations you'll need cash. Most towns have ATMs but they're often out of order.

Mobile Phones
Local SIM cards can be used in European and Australian phones. Most other phones can be set to roaming. US/ Canadian phones need to have a dual- or tri-band system.

Time
East European Time (GMT/UTC plus two hours)

When to Go

■ Dry climate
■ Warm summer, mild winter
■ Mild summer, very cold winter

Corfu
GO May-Sep

Lesvos (Mytilini)
GO Apr-Oct

Athens
GO May-Sep

Rhodes
GO May-Sep

Crete (Iraklio)
GO May-Sep

High Season
(Easter & May–Aug)

➡ Sights, tours and transport are running full tilt.

➡ Accommodation prices can double.

➡ Both crowds and temperatures soar.

Shoulder
(Apr, Sep & Oct)

➡ Accommodation prices can drop by up to 20%.

➡ Temperatures are not as blazing.

➡ Internal flights and island ferries have reduced schedules.

➡ Crowds begin to thin.

Low Season
(Nov–Mar)

➡ Many hotels, sights and restaurants shut down, especially on the islands.

➡ Accommodation rates can drop by as much as 50%.

➡ Ferry schedules are skeletal.

➡ Temperatures fall; Athens and Crete may even see snow.

Useful Websites

EOT (Greek National Tourist Organisation; www.gnto.gr) Concise tourist information.

Greek Travel Pages (www.gtp.gr) Access to ferry schedules and accommodation.

Lonely Planet (www.lonelyplanet.com/greece) Destination information, hotel bookings and traveller forum.

Ministry of Culture (www.culture.gr) For cultural events and sights.

Important Numbers

In Greece, the area code must be dialled, meaning you always dial the full 10-digit telephone number.

Country code	☑30
International access code	☑00
Ambulance	☑166
Highway rescue (ELPA)	☑10400
Police	☑100
Tourist police	☑171

Exchange Rates

Australia	A$1	€0.69
Canada	C$1	€0.69
Japan	¥100	€0.77
New Zealand	NZ$1	€0.64
UK	£1	€1.12
US	US$1	€0.86

For current exchange rates see www.xe.com.

Daily Costs

Budget: Less than €100

➡ Dorm bed and domatio (Greek B&B): less than €60

➡ Meal at markets and street stalls: less than €15

Midrange: €100–180

➡ Double room in midrange hotel: €60–150

➡ Hearty meal at a local taverna: around €20

➡ Entrance fee for most sights: less than €15

Top End: More than €180

➡ Double room in top hotel: from €150

➡ Excellent dining, some accompanied by Michelin stars: around €60

➡ Activity such as diving: certification around €400

➡ Cocktail: around €12

Opening Hours

Opening hours vary throughout the year. We've provided high-season opening hours; hours decrease significantly in the shoulder and low seasons, when many places shut completely.

Banks 8.30am–2.30pm Monday to Thursday, 8am–2pm Friday

Restaurants 11am–2pm or 3pm and 7pm–1am

Cafes 10am–midnight

Bars 8pm–late

Clubs 10pm–4am

Post offices 7.30am–2pm Monday to Friday (rural); 7.30am–8pm Monday to Friday, 7.30am–2pm Saturday (urban)

Shops 8am–3pm Monday, Wednesday and Saturday; 8am–2.30pm and 5–8pm Tuesday, Thursday and Friday

Arriving in Greece

Eleftherios Venizelos International Airport (Athens) Express buses operate 24 hours between the airport, city centre and Piraeus. Half-hourly metro trains run between the city centre and the airport from 5.30am to 11.30pm. Taxis to the city centre cost €38 (closer to €50 at night) and take about 45 minutes.

Nikos Kazantzakis International Airport (Iraklio, Crete) Bus 1 runs every 10 minutes between the airport and the city centre from 6.15am to 10.45pm. Taxis to the city centre cost €20.

Diagoras Airport (Rhodes) Buses run between the airport and Rhodes Town from 6.30am to 11.15pm (from 11.45am Sunday). Taxis from the airport to Rhodes Town cost around €30.

Getting Around

Air Domestic flights are abundant and significantly cut down travel time. In high season, flights fill up fast so book ahead.

Boat Ferries link the islands to each other and the mainland, including catamarans, well-equipped modern ferries and overnight boats with cabins. Schedules can be unreliable. Book ahead in high season.

Bus Generally air-conditioned and frequent, buses are a good way to travel between major cities.

Car Rentals are reasonably priced and found on all but the tiniest islands. They give you the freedom to explore the islands, but you'll need a good dose of bravery and road smarts.

For much more on **getting around**, see p583

First Time Greek Islands

For more information, see Survival Guide (p573)

Checklist

➡ Check your passport is valid for at least six months past your arrival date

➡ Make reservations for accommodation and travel, especially in high season

➡ Check airline baggage restrictions, including for regional flights

➡ Inform credit-/debit-card company of your travel plans

➡ Organise travel insurance

➡ Check if you'll be able to use your mobile (cell) phone

What to Pack

➡ Waterproof money belt

➡ Credit and debit cards

➡ Driving licence

➡ Phrasebook

➡ Diving qualifications

➡ Phone charger

➡ Power adapter

➡ Lock/padlock

➡ Lightweight raincoat

➡ Seasickness remedies

➡ Mosquito repellent

➡ Swimwear, snorkel and fins

➡ Clothes pegs and laundry line

➡ Earplugs

Top Tips for Your Trip

➡ If at all possible, visit in the shoulder seasons – late spring or early autumn. The weather is softer and the crowds are slim.

➡ Be sure to visit a few out-of-the-way villages where you can still find full-on, unselfconscious traditional culture. The best way to do this is to rent a car and explore. Stop for lunch, check out the local shops and test out your Greek.

➡ Go slowly. Greece's infrastructure doesn't befit a fast-paced itinerary. Visit fewer places for longer.

➡ Visit at least one local coffee shop, one seafood taverna next to a port and one traditional live-music venue. This is where you'll experience Greek culture at its most potent.

What to Wear

Athenians are well groomed and the younger crowd is trendy, so keep your most stylish clothes for the city. Nevertheless, in Athens and other big cities such as Rhodes and Iraklio, you'll still get away with shorts or jeans and casual tops. Bars or high-end restaurants require more effort – the scene is fashionable rather than dressy. Think tops and trousers rather than T-shirts and cut-offs. In summer, the heat will make you want to run naked so bring things such as quick-drying tank tops and cool dresses. Sturdy walking shoes are a must for the cobbled roads and ruins.

Sleeping

Reserving your accommodation out of season is important, as in some locations many hotels close for months on end. In high season it's equally essential as hotels can be fully booked well in advance.

Hotels Classed from A through E, with A being five-star resort-style hotels and E having shared baths and unreliable hot water.

Domatia The Greek equivalent of the British B&B, minus breakfast. Nowadays, many are purpose-built with fully equipped kitchens.

Campgrounds Found in the majority of regions and islands and often include hot showers, communal kitchen, restaurants and swimming pools.

Money

ATMs are widespread in tourist areas, and can usually be found in most towns large enough to support a bank. Most are compatible with MasterCard or Visa, while Cirrus and Maestro users can make withdrawals in major towns and tourist areas. If travelling to smaller islands, you may want to take a backup supply of cash, as many ATMs can lose their connection or (in remote areas) run out of cash at the end of the day!

It's always wise to notify your bank of your travel plans before you leave, to avoid them blocking the card as an antifraud measure after your first withdrawal abroad.

For more information, see p574.

Bargaining

Bargaining is acceptable in flea markets and markets, but elsewhere you are expected to pay the stated price.

Tipping

Restaurants If a service charge is included, a small tip is appreciated. If there's no service charge, leave 10% to 20%.

Taxis Round up the fare by a couple of euros. There's a small fee for handling bags; this is an official charge, not a tip.

Bellhops Bellhops in hotels and stewards on ferries expect a small gratuity of €1 to €3.

Language

Tourism is big business in Greece and being good businesspeople, many Greeks have learned the tools of the trade: English. In cities and popular towns, you can get by with less than a smattering of Greek; in smaller villages or out-of-the-way islands and destinations, a few phrases in Greek will go a long way. Wherever you are, Greeks will hugely appreciate your efforts to speak their language.

Etiquette

Eating and dining Meals are commonly laid in the table centre and shared. Always accept a drink offer as it's a show of goodwill. Don't insist on paying if invited out; it insults your hosts. In restaurants, service might feel slow; dining is a drawn-out experience and it's impolite to rush waitstaff.

Photography In churches, avoid using a flash or photographing the main altar, which is considered taboo. At archaeological sites, you'll be stopped from using a tripod which marks you as a professional and thereby requires special permissions.

Places of worship If you visit churches, cover up with a shawl or long sleeves and a long skirt or trousers to show respect. Some places will deny admission if you're showing too much skin.

Body language 'Yes' is a swing of the head and 'no' is a curt raising of the head or eyebrows, often accompanied by a 'ts' click-of-the-tongue sound.

Eating

Like much of Europe, the Greeks dine late and many restaurants don't open their doors for dinner until after 7pm. Outside of Athens, you will only need reservations for the most popular restaurants, and these can usually be made a day in advance.

Taverna Informal and often specialising in seafood, chargrilled meat or traditional home-style baked dishes.

Estiatorio More formal restaurant serving similar fare to tavernas or international cuisine.

Mezedhopoleio Serves mezedhes (small plates); an ouzerie is similar but serves a round of ouzo with a round of mezedhes.

Kafeneio One of Greece's oldest traditions, serving coffee, spirits and little else.

If You Like...

Ancient History

Ancient Akrotiri Phenomenal Minoan city that lay buried deep beneath volcanic ash from 1613 BC until 1967; on-site archaeologists continue to make discoveries. (p239)

Ancient Delos Once the commercial and sacred centre of Greece, these impressive ruins rest sun-bleached on a tiny, unpopulated island. (p189)

Heraklion Archaeological Museum Artefacts spanning 5500 years, but most famous for its Minoan collection, including the gobsmacking frescoes from Knossos. (p271)

Kos Town Step into the once-impregnable Castle of the Knights, check out 3rd-century mosaics and rest under the plane tree where Hippocrates taught his students. (p368)

Moni Hozoviotissis Perhaps not as ancient as some sites but certainly dramatic, this monastery from 1017 on Amorgus clings to a cliff face high above the pounding sea. (p221)

Beaches

Elafonisi Turquoise water and long, gentle dunes of pink sand await sun worshippers on Crete's southwest coast. (p313)

Lefkada's west coast Wide stretches of uninterrupted soft sand on a quiet little island – one of Greece's best-kept secrets. (p513)

Kefalos Bay A seemingly endless 12km crescent of golden sand backed by green hills and lapped by the warm Aegean. (p374)

Loutra Edipsou Take a dip at any time of year from this truly therapeutic beach, where the bay is fed by warm, thermal sulphur water. (p468)

Santorini Its volcanic past hasn't just left the island with gorgeous sunsets – beautiful beaches of red and black volcanic sand are easily reached and surprisingly quiet. (p226)

Regional Cuisine

Ottoman influence The Turkish influence is felt strongly in the kitchens of the northeastern Aegean Islands, particularly in the bakeries of Ikaria. Try kataïfi (chopped nuts inside angel-hair pastry) and loukoumadhes (doughnut balls served with honey and cinnamon). (p404)

Italian influence The Italians left behind pastas that the Greeks added to their own dishes; try makarounes (pasta with cheese and onions) and visit Corfu Town, where some of the finest homemade pasta is rolled out. (p495)

Seafood Harbourside kitchens land everything from mackerel to cuttlefish, squid and sea urchins; have yours grilled, fried, baked or stuffed with cheese and herbs. Fill yourself to the gills at 1500 BC on Santorini. (p226)

Wine The islands have a vibrant wine industry, with crisp whites made from indigenous grapes, rich dessert wines and heady reds. Sample them in the Iraklio Wine Country on Crete. (p282)

Cheese Crafted mainly from goat's and sheep's milk, there's a world of Greek cheese beyond feta: ricotta-like myzithra, provolone-style kaseri and nutty, mild, Gruyère–like graviera, best sampled on Naxos (p200) or Tinos (p166).

Art

Byzantine iconography This art thrives in galleries around Greece where artists create exquisite, gold-hued creations; check out galleries at Ouranoupoli near Mt Athos on Patmos and in Rhodes' Old Town. (p560)

National Museum of Contemporary Art A hub for the capital's flourishing modern art scene, this museum hosts regular exhibits in a neighbourhood that's home to numerous art events and galleries. (p76)

Art Space An atmospheric gallery housed in the wine caverns of one of Santorini's oldest vineyards. Showing some of the country's top current artists, it's one of Greece's largest art galleries. (p239)

Museum of Islamic Art Be mesmerised by more than 8000 pieces at one of the world's most significant collections of Islamic art, from tiles to carvings and prayer rugs. (p89)

Fish & Olive Tucked in the heart of Naxos, this gallery showcases the ceramic wizardry of local artists Katharina Bolesch and Alexander Reichardt, whose work has found its way to galleries in Helsinki and New York. (p208)

Walking

Crete's gorges Hikers flock to the spectacular Samaria Gorge, but its nearby cousins, the slender Imbros Gorge and lush Agia Irini Gorge, are equally breathtaking and less crowded. (p310)

Sifnos A network of more than 200km of trails lead to remote monasteries, beaches and mesmerising views. (p253)

Homer's Ithaki Step into the setting of Odysseus, hiking through dramatic island scenery and past archaeological sites. (p523)

Tilos Follow traditional trails along dramatic clifftops to isolated beaches for birdwatching. (p359)

Skopelos Wander deep into cool pine forests, through olive groves and clifftop plum and almond orchards. (p475)

Top: Cheese balls and honey, Mykonos (p177)

Bottom: Ancient Akrotiri (p239)

Month by Month

January

Most islands snooze during winter. However, Athens is awake and welcomes visitors with festivals not really aimed at tourists. Expect local insight and warmth from hospitality (rather than the sun).

✵ Feast of Agios Vasilios (St Basil)

The first day of January sees a busy church ceremony followed by gifts, singing, dancing and feasting. The *vasilopita* (golden glazed cake for New Year's Eve) is cut; if you're fortunate enough to get the slice containing a coin, you'll supposedly have a lucky year.

✵ Epiphany

The day of Christ's baptism by St John is celebrated throughout Greece on 6 January. Seas, lakes and rivers are all blessed, with the largest ceremony held at Piraeus.

February

While February is an unlikely time to head to Greece, if you like a party and can time your visit with Carnival, it's well worth it.

✵ Carnival Season

Carnival starts three weeks before Lent – mid-January to late February/early March. Minor events lead to a wild weekend of costume parades, floats, feasting and traditional dancing. There are regional variations: Patras' Carnival is the largest, while Skyros' features men and their male 'brides' dressed in goatskins.

🏃 Clean Monday (Shrove Monday)

On the first day of Lent (a day which is referred to as Kathara Deftera), people take to the hills throughout Greece to enjoy picnicking and kite-flying.

March

The islands are sleepy but the weather is warming up, making March a relaxed time to visit. Although the national calendar is quiet, there are countless religious festivals celebrated with great gusto in towns.

✵ Independence Day

The anniversary of the hoisting of the Greek flag by independence supporters at Moni Agias Lavras is celebrated with parades and dancing on 25 March. This act of revolt marked the start of the War of Independence.

April

The biggest day of the year is Easter, when the country – particularly the islands – shakes off its winter slumber. The holiday weekend is busy with vacationing Greeks; be sure to reserve well in advance.

✵ Orthodox Easter

Communities celebrate Jesus' resurrection with candlelit processions on Good Friday. One of the best ascends Lykavittos Hill in Athens. The 40-day fast ends on Easter Sunday with red-dyed eggs, firecrackers, feasting and dancing. Patmos' Monastery of St John is a great place to witness it.

Top: Easter procession, Corfu (p493)

Bottom: Carnival celebrations in Patras

✨ Festival of Agios Georgios (St George)

The feast day of Agios Georgios (St George), the country's patron saint and the patron saint of shepherds, falls on 23 April or the first Tuesday following Easter. It's celebrated with particular exuberance in Arahova, near Delphi. Expect dancing, feasting and a general party atmosphere.

May

If you're planning to go hiking, May is a great time to visit. Temperatures are relatively mild and wildflowers create a huge splash of colour. Local vegetables and other produce fill Greek kitchens.

🏃 May Day

The first of May is marked by a mass exodus from towns for picnics in the country. Wildflowers are gathered and made into wreaths to decorate houses. It's a day associated with workers' rights, so recent years have also seen mass walkouts and strikes.

June

For festival-goers looking for contemporary acts rather than traditional village parties, June is hopping on the mainland. Top national and international performers fill atmospheric stages with dance, music and drama.

✨ Navy Week

Celebrating their long relationship with the sea, fishing villages and ports throughout the country host historical re-enactments and parties in early June.

✿ Feast of St John the Baptist

The country is ablaze with bonfires on 24 June as Greeks light up the wreaths they made on May Day.

☆ Rockwave Festival

Rockwave has major international artists and massive crowds. It's held in late June on a huge parkland at the edge of Athens. (p96)

☆ Hellenic Festival

The most prominent summer festival features local and international music, dance and drama at the Odeon of Herodes Atticus in Athens. Events run June through August. (p96)

✿ Miaoulia Festival

Held approximately on the third weekend of June, Hydra ignites in celebration of Admiral Miaoulis and the Hydriot contribution to the War of Independence. Witness a spectacular boat burning, fireworks, boat racing and folk dancing.

July

Temperatures soar and life buzzes on the islands' beaches, while outdoor cinemas and giant beach clubs draw visitors to Athens' nightlife. If you're staying near the water, fill your belly with seafood that's hauled in daily.

🍷 Wine & Culture Festival

Held at Evia's coastal town of Karystos, this festival includes theatre, traditional dancing, music and visual-art exhibits, as well as a sampling of every local wine imaginable. (p470)

August

Respect the heat of August – do a bit less and relax a little more fully. If you're travelling mid-month, reserve well ahead as Greeks take to the roads and boats in large numbers.

☆ August Moon Festival

Under the year's brightest moon, historical venues in Athens open with free moonlit performances. Watch theatre, dance and music at venues such as the Acropolis or Roman Agora. The festival is also celebrated at other towns and sites; check locally for details.

✿ Feast of Assumption

Assumption Day is celebrated with family reunions on 15 August; the whole population is seemingly on the move on either side of the big day. Thousands also make a pilgrimage to Tinos to its miracle-working icon of Panagia Evangelistria.

September

The sun is high though less and less blazing, especially on the islands. The crowds begin to thin and some ferry schedules begin to decline mid-month. Fresh figs and grapes are in season and plentiful.

✿ Gennisis Tis Panagias

The birthday of the Virgin Mary is celebrated throughout the country on 8 September with religious services and feasting.

October

While most of the islands start to quieten down, the sunny weather often holds in October.

✿ Ohi Day

A simple 'no' (*ohi* in Greek) was Prime Minister Ioannis Metaxas' famous response when Mussolini demanded free passage through Greece for his troops on 28 October 1940. The date is now a major national holiday, with remembrance services, parades, feasting and dance.

November

Autumn sees temperatures drop. Olive-picking is in full swing in places such as Crete, and feta production picks up, giving you the opportunity to taste some seriously fresh cheese.

December

The islands may be quiet but Athens and Thessaloniki are still in full swing. Expect cooler temperatures and a chilly sea. With fewer tourists, you're likely to meet more locals.

✿ Christmas

Traditionally, Christmas marked the end of a 40-day fast with honey cookies and a roasted hog. Today you are more likely to see Christmas trees, fishing boats decorated with lights and children carolling. Families gather for a Christmas Day feast.

Itineraries

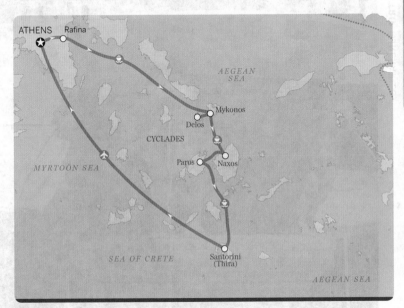

 Athens & the Cyclades

Yes, it's possible to island hop with just 10 days. Take in the must-see attractions in Athens, visit a few popular, bustling islands, and chill out in quieter havens where you can soak up that slow-paced island life. Transport between these islands and the mainland is plentiful.

Spend a couple of days in **Athens**, visiting the Acropolis, catching a play at the ancient Odeon of Herodes Atticus and wandering through the Acropolis Museum. Take in Athens' lively markets, contemporary art scene and brilliant nightlife.

Catch a ferry from **Rafina** to spend a day or two on chic **Mykonos** and enjoy the colourful harbour, vibrant bars and beaches full of sun worshippers. Take a day trip to sacred **Delos** and explore ancient ruins. Hop on a ferry to **Naxos**, the greenest of the Cyclades with its hilltop, Venetian-walled old town, quaint villages and sugar-soft beaches. Move on to **Paros**, whose cobbled capital is filled with trendy boutiques and excellent dining. Head to the seaside village of Naoussa for excellent seafood.

Lastly, visit spectacular **Santorini**, aka Thira, for stunning sunset views. Explore excellent wineries and volcanic beaches, along with the truly impressive Minoan site of Akrotiri. From here, catch a flight back to Athens.

Top: Antique fountain,
Iraklio (p271)

Bottom: Windmills on
Lasithi Plateau (p232),
Crete

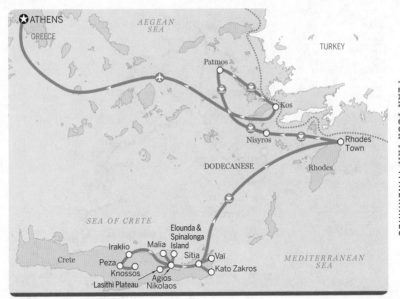

Crete & the Dodecanese

With divine beaches, atmospheric towns and jaw-dropping sights, Crete is a full destination in itself. From the eastern side, you can reach the neighbouring Dodecanese by ferry or on a short flight from Iraklio. The Dodecanese offer a wealth of diversity, and a speedy catamaran service that makes island hopping a joy.

Begin in **Iraklio**, visiting the excellent Archaeological Museum and taking a day trip to the impressive Minoan ruins of **Knossos**. En route see the surrounding **Peza wine region**, which is nestled in a landscape of shapely hills, sun-baked slopes and lush valleys. From Iraklio, head east along the northern coast to the relaxed resort town of **Agios Nikolaos**, which dishes out charm and a hip ambience in equal portions.

Agios Nikolaos is a great base for exploring the surrounding region. Join a fishing excursion from **Elounda** or take a short ferry ride across the Gulf of Mirabello to see the massive fortress on fascinating **Spinalonga Island**. Explore nearby Minoan ruins including **Malia**, a palace still filled with mysteries, and rent a bike to explore the tranquil villages of the fertile **Lasithi Plateau**, lying snugly between mountain ranges and home to Zeus' birthplace.

From Agios Nikolaos, continue east via **Sitia** to the white sand of **Vaï**, Europe's only natural palm-forest beach. You can also travel south from here to **Kato Zakros** to hike through the dramatic Valley of the Dead.

From Sitia, get settled on a 10-hour ferry ride to Rhodes. Spend a couple of days exploring the walled medieval Old Town of **Rhodes Town** and some of the surrounding beaches, fascinating Byzantine chapels and the white-sugar-cube village of Lindos. Catch one of the daily catamarans to lush **Nisyros** to explore deep within its bubbling caldera, and then carry on to **Patmos** to experience its artistic and religious vibe and to visit the cave where St John wrote the Book of Revelations. Backtrack to **Kos** to spend a final couple of days on gorgeous, sandy Kefalos Bay and to sip coffee and cocktails in Kos Town's lively squares. From Kos Town you can catch onward flights to **Athens**.

3 WEEKS — The Eastern Island Run

For intrepid travellers without a tight time schedule, Greece's eastern periphery offers languid coasts, lush scenery, amazing sights and divine beaches. Scheduled ferries are regular but not always very frequent; thankfully you won't be in any hurry to leave and many island hoppers would happily extend their exploration from three weeks to three months.

Begin your journey with a few days on **Rhodes**, wandering through the walled medieval Old Town and soaking up the contemporary, atmospheric nightlife. Visit the Acropolis of Lindos and the crumbling fairy-tale castles on the north coast with their phenomenal views. If you have time, take a day trip to **Symi** to enjoy its picturesque harbour and the ornate Moni Taxiarhou Mihail Panormiti.

From Rhodes, set sail for the remote-feeling **Tilos**, a great place for bird lovers and walkers, with ancient cobbled pathways and tiny coves only accessible on foot. Head north to **Leros** with its Italian-inspired architecture, ultra-relaxed vibe and fascinating bunker museum that reveals the island's starring role in WWII. Continue north to **Samos**, where you can hike through lush forests to secluded waterfalls and laze on idyllic beaches. From Samos, make for **Chios**, where you can get lost in the labyrinth of stone alleyways in the southern village of Mesta, and then head into the interior to hike through citrus groves under the shade of towering mountain peaks.

The next stop is **Lesvos**, aka Mytilini, birthplace of the poet Sappho and producer of some of Greece's finest olive oil and ouzo. Not surprisingly, it's also home to a hopping nightlife. Visit the island's fantastic modern-art gallery and the hilltop Byzantine monastery of Moni Ypsilou, with its glittering ancient manuscripts. Its landscape, with salt marshes, gushing hot springs, dense forests and soft beaches, is as diverse as its cultural offerings. From here hop to **Limnos** to dine on the day's catch at Myrina's waterside seafood restaurants. Carry on to secluded **Agios Efstratios** to stretch out on volcanic sand beaches before jumping on an overnight boat to **Athens**.

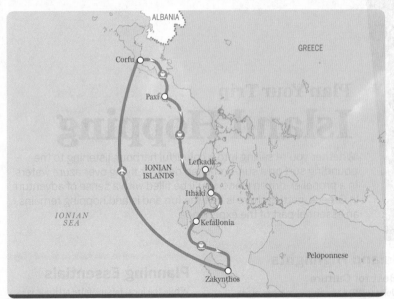

10 DAYS The Ionians

If you have a hankering for island life along with beautiful architecture, scrumptious food, flour-soft beaches and dramatic scenery, a tour of the Ionian islands will more than satisfy you. This is doubly true if you're keen to toss some outdoor activities into your trip. Both the start and end of this itinerary are reachable by short, scenic flights from Athens.

Begin your tour in **Corfu**, where you can easily spend a couple of days wandering through the amazing blend of Italian, French and British architecture in Corfu Old Town, set between two spellbinding fortresses. The arcaded promenade is a hive of cafes, boutiques and restaurants where you can indulge in gourmet cuisine that packs a heavy Italian influence. Take in the island's world-class museums and fortresses. Explore picturesque coastal villages and lounge on fantastic sandy beaches. If you want to expend a bit more energy, Corfu is also a great place for windsurfing, or try biking in the island's mountainous interior.

From Corfu, hop on a ferry to tiny **Paxi**, where ancient olive groves and windmills dot the interior while tranquil coves beckon from the coastline. Snorkel in the crystalline water and dine on seafood in colourful, Venetian-style harbour towns that beg you to stay. Drag yourself away to the west-coast beaches of **Lefkada**, where you can take water taxis to isolated stretches of sand and turquoise water. Head to the southern tip to windsurf before carrying on to sleepy **Ithaki,** where you can walk the paths of Homer and feel inspired by ancient Byzantine churches and monasteries.

Hop over to neighbouring **Kefallonia**; overnight in the picturesque village of Fiskardo, with its top restaurants. Kayak to isolated golden beaches and sample the island's unique, well-regarded local wine. Explore the Paliki Peninsula with its red clay cliffs, hilltop villages and powder-soft beaches. Catch a boat south to **Zakynthos** to take in the fabulous Byzantine Museum, then head for the verdant southern cape to escape the crowds. This island is the nesting ground of the endangered loggerhead turtle. From here you can grab a flight back to Corfu or on to Athens.

Plan Your Trip

Island Hopping

Whether you're sailing into a colourful harbour, listening to the pounding surf on a sun-drenched deck, or flying over azure waters in a propeller-driven plane, you'll be filled with a sense of adventure. In Greece, getting there is half the fun and island hopping remains an essential part of the experience.

Island Highlights

Best for Culture

Delos (p189) A stunning archaeological site.

Karpathos (p345) Experience Olymbos culture.

Patmos (p390) See the cave where St John wrote the Book of Revelations.

Naxos (p200) Roam around the Venetian Old Town.

Crete (p266) Explore the Minoan palace of Knossos.

Best for Low Season

Santorini (p226) Watch gorgeous sunsets.

Hydra (p149) Escape from Athens.

Crete (p266) Medieval cities and mountain villages.

Corfu (p493) Venetian and French architecture.

Best for Drinking & Dining

Santorini (p226) Taste-test local wine and beer.

Ikaria (p404) Have your fill of fresh lobster.

Crete (p266) Savour herb-rich Cretan specialities.

Samos (p417) Sample the famous sweet wine.

Best for Outdoors

Nisyros (p363) Explore inside the volcano.

Kefallonia (p515) Kayak to a remote cove or beach.

Lesvos (p435) Hike in a 20-million-year-old petrified forest.

Kos (p367) Ride bikes to long stretches of sand.

Planning Essentials

While the local laissez-faire attitude is worth emulating while island hopping, a little bit of planning can take you a long way. Deciding where and when you want to go and getting your head around routes and schedules before you go will take the work out of your holiday.

Travelling in Greece is that much more enjoyable when you have room to be flexible with your itinerary. Transportation schedules are always vulnerable to change, even after you've booked and paid for your ticket. Everything from windy weather to striking workers mean planes and boats are regularly subject to delays and cancellations at short notice. Ferry and airline timetables change from year to year and season to season, with ferry companies often 'winning' contracts to operate different routes annually. When island hopping, it's important to remember that no timetable is watertight.

When to Go
High Season

➡ Lots of ferries and transport links but book ahead.

➡ Water temperature is warm enough for swimming.

➡ The *meltemi* (dry northerly wind) blows south across the Aegean, sometimes playing havoc with ferry schedules.

GETTING YOUR SEA LEGS

Even those with the sturdiest stomachs can feel seasick when a boat hits rough weather. Here are a few tips to calm your tummy.

➡ Gaze at the horizon, not the sea. Don't read or stare at objects that your mind will assume are stable.

➡ Drink plenty and eat lightly. Many people claim ginger biscuits and ginger tea settle the stomach.

➡ Don't use binoculars.

➡ If possible stay in the fresh air – don't go below deck and avoid hydrofoils where you are trapped indoors.

➡ Try to keep your mind occupied.

➡ If you know you're prone to seasickness, consider investing in acupressure wristbands before you leave.

Shoulder Season

➡ Transport is less frequent but still connects most destinations.

➡ Water temperature can be chilly.

➡ The best time for sea-life spotting begins in May and runs through to September.

Low Season

➡ Planning ahead is essential as transportation can be limited.

➡ Swimming in the sea is only for those immune to cold water.

➡ Most businesses offering water sports are closed for the winter.

Travelling by Sea

With a network covering every inhabited island, the Greek ferry system is vast and varied. The slow rust buckets that used to ply the seas are nearly a thing of the past. You'll still find slow boats, but high-speed ferries are increasingly common and cover most of the popular routes. Local ferries, excursion boats and tiny, private fishing boats called caïques often connect neighbouring islands and islets to one another. You'll also find water taxis that will take you to isolated beaches and coves. At the other end of the spectrum, hydrofoils and catamarans can drastically reduce travel time. Hydrofoils have seen their heyday but continue to link some of the more remote islands and

island groups. Catamarans have taken to the sea in a big way, offering greater comfort and coping better with poor weather conditions.

For long-haul ferry travel, it's still possible to board one of the slow boats chugging between the islands and to curl up on deck in your sleeping bag to save a night's accommodation. Nevertheless, Greece's domestic ferry scene has undergone a radical transformation in the past decade and these days you can also travel in serious comfort and at a decent speed. Of course, the trade-off is that long-haul sea travel can be quite expensive. A bed for the night in a cabin from Piraeus to Rhodes can be more expensive than a discounted airline ticket.

Ticketing & Fares

As ferries are prone to delays and cancellations, for short trips it's often best not to purchase a ticket until it has been confirmed that the ferry is leaving. During high season, or if you need to reserve a car space, you should book in advance. High-speed boats such as catamarans tend to sell out long before the slow chuggers. For overnight ferries it's always best to book in advance, particularly if you want a cabin or particular type of accommodation. If a service is cancelled you can usually transfer your ticket to the next available service with that company.

Many ferry companies have online booking services or you can purchase tickets from their local offices and most

Boarding a ferry at the port of Iraklio (p271), Crete

travel agents in Greece. Agencies selling tickets line the waterfront of most ports, but rarely is there one that sells tickets for every boat, and often an agency is reluctant to give you information about a boat they do not sell tickets for. Most have timetables displayed outside; check these for the next departing boat or ask the *limenarhio* (port police).

Ferry prices are determined by the distance of the destination from the port of origin, and the type of boat. The small differences in price you may find at ticket agencies are the results of some agencies sacrificing part of their designated commission to qualify as a 'discount service'. (The discount is seldom more than €0.50.)

High-speed ferries and hydrofoils cost about 20% more than traditional ferries, while catamarans are often 30% to 100% more expensive than their slower counterparts. Caïques and water taxis are usually very reasonable, while excursion boats can be pricey but useful if you're trying to reach out-of-the-way islands. Children under five years of age travel for free while those aged between five and 10 are usually half price.

Classes

On smaller boats, hydrofoils and catamarans, there is only one type of ticket available and these days, even on larger vessels, classes are largely a thing of the past. The public spaces on the more modern ferries are generally open to all. What does differ is the level of accommodation that you can purchase for overnight boats.

A 'deck-class' ticket typically gives you access to the deck and interior, but no overnight accommodation. Aeroplane-type seats give you a reserved, reclining seat in which you will hope to sleep. Then come various shades of cabin accommodation: four-berth, three-berth or two-berth interior cabins are cheaper than their equivalent outside cabins with a porthole. On most boats, cabins are very comfortable, resembling a small hotel room with private bathroom.

Unless you state otherwise, you will automatically be given deck class when purchasing a ticket. Prices quoted are for deck-class tickets, unless otherwise indicated.

ISLAND FINDER

ISLAND	FOOD	FAMILY FRIENDLY	OFF THE BEATEN TRACK	NIGHTLIFE	BEACHES	CULTURE	ACTIVITIES	EASY ACCESS
Aegina						X		X
Alonnisos						X	X	X
Amorgos			X			X	X	
Andros			X			X	X	X
Chios	X	X			X	X	X	X
Corfu	X	X			X	X		X
Crete	X	X			X	X	X	X
Evia	X				X	X	X	X
Fourni Islands			X		X	X		
Hydra		X		X		X	X	X
Ios	X			X	X		X	X
Kalymnos		X		X		X	X	
Karpathos			X			X	X	
Kefallonia	X	X			X		X	X
Kos		X		X	X	X	X	X
Lefkada					X	X	X	X
Leros		X	X			X	X	
Lesvos	X	X			X	X	X	X
Milos		X			X	X	X	X
Mykonos				X	X			X
Naxos	X	X		X	X	X	X	X
Paros	X	X		X	X	X		X
Patmos	X	X			X	X	X	X
Paxi			X			X	X	X
Rhodes	X	X		X		X		X
Samos	X	X			X	X		X
Samothraki			X			X	X	X
Santorini	X			X	X	X	X	X
Sifnos			X			X	X	
Skiathos				X	X		X	X
Skopelos	X	X			X			X
Skyros					X	X	X	X
Small Cyclades			X		X			
Symi						X		X
Thasos		X			X	X	X	X
Zakynthos					X	X		X

PLAN YOUR TRIP ISLAND HOPPING

Taking a Car

While almost all islands are served by car ferries, they are expensive and, to ensure boarding, you'll generally need to secure tickets in advance. A more flexible way to travel is to board as a foot passenger and hire a car on each island. Hiring a car for a day or two is relatively cheap and possible on virtually all islands.

Resources

The comprehensive weekly list of departures from Piraeus put out by the EOT (known abroad as the GNTO, the Greek National Tourist Organisation) in Athens is as accurate as possible. While on the islands, the people with the most up-to-date ferry information are the local *limenarhio* (port police), whose offices are usually on or near the quayside.

You'll find lots of information about ferry services on the internet and many of the larger ferry companies have their own websites. Always check online schedules, or with operators or travel agencies for up-to-the-minute information.

A few very useful websites:

Danae Travel (www.danae.gr) A good site for booking boat tickets.

Greek Travel Pages (www.gtp.gr) Has a useful search program and links for ferries.

Greekferries (www.greekferries.gr) Allows you to search ferry schedules from countless providers, including accommodation options and multileg journeys.

Open Seas (www.openseas.gr) A reliable search engine for ferry routes and schedules.

Travelling by Air

A flight can save you hours at sea and offers extraordinary views across the island groups. Flights between the islands tend to be short and aeroplanes small, often making for a bumpy ride. The vast majority of domestic flights are handled by the merged Olympic Air and Aegean Airlines, offering regular domestic services and competitive rates. In addition to these national airlines, there are a number of smaller outfits running seaplanes or complementing the most popular routes.

Ticketing & Fares

The easiest way to book tickets is online, via the carriers themselves. You can also purchase flight tickets at most travel agencies in Greece. Olympic Air has offices in the towns that flights depart from, as well as in other major towns. There are discounts for return tickets when travelling midweek (Monday to Thursday), and bigger discounts for trips that include a Saturday night away. You'll find full details and information on timetables on the airlines' websites.

Resources

Up-to-date information on flight timetables is best found online. Airlines often have local offices on the islands.

Aegean Airlines (www.aegeanair.com) Domestic flights.

Astra Airlines (www.astra-airlines.gr) Thessaloniki-based carrier with domestic flights.

Olympic Air (www.olympicair.com) Aegean Airline's subsidiary with further domestic flights.

Sky Express (www.skyexpress.gr) Domestic flights based out of Crete.

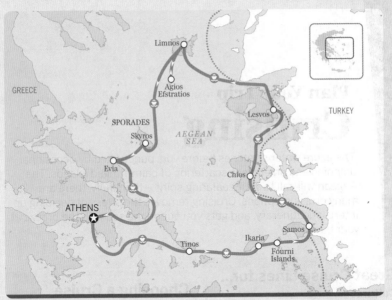

Island-Hopping Itinerary

3 WEEKS

For intrepid travellers without a tight time schedule, Greece's northeastern islands offer languid coasts, lush scenery and divine beaches, as well as some amazing historic sights. Scheduled ferries are regular but not always frequent – thankfully you won't be in any hurry to leave.

From **Athens**, hop a ferry for **Tinos** to visit the sacred Church of Panagia and explore marble-ornamented villages dotted across the terraced hillsides and misty mountaintops. Head east to **Ikaria** for isolated stretches of soft sand and lobster-rich menus. Join in the island culture of dancing, drinking and feasting during summer *panigyria* (all-night celebrations held on saints' days across the island). Afterwards take a short hop to the serene **Fourni Islands**, a former pirates' lair with surreal sunsets.

Ferry north to **Samos** where you can hike through lush forests to secluded waterfalls and laze on idyllic beaches. From Samos, head to **Chios** and get lost in the labyrinth of stone alleyways in the southern village of Mesta before venturing into the interior to hike through citrus groves under the shade of towering mountain peaks.

The next stop is **Lesvos** (Mytilini), birthplace of the poet Sappho and producer of some of Greece's finest olive oil and ouzo. Not surprisingly, it's also home to hopping nightlife. Visit the island's fantastic modern-art gallery and the hilltop Byzantine monastery of Moni Ypsilou. Lesvos' landscape, with salt marshes, gushing hot springs, dense forests and soft beaches, is as diverse as its cultural offerings.

From Lesvos, hop to **Limnos** to dine on the day's catch at Myrina's waterside seafood restaurants. Carry on to secluded **Agios Efstratios** to stretch out on volcanic-sand beaches. The village, flattened by an earthquake in 1968 and rebuilt by uninspired junta, draws few tourists meaning the beaches are yours to escape on.

Head to **Skyros** via Limnos, exploring the cobble-stoned village, Venetian fortress and many artist studios, watching for endangered Skyrian wild horses. Hop a ferry to **Evia** for a therapeutic dip in the thermal-fed bay at Loutra Edipsou before catching a final boat to Rafina on the mainland and returning to **Athens**.

Plan Your Trip

Cruising

The azure water stretches before you, punctuated by occasional dolphins and an endless scattering of palm-fringed islands. The Aegean will call to your seafaring spirit – thankfully, there are many cruising options. Cruising removes the stress of deciding an interisland itinerary, and gets you out on the sea with the breeze at your back.

Great Cruise Lines for...

Culture
Silversea Cruises (www.silverseacruises.com) Runs exclusive tours with language and cooking classes, guest lectures and entertainment from local ports.

Freedom
Azamara (www.azamaraclubcruises.com) Offers cruises at a slower pace, with top service and few organised activities.

Luxury
Seadream Yacht Club (www.seadream.com) Ultrapampering with nearly as many crew as guests.

Small & personalised trips
Variety Cruises (www.varietycruises.com) Has a maximum of 50 guests and the sea as its swimming pool.

Unconventional trips
Star Clippers (www.starclipperscruises.com) Runs cruises on the world's largest fully rigged tall ships.

Choosing a Cruise

Cruises aren't what they used to be and are certainly no longer the domain of blue rinses and slot machines. Catering to a discerning, ever-growing clientele, cruises are often geared to specific interests and niches. Greater competition also means better facilities, more varied excursions, worthwhile on-board diversions and increased dining options. Whether you're in the 30-something crowd, travelling with kids, after a little luxury or just want a no-frills adventure, if the idea of boarding a cruise ship appeals to you, chances are there's a perfect liner out there waiting.

Ship Size

Forget what you've heard, size does matter – at least when you're choosing a cruise ship. A ship's size says a lot about the experience it's offering: megaships can seem more like floating resorts, with a few thousand people on-board, while tiny liners cater to fewer than 50 passengers.

Large or Megaships

➡ Accommodate 1000-plus people.

➡ Nonstop activities and complete amenities.

➡ Casinos, restaurants, spas, theatres, children's clubs, discos, bars, cafes and shops.

➡ Often unable to squeeze into some of the smaller islands' harbours and so visit the largest, most popular ports.

CRUISE COMPANIES

COMPANY	CONTACT	SHIP SIZE	CRUISE LENGTH	DESTINATIONS	BUDGET
Azamara	www.azamaraclubcruises.com	medium	7-10 days	Greece, Turkey, Italy	$$$
Celebrity Cruises	www.celebrity.com	mega	10-13 days	Greece, Italy, Turkey, Croatia, France	$$
Celestyal Cruises	www.celestyalcruises.com	medium	3-7 days	Greece, Cyprus	$$
Costa Cruise Lines	www.costacruises.com	large	7-9 days	Greece, Italy, Turkey, Croatia, Israel	$
Crystal Yacht Cruises	www.crystalcruises.com	small	9-15 days	Greece, Italy, Turkey, Spain, Portugal	$$$
Cunard Line	www.cunard.com	large	7-14 days	Greece, Italy, Croatia, Turkey, France, Spain	$
Golden Star	www.golden-star-cruises.com	medium	3-8 days	Greece, Turkey	$
Holland America Line	www.hollandamerica.com	large	6-12 days	Greece, Italy, Spain, Croatia	$
MSC	www.msccruises.com	large	7-10 days	Greece, Turkey, Croatia, Italy, Egypt	$
Oceania Cruises	www.oceaniacruises.com	medium	10-12 days	Greece, Turkey, France, Italy, Spain	$$
Princess Cruises	www.princess.com	large & mega	7-21 days	Greece, Italy, Turkey	$$
Regent Seven Sea Cruises	www.rssc.com	medium	7-21 days	Greece, Italy, Turkey, France	$$$
Seadream Yacht Club	www.seadream.com	small	6-13 days	Greece, Turkey, Italy, Croatia	$$$
Silversea Cruises	www.silverseacruises.in	small & medium	7-12 days	Greece, Spain, Turkey, Italy	$$$
Star Clippers	www.starclipperscruises.com	small	7-14 days	Greece, Turkey, Italy	$$$

➡ Can seem to dwarf an island, with its passengers more than doubling the destination's population.

Medium or Midsized Ships

➡ Cater for 400 to 1000 passengers.

➡ Usually more focused on the destination, with more port stops, more excursions and fewer on-board activities.

➡ Spa, pool, restaurants and bars.

➡ More often able to dock in small island harbours.

Small Ships

➡ Itineraries are often more varied as they can stop at small, out-of-the-way ports.

➡ Often concentrate on a particular cruise niche, such as luxury or activity-based adventure.

➡ Don't expect a pool, spa, large cabin or plethora of dining options.

Local Cruise Lines

International cruises tend to visit Greece in combination with ports from other countries – usually Italy, Turkey and Croatia, often beginning at one port and ending at another. Greece-based cruises usually focus solely on ports within Greece and offer round-trips. These cruises are often more destination-focused, with one or two stops each day. The crew are usually Greek, adding to the feel of authenticity, and cuisine and entertainment is more locally based with a bit of international flavour thrown in.

There are some Greek-based cruise lines worth checking out.

Golden Star (www.golden-star-cruises.com) Mid-sized, short cruises taking in the Greek islands, Turkey and Italy.

Variety Cruises (www.varietycruises.com) Small, luxury cruises taking in some of the smallest Greek islands.

Celestyal Cruises (http://americas.celestyal cruises.com) Large cruises with on-board activities focusing on Greek culture and cuisine.

Excursions

Excursions are often what make cruises worthwhile and are designed to help you make the most of your sometimes-brief visits ashore. They are generally most valuable when sights are not near the port or if a cultural expert is leading the tour. Where all the sights are near the harbour, it's often just as worthwhile and more relaxing to go exploring on your own. If you plan to explore alone, it's worth double-checking before you book; some larger cruise boats dock at distant ports and it's difficult to reach the island's sights or main towns independently.

Excursions are usually booked before you depart or when you first board the ship. They are offered on a first-come, first-served basis and are generally very popular, so if you're choosing your cruise based on the excursions on offer, it's important to book as soon as possible. Tours generally range from €40 to €60 for a half-day, or €80 to €120 for a full day. Activity-based tours such as mountain biking or kayaking tend to be more, with a half-day around €100. Ensure that you factor in the cost of excursions from the get-go.

Budgeting

Cruise prices vary greatly depending on the time of year. Booking during the low season will get you good deals but it means you will probably only have the opportunity to visit the largest and busiest ports, as smaller islands virtually close out of season.

Budget cruises can be anywhere from €100 to €200 per day, midrange from €200 to €400, and luxury liners begin at around €400 and go up to as much as €650 per day. Prices on cruises include meals, on-board activities, entertainment, port fees and portage but there are sometimes additional fuel charges. You also need to budget for airfare, tips, alcohol, pre- and post-cruise accommodation and excursions. Deals to look out for include two-for-one offers, airfare- or hotel-inclusive deals, and early-bird rates.

Booking

If you know what you want from your cruise, booking online can be a straightforward option, and certainly worth it for the virtual tours and reviews. But a knowledgeable travel agent can help you through the plethora of options available and advise you on extra excursion charges and surcharges that you may miss when booking online.

There are often great rates for booking early and this allows you more choice in choosing cabins, excursions, dining options and so forth. While you can get great last-minute deals, you need to be willing to be flexible about dates and options. Booking your airfare through the cruise line may also mean you're collected at the airport and taken to the ship and if your flight or luggage is delayed, they will wait or transport you to the first port.

Choosing a Cabin

Standard cabins are akin to very small hotel rooms, with fully equipped en suites, a double bed and somewhere to unpack. The cheapest option is an 'inside cabin' (ie no window). If you get claustrophobic, you can pay significantly more for

Top: Cruise ship off the coast of Santorini (p226)

Bottom: Shipwreck Beach (p530), Zakynthos

HAVOC/SHUTTERSTOCK ©

CRUISING INDEPENDENTLY

Yachting is an amazing way to sail the seas, offering the freedom to visit remote and uninhabited islands. If you can't afford to buy a yacht, there are several other options. You can hire a bare boat (a yacht without a crew), if two of your party have sailing certificates. Prices start at €1930 per week; check out **Bare Boat Yacht Charters** (www.moorings.com). If you'd rather have someone else do the sailing for you, **Odyssey Sailing** (www.odysseysailing.gr) will add a skipper to your bare-bones boat for an additional €150 per day.

Hellenic Yachting Server (www.yachting.gr) has general information on sailing around the islands and lots of links, including information on chartering yachts.

The sailing season is from April to October, although July to September is most popular. Unfortunately, it also happens to be when the *meltemi* (dry northerly wind) is at its strongest. This isn't an issue in the Ionian Sea, where the main summer wind is the *maïstros*, a light to moderate northwesterly that rises in the afternoon and usually dies away at sunset.

an 'outside cabin' where you get either a window or porthole. Prices tend to climb with each floor on the ship but so does the ship's movement. If you suffer from seasickness, choose a lower deck where it's less rocky.

Cabin pricing is for double occupancy; if you're travelling solo you pay a surcharge, and if you're travelling as a group of three or four and willing to share a cabin, you can receive substantial discounts. Bunks are referred to as upper and lower berths, otherwise there is a double bed or twin beds that can be pushed together to make a double. Family rooms are sometimes available via connecting cabins.

Things to check are how close your cabin is located to the disco and, if you're paying extra for a window, whether or not your view is likely to be blocked by a lifeboat.

Life on Board

Embarking: What to Expect

➡ Check-in time will be two or three hours before sailing.

➡ Your passport will be taken for immigration processing.

➡ The first day's program and a deck map can be found in your cabin.

➡ You'll be offered a tour of the ship.

➡ A safety drill is legally required on all ships.

➡ You'll be able to set up an on-board credit account.

➡ Your dining-room table will be assigned.

Meals

Set mealtimes and seating assignments are still the norm on most ships and you will be able to choose your preferred dinnertime and table size when you book. Many ships continue to have formal dining evenings with dress codes. Some smaller ships have an all-casual policy, while others have alternative dining options for those not interested in attending the formal evenings.

Tipping

Firstly, don't tip the captain or officers; it would be akin to tipping your dentist or airline pilot. On the final day of your cruise, you'll likely find tipping guidelines in your cabin, usually around €8 per person per day. Tipping is not required but makes up a huge part of the wage of service staff, and is expected.

Plan Your Trip
Eat & Drink Like a Local

Greeks love eating out, sharing impossibly big meals with family and friends in a drawn-out, convivial fashion. Whether you're eating seafood at a seaside table or trying modern Greek fare under the floodlit Acropolis, dining out in Greece is never just about what you eat, but the whole sensory experience.

Food Experiences

Take a cue from the locals and go straight to the source, heading to seaside fishing hamlets for fresh fish or mountain villages for local meat. Seek out tavernas that produce their own vegetables, wine and oil, where the fried potatoes are hand-cut and recipes are passed down through generations.

Cheap Treats

Souvlaki Greece's favourite fast food, both the *gyros* and skewered meat versions wrapped in pitta bread, with tomato, onion and lashings of tzatziki.

Pies Bakeries make endless variations of *tyropita* (cheese pie) and *spanakopita* (spinach pie), plus other pies.

Street food Includes *koulouria* (fresh pretzel-style bread) and seasonal snacks such as roasted chestnuts or corn.

Cooking Courses

Well-known Greece-based cooking writers and chefs run workshops on several islands and in Athens, mostly during spring and autumn.

Glorious Greek Kitchen Cooking School (www.dianekochilas.com) Diane Kochilas runs

Meals of a Lifetime

Koukoumavlos (p234) Modern Aegean cuisine in a spectacular caldera-edge Santorini setting.

Katogi (p225) Tantalising and inventive mezedhes (small plates) in lively and delightful garden surrounds on Ios.

Klimataria (p502) Stellar example of fresh, simple food from the humble taverna, in Corfu's fishing village of Benitses.

Thalassaki (p170) Artful use of local produce and outstanding seafood in a charming seaside setting on Tinos.

Hotzas Taverna (p429) Exquisite traditional and fusion dishes in a classic stone taverna on Chios.

Marco Polo Cafe (p335) Idyllic garden courtyard with an ever-changing menu of delicious Greek and Italian-influenced dishes in Rhodes.

EATING PRICE RANGES

The following price ranges refer to the average cost of a main course (not including service charges):

€ less than €10

€€ €10–20

€€€ more than €20

week-long courses on her ancestral island, Ikaria, in spring and summer, as well as 10-day culinary tours to Ikaria, Athens, Peloponnese and Corinthia.

Kea Artisanal (www.keartisanal.com) Aglaia Kremezi and her friends open their kitchens and gardens on the island of Kea for cooking workshops.

Crete's Culinary Sanctuaries (www.cookingin crete.com) Nikki Rose combines cooking classes, organic-farm tours and cultural excursions around Crete.

Cook It at Home

Leave room in your baggage for local treats (customs and quarantine rules permitting) such as olives and extra virgin olive oil from small, organic producers; aromatic Greek thyme honey; dried oregano, mountain tea and camomile flowers; or a jar of spoon sweets (fruit preserves).

The Greek Kitchen

The essence of traditional Greek cuisine lies in seasonal homegrown produce. Dishes are simply seasoned. Lemon juice, garlic, pungent Greek oregano and extra virgin olive oil are the quintessential flavours, along with tomato, parsley, dill, cinnamon and cloves.

Mayirefta Home-style, one-pot, baked or casserole dishes. Prepared early, they are left to cool to enhance the flavours. Well-known *mayirefta* include *mousakas* (eggplant, minced meat, potatoes and cheese), *yemista* (vegetables stuffed with rice and herbs), *lemonato* (meat with lemon and oregano) and *stifadho* (sweet stewed meat with tomato and onion).

Grills Greeks are masterful with grilled and spit-roasted meats. Souvlaki – arguably the national

dish – comes in many forms, from cubes of grilled meat on a skewer to pitta-wrapped snacks with pork or chicken *gyros* done kebab-style on a rotisserie. *Paidakia* (lamb cutlets) and *brizoles* (pork chops) are also popular.

Fish & seafood Fish is often grilled whole and drizzled with *ladholemono* (lemon and oil dressing). Smaller fish such as *barbounia* (red mullet) or *maridha* (whitebait) are lightly fried. Octopus is grilled, marinated or stewed in wine sauce. Popular seafood dishes include *soupies* (cuttlefish), calamari stuffed with cheese and herbs, and *psarosoupa* (fish soup). The best way to avoid imports is to seek out tavernas run by local fishing families.

Mezedhes These small dishes (or appetisers) are often shared. Classics include tzatziki (yoghurt, cucumber and garlic), *melidzanosalata* (aubergine), *taramasalata* (fish roe), fava (split-pea purée with lemon juice) and *saganaki* (fried cheese). Also watch for *keftedhes* (meatballs), *loukaniko* (pork sausage), grilled *gavros* (white anchovies) and dolmadhes (rice wrapped in marinated vine leaves).

Greek salad This ubiquitous salad (*horiatiki* or 'village salad') is made of tomatoes, cucumber, onions, feta and olives; however, it's often garnished with local greens *(horta)*, peppers, capers or nuts. Feta is sometimes replaced by a local cheese. Beetroot salad is also popular, often served with walnuts and cheese.

Cheese Greece's regions produce many different types of cheese, most using goat's and sheep's milk, with infinite variations in taste. Apart from feta, local cheeses include *graviera* (a nutty, mild Gruyere-like sheep's-milk cheese), *kaseri* (similar to provolone), *myzithra* (ricotta-like whey cheese) and *manouri* (creamy soft cheese from the north).

Local Specialities

From cheese and olive oil to the raw ingredients on your plate, you will find many regional variations and specialities on your travels. Crete is a popular foodie destination with distinct culinary traditions, but the islands and mainland offer their own culinary treats. Be sure to ask about local dishes, cheese and produce.

Northern Greece Influenced by eastern flavours, there's less olive oil and more peppers and spices along with a strong mezes culture and Ottoman sweets.

Top: *Gyros*

Bottom: *Mezedhes and ouzo*

> ### FETA
> Greece's national cheese has been produced for about 6000 years from sheep's and goat's milk. Only feta made in Greece can be called feta, an EU ruling giving it the same protected status as Parma ham and Champagne.

Peloponnese Known for its herb-rich, one-pot dishes and *ladhera* (vegetarian, peasant-style dishes).

Cyclades A traditional reliance on beans and pulses led to the popularity of fava (split-pea purée) and *revythadha* (chickpea stew); you'll also find spaghetti with lobster and a strong sausage tradition.

Ionian Islands The Venetian influence is found in spicy braised beef, rooster *pastitsadha* (red-sauce pasta) and *sofrito* (braised veal with garlic and wine sauce).

Crete Herb-rich dishes include *anthoi* (stuffed zucchini flowers), *soupies* (cuttlefish) with wild fennel and *hohlioi bourbouristoi* (snails with vinegar and rosemary).

What to Drink

While there is coffee strong enough to stand a spoon in and ouzo that will knock you flat, thankfully Greece also has plenty of tamer options for quenching your thirst.

Coffee

The ubiquitous *kafeneio* (coffee house) is a time-honoured tradition, with older Greeks stationed over a cup of coffee, intensely debating local politics, football or gossip. They're often small and unchanged for generations, and it's well worth visiting at least one. The trendy cafes serving iced coffees are the modern answer to the *kafeneia* and are usually packed with a younger crowd.

Greek coffee is traditionally brewed in a *briki* (narrow-top pot), on a hot-sand apparatus called a *hovoli,* and served in a small cup. Order a *metrio* (medium, with one sugar) and sip slowly until you reach the mud-like grounds (don't drink them).

Ouzo

Ouzo – Greece's famous liquor – has come to embody a way of eating and socialising, enjoyed with mezedhes (small plates) during lazy, extended summer afternoons. Sipped slowly and ritually to cleanse the palate between dishes, ouzo is usually served in small bottles or *karafakia* (carafes) with a bowl of ice cubes to dilute it (turning it a cloudy white).

Ouzo is made from distilled grapes with residuals from fruit, grains and potatoes, and flavoured with spices, primarily aniseed, giving it that liquorice flavour. The best ouzo is produced on Lesvos (Mytilini).

Greek Wine

The Greek wine renaissance has been gaining international attention and awards, with first-class wines being produced from age-old indigenous varietals with unique character. The latest generation of internationally trained winemakers are producing great wines from Greece's premier wine regions, including Nemea in the Peloponnese, the vineyards of Santorini, the Iraklio Wine Country on Crete and Naoussa in the Cyclades.

Greek white varieties include *moschofilero, asyrtiko, athiri, roditis, robola* and *savatiano*; the popular reds include *xinomavro, agiorgitiko* and *kotsifali*.

House or barrel wine varies dramatically in quality (white is the safer bet), and is ordered by the kilo/carafe. Few places serve wine by the glass.

Greek dessert wines include excellent muscats from Samos, Limnos and Rhodes, Santorini's Vinsanto, Mavrodafni wine (often used in cooking) and Monemvasia's Malmsey sweet wine.

Retsina, white wine flavoured with the resin of pine trees, became popular in the 1960s and retains a largely folkloric significance with foreigners. It does go well with strongly flavoured food (especially seafood) and some winemakers make a modern version.

How to Eat & Drink

Greece's relaxed and hospitable dining culture makes it easy to get into the local spirit.

When to Eat

Greece doesn't have a big breakfast tradition, unless you count coffee and a cigarette, and maybe a *koulouri* or *tyropita* eaten on the run. You'll find English-style breakfasts in hotels and tourist areas.

While changes in working hours are affecting traditional meal patterns, lunch is still usually the big meal of the day, starting around 2pm.

Greeks eat dinner late, rarely sitting down before sunset in summer. This coincides with shop closing hours, so restaurants often don't fill until after 10pm. Get in by 9pm to avoid the crowds. Given the long summers and mild winters, al fresco dining is central to the dining experience.

Most tavernas open all day, but some upmarket restaurants open for dinner only.

Vegetarian Friendly

While vegetarians are an oddity in Greece, they are well catered for, since vegetables feature prominently in Greek cooking – a legacy of lean times and the Orthodox faith's fasting traditions.

Look for popular vegetable dishes such as *fasolakia yiahni* (braised green beans), *bamies* (okra), *briam* (oven-baked vegetable casserole) and vine-leaf dolmadhes. Of the nutritious *horta* (wild greens), *vlita* (amaranth) is the sweetest, but other common varieties include wild radish, dandelion, stinging nettle and sorrel.

Festive Food

Greece's religious and cultural celebrations inevitably involve a feast and many have their own culinary traditions.

The 40-day Lenten fast spawned *nistisima*, foods without meat or dairy (or oil if you go strictly by the book). Lenten sweets include *halva*, both the Macedonian-style version (sold in delis) made from tahini and the semolina dessert often served after a meal.

Red-dyed boiled Easter eggs decorate the *tsoureki*, a brioche-style bread flavoured with *mahlepi* (mahaleb cherry kernels) and mastic. Saturday night's post-Resurrection Mass supper includes *mayiritsa* (offal soup), while Easter Sunday sees whole lambs cooking on spits all over the countryside.

A *vasilopita* (golden-glazed cake) is cut at midnight on New Year's Eve, giving good fortune to whoever gets the lucky coin inside.

Where to Eat

Steer away from tourist restaurants and go where locals eat. As a general rule, avoid places on the main tourist drags, especially those with touts outside and big signs with photos of food. Be wary of hotel recommendations, as some have deals with particular restaurants.

Tavernas are casual, good-value, often family-run (and child-friendly) places, where the waiter arrives with a paper tablecloth and plonks cutlery on the table.

Don't judge a place by its decor (or view). Go for places with a smaller selection (where food is more likely to be freshly cooked) rather than those with impossibly extensive menus.

Restaurant Guide

Taverna The classic Greek taverna has a few specialist variations – the *psarotaverna* (serving fish and seafood) and *hasapotaverna* or *psistaria* (for chargrilled or spit-roasted meat).

Mayirio (cookhouse) Specialises in traditional one-pot stews and baked dishes *(mayirefta)*.

Estiatorio Serves upmarket international cuisine or Greek classics in a more formal setting.

Mezedhopoleio Offers lots of mezedhes (small plates).

SWEET TREATS

Greeks traditionally serve fruit rather than sweets after a meal, but there's no shortage of local sweets and cakes. Traditional sweets include baklava, *loukoumadhes* (spherical doughnuts served with honey and cinnamon), *kataïfi* (chopped nuts inside angel-hair pastry), *ryzogalo* (rice pudding) and *galaktoboureko* (custard-filled pastry). *Ghlika kutalyu* (syrupy fruit preserves, also known as 'spoon sweets') are served on tiny plates as a welcome offering but are also eaten over yoghurt.

ETIQUETTE & TABLE MANNERS

➡ Greek tavernas can be disarmingly and refreshingly laid-back. The dress code is generally casual, except in upmarket places.

➡ Service may feel slow (and patchy), but there's no rushing you out of there either.

➡ Tables generally aren't cleared until you ask for the bill, which in traditional places arrives with complimentary fruit or sweets or a shot of liquor. Receipts may be placed on the table at the start of the meal in case tax inspectors visit.

➡ Greeks drink with meals (the drinking age is 16), but public drunkenness is uncommon and frowned upon.

➡ Book for upmarket restaurants, but reservations are unnecessary in most tavernas.

➡ Service charges are included in the bill, but most people leave a small tip or round up the bill; 10% to 15% is acceptable. If you want to split the bill, it's best you work it out among your group rather than ask the server to do it.

➡ Greeks are generous and proud hosts. Don't refuse a coffee or drink – it's a gesture of hospitality and goodwill. If you're invited out, the host normally pays. If you are invited to someone's home, it is polite to take a small gift (flowers or sweets), and remember to pace yourself, as you will be expected to eat everything on your plate.

➡ Smoking is banned in enclosed public spaces, including restaurants and cafes, but this rule is largely ignored, especially on distant islands.

Ouzerie In a similar vein to the *mezedhopoleio*, the *ouzerie* serves mezedhes (traditionally arriving with each round of ouzo). Regional variations focusing on the local firewater include the *rakadhiko* (serving raki) in Crete and the *tsipouradhiko* (serving *tsipouro*) in the mainland north.

Menu Advice

➡ Menus with prices must be displayed outside restaurants. English menus are fairly standard but off the beaten track you may encounter Greek-only menus. Many places display big trays of the day's *mayirefta* or encourage you to see what's cooking in the kitchen.

➡ Bread and occasionally small dips or nibbles are often served on arrival (you are increasingly given a choice as they are added to the bill).

➡ Don't stick to the three-course paradigm – locals often share a range of starters and mains (or starters can be the whole meal). Dishes may arrive in no particular order.

➡ Frozen ingredients, especially seafood, are usually flagged on the menu (an asterisk or 'kat' on Greek menu).

➡ Fish is usually sold per kilogram rather than per portion, and is generally cooked whole rather than filleted. It's customary to go into the kitchen to select your fish (go for firm flesh and glistening eyes). Check the weight (raw) so there are no surprises on the bill.

Plan Your Trip

Outdoor Activities

Greece is graced with blue water, warm winds, undersea life, dramatic cliff faces, flourishing forests and ancient walkways – but only recently have visitors looked up from their sunloungers to notice. If you're a novice kitesurfer or avid cyclist, if you want to hike deep gorges or ski from lofty heights, opportunities abound.

Water Activities

Diving & Snorkelling

Snorkelling can be enjoyed just about anywhere along the coast of Greece and equipment is cheaply available. Especially good spots to don your fins are Monastiri on Paros, Paleokastritsa on Corfu, Xirokambos Bay on Leros and anywhere off the coast of Kastellorizo (Megisti). Many dive schools also use their boats to take groups of snorkellers to prime spots.

Greek law insists that diving be done under the supervision of a diving school in order to protect the many antiquities in the depths of the Mediterranean and Aegean Seas. Until recently dive sites were severely restricted, but many more have been opened and diving schools have flourished. You'll find schools on the islands of Corfu, Evia, Leros, Milos, Mykonos, Paros, Rhodes, Santorini, Skiathos, Crete, in Glyfada near Athens, and in Parga and Halkidiki in northern Greece.

The **Professional Association of Diving Instructors** (PADI; www.padi.com) has lots of useful information, including a list of all PADI-approved dive centres in Greece.

Best Outdoors

Hiking

Samaria Gorge (p480) Trek among towering cliffs and wildflowers.

Andros (p337) Follow well-worn footpaths across hills to deep valleys.

Nisyros (p535) Hike amid lush foliage and down into the caldera.

Samos (p594) Wander through woods and swim under waterfalls.

Skopelos (p650) Walk around olive groves and pristine meadows.

Experts

Santorini (p400) Enjoy a pathway of canyons and swim-through sand caverns for divers.

Kalymnos (p553) Climb towering limestone cliffs.

Paros (p368) Shangri-La for kitesurfing.

Novices

Vasiliki (p683) Learn how to windsurf.

Ios (p393) Dive schools catering to first-timers.

Paxi (p676) Walks through ancient olive groves.

Kos (p538) Cycle on the flat.

Hiking Mt Olympus (p446)

Windsurfing

Windsurfing is a very popular water sport in Greece. Hrysi Akti on Paros and Vasiliki on Lefkada vie for the position of the best windsurfing beach.

There are numerous other prime locations around the islands and many water-adventure outlets rent equipment. Check out Kalafatis Beach on Mykonos, Agios Georgios on Naxos, Mylopotas Beach on Ios, Cape Prasonisi in southern Rhodes, around Tingaki on Kos and Kokkari on Samos.

You'll find sailboards for hire almost everywhere. Hire charges range from €15 to €30, depending on the gear and the location. If you are a novice, most places that rent equipment also give lessons. Sailboards can be imported into Greece freely (one per passenger) provided they will be taken out of the country on departure, but always check customs regulations for your country.

Kitesurfing & Surfing

With near-constant wind and ideal conditions, Paros' Pounta beach is a magnet for kitesurfing's top talent, attracting both the

Professional Kiteboard Riders Association and the Kiteboard Pro World Tour. With a shallow side, this is also a great place to learn surfing. Mikri Vigla on Naxos is also an excellent spot, with courses off the gorgeous white-sand beach.

Waterskiing

Given the relatively calm and flat waters of most island locations and the generally warm waters of the Mediterranean, water-skiing is a very pleasant activity. August is sometimes a tricky month, when the *meltemi* (dry northerly wind) can make conditions difficult in the central Aegean. Poros is a particularly well-organised locale, with Passage (p148) hosting a popular school and slalom centre.

White-Water Rafting

The popularity of white-water rafting and other river-adventure sports has grown rapidly in recent years as more and more urban Greeks, particularly Athenians, head off in search of a wilderness experience. While spring and autumn are the best times, with high water levels and decent weather, many operators offer trips year-round on the larger rivers.

Athens Extreme Sports (www.athens extremesports.com) offers rafting on several rivers including the Ladonas and Lusios Alfios.

Land Activities

Hiking

Much of Greece is mountainous and, in many ways, a hiker's paradise. Popular routes are well walked and maintained; however, the **EOS** (Greek Alpine Club; ☑210 321 3255; www.eosathinon.gr; Lekka 23-25,

Athens) is underfunded and consequently many lesser-known paths are overgrown and inadequately marked. You'll find EOS branches in Ioannina in Epiros, Litohoro by Mt Olympus, Crete (Greek Mountaineering Association) and Evia (Halkida Alpine Club).

Northern Greece has plenty of rugged hiking terrain, especially around the Zagorohoria in the Pindos Mountains and the hill trails around Prespa Lakes. Beyond the mainland, the Lousios Gorge and the Mani, both in the Peloponnese, are two of the best places in Greece to explore on foot. With the launch of the 75km **Menalon Trail** (www.menalontrail. eu), hikers can embark on newly certified short walks or even a five-day trek along the Lousios Gorge, Mt Menalon's western

TOP ISLAND HIKES

DESTINATION, ISLAND GROUP	SKILL LEVEL	DESCRIPTION
Alonnisos, Sporades	easy	A network of established trails that lead to pristine beaches
Hydra, Saronic Gulf Islands	easy	A vehicle-free island with a well-maintained network of paths to beaches and monasteries
Paxi, Ionian Islands	easy	Paths along ancient olive groves and snaking drystone walls; perfect for escaping the crowds
Samaria Gorge, Crete	easy to medium	One of Europe's most popular hikes with 500m vertical walls, countless wildflowers and endangered wildlife (impassable mid-October to mid-April)
Zakros & Kato Zakros, Crete	easy to medium	Passing through the mysterious Valley of the Dead, this trail leads to a remote Minoan palace site
Tragaea, Naxos, Cyclades	easy to medium	A broad central plain of olive groves, unspoiled villages and plenty of trails
Sifnos, Cyclades	easy to medium	Monasteries, beaches and sprawling views abound on this freshly updated network of trails, covering 200km of island terrain
Tilos, Dodecanese	easy to medium	Countless traditional trails along dramatic clifftops and down to isolated beaches; a bird-lover's paradise
Dimosari Gorge, Evia	easy to medium	A 10km trek through a spectacular gorge of shady streams and cobbled paths ending at a small bay
Ithaki, Ionian Islands	easy to medium	Mythology fans can hike between sites linked to the Trojan War hero Odysseus
Samos, Northeastern Aegean Islands	easy to medium	Explore the quiet interior of this island with its mountain villages and the forested northern slopes of Mt Ambelos
Nisyros, Dodecanese	medium to difficult	A fertile volcanic island with hikes that lead down steep cliffs to reach steaming craters
Steni, Evia	medium to difficult	Day hikes and more serious trekking opportunities up Mt Dirfys, Evia's highest mountain

slopes and scenic villages galore. Crete's Samaria Gorge is rightly a global favourite, but western Crete boasts many gorges suitable for hikers of different skill levels.

On small islands you will encounter a variety of paths, including *kalderimia,* which are cobbled or flagstone paths that have linked settlements since Byzantine times. Other paths include *monopatia* (shepherds' or monks' trails) that link settlements with sheepfolds or link remote settlements via rough unmarked trails. Shepherd or animal trails can be very steep and difficult to navigate.

If you're venturing off the beaten track, a good map is essential. Most tourist maps are inadequate; the best hiking maps for the islands are produced by **Anavasi** (www.anavasi.gr) and **Terrain** (www.terrainmaps.gr), both Greece-based companies. Be realistic about your abilities. Always inform your guesthouse or local hiking association of your planned route before setting out.

Spring (April to June) is the best time for hiking; the countryside is green and fresh from the winter rains, and carpeted with wildflowers. Autumn (September to October) is another good time, but July and August, when temperatures rise to around 40°C (104°F), are not much fun. Whatever the season, come equipped with a good pair of walking boots to handle the rough, rocky terrain, a wide-brimmed hat, a water bottle and a high-UV-factor sunscreen.

A number of companies run organised hikes. The biggest is **Trekking Hellas** (www.trekking.gr), which offers a variety of hikes ranging from a four-hour stroll through the Lousios Valley to a week-long hike around Mt Olympus and Meteora. The company also runs hikes in Crete and the Cyclades. Many of the treks require a minimum number of participants or the price hike is steeper than the trail.

Cycling

Greece has recently established itself as a cycling destination both for mountain bikers and novices yearning to take a spin on its coastal roads. Bicycles can usually be taken on trains for free, though you may need a ticket. On ferries, mention your bike when booking tickets.

Much of Greece is very remote. Be sure to carry puncture-repair and first-aid kits with you. Motorists are notoriously fast and not always travelling in the expected lane; extra caution on corners and narrow roads is well warranted. In July and August most cyclists break between noon and 4pm to avoid sunstroke and dehydration.

Cycle Greece (www.cyclegreece.gr) Runs road- and mountain-bike tours across most of Greece for various skill levels including some sail-and-cycle tours.

Hooked on Cycling (www.hookedoncycling.co.uk/greece) Offers boat - and bike - trips through the islands plus tours of the mainland.

Bike Greece (www.bikegreece.com) Specialises in mountain biking, with various weeklong tours for beginners and the experienced.

Skiing & Snowboarding

Greece's main skiing areas are Mt Parnassos (1600m to 2250m), 195km northwest of Athens, and Mt Vermio (1420m to 2005m), 110km west of Thessaloniki. The best action is in the north, with Metsovo, Konitsa or the Zagori villages all possible bases for snow sports around Vasilitsa in the Pindos Mountains.

Resorts are used mainly by Greeks and can be a pleasant alternative to western Europe's expensive resorts. If you want to combine city and snow, ski Vigla-Pisoderi as a day trip from Florina or head to Mt Vermio from Veria.

The season depends on snow conditions but runs approximately from January to the end of April. Get information from the **Hellenic Skiing Federation** (210 323 0182; www.eox.gr) and check conditions and ski centres at **Snow Report** (www.snowreport.gr).

Plan Your Trip

Travel with Children

While Greece doesn't cater to kids the way that some countries do, children will be welcomed and included wherever you go. Greeks generally make a fuss over children, who may find themselves receiving many gifts and treats. Teach them some Greek words and they'll feel even more appreciated.

Greece for Kids

Sights & Activities

While even the most modern Greek museums are often filled to the gills with relics and objects that not all children will appreciate, the ancient palace-like settings can be intriguing for kids to wander through. The stories behind the objects can also captivate their imaginations – ancient statues hauled up from the depths of the sea or helmets worn by gladiators. Generally more popular than the museums are the many ancient sights where kids enjoy climbing and exploring.

The beach is one of the best sources of entertainment for children in Greece. In summer, many of the larger, popular beaches have bodyboards, surfboards, snorkelling gear and windsurfing equipment for rent. Many also offer lessons or trips on boats or giant, rubber, air-filled bananas. While some beaches have steep drop-offs or strong currents, there is generally a calmer side to each island or a shallow, protected bay that locals can direct you to.

Most towns will have at least a small playground, while larger cities often have fantastic, modern play parks. In many cases, you can admire children's innate ability to overcome language barriers

Best Regions for Kids

Athens

With ruins to clamber over, plus museums and child-geared sights to explore, Athens is great for kids. You'll also find big parks and gardens, a variety of cuisines and family-friendly hotels.

Crete

The island's beaches are long and sandy, Knossos ignites kids' imaginations, and you can explore from a single base, side-stepping the need to pack up and move around.

Dodecanese

The magical forts and castles, glorious beaches, laid-back islands, and speedy catamarans linking the Dodecanese daily make it ideal for families. And the Italian influence means an abundance of kid-friendly pasta dishes.

through play while you enjoy a coffee and pastry at the park's attached cafe. Some of the larger and more popular locations (such as Rhodes, Crete and Athens) also have water parks.

Dining Out

Greek cuisine is all about sharing; ordering lots of mezedhes (small dishes) lets your children try the local cuisine and find their favourites. You'll also find lots of kid-friendly options such as pizza and pasta, omelettes, chips, bread, savoury pies and yoghurt.

The fast service in most restaurants is good news when it comes to feeding hungry kids. Tavernas are very family-friendly affairs and the owners will generally be more than willing to cater to your children's tastes. Ingredients such as nuts and dairy find their way into lots of dishes so if your children suffer from any severe allergies, it's best to ask someone to write this down for you clearly in plain Greek to show restaurant staff.

Accommodation

Many hotels let small children stay for free and will squeeze an extra bed in the room. In all but the smallest hotels, travel cots can be found, but it's always best to check in advance. Larger hotels and resorts often have package deals for families and these places are generally set up to cater to kids with childcare options, adjoining rooms, paddling pools, cots and high chairs.

Safety

Greece is a safe and easy place to travel with children. Greek children are given a huge amount of freedom and can often be seen playing in village squares and playgrounds late into the night. Nevertheless, it's wise to be extra vigilant with children when travelling, and to ensure they always know where to go and who to approach for help. This is especially true on beaches or in playgrounds where it's easy for children to become disoriented. It's also prudent not to have your children use bags, clothing, towels etc with their name or personal information (such as national flag) stitched onto them; this kind of information could be used by potential predators to pretend to know you or the child.

Dangers children are far more likely to encounter are heatstroke, water-borne bugs and illness, mosquito bites, and cuts and scrapes from climbing around on ancient ruins and crumbling castles. Most islands have a clinic of some sort, although hours may be irregular so it's handy to carry a first-aid kid with basic medicine and bandages.

Children's Highlights

Keep Busy

Boat trips Whether it's zipping over the sea in a catamaran, bobbing up and down in a fishing boat or sailing on a day trip to a secluded bay.

Kayaking Paddle alongside dolphins and visit pirate coves off Kefallonia.

Beach time Jump waves, build sandcastles and snorkel. Always ask locally for kid-friendly beaches; Patmos is a great place to start.

Cycling Use pedal-power along the flat, bike-friendly roads of Kos.

Playgrounds Every city has one and they are most often well maintained and shady.

Explore

Acropolis (p67) The home of the Greek gods is perfect for exploring early in the day.

Rhodes' medieval castles (p328) The island of Rhodes is packed with crumbling castles perched on cliffs above the sea – perfect for climbing and make-believe.

Knossos (p278) Young imaginations go into overdrive when let loose in this labyrinth.

Nisyros' volcano (p366) See it hiss and hear it bubble.

Eat Up

Yemista Veggies (usually tomatoes) stuffed with rice.

Pastitsio Buttery macaroni baked with minced lamb.

Tzatziki A sauce or dip made from cucumber, yoghurt and garlic.

WHAT TO PACK

➡ Travel high chair (either an inflatable booster seat or a cloth one that attaches to the back of a chair; these are light and easy to pack away)

➡ Lightweight pop-up cot for babies (if travelling to remote locations)

➡ Car seats (rental agencies don't always offer these)

➡ Plastic cups and cutlery for little ones

➡ Medicine, inhalers etc along with prescriptions

➡ Motion-sickness medicine and mosquito repellent

➡ Hats, waterproof sunscreen, sunglasses and water bottles

Loukoumadhes Ball-shaped doughnuts served with honey and cinnamon.

Galaktoboureko Custard-filled pastry.

Politiko pagoto Constantinople-style (slightly chewy) ice cream made with mastic.

Cool Culture

Carnival season Fancy dress, parades and traditional dancing will keep even the oldest kids enthralled.

Football Snag tickets for a game to catch some national spirit. Athens and Thessaloniki stadiums draw the biggest crowds.

Hellenic Children's Museum (p88) Build, bake and investigate alongside Athenian kids in this museum's brand-new location.

Planning

The shoulder seasons (April to May and September to October) are great times to travel with children because the weather is milder and the crowds thinner.

An excellent way to prepare your kids for their holiday and to encourage an active interest in the destination is by introducing them to some books or DVDs ahead of time. Lots of younger children enjoy stories of Greek gods and Greek myths while slightly older kids will enjoy movies like *Mamma Mia* or *Lara Croft: Tomb Raider* for their Greek settings. You can also find children's books about life in Greece that include a few easy phrases that your kids can try out.

Fresh milk is available in large towns and tourist areas, but harder to find on smaller islands. Supermarkets are the best place to look. Formula is available almost everywhere, as is heat-treated milk. Disposable nappies are also available everywhere, although it's wise to take extra supplies of all of these things to out-of-the-way islands in case of local shortages.

Travel on ferries, buses and trains is free for children under four. For those up to age 10 (ferries) or 12 (buses and trains) the fare is half. Full fares apply otherwise. On domestic flights, you'll pay 10% of the adult fare to have a child under two sitting on your knee. Kids aged two to 12 travel with half-fare. If you plan to hire a car, it's wise to bring your own car seat or booster seat as rental agencies are not always reliable for these, particularly on small islands or with local agencies.

If your kids aren't old enough to walk on their own for long, consider a sturdy carrying backpack; pushchairs (strollers) are a struggle in towns and villages with slippery cobblestones and high pavements. Nevertheless, if the pushchair is a sturdy, off-road style, with a bit of an extra push you should be OK.

Online Resources

My Little Nomads (www.santorinidave.com/greece-with-kids) For plenty of recommendations and hearty discussion on visiting Greece with kids, visit David Hogg's site.

Travel Guide to Greece (www.greektravel.com) Matt Barrett's website has lots of useful tips for parents

Greece 4 Kids (www.greece4kids.com) Matt Barrett's daughter Amarandi has put together some tips of her own.

Regions at a Glance

If you're after knockout sites, Crete, the Dodecanese, the Ionians and the Cyclades have atmospheric architecture and ancient ruins that draw crowds. If you fancy getting active, these same regions offer diving, surfing, rock climbing, hiking and kayaking. They're well set up for tourists – and receive lots.

For a beach scene head to Corfu, Mykonos or Kos. Thankfully, isolated pockets of sandy bliss can be found within almost all of the island groups, but to really escape, head to the northeastern Aegean.

Some island groups, including the Dodecanese and Cyclades, have strong transport links that zip you easily from one harbour to the next. Others, such as the northeastern Aegean Islands, require you to take more time and be more intrepid in manoeuvring to and from.

Athens & Around

Ruins
Museums
Nightlife

Ancient Greece

The Acropolis is an experience not to be missed. But don't stop there – the capital and surrounding region are littered with more ruins to explore, from the ancient Agora in the city's heart to the Temple of Poseidon on Cape Sounion.

Art & Ancient Treasures

From the eclectic Benaki Museum to the ultra-modern Acropolis Museum, Athens is a major contributor to the world's museum scene. Regardless of your interests, you're sure to find one to wow you.

Rembetika Bars & Beach Clubs

This city refuses to snooze, with glamorous beachside clubs, intimate *rembetika* (Greek blues) bars and everything in between.

p60

Saronic Gulf Islands

Activities
Museums
Architecture

Diving & Hilltops

Diving is magical in these waters, which offer amazing sea life, sunken pirate ships and underwater caves. The peaceful interiors of Poros, Hydra and Spetses offer forests and hilltops to explore.

Nautical Collections

The museums here are small and relaxed. See fully restored mansions, eclectic naval collections, traditional seafarers' homes and a museum of sea craft with caïques and yachts.

Traditional Buildings

Hydra is picture-perfect, with tiers of traditional buildings sweeping down to the harbour. Spetses' Old Harbour shows off traditional boatbuilding, while mansions are scattered across the island.

p139

Cyclades

Cuisine
Nightlife
Ancient Ruins

Local Food

Smoked eel and ham, Mykonian prosciutto, soft cheeses and wild mushrooms are gathered locally and fill the menus on Mykonos and Paros, with creative, modern takes on traditional food.

Raising the Roof

The nightlife on Mykonos is legendary, sometimes frantic, at other times all gloss and glitter. Ios' scene is less swanky but very full on, while Santorini has cocktail bars over the caldera.

Sacred Relics

The sacred relics of Delos, with their own private island, are one of Greece's most important sites. On Santorini, Thira has mosaics and phenomenal views, while atmospheric Akrotiri lets you explore the ruins of an ancient Minoan city.

p159

Crete

Activities
Ruins
Beaches

Canyons

A footpath winds down between the steep canyon walls of Samaria Gorge, Europe's longest gorge and one of Crete's most popular draws. There are quieter, equally dramatic gorges for trekking and rock climbing and a mountainous interior concealing hermit caves and a 'haunted' woodland.

Minoan Sites

Splendid Minoan ruins grace the island. The impressive, restored palace of Knossos is the star, with its famous labyrinth.

Unending Sand

Crete has some of Greece's top beaches, palm-fringed stretches of powder-soft sand. Others are lapped by the crystal-clear Libyan Sea or backed by charismatic old towns. All are worth sinking your toes into.

p266

Dodecanese

Architecture
Cuisine
Activities

Churches & Castles

Architectural eye candy galore, with fairy-tale castles, frescoed Byzantine churches and a walled medieval city. Find mountain villages hidden from pirates, ancient temple ruins and Italian-inspired harbour towns.

Italian Influence

Traditional Greek cuisine stirred up with an Italian influence equals scrumptious results. Creative pizzas, pastas, stews and stuffed veggies, lots of fresh cheeses, honey, wild greens and herbs, seafood and grilled meats.

Outdoor Action

World-class rock climbing, kitesurfing, beachcombing, diving and walking are all here. Follow ancient footpaths, hike into the caldera of a smoking volcano or surf the waves.

p325

Northeastern Aegean Islands

Cuisine
Beaches
Activities

Fresh Seafood

Dining daily on fresh seafood is a way of life here. Venus clams, sea urchins, crayfish, grilled cod and lobster are all washed down with ouzo and Samos' sweet wine. Wherever you go, you'll be greeted with locally sourced, homemade meals.

Hidden Coves

From the remote, white-pebbled coast on Ikaria to hidden coves on the Fourni Islands, pristine sandy stretches on Chios and seaside resorts on Samos, you're never far from a beach gently lapped by the Aegean.

Swimming

Dive into the clear water that laps these islands. You'll be beckoned by waterfalls, rivers and old-growth forests to explore by foot or cycle.

p402

Evia & the Sporades

Nightlife
Cuisine
Activities

Live Music

Nightlife here is about listening to some of the country's top bouzouki players and watching the sun sink over the horizon from low-key wine bars.

Local Produce

Don't leave without trying the local honey, especially the *elatos* (fir) and *pefko* (pine) varieties. Also try the amazingly fresh fish – choose it from the nets and dine on the dock. Locally grown veggies and pressed olive oil means home cooking just like *yiayia* (grandma) makes it.

Water Sports

Soak in thermal waters, watch for dolphins as you tour a marine park, and hike through olive groves. This region's watery depths are renowned for scuba-diving, with opportunities for beginners and pros.

p463

Ionian Islands

Cuisine
Activities
Architecture

Corfiot Flavours

Soft-braised meat, plenty of garlic, home-made bread, seafood risottos and hand-rolled pasta allude to an Italian influence. Without a history of Turkish rule, Corfiots have a distinct cuisine.

Kayaking & Rambling

Kayak to remote coves, windsail across the deep-blue Aegean and trek through the mountains. Continuous stretches of gorgeous coastline and quiet interiors lure the adventurous here.

Mansions & Windmills

Corfu Town is a symphony of pastel-hued Venetian mansions, French arcades and British neoclassical architecture. Neighbouring islands have traditional white-washed villages and ancient windmills.

p491

On the Road

Athens & Around

Best Places to Eat

➡ Mani Mani (p101)

➡ Ta Karamanlidika tou Fani (p107)

➡ Telis (p106)

➡ Mavro Provato (p110)

➡ Funky Gourmet (p105)

Best Places to Stay

➡ Grande Bretagne (p99)

➡ NEW Hotel (p99)

➡ Hera Hotel (p97)

➡ Athens Was (p98)

➡ City Circus (p100)

Why Go?

With equal measures of grunge and grace, Athens is a heady mix of history and edginess. Cultural and social life plays out amid, around and in ancient landmarks. The magnificent Acropolis, visible from almost every part of the city, reminds Greeks daily of their heritage and the city's many transformations.

Although individuals have endured difficult circumstances since the start of the economic crisis in 2009, the city is on the rise. There is crackling energy in galleries, political debates and even on the walls of derelict buildings. This creates a lively urban bustle, but at the end of the day, Athenians build their own villages in the city, especially in open-air restaurants and bars where they linger for hours.

Beyond Athens, down the Attica peninsula, are more spectacular antiquities, such as the Temple of Poseidon at Sounion, as well as very good beaches, such as those near historic Marathon.

When to Go
Athens

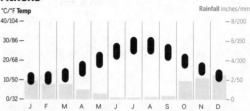

May Perfect weather for sightseeing and open-air attractions such as cinemas and restaurants.

Jun–Aug The Athens & Epidaurus Festival lights up venues with drama and music.

Sep–Oct Weather cools and the social scene heats up as residents return from the islands.

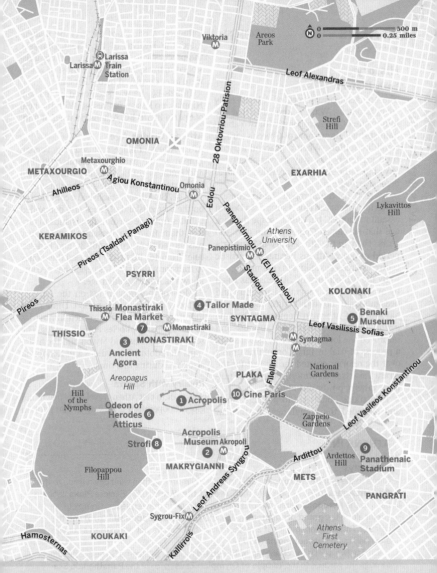

Athens & Around Highlights

1 Acropolis (p67) The awe-inspiring ancient site.

2 Acropolis Museum (p73) Enjoying the majesty of the Parthenon sculptures.

3 Ancient Agora (p76) Strolling in the historic centre.

4 Tailor Made (p111) Staying out till the wee hours at lively cafe-bars.

5 Benaki Museum (p89) Admiring superb antiquities and other legacies of Greece.

6 Odeon of Herodes Atticus (p73) Catching a summer festival show.

7 Monastiraki Flea Market (p124) Picking through flea-market antiques and finding a bargain.

8 Strofi (p101) Dining out at restaurants with views of the floodlit Acropolis.

9 Panathenaic Stadium (p92) Revelling in ancient feats of strength.

10 Cine Paris (p116) Watching a movie at a historic outdoor theatre with views of the Acropolis.

ATHENS AΘHNA

POP 3.1 MILLION

History

Early History

The archaeological record of Athens' early years is patchy. What is known is that the hilltop site of the Acropolis, with two abundant springs, drew some of Greece's earliest Neolithic settlers. When a peaceful agricultural existence gave way to war-orientated city states, the Acropolis provided an ideal defensive position.

By 1400 BC the Acropolis had become a powerful Mycenaean city. It survived a Dorian assault in 1200 BC but didn't escape the dark age that enveloped Greece for the next 400 years. Then, in the 8th century BC, during a period of peace, Athens became the artistic centre of Greece, excelling in ceramics.

By the 6th century BC, Athens was ruled by aristocrats and generals. Labourers and peasants had no rights until Solon, the harbinger of Athenian democracy, became *arhon* (chief magistrate) in 594 BC and improved the lot of the poor by establishing a process of trial by jury. Continuing unrest over the reforms created the pretext for the tyrant Peisistratos, formerly head of the military, to seize power in 560 BC.

Peisistratos built a formidable navy and extended the boundaries of Athenian influence. A patron of the arts, he inaugurated the Festival of the Great Dionysia, the precursor to Attic drama, and commissioned many splendid works, most of which were later destroyed by the Persians.

In 528 BC, he was succeeded by his son, Hippias, no less an oppressor. With the help of Sparta in 510 BC, Athens rid itself of him.

Athens' Golden Age

After Athens finally repulsed the Persian Empire at the battles of Salamis (480 BC) and Plataea (479 BC) – again, with the help of Sparta – its power knew no bounds.

In 477 BC Athens established a confederacy on the sacred island of Delos and demanded tributes from the surrounding islands to protect them from the Persians. The treasury was moved to Athens in 461 BC and Pericles, ruler from 461 BC to 429 BC, used the money to transform the city. This period has become known as Athens' golden age.

Most of the monuments on the Acropolis today date from this period. Drama and literature flourished due to such luminaries as Aeschylus, Sophocles and Euripides. The sculptors Pheidias and Myron and the historians Herodotus, Thucydides and Xenophon also lived during this time.

Rivalry with Sparta

Sparta didn't let Athens revel in its newfound glory. Cooperation gave way to competition

---

ATHENS IN...

Two Days

Climb to the glorious **Acropolis** (p67) in the early morning, then wind down through the **Ancient Agora** (p76), or pop in to the **Tower of the Winds** (p77). Explore **Plaka**, looping back to the **Acropolis Museum** (p73) for the Parthenon masterpieces. Complete your circuit along the **grand promenade** (p75), then up to **Filopappou Hill** (p75) and the cafes of **Thisio** before dinner at a restaurant with Acropolis views – or grab a souvlaki and head to an **outdoor movie** (p117).

On day two, watch the **changing of the guard** (p83) at Syntagma Sq before heading through the gardens to the **Temple of Olympian Zeus** (p75) or the **Panathenaic Stadium** (p92). Take a trolleybus to the **National Archaeological Museum** (p89), then catch an evening show at the historic **Odeon of Herodes Atticus** (p73), or head to the **Plateia Agia Irini** area in Monastiraki for dinner and nightlife.

Four Days

Visit the **Benaki Museum** (p89), the **Museum of Cycladic Art** (p89) and the **Byzantine & Christian Museum** (p90) before lunch in **Kolonaki**. Take the *teleferik* (funicular railway) or climb **Lykavittos Hill** (p90) for panoramic views. Hit a **rembetika club** (p117) in winter, or bar-hop around Exarhia in summer.

On day four explore the dynamic **central market** (p123) and **Kerameikos** (p85). Trip along the coast to Cape Sounion's **Temple of Poseidon** (p136), or save your energy for nightlife at Glyfada's **beach bars** (p111).

and the Peloponnesian Wars, which began in 431 BC and dragged on until 404 BC. Sparta gained the upper hand and Athens never returned to its former glory. The 4th century BC did, however, produce three of the West's greatest orators and philosophers: Socrates, Plato and Aristotle.

In 338 BC Athens, along with the other city-states of Greece, was conquered by Philip II of Macedon. After Philip's assassination, his son Alexander (soon to be known as the Great) favoured Athens over other city-states. But after Alexander's untimely death, Athens passed in quick succession through the hands of his generals.

Roman & Byzantine Rule

The Romans defeated the Macedonians, and in 186 BC attacked Athens after it sided against them in a botched rebellion in Asia Minor. They destroyed the city walls and took precious sculptures to Rome. During three centuries of peace under Roman rule, known as the 'Pax Romana', Athens continued to be a major seat of learning. The Romans adopted Hellenistic culture: many wealthy young Romans attended Athens schools and anyone who was anyone in Rome spoke Greek. The Roman emperors, particularly Hadrian, graced Athens with many grand buildings.

In the late 4th century, Christianity became the official religion of Athens and worship of the 'pagan' Greek gods was outlawed. After the subdivision of the Roman Empire into east and west, Athens remained an important cultural and intellectual centre until Emperor Justinian closed its schools of philosophy in AD 529. Athens declined and, between 1200 and 1450, was continually invaded – by the Franks, Catalans, Florentines and Venetians, all preoccupied with grabbing principalities from the crumbling Byzantine Empire.

Ottoman Rule & Independence

Athens was captured by the Turks in 1456, and nearly 400 years of Ottoman rule followed. The Acropolis became the home of the Turkish governor, the Parthenon was converted to a mosque and the Erechtheion became a harem.

On 25 March 1821, the Greeks launched the War of Independence, declaring independence in 1822. Fierce fighting broke out in the streets of Athens, which changed hands several times. Britain, France and Russia eventually stepped in and destroyed

> ## CONTEST FOR ATHENS
>
> The founding of Athens is enshrined in myth. Phoenician king Kekrops, the story goes, founded a city on a huge rock near the sea. The gods of Olympus proclaimed that it should be named for the deity who could provide the most valuable legacy for mortals. Athena (goddess of wisdom, among other things) produced an olive tree, symbol of peace and prosperity. Poseidon (god of the sea) struck a rock with his trident, creating a saltwater spring, to signify great maritime power. It was a close contest, but the gods judged that Athena's gift, which would provide food, oil and fuel, would better serve the citizens – though of course Athens today draws its wealth from Poseidon's domain as well.

the Turkish–Egyptian fleet in the famous Battle of Navarino in October 1827.

Initially the city of Nafplio was named Greece's capital. After elected president Ioannis Kapodistrias was assassinated in 1831, Britain, France and Russia again intervened, declaring Greece a monarchy. The throne was given to 17-year-old Prince Otto of Bavaria, who transferred his court to Athens. It became the Greek capital in 1834, though was little more than a sleepy town of about 6000, as so many residents had fled after the 1827 siege. Bavarian architects created imposing neoclassical buildings, tree-lined boulevards and squares.

Otto was overthrown in 1862 after a period of power struggles, including the British and French occupation of Piraeus, aimed at quashing the 'Great Idea' – Greece's doomed expansionist goal. The imposed sovereign was Danish Prince William, crowned as Prince George in 1863.

The 20th Century

Throughout the latter half of the 19th century and the beginning of the 20th, Athens grew steadily – and then quite suddenly in 1922 and 1923, when more than a million refugees arrived in the city, first from the burning of Smyrna (Izmir), then due to the population exchange mandated by the Treaty of Lausanne the next spring.

During the German occupation of WWII, Athens suffered appallingly. More Athenians

Greater Athens

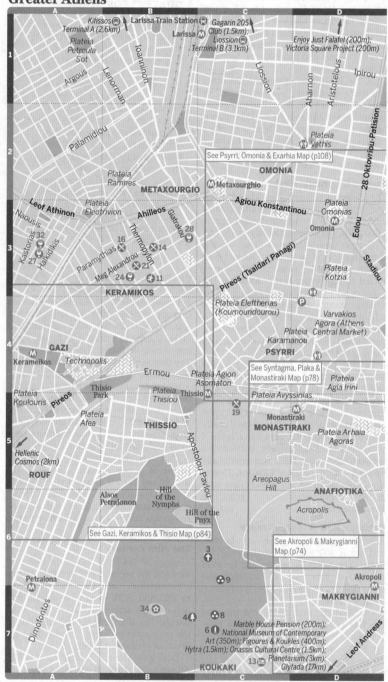

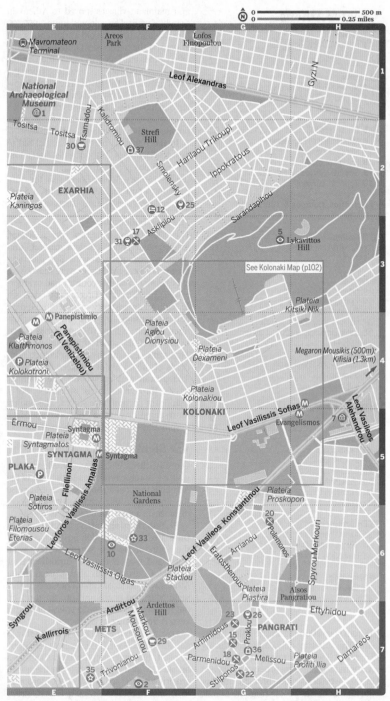

Greater Athens

died from starvation than were killed by the enemy. The suffering only continued during the bitter civil war that followed.

A '50s industrialisation program, launched with the help of US aid, brought another population boom, as people from the islands and mainland villages moved to Athens in search of work. The colonels' junta (1967–74) tore down many of the old Turkish houses of Plaka and the neoclassical buildings of King Otto's time, but failed to tackle the chronic infrastructure problems resulting from the rapid growth of the 1950s. The elected governments that followed didn't do much better, and by the end of the 1980s the city had a reputation as one of the most traffic-clogged, polluted and dysfunctional in Europe.

In the 1990s, as part of an initial bid to host the Olympics, authorities embarked on an ambitious program to drag the city into the 21st century. Athens finally won the competition to host the 2004 Olympics, a deadline that fast-tracked infrastructure projects.

The New Millennium

The 2004 Olympics legacy was a cleaner, greener and more efficient capital, and booming economic growth. But the optimism and fiscal good times were short-lived, as it became clear the country had overborrowed. In 2010, the Greek debt crisis set in, with strict austerity measures including cutting pensions by half. The unemployment rate hit 28% in 2014 and banks closed briefly in 2015 amid dramatic elections. That same year, Athens also welcomed hundreds of thousands of refugees from Syria, Afghanistan and elsewhere. The majority passed through to northern Europe, but a significant portion have stayed. The bounty represented by Athena's olive tree persists, despite this period of adversity.

◉ Sights

Central Athens is relatively small: you can walk a leisurely circuit around the base of the Acropolis in about an hour. However, because the city is quite hilly, what looks like a short distance on a map can be a hike in real life.

Plateia Syntagmatos (Syntagma Sq; translated as Constitution Sq) is considered the centre of modern Athens. A short walk south and west is the old Turkish quarter in **Plaka**, virtually all that existed when Athens was declared capital of Greece. This neighbourhood is ground zero for tourism, but lifelong residents and a splash of graffiti keep it from losing its character.

Due west from Syntagma is **Monastiraki** and just north, **Psyrri**. They're both very lively at night, but some emptier blocks can be a bit sketchy at night, especially in the northern fringes of Psyrri. West of the Acropolis, in **Thisio**, Apostolou Pavlou is a lovely green pedestrian promenade with a host of cafes and youth-filled bars, with residential blocks to either side. Further west, **Gazi** was for years the edgy neighbourhood; now it's decidedly the centre, mostly for nightlife and a strong gay scene. The urban fringes, where new bars and creative endeavours pop up, are now **Keramikos** and **Metaxourgio**, where car-repair shops mix with abandoned mansions.

East and north of Syntagma, **Kolonaki** is Athens' poshest central neighbourhood. Behind the Panathenaic Stadium, **Pangrati** and neighbouring **Mets** are unpretentious residential areas, with low-key-cool places to eat. The quiet neighbourhoods of **Makrygianni** and **Koukaki**, south of the Acropolis, are relatively untouristed as well.

Heading north from Syntagma, you pass the 'neoclassical trilogy' of elaborate, formal late-19th-century buildings on Stadiou. Up the hill behind, **Exarhia**, covered in more graffiti than the rest of the city, is known for its lively squat scene, with frequent rallies on Plateia Exarhia. **Omonia**, once one of the city's smarter areas, can be seedy at night – although the square itself, focus of police vigilance, is relatively fine. North from here, you reach **Viktoria**, **Kypseli** and **Plateia Amerikis**, all home to many recent immigrants.

Athens is somewhat constrained by the surrounding mountains, though it is eating its way up the slopes. Far to the north is Mt Parnitha; the northeast is marked by Mt Pendeli, the west by Mt Egaleo and the east by Mt Hymettos. Downtown Athens is dominated by its much smaller hills.

⊙ Acropolis

★**Acropolis**   HISTORIC SITE
(Map p78; ☑ 210 321 4172; http://odysseus.culture. gr; adult/concession/child €20/10/free; ⊗ 8am-8pm Apr-Oct, to 5pm Nov-Mar, last entry 30min before closing; Ⓜ Akropoli) The Acropolis is the most important ancient site in the Western world. Crowned by the Parthenon, it stands sentinel over Athens, visible from almost everywhere within the city. Its monuments and sanctuaries of white Pentelic marble gleam in the midday sun and gradually take on a honey hue as the sun sinks, while at night they stand brilliantly illuminated above the city. A glimpse of this magnificent sight cannot fail to exalt your spirit.

Inspiring as these monuments are, they are but faded remnants of the city of Pericles, who spared no expense – only the best materials, architects, sculptors and artists were good enough for a city dedicated to Athena. It was a showcase of lavishly coloured colossal buildings and of gargantuan statues, some of bronze, others of marble plated with gold and encrusted with precious stones.

The Acropolis was first inhabited in Neolithic times (4000–3000 BC). The earliest temples were built during the Mycenaean era, in homage to the goddess Athena. People lived on the Acropolis until the late 6th century BC, but in 510 BC the Delphic oracle declared that it should be the province of the gods.

After all the buildings on the Acropolis were reduced to ashes by the Persians on the eve of the Battle of Salamis (480 BC), Pericles set about his ambitious rebuilding program. He transformed the Acropolis into a city of temples, which has come to be regarded as the zenith of Classical Greece.

Ravages inflicted during the years of foreign occupation, pilfering by foreign archaeologists, inept renovations following Independence, visitors' footsteps, earthquakes and, more recently, acid rain and pollution have all taken their toll on the surviving monuments. The worst blow was in 1687, when the Venetians attacked the Turks, opening fire on the Acropolis and causing an explosion in the Parthenon – where the Turks had been storing gunpowder – and damaging all the buildings.

Major restoration programs are continuing and most of the original sculptures and friezes have been moved to the Acropolis Museum (p73) and replaced with casts. The Acropolis became a World Heritage–listed site in 1987.

The one modern detail on the hill (aside from the ever-present scaffolding and cranes) is the large Greek flag at the far east end. From here, you can look down into the Temple of Olympian Zeus. In 1941, early in the Nazi occupation, two teenage boys climbed up here and pulled down the Nazi flag and raised the Greek one; their act of resistance is commemorated on a brass plaque nearby.

A combined ticket permits entry to the Acropolis and six other sites within five days. On the first Sunday of the month from November to March, admission is free.

Beulé Gate   ARCHITECTURE
(Map p78) Inside the main entrance of the Acropolis site, the path leads you up through the Beulé Gate, named after the French archaeologist Ernest Beulé, who uncovered

ATHENS & AROUND ATHENS

Acropolis

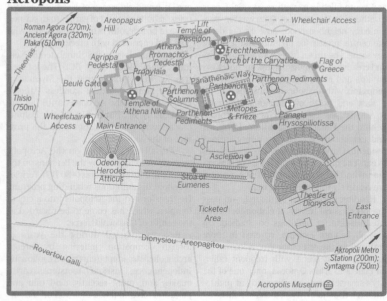

it in 1852. The 8m-high pedestal on the left, halfway up the stairs leading to the Propylaia, was once topped by the Monument of Agrippa, a bronze statue of the Roman general riding a chariot, erected in 27 BC after victory in the Panathenaic Games.

Propylaia   ARCHITECTURE
(Map p78) The Propylaia formed the monumental entrance to the Acropolis (p67). Built by Mnesicles between 437 BC and 432 BC, it ranks in architectural brilliance with the Parthenon. It consists of a central hall with two wings on either side; each section had a gate, and in ancient times these five gates were the only entrances to the 'upper city'. The middle gate, the largest, opened on to the Panathenaic Way, the route for the great Panathenaic Procession.

As you walk through on the central boardwalk, admire the thick panels of marble cladding, and as you pass the northeastern section (once used as a *pinakothiki,* or art gallery), look up to see the marble ceiling panels. These were once painted with gold stars on a blue field. Up ahead, beyond the Propylaia to the right, near the Parthenon, the path leads past (new) ceiling panels, stored upright. They are startlingly huge, giving a sense of the true height of the Propylaia's columns.

Temple of Athena Nike   TEMPLE
(Map p78) The small but exquisitely proportioned Temple of Athena Nike sits at the southwest edge of the Acropolis (p67), jutting in front and to the right of the Propylaia. Designed by Kallicrates, the temple was built of white Pentelic marble between 427 BC and 424 BC. The building is almost square, with four graceful Ionic columns at either end.

Only fragments remain of the frieze and relief sculptures, now replicas; the originals are in the Acropolis Museum (p73). The frieze shows scenes from mythology, the Battle of Plataea (479 BC) and Athenians fighting Boeotians and Persians. An additional relief sculpture shows Athena Nike fastening her sandal. The temple housed a wooden statue of Athena.

The temple was dismantled in 1686, when the Turks used its stones to build a bastion against the Venetians. From 1836–42, it was carefully reconstructed, but this and later interventions had to be corrected starting in 2003. The temple was once again dismantled, piece by piece, and painstakingly rebuilt without corrosive iron and using new marble from ancient quarries to fill in gaps; this gleams white in contrast with the old stones.

Statue of Athena
Promachos & Pedestals   RUINS

(Map p78) As you walk beyond the Propylaia into the Acropolis (p67) site, along the Panathenaic Way, you will see to your left the foundations of pedestals for the statues that once lined the path, including one that held Pheidias' 9m-high statue of Athena Promachos (*promachos* means 'champion'). Symbolising Athenian invincibility against the Persians, the helmeted goddess held a shield in her left hand and a spear in her right.

The statue was carted off to Constantinople by Emperor Theodosius in AD 426. By 1204 it had lost its spear, so the hand appeared to be gesturing. This led the inhabitants to believe that the statue had beckoned the Crusaders to the city, so they smashed it to pieces.

★ Parthenon   TEMPLE

(Map p78) More than any other monument, the Parthenon epitomises the glory of Ancient Greece. Meaning 'virgin's apartment', it's dedicated to Athena Parthenos, the goddess embodying the power and prestige of the city. The largest Doric temple ever completed in Greece, and the only one built completely of white Pentelic marble (apart from its wooden roof), it took 15 years to complete. It was designed by Iktinos and Kallicrates and completed in time for the Great Panathenaic Festival (p76) of 438 BC.

Designed to be the pre-eminent monument of the Acropolis (p67) and built on its highest ground, the Parthenon had a dual purpose: to house the great statue of Athena commissioned by Pericles and to serve as the new treasury. It was built on the site of at least four earlier temples dedicated to Athena.

The temple consisted of eight fluted Doric columns at either end and 17 on each side. To achieve perfect form, its lines were ingeniously curved to create an optical illusion – the foundations are slightly concave and the columns are slightly convex to make both look straight. Supervised by Pheidias, the sculptors Agoracritos and Alcamenes worked on the architectural sculptures of the Parthenon, including the pediments and friezes, which were brightly coloured and gilded.

The metopes (the decorative panels on the frieze) on the eastern side depicted the Olympian gods fighting the giants; on the western side they showed Theseus leading the Athenian youths into battle against the Amazons. The southern metopes illustrated the contest of the Lapiths and Centaurs at a marriage feast, while the northern ones depicted the sacking of Troy.

Much of the frieze depicting the Panathenaic Procession was either damaged in the Turkish gunpowder explosion of 1687 or later defaced by the Christians, but the greatest existing part (over 75m long) consists of the controversial Parthenon Marbles, taken by Lord Elgin and now in the British Museum in London. The British government continues to ignore campaigns for their return.

The ceiling of the Parthenon, like that of the Propylaia, was painted blue and gilded with stars. At the eastern end was the holy cella (inner room of a temple), into which only a few privileged initiates could enter. Here stood the statue for which the temple was built: the Athena Polias (Athena of the City), considered one of the wonders of the ancient world. Designed by Pheidias and completed in 432 BC, it was gold-plated over an inner wooden frame and stood almost 12m high on its pedestal. The face, hands and feet were made of ivory, and the eyes were fashioned from jewels. Clad in a long gold dress with the head of Medusa carved in ivory on her breast, the goddess held a statuette of Nike (the goddess of victory) in her right hand; in her left, a spear with a serpent at its base. On top of her helmet was a sphinx, with griffins in relief at either side.

Erechtheion   TEMPLE

(Map p78) Although the Parthenon was the most impressive monument of the Acropolis (p67), it was more showpiece than working sanctuary. That role fell to the Erechtheion. Named after Erechtheus, a mythical king of Athens, the temple housed the cults of Athena and Poseidon. It was here that, the myths told, the god and goddess had a contest for the city's affections. Poseidon struck the ground with his trident, making a salt spring, but Athena won by producing an olive tree.

The Erechtheion was part of Pericles' plan for rebuilding after the Persian attack, but the project was postponed after the outbreak of the Peloponnesian Wars. Work did not start until 421 BC, eight years after his death, and was completed around 406 BC.

It is the most unusual monument of the Acropolis, a supreme example of Ionic architecture ingeniously built on several levels to compensate for the uneven bedrock. The main temple is divided into two cellae – one dedicated to Athena, the other to Poseidon – representing a reconciliation of the two deities after their contest.

The Acropolis

A WALKING TOUR

Cast your imagination back in time, two and a half millennia ago, and envision the majesty of the Acropolis. Its famed and hallowed monument, the Parthenon, dedicated to the goddess Athena, stood proudly over a small city, dwarfing the population with its graceful grandeur. In the Acropolis' heyday in the 5th century BC, pilgrims and priests worshipped at the temples illustrated here (most of which still stand in varying states of restoration). Many were painted brilliant colours and were abundantly adorned with sculptural masterpieces crafted from ivory, gold and semiprecious stones.

As you enter the site today, elevated on the right perches one of the Acropolis' best-restored buildings: the diminutive ❶ **Temple of Athena Nike**. Follow the Panathenaic Way through the Propylaia and up the slope towards the Parthenon – icon of the Western world. Its ❷ **majestic columns** sweep up to some of what were the finest carvings of their time: wraparound ❸ **pediments, metopes and a frieze**. Stroll around the temple's exterior and take in the spectacular views over Athens and Piraeus below.

As you circle back to the centre of the site, you will encounter those renowned lovely ladies, the ❹ **Caryatids** of the Erechtheion. On the Erechtheion's northern face, the oft-forgotten ❺ **Temple of Poseidon** sits alongside ingenious ❻ **Themistocles' Wall**. Wander to the Erechtheion's western side to find Athena's gift to the city: ❼ **the olive tree**.

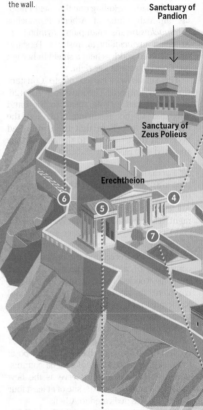

Themistocles' Wall
Crafty general Themistocles (524–459 BC) hastened to build a protective wall around the Acropolis and in so doing incorporated elements from archaic temples on the site. Look for the column drums built into the wall.

Sanctuary of Pandion

Sanctuary of Zeus Polieus

Erechtheion

Temple of Poseidon
Though he didn't win patronage of the city, Poseidon was worshipped on the northern side of the Erechtheion, which still bears the mark of his trident-strike. Imagine the finely decorated coffered porch painted in rich colours, as it was in the past.

VWB PHOTOS / GETTY IMAGES ©

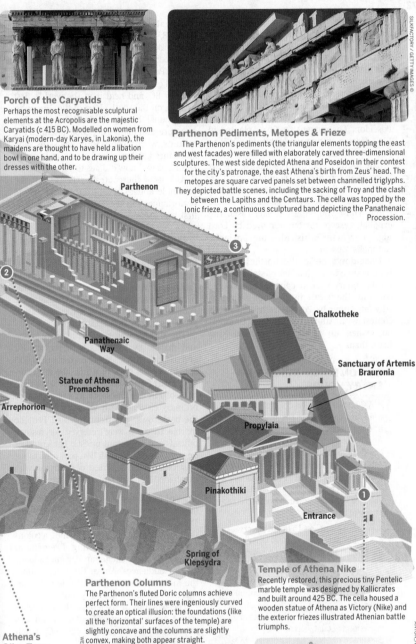

Porch of the Caryatids

Perhaps the most recognisable sculptural elements at the Acropolis are the majestic Caryatids (c 415 BC). Modelled on women from Karyai (modern-day Karyes, in Lakonia), the maidens are thought to have held a libation bowl in one hand, and to be drawing up their dresses with the other.

Parthenon Pediments, Metopes & Frieze

The Parthenon's pediments (the triangular elements topping the east and west facades) were filled with elaborately carved three-dimensional sculptures. The west side depicted Athena and Poseidon in their contest for the city's patronage, the east Athena's birth from Zeus' head. The metopes are square carved panels set between channelled triglyphs. They depicted battle scenes, including the sacking of Troy and the clash between the Lapiths and the Centaurs. The cella was topped by the Ionic frieze, a continuous sculptured band depicting the Panathenaic Procession.

Parthenon

Chalkotheke

Panathenaic Way

Sanctuary of Artemis Brauronia

Statue of Athena Promachos

Arrephorion

Propylaia

Pinakothiki

Entrance

Spring of Klepsydra

Parthenon Columns

The Parthenon's fluted Doric columns achieve perfect form. Their lines were ingeniously curved to create an optical illusion: the foundations (like all the 'horizontal' surfaces of the temple) are slightly concave and the columns are slightly convex, making both appear straight.

Temple of Athena Nike

Recently restored, this precious tiny Pentelic marble temple was designed by Kallicrates and built around 425 BC. The cella housed a wooden statue of Athena as Victory (Nike) and the exterior friezes illustrated Athenian battle triumphs.

Athena's Olive Tree

The flourishing olive tree next to the Erechtheion is meant to be the sacred tree that Athena produced to seize victory in the contest for Athens.

SILKFACTORY / GETTY IMAGES ©

ANTON_IVANOV / SHUTTERSTOCK ©

WESTEND61 / GETTY IMAGES ©

In **Athena's cella** stood an olive-wood statue of Athena Polias holding a shield adorned with a gorgon's head. It was this statue on which the sacred *peplos* (shawl) was placed at the culmination of the Great Panathenaic Festival (p76). In front of the temple grows an olive tree, held to be a cutting of the one that sprang forth at Athena's behest when she won the contest against Poseidon. The current tree was planted in 1952, from a cutting made during WWII to protect the tree from the Germans.

The southern portico is supported by six larger-than-life maiden columns, the Caryatids, modelled on women from Karyai – modern-day Karyes, in Lakonia, hence the name. Those you see are plaster casts. The originals (except for one removed by Lord Elgin, now in the British Museum) are in the Acropolis Museum.

Poseidon's cella, the northern porch, is accessible by a small set of stairs against the boundary wall. It consists of six Ionic columns; the fissure in the floor is supposedly left either by Poseidon's trident in his contest with Athena, or by Zeus' thunderbolt when he killed the mythical king Erechtheus.

ℹ COMBINED TICKETS & ENTRY HOURS

➡ A €30 unified ticket covers entry to the Acropolis and Athens' other main ancient sites: Ancient Agora, Roman Agora, Hadrian's Library, Kerameikos, the Temple of Olympian Zeus and Aristotle's Lyceum. It pays off if you're planning to see the Acropolis (€20 alone) and at least two other sites. The ticket is valid for five days and can be purchased at any of the included sites.

➡ For museums, a €15 ticket covers the National Archaeological Museum, the Byzantine & Christian Museum, the Epigraphic Museum and the Numismatic Museum. It's valid for three days.

➡ Hours for many sites can be cut back in winter, closing sometimes as early as 2pm. Additionally, budget cuts have occasionally curtailed opening times. Be sure to double-check hours before making a special trip.

➡ Box offices close 15 to 30 minutes before the sites close. Check www.culture.gr for free-admission holidays.

★ Theatre of Dionysos
THEATRE

(Map p78; ☎ 210 322 4625; Dionysiou Areopagitou; adult/child €2/free, with Acropolis pass free; ⊙ 8am-8pm, reduced hours low season; Ⓜ Akropoli) The tyrant Peisistratos introduced the annual Festival of the Great Dionysia during the 6th century BC, and held it in the world's first theatre, on the south slope of the Acropolis. The original theatre on this site was a timber structure, and masses of people attended the contests, where men clad in goatskins sang and danced, followed by feasting and revelry. Drama as we know it dates to these contests.

At one of the contests, Thespis left the ensemble and took centre stage for a solo performance, an act considered to be the first true dramatic performance – hence the term 'thespian'.

During the golden age in the 5th century BC, the annual festival was one of the state's major events. Politicians sponsored dramas by writers such as Aeschylus, Sophocles and Euripides, with some light relief provided by the bawdy comedies of Aristophanes. People came from all over Attica, with their expenses met by the state.

The theatre was reconstructed in stone and marble by Lycurgus between 342 BC and 326 BC, with a seating capacity of 17,000 spread over 64 tiers, of which about 20 survive. Apart from the front row, the seats were built of Piraeus limestone and occupied by ordinary citizens, with women confined to the back rows. The front row's 67 Pentelic marble **thrones** were reserved for festival officials and important priests. The grandest one – in the centre, with lion-paw armrests – was reserved for the Priest of Dionysos, who sat shaded from the sun under a canopy.

Stoa of Eumenes & Asclepion
RUINS

(Map p78) From the stage of the Theatre of Dionysos, the path leads uphill and west to the top of the long Stoa of Eumenes, a colonnade built by Eumenes II, King of Pergamum (197–159 BC), as a shelter and promenade for theatre audiences. Above the stoa, against the hillside, the Asclepion is a temple that was built around a sacred spring.

The worship of Asclepius, the physician son of Apollo, began in Epidavros and was introduced to Athens in 429 BC, when plague was sweeping the city.

Panagia Hrysospiliotissa
HISTORIC SITE

(Map p78) Above the Theatre of Dionysos, accessible by a path east from the Asclepion, is a grotto in the cliff face that Thrasyllos

ℹ️ ACROPOLIS LOGISTICS

➡ The main entrance is at the southwest side of the hill. Tour groups enter here and if you have a large bag (or camera bag), you must check it at the cloakroom. You can also hire a tour guide here.

➡ The east entrance is by the Theatre of Dionysos and the Akropoli metro station. It's recommended for individuals as it's less crowded.

➡ Tour groups start massing around 9am; arrive earlier to get a head start. Or go in the last two hours, when crowds thin out.

➡ Sight clearance starts 15 minutes before closing. At this time, you must go out via the main (west) entrance.

➡ The site closes before sunset, but Aeropagus Hill, outside the main gate, is a nice (if busy) place to watch the light show.

➡ Wear shoes with grippy rubber soles, as the paths around the site are uneven and slippery.

➡ People with mobility issues can access the site via a cage-lift rising vertically up the rock face on the north side. It's best to call ahead (📞 210 321 4172) to arrange. When you arrive, first go to the main entrance for guidance.

➡ There are restrooms near the main entrance (outside the ticket gate) and at the top of the hill, east of the Parthenon. Several water fountains are around the site.

➡ Phones get poor reception at the top. Take paper or download information.

converted to a Dionysian temple in 320 BC. In the Christian era, it became the Chapel of Our Lady of the Cavern; old pictures and icons cover the walls. Above the chapel, two slender Ionic columns are the remains of Thrasyllos' temple. It's open only on 15 August, the day of the Dormition of the Virgin.

👁 South Slope of the Acropolis & Makrygianni

⭐ **Odeon of Herodes Atticus** THEATRE
(Map p78; 📞 210 324 1807; Ⓜ Akropoli) This large amphitheatre was built in AD 161 by wealthy Roman Herodes Atticus in memory of his wife Regilla. It was excavated in 1857–58 and completely restored from 1950–61. The Athens & Epidaurus Festival (p96) holds drama, music and dance performances here in summer.

⭐ **Acropolis Museum** MUSEUM
(Map p74; 📞 210 900 0900; www.theacropolis museum.gr; Dionysiou Areopagitou 15, Makrygianni; adult/child €5/free; ⊗8am-4pm Mon, to 8pm Tue-Sun, to 10pm Fri Apr-Oct, 9am-5pm Mon-Thu, to 10pm Fri, to 8pm Sat & Sun Nov-Mar; Ⓜ Akropoli) This dazzling modernist museum at the foot of the Acropolis' southern slope showcases its surviving treasures still in Greek possession. While the collection covers the Archaic and Roman periods, the emphasis is on the Acropolis of the 5th century BC, considered the apotheosis of Greece's artistic achievement. The museum cleverly reveals layers of history, floating over ruins with the Acropolis visible above, showing the masterpieces in context. The surprisingly good-value **restaurant** has superb views; there's also a fine museum **shop**.

Designed by US-based architect Bernard Tschumi with Greek architect Michael Photiadis, the €130-million museum includes items formerly held in other museums or in storage, as well as pieces returned from foreign museums.

As you enter the museum grounds, look through the plexiglass floor to see the **ruins of an ancient Athenian neighbourhood**, which were artfully incorporated into the museum design after being uncovered during excavations.

Finds from the slopes of the Acropolis are on display in the **foyer gallery**, which has an ascending glass floor emulating the climb up to the sacred hill, while allowing glimpses of the ruins below. Exhibits include painted vases and votive offerings from the sanctuaries where gods were worshipped, and more recent objects found in excavations of the settlement, including two clay statues of Nike at the entrance.

Bathed in natural light, the 1st-floor **Archaic Gallery** is a veritable forest of

Akropoli & Makrygianni

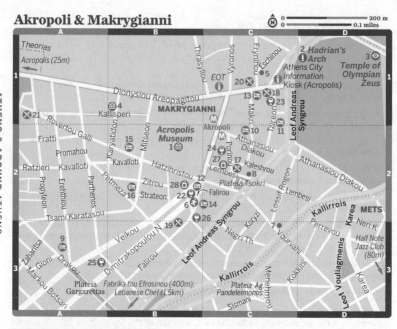

Akropoli & Makrygianni

statues, mostly votive offerings to Athena. These include stunning examples of 6th-century *kore* – statues of young women in draped clothing and elaborate braids, usually carrying a pomegranate, wreath or bird. Most were recovered from a pit on the Acropolis, where the Athenians buried them after the Battle of Salamis. The 570 BC statue of a youth bearing a calf is one of the rare male statues found. There are also bronze figurines and artefacts from temples predating the Parthenon (destroyed by the Persians), including wonderful pedimental sculptures such as Hercules slaying the Lernaian Hydra and a lioness devouring a bull. Also on this floor are five **Caryatids**, the maiden columns that held up the Erechtheion (the sixth is in the British Museum).

The museum's crowning glory is the top-floor **Parthenon Gallery**, a glass atrium housing the temple's 160m-long frieze. It's mounted as it once was, following the layout of the building, and you can stroll along, as though atop the columns, and examine the fragments at eye level. The frieze depicts the Panathenaic Procession, starting at the southwest corner of the temple, with two groups splitting off and meeting on the east side for the delivery of the *peplos* to Athena. (It helps a bit to see the movie that is screened on this floor.) Interspersed between the golden-hued originals are stark-white plaster replicas of the missing pieces – the Parthenon Marbles hacked off by Lord Elgin in 1801 and later sold to the British Museum (more than half the frieze is in London).

Filopappou Hill PARK

(Map p64; M Akropoli) Also called the Hill of the Muses, Filopappou Hill – along with the Hills of the Pnyx and the Nymphs – was, according to Plutarch, where Theseus and the Amazons did battle. Inhabited from prehistoric times to the post-Byzantine era, today the pine-clad slopes are a relaxing place for a stroll. They offer excellent views of Attica and the Saronic Gulf, well-signed ruins and some of the very best vantage points for photographing the Acropolis.

The hill, to the southwest of the Acropolis, is identifiable by the **Monument of Filopappos** (Map p64) crowning its summit; it was built between AD 114 and 116 in honour of Julius Antiochus Filopappos, a prominent Roman consul and administrator. The paved path to the top starts near the *peristera* (kiosk) on Dionysiou Areopagitou. After 250m, it passes the excellent **Church of Agios Dimitrios Loumbardiaris** (Map p64), which contains fine frescoes, and continues past **Socrates' prison** (Map p64), the **Shrine of the Muses** (Map p64) and on up to the top.

Areopagus Hill PARK

(Map p78; M Monastiraki) This rocky outcrop below the Acropolis has great views over the Ancient Agora. According to mythology, it was here that Ares was tried by the council of the gods for the murder of Halirrhothios, son of Poseidon. The council accepted his defence of justifiable deicide on the grounds that he was protecting his daughter, Alcippe, from unwanted advances.

The hill became the place where murder, treason and corruption trials were heard before the Council of the Areopagus. In AD 51, St Paul delivered his famous 'Areopagus Sermon' here: 'As I...looked carefully at your objects of worship, I even found an altar with this inscription: to an unknown god. So you are ignorant of the very thing you worship.' (The words are in Greek on a brass plaque on the hillside.) From this St Paul gained his first Athenian convert, Dionysos, who became the city's patron saint.

Hill of the Pnyx PARK

(Map p84; M Thissio) North of Filopappou Hill, the Pnyx is a rocky outcropping that was the official meeting place of the Democratic Assembly in the 5th century BC – really, the first site of democracy. You can see the speakers' steps, where the great orators Aristides, Demosthenes, Pericles and Themistocles addressed assemblies. More generally, the hill is less visited than other central sites and a peaceful place to walk.

Hill of the Nymphs PARK

(Map p84; M Thissio) Northwest of Hill of the Pnyx, this hill is home to the **old Athens observatory**, built in 1842.

★ **Temple of Olympian Zeus** TEMPLE

(Olympieio; Map p74; ☎ 210 922 6330; http://odysseus.culture.gr; Leoforos Vasilissis Olgas, Syntagma; adult/student/child €6/3/free, with Acropolis pass free; ⊙ 8am-3pm Oct-Apr, to 8pm May-Sep, final admission 30min before closing; M Akropoli,

---

ANCIENT PROMENADE

One major lasting benefit of the 2004 Olympics was the transformation of the once traffic-choked streets around Athens' historic centre into a spectacular 3km-long pedestrian promenade, one of Europe's longest. Locals and tourists alike come out in force for an evening *volta* (stroll) along the interesting heritage trail, which passes many of the best historic sites.

The grand promenade starts at Dionysiou Areopagitou, opposite the Temple of Olympian Zeus, and continues along the southern foothills of the Acropolis, all the way to the Ancient Agora, branching off from Thisio to Keramikos and Gazi, and north along Adrianou to Monastiraki and Plaka.

PANATHENAIC PROCESSION

The biggest event in ancient Athens was the Panathenaic Procession, the climax of the Panathenaic Festival held to venerate the goddess Athena. Colourful scenes of the Procession are depicted in the 160m-long Parthenon frieze in the **Acropolis Museum** (p73).

There were actually two festivals, a lesser one to mark Athena's birthdate every year, and the Great Panathenaic Festival, every fourth year. This began with dancing, followed by athletic, dramatic and musical contests. On the final day, the Panathenaic Procession began at **Kerameikos** (p85), led by men carrying animals sacrificed to Athena, followed by maidens carrying *rhytons* (horn-shaped drinking vessels) and musicians playing a fanfare for the girls of noble birth who held aloft the sacred *peplos*, a glorious saffron-coloured shawl. The parade followed the Panathenaic Way, which cuts across the middle of the Acropolis. In the festival's grande finale, the *peplos* was placed on the statue of Athena Polias in the **Erechtheion** (p69).

Syntagma) A can't-miss on two counts: it's a marvellous temple, the largest in Greece, and smack in the centre of Athens. The temple is impressive for the sheer size of its 104 Corinthian columns (17m high with base diameter of 1.7m), of which 15 remain – the fallen column was blown down in a gale in 1852.

Begun in the 6th century BC by Peisistratos, the temple was abandoned for lack of funds. Various other leaders took a stab at completing it, but it was left to Hadrian to finish the job in AD 131, thus taking more than 700 years in total to build. In typically immodest fashion, Hadrian built not just a colossal statue of Zeus in the cella, but also an equally large one of himself.

★ **Hadrian's Arch** MONUMENT
(Map p74; cnr Leoforos Vasilissis Olgas & Leoforos Vasilissis Amalias, Syntagma; M Akropoli, Syntagma) FREE The Roman emperor Hadrian had a great affection for Athens. Although he did his fair share of spiriting its Classical artwork to Rome, he also embellished the city with many monuments influenced by Classical architecture. His arch is a lofty monument of Pentelic marble that stands on the edge of one of Athens' busiest avenues. Hadrian erected it in AD 132, probably to commemorate the consecration of the Temple of Olympian Zeus.

The inscriptions show that it was intended as a dividing point between the ancient and Roman city. The northwest frieze reads, 'This is Athens, the Ancient city of Theseus', while the southeast frieze states, 'This is the city of Hadrian, and not of Theseus'.

**National Museum of
Contemporary Art** MUSEUM
(EMST; ☑ 211 101 9000; www.emst.gr; Kallirrois & Frantzi, Koukaki-Syngrou; adult/student/child €8/4/

free, 5-10pm Thu free; ⊙ 11am-8pm Tue-Sun, to 11pm Thu; M Sygrou-Fix) Set in the former Fix Brewery (though you'd never know it, following the flashy renovation unveiled in 2015), the city's most prestigious contemporary museum shows exhibitions of Greek and international art in all media, from painting to video to experimental architecture. The Greek scene is still evolving, so shows can be hit or miss. The building layout is not very welcoming, with each exhibit hall behind closed doors, and a rather too-accessible fire-escape stairwell.

Onassis Cultural Centre CULTURAL CENTRE
(☑ info & tickets 210 900 5800; www.sgt.gr; Leoforos Syngrou 107-109, Neos Kosmos; ☑ 10 or 550 to Panteio, M Sygrou-Fix, ☑ Kassomouli) The eye-catching visual- and performing-arts centre livens up the dull urbanity of Leoforos Syngrou. Cloaked in a net of white marble, it glows at night when it hosts big-name productions, installations and lectures. Check the schedule for free events. It's 1.5km southwest of the Sygrou-Fix metro station.

⊙ Syntagma, Plaka & Monastiraki

★ **Ancient Agora** HISTORIC SITE
(Map p78; ☑ 210 321 0185; http://odysseus.culture.gr; Adrianou 24, Monastiraki; adult/student/child €8/4/free, with Acropolis pass free; ⊙ 8am-8pm daily May-Oct, to 3pm Nov-Apr; M Monastiraki) The heart of ancient Athens was the Agora, the lively focal point of administrative, commercial, political and social activity. Socrates expounded his philosophy here, and in AD 49 St Paul came here to win converts to Christianity. The site today is a lush, refreshing respite, with beautiful monuments, the grand **Temple of Hephaistos** (Ancient Agora, Monastiraki), a fascinating **museum** (Map

p78) and the late-10th-century Byzantine **Church of the Holy Apostles**, trimmed in faux-Kufic brick patterns, in imitation of an Islamic style of decoration.

First developed as a public site in the 6th century BC, the Agora was devastated by the Persians in 480 BC, but a new one was built in its place almost immediately. It was flourishing by Pericles' time and continued to do so until AD 267, when it was destroyed by the Herulians, a Gothic tribe from Scandinavia. The Turks built a residential quarter on the site, but this was demolished by archaeologists after Independence and later excavated to Classical and, in parts, Neolithic levels.

★**Roman Agora & Tower of the Winds**   HISTORIC SITE
(Map p78; ☑210 324 5220; http://odysseus. culture.gr; Dioskouron, Monastiraki; adult/student/ child €6/3/free, with Acropolis pass free; ☺8am-5pm, reduced hours in low season; Ⓜ Monastiraki) The most dramatic remains of the **Roman Agora** (Map p78; cnr Pelopida & Eolou, Monastiraki; Ⓜ Monastiraki) are at the entrance, where the

ART GALLERIES

Get the 'Athens Contemporary Art Map', a list of art spaces and events, at www.athens artmap.net. Alternatively, pick up a paper copy at galleries and cafes around town.

Depot Gallery (Map p102; ☑210 364 8174; www.depotgallery.gr; Neofytou Vamva 5, Kolonaki; ☺noon-9pm; Ⓜ Evangelismos) Located in Kolonaki, this is a newer gallery in the city's contemporary-art scene. The whitewashed space celebrates 'the line between art and design' and holds popular events. It features both Greek artists (including George Raptis, Vasilis Geros and Faye Tsakalides) and international names such as Frederic Bootz. Exhibitions change monthly.

Theocharakis Foundation for the Fine Arts & Music (Map p102; ☑210 361 1206; www.thf.gr; Leoforos Vasilissis Sofias 9, Kolonaki; adult/child €6/free; ☺10am-6pm Mon-Wed & Fri-Sun, to 8pm Thu Sep-Jul; Ⓜ Syntagma) This excellent centre has three levels of exhibition space featuring local and international 20th- and 21st-century artists, a theatre, an art shop and a pleasant cafe. Music performances are held between September and May.

Metamatic:TAF (The Art Foundation; Map p78; ☑210 323 8757; www.theartfoundation.gr; Normanou 5, Monastiraki; ☺noon-9pm Mon-Sat, to 7pm Sun, cafe-bar open late; Ⓜ Monastiraki) The central courtyard at TAF, surrounded by crumbling 1870s brick buildings, is a cafe-bar that fills with an eclectic young crowd. The surrounding space hosts art, music and theatre, often free.

CAN (Map p102; ☑210 339 0833; www.can-gallery.com; Anagnostopoulou 42, Kolonaki; ☺11am-3pm & 5-8pm Tue-Fri, 11am-4pm Sat Sep-Jul; Ⓜ Syntagma) The brainchild of Christina Androulidaki, this entry on the Kolonaki gallery scene has a stable of emerging contemporary Greek artists.

A.antonopoulou.art (Map p108; ☑210 321 4994; www.aaart.gr; Aristofanous 20, 4th fl, Psyrri; ☺2-8pm Wed-Fri, noon-6pm Sat; Ⓜ Monastiraki) One of the original galleries to open in Psyrri's warehouses, this impressive art space hosts exhibitions of contemporary Greek and international art, including installations, video art and photography.

Medusa Art Gallery (Map p102; ☑210 724 4552; www.medusaartgallery.com; Xenokratous 7, Kolonaki; ☺11am-2.30pm & 6.30-9.30pm Tue-Fri, closed Aug; Ⓜ Evangelismos) Since 1979, this Kolonaki stalwart has shown excellent Greek contemporary painting, sculpture, installations and photography.

Qbox Gallery (Map p108; ☑211 119 9991; www.qbox.gr; Armodiou 10, Monastiraki; ☺noon-6pm Tue-Fri, to 4pm Sat; Ⓜ Omonia, Monastiraki) Myrtia Nikolakopoulou directs this gallery, which promotes young, emerging local and visiting artists on the international scene. Great for a taste of Greece's cutting edge.

Bernier/Eliades (Map p84; ☑210 341 3935; www.bernier-eliades.gr; Eptachalkou 11, Thisio; ☺10.30am-6.30pm Tue-Fri, noon-4pm Sat; Ⓜ Thissio) This well-established gallery showcases prominent Greek artists and an impressive list of international artists, from abstract American impressionists to British pop.

Syntagma, Plaka & Monastiraki

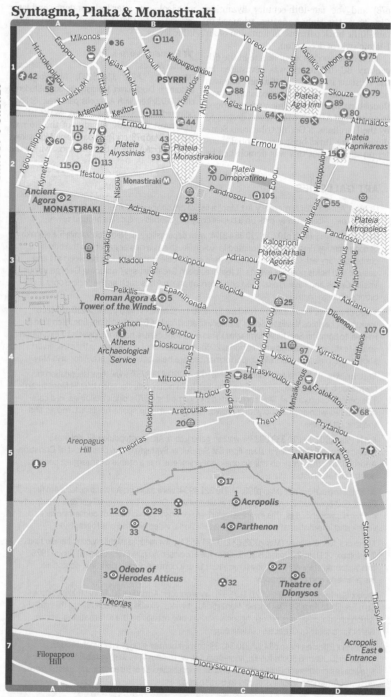

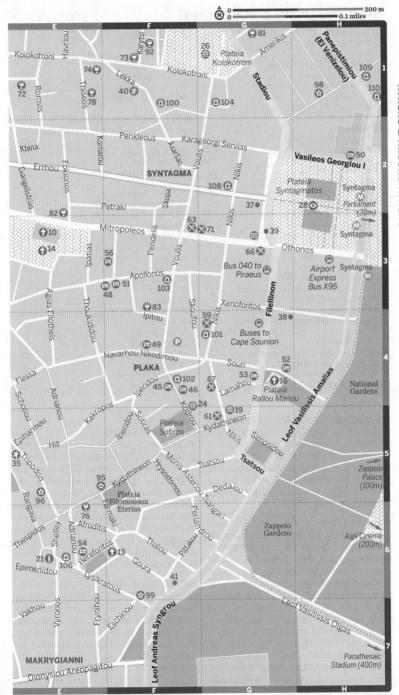

Syntagma, Plaka & Monastiraki

well-preserved **Gate of Athena Archegetis** is flanked by four Doric columns. It was financed by Julius Caesar and erected sometime during the 1st century AD. The real attraction here is the ingenious and beautiful **Tower of the Winds** (Map p78). You can see a lot from outside the fence, but it's worth going inside.

Hadrian's Library   RUINS
(Map p78; ☎210 324 9350; http://odysseus.culture.gr; Areos 3, Monastiraki; adult/child €4/free, with Acropolis pass free; ⊙8am-3pm, reduced hours in low season; Ⓜ Monastiraki) North of the Roman Agora are the remains of the largest structure erected by Hadrian, in the 2nd century AD. The library, which also held music and lecture rooms, was set next to a courtyard bordered by 100 columns, with a pool in the centre. However, today only one restored wall remains and the site is dominated by an 11th-century church. If you have the Acropolis pass, pop in – but only specialists will make a special trip.

**Museum of Greek
Popular Instruments**   MUSEUM
(Map p78; ☎210 325 4119; http://odysseus.culture.gr; Diogenous 1-3, Plaka; ⊙10am-2pm Tue & Thu-Sun, noon-6pm Wed; Ⓜ Monastiraki) FREE More than 1200 folk instruments, most collected by a single avid ethnomusicologist, fill three floors of this museum. Some instruments date to the 18th century. Headphones let visitors listen to the sounds of the *gaida* (Greek goatskin bagpipes) and Byzantine mandolins, among others. Musical performances are held in the lovely garden in summer.

Athens Cathedral   CHURCH
(Map p78; ☎210 322 1308; Plateia Mitropoleos, Monastiraki; ⊙7am-7pm, Mass Sun 6.30am; Ⓜ Monastiraki) The ornate 1862 Athens Cathedral is the seat of the archbishop of the Greek Orthodox Church of Athens. However, far more significant, both historically and architecturally, is the small, 12th-century, cruciform-style marble church next to the cathedral, known as the **Little Metropolis**

(p87) built of bits and pieces of ancient temples and earlier Christian monuments.

Church of Kapnikarea
CHURCH

(Map p78; Ermou, Monastiraki; ⊘8am-2pm Tue, Thu & Fri; Ⓜ Monastiraki, Syntagma) This small 11th-century structure stands smack in the middle of the Ermou shopping strip. It was saved from the bulldozers and restored by Athens University. Its dome is supported by four large Roman columns.

Bath House of the Winds
MUSEUM

(Map p78; ☎210 324 4340; www.melt.gr; Kyrristou 8, Monastiraki; adult/child €2/free, free Sun Nov-Mar; ⊘8am-3pm Wed-Mon; Ⓜ Monastiraki) This 17th-century *hammam* (Turkish baths) is one of the few remnants of Ottoman times, and the only surviving public bath building in Athens. A helpful free audio tour takes you back to its glory days, through multiple levels, including the furnaces in the basement. It's beautiful, but of course it would be nicer if it were functional.

Kanellopoulos Museum
MUSEUM

(Map p78; ☎210 321 2313; http://odysseus.culture.gr; Theorias 12, cnr Panos, Plaka; adult/child €2/1; ⊘8am-3pm Tue-Sun, reduced hours in low season; Ⓜ Monastiraki) FREE In 1972, Paul and Alexandra Kanellopoulos bequeathed to the Greek state the jewellery, clay and stone figurines, weapons, Byzantine icons and assorted objets d'art they'd amassed in their lifetime. The mansion setting is lovely, and as it's often empty of other visitors, it can feel like you're touring your own private eclectic collection.

Agios Nikolaos Rangavas
CHURCH

(Map p78; ☎210 322 8193; Prytaniou 1, cnr Epiharmou, Plaka; ⊘8am-noon & 5-8pm; Ⓜ Akropoli, Monastiraki) This lovely 11th-century church was part of the palace of the Rangavas family, who counted among them Michael I, emperor of Byzantium. The church bell was the first installed in Athens after liberation from the Turks (who had banned them), and was the first to ring in 1833 to announce the freedom of Athens.

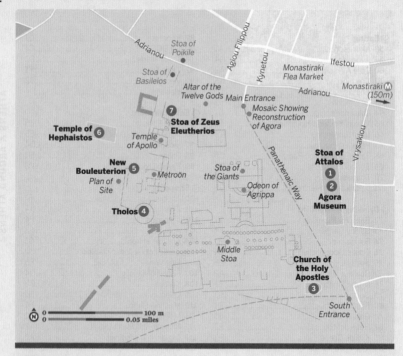

Site Tour
Ancient Agora

LENGTH TWO HOURS

As you enter the Agora, make your way to the magnificent ❶ **Stoa of Attalos**, built by the king of Pergamum in the 2nd century BC. Originally its facade was painted red and blue. People gathered here to watch the Panathenaic Procession (p76). It was also the first-ever shopping arcade, for which the word stoa is still used today.

The excellent ❷ **Agora Museum**, inside the stoa, is a good place to make sense of the site. It holds a model of the Agora, and is surrounded by ancient statues of the gods.

Continue to the southern end of the site to the charming ❸ **Church of the Holy Apostles**, built in the early 10th century to commemorate St Paul's teaching in the Agora. From 1954–57 it was stripped of 19th-century additions and restored to its original form. It contains 17th-century frescoes. The exterior patterns are an imitation of Islamic Kufic-style decoration, showing the cross-pollination of style in this period.

Walking northwest across the site, you'll pass the circular ❹ **Tholos**, where the heads of government met, and what was the ❺ **New Bouleuterion**, where the Senate met.

On the Agora's western edge is the striking ❻ **Temple of Hephaistos**, god of the forge, which was surrounded by foundries and metalwork shops. It was one of the first buildings of Pericles' rebuilding program and is the best-preserved Doric temple in Greece. Built in 449 BC by Ictinus, one of the Parthenon architects, it has 34 columns and a frieze on the eastern side depicting nine of the Twelve Labours of Hercules. In AD 1300 it was converted into the Church of Agios Georgios. The last service held there was in 1834, to honour King Otto's arrival in Athens.

In 1922–23, the temple sheltered refugees from Asia Minor. Photos from that period show families hanging laundry among the pillars, and tents erected along the temple's base.

Northeast of the temple, you'll pass the foundation of the ❼ **Stoa of Zeus Eleutherios**, one of the places where Socrates expounded his philosophy.

Jewish Museum
MUSEUM

(Map p78; ☑ 210 322 5582; www.jewishmuseum. gr; Nikis 39, Plaka; adult/child €6/free; ⊙ 9am-2.30pm Mon-Fri, 10am-2pm Sun; Ⓜ Syntagma) This small museum traces the history of the Jewish community in Greece – starting with the deeply rooted Romaniote community established in the 3rd century BC, through the arrival of Sephardic Jews and beyond the Holocaust. The documents, religious art and folk objects are beautifully presented. It's worth visiting to learn the story of the bishop and the mayor of Zakynthos, the only Greek leaders who managed to save the Jewish community from Nazi round-ups.

Church of Sotira Lykodimou
CHURCH

(Map p78; Fillelinon, Plateia Rallou Manou, Plaka; Ⓜ Syntagma) First built in the 11th century and now the Russian Orthodox Cathedral, this is the only Byzantine church built to an octagonal plan. It's quite small but topped with a high dome, so the whole space, glittering with gold stars and icons, soars upward. It's open more frequently than other churches, so it's worth crossing the street to peek inside.

Lysikrates Monument
MONUMENT

(Map p78; cnr Sellei & Lysikratous, Plaka; Ⓜ Akropoli, Syntagma) FREE Chorus leader and musical patron Lysikrates built this tower in 334 BC to commemorate the victory of his sponsored chorus in the dramatic contests of the Dionysia. The trophy, a bronze tripod, was set atop the pedestal. It's the earliest-known monument using Corinthian capitals externally, a style that is imitated in many modern monuments. The reliefs depict the battle between Dionysos and the Tyrrhenian pirates, whom the god had transformed into dolphins.

Plateia Syntagmatos
SQUARE

(Syntagma Sq; Map p78; Ⓜ Syntagma) Generally considered the centre of Athens, this square is a transport hub and general hang-out spot, especially on warm summer evenings when young people and families lounge around the central fountain. Parliament, where the syntagma (constitution) was granted in 1843, is directly across the road, so the square is also the epicentre for any demonstrations or strikes.

★ Parliament & Changing of the Guard
NOTABLE BUILDING

(Map p102; Plateia Syntagmatos; Ⓜ Syntagma) FREE In front of the parliament building on Plateia Syntagmatos, the traditionally costumed *evzones* (guards) of the Tomb of the Unknown Soldier change every hour on the hour. On Sunday at 11am, a whole platoon marches down Vasilissis Sofias to the tomb, accompanied by a band.

★ National Gardens
GARDENS

(Map p102; cnr Leoforos Vasilissis Sofias & Leoforos Vasilissis Amalias, Syntagma; ⊙ 7am-dusk; Ⓜ Syntagma) FREE Formerly the royal gardens, designed by Queen Amalia in 1938, this park makes a delightful, shady refuge, especially when summer heat and traffic turn intense. Tucked among the trees is a cafe, a large playground and ponds for turtles and ducks, as well as a tiny, slightly dispiriting zoo.

Zappeio Gardens
GARDENS

(Map p64; Syntagma; Ⓜ Syntagma) FREE These gardens sit between the National Gardens and the Panathenaic Stadium (p92) and are laid out in a network of wide walkways around the grand Zappeio Palace. The palace was built in the 1870s and hosts conferences and exhibitions. A pleasant cafe, restaurant and the open-air Aigli Cinema (p116) are alongside the palace.

National Historical Museum
MUSEUM

(Map p78; ☑ 210 323 7617; www.nhmuseum.gr; Stadiou 13, Syntagma; adult/child €3/free, Sun free; ⊙ 8.30am-2.30pm Tue-Sun; Ⓜ Syntagma) Specialising in memorabilia from the War of Independence (1821–27), this museum houses Byron's helmet and sword, a series of paintings depicting events leading up to the war and a collection of photographs and royal portraits. The museum is housed in the old Parliament building, where Prime Minister Theodoros Deligiannis was assassinated on the front steps in 1905.

Church of Agii Theodori
CHURCH

(Map p108; cnr Dragatsaniou & Agion Theodoron, Syntagma; Ⓜ Panepistimio) FREE Even if it's locked, this church is worth a detour just to see it still existing, as it has since the 11th century, amid all the modern office buildings. If you get in, you'll see a tiled dome and walls decorated with a pretty terracotta frieze of animals and plants.

◉ Gazi, Keramikos & Thisio

★ Benaki Museum Pireos Annexe
MUSEUM

(Map p84; ☑ 210 345 3111; www.benaki.gr; Pireos 138, cnr Andronikou, Rouf; €6-8; ⊙ 11am-9pm Tue-Sun, to 11pm Thu; Ⓜ Kerameikos) While the main

Gazi, Keramikos & Thisio

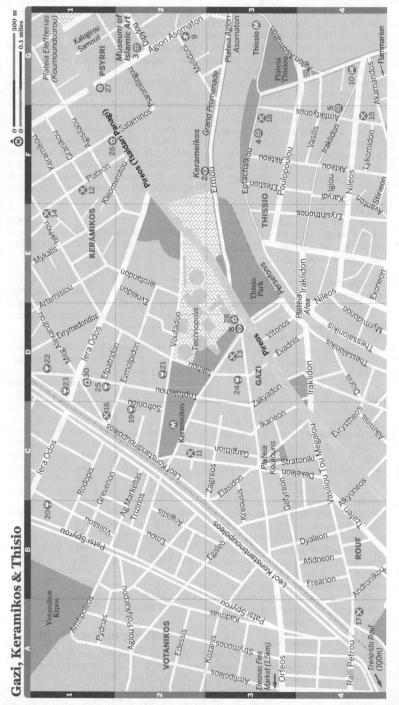

Plateia Eleftherias
(Koumoundourou)

Kalogirou
Samouil

PSYRRI 27

Museum of
Islamic Art 3

Diplon

Agion Asomaton 9

Plateia Agion
Asomaton

Thissio M

Agion Asomaton

Plateia
Thissiou

10

Antikyonos 5

18

Vasilis

Iraklidon

Lykomidon 15

Akamandos — Flammarion

Akteou

Elef sion

Nileos

Karydi

Strieon

Avanton

Poulopoulou

Eftalou

Akteou

Epthalikou

THISSIO

Erysithonos

Paregeionis

Thisio
Park

Plateia Iraklidon

Afea

Nileos

Exoneon

Myrmidon

Vitonos

Evadnis

Thessalonikis

Thessalonikis

Dions

Iraklidon

Evrystheos

Alkimnis

Piraeos (Tsaldari Panou) 26

Salaminos

Geraniou

Aristidou

Plateon 12

Kleomvrotou

Keramikos
2

Ermou

Grand Promenade

Grand Promenade

Technopolis

8   28

13

Voutadon

Iachon

24   GAZI

Zakyadon

Ikarieon

Plateia
Koulouris

Stratoniki

Dekeleon

Vasiliou Tou Megalou

Getyreon

Mykalis

Mavromichali

Mavromichali

Evrymedondos

Artemisiou

Ierodandon

Evneidon

Iera Odos

Mela

Eipatridon

Evmolpidon

25   30

22

23

16

19

Sofroniou

Keramikos M

11

Gargition

Pireos

Evadnis

KERAMIKOS

Mykalis

Ioullel

14

Iera Odos

Leof Konstantinoupoleos

Rodopis

Grevenon

Ag. Markellas

Trizinos

Angistis

Emou

Zagreos

Elasidon

Kreousis

Egaleo

Patsi Spyrou

Kadmias

Volissou

Patsi Spyrou

Amfipoleos

Pydnas

Agiou Polykarpou

VOTANIKOS

Edessis

Kozanis

Strymonos

Amfipoleos

Orfeos

Eleonas Flea
Market (1.5km)

Votanikos
Kipos

20

Dyaleon

Afidneon

Frearion

ROUF

Andronikou

Tzaferi

Alkyoneos

Ralli Petrou

Trenosto Rouf
(100m)

17

200 m
0.1 miles

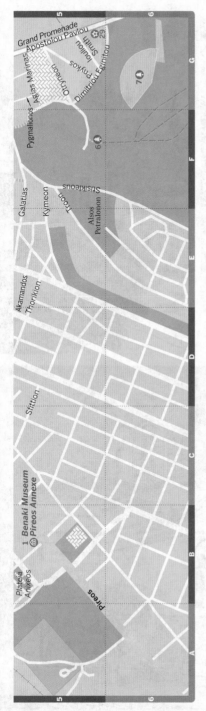

Gazi, Keramikos & Thisio

Benaki Museum (p89) displays the Classical and traditional, this mammoth annex focuses on all that is new and inventive. It's a major hub in the contemporary-art scene, and often hosts major international artists, as well as musical performances in its garden. It has an airy **cafe** and excellent **gift shop**.

★ Kerameikos
HISTORIC SITE

(Map p84; ☎ 210 346 3552; http://odysseus.culture.gr; Ermou 148, Keramikos; adult/child incl museum €8/free, with Acropolis pass free; ⏱ 8am-8pm, reduced hours in low season; Ⓜ Thissio) This site is named for the potters who settled the area in

1. Architectural details, Church of Eleftherios 2. Moni Kaisarianis
3. Church of the Holy Apostles 4. Mosaic, Moni Dafniou

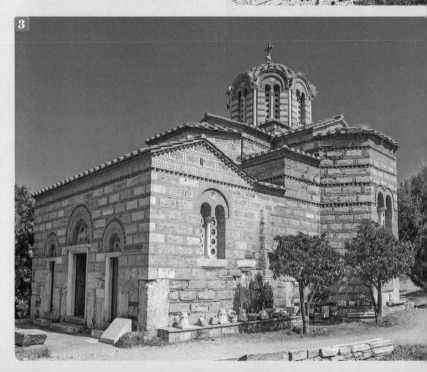

ELGREKO/SHUTTERSTOCK ©

Byzantine Athens

The city is dotted with churches that just happen to be a thousand years old, dating from the high point of the Byzantine Empire. Few churches open regularly, but the ones that do are gold-bedecked portals to the past. Don't miss the outstanding Byzantine & Christian Museum (p90), as well as the great icons at the Benaki Museum (p89).

Moni Dafniou

The area's most important Byzantine building is the World Heritage–listed 11th-century **Moni Dafniou** (☏210 581 1558; http://whc.unesco.org/en/list/537; Dafni; ⊘9am-2pm Tue & Fri; ☐811, 866 or A16 to Psychiatreion) FREE at Dafni, 10km northwest of Athens. Many of the church's elaborate mosaics, wrought by artisans from Constantinople, have been beautifully restored and more work is underway. The octagonal structure incorporates part of a wall from a 6th-century church.

Moni Kaisarianis

Nestled on the slopes of Mt Hymettos, 5km east of Athens, beautiful 11th-century **Moni Kaisarianis** (Monastery of Kaisariani; ☏210 723 6619; Mt Hymettos; adult/child €2/free; ⊘8.30am-2.45pm, grounds to sunset, Tue-Sun) is a peaceful walled sanctuary. The domed *katholikon* (main church), supported by four columns from an ancient temple, has well-preserved frescoes from the 17th and 18th centuries.

Church of the Holy Apostles

One of the oldest churches in Athens is the late-10th-century Church of the Holy Apostles in the Ancient Agora (p77), a tribute to the place where St Paul once taught. It bears decorative details that are now seen as Islamic but were a product of artisans who worked across the eastern Mediterranean.

Church of Eleftherios (Little Metropolis)

Look closely at this 12th-century **church** (Plateia Mitropoleos, Monastiraki), and you'll see it's a historical collage of medieval stonework and ancient Pentelic marble. Its facade sports both medieval lions and Classical athletes, a portion of a delicate ancient marble frieze. It was even built on the ruins of an ancient temple.

around 3000 BC, then on the clay-rich banks of the Iridanos river. But its real finds come from its long later use as a cemetery, through the 6th century AD, under the Romans. Rediscovered in 1861 during the construction of Pireos St, the site is now lush and tranquil, with a small but excellent **museum** containing remarkable *stelae* (stone slabs) and sculptures, vases and terracotta figurines.

Once inside, head for the small knoll ahead to the right, where you'll find a **plan of the site**. A path leads down to the right from the knoll to the remains of the **city wall** built by Themistocles in 479 BC, and rebuilt by Konon in 394 BC. The wall is broken by the foundations of two gates; tiny signs mark each one.

The first, the **Sacred Gate**, spanned the Sacred Way and was the gate by which pilgrims from Eleusis entered the city during the annual Eleusian procession. To the northeast is the **Dipylon Gate** – the city's main entrance and where the Panathenaic Procession (p76) began. It was also where the city's prostitutes gathered to offer their services to travellers. From a platform outside the Dipylon Gate, Pericles gave his famous speech extolling the virtues of Athens and honouring those who died in the first year of the Peloponnesian Wars.

Between the Sacred and Dipylon Gates are the foundations of the **Pompeion**, used as a dressing room for participants in the Panathenaic Procession.

Leading off the Sacred Way to the left as you head away from the city is the **Street of Tombs**. This avenue was reserved for the tombs of Athens' most prominent citizens. The surviving *stelae* are now in the National Archaeological Museum, so what you see are mostly replicas. The astonishing array of funerary monuments and their bas-reliefs warrant close examination. Ordinary citizens were buried in the areas bordering the Street of Tombs. One well-preserved *stela* (up the stone steps on the northern side) shows a little girl with her pet dog. The site's largest *stela* is of sisters Demetria and Pamphile.

ATHENS WITH CHILDREN

Athens is short on playgrounds, but there's plenty to keep kids amused and children are welcome everywhere. The National Gardens (p83) has a playground, duck pond and small, somewhat dismal, zoo. There is also an enclosed, shaded playground in the Zappeio Gardens (p83). A tram ride south gets you to the much bigger facilities at Stavros Niarchos Park (p92) and **Flisvos Park** (Palaio Faliro; 🚊; 🚊 Parko Flisvou) FREE; the latter also has an outdoor cinema and an excellent shadow-puppet theatre (p120).

The **Museum of Greek Children's Art** (Map p78; ☎ 210 331 2621; www.childrens artmuseum.gr; Kodrou 9, Plaka; €3; ⊙ 9am-2pm Tue-Sat Sep-Jul; Ⓜ Syntagma) FREE has a room set aside where children can learn about Ancient Greece. The **Hellenic Children's Museum** (Map p102; ☎ 210 331 2995; www.hcm.gr; Vasileos Georgos II 17-19, Athens Conservatory; ⊙ 11am-7pm Wed, to 3pm Thu-Sun; Ⓜ Evangelismos) FREE was in the process of moving in 2017, and the new facility was developing exhibits.

Attica Zoological Park (☎ 210 663 4724; www.atticapark.gr; Yalou, Spata; adult/child €18/14; ⊙ 9am-sunset) has an expanding collection of big cats, birds, reptiles and other animals, including a monkey forest and 'Cheetahland'. It's near the airport.

Escape the heat and amuse the kids with a virtual-reality tour of Ancient Greece at the **Hellenic Cosmos** (Cultural Centre of the Foundation for the Hellenic World; ☎ 212 254 0000; www.hellenic-cosmos.gr; Pireos 254, Tavros; per show adult €5-10, child €3-8, day pass adult/child €15/12; ⊙ 10am-3pm Mon-Fri & Sun, earlier hours in winter, closed 2 weeks mid-Aug; Ⓜ Kallithea), or explore the universe at the impressive **Planetarium** (☎ 210 946 9600; www.eugenfound. edu.gr; Leoforos Syngrou 387, Palaio Faliro; adult €6-8, child €4-5; ⊙ 5.30-8.30pm Wed-Fri, 10.30am-8.30pm Sat & Sun late Aug–mid-Jul; 🚌 550 or B2 to Onassio, Ⓜ Sygrou-Fix). At the **War Museum** (Map p102; ☎ 210 725 2975; www.warmuseum.gr; Rizari 2, cnr Leoforos Vasilissis Sofias, Kolonaki; adult/child €4/2; ⊙ 9am-7pm Tue-Sun Jun-Aug, to 5pm Sep-May; Ⓜ Evangelismos), kids can climb into the cockpit of a WWII plane and other aircraft.

Head 6km west of Syntagma Sq for the enormous **Allou Fun Park & Kidom** (☎ 210 809 2888; www.allou.gr; cnr Leoforos Kifisou & Petrou Rali, Renti; passes from €12; ⊙ 5-10.30pm Mon-Fri, 10am-11.30pm Sat, to 11pm Sun; 🚌 21 or B19 to Kan Kan, 803 to Nekrotafeio, Ⓜ Egaleo), Athens' biggest amusement-park complex. Kidom is aimed at younger children.

Industrial Gas Museum NOTABLE BUILDING
(Technopolis; Map p84; ☑ 210 347 5535; www.tech-nopolis-athens.com; Pireos 100, Gazi; adult/child €1/free; ⊙ 10am-8pm Tue-Sun, to 6pm mid-Oct– mid-Apr; Ⓜ Kerameikos) A walking route runs through the old gasworks in Gazi, a complex of furnaces and industrial buildings from the mid-19th century. The atmosphere is cool, and so are the old photos and film clips. There's a pleasant cafe, and the space is often used for music and other events.

Herakleidon Museum MUSEUM
(Map p84; ☑ 210 346 1981; www.herakleidon-art.gr; Iraklidon 16, Thisio; adult/child €6/free; ⊙ 10am-2pm Sun for permanent exhibit; Ⓜ Thissio) This eclectic private museum examines the interrelation of art, mathematics and philosophy. The main building, a restored mansion, holds a kid-oriented permanent science exhibit. An annex, around the corner at Apostolou Pavlou 37, is dedicated to eclectic rotating shows (with varied hours and admission), on topics from shipbuilding to printmaking. The museum also holds one of the world's biggest collections of MC Escher artworks (though it is not always on view).

◎ Psyrri, Omonia & Exarhia

★**National Archaeological Museum** MUSEUM
(Map p64; ☑ 213 214 4800; www.namuseum.gr; 28 Oktovriou-Patision 44, Exarhia; adult/child €10/ free; ⊙ 1-8pm Mon, 8am-8pm Tue-Sun Apr-Oct, 1-8pm Mon, 9am-4pm Tue-Sun Nov-Mar; ☐ 2, 3, 4, 5 or 11 to Polytechnio, Ⓜ Viktoria) This is one of the world's most important museums, housing the world's finest collection of Greek antiquities. Treasures offering a view of Greek art and history – dating from the Neolithic era to Classical periods, including the Ptolemaic era in Egypt – include exquisite sculptures, pottery, jewellery, frescoes and artefacts found throughout Greece. The beautifully presented exhibits are displayed mainly thematically. Allow plenty of time to view the vast and spectacular collections (more than 11,000 items) housed in this enormous (8000-sq-metre) 19th-century neoclassical building.

A joint ticket with the Byzantine & Christian Museum (p90) and two others is €15.

★**Museum of Islamic Art** MUSEUM
(Map p84; ☑ 210 325 1311; www.benaki.gr; Agion Asomaton 22 & Dipylou 12, Keramikos; adult/ student/child €9/7/free; ⊙ 10am-6pm Thu-Sun; Ⓜ Thissio) This is one of the world's most significant collections of Islamic art. Housed in two restored neoclassical mansions near Keramikos, it exhibits more than 8000 items representing the 12th to 19th centuries, including weavings, carvings, prayer rugs, tiles and ceramics. On the 3rd floor is a 17th-century reception room with an inlaid marble floor from a Cairo mansion. In the basement, part of Athens' ancient Themistoklean wall is exposed.

◎ Kolonaki & Around

★**Benaki Museum** MUSEUM
(Map p102; ☑ 210 367 1000; www.benaki.gr; Koumbari 1, cnr Leoforos Vasilissis Sofias, Kolonaki; adult/ student/child €9/7/free, Thu free, pass to all Benaki museums €20; ⊙ 9am-5pm Wed & Fri, to midnight Thu & Sat, to 3pm Sun; Ⓜ Syntagma, Evangelismos) Antonis Benakis, a politician's son born in Alexandria, Egypt, in the late 19th century, endowed what is perhaps the finest museum in Greece. Its three floors showcase impeccable treasures from the Bronze Age up to WWII. Especially gorgeous are the Byzantine icons and the extensive collection of Greek regional costumes, as well as complete sitting rooms from Macedonian mansions, intricately carved and painted.

The variety of displays here, including Classical Greek masterpieces, mean it's great for a group with varied interests. Late opening hours are another plus. Note also (to avoid confusion) that there are two other major branches: the Pireos Annexe (p83), for contemporary art, and the Museum of Islamic Art in Keramikos, as well as several smaller museums; a €20 pass is valid for three months.

★**Museum of Cycladic Art** MUSEUM
(Map p102; ☑ 210 722 8321; www.cycladic.gr; Neofytou Douka 4, cnr Leoforos Vasilissis Sofias, Kolonaki; adult/child €7/free, Mon half-price, special exhibits €10; ⊙ 10am-5pm Mon, Wed, Fri & Sat, to 8pm Thu, 11am-5pm Sun; Ⓜ Evangelismos) The 1st floor of this exceptional private museum is dedicated to the iconic minimalist marble Cycladic figurines, dating from 3000 BC to 2000 BC. They inspired many 20th-century artists, such as Picasso and Modigliani, with their simplicity and purity of form. Most are surprisingly small, considering their outsize influence, though one is almost human size. The rest of the museum features Greek and Cypriot art dating from 2000 BC to the 4th century AD.

Overall, there's an interesting focus on how these objects were used, culminating in the 4th-floor exhibit, *Scenes from Daily Life in Antiquity,* where objects are set in photo recreations of ancient scenes.

★**Byzantine & Christian Museum**   MUSEUM
(Map p102; ☑213 213 9500; www.byzantine museum.gr; Leoforos Vasilissis Sofias 22, Kolonaki; adult/child €8/free; ⊙8am-8pm Apr-Oct, reduced hours Nov-Mar; Ⓜ Evangelismos) This outstanding museum – on the grounds of former Villa Ilissia, an urban oasis – presents a priceless collection of Christian art from the 3rd to 20th centuries. Thematic snapshots of the Byzantine and post-Byzantine world are exceptionally presented in expansive, well-lit, multilevel galleries, clearly arranged chronologically with English translations. The collection includes icons, frescoes, sculptures, textiles, manuscripts, vestments and mosaics.

Aristotle's Lyceum   RUINS
(Lykeion; Map p102; http://odysseus.culture.gr; cnr Rigillis & Leoforos Vasilissis Sofias; adult/child €4/free; ⊙8am-8pm Mon-Fri; Ⓜ Evangelismos) Unearthed when the site was cleared to build a museum of contemporary art, the Lyceum where Aristotle founded his school in 335 BC was excavated only in 2011. The Lyceum, which used to lie outside the city walls, was a *gymnasio* where Aristotle taught rhetoric and philosophy. It was also known as a Peripatetic School, because teacher and pupils would walk as they talked.

Lykavittos Hill   LANDMARK
(Map p64; Kolonaki; Ⓜ Evangelismos) The summit of Lykavittos – 'Hill of Wolves', from ancient times, when it was wilder than it is now – gives the finest panoramas of the city and the Attic basin, *nefos* (pollution haze) permitting. Perched on the summit is the little **Chapel of Agios Giorgios** (Map p102), floodlit like a beacon over the city at night. Walk up the path from the top of Loukianou in Kolonaki, or take the 10-minute funicular railway (p128), or *teleferik,* from the top of Ploutarhou.

National Sculpture & Art Gallery   MUSEUM
(National Glyptotheque; ☑210 723 5857; www. nationalgallery.gr; Army Park – Alsos Stratou, Goudi; adult/child €5/free; ⊙9am-8pm Mon & Wed-Fri, to 4pm Sat & Sun; Ⓜ Katehaki) While the more central building of the **National Gallery** (Map p64; ☑210 723 5937; Leoforos Vasileos Konstantinou 50, Kolonaki; Ⓜ Evangelismos) is being rebuilt, a portion of the collection has moved alongside the National Sculpture Gallery, in the former royal stables in Goudi. Although a

🏃 Museum Tour
National Archaeological Museum

....

LENGTH TWO HOURS

....

Straight ahead as you enter the museum is the ❶ **Prehistoric collection**, showcasing the fabulous collection of ❷ **Mycenaean antiquities** (gallery 4). The first cabinet holds the celebrated gold ❸ **Mask of Agamemnon**, unearthed at Mycenae, and bronze daggers with intricate representations of the hunt. The exquisite ❹ **Vaphio gold cups**, with scenes of men taming wild bulls, are regarded as among the finest surviving examples of Mycenaean art.

The ❺ **Cycladic collection** (gallery 6) includes superb figurines of the 3rd and 2nd millennia BC, which inspired modern artists such as Picasso.

The galleries to the left of the entrance house the oldest, most significant pieces of the sculpture collection. The colossal, Naxian marble ❻ **Sounion Kouros** (room 8), carved in 600 BC, stood before Poseidon's temple in Sounion. In artistic terms, it's a link between Ancient Egypt's rigid monumental statues and the Greeks' later life-size, naturalistic sculpture. Gallery 15 is dominated by the incredible 460 BC bronze ❼ **statue of Zeus or Poseidon**, found in the sea off Evia. It depicts one of the gods with his arms outstretched.

The 200 BC ❽ **statue of Athena Varvakeion** (gallery 20) is the most famous copy of the colossal statue of Athena Polias by Pheidias that stood in the Parthenon.

In gallery 21, the striking ❾ **statue of horse and young rider** (2nd century BC), recovered from a shipwreck off Cape Artemision in Evia, stands opposite exquisite works such as the ❿ **statue of Aphrodite**.

On the upper level, straight ahead from the stairs, are the spectacular ⓫ **Minoan frescoes** from Santorini (Thira). They were uncovered in the prehistoric settlement of Akrotiri, which was buried by a volcanic eruption in the late 16th century BC.

Also upstairs is a superb ⓬ **pottery collection**, from the Bronze Age through Attic red-figured pottery (late 5th to early 4th centuries BC). Among the treasures are six amphorae presented to the winners of the Panathenaic Games.

NATIONAL ARCHAEOLOGICAL MUSEUM

Pottery Collection

Cypriot Collection

Pottery Collection

12

Panathenaic Amphorae

Thira Gallery

Lift

Minoan Frescoes

11

1st Floor

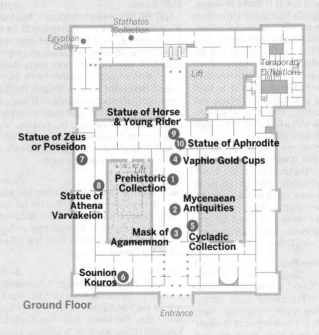

Stathatos Collection

Egyptian Gallery

Lift

Temporary Exhibitions

Statue of Horse & Young Rider

9

Statue of Zeus or Poseidon

7

10 **Statue of Aphrodite**

4 **Vaphio Gold Cups**

Lift

Prehistoric Collection **1**

Statue of Athena Varvakeion

8

Mycenaean Antiquities

2

5

Cycladic Collection

Mask of Agamemnon

3

Sounion Kouros

6

Ground Floor

Entrance

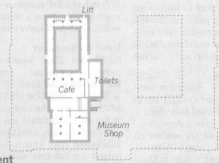

Lift

Toilets

Cafe

Museum Shop

Basement

bit far from the centre, the museum is a nice break from the classics. The modern sculpture exhibit begins in the early 19th century, when figurative marble carving was taken up again. In the other building are the gallery's prize El Grecos, plus some compelling portraiture.

◉ Pangrati & Mets

★ **Panathenaic Stadium**   HISTORIC SITE

(☏ 210 752 2984; www.panathenaicstadium.gr; Leoforos Vasileos Konstantinou, Pangrati; adult/student/child €5/2.50/free; ☉ 8am-7pm Mar-Oct, to 5pm Nov-Feb; ☐ 2, 4, 11 to Stadio, Ⓜ Akropoli, ☐ Zappeio) Originally built in the 4th century BC as a venue for the Panathenaic athletic contests, this stadium has had several lives. It's said that at Hadrian's inauguration in AD 120, a thousand wild animals were sacrificed in the arena. Later, the seats were rebuilt in Pentelic marble by Herodes Atticus. In 1895, after centuries of disuse, the stadium was restored by wealthy Greek benefactor Georgios Averof to host the first modern Olympic Games the following year.

This 19th-century rendition is a faithful replica of the original. It seats 70,000 spectators around the running track and field – which is not, unfortunately, modern Olympic-size, so the stadium could be used only for archery and the marathon finish in the 2004 games. Now it's occasionally used for concerts and public events. Morning joggers are welcome here from 7.30am to 9am.

Stavros Niarchos Park   PARK

(www.snfcc.org; Synggrou 364, Kallithea; ☉ 6am-midnight Apr-Oct, to 8pm Nov-Mar; ☐ 550 to Onasseio, 10 to Epaminonda) FREE Athens is short on green spaces, so this vast park, opened in 2016, is a true breath of fresh air. A large central lawn hosts free dance and exercise classes (a fine way to learn some Greek!), while rambling paths cut through patches of lavender and rows of olive trees. A playground, interactive sound installations and rental bikes (€1 per hour) add to the fun.

Athens' First Cemetery   CEMETERY

(Map p64; Longinou, Mets; ☉ 8am-5pm winter, 7am-8pm summer; Ⓜ Sygrou-Fix) FREE Under Ottoman rule, Greeks buried their dead at their local church. Only after independence in 1821 was this city cemetery established. It's a peaceful place to explore, with beautiful neoclassical sculptures, including *Sleeping Maiden* by Yannoulis Chalepas, the most admired Greek sculptor of the modern era. Famous people buried here include the Benaki family and the archaeologist Heinrich Schliemann (1822–90), whose mausoleum is decorated with scenes from the Trojan War.

🏃 Activities

For all the time its residents spend in cafes, Athens is a fairly active city and loves its sports. Visitors can also hit the streets with a number of good walking tours.

Beaches & Water Sports

Astir Beach   BEACH

(☏ 210 890 1621; www.astir-beach.com; Apollonus 40, Vouliagmeni; adult/child Mon-Fri €18/10, Sat & Sun mid-Jun–mid-Sep €28/15, reduced prices rest of year; ☉ beach 8am-9pm, restaurants to midnight; ☐ 114 from Glyfada or Voula tram stops) Astir is the most exclusive summer beach playground (giveaway: there's a helipad, for the most elite Athenian commuters). It has all the water sports, shops and restaurants you could want (plus, oddly, a TGI Fridays). It's 19.5km south of Athens, 7.5km south of Glyfada. If it all gets too flashy for you, there's a nice public beach across the road.

Limanakia   BEACH

(☐ 117, 122) The rocky coves below the bus stop at Limanakia B (near Varkiza on the Apollo Coast) are a popular nudist hang-out with a slight gay slant. Take the tram or A2/E2 express bus to Glyfada, then bus 117 or 122 to the Limnakia B stop.

Yabanaki   BEACH

(☏ 210 897 2414; www.yabanaki.gr; Varkiza; adult/child Mon-Fri €5/3.50, Sat & Sun €6/3.50; ☉ 8am-7pm Jun-Aug, 9am-5pm May; ☐ 122) Slightly less flashy than the beach clubs near Glyfada, Yabanaki (21km south of Syntagma) nonetheless has a full complement of entertainment options, from a restaurant to beach volleyball. Great if you're travelling with kids.

Limni Vouliagmenis   SWIMMING

(☏ 210 896 2239; www.limnivouliagmenis.gr; Leoforos Vouliagmenis; adult/child Mon-Fri €12/5.50, Sat & Sun €13/6; ☉ 7.30am-8pm; 👣; ☐ 114, 115 or 149, ☐ A2 or E2) This lightly salty lake, at the base of a huge cliff, is connected to the sea underground and fed by mineral-rich warm springs, so its temperature never falls below 21°C. This makes it a friendly habitat for fish that nibble the dead skin from your feet – an exfoliating treat for some, or a nightmare for the ticklish.

The loyal clientele of bathing-cap-clad elderly citizens tout the water's healing properties. There's a modern spa-cuisine cafe (lunch from €12) at the edge, where you can eat without paying the lake admission, plus sunbeds, a playground and showers. Take the A2 bus (E2 express in summer) to Plateia Glyfada, then take bus 114, 115 or 149.

Planet Blue Dive Centre   DIVING
(📞 210 418 0174; www.planetblue.gr; Velpex Factory, Lavrio; PADI certification from €300, dives €35-80) Popular with seasoned divers, but caters to all levels at sites around Cape Sounion.

Hellenic Windsurfing Association   WINDSURFING
(www.speedsslalom.gr) No offices in Athens, but can be reached via windsurfing spots around Athens, such as Loutsa.

Bathhouses

Al Hammam Baths   BATHHOUSE
(Map p78; 📞 211 012 9099; www.alhammam. gr; Tripodon 16 & Ragava 10, Plaka; 45min bath €25, bath-scrub combos from €35; ⊙ 11am-9pm; Ⓜ Acropolis) Like the other two Turkish-style baths in Athens, this one is a bit small, but it is beautifully decorated, in marble and tile and coloured chandeliers, to conjure an old-Ottoman atmosphere. Moreover, it's set in a nice old house in Plaka, so after your steam and skin scrub, you can have tea on the terrace and admire the Acropolis.

Polis Hammam   BATHHOUSE
(Map p78; 📞 210 321 2020; www.polis-hammam. gr; Avliton 6, Psyrri; 1½hr bath €20, bath-scrub combos from €27; ⊙ noon-11pm Mon-Fri, from 11am Sat & Sun; Ⓜ Thissio) The best value of Athens' three Turkish-style baths. There's also space for other treatments, such as Thai massage and cupping. The only complaint is the mood music. Look for it down a tiny alley, sharing with a theatre.

Hammam   SPA
(Map p84; 📞 210 323 1073; www.hammam.gr; Melidoni 1, cnr Agion Asomaton, Thisio; 1hr €25, bath-scrub combos from €45; ⊙ 12.30-10pm Mon-Fri, 10am-10pm Sat & Sun; Ⓜ Thissio) The marble-lined Turkish-style steam room here is small; the real attraction is the added scrubs and massages. Tuesday is women only.

Cycling & Skating

Cycle Greece   CYCLING
(📞 210 921 8160; www.cyclegreece.com; Aristotelous 13, Moschato) This excellent company, run by a husband–wife team, offers a great

---

BASKETBALL

'Basket' is one of Athens' most popular sports, with a number of men's and women's pro teams in Athens (Panathinaikos and AEK are the biggest) and Piraeus (Olympiacos). For schedules, see the website of the **Hellenic Basketball Federation** (EOK; www. basket.gr). Games are often at the 18,000-seat stadium at the **Athens Olympic Complex** (OAKA; 📞 210 683 4777; www.oaka.com.gr; Marousi; Ⓜ Irini).

range of trips, from day rides outside Athens, including a tour of Attica wineries, to multiday tours that combine biking and sailing. Very well-planned self-guided itineraries too.

Funky Rides   CYCLING
(Map p74; 📞 211 710 9366; www.funkyride.gr; Dimitrakopoulou 1, Koukaki; 3hr/day €7/15; Ⓜ Akropoli) Rents bikes near the Acropolis.

Solebike   CYCLING
(Map p74; 📞 210 921 5620; www.solebike.eu; Lembesi 11, Makrygianni; 2hr from €12; ⊙ 9am-5pm Mon-Sat Apr-Nov, 10am-4pm Mon-Sat Sep-Mar; Ⓜ Akropoli) Hires out electric bikes, and offers tours (from €39).

Latraac   SKATING
(Map p64; www.facebook.com/latraac; Leonidou 63-65, Keramikos; ⊙ skating noon-3pm & 5.30-10.30pm, cafe to 1am) **FREE** If you ever thought the problem with skateboarding was that there was nowhere to drink a coffee while you did it, the Greeks have solved this for you. A wooden skate bowl occupies one half of a city lot; picnic benches take up the other. The crowd skews adult and arty, but kids are welcome. Food is good too.

Outdoor Adventure

Alpin Club   ADVENTURE
(📞 210 675 3514; www.alpinclub.gr) For kayaking, rafting, canyoning and mountain biking – just to name a few. In Athens but operates out of Karitena in the Peloponnese.

Trekking Hellas   OUTDOORS
(📞 210 331 0323; www.trekking.gr; Gounari 96, Marousi) Array of activities tours ranging from Athens walking tours (€50) to caving, cycling, or trekking in the Peloponnese and the islands.

EOS

HIKING

(Greek Alpine Club; Map p78; 210 321 3255; www.eosathinon.gr; Lekka 23-25) The EOS runs weekly hiking trips outside the city (information only in Greek) and maintains trails on Mt Hymettos and around Attica. It's not really geared to tourists, but it is the place to ask for advice on longer trips and lesser-known trails.

Hellenic Skiing Federation

SKIING

(210 323 0182; www.eox.gr) Information about skiing in Greece.

Tours

Three main companies run almost identical air-conditioned city coach tours, as well as excursions to nearby sights: **CHAT** (Map p78; 210 323 0827; www.chatours.gr; Xenofontos 9, Syntagma; 5hr tour €68; Syntagma), **GO Tours** (Map p74; 210 921 9555; www.gotours.com.gr; Kallirrois 12, Makrygianni; Akropoli) and **Hop In Sightseeing** (Map p78; 210 428 5500; www.hopin.com; Leoforos Vasilissis Amalias 44, Makrygianni; 6.30am-10pm; Akropoli).

Tours include a half-day sightseeing tour of Athens (from €78), usually doing little more than pointing out all the major sights and stopping at the Acropolis. There are also half-day trips to Ancient Corinth (€62) and Cape Sounion (€49); day tours to Delphi (€93), the Corinth Canal, Mycenae, Naflio and Epidavros (€100); and **cruises** to Aegina, Poros and Hydra (including lunch €109). Hotels act as booking agents and often offer discounts.

CitySightseeing Athens

BUS

(Map p78; 210 921 4174; www.city-sightseeing.com; Plateia Syntagmatos, Syntagma; adult/child €20/8; every 30min 9am-9pm Apr-Oct, to 6.30pm Nov-Mar; Syntagma) Open-top double-decker buses cruise around town on a 90-minute circuit starting at Syntagma. With the basic ticket, you can get on and off at 15 stops in 24 hours; add on Piraeus and/or the beaches, and extend duration to 48 or 72 hours.

Athens Walking Tours

TOURS

(210 884 7269; www.athenswalkingtours.gr; Heyden 2, Viktoria; Viktoria) Runs a full range of guided tours around and outside the city, but especially notable for its cooking class (€77) in a Thisio taverna, which cuts no corners and even shows you how to roll out your own filo for *spanakopita* (spinach pie) and other pies.

Walking Tour
Central Athens

START PLATEIA SYNTAGMATOS
END MONASTIRAKI FLEA MARKET
LENGTH 3.5KM; TWO HOURS

Start in ① **Plateia Syntagmatos** (p83). The square has been a favourite place for protests ever since the rally that led to the granting of a constitution on 3 September 1843. In 1944 the first round of the civil war began here after police, under British direction, opened fire on a communist rally. In 1954 it was the location of the first demonstration demanding the *enosis* (union) of Cyprus with Greece.

The historic Hotel Grande Bretagne, the most illustrious of Athens' hotels, was built in 1862. During WWII, the Nazis made it their headquarters, and the British moved in after. Resistance fighters laid dynamite to blow up the building, but the operation was halted when Winston Churchill arrived unexpectedly; the fighters weren't willing to assassinate him.

On the north side of the square is a section of the ② **Peisistratos aqueduct**, unearthed during metro excavations.

Across the road, in front of ③ **Parliament**, the much-photographed *evzones* (presidential guards) stand sentinel at the Tomb of the Unknown Soldier. The changing of the guard takes place every hour.

Walk through the lush ④ **National Gardens** (p83) and exit to the Zappeio Palace, opened in 1888 in preparation for the first modern Olympic games in 1896, for which part was used as a fencing hall. Follow the road south, passing the playground. Turn left and walk until you see the crossing to the ⑤ **Panathenaic Stadium** (p92), the main site of the 1896 Olympic Games.

Walk back along the south edge of the gardens to the striking ⑥ **Temple of Olympian Zeus** (p75), the largest temple ever built. Teetering on the edge of the traffic alongside the temple is ⑦ **Hadrian's Arch** (p76), the ornate gateway erected to mark the boundary of Hadrian's Athens.

Cross Leoforos Vasilissis Amalias and head right towards Lysikratous, where you turn left into Plaka. Ahead on your right are the ruins of a Roman monument in the forecourt of the ⑧ **Church of Agia Ekaterini**.

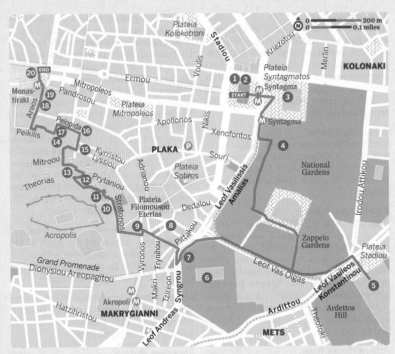

Ahead on the left is the ⑨ **Lysikrates Monument** (p83), built in 334 BC, the only remaining example of monuments that lined this street to the Theatre of Dionysos, site of dramatic contests. The monument commemorates one chorus's victory, with reliefs showing Dionysos battling the Tyrrhenian pirates, transformed into dolphins. It's the earliest-known monument using Corinthian capitals externally, a style imitated in many modern monuments.

Facing the monument, turn left and then right into Epimenidou. At the top of the steps, turn right into Stratonos, which skirts the Acropolis. Just ahead you'll see the ⑩ **Church of St George of the Rock**, which marks the entry to the ⑪ **Anafiotika quarter**. The picturesque maze of little white-washed houses is the legacy of stonemasons from the small Cycladic island of Anafi, who were brought in to build the king's palace after Independence. It's a peaceful spot, with brightly painted olive-oil cans brimming with flowers in the tiny gardens in summer.

Continue past the tiny ⑫ **Church of Agios Simeon**. The street looks like a dead end but persevere and you'll emerge at the Acropolis road. Turn right, then left into Prytaniou, veering right after 50m into Tholou. The yellow-ochre building at Tholou 5 is the ⑬ **old Athens University**, from 1837–41. Built by the Venetians, it was used by the Turks as public offices; it's now a history museum.

Continue down to the ruins of the ⑭ **Roman Agora** (p77). To the right of the Tower of the Winds on Kyrristou is the ⑮ **Bath House of the Winds** (p81), a historic (but nonfunctional) Turkish *hammam*. Meanwhile, the ⑯ **Museum of Greek Popular Instruments** (p80), on Diogenous, is filled with more than a thousand ways to make music. Turning on to Pelopida, you'll see on the right the gate of the 1721 Muslim Seminary, the only remains after the complex was destroyed in a fire in 1911. Ahead on the left, the 17th-century ⑰ **Fethiye Mosque** is on the site of the Agora.

Follow the road around the Agora to the ruins of ⑱ **Hadrian's Library** (p80). Next to them is the 1759 ⑲ **Mosque of Tzistarakis**, only very occasionally open as a ceramics museum; after Independence it lost its minaret and was used as a prison.

You're now in Monastiraki, the colourful, chaotic square teeming with street vendors. To the left is ⑳ **Monastiraki Flea Market** (p124).

Alternative Athens TOURS

(Map p78; ☑ 6951518589; www.alternative athens.com; Karaiskaki 28) As the name promises, this company offers tours with less-typical slants. There's a very good three-hour street-art tour (€40), and another visiting Athenian designers (€50), as well as an LGBTQ bar crawl, food tours and even day trips out of the city.

This Is My Athens TOURS

(http://myathens.thisisathens.org) **FREE** Excellent city-run program that pairs you with a volunteer local to show you around for two hours. You must book online 72 hours ahead.

Athens Adventures TOURS

(Map p74; ☑ 210 922 4044; www.athensadventures.gr; Veikou 3a, Makrygianni; walking tour €7; ☺ walking tour 10am Mon & Wed-Sat) Run by the team at Athens Backpackers, this group offers a very popular Athens walking tour, departing from **Athens Sports Bar** (Map p74; www.athenssportsbar.com; Veikou 3a, Makrygianni; ☺ 7.30am-late; Ⓜ Akropoli). In high season, it also runs day trips to Nafplio, Delphi and Sounio.

Athens Happy Train TOURS

(Map p78; ☑ 213 039 0888; www.athenshappytrain.com; Plateia Syntagmatos, Syntagma; adult/child €6/4; ☺ every 30min 9am-11pm Jun-Sep, to 9pm Oct-May; Ⓜ Syntagma) This little red train-on-wheels is a bit goofy, but at least it's more city-friendly than a massive double-decker tour bus. Stops include the Acropolis, Monastiraki and the Panathenaic Stadium. Tours take one hour nonstop, or you can get on and off over five hours. Trains leave from the top of Ermou every 30 minutes.

Athens Segway Tours TOURS

(Map p74; ☑ 210 322 2500; www.athenssegwaytours.com; Eschinou 9, Plaka; 2hr tour €59; Ⓜ Akropoli) Zip through town on a Segway.

🎉 Festivals & Events

Athens & Epidaurus Festival PERFORMING ARTS

(Hellenic Festival; ☑ 210 928 2900; www.greekfestival.gr; ☺ Jun-Aug) The ancient Theatre of Epidavros (p153) and Athens' Odeon of Herodes Atticus (p73) are the headline venues for Greece's annual cultural festival featuring a top line-up of local and international music, dance and theatre.

Major shows in its **Athens Festival** take place at the Odeon of Herodes Atticus (p73), one of the world's prime historic venues,

with the Acropolis as a backdrop. Events are also held in modern venues around town.

Its **Epidavros Festival** presents local and international productions of Ancient Greek drama at the famous ancient Theatre of Epidavros in the Peloponnese, two hours west of Athens, on Friday and Saturday nights in July and August. Check the festival website for special KTEL buses (p125) to Epidavros.

As box-office queues can be long and events often sell out, it's best to book tickets online, by phone, at the **box office** (Map p108; ☑ 210 327 2000; Stoa Pesmatzoglou, Panepistimiou 39, Panepistimio; ☺ 10am-4pm Mon-Fri, to 3pm Sat; Ⓜ Panepistimio), or at Public and Papasotiriou stores. Half-price student discounts (with ID) are available for most performances.

August Moon Festival PERFORMING ARTS

(☺ Aug) Every August on the night of the full moon, major historic sites such as the Acropolis and the Roman Agora are open all night and host musical performances.

Athens International Film Festival FILM

(☑ 210 606 1413; www.aiff.gr; ☺ Sep) Features retrospectives, premieres and international art films and documentaries.

Rockwave Festival MUSIC

(☑ 210 882 0426; www.rockwavefestival.gr; ☺ late May-Jul) Annual international rock show held at Terra Vibe, a parkland venue on the outskirts of Athens in Malakasa. Special buses from town. Sometimes cheap camping is offered.

Athens Pride PARADE

(www.athenspride.eu; ☺ early Jun) Athens Pride is an annual LGBTQ event, usually celebrated in early June, culminating in a parade that starts on Syntagma.

Athens Technopolis Jazz Festival MUSIC

(www.technopolisjazzfestival.com; ☺ late May-early Jun) Annual early-summer jazz festival at Technopolis (p121), the converted gasworks in Gazi, as well as at the Onassis Cultural Centre (p76).

🛏 Sleeping

Athens lodging covers the full range, from hostels to five stars, but can be a bit basic for the price, especially in the midrange. Non-smoking rules are often laxly enforced. For the best selection in July and August, book several months ahead.

Boutique Athens (☑ 6985083556; www.boutiqueathens.com; 1-/2-/4-bedroom apt from

IMMIGRANT ATHENS

Starting in the early 1990s, Greece saw an influx of immigrants, at least 600,000 people in a decade, most of whom came to Athens: migrant agricultural labourers from Punjab, domestic help from the Philippines, Albanians fleeing the postcommunist collapse, asylum seekers from all over. And since 2015, the city has been actively working to absorb another estimated 100,000 refugees from Syria, Afghanistan, Congo and other countries, from the sudden influx of people on boats from Turkey.

City government has embraced the change, stating that immigration is not a problem but an opportunity for growth. And indeed, it has reinvigorated previously tired neighbourhoods and brought new businesses – and foods. In the centre, **Psyrri**, just south of Omonia, has a few blocks of Pakistani and Bangladeshi businesses, established in the 1990s.

Newer arrivals have enlivened the squat scene in **Exarhia** – **Steki Metanaston** (Map p64; www.facebook.com/stekimetanaston; Tsamadou 13a, Exarhia; ⊗ late morning–midnight; Ⓜ Polytehnion) is a great social centre – as well as the **Viktoria** neighbourhood, where **Victoria Square Project** (www.facebook.com/victoriasquareproject; Elpidos 13, Viktoria; ⊗ 9am-4pm Mon-Sat; Ⓜ Victoria) FREE is a good place to start exploring. Also don't miss **Enjoy Just Falafel** (p106) nearby. Further north, the blocks around **Plateia Amerikis** have attracted immigrants from West Africa and Eritrea.

€80/140/430; ✳ 🛜) rents renovated spacious apartments and whole houses all over town.

🛏 Akropoli, Makrygianni & Koukaki

★ Athens Backpackers HOSTEL €
(Map p74; ☎ 210 922 4044; www.backpackers.gr; Makri 12, Makrygianni; dm incl breakfast €27-30; ✳ @ 🛜; Ⓜ Akropoli) The popular rooftop bar with cheap drinks and Acropolis views is a major draw at this modern and friendly Australian-run backpacker favourite. There's a barbecue in the courtyard, a well-stocked kitchen and a busy social scene. Spotless dorms with private bathrooms and lockers have bedding, but towel use costs €2. Management also runs well-priced Athens Studios (p98), with modern apartments nearby.

Marble House Pension PENSION €
(☎ 210 923 4058; www.marblehouse.gr; Zini 35a, Koukaki; d/tr €49/59, d/tr/q with shared bathroom €45/50/69; ✳ @ 🛜; Ⓜ Sygrou-Fix) In a quiet cul-de-sac is one of Athens's best-value budget hotels. Rooms have been artfully updated, with wrought-iron beds, and bathrooms are sleek marble. All rooms have fridge and ceiling fan and some have air-con (€9 extra). It's a fair walk from the tourist drag, but close to the metro. Breakfast available (€5).

Art Gallery Hotel PENSION €
(Map p74; ☎ 210 923 1933; www.artgallery hotel.gr; Erehthiou 5, Koukaki; s/d/tr/q from €70/75/100/120; ✳ 🛜; Ⓜ Sygrou-Fix) This family-run place is an ideal combo: close to

tourist zones, but set on a pretty residential block, so you feel you're in a home, inside and out. Some rooms are a bit small and can show their age, but the upstairs balcony is a fine breakfast spot. The cheapest rooms have bathrooms across the hall (private, though, not shared).

★ Hera Hotel BOUTIQUE HOTEL €€
(Map p74; ☎ 210 923 6682; www.herahotel.gr; Falirou 9, Makrygianni; d incl breakfast €160-190, ste €250; ✳ @ 🛜; Ⓜ Akropoli) Behind its elegant neoclassical facade, this boutique hotel was totally rebuilt. But the formal interior design stays true to exterior style, with lots of brass and dark wood. It's a short walk to the Acropolis and Plaka, and the rooftop Peacock restaurant and bar have fine views and good service. North-side rooms, away from an adjacent music bar, are preferable.

★ Herodion HOTEL €€
(Map p74; ☎ 210 923 6832; www.herodion.gr; Rovertou Galli 4, Makrygianni; d incl breakfast from €165; ✳ @ 🛜; Ⓜ Akropoli) This smart four-star hotel is geared towards the well-heeled traveller and business travellers. Rooms are small but decked out with all the trimmings and have supercomfortable beds. The rooftop spa and lounge have unbeatable Acropolis and museum views.

Philippos Hotel HOTEL €€
(Map p74; ☎ 210 922 3611; www.philipposhotel. com; Mitseon 3, Makrygianni; d incl breakfast from €145; ✳ @ 🛜; Ⓜ Akropoli) A popular favourite, under the same ownership as the larger

Herodion nearby, Philippos offers small, well-appointed rooms near the Acropolis. The double on the roof has a private terrace.

Athens Studios
APARTMENT €€

(Map p74; ☑ 210 923 5811; www.athensstudios. gr; Veïkou 3a, Makrygianni; apt incl breakfast €105; @ 🛜; M Akropoli) Run by the folk from Athens Backpackers (p97), these relaxed apartments are spacious, with kitchenettes, colourful bathrooms and a lounge area with shared balcony (top-floor balconies are largest). The bedroom has either two beds or four bunks, making it a well-priced alternative to dormitory living. Another perk: a laundry on the ground floor.

Athens Was
BOUTIQUE HOTEL €€€

(Map p74; ☑ 210 924 9954; www.athenswas.gr; Dionysiou Areopagitou 31-39, Makrygianni; d €198-365, ste from €350; ✲ @ 🛜; M Akropoli) The location, a three-minute walk to the Acropolis gate, couldn't be better. Staff is friendly, adding a warm touch to the minimalist decor, and standard rooms have big balconies overlooking the pedestrian street. Korres amenities are another plus. Breakfast is excellent and the terrace has a magnificent view. Suites on the 5th and 6th floors also have Acropolis views.

Athens Gate
BUSINESS HOTEL €€€

(Map p74; ☑ 210 923 8302; www.athensgate.gr; Leoforos Syngrou Andrea 10, Makrygianni; d incl breakfast €205-280; ✲ @ 🛜; M Akropoli) With stunning views over the Temple of Olympian Zeus from the spacious front rooms, and a central (if busy) location, this old reliable hotel was improved with a 2007 renovation. The chic, stylish rooms are immaculate and have all the mod cons; staff are friendly and breakfast is served on the superb rooftop terrace with 360-degree Athens views.

🛏 Syntagma, Plaka & Monastiraki

Phaedra
HOTEL €

(Map p78; ☑ 210 323 8461; www.hotelphaedra. com; Herefontos 16, Plaka; s/d/tr from €60/80/90; ✲ @ 🛜; M Akropoli) All the rooms at this small, family-run hotel have balconies overlooking a church or the Acropolis. The rooms are basic and range from small to snug; a few have private bathrooms across the hall.

Morning trash collection on the corner can be a bit noisy, but given the rooftop terrace, the friendly staff and the unbeatable location, it's still one of the better deals in Plaka.

Cecil
HOTEL €

(Map p108; ☑ 210 321 7079; www.cecilhotel.gr; Athinas 39, Monastiraki; s/d/tr/q incl breakfast from €60/75/120/155; ✲ @ 🛜; M Monastiraki) This charming old hotel on busy Athinas has beautiful high, moulded ceilings, polished timber floors and an original cage-style lift. The simple rooms are tastefully furnished, but don't have fridges. Two connecting rooms with a shared bathroom are ideal for families.

Tony
APARTMENT €

(Map p64; ☑ 210 923 0561; www.hoteltony.gr; Zaharitsa 26, Koukaki; studios €65-130; ✲ @ 🛜; M Sygrou-Fix) After a total renovation in 2015, Hotel Tony offers spacious, clean and modern studios, all with kitchenette. Great for groups as, for instance, the 'superior family room' has three balconies. Bathrooms boast walk-in showers and sleek tiles all around. It's about 1km southwest of the Acropolis. The only small shame is the treeless block, but Filopappou is just uphill.

Tempi Hotel
HOTEL €

(Map p78; ☑ 210 321 3175; www.tempihotel.gr; Eolou 29, Monastiraki; d/tr €59/72, s/d with shared bathroom €39/52; ✲ 🛜; M Monastiraki) Location and affordability are the strengths of this older, family-run place on pedestrian Eolou. Front balconies overlook Plateia Agia Irini, the scene of some of Athens' best nightlife; side views get the Acropolis. Basic rooms have satellite TV, but bathrooms are primitive. Top-floor rooms are small and quite a hike. There is a communal kitchen.

InnAthens
BOUTIQUE HOTEL €€

(Map p78; ☑ 210 325 8555; www.innathens.com; Souri 3, Syntagma; d incl breakfast €165; ✲ @ 🛜; M Syntagma) This 22-room hotel is minutes from Syntagma, but you'd never know it once you're inside its cocoon, down the end of a shopping arcade. All rooms look down on to a pretty interior courtyard, and the restfulness is reinforced with soothing grey-and-white decor and excellent Coco-Mat beds.

Sweet Home Hotel
BOUTIQUE HOTEL €€

(Map p78; ☑ 210 322 9029; www.sweethome hotel.com; Patroou 5, Plaka; s/d incl breakfast from €140/150; ✲ @ 🛜; M Syntagma) Just a stone's throw from all the major Athens sights, this 15-room place in a converted old mansion has cosy, well-appointed rooms that are a good mix of old (wood floors, chandeliers) and new (sleek, if tiny, bathrooms). The attic room has a nice wood ceiling, and an Acropolis view if you stretch.

Central Hotel
BUSINESS HOTEL €€

(Map p78; ☎ 210 323 4357; www.centralhotel. gr; Apollonos 21, Plaka; d/tr incl breakfast from €135/160; ✸@🖥; MSyntagma) This low-key stylish hotel has comfortable rooms done in light, contemporary tones, with good bathrooms. The roof terrace has the requisite Acropolis view (as do some rooms), plus a small spa and sunloungers. As its name suggests, Central Hotel is in a great location between Syntagma and Plaka. The cheapest rooms (from €111) look on to an air shaft.

Adonis
HOTEL €€

(Map p78; ☎ 210 324 9737; www.hotel-adonis.gr; 3 Kodrou St, Plaka; s/d/tr incl breakfast €75/95/105; ✸@🖥; MSyntagma) This comfortable pension on a quiet pedestrian street in Plaka has basic, clean rooms with TV. Bathrooms are small but have been excellently renovated. Take in great Acropolis views from 4th-floor rooms and the rooftop terrace (where breakfast is served). No credit cards.

Hermes
HOTEL €€

(Map p78; ☎ 210 323 5514; www.hermeshotel. gr; Apollonos 19, Plaka; s/d/q incl breakfast €104/150/251; ✸@🖥; MSyntagma) Hermes offers modern amenities with snug but comfortable rooms, including two interconnecting rooms for families. No real Acropolis views, but sister hotel Plaka has them, and guests are welcome to visit the rooftop bar there.

Plaka Hotel
HOTEL €€

(Map p78; ☎ 210 322 2096; www.plakahotel.gr; Kapnikareas 7, cnr Mitropoleos, Monastiraki; d incl breakfast from €181; ✸🖥; MMonastiraki) It's hard to beat the Acropolis views from the rooftop garden, as well as those from top-floor rooms. Tidy rooms have light timber floors and furniture, and satellite TV, though bathrooms are on the small side. Though called the Plaka, it's actually closer to Monastiraki.

Adrian Hotel
HOTEL €€

(Map p78; ☎ 210 322 1553; www.douros-hotels. com; Adrianou 74, Plaka; s/d/tr incl breakfast from €120/145/160; ✸@🖥; MMonastiraki) This tiny hotel right in the heart of Plaka serves breakfast on a lovely shady terrace with Acropolis views. The well-equipped rooms are pleasant, if a bit worn. Third-floor rooms are the best, with large balconies overlooking the square.

Acropolis House Pension
PENSION €€

(Map p78; ☎ 210 322 2344; www.acropolis house.gr; Kodrou 6-8, Plaka; d/tr/q incl breakfast from €89/119/149; ✸🖥; MSyntagma) This family-run pension is in a beautifully preserved, 19th-century house, which retains many original features and has lovely painted walls. There are discounts for stays of three days or more. The cheapest rooms (from €83) have private bathrooms across the hall. Avoid the street level, due to noise.

★Grande Bretagne
LUXURY HOTEL €€€

(Map p78; ☎ 210 333 0000; www.grande bretagne.gr; Vasileos Georgiou I 1, Syntagma; r/ ste from €400/700; P✸@🖥⊠; MSyntagma) If you aspire to the best, *the* place to stay in Athens is – and always has been – the Grande Bretagne, right on Syntagma Sq. Built in 1862 to accommodate visiting heads of state, it ranks among the grandest hotels in the world. Though renovated some years ago, it still retains its old-world grandeur.

There is a divine spa, and the rooftop restaurant and bar are worth a visit, even if you aren't a guest.

★Electra Palace
LUXURY HOTEL €€€

(Map p78; ☎ 210 337 0000; www.electrahotels.gr; Navarhou Nikodimou 18, Plaka; d/ste incl breakfast from €270/375; P✸@🖥⊠; MSyntagma) Plaka's smartest hotel is one for the romantics – have breakfast under the Acropolis on your balcony (in higher-end rooms) and dinner in the chic rooftop restaurant. Completely refurbished with classic elegance, the well-appointed rooms are buffered from the sounds of the city streets. There's a gym and an indoor swimming pool, as well as a rooftop pool with Acropolis views.

★NEW Hotel
DESIGN HOTEL €€€

(Map p78; ☎ 210 327 3000; www.yeshotels.gr; Filellinon 16, Plaka; d from €218; P✸@🖥; MSyntagma) Brazilian designers, the Campana designers, melded their signature scraps-to-art style with Greek-folk touches and old Athens photos, creating a space that's full of fun eye candy. More practically, the rooms are cushy (lots of pillow options) and there's a good roof lounge. Location is prime but loud; upper floors are better.

A for Athens
HOTEL €€€

(Map p78; ☎ 210 324 4244; www.aforathens.com; Miaouli 2, Monastiraki; d from €213; ✸🖥; MMonastiraki) Modern and simple, A for Athens is a good, central base – and its location just across from the Monastiraki metro makes it a straight shot from the airport. The rooftop **cafe-bar** is grand, with sweeping 360-degree views that take in the Acropolis (as do some of the rooms). But it can get a bit rowdy on weekends.

360 Degrees HOTEL €€€
(Map p78; ☎210 324 0034; www.360hotelathens.com; Plateia Monastirakiou, Monastiraki; d incl breakfast €190; ❄📶; Ⓜ Monastiraki) The raison d'etre of this hotel is in its name: the super roof restaurant gives a view around the whole city. The rooms are basic, with a light sprinkling of hipster-rustic wood and Edison light bulbs. The location on Monastiraki Sq is handy (especially for the metro from the airport), but potentially noisy. Request an upper floor, away from the square.

Thisio

Phidias Hotel HOTEL €€
(Map p84; ☎210 345 9511; www.phidias.gr; Apostolou Pavlou 39, Thisio; s/d/tr incl breakfast from €170/180/190; ❄📶; Ⓜ Thissio) Midway along Thisio's grand pedestrianised promenade, this hotel is in a lovely location. A 2016 makeover to the rooms boosted prices substantially, but you can still find substantially better deals online. The cheapest rooms (single/double €105/115) have only windows on an air shaft – not as grim as it sounds, and cool in summer.

Psyrri, Omonia & Exarhia

★ **City Circus** HOSTEL €
(Map p108; ☎213 023 7244; www.citycircus.gr; Sarri 16, Psyrri; dm incl breakfast €27-31.50, s/d from €47.50/95; ❄@📶; Ⓜ Thissio, Monastiraki) It's not the cheapest hostel going, but with its jaunty style and helpful staff, City Circus does lift the spirit more than most ultrabudget lodgings. Its bright, well-designed rooms have modern bathrooms; some have kitchens. Book at its website for free (and good) breakfast.

★ **Athens Quinta Hostel** HOSTEL €
(Map p64; ☎213 030 5322; www.facebook.com/athensquinta; Methonis 13, Exarhia; dm €25; 📶; Ⓜ Panepistimio) Set in an old mansion, complete with velvet sofas and patterned tile floors, this friendly place is pleasantly homey and a nice change from slicker, busier hostels. There's a nice backyard for lounging. The location in cool Exarhia is a plus for neighbourhood vibe, but it is far from the main sights.

Evripides HOTEL €
(Map p108; ☎210 321 2301; www.evripideshotel.gr; Evripidou 79, Psyrri; s/d incl breakfast €65/75; ❄@📶; Ⓜ Monastiraki, Omonia, Thissio) Excellent and clean 62-room budget hotel on a somewhat divey block. Most rooms have a little balcony, and all have minifridges, handy for longer stays. Book early, and you might score a room with an Acropolis view and bigger balcony, for only a tiny bit more. Failing that, everyone can enjoy the view from the rooftop breakfast terrace and bar.

Exarchion HOTEL €
(Map p108; ☎210 380 0731; www.exarchion.com; Themistokleous 55, Exarhia; s/d/q incl breakfast from €45/58/90; ❄@📶; Ⓜ Omonia) What this 1960s high-rise hotel lacks in character, the surrounding neighbourhood of Exarhia makes up for. Rooms are clean and comfortable, and some have balconies. There's a rooftop cafe-bar, though most guests will head straight out to the action of Plateia Exarhia out front, and the numerous nearby dining and entertainment options.

Fresh Hotel BOUTIQUE HOTEL €€
(Map p108; ☎210 524 8511; www.freshhotel.gr; Sofokleous 26, cnr Klisthenous, Omonia; s/d/ste incl breakfast from €160/180/310; ❄📶; Ⓜ Omonia) A hip hotel in the gritty south-of-Omonia area, this is a cool place so long as you're happy to ignore the working girls in the streets outside. Expect chic design and brightly coloured rooms plus a fantastic Acropolis-view rooftop with pool, bar and restaurant. Front rooms have balconies, but if you need quiet, go for the back.

Attalos HOTEL €€
(Map p108; ☎210 321 2801; www.attaloshotel.com; Athinas 29, Psyrri; s/d/tr/q from €81/91/113/179; ❄@📶; Ⓜ Monastiraki) Decor can be an odd mix of antique and late-'90s-chain-hotel, but nonetheless this 78-room place is comfortable, clean and central. Its best feature remains the rooftop bar with wonderful views of the Acropolis. Rooms at the back have balconies with Acropolis views.

Ochre & Brown BOUTIQUE HOTEL €€€
(Map p108; ☎210 331 2940; www.oandbhotel.com; Leokoriou 7, Psyrri; d/ste from €196/330; ❄📶; Ⓜ Thissio) As the name promises, this boutique hotel is all about the earth tones, with

subdued, somewhat small rooms. They are quiet, however, and the style is not painfully trendy. Very friendly staff. A bit overpriced at the standard rate, but potentially excellent value if you score a deal on the website.

Kolonaki

Periscope BOUTIQUE HOTEL €€
(Map p102; ☎ 210 729 7200; www.yeshotels.gr; Haritos 22, Kolonaki; s/d from €149/168; ❄ �﹖; Ⓜ Evangelismos) On a small street lined with tiny, creative boutiques, this sleek, grey-tone hotel is the essence of new Kolonaki. Clever gadgets are sprinkled throughout, including the lobby slide show and aerial shots of the city on the ceilings. Korres toiletries and the trendy **Pbox** restaurant add to the vibe. The penthouse's private rooftop spa has sensational views.

Coco-Mat BOUTIQUE HOTEL €€€
(Map p102; ☎ 210 723 0000; www.cocomat athens.com; Patriarhou Ioakeim 36, Kolonaki; d incl breakfast from €195; ❄ ❄ ﹖ ﹖; Ⓜ Evangelismos) A literal boutique hotel, this place adjoins the showroom for Coco-Mat beds, the excellent Greece-made all-natural mattresses. Tiny 'Sleep Tight' (appropriate!) rooms are suitable only for solo travellers; 'Urban' rooms have little balconies. There's a nice honour bar and good breakfast. Overall, rooms are small for the price – but, oh, those beds!

St George Lycabettus BOUTIQUE HOTEL €€€
(Map p102; ☎ 210 741 6000; www.sglycabettus. gr; Kleomenous 2, Kolonaki; s/d from €157/201; ❄ @ ﹖ ﹖; Ⓜ Evangelismos, Syntagma) A high-end clientele bunks here for excellent service and posh, if a bit staid, rooms. Newer 'eco-chic' rooms have organic bedding and comfy Coco-Mat beds. Up the hill in Kolonaki, it's a bit remote, but this pays off in views of the city and a good price for a pool. Plenty of promo rates online.

Eating

Eating, drinking and talking is the main entertainment for Athenians. The vibrant restaurant scene is marked by a delightful culture of casual, convivial al fresco dining. Many nouveau-Greek restaurants have real substance while neighbourhood tavernas have become less reliable, with quality sometimes compromised to keep prices low. *Ouzeries* and *mezedhopoleia,* serving small plates with drinks, are popular for those with limited budgets.

Reservations are essential on weekends for higher-end restaurants; book through E-table (www.e-table.gr).

Akropoli, Makrygianni & Koukai

Fresko Yogurt Bar DESSERTS €
(Map p74; ☎ 210 923 3760; www.freskoyogurt bar.gr; Dionysiou Areopagitou 3, Makrygianni; yoghurt from €2.20; ⊙ 9am-9pm; Ⓜ Akropoli) Delicious Greek yoghurt is the base of all things here. Either fresh or in smoothie form, you can pair it with any number of toppings, from chocolate to black-cherry spoon sweets. A perfect cool-off after seeing the Acropolis.

★ **Mani Mani** GREEK €€
(Map p74; ☎ 210 921 8180; www.manimani.com.gr/ english.html; Falirou 10, Makrygianni; mains €15-20; ⊙ 2-11pm Mon-Sat, 1-6pm Sun; Ⓜ Akropoli) Head upstairs to the relaxing, cheerful dining rooms of this delightful modern restaurant, which specialises in herb-filled cuisine from the Mani region in the Peloponnese. Standouts include the ravioli with Swiss chard and the tangy sausage with orange. Good for a late lunch, as before 6pm weekdays dishes can be ordered as half portions, allowing you to sample widely.

★ **Strofi** GREEK €€
(Map p74; ☎ 210 921 4130; www.strofi.gr; Rovertou Galli 25, Makrygianni; mains €11-15; ⊙ noon-1am; Ⓜ Akropoli) Book ahead for a Parthenon view from the rooftop of this exquisitely renovated townhouse. Food is simple grilled meats and fish, but the setting, with elegant white linen and sweet service, elevates the experience to romantic levels.

Lebanese Chef SYRIAN €€
(☎ 211 184 4606; Syngrou 184, Kallithea; mains €8-15; ⊙ 12.30pm-1am; ☐ 10 to Sostis) The location on unscenic Sygrou is misleading, and so is the name: inside it's all warmth and hospitality, and excellent food by a recently arrived Syrian-refugee chef.

Fabrika tou Efrosinou GREEK €€
(Zini 34, Koukaki; mains €8-17; ⊙ 1.30-11pm Tue-Thu, to midnight Fri & Sat, 1-10pm Sun; Ⓜ Sygrou-Fix, ☐ Fix) Named for the patron saint of cooks, this 'factory' is really a homey-feeling bilevel restaurant focusing on good ingredients and rarer Greek recipes. Service can

Kolonaki

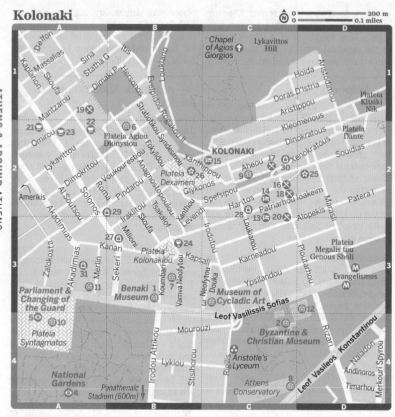

be a little patchy (all those stairs), but when everything is swinging, it's the perfect combination of bountiful, healthy food, excellent wine (a co-owner is a winemaker) and great atmosphere. Book ahead on weekends.

Aglio, Olio & Peperoncino ITALIAN €€
(Map p74; ☑ 210 921 1801; Porinou 13, Makrygianni; mains €15-25; ☺ 8pm-12.45am Tue-Sat, 2-6.45pm Sun; Ⓜ Akropoli) The food at this cosy Italian trattoria is simple pastas and the like, satisfying and reasonably priced. It's enhanced by the satisfaction of evading all the restaurant touts facing the nearby Acropolis Museum and finding this place on a quiet side street.

Hytra MEDITERRANEAN €€€
(☑ 210 331 6767, 217 707 1118; www.hytra.gr; Syngrou 107-109, Onassis Cultural Centre; mains €27-32, 8-course tasting menu €59; ☺ 8pm-midnight Mon, Tue & Sun, to 1am Fri & Sat; ☐ 10, 550 to Panteio, Ⓜ Sygrou-Fix, ☐ Kassomouli) Head to

Hytra at the Onassis Cultural Centre (p76) for exquisitely presented Greek food with a modern twist. Though portions are small, flavours are large, which is how it earned its Michelin star. In summer, the restaurant moves to the 7th floor, for amazing Acropolis views.

✕ Syntagma, Plaka & Monastiraki

★ Avocado VEGETARIAN €
(Map p78; ☑ 210 323 7878; www.avocadoathens. com; Nikis 30, Plaka; mains €8-13; ☺ noon-11pm Mon-Fri, 11am-11pm Sat, noon-7pm Sun; 🛜 ✎; Ⓜ Syntagma) This excellent, popular cafe offers a full array of vegan, gluten-free and organic treats – a rarity in Greece. Next to an organic market, and with a tiny front patio, you can enjoy everything from sandwiches to quinoa with eggplant or mixed-veg coconut

Kolonaki

curry. Fresh juices and mango lassis are all made on the spot.

★**Kalderimi**　　　　　　　　TAVERNA €
(Map p108; ☑ 210 331 0049; Plateia Agion Theodoron, cnr Skouleniou, Monastiraki; mains €5-8; ⏰ 11am-7pm Tue-Sat; ☎; Ⓜ Panepistimio) Look behind the Church of Agii Theodori for this open-air taverna offering Greek food at its most authentic. Everything is freshly cooked and delicious: you can't go wrong. Hand-painted tables edge a pedestrian street, for a feeling of peace in one of the busiest parts of the city. (It helps that it closes just before nearby bars get rolling.)

Thanasis　　　　　　　　　　KEBAB €
(Map p78; ☑ 210 324 4705; Mitropoleos 69, Monastiraki; gyros €2.50; ⏰ 8.30am-2.30am; Ⓜ Monastiraki) In the heart of Athens' souvlaki hub, just off Plateia Monastiraki, Thanasis is a good place to settle in and watch the street parade. It's known for its kebabs on pitta with grilled tomato and onions.

Cremino　　　　　　　　　ICE CREAM €
(Map p78; Nikis 50a, Plaka; scoops €1.50; ⏰ 11am-11pm, to midnight Sat Jun-Aug, reduced hours Sep-May; Ⓜ Syntagma, Akropoli) The lovely proprietress at Cremino makes all the ice cream from scratch, using cow and buffalo milk and popular Greek recipes.

★**Tzitzikas kai Mermigas**　　MEZEDHES €
(Map p78; ☑ 210 324 7607; www.tzitzikasmermi gas.gr; Mitropoleos 12-14, Syntagma; mezedhes €6-12; ⏰ noon-11pm; Ⓜ Syntagma) Greek merchandise lines the walls of this cheery, modern *mezedhopoleio* that sits smack in the middle of central Athens. It serves a tasty range of delicious and creative mezedhes (appetisers), such as honey-drizzled, bacon-wrapped Naxos cheese, to a bustling crowd of locals and tourists.

Meatropoleos 3　　　　　　　GREEK €
(Map p78; ☑ 210 324 1805; www.meatropoleos3. com; Mitropoleos 3, Syntagma; mains €6-12, souvlaki €1.50; ⏰ noon-midnight; Ⓜ Syntagma) A blessing amid the multistorey fast-food joints on Syntagma, this sleek little restaurant does a great array of grilled meats, including good housemade sausage and a hefty burger, as well as the usual souvlaki to offset a night on the town. You'll also find good salads, seasonal pies and other Greek staples.

Palia Athina　　　　　　　　TAVERNA €
(Map p78; ☑ 210 324 5777; www.paliaathina.gr; Nikis 46, Syntagma; mains €6-12; ⏰ noon-midnight; Ⓜ Syntagma) No muss, no fuss, no music or show: just a quiet little family-run taverna with excellent prices, especially for the area. The stews and casseroles are solid; if you can't read the menu, you can go to the kitchen and

point. Also does delivery or takeaway, if you're too tired to leave the hotel room.

Mikro Politiko   FAST FOOD €
(Map p74; ☑ 210 321 7879; Dionysiou Areopagitou 8, Makrygianni; souvlaki €1.70; ⊙ 11am-midnight; Ⓜ Akropoli) Just the thing to stave off post-Acropolis collapse: a quick souvlaki or falafel from this little takeout place. It's markedly better than other snack options in the area, with fresh ingredients and good salads too. Nowhere to sit, but the sweet staff can pack food to go. Order inside at the cash register.

Lukumades   SWEETS €
(Map p78; ☑ 210 321 0880; Eolou 21, Monastiraki; portion €2.70; ⊙ 8am-1am, to 3am Fri & Sat; Ⓜ Monastiraki) What's not to love about fried dough? *Loukoumadhes* (from Arabic *lu'mat al-qadi,* 'the judge's morsel') are served here as crunchy round balls, doused either in traditional honey and cinnamon or with all manner of 'modern' innovations, such as chocolate, fruit or ice cream. You can even get them filled, for maximum morseliciousness. Open late, to bar-goers' delight.

Le Greche   ICE CREAM €
(Map p78; ☑ 216 700 6458; Mitropoleos 16, Syntagma; ice cream from €2.50; ⊙ 8.30am-1am Mon-Thu, 8.30am-2am Fri, 10am-2am Sat, 10am-midnight Sun; Ⓜ Syntagma) Gem of a gelato shop, with espresso and little cakes as well. Gelato flavours mix traditional (intense, not-too-sweet pistachio) and novel (bergamot peel and Aperol).

Kallipateira   MEZEDHES €
(Map p108; ☑ 210 321 4152; www.kallipateira.gr; Astingos 8, Monastiraki; dishes €4-10; ⊙ lunch & dinner; Ⓜ Monastiraki) In a neoclassical building overlooking an archaeological dig, this restaurant is a good stop for mezedhes and carafes of ouzo – and live *rembetika* (Greek blues music) Saturday and Sunday afternoons starting at 2.30pm. Daily specials are a very good deal.

Kuzina   GREEK €€
(Map p64; ☑ 210 324 0133; www.kuzina.gr; Adrianou 9, Monastiraki; mains €12-25, set menu €20; ⊙ 11am-late; Ⓜ Thissio) This comfortably elegant restaurant does upscale Greek, with novel creations and rarer traditional dishes such as Cretan pappardelle or chicken with figs and sesame. It's cosy in winter, as light streams in, warming the crowded tables. In summer, book ahead for a rooftop-terrace

table. A fine second choice is an outside table on the pedestrian street.

Manas Kouzina-Kouzina   GREEK €€
(Map p78; ☑ 210 325 2335; www.manaskouzina kouzina.gr; Aiolou 27a, Monastiraki; mains from €10; ⊙ 8am-midnight; Ⓜ Monastiraki) 'Mother's kitchen' brings the slow-cooked, traditional Greek recipes called *magirefta* to the forefront. Incorporating locally sourced ingredients, lunch is a cafeteria-style selection of dishes from around the country. In the evening, the selection is à la carte, always seasonal and featuring some interesting rarer dishes.

Café Avyssinia   MEZEDHES €€
(Map p78; ☑ 210 321 7047; Kynetou 7, Monastiraki; mains €10-16; ⊙ 11am-1am Tue-Sat, to 7pm Sun; Ⓜ Monastiraki) This antiques-bedecked place on Plateia Avyssinias, in the middle of the flea market, has been legendary since the 1980s for its boisterous live music and varied mezedhes. But on a slow day, it can feel a bit stuffy. Either take a midday break from the market, or go late on a weekend night. In summer, snag fantastic Acropolis views upstairs.

Black Duck Garden   CAFE €€
(Map p108; ☑ 210 325 2396; www.blackduck garden.gr; Paparigopoulou 5-7, Plateia Klafthmonos; mains from €10; ⊙ 10am-1am; Ⓜ Panepistimio) The cafe at the Museum of the City of Athens (Map p108; ☑ 210 323 1397; www.athens citymuseum.gr; Paparigopoulou 7, Syntagma; adult/child €5/3; ⊙ 9am-4pm Mon & Wed-Fri, 10am-3pm Sat & Sun; Ⓜ Panepistimio) occupies a lovely courtyard of potted plants, marble sculptures and shady trees. By day a full menu of brunch, Greek specialities, coffee and dessert is served. It's also an evening retreat for dinner or cocktails among the romantically lit greenery, often with live jazz.

Palia Taverna tou Psara   TAVERNA €€
(Map p78; ☑ 210 321 8734; www.psaras-taverna. gr; Erechtheos 16, Plaka; mains €12-24; ⊙ 11am-12.30am Wed-Mon; Ⓜ Akropoli) Away from the main hustle of Plaka, this taverna is a cut above the rest and fills tables cascading across the street. It's known as the best seafood taverna in Plaka (fish €65 per kilogram).

School Pizza Bar   ITALIAN €€
(Map p78; ☑ 210 325 1444; Plateia Agia Irini 8, Monastiraki; pizzas from €10; ⊙ 9am-4am; Ⓜ Monastiraki) Settle into a desk like the old days, and check out the chalkboard. This time

round though, school is a party. Topping options for the thin-crust pizzas include good Greek products, such as cured pork from Crete. At night, it's the choice hang-out near trendy Plateia Agia Irini for excellent drinks and cocktails and lounge music by top local DJs.

Gazi, Keramikos & Thisio

To Steki tou Ilia   TAVERNA €
(Map p84; 210 345 8052; Eptahalkou 5, Thisio; chops per portion/kg €9/30; noon-late; Thisio) It's worth joining the line to dine at this *psistaria* (restaurant serving grilled food) that's famous for its grilled lamb and pork chops. In summer, the operation moves across the street into a hidden garden over the train tracks. It's a no-frills place with barrel wine and simple dips, chips and salads.

Elvis   GREEK €
(Map p84; 210 345 5836; Plataion 29, Keramikos; skewers €1.50; noon-3am, to 5am Fri & Sat; Keramikos or Thissio) This souvlaki joint is mobbed, and not just because the counter staff slide you a shot of booze while you're waiting. The meat quality is high, the prices are right and the music is great. Souvlaki comes with good chewy bread (NYC-style; an owner is from Queens). A branch in Pangrati, next to Chelsea Hotel (p116), applies the same winning formula.

Kanella   TAVERNA €
(Map p84; 210 347 6320; www.kanellagazi.gr; Leoforos Konstantinoupoleos 70, Gazi; dishes €7-11; 1.30pm-late; Keramikos) Housemade village-style bread, mismatched retro crockery and brown-paper tablecloths set the tone for this modern taverna serving regional Greek cuisine. Friendly staff serve daily specials such as lemon lamb with potatoes, and an excellent zucchini and avocado salad.

Gevomai Kai Magevomai   TAVERNA €
(Map p84; 210 345 2802; Nileos 11, Thisio; mains €6-14; lunch & dinner; ; Thissio) Stroll off the pedestrian way to find this small corner taverna with marble-topped tables. Neighbourhood denizens know it as one of the best for home-cooked, simple food with the freshest ingredients. Menu changes constantly.

Skoufias   TAVERNA €
(Map p84; 210 341 2252; Vasiliou tou Megalou 50, Rouf; mains €5-9; 9pm-late Oct-May; Kerameikos) This gem of a winter-only taverna

near the railway line is off the beaten track but worth seeking out. The menu has Cretan influences and an eclectic selection of regional Greek cuisine, including dishes you won't find in any tourist joint, from superb rooster with ouzo to lamb *tsigariasto* (braised) with *horta* (wild greens) and potato salad with orange.

★Athiri   GREEK €€
(Map p84; 210 346 2983; www.athirirestaurant.gr; Plateon 15, Keramikos; mains €14-19; 8pm-1am Tue-Sat, 1-5pm Sun; Thissio) Athiri's lovely garden courtyard is a verdant surprise in this pocket of Keramikos. The small but innovative menu plays on Greek regional classics, with seasonal specialities. This might include Santorini fava and hearty beef stew with *myzithra* (sheep's-milk cheese) and handmade pasta from Karpathos.

Butcher & Sardelles   INTERNATIONAL €€
(Map p84; 210 341 3440; Persefonis 19, Gazi; mains €10-17; 7-11.30pm; Kerameikos) Surf or turf? No need to choose at this modern restaurant where the menu is split between meat and seafood. It's in a scenic spot alongside the Gazi gasworks arts centre and has tables outside.

A Little Taste of Home   GREEK €€
(Map p84; 210 341 0013; www.facebook.com/alittletasteofhomeathens; Dekeleon 3, Gazi; mains €8-11; 6pm-1am Mon-Thu, to 2am Fri & Sat, 2-10pm Sun) You might expect a restaurant owned by a Syrian refugee to serve Syrian food, but this is solid Greek, plus creative salads – all good and fresh, and indeed, a nice homey place in the middle of party-scene Gazi. Ahmed is an excellent host.

★Aleria   MEDITERRANEAN €€
(Map p64; 210 522 2633; www.aleria.gr; Megalou Alexandrou 57, Metaxourgio; mains €20-28, set menus from €64; 7.30-11.30pm Mon-Sat, closed late Aug; Metaxourghio) This contemporary, elegant restaurant in a restored mansion feels a bit out of place in the otherwise scruffy Metaxourgio neighbourhood. Still, it does lovely things with Greek ingredients.

★Funky Gourmet   MEDITERRANEAN €€€
(Map p64; 210 524 2727; www.funkygourmet.com; Paramythias 13, cnr Salaminas, Keramikos; set menu from €145; 7.30pm-1am Tue-Sat, last order 10.30pm; Metaxourghio) Greek food gets the molecular gastronomy treatment at this two-Michelin-star restaurant. The two chefs seem to take absolute glee in devising

mind-bending versions of familiar flavours. It's most famous for its somewhat macabre 'Silence of the Lamb' presentation. A worthwhile stop for any foodie. Book ahead.

Psyrri, Omonia & Exarhia

★ Telis
TAVERNA €

(Map p108; ☑ 210 324 2775; Evripidou 86, Psyrri; meal with salad €13; ⊗ 8am-2am Mon-Sat; Ⓜ Thissio) A fluorescent-lit beacon of good food and kind service on a grimy block, Telis has been serving up simplicity since 1978. There's no menu, just a set meal: a small mountain of charcoal-grilled pork chops atop chips, plus a side vegetable. Greek salad is optional, as is rough house wine or beer.

★ Varvakios Agora
MARKET €

(Athens Central Market; Map p108; Athinas, btwn Sofokleous & Evripidou, Omonia; ⊗ 7am-6pm Mon-Sat; Ⓜ Monastiraki, Panepistimio, Omonia) The streets around the colourful and bustling Varvakios Agora are a sensory delight. The meat and fish market (p123) fills the historic building on the eastern side, and the fruit and vegetable market (p123) is across the road. The meat-market **tavernas** are an Athenian institution. Clients range from hungry market workers to elegant couples emerging from nightclubs in search of hangover-busting *patsas* (tripe soup).

★ Diporto Agoras
TAVERNA €

(Map p108; ☑ 210 321 1463; cnr Theatrou & Sokratous; plates €5-7; ⊗ 7am-7pm Mon-Sat, closed 1-20 Aug; Ⓜ Omonia, Monastiraki) This quirky old taverna is an Athens' dining gem. There's no signage – two doors lead to a rustic cellar where there's no menu, just a few dishes that haven't changed in years. The house speciality is *revythia* (chickpeas), usually followed by grilled fish and paired with wine from one of the giant barrels lining the wall.

Nikitas
TAVERNA €

(Map p108; ☑ 210 325 2591; Agion Anargyron 19, Psyrri; mains €7-10; ⊗ noon-6.30pm Sun-Tue, to 11.30pm Wed-Sat; Ⓜ Monastiraki) Locals swear by this tried-and-true taverna that has been serving reasonably priced, refreshingly simple and tasty traditional food since well before Psyrri became a hotspot. It's the only place busy on weekdays.

Hypovrihio
GREEK €

(Map p64; ☑ 210 409 0058; Asklipiou 53, Arahovis, Exarhia; small plates €4-10; ⊗ 4pm-4am Sun-Fri, noon-4pm Sun) The 'Submarine' is a typical Exarhia hang-out, colourful and cramped. Raki (Cretan fire water) is encouraged, but the booze is offset with a big range of home-cooked Greek standards (pork chops, Cretan rusk salads, lots of veg options) and pastas that meet Italian standards of toothiness. Food comes in 'small' portions, great for solo diners or tasting a range of things.

Kimatothrafstis
TAVERNA €

(Map p108; ☑ 213 030 8274; Harilaou Trikoupi 49, Exarhia; small/large plate €4/7; ⊗ 8am-11pm, closed dinner Sun; 🖥🍴; Ⓜ Omonia) This great-value, bright and casual little cafe dishes out a range of home-style Greek cooking and alternative fare. Choose from the day's offerings at the cafeteria-style display. Plates come in two sizes: big or small.

Nancy's Sweet Home
CAFE €

(Map p108; ☑ 210 321 1323; www.nancysweethome.gr; Plateia Iroön 1, Psyrri; cakes from €10; ⊗ 9am-midnight; Ⓜ Monastiraki) Get your sugar fix at this place on a bustling *plateia*. It's famous for its extra-large cakes swimming in melted chocolate and giant dollops of ice cream. Also has syrup-soaked Greek pastries; a local favourite is the *kunefe*, a sweet cheese pastry served with a generous helping of mastic-flavoured ice cream.

Enjoy Just Falafel
SYRIAN €

(Aristotelous 98, Viktoria; sandwiches from €2; ⊗ 8am-8pm Mon-Fri, 11am-7pm Sat; 🍴; Ⓜ Viktoria) Sweet little falafel-and-salad shop run by a Syrian immigrant who came to Greece in the late 1990s. Good food and information about this interesting neighbourhood.

Barbagiannis
TAVERNA €

(Map p108; ☑ 210 330 0185; Emmanuel Benaki 94, Exarhia; mains €5-8; ⊗ lunch & dinner; Ⓜ Omonia) An Exarhia institution, this low-key *mayirio* (cookhouse) is popular with students and those wanting good-value, home-style Greek food.

Ivis
MEZEDHES €

(Map p108; ☑ 210 323 2554; Navarhou Apostoli 19, Psyrri; mezedhes €4-10; ⊗ noon-2am Tue-Sat, to 8pm Sun; Ⓜ Thissio) This cosy corner *mezedhopoleio*, with its bright, arty decor, has a small but delicious range of simple, freshly cooked mezedhes that change daily. A good ouzo and raki selection lights things up.

Rozalia
TAVERNA €

(Map p108; ☑ 210 330 2933; www.rozalia.gr; Valtetsiou 58, Exarhia; mains €5-11; Ⓜ Omonia) An Exarhia favourite on a lively pedestrian strip, this family-run taverna serves grills and home-style fare. Mezedhes are brought around on a tray, so you can point and pick. Pavement tables are tempting, but better to sit in the garden where the ground is level.

Oxo Nou CRETAN €
(Map p108; ☑ 210 380 1778; www.facebook.com/oxonouathens; Emmanuel Benaki 63-65, Exarhia; mains €8-11; ⊗1pm-1.30am; ☏; ⓜOmonia) This was one of the trailblazers for supercasual and superdelicious Cretan food and it still delivers, often with a free shot of island booze to start.

★**Akordeon** MEZEDHES €€
(Map p78; ☑ 210 325 3703; Hristokopidou 7, Psyrri; dishes €6-18; ⊗7pm-2am Tue-Sat, 1-7pm Sun Sep-May; ⓜMonastiraki, Thissio) Slide into this charming butter-yellow house across from a church in a quiet Psyrri side street for a warm welcome by musician-chefs Pepi and Achilleas (and their spouses), who run this excellent venue for local music and mezedhes. They'll help you order authentic Greek fare, then (at night and on weekends) surround you with their soulful songs.

★**Ta Karamanlidika tou Fani** GREEK €€
(Map p108; ☑ 210 325 4184; www.karamanlidika.gr; Sokratous 1, Psyrri; dishes €7-18; ⊗11am-midnight; ⓜMonastiraki) At this modern-day *pastomageireio* – a combo tavern-deli – tables are set alongside the deli cases, and staff offer tasty morsels while you're looking at the menu. Beyond the Greek cheeses and cured meats, there's good seafood, such as marinated anchovies, as well as rarer wines and craft beers. Service is excellent, as is the warm welcome from Fani herself.

★**Yiantes** TAVERNA €€
(Map p108; ☑ 210 330 1369; Valtetsiou 44, Exarhia; mains €10-18; ⊗1pm-midnight; ☏; ⓜOmonia) This lovely garden restaurant is upmarket for Exarhia, but the food is superb and made with largely organic produce. Expect interesting seasonal greens such as *almirikia*, perfectly grilled fish or delicious mussels and calamari with saffron.

Kolonaki

★**Oikeio** MEDITERRANEAN €
(Map p102; ☑ 210 725 9216; Ploutarhou 15, Kolonaki; mains €8-12; ⊗12.30pm-midnight Mon-Thu, to 1am Fri & Sat, to 6pm Sun; ⓜEvangelismos) With excellent home-style cooking, this modern taverna lives up to its name (meaning 'homey'). It's decorated like a cosy bistro, and tables on the footpath allow people-watching without the normal Kolonaki bill. Pastas, salads and international fare are tasty, but try the daily *mayirefta* (ready-cooked meals), such as the excellent stuffed zucchini. Book ahead.

Mia Zoe tin Ehoume MEZEDHES €
(Map p64; ☑ 6987854164; www.ikalizoi.gr/miazoit-inexoume; Sfaktirias 20, Keramikos; ⊗5pm-late; ⓜKerameikos, Thisso or Metaxourghio) 'We have but one life', as the name of this neighbourhood taverna says, and this is a fine place to enjoy it. The summer yard is a ramshackle mix of sofas, lanterns and rusting oddities. In winter, there's a cosy wood stove. Drink and snack till late, with live music on weekends.

Filippou TAVERNA €
(Map p102; ☑ 210 721 6390; Xenokratous 19, Kolonaki; mains €8-12; ⊗1-5pm & 7-11pm Mon-Fri, 1-5pm Sat; ⓜEvangelismos) Why mess with what works? Filippou has been dishing out Greek goodness – heavy on the garlic and hearty meats – since 1923, and it's still a go-to for the neighbourhood. You can get this food elsewhere and for less, but here you get white linen and a gracious older long-lunching clientele, in the heart of Kolonaki.

Kalamaki Kolonaki GREEK €
(Map p102; ☑ 210 721 8800; Ploutarhou 32, Kolonaki; mains €7; ⊗1pm-midnight; ⓜEvangelismos) Order by the *kalamaki* (skewer; €1.70), add some salad and pittas, and you have great quick eats at this standout souvlaki joint. It's small, but there's pavement seating, for the requisite people-watching. And because it's Kolonaki, it's just a little more chic than average.

Benaki Museum Cafe GREEK €€
(Map p102; Koumbari 1, Kolonaki; mains €12-16; ⓜEvangelismos) Traditional Greek food gets dressed up to match the museum setting, with an open dining room and terrace with a view of the national gardens and the Acropolis. It feels a bit clubby, with older locals meeting for lunch, and it's open as late as the museum is, so you can have dinner or even just a late drink here.

Nice N' Easy CAFE €€
(Map p102; ☑ 210 361 7201; www.niceneasy.gr; Omirou 60, Kolonaki; mains €8-18; ⊗9am-1.30am; ☏; ⓜPanepistimio) ☏ Dig into organic, fresh sandwiches, salads and brunch treats such as huevos rancheros beneath images of

Psyrri, Omonia & Exarhia

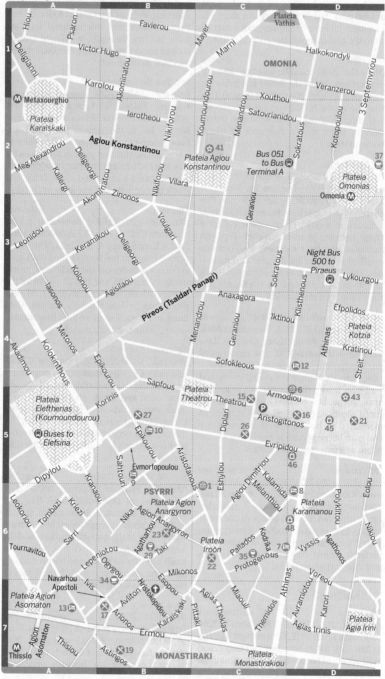

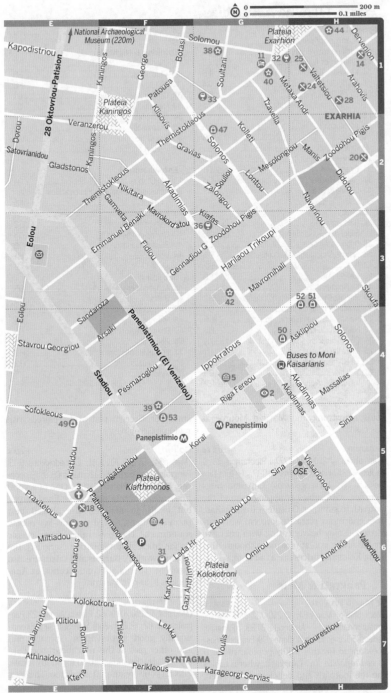

Psyrri, Omonia & Exarhia

Louis Armstrong and Marilyn Monroe at this casual cafe.

Capanna　　　　　　　　　　ITALIAN €€
(Map p102; ☑210 724 1777; Ploutarhou 38 & Haritos 42, Kolonaki; mains €10-17; ◷1pm-1am Tue-Sun; ☜; ⓜEvangelismos) Capanna hugs a corner, with tables wrapping around the footpath in summer. Cuisine is fresh Italian, from enormous pizzas to gnocchi with gorgonzola. Enjoy hearty eating with attentive service and a goblet of wine, although, this being Kolonaki, prices are a tad high.

✗ Pangrati & Mets

★**Mavro Provato**　　　　　　MEZEDHES €
(Black Sheep; Map p64; ☑210 722 3466; www.tomauroprovato.gr; Arrianou 31-33, Pangrati; dishes €5-12; ◷lunch & dinner; ⓜEvangelismos) Book ahead for this wildly popular modern *mezedhopoleio* in Pangrati, where tables line the footpath and delicious small (well,

small for Greece) plates are paired with regional Greek wines.

Colibri　　　　　　　　　　　PIZZA €
(Map p64; ☑210 701 1011; Embedokleous 9-13, Pangrati; small pizzas €6-12, mains €5-9; ◷noon-late; ☒2, 4, 11 to Plateia Plastira) One of several fine cafes on this quiet, tree-lined street, but locals go here for the alleged best pizza in Athens, served to a low-key reggae soundtrack. The pies range from classic Italian to creative vegetarian (seriously, the yoghurt works!). Burgers and salads are also excellent. There's a second location at Anapafseos 9, also in Pangrati.

Kallimarmaro　　　　　　　BAKERY €
(Map p64; ☑210 701 9062; Plateia Varnava 22, Pangrati; pita €2; ◷8am-8pm Mon-Sat; ☒) Exceptionally good *spanakopita* (spinach pie) and other pies at this neighbourhood bakery – it's the breakfast go-to for many locals. Fills all your cream-puff needs too. There's a

second one nearby in Mets, across from the Odeon Cafe (p116).

Vyrinis
TAVERNA €

(Map p64; ☑ 210 701 2021; Arhimidous 11, Pangrati; mains €6-8; ⊗ 7-11pm Mon-Fri, noon-3pm & 7-11pm Sat & Sun; ☐ 2, 4, 11 to Plateia Plastira) Just behind the old Panathenaic stadium, this popular neighbourhood spot has been modernised a bit, but maintains its essential taverna-ness, with home-style Greek food and reliable house wine at reasonable prices. On warm nights, all activity moves to the lovely courtyard garden, just up the side street.

★ Spondi
MEDITERRANEAN €€€

(Map p64; ☑ 210 756 4021; www.spondi.gr; Pyrronos 5, Pangrati; mains €44-52, set menus from €73; ⊗ 8pm-late; ☐ 209 to Plateia Varnava, ☐ 2, 4 or 11 to Plateia Plastira) Athenians frequently vote two-Michelin-starred Spondi the city's best restaurant, and its Mediterranean haute cuisine, with a strong French influence, is indeed excellent. Visitors to the city might want something a bit more distinctly Greek, however. Either way, it's a lovely dining experience, in a relaxed setting in a charming old house with a bougainvillea-draped garden. Book ahead.

🍷 Drinking & Nightlife

In Athens, the line between cafe and bar is blurry. Most places serving coffee by day segue to drinks, and maybe music and a DJ, at night. Many cafes and bars also serve food – although places that serve only drinks are more common in the economic crisis (you can bring your own snacks).

Akropoli, Makrygianni & Koukaki

Tiki Athens
BAR

(Map p74; ☑ 210 923 6908; www.tikiathens.com; Falirou 15, Makrygianni; ⊗ 6pm-late; Ⓜ Akropoli) Kitschy bachelor-pad decor, a whole roster of live music, an Asian-inspired menu and an alternative young crowd make this two-storey spot a fun place for a drink.

Sfika
BAR

(Map p74; ☑ 210 922 1341; Stratigou Kontouli 15, Makrygianni; ⊗ 9am-late; Ⓜ Akropoli) Glowing yellow inside (perhaps for its namesake; *sfika* means 'wasp'), this small neighbourhood cafe-restaurant-bar has an alternative/student vibe and occasional live music.

SUMMER BEACH CLUBS

In summer, much of the city's serious nightlife moves to glamorous, enormous seafront clubs radiating out from Glyfada (p133). Many sit on the tram route, which runs to 2.30am on Friday and Saturday. If you book for dinner you don't pay cover; otherwise admission ranges from €10 to €20 and includes one drink. Glam up to get in.

Duende
BAR

(Map p74; Tzireon 2, Makrygianni; ⊗ 8pm-3am; Ⓜ Akropoli) With the golden glow of a Parisian brasserie, this intimate pub is a good place for a grown-up glass of wine or whisky (though not so much for food or cocktails). It's especially welcome as a respite from the tourist bustle nearby.

Syntagma, Plaka & Monastiraki

The best central bars are around Kolokotroni St, north of Syntagma, and around Plateia Agia Irini in Monastiraki. Look especially at the ends of shopping arcades for old-style bars staffed with smart barkeeps and DJs. Multiuse spaces such as Metamatic:TAF (p77) and Six DOGS (p112) combine gallery, cafe and overflowing bar. Some hotel bars, such as Grande Bretagne (p99) and A for Athens (p99), have super Acropolis views.

★ Tailor Made
BAR

(Map p78; ☑ 213 004 9645; www.tailormade.gr; Plateia Agia Irini 2, Monastiraki; ⊗ 8am-2am; Ⓜ Monastiraki) Arguably the best third-wave coffee operation in Athens, with its own microroastery and hand-pressed teas, this place has outdoor tables alongside the flower market. At night it turns into a happening cocktail and wine bar. Menu includes homemade desserts (€5) and sandwiches (€6) too.

★ Tall's Toy
COCKTAIL BAR

(Map p78; ☑ 210 331 1555; www.facebook.com/tallstoybar; Plateia Karytsi 10, Syntagma; ⊗ noon-4am; Ⓜ Syntagma) With jewel-toned walls, old-fashioned wood fittings, open windows to the street and a usually chill DJ, this might be the ideal small downtown bar. The crowd is usually 30-something and older.

Dude
BAR

(Map p78; ☎ 210 322 7130; www.facebook.com/thedudebar; Kalamiotou 14, Monastiraki; ⊗2pm-5am, to 6am Sat & Sun; Ⓜ Monastiraki) Exceptionally good music – obscure funk and soul that makes you feel like you're living a Quentin Tarantino soundtrack – at this little bar on a pedestrian street. Moreover, the Dude abides till practically dawn.

Couleur Locale
BAR

(Map p78; ☎ 216 700 4917; Normanou 3; ⊗10am-4am; Ⓜ Monastiraki) Tucked in a narrow pedestrian lane in Monastiraki, Couleur Locale is a great secret. At ground level, it's a pretty enough bar, but often completely empty. That's because everyone has taken the elevator to the 3rd-floor rooftop. It's a go-to spot for Athenians who love to sip a coffee or drink with a chill vibe and a view of their beloved Acropolis.

Baba Au Rum
COCKTAIL BAR

(Map p78; ☎ 211 710 9140; www.babaaurum.com; Klitiou 6, Monastiraki; ⊗7pm-3am Sun-Fri, 1pm-4am Sat; Ⓜ Syntagma, Monastiraki) As the name implies, the focus here is on rum drinks, with an excellent selection of rarer Caribbean rums and a whole range of cocktails, from classic tiki drinks to new inventions. This is just one of a handful of good little bars in this strip.

Noel
BAR

(Map p78; ☎ 211 215 9534; www.noelbar.gr; Kolokotroni 59b, Monastiraki; ⊗11am-4am; Ⓜ Monastiraki) The bar's slogan is 'where it's always

Christmas' and Noel is going for the candle-lit cocktail-party kind of Christmas, no Santa suits required. The downright beautiful place is decked out with period furniture and softly glimmering chandeliers. Smartly suited bartenders serve some of the most creative cocktails in town. Music is a mix of '80s, '90s and jazz.

Barley Cargo
BAR

(Map p78; ☎ 210 323 0445; Kolokotroni 6, Syntagma; ⊗11am-3am; Ⓜ Syntagma) If you think Greek beer stops at Alpha, head here to learn more. The big open-front bar stocks the products of many Greek microbreweries, as well as more than 100 international beers. Live music is a bonus.

Galaxy Bar
BAR

(Map p78; ☎ 210 322 7733; Stadiou 10, Syntagma; ⊗1pm-late Mon-Sat; Ⓜ Syntagma) Once upon a time (the early 1970s, to be exact), this was a modern bar – the sort with an actual European-style *bar*. Now it's a beautiful, subdued time capsule with gallant bartenders who respect the spirit of the place, which can be summarised in the framed photos of the Rat Pack and Franz Kafka. At the end of the arcade.

Six DOGS
BAR

(Map p78; ☎ 210 321 0510; www.sixdogs.gr; Avramiotou 6-8, Monastiraki; ⊗10am-late; Ⓜ Monastiraki) The core of this supercreative events space is a rustic back garden, a great place for quiet daytime chats over coffee or a relaxed drink. From there, you can head in to one of several adjoining buildings to see a band, art show or other general cool happening.

Klepsidra
CAFE

(Map p78; ☎ 210 321 2493; Klepsydras & Thrasyvoulou, Plaka; snacks €4; ⊗9am-1am; Ⓜ Monastiraki) Tucked away in a delightfully quiet spot on the west end of Plaka, with shady outdoor tables and friendly service, Klepsidra is a favourite with locals before and after work and an ideal rest spot after serious sightseeing. It has a small selection of snacks, such as *spanakopites* (spinach pies), though it's really about the atmosphere.

Clumsies
BAR

(Map p108; ☎ 210 323 2682; www.theclumsies.gr; Praxitelous 30, Syntagma; ⊗10am-2am, to 4am Fri & Sat; Ⓜ Syntagma) Look for the red neon in the hallway of this unsigned bar that fills your coffee and creative cocktail needs. Founded by three award-winning

> ### ⓘ TOP NIGHTLIFE TIPS
>
> ➡ Bars begin filling after 11pm and uually stay open till 3am or 4am.
>
> ➡ Transit stops or slows after midnight, but cabs are very cheap.
>
> ➡ Athenians drink plenty, but public drunkenness is rarely seen. If you're visibly intoxicated, you're a clear target for pickpockets or worse.
>
> ➡ Gazi and Kolonaki tend towards slick and bigger-budget clubs. For cheaper drinks and live music, head for Keramikos or Exarhia. Monastiraki and north of Syntagma are the best central areas for more interesting bars.
>
> ➡ For the best dancing in summer, head to beach clubs (p111) along the coast near Glyfada – city locations close earlier.

bartenders, it is very serious about its drinks, but the atmosphere is definitely fun, and full of handsome types on the weekends.

Drunk Sinatra
COCKTAIL BAR

(Map p78; ☑210 331 3733; Thiseos 16, Syntagma; ☺10am-late; Ⓜ Syntagma) Look for the movie marquee on a small side street to find this hipster hang. It serves a mean cocktail.

Brettos
BAR

(Map p78; ☑ 210 323 2110; www.brettosplaka. com; Kydathineon 41, Plaka; ☺10am-3am; Ⓜ Akropoli) You won't find any happening bars in Plaka, but Brettos is a delightful old bar and distillery with a stunning wall of colourful bottles and huge barrels. Sample its home brands of wine, ouzo, brandy and other spirits.

Faust
BAR

(Map p78; ☑210 323 4095; www.faust.gr; Kalamiotou 11 & Athinaidos 12, Monastiraki; ☺Sep-May; Ⓜ Monastiraki) Loud, raunchy, funny, just plain quirky – eclectic and popular bar Faust probably hosts it on its small stage.

Heteroclito
WINE BAR

(Map p78; ☑210 323 9406; www.heteroclito. gr; Fokionos 2, Monastiraki; ☺12.30pm-midnight Mon-Thu, to 1.30am Fri & Sat, 6pm-midnight Sun; Ⓜ Monastiraki) This relaxed wine bar with a French bistro-like setting showcases the best of Greek wines. The petite, yet charming, venue has a vintage feel with mismatched period furniture and a mix of warm wood and cool marble details. The wines can be paired with Greek cheeses and cold cuts. Heteroclito periodically organises tasting events.

Booze Cooperativa
BAR

(Map p78; ☑211 405 3733; www.boozecooperativa.com; Kolokotroni 57, Monastiraki; ☺11am-late; ☏; Ⓜ Monastiraki) By day, this art mansion is full of young Athenians playing chess and backgammon and working on their Macs. Later it transforms into a happening bar that rocks till late. The basement hosts art exhibitions and there's a theatre upstairs.

Bartesera
BAR

(Map p78; ☑210 322 9805; Kolokotroni 25, Syntagma; ☺10am-late, 6pm-late Sun; Ⓜ Syntagma) This casual bar-cafe with great music hides at the end of the narrow Praxitelous arcade.

Yiasemi
CAFE

(Map p78; ☑213 041 7937; www.yiasemi.gr; Mniskleous 23, Plaka; ☺10am-3am; Ⓜ Monastiraki) Proof that Plaka is still very much a Greek neighbourhood, despite the tourists: this cafe attracts a good mix of young Athenians, who set up for hours in the big armchairs or out on the scenic steps. It's better by day and on weeknights, when it's not overwhelmed by the night scene at nearby restaurants.

Gin Joint
COCKTAIL BAR

(Map p108; ☑210 321 8646; Christou Lada 1, Syntagma; ☺noon-2am; Ⓜ Syntagma) Just what the name promises: sample 60 gins or other fancy beverages, some with historical notes on their origin. It's a tiny place, but like so many downtown bars, the crowd can expand into the adjacent arcade.

Kiki de Grece
WINE BAR

(Map p78; ☑210 321 1279; www.facebook.com/ kikidegrece; Ipitou 4; ☺noon-1am; Ⓜ Syntagma) Man Ray's muse, Kiki de Montparnasse, declared that in hard times, all she needed was bread, an onion and a bottle of red wine. This pedestrian-street bar also takes her as its muse, and offers plenty more than a bottle of red. There's a huge range from Greece's vintners, paired with seasonal dishes from various regions in Greece.

Poems & Crimes Art Bar
CAFE

(Map p78; ☑210 322 8839; www.poemsandcrimes.gr; Agias Irinis 17, Monastiraki; ☺9am-midnight; Ⓜ Monastiraki) Set in a 19th-century neoclassical building, Poems & Crimes is the local writers' and book lovers' haunt. The quiet bookshop is also the office for a Greek publishing house and a coffee shop. Various book and poetry readings are often scheduled, and a little backyard turns into a cafe and music performance space in summer.

Hitchcocktales
COCKTAIL BAR

(Map p74; ☑210 921 0023; www.facebook.com/ hitchcock.athens; Porinou 10; ☺9am-2am; Ⓜ Acropolis) Famous Hitchcock film scenes are spray-painted on the wall in front of this bar on a quiet street that gathers a crowd that loves creative drinks and candlelight. The bartenders are polished, and the soundtrack can be lively swing, jazz, soul and funk. The noise level, in the industrial-look raw-concrete space, can spike later in the night.

🔖 Gazi, Keramikos & Thisio

Once touted as the 'edgy' neighbourhood, Gazi is now fairly mainstream and particularly well known for its gay scene. In Thisio, cafes along the pedestrian promenade Apostolou Pavlou have great Acropolis views; those along pedestrianised Iraklidon pack 'em in at night. More creative, fringier bars are found in Keramikos and adjoining Metaxourgio – pedestrian-only Salaminos is especially nice.

★ Gazarte   BAR
(Map p84; ☑ 210 346 0347; www.gazarte.gr; Voutadon 32-34, Gazi; Ⓜ Kerameikos) At this varied arts complex, you'll find a cinema-sized screen playing videos, amazing city views taking in the Acropolis, mainstream music and a trendy 30-something crowd. At ground level is a large theatre that hosts music and comedy. There's occasional live music and a restaurant to boot.

Alphaville   BAR
(Map p64; ☑ 215 505 2001; Salaminos, cnr Sfaktirias, Metaxourgio; ⊙ 11am-3am; Ⓜ Thissio, Kerameikos or Metaxourghio) Just one in a strip of near-perfect bohemian bars on the pedestrian street of Salaminos, the heart of the cool Keramikos scene. All with a good mix of music, inexpensive drinks and loads of *kefi* (atmosphere), plus a dramatic graffiti backdrop on the derelict buildings. Start here and wander.

A Liar Man   BAR
(Map p84; ☑ 210 342 6322; www.facebook.com/aliarmanathens; Sofroniou 2, Gazi; ⊙ 5pm-2am Mon-Thu, to 4am Fri & Sat, 2pm-1am Sun mid-Sep–mid-Jun; Ⓜ Kerameikos) A tiny hideout with a more hushed vibe – a very nice antidote to other top-volume bars and clubs nearby. It closes in summer.

Laika   BAR
(Map p64; ☑ 215 501 3801; Pellis 30, Gazi; ⊙ noon-2am Tue-Sun; Ⓜ Kerameikos) Out on the fringes of Gazi, amid car workshops and the occasional experimental theatre, this hip little cafe-bar is a treat. There's a good food menu, and often music at night.

🔖 Psyrri, Omonia & Exarhia

Exarhia is a good bet for youthful, lively bars on Plateia Exarhion and side streets; many have live music. The cheap-bar precinct on nearby Mesolongiou is popular with students and anarchists. At night, the actual square of Omonia is less seedy than it was, but drug-dealing and the like have simply been pushed south into Psyrri, west of the market; stay alert here.

Veneti   CAFE
(Map p108; ☑ 210 523 0740; Plateia Omonias 7, Omonia; ⊙ 7am-11pm; Ⓜ Omonia) Legendary cafe Neon, famous haunt of Athens literati, fell victim to the crisis. But the cavernous space got a decent new tenant in Veneti (aka Beneth, if you read the letters in English), which has filled the lower level with good-quality pastries, cookies, pies and even hot meals. There's seating upstairs and out on the square. Excellent service.

There are several other branches of Veneti around town, including one on Monastiraki (Map p78; ☑ 210 323 3122; Monastiraki 10; ⊙ 7am-midnight; Ⓜ Monastiraki).

Little Kook   CAFE
(Map p78; ☑ 210 321 4144; www.facebook.com/littlekookgr; Karaiskaki 17, Psyrri; ⊙ 11am-midnight, from 10am Sat & Sun; 🐾; Ⓜ Monastiraki) Nominally, this place sells coffee and cake. But it's really about its dazzling decor, which conjures an odd childhood fantasy. Precisely which one depends on the season, as the theme changes regularly. Everywhere are dolls, props, paintings and table decorations. You'll know you're getting close when you see party streamers over the street. Kids will be dazzled; Instagrammers will swoon.

Blue Fox   BAR
(Map p64; ☑ 6942487225; Asklipiou 91, Exarhia; ⊙ 9pm-3am Thu-Sat; Ⓜ Panepistimio) Athens supports a small but lively swing and rockabilly scene, and Blue Fox, with its big wooden dance floor, is one of its hubs. Weekend nights, you'll likely spot it from the Vespas parked outside.

Cinque   WINE BAR
(Map p108; ☑ 215 501 7853; www.cinque.gr; Agatharhou 15, Psyrri) Painted dark purple, this place feels like a jewel box, and the assorted Greek wines are the gems. Also a good place for light food, with platters of meats and cheeses.

Tralala   BAR
(Map p64; ☑ 210 362 8066; Asklipiou 45, Exarhia; ⊙ 11pm-3am; Ⓜ Panepistimio, Omonia) Actors frequent cool Tralala, with its original artwork, lively owners and gregarious atmosphere.

Revolt BAR
(Map p108; ☎210 380 0016; Kolleti 29, Exarhia; ⏱11am-2am; Ⓜ Omonia) This small, simple bar with tables spilling out on to a pedestrianised square anchors a few solid blocks of good nightlife. The vibrant murals out front are super. Start here and explore.

Tsin Tsin COCKTAIL BAR
(Map p108; ☎210 384 1460; Kiafas 6, Exarhia; ⏱7pm-late; Ⓜ Omonia) Teeny, tiny and a bit out of the way on a little lane. The bartender knows the craft and the loungey feel is relaxing.

Tranzistor BAR
(Map p108; ☎210 322 8658; Protogenous 10, Psyrri; ⏱9am-midnight; Ⓜ Monastiraki) Sidle up to the backlit bar or relax at tables outside at this small, cool spot. It's one of a few good mellow bars on this narrow street.

Spiti Mas CAFE
(Map p108; ☎210 331 4751; Navarhou Apostoli 10, Psyrri; ⏱9am-6pm; Ⓜ Thissio, Monastiraki) Fancy breakfast in bed? You can have it at 'Our House', a cafe set up like a hip apartment, complete with a single bed. The whole operation might be unbearably twee if it weren't for the good, fresh food and the genuinely sweet staff.

Ginger Ale BAR
(Map p108; ☎210 330 1246; Themistokleous 74, Exarhia; ⏱8am-late; Ⓜ Omonia) This place cultivates a poppy '60s kitsch vibe. By day, it's a good place to sip coffee and watch the scene on Plateia Exarhia.

GAY & LESBIAN ATHENS

Athens' gay and lesbian scene is relatively low-key. Athens Pride (p96), held in June, has been an annual event since 2005; there's a march and a concert on Syntagma.

For nightlife, Gazi has become Athens' gay and lesbian hub. Gay and gay-friendly clubs around town are also in Plateia Agia Irinis, Metaxourgio and Exarhia. Check out www.athensinfoguide.com.

Rooster (Map p78; www.roostercafe.gr; Plateia Agia Irini 4, Monastiraki; ⏱9am-3am; Ⓜ Monastiraki) This wonderfully packed gay cafe on lively Plateia Agia Irini is straight-friendly, too, and so fills with chatting locals.

Loukoumi (Map p78; www.loukoumibar.gr; Plateia Avyssinias 3, Monastiraki; ⏱11am-2am; Ⓜ Monastiraki) This creative, gay-friendly cafe and arts space occupies two buildings facing each other across Plateia Avyssinias. It covers everything from daytime coffee and snacks to night-time DJs to drag queens, plus a vintage shop and gallery space.

S-Cape (Map p84; www.s-capeclub.gr; Iakhou 32, Gazi; ⏱11.30pm-5am; Ⓜ Ke{rameikos) Stays packed with the younger gay, lesbian and transgender crowd. Check theme nights online.

Trap (Map p64; ☎210 922 2248; Korytsas 15, Gazi; ⏱11pm-8am Mon & Wed-Sun) This club is out on the fringes of Gazi and has a laid-back atmosphere to match.

Sodade2 (Map p84; ☎210 346 8657; Triptolemou 10, Gazi; ⏱11pm-6am; Ⓜ Kerameikos) Open since 2000, before Gazi was any kind of nightlife destination, this club remains superfun for dancing. Weeknights are pop, weekends are EDM. Mondays are Greek-music nights.

Noiz Club (Map p84; ☎210 346 7850; www.facebook.com/noizclubgaz; Konstantinoupoleos 78, Gazi; Ⓜ Kerameikos) Athens' main lesbian club has retro dance nights.

Myrovolos (Map p64; ☎210 522 8806; Giatrakou 12, Metaxourgio; ⏱noon-4am Mon-Fri, 11am-4am Sat & Sun; Ⓜ Metaxourghio) Popular lesbian cafe-bar-restaurant on a vast and somewhat unkempt *plateia*, with a motorcycle clubhouse (unrelated) upstairs. Archetypal Metaxourgio, in other words.

BIG (Map p84; ☎6946282845; www.barbig.gr; Falesias 12, Gazi; ⏱10pm-3am Tue, Thu & Sun, to 5am Fri & Sat; Ⓜ Kerameikos) Cosy hub for Athens' lively bear scene.

Moe Club (Map p84; www.moeclub-gazi.blogspot.com; Keleou 5, Gazi; ⏱1am-6am; Ⓜ Kerameikos) After-hours hang-out with occasional special parties. Next door is the Moe Bear Garage, which opens earlier.

By night, it's all tiki cocktails and rock music.

Kolonaki

Kolonaki has two main nightlife strips: sprawling bar-cafes, most quite slick and sceney, around the north end of Skoufa, and a cluster of tiny, crowded bars along Haritos.

Rock'n'Roll BAR
(Map p102; ☑ 210 722 0649; www.facebook.com/rockathens; Plateia Kolonakiou, Kolonaki; ⊗ Sep-Jun; Ⓜ Evangelismos) A Kolonaki classic, this upscale crowd-pleaser lives up to its name at night, when dance parties get wild. Popular with the trendy Kolonaki crowd, it has a good vibe, but 'face control' can be strict. During the day it's a busy, but more relaxed cafe lining Kolonaki's main square. In summer, it closes in favour of a beach location.

Filion CAFE
(Map p102; ☑ 210 361 2850; Skoufa 34, Kolonaki; ⊗ 8am-midnight; ☎; Ⓜ Syntagma) Holding strong against modern glitz in Kolonaki, Filion is a pleasantly dowdy old-school cafe, frequented by older members of the intellectual establishment and the occasional younger artist or writer.

Dark Side of Chocolate CAFE
(Map p102; ☑ 210 339 2348; Solonos 49; ⊗ 8am-11pm; Ⓜ Syntagma) This tiny cafe in Kolonaki has made a name for itself for its hot chocolate and handmade truffles, displayed like gems in a glass case. It's a tiny, cosy place for some restorative caffeine (there's coffee too) and a sweet to nibble.

Petite Fleur CAFE
(Map p102; www.petite-fleur.gr; Omirou 44, Kolonaki; ⊗ 8am-11pm; Ⓜ Panepistimio) Petite Fleur serves up large mugs of hot chocolate and speciality cappuccinos in a quiet, almost-Parisian ambience.

Pangrati & Mets

Chelsea Hotel BAR
(Map p64; ☑ 210 756 3374; Arhimidous 1, cnr Proklou, Pangrati; ⊗ 9.30am-late; ☎; 🚌 2, 4, 11 to Plateia Plastira) When people talk about the cool but mellow scene in Pangrati, they're probably thinking of this busy cafe-bar on Plateia Plastira. By day, it's coffee, books and the occasional laptop. When the sun sets, every seat, inside and out, is filled with young Athenians aspiring to be as artistic

and bohemian as residents of the bar's NYC namesake.

Odeon Cafe CAFE
(Map p64; ☑ 210 922 3414; Markou Mousourou 19, Mets; ⊗ 8.30am-late; Ⓜ Akropoli) This delightful slice of local Athens life is a simple corner cafe-bar where quietly chatting friends sit beneath ivy winding over the footpath. Extra-friendly staff, plus snacks and drinks, and occasional live music at night.

☆ Entertainment

English-language entertainment information appears daily in the *Kathimerini* supplement in the *International New York Times*. Athens' thriving multiuse art spaces host all manner of goings-on. For comprehensive events listings, with links to online ticket-sales points, try the following:

www.thisisathens.gr Athens tourism site.

www.elculture.gr Arts and culture listings.

www.tickethour.com Also has sports matches.

www.tickethouse.gr Rockwave and other festivals.

www.ticketservices.gr Range of events.

Cinema

★ Cine Paris CINEMA
(Map p78; ☑ 210 322 0721; www.cineparis.gr; Kydathineon 22, Plaka; Ⓜ Syntagma) The Paris was the very first outdoor cinema in Athens, established in the 1920s. It's still a magical place to see a movie, on a rooftop in Plaka, with great views of the Acropolis from some seats.

Thission CINEMA
(Map p84; ☑ 210 342 0864; www.cine-thisio.gr; Apostolou Pavlou 7, Thisio; Ⓜ Thissio) Across from the Acropolis, this is a lovely old-style outdoor cinema in a garden setting. Sit towards the back if you want to catch a glimpse of the glowing edifice.

Aigli Cinema CINEMA
(Map p64; ☑ 210 336 9369; www.aeglizappiou.gr; Zappeio Gardens, Syntagma; €8.50; ⊗ films at 9pm & 11pm; Ⓜ Syntagma) Historic open-air cinema in the verdant Zappeio Gardens (p83).

Vox CINEMA
(Map p108; ☑ 210 331 0170; Themistokleous 82, Exarhia; Ⓜ Omonia) Vox open-air cinema on

Exarhia's main square rivals the Paris in Plaka as one of the older cinemas in the city. It has fortunately received historic-building designation. Still, it has the rough-and-ready vibe you'd expect in this neighbourhood.

Cine Athinaia CINEMA
(Map p102; ☑ 210 721 5717; www.facebook.com/cineathinaia; Haritos 50, Kolonaki; Ⓜ Evangelismos) This summer-only open-air cinema in Kolonaki lists what's playing on its Facebook page.

Dexameni CINEMA
(Map p102; ☑ 210 362 3942; www.facebook.com/cine-dexameni; Plateia Dexameni, Kolonaki; Ⓜ Evangelismos) This classic open-air cinema is in a lovely spot in the quieter reaches of Kolonaki, with a wall of cascading bougainvillea, deckchairs and little tables to rest your beer on.

Greek Music

Athens has some of the best *rembetika* in intimate, evocative venues. Performances usually include both *rembetika* and *laïka* (urban popular music), start at around 11.30pm and do not have a cover charge, though drinks can be more expensive than at bars. Most close May to September, so in summer try live-music tavernas around Plaka and Psyrri, or small bars in Exarhia.

Stoa Athanaton TRADITIONAL MUSIC
(Map p108; ☑ 210 321 4362; Sofokleous 19, Central Market, Omonia; ☺ 3-6pm & midnight-6am Mon-Sat Oct-May; Ⓜ Monastiraki, Panepistimio, Omonia) This legendary club occupies a hall above the central meat market (p123). Popular for classic *rembetika* and *laïka* from a respected band of musicians, it often starts from midafternoon. Access is by a lift in the arcade. Food is not the attraction.

Perivoli tou Ouranou TRADITIONAL MUSIC
(Map p78; ☑ 210 323 5517; www.perivolitouranou.gr; Lysikratous 19, Plaka; ☺ 9pm-late Fri & Sat, noon-6pm Sun Oct-Jun; Ⓜ Akropoli) A favourite rustic, old-style Plaka music haunt with dinner (mains €18 to €29).

Boemissa TRADITIONAL MUSIC
(Map p84; ☑ 210 383 8803; www.boemissa.gr; Pireos 69, Thisio; ☺ 10pm-late Thu-Sat; Ⓜ Omonia) For decades in Exarhia, this budget-friendly music joint moved across town and lost some of its accumulated divey-ness. But the young audience, fuelled by a €15 'crisis special' meal and unlimited wine, makes up for lost time when singers belt the classic heart-rending *rembetika* and *laïka*.

DON'T MISS

SUMMER CINEMA

One of the delights of Athens is the enduring tradition of open-air cinema, where you can watch the latest Hollywood or art-house flick in the warm summer air. Many original outdoor cinemas have been refurbished and are still operating in gardens and on rooftops around Athens, with modern sound systems.

Plaka's rooftop **Cine Paris** and Exarhia's **Vox** both claim to be the oldest, though Cine Paris has an advantage with Acropolis views, as does **Thission**. **Aigli**, in the verdant Zappeio Gardens, is a bit away from traffic noise, and you can watch a movie in style with a glass of wine. Kolonaki's **Dexameni** is in a peaceful square.

Kavouras TRADITIONAL MUSIC
(Map p108; ☑ 210 381 0202; Themistokleous 64, Exarhia; ☺ 11pm-late Thu-Sat Sep-Jun; Ⓜ Omonia) Above Exarhia's popular souvlaki joint, this lively club usually plays until dawn for a student crowd.

Mostrou TRADITIONAL MUSIC
(Map p78; ☑ 210 322 5558; www.mostrou.gr; Mnisikleous 22, cnr Lyssiou, Plaka; ☺ 6pm-2am Thu-Sun; Ⓜ Monastiraki) This is the postcard scene of an Athens taverna, with tables set up on Plaka's famous stair-street, Acropolis views and a band playing all the bouzouki hits. As a result, it's thronged with tourists, but the music and food are still good. In winter, it's even rowdier, with a dance floor inside.

Rock & Jazz Music

Athens has a healthy rock-music scene and many European tours stop here. In summer, check Rockwave and other festival schedules.

★**Half Note Jazz Club** JAZZ
(Map p64; ☑ 210 921 3310; www.halfnote.gr; Trivonianou 17, Mets; Ⓜ Akropoli) Athens' most serious jazz venue is a stylish place that hosts Greek and international musicians. Check the schedule ahead of your trip, as it's not open every night and closes entirely in summer.

Gagarin 205 Club LIVE MUSIC
(☑ 211 411 2500; www.gagarin205.gr; Liossion 205, Thymarakia; Ⓜ Agios Nikolaos) Friday- and Saturday-night gigs feature leading rock and underground bands.

The Olympic Games

The Olympic Games were undoubtedly the ancient world's biggest sporting event and remain for most athletes today the biggest of dreams. Then, as now, the Games made warring states temporarily halt their squabbles, and victorious competitors won great fame and considerable fortune.

Origins of the Games

Some Ancient Greek texts attribute the founding of the Games to the hero Pelops; others name Hercules as the founder who made Zeus the patron god of the Olympic sanctuary. The first official quadrennial Olympic Games were declared in 776 BC by King Iphitos of Elis, took place around the first full moon in August, and reached the height of their prestige in 576 BC.

During the ancient Games, writers, poets and historians read their works to large audiences; traders clinched business deals; and city-state leaders attempted to resolve differences through diplomacy.

Olympic Qualifications

In Ancient Greece only free-born Greek males were allowed to compete in the Games; the Romans changed the rules to include Roman citizens. Slaves and women were not allowed to enter the Olympic sanctuary even as spectators; women trying to sneak in were thrown from Mt Typaion. Today's Summer Olympics include athletes from 204 countries, with 88 countries competing in the Winter Olympics.

Demise & Rebirth

During Roman times the Games declined. Held for the last time in AD 393, they were banned by Emperor Theodosius I as part of a purge of pagan festivals.

1. Ancient pottery depicting Olympic wrestlers
2. Ruins of the Temple of Hera (p190), Olympia Town
3. Statue of a discus thrower

The modern Olympic Games were instituted in 1896 and, except during WWI and WWII, have been held every four years around the world ever since. The Olympic flame is lit at the ancient site and carried by runners to the city where the Games are held.

Scandal & Controversies

Throughout history the Olympics have been marred by scandals. These range from the farcical – Emperor Nero entering the chariot race in AD 67 with 10 horses, ordering that other competitors could only have four, falling off and still being declared winner – to the serious, including Israeli athletes being murdered by Palestinian group Black September in 1972, and Hitler refusing to award gold medals to African American sprinter Jesse Owens in 1936.

ANCIENT OLYMPICS VS MODERN OLYMPICS

➡ Contemporary opening ceremonies may involve such displays as James Bond parachuting in. In Ancient Greece, it was all about sacrificing oxen to Zeus.

➡ Ancient Greek events included wrestling, chariot and horse racing, the pentathlon (three foot races, the long jump and the discus), javelin, boxing and pankration (few-holds-barred fighting). Today's Summer Olympics have been joined by the Winter Olympics; a total of 56 events across both games include modified sprinting, equestrian, boxing and wrestling.

➡ Victorious ancient Olympians were crowned with sacred olive branches and enjoyed tax exemption and other privileges. Modern Olympians receive medals, TV fame and sponsorship fortune.

AN Club
LIVE MUSIC

(Map p108; ☑ 210 330 5056; www.anclub.gr; Solomou 13-15, Exarhia; Ⓜ Omonia) A spot for lesser-known international and local rock bands.

Bios
LIVE MUSIC, GALLERY

(Map p84; ☑ 210 342 5335; www.bios.gr; Pireos 84, Gazi; ⊙ 11am-late; Ⓜ Thissio) Occupying a Bauhaus apartment building, this multilevel warren has a ground-floor bar, a basement club, a tiny art-house cinema and a roof deck. Expect live performances, art and new-media exhibitions, or at the very least a solid DJ and an Acropolis view.

Theatre & Performing Arts

Athens, as the birthplace of live theatre, has an excellent scene – but it's unfortunately accessible only to Greek speakers; subtitling and English performances are rare. In summer the main cultural happening is the Athens & Epidaurus Festival (p96), which includes dance and music programming.

Theatro Skion Tasou Konsta
PUPPET THEATRE

(☑ 6948852493; www.fkt.gr; Floibos Park, Palaio Faliro; €3.50; ⊙ 8.30pm Fri-Sun; ⊞; ⬚ Park Flisvou) Greece's wise fool, Karagiozis, gave his name to the art of shadow puppetry (*karagiozi*), and they're on beautiful display in this tiny outdoor theatre every summer. Sure it's all in Greek, but the humour is slapstick and there's plenty of music in the various shows. After the 45-minute show, kids can file backstage to see how the magic happens.

Figoures & Koukles
PUPPET THEATRE

(Map p78; ☑ 210 322 7507; www.fkt.gr; Tripodon 30, Plaka; €3.50; ⊙ shows Sun morning) This puppet workshop gives weekly *karagiozi* shows in winter in its sweet 50-seat theatre. The husband-and-wife team are happy to show how the shadow-puppet set-up works and how the figures are made. Check the site for the winter schedule. In summer, they mount more frequent shows in the Theatro Skion Tasou Konsta, in the park in Palaio Faliro.

Treno sto Rouf
ARTS CENTRE

(☑ 210 529 8922; www.totrenostorouf.gr; Konstantinoupoleos, Rouf; ⊙ 8pm-late Tue-Sat Sep-Jul; ⬚ 21 or B16 to Rouf, Ⓜ Kerameikos) Look for the glowing headlight on a steam locomotive behind Rouf station. Attached is a string of old train cars converted into a restaurant, bar-cafe, music club and theatre. Even on a night when nothing's scheduled, it's a cool place to have a drink and a snack (€6 to €15) and imagine yourself on the Orient Express.

Stavros Niarchos Foundation Cultural Center
CULTURAL CENTRE

(☑ 216 809 1001; www.snfcc.org; Leoforos Syngrou 364, Kallithea; ⬚ 550 to Onasseio, 10 to Epaminonda) FREE Spreading its winged roof on a hill above Faliron Bay, this Renzo Piano building, surrounded by a vast park (p92), made a big splash on the Athens cultural scene when it opened in 2017. Architecture buffs will love seeing the structure. Otherwise, check the schedule for arts events by the grand pool or at the National Opera of Greece, inside the complex.

National Theatre
THEATRE

(Map p108; ☑ 210 528 8100; www.n-t.gr; Agiou Konstantinou 22-24, Omonia; Ⓜ Omonia) Performances of contemporary plays and ancient theatre in one of the city's finest neoclassical buildings, as well as in venues around town and, in summer, in ancient theatres across Greece. Happily for tourists, some of the productions are surtitled in English.

Pallas
THEATRE

(Map p78; ☑ 210 321 3100; www.ellthea.gr; Voukourestiou 5, Syntagma; Ⓜ Syntagma) One of Athens' premier theatres, the Pallas is centrally located and stages large productions, often in Greek. The Mikro Pallas is a smaller, basement theatre in the same complex, connected via an indoor strip of sleek bars and cafes.

Megaron Mousikis
PERFORMING ARTS

(Athens Concert Hall; ☑ 210 728 2333; www.megaron.gr; Kokkali 1, cnr Leoforos Vasilissis Sofias, Ilissia; ⊙ box office 10am-6pm Mon-Fri, to 2pm Sat, later on performance days; Ⓜ Megaro Mousikis) The city's state-of-the-art concert hall presents a rich winter program of operas and concerts featuring world-class international and Greek performers. In summer, it has shows in the back garden.

Dora Stratou Dance Theatre
DANCE

(Map p64; ☑ 210 921 4650; www.grdance.org; Filopappou Hill; adult/child €15/5; ⊙ performances 9.30pm Wed-Fri, 8.30pm Sat & Sun Jun-Sep; Ⓜ Petralona, Akropoli) Every summer this company performs its repertoire of Greek folk dances at its open-air theatre on the western side of Filopappou Hill. It also runs folk-dancing workshops in summer.

Greek National Opera
OPERA

(Ethniki Lyriki Skini; ☑ 210 366 2100; www.nationalopera.gr; Leoforos Syngrou 364, Kallithea) The season runs from November to June. Performances are usually held at the grand

Renzo Piano building at the Stavros Niarchos Foundation Cultural Center, plus the Odeon of Herodes Atticus (p73) in summer. The opera's former home, the Olympia Theatre, is also still used, and is a central place to buy tickets.

Olympia Theatre
PERFORMING ARTS

(Map p108; ☑ 210 361 2461; Akadimias 59, Exarhia; Ⓜ Panepistimio) From November to June; ballet, symphony and some opera.

Technopolis
PERFORMING ARTS

(Map p84; ☑ 210 346 7322; www.technopolisathens.com; Pireos 100, Gazi; Ⓜ Kerameikos) There's always something on at the city's old gasworks, the impressively restored 1862 complex of furnaces and industrial buildings. It hosts multimedia exhibitions, concerts, festivals and special events and has a pleasant cafe.

🔒 Shopping

Central Athens is one big shopping hub, with an eclectic mix of stores, many still organised roughly by category – lace and buttons on one block, light bulbs on the next. The main (if generic) shopping street is pedestrianised Ermou, running from Syntagma to Monastiraki.

Books, Maps & Music

Politeia
BOOKS

(Map p108; ☑ 210 360 0235; www.politeianet.gr; Asklipiou 1-3, Panepistimio; ⊙ 9am-9pm Mon-Fri, to 8pm Sat; Ⓜ Panepistimio) Large bookstore that occupies four storefronts. While it doesn't have a dedicated English section, it does stock English-language books, filed in the relevant sections. And because it's on the edge of Exarhia, it stocks communist theory in the impulse-buy section by the checkout.

Anavasi
MAPS, BOOKS

(Map p78; ☑ 210 321 8104; www.anavasi.gr; Voulis 32, cnr Apollonos, Syntagma; ⊙ 9.30am-5.30pm Mon & Wed, to 8.30pm Tue, Thu & Fri, 10am-4.30pm Sat; Ⓜ Syntagma) Great travel bookshop with an extensive range of Greece maps and walking and activity guides.

Yiannis Samouelin
MUSIC

(Map p78; ☑ 210 321 2433; www.musicshop.gr; Ifestou 36, Monastiraki; ⊙ 9am-7pm; Ⓜ Monastiraki) Wedged between more modern, generic shops on Ifestou, this shop is the place to buy the bouzouki of your dreams. It has been dealing in musical instruments from around the world since 1928.

Xylouris
MUSIC

(Map p108; ☑ 210 322 2711; http://xilouris.gr; Stoa Pesmatzoglou, Panepistimiou 39, Panepistimio; ⊙ 9am-4pm Mon, Wed & Sat, to 8pm Tue, Thu & Fri; Ⓜ Panepistimio) Set in an arcade with several other music shops, this treasure trove is run by the family of legendary Cretan composer Nikos Xylouris. They can guide you through the comprehensive range of Greek music. Also has a branch at the Museum of Greek Popular Instruments (p80).

Comicon Shop
COMICS

(Map p108; ☑ 213 008 0255; www.comicon-shop.gr; Solonos 128, Exarhia; Ⓜ Omonia) Browse a full range of Greek indie comics, graphic novels and zines.

Travel Bookstore
BOOKS

(Map p108; ☑ 210 361 6943; www.travelbookstore.gr; Solonos 71, Panepistimio; ⊙ 8.30am-4.30pm Mon, Wed & Sat, to 8.30pm Tue, Thu & Fri) Good central place for maps.

Syd
MUSIC

(Map p78; ☑ 210 321 8374; www.sydrecords.com; Protogenous 13, Monastiraki; ⊙ noon-8pm; Ⓜ Monastiraki) Not just vinyl records, but the whole 'vinyl culture' – whatever that entails. Lots of new and interesting stuff, plus tickets to local shows.

Tsigaridas
BOOKS

(Map p108; ☑ 210 271 7521; www.tsigaridasbooks.gr; Alikarnassou 19, Panepistimio; ⊙ 8am-5pm Mon, to 8pm Tue-Fri, to 3pm Sat; Ⓜ Panepistimio) The best selection of English books – in fact, books in all languages – in central Athens.

Fashion & Jewellery

Korres
COSMETICS

(Map p78; ☑ 210 321 0054; www.korres.com; Ermou 4, Syntagma; ⊙ 9am-9pm Mon-Fri, to 8pm Sat; Ⓜ Syntagma) Most pharmacies stock at least some of this popular natural-beauty-product line, but you can get the full range at the company's original homeopathic pharmacy – at a fraction of the price you'll pay in London or New York. There's also a branch at the airport and one near the Panathenaic Stadium.

Fanourakis
JEWELLERY

(Map p102; ☑ 210 721 1762; www.fanourakis.gr; Patriarhou Ioakeim 23, Kolonaki; ⊙ 10am-5pm Mon, Wed & Sat, to 9pm Tue, Thu & Fri; Ⓜ Syntagma) One of the most creative Greek jewellers, Fanourakis designs delicate pieces of folded gold, encrusted rings, bows and other unique creations. The forms are sheer art, a factor that is also reflected in the prices (though it now has a more inexpensive line as well).

El.Marneri Galerie
JEWELLERY, ART

(Map p74; ☑ 210 861 9488; www.elenimarneri. com; Lembesi 5-7, Makrygianni; ⊙ 11am-8pm Tue, Thu & Fri, to 4pm Wed & Sat; Ⓜ Akropoli) Sample rotating exhibitions of local modern art and some of the best jewellery in the city. Handmade, unusual and totally eye-catching.

Lovecuts
CLOTHING

(Map p74; ☑ 215 501 1526; Veikou 2, Makrygianni; ⊙ 10am-2pm Mon, 4-8pm Tue, noon-4pm Wed, 11am-2.30pm & 5.30-8.30pm Thu & Fri, 10am-3pm Sat; Ⓜ Akropoli) A young Greek designer makes all the cute, affordable cotton clothing here, such as reversible hoodies and skirts in fun prints. One of several creative, small-scale boutiques on this street.

Rien
FASHION & ACCESSORIES

(Map p84; ☑ 210 342 0622; www.rien.gr; Triptolemou 2-4, Gazi; ⊙ 4-8pm Wed-Sat, or by appointment; Ⓜ Kerameikos) Penny Vomva designs stylish, sexy clothes with naturalistic lines. Her handbags are colourful leather fancies.

Melissinos Art
SHOES

(Map p78; ☑ 210 321 9247; www.melissinos poetsandalmaker.com; Agias Theklas 2, Psyrri; ⊙ 10am-8pm, to 6pm winter; Ⓜ Monastiraki) Pantelis Melissinos continues the sandal-making tradition of his famous poet/cobbler father Stavros, who built his reputation by crafting Classical-inspired shoe designs for Hollywood stars. The shop can get a bit crowded, as people come for the character of Pantelis himself. But the prices are reasonable – and where else can you get sandals adjusted just to your feet?

Olgianna Melissinos
SHOES

(Map p78; ☑ 210 331 1925; www.melissinos-sandals.gr; Normanou 7, Monastiraki; ⊙ 10am-6pm Mon, Wed, Sat & Sun, to 8pm Tue, Thu & Fri; Ⓜ Monastiraki) Another scion of the legendary Stavros Melissinos, Olgianna has a line of custom-fitted sandals as well as smart belts and bags. She can also make designs to order.

Vassilis Zoulias
CLOTHING

(Map p102; ☑ 210 338 9924; www.vassiliszoulias. com; Akadimias 4, Kolonaki; ⊙ 10am-5pm Mon, Wed & Sat, to 9pm Tue, Thu & Fri; Ⓜ Syntagma) An exquisite range of elegant, feminine shoes can be found at the boutique store of Greece's Manolo Blahnik. Some of these designs are works of art inspired by '50s and '60s films, as is his couture line.

Lalaounis
JEWELLERY

(Map p78; ☑ 210 361 1371; www.iliaslalaounis. eu; Panepistimiou 6, cnr Voukourestiou, Syntagma; ⊙ 10am-4.30pm Mon, Wed & Sat, to 8pm Tue, Thu & Fri; Ⓜ Syntagma) Leading Greek jeweller Lalaounis' exquisitely crafted creations reflect ancient Greek motifs and draw inspiration from other cultures, biology, nature and mythology. If you like his work, you may also appreciate his museum (Map p74; ☑ 210 922 1044; www.lalaounis-jewelrymuseum.gr; Kallisperi 12, cnr Karyatidon, Makrygianni; adult/child €5/free; ⊙ 9am-3pm Tue-Sat, 11am-4pm Sun; Ⓜ Akropoli).

Actipis
JEWELLERY

(Map p78; ☑ 210 323 6907; www.actipis.com; Lekka 20, Syntagma; ⊙ 11.30am-8pm Mon-Fri, to 5pm Sat Nov-Apr; Ⓜ Syntagma) Spiros Actipis designs elegant jewellery using smooth pebbles, gleaming silver and raw leather. The shop closes in summer.

Food

Bahar
FOOD

(Map p108; ☑ 210 321 7225; www.bahar.gr; Evripidou 31, Omonia; ⊙ 7am-3pm Mon-Thu & Sat, to 6pm Fri; Ⓜ Omonia, Monastiraki) Evripidou, just south of the central market, is Athens' traditional street for spices, a couple of highly aromatic blocks of Mediterranean herbs and imported seeds, barks and other wonders. Bahar is just one of half a dozen shops here, all overflowing with hundreds of ways to add flavour and fragrance to your life.

Pantopoleion
FOOD & DRINKS

(Map p108; ☑ 210 323 4612; www.atenco.gr; Sofokleous 1, Omonia; ⊙ 8am-7pm; Ⓜ Panepistimio) Enormous store selling traditional food products from all over Greece, from Santorini capers and boutique olive oils to Cretan rusks, jars of goodies for edible souvenirs and Greek wines and spirits.

Bakaliko
FOOD & DRINKS

(Map p64; ☑ 210 756 0055; Proklou 31, Pangrati; ⊙ 9am-3pm Mon, Tue & Sat, to 6pm Wed, Thu & Fri; 🚌 2, 4, 11 to Plateia Plastira) One-stop shopping for the best Greek food products: the store has won awards for its dedication and stock of traditional oil, wine, cheese, yoghurt and honey. Herbs hang in bunches, lentils fill sacks, beans are dazzling in their freshness and variety.

Aristokratikon
FOOD

(Map p78; ☑ 210 323 4373; www.aristokratikon. com; Voulis 7, Syntagma; ⊙ 8am-9pm Mon-Fri, to 4pm Sat; Ⓜ Syntagma) Since 1928, this shop has been making fine chocolates. One of its specialities is dried fruits and candied citrus peel dipped in dark chocolate. It's in the tiny nuts-and-sweets district on Karageorgi Servias; look for it just inside an arcade.

Gusto di Grecia
FOOD & DRINKS

(Map p102; ☑ 210 362 6809; Pindarou 16-20, Kolonaki; ⊙ 8am-9pm Mon-Sat, 10am-6pm Sun; Ⓜ Syntagma) Shop for the best treats from all over Greece, from cheese to local honeys, cold cuts, olive oil and wine.

Fine Wine
WINE

(Map p78; ☑ 210 323 0350; www.finewine.gr; Lysikratous 3, Plaka; ⊙ noon-9pm; Ⓜ Akropoli) In the winding streets of Plaka, the finest wines can be found in this small terracotta-hued building. It's a welcoming destination for the curious and for local wine lovers who come to browse the rows of vintage Greek wines.

Gifts & Souvenirs

★ Forget Me Not
GIFTS & SOUVENIRS

(Map p78; ☑ 210 325 3740; www.forgetmenot athens.gr; Adrianou 100, Plaka; ⊙ 10am-10pm May-Sep, to 8pm Oct-Apr; Ⓜ Syntagma, Monastiraki) This impeccable small store stocks supercool design gear, from fashion to housewares and gifts, all by contemporary Greek designers. Great for gift shopping – who doesn't want a set of cheerful 'evil eye' coasters or some Hermes-winged beach sandals?

Centre of Hellenic Tradition
ARTS & CRAFTS

(Map p78; ☑ 210 321 3023; www.kelp.gr; Pandrosou 36, Monastiraki; ⊙ 9am-8pm Apr-Nov, to 6pm Oct-Mar; Ⓜ Monastiraki) If you like traditional crafts, make this one of your first stops, to see the range and skill of Greek artisans. This organisation collects excellent work and stocks its shop with ceramics, sculpture and handicrafts from around the country. There's an old-style *kafeneio* (coffee house) upstairs (open till midnight) that makes a nice break from the Monastiraki shopping frenzy.

Mompso
ARTS & CRAFTS

(Map p108; ☑ 210 323 0670; www.mompso.com; Athinas 33, Psyrri; ⊙ 10am-6pm Mon-Sat; Ⓜ Monastiraki) The curators of Mompso have put a refined spin on all things rural, so it has the most elegant and excellent-quality equestrian supplies and traditional accessories for donkeys (beaded headdresses), shepherds (bronze bells) and country folk (walking sticks).

Mastiha Shop
FOOD, BEAUTY

(Map p78; ☑ 210 363 2750; www.mastihashop.com; Panepistimiou 6, Syntagma; ⊙ 9am-8pm Mon & Wed, to 9pm Tue, Thu & Fri, to 5pm Sat; Ⓜ Syntagma)

Mastic, the medicinal resin from rare trees only on the island of Chios, is the key ingredient in everything in this store, from natural skin products to a liqueur that's divine when served chilled.

Amorgos
ARTS & CRAFTS

(Map p78; ☑ 210 324 3836; www.amorgosart.gr; Kodrou 3, Plaka; ⊙ 11am-8pm Mon-Fri, to 7pm Sat; Ⓜ Syntagma) Charming store crammed with wooden toys, *karagiozis* puppets, ceramics, embroidery and other folk art, as well as carved wooden furniture made by the owner.

Apivita
COSMETICS

(Map p102; ☑ 210 364 0560; www.apivita.com; Solonos 6, Kolonaki; ⊙ 10am-9pm Tue, Thu & Fri, to 5pm Mon, Wed & Sat, spa closed Mon & Sun; Ⓜ Syntagma) Honey, propolis and other bee-made stuff are the wonder ingredients in many of Apivita's natural beauty products. You can also try Greek herbal teas or head upstairs to the spa. There's also a branch at the airport.

Aidini
ARTS & CRAFTS

(Map p78; ☑ 210 323 4591; Nikis 32, Syntagma; ⊙ 10.30am-5pm Mon & Wed, to 9pm Tue, Thu & Fri, to 4pm Sat; Ⓜ Syntagma) Artisan Errikos Aidini's unique metal creations are made in his workshop at the back of this charming store, including small mirrors, candlesticks, lamps, planes and his signature bronze boats.

Markets

Athens Central Market
MARKET

(Varvakios Agora; Map p108; Athinas, btwn Sofokleous & Evripidou; ⊙ 7am-3pm Mon-Sat; Ⓜ Monastiraki, Panepistimio, Omonia) The hectic, colourful Athens *agora* (market; also referred to as the Varvakios Agora) is the highlight of the vibrant Athinas market district. It's a sensory and gastronomic delight, with an amazing range of olives, spices, cheeses and deli treats. The historic **meat market** (Map p108; ⊙ 7am-6pm Mon-Sat), with hanging carcasses illuminated by swinging light bulbs, is a highlight. **Fruits and vegetables** (Map p108; Athinas, btwn Sofokleous & Evripidou, Omonia; ⊙ 7am-6pm Mon-Sat) are across Athinas.

Kolonaki Weekly Market
MARKET

(Map p102; www.laikesagores.gr; Xenokratous, Kolonaki; ⊙ 7am-2pm Fri; Ⓜ Syntagma) Most Athens neighbourhoods have a weekly *laïki agora*, a street market for fruit, veg and household miscellany, and Kolonaki's is a good one. Leafy Xenokratous is blocked off to traffic from Friday morning to early afternoon. Local regulars come to buy fresh fruit, vegetables, fish, honey, handmade products and flowers.

Exarhia Weekly Market   MARKET
(Map p64; www.laikesagores.gr; Kalidromiou, Exarhia; ☉6am-2pm Sat; 🚋026, Ⓜ Omonia) With rowdy traders working against lovely neoclassical buildings, this is one of the most atmospheric renditions of the *laïki agora*, the weekly market that takes over a street in each big neighbourhood every week. Visitors won't have much practical use for the produce and household goods, but look for the roving ouzo seller. Or camp at a cafe and spectate.

★Monastiraki Flea Market   MARKET
(Map p78; btwn Adrianou, Ifestou & Ermou, Monastiraki; ☉daily May-Oct, Sun-Wed & Fri Nov-Apr; Ⓜ Monastiraki) What's touted as a 'flea market' is now mostly souvenir shops, though there are still a few good artisans, as well as *palaiopoleia* ('old-stuff sellers'). For the best rummaging, come Sunday mornings, when dealers of jewellery, handicrafts and bric-a-brac set up tables on Plateia Avyssinias.

Eleonas Flea Market   MARKET
(Pazari; Agias Annis, Eleonas; ☉dawn-2pm Sun; Ⓜ Eleonas) The so-called 'Gypsy market' is not for everyone. The city's trash-pickers and junk dealers, plus sellers of vegetables, new clothes and bulk items, lay out their wares in several warehouses and parking lots in this industrial part of town. The brave of heart can find some bargains, collectables and kitsch delights among the junk.

❶ Information

DANGERS & ANNOYANCES
During the financial crisis, crime has risen in Athens. But this is a rise from almost zero, and violent street crime remains relatively rare. Nonetheless, travellers should be alert. Stay aware of your surroundings at night, especially in streets around Omonia, where prostitutes and junkies gather, as well as by the Mavromateon bus terminal, as the adjacent park is a rather grim homeless encampment.

EMERGENCY
Athens' landline numbers begin with 210. Mobile phones begin with 6.

ELPA (Elliniki Leschi Aftokinitou kai Periigiseon; 🖉210 606 8800, 24hr roadside assistance 10400; Leoforos Mesogion 541, Agia Paraskevi, Athens) Nationwide roadside assistance.

Police station (🖉210 770 5711, emergency 100; www.astynomia.gr; Leoforos Alexandras 173, Ambelokipi; Ⓜ Ambelokipi); **Syntagma**

station (🖉210 725 7000, emergency 100; Mimnermou 6-8; Ⓜ Syntagma)

Tourist Police (🖉210 920 0724, 24hr 171; Veïkou 43-45, Koukaki; ☉8am-10pm; Ⓜ Sygrou-Fix, Akropoli)

MEDICAL SERVICES
Check pharmacy windows for details of the nearest duty pharmacy, or call 🖉1434 (Greek only). There's a 24-hour pharmacy at the airport.

SOS Doctors (🖉210 821 1888, 1016; www.sosiatroi.gr; ☉24hr) Pay service with English-speaking doctors.

MONEY
Major banks have branches around Syntagma. ATMs are plentiful enough in commercial districts, but harder to find in more residential areas.

National Bank of Greece (🖉210 334 0500; cnr Karageorgi Servias & Stadiou, Syntagma; Ⓜ Syntagma) Has a 24-hour automated exchange machine.

Onexchange Currency and money transfers. Branches: **Syntagma** (🖉210 331 2462; www.onexchange.gr; Karageorgi Servias 2, Syntagma; ☉9am-9pm; Ⓜ Syntagma), **Monastiraki** (🖉210 322 2657; www.onexchange.gr; Areos 1, Monastiraki; ☉9am-9pm; Ⓜ Monastiraki).

POST
Athens Central Post Office (Map p108; Eolou 100; ☉7.30am-8.30pm Mon-Fri, to 2.30pm Sat; Ⓜ Omonia)

Parcel Post Office (Map p78; Mitropoleos 60, Monastiraki; ☉7.30am-8.30pm Mon-Fri; Ⓜ Monastiraki)

Syntagma Post Office (Map p78; Plateia Syntagmatos, Syntagma; ☉7.30am-8.30pm Mon-Fri, to 2.30pm Sat, 9am-1.30pm Sun; Ⓜ Syntagma)

TOURIST INFORMATION
EOT (Greek National Tourism Organisation; Map p74; 🖉210 331 0347, 210 331 0716; www.visitgreece.gr; Dionysiou Areopagitou 18-20, Makrygianni; ☉8am-8pm Mon-Fri, 10am-4pm Sat & Sun May-Sep, 9am-7pm Mon-Fri Oct-Apr; Ⓜ Akropoli) Free Athens map, transport information and *Athens and Attica* booklet. There's also a desk at **Athens Airport** (☉9am-5pm Mon-Fri, 10am-4pm Sat).

Athens Airport Information Desk (☉24hr) This 24-hour desk has Athens info, booklets and the free Athens Spotlighted discount card for restaurants and attractions.

Athens City Information Kiosks Airport (🖉210 353 0390; www.thisisathens.org; ☉8am-8pm; Ⓜ Airport), **Acropolis** (Map p74; 🖉210 321 7116; www.thisisathens.org; Dionysiou Areopagitou & Leoforos Syngrou; ☉9am-9pm May-Sep; Ⓜ Akropoli) Maps, transport information and all Athens info.

ⓘ Getting There & Away

AIR

Modern **Eleftherios Venizelos International Airport** (ATH; ☑ 210 353 0000; www.aia.gr), at Spata, 27km east of Athens, has all the modern conveniences, including 24-hour luggage storage in the arrivals hall, a children's playroom and even a small archaeological museum. It's served by many major and budget airlines as well as high-season charters.

Average domestic one-way fares range from €56 to €140, but vary dramatically depending on season. Between Aegean Airlines and Olympic Air (which have merged but still run separate routes), there are flights to all islands with airports.

Aegean Airlines (www.aegeanair.com)

Air Berlin (AB; ☑ 210 353 5264; www.airberlin. com)

Astra Airlines (☑ 800 700 7466, 2310 489 392; www.astra-airlines.gr) Thessaloniki-based, but with a few flights from Athens to Kozani/Kastoria, Chios and Samos.

British Airways (☑ from landline only 800 4414 6798; www.ba.com)

Olympic Air (☑ 801 801 0101, 210 355 0500; www.olympicair.com)

Sky Express (GQ; ☑ 28102 23800; www.sky express.gr) Crete-based. Beware harsh baggage restrictions.

BOAT

Most ferry, hydrofoil and high-speed catamaran services to the islands leave from the massive port at Piraeus, southwest of Athens.

Purchase tickets online at **Greek Ferries** (☑ 28105 29000; www.greekferries.gr), over the phone or at booths on the quay next to each ferry. Travel agencies selling tickets also surround each port; there is no surcharge.

BUS

Athens has two main intercity bus stations, 5km and 7km north of Omonia, plus a small bay for buses bound for south and east Attica. Pick up timetables at the tourist office, or see the relevant KTEL operator's website. Find a master list of KTEL companies at www.ktelbus.com; **KTEL Attikis** (☑ 210 880 8000; www.ktelattikis.gr) covers the Attica peninsula.

For international buses (from Bulgaria, Turkey etc), there is no single station; some come to Kifissos, while others stop at Plateia Karaïskaki or near Omonia.

Kifissos Terminal A (☑ 210 515 0025; Leoforos Kifisou 100, Peristeri; Ⓜ Agios Antonios) Buses to Thessaloniki, the Peloponnese, Ionian Islands and destinations in western Greece such as Igoumenitsa, Ioannina, Kastoria and Edessa. Local bus 051 goes to central Athens (junction of Zinonos and Menandrou, near Omonia) every 20 minutes from 5am to midnight. Local bus X93 goes to/from the airport. Local bus 420 goes to/from Piraeus (junction of Akti Kondili and Thermopilon). Taxis to Syntagma cost about €16 (€28 at night).

Liossion Terminal B (☑ 210 831 7153; Rikaki 6, Thymarakia; Ⓜ Agios Nikolaos, Attiki) Buses to central and northern Greece, such as Trikala (for Meteora), Delphi, Larissa, Thiva and Volos. To get here, take the metro to Attiki and catch any local bus north on Liossion. Get off the bus at Liossion 260 (stop labelled 'Stathmos Iperastikon Leof'), backtrack to Gousiou and turn left, and you'll see the terminal. Between 11.40pm and 5am, there are no buses to the centre; taxis to Syntagma cost about €15 at night (€9 by day). Local bus X93 connects Kifissos Terminal A, Liossion Terminal B and the Athens Airport.

Mavromateon Terminal (Map p64; ☑ 210 822 5148, 210 880 8000; www.ktelattikis.gr; cnr Leoforos Alexandras & 28 Oktovriou-Patision, Pedion Areos; ☐ 2, 4, 5 or 11 to OTE, Ⓜ Viktoria) About 250m north of the National Archaeological Museum, with buses for around Attica. For Cape Sounion, look for the stop just north of Leoforos Alexandras. Ticket booths and buses for Rafina, Lavrio and Marathon are just north, on Mavromateon.

KTEL Buses to Epidavros (☑ 210 513 4588; www.ktelargolida.gr; 1-way €13)

Tourist Service (www.tourist-service.com) Buses from Piraeus and Athens to Bulgaria.

Key Buses From Kifissos Terminal A

DESTINATION	DURATION	FARE (€)	FREQUENCY
Alexandroupoli	11hr	77	5 daily
Corfu*	9hr	59	3 daily
Epidavros	2½hr	13	2 daily
Igoumenitsa	7½hr	49	3 daily
Ioannina	6¼hr	43	6 daily
Ithaki*	8½hr	52	1 daily
Kalavryta	3hr	18	1 daily
Kefallonia*	7hr	38	4 daily
Lefkada	5¼hr	37	4 daily (5 Jul-Aug)
Monemvasia	6hr	32	4 daily
Nafplio	2½hr	14	hourly
Olympia	5½hr	33	2 daily
Patra	3hr	22	half-hourly
Thessaloniki	7hr	45	9 daily
Zakynthos*	6hr	38	3 daily

* quoted price includes ferry ticket

Key Buses From Liossion Terminal B

DESTINATION	DURATION	FARE (€)	FREQUENCY
Agios Konstantinos	2½hr	17	8 daily
Delphi	2½hr	17	4 daily
Halkida	1¼hr	8	half-hourly
Karpenisi	4½hr	27	2 daily
Paralia Kymis	4½hr	23	2 daily (Jul-Aug)
Trikala (for transfer to Meteora)	4½hr	30	6 daily
Volos	4½hr	30	10 daily

Key Buses From Mavromateon Terminal

DESTINATION	DURATION	FARE (€)	FREQUENCY
Cape Sounion (coastal road)	2hr	6.90	hourly
Lavrio port	1½hr	5.30	half-hourly
Marathon	1½hr	4.10	half-hourly
Rafina port	1hr	2.60	half-hourly

CAR & MOTORCYCLE

Attiki Odos (Attiki Rd), Ethniki Odos (National Rd) and various ring roads facilitate getting in and out of Athens.

The airport has all major car-hire companies, and the top end of Leoforos Syngrou, near the Temple of Olympian Zeus, is dotted with firms. Local companies tend to offer better deals than multinationals. Expect to pay €45 per day, less for three or more days.

Avis (☑ 210 322 4951; www.avis.gr; Leoforos Syngrou 23, Makrygianni; ⊘ 7.30am-9pm; Ⓜ Akropoli)

Budget (☑ 210 922 4200; www.budget.gr; Leoforos Syngrou 23, Makrygianni; ⊘ 7.30am-9pm; Ⓜ Akropoli)

Europcar (☑ 210 921 1444; www.europcar-greece.gr; Leoforos Syngrou 25, Makrygianni; ⊘ 8.30am-9pm; Ⓜ Akropoli)

Hertz (☑ 210 922 0102; www.hertz.gr; Leoforos Syngrou 12, Makrygianni; ⊘ 8am-9pm; Ⓜ Akropoli)

Kosmos (☑ 210 923 4695; www.kosmos-carrental.com; Leoforos Syngrou 5, Makrygianni; ⊘ 8am-8.30pm; Ⓜ Akropoli)

Motorent (☑ 210 923 4939; www.motorent.gr; Kavalloti 4, Makrygianni; ⊘ 9am-6pm Mon-Fri, 9.30am-3pm Sat; Ⓜ Akropoli) From 50cc to 250cc (from €20 per day); must have motorcycle licence (and nerves of steel).

TRAIN

Intercity (IC) trains to central and northern Greece depart from the central **Larisis train station** (Stathmos Larisis; ☑ €1 per min 6am-11pm 14511; www.trainose.gr; Ⓜ Larissa Station), about 1km northwest of Plateia Omonias.

For the Peloponnese, take the **suburban rail** (☑ 14511; www.trainose.gr) to Kiato and change for a bus there. At the time of research, the Patra train line was closed for repairs, so OSE buses replace its services. It's easier to just take a bus from Athens' Kifissos Bus Terminal A to your ultimate destination.

At the time of research, Greece's train system was in a state of flux due to the financial crisis. Domestic schedules/fares should be confirmed online or at **OSE** (☑ 210 362 4406, 210 362 4402, €0.99 per min 6am-11pm 14511; www.trainose.gr; Sina 6, Syntagma; ⊘ 8am-3pm Mon-Fri; Ⓜ Panepistimio). Tickets can be bought online.

Consult www.seat61.com for tips on international trains to/from Greece; all service goes via Thessaloniki.

DESTINATION	DURATION	FARE (€)	FREQUENCY
Alexandroupoli	12¼hr	40	1 daily (overnight)
Alexandroupoli (IC)	11hr	65	1 daily (via Thessaloniki)
Corinth (suburban rail)	1hr 20min	8	13 daily
Kalambaka (for Meteora)	5hr	30	1 daily direct, 4 via Paleofarsalos (€18)
Kiato (suburban rail)	1hr 40min	8	13 daily
Thessaloniki	7hr	25	1 daily
Thessaloniki (IC)	5½hr	45	5 daily
Volos (IC)	5hr	30	6 daily (via Larissa)

❶ Getting Around

TO/FROM THE AIRPORT

The metro and suburban rail provide quick connections to central Athens. The bus is cheapest, though it takes longer. The suburban rail also goes to Piraeus and Larisis stations.

Bus

Express buses operate 24 hours between the airport and the city centre, Piraeus and KTEL bus terminals. At the airport, buy tickets (€6; not valid for other forms of public transport) at the booth near the stops.

Plateia Syntagmatos Bus X95 (Map p78; tickets €5; 1-1½ hours, every 30 minutes, ⊘24hrs). The Syntagma stop is on Othonos St.

Kifissos Terminal A bus station Bus X93 (1 hour; every 30 minutes by day, 60 minutes at night; ⊘24hrs).

Piraeus Bus X96 (1½ hours; every 20 minutes; ⊘24hrs). To Plateia Karaïskaki.

Metro

Metro line 3 goes to the airport. Some trains terminate early at Doukissis Plakentias; disembark and wait for the airport train (displayed on the train and platform screen). Trains run every 30 minutes, leaving Monastiraki between 5.50am and midnight, and the airport between 5.30am and 11.30pm, on the hour and half-hour.

Airport tickets cost €10 per adult or €18 return (return valid seven days). The fare for two/three or more passengers is €9/8 each, so purchase tickets together (same with suburban rail). Tickets are valid for all forms of public transport for 90 minutes (revalidate your ticket on the final mode of transport).

Suburban Rail

Take the suburban rail (one hour) from central Athens (Larisis train station), then change trains for the airport at Ano Liosia, or Neratziotissa (on metro line 1); it's the same price as the metro but the return ticket is valid for a month. The metro also connects with the suburban rail at Doukissis Plakentias (line 3). Trains to the airport run from 6am to midnight; trains from the airport to Athens run from 5.10am to 11.30pm; trains run every 15 minutes from Neratziotissa.

Suburban rail also goes from the airport to Piraeus (change trains at Neratziotissa) and Kiato in the Peloponnese (via Corinth).

Taxi

Fares are fixed between the airport and the centre (both directions): day/night (midnight to 5am) €38/54. For Piraeus, expect day/night €50/60 to Piraeus. It's around 30 to 45 minutes to the centre and an hour to Piraeus.

To prebook a taxi, contact **Welcome Pickups** (www.welcomepickups.com), at the same flat rate as regular taxis, with local English-speaking drivers.

Even experienced cyclists might find Athens' roads a challenge, with no cycle lanes, often reckless drivers and loads of hills – but some hardy locals do ride. Work is progressing on a 27km bike route between Kifisia in the north and Faliro in the south, but only small stretches are open, south of Thisio. A few outfits offer bicycle hire, such as Funky Rides (p93).

CAR & MOTORCYCLE

Athens' notorious traffic congestion, confusing signage, impatient/erratic drivers and narrow one-way streets make for occasionally night-marish driving.

Contrary to what you see, parking is actually illegal alongside kerbs marked with yellow lines, on footpaths and in pedestrian malls. Paid parking areas require tickets available from kiosks.

PUBLIC TRANSPORT

Athens has an extensive and inexpensive integrated public-transport network of metro, electric trolleybuses and regular buses. Visitors are most likely to use the metro and the trolleys, which run roughly north–south. Bus routes are extensive, but no printed maps exist; information is very well integrated with mobile-app trip planners, though. You can also use the trip planner at the website of bus company **OASA** (Athens Urban Transport Organisation; ☑11185; www.oasa.gr; ⊘6.30am-11.30pm Mon-Fri, from 7.30am Sat & Sun).

Tram and metro extensions are under way, but will likely not be used much by visitors; the waterfront tram will reach Piraeus by 2018, and metro line 3 will eventually reach the commercial port southwest of the city.

Tickets

In 2017, the Athens transport network was shifting away from paper tickets to stored-value swipe cards. But at the time of research, there was no date set for the transition.

In the meantime, paper tickets good for 90 minutes (€1.40) and a 24-hour/five-day travel pass (€4/10) are valid for all forms of public transport except for airport services. The three-day tourist ticket (€22) includes one round-trip airport ride. Children under six travel free; people under 18 and over 65 pay half-fare.

Buy tickets in metro stations or transport kiosks or most *periptera* (kiosks). Validate the ticket in the machine as you board your transport of choice.

Bus & Trolleybus

Local express buses, regular buses and electric trolleybuses operate every 15 minutes from 5am to midnight. The OASA website's trip planner shows routes.

Buses to Cape Sounion (Map p78; www.ktelattikis.gr)

Buses to Elefsina (Map p108)

Buses to Moni Kaisarianis (Map p108)

The metro is preferable, but after it stops at midnight, you can still get to Piraeus on the bus:

From Syntagma Bus 040 (Map p78). On Filellinon just south of Syntagma to Akti Xaveriou (every 10 to 20 minutes 6am to midnight, half-hourly after).

From Omonia Bus 500 (Map p108) Opposite the town hall south of Omonia to Plateia Themistokleous (hourly midnight to 5am, starting in Kifisia).

Metro

The metro works well and posted maps have clear icons and English translations. Trains operate from 5am to midnight, every four minutes during peak periods and every 10 minutes off-peak. On Friday and Saturday, lines 2 and 3 run till 2am. Get information at www.stasy.gr. All stations have wheelchair access.

Line 1 (Green) The oldest line, Kifisia–Piraeus, known as the Ilektriko, is slower than the others and above ground. Transfer at Omonia and Attiki for line 2, Monastiraki for line 3 and Neratziotissa for suburban rail. The hourly all-night bus service (bus 500, Piraeus–Kifisia) follows this route, stopping outside the metro stations.

Line 2 (Red) Runs from Agios Antonios in the northwest to Agios Dimitrios in the southeast. Attiki and Omonia connect with line 1; Syntagma connects with line 3.

Line 3 (Blue) Runs northeast from Egaleo to Doukissis Plakentias, with airport trains continuing on from there. Transfer for line 1 at Monastiraki; for line 2 at Syntagma.

Train

Fast suburban rail (p126) links Athens with the airport, Piraeus, the outer regions and the northern Peloponnese. The airport–Kiato line (€14, 1½ hours) connects to the metro at Doukissis Plakentias and Neratziotissa. Two other lines cross the metro at Larissa station.

Funicular Railway (Teleferik; ☑ 210 721 0701; return/1-way €7.50/5; ☉ every 30min 9am-3am) For Lykavittos Hill.

Tram

Athens' **tram** (www.stasy.gr) offers a slow, scenic coastal journey to Faliro and Voula, via Glyfada.

Trams run from Syntagma, opposite the National Gardens, to the coast, then split: east to Voula (one hour) and west to Faliro (45 minutes). (The western line is being extended to Piraeus but most visitors will find the metro a faster option.) Service is from 5.30am to 1am Sunday to Thursday (every 10 minutes), and to 2.30am on Friday and Saturday (every 40 minutes). Ticket vending machines are on the platforms.

TAXI

Athens' taxis are excellent value and can be the key for efficient travel on some routes. But it can be tricky getting one, especially during rush hour. Thrust your arm out vigorously...you may still have to shout your destination to the driver

to see if he or she is interested. Make sure the meter is on. It is better to use the mobile app **Taxibeat** (www.taxibeat.gr) – you can book from abroad and pay in cash. It also does deliveries. Uber also operates in Athens. Or call a taxi from dispatchers such as **Athina 1** (☑ 210 921 0417, 210 921 2800; www.athens1.gr), **Enotita** (☑ 6980666720, 18388, 210 649 5099; www.athensradiotaxienotita.gr) or **Parthenon** (☑ 210 532 3300; www.radiotaxi-parthenon.gr).

ATHENS PORTS

Piraeus   Πειραιάς

POP 163,688

Ten kilometres southwest of central Athens, Piraeus is dazzling in its scale, its seemingly endless quays filled with ferries, ships and hydrofoils. It's the biggest port in the Mediterranean (with more than 20 million passengers passing through annually), the hub of the Aegean ferry network, the centre of Greece's maritime trade and the base for its large merchant navy. While technically its own city, it melds into the Athens sprawl, with close to half a million people living in the greater area.

Shabby and congested, central Piraeus is not a place where visitors choose to linger. Beyond its shipping offices, banks and public buildings are a jumble of pedestrian precincts, shopping strips and rather grungy areas. The most attractive quarter lies east around **Zea Marina** and **Mikrolimano** harbours. The latter is lined with cafes, restaurants and bars often filled with people who've disembarked from cruise ships for the day.

◉ Sights

Electric Railways Museum   MUSEUM
(☑ 210 412 9503, 210 414 7552; www.museum-synt-isap.gr; Loudovikou 1; ☉ 9am-2pm Mon-Fri; Ⓜ Piraeus) **FREE** Tucked inside the Piraeus station, this museum is a trove of old switches, nifty models and cool machinery, including a gleaming old wooden train car. It's a passion project of a former railway employee, and he and the other staff are full of interesting facts.

Piraeus Archaeological Museum   MUSEUM
(☑ 210 452 1598; http://odysseus.culture.gr; Harilaou Trikoupi 31; adult/child €4/free; ☉ 8am-3pm Tue-Sun) The museum's star attraction is the magnificent **statue of Apollo**, the *Piraeus Kouros*, the larger-than-life, oldest hollow

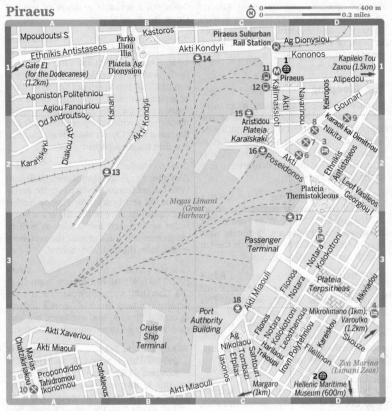

Piraeus

N 0 ——————— 400 m
0 ——————— 0.2 miles

ATHENS & AROUND PIRAEUS

Piraeus

◉ Sights
1 Electric Railways Museum	C1
2 Piraeus Archaeological Museum	D4

🛏 Sleeping
3 Hotel Triton	D2
4 Phidias Piraeus	D4
5 Piraeus Dream City Hotel	D3

🍴 Eating
6 Captain's Grill	D2
7 General Market	D2
8 Mandragoras	D2
9 Rakadiko	D2
10 Yperokeanio	A4

ℹ Transport
11 Bus X96 to/from Airport	C1
12 Ferry Port Shuttle Bus	C1
13 Gate E2 (for Crete & Northeastern Aegean Islands)	B2
14 Gate E4 (for Kythira)	C1
15 Gate E7 (for the Western & Central Cyclades)	C1
16 Gate E8 (for the Saronic Gulf Islands)	C2
17 Gate E9 (for the Cyclades, Samos, Ikaria)	D3
18 Piraeus Port Authority	C4

bronze statue yet found. It dates from about 520 BC and was discovered buried in rubble in 1959. Other important finds from the area include fine tomb reliefs from the 4th to 2nd centuries BC.

Hellenic Maritime Museum   MUSEUM
(☏ 210 451 6264; http://hmmuseum.gr; Akti Themistokleous, Plateia Freatidas, Zea Marina; €4; ⊙9am-2pm Tue-Sat) As nautical museums go, this unfortunately isn't one of the best,

despite Greece's long maritime history. Still, it does have all the requisite models of ancient and modern ships, seascapes by leading 19th- and 20th-century Greek painters, guns, flags and maps, and even part of a submarine.

🛏 Sleeping

If you're catching an early ferry, it can make sense to stay in Piraeus instead of central Athens, but be wary of the cheapest hotels, as they are often aimed at sailors and clandestine liaisons. Don't sleep outside: Piraeus is probably one of the most dangerous places in Greece to do so.

Piraeus Dream City Hotel
HOTEL €

(☎210 411 0555; www.piraeusdream.gr; Notara 78; d/tr from €75/95; ❋@🛜; ⓂPiraeus) This renovated hotel is about a 10-minute walk from the metro; quiet rooms start on the 4th floor. It has a rooftop restaurant.

Hotel Triton
HOTEL €

(☎210 417 3457; www.htriton.gr; Tsamadou 8; s/d/tr from €58/90/95; ❋@🛜; ⓂPiraeus) This simple, conveniently located hotel with helpful staff is a treat compared to some of the other run-down joints in Piraeus. Some rooms overlook the bustling market square. There's one family suite (€148).

Phidias Piraeus
HOTEL €€

(☎210 429 6480; www.hotelphidias.gr; Kountouriotou 189, Zea Marina; s/d/tr from €49/79/119; ❋@🛜; 🚌040 to Terpsithea) A far cry from standard Piraeus grunge, this place is also a bit far from the metro (20-minute walk) and the ferry port. But it runs a free shuttle and you're close to the prettier leisure port, for an evening's stroll. Rooms are simple and new, with cute wallpaper. Full breakfast is an extra €7.

🍴 Eating

The Great Harbour is backed by lots of gritty cafes and fast-food joints; better food and ambience hide away in the backstreets – or further afield around Mikrolimano, Zea Marina and along the waterfront promenade at Freatida.

★ Mandragoras
DELI €

(☎210 417 2961; Gounari 14; ⊙7.45am-4pm Mon, Wed & Sat, to 8pm Tue, Thu & Fri; ⓂPiraeus) This superb delicatessen and spice shop offers a fine selection of gourmet cheeses, readymade mezedhes, olive oils and preserved foods. It's a veritable museum of regional Greek foodstuffs.

Yperokeanio
MEZEDHES €

(☎210 418 0030; Marias Hatzikiriakou 48; dishes €6-12; ⊙noon-11.30pm) Grab a cab to this fantastic seafood *mezedhopoleio*, where you can tuck into small plates of grilled sardines or steamed mussels. For dessert there's *kaimaki* ice cream – an old Asia Minor recipe made chewy with *sahlep* (orchid root) and flavoured with Chios mastic. Book ahead, if possible; it's often packed.

General Market
MARKET €

(Dimosthenous; ⊙6am-4pm Mon-Fri; ⓂPiraeus) With the sea breezes blowing over the morning hustle and bustle, the Piraeus market is an excellent slice of life. There's a broad range of food and bric-a-brac, as well as cheap bars and cafes around the periphery, especially in the back alley behind.

Captain's Grill
GREEK €

(☎210 417 6242; Akti Poseidonos 8; mains €6-12; ⊙9.30am-11pm) A reputable place for an inexpensive and tasty lunch of Greek standards in central Piraeus. Nothing fancy, but very nice owners and superconvenient location.

To Kapileio Tou Zaxou
TAVERNA €€

(☎210 481 3325; Komotinis 37; mains from €15; ⊙noon-1am; 🚌16) It may be a bit inland, but this family-run Greek fish taverna still conveys the spirit of the sea. Choose from grilled catches of the day, calamari and octopus. House wine comes from the big barrels shelved above the tables, as it ought to in a traditional place. A favourite among locals for its reasonable prices and generous portions.

Margaro
SEAFOOD €€

(☎210 451 4226; Marias Hatzikiriakou 126; mains €6-21; ⊙noon-midnight Mon-Sat, to 5.30pm Sun Sep-Jul; 🚌904) This port restaurant is the picture of simplicity, with a menu that comprises exactly three things: salad, fried shrimp and fried red mullet. Although it's tucked away by the naval academy, it's no secret, and can be very crowded on weekends. Take the bus here from the Piraeus metro, or a taxi.

Rakadiko
TAVERNA €€

(☎210 417 8470; www.rakadiko.gr; Karaoli kai Dimitriou 5, Stoa Kouvelou; mains €7-18; ⊙noon-midnight Mon-Sat, 1-6pm Sun; ⓂPiraeus) A spot of calm: head back into this renovated old shopping arcade to dine under grapevines on mezedhes or classic dishes from all over Greece. There's live *rembetika* on weekends. If you're not hungry for a full meal, stop at the adjacent sweets shop for ice cream or very good orange-blossom-scented fried *loukoumadhes*.

★ **Varoulko**   SEAFOOD €€€
(🖂 210 522 8400; www.varoulko.gr; Akti Koumoundourou 52, Mikrolimano; mains €45-65; ⊙1pm-1am) Chef Lefteris Lazarou, a Piraeus native, has been shaping Greek tastes since the 1980s, when he brought fish to the fine-dining menu. For years he had a Michelin-starred restaurant in Athens, but moved back to his roots in 2014. Michelin still approves, and his cooking remains elegant and creative. The setting in Mikrolimano, where sailboats bob, is lovely.

ℹ️ Information

There are luggage lockers at the metro station (€3 for 24 hours, maximum 15 days).

ATMs and money changers line the Great Harbour.

Alpha Bank (🖂 210 412 1721; Ethnikis Antistasseos 9; ⊙8am-2pm Mon-Fri)

National Bank of Greece (🖂 210 414 4311; cnr Antistaseos & Makras Stoas; ⊙8am-2.45pm Mon-Fri)

ℹ️ Getting There & Away

The metro and suburban rail from Athens terminate at the northeastern corner of the Great Harbour on Akti Kalimassioti. Airport bus X96 stops out front. A few ferry departure points are just across the road; for further gates, you'll need a port-run bus (free) or a taxi (cheap).

The Athens tramway is extending its line from Faliro to the harbour, with a terminus just south of the metro stop; it's expected to be completed in 2018.

BOAT

Piraeus is the busiest port in Greece, with daily service to most island groups. The exceptions are the Ionians, with boats only to Kythira (for the other islands, sail from Patra and Igoumenitsa) and the Sporades, plus Kea (Tzia) and Andros in the Cyclades (which sail from Rafina and Lavrio). Piraeus ferries also serve the Peloponnese (Methana, Ermioni, Porto Heli, Monemvasia and Gythio).

Always check departure docks with the ticketing agent.

Note that there are two departure points for Crete: ferries for Iraklio leave from the western end of Akti Kondyli, while ferries for other Cretan ports occasionally dock there as well, or in other places.

Schedules & Tickets

Ferry schedules are reduced in April, May and October, and radically cut in winter, especially to smaller islands. Find schedules and buy tickets online (www.greekferries.gr, www.openseas.gr, www.ferries.gr or company websites), or buy in person at travel agents or at each ferry company's kiosk in front of the boat (open about two hours before sailing). **Piraeus Port Authority** (🖂 210 455 0000, €0.89 per 1min 14541; www.olp.gr) also has schedule information.

In this book, we list ferry schedules in the relevant island/destination chapters.

BUS

The **X96 Piraeus–Athens Airport Express** (Plateia Karaïskaki; tickets €5) stops in front of the metro. It runs around the outside of the port also, but stops rarely, so it's better to take the inside-port shuttle to your gate. Bus 040 goes to Athens from Lambraki at the corner of Vasileos Georgiou II. Arriving, you'll come down Polytehniou; get off at Plateia Korai.

METRO

The fastest and most convenient link between the Great Harbour and Athens is the metro (€1.40, 30 minutes, every 10 minutes, 5am to midnight), near the ferries at the northern end of Akti Kalimassioti.

SUBURBAN RAIL

Piraeus is connected to the suburban rail – the terminus is next to the metro station. To get to the airport or to Kiato in the Peloponnese, you need to change trains at Nerantziotissa.

ℹ️ Getting Around

The port is massive, so a free shuttle bus runs regularly along the quay inside the port from gate E7 to E1; cross over from the metro and you'll see it. For gate E9, look for buses outside the port, with route numbers starting with 8.

The Piraeus city buses most likely to interest travellers are 904 and 905 between Zea Marina and the metro station.

The continuing Athens tramway and metro extensions have made the port area a zoo of blocked streets and redirected traffic.

Rafina   Ραφήνα

POP 13,091

Rafina, on Attica's east coast, is a port town with passenger ferries to the northern Cyclades. If this is your destination, it's a good alternative to Piraeus, as it's smaller (hence, less confusing), and fares are about

20% cheaper. It's also a pleasant place to spend a night if ferry schedules require it.

🛏 Sleeping

Avra   HOTEL €€
(☏ 22940 22780; www.hotelavra.gr; Arafinidon Alon 3; d from €90) Set on one end of Rafina's pretty crescent port, Avra is a big and functional hotel that helps make this town a pleasant stop midtransit. (It also runs a free shuttle to the airport, about 30 minutes away.) Rooms are modern and comfortable, with balconies for watching the ships come in.

❶ Getting There & Away

Rafina is close to Athens airport, so if you're headed to the northern Cyclades (Mykonos, Naxos etc), consider coming here directly, bypassing Athens and Piraeus completely.

BUS

Frequent KTEL buses (p125) run from Athens to Rafina (€2.60, one hour) between 5.45am and 10.30pm, departing from Athens' Mavromateon bus terminal. Buses from Athens airport (€3, 45 minutes) leave from in front of the arrivals hall near the Sofitel, between 4.40am and 10.20pm; buy tickets on board. Both stop on the Rafina quay.

BOAT

Rafina Port Authority (☏ 22940 28888; www. rafinaport.gr) and www.openseas.gr have information on ferries.

Lavrio   Λαύριο
POP 10,370

Lavrio, on the coast 60km southeast of Athens, is the port for ferries to Kea and Kythnos and high-season catamarans to the western Cyclades. It is, unfortunately, not an exciting place to spend the night. The long beach north of the ferry port is a bit of a windsurfing scene, but that same wind is somewhat wearing if you're not on the water. It has a grand industrial past – from silver mining in antiquity to massive late-19th-century steam-powered mining works – but there's not much happening now. (The sprawling ruins of the more recent industry are awesome, but open only to Athens Technical University students.)

◉ Sights

Mineralogical Museum   MUSEUM
(☏ 22920 26270; Iroön Polytehniou, Lavrio; adult/child €2/free; ⊙ 10am-noon Fri-Sun) If you happen to be in town during the museum's limited opening hours, peek in to see fabulous crystals and metals mined from the area, plus a bit about the region's rich mining history. Outside are the ruins of the town's old steam-powered ore-washing facility.

Archaeological Museum   MUSEUM
(☏ 22920 22817; http://odysseus.culture.gr; cnr Agias Paraskevis & Leoforos Souniou; adult/child €2/free; ⊙ 8am-3pm Tue-Sun) Lavrio's small

BOAT SERVICES FROM RAFINA

DESTINATION	COMPANY	DURATION	FARE (€)	FREQUENCY
Andros	Fast Ferries, Golden Star	2½hr	19	4-6 daily
Ios	Golden Star	6hr	48	6 weekly
Mykonos	Fast Ferries, Golden Star	4½hr	29	2-3 daily
Mykonos*	Sea Jets	2¼hr	33	2 daily
Naxos	Fast Ferries	6hr	30	6 weekly
Naxos*	Golden Star, Sea Jets	4hr	33	3 daily
Paros*	Golden Star, Sea Jets	3½hr	30	3 daily
Santorini (Thira)*	Golden Star	6¾hr	48	1 daily
Tinos	Fast Ferries, Golden Star	3¾hr	27	6-9 daily
Tinos*	Sea Jets	2hr	39	2 daily

*high-speed services

archaeological museum holds finds from the area – mostly stone carvings. Some date to 5000 BC. Entrance and parking is on the small branch of Agias Paraskevis on the south side of the building.

❶ Getting There & Away

BUS

KTEL buses (p125) to Lavrio (€5.30, two hours, every 30 minutes) run from the Mavromateon terminal in Athens. Airport buses leave from the front of the arrivals hall near the Sofitel; you must change buses at Markopoulo. Both stop on the Lavrio quay.

BOAT

Lavrio Port Authority (☑ 22920 25249) and www.openseas.gr have ferry information.

TAXI

Taxi Posidon (☑ 22920 24200; www.taxi poseidon.gr) can run you to the airport (day/night €40/55, 30 minutes) and central Athens (€60/80, one hour); fares are higher for pick-up in Athens or the airport. Lavrio to Cape Sounion is €12.

AROUND ATHENS

An agricultural region with several large population centres, the southern Attica peninsula has some fine beaches, particularly along the Apollo Coast and at Shinias, near Marathon. It's also known for its wine production; a group of five **wineries** have information online (www.winesofathens. com), including a downloadable map. Cycle Greece (p93) runs an excellent day-trip bike ride to some.

Until the 7th century, Attica was home to a number of smaller kingdoms, such as those at Eleusis (Elefsina), Ramnous and Brauron (Vravrona). In pure visual terms, the remains of these cities pale alongside the superb Temple of Poseidon at Cape Sounion, but any of them can be nice to visit simply because you'll probably have the place to yourself.

Apollo Coast

Glyfada, about 17km southeast of Athens, is an upscale suburb of Athens that marks the beginning of the Apollo Coast (sometimes called the Athenian Riviera), a 48km stretch down to Cape Sounion of fine beaches, resorts and summer nightlife. It is

❶ APOLLO COAST TOP TIPS

➡ To avoid heavy traffic on weekends in summer, set out by 9am; without much traffic, the drive from Glyfada to Sounion should take about an hour.

➡ Beaches closest to Glyfada can be reached from Athens by tram. To get further south, change in Glyfada or Voula for a coastal bus.

➡ Pack evening wear in your beach bag in case an all-day sun-fest leads to nightclubbing on the beach.

➡ There are free beaches and rocky coves near Palaio Faliro (Edem), Kavouri, Glyfada and south by Varkiza. Look for areas where locals have parked their cars by the side of the road.

a refreshing getaway from Athens and easily reached by bus.

The coast road (Poseidonos Ave, often just called *paraliaki*) leads from Glyfada to **Voula**, **Kavouri** and then bustling and popular **Vouliagmeni** and ritzy Astir Beach. In general, the coast is a bit expensive, but the further south you go, the cheaper and less built-up it becomes. Of note are the natural mineral waters at **Limni Vouliagmenis** and the gay and nudist beaches tucked in the rocky coves at **Limanakia**.

There is better (free) swimming northeast and east of Athens, at Shinias, Marathon and Vravrona, though these take longer to get to and are best reached by car.

🏃 Activities

Most of the Apollo Coast beaches are privately run and charge admission (€5 to €15 per adult). They're usually open from 8am to dusk, May to October (later during heatwaves), and have sunbeds and umbrellas (additional charge in some places), changing rooms, children's playgrounds and cafes. Many morph into summer nightclubs (p111) as well.

Akti tou Iliou BEACH

(☑ 210 985 5169; www.aktitouiliou.gr; Leoforos Poseidonos, Alimos; adult/child Mon-Fri €5/3, Sat & Sun €6/3; ⊗ 8am-8pm; ☐ Zefyros) Relatively laid-back, with a slew of sunloungers and some reed-roofed beach bars, it's one of the closer beaches to Athens (just 7.5km south).

Attica

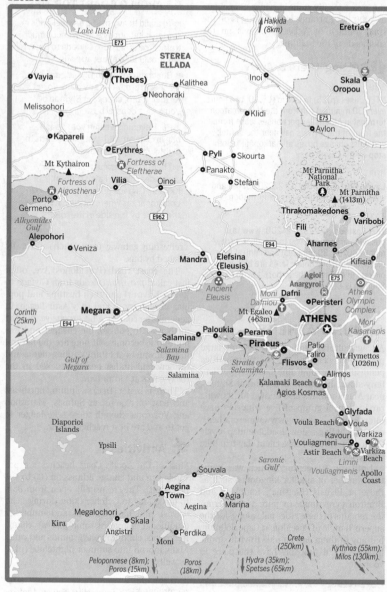

Asteras Beach BEACH
(📞 210 894 1620; www.asterascomplex.com; Glyfada; adult/child Mon-Fri €6/3, Sat & Sun €7/3; ⏱ beach 8.30am-8pm; 🚌 790 from Syntagma, 🚊 T5 to Asteria) Swanky Asteras, convenient to Glyfada and the tram, is a resort without the hotel: a complex of waterfront cafes, play zones, bars and the see-and-be-seen **Balux** (📞 210 894 1620; www.baluxcafe.com; Leoforos Poseidonos 58, Glyfada; 🎵; 🚊 T5 to Asteria) restaurant. If the megabeach with sunloungers for thousands isn't enough, there's also a pool.

🛏 Sleeping

Spending the night along the Apollo Coast can be a bit pricey, and for this reason (and the proximity to Athens), visitors often limit themselves to day outings. But there are a couple of good-value options if you do want to stay the night as part of a road trip.

Villa Orion   HOTEL €

(☑210 895 8000; www.villaorionhotel.gr; Ioanni Metaxa 4, Voula; d/tr incl breakfast €70/85; ❋ 🛜; 🚌A1, A2, 122, 🚌Asklipiio Voulas) This simple hotel has been dressed up with a bit of creative interior decor, but its real attraction is its great value. It's a few blocks inland, yes, but convenient to all the beaches. Rooms have little balconies and breakfast is served outside in a small garden.

Hotel Vouliagmeni Suites   HOTEL €€€

(☑210 896 4901; www.vouliagmenisuites.com; Panos 8, Vouliagmeni; s/d incl breakfast from €172/183; 🚌122 to Agia Pantelimon) This posh pad a bit back from the beach has quirkily decorated luxe rooms, some with sea views.

🍴 Eating

Trigono   TAVERNA €

(☑22990 48540; Athinon 36, Kalyvia; mains €8-15; ☉lunch & dinner) At this casual grill house, the pork chops are flawless and flow nonstop – thanks to an in-house butcher, an exceedingly rare feature in Greece. As it's just off the highway back to Athens, it's a popular family pit stop on weekend afternoons. Go early to avoid the epic post-lunch lull, when it feels like an army has just marched out.

Family   AMERICAN €€

(☑212 104 3411; www.family-voula.gr; Vasileos Pavlou 74, Voula; mains €9-15; ☉9am-2am; 🚌Asklipiio Voulas) The restaurant lives up to its name with affectionate service and a nice homey atmosphere in an old mansion. It has a wide-ranging, family-friendly menu: eggs, burgers, pizzas and plenty more. It's on Voula's pleasant little downtown strip, calmer than Glyfada. It's about a 20-minute walk from the last tram stop.

Moouu Quality Meats   STEAK €€

(☑211 409 6295; Foivis 17, Glyfada; mains €10-25; ☉12.30pm-2am; 🚌Platia Espiridon) Dig in to grilled meats at this steakhouse *du jour* in the heart of Glyfada's restaurant and cafe district.

The restaurants are expensive for Greece (coffee €4.50, mains from €15), but if you don't take a seat, you can order from a basic menu of coffee, water and toasted sandwiches for less than €2.

❶ Getting There & Away

The Athens tram (p128) runs all the way to Voula, via Glyfada. For Vouliagmeni and beyond, you can take buses from the end of the tram line or (faster but less scenic) buses direct from Athens.

Cape Sounion
Ακρωτήριο Σούνιο

The Ancient Greeks knew how to choose a site for a temple. At Cape Sounion, 70km south of Athens, the Temple of Poseidon (☑ 22920 39363; http://odysseus.culture.gr; Cape Sounion; adult/child €8/4; ☉ 9am-sunset) stands on a craggy spur that plunges 65m to the sea. Built in 444 BC – same year as the Parthenon – of marble from nearby Agrilesa, it is a vision of gleaming white columns. Sailors in ancient times knew they were nearly home when they saw the first glimpse of white, and views from the temple are equally impressive.

It is thought that the temple was built by Iktinos, the architect of the Temple of Hephaestus in Athens' Ancient Agora. Sixteen of the slender Doric columns remain. The site also contains scant remains of a propylaeum, a fortified tower and, on a lower hill to the northeast, a 6th-century temple to Athena.

As with all major sites, it's best to visit first thing in the morning, or head there for sunset to enact Byron's lines from *Don Juan*: 'Place me on Sunium's marbled steep/ Where nothing save the waves and I/May hear our mutual murmurs sweep.'

Byron was so impressed by Sounion that he carved his name on one of the columns (sadly, many other not-so-famous travellers followed suit).

There is a decent cafe-restaurant at the site, and from the parking lot at the Athena temple, a steep path leads down to a small beach. If you want more room or variety, you'll need a car, or a short bus ride, to reach the nearby bigger beaches and tavernas. (There is a pretty, if busy, beach near the site to the west, plus some nice wilder areas along the west-coast road towards Sounio town.)

The site is a common package day trip from Athens, and this is the easiest way to visit. KTEL also runs frequent buses from the Mavromateon Terminal (p125) in Athens; the buses also stop near Syntagma (p127). The ride along the coast road takes about two hours.

Mt Parnitha
Πάρνηθα

Mt Parnitha National Park (☑ 210 243 4061; www.parnitha-np.gr/welcome.htm; Aharnes), about 25km north of Athens, comprises a number of smaller peaks, the highest of which is Karavola (1413m), tall enough to get snow in winter. The forest was badly burned in 2007 but has rebounded well. There are many caves and much wildlife, including red deer. The park is criss-crossed by hiking trails, with two large, full-featured hiking lodges. It's popular for mountain biking as well.

The easiest way to explore is on the path (about a 45-minute walk) through Tatoi, the 4000-hectare grounds of the former summer palace (closed); follow Tatoi Rd out of Varibobi and look for a small trail sign on the right. For other common trails, see Activities on the park website, or contact EOS (p94) in Athens for more current advice (the site is not well maintained).

For a meal with a view, wind past the posh country estates of Varibobi and up the foothills of Mt Parnitha to reach busy taverna Agios Merkourios (☑ 210 816 9617; Varibobi; starters €4-6, lamb per kg €33; ☉ 1pm-midnight Tue-Sun). Weekends, it's packed with Athenians making the pilgrimage for a big family meal. You'll see all sorts of meat on the menu, but charcoal-grilled lamb chops are the order of the day.

Marathon & Around
Μαραθώνας

The town of Marathon, northeast of Athens, may be small and unremarkable, but in 490 BC the surrounding plain was the site of one of the most celebrated battles in world history. All over the area, you can see traces of the event – even in the road signs that mark the historic route of Pheidippides, the courier who ran to Athens to announce victory, and thus gave the name to the 42km race. The Marathon battlefield, directly south of town, is where the Athens Marathon (www.athensauthenticmarathon.gr) begins.

◎ Sights & Activities

Marathon
Archaeological Museum MUSEUM
(☑ 22940 55155; http://odysseus.culture.gr; Plataion 114; museum & Marathon Tomb site adult/child €6/3; ☉ 8.30am-3pm Tue-Sat) South of Marathon town, this excellent museum displays local

discoveries from various periods, including Neolithic pottery from the Cave of Pan and finds from the Tomb of the Athenians. The showpieces are several larger-than-life statues from an **Egyptian sanctuary** in nearby **Brexiza**. Next to the museum is a **prehistoric grave circle site**, which has been preserved under a hangar-like shelter, with raised platforms and walkways. Another hangar on the road to the museum contains an early Helladic **cemetery site**.

The admission fee covers entrance to the Marathon Battlefield & Tomb area, a few kilometres southeast.

Ramnous   RUINS
(☎22940 63477; http://odysseus.culture.gr; adult/child €4/2; ◎8.30am-3pm Tue-Sun) The evocative, overgrown and secluded ruins of the ancient port of Ramnous, about 10km northeast of Marathon, stand on a picturesque plateau overlooking the sea. Among the ruins are the remains of the Doric **Temple of Nemesis** (435 BC). Another section of the site leads 1km down a track to a clifftop with the relatively well-preserved town **fortress** and the remains of the city, a temple, a gymnasium and a theatre. There is no public transport to the site.

Marathon Battlefield & Tomb   MONUMENT
(☎22940 55155; http://odysseus.culture.gr; site & archaeological museum adult/child €6/3; ◎8am-3pm Tue-Sat) This 10m-high tumulus, or burial mound, sits 4km south of the town of Marathon, just east of the Athens–Marathon road. Traditionally in Ancient Greece, bodies of those killed in battle were returned to their families for private burial. But after the Battle of Marathon, as a sign of honour, the 192 men who fell were cremated and buried in this collective tomb. The site has a model of the battle and historical information.

Shinias   BEACH
A long, gold-sand beach, Shinias is backed by a brushy pine forest. There are sunloungers and a taverna, but no other major developments around, making it the most relaxed and prettiest place to swim in this part of Attica. It's very popular at weekends.

🛏 Sleeping & Eating

Ramnous Camping   CAMPGROUND €
(☎22940 55855; www.ramnous.gr; Leoforos Poseidonos 174, Shinias; campsites per adult/child €6/4; ◎Apr-Oct; 🅿🛜) About 1km south of Shinias Beach, this is the most pleasant camp-

ground in Attica, with sites nestled among shrubs and trees and long-stay residents who maintain a calm atmosphere. There's a minimarket, playground, laundry and a nice bar-restaurant, **Octopus** (mains €4 to €14). Casual campers can rent a tent (€6 per night). Buses to Athens go right by out front.

🛈 Getting There & Away

Given that most of the traces of ancient Marathon are spread around the area, it is easiest to visit by car (and you can also pass by the large dam at Lake Marathon). But the tomb and museum, at least, are a short walk from bus stops. Service is hourly (half-hourly in the afternoon), from Athens' Mavromateon terminal (€4.10, 1¼ hours).

Vravrona   Βραυρώνα
The **Sanctuary of Artemis** (Archaeological Museum at Brauron; ☎22990 27020; http://odysseus.culture.gr; Vravron, Markopoulou; adult/child €6/free; ◎8am-2.45pm Tue-Sun), a partially restored temple to the goddess of the hunt, dates from approximately 420 BC, with some earlier remains. Most remarkable is an ancient stone bridge over the river (now rerouted), cut through with wagon-wheel tracks. Entrance is via a very good museum, which shows remarkable votive gems and statues of children (Artemis was their protector). Then a pleasant path leads to the site through lush marshland with lots of birds. Another path leads to a quiet stretch of beach.

From Athens, take metro line 3 to Nomismatikopio, then bus 304 to Artemis (Vravrona). It's a 10-minute taxi ride from there.

Peania   Παιανία

👁 Sights

Vorres Museum   MUSEUM
(☎210 664 2520; www.vorresmuseum.gr; Parodos Diadohou Konstantinou 4, Peania; adult/child €5/free; ◎10am-2pm Sat & Sun; 🚌125 or 308 to Koropi-Peania, Ⓜ Nomismatikopio) This hodgepodge of a museum is set on a rambling 32-hectare estate, once the home of Ion Vorres. Vorres migrated to Canada as a young man, but built his home here in 1963 and began collecting contemporary art, furniture, artefacts, textiles and historic objects from around Greece to preserve the national heritage. Like many personal collections, it's

a bit erratic, but a pleasant place to spend an hour or two.

Take bus 125 or 308 to Koropi-Peania from Athens' Nomismatikopio metro station.

Koutouki Cave CAVE
(Σπήλαιο Κουτούκι Παιανίας; ☑ 210 664 2910; http://odysseus.culture.gr; Peania; adult/child €2/free; ☉ 8.30am-3pm Mon-Fri, to 2.30pm Sat & Sun) This cave is not particularly large, but the winding path goes past some interesting formations and the whole place is tinged rust-red from iron deposits. The guided tour takes about a half-hour.

The cave is best visited by car. Buses 125 and 308 from outside Athens' Nomismatikopio metro station can take you as far as Peania, but it's a further 4.5km to the cave.

Elefsina Ελευσίνα

POP 29,902

Sights

Old Oil Mill ARTS CENTRE
(Palaio Elaiourgeio; Kanellopoulou 1, Paralia Elefsinas; ☉ 5-9pm Mon-Fri, 10.30am-7pm Sat & Sun) FREE Elefsina's current culture revolves around this vast, ruined soap factory, a space constantly in flux as various arts and performance groups adapt it to their uses. The big event of the year is the summer **Aeschylia Festival** (☑ 210 556 5613; www.aisxlia.gr; ☉ Jun & Jul); it's also a venue for some events in the Athens & Epidaurus Festival (p96).

Ancient Eleusis RUINS
(☑ 210 554 6019; Sotiriou Gkioka; adult/child €6/free; ☉ 8am-8pm Tue-Sun; ☐ A16 or B16 from Plateia Eleftherias, Koumoundourou) Eleusis occupies a great site on the slopes of a low hill, close to the shore of the Saronic Gulf. Although little has been restored, the scale of its construction is impressive, as enormous pieces of columns and building blocks are scattered all over. The core of the site is the **Sanctuary of Demeter**, dating to Mycenaean times, when the goddess's cult was one of the most important in Ancient Greece.

By Classical times, until the 4th century AD, Demeter was celebrated with a huge annual festival that attracted thousands of pilgrims seeking initiation to the Eleusinian mysteries. They walked in procession from the Acropolis to Eleusis along the Sacred Way, which was lined with statues and votive monuments. Initiates were sworn to secrecy on punishment of death; during the 1400 years that the sanctuary functioned, its secrets were never divulged.

Saronic Gulf Islands

Best Places to Eat

➡ On the Verandah (p158)

➡ Techne (p155)

➡ Oraia Hydra (p153)

➡ Aspros Gatos (p149)

➡ Miltos (p145)

➡ Akrogialia (p158)

Best Places to Stay

➡ Poseidonion Grand Hotel (p157)

➡ Hydra Hotel (p151)

➡ Rosy's Little Village (p145)

➡ Orloff Resort (p158)

➡ Sirene Blue Resort (p148)

Why Go?

The Saronic Gulf Islands (Νησιά του Σαρωνικού) dot the waters nearest Athens and offer a fast track to Greek island life. As with all Greek islands, each of the Saronics has a unique feel and culture, so you can hop between classical heritage, resort beaches, exquisite architecture and remote escapism.

Aegina is home to a spectacular Doric temple and ruined Byzantine village, while nearby pine-clad Angistri feels protected and peaceful outside of the booming midsummer months. Further south, Poros, with its forested hinterland, curves only a few hundred metres from the Peloponnese. The Saronic showpiece, Hydra, is a gorgeous car-free island with a port of carefully preserved stone houses rising from a chic, history-charged harbour. Deepest south of all, pine-scented Spetses also has a vibrant nautical history and pretty town architecture, plus myriad aqua coves only minutes from the Peloponnese.

When to Go
Hydra

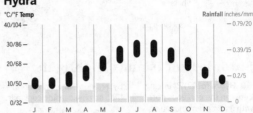

Apr & May The islands awaken after winter; come for flower-filled Easter.

Jun Celebrate Miaoulia in Hydra with sparkling waters and warm weather.

Sep The best-kept secret: clear skies, thinning crowds and Spetses' Armata celebration.

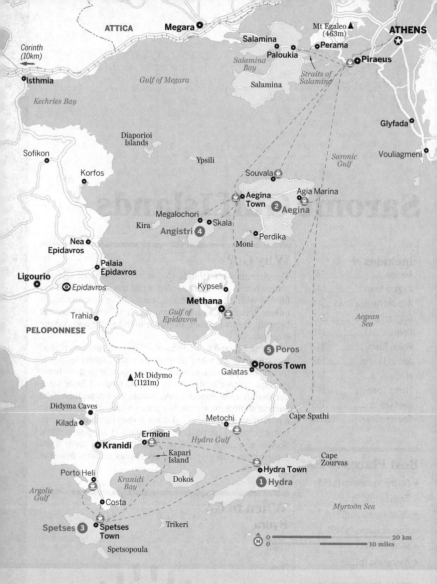

Saronic Gulf Islands Highlights

1 Hydra (p149) Bouncing between the gorgeous port, with its excellent museums and stylish scene, and the island's deserted trails and ubiquitous swimming rocks.

2 Aegina (p141) Delving into ancient history at the beautiful Temple of Aphaia and

Byzantine village, Paleohora, then sipping seaside cocktails.

3 Spetses (p155) Taste testing your way through top restaurants, tracing the region's history in the town's museums, or cycling the island's ring road to dip into sparkling bays.

4 Angistri (p145) Getting away from it all in the low season, when the beaches are most tranquil.

5 Poros (p146) Exploring the peaceful, forested interior and strolling the cafe-lined quay in town, or trying out the family-run tavernas.

AEGINA ΑΙΓΙΝΑ

POP 13,056

Beyond its bustling port, Aegina has the seductive, easygoing character of a typical Greek island, but with the added bonus of more than its fair share of prestigious ancient sites. Weekending Athenians spice up the mix of laid-back locals and island-dwelling commuters who use the island like an Athens suburb. Unique Aegina treats include a special – and delicious – pistachio nut, the splendid 5th-century Temple of Aphaia and the magical Byzantine Paleohora ruins.

Aegina was the leading maritime power of the Saronic Gulf during the 7th century BC, when it grew wealthy through trade and political ascendancy. The island made a major contribution to the Greek victory over the Persian fleet at the Battle of Salamis in 480 BC. Despite this solidarity with the Athenian state, the latter invaded in 459 BC out of jealousy of Aegina's wealth and status, and of its liaison with Sparta. Aegina never regained its glory, although in the early 19th century it played a bold part in the defeat of the Turks and was the temporary capital of a partly liberated Greece from 1827 to 1829.

ⓘ Getting There & Away

Aegina's main port, Aegina Town, has conventional ferries that you book online at www.saronicferries.gr. They are operated by **Hellenic Seaways** (☑ conventional ferry 22970 22945, high-speed ferry 22970 26777; www.hsw.gr), **Nova Ferries** (☑ 22970 24200; www.novaferries.gr), **Agios Nektarios** (ANES Ferries; ☑ Aegina 22970 25625, Piraeus 21042 25625; www.anes.gr), 2wayferries and Leves Lines. Book high-speed hydrofoils with Hellenic Seaways and **Aegean Flying Dolphins** (☑ 22970 25800) to/from Piraeus and Angistri. Ferries dock at the large outer quay, with hydrofoils at the smaller inner quay.

Evoikos Lines (☑ Agia Marina 22970 32234, Piraeus 21048 21002, Souvala 22970 52210; www.evoikoslines.gr) serves Aegina's smaller ports Agia Marina and Souvala, and Piraeus in high season only.

Even in winter, high-speed ferries from Piraeus get fully booked for weekends: book ahead.

Angistri Express (p146) makes several daily trips in high season to Skala and Mylos on Angistri. It leaves from midway along Aegina harbour, where timetables are displayed.

Water taxis (☑ 6944535659, 6972229720, 22970 91387) to Piraeus cost about €40 one way, regardless of the number of people.

ⓘ Getting Around

BUS

Buses from Aegina Town run several times a day on three routes across the island. Departure times are displayed outside the ticket office on Plateia Ethnegersias (Ethnegersias Sq); you must buy tickets there. Visit www.aeginagreece.com for details.

Agia Marina (€2, 30 minutes), via Paleohora (€2, 15 minutes) and Temple of Aphaia (€2, 25 minutes)

Perdika (€1.80, 15 minutes)

Vagia (€1.80, 25 minutes) via Souvala (€1.80, 20 minutes)

CAR, MOTORCYCLE & BICYCLE

Numerous outfits hire out vehicles. Prices start from €35 per day for cars, €17 for a 50cc motorcycle and €8 for bicycles.

Karagiannis Travel (☑ 22970 28780; www.aeginatravel.gr; Pan Irioti 44; ⊙ 9am-2pm & 5-9pm) Rents vehicles and arranges tours and tickets.

Sklavenas Rent A Car (☑ 22970 22892; Kazantzaki 5; ⊙ 9am-2pm & 5-9pm) For cars,

BOAT SERVICES FROM AEGINA

DESTINATION	PORT	DURATION	FARE (€)	FREQUENCY
Angistri (Skala)	Aegina Town	20min	2.80	1-2 daily
Angistri (Skala)*	Aegina Town	10min	6	4-6 daily
Angistri (Mylos)*	Aegina Town	10min	6	5 daily
Methana	Aegina Town	40min	5.70	2-3 daily
Piraeus	Aegina Town	1hr 10min	8-10	hourly
Piraeus*	Aegina Town	40min	14	6 daily
Piraeus	Agia Marina	1hr	10	3-4 daily, summer
Piraeus	Souvala	1hr 35min	8	3-4 daily, summer
Poros	Aegina Town	1hr 50min	8.50	2-3 daily

*high-speed services

Aegina & Angistri

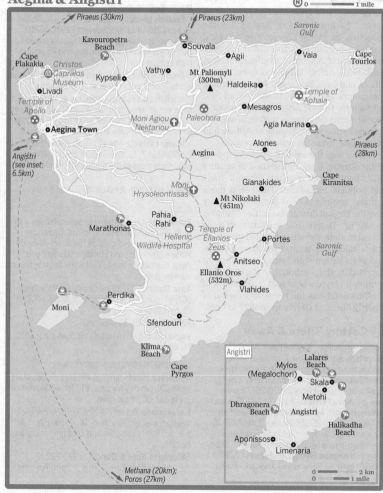

4WDs, scooters, quads and bikes. In Aegina Town, located on the road near the Temple of Apollo. Also has a branch in Agia Marina.

TAXI

Taxi (☎ Aegina Town 22970 22010, Agia Marina 22970 32107) Taxis around Aegina island.

Aegina Town   Αίγινα

POP 8905

Aegina Town's sparkling harbour is backed by a buzzing promenade of people, motorbikes, cafes and restaurants. As you wander back into the narrow town streets, with kids riding

bikes and laundry strung from balconies, small-town Greek life takes over again.

The parallel streets backing the harbour, Irioti and Rodi, are crammed with shops of every kind and a few 19th-century neoclassical buildings intermix with whitewashed houses. Ancient Greece is represented by the impressive ruins of the Temple of Apollo, just north of the harbour.

◉ Sights

Temple of Apollo   RUINS
(Kolona; ☎ 22970 22248; http://odysseus.culture. gr; adult/child €3/free; ⊗ 8.30am-3pm Tue-Sun May-Oct, reduced hours Nov-Apr) Northwest of

the port, ruined walls, cisterns and broken pillars in honey-coloured stone are lorded over by a solitary surviving column. It's all that's left of a 5th-century-BC temple that was once part of an ancient acropolis (built on a prehistoric site). The informative Sanctuary Museum has translations in English and German.

Folklore Museum MUSEUM
(☑22970 26401; http://laografiko.gr; S Rodi; €2; ☉10am-12.30pm & 5.30-8.30pm Fri & Sat) Peruse historic clothing, housewares and artwork re-creating the mood of old-time island life.

✯ Festivals & Events

Aegina Fistiki Fest FOOD & DRINK
(www.aeginafistikifest.gr; ☉Sep) *Fistiki* means 'pistachio' and this three-day brouhaha celebrates Aegina's famous Protected Designation of Origin (PDO) pistachio through music, art and culinary contests.

🛏 Sleeping

Aegina offers a range of solid, simple guesthouses, apartment complexes and a handful of hotels. Book ahead at weekends.

Electra Pension PENSION €
(☑22970 26715; www.aegina-electra.gr; Leonardou Lada 25; r €45; ☒🖥) There are no views from this small whitewashed pension, but rooms are impeccable and comfy in a quiet corner of the town centre. It outclasses nearby hotels by a long way.

Marianna Studios PENSION €
(☑22970 25650; www.aeginastudiosmarianna. com; Kiverniou 16-18; s/d €35/40, d/tr with kitchen €40/45; ☒) Simple, basic rooms and very friendly owners create a top-notch budget choice. Some rooms have balconies or overlook a quiet, leafy garden alongside an interior courtyard. One room has a kitchen.

★Hotel Rastoni HOTEL €€
(☑22970 27039; www.rastoni.gr; Odos Stratigou Dimitri Petriti 31; d/tr/q €80/120/130; P☒@🖥) Spacious rooms have balconies overlooking a lovely garden and the Temple of Apollo. Generous breakfasts and friendly staff round out the experience. Find it in a residential neighbourhood a few minutes north of the harbour.

Aegina Hotel HOTEL €€
(☑22970 28501; www.aeginahotel.gr; Stratigou Dimitriou Petriti 23; d/tr from €60/70; ☒🖥) This 19-room hotel sits about 500m back from the harbour and has clean, well-appointed rooms with refrigerators and TVs.

Aeginitiko Archontiko PENSION €€
(☑22970 24968; www.aeginitikoarchontiko.gr; cnr Ag Nikolaou & Thomaidou 1; s/d/tr/ste incl breakfast from €50/60/70/100; ☒🖥) The rich character of this centrally located old mansion translates through period 19th-century features, a charming salon and courtyard and a splendid breakfast. Rooms, however, are a bit cramped and worn, and bathrooms are basic. Sea views from the rooftop terrace.

Fistikies Holiday Apartments APARTMENT €€
(☑22970 23783; www.fistikies.gr; Logiotatidou 1; studios €90, 4-person apts €120; P☒🖥☒) This complex of tidy, family-friendly apartments was built in 2007 on the southern edge of town, inland from the football field. Spacious apartments have DVD players and terraces overlooking the pool.

🍴 Eating

The harbourfront restaurants make for lazy world-watching, but are not outstanding, unless you hit the unvarnished *ouzeries* (places serving ouzo and light snacks). Aegina's pistachio nuts are on sale everywhere (from €7 for 500g, depending on quality).

Elia MEDITERRANEAN €
(☑22975 00205; Koumoundourou 4; mains €6-9; ☉noon-4pm & 6-11pm, hours reduced winter) Burrow into the backstreets to find this excellent restaurant that's popular with locals. Imaginative, fresh specialities include its pistachio pesto and the pittas of the day.

Gelladakis MEZEDHES €
(☑22970 27308; Pan Irioti 45; dishes €7-12; ☉lunch & dinner) Ensconced behind the noisy midharbour fish market, this vibrant joint is always thronged with people tucking into charcoal-fired octopus or sardines, plus other classic mezedhes (appetisers).

Tsias TAVERNA €
(☑22970 23529; Dimokratias 47; mains €7-10; ☉lunch & dinner) Harbourside eating at its best. Try shrimps with tomatoes and feta, or one of the daily specials.

Kriton Gefsis CRETAN €€
(☑22970 26255; www.facebook.com/kritongefsis; cnr Pan Irioti & Damanos; dishes €5-15; ☉10am-2am) Cretan ingredients and flavours are the order of the day at this lively taverna, with fresh seafood featuring; also has live music.

Bakalogatos MEZEDHES €€
(☑22975 00501; cnr Pan Irioti & Neoptolemou; mains €7-13; ☉lunch & dinner Tue-Sun) Fresh, well-crafted mezedhes in an elegant setting,

SARONIC GULF ISLANDS AEGINA

with faux-finished tables and traditional products on the walls.

Drinking & Nightlife

International Corner   BAR
(☑ 22970 26564; cnr I Katsa & S Rodi; ☺ noon-late) Get off the main strip and head to this character-filled, wood-panelled bar room. The gregarious owner takes requests, from top 40 to fantastic Greek music.

Avli   BAR
(☑ 22970 26438; Pan Irioti 17; ☺ 9am-late) This lively restaurant and bar plays tunes from '60s to Greek pop, and has a covered garden that bubbles with activity.

Remvi   BAR
(☑ 22970 28605; Dimokratias 51; ☺ 8am-late; ☎) A popular music cafe-bar that hops day and night.

❶ Information

Harbour-front banks have ATMs. Aegina has no tourist office. Check Karagiannis Travel (p141) for car hire, tours and non-Aegina boats.
Hospital (☑ 22970 24489, emergency 22970 22251; Agios Dionisios Nosokomeiou 4)
Port Authority (☑ 22970 22328; Dimokratias) At the entrance to the ferry quays.
Tourist Police (☑ 22970 27777; Leonardou Lada) Up a lane opposite the hydrofoil dock.

❶ Getting There & Away

Aegina's main port is located in Aegina Town: it's served by both conventional ferries (book online at www.saronicferries.gr) and high-speed hydrofoils operated by Hellenic Seaways (p141) and Aegean Flying Dolphins (p141).

❶ Getting Around

There is a hub of local buses and water taxis at the main port.

---

❶ ISLAND HOPPING

No direct ferries connect Aegina and Angistri with Hydra and Spetses; go via Piraeus or Poros. For day trips, take the Hydra–Poros–Aegina cruise from Piraeus with **Athens One Day Cruise** (☑ 210 451 6106; www.athensonedaycruise. com; cruise adult/child €99/56, with transfers €109) or **Evermore Cruises** (☑ 211 188 2220; www.evermorecruises.com; cruise adult/child €99/56, with transfers €109). Pegasus Cruises goes from Nafplio to Spetses and Hydra.

Around Aegina Town

Aegina is lush and wildflower-laden in spring, and year-round offers some of the best archaic sites in the Saronic Gulf. The interior hills and mountains add drama to the small island, but beaches are not its strongest suit. The east-coast town of Agia Marina is the island's main package resort. It has a shallow-water beach that is ideal for families, but it's backed by a fairly crowded main drag. A few thin, sandy beaches, such as Marathonas, line the roadside between Aegina Town and Perdika.

◉ Sights

★ **Paleohora**   CHURCH, RUIN
(Παλαιοχώρα) [FREE] This enchanting remote hillside is dotted with the remains of a Byzantine village. More than 30 surviving churches punctuate the rocky heights of the original citadel, and several have been refurbished. They are linked by a network of paths, carpeted with wildflowers in spring. The ancient town of Paleohora was Aegina's capital from the 9th century through the medieval period and was only abandoned during the 1820s.

Paleohora is 6.5km east of Aegina Town, near enormous modern church Moni Agiou Nektariou. Buses from Aegina Town to Agia Marina stop at the turn-off to Paleohora (10 minutes); taxis cost €8 one way.

★ **Temple of Aphaia**   TEMPLE
(☑ 22970 32398; http://odysseus.culture.gr; adult/child €4/free; ☺ 9.30am-4.30pm, museum 10.30am-1.30pm Tue-Sun) The well-preserved remains of this impressive temple stand proudly on a pine-covered hill with far-reaching views over the Saronic Gulf. Built in 480 BC, it celebrates a local deity of pre-Hellenic times. The temple's pediments were originally decorated with splendid Trojan War sculptures, most of which were stolen in the 19th century and now decorate Munich's Glyptothek. Panels throughout the site are also in English.

Aphaia is 10km east of Aegina Town. Infrequent buses to Agia Marina stop here (20 minutes); taxis cost about €12 one way.

Christos Capralos Museum   MUSEUM
(☑ 22970 22001; Nikou Kazantzaki (Coast Rd), Livadi; €2; ☺ 10am-2pm & 6-8pm Tue-Sun Jun-Oct, 10am-2pm Fri-Sun Nov-May) The home and studio of acclaimed sculptor Christos Capralos (1909–93), on the coast near Livadi, 1.5km north of Aegina Town, has been made into a

PERDIKA ΠΕΡΔΙΚΑ

The quaint fishing village of Perdika lies about 9km south of Aegina Town on the southern tip of the west coast and makes for a relaxed sojourn.

Perdika's harbour is very shallow so, for the best swimming, catch one of the regular caïques (little boats; return adult/child €5/free) to the small island of Moni, a few minutes offshore. A nature reserve, it has a tree-lined beach and summertime cafe.

Tavernas line Perdika's raised harbour-front terrace, and sultry sunset relaxation makes way for buzzing nightlife when late-night music bars rev into gear during summer.

Villa Rodanthos (☑6944250138, 22970 61400; www.villarodanthos.com; studios from €55; ❉⚑) is a gem of a place, not least because of its charming owner. Each room has its own colourful decor and a kitchen.

The most locally popular of Perdika's quayside tavernas, **Miltos** (☑22970 61051; mains €12-15; ⊙noon-4pm & 6pm-late) is known for the highest-quality seafood and no-nonsense Greek staples.

museum displaying many of his fluid, powerful works. Monumental sculptures include the 40m-long *Pindus Frieze*.

ANGISTRI ΑΓΚΙΣΤΡΙ

POP 1142

Tiny Angistri lies a few kilometres off the west coast of Aegina and, out of high season, its mellow lanes and azure coves make a rewarding day trip or longer escape.

The port-resort village of Skala is crammed with small hotels, apartments, tavernas and cafes, but life, in general, still ticks along gently. A right turn from the quay leads to the small harbour beach and then to a church on a low headland. Beyond lies the best beach on the island, but it disappears beneath sun loungers and broiling bodies in July and August. Turning left from the quay at Skala takes you south along a dirt path through the pine trees to the pebbly and clothing-optional Halikadha Beach.

About 1km west from Skala, Angistri's other port, Mylos (Megalochori), has an appealing traditional character, rooms and tavernas, but no beach.

Aponissos has turquoise waters, a small offshore island and a reliably tasty taverna. Limenaria has deeper green waters. The entire island is supersleepy in low season.

🛏 Sleeping & Eating

Book ahead, especially for August and summer weekends. A board on Skala's quay lists a range of small guesthouses and hotels.

Alkyoni Inn PENSION €
(☑22970 91378; www.alkyoni-agistri.com; s/d/ maisonettes from €30/45/60; ⊙Easter-Sep;

❉⚑) This recently refurbished pension offers some sea-facing rooms with fabulous, unobstructed views. Two-storey family maisonettes sleep up to four. Its taverna is very popular too.

★ **Rosy's Little Village** PENSION €€
(☑22970 91610; www.rosyslittlevillage.com; s/d/ tr/q from €65/73/83/108; ❉⚑) A complex of simple Cycladic-style cubes steps gently down to the sea, a short way east of Skala's quay. Full of light and colour, with built-in couches and tiny balconies with sea views, Rosy's also offers mountain bikes, summer courses, weekly picnics and live-music evenings. Its restaurant (mains €8 to €18, open lunch and dinner) emphasises organics.

Akrogiali Hotel HOTEL €€
(☑22970 91354; www.akrogiali-agistri.gr; Skala; d from €65; ⊙Apr-Oct; ❉⚑) Just a quick hop from the ferry dock, this modern beachfront hotel has tidy rooms with colourful, tasteful decor.

Nontas Hotel HOTEL €€
(☑22970 91212; www.facebook.com/NontasHotel Agistri/; Mylos; d from €65; ⊙Apr-Oct; ❉⚑) This space-age-looking hotel is best for its sea-facing modern rooms and proximity to local cafes and tavernas.

Alkyoni Inn TAVERNA €
(☑22970 91378; www.alkyoni-agistri.com; mains €7-15; ⊙8am-10pm Easter-Sep; ❉⚑🚲) The welcoming, family-run Alkyoni is a 10-minute stroll southeast of Skala's quay. The popular taverna dishes up well-prepared fish and meat, while the refurbished pension offers sea-facing rooms and family maisonettes.

ⓘ Information

There's a bank with ATM on Skala's main street. Visit www.agistri.com.gr for island information.

ⓘ Getting There & Away

Fast Aegean Flying Dolphins (p141) and Hellenic Seaways (p141) hydrofoils and car ferries (www.saronicferries.gr) come from Piraeus (hydrofoil/ferry €14.50/10.90, 55 minutes/1½ hours) via Aegina (hydrofoils €6, 10 minutes, four to six daily; ferry €2.80, 20 minutes, one to two daily) to either Skala or Mylos. **Angistri Express** (☎ 6934347867) serves Aegina several times daily, Monday to Saturday.

Water taxis (p141) cost €45 one way between Aegina and Angistri.

ⓘ Getting Around

Several **buses** (☎ 6973016132, 22970 91244; Skala) a day during summer run from Skala and Mylos (Megalochori) to Limenaria and Dhragonera Beach. It's worth hiring a scooter (€15) or sturdy bike (€7) to explore the coast road.

You can also follow tracks from Metohi overland through cool pine forest to reach Dhragonera Beach. Take a compass; tracks divide often and route-finding can be frustrating.

Kostas Bike Hire (☎ 22970 91021; Skala)

Takis Rent a Bike & Bicycles (Logothetis; ☎ 22970 91001; www.agistri.com.gr/logothetis; Mylos)

Taxi (☎ 6977618040, 22970 91455; Skala)

POROS ΠΟΡΟΣ

POP 3800

Poros is separated from the mountainous Peloponnese by a narrow sea channel, and its protected setting makes the main settlement of Poros Town seem like a cheery lakeside resort. Its pastel-hued houses stack up the hillside to a clock tower and make a vibrant first impression.

Poros is made up of two land masses connected by a tiny isthmus: Sferia, which is occupied mainly by the town of Poros; and

Poros

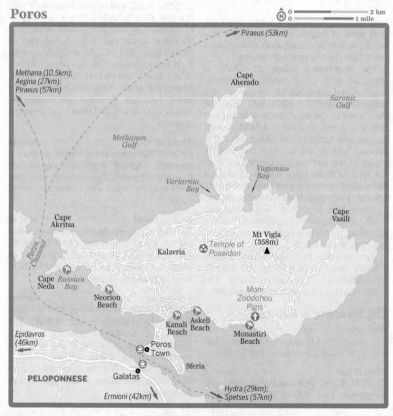

the much larger and mainly forested Kalavria, which has the island's beaches and seasonal hotels scattered along its southern shore. Poros still maintains a sense of remoteness in its sparsely populated, forested interior.

The Peloponnesian town of Galatas lies on the opposite shore, making Poros a useful base from which to explore the ancient sites of the Peloponnese. For example, the exquisite ancient theatre of Epidavros is within reach by car or taxi (☑ in Galatas 22980 42888).

❶ Getting There & Away

Daily ferries (www.saronicferries.gr) connect Piraeus to Poros in summer (reduced timetable in winter). High-speed Hellenic Seaways (p141) ferries continue south to Hydra, Spetses, Ermioni and Porto Heli. Conventional ferries connect Aegina to Poros and Methana on the mainland. Travel agents (p148) sell tickets.

Caïques shuttle constantly between Poros and Galatas (€1, five minutes). They leave from the quay opposite Plateia Iroön, the triangular plaza near the main ferry dock in Poros Town. Hydrofoils dock about 50m north of here. Car ferries to Galatas (per person/car €1/6, from 7.30am to 10.40pm) leave from the dock several hundred metres north again, on the road to Kalavria.

You can also do a one-way rental between branches of **Pop's Car** (☑ in Galatas 22980 42910; www.popscar.gr) at Athens Airport and Galatas (or Ermioni).

❶ Getting Around

BOAT
Caïques go to beaches around the island during summer.

BUS
A bus (€3) operates mid-June to October every hour from 7am until midnight on a route that starts next to the kiosk at the eastern end of Plateia Iroön. It crosses to Kalavria and goes east along the south coast for ten minutes as far as Moni Zoödohou Pigis (p148), then turns around and heads west to Neorion Beach (15 minutes). Buy tickets from the kiosk.

MOTORCYCLE & BICYCLE
Several places on the road to Kalavria rent out bicycles, scooters and all-terrain vehicles (ATVs; per day from €6/20/30).
Moto Fotis (☑ 22980 25873; www.motofotis-poros.gr; Kanali; ⊙ 9am-9pm) Rents bicycles, motorbikes and ATVs.
Moto Stelios (☑ 22980 23026; www.moto stelios.gr; Harbour, Poros Town; ⊙ 9am-9pm) Rents ATVs, scooters and bicycles in Poros harbour and Askeli beach.

TAXI
Taxi (☑ 22980 23003) Standard taxi fares are posted at the main stand on the quay.

Poros Town   Πόρος

POP 3651

Zippy Poros Town is a mishmash of charming ice-cream-coloured houses that look out across the narrow channel at Galatas and the shapely mountains of the Peloponnese. Sailing boats bob along the lengthy quay, while ferries glide through the channel and smaller vessels scurry to and fro. Behind the harbour, *plateíes* (squares) and tavernas hide from view and a rocky bluff rises steeply to a crowning clock tower.

⊙ Sights

Archaeological Museum of Poros   MUSEUM
(☑ 22980 23276; http://odysseus.culture.gr; Harbourfront, Plateia Koryzi; €2; ⊙ 8.30am-3pm Tue-Sun) This small museum on the waterfront shows a beautiful collection of classic Greek sculpture from the area.

Citronne   GALLERY
(☑ 22980 22401; www.citronne.com; Leof Papadopoulou; ⊙ 10am-3pm Mon-Sat Jun-Aug) This bright and cheerful local gallery shows artists from around Greece.

🛏 Sleeping

★**Seven Brothers Hotel**   HOTEL €
(☑ 22980 23412; www.7brothers.gr; Poros Harbour; s/d/tr €50/55/60; 🕸 🛜) Conveniently close to the hydrofoil quay, this modern hotel has bright, comfy rooms with superduper bathrooms. Some have small balconies, some sea views.

Georgia Mellou Rooms   PENSION €
(☑ 22980 22309; http://porosnet.gr/gmellou; Plateia Georgiou; d/tr €40/45; 🕸🛜) Simple, old-fashioned rooms tucked into the heart of the old town, next to the cathedral, high above the harbour. The charming owner keeps everything shipshape. Book ahead for fantastic views from the west-side rooms.

Hotel Manessi   BUSINESS HOTEL €
(☑ 22980 22273; www.manessi.com; Harbourfront; d from €55; 🕸 @ 🛜) Well placed at the midpoint of the harbour, the Manessi is a bit worn in places, but offers clean business-style rooms, some with sea views.

Sto Roloi   APARTMENT €€
(☑ 6932427267, 22980 25808; www.storoloi-poros.gr; studio/apt/houses from €63/105/155; 🕸)

Roloi is a good source for tidy apartments and houses around Poros Town.

Eating

Dimitris Family Taverna
TAVERNA €

(☎22980 23709; www.dimitrisfamily-poros.gr; mains €6-14; ☺6-10pm or 11pm) Renowned for its meat, this taverna's owners have a butchering business, so cuts of pork, lamb and chicken are of the finest quality. It's up the hill in the centre of town; ask a local for directions.

Taverna Karavolos
TAVERNA €

(☎22980 26158; www.karavolos.com; mains €6-12; ☺7-11pm) Karavolos means 'big snail' and snails are a house speciality at this quaint eatery on a backstreet. Friendly proprietors also offer classic Greek meat dishes and some fish, as well as **rooms** (double/triple €35/45) upstairs.

Poseidon
SEAFOOD €€

(☎22980 23597; www.poseidontaverna.gr; Harbourfront; mains €7-15; ☺9.30am-12.30am Easter-Oct) A quayside favourite for delicious seafood, friendly service and occasional Greek dancing.

Oasis
TAVERNA €€

(☎22980 22955; Harbourfront; mains €7-14; ☺10am-1am) Hang out harbourside and feast on home-cooked Greek staples and seafood.

ⓘ Information

Banks on Plateia Iroön have ATMs. Poros has no tourist office. Harbour-front agencies arrange accommodation, car hire, tours and cruises.

Family Tours (☎22980 23743; www.family tours.gr; Harbourfront; ☺9am-2pm & 5-10pm) Sells conventional-ferry tickets.

Marinos Tours (☎22980 23423; www.marinos tours.gr; Harbourfront; ☺7am-9.30pm Apr-Oct, to 7pm Nov-Mar) Across from the hydrofoil quay; sells hydrofoil tickets.

Tourist Police (☎22980 22256; Dimosthen-ous 10) Behind the high school.

Around Poros

◉ Sights & Activities

Poros' best beaches include the pebbly Kanali Beach, on Kalavria islet 1km east of the bridge, and the long, sandy Askeli Beach, about 500m further east.

Neorion Beach, 3km west of the bridge, has waterskiing, and banana-boat and air-chair rides. The best beach is at Russian Bay, 1.5km past Neorion.

Temple of Poseidon
RUINS

(☎22980 23276; ☺8.30am-3pm) **FREE** There's very little left of this 6th-century temple. Once it was a magnificent building giving sanctuary to fugitives and wrecked sailors, but in the 18th century it was mostly dis-mantled and the materials used to build a monastery on Hydra. Still, the walk or drive to the site gives superb views of the Saronic Gulf and the Peloponnese.

With your own wheels, from the road near Moni Zoödohou Pigis, head inland to reach the ruins. Then you can continue along the road and circle back to the bridge onto Sferia. It's about 6km in total.

Moni Zoödohou Pigis
MONASTERY

(☺9am-noon & 2.30-6pm) The 18th-century 'Monastery of the Life-giving Spring', well signposted 4km east of Poros Town, has a beautiful gilded iconostasis (a screen bear-ing icons) from Asia Minor.

Passage
WATER SPORTS

(☎22980 42540; www.passage.gr; Neorion Bay; lesson from €45) A popular waterskiing school and slalom centre.

🛏 Sleeping & Eating

★ Sirene Blue Resort
RESORT €€

(☎22980 22741; www.sireneblueresort.gr; Monas-tiri Beach; d/tr incl breakfast from €120/150; ❈ 🛜 🏊) Sirene Blue Resort offers a deluxe

BOAT SERVICES FROM POROS

DESTINATION	DURATION	FARE (€)	FREQUENCY
Aegina	1¼hr	8.50	2-5 daily
Hydra*	30min	13.50	4-5 daily
Methana	30min	4.30	2-3 daily
Piraeus	2½hr	11.50-14	2-3 daily
Piraeus*	1hr	24.50	4-5 daily
Spetses*	1½hr	16	4 daily

*high-speed services

seaside vacation, from sparkling pool to crisp linens. Find it at Monastiri Beach, near Moni Zoödohou Pigis.

Hotel New Aegli   HOTEL **€€**
(☑ 22980 22372; www.newaegli.com; Askeli Beach; d from €95; ⊘ Apr-Oct; ❄ @ 🅿 ⛱) Poros' best beaches include the long, sandy Askeli Beach. Hotel New Aegli, across the road from the beach, is a decent resort-style hotel and offers good, modern rooms, many with sea views.

★**Aspros Gatos**   SEAFOOD, TAVERNA **€€**
(☑ 22980 24274; Labraki 49; mains €6-15; ⊘ noon-11pm Easter-Oct) A short walk from town, 400m west of the bridge on the road to Neorion Beach, Poros' best seafood taverna sits smack out over the water. Watch the local kayaking team do its thing as the jolly owner provides anything from bolognese to the catch of the day.

HYDRA   ΥΔΡΑ

POP 1966

Hydra is truly the gem of the Saronic Gulf and stands alone among Greek islands as the one free of wheeled vehicles. No cars. No scooters. Just tiny marble-cobbled lanes, donkeys, rocks and sea. Artists (Brice Marden, Nikos Chatzikyriakos-Ghikas, Panayiotis Tetsis), musicians (Leonard Cohen), actors and celebrities (Melina Mercouri, Sophia Loren) have all been drawn to Hydra over the years. In addition to the island's exquisitely preserved stone architecture, criss-crossing rural paths and clear, deep waters, you can find a good cappuccino along the harbour, which is great for people-watching.

History

Hydra was sparsely populated in ancient times and is just mentioned in passing by Herodotus. The most significant evidence of settlement dates from Mycenaean times. But in the 16th century, Hydra became a refuge for people fleeing skirmishes between the Venetians and the Ottomans. Many hailed from the area of modern-day Albania.

By the mid-1700s the settlers began building boats and took to the thin line between maritime commerce and piracy with enthusiasm. They travelled as far as Egypt and the Black Sea and ran the British blockade (1803–15) during the Napoleonic Wars. As a result of steady tax paying, the island experienced only light interference under the Ottoman Empire. By the 19th century,

Hydra had become a full-blown maritime power, and wealthy shipping merchants had built most of the town's grand mansions. At its height in 1821, the island's population reached 28,000. Hydra supplied 130 ships for a blockade of the Turks during the Greek War of Independence and the island bred such leaders as Admiral Andreas Miaoulis, who commanded the Greek fleet, and Georgios Koundouriotis, president of Greece's national assembly from 1822 to 1827.

ⓘ Getting There & Away

High-speed **Hellenic Seaways** (www.hsw.gr) ferries link Hydra with Poros, Piraeus and Spetses, and Ermioni and Porto Heli on the Peloponnese. Service is greatly reduced in winter. Buy tickets from **Hydreoniki Travel** (☑ 22980 54007; www.hydreoniki.gr; ⊘ 7am-10pm or around ferry departures), up the lane to the right of the Alpha Bank in Hydra Town.

Freedom (☑ 6947325263, 6944242141; www.hydralines.gr) boats run between Hydra and Metohi (little more than a car park) on the mainland (€6.50, 15 minutes, five to 11 daily). The schedule is posted on the quay and online.

ⓘ Getting Around

Generally, people get around Hydra by walking.

The island is vehicle-free, and mules and donkeys are the main means of heavy transport. Donkey owners are clustered around the port; they transport luggage to the hotels and provide quick donkey rides around the port. Note that animal rights groups urge people to consider whether the animals are maltreated before deciding to take a ride.

In summer, caïques (little boats) from Hydra Town go to the island's beaches. **Water-taxi** (☑ 22980 53690) fares are posted on the quay (Kamini €10, Vlyhos €15).

Hydra Town   Υδρα

POP 1900

Life in Hydra centres around the gorgeous port. Whether you sail or ferry in, the sparkling boat-filled harbour and the bright light striking the tiers of carefully preserved stone houses make a lasting impression. The harbour in high season is an ecosystem of its own, with yachts, caïques (little boats) and water taxis zipping in and out. The marble quay is a surging rhythm of donkeys, visitors, cafe denizens and boat-taxi hawkers. By night the scene becomes a promenade: grab a chair, order a drink and watch the world go by.

Hydra

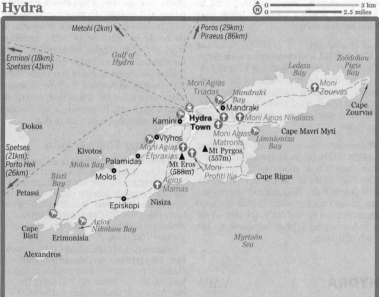

If you head back into the warren of portside houses, to the steep slopes banking away from the town centre, you get a different view on Hydriot life. Grandmothers chat in quiet lanes about what's for dinner, and roads peter out into dirt paths that head into the mountains, ever-changing in colour, depending on the time of day.

⊙ Sights

Melina Mercouri Exhibition Hall and Deste Foundation host high-season art shows.

★ Kimisis Tis Theotokou Cathedral
CHURCH
(Metropolis; Harbour; ⊙7am-7pm) Housed in the peaceful monastery complex on the harbour, this lovely cathedral dates from the 17th century and has a Tinian-marble bell tower. Its **Ecclesiastical Museum** (⌨22980 54071; www.imhydra.gr/mouseio_main.htm; adult/child €2/free; ⊙10am-5pm Tue-Sun Apr-Nov) contains a collection of icons and vestments. The monastery complex is also known as Faneromeni. Dress appropriately (covered shoulders, long skirts or pants) to enter.

★ Deste Foundation
GALLERY
(www.deste.gr) **FREE** Deste Foundation hosts an annual Hydra exhibit at the small former slaughterhouse on the sea.

★ Lazaros Koundouriotis Historical Mansion
MUSEUM
(⌨22980 52421; www.nhmuseum.gr; adult/child €4/free; ⊙10am-4pm Tue-Sun Mar-Oct) Hydra's star cultural attraction is this handsome ochre-coloured *arhontiko* (stone mansion) high above the harbour. It was home to one of the major figures in the Greek independence struggle and is an exquisite example of late 18th-century traditional architecture, featuring original furnishings, folk costumes, handicrafts and a painting exhibition.

Historical Archives Museum of Hydra
MUSEUM
(⌨22980 52355; www.iamy.gr; Harbour; adult/child €5/3; ⊙9am-4pm) This fine harbourfront museum houses an extensive collection of portraits and naval artefacts, with an emphasis on the island's role in the War of Independence. It hosts temporary exhibitions in summer, and concerts on the rooftop terrace.

☆ Activities

Harriet's Hydra Horses
HORSE RIDING
(⌨6980323347; www.harrietshydrahorses.com; 1/2/8hr tour €25/55/175) Harriet, a friendly, bilingual British-Greek local, guides licensed horse-riding tours (from one to eight hours) around the island, to the monasteries and to the beaches.

Vasilis Kokkos BOATING
(☏ 6977649789; bkokkos@yahoo.com) Vasilis Kokkos, proprietor of Caprice (p153) restaurant and boat captain, rents speedboats (per day €80 to €250) and a sailing boat (by prior arrangement; one-week minimum from €900). Licence required.

✦ Festivals & Events

Miaoulia Festival CULTURAL
(☉ weekend around 21 Jun) Celebration of Admiral Miaoulis and the Hydriot contribution to the War of Independence, with a spectacular boat burning (with fireworks) in Hydra harbour.

🛏 Sleeping

Accommodation in Hydra is of a high standard, but you pay accordingly. Most owners will meet you at the harbour and organise luggage transfer.

Piteoussa PENSION €
(☏ 22980 52810; www.piteoussa.com; Kouloura; d €50-70; 🕸 🛜) Jolly owners maintain beautiful rooms in two buildings on a quiet, pine-tree-lined street. Rooms in the restored corner mansion have period character and all the modern amenities you need, while the smaller rooms in the second building were renovated in 2010 and have a mod feel.

Pension Erofili PENSION €
(☏ 22980 54049; www.pensionerofili.gr; Tombazi; s/d/tr from €45/55/97; 🕸 🛜) Tucked in the inner town, these pleasant, unassuming rooms are a good deal for Hydra. Also has a studio with kitchen.

Hotel Sophia BOUTIQUE HOTEL €€
(☏ 22980 52313; www.hotelsophia.gr; Harbourfront; d incl breakfast €85-115; ☉ Apr-Oct; 🕸 🛜) Gorgeous small rooms sit right on the harbour and some have balconies. Each has been painstakingly outfitted with all the mod cons, and bathrooms are luscious marble. Some rooms are two storeys.

Angelica Hotel BOUTIQUE HOTEL €€
(☏ 22980 53202; www.angelica.gr; Miaouli; d/tr/q incl breakfast from €130/180/220; 🕸 🛜) An attractive boutique hotel in a quiet location, the Angelica is popular for its comfortable, luxurious rooms and spacious, impeccable bathrooms. Superior rooms have balconies. Relax in the spa or courtyard.

Mastoris Mansion BOUTIQUE HOTEL €€
(Ξενώνας Αρχοντικό του Μάστορη; ☏ 22980 29631; www.mastoris-hydra.gr; d/tr from €100/150) One of the most recent entries on Hydra's hotel scene, this renovated stone building in the centre of town offers plush doubles and triples. While convenient to harbour action, rooms don't have views.

Nereids PENSION €€
(☏ 22980 52875; www.nereids-hydra.com; Kouloura; d from €70; 🕸 🛜) This carefully restored stone house contains lovely rooms of exceptional value and quality. Spacious, peaceful and with beautiful decor, rooms have open views to Hydra's rocky heights and top-floor rooms have sea views.

Amaryllis Hotel HOTEL €€
(☏ 22980 53611; www.amarillishydra.gr; Tombazi 15; s/d €45/60; 🕸 🛜) Simple rooms, a friendly owner and a super location right in the heart of town make this a safe midrange bet. Shared kitchen too.

★ Cotommatae BOUTIQUE HOTEL €€€
(☏ 22980 53873; www.cotommatae.gr; d/f incl breakfast from €170/250; 🕸) This restored mansion has retained the character and some of the memorabilia of the original family while adding impeccable modern touches. Some suites have private terraces or a spa.

★ Hydra Hotel APARTMENT €€€
(☏ 6985910717, 22980 53420; www.hydra-hotel.gr; Petrou Voulgari 8; studio incl breakfast €175-265, maisonettes €255; 🕸 🛜) Climb high on the south side of the port to swishy, top-of-the-line apartments in an impeccably renovated ancient mansion with kitchenettes and

BOAT SERVICES FROM HYDRA

DESTINATION	DURATION	FARE (€)	FREQUENCY
Ermioni*	20-40min	8	3 daily
Piraeus*	1¾hr	28	4-6 daily
Poros*	30min	13	4 daily
Porto Heli*	1hr	16.50	4 daily
Spetses*	40min	11.50	4-5 daily

*high-speed services

Hydra Town

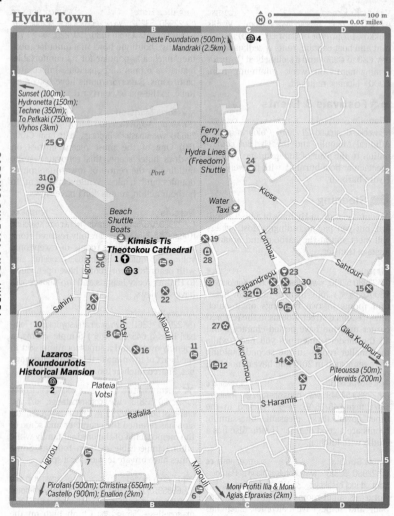

sweeping views. Get room 202 for a tiny balcony with panoramas to die for.

Leto Hotel HOTEL €€€
(☑22980 53385; www.letohydra.gr; Rigillis 8; d/ste from €177/485) This proper hotel is family-owned with formal rooms and all the services. It also offers a rarity in Greece: a wheelchair-accessible room, served by ramps all the way from the harbour.

Douskos Guest House PENSION €€€
(☑22980 53845; www.douskosguesthouse.gr; d/tr from €180/190) Clean lines and clock-tower views are part of this new guesthouse just back from the harbour. Bathrooms are top-

notch and owners also operate a popular local restaurant.

✗ Eating

Flora's SWEETS €
(Anemoni; ☑22980 53136; Plateia Votsi; sweets from €1; ⊙9am-late) Flora's sweet shop on inland Plateia Votsi makes *galaktoboureko* (custard slice), rice pudding and ice cream from local goats' milk.

Zefyros TAVERNA €
(☑22980 52008; Miaouli; mains €5-9; ⊙noon-10pm) Lovely Amalia and her family serve up classic Greek dishes in a low-key dining room

Hydra Town

just back from the port. Look in the glass case to see the day's specials. German expats also say it's got the best schnitzel on the island.

Ke Kremmidi GREEK €
(☑22980 53099; Tombazi; gyros €2.50, mains €6-9; ⊙noon-late) This friendly souvlaki joint has tables spilling out onto a busy pedestrian way and offers up good salads and grilled-meat plates as well.

Ostria TAVERNA €
(Stathis & Tassoula; ☑22980 54077; mains €5-8; ⊙noon-4pm & 6.30pm-late) Often referred to by just the gregarious owners' names 'Stathis & Tassoula', this year-round taverna serves only what's fresh: put the menu to one side and ask. You might be served chicken cutlets or fava or zucchini balls. Stathis catches his own sweet and delicious calamari.

Paradosiako TAVERNA €
(☑22980 54155; Tombazi; mains €5-15; ⊙noon-11.30pm Easter-Nov) This little streetside spot is traditional Greek personified. Sit on the corner terrace to watch the people parade as you dig into classic mezedhes – perhaps beetroot salad with garlic dip – or meats and seafood, such as fresh, filleted and grilled sardines.

★**Oraia Hydra** GREEK €€
(☑22980 52556; Harbourfront; mains €9-18; ⊙noon-midnight) Oraia Hydra translates as 'Beautiful Hydra' and this small bistro lives right up to its name. You'll dine on the harbour with sailboats bobbing alongside and

enjoy Greek dishes elevated by top ingredients and creative twists.

★**Il Casta** ITALIAN €€
(☑22980 52967; Tombazi; mains €10-22; ⊙noon-11pm) Dine al fresco and enjoy authentic Italian food like owner Pietro's Neapolitan grandmother used to make. Menus change daily. Reserve in high season.

★**Sunset** MEDITERRANEAN €€
(☑22980 52067; mains €9-25; ⊙noon-11pm Easter-Oct) Famed for its splendid panoramic spot near the cannons to the west of the harbour, Sunset has fine, fresh cuisine. Tasty salads, inventive pastas and local fish are prepared with flair and a hint of elegance.

Barba Dimas MEZEDHES €€
(☑22980 52967; Tombazi; small dishes €4-12; ⊙6-11pm) Tables line a small lane, back from the portside fray, and dishes run the gamut of Greek mezedhes, from tender calamari to greens picked from the mountains.

Caprice ITALIAN €€
(☑22980 52454; Sahtouri; mains €9-15; ⊙6pm-midnight Apr-Oct) A chance for romantic candlelit dining with a solid repertoire of Italian dishes, some using freshly made pasta.

■ Drinking & Nightlife

Prices are high, but lively people-watching comes with your coffee or cocktail. The harbour revs up after midnight.

★**Pirate** CAFE

(📞 22980 52711; www.thepiratebar.gr; Harbourfront; ⊙8am-late) Friendly Wendy and Takis and their kids, Zeus and occasionally Zara, run this daytime cafe with first-rate coffee, some of the island's most delicious breakfasts and home-cooked lunches (9am to 5pm), then morph it into a raging party place at night. Music changes with the crowd and the mood.

★**Hydronetta** BAR

(📞 22980 54160; www.hydronetta.gr; ⊙noon-11pm Easter-Oct) You can't beat this gorgeous waterfront location to the far west of the harbour. Brothers Andreas and Elias provide snazzy cocktails and lunch (high season only) with a smile.

Papagalos BAR

(📞 22980 52626; Harbourfront; ⊙9am-late) Papagalos is just that bit away from the madding crowd, on the quieter side of the harbour. By day, it offers coffee and basic food, and by night, cocktails and a clear view of the moonrise.

Isalos CAFE

(📞 22980 29661; www.isaloshydra.gr; Harbourfront; ⊙7am-late) Isalos makes exceptional coffee and a solid run of sandwiches and pastas.

Amalour COCKTAIL BAR

(📞 22980 53800; Tombazi; ⊙7pm-late Jun-Aug, reduced hours Sep-May) A lively line in cocktails, relaxed outdoor seating and dancing inside after midnight.

☆ **Entertainment**

Cinema Club of Hydra CINEMA, THEATRE

(📞 22980 53105; http://cineclubhydras.blogspot. com; Oikonomou) In July and August the open-air cinema screens blockbusters and indie flicks. It also organises excursions to plays at the ancient theatre of Epidavros.

🔒 **Shopping**

Sirens CLOTHING

(📞 22980 53340; Harbourfront; ⊙10am-10pm Easter-Oct) Charming owner Elena offers unique island-friendly, high-end fashion and Greek-designed jewellery.

Sugarfree CLOTHING

(📞 22980 53352; www.sugarfreeshops.com; Tombazi; ⊙11am-11pm May-Nov) Youthful beach-and loungewear created by Greek designers fill this sparkling white shop just back from Amalour bar, on the way to the Bratsera Hotel. Prices are reasonable by local standards and the colours dazzling.

Svoura ARTS & CRAFTS

(📞 22980 29784; Harbourfront; ⊙10am-11pm Apr-Oct) Carefully curated ceramics from all over Greece plus a smattering of fashion make this one of Hydra's top shops.

Elena Votsi JEWELLERY

(📞 22980 52637; www.elenavotsi.com; Harbourfront; ⊙10am-11.30pm) Hydra native Votsi is renowned for her original, bold designs using exquisite semiprecious stones, which sell in New York and London. She designed the Athens Olympic Games medal.

Turquoise FASHION & ACCESSORIES

(📞 22980 54033; www.turquoise.gr; ⊙10am-10pm Jun-Aug, reduced hours Sep-May) Local designer Dimitris creates an annual line of womenswear and accessories using intricate Indian block prints.

ℹ️ **Information**

ATMs are at harbour-front banks. There's no tourist office on Hydra.

Hospital (📞 22980 53150; Votsi) Basic hospital with an X-ray machine.

Post Office (⊙7.30am-2pm Mon-Fri) On the small, internal market square.

Tourist Police (📞 22980 52205) Shares an office with regular police.

Around Hydra

Hydra's mountainous, arid interior makes a robust but peaceful contrast to the clamour of the quayside. A useful map for walkers is Anavasi's *Hydra* map. A map is posted on the quay, and several marked trails extend across the island. Once you leave the villages of Hydra/Kamini/Vlyhos there are no services. Take plenty of water.

An unbeatable experience is the long haul up to Moni Profiti Ilia. The wonderful monastery complex contains beautiful icons and boasts super views. It's a solid hour or more through zigzags and pine trees to panoramic bliss on top.

A smaller monastery, Moni Agias Efpraxias, sits just below Profiti Ilia and is run by nuns.

Other paths lead to Mt Eros (588m), the island's highest point, and east and west along the island spine, but you need advanced route-finding skills or reliable directions from knowledgable locals.

The coastal road turns into a partially cobbled, beautiful trail about 1.5km west of the port, after Kamini. Kamini has a tiny fishing port, several good tavernas, swimming rocks and a small pebble beach. In fact, Hydra's shortcoming – or blessing – is its lack of sandy beaches to draw the crowds. People usually swim off the rocks, but if you go as far as Vlyhos, 1.5km after Kamini, this last little hamlet before the mountains offers two slightly larger pebble beaches (one called Vlyhos and the other, the more pristine Plakes), tavernas and a restored 19th-century stone bridge.

The coastal road leads 2.5km east from the port to a pebble beach at Mandraki.

Boats run from the harbour to all of these places, and you certainly need them to reach Bisti Bay or Agios Nikolaos Bay, in the island's southwest, with their remote but umbrella-laden pebble beaches and green waters.

✗ Eating

Christina   TAVERNA €
(☏ 22980 53516; Kamini; mains €6-12; ⊘ noon-4pm & 6-10pm Thu-Tue Easter-Oct) Just inland from the port in Kamini, Mrs Christina and her kids dish out some of the island's best Greek dishes and fresh fish.

To Pefkaki   SEAFOOD, MEZEDHES €
(☏ 6973535709; Kamini; dishes €5-10; ⊘ noon-4pm & 6.30-10pm Thu-Tue Easter-Oct) Worth the short walk along the coast to Kamini for a laid-back lunch of mezedhes and fresh seafood (delicious fried anchovies).

★ Techne   INTERNATIONAL €€
(☏ 22980 52500; www.techne-hydra.com; Coast Rd, Avlaki; mains €13-23; ⊘ 10am-midnight) Spread across several terraces and overlooking a broad sweep of sea and sunset, this elegant cafe and restaurant serves lighter fare by day and full, well-conceived, delicious and thoughtfully served meals at night. Book ahead on weekend evenings to nab a table, perfect for date night.

Four Seasons   TAVERNA €€
(☏ 22980 53698; www.fourseasonshydra.gr; Plakes Beach; mains €6-15; ⊘ noon-10pm Easter-Oct; ☏) This tasty seaside taverna offers a different face of Hydra: the sound of the breeze and the waves instead of the portside buzz. Don't miss the *taramasalata* (fish-roe dip) with bread and whatever else tickles your fancy. It also has handsome suites (from €240, including breakfast).

Enalion   TAVERNA €€
(☏ 22980 53455; www.enalion-hydra.gr; Vlyhos; mains €6-12; ⊘ noon-10pm Easter-Oct) Perhaps the best seaside option at Vlyhos Beach, with traditional Greek fare.

Pirofani   INTERNATIONAL €€
(☏ 22980 53175; www.pirofani.com; Kamini; mains €10-16; ⊘ 7.30pm-midnight Wed-Sun late May-Sep) Gregarious Theo creates an eclectic range of dishes, from a beef fillet with rose-pepper sauce to a spicy Asian curry.

Castello   MEDITERRANEAN €€€
(☏ 22980 54101; www.castellohydra.gr; Kamini; snacks €7-15, mains €15-30; ⊘ 1pm-late Jun-Sep) In a renovated 18th-century bastion and spilling onto the beach, Castello offers waterfront snacks at its daytime beach bar, gourmet seaside dining at its refined restaurant and sunset cocktails at its bar. Amazing views.

SPETSES   ΣΠΕΤΣΕΣ

POP 4027

Spetses stands proudly just a few kilometres from mainland Peloponnese, but there is a stronger sense of carefree island Greece here than in other Saronic Gulf destinations. The lively, historic old town is the only village on the island; the rest, ringed by a simple road, is rolling hills, pine forests and crystal-clear coves. Relaxed Spetses Town has great nightlife, some of the Saronic's best restaurants and gorgeous, easily accessible swimming spots. With a rich naval history, it is still incredibly popular with yachties, and with its vibrant culture, it attracts artists, intellectuals and lovers of a good island party.

History

In Spetses Town there's evidence of early Helladic settlement near the Old Harbour and around the Dapia Harbour. Roman and Byzantine remains have been found in the area behind Moni Agios Nikolaos, halfway between the two.

From the 10th century, Spetses is thought to have been uninhabited for almost 600 years, until the arrival of Albanian refugees fleeing the fighting between Turks and Venetians in the 16th century.

Spetses, like Hydra, grew wealthy from shipbuilding. Island captains busted the British blockade during the Napoleonic Wars and refitted their ships to join the Greek fleet during the War of Independence. In the process they immortalised one local woman (albeit originally from Hydra) the formidable Laskarina Bouboulina, ship commander and fearless fighter.

The island's hallmark forests of Aleppo pine, a legacy of the far-sighted philanthropist Sotirios Anargyros, have been devastated

Spetses

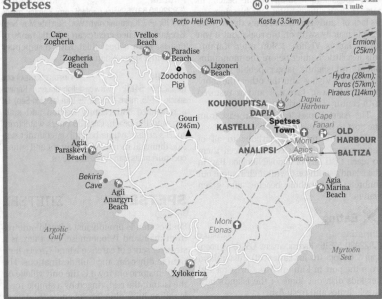

by fires several times in the past 20 years. The trees are steadily recovering.

ⓘ Getting There & Away

High-speed ferries link Spetses with Hydra, Poros and Piraeus, and Ermioni and Porto Heli on the Peloponnese. In summer caïques (per person €4) and a car ferry (€2) go from the harbour to Kosta on the mainland. Note: only locally owned cars are allowed on Spetses. Park yours in Kosta. Get tickets at Bardakos Tours (p158).

ⓘ Getting Around

BICYCLE

Bike Center (☏22980 72209; http://spetses bikecenter.blogspot.com; ⊘10am-3.30pm & 5.30-10pm) Behind the fish market; rents out bikes (per day €8), including baby seats.

BOAT

In summer caïques serve the island's beaches (return €13). **Water-taxi** (☏22980 72072; Dapia Harbour; ⊘24hr) fares are displayed on a board at the quay. All leave from the quay opposite Bardakos Tours (p158).

BUS

Two routes start over Easter and increase in frequency to three or four daily from June to September. Departure times are displayed on boards by the bus stops and around town.

One goes from Plateia Agiou Mama in Spetses Town to Agia Paraskevi (€6, 40 minutes), travelling via Agia Marina and Agii Anargyri. The other leaves from in front of Poseidonion Grand Hotel, going to Vrellos (€4) via Ligoneri.

CAR & MOTORCYCLE

Only locally owned autos are allowed on Spetses, and those are not permitted in the centre of town. The transport of choice tends to be scooters. Motorbike- and quad-bike-hire shops abound (per day €15 to €35). Taxis are another option.

Spetses Town Σπέτσες

POP 4001

Bustling Spetses Town stretches along a meandering waterfront encompassing several quays and beaches. The main Dapia Harbour, where ferries arrive, and the area around adjacent Plateia Limenarhiou and inland Plateia Orologiou (Clocktower Sq) teem with chic tourist shops and cafes.

As you head further inland on the quieter lanes, or go left along the harbour-front road of Sotiriou Anargyriou, past the town beach and Plateia Agiou Mama, impressive old arhontika (mansions) illustrate Spetses' historic (and ongoing) wealth.

Passing the church of Moni Agios Nikolaos you arrive at the attractive Old Harbour (Palio Limani) and the interesting Baltiza yacht anchorage and boat-building area.

From the north side of Dapia Harbour a promenade and road lead through the seafront Kounoupitsa area.

◉ Sights

Bouboulina's Museum   MUSEUM
(☑22980 72416; www.bouboulinamuseum-spetses. gr; adult/child €6/2; ☉tours daily Apr-Oct) The mansion of Spetses' famous daughter, the 19th-century seagoing commander Laskarina Bouboulina, has been converted into a museum. Entry is via 40-minute guided tours (billboards around town advertise starting times, also posted online). The museum hosts occasional concerts. There's an impressive statue of Bouboulina on the harbour, opposite the Poseidonion Grand Hotel.

Spetses Museum   MUSEUM
(☑22980 72994; http://odysseus.culture.gr; adult/ child €3/free; ☉8am-3pm Tue-Sun) Small, fascinating collections are housed in the old mansion of Hatzigiannis Mexis (1754–1844), a shipowner who became the island's first governor. They include island artefacts, traditional costumes and portraits of the island's founding fathers.

★ Festivals & Events

★Armata   CULTURAL
(☉early Sep) This week-long celebration culminates on 8 September in a commemoration of Spetses' victory over the Turks in a key 1822 naval battle, with an enormous water-borne re-enactment and fireworks.

🛏 Sleeping

Villa Christina Hotel   PENSION €
(☑22980 72218; www.villachristinahotel.com; s/d/ tr/f incl breakfast from €50/55/70/90; ❄ 🕾) Located about 200m uphill on the main road inland from the harbour, these well-kept rooms and lovely garden are back from the worst traffic noise.

Villa Marina   PENSION €
(☑22980 72646; www.villamarinaspetses.com; Agios Mamas; d €55-60; ❄ 🕾) Superbasic, clean rooms have refrigerators and there is a well-equipped communal kitchen downstairs. Just to the right of Plateia Agiou Mama.

Hotel Kamelia   PENSION €
(☑6939095513; http://hotelkamelia.gr; Agias Mamas; s/d from €40/45; ☉Easter-Oct; ❄🕾) Good-value airy rooms are tucked away from the busy seafront in the Agios Mamas area, with a bougainvillea-draped terrace.

Economou Mansion   PENSION €€
(☑22980 73400; www.economouspetses.gr; d incl breakfast from €130; ❄🕾❄) This beautiful pension on the ground floor of a restored captain's mansion sits right on the waterfront, about 500m north of Dapia Harbour, and offers a homey, relaxed hideaway combining antique decor and modern amenities such as swimming pool, TV, hairdryer and safe. Breakfast is bountiful.

Kastro Hotel   APARTMENT €€
(☑22980 75319; www.kastrohotel-spetses.gr; studios/4-person apt incl breakfast €120/165; ❄🕾❄) A private, quiet complex encloses these studios and apartments close to the centre of town. Low-key decor and modern amenities combine with extensive terraces.

Klimis Hotel   HOTEL €€
(☑22980 73725; www.klimishotel.gr; Dapia Harbour; s/d/apt incl breakfast from €75/95/170; ❄🕾) Sleek rooms, some with seafront balconies, at this standard hotel sit above a ground-floor cafe-bar and patisserie.

★Poseidonion Grand Hotel   LUXURY HOTEL €€€
(☑22980 74553; www.poseidonion.com; Dapia Harbour; d/ste incl breakfast from €280/670; ❄🕾❄) Here's your chance to live like a wealthy dame or gent in the roaring '20s. This grand old hotel has been totally renovated and every centimetre, from the chic rooms to the gracious lobby bar and grand

BOAT SEVICES FROM SPETSES

DESTINATION	DURATION	FARE (€)	FREQUENCY
Ermioni*	20-30min	8	2 daily
Hydra*	40min	11.50	4-5 daily
Piraeus*	2hr 10min	38.50	5 daily
Poros*	1½hr	16	4-5 daily
Porto Heli*	15min	6	3-4 daily

*high-speed services

pool, drips with luxury. Oh, and it also has one of the island's best restaurants.

★ **Orloff Resort** BOUTIQUE HOTEL €€€
(☑22980 75444; www.orloffresort.com; Old Harbour; d/studios/apt incl breakfast from €210/225/410; ☉Mar-Oct; ❄☎❄) On the edge of town, along the road to Agia Marina and near the old port, the pristine Orloff hides behind high white walls. Enjoy stylish rooms and a crystal-clear pool.

✗ Eating

★ **Akrogialia** SEAFOOD, TAVERNA €€
(☑22980 74749; www.akrogialia-restaurant.gr; Kounoupitsa; mains €9-17; ☉11am-midnight) This superb restaurant is on the Kounoupitsa seafront and matches its delicious food with friendly service and a bright setting. Tasty options include oven-baked *melidzana rolos* (eggplant with creamy cheese and walnuts). Enjoy terrific fish risotto or settle for a choice steak. All are accompanied by a thoughtful selection of Greek wines. Book ahead on weekends.

To Nero tis Agapis MEDITERRANEAN €€
(☑22980 74009; www.nerotisagapis.gr; Kounoupitsa; mains €9-22; ☉11am-midnight) The sweetly named 'Water of Love' offers gourmet meat as well as fish dishes. The crayfish tagliatelle is worth every bite, as is the *zarzuela* (fish stew). There's a selection of creative salads. Book ahead for the romantic tables with the best sea views.

Patralis SEAFOOD €€
(☑22980 75380; www.patralis.gr; Kounoupitsa; mains €7-15; ☉10am-midnight Jan-Oct) Operating for more than 70 years and known islandwide for its outstanding seafood, Patralis sits smack on the seafront in Kounoupitsa.

Orloff MEDITERRANEAN €€
(☑22980 75255; www.orloffrestaurant.com; Old Harbour; mains €14-21; ☉6.30pm-1am Jun-Sep, 6.30pm-1am Fri, 12.30pm-1am Sat, 12.30-6pm Sun May & Oct) Fresh fish and specialities such as seafood linguine or pork fillet with aubergine purée are hallmarks of the popular Orloff. The terrace sits above the water at a bend in the road just north of the Old Harbour.

★ **On the Verandah** MEDITERRANEAN €€€
(☑6957507267;www.poseidonion.com/en/Dining-On-the-Verandah; Poseidonion Hotel; 4-course dinner €38; ☉7.30pm-midnight Jul & Aug, reduced hours May, Jun & Sep) One of the Saronic Gulf's top dining experiences, the Verandah at the Poseidonion Hotel is the dining space for the high-concept cuisine of chef Stamatis

Marmarinos. Ingredients are locally sourced and comprise exquisitely presented, creative Mediterranean dishes. Book ahead.

★ **Tarsanas** SEAFOOD €€€
(☑22980 74490; www.tarsanas-spetses.gr; Old Harbour; mains €17-26; ☉11am-midnight) A hugely popular *psarotaverna* (fish taverna) on the water at the Old Harbour, this family-run place deals almost exclusively in fish dishes. It can be pricey, but the fish soup (€7) alone is a delight and other starters, such as anchovies marinated with lemon, start at €6.

🍷 Drinking & Nightlife

Mourayo BAR
(☑22980 73700; Old Harbour; ☉8pm-2am) You can come for the food, but be sure to stay for a sunset or late-night waterfront cocktail and dancing.

La Luz BAR
(☑22980 75024; www.laluzspetses.gr; Old Harbour) La Luz often has live music and always sports super sea views in the Old Harbour area of Spetses.

Ariston CAFE
(☑22980 73803; Dapia Harbour; ☉9am-late; ☎) A touch of class on the waterfront, with coffee by day and sundowners by evening.

Bar Spetsa BAR
(☑22980 74131; www.barspetsa.org; Agios Mamas; ☉8pm-late Mar-Oct) One of life's great little bars, this Spetses institution never loses its easygoing atmosphere. Find it 50m beyond Plateia Agiou Mama, on the road to the right of the kiosk.

Roussos CAFE
(☑22908 72819; Dapia Harbour; ☉7.30am-late) Old-time Spetsiot coffee house with pastries, on the harbour.

ℹ️ Information

Banks at Dapia Harbour have ATMs.

Bardakos Tours (☑22980 73141; hswbarda@yahoo.gr; Dapia Harbour; ☉8am-9pm Jun-Aug, reduced hours Sep-May) Sells ferry tickets and assists with other arrangements.

Municipal Information Kiosk (www.spetses.com.gr; ☉10am-9pm May-Sep) On the quay; seasonal staff provide answers to general questions about the island.

Port Authority (☑22980 72245; Dapia) Just inland from the cafe terrace overlooking Dapia Harbour.

Tourist Police (☑Police 22980 73100, Tourist Police 22980 73744; Dapia; ☉mid-May–Sep) Housed with the port authority.

Cyclades

Best Places to Eat

➡ Doukato (p206)
➡ M-Eating (p183)
➡ Captain Dimos (p219)
➡ Cayenne (p256)
➡ Theoni's Kitchen (p233)
➡ O Ntinos (p171)

Best Places to Stay

➡ Red Tractor Farm (p263)
➡ Pension Sofi (p205)
➡ Windmill of Karamitsos (p250)
➡ Stelios Place (p239)
➡ Francesco's (p224)

Why Go?

On a quest to find the Greek islands of your dreams? Start, here, in the Cyclades (Κυκλάδες). Rugged, sun-drenched outcrops of rock, anchored in azure seas and liberally peppered with snow-white villages and blue-domed churches, this is Greece straight from central casting, with stellar archaeological sites and dozens of postcard-worthy beaches. Throw in a blossoming food scene, some renowned party destinations and a good dose of sophistication, and you really do have the best of Greece's ample charms.

The biggest surprise may be the variety found within this island group. Chase hedonism on Mykonos or Ios, history on Delos, hiking trails on Andros or Amorgos. Want a romantic break? Try Santorini. To escape reality? Pick Donousa or Anafi. You can ferry-hop to your heart's content, enjoy long, lazy lunches at waterside tavernas, or simply lay claim to a sunbed by a spectacular beach. You're living the dream.

When to Go
Mykonos Town

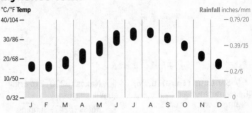

Apr–Jun Catch the early-season sun without overheating, and boats without overcrowding.

Jul & Aug Pros: sun, sea and sand, plus balmy nights and lively company. Cons: peak crowds and prices.

Sep & Oct Quieter beaches, open spaces, the sweet scent of herbs, and great walks on island hills.

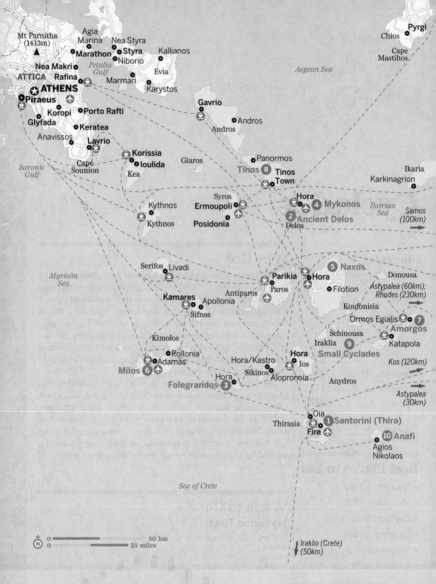

Cyclades Highlights

1 Santorini (Thira) (p226) Being mesmerised by the dramatic volcanic cliffs.

2 Ancient Delos (p189) Immersing yourself in history on this sacred island.

3 Folegandros (p243) Wandering the streets of Hora.

4 Mykonos (p177) Partying until dawn.

5 Naxos (p200) Exploring quaint villages.

6 Milos (p247) Sunning yourself on stone cliffs or lazing in sandy coves.

7 Amorgos (p217) Marvelling at the dazzling cliffside monastery.

8 Tinos (p166) Exploring

marble villages and gorgeous dovecote valleys.

9 Small Cyclades (p211) Slipping away to serenity on these remote-feeling islands.

10 Anafi (p240) Enjoying a slow-paced traditional lifestyle on this far-flung isle.

History

The Cyclades are said to have been inhabited since at least 7000 BC. Around 3000 BC there emerged a cohesive Cycladic civilisation that was bound together by seagoing commerce and exchange. During the Early Cycladic period (3000–2000 BC), the tiny but distinctive Cycladic marble figurines, mainly stylised representations of the naked female form, were sculpted. Recent discoveries on Keros, an uninhabited island near Koufonisia in the Small Cyclades, indicate that the island was a possible pilgrimage site where figurines that had been broken up as part of rituals were deposited.

During the Middle Cycladic period (2000–1500 BC), many of the islands were occupied by the Minoans, who probably colonised from Crete. At Akrotiri, on Santorini, a Minoan town has been excavated, and artefacts from the site have all the distinctive beauty of those from Crete's Minoan palaces. At the beginning of the Late Cycladic period (1500–1100 BC), the archipelago came under the influence of the Mycenaeans of the Peloponnese, who were supplanted by northern Dorians in the 8th century BC.

By the mid-5th century BC the Cyclades were part of a fully fledged Athenian empire. In the Hellenistic era (323–146 BC), they were governed by Egypt's Ptolemaic dynasties, and later by the Macedonians. In 146 BC the islands became a Roman province, and lucrative trade links were established with many parts of the Mediterranean.

The division of the Roman Empire in AD 395 resulted in the Cyclades being ruled from Byzantium (Constantinople), but after the fall of Byzantium in 1204, they came under a Venetian authority that doled out the islands to opportunistic aristocrats. The most powerful of these was Marco Sanudo (the self-styled Venetian Duke of Naxos), who acquired a dozen of the larger islands – including Naxos, Paros, Ios, Sifnos, Milos, Amorgos and Folegandros – introducing a Venetian gloss that survives to this day in island architecture.

The Cyclades came under Turkish rule in 1537, although the empire had difficulty in managing, let alone protecting, such scattered dependencies. Cycladic coastal settlements suffered frequent pirate raids, a scourge that led to many villages being relocated to hidden inland sites. They survive as the 'Horas' (capitals, also often written as

'Chora') that are such an attractive feature of the islands today. Ottoman neglect, piracy and shortages of food and water often led to wholesale depopulation of more remote islands, and in 1563 only five islands were still inhabited.

The Cyclades played a minimal part in the Greek War of Independence, but became havens for people fleeing from other islands where insurrections against the Turks had led to massacres and persecution. Italian forces occupied the Cyclades during WWII. After the war, the islands emerged more economically deprived than ever. Many islanders lived in deep poverty, while many more gave up the struggle and headed to the mainland, or to America and Australia, in search of work.

The tourism boom that began in the 1970s revived the fortunes of the Cyclades. The challenge remains, however, of finding alternative and sustainable economies that will not mar the beauty and appeal of these remarkable islands.

❶ Getting There & Away

AIR

Of the 24 Cyclades islands, six have airports – Mykonos, Syros, Paros, Naxos, Santorini and Milos – all with daily links to Athens. Some have direct links with European cities in summer (charter flights, plus scheduled services to Mykonos and Santorini). There are rarely direct links between islands, so to fly from Mykonos to Santorini, you'll almost certainly need to go via Athens.

BOAT

The key to sculpting an itinerary through the islands is knowing which ferries go where – and when they're going. The peak ferry services run in July and August, but in winter services are reduced or nonexistent on some routes.

A host of companies offer connections throughout the Cyclades. They depart from the main ports of Attica: Piraeus (the largest port, with services to most islands), Rafina (particularly good for Mykonos, Andros and Tinos) and Lavrio (for Kythnos and Kea).

Three extremely useful websites are:

http://ferries.gr For checking dates and times, and buying tickets online.

www.ferriesingreece.com/live-boat-traffic. htm See ferry locations in real time and check if they are likely to turn up on time.

www.vesselfinder.com If you know your ferry's name, check here to see where it is.

ANDROS ΑΝΔΡΟΣ

POP 9221

Andros, the second-largest island of the Cyclades, has a long and proud seafaring tradition and is also a walker's paradise. Its wild mountains are cleaved by fecund valleys with bubbling streams and ancient stone mills. A lush island, springs tend to be a feature of each village, and waterfalls cascade down hillsides most of the year. It's worth renting a car to get out to the footpaths, many of them stepped and cobbled, which will lead you through majestic landscapes, wildflowers and archaeological remnants. The handsome main town of Hora, also known as Andros, is a shipowners' enclave packed with neoclassical mansions.

ⓘ Getting There & Away

Reach Andros from the mainland port of Rafina via regular ferries that continue south to Tinos and Mykonos. Direct services run to/from Syros a few times a week, from where easy onward links can be made (or you can reach Syros daily, by changing ferry in Tinos).

Buy tickets at Ploes Travel (p165) in Hora or Batsi Travel in Gavrio.

Boat Services from Andros

DESTINATION	DURATION	FARE (€)	FREQUENCY
Kea	6hr	13	Thu
Kythnos	4¾hr	18	Thu
Mykonos	2½hr	18-19	2-4 daily
Naxos	3¾-4hr	26-28	daily
Rafina	2hr	22-23	2-4 daily
Syros	2hr	12	Thu
Tinos	1½-2hr	12-17	2-4 daily

ⓘ Getting Around

KTEL Andros (☑ 22820 22316) has up to nine buses daily (fewer on weekends) linking Gavrio and Hora (€4, 55 minutes) via Batsi (€2, 15 minutes), and Gavrio and Korthi (€5, 1¼ hours, two to three daily). Schedules are posted at the bus stops in Gavrio and Hora. Low-season buses are usually timed to meet Rafina ferries.

Taxis (☑ Batsi 22820 41081, Gavrio 22820 71561, Hora 22820 22171) from Gavrio to Batsi cost about €12, and to Hora €40.

Roads can be rough and narrow, but many walking paths and sights are only accessible by car. **Escape in Andros** (☑ 22820 29120; www.escapeinandros.gr) can arrange to meet you at the port with a rental car (from about €40 per day in August, €25 in low season). There are a couple of scooter and ATV rental agencies on the waterfront in Gavrio.

Gavrio Γαύριο

POP 1199

Sleepy Gavrio on the west coast is the main port of Andros. The waterfront is lined with services (ATMs, ticket agencies, car and scooter hire), but the town isn't the most interesting part of the island to base yourself – there are some stretches of beach to the south (en route to Batsi) that are more appealing.

🛏 Sleeping & Eating

Standard tavernas line Gavrio's waterfront. Gavrio is used as the jumping-off point to visit Andros' most celebrated restaurant in the north part of the island.

Andros Camping CAMPGROUND €
(☑ 22820 71444; www.campingandros.gr; campsite per adult/tent/car €7/4/4; ☺ May-Sep; 🐾) A rustic site set among olive trees about 400m behind the harbour. Follow the signs from the road to Batsi, turning at the Escape in Andros travel agency.

Allegria Family Hotel HOTEL €€
(☑ 22820 72110; www.allegria-andros.com; Agios Petros Beach; d/f €75/85; ☺ Apr-Sep; ❄🔊) Nicely geared to families and close to the beach at Agios Petros, a few kilometres south of Gavrio. Studios have kitchenettes, and some have bunks for kids, all set in a pretty garden.

ⓘ Information

There's a full range of services along the waterfront, including three ATMs and two banks.
Kyklades Travel (☑ 22820 72363; ☺ 9am-9pm) and **Batsi Travel** (☑ 22820 71489; ☺ 9am-9pm) sell ferry tickets and can arrange accommodation.

Batsi Μπατσί

POP 957

Batsi lies 7km southeast of Gavrio on the overbuilt shores of a handsome bay with a long beige-sand beach. The island's main resort, it revs up through July and August. A couple of good, short hiking trails start from town.

🛏 Sleeping & Eating

Cavo D'Oro GUESTHOUSE €
(☑ 22820 41776; www.andros-cavodoro.gr; d €50; ❄🔊) The handful of simple, pleasant rooms

Andros

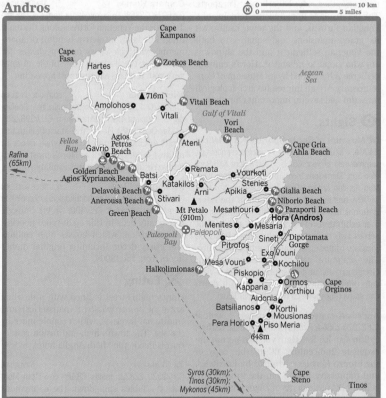

Cape Kampanos
Cape Fasa
Hartes
Zorkos Beach
▲716m
Amolohos
Vitali
Vitali Beach
Aegean Sea
Gulf of Vitali
Vori Beach
Ateni
Fellos Bay
Agios Petros Beach
Gavrio
Cape Gria
Ahla Beach
Rafina (65km)
Golden Beach
Agios Kyprianos Beach
Batsi
Remata
Vourkoti
Stenies
Katakilos
Arni
Apikia
Gialia Beach
Delavoia Beach
Niborio Beach
Anerousa Beach
Stivari
Mt Petalo (910m)
Mesathouri
Paraporti Beach
Green Beach
Hora (Andros)
Menites
Mesaria
Paleopoli Bay
Paleopoli
Sineti
Dipotamata Gorge
Pitrofos
Exo Vouni
Kochilou
Mesa Vouni
Halkolimionas
Piskopio
Kapparia
Ormos Korthiou
Cape Orginos
Aidonia
Batsilianos
Korthi
Mousionas
Pera Horio
Piso Meria
648m
Syros (30km);
Tinos (30km);
Mykonos (45km)
Cape Steno
Tinos

CYCLADES ANDROS

at Cavo D'Oro are excellent value. It's located above a restaurant across the road from the beach.

Krinos Suites Hotel   BOUTIQUE HOTEL €€€
(☎ 22820 42038; www.krinoshotel.com; ste incl breakfast from €180; ⊗ late May–Sep; 🅿️🅿️) One of Andros' high-end entries, housing nine well-kitted-out suites and a smart 'art cafe'. Some rooms have sea-view balconies.

★ Themelos   CYCLADIC €
(☎ 22820 29426; www.facebook.com/themelos andros; Dionisou; dishes €5-8; ⊗12.30-11pm; 🅿️) Head up the stairs from the waterfront to find this delightful little cafe tucked away on a tiny pedestrian street. Works by local artists liven up the interior, and the menu is full of local mezedhes – smoked baby mackerel, slightly fermented local *kopanisti* cheese, locally made sausage, wild artichokes. Wash it down with a sour cherry juice.

Stamatis Taverna   GREEK €€
(☎ 22820 41283; mains €7-17; ⊗ noon-11pm; 🅿️) Next to the harbour, this restaurant's interior is a charming time warp, and the food is renowned for its authenticity: Andros lamb and stuffed chicken are specialities, as is the fresh fish. Reserve ahead for the Wednesday night slow-cooked lamb.

🛈 Information

Greek Sun Holidays (☎ 22820 41198; www.andros-greece.com) Arranges accommodation, car hire, ferry tickets and island walks and excursions.

Hora (Andros)
Χώρα (Ανδρος)
POP 1665

Hora perches dramatically on a rocky promontory and has surprising views through the neoclassical mansions to two vibrant bays on either side: Niborio and Paraporti. The peninsula is tipped by the remains of a Venetian fortress, and the town itself owes its grand mansions and squares to both the Venetian settlement and the shipowners who came to inhabit it. Hora's cultural pedigree is burnished by its Museum of Contemporary Art, an impressive archaeological museum and several important churches.

☉ Sights

★ **Museum of Contemporary Art**   MUSEUM
(MOCA; ☑ 22820 22444; www.moca-andros.gr; summer/rest of year €5/3; ☉ 11am-3pm & 6-9pm Wed-Sun, 11am-3pm Mon Jul-Sep, 10am-2pm Wed-Mon Apr-Jun & Oct, 10am-2pm Sat-Mon Nov-Mar) MOCA has earned a reputation in the international art world for its outstanding summer exhibitions of world-famous artists. Split across two buildings, exhibits have included Picasso, Matisse, Toulouse-Lautrec and Miró. The sculpture gallery features prominent Greek artists, and a summertime sea-view cafe offers homemade sweets. Find it down the steps (signposted) from Plateia Kaïri.

Andros Archaeological Museum   MUSEUM
(☑ 22820 23664; Plateia Kaïri; adult/child €3/free; ☉ 9am-4pm Tue-Sat) Here you can peruse the exquisite 2nd-century BC marble copy of the bronze *Hermes of Andros* by Praxiteles, and impressive finds from the 9th- to 5th-century BC settlements of Zagora and Paleopoli on Andros' west coast.

Afanis Naftis   MONUMENT
(Plateia Riva) The huge bronze sailor, donated by the Soviet Union, stands in the square at the tip of the promontory and celebrates Hora's seagoing traditions.

Venetian Fortress   RUINS
The picturesque ruins of a Venetian fortress stand on an island linked to the tip of the headland by the worn remnants of an arched stone bridge. Don't attempt to scramble over in the manner of locals.

⊨ Sleeping

★ **Anemomiloi Studios**   APARTMENT €€
(☑ 22820 24084; www.anemomiloi.gr; d/q from €95/105; ❄☎✿) This popular complex of bright, spic-and-span studios, split between two buildings, sits at the southern end of town enjoying views over green fields from all its balconies. There's friendly, helpful service from the owners, and a quiet poolside patio. Off-peak rates drop considerably.

Camara Homes   APARTMENT €€
(☑ 6972028853; Empeirikou; apt from €60; ❄☎) Towards the Venetian fortress along the main drag, this is an attractive handful of apartments, with sea views and spyglasses for peering at the horizon. The split-level ones with roof terraces are the most appealing.

Micra Anglia   BOUTIQUE HOTEL €€
(☑ 22820 22207; www.micra-anglia.gr; Goulandri 13; d/tr/ste incl breakfast from €117/198/270; ☉ May-Oct; ❄☎) Hora's five-star offering has a raft of chic amenities and stylish decor in neutral shades, as well as Hora's most imaginative restaurant. Discounts available online.

Archontiko Eleni   BOUTIQUE HOTEL €€
(☑ 2282022270; www.archontikoeleni.gr; Empirikou 9; s/d incl breakfast €85/100; ❄☎) Snuggle into comfy beds in this eight-room neoclassical mansion, which boasts high ceilings and classy decor, including original timber floors from the 1890s.

✗ Eating

Hora's main street is lined with a dazzling array of *zaharoplasteia* (patisseries) and traditional tavernas, with a couple more by the sea. The town's high-end fusion restaurant is inside the Micra Anglia hotel.

Ta Skalakia   TAVERNA €
(☑ 22820 22822; mains €8-12; ☉ 6-11pm Mon-Sat; ☎) Tables spill down the eponymous stairs from this buttercup-yellow restaurant. Inside feels more like a bistro, with quaint bric-a-brac. There's a short, tasty menu offering the likes of oregano-flavoured pork, meatballs and roasted feta.

I Parea   TAVERNA €
(☑ 22820 23721; Plateia Kaïri; mains €7-13; ☉ noon-10pm; ☎) Long-established and popular with locals, central Parea boasts a super terrace overlooking Paraporti Beach. Head inside to see what's been freshly cooked.

★ **Dolly's Bar Restaurant**   FUSION €€
(☑ 22820 22207; Goulandri 13; mains €16-25; ☉ 7.30pm-late; ❄☎) In the basement of the Micra Anglia hotel, this is the most stylish and imaginative restaurant in town. Go for tabbouleh topped with grilled giant prawns or the impeccably grilled steak.

Endochora   CYCLADIC €€
(☑ 22820 23207; www.endochora.com; Empirikou; mains €9-17; ☉ noon-10pm May–mid-Sep, weekends only rest of year; ☎) Endochora is a stylish

hotspot on the main drag, offering a fresh twist on Greek classics and a great vantage point for people-watching. Salads showcase prime local produce like capers, tomatoes, figs and cheeses. It was under refurbishment on our last visit.

❶ Information

The pedestrianised marble main street, leading downhill to the Venetian *kastro* (fortress), is lined with numerous banks.

See http://andros.gr/en for more info.

Ploes Travel (☑ 22820 29220; Empirikou; ☻9am-1pm & 3-9pm) Can arrange guided hikes and scooter and car rental. Also sells ferry tickets.

Around Andros

It's well worth renting a car or scooter to explore Andros' vast mountains and sprinkling of picturesque villages. Its mountain drives are panorama-filled.

The north of the island, with the lush watershed around **Arni**, gives way to raw, windswept hills as the road zigzags to **Vourkoti** and **Agios Nikolaou** with its sweeping views.

Paleopoli, 7km south of Batsi on the coast road, is the site of Ancient Andros and its sunken harbour. Only rubble remains but the small roadside **Archaeological Museum of Paleopoli** (☑ 22829 41985; ☻9am-4pm Tue-Sun) FREE displays finds.

The island is cleaved by a sweeping agricultural valley, and loads of small villages with springs, often marked by marble lions' heads and the like, surround Hora. The road winds through **Sariza**, **Stenies**, **Mesathouri**, **Strapouries** and **Menites** – all fun to explore.

In the south, visit quaint agricultural villages like **Livadia**, **Kochilou**, **Piskopio**, and **Aidonia**, which has ruined tower houses. The area's charming landscape of fields and cypresses encircle **Ormos Korthiou**, an uninspiring bayside village.

❍ Sights & Activities

Walking

There are 18 wonderful waymarked trails criss-crossing Andros, which range in duration from 30 minutes to six hours, and are labelled in difficulty level from easy to average. Wear hiking boots and trekking pants, as there are some (shy) snakes.

The best investment you can make is the *Andros Hiking Map* (€6) published by the marvellous **Andros Routes** (www.androsroutes.gr) project, in conjunction with Anavasi mapping company. It's available at bookshops and gift shops on the island. The Andros Routes website outlines the paths they maintain and has good advice for hiking on the island.

Locals recommend the areas north of Hora for great walks, including the villages of Stenies and Apikia. For a lovely short walk, **Pithara** is a shady glade of streams accessed from Apikia. For a longer ramble, hike up the dramatic **Dipotamata Gorge**, signposted as you drive inland, after Sineti (southeast of Hora). The trail is cobbled part of the way and leads past ancient bridges and water mills and through vivid foliage, water burbling below.

Better yet, book a guided walk with **Trekking Andros** (☑ 22820 61368; www.trekkingandros.gr; guided walk per person from €20), a company that arranges and guides a menu of activities on the island, including hiking, mountain biking, boat trips, yoga, cooking or painting classes.

🏃 Beaches

Between Gavrio and Paleopoli Bay excellent beaches include **Golden Beach** (Hrisi Ammos), **Delavoia** (one half of which is naturist), **Anerousa**, and **Green Beach**. Near Hora, check out lovely Gialia Beach.

Spectacular **Halkolimionas** – with tawny sand and a tiny church – sits 2km down a stone-terraced valley near the junction for Hora. A small beach bar sets up here in summer.

Many of the best beaches, such as **Ahla**, **Vori** and **Vitali** (all in the northeast), are only reached by 4WD, ATV or boat. Boat trips can usually be arranged (or boats hired) in Batsi and Nimborio.

🛏 Sleeping

Perrakis   HOTEL **€€**
(☑ 22820 71456; www.hotelperrakis.com; Chrissi Ammos; s/d incl breakfast from €75/100; ❋🅿️🛜🏊) Across the road from the sweep of Golden Beach, about 3km south of Gavrio, are super views and swell rooms – the superior rooms are lovely and have big balconies. A dive centre is based here, and there's a restaurant. Off-peak rates can drop by 50%.

★ **Onar Residence** COTTAGE €€€

(☑ 210 625 1052, 6932563707; www.onar-andros.gr; Ahla Beach; 3-/5-/7-person cottage €220/370/680; ☺ May-Oct; ✻ 🐾) 🏄 Ecofriendly, unique and luxurious secluded cottages in wetlands behind the stunning remote beach at Ahla. The resort has an organic restaurant for guests. Details on how to reach the resort are on the website (access road is 4WD only; transfers can be arranged).

✗ Eating

Gialia GREEK €

(☑ 22820 24452; mains €8-12; ☺ noon-10pm Apr-Oct; 🐾) A few kilometres from Hora is the delightful crystal-clear blue of Gialia Beach, where this excellent restaurant serves snacks and Greek classics to hungry beachgoers or island explorers. There's no English menu, but the waiter can give you the rundown. Try the delicious (and ample) Andros salad topped with local *kopanisti* cheese.

Tou Josef TAVERNA €

(☑ 22820 51050; Pitrofos; mains €7-12; ☺ noon-3pm & 6-10pm) Gregarious Katerina Remoundou welcomes you to her sitting room or her tree-lined courtyard like she's your long-lost auntie. She chats with guests as they dine on seasonal Andriot fare like cheese and onion pie or stewed kid. Meals are rustic and delicious, and ingredients all sourced locally. The restaurant is in Pitrofos village, about 7km southwest of Hora; call ahead.

A BENT FOR CYCLADIC TRAVEL

Long before the hip lotus-eaters of the 1960s discovered their dream world in the Greek islands, a redoubtable pair of travellers had been thoroughly 'doing' the Cyclades during the late 19th century. James Theodore Bent and his wife, Mabel, travelled extensively throughout the Aegean, 'researching' the cultural life of the islands as much as their archaeology. J Theodore's 1885 island-by-island book, *The Cyclades, Or Life Among the Insular Greeks,* is a quirky masterpiece that describes the sights and cultural realities of the islands in the late 19th century – along with Bent's often eccentric reflections. Look for it online, and in bookshops on bigger islands such as Santorini.

★ **O Kossis** CYCLADIC €€

(☑ 6972002975; Gavrion; mains €9-17; ☺ noon-11pm; 🐾) Renowned throughout Andros as the island's best 'meatery', O Kossis is located in the middle of nowhere, in the hills above Gavrio, signposted beyond Epano Fellos. Attached to stables and festooned with vines, this family-run taverna's speciality is melt-in-your-mouth lamb chops, though diners swear by their other meaty delights as well. Complimentary ouzo shot. Call ahead.

Sea Satin Nino CYCLADIC €€

(☑ 22820 61196; www.facebook.com/Sea.Satin.Nino.Andros; Ormos Korthiou; mains €8-17; ☺ 7am-2am; 🐾) Shaded by overhanging vines on a tiny square, this place uses local ingredients to great effect. Homemade pasta, fish dishes and a smattering of beautifully done Greek standards grace the short but sweet menu.

TINOS ΤΗΝΟΣ

POP 8636

Tinos is one of those sleeper hit islands. It's known widely for its sacred Greek Orthodox pilgrimage site: the Church of Panagia Evangelistria, in the main town, Hora. But as soon as you leave the throngs in town, Tinos is a wonderland of natural beauty, dotted with more than 40 marble-ornamented villages found in hidden bays, on terraced hillsides and atop misty mountains. Also scattered across the brindled countryside are countless ornate dovecotes, a legacy of the Venetians.

There's a strong artistic tradition on Tinos, especially for marble sculpting, as in the sculptors' village of Pyrgos in the north, near the marble quarries. The food, made from local produce (cheeses, sausage, tomatoes and wild artichokes), is some of the best you'll find in Greece.

➊ Getting There & Away

Year-round ferries serve the mainland ports of Rafina and Piraeus and the islands Syros, Andros and Mykonos. Summer high-speed services include Tinos on their passage south from Rafina to major islands such as Mykonos, Paros, Naxos, Ios and Santorini. Get tickets at Malliaris Travel (p169), on the waterfront in Hora.

Hora has two ferry departure quays. The New (or Outer) Port is located 300m to the north of the main harbour and serves conventional and larger fast ferries. The Old (or Inner) Port, at the northern end of the town's main harbour, serves smaller fast ferries.

Boat Services from Tinos

DESTINATION	DURATION	FARE (€)	FREQUENCY
Andros	1½-2hr	12-17	up to 3 daily
Ios	3½hr	54	1-2 daily
Kea	8hr	16	Thu
Mykonos	20-40min	11-25	2-6 daily
Naxos	2hr-2hr 20min	24-52	1-2 daily
Paros	1hr-1hr 20min	12-53	1-3 daily
Piraeus	1¾-4¾hr	31-39	daily
Rafina	1¾-4¾hr	31-39	2-4 daily
Santorini	4½hr	52	1-2 daily
Syros	30min	12	4 weekly

ⓘ Getting Around

Between May and September, **KTEL Tinos buses** (☑ 22830 22440; www.kteltinou.gr) run from Hora to nearby Kionia (€1.80, 10 minutes, frequent), and northwest to Panormos (€4.50, one hour, several daily) via Kambos (€1.80, 15 minutes) and Pyrgos (€3.60, 50 minutes). The Hora bus station is on the harbour near the port. Buy tickets on board.

Hire motorcycles (€15 to €20 per day) and cars (€40 per weekday, €60 on weekends in high season) along the Hora waterfront. **Vidalis Rent a Car & Bike** (☑ 22830 23400; www.vidalis-rentacar.gr) has four outlets in Hora.

Phone for a **taxi** (☑ 22830 22470).

Hora (Tinos) Χώρα (Τήνος)

POP 4762

Hora, also known as Tinos, is the island's welcoming capital and port. Though the harbourfront is lined with cafes and hotels, and the narrow backstreets are packed with restaurants, Hora's crowning glory is its Church of Panagia Evangelistria, perhaps the most important pilgrimage site for the Greek Orthodox religion.

Two main streets lead up to the church. Evangelistria is lined with shops and stalls crammed with souvenirs and religious wares, while Leoforos Megalocharis has a carpeted strip down the side, used by pilgrims crawling towards the church and pushing long candles before them. Religion certainly takes centre stage in Hora (woe betide the tourist looking for a room on one of the high holy days), but the town still hums with the vibrancy of a low-key island port.

◎ Sights

★ Church of Panagia Evangelistria   CHURCH

(Church of the Annunciation; ☑ 22830 22256; www.panagiatinou.gr; ⊙ 8am-8pm) **FREE** Tinos' religious focus is this neoclassical church and its icon of the Virgin Mary. The hallowed icon was found in 1822 on land where the church now stands, after a nun in Tinos, now St Pelagia, was visited by visions from the Virgin instructing her where to find it. From the start, the icon was said to have healing powers, thus encouraging mass pilgrimage. Our Lady of Tinos became the patron saint of the Greek nation.

As you enter the church, the icon is on the left of the aisle, and is totally draped in jewels. Hundreds of silver lamps hang from the ceiling, each dangling a votive offering: a ship, a cradle, a heart, a pair of lungs, a chainsaw.

The church, built of marble from the island's Panormos quarries, lies within a pleasant courtyard flanked by cool arcades. The complex has sweeping views all around and museums (with variable hours) that house collections of religious artefacts, icons and secular art.

Respectful attire must be worn.

Cultural Foundation of Tinos   GALLERY

(☑ 22830 29070; www.itip.gr; adult/child €3/free; ⊙ 9am-3pm Mon-Thu, 10am-2pm & 5-8.30pm Fri, 10am-2pm Sat) This excellent cultural centre in a handsome neoclassical building on the southern waterfront houses a superb permanent collection of the work of famous Tinian sculptor Yannoulis Chalepas. A second gallery has rotating exhibitions. Musical events are staged in summer, and there's a gift shop and harbourfront cafe.

Archaeological Museum   MUSEUM

(☑ 22830 29063; Leoforos Megalocharis; adult/child €2/free; ⊙ 8am-3pm Tue-Sun) Just downhill from the Church of Panagia Evangelistria, this museum has a collection that includes impressive clay *pithoi* (large Minoan storage jars).

Sanctuary of Poseidon & Amphitrite   ARCHAEOLOGICAL SITE

(€2; ⊙ 8.30am-3pm Tue-Sun) Kionia, 3km northwest of Hora, has the remains of the 4th-century BC Sanctuary of Poseidon and his wife Amphitrite, a once-enormous complex that drew pilgrims with the deities' healing powers.

CYCLADES TINOS

Tinos

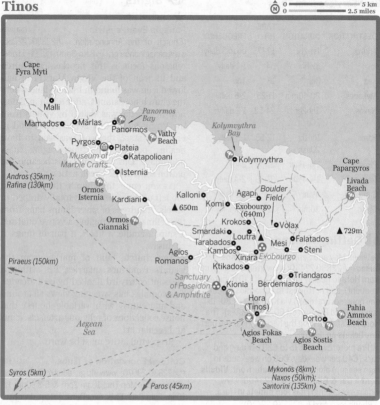

🏃 Activities

KTEL Tours BUS
(☏ 22830 22440; www.poseidontravel-tinos.com; full-day tour €12) In summer, ask at the bus station about the daily tour that takes in a number of the island's villages, including Volax, Loutra, Pyrgos, Panormos and Tarambados. It's a great way to see the sights in a day. Tours departs the bus station at 11am, returning around 5pm.

✨ Festivals & Events

Assumption of the Virgin Mary RELIGIOUS
(Feast of the Assumption) On 15 August the town is beyond full for the Virgin's feast day.

🛏 Sleeping

Hora is overcrowded on 25 March (Annunciation), Greek Easter, 15 August (Feast of the Assumption) and 15 November (Advent).

Book months ahead or join devotees sleeping in the street.

Nikoleta PENSION €
(☏ 22830 25863; www.nikoletarooms.gr; Kapodistriou 11; s/d from €35/45; ❉ ☎) Little Nikoleta is a short walk inland from the southern end of town, but it's one of the best-value options. There's a lovely garden, and some rooms have kitchens.

★ Studios Eleni II GUESTHOUSE €€
(☏ 22830 24352; www.studio-eleni.gr; Ioannou Plati 7; d/tr €90/120; ❉ ☎) A stone's throw from the Church of Panagia Evangelistria, pocket-rocket Eleni runs this beautiful guesthouse, all whitewashed walls, pale linen and a supremely photogenic Cycladic courtyard. Rooms each have a fridge, and share a small kitchenette.

Eleni also runs Studios Eleni I, which is of an equally high standard at the southern end of town, close to Agios Fokas Beach. Port transfer is offered by both properties.

Hotel Tinion
HISTORIC HOTEL €€

(☑ 22830 22261; www.tinionhotel.gr; Eleftherias Sq; s/d/tr incl breakfast €60/75/90; ❈ 🌐) This old-school central hotel dates from the 1920s, and has a broad verandah and sweeping stairs leading to comfortable, high-ceilinged rooms. They are a little dated in decor but not without charm, especially for the price; try to score a balcony with sea views. Breakfast is bumper.

Altana Hotel
BOUTIQUE HOTEL €€

(☑ 22830 25102; www.altanahotel.gr; s/d/ste incl breakfast from €80/90/120; ⊙ May-Oct; ❈ 🌐 ❄) Located about a 10-minute walk north of the town centre en route to Kionia Beach, this agreeable hotel has a modernist Cycladic style, with snow-white walls and cool interiors incorporating distinctive Tinian motifs.

✗ Eating

Tinian food tends to be fresh and creative, using local products. Beer lovers should look for Tinos' own artisanal Nissos beer (p171). Hora may have the widest range of restaurants, but some of most celebrated tavernas are found in remoter parts of the island.

Mesklies
CAFE €

(☑ 22830 22151; www.mesklies.gr; snacks €3.50-7; ⊙ 9am-late) This harbourfront cafe does a fine line in breakfasts, but it's the patisserie's delectable sweets that catch most people's eyes. From the homemade ice cream (try the bitter chocolate) to traditional sweets like *liknaraki* (sweet cheese cupcakes) and almond cookies, you'll find something to like.

★ Marathia
CYCLADIC €€

(☑ 22830 23249; www.marathiatinos.gr; Ir Politechniou; mains €10-25; ⊙ noon-midnight; 🌐) Grilled red mullet with capers and lemon. Wild artichokes, baked on coals. A glass of crisp white. Waves lapping at the beach. Pretty flawless, as far as combinations go. Super-fresh ingredients, family recipes and a deep appreciation for Tinian cuisine make this seafront restaurant a special place.

San To Alati
CYCLADIC €€

(☑ 22830 29266; www.facebook.com/santoalati; Ir Politechniou; mains €10-17; ⊙ noon-midnight; 🌐) Meaning 'like salt', this cute seaside taverna takes its name from a royal-themed fairy tale (hence the crowns and salt shakers). The place lives up to its Aegean cuisine

label, with extensive use of local produce, from local cheeses to just-out-of-the-sea *kalamari*, octopus and catch of the day.

Tarsanas
SEAFOOD €€

(☑ 22830 24667; Kazanova 5; mains €9-20, fish by kg; ⊙ noon-11pm; 🌐) The owner grills out front of this friendly, rustic spot, tucked away at the southern end of the harbour. It specialises in seafood: try smoked fish dip and anchovies wrapped in vine leaves, or splurge on lobster spaghetti.

Itan Ena Mikro Karavi
MEDITERRANEAN €€

(☑ 22830 22818; Trion Ierarchon; mains €13-27; ⊙ lunch & dinner; 🌐) Named for the opening line of a children's tale ('There was a little boat...'), this elegant indoor-outdoor eatery serves Greek fare with creative Mediterranean flair. Dishes like slow-cooked pork and rabbit ravioli are made with impeccably sourced local ingredients, and the setting and service are first-class.

To Koutouki Tis Elenis
TAVERNA €€

(☑ 22830 24857; G Gagou 5; mains €9-22; ⊙ noon-11pm; 🌐) This colourful, rustic little place is on the narrow taverna-packed lane veering off the bottom of Evangelistria. The menu bursts with local flavours. Try fresh cheeses, fish soup, artichoke pie or the delicious fritters made from fennel leaf.

ℹ Information

Malliaris Travel (☑ 22830 24242; www.malliaristravel.gr; ⊙ 9am-9pm) Sells ferry tickets.

Around Tinos

The countryside of Tinos is a glorious mix of broad terraced hillsides, mountaintops crowned with crags, unspoiled villages, fine beaches and fascinating architecture that includes picturesque dovecotes. Rent wheels to see it all.

Kionia, 3km northwest of Hora, has several small beaches and the scant remains of the 4th-century BC Sanctuary of Poseidon & Amphitrite (p167), a once-enormous complex that drew pilgrims.

First along the way north of town, beautiful **Ktikados** perches in a hanging valley and has a matched set of blue-topped church and campanile. **Drosia** is tops for local lunches and magnificent views.

Kambos sits on the top of a scenic hill surrounded by fields and is home to the **Costas Tsoclis Museum** (☑ 22830 51009;

DON'T MISS

MARVELLOUS MARBLE

On the slopes above Pyrgos is the outstanding **Museum of Marble Crafts** (☑ 22830 31290; www.piop.gr; adult/child €3/free; ☉ 10am-6pm Mar–mid-Oct, to 5pm mid-Oct–Mar, closed Tue year-round), a modern, well-curated complex that creatively explains quarrying and sculpting techniques. It includes films and beautifully illustrated displays with English translations, along with top examples of artefacts and architectural features shaped from Tinian marble. The films of some of the last living quarrymen plying their trade are fascinating.

Kambos; ☉ 10am-1.30pm & 6-9pm Wed-Mon Jun-Sep) FREE, home to works by the renowned contemporary artist.

Don't miss **Tarabados**, a fun maze of small streets decorated with marble sculptures and leading to a breezy valley lined with dovecotes (look for the sign 'Pigeon Houses' Area'). Explore!

About 17km northwest of Hora, lovely **Kardiani** perches on a steep cliff slope enclosed by greenery. Narrow lanes wind through the village, and the views towards Syros are exhilarating.

Pyrgos is a stunning, church-dotted hamlet where even the cemetery is a feast of carved marble, and the perfect village square looks like a film set. During the late 19th and early 20th centuries, Pyrgos was the centre of a remarkable sculpture enclave sustained by the supply of excellent local marble.

At the main entrance to Pyrgos, the fascinating **Museum House of Yannoulis Chalepas** (adult/child €3/free; ☉ 11am-3pm & 5.30-7.30pm Apr–mid-Oct) preserves the sculptor's humble rooms and workshop.

Further north of Pyrgos the main road ends at **Panormos**, a popular excursion destination for its photogenic fishing harbour lined with fish tavernas.

About 12km north of Hora on the north coast is emerald **Kolymvythra Bay**, where **Tinos Surf Lessons** (www.tinossurflessons.com; surfing lesson from €20 per person; ☉ 10am-9pm) takes advantage of the breaks at two excellent sandy beaches. It offers surf tuition, plus rentals of surfboards, bodyboards, kayaks and canoes.

A worthwhile detour inland takes you to **Agapi**, in a lush valley of dovecotes. Ethereal

and romantic, it lives up to its name (meaning 'love' in Greek).

Pass eye-catching **Krokos** with its Evangelismou tis Panagias, an enormous Catholic church, to reach **Volax**, about 6km directly north of Hora. This hamlet sits at the heart of an amphitheatre of low hills festooned with hundreds of enormous, multicoloured boulders.

The ruins of the Venetian fortress of **Exobourgo** lie 2km south of Volax, on top of a mighty 640m rock outcropping.

The northeast coast beach at **Livada** is spectacular, but the ones east of Hora, like Porto and Pahia Ammos, can seem comparatively built-up.

🛏 Sleeping & Eating

⭐**Tinos Habitart**   COTTAGE €€€
(☑ 22830 41907; www.tinos-habitart.gr; Triantoros; 4-person house from €200; 🛜🏊) The cleverly designed complex lies in a village 6km northeast of Hora, and gives you a taste of traditional island life. Five houses incorporate local stone and marble and are fully equipped with kitchen, living spaces and outdoor areas (most with private pool). Our favourite is the dovecote irresistibly transformed into a three-bedroom villa.

Volax   TAVERNA €
(☑ 22830 41021; mains €7-12; ☉ noon-3pm & 6-10pm) Volax is a scenic hamlet about 6km directly north of Hora, surrounded by low hills festooned with hundreds of enormous, multicoloured boulders. The taverna Volax serves reliable Tinian favourites like wild artichokes with lemon.

Drosia   TAVERNA €
(☑ 22830 21807; Ktikados; mains €9-13; ☉ noon-3pm & 6-10pm Easter-Oct; 🛜) At Drosia, in the pretty village of Ktikados, you can dine on fish or lamb and take in the magnificent views.

⭐**Thalassaki**   GREEK €€
(☑ 22830 31366; Ormos Isternia; mains €9-18, fish by kg; ☉ noon-10pm Easter-Oct; 🛜) Come to Ormos Isternia, a stony beach set among plunging hills south of Pyrgos, on a foodie pilgrimage. The seafront taverna crafts local cheese, tomatoes, wild artichokes and the like into veritable works of art and has outstanding seafood prepared in deliciously creative fashion (eg octopus baked in grape molasses, mussels with wine and fennel). Book ahead in high season.

★ **O Ntinos** CYCLADIC €€
(☑ 22830 31673; mains €8-16; ☎) Superlative home-cooked island specialties, served on a sunny terrace overlooking Giannaki Bay.

🍷 Drinking & Nightlife

Nissos Cyclades Microbrewery at Tinos Island MICROBREWERY
(☑ 22830 26333; http://nissos.beer; ☉ tours mid-Jun–mid-Sep on Mon, Thu & Sat) It's well worth visiting this microbrewery to familiarise yourself with the mysteries of brewing and to sample Nissos' beer collection.

SYROS ΣΥΡΟΣ

POP 21,507

Endearing little Syros merges traditional and modern Greece. One of the smallest islands of the Cyclades and relatively rural outside the capital, it nevertheless has the highest population since it's the legal and administrative centre of the entire archipelago. It's also the ferry hub of the northern islands and home to Ermoupoli, the grandest of all Cycladic towns, with an unusual history. As the Cyclades' capital, it pays less heed to tourism, and its beaches never get as crowded as those of the neighbouring islands. It buzzes with life year-round, boasts great eateries and showcases the best of everyday Greek life.

History

Excavations of an Early Cycladic fortified settlement and burial ground at Kastri in the island's northeast date from the Neolithic era (2800–2300 BC).

During the 17th and 18th centuries, Capuchin monks and Jesuits settled on the island. Becoming overwhelmingly Catholic, Syros even called upon France for help during Turkish rule.

During the War of Independence, thousands of Orthodox refugees from islands ravaged by the Turks fled to Syros. They brought an infusion of Greek Orthodoxy and a fresh entrepreneurial drive that made Syros the commercial, naval and cultural centre of Greece during the 19th century. Syros' position declined in the 20th century, but you still see shipyards, textile manufacturing, thriving horticulture, a sizeable administrative sector, a university campus and a continuing Catholic population.

ℹ️ Getting There & Away

AIR

Sky Express (☑ 28102 23800; www.skyexpress.gr) flies daily from Athens (€90, 35 minutes) to **Syros airport** (JSY; ☑ 22810 81900), 5km south of Ermoupoli.

BOAT

Year-round ferries serve the mainland port of Piraeus. As the island group's capital, Syros theoretically has fair to good year-round ferry links with all the Cyclades islands. Check www.openseas.gr due to ever-changing schedules.

Most boats leave from the **main ferry quay**. There's a weekly **Blue Star** (www.bluestarferries.com) ferry linking Syros with each of the Small Cyclades islands and then Amorgos (Aegiali port). A few times a week, Blue Star links Syros with Dodecanese islands, including Patmos, Leros, Kos and Rhodes. There are weekly **Hellenic Seaways** (www.hellenicseaways.gr) links with the northeastern Aegean islands, including Patmos, Ikaria, Samos, Lesvos and Limnos. **Sea Jets** (www.seajets.gr) serve Kea, Kythnos and Lavrio.

Buy tickets at **Teamwork Holidays** (p176) or **Vassilikos** (p176) in Ermoupoli. Ask where your ferry will depart from, as it may dock anywhere on the western part of the port. Both agencies have the week's ferry schedule on their websites.

Boat Services from Syros

DESTINATION	DURATION	FARE (€)	FREQUENCY
Chios	8½hr	55	Tue
Ios	6½hr	21	Fri
Kos	6hr	47	Mon, Wed & Fri
Leros	5½hr	42	Mon & Wed
Mykonos	45-75min	11-17	1-3 daily
Naxos	4½hr	13	1-4 weekly
Paros	1hr-10½ hr	11-17	5-6 weekly
Patmos	4hr	39	Mon & Wed
Piraeus	3¼-5hr	24-37	1-3 daily
Rhodes	9-11hr	52	Mon, Wed & Fri
Santorini	9½hr	24	Tue & Sat
Tinos	30min	8-12	4 weekly

ℹ️ Getting Around

Regular **buses** (☑ 22810 82575; www.ktel-syrou.gr) loop from Ermoupoli bus station beside the ferry quay, taking in Galissas, Finikas,

Syros

N 0 ——————— 2 km
  0 ——————— 1 mile

Kythnos (55km); Kea (60km);
Lavrio (80km); Piraeus (130km)

Cape
Trimeson

Cape
Diapori

Aegean
Sea

Grammata
Beach

Kampos

Lia Beach

San Michalis

Tinos (20km);
Mykonos (35km);
Andros (50km)

Aetos Beach

▲ 431m

Varvarousa

Aegean
Sea

Delfini Beach

Mytikas

Pyrgos
(440m) ▲

Agios
Georgios
Cathedral

To Leros (180km);
Kos (200km);
Rhodes (300km)

Kini
Kini Beach

Ano Syros

Vrodado

Ermoupoli

Cape
Katakefalos

Danakos

▲
Mt Volakas
(312m)

Paros (40km);
Naxos (50km);
Ios (95km);
Santorini
(135km)

Lazareto

Galissas
Bay

Armeos Beach

Galissas

Pagos

Parakopi

Mesaria

Ano
Manno

Manna

Azolimnos
Beach

Vissa

Adiata

Hrousa

Atelio

Finikas
Beach

Finikas

▲
Mt Axachas
(319m)

Vari

Fabrika
Beach

Finikas Bay

Posidonia
Beach

Angathopes
Beach

Posidonia

Vari Beach

Nisi

Vari
Bay

Shinonisi

Komito
Beach

Strongylo

Megas
Gialos

Megas Gialos
Beach

Cape
Viglostasi

Posidonia, Megas Gialos and Vari. The full loop takes about an hour, and buses run hourly in both directions, with a maximum fare of €1.70. About five buses go to Kini (€1.60, 35 minutes) or to Ano Syros (€1.60, 15 minutes) every day except Sunday. Schedules are posted at the waterfront bus station.

A free bus traverses the harbour between the car parks at the northern and southern ends of Ermoupoli (half-hourly 7am to 10pm Monday to Friday, to 4pm Saturday and Sunday).

You can hire cars (from €40 per day) and scooters (from €15) at waterfront agencies. Avoid driving in central Ermoupoli, as it's mostly stairs or pedestrianised ways.

From the port, **taxis** (⊉ 22810 86222) charge around €4 to Ano Syros, €12 to Galissas and €12 to Vari.

Several rental agencies along the waterfront rent scooters (€18) and cars (€35).

Ermoupoli   Ερμούπολη

POP 11,407

As you sail into striking Ermoupoli, named after Hermes and formerly Greece's main port, its peaked hilltops emerge, each topped by a dazzling church. The Catholic settlers built on high ground, and the 19th-century Orthodox newcomers built from below. Now buildings spread in a pink and white cascade over it all, and the centre is a true maze of stairways, pedestrianised shopping streets and neoclassical mansions all radiating out from the grand Plateia Miaouli, with its impressive town hall.

Catholic **Ano Syros** and Greek Orthodox **Vrodado** spill down from high hilltops to the northwest and northeast of town, with even taller hills rising behind.

◉ Sights

★ Industrial

Museum of Ermoupoli   MUSEUM
(⊉ 22810 84762; www.ketepo.gr; George Papandreou 11; €3; ⊙ 9am-5pm Mon-Fri Oct-Mar, 10am-3.30pm Mon-Fri, 10am-3.30pm & 6-8pm Sat, 10am-3pm Sun Apr-Sep) This excellent chronicle of Syros' industrial and shipbuilding traditions occupies a restored factory packed with more than 300 well-labelled items relating to sewing, printing, spinning, engines, ships and more. Ask if the Aneroussis lead shot factory is open – it's fascinating. Find the museum about 1km south of the centre, opposite the hospital on the road to Kini. At research time, there was talk about moving to a new location.

Apollo Theatre   THEATRE
(⊉ 2281085192; www.facebook.com/apollontheater; Plateia Vardaka; €2; ⊙ 10am-4pm & 6-10pm Mon, 10am-10pm Tue-Sat, 10am-2pm & 6-10pm Sun) Built in the 1860s, this venerable theatre was partly modelled on La Scala in Milan. Keep an eye out for regular theatre performances (in Greek), or pop in to take a look around.

Vaporia   AREA
Stroll the Vaporia district, east and northeast of Plateia Miaouli, for palm-lined squares and elegant shipowners' mansions (some now home to boutique hotels). The shipowners' wealth is evident in the grand Orthodox **Agios Nikolaos** (Vaporia District) loaded with fine murals, icons, gilt and chandeliers.

Plateia Miaouli   SQUARE
This great square is perhaps the finest urban space in the Cyclades. Once situated immediately upon the seashore, today it sits well inland and is dominated by the dignified neoclassical **town hall** (Plateia Miaouli), designed by Ernst Ziller. Flanked by palm trees and lined along all sides with cafes and bars, the square and accompanying statue are named for Hydriot naval hero Andreas Miaoulis.

The town's small, unremarkable **archaeological museum** (⊉ 22810 88487; Benaki; adult/child €2/free; ⊙ 8.30am-8pm) is housed in the rear of the town hall. A couple of elegant old-world cafes are found in the hall's wings, with al fresco seating for great people-watching.

🛏 Sleeping

Most budget options cluster above the ferry quay, while boutique hotels in renovated mansions dot the Vaporia district. Much accommodation is open year-round, with discounts in low season.

Hermoupolis Rooms   PENSION €
(⊉ 22810 87475; www.hermoupolis-rooms.gr; Naxou; s/d/tr from €35/40/50; ❊ 🛜) There's a cheerful welcome at these well-kept self-catering rooms, a short climb from the waterfront. Front rooms open onto tiny, bougainvillea-cloaked balconies.

★ 1901

Hermoupolis Maison   BOUTIQUE HOTEL €€
(⊉ 22810 84680; www.1901.gr; Palaion Patron Germanou 37-39; r from €75; ❊ 🛜) Housed in a 19th-century stone mansion, this delightful boutique hotel comprises just five rooms,

presided over by the ever-helpful Konstantinos and his wife. Rooms come with super-comfortable beds and free-standing tubs with Molton Brown toiletries, with quirky objects scattered throughout – antique telephones, an olive press, a Singer sewing machine. Terrific breakfast too.

Lila Guesthouse GUESTHOUSE €€
(📲 22810 82738; www.guesthouse.gr; Kosma; s/d/tr incl breakfast €80/100/120, ste from €160; ❄️🌐) In the former French consulate, these elegantly renovated rooms and suites are kitted out with impeccable modern decor and top-notch bathrooms. Suites are spacious, with dining tables and antiques. A bumper breakfast is served by the genial proprietors in the airy common area. Port pick-ups available.

Ethrion HOTEL €€
(📲 22810 89066; www.ethrion.gr; Kosma 24; r €90-135; ❄️🌐) The eight rooms and studios at family-run Ethrion are comfortable and well equipped. Opt for the ones with sea view if you can, and bear in mind that the ground-floor studio is on the dark side.

★ Wind Tales BOUTIQUE HOTEL €€€
(📲 6946771400; www.windtales.gr; Agiou Aloisiou; r from €150; ❄️🌐) If you wish to linger after the madding crowd has gone and wander Ano Syros' labyrinthine lanes at your leisure, then try the Wind Tales' three gorgeous, individually designed rooms, one of them carved into natural rock. The service is wonderfully personalised, breakfast makes extensive use of local produce, and sipping cocktails on the terrace overlooking Ermoupoli is pure magic.

★ Ploes Hotel BOUTIQUE HOTEL €€€
(📲 22810 79360; www.hotelploes.com; Apollonos 2; d from €200, ste €600; 🕐 Apr-Oct; ❄️🌐) Unremitting elegance and attention to detail are hallmarks of this boutique beauty, inside a restored banker's mansion. Soaring ceilings, original artworks and designer furniture make the seven rooms here shine, and there's a private pavilion giving direct sea access to swimmers.

✖ Eating & Drinking

Restaurants and cafe-bars throng the waterfront, especially along Akti Petrou Ralli – these fire up late, full of party people. Another great area for dining is the bougainvillea-bedecked laneways of Emmanouil Roidi and Kyparissou.

★ Kouzina MEDITERRANEAN €€
(📲 22810 89150; Androu 5; mains €12-26; 🕐 7pm-12.30am Wed & Thu, 1pm-12.30am Fri & Sat, 1-6pm Sun; 🌐) In this colourfully lit, intimate dining room, fresh local ingredients are the building blocks of creative Mediterranean cuisine, from slow-cooked baby goat and smoked *mousakas* to *kalamari* with Cretan smoked pork. Decent wine list and craft beer to boot.

Sta Vaporia CAFE
(📲 22810 76486; 🕐 10am-3am) Down a signposted set of stairs behind Agios Nikolaos is this perfectly positioned all-day cafe. It's a cruisy terrace with postcard panoramas and a menu of coffee, cocktails, homemade lemonade and sangria, and snacks, large and small. Down below are popular seaside swimming platforms (so bring your swimsuit).

Kouchico COCKTAIL BAR
(📲 22813 00880; www.facebook.com/kouchico; Ioannou Lavrentiou Ralli 15; 🕐 7.30am-3am; 🌐) A hip spot to sip a coffee by day, Kouchico turns into a buzzy cocktail bar at night, with a trendy young crowd spilling out of its doors. The signature cocktails are not all to our taste, but involve quality ingredients.

ANO SYROS ΑΝΩ ΣΥΡΟΣ

The narrow lanes and whitewashed houses of Ano Syros, originally a medieval Catholic settlement, tower above Ermoupoli. From the bus terminus, head into the delightful maze and search out the finest of the Catholic churches, the 13th-century **Agios Georgios Cathedral**, with its star-fretted barrel roof and baroque capitals (still under renovation at the time of research). Continue past stunning viewpoints to reach the main street; the sweet **Our Lady of Mt Carmel**; the **Vamvakaris Museum** (€2; 🕐 12.30-6.30pm Sat & Sun), celebrating locally born patriarch of *rembetika* (blues) Markos Vamvakaris; and the **monasteries** of the Jesuits and the Capuchins. Prepare to get lost, but try to find your way back to the view-enriched terraces of the handful of cafes and taverna along the main laneway.

Ermoupoli

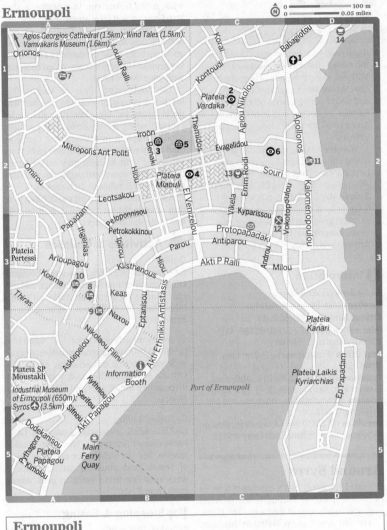

CYCLADES SYROS

WORTH A TRIP

SAN MICHALIS
ΣΑΝ ΜΙΧΑΛΗΣ

If you have your own wheels, don't miss the drive to the northern village of San Michalis, along the spine of Syros, with spectacular views of unspoilt valleys and neighbouring islands on either side. Famous for its cheese, San Michalis is now a small hamlet of stone houses and vineyards.

Walk the winding rock path to the hilltop church and get Syran food at its best at **Plakostroto** (📞 6973980248; www.plakostroto.gr; mains €9-16; ☉ lunch & dinner May-Oct, Sat & Sun Nov-Apr; 🗣). It serves local cheese plus rooster, lamb or rabbit grilled on the open wood fire. Views sweep down the hillside to Kea, Kythnos and beyond.

ⓘ Information

Alpha Bank (El Venizelou)
Eurobank (Akti Ethnikis Antistasis)
Piraeus Bank (Akti Petrou Ralli)
Information Booth (📞 22810 80485; Akti Ethnikis Antistasis; ☉ hr vary)
Post Office (Protopapadaki; ☉ 9am-5pm Mon-Fri)
Teamwork Holidays (📞 22810 83400; www. teamwork.gr; Akti Papagou 18; ☉ 9am-9pm) Arranges accommodation and excursions and sells ferry tickets.
Vassilikos (📞 22810 84444; www.vassilikos.gr; Akti Papagou 10; ☉ 9am-9pm) Ferry tickets.

Around Syros

Outside Ermoupoli, Syros comprises a series of hills and valleys folding down to small bays and beaches, most well served by buses.

The old resort town **Galissas** has seen better days, but it has an appealing beach and is still popular with French travellers, and has a couple of excellent tavernas. Behind the Dolphin Bay Hotel is **Armeos**, the nudist beach.

South of Galissas, reachable via a short bus ride or a 40-minute walk, **Finikas** has a long, narrow strip of sand against a backdrop of tamarisk trees. South of the headland is **Posidonia**, another narrow, sandy beach, beyond which lies the delightful and popular **Agathopes** beach, with calm waters and a smattering of tavernas. Another 10-minute

walk south brings you to **Komito**, a sheltered bay backed by olive groves.

The beaches south of Galissas all have domatia, and some have hotels. It takes only about an hour to do a loop drive from Galissas around the south coast, so go exploring with your own wheels.

The south-coast town of **Megas Gialos** has a couple of roadside beaches with pedal boats for hire, but they are rather exposed when the *meltemi* (dry northerly wind) sweeps in in the summer. Gorgeous (and sheltered) **Vari Bay**, further east, is the better bet with its light grey sandy beach, though the waterfront and tavernas get packed with families in high season.

Kini Beach, on the west coast, has a long, thin stretch of beach popular with families due to its shallow waters.

🏃 Activities & Courses

Omilo LANGUAGE
(📞 Athens 210 612 2896; www.omilo.com/syros) Offers summertime Greek language and culture courses on Syros and Andros. Courses take place in Azolimnos, 4km south of Ermoupoli.

Syros Windsurfing School WINDSURFING
(📞 6936713547; www.facebook.com/SyrosWindsurfingSchool; stand-up paddleboarding per hr €25) Organises windsurfing and stand-up paddleboarding for all ages and levels. Based at Finikas.

Cyclades Sailing BOATING
(📞 22810 82501; www.cyclades-sailing.gr) Large yacht-charter company, based at Finikas marina. See the website for the huge range of vessels and potential sailing areas. A week-long four-berth yacht in peak season costs from €1420.

🛏 Sleeping & Eating

Krinakia Agathopes APARTMENT €
(📞 22810 42375; apt from €50; ☉ May-Sep; ❄ 🗣) Quiet, spacious, well equipped apartments overlooking Agkathopes Beach. Popular with families.

Hotel Alkyon HOTEL €€
(📞 22810 61761; www.alkyonsyros.gr; r from €60; ☉ Apr-Oct; ❄ 🗣 ⛱) Inland and about 1.5km from Megas Gialos is peaceful Hotel Alkyon, run by a charming French-Greek couple, with a large pool and spotless rooms. Hosts arrange seminars and activities that include painting and Greek gastronomy.

Blue Harmony Hotel HOTEL €€

(☑ 22810 71570; www.blueharmony.gr; r/tr from €126/135; ✳ 🏠) This waterfront hotel at Kini Beach makes a fine choice, with bright, well equipped rooms and a funky slate facade.

Hotel Benois HOTEL €€

(☑ 22810 42833; www.benois.gr; s/d/tr/f incl breakfast €70/77/90/121; ⊘ Easter-Oct; ✳ 🏠 ☀) A well-run hotel at the northern entrance to the village, the Benois has spick-and-span rooms that are all minimalist charm and neutral shades. It has relaxing and spacious public areas and an inviting swimming pool.

Allou Yialou SEAFOOD €€

(☑ 22810 71196; Kini Beach; mains €8-22; ⊘ noon-10pm May-Sep; 🏠) Tops for eats on Kini Beach is Allou Yialou, absolutely waterfront and with excellent fish stew and other seafood. It's a prime sunset spot.

Iliovasilema CYCLADIC €€

(☑ 22810 43325; mains €8-16; ⊘ noon-10pm Apr-Oct; 🏠) The name means sunset, and this west-coast fish-heavy restaurant is a fine choice for watching it. The menu is an ode to local produce. Try the *kakavia* (traditional fish soup) or the fennel pie.

MYKONOS ΜΥΚΟΝΟΣ

POP 10,134

Mykonos is the great glamour island of Greece and happily flaunts its sizzling St-Tropez-meets-Ibiza style and party-hard reputation.

The high-season mix of hedonistic holiday-makers, cruise-ship crowds and posturing fashionistas throngs Mykonos Town (aka Hora), a traditional whitewashed Cycladic maze, delighting in its authentic cubist charms and its chichi cafe-bar-boutique scene.

The number of tourists (and cashed-up A-listers) visiting Mykonos is booming, and hip new hotels, beach bars and restaurants are mushrooming. In July and August, come only if you are prepared to pay and are intent on joining the jostling street crowds, the oiled-up lounger lifestyle at the packed main beaches and the relentless party. Out of season, devoid of gloss and preening celebrities, find more subdued local life, the with occasional pelican wandering the empty streets and beaches that you will have largely to yourself.

Mykonos is also the jumping-off point for the archaeological site of the nearby island of Delos.

ℹ Getting There & Away

BOAT

Year-round ferries serve mainland ports Piraeus and Rafina (the latter is usually quicker if you are coming directly from Athens airport), and nearby islands Tinos and Andros. In the high season, Mykonos is well connected with all neighbouring islands, including Paros and Santorini. Hora is loaded with ticket agents.

Mykonos has two ferry quays: the Old Port, 400m north of town, where some smaller fast ferries dock, and the New Port, 2km north of town, where the bigger fast ferries and all conventional ferries dock. When buying outgoing tickets, double-check which quay your ferry leaves from.

Excursion boats for Delos depart from the quay just off the waterfront of Mykonos Town.

Boat Services from Mykonos

DESTINATION	DURATION	FARE (€)	FREQUENCY
Andros	2hr 20min	18-19	1-2 daily
Folegandros	3½-6½	18-63	daily
Ios	2-3hr	52-57	3 daily
Iraklio	5hr	89	2 daily
Naxos	1hr 20min-3hr	13-53	3 daily
Paros	45-50min	35-53	up to 3 daily
Piraeus	2½-4½	32-63	2-3 daily
Rafina	2½-4½hr	32-52	3-4 daily
Santorini (Thira)	2½-4hr	52-71	up to 4 daily
Syros	45min-75min	11-17	1-2 daily

AIR

Mykonos Airport (☑ 22890 79000; www.mykonos-airport.com), 3km southeast of the town centre, has flights year-round to Athens with Sky Express (www.skyexpress.gr) and Aegean Airlines (www.aegeanair.com), among others, and to Thessaloniki with Astra Airlines (www.astra-airlines.gr) and Aegean Airlines.

From May to mid-September, direct European connections are plentiful, including easyJet flights from London, Geneva, Paris, Rome and Milan, and Air Berlin flights from German and Austrian hubs.

Mykonos

Tinos (15km);
Syros (30km);
Andros (70km);
Rafina (135km);
Piraeus (175km)

0   2.5 miles
0   5 km

Dragonisi

Cape Evros

Cape Goni

Profitis Ilias
Anomeritis
(351m)

Merhias Bay

Aegean Sea

Lia Beach

Kalafatis Beach

Cape Kalafatis

Cape Mavros

Mersini Bay

Mersini Beach

Fokos Beach

Kalo Livadi Beach

Cape Mavrokefalas

Agios Sostis Beach

Panormos Beach

Panormos Bay

Ftelia Beach

Ano Mera

Tourliani Monastery

Elia Beach

Elia

Agrari Beach

Cape Armenistis

Lake Marathi

Marathi

275m

Super Paradise Beach

Paradise Beach

Excursion Boats

372m

Vothonas

Paraga Beach

Houlakia Beach

Agios Stefanos

New Port

Tourlos

Old Port

Platys Gialos

Platys Gialos Beach

Agios Stefanos Beach

Tourlos Beach

Hora
(Mykonos Town)

Vrissi

Ornos

Psarou

Psarou Beach

Korfos

Nea Mykonos

Kapari Beach

Kapari

Agios Ioannis Beach

Cape Alogomandra

Naxos (35km);
Paros (45km); Ios (80km);
Santorini (120km)

Delos (3km);
Rafina

Excursion Boat

⊙ Getting Around

TO/FROM THE AIRPORT

Buses from the southern bus station serve Mykonos' airport (€1.60). Some hotels and guesthouses offer free airport and port transfers. Otherwise, arrange airport transfer with your accommodation (around €7) or take a taxi to town (€10).

BOAT

Mykonos Cruises (☑ 22890 23995; www. mykonos-cruises.gr; ⊙8am-7pm Apr-Oct) An association of sea-taxi operators offering services to the island's best beaches. See the timetables online. The main departure point is Platys Gialos, with drop-offs and pick-ups at Ornos, Paraga, Paradise, Super Paradise, Agrari and Elia beaches (return trip costs between €5 and €7). Cruises and personalised itineraries can also be arranged.

Sea Bus (☑ 6978830355; www.mykonos-seabus.gr; one-way €2.50) This water-taxi service connects the New Port with Hora, running hourly from 9am to 10pm (more frequently when a cruise ship is in port).

BUS

The **KTEL Mykonos** (☑ 22890 23360, 22890 26797; www.mykonosbus.com) bus network has two main terminals plus pick-up points at the Old and New Ports.

Low-season services are much reduced, but buses in high season run frequently; the fare is €1 to €2 depending on the distance travelled. Timetables are on the website. In July and August, some bus services run until 2am or later from the beaches.

Terminal A, the **southern bus station** (Fabrika Sq), known as Fabrika, serves Ornos and Agios Ioannis Beach, Platys Gialos, Paraga and Super Paradise Beaches.

Terminal B, the northern bus station, sometimes called Remezzo, is behind the OTE office and has services to Agios Stefanos via Tourlos, Ano Mera, and Kalo Livadi, Kalafatis and Elia beaches. Buses for Tourlos and Agios Stefanos stop at the Old and New Ports.

A regular bus connects the New Port with the southern bus station, and there are buses running between the southern bus station and the nearby airport. In summer there's a bus to Paradise Beach from the Old Port.

Private transfer buses operate in summer's peak every hour (11am to 11pm) from the Old Port to Paradise Beach (via Fabrika). There are also frequent shuttles to Super Paradise Beach.

CAR & MOTORCYCLE

Cars start at €45 per day in high season and €30 in low season. Scooters/quads are around €20/40 in high season and €15/30 in low season.

Avis and Sixt are among the agencies at the airport, and there are dozens of hire places all over the island, particularly near the ports and bus stations (which is where the large public car parks are found – you can't drive into Hora proper). You can rent from Mykonos Accommodation Centre (p185).

Apollon (☑ 22890 24136; www.apollonrentacar.com; Epar. Od. Mikonou; ⊙9am-8pm) One of several agencies near Hora's southern bus station.

OK Rent A Car (☑ 22890 23761; www. okmykonos.com; Agios Stefanos) Near New Port.

TAXI

Taxis (☑ 22890 23700, 22890 22400) queue at Hora's Plateia Manto Mavrogenous (Taxi Sq), bus stations and ports, but waits can be long in high season. All have meters, and the minimum fare is €3.50 (plus €0.50 per bag, €3.30 for phone booking).

Approximate fares from Hora include New Port (€6), Ornos (€10), Platys Gialos (€10), Paradise (€11), Kalafatis (€18) and Elia (€18).

Hora (Mykonos)
Χώρα (Μύκονος)

POP 8397

Hora (also known as Mykonos), the island's well-preserved port and capital, is a warren of narrow alleyways and whitewashed buildings overlooked by the town's famous windmills. In the heart of the waterfront Little Venice quarter, which is spectacular at sunset, tiny flower-bedecked churches jostle with glossy boutiques, and there's a cascade of bougainvillea around every corner. High-season streets are crowded with chic stores, cool galleries, jangling jewellers and both languid and loud music bars – plus a catwalk cast of thousands.

⊙ Sights

★**Aegean Maritime Museum** MUSEUM
(☑ 22890 22700; Enoplon Dynameon 10; adult/student €4/2; ⊙10.30am-1pm & 6.30-9pm Apr-Oct) Amidst the barnacle-encrusted amphorae, ye olde nautical maps and navigation instruments, there are numerous detailed models of various famous sailing ships and paddle steamers. You can also learn the difference between an Athenian trireme, a Byzantine dromon and an ancient Egyptian

seagoing ship. There's an enormous Fresnel lighthouse lantern in the courtyard.

★ Panagia Paraportiani   CHURCH

(Paraportiani) Mykonos' most famous church, the whitewashed, rock-like Panagia Paraportiani, comprises four small chapels – plus another on an upper storey reached by an exterior staircase. It's usually locked but the fabulously photogenic whitewashed exterior is the drawcard.

Rarity Gallery   GALLERY

(☑ 22890 25761; www.raritygallery.com; Kalogera 20; ☺ 10am-midnight) FREE This little gallery is well worth a peek for its temporary exhibitions that showcase paintings, sculpture and photography by the likes of Paul Rousso, Yigal Ozeri and George Pousenkoff.

Windmills   LANDMARK

(off Plateia Alefkandra) Constructed in the 16th century by the Venetians for the milling of wheat, seven of Mykonos' iconic windmills are picturesquely situated on a small hill overlooking the harbour.

Archaeological Museum   MUSEUM

(☑ 22890 22325; Agiou Stefanou; adult/child €4/ free; ☺ 9am-4pm Tue-Sun) Peruse pottery from Delos, dating back to the 9th century BC, and grave *stelae* (pillars) and jewellery from the island of Renia (Delos' necropolis). Chief exhibits include a statue of Hercules in Parian marble.

Lena's House   MUSEUM

(☑ 22890 22591; Enoplon Dynameon 10; ☺ 6-9pm May–mid-Oct) FREE This charming late-19th-century, middle-class Mykonian house (with furnishings intact) takes its name from its last owner, Lena Skrivanou. It's next door to the Aegean Maritime Museum.

ⓘ NAVIGATING HORA (MYKONOS)

Without question, you will soon pass the same junction twice. It's entertaining at first, but can become frustrating amid throngs of equally lost people and fast-moving locals. For quick-fix navigation, familiarise yourself with Plateia Manto Mavrogenous (Taxi Sq), and the three main streets of Matogianni, Enoplon Dynameon and Mitropoleos, which form a horseshoe behind the waterfront.

Mykonos Folklore Museum   MUSEUM

(☑ 22890 22591; Paraportianis; ☺ 10.30am-2.30pm & 5.30-8.30pm Jun-Sep) FREE This folklore museum, housed in an 18th-century sea captain's house, features a large collection of furnishings and other artefacts, including old musical instruments.

🏃 Activities & Tours

Mykonos Accommodation Centre (p185) organises excursions and guided tours, and arranges private tours and charters. Tours go to Delos (adult/child €50/25), including the return boat trip, admission fee and guide, and Tinos (€70/45) to see its holy church and island sights. It also organises a walking tour of Hora and a bus tour around the island (€40/25). A full-day island cruise along the south coast (€70/40), a sunset cruise (€45/30) and a 4WD safari to isolated beaches (€65/35) are also available.

Mykonos Cruises (p179) runs sea-taxis to various south-coast beaches and can arrange fishing trips and private cruises.

Mykonos Tour & Excursions   WALKING

(☑ 22890 79376; www.mykonos-web.com; €69) This four-hour tour of the island takes in a couple of beaches and the monastery of Ano Mera by bus, and the highlights of Mykonos Town - Little Venice, the windmills, Paraportiani church - on foot. Knowledgeable guides.

Mykonos On Board Sailing   SAILING

(☑ 6932471055; www.mykonosonboard.com) Highly recommended private and semi-private yachting excursions around Mykonos and to nearby islands Delos and Rhenia.

🛏 Sleeping

MyCocoon Hostel   HOSTEL €

(☑ 22890 23168; www.hostelmykonos.com; Kaminaki; dm/q €50/350; 🕸 🛜) A lot of thought has gone into this stylish new hostel, from the custom-made bunks which are like Cycladic houses in miniature, allowing dorm guests some privacy, to ample storage space for luggage and a good ratio of guests per bathroom. It's a block from the Old Port.

Andriani's Guest House   GUESTHOUSE €€

(☑ 22890 23091; www.andrianis.com.gr; d/apt €108/152; 🅿 🕸 🛜) This clutch of typical Cycladic rooms and studios sits above the School of Fine Arts a few minutes' walk from the heart of Hora. There's a peaceful garden, and free pick-up and drop-off.

Hotel Jason
HOTEL €€

(☎22890 23481; www.hoteljason-mykonos.gr; d/tr €130/110; P❄❅🌐🅿) With spotless, tiled rooms, some with heavy wooden beams, some with kitchenettes, this friendly budget hotel is an easy walk from Ornos Beach and a short ride from Hora. Doubles are nicer than the triple rooms.

Town Suites
APARTMENT €€

(☎22890 23160; www.mykonos-accommodation.com; d/tr €240/315; ❅🌐) Owned by John, the man behind the info-rich Mykonos Accommodation Centre (p185), this hidden complex of six bright, high-beamed suites and apartments makes a splendid choice. Each has well-equipped kitchen and sunny outdoor space. Gay-friendly, and in a quiet area. Check in at MAC and you'll be guided to the unsigned complex. Low-season rates are a marvellous €70.

Fresh Hotel
BOUTIQUE HOTEL €€

(☎22890 24670; www.hotelfreshmykonos.com; Kalogera 31; s/d incl breakfast €160/170; ⊘mid-May–Oct; ❅🌐) In the heart of town, with a lush and leafy garden and highly regarded on-site restaurant, Fresh is indeed very fresh, with compact and stylishly minimalist rooms. Rates fall to €70/80 in the low season.

Hotel Lefteris
PENSION €€

(☎22890 23128; www.lefterishotel.gr; Apollonas 9; d from €130; ❅🌐) Tucked uphill and away from the crowds, a colourful entrance-way leads to pristine, compact rooms and a warm welcome. A young family now runs this eight-room guesthouse (established by the owner's grandfather in the 1970s). Individually styled rooms have TV and air-con, and there's a roof terrace with views. Winter prices drop to €35.

★ Semeli Hotel
HOTEL €€€

(☎22890 27466; www.semelihotel.gr; off Rohari; d incl breakfast from €460; ❄❅🌐🅿) Expansive grounds, a glamorous restaurant terrace and swimming pool, and stylish, contemporary rooms combine to make this one of Mykonos' loveliest (and more affordable) top-end hotels. Low-season rates make it considerably more accessible.

Portobello Boutique Hotel
BOUTIQUE HOTEL €€€

(☎22890 23240; www.portobello-hotel.gr; Kaminaki; s/d/ste €169/289/589; ❄🌐🅿) In an elevated location on the edge of Mykonos

ℹ SLEEPING ON MYKONOS

In July and August, a no-frills double room with private bathroom in Hora costs about €100; midrange options cost €100 to €250. The sky's the limit for the top-end category. It's best not to arrive in July or August without a reservation, as there will be few vacancies. Some places insist on a minimum stay during the peak period. Noise levels in Hora and popular resorts are high in summer.

Town overlooking a ruined windmill, this welcoming hotel is a prime sunset-viewing spot. Delicious breakfast includes homemade yoghurt, and the staff are more than happy to help you plan your stay.

✖ Eating

Sakis Grill House
KEBAB €

(☎22890 24848; Grecia; mains from €5; ⊘24hr) Sometimes you want a fancy meal, and sometimes there's nothing better than tucking into a heaped portion of lamb or chicken souvlaki, or a bounty of doner kebab spilling out of pitta bread. Caters to clubbing night owls.

Taste Diaries
CRÊPES €

(☎22890 29117; www.facebook.com/TheTaste Diaries; mains €6-10; ⊘24hr; 🌐) Sandwiches and crêpes are served at all hours on the waterfront. Build your own from gourmet ingredients, or go with fab menu suggestions like a sweet crêpe of white praline, almond slices, caramel and kiwi.

Nice n Easy
FUSION €€

(☎22890 25421; www.niceneasy.gr; Little Venice; mains €12-25; ⊘9am-1am; 🌐🍴) With a great view of Mykonos' windmills from its seafront terrace, this Athenian outpost specialises in organic fusion dishes. The chef has spent time in California, and as a result healthy options like egg-white omelettes, quinoa salad and various vegan offerings appear on the menu.

Joanna's Nikos Place Taverna
GREEK €€

(☎22890 24251; mains €8-17; ⊘10am-11pm; 🌐) Run by the delightful Joanna herself and overlooking the beach just a few minutes' walk south of Mykonos Town, this taverna focuses on Greek standards and it does them very well, particularly the meze and the mixed grill.

Hora (Mykonos)

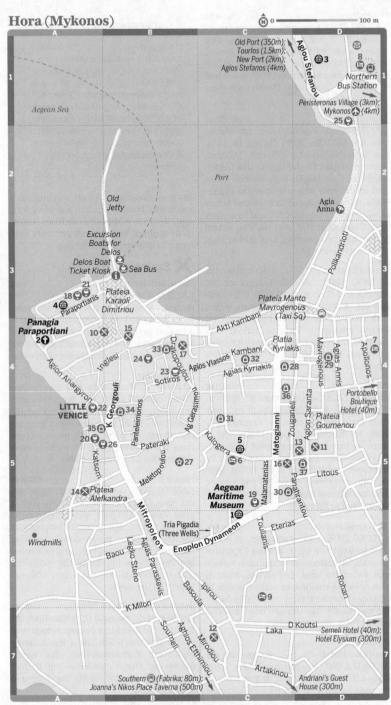

Hora (Mykonos)

Eva's Garden GREEK €€

(☏ 22890 22160; www.evas-garden.gr; Plateia Goumenou; mains €12-19; ⊘ 6.30pm-midnight; 🛜) Its patio shaded by hanging vines, this tempting corner of Eden focuses on traditional Greek specialities, such as *spaniko-pita* (spinach pie), moussaka and plenty of grilled fish.

Nikos Taverna GREEK €€

(☏ 22890 24320; www.tavernanikos.gr; Mavrou Markou; mains €13-20; ⊘ 11.30am-1.30am) Still going strong after more than 40 years, this casual taverna serves heaped platters of seafood, as well as Greek standards, such as lamb *kleftiko*. Great value, and there's a semi-resident pink pelican who hangs around in hope of fish.

★ Funky Kitchen FUSION €€€

(☏ 22890 27272; www.funkykitchen.gr; mains €18-31; ⊘ 6pm-1am; 🛜) The open kitchen of this contemporary restaurant brings forth beautifully presented Mediterranean fusion dishes such as seared tuna with smoky aubergine mousse, octopus carpaccio with pink peppercorns and rack of lamb with cumin fava, the likes of which will tempt you back until you drift into insolvency. The chocolate nirvana is orgasm on a plate. Book ahead.

★ M-Eating MEDITERRANEAN €€€

(☏ 22890 78550; www.m-eating.gr; Kalogera 10; mains €17-38; ⊘ 7pm-1am daily; 🛜) Attentive service, soft lighting and relaxed luxury are the hallmarks of this creative restaurant specialising in fresh Greek produce prepared with flair. Sample anything from sea bass tartare to rib-eye veal with honey truffle. Don't miss the dessert of Mykonian honey pie.

Daniele & Alessandro ITALIAN €€€

(☏ 22890 25852; Agia Moni Square; mains €15-39; ⊘ noon-11pm; 🛜) After the runaway success of their **restaurant** (☏ 22890 71513; mains €16-39; ⊘ noon-midnight; 🛜) in Ano Mera, this Italian couple have brought their superlative Italian cuisine to Hora. The menu is short and sweet – standouts include penne with homemade pesto and tender beef tagliata.

🍷 Drinking & Nightlife

Night action in town starts around 11pm and warms up by 1am. Hora's Little Venice is a swath of colourful bars; behind them are some excellent clubs. Another prime spot is the Tria Pigadia (Three Wells) area on Enoplon Dynameon.

★ Popolo COFFEE

(☏ 22890 22208; www.popolomykonos.com; Drakopoulou 18; ⊘ 8.30am-2.30am; 🛜) Hidden in Hora's labyrinthine depths, this tiny cafe has gained a reputation as the best place for coffee on Mykonos. Freshly cooked breakfasts, plus salads, sandwiches and juices throughout the day seal the deal.

Galleraki   BAR

(☑ 22890 27188; www.galleraki.com; Little Venice; ☺8am-late; ☎) Choose plum waterfront seating or the upstairs balcony at this friendly cafe-bar, and order one of its ace fresh-fruit cocktails (like the signature 'katerinaki', made with melon) or a champagne mix.

Piano Bar   COCKTAIL BAR

(☑ 22890 23719; www.thepianobar.com; Agion Anargyron 24; ☺7pm-3am; ☎) With the sunset lighting up Mykonos' windmills, this Little Venice bar is a perfect place for watching the greatest free show on earth while sipping a reasonably priced cocktail. Cabaret and live music take over once the sun goes down.

Cosi   BAR

(☑ 22890 27727; Matoghiannia; ☺10am-6am; ☎) This, erm, cosy nook with bohemian lampshades is a cafe by day with a few al fresco tables. By night it morphs into a lively little bar with occasional DJ sets.

Semeli   COCKTAIL BAR

(☑ 22890 26505; http://semelithebar.gr; Little Venice; ☺9am-late) Recently refurbished by renowned Greek architect Pavlos Ninios, this funky cocktail bar in the heart of Little Venice draws the bold and the beautiful with its signature cocktails and DJ sets.

Remezzo   CLUB

(☑ 22890 25700; https://remezzo-mykonos.com; Polikandrioti; ☺6pm-4am) International hits pump until the wee hours of the morning, with plenty of beautiful people burning up the dance floor.

☆ Entertainment

★ Cine Manto   CINEMA

(☑ 22890 26165; www.cinemanto.gr; Meletopoulou; adult/child €8/6; ☺9pm & 11pm Jun-Sep) Need a break from the bars and clubs? Seek out this gorgeous open-air cinema, in a perfect garden setting. There's a cafe here too. Movies are shown in their original language; view the program online.

🔒 Shopping

Fashion boutiques and art galleries vie for attention. Mavrogenous St is good for art, Matogliani is best for luxe brands and excellent Greek designers, while the streets of Little Venice mix fashion with jewellery and tat. Most stores close in the winter (November to March).

★ Eliza's Art Gallery   ARTS & CRAFTS

(☑ 22890 24461; www.elizasgallery.com; Mavrogenous 15; ☺10am-10pm) Gorgeous glass creations, quirky lamps, jewellery and works by renowned Naxos sculptor Yiannis Nanouris.

★ iMuseum Shop   ART

(☑ 22890 77370; www.i-museumshop.com; Dilou 8; ☺10am-10pm) An elegant and innovative boutique, selling approved hand-crafted replicas of pieces showcased in the most important museums of Greece – including classic art, jewellery, ceramics and figurines.

HEEL Athens Lab   FASHION & ACCESSORIES

(☑ 22890 77166; www.heel.gr; Panahrantou; ☺11am-2am) 🌿 Ecologically friendly garments made from organic cotton and other sustainable fibres, as well as one-of-a-kind jewellery made from recycled materials.

Mayonaisa Darling   JEWELLERY

(☑ 6975592478; www.mayonaisadarling.com; Drakopoulou 6; ☺10am-9pm) Worth buying for the designer's name alone, this collection of original handmade jewellery uses hypoallergenic materials, semi-precious stones and recycled pieces, such as gears from vintage clocks.

Delaros Fashion D-Tales   FASHION & ACCESSORIES

(☑ 22890 79359; www.delaros.gr; Matheou Andronikou 9; ☺10am-midnight) Gladiator sandals, handmade loom bags, wrap jumpsuits, beachwear, butterfly air maxi dresses, geometric Grecian-style jewellery and more by Greek designers such as Nadia Rapti, Milk & Honey, Monochrome, Park House, Noilence, Most Chic, Kyma Sandals and Thalatta.

Olive Oil Shop   GIFTS & SOUVENIRS

(☑ 22890 23598; Matogianni 15; ☺10am-midnight) Going strong for more than 20 years, this cute shop specialises in all things olive oil – soap, skincare products, the oil itself, plus olivewood kitchen implements and locally produced honey and herbs.

TЯUE Image   FASHION & ACCESSORIES

(☑ 22890 44432; Kalogera 11; ☺10am-11.30pm) These hand-printed T-shirts with a design of your choice are a good alternative to the corny, mass-produced tat sold nearby. Funky hand-printed shoes too.

Mykonos
Leather Shop   FASHION & ACCESSORIES
(✆22890 78660; K Georgouli 37; ⊘9.30am-10pm)
Gorgeous, colourful handmade leather
purses, bags, belts and accessories.

Mykonos Sandals   SHOES
(✆22890 22451; www.mykonos-sandals.gr; Little
Venice; ⊘10am-10pm) Come for the sunset
cocktails and stay for the handmade leather
sandals.

International Press   BOOKS
(Kambani 5; ⊘10am-9pm) International news-
papers, magazines and books.

❶ Information

Mykonos has no tourist office; visit travel agencies instead. Online, visit www.inmykonos.com
and www.mykonos.gr for more information.

There is information online at www.inmykonos.
com and www.mykonos.gr.

Mykonos Accommodation Centre (MAC;
✆22890 23408; www.mykonos-accommoda-
tion.com; 1st fl, Enoplon Dynameon 10; ⊘9am-
1pm & 4-9pm) Helpful for all things Mykonos.
Sea & Sky (✆22890 22853; www.seasky.gr;
Akti Kambani; ⊘9am-9pm) Sells ferry tickets.
Delia Travel (✆22890 22322; Akti Kambani;
⊘9am-9pm) Ferry tickets.
Police Station (✆22890 22716) On the road
to the airport.
Post Office (⊘9am-5pm Mon-Fri)

Around Mykonos

Aside from Hora, the island's only other village of any size is Ano Mera, which has the
attractive **Tourliani Monastery** (Ano Mera;
€1; ⊘9am-1pm & 3.30-7pm Mon-Sat, 11am-1pm &
3.30-7pm Sun) on its taverna-lined square.

🏖 Beaches

Mykonos' golden-sand beaches in their
formerly unspoilt state were the pride of
Greece. Now most are jammed with umbrellas and backed by beach bars, but they do
make for a hopping scene that draws floods
of beachgoers. Moods range from the simply hectic to the outright snobby, and nudity
levels vary.

Without your own wheels, catch buses
from Hora or caïques from Ornos and Platys
Gialos to further beaches. Mykonos Cruises
(p179) has an online timetable of its sea-taxi
services.

The nearest beaches to Hora were over-
taken by the construction of the New Port.

That leaves little **Agios Stefanos** (4km
north of Hora), within sight of docking
cruise ships. There's a tiny strip of sand in
town, **Agia Anna**.

About 5km southwest of Hora are family-
oriented **Agios Ioannis** (where *Shirley Valentine* was filmed) and **Kapari**. The nearby
packed and noisy **Ornos** and the package-
holiday resort of **Platys Gialos** have boats for
the glitzier beaches to the east. In between
these two is **Psarou**, a magnet for the Greek
cognoscenti.

Approximately 1km south of Platys Gialos
you'll find **Paraga Beach**, which has a small
gay section. Party people should head about
1km east to famous **Paradise**, which is not
a recognised gay beach but has an action-
packed younger scene, a camping resort
(www.paradisemykonos.com) and nightlife
that doesn't quit. Down a steep access road,
Super Paradise (aka Plintri or Super P) has
a fully gay section (including the JackieO'
beach club) and a huge eponymous club.

Mixed and gay-friendly **Elia** is a long,
lovely stretch of sand and is the last caïque
stop. A few minutes' walk west from here is
the secluded **Agrari**.

Further east, **Kalafatis** is a hub for water
sports (including diving and windsurfing),
and **Lia** has a remote, end-of-the-road feel.

North-coast beaches can be exposed to the
meltemi, but **Panormos** and **Agios Sostis**
with their golden sand are fairly sheltered
and less busy than the south-coast beaches.

For out-of-the-way beaching you'll need
tough wheels to reach the likes **Fokos** and
Mersini on the northeast coast.

🏃 Activities

There's good diving around Mykonos, with
wrecks, caves and walls to explore, and
scuba diving operators on Paradise Beach
and Lia Beach. Kalafatis Beach and Ftelia
Beach are good for windsurfing, while Platys
Gialos is the place to try flyboarding or rent
a stand-up paddleboard or kayak.

⭐**Yummy Pedals**   MOUNTAIN BIKING
(✆6972299282, 22890 71883; www.yummy
pedals.gr; 2hr tour from €40) A world away from
the beach bars, multilingual Dimitra offers
you guided mountain-biking tours through
the backroads of Mykonos. The duration
and route is personalised to fit your skill
level, but may take in farms, villages and
quiet beaches (with swimming and snack-
ing stops). Tours begin and end at Dimitra's

MILA ATKOVSKA/SHUTTERSTOCK ©

1. Ancient Delos (p190)
Once home to a magnificent city, Delos is now one of Greece's most important archaeological sites.

2. Naxos (p200)
A colourful, lively island with a strong cultural heritage.

3. Oia (p236), Santorini
Postcard-perfect Cycladic scenery.

4. Kleftiko (p249), Milos
A stunning coastline of rock formations and beaches.

family's vineyard, with the option of food and wine.

⭐**Platys Gialos Watersports**   WATER SPORTS
(☎6977279584; www.mykonoswatersports.gr; Platys Gialos Beach; stand-up paddleboard 1hr €30; ⏱9am-9pm) This operator specialises in adrenalin-packed water sports and arranges wakeboarding, wakeskating, waterskiing and wakesurfing sessions. They can also introduce you to the new flyboard craze, and rent sea kayaks and stand-up paddleboards.

GoDive Mykonos   DIVING
(☎6942616102; www.godivemykonos.com; Lia beach; 1-/2-tank dives €70/115; ⏱9.30am-6pm; ⛵) This highly professional operator is based on Lia beach and offers a full range of activities below the waves, from multi-day scuba safaris to night dives, PADI courses, snorkelling trips and Bubblemaker inductions for kids over eight.

Mykonos Diving Centre   DIVING
(☎22890 24808; www.diveadventures.gr; Paradise Beach; 1-/2-tank dive €65/115; ⛵) Based at Paradise Beach, this reputable operator offers a range of PADI courses, as well as night dives, Discover Scuba outings and Bubblemaker for kids over eight.

Windsurf Centre Mykonos   WINDSURFING
(☎22890 72345; www.pezi-huber.com; Kalafatis Beach; 1hr/day windsurf rental €35/90, 1hr private lesson €65; ⏱mid-May-Sep) Offers windsurf rental and private lessons at Kalafatis Beach.

🛏 **Sleeping**

Peristeronas Village   HOTEL €
(☎22893 00408; http://mykonos-pv.gr; r from €55; P❄🛜🏊) Around 2km from Mykonos Town and by the turn-off for Agios Sostis and Panormos beaches, this is a self-contained place that's equally popular with the young and the beautiful lying around the gorgeous pool or sipping cocktails by the bar, and holidaying middle-aged couples. Friendly young staff and free pick-up and drop-off are all boons.

Paradise Beach Camping   CAMPGROUND €
(☎22890 22852; www.paradisemykonos.com; campsites per tent/adult/child €5/10/5; @🛜🏊) There are lots of options here, including camping, beach cabins and apartments, as well as bars, a swimming pool, games and so on. It is skin-to-skin mayhem in summer, with a real party atmosphere.

Artemoulas Studios Mykonos   APARTMENT €€
(☎22890 22174; www.artemoulas-mykonos.gr; 2-/3-/4-person apt €180/210/270; P❄🛜🏊) Funky decor and a hillside location a few minutes' walk from two of Mykonos' most popular beaches. The spacious, self-contained apartments make this a solid midrange choice.

MYKONOS' GAY SCENE

Mykonos is a gay travel mecca. Most gay-centric bars and hang-outs welcome a mixed crowd too. The waterfront area, between the Old Harbour and the Church of Paraportiani, is a focus for the late-night gay scene.

Check out coverage of the island's many hotspots (including beaches) on www.gayguide.gr.

Party people should visit in mid-August for **XIsior** (www.xlsiorfestival.com), a huge gay clubbing festival that draws some 30,000 partiers.

Hotel Elysium (☎22890 23952; www.elysiumhotel.com; School of Fine Arts District; d from €260; ⏱Apr-Oct; ❄🛜🏊) Probably the most famous gay property on the island, this flash hotel sits high above the main town of Hora. Its high-camp sunset cabaret shows by the pool bar are an essential start to a night of partying (book a table). It's uphill from the Belvedere Hotel, in the town's southwest.

Porta (☎22890 27807; Ioanni Voinovich; ⏱8pm-4am) Porta's cruisey ambience fills small-scale rooms where things get crowded and close towards midnight.

JackieO' (☎22890 77168; www.jackieomykonos.com; Old Harbour; ⏱from 8pm) One of Mykonos' main gathering points for gay and straight alike. Throngs circulate from the retro-chic interior to the harbourfront, starting in early evening. There is a fab all-day outpost at Super Paradise Beach featuring restaurant, bar, pool and Jacuzzi.

Babylon (☎22890 25152; Old Harbour; ⏱7.30pm-5.30am) Gay-friendly masses party pierside next to JackieO'.

★ Nissaki

Boutique Hotel BOUTIQUE HOTEL €€€
(☑ 22890 27666; www.hotelnissaki.gr; Platys Gialos
beach; d/ste from €600/750; P✳❋☀) With its
pool overlooking the bay, this is one of the
loveliest Mykonos retreats. Whitewashed
rooms are livened up with touches of contemporary art, floor-to-ceiling windows let in
plenty of light, and suites come with hot tubs.
A spa, romantic dining and the pearly light
dancing on the water after sunset make this
an ideal place to canoodle with your sweetie.

✗ Eating

★ Kiki's Taverna CYCLADIC €€
(☑ 6940759356; Agios Sostis Beach; mains €8-22;
☺1-7pm; ☎) Every day around noon customers begin lining up outside Kiki's, helping
themselves to complimentary wine spritzers
as they wait. Their prize? Enormous portions of solid local food off the grill: pork
chops, octopus, swordfish, feta cheese,
accompanied by epic salads and served
beneath a shady vine trellis on a terrace
overlooking the sea.

Indian Palace INDIAN €€
(☑ 22890 78044; Paradise Beach; mains €12-20;
☺12.30pm-midnight; ❋☎✐) Athens' loss is
Mykonos' gain. Chef Manu Bhai abandoned
the capital's renowned Jaipur Palace to open
his own place overlooking Paradise Beach.
Beachgoers and clubbers find it hard to resist
the siren song of curries and crispy naan
bread after a diet of grilled fish and tzatziki.

Kalosta MEDITERRANEAN €€
(☑ 22890 78589; www.facebook.com/Kalosta
RestaurantPanormos; Panormos Beach; mains
€9-22; ☺noon-10pm; ☎) Drunk with sunshine
and skin tangy with sea salt, beachgoers make
their way up to Kalosta's shady terrace overlooking the Aegean. Bask in the afterglow of
a long, lazy day at the beach and feast on its
seafood-heavy mix of Mediterranean and local
dishes.

★ Buddha Bar JAPANESE €€€
(☑ 22890 23220; www.buddhabarbeachmykonos.
gr; Ornos; mains €16-28; ☺1-6.30pm & 7pm-1am;
☎) On the premises of the luxurious Santa
Marina resort, this elegant beachfront restaurant and bar is hands down the best place
in Mykonos for refined takes on Japanese
food and fishy delights such as ceviche. Portions are dainty, the service seamless and the
wonderful signature cocktails an expensive
temptation. Reservations recommended.

🍷 Drinking & Nightlife

Super Paradise CLUB
(☑ 22890 24702; http://superparadise.com.gr;
☺9am-late; ☎) Dominating its namesake
beach, this beach bar and club is synonymous with hedonism. Celebrity sightings,
a crush of scantily-clad young bodies heaving to the DJs' beats, cocktails by the sea –
yep, it's got all that. Music kicks off in the
afternoons and pumps until the wee hours.
Numerous free shuttle buses from Hora.

Paradise Club CLUB
(☑ 6949468227; www.paradiseclubmykonos.com;
Paradise Beach; ☺8pm-5am) Big-name international DJs and white-on-white decor that
sets off all that bronzed skin in the island's
biggest club.

Cavo Paradiso CLUB
(☑ 22890 26124; www.cavoparadiso.gr; Paradise
Beach; ☺11.30pm-7am) When dawn gleams
just over the horizon, hard-core bar-hoppers
move from Hora to Cavo Paradiso at Paradise
Beach, the open-air clifftop mega-club that
has featured top international DJs since 1994.

Kalua Beach Bar CLUB
(☑ 22890 23397; https://kalua.gr; Paraga Beach;
☎) Originally made famous by the 1970s
hippie generation and renowned for its
beach parties that carry on until sunrise,
this bar pretty much takes over Paraga
Beach after sundown. During the day, it's a
chilled-out cocktail haunt.

DELOS ΔΗΛΟΣ

The Cyclades fulfil their collective name
(*kyklos* means circle) by encircling the sacred
island of **Delos** (☑ 22890 22259; museum & site
adult/child €12/free; ☺8am-8pm Apr-Oct, to 3pm
Nov-Mar). The mythical birthplace of twins
Apollo and Artemis, splendid Ancient Delos
was a shrine turned sacred treasury and commercial centre. This Unesco World Heritage
Site is one of the most important archaeological sites in Greece. Cast your imagination
wide to transform this sprawling ruin into
the magnificent city it once was.

The island, just 5km long and 1300m
wide, has no permanent population, so it
offers a soothing contrast to Mykonos, from
where Delos can be visited. Overnight stays
are forbidden, and boat schedules allow a
maximum of four hours at Delos. Wear a
hat, sunscreen and walking shoes.

190

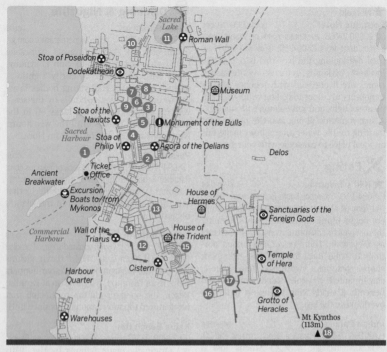

🏃 Site Tour
Ancient Delos

START & END BOAT DOCK
LENGTH THREE HOURS

Excursion boats from Mykonos dock on a bay south of the tranquil **①Sacred Harbour**. The narrow spit dividing the two bays was man-made. Follow the arrowed path past the ruins of the **②South Stoa**, or portico, built after the mid-3rd century BC with 28 Doric columns, and used to house shops and workshops. Continue to the **③Sanctuary of Apollo**, northeast of the harbour. The Sacred Way (a wide, paved path used by ancient pilgrims) enters the complex through the **④Propylaia**, to a compound of magnificent temples and treasuries. Three were dedicated to Apollo: **⑤Temple of the Delians**, **⑥Temple of the Athenians** and **⑦Poros Temple**. The Sanctuary also housed the classical **⑧treasuries** and the **⑨Artemision**, a sanctuary of Artemis.

North of the sanctuary is the much-photographed **⑩Terrace of the Lions**. To the northeast, the now-empty **⑪Sacred**

Lake is where Leto gave birth to Apollo and Artemis.

Next, head south to the **⑫Theatre Quarter**, where Delos' wealthiest inhabitants lived in houses surrounded by peristyle courtyards, with intricate, colourful mosaics. The most lavish include the **⑬House of Dionysos**, named after its mosaic depicting the wine god riding a panther, and the **⑭House of Cleopatra**.

The **⑮theatre** dates from 300 BC and had a large cistern which supplied much of the town's water.

The **⑯House of the Masks** has another mosaic of Dionysos astride a panther between two centaurs. The extraordinary mosaic at the **⑰House of the Dolphins** incorporates lions, griffins and dolphins.

⑱Mt Kynthos (113m) rises to the southeast of the harbour. It's worth the steep climb: on clear days there are terrific views of the encircling islands. It also has monuments such as the Sanctuaries of Zeus Kynthios and Athena Kynthia, and the Temple of Hera.

History

Delos won early acclaim as the mythical birthplace of the twins Apollo and Artemis, and was first inhabited in the 3rd millennium BC. From the 8th century BC it became a shrine to Apollo, and the oldest temples on the island date from this era. The dominant Athenians had full control of Delos – and thus the Aegean – by the 5th century BC.

In 478 BC Athens established an alliance known as the Delian League, which maintained its treasury on Delos. A decree ensured that no one could be born or die on Delos, strengthening Athens' control over the island by expelling the native population.

Delos reached the height of its power in Hellenistic times, becoming one of the three most important religious centres in Greece and a flourishing centre of commerce. Many of its inhabitants were wealthy merchants, mariners and bankers from as far away as Egypt and Syria. They built temples to their homeland gods, but Apollo remained the principal deity.

The Romans made Delos a duty-free port in 167 BC. This brought even greater prosperity, due largely to a lucrative slave market. During the following century, as ancient religions diminished and trade routes shifted, Delos began a long decline. By the 3rd century AD there was only a small Christian settlement on the island, and in the following centuries the ancient site was a hideout for pirates and was looted of many of its antiquities. It wasn't until the Renaissance that its antiquarian value was recognised.

Every now and then fresh discoveries are unearthed: in recent years a gold workshop was uncovered alongside the Terrace of the Lions.

The ticket office sells detailed Delos guidebooks, and Mykonos bookshops sell some with reconstructions which are helpful for picturing the ruins in their heyday.

Visitors are given a map of the site with three self-guided walking tours marked on it, taking from 1½ to five hours, depending on the route.

☞ Tours

It pays to tour the site with a guide, to give context to the various neighbourhoods and buildings. Mykonos Accommodation Centre (p185) in Hora (Mykonos) organises multilingual guided tours to Delos (adult/child €50/25) including boat, entrance fee and guide. Licensed guides may tout for business

---

SANCTUARIES OF THE FOREIGN GODS

Delos was a place of worship for many cultures beyond the Greeks, and their temples are concentrated in the area called the Sanctuaries of the Foreign Gods.

Shrine to the Samothracian Great Gods Here people worshipped the Kabeiroi (twins Dardanos and Aeton).

Sanctuary of the Syrian Gods There are remains of a theatre used for mystical rites (some say ritual orgies) here.

Shrine to the Egyptian Gods Honoured deities including Serapis and Isis.

---

as you disembark the boat; they charge around €10 per person.

❶ Getting There & Away

Boats for Delos (return adult/child €20/10, 30 minutes) leave Hora (Mykonos) four times daily in high season starting around 9am, with the last outward boat about 5pm. Boats return between 12.15pm and 8pm. There are fewer boats from November to March.

Departure/return times are posted at the **Delos Boat Ticket Kiosk** (☎ 22890 23051; www.delostours.gr; adult/child return ticket €20/10), located at the foot of the jetty at the southern end of the old harbour, as well as online. Buy tickets online or from the kiosk or various travel and transport agencies. When buying tickets, establish which boat you can return on.

PAROS ΠΑΡΟΣ

POP 14,920

Paros rests nonchalantly in the shadows of the limelight. Long tagged as primarily a ferry hub, its stylish capital, fashionable resort towns and sweet rural villages are all the more charming for their relative lack of crowds and tourist kudos. For holidaymakers looking for Mykonos without the hype and price tag, this might be the spot. But word is spreading. There's plenty to do, with good walks, plus excellent windsurfing, kite-surfing and diving.

Geologically speaking, Paros has long been a Greek star; white marble drawn from the island's interior made the island prosperous from the Early Cycladic period onwards. Most famously, the *Venus de Milo* was carved from Parian marble, as was Napoleon's tomb.

The smaller island of Antiparos, 1km southwest of Paros, is easily reached by car ferry or excursion boat. To Paros' east is Naxos, separated by an 8km channel.

❶ Getting There & Away

Paros is a major ferry hub for onward travel to other islands in the Aegean. It is well-served by regular ferries from Piraeus and by connections to most of the other islands of the Cyclades, and also to Thessaloniki, Crete and the Dodecanese.

New Paros Airport opened in 2016, a few kilometres north of the old airport (south of Parikia). Despite 'I'll believe it when I see it' comments from locals, scheduled international flights appear to be on the horizon. There are daily flights from Athens to Paros (€95, 40 minutes) with **Olympic Air** (www.olympicair.com).

Boat Services from Paros

DESTINATION	DURATION	FARE (€)	FREQUENCY
Amorgos	3hr-4hr	19	1 daily
Anafi	4hr 50min	20	2 weekly
Astypalea	4hr 50min	34	5 weekly
Donousa	2¼hr	14	4 weekly
Folegandros	4½hr	18	1 weekly
Ios	2¼hr	16	2-4 daily
Ios*	1-1½hr	29	2-3 daily
Iraklia	2hr	16	3 weekly
Iraklio*	3¾hr	69	1 daily
Koufonisia	3hr	19	3 weekly
Koufonisia*	1hr 20min	28	1 daily
Mykonos	1hr 20min	16	1 daily
Mykonos*	40-50min	29	3 daily
Naxos	45-50min	10	4-5 daily
Naxos*	30min	18	3 daily
Piraeus	4-5hr	33	2-5 daily
Piraeus*	2¾hr	51	1 daily
Rafina	5hr	30	1 daily
Rafina*	3¼hr	50	2 daily
Santorini (Thira)	3-3½hr	20	1-2 daily
Santorini (Thira)*	2-2¼hr	46	2-3 daily
Schinousa	2hr 20min	13	3 weekly
Syros	1½hr	12	3 weekly
Tinos*	1hr 20min	28	2 daily

* high-speed services

❶ Getting Around

BOAT

Sea-taxis leave from the Parikia quay for beaches around Paros and to Antiparos. Tickets range from €8 to €15 and are available on board.

BUS

Frequent **buses** (☎22840 21395; http://ktelparou.gr) link Parikia and Naoussa (€1.80) directly. Buses also run from Parikia to east-coast beaches such as Piso Livadi (€2.40), Hrysi Akti (Golden Beach; €3) and Dryos (€3). Some of these services run via Naoussa, some via Lefkes (€1.80).

There are frequent buses to Pounta (for the Antiparos ferry; €1.80) and Aliki (€1.80).

Tickets can be purchased from machines at the bus terminals, and at kiosks and minimarkets island-wide, or from the driver at a slightly higher rate.

CAR & MOTORCYCLE

There are rental outlets along the waterfront in Parikia and all around the island. In high season the minimum cost is about €45 per day for car hire and €20 for a motorbike. A good outfit is **Acropolis** (☎22840 21830; www.acropolis paros.com; Waterfront, Parikia).

TAXI

Taxis (☎22840 21500) gather beside the roundabout in Parikia. Fares include the airport (€20), Naoussa (€13), Pounta (€12), Lefkes (€14) and Piso Livadi (€22). Add €1 if going from the port. There are extra charges for booking ahead, and for luggage.

Parikia   Παροικιά

POP 6100

For its small size, Parikia packs a punch. Its labyrinthine old town is pristine and filled with boutiques, cafes and restaurants. You'll also find a handful of impressive archaeological sites, a waterfront crammed with tavernas and bars, first-class midrange accommodation, and sandy stretches of beach – particularly popular is Livadia, a short walk north of town.

◉ Sights

★ Archaeological Museum   MUSEUM
(☎22840 21231; €2; ◷8am-3pm Tue-Sun) Behind the Panagia Ekatontapyliani, this museum is a cool escape into the island's past. It harbours some marvellous pieces, including a 5th-century BC Nike on the

point of alighting and a 6th-century BC Gorgon also barely in touch with the earth. A major exhibit is a fragment slab of the 3rd-century BC Parian Chronicle, which lists the most outstanding personalities and events of Ancient Greece.

Panagia Ekatontapyliani CHURCH
(www.ekatontapyliani.gr; ⊙8am-9pm) The Panagia Ekatontapyliani, which dates from AD 326, is one of the finest churches in the Cyclades. The building is comprised of three distinct churches: Agios Nikolaos, the largest, with superb columns of Parian marble and a carved iconostasis in the east of the compound; the ornate Church of Our Lady; and the ancient Baptistery. The name translates as Our Lady of the Hundred Doors. The **Byzantine Museum** (€2; ⊙9am-10pm Apr-Oct), within the compound, has a collection of icons and other artefacts.

Frankish Kastro RUINS
Check out the outer walls of this fortress, built by the Venetian Duke Marco Sanudo of Naxos in AD 1260. Built with the stones from ancient buildings that once stood on this site, you can find remnants from the archaic temples of Athena and an Ionic temple from the 5th century BC.

Ancient Cemetery RUINS
North along the waterfront is a fenced ancient cemetery dating from the end of the 8th century BC. It was in use until the 3rd century AD. Excavations in 1983 discovered graves, burial pots and sarcophagi.

🏃 Activities & Tours

Paros Hikes HIKING
(☏6972288821; www.paroshikes.com) Chris guides ecotours to explore the lesser-known sides of Paros and Antiparos, from countryside walks to mountain hiking adventures. Tours can be tailor-made, or you can join

Paros & Antiparos

0 ─── 5 km
0 ─── 2.5 miles

Parikia

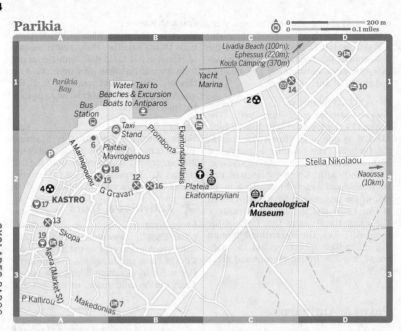

Parikia

him for scheduled walks. Upcoming events are outlined on the website, along with routes, departure info and prices. There are also Bike & Hike and Sail & Hike combos.

Travel to Paros TOURS
(☎22840 24245; http://traveltoparos.gr) Opposite the bus terminal, this efficient company can book bus tours of Paros (€37), cruises around Antiparos (€50-100) and full-day excursions to Mykonos and Delos (€50), Santorini (€65), and the beaches of Iraklia and Koufonisia (€45).

🛏 Sleeping

Rooms Mike PENSION €
(☎22840 22856; http://roomsmike.com; r from €60; ✳🛜) A popular and friendly place, Mike's offers a great location within view of the ferry quay, and good local advice. Options range from shared facilities to self-contained units with kitchens. Mike's sign is easy to spot from the quay – away to the left. A decent budget option, if a tad dated.

Koula Camping   CAMPGROUND **€**
(☑ 22840 22081; www.campingkoula.gr; Livadia Beach; campsite per adult/child/tent €8/3/4, tent rental €7; ☺ May-Oct; ☎) With plenty of trees and just footsteps from the sea, this is a decent (if slightly ramshackle) place to pitch your tent. It's at the northern end of the Parikia waterfront on Livadia Beach. Free transfers to/from town are available, though it's only a 10-minute walk. There's a cafe and minimarket.

★**Pension Sofia**   PENSION **€€**
(☑ 22840 22085; http://pension-sofia.gr; d/tr €80/120; ☺ Apr-Oct; ✳☎) A few blocks behind the waterfront, Sofia's verdant garden alone makes it worth the stay. Rooms are immaculate, and some are decorated with the owner's artwork. Breakfast is available for €8; take it on your balcony or in the garden. Sofia is inland, 400m east of the ferry quay.

La Selini   GUESTHOUSE **€€**
(☑ 22840 23106; www.laselini.com; s/d/tr €70/90/110; ☺ Apr-Oct; ✳☎) La Selini shines under the care of its North American owner, Lou Ann. A short walk from Livadia Beach, the cheerful complex offers bright, comfy rooms and studios sleeping up to four. Upper rooms have a sea view.

Hotel Dina   HOTEL **€€**
(☑ 22840 21325; www.hoteldina.com; Agora (Market St); s/d €70/80; ☺ May-Oct; ✳☎) Smack-bang in the heart of the Old Town, these eight family-run rooms are a find. With whitewashed walls and wrought-iron beds, they are spotless and comfortable. Each room has a small balcony, some looking out over Market St, with shared courtyards and verandahs in the traditional building's centre. Hostess Dina is a mine of information.

Angie's Studios   APARTMENT **€€**
(☑ 22840 23909; www.angies-studios.gr; Makedonias; d €90; ☺ Apr-Oct; ✳☎) South beyond the Old Town, but just a short walk to Market St, Angie's is a worthwhile place to lay your head. Spacious, immaculate rooms with flagstone floors and lots of local touches are set within a garden glowing with bougainvillea. Each room has a private balcony and a kitchenette, and the staff are warm. Call ahead for pick-up from the dock.

✖ Eating

★**Symposium**   CAFE **€**
(☑ 22840 24147; http://cafesymposium.gr; mains from €8; ☺ 9am-3.30pm & 6pm-midnight) A gor-

geous location under a massive bougainvillea tree adds to the delicious light meals, sophisticated atmosphere and tasteful jazz and classical music to make this a top place to hang out in Parikia. Head into the back of town to find this haven away from the full-on hustle and bustle.

★**Cafe Distrato**   CAFE **€**
(☑ 22840 25175; G Gravari; mains €3-10; ☺ 8am-late) Dine outside under a leafy canopy at this friendly place that will draw you back time and again. This casual all-day cafe exudes wholesomeness, and is attached to a shop selling local food products. The crowd-pleasing menu lists crêpes, sandwiches, burgers, pastas and salads, plus coffee, cocktails and local wines. Look for the huge tree over the street.

Ragoussis   BAKERY **€**
(☑ 22840 21573; https://ragoussisbakery.com; Plateia Mavrogenous; ☺ 8am-11pm) An ode to deliciousness, this bakery-patisserie just off the main square and next to Hotel Argonauta has cabinets full of baklava, cake and traditional biscuits, plus perfect beach picnic fodder like sandwiches. So, so much to choose from.

Little Green Rocket   INTERNATIONAL **€€**
(☑ 22840 27560; www.facebook.com/thelittlegreenrocket; mains €10-15; ☺ 6pm-late) Fresh and fun waterfront restaurant-bar, with a small but varied menu grabbing influences from all over (yakitori, curry, burritos). It's a good spot for a lazy drink too. Panos and his team have got things working well. Just past the post office on the way to Livadia Beach.

Ephessus   GREEK **€€**
(☑ 22840 22520; www.parosweb.com/ephessus; Livadia Beach; mains €7-15; ☺ 10am-late) Sit in the beachfront, lantern-filled garden, then dig into a dish of Greek or Anatolian cuisine from Ephessus' wood-fired oven, and you'll understand why this restaurant is so popular. Setting, service and food are tops. Try the *manti* (Anatolian ravioli), the *peinirli* (traditional pizza) or take a look at the specials the chef has cooked up for the day.

Levantis   GREEK **€€**
(☑ 22840 23613; www.levantisrestaurant.com; Agora (Market St); dishes €13-22; ☺ dinner May-Oct) A vine-covered courtyard and simple, whitewashed interior with splashes of modern art create a polished setting for some of the Cyclades' finest contemporary Greek

cuisine. The menu makes for hungry reading – choose from inspired flavour combinations like chicken and pistachio dolmades, slow-braised honey-spiced lamb and dark chocolate mocha soufflé.

 Drinking & Nightlife

The southwestern waterfront is peppered with bars, popular with both locals and visitors. Old Town also has its fair share of drinking holes.

Bebop BAR

(☑22840 28075; ☺9am-4am) Climb the steps up to this cool-cat waterfront spot with no shortage of outdoor areas, including a sunset-primed rooftop terrace. There's a long list of coffee and cocktail options, as well as fine sangria. Keep an eye out for live-music events, especially jazz. Look up as you head down the waterfront passing the *kastro*.

Koukoutsi BAR

(☑6933020592; Plateia Mavrogenous; ☺8am-late) On the inland back corner of the main square, this local hangout is a gem. Small and lively, with walls covered in posters and wooden benches filled with cushions, come here to mix with locals, nibble on mezedhes and sip juices, coffees, beer or a shot of ouzo.

Pirate BAR

(☑6970024122; Agora (Market St); ☺9am-late) Ultracool and cave-like, Pirate is an ideal refuge within the Old Town. It's been a favourite with locals since 1983.

ⓘ Information

On the waterfront opposite the bus terminal, **Travel to Paros** (p194) sells ferry tickets, can advise on accommodation and car hire, and has luggage storage. You can also book various tours here.

Post Office Located 400m east of the ferry quay.

Naoussa Ναούσα

POP 2870

Naoussa has gradually turned from a quiet fishing village into an increasingly stylish resort and visitor destination. Perched on the shores of the large Plastira Bay, there are good beaches nearby, excellent restaurants and an ever-expanding number of chic beachside hotels, cafes and bars. Behind the waterfront is a maze of narrow, white-washed streets.

 Sights & Activities

The fun of Naoussa is to get lost wandering the streets of Old Town, and admire the crumbling remains of the 15th-century Venetian *kastro* guarding the port area.

The best beaches in the area are **Kolimbythres**, set among fabulous rock formations, and **Monastiri**, which has some good snorkelling. Low-key **Lageri** is also worth seeking out. **Santa Maria**, on the other side of the eastern headland, is ideal for windsurfing. These beaches can all be reached by road, but caïques go from Naoussa to each of them during July and August.

Paros Park PARK

(☑22840 53573; www.parospark.com; Agios Ioannis Detis Peninsula) This 80-hectare park north of Naoussa features impressive rock formations, caves, hidden coves and gorgeous beaches. There's three established walking trails, a museum, a monastery, a cafe and the extremely popular open-air Cine Enastron. There's also a lot of history – the Russian fleet was based here during the Russo-Turkish War (1768–74). The park is a 10-minute drive west, then north from Naoussa on the Agios Ioannis Detis Peninsula.

★Moraitis Winery WINERY

(☑22840 51350; www.moraitiswines.gr; tastings from €5; ☺10am-3pm, to 8pm in summer) Pressing grapes since 1910, the Moraitis family has it down to a fine art. Wander the original stone cellars before sidling up to the bar for a taste of up to 14 wines. Anything made with the island's indigenous grape, Monemvasia, is particularly worth a try. The winery is an easy walk southeast of the centre.

Michael Zeppos BOATING

(☑6947817125; www.mzeppos.gr) Operating primarily from Naoussa (and also from Aliki), this company offers full-day sailing itineraries taking in the beaches of Paros, Antiparos and potentially calling at Naxos. There are also sunset and fishing options. See the website for details; prices depend on numbers.

Kokou Riding Centre HORSE RIDING

(☑22840 51818; www.horseridingparos.com) The well-established Kokou has 2½-hour morning rides (€60), venturing into the sea, and 1½-hour evening rides (€40). Pick-up is available from Naoussa's main square for €3.

🛏 Sleeping

Hotel Kalypso
HOTEL €€

(☑ 22840 51488; www.kalypso.gr; Agii Anargiri Beach; r from €110; ☺ Apr-Oct; ❄ @ ☎) This cheerful complex has a fresh feel thanks to attentive care and upgrades from its owners. Inside there's a surprisingly chic lounge and simple, spotless rooms, studios and apartments with colourful touches. Outside is the winner, though: a sunlounger-filled garden, right on the beach.

Katerina Mare
APARTMENT €€

(☑ 22840 51642; www.katerinamare.com; d/tr incl breakfast €130/150, apt from €170; ❄ ☎) In a word: lovely. Light-filled suites are classy and pristine, each with a great view and every convenience, including kitchenette. Service is stellar. It's on a hillside southwest of the town centre, with many accommodation options as neighbours.

Hotel Galini
HOTEL €€

(☑ 22840 51210; www.hotelgaliniparos.com; d €80-90, tr €100; ❄ ☎) Run by a local family for three generations, this spic-and-span hotel has simple, comfortable rooms. Ask for a balcony and a sea view. It's opposite the blue-domed local church, on the main road into town from Parikia. Rooms cost €50 outside July and August.

Lilly Residence
BOUTIQUE HOTEL €€€

(☑ 22840 51377; www.lillyresidence.gr; r incl breakfast from €285; ☺ May-Oct; P ❄ ☎ ☑) Naoussa's most stylish hotel, where stone, wood and wicker combine to great effect and white is the unifying theme. The place is discreetly luxurious (eg Hermes toiletries) and grown-up (no kids under 12). Just back from the water, all 11 suites have sea views, or you can enjoy the eye-candy pool area.

✗ Eating

Naoussa knows how to do waterfront dining. Tables fill every waterfront spot, creating a superbly convivial atmosphere just inches from moored boats or the beach.

★ Sousouro
CAFE €

(☑ 22840 53113; www.facebook.com/Sousouro CafeBar; breakfast €4-6; ☺ 9am-3am) Occupying a small corner in the Old Town, this cafe is big on flavour. It has one of the islands' best breakfasts: superfood smoothies and shakes, homemade granola with sheep's-milk yoghurt and thyme honey, and toast topped with avocado or cacao hazelnut butter and banana. At night the wholesomeness makes way for killer cocktails.

To Paradosiako
SWEETS €

(loukoumadhes €4-5; ☺ 6pm-midnight) An essential evening stop for a serve of To Paradosiako's legendary fresh doughy balls of goodness known as *loukoumadhes* (Greek doughnuts). It's a self-service operation: add honey, chocolate sauce and/or ice cream.

Glafkos
MEDITERRANEAN €€

(☑ 22840 52100; mains €8-16; ☺ lunch & dinner) With tables practically on the sand on Agios Dimitrios Beach, it's not surprising that this tucked-away place specialises in seafood. Try steamed mussels and grilled calamari, or dig into shrimp *saganaki* or black risotto with cuttlefish – all are great paired with local white wine.

🍷 Drinking & Nightlife

★ Sommaripa Consolato
BAR

(☑ 22840 55233; www.facebook.com/Sommaripa Consolato; ☺ 10am-late) The owner opened this elevated cafe-bar in the former home of his grandparents – how fortunate that it's right in the hub of Naoussa's small port (above Mario's restaurant), making for great people-watching from the terraces. First-class drinks, snacks and service too.

To Takimi
BAR

(Music Cafe; ☑ 22840 55095; ☺ 5pm-late) Just south of the main square, this is where locals come to drink beer or ouzo and listen to live music, often played on the traditional string instruments waiting on the walls. Everything from *rembetika* (blues) to rock goes down here.

☆ Entertainment

Cine Enastron
CINEMA

(☑ 22840 53573; www.parospark.com/cine-enastron; Paros Park; free; ☺ 9.30pm Jul-Sep) As good as it gets! Watch retro movies under the stars by the sea in this classic open-air cinema in Paros Park, a 10-minute drive around the coast, north of Naoussa. You'll want a rental car to get here. Check the website for a schedule of what's on. Movies are in English with Greek subtitles.

ⓘ Information

The bus from Parikia terminates some way inland from the waterfront, where there's a large public car park (most of the Old Town area is pedestrian-only). The Old Town is east of here.

Erkyna Travel (☎22840 53180; www.erkynatravel.com) Sells ferry tickets and can help with accommodation, car hire, excursions, water sports and boat trips to other islands. It's on the main road into town.

Around Paros

On the southeast coast is Paros' top beach, **Hrysi Akti** (Golden Beach), with good swimming, windsurfing and diving operations.

Paros' west coast, around **Pounta**, is the hub for top water sports activities: a long shallow-water shoreline and perfect sideshore wind conditions make it perfect for all skill levels of kiteboarder or windsurfer.

🏃 Activities

Walking

Paros is popular with walkers, and there are excellent tracks all over the island. See www.parosweb.com/guide for more information. One particularly popular trail is the **Byzantine path** from Lefkes to Prodromos to Marpissa, taking a bit over an hour. In places, the path is paved with marble as it heads out west from Lefkes in the mountains.

Terrain (http://terrainmaps.gr) has an excellent Paros/Antiparos map which covers both islands, including walking tracks.

Water Sports

Force7 Surf Centre   WINDSURFING
(☎22840 41789; www.force7paros.gr) Force7 Surf Centre is a well-run centre on Hrysi Akti offering windsurfing courses and rental (including classes for kids), plus kayaking, stand-up paddleboard and catamaran rentals.

Paros Kite   KITESURFING
(☎22840 93018; www.paroskite.gr; 90min intro €90) At this slick, professionally run complex at Pounta it's all about the wind: kitesurfing and windsurfing instruction and gear rental are offered, plus there's a surf shop, beach bar-cafe, massage and yoga. Local accommodation can be arranged.

Aegean Diving College   DIVING
(☎22840 43347; www.aegeandiving.gr; shore dive from €80) At Hrysi Akti, the Aegean Diving College offers a range of dives to places of archaeological and ecological interest. Dive courses are also available.

🛏 Sleeping

Golden Beach Hotel   HOTEL €€
(☎22840 41366; www.goldenbeach.gr; Hrysi Akti; d incl breakfast €125, 4-person apt €250; ◷Apr–mid-Oct; ❄☎) Right on Hrysi Akti, this top spot offers simple, appealing rooms and apartments in pastel colours. More important is what's outside the rooms: a splendid grassy lawn down to the shore, plus restaurant, beach bar and oodles of beach activities. Lots of fun to be had on Paros' east coast.

ANTIPAROS   ΑΝΤΙΠΑΡΟΣ
POP 1200

Antiparos lies dreamily offshore from Paros. As soon as your ferry docks, you feel a distinct slowing down in the pace of things. The main village and port (also called Antiparos) are relaxed. There's a touristy gloss around the waterfront and main street, but the village runs deep inland to quiet squares and alleyways that give way suddenly to open fields.

The rest of the island runs to the south of the main settlement through quiet countryside. There are several decent beaches, especially at Glyfa and Soros, and one of Greece's most celebrated caves. There's also a 'secret getaway' factor to the island that puts it on the radar of those who don't like to be disturbed: Euro royalty, Hollywood stars (Tom Hanks has a villa on the island) and A-list rock stars holiday here.

◉ Sights & Activities

Antiparos Town   VILLAGE
The main town is well worth a wander. Its long pedestrianised main street is lined with services and a whole lot of stylish boutiques, bars and restaurants. Follow it to the end, to the distinctive, giant plane tree of Plateia Agios Nikolaou. From here, a narrow lane leads to the intriguing remnants of the old Venetian *kastro*, entered through an archway. This old fortified settlement dates from the mid-15th century.

★ Cave of Antiparos   CAVE
(http://antiparos.gr; adult/child €5/2.50; ◷10am–6pm Jul & Aug, to 5pm Jun, to 4pm May & Sep, to 3pm Apr) About 10km south of the port, this huge and atmospheric cave remains impressive despite much looting of stalactites and stalagmites in the past (check out the ancient graffiti from past visitors; one dates from

1776). Descending the 400-plus concrete steps into the well-lit cave is an enthralling experience – beware the climb out! To get to the cave, follow the coastal road south until you reach a signposted turn-off. A bus runs here from the port (€1.80).

Anti Art Gallery GALLERY

(☑ 22840 61544; https://antiartgallery.gr; ☺ 7pm-12.30am Jun-Sep) In true Antiparos fashion, the 'anti' Art Gallery has late hours and an excellent run of scheduled exhibitions, detailed on its website. The brainchild of curator Mary Chatzaki, it plays an entertaining, educational role in island life.

Historical & Folklore
Museum of Antiparos MUSEUM

(☑ 22840 61417; €3; ☺ 10am-9pm summer) This tiny new museum on the main street shows off intriguing old photographs, maps, manuscripts and all sorts of bits and pieces associated with life on the island.

🏃 Activities

Captain Sargos Boat Trips BOATING

(☑ 6973794876; www.sargosantiparos.gr; per person €25) Operating out of Agios Georgios, Yorgos runs three-to-four-hour boat trips that include a visit to the archaeological site on nearby Despotiko island, time to swim or laze on the island's spectacular beach, and a cruise through local sea caves. Also available for local charters.

Blue Island Divers DIVING

(☑ 22840 61767; www.blueisland-divers.gr; dives from €60, PADI certification from €240) On the northern waterfront is this operator, offering fun dives, PADI courses, and information on the island.

🛏 Sleeping

Camping Antiparos CAMPGROUND €

(☑ 22840 61221; www.camping-antiparos.gr; campsite per adult/child/tent €8/4/3; ☺ May-Sep; 🛜) This chilled-out beachside campground is planted with bamboo 'compartments' and cedars. There's a bar, minimarket and free wi-fi. It's 1.5km north of the port (pick-up is available).

★ Artemis Hotel HOTEL €€

(☑ 22840 61460; www.artemisantiparos.com; d incl breakfast €80-90; ☺ Apr–mid-Oct) The elegant, marble-lined rooms at Artemis (at the far northern end of the harbour) are compact but well priced, and have lovely private terraces (opt for a sea-view room). The common areas are stylishly appealing, and rates include a good breakfast. Family-run and friendly, rates halve out of the high season.

Beach House Antiparos RESORT €€€

(☑ 22840 64000; http://beachhouseantiparos.com; ste from €220; ☺ mid-May–Sep; ❄🛜) This is a glossy boutique resort on Apandima beach, with a 'beach house' housing nine suites (some family-sized). There's an upmarket beachside restaurant serving brunch, lunch and dinner, a beach bar and sunbeds, all open to nonguests. From the beach, arrange a massage, charter a boat or peek in the concept store.

🍴 Eating

Elia Kafenes CAFE €

(☑ 22840 61704; mains from €7; ☺ 9am-2am) A handwritten menu details the day's offerings at this cool little cafe-bar just back from the waterfront on the main street. Stop by for a tasty breakfast or for tapas and drinks.

★ Margarita Cafe CAFE €€

(☑ 22840 61491; www.facebook.com/margarita antiparos; mains from €10; ☺ 9am-late; 🛜) Strolling down Antiparos' main street, you'll find it hard to continue on past the Margarita Cafe – shaded seating both on the street and on the verandah under a huge palm tree make this the spot. There are snacks and sandwiches during the day, pastas, risottos and seafood for dinner, plus a good range of beer and wine. Free wi-fi and extremely friendly service.

★ Captain Pipinos TAVERNA €€

(☑ 22840 21823; http://captainpipinos.com; mains €6-15, fish by kg; ☺ lunch & dinner) In the island's south, right on the water at Agios Georgios and with panoramas of neighbouring uninhabited Despotiko, Captain Pipinos is a gloriously old-school fish taverna. Octopus dishes are a top pick (you'll see them drying), as is anything with fresh fish.

ℹ Information

From the ferry quay, go right along the waterfront. The main street, Agora, heads inland just by the Anarghyros Restaurant, and you'll find most services you need here, including groceries and banks. To reach the central square turn left at the top of the main street and then right. See www.antiparos.gr for more information.

There are several tour and travel agencies, including **Oliaris Tours** (☑ 22840 61231; www.

LEFKES ΛΕΥΚΕΣ

Lovely Lefkes clings to a natural amphitheatre amid hills whose summits are dotted with old windmills. Siesta is taken seriously here and the village has a general air of serenity. Just 9km southeast of Parikia on the cross-island road, it was the capital of Paros during the Middle Ages. The village's main attraction is wandering through its pristine alleyways. Consider walking here on the Byzantine path (p198) east to Marpissa.

The **Cathedral of Agia Triada** is an impressive structure with unique bell towers. On the square in front of the cathedral is **Kafeneio tis Marigos** (☎22840 44014; Lefkes; snacks from €4; ☺9am-late), a delightfully retro cafe run by Kostas serving up mama-made meatballs and cakes. The old photos inside are fascinating.

Out on the main road, the **Lefkes Ceramic Workshop** (☎22840 43255; ☺10am-midnight) features Kostas Fifas and his award-winning crackle-style ceramics. The style, passed down by Kostas' father, is unique and you can watch him at work and purchase his finished products.

antiparostravel.gr), where you can ask about the local bus.

ⓘ Getting There & Away

In summer, frequent small passenger boats depart for Antiparos from Parikia (€5), and numerous operators offer day cruises taking in the beaches of both islands, departing from Parikia, Pounta, Aliki and Naoussa.

There's also a regular car ferry that runs from Pounta on the west coast of Paros to Antiparos (one-way €1.10, per scooter €1.40, per car €5.90, one or two services hourly, 10 minutes). You can take a car rented on Paros to Antiparos on this ferry.

ⓘ Getting Around

A bus service runs from the port to the cave, and another services the east-coast beaches as far as Agios Georgios; tickets cost €1.80. The schedule varies with the season; in theory, buses run from April to September.

Wheels can be hired from **Aggelos** (☎22840 61626; http://antiparosrentacar.com), the first office as you come from the ferry quay. Cars start at about €40 per day (high season), scooters €15 and bicycles €5.

NAXOS ΝΑΞΟΣ

POP 18,900

The largest of the Cyclades, Naxos packs a lot of bang for its buck. Its main city of Hora (known also as Naxos) has a gorgeous waterfront and a web of cobbled alleys below its hilltop *kastro*, all filled with the hubbub of tourism and shopping. You needn't travel far, though, to find isolated beaches, atmospheric mountain villages and ancient sites.

Naxos was a cultural centre of Classical Greece and Byzantium, and Venetian and Frankish influences also left their mark. Its high mountains form rain clouds, and consequently Naxos is more fertile and green than most of the other Cyclades islands. It produces olives, grapes, figs, citrus fruit, corn and potatoes. Mt Zeus (also known as Mt Zas; 1004m) is the Cyclades' highest peak and is the central focus of the island's mountainous interior, where you will find enchanting villages such as Halki and Apiranthos.

ⓘ Getting There & Away

BOAT

Like Paros, Naxos is something of a ferry hub in the Cyclades, with a similar number of conventional and fast ferries making regular calls to/from Piraeus, plus links to/from the mainland port of Rafina via the northern Cyclades.

AIR

There are daily flights to/from Athens (€95, 45 minutes) with **Olympic Air** (www.olympicair.com).

ⓘ Getting Around

TO/FROM THE AIRPORT

The **airport** (JNX; www.naxos.net/airport) is 3km south of Hora. There's no shuttle bus, but buses to Agios Prokopios Beach and Agia Anna pass close by. A taxi costs €10 to €15 depending on the amount of luggage you have, the time of day and if booked.

BUS

Frequent buses run to Agios Prokopios Beach (€1.60) and Agia Anna (€1.60) from Hora. Seven buses daily serve Filoti (€2.30) via Halki

(€2); five serve Apiranthos (€3.10) via Filoti and Halki; and at least two serve Apollonas (€6.20), Pyrgaki (€2.30) and Melanes (€1.60). There are less frequent departures to other villages.

Buses leave from the end of the ferry quay in Hora; timetables are posted outside the **bus information office** (☑ 22850 22291; www. naxosdestinations.com; Harbour), diagonally left and across the road from the bus stop. You have to buy tickets from the office or from the machine outside (not from the bus driver).

CAR & MOTORCYCLE

August rates for hire cars range from about €45 to €65 per day, and quad bikes from €30. Hire from **Naxos Auto Rent** (☑ 22850 41350; http://naxosautorent.com), **Rental Center** (☑ 22850 23395; www.rentalcenter.com.gr; Plateia Evripeou), **Auto Tour** (☑ 22850 25480; www.naxosrentacar.com) or **Fun Car** (☑ 22850 26084; www.funcarandrides.com).

TAXI

Due to its large size, most visitors to Naxos rely on buses or their own wheels to travel around.

BOAT SERVICES FROM NAXOS

DESTINATION	DURATION	FARE (€)	FREQUENCY
Amorgos	2-6hr	11	2-5 daily
Amorgos*	1hr-1½hr	24	2 daily
Anafi	3¾hr	19	2 weekly
Astypalea	3¾hr	34	5 weekly
Donousa	1-4hr	7	7 weekly (note: not daily)
Folegandros	3hr 10min	17	1 weekly
Folegandros*	2½hr-4hr	49	6 weekly
Ios	1-2hr	14	1-2 daily
Ios*	50min	25	1-2 daily
Iraklia	1-1½hr	7	1-2 daily
Iraklio*	3hr 40min	70	1 daily
Kimolos	4hr 40min	17	1 weekly
Koufonisia	2½hr	8	1-2 daily
Koufonisia*	40-50min	19	1-2 daily
Milos	6hr	21	1 weekly
Milos*	3½-5½hr	59	6 weekly
Mykonos	2½hr	18	1 daily
Mykonos*	40min-1½hr	29	4-5 daily
Paros	50hr	10	4-5 daily
Paros*	30min	16	3 daily
Piraeus	5¼hr	34	2-4 daily
Piraeus*	3½hr	57	2 daily
Rafina	6hr	32	1 daily
Rafina*	4hr	52	2 daily
Santorini (Thira)	2hr	19	1-2 daily
Santorini (Thira)*	1hr 35min	38	4-5 daily
Schinousa	1¼hr-2hr	7	1-2 daily
Sikinos	2hr 20min	13	1 weekly
Syros	3h 10min	15	1 weekly
Tinos*	2hr	29	2 daily

* high-speed services

Note: journey times vary with vessel type and routing.

Naxos

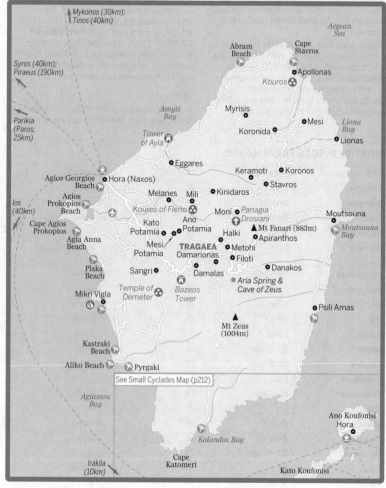

Taxis (☑ 22850 22444) are an option for shorter trips (eg Hora to Agios Prokopios Beach or Agia Anna for around €10). Taxis cluster at the port, or you can call one.

Hora (Naxos) Χώρα (Νάξος)

POP 6700

Hora has the colour and bustle you'd expect of the island's port and capital. Settled on the west coast, the old town is a tangle of steep footpaths and is divided into two historic Venetian neighbourhoods: Bourgos, where the Greeks lived, and the hilltop Kastro, where the Roman Catholics lived.

Despite being fairly large, Hora can still be easily managed on foot. It's almost impossible not to get lost in the old town, however, and maps are of little use.

◉ Sights

★ Kastro

AREA

The most alluring part of Hora is the 13th-century residential neighbourhood of Kastro, which Marco Sanudo made the capital of his duchy in 1207. Behind the waterfront, get lost in the narrow alleyways scrambling up to its spectacular hilltop location. Venetian mansions survive in the centre of Kastro, and you can see the remnants of the castle, the **Tower of Sanoudos**. To see the Bourgos area of the old town, head into the winding backstreets behind the northern end of Paralia.

★ **Temple of Apollo** ARCHAEOLOGICAL SITE
(The Portara) FREE From Naxos Town harbour, a causeway leads to the Palatia islet and the striking, unfinished Temple of Apollo, Naxos' most famous landmark (also known as the Portara, or 'Doorway'). Simply two marble columns with a crowning lintel, it makes an arresting sight, and people gather at sunset for splendid views.

Della Rocca-Barozzi Venetian Museum MUSEUM
(☑ 22850 22387; www.naxosfestival.com; €5; ⊙ 10am-10pm) This atmospheric museum is in a handsome old tower house of the 13th century, within the *kastro* ramparts (by the northwest gate). Wander through the rooms to see how the original Italian aristocrat owners lived, what they wore and how they furnished their rooms. There are changing art exhibitions in the vaults. Concerts (p207) and other events are frequently staged in the museum and its grounds.

Agios Georgios Beach BEACH
Conveniently just south of the waterfront is sandy Agios Georgios, Naxos' town beach. It's backed by hotels and tavernas at the town end (where it can get crowded), but it runs for some way to the south, where you can spread out a little. Its shallow waters make it great for families.

Mitropolis Museum MUSEUM
(☑ 22850 24151; Plateia Mitropolis; ⊙ 8.30am-3pm Tue-Sun) FREE Behind the northern end of the waterfront are several churches and chapels, as well as the Mitropolis Museum. It features fragments of a Mycenaean city (13th–11th centuries BC) that was abandoned because of the threat of flooding. Glass panels underfoot reveal ancient foundations.

Archaeological Museum MUSEUM
(☑ 22850 22725; Kastro; adult/child €3/free; ⊙ 8.30am-3pm Tue-Sun) This museum in Kastro is housed in the former Jesuit school where novelist Nikos Kazantzakis was briefly a pupil. It's slightly musty but contains fascinating finds from the Ionic and Doric eras, and some splendid Early Cycladic marble figurines.

Folk Museum Collection MUSEUM
(☑ 22850 25561; www.naxosfolkmuseum.com; Old Market St; €3; ⊙ 10am-2pm & 7-10pm) This small but well-curated collection gives a digestible account of the elements that make Naxos' history special: succinct displays cover farming, bee-keeping, weaving, bread-making, winemaking and cheese production. It's a privately owned collection and worth a stop.

🏃 Activities & Tours

★ **Naxos Bike** CYCLING
(☑ 22850 25887, 6932795125; www.naxosbikes.com; bike hire per day from €10) Get all of your equipment here, from electric-, road-, mountain- and trekking-bikes to children's seats. Local expert Giannis knows everything there is to know about bikes, and can set you up with maps to get you exploring. He also leads three-hour tours (per person €30, minimum two people).

Flisvos Sport Club WINDSURFING
(☑ 22850 24308; www.flisvos-sportclub.com; Agios Georgios Beach) Well-organised beach club offering a range of windsurfing courses (one-hour private lesson from €40), catamaran sailing (one-hour rental from €40) and mountain-bike rental (from €15 per day). It also has a cool cafe, accommodation and the options of beach volleyball, a fitness centre and yoga.

Naxos Horse Riding HORSE RIDING
(☑ 6948809142; www.naxoshorseriding.com; 2/3hr ride €45/55; ⊙ Mon-Sat) Organises daily morning, afternoon and sunset horse rides inland and on beaches. Staff can arrange pick-up and return to and from the stables. Beginners, young children and advanced riders are all catered for.

Naxos Tours TOURS
(☑ 22850 24000; www.naxostours.net; island bus tour adult/child €30/15; ⊙ 8am-10pm) Call into this agency on the waterfront to find out about its array of tours and excursions, including an island tour by bus, guided walks and daily cruises. There are frequent excursion boats to Delos and Mykonos (adult/child €45/20), Santorini (€55/30), and Iraklia and Koufonisia (€40/20), plus sailing explorations of various parts of Naxos.

Hora (Naxos)

Temple of
Apollo (250m)

Pension Sofi (150m);
Hotel Grotta (350m);
Eggares (8km);
Apollonas (34km)

Amyti
Bay

Bus Information
Office

Bus
Station

8 Mitropoleos
6 Plateia
Kondyli Mitropolis

15 19 16
Agiou
5
Plateia
Mandilara
23
BOURGOS
24

Protopapadaki (Paralia)

10

22
27
Apollonos

Small Cyclades Line
Ferry to Small
Cyclades & Amorgos

18 28
4
25

Kastro
1
7
Kazantzaki

3
Delaroca

Neohytou

Iossif

20

17

Aegean
Sea

21

Protopapadaki (Paralia)

29
9
Plateia
Pigadakia

13
Exarhopoulou

Prantouna

Alexinoros

Dionyssou

26
Papavasiliou

Halki (15km);
Filoti (19km);
Apiranthos (26km)

P

Plateia Evripeou
(Main Square)

P

Agios Georgios

Cemetery

Paparrigopoulou

Anadnis

Odos Komiakis

Aigiou Arseniou

11

14

12
2

Ippokampos
Beachfront
Hotel (50m)

Flisvos Sport Club
(1.2km)

N 0 ———————— 100 m

Hora (Naxos)

🛏 Sleeping

Hora has plenty of accommodation places (the majority open year-round), including numerous options backing the town beach, Agios Georgios. Book early for July and August.

The best campgrounds are at the beaches south of Hora (Agia Anna and Plaka); minibuses from these grounds will meet the ferries.

Despina's Rooms   PENSION €
(☑ 22850 22356; www.despinarooms.gr; Kastro; d €60; ❋ 🛜) Despina has been renting simple, comfy rooms for more than 50 years, and they're a steal. Tucked away in the heart of Kastro (reached with a climb), some have sea views. Rooms on the roof terrace are popular despite their smaller size. There's a communal kitchen.

★ Pension Sofi   PENSION €€
(☑ 22850 23077; www.pensionsofi.gr; r €90; 🅿 ❋ 🛜) Run by members of the friendly Koufopoulos family, guests at Pension Sofi are met with family-made wine or cake and immaculate rooms, each with a freshly renovated bathroom and a basic kitchen. Sofi is a short walk back from the waterfront. Let them know your arrival details for a complimentary pick-up at the port. Rates halve out of high season.

★ Hotel Grotta   HOTEL €€
(☑ 22850 22215; www.hotelgrotta.gr; off Kontoleontos; d incl breakfast €110-135; ❋ 🛜) Located on high ground overlooking the *kastro* and main town, this excellent hotel has immaculate rooms, great sea views from the front, spacious public areas and a cool indoor Jacuzzi area. It's made even better by the cheerful, attentive atmosphere. A rooftop garden bar and complimentary port and airport transfers make Hotel Grotta a top choice.

**Ippokampos
Beachfront Hotel**   BOUTIQUE HOTEL €€
(☑ 22850 24648; www.ippokampos-naxos.com; Agios Georgios Beach; r incl breakfast from €105; ⊙ mid-Apr–mid-Nov; 🅿 ❋ 🛜) Part of a stylish all-white beachfront complex that includes a restaurant-bar, this nine-room hotel offers accommodation kitted out with a dash of panache. Cheaper economy rooms are smaller. All share a fab terrace, and the gorgeous beach is right outside your door.

Nikos Verikokos Studios   HOTEL €€
(☑ 22850 22025; www.nikos-verikokos.com; Naxos Town; s/d/tr €90/100/120; ❋ 🛜) Friendly Nikos maintains these immaculate rooms in the heart of the old town. Some have balconies and sea views, most have little kitchenettes. They offer port pick-up with pre-arrangement.

CYCLADES NAXOS

DRINKING IN THE HISTORY

It was on Naxos that an ungrateful Theseus is said to have abandoned Ariadne after she helped him escape the Cretan labyrinth. She didn't pine long, and was soon entwined with Dionysos, the god of wine and ecstasy, and the island's favourite deity. Naxian wine has long been considered a useful antidote to a broken heart.

Hotel Galini
HOTEL €€

(☑ 22850 22114; www.hotelgalini.com; d incl breakfast from €90; 🕸 🛜) A nautical theme lends this super-friendly place loads of character. Updated, spacious rooms have small balconies and wrought-iron beds, plus great decor creatively fashioned from seashells and driftwood. The location is first-rate – close to the old town and the beach – and the breakfast is hearty.

Hotel Glaros
BOUTIQUE HOTEL €€€

(☑ 22850 23101; www.hotelglaros.com; Agios Georgios Beach; d €150-180; ☺ Apr-Oct; 🕸 @ 🛜) Edgy yet homey, simple yet plush, this well-run and immaculate 13-room hotel has a seaside feel in its boutique fit-out. Service is thoughtful, there's an indoor Jacuzzi, the beach is only a few steps away and it's adults only. Breakfast is €10.

✖ Eating

Hora has fantastic dining. For the freshest seafood, head to the tavernas on the waterfront where the fishermen hang out and sample their catch. Naxian cheeses, sausages and potatoes are also well worth taste-testing.

★ Doukato
GREEK €

(☑ 22850 27013; www.facebook.com/doukato naxos; Old Town; mains from €8; ☺ 6pm-late) In a magical setting that has been a monastery, church and a school, Doukato is capturing plenty of attention on the Naxos dining scene. Its award-winning chef produces top Naxian specialities such as *gouna* (sun-dried mackerel), *kalogeras* (beef, eggplant & cheese) and their unbelievably delicious Doukato 'Special' souvlaki. A lot of pride at the heart of the Old Town.

Anna's Garden Café
CAFE €

(☑ 22850 26774; http://annasorganicnaxos.blog spot.com; Paparrigopoulou; dishes €5-10; ☺ 9am-

2pm & 6-9pm May-Sep; ☑ 🛗) Entirely earthy feeling and 100% organic, Anna's creates a lunchtime dish of the day, driven by local, seasonal produce. Breakfasts are good: think homemade muesli and yoghurt, spelt bread or omelettes. Anna's also supplies picnic baskets if ordered a day in advance.

Labyrinth
GREEK €€

(☑ 22850 22253; mains €10-17; ☺ lunch & dinner) It's a toss-up as to which is more welcoming here: the warm interior or the pretty, private courtyard. Munch through marinated veggies with grilled *manouri* (soft cheese from the north), swordfish with herbs, or seafood risotto with ouzo sauce. The name is apt: it has a sign, but is easiest to find if you enter the winding alleys from the north.

L'Osteria
ITALIAN €€

(☑ 22850 24080; www.osterianaxos.com; mains €10-16; ☺ 7pm-midnight) This authentic Italian eatery is tucked away in a small alley uphill from the harbour, beneath the *kastro* walls. Grab a table in the cute courtyard and prepare to be impressed: the appetising menu changes daily, but there's also an unchanging list of bruschetta, salads and delectable antipasti.

O Apostolis
GREEK €€

(☑ 22850 26777; Old Market St; mains €8-15; ☺ lunch & dinner) Right at the heart of labyrinthine Bourgos, O Apostolis serves up tasty dishes in its pretty flagstone courtyard. The *kleftiko* (lamb wrapped in filo pastry), with sautéed vegetables and feta cheese, is delicious.

Meze 2
SEAFOOD €€

(☑ 22850 26401; mains €6-15; ☺ lunch & dinner) It would be easy to dismiss this waterfront restaurant at the harbour as a tourist trap, but don't. Its Cretan and Naxian menu and fantastic service make it stand out from the bunch. The seafood is superb – try squid stuffed with local cheese, grilled sardines, or mussels in ouzo and garlic.

🍷 Drinking & Nightlife

There are a few large, louder clubs at the southern end of the waterfront, and some great bars offering big views and cocktails from upper floors along the waterfront.

★ The Rum Bar
BAR

(☑ 6948592718; ☺ 8pm-late) Perched upstairs above Hora's busy waterfront, this newbie has lovely sunset views looking out over the yacht harbour. Open year-round, Rum Bar plays rock classics and occasionally features live music. Original cocktails are the name of the game here – try the Isla Tropical, which includes a healthy dose of Naxos *kitron*.

Naxos Cafe
BAR

(☑ 22850 26343; Old Market St; ⊘ 8pm-2am) If you want to drink but don't fancy the club scene, here's your answer. This atmospheric, traditional bar is small and candlelit and spills into the cobbled Bourgos street. Drink Naxian wine with the locals.

520
BAR

(☑ 6976251135; ⊘ 9am-late) With a deck overlooking the harbour, this cool, comfortable bar whips up the most divine cocktails. Have breakfast, read a newspaper or party – it's all possible in this chic, cushioned interior.

La Vigne
WINE BAR

(☑ 22850 27199; www.lavignenaxos.com; ⊘ 7pm-1am) For a relaxed take on Naxian nightlife, head for this cheerful wine bar just behind Plateia Mandilara. It's run by two French expats who know more than a thing or two about fine wines and good conversation. Excellent fusion food too.

Citron Cafe
CAFE

(☑ 22850 27055; Protopapadaki; ⊘ 8am-late) You can begin your day on a sofa here, with coffee and a harbour view, and end it with a glass of local wine or *kitron* (liqueur made from the leaves of the citron tree) from Halki's distillery (p208). Check out the *kitron*-based cocktails (€6) for local flavour.

DaCosta
CLUB

(☑ 6975939104) Right behind the port police, this sleek club brings well-known guest DJs from Athens to play dance music into the wee hours. All white and wood and chic, it has a loungy feel, which gives you somewhere to relax while you contemplate the well-stocked bar.

☆ Entertainment

★ Della Rocca-
Barozzi Venetian Museum
LIVE MUSIC

(☑ 22850 22387; www.naxosfestival.com; Kastro; event admission €15-20; ⊘ 8pm Apr-Oct) Special evening cultural events are held outside at the museum, almost nightly in summer. Posters around town advertise what's on the horizon. It may be traditional music and dance concerts, classical piano recitals, bouzouki, or jazz and blues. There may even

be screenings of *Zorba the Greek*. There's an inside venue on the off-chance it rains.

🛍 Shopping

Kohili Jewels
GIFTS & SOUVENIRS

(☑ 22850 22557; ⊘ 10am-11pm) Hidden in the maze of small streets behind the waterfront, Kohili is chock-full of goodies. This is a good spot to purchase jewellery made from the Eye of Naxos, the hard shell that develops in the hole of a shellfish. The eye in the beautiful rings, necklaces, earrings and bracelets is said to bring good luck and fortune.

Papyrus Jewellery & Used Books
BOOKS

(☑ 22850 23039) What began as a box of books left by a traveller has turned into a shockingly organised collection of over 10,000 second-hand books, covering multiple languages and genres. It's uphill from the port, behind Meze 2.

Kiriakos Tziblakis
FOOD & DRINKS

(☑ 22850 22230; Papavasiliou) The pungent aromas will bowl you over as soon as you get through the door of this colourful wonderland, a family store dating from 1938. It's where locals come to buy bulk spices, olives, honey and cheese, and it's crammed with a photogenic jumble of local produce and goods, from pots to brushes, soaps to ouzo and raki.

Zoom
BOOKS

(☑ 22850 23675; Paralia; ⊘ 10am-10pm) A large, well-stocked newsagent and bookshop that has most international newspapers the day after publication and perhaps the best collection of postcards in Greece.

ℹ Information

There's no official tourist office on Naxos. Travel agencies can deal with most queries. Handy online resources include www.naxos.gr.

Alpha Bank (cnr Paralia & Papavasiliou) Has an ATM.

Hospital (☑ 22850 23550; Prantouna) On the eastern edge of town.

Information Booth At the ferry quay in summer. Opens when ferries arrive.

National Bank of Greece (Paralia) Has an ATM.

Naxos Tours (☑ 22850 24000; www.naxos tours.net; Paralia; ⊘ 8am-10pm) Sells ferry tickets and organises accommodation, excursions and car hire.

Police Station (☑ 22850 22100; Paparrigopoulou) Southeast of Plateia Evripeou.

Post Office (Agios Georgios) Go past the OTE, across Papavasiliou, and left at the forked road.
Zas Travel (☑ 22850 23330; www.zastravel. com; ☉ 9am-9pm) Sells ferry tickets and organises accommodation, tours and car hire. Shorter hours in winter. Located on the harbourfront.

Around Naxos

Southwest Beaches

Beaches south of Agios Georgios (Hora's town beach) include beautiful **Agios Proko-pios**, which is sandy and shallow and lies in a sheltered bay to the south of the headland of Cape Mougkri. It merges with **Agia Anna**, a stretch of white sand, quite narrow but long enough to feel uncrowded. Development is fairly solid at Prokopios and the northern end of Agia Anna.

Sandy beaches continue as far as Pyrgaki, passing the beautiful turquoise waters of the long, dreamy **Plaka Beach** and gorgeous sandy bays punctuated with rocky outcrops. You'll find plenty of restaurants, accommodation and bus stops along this stretch – it's an idyllic place for a chilled-out beach stay. **Maragas Beach Camping** (☑ 22850 42552; www.maragascamping.gr; Agia Anna Beach; campsites per adult/tent €9/2, d/studio from €40/€60) has a good set-up across from a long sandy

---

DON'T MISS

LOCAL LIQUEUR

The citron fruit (Citrus medica) looks like a very large, lumpy lemon and is barely edible in its raw state. The rind is quite flavoursome when preserved in syrup, however, and *kitron*, a strong liqueur made from citron leaves, has been a hallmark of Naxos since the late 19th century.

Leaves are collected from October to February, dried, dampened and distilled up to three times with water and sugar. Dye is then added to mark its strength: yellow is the strongest and green is the lightest and sweetest. Clear is somewhere in the middle.

Visit the **Vallindras Distillery** (☑ 22850 31220; ☉ 10am-10pm Jul & Aug, to 6pm May-Jun & Sep-Oct) in Halki to sample all three, or try **Citron Cafe** (p207) in Hora.

---

strand south of Agia Anna: camping, studios and rooms, a supermarket and a taverna. There's a regular bus from Hora that stops out front.

At **Mikri Vigla** (http://mikrivigla.com), golden granite slabs and boulders divide the beach into two. This beach is becoming an increasingly big fish on the kitesurfing scene, with reliable wind conditions. **Flisvos Kite Centre** (☑ 6945457407; www. flisvos-kitecentre.com) offers kite- and windsurfing classes and rents equipment to certified surfers. You can stay next door at **Orkos Beach Hotel** (☑ 22850 75194; www.orkosbeach. gr; s/d/apt incl breakfast €75/105/166; ☉ mid-May–Sep; ✳ ☎ ✿), where rooms are clean and comfy but will hardly see you as you'll be too busy on the beach.

Halki   Χάλκη
POP 480

This village is a vivid reflection of historic Naxos, with the handsome facades of old villas and tower houses a legacy of its wealthy past as the island's long-ago capital. Today it's home to a small but fascinating collection of shops and galleries, drawing artists and culinary wizards. Halki lies at the heart of the Tragaea mountainous region, about 20 minutes' drive (15km) from Hora.

The main road skirts Halki, with parking areas near the entry (from Hora) and exit of town (the latter by the schoolyard). Pedestrian lanes lead off the main road to the picturesque square at the heart of Halki.

Paths radiate from Halki through peaceful olive groves and flower-filled meadows. The atmospheric 11th-century **Church of St Georgios Diasorites** lies a short distance to the north of the village. It contains some splendid frescoes.

◉ Sights

Fish & Olive   GALLERY
(☑ 22850 31771; www.fish-olive-creations.com; ☉ May–mid-Oct) This gallery displays the exquisite work of Naxian potter Katharina Bolesch and her partner, artist and craftsman Alexander Reichardt. Each piece of work reflects ancient Mediterranean themes of fish and olives, motifs that frame the edges of shining plates, tumble down the sides of elegant jugs and bowls and dart across platters. The artists' work has been exhibited nationally and internationally. There's also a boutique selling their works a few metres from the gallery.

TRAGAEA & MT ZEUS

Naxos' lovely inland Tragaea (Τραγαία) region is a vast plain of olive groves and unspoilt villages high in the mountains, harbouring numerous little Byzantine churches. The Cyclades' highest peak, Mt Zeus (1004m; also known as Mt Zas), dominates the landscape. Filoti, on the slopes of Mt Zeus, is the region's largest village.

To climb Mt Zeus from Filoti, walk 40 minutes up to Aria Spring, a verdant fountain and picnic area, carry on another 20 minutes to the Cave of Zeus, and then climb to the summit in another 45 minutes.

Alternatively, if you have a car and want to shorten the walk, there's a junction signposted to Aria Spring and Zas Cave, about 800m up from Filoti on the main road. This side road ends after 1.3km. From the road-end parking it's a short walk to Aria Spring, and you can carry on to the cave and summit from there.

An option for the descent, if you hike up via the cave, is to walk down via the little chapel of Agia Marina to Filoti. You can walk down this route on waymarked track Number 2 in about 1½ hours.

Make sure to take good walking shoes, water and sunscreen.

Phos Gallery GALLERY
(☑ 22850 31118; www.phosgallery.gr; ⊙ May-Oct) See the island through the lens of talented photographer Dimitris Gavalas. Stunning landscapes – mostly of Naxos – grace the walls of this gallery, along with a handful of conceptual prints.

 Eating

Dolce Vita BAKERY, CAFE €
(☑ 6981467240; snacks €3-7; ⊙ breakfast, lunch & dinner) Cool and inviting, with dark wood and a gramophone daring to be wound, this is the place to lounge over homemade baking, coffee and ice cream.

Giannis Taverna TAVERNA €
(☑ 22850 31214; dishes €5-12; ⊙ lunch & dinner) With tables filling Halki's pretty central square under a leafy overhang, Giannis is well known for traditional fare. Try moussaka, pork souvlaki, savoury pies or village sausage.

Il Basilico ITALIAN €€
(☑ 22859 31140; mains €10-25; ⊙ dinner Jun-Sep) Near the entrance to Halki coming from Hora, this lively restaurant offers an excellent, changing menu, sourcing ingredients daily. The garden patio and colourful tiles add to the atmosphere (as do the excellent Italian wines).

Shopping

Penelope ARTS & CRAFTS
(☑ 22850 31754) The know-how has been passed down to Penelope through at least four generations, and her fingers and feet fly on the loom. Watch her incorporate traditional designs into hats, scarves, bags and tablecloths that make fab souvenirs. You'll notice a lot of red and blue – the traditional colours of Naxos.

Era Jam Workshop FOOD
(☑ 22859 31009) A visit to this shop gives you a peek into the open workshop where more than 20kg of delicious marmalade, jam and spoon desserts are made every day. This stuff is only sold on the island; taste it while you can!

Panagia Drosiani
Παναγία Δροσιανή

Located 2.5km north of Halki, just below Moni, the small, peaceful **Panagia Drosiani** (donations appreciated; ⊙ 10am-7pm May–mid-Oct) is among the oldest and most revered churches in Greece. Inside is a series of cave-like chapels. In the darkest chapels, monks and nuns secretly taught Greek language and religion to local children during the Turkish occupation. Several frescoes still grace the walls, and date from the 7th century. Look for the depiction of Mary in the eastern chapter; the clarity and expression is incredible.

Sangri
Σαγκρί

Temple of Demeter TEMPLE
(Dimitra's Temple) About 2km south of the village of Sangri is the 6th-century BC Temple of Demeter. The ruins and reconstructions are not large, but they are historically interesting. Demeter was the goddess of grain,

and temples were built to her in fertile areas such as the valley running south from Sangri; the remains were discovered in 1949. Signs point the way from Sangri.

Bazeos Tower
TOWER

(✆ 22850 31402; www.bazeostower.gr) The handsome Bazeos Tower stands prominently in the landscape about 2km east of Sangri. It was built in its original form as a monastery during the 17th century, and was later bought by the Bazeos family, whose modern descendants have refurbished the building with skill and imagination. The castle now functions as a cultural centre and stages art exhibitions and the annual Naxos Festival in July and August, when concerts, plays and literary readings are held.

Melanes   Μέλανες

Sights

Marble Quarries
LANDMARK

The area between Melanes and Kinidaros has been the island's marble quarry since ancient times. Marble is still collected from this region, and you'll see sides of the mountains sliced open and looking like huge slabs of feta.

Kouros of Flerio
MONUMENT

In Flerio, near Mili, is an ancient marble-working area. There remain two examples of *kouroi*, large marble statues created in the 7th and 6th centuries BC. Each measures about 5.5m and both are in a broken state (the theory being that they were damaged during transportation or were simply left unfinished by dissatisfied sculptors). The first *kouros* you come to is lying on its back under a tree; the second is on a hillside about 800m away.

Eggares Olive Press
MUSEUM

(✆ 22850 62021; www.olivemuseum.com; ⊙ 9am-6pm May-Sep) FREE A worthy side-trip is to this sweet set-up in the village of Eggares, 7km from Hora. A guide explains the workings of this small olive press (in operation from 1850 to 1960), and there are free tastings of olive-based products. The store here sells oil, pastes, soaps and unguents, plus cake and coffee.

Apiranthos   Απείρανθος

Apiranthos seems to grow out of the stony flanks of rugged Mt Fanari (883m), about 25km east of Hora (or 10 winding kilometres

from Halki). The village's unadorned stone houses and marble-paved streets reflect a rugged individualism that is matched by the villagers themselves. Many of them are descendants of refugees who migrated from Crete, and today the village's distinctive form of the Greek language has echoes of the 'Great Island'. Apiranthos people have always been noted for their spirited politics and populism, and the village has produced a remarkable number of academics. These days, the village is peppered with quirky shops, galleries and cafes, and it's a lovely place to spend an afternoon.

Eating

Taverna O Platanos
GREEK €

(✆ 22850 61192; mains €6-13; ⊙ lunch & dinner) Set beneath the shade of its namesake plane tree, this lively family restaurant serves up everything from yoghurt and homemade cheeses to grilled local meat. Try the hearty traditional dish of 'rosto' pork in tomato sauce. They've also got seating on a terrace with glorious views out over the valley – and some intriguing old weaponry on display.

Lefteris
GREEK €€

(✆ 22850 61333; www.stoulefteri.gr; mains €10-22; ⊙ lunch & dinner May-Oct) With a deck taking in a phenomenal view, this charming, well-regarded place has the look and feel of an old country kitchen. Not much has changed here in a while! The short menu homes in on local cheeses and grilled meats – try lamb, steak or a burger stuffed with cheese and tomato.

The North

Heading north from the mountains inland, the roads wind and twist like spaghetti, eventually taking you to the somewhat scrappy seaside village of **Apollonas**. In an ancient quarry on the hillside above the village is a colossal 7th-century BC **kouros**, much larger and easier to find than the Kouros of Flerio. Follow the small signs to get here.

Apollonas' beach isn't great but the seafood is. Tavernas line the waterfront and serve the freshest of fish.

A worthy side-trip is to **Lionas**, where a scenic 8km drive past old emery mines leads you to a lovely stony beach and a couple of tavernas. **Delfinaki** (✆ 22850 51290; www.delfinaki.gr; Lionas; mains from €8) is super-friendly, serving up great home cooking and farm-fresh ingredients. Vassiliki, the hostess, sells home-made jams, 'spoon sweets' and wines.

With your own transport you can return to Hora via the northwest-coast road, passing through wild and sparsely populated country with awe-inspiring sea views. En route, stop for a look at the **Tower of Ayia**, the majestic ruins of a castle with a spectacular ocean backdrop.

SMALL CYCLADES
ΜΙΚΡΕΣ ΚΥΚΛΑΔΕΣ

The tiny islands that lie between Naxos and Amorgos are like miniature outposts of calm. In the days of antiquity, all were densely populated, revealed by the large number of ancient graves that have been uncovered. During the Middle Ages, only wild goats and even wilder pirates inhabited these islands. Post-independence, intrepid souls from Naxos and Amorgos recolonised the Small Cyclades, and today four have permanent populations – Iraklia, Schinousa, Ano Koufonisi and Donousa. Recently, the islands have welcomed a growing number of independent-minded tourists.

The Small Cyclades are officially under the administration of Naxos. Donousa is the northernmost of the group and the furthest from Naxos; the others are clustered near the larger island's southeast coast.

ⓘ Getting There & Away

There are several connections a week between Piraeus and the Small Cyclades via Naxos, and daily connections to/from Naxos. The Small Cyclades are off most tourists' radars, and unplanned old-fashioned island-hopping is still possible here outside high season; you'll have no problem finding a room at a reasonable rate. Make sure to book ahead for high season, though. For ferry schedules, visit http://ferries.gr.

Blue Star Ferries (www.bluestarferries.gr) serves the Small Cyclades year-round. It has two routes, both beginning in Piraeus and calling at Paros and Naxos. From Naxos, three times a week the ferry calls at Donousa, then Amorgos (Aegiali) and terminates at Astypalea (in the Dodecanese). Three times a week from Naxos the ferry stops at Iraklia, Schinousa and Koufonisia before terminating at Amorgos (Katapola).

The **Small Cyclades Line** runs the mainstay service, weather permitting in winter. Their sturdy little *Express Skopelitis* has been plying these waters for 35 years and is due for retirement. It is expected a new vessel will be ready

for the 2018 season, but don't be surprised to see the *Skopelitis* back. It leave from Naxos in the afternoon daily Monday to Saturday, and calls at the Small Cyclades and Amorgos (often to both ports, Aegiali and Katapola). It then returns to Naxos early the following morning.

Iraklia   Ηρακλεία
POP 140

Iraklia is only 19 sq km in area, a little Aegean gem dozing in the sun. Dump the party gear and spurn the nightlife, the sightseeing and the souvenir shops. Instead, brace yourself for a serene and quiet life, and Iraklia will not disappoint. Only in July and August will you have to share the idyll with like-minded others.

The port and main village of Iraklia is **Agios Georgios**. It has an attractive cove-like harbour, complete with a sandy beach.

Boat Services from Iraklia

DESTINATION	DURATION	FARE (€)	FREQUENCY
Amorgos	1¾-4¾hr	8	1-2 daily
Donousa	2¼hr	8	3 weekly
Koufonisia	55min	5	1-2 daily
Naxos	1hr-1½hr	7	1-2 daily
Paros	2¼hr	12	3 weekly
Piraeus	8hr	35	3 weekly
Schinousa	10min	4	1-2 daily

◎ Sights & Activities

A surfaced road leads off to the left of the ferry quay, and after about 1km you'll reach **Livadi**, the island's best beach. A steep 2.5km further on is **Hora** (also called Panagia). From Hora, a surfaced road carries on to **Tourkopigado Beach**.

Walking

There are well-marked hiking trails of varying length all over the island. Get a map, make sure to take plenty of water.

Follow tracks 7, 4 and 3 from Agios Georgios to get to the **Cave of the Sacred Icon of Agios Giannis** in about two hours. Alternatively, follow track 3 from Hora to get there in one hour.

Beyond the cave, a path leads to the beach at Alimina, which is also served by **boat** (☑ 22850 71145; ⊙ Jun-Sep) from Agios Georgios in summer (offering a shortcut to the cave).

Small Cyclades

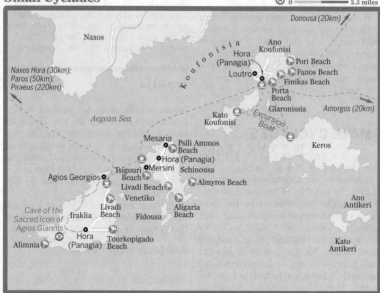

For a shorter walk from Agios Georgios, take track 8 for 30 minutes to reach the gorgeous cove of **Vorini Spilla** and a refreshing swim.

🛏 Sleeping

Maïstrali ROOMS €

(☑ 22850 71807; www.bluehotels.gr; r from €60; 🛜) In Agios Georgios, a few hundred metres up from the port, Maïstrali offers a range of simple, good-value rooms and apartments with rates that tumble to €30 out of high season. It also features a shady elevated terrace **taverna** that has all the Greek standards covered and is open for breakfast, lunch and dinner. A good budget option.

Anna's Place PENSION €

(☑ 22850 74234; www.annasplace.gr; d/q €60/80; ❄🛜) Located on high ground above the port is this lovely, well-run complex, set in pretty gardens and with balconies taking in sweeping views. Inside, each super-clean, comfortable room has a kitchenette; some are well suited to families. Transfers from and to the port are complimentary.

Speires Hotel BOUTIQUE HOTEL €€

(☑ 22850 77015; www.speires.gr; d incl breakfast €125; ☉ May-Oct; ❄🛜) This stylish boutique is a short walk uphill from the port, with white decor and flash bathrooms with all the mod-cons. Superior double rooms can fit a family. The terrace at the elegant on-site **cafe** and **wine bar** is a fine place to engage in a toast to holidaymaking.

🍷 Drinking & Nightlife

⭐ **En Lefko** CAFE

(☑ 22850 77027; www.facebook.com/en.leuko. iraklia; ☉ 9am-late May-Sep) This rooftop bar on top of Perigiali Supermarket is lovingly run by a local couple. There are brunch menus plus cocktails, drinks and snacks until the wee hours. One of few options in Iraklia if you feel the urge to have a late night.

❶ Information

There is an ATM by the harbour beach.

Schinousa Σχοινούσα

POP 250

Like its neighbours, Schinousa has an easy-going pace and a sense of timelessness, although high season can be lively. With an area of only 8.5 sq km, it has a gentle landscape and is known for its beaches.

The major settlement **Hora (Panagia)** has a long, narrow main street lying along the breezy crest of the island. Ferries dock at the fishing harbour of **Mersini**. Hora is a 1km walk uphill from there.

Boat Services from Schinousa

DESTINATION	DURATION	FARE (€)	FREQUENCY
Amorgos	1½-4½hr	7	1-2 daily
Donousa	2hr	7	3 weekly
Iraklia	10min	4	1-2 daily
Koufonisia	30min	5	1-2 daily
Naxos	1hr 20min	7	1-2 daily
Paros	2hr 35min	13	3 weekly
Piraeus	8½hr	35	3 weekly

⊙ Sights & Activities

Dirt tracks lead from Hora to beaches around the coast. The nearest are sandy **Tsigouri** and **Livadi**, both uncrowded outside August. Haul a little further southeast to decent beaches at **Almyros** with its shallow water and the small bays of **Aligaria**. Tsigouri, Livadi and Almyros have tavernas and/or beach bars. Just east of Mesaria in the north is **Psili Ammos** beach, good when a southerly is blowing.

Aeolia   BOATING
(☑ 6979618233; boat trip €15-35) From June to September, the Aeolia tour boat runs various daily trips, including around the beaches of the island, or to Iraklia and Koufonisia. Private trips can also be arranged. Ask about the week's schedule where you are staying.

🛏 Sleeping & Eating

There are rooms down at Mersini (the port) and plenty of options in Hora. Domatia owners, with transport, meet ferries from about May onwards and will always meet booked guests. Book ahead in July and August.

★ Meltemi   PENSION €€
(☑ 22850 71947; www.pension-meltemi.gr; d €70-80; ❄ 🛜) Warm hospitality is the hallmark of this family-run pension and restaurant in the heart of Hora. Rooms are comfy and simple. You have a choice between older rooms in the Meltemi 1 building or newer rooms in Meltemi 2. Both are good. The on-site restaurant serves up delicious homemade meals. Free port and beach transfers too!

Iliovasilema   HOTEL €€
(☑ 22850 71948; www.iliovasilemahotel.gr; Hora; d incl breakfast €80; ☺ mid-May–Sep; ❄ 🛜) In

Hora, but perched at the port end of town with king-of-the-castle sunset views (*iliovaselima* means sunset), rooms here are small, simple and spotless. The views out towards Iraklia from the balconies are fab, and the service is warm. Rates include a good buffet breakfast.

Kafe stou Peri   CAFE €
(☑ 22850 76030; dishes €2-8; ☺ 7am-late) Open year-round, this colourful and friendly little cafe on the main street of Hora has crêpes, waffles, sandwiches and fresh salads, as well as breakfast options. There is also a well-stocked bar that keeps things pumping in the evening.

★ Fish Tavern & Rooms Mersini   SEAFOOD €€
(☑ 22850 71159; www.mersini.gr; mains €8-18; ☺ May-Sep; ❄ 🛜) Down at the port, Mersini woos diners with a stylish white fit-out, in a garden setting with great harbour views. It seals the deal with excellent seafood (especially squid). The five chic all-white rooms behind the taverna are some of the nicest on the island (double €80 to €100). Straight ahead 200m from the quay.

Deli Restaurant & Cafe-Bar   GREEK €€
(☑ 22850 74278; restaurant mains €15-25; ☺ lunch & dinner Mar-Oct) Deli's upper floor features a top-notch restaurant with views out to Ios and Iraklia, while the ground floor houses a cool cafe-bar. On offer upstairs is a gourmet menu from the Cretan owner-chef using locally sourced ingredients, plus a wine list boasting some fine Greek vintages. Downstairs you'll find homemade sweets, coffees, drinks and cocktails and a cool crew.

ⓘ Information

For more information see www.schinousa.com and www.naxos.gr.

There's an ATM outside Hora's Paralos Travel.
Paralos Travel (☑ 22850 71160; sparalos@ otenet.gr) Halfway along Hora's main street. It sells ferry tickets and also doubles as the post office and newsagent in season.

Koufonisia   Κουφονήσια
POP 400

Koufonisia's star is on the rise; it is becoming a fashionable island for in-the-know visitors and is referred to by locals as 'the Mykonos of the Small Cyclades'.

BOAT SERVICES FROM KOUFONISIA

DESTINATION	DURATION	FARE (€)	FREQUENCY
Amorgos	40min-3½hr	7	1-2 daily
Amorgos*	25min	14	1-2 daily
Donousa	1hr 10min	6	3 weekly
Folegandros*	2¼-5½hr	69	6 weekly
Iraklia	50min	5	1-2 daily
Milos*	3¼hr-6½hr	69	6 weekly
Mykonos*	1hr 40min	55	3 weekly
Naxos	2-2½hr	7	1-2 daily
Naxos*	40-50min	19	1-2 daily
Paros	3hr 20min	19	3 weekly
Paros*	1hr 25min	30	1 daily
Piraeus	9hr	35	3 weekly
Piraeus*	4¼hr-5hr	59	1-3 daily
Santorini*	1-4hr	50	6 weekly
Schinousa	30min	5	1-2 daily
Serifos*	2hr	48	1 daily
Sifnos*	1½hr	45	1 daily

* high-speed services

It's made up of three main islands, two of which, Kato Koufonisi and Keros, are uninhabited. The three cover a total of 26 sq km. You'll arrive at the populated, low-lying **Ano Koufonisi**. It sees a flash-flood of tourism each summer thanks to its superb beaches, good hotels and chic restaurants, and it welcomes a growing number of summer high-speed ferries from other Cycladic islands. The main street is a joy to wander along.

Still, the island retains its low-key charm, and a substantial fishing fleet sustains a thriving local community outside the fleeting summer season.

☉ Sights

Koufonisia's only settlement spreads out behind the ferry quay. The older part of town, the **Hora**, sprawls along a low hill above the harbour, parallel to the coast, and is one long whitewashed main street lined with restaurants and cafes.

At the western end of the main street, you'll reach **Loutro**, with a stony cove, small boatyard, windmill and whitewashed church.

☉ Other Islands

The flat profile of uninhabited **Kato Koufonisi** is just to the south of Ano Koufonisi and a short caïque ride away. If you've come by ferry from Schinousa, you'll have passed its entire length on your way to Ano Koufonisi. Kato Koufonisi has some beautiful beaches and a lovely church.

East of here is the dramatic **Keros**, a rugged mountain of an island with towering cliffs. Archaeological digs on Keros have uncovered more than 100 Early Cycladic figurines, including the famous harpist and flautist now on display in Athens' National Archaeological Museum.

🏊 Beaches

An easy 2km walk along the sandy coast road east of the port leads to **Porta**, **Finikas** and **Fanos** beaches. All tend to become swamped with grilling bodies in July and August, and nudity becomes more overt the further you go.

Beyond Fano, a walking path leads to several rocky swimming places, including the glorious **Piscina**, a swimming hole surrounded by rock that is linked to the sea. The path then continues to the great bay at **Pori**, where a long crescent of sand slides effortlessly into the dreamy clear sea. Pori can also be reached by an inland road from Hora.

☘ Activities & Tours

Bike Hire
CYCLING

(☑6989637046; per day €4-10) Bike hire is available from this shop at the eastern end of the town beach. Koufonisia is relatively flat, so cycling is a good option. Look for the sign on the end of the building.

Captain Kostas
BOATING

(☑22850 71438, 6945042548; www.roussetos hotel.gr; ☻ Jun-Sep) Head to the marina and hop on Captain Kostas' boat to transfer to/from various beaches around the island (€3-5 return depending on the beach) and Kato Koufonisi (€5 return). There's a ticket kiosk at the port, or inquire at Prasinos travel agency.

Koufonissia Tours
BOATING

(☑22850 74435; www.koufonissiatours.gr; Villa Ostria) Based at Villa Ostria, Koufonissia Tours organises sailing, diving and sea-kayaking trips around Koufonisia and the Small Cyclades.

⛺ Sleeping

★Ermis Rooms
PENSION €€

(☑22850 71693, 6972265240; www.koufonisia. gr/?page_id=1255&lang=en; d €70-80; ❋ ☎) These immaculate rooms are in a quiet location, behind a pretty white-and-lilac exterior and a flowering garden. Ask Sofia for a balcony with sea view. At the port end of the beach, take the road uphill to the left of Roussetos Hotel. Ermis Rooms is next to the pale green post office, also run by Sofia.

Anna Villas
PENSION €€

(☑22850 71697; www.annavillas.gr; d incl breakfast €100; ❋ ☎) In a quiet location, these fresh, bright studios are charming and run with warmth. All have balconies and kitchenettes. It's a family-friendly spot, with a lovely reading nook and summertime cafe. Take the first left after the rental bike sign at the eastern end of the beach and climb the hill. On the left immediately after Villa Ostria.

Villa Ostria
HOTEL €€

(☑22850 71671; www.ostriavilla.gr; r/studio €75/95; ❋ ☎) One of several hotels on the high ground east of the beach, colourful Ostria has attractive rooms and studios with some quirky decor made from seashells and driftwood. Rooms have kitchenettes; spacious studios have kitchens. Take the first left after the rental bike sign at the eastern end of the beach and climb the hill.

✗ Eating & Drinking

Gastronautis
MEDITERRANEAN €

(☑22850 71468; mains €5-10; ☻lunch & dinner May-Sep) Found on the narrow, whitewashed main street, this is one of a new breed of fashionable eateries. There's a beachside-chic interior and a well-priced fusion menu. Try tuna tartar, zucchini cake or pork chops in barbecue sauce.

Karnagio
TAVERNA €

(Loutro; mains from €8; ☻dinner Jun-Sep) This tiny taverna at Loutro, where the tables skirt the small harbour, has a magical setting. *Karnagio* means 'boatyard', and the taverna is owned by the same guy who fixes the boats. Expect good local food and a convivial atmosphere right on the water.

Capetan Nikolas
SEAFOOD €€

(☑22850 71690; Loutro; mains €5-18; ☻dinner May-Oct) One of the best seafood places around, this cheerful restaurant overlooks the harbour at Loutro. Let the welcoming owners show you what's been freshly cooked, or help you select a fish for grilling. The lobster salad is famous and the seafood pasta delicious. Locally caught fish, such as red mullet and sea bream, are priced by the kilogram.

Scholio
BAR

(☑22850 71837; ☻7pm-3am; ☎) A cosy bar and crêperie, Scholio plays to the crowd with jazz, blues or rock. It's at the western end of the main street above Loutro. The owners are accomplished photographers and often have exhibitions of their work on show.

❶ Information

The post office has an ATM; it's up the road to the left of Roussetos Hotel.

For more information, check out www.koufo nisia.net and www.naxos.gr.

Prasinos (☑22850 71438; ☻7am-11pm in summer) sells ferry tickets and tours on Hora's main street.

Donousa
Δονούσα

POP 160

Donousa is the wonderfully out-on-a-limb island where you stop bothering about which day it is. In late July and August the island can be swamped by holidaymaking Greeks and sun-seeking northern Europeans, but out of season be prepared to linger – quietly.

Stavros is Donousa's main settlement and port. It's a cluster of whitewashed buildings around a handsome church, overlooking the ferry quay and a small sandy bay. Little has changed here over the years. There's an excellent **beach**, which also serves as a thoroughfare for foot traffic to a clutch of homes, rental rooms and a taverna on the far side of the sands.

For active types, Donousa offers up plenty to do, with good walking trails and attractive beaches.

Boat Services from Donousa

DESTINATION	DURATION	FARE (€)	FREQUENCY
Amorgos	40min-2¼hr	8	1-2 daily
Astypalea	2hr 20min	14	3 weekly
Iraklia	2hr	7	3 weekly
Koufonisia	1hr	5	3 weekly
Naxos	1hr 10min-3hr 40min	7	1 daily
Paros	2hr 25min	16	3 weekly
Piraeus	9hr 10min	35	3 weekly
Schinousa	1hr 50min	7	3 weekly

⊙ Sights

Kendros, 1.25km southeast of Stavros, best reached by a stepped track, is a sandy and secluded beach with a seasonal taverna and free camping. **Livadi**, an hour's hike further east, sees even fewer visitors. A steep 20-minute walk up from Livadi is the excellent taverna I Kori tou Mihali in the village of Mersini. Both Kendros and Livadi are popular with naturists.

At the end of the road on the northeast coast, the tiny village of **Kalotaritissa** boasts three gorgeous little beaches and a seasonal taverna. Get here by minibus or the boat *Margissa* in summer – or hike over the hill from Stavros in 90 minutes.

🛏 Sleeping & Eating

Aposperitis Rooms PENSION **€**
(☑ 22850 51586; www.aposperitis-rooms.com; d/tr/apt €45/60/65; ⊙ mid-May–Sep; ❋ 🛜) Super-central to the beach and village (right on the town beach!), this guesthouse has a range of simple double rooms, triple studios (with kitchen) and family-sized apartments. Decor is dated, but balconies with sea views compensate.

★**Makares** APARTMENT **€€**
(☑ 22850 79079; www.makares-donoussa.gr; r & apt €80-140; ⊙ May-Oct; ❋ 🛜) Loukas is an excellent host at Makares, a complex of self-catering studios and apartments at the end of Stavros bay (across the beach from the port). It's a short walk to the beach and village, the views are fabulous, the decor simple and elegant, and the feeling of seclusion (with the required luxuries) is first-rate.

Captain George Restaurant GREEK **€**
(☑ 22850 51867; mains from €7.50; ⊙ lunch & dinner) A mainstay in Stavros as it's open year-round, this taverna above the port serves up Greek staples with everything from *gyros* to Greek salads to fish. The outlook is superb and, out of season, locals hang out here, eating and chatting. In high season you might be battling for a table. Nothing flashy, but it's a solid place to eat.

★**I Kori tou Mihali** TAVERNA **€€**
(☑ 22851 00006; mains €8-17; ⊙ lunch & dinner) At this welcoming taverna in Mersini village, 6km from Stavros by road, Koula conjures up excellent Greek cuisine with a modern twist: wild goat from the island, pork in honey and yoghurt, and smoky eggplant dip. It's worth the visit, for the food and the knockout views. Bathers at Livadi Beach hike 20 minutes up to eat here.

★**Skantzoxiros** CAFE-BAR
(☑ 22850 51880; ⊙ 9am-late Jun-Sep) Up the stone steps at the port, this cafe-bar serves the younger crowd year-round. Out of season, it opens at 5pm, has Monday night movies and various locals' nights. In high season, it opens at 9am and is raging until the wee hours. Snacks, coffees, drinks and cocktails in a very convivial setting.

ℹ Information

There's an ATM next to a small shop on the harbour road (it's sometimes hidden behind a blue shutter for protection from blown sand), but be sure to bring sufficient cash in high season.

There's good information online at www.donoussa.gr and www.naxos.gr.

Medical Centre (☑ 22850 51506) Just below the church.

Sigalas Travel (☑ 22850 51570) is the ticket agency for all ferries, with a main office in Stavros (behind the bakery) and a branch at the Iliovasilema restaurant complex on the far side of the town beach. The main office opens most evenings, plus 40 minutes before ferry arrivals.

AMORGOS ΑΜΟΡΓΟΣ

POP 1980

Dramatic Amorgos is shaped like a seahorse swimming its way east towards the Dodecanese. As you approach by sea, its long ridge of mountains appears to stretch ever skyward.

Amorgos is just 30km from tip to toe but reaches more than 800m at its highest point. The southeast coast is unrelentingly steep and boasts an extraordinary monastery built into the base of a soaring cliff. The opposite coast is just as spectacular, but softens a little at the narrow inlets where the main port and town of Katapola and the second port of Aegiali lie. The enchanting Hora (also known as Amorgos) lies amid a rocky landscape high above Katapola. All three towns have plenty of appeal as a base.

Amorgos is more about archaeology and activities than beach-going – there's great walking, diving and a burgeoning rock-climbing scene.

ⓘ Getting There & Away

Connections from Naxos are good, with the **Small Cyclades Line** (www.ferries.gr/small cycladeslines) operating each day (except Sunday), connecting Naxos with the two Amorgos ports by way of the Small Cyclades.

Blue Star Ferries (www.bluestarferries.gr) has three useful routes: two run regularly from Piraeus via Paros, Naxos and the Small Cyclades, ending at either Aegiali or Katapola port. The third route sails weekly from Piraeus to Katapola and eastwards to Patmos, Leros, Kos and Rhodes.

Ferries dock at either Katapola or Aegiali (sometimes both) so it's important to check both port schedules and to know which port you're arriving at or departing from.

Purchase your tickets from **Nautilos** (☑ Aegiali 22850 73032, Katapola 22850 71201), a ticket agency with offices close to both harbours.

ⓘ Getting Around

The **Amorgos Bus Company** (☑ 6936671033; http://amorgosbuscompany.com) has timetables and ticket prices online. Summer buses go regularly from Katapola to Hora (€1.80) and Moni Hozoviotissis and Agia Anna Beach (€1.80), and less often to Aegiali (€2.80, 30 minutes). There are also buses from Aegiali up to Langada (€1.80).

Without doubt, the easiest way to get around is by rental car. Cars and motorcycles are available for hire from **Thomas Rental** (☑ Aegiali 22850 73444, Katapola 22850 71777; www.thomas-rental.gr) or **Evi's Cars** (☑ 22850 71066; www.eviscars.gr). Expect to pay from €40 per day for a small car in August. There are only two petrol stations: one 1.5km inland from Katapola, the other in Aegiali.

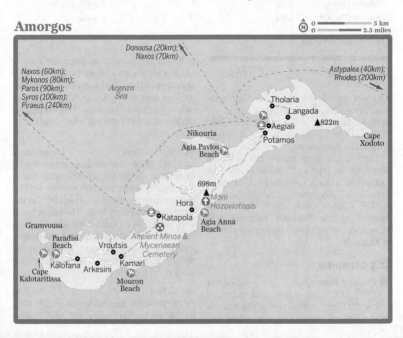

Amorgos

N 0 ———— 5 km
0 ———— 2.5 miles

Donousa (20km);
Naxos (70km)

Naxos (60km);
Mykonos (80km);
Paros (90km);
Syros (100km);
Piraeus (240km)

Aegean
Sea

Astypalea (40km);
Rhodes (200km)

Tholaria
Langada
Aegiali ▲822m
Nikouria
Potamos
Cape
Xodoto
Agia Pavlos
Beach

698m
▲
Moni
Hozoviotissis
Hora
Katapola
Agia Anna
Beach

Gramvousa
Paradisi
Beach
Vroutsis
Ancient Minoa &
Mycenaean
Cemetery
Kalofana
Arkesini
Kamari
Cape
Kalotaritissa
Mouron
Beach

BOAT SERVICES FROM AMORGOS

DESTINATION	DURATION	FARE (€)	FREQUENCY
Astypalea	1½hr	12	4 weekly
Donousa	2½hr	6	1 daily
Folegandros*	2hr 35min	69	5 weekly
Ios	5hr 20min	12	1 weekly
Iraklia	1¾-4½hr	8	1-2 daily
Kos	5hr	8	1 weekly
Koufonisia	40min-3½hr	6	1-2 daily
Koufonisia*	25min	14	1-2 daily
Leros	3hr 10min	2	1 weekly
Milos*	3¾hr	69	5 weekly
Mykonos*	2¼hr	55	3 weekly
Naxos	2-6hr	11	1-3 daily
Naxos*	1hr 20min	24	1-2 daily
Paros	3½-4½hr	19	7 weekly (note: not daily)
Paros*	2hr	29	1 daily
Patmos	2hr	21	1 weekly
Piraeus	8-10hr	35	7 weekly (note: not daily)
Piraeus*	5-6hr	62	1-3 daily
Rhodes	8hr	31	1 weekly
Schinousa	1½-4¼hr	7	1-2 daily
Santorini (Thira)	3¼hr	14	1 weekly
Santorini (Thira)*	1-4hr	50	5 weekly

* High-speed services

Katapola   Κατάπολα

POP 620

Katapola sprawls round the curving, yacht-filled shoreline of a picturesque bay in the most verdant part of the island. It's a bustling port town and there is a lot of activity around the ferry quay.

The remains of the ancient city of **Minoa** lie above the port and can be reached by footpath or a steep, concrete road, although there is no information. Amorgos has also yielded many Cycladic finds: the largest figurine in the National Archaeological Museum in Athens was found in the vicinity of Katapola.

Sleeping

★ Pension Amorgos   PENSION €€

(22850 71013; www.pension-amorgos.com; d €70;) There's a good deal of character in this traditional guesthouse, with bright and well-kept rooms right on the waterfront. It has the same owner as Emprostiada (p219) in Amorgos' Hora, and a similarly high quality. Very reasonable, Katapola's tavernas are only a short stumble away. You won't miss the morning ferry staying here – it parks up right outside.

Villa Katapoliani   PENSION €€

(22850 71664; www.villakatapoliani.gr; d €80-85, q €120;) Owner Stamatia has a high-quality collection of rooms, studios and apartments, handily located behind the waterfront and ferry quay. The balconies at Villa 1 overlook a garden filled with bougainvillea and the scattered ruins of the ancient temple of Apollo. Or scoot upstairs to the rooftop terrace for sea views. Apartments sleep up to four.

Minoa Hotel   HOTEL €€

(22850 74055; www.hotelminoa.gr; d/tr €90/100;) On the waterfront, this family-run place couldn't be more convenient for early-morning ferries. Service is friendly, and the sweet, neat rooms have tidy bathrooms and balconies overlooking a tree- and bird-filled garden. The lobby shares space with the family's Sweets by Pothiti cafe and patisserie.

✖ Eating

Honey & Cinnamon BAKERY €
(☑ 22850 71485; Katapola; ⊙ 8am-11pm) Look for the bright red window shutters and follow your nose. This tiny patisserie, a block back from the waterfront, bakes up cakes, pastries and lots of local cookies. Try the ones made with the local liquor, *psimeni raki,* or simply grab a coffee or a gelato.

★ Captain Dimos GREEK €€
(☑ 22850 71020; mains €6-16; ⊙ lunch & dinner) The captain, who is seriously into food, whips up mouthwatering dishes on his convivial harbourside patio. Crowding the tempting menu are dishes like octopus cooked in ouzo with lemongrass and ginger, and pork cooked with beer, apples and prunes. Creative pastas and pizza too. Sit back, enjoy and watch the world go by.

Karamel MEDITERRANEAN €€
(☑ 22850 71516; dishes €4-12; ⊙ lunch & dinner) Pass the beach and head to the far side of the harbour from the ferry quay to find some enticing dining options, including this colourful, French-run bistro. Sip wine at the waterfront tables and choose between daily dishes like chicken à la marocaine, carrots caramélisées and juicy octopus, which deliciously marry Greek and French flavours.

ℹ Information

Boats dock right on the waterfront. The bus station is a few minutes' walk inland along the water.

A bank (with ATM) is mid-waterfront.

N Synodinos (☑ 22850 71201; synodinos@nax.forthnet.gr) Sells ferry tickets and has a money exchange on the waterfront.

Hora (Amorgos)
Χώρα (Αμοργός)

The old capital of Hora sparkles like a snow-drift across its rocky ridge. It's capped by a 13th-century *kastro* and guarded by windmills that stand sentinel on the surrounding cliffs. There's a veneer of sophistication in the handful of fashionable bars and stores that enhance Hora's appeal without eroding its timelessness. The main activity here is wandering, rewarded with beautiful village settings around each corner.

The bus stop is on a small square at the edge of town, with car parking. There's also an ATM next to a minimarket right at the entrance to Hora and a post office.

◉ Sights

Archaeology Collection MUSEUM
(⊙ 9am-1pm & 6-8.30pm Tue-Sun) **FREE** Hora's Archaeology museum has some interesting pieces excavated on the island, including remnants of the Minoan civilisation which existed here more than 4000 years ago.

🛏 Sleeping & Eating

Pension Ilias PENSION €
(☑ 22850 71277; www.iliaspension.gr; d/apt €60/100; ❄ 🕾) Tucked away amid a jumble of traditional houses not far from the bus stop is this friendly family-run place with pleasant, comfortable rooms. The apartments can accommodate four people.

★ Emprostiada GUESTHOUSE €€
(☑ 22850 71814; http://emprostiada.gr; d €100, ste €130-150; ⊙ Mar-Nov; ❄ 🕾) There's charm in abundance at this traditional guesthouse, where private, characterful suites are housed in an old merchant's home. It's a postcard scene in a peaceful setting at the back of the village. Choose from spacious doubles, maisonettes and suites. Doubles are a bargain €50 outside the July and August peak. Free port transfers from Katapola or Aegiali.

Jazzmin CAFE €
(☑ 22850 74017; breakfast €6-13, snacks €3-6; ⊙ 9am-late) Down some stairs from the main pedestrian street, Jazzmin spreads through the cosy rooms of a traditional home. Perch in a window seat or lounge on the roof deck. Breakfast choices are good, as are smoothies, juices and herbal teas. The list of cocktails hints at the impressively stocked bar, and jazz and other smooth tunes provide a chilled-out soundtrack.

Triporto CAFE €
(☑ 22850 73085; breakfast €8, snacks €3-5; ⊙ 9am-late) Once the village bakery, this cafe has a strong traditional feel, plumped up with some colourful, hip decor. Come for breakfast to create an omelette from

ingredients like olive sauce and hot paprika cream, or snack on salads, sandwiches and sweets. The friendly owner is a virtual encyclopaedia of local knowledge.

Kath Odon GREEK €
(☑ 22850 74148; mains €5-10; ⊙ lunch & dinner) The setting is idyllic: tables under trees in a lovely little *plateia* at the top end of the main street, nestled between whitewashed churches. The menu of this unpretentious bistro presents tasty Amorgon produce, including goat, sausage, cheese, and some excellent zucchini balls.

Aegiali Αιγιάλη

POP 520

Aegiali is Amorgos' second port and sees fewer yachts and a bit more of the holidaymaker scene. It's a vibrant village with plenty going on. A sweep of sand lines the inner edge of the bay on which the village stands.

🏃 Activities & Tours

Amorgos Diving Center DIVING
(☑ 6932249538, 22850 73611; www.amorgos-diving.com) Enthusiastic and friendly instruction can be had at this well-run centre on the beach. Dives (with equipment) start at €50, with night dives, wreck dives and PADI courses available. It also offers a Bubblemaker class for kids, and snorkelling tours (€20).

Special Interest Holidays WALKING
(www.walkingingreece.com) Based at Langada, this outfit organises walking holidays (guided or self-guided) with experienced, knowledgeable hosts: Paul and Henrietta Delahunt-Rimmer, an English couple who have written the excellent resource *Amorgos: A Visitor's and Walker's Guide*. See the website for full details.

🛏 Sleeping

Apollon Studios GUESTHOUSE €
(☑ 22850 73297; www.apollon-amorgos.com; studio d/q €55/85; ❄ 🕏) With a nautically themed lobby, this guesthouse in the heart of the village has studios with well-equipped kitchens and harbour-view balconies. Rooms aren't fussy, but they're comfortable and reasonably priced. This place draws lots of repeat guests and families. Lots of places to eat right out the front door.

Aegiali Camping CAMPGROUND €
(☑ 22850 73500; www.aegialicamping.gr; campsite per adult/child/tent €5.50/2/4; ⊙ May–mid-Oct; P 🕏) Basic facilities a block back from the beach, with tents under the vines. There are showers, toilets and free wi-fi. Rent a tent for €6. On-site taverna and bar, too.

Yperia HOTEL €€
(☑ 22850 73084; www.yperia.com; d €105-115, f €168, all incl breakfast; ⊙ Apr-Oct; ❄ 🕏 🏊) Yperia's modern rooms have warm, artsy touches, handmade wood and iron furnishings, big bathrooms and excellent sea views. The pool overlooks the ocean, and the hotel is just a block from the beach. Staff are friendly and accommodating.

Aegialis Hotel & Spa HOTEL €€€
(☑ 22850 73393; www.amorgos-aegialis.com; d from €195; ❄ 🕏 🏊) High on a hill and with magical views over Aegiali Bay and village, this is one of the island's smartest options. Rooms are good, but it's the facilities that make this place shine: pool and pool bar, a bliss-out day spa and indoor pool, restaurants – oh, and did we mention the view? Decent off-peak rates; book online.

🍴 Eating

★ Amorgis CAFE €
(☑ 22850 73606; meals €3-10; ⊙ 9am-late; 🕏) On the steps leading up from the ferry quay, Amorgis is open from morning until late. Sunset drinks here are a fine idea. Family-friendly, it's as pretty as a picture, full of pastel colours and hanging pot plants. The menu offers enticements like fresh juices, cool cocktails, baguettes, salads and tortillas. A lovely place to relax and stare out to sea.

Falafel INTERNATIONAL €
(☑ 6936808038; dishes €4-12) Up an alley from the waterfront, Falafel is a fresh-faced, laid-back eating and drinking venue with a menu that's a grab-bag of world cuisines (spring rolls, falafel, summer salads, curries). It's an easy place to while away some time away from the main street.

To Limani TAVERNA €€
(☑ 22850 73269; http://tolimani.weebly.com; dishes €5-15; ⊙ breakfast, lunch & dinner) This popular restaurant carries its traditional atmosphere comfortably, up from the main street. Using home-grown produce, the cooks whip up hefty portions of great local dishes: try the fish soup, *patatao* (lamb with potatoes in tomato sauce), or anything with

local cheese. And save room for some home-made orange pie.

ⓘ Information

Aegialis Tours (☎ 22850 73393; http://amorgos-aegialis.com/services), based at Aegialis Hotel & Spa, can help arrange local tours and experiences (hiking, cultural excursions, cooking classes etc).

Around Amorgos

Agia Anna Beach is the nearest beach to Hora, but it's tiny and rocky; the car park is bigger. It's popular for its starring role in the French film *Le Grand Bleu*, and is known for its dramatic location and photogenic whitewashed chapel. There's a small cantina next to the car park on the clifftop, selling food and drinks.

Amorgos is a popular walking destination, and the island has a selection of well-marked numbered walking tracks. Check these routes out online at www.amorgos.gr. Cartography company Terrain (http://terrainmaps.gr) produces an excellent hiking map for Amorgos.

The lovely villages of **Langada** and **Tholaria** nestle amid the craggy slopes above Aegiali, each about 3km from the town. The two are linked to each other, and to Aegiali, by a signposted 9km circular path that takes 2½ to three hours to walk.

🛏 Sleeping & Eating

Pagali Hotel   HOTEL **€€**
(☎ 22850 73310; www.pagalihotel-amorgos.com; Langada; d €73-110; ❄🅿) Pagali Hotel is tucked away in Langada village, with superb views. Rooms and studios are comfortable, and the year-round hotel offers alternative agritourism activities like grape or olive harvesting and winemaking, and activities including rock climbing, hiking, yoga and art workshops. The hotel sits in a cute family-run pocket of Langada, next to the excellent Nikos Taverna and Vassalos Bakery.

IOS   ΙΟΣ

POP 2030

Ios' image has long been linked to holiday sun, sea and sex, with a reputation for non-stop booze-fuelled partying. It's partly true: there's no denying that from June to August, the island is the much-loved stomping

ground of youth and hedonism. But it's so much more – if you want it to be – and the partying doesn't infiltrate every village or beach.

Spend your days exploring the winding footpaths of the traditional hilltop old town or ensconced on a sandy beach. Discover the isolated interior or sandy beaches such as Manganari in the south, and then return to town in time for the party. Or visit in the shoulder season for a quieter pace, when Ios draws families and more mature travellers. It's pretty easy to escape the crowds: simply rent a car and venture into the countryside of goat farms, honey boxes and dramatic views.

ⓘ Getting There & Away

Ios lies conveniently on the Mykonos to Santorini ferry axis and has regular connections with Piraeus. Purchase tickets at **Acteon Travel** (p226) in Ormos, or its smaller branch in Hora.

ⓘ Getting Around

In summer crowded **buses** (☎ 22860 92015; www.ktel-ios.gr) run between Ormos, Hora and Mylopotas Beach (all fares €1.80) about every 20 minutes. Schedules are posted at the main village bus stops and online. In summer, additional buses run frequently to Koubara, and less frequently to beaches at Agia Theodoti, Psathi and Manganari. For taxis call **Ios Taxi Service** (☎ 6977760570); it's €5 from the port to Hora, €5 from Hora to Mylopotas.

Summertime caïques travel from Ormos to Manganari via Mylopotas and cost about €12 per person for a return trip.

BOAT SERVICES FROM IOS

DESTINATION	DURATION	FARE (€)	FREQUENCY
Amorgos	3hr	12	1 weekly
Anafi	2hr 25min	11	2 weekly
Folegandros	1hr 20min	10	4 weekly
Folegandros*	25min	44	2 weekly
Iraklio*	2hr 40min	64	2 daily
Kimolos	2hr 50min	16	3 weekly
Milos	3-4hr	16	2 weekly
Milos*	1¾hr	49	1 daily
Mykonos	4hr	24	1 daily
Mykonos*	1hr 50min-3hr 50min	48	4 daily
Naxos	1-1¾hr	14	1-3 daily
Naxos*	45min	25	1-2 daily
Paros	2hr 20min	16	1-3 daily
Paros*	1-1½hr	28	3 daily
Piraeus	7hr	36	6 weekly
Piraeus*	3hr 40min-5hr	59	2 daily
Rafina	7½hr	35	1 daily
Rafina*	5-6hr	62	2 daily
Santorini (Thira)	1-1½hr	12	6 weekly
Santorini (Thira)*	40-50min	29	4-7 daily
Serifos	4hr 50min	19	1 weekly
Sifnos	4-5½hr	18	3 weekly
Sifnos*	3hr	54	1 daily
Sikinos	25min	5	4 weekly
Syros	5hr 10min	18	1 weekly
Tinos*	3-4½hr	38	2 daily

* high-speed services

Ormos, Hora and Mylopotas Beach all have car, motorcycle and four-wheeler hire. You can book through Acteon Travel (p226).

Hora, Ormos & Mylopotas
Χώρα, Ορμος & Μυλοπότας

Ios' three main centres sit nearly on top of one another on the west coast. The port, Ormos, is lined with tavernas and cafes and stretches out into sandy **Gialos Beach**, backed by beach bars. Just 2km uphill (or 1.2km up a stone staircase) sits the capital of Hora, a stunning traditional village and nightlife hub. From here, the road winds south to the brown-sugar sand of **Mylopotas Beach**, with upscale and backpacker-style resorts. You'll find places to eat, sleep, drink and dance in all three settlements. Grocery stores are also found in each.

Hora's central square is Plateia Valeta, buried deep in the old town. The road straight ahead from Hora's bus stop leads 3km to Mylopotas Beach.

☉ Sights & Activities

Hora is a charming Cycladic village with a labyrinth of narrow lanes and cubist houses. Visit during the day and wander from the main streets into the quiet residential quarters to get a glimpse of village life that carries on behind the tourist hype scene.

Skarkos　　　　　　　　ARCHAEOLOGICAL SITE
(The Snail; €4; ☉8am-3pm Tue-Sun May-Sep) Crowning a low hill just north of Hora, this Early to Late Bronze Age settlement has restored walled terraces and the low

ruins of several Cycladic-style buildings to explore. A small visitor centre and interpretation boards in Greek and English help out. If driving, take the signed turn-off between Ormos and Hora. To walk, follow the traditional stone footpath from the back of Hora, passing goats and farmhouses. The pleasant walk takes around 15 minutes.

Archaeological Museum
MUSEUM

(📞 22860 91246; Hora; €2; ⏲ 8.30am-3pm Tue-Sun) Finds from Skarkos are displayed at this thorough, if slightly dry, museum in the town hall next to the bus stop in Hora. There are also exhibits from island excavations in general.

Mylopotas Watersports & New Dive
WATER SPORTS, DIVING

(📞 22860 92340; http://mylopotas-watersports.gr; Mylopotas; ⏲ May–mid-Oct) A thousand ways to fill your day: try a discover scuba-diving session (€55) or more intensive PADI courses

from €270. There are also wreck dives and night dives. Join a three-hour boat snorkelling trip for €35, or rent a long list of gear: windsurfing kit, kayaks, sailboats and more. Take a tube ride or do some waterskiing. Sea-taxi services too.

Meltemi Watersports & Dive Centre
WATER SPORTS, DIVING

(📞 6980386990; www.meltemiwatersports.com; Mylopotas) Based at the Far Out Beach Club (p224), with a ready flow of keen customers, Meltemi has a smorgasbord of ways to get wet: try out a diving sampler (€55) or full PADI courses, then check out wreck, cave and night dives. Learn to windsurf, waterski and wakeboard, hire a stand-up paddleboard, join a canoe safari or take a boat excursion.

Yialos Watersports
WATER SPORTS

(📞 22860 92463, 6974290990; www.yialoswatersports.com; Gialos Beach) Mylopotas isn't the

Ios

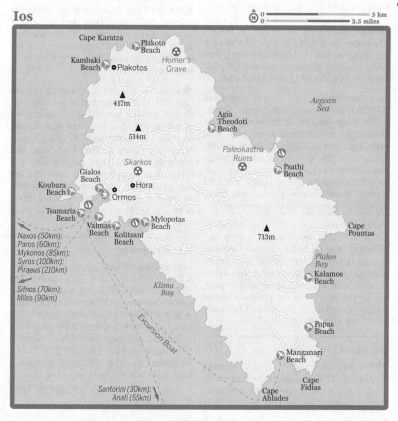

0 — 5 km
0 — 2.5 miles

- Cape Karatza
- Plakoto Beach
- Homer's Grave
- Kambaki Beach
- Plakotos
- ▲ 417m
- ▲ 514m
- Agia Theodoti Beach
- Aegean Sea
- Paleokastro Ruins
- Skarkos
- Psathi Beach
- Gialos Beach
- Koubara Beach
- ● Hora
- Ormos
- Tsamaria Beach
- Valmas Beach
- Kolitsani Beach
- Mylopotas Beach
- ▲ 713m
- Cape Pountas
- Naxos (50km); Paros (60km); Mykonos (85km); Syros (100km); Piraeus (210km)
- Sifnos (70km); Milos (90km)
- Klima Bay
- Plakes Bay
- Kalamos Beach
- Excursion Boat
- Papas Beach
- Manganari Beach
- Cape Fidias
- Santorini (30km); Anafi (55km)
- Cape Ahlades

only beach full of activity. At Gialos Beach, this company can get you afloat with windsurfing (lessons and gear), stand-up paddleboarding, waterskiing, wakeboarding, banana rides, canoes, snorkelling gear – you name it. There are mountain bikes for the landlubbers, too, or simply sunbeds if you're worn out from all the activities.

🛏 Sleeping

Ormos is considerably quieter than Hora or Mylopotas. If you're here to party, Hora is the best place to stay. Book early for July and August. Outside those months, prices fall by 50% or more.

🛏 Ormos

Yialos Ios Hotel HOTEL **€€**
(☑22860 91421; www.yialosioshotel.gr; Ormos; s/d €80/100, studio €130-170, all incl breakfast; ☀May-Sep; ❋🗐🛏) Just a block back from the port, this newly restored, 200-year-old stone building feels like the home you wish you had. Crisp, characterful rooms, beamed ceilings, traditional beds and a flower-filled poolside give it the edge. The owners are attentive, and the breakfast room is just like your Greek grandma's kitchen. Off-peak rates are excellent (doubles around €50).

Avra Pension PENSION **€€**
(☑22860 91985; www.avrapension.gr; Ormos; r €65; ☀Apr–mid-Oct; ❋🗐) Down a lane behind the yacht marina at the port, Katerina runs this delightful guesthouse with warmth and efficiency, and at bargain prices (outside the short summer peak, rooms fall to €30). Colourful potted plants, a restful terrace, homey common areas and fresh, appealing rooms add up to super value.

Pension Irene PENSION **€€**
(☑22860 91023; www.iosirene.gr; r from €80; ☀Jun-Oct; ❋🗐🛏) Just back from the yacht marina in Ormos, with double rooms right through to a two-bedroom apartment. Quiet location with a sparkling swimming pool; ask for the top view to get a massive shared terrace. Reception is like a small museum, with some great old photos of Ios.

🛏 Hora

★Francesco's HOSTEL **€€**
(☑22860 91223; www.francescos.net; Hora; dm/d/tr/q €20/70/105/140; ☀Apr–mid-Oct; ❋🗐🛏) Former backpackers are now sending their own 18-year-olds to Francesco's, which is still going strong. Rooms are spotless, views are dreamy and it's within stumbling distance of Hora's nightlife. There's a global feel and a roll-call of happy-traveller features: terrace bar, pool and cheap breakfast menu. Head towards the main square and turn left down Odos Scholarhiou for 200m. Or ask anyone.

Pavezzo GUESTHOUSE **€€**
(☑6977046091; www.iospavezzo.com; Hora; d €70-100; P🗐) This place is just steps from Hora but away from the night-time noise, on a quiet side road to Kolitsani Beach. The seven rooms are a steal; clean and comfortable, they feature country-style decor and private, sea-view patios. Suites have well-stocked kitchens, and the hosts are welcoming and attentive.

Avanti Hotel HOTEL **€€**
(☑22860 91165; www.avanti-hotelios.com; Hora; d incl breakfast €130-150; ☀mid-Apr–mid-Oct; ❋@🗐🛏) These fresh, sparkling rooms are a short stroll out of Hora, but far enough away to offer a little peace. Private balconies and a beautiful pool and outdoor area are the icing on the cake. Rates halve outside the summer peak.

★Liostasi BOUTIQUE HOTEL **€€€**
(☑22860 92140; www.liostasi.gr; Hora; d/ste incl breakfast from €150/280; ☀May-Sep; ❋@🗐🛏) Step into the lobby of this place and you may never want to leave. A contemporary Greek design blends chic and comfy in just the right proportions. The on-site spa, restaurant and pool area are top quality, and the rooms are crisp with splashes of colour and gorgeous sea views. Service is impeccable. It's halfway between Ormos and Hora.

🛏 Mylopotas

Far Out Beach Club & Beach Resort HOSTEL, CAMPGROUND **€**
(☑22860 91468; www.faroutclub.com; Mylopotas; campsite per person €10, dm €15, d/q €90/180; P@🗐🛏) Nearly on top of the beach is this backpacker party haven with poolside bars, restaurants and everything from laundry to tattooing, a sushi bar, yoga and gym. There's an enormous array of sleeping options, from tents to dorm beds, including en-suite rooms. Far Out even has a hotel and luxury villas nearby.

Eating

Ormos

La Randa ITALIAN €
(☑22860 92448; www.facebook.com/larandaios; Ormos; mains €7-14; ☺9am-1am; 🐾) Right on the port where the ferries dock, this place is fabulous for Italian cuisine. The owner has shipped an authentic oven over from Italy and makes drool-worthy pizzas and pasta dishes in homemade tomato sauce.

Akrogiali TAVERNA €€
(☑22860 91096; Ormos; mains from €8; ☺lunch & dinner) In the complex across the road from the ferry quay, Akrogiali is a superb, well-priced seafood taverna. The locals eat here, which gives it a tick from the start. Try the *salatouri* (stingray salad) or the octopus in red wine sauce.

Hora

★**Katogi** MEZEDHES €
(☑6983440900; www.facebook.com/katogios; Hora; dishes €4-11; ☺dinner) Full of life, entering Katogi feels like you've walked into a party in someone's living room, where bright, homey decor flows into a gorgeous garden and the music selection rocks. More importantly, the food is divine. Try haloumi bites with cherry tomatoes, pork bites in whisky sauce or pasta purses filled with cheese and pear.

Thai Smile THAI €
(☑22860 91925; Hora; mains €7-12; ☺dinner) Ignore the international dishes and go for the authentic Thai flavours, created by the Thai owner-chef. A backstreet spot with plenty of atmosphere, serving plates overflowing with phad thai noodles, Massaman curry and tom yum soup.

The Nest GREEK €€
(☑22860 91778; www.facebook.com/thenestios; Hora; mains €6-18; ☺lunch & dinner) The Nest feels authentic, right down to the *rembetika* music and the tables of older men deep in discussion over rounds of raki. Local garlic sausage, chicken souvlaki, stuffed eggplant and lamb *kleftiko* are served with bowls of tzatziki, olives and fresh bread. Wine is served by the jug, and the veggies come from the owner's garden.

Lord Byron MEDITERRANEAN €€
(☑22860 92125; www.lordbyronios.gr; dishes €7-14; ☺dinner) An explosion of colour and quirky decor near the square in Hora, this laid-back, lively restaurant is as pleasing to the stomach as it is to the eye. Enjoy huge portions of creative salads and mains, with dishes like cheese pies with orange and honey mustard dip, or barbecued crab. Service gets five stars.

Mylopotas

Cantina del Mar CAFE €
(☑22860 91016; http://cantinadelmar.gr; Mylopotas; sandwiches & salads €2-8; ☺breakfast, lunch & dinner) Come here, at the entrance to Mylopotas, to chill out next to the beach over bumper brunches, sandwiches and wraps. Choose from a long, healthy-sounding list of juices and smoothies (can the hangover juice of lemon, orange and carrot really do the trick?) or wine and cocktails for when you're feeling well again. The music selection soothes.

🍷 Drinking & Nightlife

Nightlife at the heart of Hora is full-on and radiates from the tiny main square, where it gets so crowded by midnight that you won't be able to fall down, even if you need to.

There's everything from jazz bars to frantic backpacker bars that dole out cheap shooters, though venues open and close regularly.

★**Blue Note Club** CLUB
(☑22860 92271; www.facebook.com/bluenote official; ☺11.15pm-late May-Oct) This Hora favourite has been thumping for decades and is still the hottest spot on the island. Catering to a young crowd, if you were under the impression Ios was a party island before you came, Blue Note will reinforce those thoughts. Head straight through the square and turn left at Katogi.

Free Beach Bar BAR
(☑22860 28357; http://freebeachbar.gr; ☺10am-1am May-Sep) Offering dozens of colourful, ways to lounge and recline, this beach bar sits in the middle of Mylopotas Beach and sends a siren call via its dusk cabanas and pool, surrounded by hanging beds and cushioned pods. Aside from all-day drinks, snacks are on offer (club sandwich, pizza). Chill out or dig the DJ-fired action.

Fun Pub
PUB

(☑ 22860 92022; www.facebook.com/funpubios; ☺11am-late Apr-Oct) If you can't find your tribe on Hora's main square, they might be here – at the Irish-owned Fun Pub, on the main road through the town. It does what it says on the label, with fun in various guises: music, dancing, food, live sports, pool tables and plenty of mingling. Pub grub and a Sunday roast.

Foiniki Art Cafe
BAR

(☑ 22860 92247; Hora; 9am-late) It's easy to settle into this funky little bar, with its friendly owners, rich colours, stacks of magazines and hand-crafted beer from around Greece. Tucked behind Lord Byron (p225), it's a great spot for a morning coffee or pre-dinner tipple.

Ios Club
COCKTAIL BAR

(☑ 6985720049; www.iosclub.gr; ☺7pm-3am Apr-Oct) A deliciously sophisticated cocktail bar that's perfect for sunset cocktails and sweeping views on the chic terrace. It's along the pathway by Sweet Irish Dream, on the right as you head into Hora from Ormos.

☆ Entertainment

★ Cine Liostasi
CINEMA

(☑ 22860 92140; www.liostasi.gr/cine-liostasi) FREE Outside at Liostasi Hotel & Suites, halfway between Ormos and Hora, this lovely setting hosts nightly outdoor cinema under the stars. The aim is to become the top outdoor cinema in Greece and, indeed, this spot is hard to beat. Watch classic and modern movies in loungers while sipping signature cocktails with a gorgeous view as background to the screen.

ⓘ Information

There's an ATM right by the kiosks at the ferry quay in Ormos. In Hora, the National Bank of Greece, behind the church, has an ATM.

In Hora there is a seasonal information kiosk at the bus stop, across the road from the big cathedral. Online, check out http://ios.gr for more info.

Acteon Travel (☑ 22860 91343; www.acteon. gr; ☺8am-10pm) Purchase ferry tickets at Acteon Travel in Ormos, or its smaller branch in Hora.

Hospital (☑ 22863 60000) On the way to Gialos, 250m northwest of the quay.

Dr Yannis Kalathas (☑ 6932420200, 22860 91137; ☺24hr) Your best contact in case of medical emergency.

Around Ios

Head to Cape Gero Angeli, at the northernmost tip of the island and 12km from Hora, to the believed site of **Homer's Grave**. There's nothing much to see here but the panoramic sea views are fabulous.

En route to Psathi is **Paleokastro**, the remains of a Byzantine castle perched atop a seaside cliff. Follow the stone pathway from the roadside; it'll likely just be you and the goats here.

Ios is well known for its beaches. Vying with Mylopotas for first place is **Manganari**, a long swath of fine white sand on the south coast, reached by bus or by caïque in summer. **Agia Theodoti** has the bluest of blue water and is favoured by Greek families in summer. Nearby **Psathi** is quieter.

SANTORINI (THIRA)
ΣΑΝΤΟΡΙΝΗ (ΘΗΡΑ)

POP 15,550

With multicoloured cliffs soaring above a sea-drowned caldera, Santorini looks like a giant slab of layered cake. The main island of Thira will take your breath away with its snow-drift of white Cycladic houses lining the cliff tops and, in places, spilling like icy cornices down the terraced rock. When the sun sets, the reflection on the buildings and the glow of the orange and red in the cliffs can be truly spectacular.

Santorini is no secret and draws crowds for much of the year, yet it wears its tourism crown well. The island's intrigue reaches deep into the past, with the fascinating Minoan site of Akrotiri and the gorgeous traditional hilltop village of Oia. It also glides effortlessly into the future with accomplished artists, excellent wineries, a unique microbrewery and some of the Cyclades' finest accommodation and dining experiences. The multicoloured beaches are simply the icing on the cake.

History

Minor eruptions have been the norm in Greece's earthquake-prone history, but Santorini has a definite history of overachieving – eruptions here were genuinely earth-shattering, and so wrenching they changed the shape of the island several times.

Dorians, Venetians and Turks have occupied Santorini, but its most influential early

Santorini (Thira)

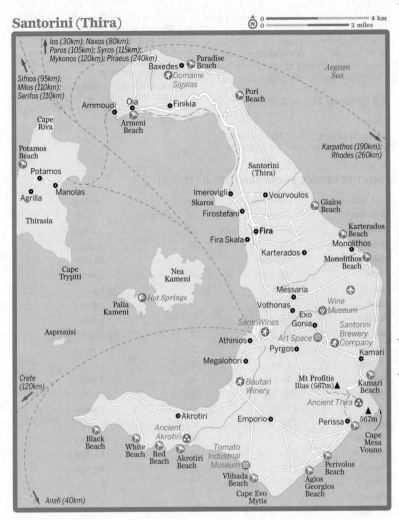

inhabitants were Minoans. They came from Crete some time between 2000 BC and 1600 BC, and the settlement at Akrotiri dates from the peak years of their great civilisation.

The island was circular then and was called Strongili (Round One). Thousands of years ago, a colossal volcanic eruption caused the centre of Strongili to sink, leaving a caldera with towering cliffs along the east side – a truly dramatic sight. The latest theory, based on carbon dating of olive-oil samples from Akrotiri, places the event 10 years either side of 1613 BC.

Santorini was recolonised during the 3rd century BC, but for the next 2000 years sporadic volcanic activity created further physical changes that included the formation of the volcanic islands of Palia Kameni and Nea Kameni at the centre of the caldera.

As recently as 1956, a major earthquake devastated Oia and Fira, yet by the 1970s the islanders had embraced tourism as tourists embraced the island, and today Santorini is a destination of truly spectacular global appeal, drawing honeymooners, backpackers, the jet set, cruise-boat passengers, Chinese bridal parties (in part due to the success of *Beijing Love Story,* filmed partly on Santorini) and everyone else too.

For better or worse, Santorini and Mykonos have become the poster-children for the Greek islands. As well as bigger crowds, that also means considerably higher prices.

ℹ Getting There & Away

AIR

Santorini Airport (JTR; ☑ 22860 28400; www.santoriniairport.com) has flights year-round to/from Athens (from €65, 45 minutes) with **Olympic Air** (www.olympicair.com) and **Aegean Airlines** (www.aegeanair.com). Seasonal European connections are plentiful, including, among others, easyJet from London, Rome, Geneva and Milan.

Give yourself plenty of time when flying back out as tourism infrastructure hasn't kept up with the island's growing popularity and the airport terminal can be mayhem.

BOAT SERVICES FROM SANTORINI (THIRA)

DESTINATION	DURATION	FARE (€)	FREQUENCY
Amorgos*	1-4¼hr	49	6 weekly
Anafi	1hr 10min-1hr 40min	7	4 weekly
Folegandros	3hr	12	3 weekly
Folegandros*	45-80min	44	1-2 daily
Halki	12½-15½hr	26	2 weekly
Ios	1-2hr	12	1 daily
Ios*	35-45min	29	4-6 daily
Iraklio*	1¾hr	60	2 daily
Karpathos	8½-11½hr	25	2 weekly
Kasos	6¾-9½hr	25	2 weekly
Kimolos	4½hr	16	2 weekly
Kos	4½hr	34	4 weekly
Koufonisia*	1½-3½hr	49	6 weekly
Milos	3½hr	17	2 weekly
Milos*	2hr	52	2 daily
Mykonos*	2-3hr	60	5-6 daily
Naxos	2hr	19	1-2 daily
Naxos*	1½hr	38	4-5 daily
Paros	3-3½hr	20	1-2 daily
Paros*	2-2¼hr	46	3 daily
Piraeus	5½-12hr	36	2-3 daily
Piraeus*	4½-6hr	59	3-4 daily
Rafina*	5¾hr	64	2 daily
Rethymno (Crete)*	2hr 20min	65	2 weekly
Rhodes	8-17¾hr	27	5 weekly
Serifos	6½hr	19	1 weekly
Sifnos	5-7¼hr	18	3 weekly
Sifnos*	3-4hr	54	1-2 daily
Sikinos	2hr	9	3 weekly
Sitia (Crete)	6hr	26	1 weekly
Tinos*	3½-4hr	40	2 daily

* high-speed services

Note: differences in durations are on account of vessel type and/or route.

BOAT

There are plenty of ferries each day to and from Piraeus and many Cyclades islands.

Thira's main port, Athinios, stands on a cramped shelf of land at the base of sphinx-like cliffs and is a scene of marvellous chaos that always seems to work itself out when ferries arrive. Buses (and taxis) meet all ferries and then cart passengers up the towering cliffs through an ever-rising series of S-bends to Fira. Accommodation providers can usually arrange transfers (to Fira per person is around €10).

ⓘ Getting Around

TO/FROM THE AIRPORT

There are frequent bus connections between Fira's bus station and the airport, located 5km east of Fira (€1.80, 20 minutes, 7am to 9pm). Most accommodation providers will arrange paid transfers.

Bus

KTEL Santorini Buses (☑ 22860 25404; http://ktel-santorini.gr) has a good website with schedules and prices. Tickets are purchased on the bus.

In summer buses leave Fira regularly for Oia, with more services pre-sunset (€1.80). There are also numerous daily departures for Akrotiri (€1.80), Kamari (€1.80), Perissa and Perivolos Beach (€2.40), and a few to Monolithos (€1.80).

Buses leave Fira for the port of Athinios (€2.30, 30 minutes) a half-dozen times per day, but it's wise to check times in advance. Buses for Fira meet all ferries, even late at night.

Car & Motorcycle

A car is the best way to explore the island during high season, when buses are intolerably overcrowded and you'll be lucky to get on one at all. Be very patient and cautious when driving – the narrow roads and heavy traffic, especially in and around Fira, can be a nightmare.

There are representatives of all the major international car-hire outfits, plus dozens of local operators in all tourist areas. A good local hire outfit is **Damigos Rent a Car** (☑ 22860 22048; www.santorini-carhire.com). You'll pay from around €50 per day for a car and €25/30 for a scooter/four-wheeler in high season, but it pays to shop around. Note: scooter hire requires you to have a motorbike licence, while four-wheelers require just a car licence. Check this website for details: www.santorini.com/rentals/motorbikes.

Taxi

Fira's **taxi stand** (☑ 22860 23951, 22860 22555) is on Dekigala just around the corner from the bus station. A taxi from the port of Athinios to Fira costs €10 to €15, and a trip from Fira to Oia about €15. Expect to add €2 if the taxi is booked ahead or if you have luggage. A taxi to Kamari is about €15, to Perissa €18 and to Ancient Thira about €25 one-way.

Santorini Transport (☑ 6984637383; www.santorinitransport.com) is a good option for arranging fixed-price transfers to/from the airport or Athinios port.

Fira Φήρα

POP 2300

Santorini's main town of Fira is a vibrant, bustling place, its caldera edge layered with hotels, cave apartments, infinity pools and swish restaurants, all backed by a warren of narrow streets full of shops and even more bars and restaurants. A multitude of fellow admirers cannot diminish the impact of Fira's stupendous landscape; this is one of the few places in the world that actually looks better than the postcards! Views over the multicoloured cliffs are breathtaking, and at night the caldera edge is a frozen cascade of lights.

While Fira's population is only a tad over 2000, it sprawls north and merges into two more villages: **Firostefani** (about a 15-minute walk from Fira) and **Imerovigli** (the highest point of the caldera edge, about a half-hour walk from Fira). A path runs through these villages and is lined with glorious hotels, restaurants and endless photo opportunities.

◎ Sights

★**Museum of Prehistoric Thera** MUSEUM
(☑ 22860 22217; www.santorini.com/museums; Mitropoleos; adult/child €3/free; ◷ 8.30am-3pm Wed-Mon) Opposite the bus station, this well-presented museum houses extraordinary finds excavated from Akrotiri and is all the more impressive when you realise just how old they are. Most remarkable is the glowing gold ibex figurine, dating from the 17th century BC and in mint condition. Also look for fossilised olive tree leaves from within the caldera, which date back to 60,000 BC.

Archaeological Museum MUSEUM
(☑ 22860 22217; M Nomikou; adult/child €3/free; ◷ 8.30am-3pm Tue-Sun) Near the cable-car station, this museum houses impressive finds from Akrotiri and Ancient Thira, such as unbelievably detailed clay statuettes from the latter site, including a donkey, pig, ram

Fira

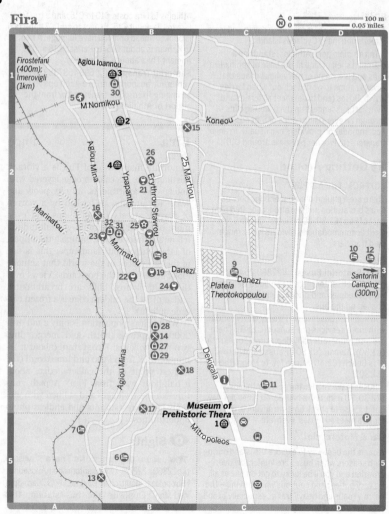

CYCLADES SANTORINI (THIRA)

and birds. Check out the chariot-racing images on some of the pottery. The content is strong, though the museum itself is in need of a little TLC.

Santozeum MUSEUM
(☎ 22860 21722; www.santozeum.com; Ypapantis; adult/child €5/3; ☉ 10am-6pm May-Oct) Around the corner from the Archaeological Museum, this modern cultural centre is home to the 'Wall Paintings of Thera' exhibition, a collection of life-size reproductions of the finest Akrotiri murals. Be sure to watch the short video on the work of

conservators – it is fascinating. There's no labelling, so be sure to ask for the information sheet for context.

Megaro Gyzi Cultural Centre MUSEUM
(☎ 22860 23077; www.megarogyzi.gr; Erythrou Stavrou; adult/child €3/free; ☉ 10am-9pm Mon-Sat, 10.30am-4.30pm Sun May-Oct) Escape the crowds to this quiet museum in the town's north to take in fascinating before-and-after photographs of the 1956 earthquake in Fira, along with a collection of maps, engravings, paintings and 15th-century manuscripts.

🏃 Activities

Walks in and around Fira are spectacular, particularly heading north to Firostefani and Imerovigli along the caldera-edge pathway. This is about a 30-minute walk, one-way. If you want to keep walking, you can eventually reach **Oia**, but be aware that this is no small undertaking, and the trail beyond Imerovigli can be rough. It's about 9km in all, and a good three to four hours' walk one-way. It's best not to undertake it in the heat of the day.

Other options include walking down to (or up from) the small port known as **Fira Skala**, from where volcanic island cruises leave (and where cruise-ship passengers come ashore). It's around 600 steps each way. You can make a more leisurely, and aromatic, upward trip by donkey (€5) – although animal-rights groups strongly urge travellers not to, due to the cruelty involved. You can also go by the **Santorini Cable Car** (https://scc.gr/cablecar.htm; one-way €6; ⊙7am-10pm May-Sep; reduced hr Oct-Apr) that hums quickly and smoothly (every 20 minutes 6.30am to 11pm June to August) between Fira and Fira Skala. Less frequent services operate outside the peak season; there is an additional charge to take luggage (€2.50).

From Imerovigli, a sign at Mezzo restaurant leads west to Skaros, a rocky headland with great views and a perfectly situated church. From Imerovigli it's about 20 minutes one-way.

🏃 Tours

Any tour your heart desires can be organised on Santorini – there are dozens of agencies primed and ready to help with winery visits, archaeology tours, traditional villages, sunset-watching and other activities.

Another option is a cruise, and the most popular itinerary takes in the caldera's volcanic islands of Nea Kameni and Palia Kameni, including a stop at the former's crater and the latter's hot springs. Some tours will also call at Thirasia, and/or a port below Oia. Sunset-watching from a boat, drink in hand, is also in demand.

Departures are from Fira Skala, below Fira. Book with one of the agencies around town. Vessels vary, from replica schooners to sleek catamarans and yachts – therefore prices vary wildly.

The starting rate for a basic full-day excursion is around €30. Before booking, ask about the itinerary, inclusions (eg lunch or drinks) and the number of fellow passengers.

🛏 Sleeping

Pension Petros
PENSION €

(☎ 22860 22573; www.hotelpetros-santorini.gr; r from €90; ❄️ 🛜 🏊) Three hundred metres east of the square in Fira, Petros offers decent rooms at good rates, but no caldera views. This is a friendly, family-run operation and makes an affordable option, especially outside high season, when rates are less than half. Cute pool too!

Santorini Camping
HOSTEL, CAMPGROUND €

(☎ 22860 22944; www.santorinicamping.gr; Fira; dm/d €25/70, campsite per person €12.50; ☺ Mar-Nov; 🅿️ ❄️ @ 🛜 🏊) On the eastern outskirts of town, this hostel and campground has some shade and decent facilities. You get what you pay for with the rooms, which are clean but quite basic. There's a self-service restaurant, minimarket, bar and pool.

Villa Roussa
HOTEL €

(☎ 22860 23220; www.villaroussa.gr; Dekigala; s/d/tr from €80/100/120; 🅿️ ❄️ 🛜 🏊) This place is all about location. Minutes from the caldera (without the prices to match) and seconds from the bus station (but thankfully out of earshot), it has fresh, immaculate rooms and helpful staff.

Hotel Sofia
HOTEL €

(☎ 22860 22802; www.sofiahotelsantorini.com; Firostefani; d €110; ☺ May-Oct; ❄️ 🛜 🏊) Comfortable, with a touch of character, these half-dozen petite rooms at the heart of Firostefani are a great alternative to the bustle of Fira. There's no caldera view, but it's literally outside your door. The rates are a near-steal (book early) and the small, lovely pool and verandahs are a bonus. Fira's centre is about 800m south.

★ Aroma Suites
BOUTIQUE HOTEL €€

(☎ 22860 24112; www.aromasuites.com; Agiou Mina; d from €240; ❄️ @ 🛜) Overlooking the caldera at the quieter southern end of Fira, and more accessible than similar places, this boutique hotel has charming service and six plush, beautiful suites. Built into the side of the caldera, the traditional interiors are made all the more lovely with monochrome decor, local art, books and stereos. Balconies offer a feeling of complete seclusion.

Kavalari Hotel
HOTEL €€

(☎ 22860 22455; www.kavalarihotel-santorini.com; r from €180; ♿ ❄️ 🛜) One of Fira's top-value hotels, Kavalari is at the heart of the action and offers standard rooms and cave apartments. The central location, views and spotless rooms make this an affordable option when surrounding hotel rates are taken into consideration. An excellent breakfast is included.

Pelican Hotel
HOTEL €€

(☎ 22860 23113; www.pelicanhotel.gr; Danezi; s/d/tr €90/110/130; ❄️ 🛜) There's no caldera view, but you're just metres from the heart of the action in this long-standing hotel with a homey feel. Two of its best attributes are the restaurant next door and the delightful garden setting.

Hotel Keti
HOTEL €€

(☎ 22860 22324; www.hotelketi.gr; Agiou Mina, Fira; d from €170; ❄️ 🛜) Hotel Keti is one of the smaller 'sunset view' hotels in a peaceful caldera niche. Its attractive traditional rooms are carved into the cliffs, half of which have Jacuzzis. Two-night minimum in high season.

Villa Soula
HOTEL €€

(☎ 22860 23473; www.santorini-villasoula.gr; Fira; r from €100; ❄️ 🛜 🏊) Cheerful and spotless, this hotel is a great deal. Rooms aren't large but are freshly renovated with small, breezy balconies. Colourful public areas and a small, well-maintained undercover pool give you room to spread out a little. It's a short walk from the town centre.

★ Mill Houses
BOUTIQUE HOTEL €€€

(☎ 22860 27117; www.millhouses.gr; Firostefani; d incl breakfast from €350; ❄️ 🛜 🏊) Built right into the side of the caldera at Firostefani, down a long flight of steps, these superb studios and suites are chic and plush. Lots of white linen and whitewashed walls fill them with light. King-sized beds, Bulgari toiletries and private patios looking out over the Aegean are just a few of the lavish touches.

Anteliz Suites
BOUTIQUE HOTEL €€€

(☎ 22860 28842; www.anteliz.gr; r from €285; ♿ ❄️ 🛜 🏊) North of Fira on the path that runs to Firostefani, Anteliz offers an amazing pool, sun terrace and oh, those views. Relax in the open-air hot tub and take it all in. The suites feature white-marble floors and a high degree of elegance and style – definitely one of Fira's top places to stay.

🍴 Eating

Overpriced, indifferent food geared towards tourists is still an unfortunate feature of summertime Fira; thankfully, there are many excellent exceptions.

ℹ️ SLEEPING ON SANTORINI

There's so much to choose from in Fira and Oia that confusion can set in. Away from these main towns, the biggest concentration of rooms can be found in and around Kamari and Perissa. The latter is a good option if you are on a budget. High-season rates are as follows:

€ less than €100

€€ €100-250

€€€ over €250

Things to know about Santorini accommodation:

➡ Few of Fira's sleeping options are cheap. For a caldera view, expect to pay a premium.

➡ The sky is the limit here and in Oia: luxury accommodation is everywhere, with all the trimmings (private terrace, plunge pool etc).

➡ Consider accommodation in Firostefani and Imerovigli if you don't mind a walk into Fira. There are plenty of quality hotels and restaurants with caldera views here too.

➡ Many hotels on the caldera rim cannot be reached by vehicle and may involve several flights of steps. Many hotels have porters who can help with luggage.

➡ Some domatia touts at the port may claim that their rooms are in town, when they're actually a long way out; ask to see a map showing the exact location.

➡ Some places may offer free transfer to the port or airport; other places may charge €12 upwards for a transfer.

In general, there's a price hike for a caldera view, while cheap eats surround the central square. Book ahead in July and August.

⭐ **Theoni's Kitchen** GREEK €
(☏ 22860 25680; www.theoniskitchen.com; Dekigala; mains from €7; ☺ noon-midnight) Theoni's isn't fancy and you won't be gazing out over the caldera, but this is the best 'momma's kitchen' home-cooked Greek food you'll find, with smiling, friendly owners and good service. Expect decent-sized portions of Greek classics and daily specials that may well have you returning for more. The Greek salad here is exceptional.

Galini Cafe CAFE €
(☏ 22860 22095; www.galinicafesantorini.com; mains €6-14; ☺ 8am-midnight) Just as you reach Firostefani, this breezy cafe welcomes you with brightly coloured flowerpots and a hand-crafted school of fish swimming overhead. Chilled out and friendly, with unparalleled caldera views, it's a great place for breakfast or a light meal and cocktail at sunset. Gorgeous views.

To Ouzeri TAVERNA €
(☏ 22860 21566, 6945849921; http://ouzeri-santorini.com; Fabrika Shopping Centre; mains €7-15; ☺ lunch & dinner) Central and cheerfully dressed in red gingham, this terrace restaurant has surprisingly reasonable prices. It's a long-standing favourite with locals and tourist alike, with top traditional dishes like mussels *saganaki,* baked feta and stuffed calamari.

Cacio e Pepe ITALIAN €€
(☏ 22860 24971; www.cacioepepe.gr; 25 Martiou; mains from €10; ☺ noon-midnight) You're up for pizzas, pastas, meats, seafood and all kinds of Italian favourites at this proud place out on 25 Martiou. There's a full-on Italian wine list and they're especially proud of the signature dishes – the ravioli tartufo and the cacio e pepe (cheese and pepper) spaghetti.

Fanari GREEK €€
(☏ 22860 25107; www.fanari-restaurant.gr; dishes €7-20) Tasty traditional Greek dishes and superlative views are on offer at this place overlooking the caldera on the steps down to the Old Port. Along with unique local recipes, seafood and fresh fish, there are local dessert favourites such as Santorini pudding and *meletinia,* made of skimmed-milk cheese and scented with mastic and vanilla.

Assyrtico Wine Restaurant GREEK €€
(☏ 22860 22463; www.assyrtico-restaurant.com; Fira; mains €15-30; ☺ lunch & dinner) Settle in on this terrace above busy Ypapanti for polished

ℹ️ SANTORINI ON A BUDGET

Santorini doesn't need to blow your budget. If you don't need caldera views from your room and you'd rather have euros in your pocket, consider staying in Perissa on Santorini's southeast coast. It's all here at reasonable prices, and frantic Fira is only a €2.40 bus ride away.

Perissa, with its sizzling black pebbly sand, is arguably Santorini's top beach. **Stelios Place** (p239) is only a couple of minutes' walk back from the sand, with sparkling rooms that are a steal. Stay three nights and Stelios will pick you up and drop you off at the port or airport. Eateries such as **Fratzeskos Fish Tavern** (☎22860 83488; www.facebook.com/fishtavernfrageskos1; mains from €8; ☺lunch & dinner) and **Apollon Taverna** (☎22860 85340; mains from €8; ☺10am-midnight) line the beach – and don't worry, you won't miss out on nightlife, as **The Beach Bar** (www.thebeachbar.gr; ☺24hr; 🛜) is open 24 hours a day in high season. **Santosun Travel** (☎22860 81456; ☺9am-9pm) on Perissa's main drag can meet all your travel requirements with rental cars, ferry tickets and tours.

local flavours accompanied by caldera views. Start with, say, the *saganaki* wrapped in a pastry crust, and follow with the deconstructed *gyros* or the white eggplant moussaka. Service is relaxed and friendly; the wine list is big.

★1500 BC
SEAFOOD €€€

(☎22860 21331; www.1500bc.gr; mains €22-39; ☺lunch & dinner) With top views south across the caldera, this elegant patio serves top-quality food. Braised lobster, royal crab legs with green olive oil, and chateaubriand veal fillet are just a few of the mouthwatering choices. Service is impeccable – they'll debone the fish at your table and bring you a shawl if you're chilly.

★Koukoumavlos
GREEK €€€

(☎22860 23807; www.koukoumavlos.com; mains €28-34; ☺dinner Apr–mid-Oct) This terrace is filled with gleeful diners partaking of award-winning fresh, modern Aegean cuisine (including a worthwhile degustation at €74). Creativity reigns and the menu is poetic, elevating dishes to new heights: 'slow-cooked shoulder of lamb with potato mousseline flavoured with jasmine, fig and Greek coffee sauce'. Look for the pink building and wooden doorway. Book ahead.

Mylos
GREEK €€€

(☎22860 25640; www.mylossantorini.com; Firostefani; mains €22-26; ☺lunch & dinner) Located in a converted windmill on the caldera edge in Firostefani, this uber-glam venue has upscale food that's ambitious in its techniques and beautifully presented. Try crispy fish 'covered with sea snow', or Greek black pork with Romesco sauce. Book ahead.

🍷 Drinking & Nightlife

After midnight, Erythrou Stavrou fires up as the clubbing caldera of Fira, while Marinatou is lined with fabulously chic drinking spots.

Kira Thira
BAR

(☎22860 22770; Erythrou Stavrou; ☺9pm-6am Wed-Sun) The oldest bar in Fira and one of the best. Dark wood and vaulted ceilings give it an intimate, cave-like atmosphere, with smooth cocktails and smoother jazz. With a huge viola hanging on the ceiling, this tiny bar is so popular it often gets swamped, especially when there is live music on offer.

Crystal Cocktail Bar
COCKTAIL BAR

(☎22860 22480; www.loucashotelsantorini.com; ☺10am-1am) With views to die for, relax at Crystal with coffee in the morning and cocktails as your day evolves. This is one of those spots that you won't want to leave. Part of Loucas Hotel, Crystal is a top spot for romance, with stupendous sunsets.

Two Brothers Bar
BAR

(☎22860 23061; www.2brothersbarsantorini.com; ☺10am-6am) Originally started by brothers Dimitris and Giannis in 1983, this Fira institution is now run by their sons, Jack and Leuteris. Expect a party vibe and when things really wind up, little room to move. Two-for-one cocktails from 4pm to 7pm and 9pm to midnight at this island favourite.

MoMix Bar Santorini
BAR

(☎6974350179; www.facebook.com/MoMixBar Santorini; Marinatou; ☺8pm-5am) It might take a minute to get your head around this, but MoMix is short for Molecular Mixology. This popular party spot offers innovative cocktails (to help your mind travel) and cool interior colours in its cave-like bar. Head outside for stunning caldera views.

Tango Champagne & Cocktail Bar BAR
(📞 6947453999; www.tangosantorini.gr; Marinatou; ⊙ 8pm-5am) This is edge-of-the-caldera stuff, with stupendous views, delicious cocktails, a fashionable crowd and brilliant tunes that get louder and funkier as the sun goes down. Come for sunset and stay for hours – or until your wallet is empty.

Koo Club CLUB
(📞 22860 22025; www.kooclub.gr; Erythrou Stavrou; ⊙ 10pm-5am Jun-Sep) Hang out with your new best friends on the sofa-strewn, multi-tiered outdoor balconies while sipping cocktails to live DJs.

☆ Entertainment

The White Door Theatro THEATRE
(📞 22860 21770; www.whitedoorsantorini.com; €49; ⊙ May-Oct) Fira's popular *Greek Wedding Show* is a hit with visitors, featuring lots of traditional music, dance, fun and audience participation. Small plates (mezedhes) and local wine are included in the ticket, which can be booked online – advisable in the high season. The show is in an atmospheric open-air courtyard surrounded by whitewashed buildings.

Casablanca Soul Bar LIVE MUSIC
(📞 6977575191; www.facebook.com/casablanca soul; Ypapantis; ⊙ 9.30pm-5.30am) This cocktail and absinthe bar is a Fira, hotspot with live bands, visiting DJs and soul well into the wee hours. Expect tasty cocktails and a relaxed vibe.

🛍 Shopping

Mati Art Gallery ARTS & CRAFTS, JEWELLERY
(📞 22860 23814; www.matiartgallery.com; Cathedral Plateau) The installation pieces outside are sure to catch your attention before you even step inside this gallery. This is the main exhibition space of Yorgos Kypris, an internationally celebrated artist who takes much of his inspiration from Santorini. Take in his larger sculptures (incredible fish) and then consider home items, pendants and jewellery that are hard to resist.

Orion Art Gallery ART
(📞 22860 21616; www.artoftheloom.gr; Kamares; ⊙ 9am-10pm) This new gallery and shop next to the Megaro Gyzi Cultural Centre (p230) at the northern end of town displays gorgeous pieces by some of the island's top artists. Expect everything from fusion glass to modern bronze statues, handmade jewellery and colourful ceramics. Everything can be packed and sent overseas.

AK Art Gallery ART
(📞 22860 23041; www.ak-galleries.com) AK, Santorini's first art gallery, was founded in 1980 by local artists, painter Christopher Asimis and his wife, Eleni Kolaiti, who specialises in jewellery and sculptures. The stunningly white gallery, near the Orthodox Cathedral, was formerly a flour mill and features impressive art inspired by the beauty of the island. AK also has galleries in Oia and on the Fira–Pyrgos road.

Greco Gold Santorini JEWELLERY
(📞 22860 22460; http://grecogoldsantorini.gr; ⊙ 10am-11pm) Just north of the cathedral, Greco Gold has been around for over four decades, selling the well-known Greek brand Konstantino, handmade Byzantine-style jewellery and contemporary pieces designed and made by Greco Gold itself.

the White, Santorini FASHION & ACCESSORIES
(📞 22860 36217; www.thewhitesantorini.com) This small fashion boutique, run by designer Sophia Hatzigeorgiou, draws inspiration from Santorini's unique landscapes, colours and lifestyle. The clothing is hand-sewn in Greece and, as the name suggests, collections feature plenty of options in white. There's a second store out at Kamari Beach.

Theta 8 FASHION & ACCESSORIES
(📞 22866 72935; Marinatou; ⊙ 9am-midnight) The new kid on the block is a chic boutique in a white-cave shop on the steps down to the Old Port. It offers colourful leather bags handmade in Greece, plus appealing accessories. Owned and operated by three local women, expect friendly smiles and service.

ℹ Information

There are numerous ATMs scattered around town.

Alpha Bank (Plateia Theotokopoulou) Has an ATM.

Central Clinic of Santorini (📞 22860 21728; www.santorinicentralclinic.gr) Health clinic just east of the town centre. Open 24 hours for emergencies.

Dakoutros Travel (📞 22860 22958; www.dak outrostravel.gr; Fira; ⊙ 8.30am-10pm) Travel agency on the main street, just before Plateia Theotokopoulou. Ferry and air tickets sold;

SAMPLING SANTORINI

Beyond caldera views, infinity pools and black-sand beaches, Santorini is cultivating a reputation for wine and food tourism. It's a side of the island well worth exploring.

Food

Food-wise, the island is best known in Greece for its white eggplants, capers, cherry tomatoes and fava (yellow split peas, not unlike lentils). Cooked and puréed, the popular fava dish is traditionally eaten warm, as an appetiser (or dip), or accompanying a main course of meat or fish. Santorini was 'tomato island' before the tourism boom, though only one of 13 former tomato processing factories is still in operation.

Tomato Industrial Museum (☑ 22860 85141; www.tomatomuseum.gr; Vlihada; €5; ⊗ 10am-6pm Tue-Sun) Despite the dry-sounding name, this is a unique look inside an old tomato factory in Vlihada. Tomato processing was a major industry on the island, and the video interviews of elderly former factory workers is fascinating. The seaside museum is part of the cool **Santorini Arts Factory** (www.santoriniartsfactory.gr), which hosts exhibitions, concerts and theatre; check its program online.

Selene (☑ 22860 22249; www.selene.gr; Pyrgos) Acclaimed restaurant **Selene** (☑ 22860 22249; www.selene.gr; Pyrgos; mains restaurant €30-40, bistro €9-16; ⊗ restaurant dinner, bistro lunch & dinner) offers a program of cooking demonstrations, wine-tasting and hands-on cooking courses, with plenty of opportunity for sampling the wares. Courses include a tour of the on-site **Cultural Village** (☑ 22860 31101; www.santorinimuseum.com; Pyrgos; €4; ⊗ 10am-4pm & 6-8pm Mon-Sat), which explores culinary, agricultural and other island traditions. See the website for details.

Wine

Santorini's lauded wines are its crisp dry whites, and the amber-coloured, unfortified dessert wine known as Vinsanto. Both are made from the indigenous grape variety, Assyrtiko. Most local vineyards host tastings (usually for a small charge), and some offer food, with scenery and local produce combining to great effect.

assistance with excursions, accommodation and transfers.

Information Kiosk (⊗ 9am-8pm Mon-Fri May-Sep) Seasonal information kiosk.

National Bank of Greece (Dekigala) South of Plateia Theotokopoulou, on the caldera side of the road. Has an ATM.

Police Station (☑ 22860 22649) In the centre of Fira.

Post Office (Dekigala)

Oia   Οία
POP 670

Perched on the northern tip of the island, the village of Oia reflects the renaissance of Santorini after the devastating earthquake of 1956. Restoration work has whipped up beauty, and you will struggle to find a more stunning Cyclades village. Built on a steep slope of the caldera, many of its dwellings nestle in niches hewn into the volcanic rock.

Not surprisingly, Oia draws enormous numbers of tourists, and overcrowding is the price it pays for its good looks. Try to visit in the morning or spend the night here; afternoons and evenings often bring busloads from the cruise ships moored in the bay. At sunset the town feels like a magnet for every traveller on the island.

◉ Sights & Activities

★**Ammoudi**   PORT
This tiny port full of colourful fishing boats lies 300 steps below Oia. It's a hot haul down and up again but the effort is well worth it for the views of the blood-red cliffs, the harbour and back up to Oia. Once you're down there, have lunch at one of the excellent, if pricey, fish tavernas right on the water's edge. In summer, boats and tours go from Ammoudi to Thirasia daily; check with travel agencies in Fira for departure times.

Santorini Wine Adventure (☑ 22860 34123; www.winetoursantorini.com; half-day tours from €100) Runs wine- and food-focused tours, including Santorini Wine Adventure, Wine & Food Lover Tour and Trails of History & Wine Tour.

Santorini Wine Tour (☑ 22860 28358; www.santoriniwinetour.com; ⊙ half-day tour from €100) Food- and wine-focused tours of Santorini.

SantoWines (☑ 22860 22596; www.santowines.gr; tours & tastings from €12.50; ⊙ 9am-9pm) The best place to start your wine adventure is at Santorini's cooperative of grape growers, a large tourist-focused complex on the caldera edge near the port. It has short tours of the production process and lots of tasting options. There are also superb views, a wine bar with food and a shop full of choice vintages as well as gourmet local products.

Domaine Sigalas (☑ 22860 71644; www.sigalas-wine.com; Oia) A polished, peaceful patch not far from Oia, with wine samples and platters among the vines. On the road between Finikia and the coast, you'll want to join a tour or use rental wheels to get here.

Boutari (☑ 22860 81011; www.boutari.gr; Megalohori; ⊙ 10am-7pm) A relaxed winery on the way south to Akrotiri with 40 great wines to sample in a number of packages. Simple local dishes on offer too. This is one of seven Boutari wineries around Greece.

Wine Museum (☑ 22860 31322; www.winemuseum.gr; €9.50; ⊙ 10am-5pm Apr-Oct, 9am-4.30pm Mon-Sat Nov-Mar) At the Koutsoyannopoulos Winery en route to Kamari, this heavily promoted attraction has a pricey, slightly kitsch museum in a traditional *canava* (winery). Admission includes tastings of four wines.

Beer

Santorini Brewery Company (☑ 22860 30268; www.santorinibrewingcompany.gr; ⊙ 11am-5pm Mon-Sat summer, shorter hr rest of year) The home of the island's in-demand Donkey beers (you may have seen the eye-catching logo on your travels) is well worth a stop. Sample the Yellow Donkey (golden ale), Red Donkey (amber ale), the Crazy Donkey (IPA) and the White Donkey (wheat with a touch of orange peel). All are unfiltered, unpasteurised and extremely palatable. Free tastings, plus cool merchandise that makes a fun souvenir.

Maritime Museum MUSEUM
(☑ 22860 71156; €3; ⊙ 10am-2pm & 5-8pm Wed-Mon) This museum is located along a narrow lane that leads off north from Nikolaou Nomikou. It's housed in a renovated and converted 19th-century mansion and has endearing displays on Santorini's maritime history. Oia's prosperity was based on its merchant fleet, which serviced the eastern Mediterranean, especially between Alexandria and Russia.

🛏 Sleeping

Oia is known for its glorious luxury villas and suites cascading down the caldera. Book well ahead. If you're on a budget, consider staying elsewhere.

Maria's Place HOTEL €€
(☑ 22860 71221; www.mariasantorini.com; d studio €120; ✳ 🛜 🌊) Excellent midrange option, inland from town on the road to Finikia and a 10-minute walk to the caldera. Peaceful (no kids under 16), great hosts, lovely pool and very reasonable off-peak rates.

Zoe Houses APARTMENT €€
(☑ 22860 71466; www.zoe-aegeas.gr; studio/apt €190/260; ✳ @ 🛜) Traditional houses built into the caldera's edge with all the comforts of home. Classy decor, amazing views and unrivalled hospitality mean that this place gets a lot of happily returning guests. Book ahead. Each suite is different; some can sleep up to six.

Chelidonia Traditional Villas APARTMENT €€
(☑ 22860 71287; www.chelidonia.com; Nikolaou Nomikou; studio €215, villa from €245; ✳ 🛜) Traditional cliffside dwellings that have been in the owner's family for generations and offer a grand mix of old and new. Modern niceties are offset with traditional wooden furniture, and private patios offer uninterrupted caldera views.

DON'T MISS

CINEKAMARI

After the caldera sunset, **CineKamari** (☑ 22860 33452; www.cinekamari.gr; Kamari; €8; ⊙ 9.30pm) is one of the finest ways to spend a Santorini evening. On the road into Kamari, this tree-surrounded, open-air cinema screens movies in their original language throughout the summer. Pull up a deckchair, request a blanket if you're feeling chilly, and relax. Drinks and snacks available.

✕ Eating

Lolita's Gelato
ICE CREAM €

(☑ 22860 71279; www.lolitasgelato.com; cones €3-6) Near the bus station, Lolita's sells scoopfuls of homemade heaven, including classics like blueberry or pistachio, plus original flavours like rosewater and red pepper. Take a break while you wait for the bus.

Krinaki
TAVERNA €€

(☑ 22860 71993; www.krinaki-santorini.gr; Finikia; mains €12-22; ⊙ noon-late) All-fresh, all-local ingredients go into top-notch taverna dishes at this homey spot in tiny Finikia, just east of Oia. Local beer and wine, plus a sea (but not caldera) view looking north to Ios.

Karma
GREEK €€

(☑ 22860 71404; www.karma.bz; mains €11-17; ⊙ dinner) With fountains, flickering candles, golden-coloured walls and wine-coloured cushions, this courtyard restaurant feels rather royal and august. The food is traditional and hearty, and as Karma is away from the caldera, the prices are considerably more relaxed.

Skala
GREEK €€

(☑ 22860 71362; www.facebook.com/skalarestaurantoia; Nikolaou Nomikou; dishes €8-18; ⊙ lunch & dinner) Watch life pass up and down to Armeni Bay from the high ground of Skala's relaxed terrace. Traditional dishes like souvlaki, baked eggplant and cheese pies fill the crowd-pleasing menu.

1800
GREEK €€€

(☑ 22860 71485; www.oia-1800.com; Nikolaou Nomikou; mains €13-35) Housed in a restored sea captain's mansion, the artistically prepared modern Greek cuisine has won this restaurant accolades for years. Sea bass with an aromatic spell of quinoa, artichoke and fennel purée or grilled lamb with sweet-and-sour green apple sauce give you a glimpse at the creative menu. Dine inside or on the caldera-view rooftop.

🔒 Shopping

Iatis Workshop
JEWELLERY, CERAMICS

(☑ 22860 72127; www.facebook.com/IatisWorkshop; Nikolaou Nomikou) With his studio at the back of the gallery, Christos Papageorgiou wows passers-by with his contemporary designs. Stunning silver and gold jewellery is professionally crafted and shimmers next to the artist's striking pottery.

Atlantis Books
BOOKS

(☑ 22860 72346; www.atlantisbooks.org; Nikolaou Nomikou; ⊙ 11am-8pm) This amazing little bookstore is a destination in itself. Follow quotes and words that wind their way down the stairs into a hobbit hole that appears to be held up by row upon row of books. Staff are friendly and knowledgeable, and musicians and other events are hosted on the rooftop.

ℹ Information

ATMs can be found on Nikolaou Nomikou and also by the bus terminus.

Travel agencies such as **NS Travel** (☑ 22860 71199; www.nst-santorinitravel.com) are found by the bus area.

Around Santorini

There's more than just the spectacular caldera and sunset views to keep visitors busy on Santorini. Head out to visit impressive ancient sites, black-sand beaches, wineries (and a brewery) or take a boat tour to an active volcanic island in the caldera.

⊙ Sights & Activities

Santorini's best beaches are on the east and south coasts. Sunbeds, beach bars and water sports operators are here to serve.

The long stretch of black sand, pebbles and pumice stones at **Perissa**, **Perivolos** and **Agios Georgios** is backed by bars, tavernas, hotels and shops and remains fairly relaxed.

Red (Kokkini) Beach, near Ancient Akrotiri in the south, has impressive red cliffs. Caïques from **Akrotiri Beach** can take you there and on to **White (Aspri)** and **Black (Mesa Pigadia) Beaches** for about €5 return.

Vlihada, also on the south coast, has a beach backed by weirdly eroded cliffs as well as tavernas; it also has a photogenic fishing harbour.

Kamari is Santorini's best-developed resort, with a long beach of black sand. The beachfront road is dense with restaurants and bars, and things get extremely busy in high season. Boats connect Kamari with Perissa in summer.

Note: at times, Santorini's black-sand beaches become so hot that a sunlounge or mat is essential.

★ **Ancient Akrotiri**   ARCHAEOLOGICAL SITE
(✐ 22860 81366; http://odysseus.culture.gr/h/3/eh351.jsp?obj_id=2410; adult/child €12/free; ⊙ 8am-8pm Apr-Oct, 8am-3pm Nov-Mar) In 1967, excavations uncovered an ancient Minoan city buried deep beneath volcanic ash from the catastrophic eruption of 1613 BC. Housed within a cool, protective structure, wooden walkways allow you to pass through the city. Peek inside three-storey buildings that survived, and see roads, drainage systems and stashes of pottery. The vibe of excitement still courses through the site, with continued excavations and discoveries. Guided tours are available (per person €10) and help to give context.

Ancient Thira   ARCHAEOLOGICAL SITE
(✐ 22860 23217; http://odysseus.culture.gr/h/3/eh351.jsp?obj_id=2454; adult/child €4/free; ⊙ 8am-3pm Tue-Sun) First settled by the Dorians in the 9th century BC, Ancient Thira consists of Hellenistic, Roman and Byzantine ruins and is an atmospheric and rewarding site to visit. The ruins include temples, houses with mosaics, an *agora* (market), a theatre and a gymnasium. Views are splendid. If you're driving, take the narrow, switchbacked road from Kamari for 3km. From Perissa, a hike up a dusty path takes a bit over an hour to reach the site.

★ **Art Space**   GALLERY
(✐ 22860 32774; www.artspace-santorini.com; Exo Gonia; ⊙ 11am-sunset) **FREE** This unmissable, atmospheric gallery is on the way to Kamari, in Argyros Canava, one of the oldest wineries on the island. The atmospheric old wine caverns are hung with superb artworks, while sculptures transform lost corners and niches. The collection features some of Greece's finest modern artists. Winemaking is still in the owner's blood, and part of the complex produces some stellar vintages under the Art Space Wines label. Tastings (€5) enhance the experience.

🛏 Sleeping

🛏 Karterados

★ **Karterados Caveland Hostel**   HOSTEL €
(✐ 22860 22122; www.cave-land.com; Karterados; dm/d incl breakfast €25/90; ⊙ Mar-Oct; 🅿 ❄ 🛜 ≋) This fabulous, chilled-out hostel is based in an old winery complex in Karterados about 2km from central Fira (see website for directions). Accommodation is in the big old wine caves, all of them with creative, colourful decor and good facilities. The surrounding garden is relaxing, and there are weekly barbecues, tennis courts, a swimming pool and yoga too.

🛏 Kamari

Narkissos Hotel   HOTEL €
(✐ 22860 34205; www.narkissoshotel.com; Kamari; r incl breakfast €75; ⊙ Apr-Nov; ❄ 🛜) A decent budget option at the southern end of Kamari, close to the beach and with well-kept rooms. Outside the summer peak, room prices tumble (€30).

Hippocampus Hotel   HOTEL €€
(✐ 22860 32050; www.hippocampus-hotel.gr; Kamari; d/tr/q €140/160/180; ⊙ May-Oct; ❄ 🛜 ≋) Just steps from Kamari's beachfront, this friendly place has a sparkling collection of rooms and studios, with added extras like hand-painted wall murals and a commitment to ecopractices. Good family-sized studios too.

🛏 Perissa

★ **Stelios Place**   HOTEL €
(✐ 22860 81860; www.steliosplace.com; Perissa; d/tr/q €88/110/130; ❄ @ 🛜 ≋) This small, family-run hotel has a great position set

---

DISAPPEARING ACT

No one knows what happened to the Minoan people of Akrotiri as no human remains have been found at the site. Some believe that residents fled the city following the earthquake that took place two or three weeks before the volcanic eruption and are buried elsewhere on the island, beneath tonnes of ash. Others speculate that they recognised signs of impending doom and fled by boat towards Crete.

THIRASIA & VOLCANIC ISLETS
ΘΗΡΑΣΙΑ & ΗΦΑΙΣΤΕΙΑΚΕΣ ΝΗΣΙΔΕΣ

Relatively untouched in terms of tourism, **Thirasia** (population 160) was separated from Santorini by an eruption in 236 BC. Clifftop **Manolas**, the main town, has tavernas and domatia. It's an attractive place, noticeably more relaxed and reflective than Fira could ever be. Thirasia is a stop on a couple of ferry routes to/from Athinios a few times a week, or take one of the regular boats from Ammoudi, below Oia (€5). Ask at central travel agencies for the schedule.

The unpopulated islets of **Palia Kameni** and **Nea Kameni** in the middle of the caldera are still volcanically active and can be visited on various boat excursions from Fira Skala and Athinios. A day's excursion taking in Nea Kameni, the **hot springs** on Palia Kameni (more lukewarm than hot), Thirasia and Oia starts at about €30.

back from the main drag in Perissa, one block from the beach. Well-equipped rooms sparkle with cleanliness, as does the swimming pool. Breakfast is available. Free airport or port transfers for those staying three nights or longer; note that off-peak rates fall to a bargain €35.

Zorzis Hotel   BOUTIQUE HOTEL €
(☑ 22860 81104; www.santorinizorzis.com; Perissa; d incl breakfast from €90; ❄ 🛜 🏊) Behind a huge bloom of geraniums on Perissa's main street, Hiroko and Spiros (a Japanese-Greek couple) run an immaculate 10-room hotel. It's a pastel-coloured sea of calm (no kids), with delightful garden, pool and mountain backdrop.

🍴 Eating

Brusco   CAFE €
(☑ 22860 30944; Pyrgos; mains from €7) In Pyrgos, Brusco offers coffee, wine and local flavours in a sweet rustic cafe-deli, with plenty of outdoor space. Stop by for the warm welcome, homemade cakes (including baklava) and platters of great Santorini produce (fava, tomatoes, eggplant, capers and more).

★ Metaxi Mas   TAVERNA €€
(☑ 22860 31323; www.santorini-metaximas.gr; Exo Gonia; mains €8-19; ⏱ lunch & dinner) The raki flows at this convivial taverna, a favourite among locals and authenticity-seeking travellers. In the central village of Exo Gonia (on the steep winding road between Pyrgos and Kamari), park by the large church and walk down some steps to reach it. Enjoy sweeping views and a delicious menu of local and Cretan specialities.

ANAFI   ΑΝΑΦΗ

POP 270

Anafi lies a mere 22km east of Santorini, a tiny island perched on a distant horizon, with a slow-paced traditional lifestyle and striking Cycladic landscapes. There are few visitors outside high summer, which is a big part of its charm. Come to Anafi if you're looking for a quiet Greek island escape.

The port of **Agios Nikolaos** is on the south coast, with the main town of **Hora** a steep 2km by road above to the north.

ℹ Getting There & Away

Anafi is out on a limb and you may face challenges getting there, but in July and August the island has reasonable ferry connections. Plan well, especially outside the high season, and consult http://ferries.gr for up-to-date ferry information. Because of its proximity to Santorini, to visit Anafi you will in all likelihood take a ferry from there. Don't make travel connections that are too tight as ferries from Anafi are notoriously late.

Buy ferry tickets at **Roussou Travel** (☑ 22860 61220) in Hora's main street or at an office on the harbourfront one hour before ferries are due.

ℹ Getting Around

The island's port is Agios Nikolaos. From here, the main village, Hora, is a 10-minute bus ride (€1.80) up a winding road, or a 1km hike up a less winding but steep walkway. In summer a bus runs regularly and usually meets boats; buses also run east to the monastery (€2.60).

Summertime caïques serve various beaches and nearby small islands.

In Hora, **Manos** (☑ 22860 61430; www.rentacarmanos.com) has cars, scooters and four-wheelers for rent.

⊙ Sights & Activities

The monastery **Zoodochos Pigi** is 9km from Hora by road, or reached by a 7km walk along the south-coast trail. The monastery lies in the east of the island, on the isthmus connecting Anafi to the imposing 463m **Kalamos** (or Monastery Rock), which has the uninhabited **Kalamiotissas Monastery** at its peak. Locals claim Kalamos as the second-largest rock in the Mediterranean after the Rock of Gibraltar.

There are several lovely beaches near Agios Nikolaos. **Klissidi**, a 1.5km walk east of the port and visible from the ferry when you arrive, is the closest and most popular. The south-coast walking trail that goes to Zoodochos Pigi Monastery gives access to more strands, including the long, sandy **Roukounas Beach**.

🛏 Sleeping

Many of the rooms on Hora's main pedestrian street have good views across Anafi's rolling hills to the sea and to the great summit of Kalamos. Beachgoers should stay at Klissidi Beach. Book early for July and August; outside these two months, accommodation is cheap.

★ Margarita's Rooms   PENSION €
(📞 22860 61237; www.margarita-anafi.gr; d from €60; 🛜) Just above Klissidi beach, these simple, beloved family-run rooms hark back to the Greek island life of quieter times. Nothing luxurious here, but if you're after an affordable island escape next to a lovely beach, you can't really go wrong. It's a tad isolated, but all you need is here, including Margarita's taverna. Port transfers included.

Villa Kalamiotissa   APARTMENT €€
(📞 22860 61415; www.villakalamiotissa.gr; d €100; ⊙Apr-Oct; ❄🛜) A handsome complex of rooms and studios, all white and pale blue with lovely stonework. It sits on a quiet edge of Hora, with spectacular views south from each verandah. Studios sleep three and have kitchens. Entry is from the ring road around Hora.

Apollon Village Hotel   APARTMENT €€
(📞 22860 28739; http://apollonvillagehotel.com; d/studio/apt from €70/95/120; ⊙May-Sep; ❄🛜) Rising in tiers above Klissidi Beach, these individual rooms, studios and apartments with glorious views are each named after a Greek god and remain outstanding value. The Blue Cafe-Bar is a cool adjunct to the hotel, with homemade sweets and pastries. Entry is from the port to Hora road.

✕ Eating & Drinking

★ Margarita's   TAVERNA €
(📞 22860 61237; www.margarita-anafi.gr; Klissidi; mains €6-12; ⊙breakfast, lunch & dinner; 🛜) A sunny little terrace overlooking the bay at Klissidi makes for an idyllic dining experience. Margarita's fresh-baked bread, hand-made pasta and meatballs are staples; fava, goat stew and cheese pies are all full of local flavour. There are rooms here too.

Armenaki   TAVERNA €€
(📞 22860 61234; mains €7-15; ⊙lunch & dinner Jun-Sep) Tuna and swordfish are the go-to dishes at this traditional taverna in Hora, enhanced by an airy terrace, splendid views and occasional live music. Head down the small street opposite the bakery in central Hora to find it.

Liotrivi   TAVERNA €€
(📞 22860 61209; www.facebook.com/liotrivirest; mains from €7; ⊙lunch & dinner May-Oct) A classy old-school taverna on the main street in Hora, where fresh fish is brought in from the family's boat, while just about everything else, from eggs to vegetables and honey, comes from their garden. Huge views from the terrace seating.

Glaros   BAR
(⊙Jun-Sep) In Hora, be sure to stop for a drink at this local institution. If you're lucky, you'll stumble across some live music – if not, the views won't disappoint. Carry on down the main street past the market to find it.

ℹ Information

Find more information online at www.anafi.gr.

SIKINOS   ΣΙΚΙΝΟΣ

POP 280

A stone's throw from Santorini, Sikinos is really worlds away – and decidedly off the tourist radar. Quiet and remote, this is the place to come if you want to experience traditional island life at its least commercial. With a charming old town and terraced hills that sweep down to sandy beaches, Sikinos offers a true escape.

The main clusters of habitation are the port of Alopronia and the linked inland villages of Horio and Kastro (collectively known as the Hora). Kastro has homes and businesses, Horio is purely residential. They are reached by a 3.4km road winding up from the port. There's a post office at the eastern edge of Kastro, and an ATM in Kastro's central square.

July and August see lots of Greek visitors turn up, but if you arrive before mid-May, don't expect there to be much going on.

Getting There & Away

Ferry tickets can be bought at the port at **Kountouris Travel** (☑ 6981594106, 22860 51232). Out of high season, boat services are skeletal.

Boat Services from Sikinos

DESTINATION	DURATION	FARE (€)	FREQUENCY
Folegandros	45min	5	4 weekly
Ios	25min	5	4 weekly
Kimolos	2¼hr	13	4 weekly
Milos	3hr 25min	13	2 weekly
Naxos	2hr 25min	12	1 weekly
Paros	3hr 50min	14	1 weekly
Piraeus	7½–9½hr	39	4 weekly
Serifos	4¼hr	18	1 weekly
Sifnos	2¾hr–5hr	16	4 weekly
Santorini (Thira)	2hr	7	3 weekly
Syros	6hr	13	1 weekly

Getting Around

The local bus meets ferry arrivals and runs between Alopronia and Horio/Kastro (€1.80) every half-hour in August, but less frequently at other times. A timetable is posted at the terminus, just inland from the port. If you're out of season and nothing is going on, talk to English-speaking Flora in the minimarket at Alopronia – she'll call the bus driver, who'll come to get you in her car and take you to Hora for the same price as the bus!

There is a small agency at the port, **RaC** (☑ 21040 80300; www.rentacar-sikinos.gr), hiring out cars and scooters.

Sights & Activities

The beach at the port of **Alopronia** is lovely – sandy, with some shade and a children's playground. It looks straight out at Santorini.

A narrow, dramatic bay with a small sandy patch, **Agios Nikolaos Beach** is a 20-minute walk through the countryside from the port. To find it, follow signs to Dialiskari. A path leads further on to **Agios Georgios**, or you can reach it by sealed road (7km).

Summertime caïques (about €6) run to beaches, including **Malta** in the north (which boasts ancient ruins on the hill above) and **Kara** in the south.

Sikinos is popular with walkers, and the island has set up seven **Paths of Culture**, a network of well-signposted paths all over the island. Keen walkers should purchase Terrain's (http://terrainmaps.gr) excellent hiking map for Sikinos.

★**Moni Zoödohou Pigis**   MONASTERY
(☑ 6975743928; ☺10am-noon & 4-6pm) **FREE**
A flight of whitewashed steps leads to the fortified monastery of Moni Zoödohou Pigis, high above the Kastro. Originally built as a women's monastery in 1690, this is where the nuns and villagers would hide out during pirate attacks. The monastery has recently opened to the public, and you can go into the church and the visitors' room, or check out the amazing views. Don't miss the nuns' emergency escape route, by rope down the cliffs out the back.

Kastro   VILLAGE
A Venetian fortress that stood here in the 13th century gave Kastro its name. Today it is a charming, lived-in place, with winding alleyways between brilliant white houses. At its heart is the main square and the Church of Pantanassa. Check out the buildings surrounding the church, which were homes to the town's wealthy merchants: two-storey affairs with remnants of ornate stonework around the windows.

Horio   VILLAGE
Just west of Kastro, above steeply terraced fields and reached by a flight of whitewashed steps, is the reclusive, beautiful Horio. Still home to a dozen or so residents, it's a patchwork of derelict and well-tended houses and is definitely worth a wander.

Moni Episkopis   MONASTERY
FREE From the saddle between Kastro and Horio, a surfaced road leads southwest to Moni Episkopis. The remains here are believed to be those of a 3rd-century AD Roman mausoleum that was transformed into a church in the 7th century and a monastery 10 centuries later.

Manalis Winery
WINERY

(☑ 6932272854; www.manaliswinery.gr; ☺ 6pm-late summer) On the road to Moni Episkopis, Manalis Winery produces Sikinos wine using self-sustaining, traditional methods. You can easily spend an hour or two here nibbling on snacks, sipping wine and trying out the traditional menu on the view-filled patio.

🛏 Sleeping

Rooms Kaminia
PENSION €

(☑ 22860 51304; Kastro; d €60; ❄ 🐧) A white-washed staircase next to the post office in Kastro leads up to this complex of four simple studios – large and spotless, with kitchen facilities, new bathrooms and splendid views. It's open year-round, with low-season prices a steal at €30.

Stegadi Apartments
APARTMENT €€

(☑ 22860 51305; www.stegadi.com; Kastro; d €90; ❄ 🐧) Near the heart of Kastro, these traditional apartments sleep up to four and are individually decorated with modern furnishings and splashes of vibrant colour. The balconies have views across to the sea.

Ostria Studios
PENSION €€

(☑ 22860 51062; www.ostriastudios-sikinos.gr; Alopronia; d from €75; ❄ 🐧) These comfy rooms and studios are lovingly decorated. Margarita has three sets of rooms – Ostria Studios Spilia, Agnanti and Molos; Spilia is on the far side of the bay from the ferry quay. The rooms are right on the water, and you can swim below your room. They have sea-view balconies and plenty of peace.

🍴 Eating

★ Anemelo
CAFE €

(☑ 22860 51216; Kastro; mains €4-8; ☺ 10am-3pm & 5pm-late) This is Kastro's most atmospheric place to grab a local tea, beer or simple crêpe-and-salad lunch. Locals chat at the tables over chess games or lounge over coffee at the tables outside. Take the *tiny* staircase up to the terrace for ace views. The killer Traditional Sandwich (€5) features olive paste, feta, capers and tomato.

Kapari
GREEK €

(☑ 22860 51070; Kastro; mains from €7.50; ☺ 8am-2.30am) Your go-to place if you arrive out of season or are staying at Alopronia and absolutely nothing is open. It's on the main road in Hora – Flora at the minimarket in Alopronia will figure out how to get you here if you're stuck. These guys have good solid

Greek staples, including their own uniquely named 'beer salad' and 'sinful meatballs'.

Klimataria
GREEK €€

(☑ 22860 51065; Kastro; mains €8-13; ☺ lunch & dinner May-Oct; 🐧) A cute leafy laneway shades a couple of traditional eateries, including this friendly spot, where you can indulge in platters heaped with mixed grills.

FOLEGANDROS
ΦΟΛΕΓΑΝΔΡΟΣ

POP 765

Folegandros lies on the southern edge of the Cyclades, with the Sea of Crete sweeping away to its south. The island has a bewitching beauty that is amplified by its alluring clifftop Hora, perhaps the most appealing village in the Cyclades.

Folegandros is barely 12km by 4km but shoulders a somewhat dark past. The remoteness and ruggedness of the island made it a place of exile for political prisoners from Roman times to the 20th century, as late as the military dictatorship of 1967–74. Today the seductive charm of Folegandros has left its grim history behind.

Boats dock at the little harbour of **Karavostasis**, on the east coast. Aside from it and Hora, the only other settlement of any size is **Ano Meria**. There are some good beaches, but be prepared for strenuous walking to reach some of them (or the easy option: take a boat).

❶ Getting There & Away

Once poorly served by ferries, Folegandros has good connections (at least in summer) with Piraeus through the western Cyclades route. It has connections to Santorini and is part of a Ios-Sikinos-Folegandros link, with regular ferries passing through.

❶ Getting Around

The local bus meets all ferry arrivals and takes passengers to Hora (3km; €1.80). From Hora there are buses to the port one hour before ferry departures. Buses from Hora run hourly in summer to Ano Meria (€1.80) and divert to Angali Beach (€2.20). The bus terminus is at the entrance to Hora from the south, behind the post office.

There is a **taxi service** (☑ 6944693957) on Folegandros. Fares to the port are about €7 to €10, to Ano Meria €10 and to Angali Beach €10 to €14.

BOAT SERVICES FROM FOLEGANDROS

DESTINATION	DURATION	FARE (€)	FREQUENCY
Amorgos*	2-5½hr	69	6 weekly
Ios	1hr 20min	10	4 weekly
Ios*	20min	44	2 weekly
Kimolos	1¼hr-2¾hr	13	4 weekly
Koufonisia*	1¾hr-5hr	69	6 weekly
Milos	2½hr	13	2 weekly
Milos*	1hr	39	1-2 daily
Mykonos*	3-3½hr	59	6 weekly
Naxos*	2hr 40min	49	6 weekly
Piraeus	6½-9hr	36	4 weekly
Piraeus*	3½hr-5hr	59	1-2 daily
Santorini (Thira)	3hr	12	3 weekly
Santorini (Thira)*	40-70min	44	1-2 daily
Serifos	3hr 20min	18	1 weekly
Sifnos	2-4hr	16	4 weekly
Sifnos*	2hr	49	3 weekly
Sikinos	45min	7	5 weekly
Syros	6¾hr	18	1 weekly

* high-speed services

You can hire cars/motorbikes from a number of outlets in high season for about €60/25 per day. Rates can drop by half outside high season. **Tomaso** (☑ 22860 41600; www.tomaso.gr) in Hora is a good option.

In summer, small boats regularly run between beaches.

Karavostasis Καραβοστάσις

POP 90

Folegandros' port is a sunny place with a pleasant pebble beach. Within a kilometre north and south lie a series of other beaches, all enjoyable and easily reached by short walks. In high season, boats leave Karavostasis for beaches further afield. If beaches are your allure, stay here – for our money, however, Hora, 3km up the road, is where the magic is.

🛏 Sleeping & Eating

Aeolos Beach Hotel　　　　HOTEL €€
(☑ 22860 41205; www.aeolos-folegandros.gr; s/d €70/100; ⊗ May-Sep; ❊ 🎅) Settle in right on the beach here at Aeolos. Rooms have sea or mountain views and are each unique, with varying degrees of character. There's

a minimum three-night stay in July and August; breakfast costs €8.

★**Anemi**　　　　LUXURY HOTEL €€€
(☑ 22860 41610; www.anemihotel.gr; d/ste incl breakfast from €275/430; ⊗ late May-Sep; ❊ 🎅 🏊) Oh so modern and entirely luxurious, this is a place for pampering. Rooms are plush but sleek, brought to life by modern artwork that doubles as headboards. The pool is a large, beckoning sheet of blue (some of the suites have a private pool) and there's an enviable roll-call of extras, including family-friendly ones.

Meltemi　　　　TAVERNA €
(☑ 22860 41287; mains from €7; ⊗ 9am-late Apr-Oct) Perched above the port with lovely views, Meltemi stands out with its lovely terrace with blue balustrades. This is a mama's cooking, family-run place with Greek staples, seafood and grilled meats.

Hora (Folegandros) Χώρα (Φολέγανδρος)

POP 425

Hora (Folegandros) has had some high-profile television coverage of late, and the secret is now out – this village is probably the most charming in the Cyclades. Its meandering main street, winding happily from leafy square to leafy square, where al fresco tables buzz with life, is a joy to behold. Its marvellous natural stone buildings, mixed among those in Cycladic white and blue, stylishly impress.

◉ Sights

The village proper starts at **Plateia Pounta**; on its north side, it stands on the edge of a formidable cliff. Just west of here is the medieval **kastro**, a small tangle of narrow alleys spanned by low archways. It dates from when Marco Sanudo ruled the island in the 13th century. The balconies of the traditional houses blaze with bougainvillea, and a few whitewashed chapels add charm.

Panagia   CHURCH

(◉6-9pm) From Plateia Pounta, a zigzag path leads up to the large Church of the Virgin, Panagia, which sits perched on the side of a hill above the town and acts as a mecca for sunset-watchers. It's an easy 20-minute walk without steps on a wide concrete path, offering spectacular views down to Hora, cliffs and pounding waves along the way.

☞ Tours

Given the tough-to-access nature of many beaches, a popular excursion is the six-hour boat trip around the island (adult/child €40/15). The price includes lunch and plenty of swimming stops. The tour leaves Karavostasis at 11am, and can be booked through Diaplous Travel (p246). Private boat trips can also be arranged.

⌂ Sleeping

In July and August, most domatia and hotels will be full, so book well in advance. Free port transfers (3km to the port) are generally included with most sleeping options.

★ Ampelos   BOUTIQUE HOTEL €€

(☑22860 41544; http://ampelosresort.com; s/d/tr €100/110/120; ◉May-Oct; ❊⊛☒) Theo and Areti's place is a gorgeous family-run operation with a sparkling pool, tasteful colours and lovely rooms. It's an easy 10-minute stroll into the centre of Hora from just south of town. There are free port transfers, complimentary coffee, rates that halve outside the peak season and friendly smiles.

Hotel Odysseus   HOTEL €€

(☑22860 41276; www.hotelodysseus.com; s/d €85/110; ◉mid-May–Sep; ❊⊛☒) Tucked away in a quiet corner of town with some

Folegandros

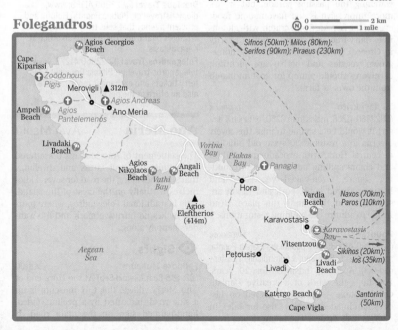

dramatic views and colourful green doors, Odysseus has pretty, compact rooms with sweet terraces, and a lovely pool area that's shared with Aria Boutique Hotel next door. Low-season prices are ace (doubles €60) but breakfast is an additional €12.

Folegandros Apartments APARTMENT €€
(☑ 22860 41239; www.folegandros-apartments. com; d from €140; ☺ May-Sep; ❋ 🛜 🌊) This lovely complex of studios and apartments (the largest can sleep seven) is set in well-kept gardens around a pristine pool just above Plateia Pounta in Hora. It's only a couple of minutes' stroll into the village.

Anemomilos Apartments HOTEL €€€
(☑ 22860 41309; www.anemomilosapartments. com; d incl breakfast from €270; ☺ May-Sep; ❋ 🛜 🌊) A prime clifftop location just above Plateia Pounta in Hora grants awesome views from this stylish complex and its lovely terraces. Rooms are elegant and embellished with antiques. The pool is divine, and service comes with wonderful attention to detail.

✖ Eating & Drinking

★ Chic GREEK €
(☑ 22860 41515; mains €6.50-13; ☺ dinner Easter-Oct; ✔) Chic is perfectly placed for watching the passing parade, but what's more impressive is the flavoursome food: everything is made from scratch, with gluten-free, dairy-free and vegan options (a rarity in Greece). Veggie dishes (featuring home-grown veggies and herbs) are plentiful; carnivores should plump for goat and lamb from the owners' farm.

To Asygkrito TAVERNA €
(☑ 22860 41266; mains from €7.50; ☺ lunch & dinner) It would be a shame to miss this lovely taverna in a restored 300-year-old building in central Hora, with avocado-green tables and chairs spilling out into the surrounding square. Oven-baked vegetables and home-produced lamb, pork and rabbit are specialities at this family-run place. Head inside to admire the building restorations.

Pounta TAVERNA €€
(☑ 22860 41063; www.pounta.gr; Plateia Pounta; mains €6-12; ☺ 8am-3pm & 6pm-midnight Easter–mid-Oct) A family business for 20 years, Pounta is the work of a creative Danish-Greek couple – dishes are served on Lisbet's handmade ceramics (also for sale), in a large, lush garden. The menu ranges from breakfast yoghurt to grilled octopus by way of rabbit *stifadho* (meat with onions in a tomato purée) and baked eggplant. Right on Plateia Pounta in Hora.

Eva's Garden MEDITERRANEAN €€€
(☑ 22860 41110; www.facebook.com/evasgarden folegandros; mains €10-25; ☺ dinner May-Sep) Eva's is a sophisticated spot that puts a gourmet spin on Greek cuisine (with portions that may seem small if you've been eating at tavernas!). Starters include octopus carpaccio or sautéed shrimp, while mains tempt with sea bass fillet or rib-eye on the grill. Turn left after Plateia Piatsa.

★ Rakentia BAR
(☑ 22860 41581; www.rakentia.gr; ☺ 10.30am-3pm & 6.30pm-1am May-Sep) Head west and look for a signed laneway beside the Anemousa Hotel to find this gem, a cafe-bar with cool music and cooler views. Watch birds soar at dusk over cocktails and creative tapas dishes.

ℹ Information

ATMs are at the post office (as you reach town from the port) and on Plateia Dounavi.

Travel agencies are good sources of information. There's information (and a downloadable app) at www.folegandros.com.
Diaplous Travel (☑ 22860 41158; www. diaploustravel.gr; Plateia Pounta) Helpful and efficient agency that sells ferry tickets and arranges boat trips. There's also an office at Karavostasis.
Folegandros Travel (☑ 22860 41273; www. folegandros-travel.gr; Plateia Dounavi) Sells ferry tickets and exchanges money. There's also an office at the port.

Ano Meria Ανω Μεριά
POP 240
The settlement of Ano Meria is a scattered community of small farms and dwellings that stretches along the road for several kilometres, virtually on the crest of the island. This is traditional Folegandros, where tourism makes no intrusive mark and life wanders happily along.

◉ Sights

Folklore Museum MUSEUM
(€2; ☺ 5-8pm Jul–mid-Sep) At the Hora end of Ano Meria village, this tiny museum is up a side road, indicated by a peeling, faded, hand-painted sign on the main road. It

provides a glimpse of Folegandros village life. Ask the bus driver to drop you off nearby. If no one is there, an old woman may mysteriously appear and open up for you.

✗ Eating

★I Synantisi
TAVERNA €

(☏22860 41208; mains from €6; ⊙lunch & dinner May-Sep) Also known as Maria's, I Synantisi is at the far end of the strung-out village, so much so that you may think you've missed it. With pale blue colours, it was originally opened in 1920 by the proprietor's grandfather. This is a great spot to try *matsata* (local pasta) and Greek salad with local Folegandros cheese.

Mimis
TAVERNA €

(☏22860 41377; ⊙lunch & dinner May-Sep) Towards the far end of Ano Meria village, Mimis specialises in *matsata,* the local hand-made pasta dish, but everything else on the menu is good too.

Around Folegandros

For **Livadi Beach**, 1.2km southeast of Karavostasis, take the 'bypass' road just past the Anemi Hotel and follow it around the coast. There is camping here (see www.folegandros.org).

Katergo Beach is on the southeastern tip of the island and is best reached by boat from Karavostasis. Boats leave regularly (weather permitting), for €8 return.

The sandy and pebbled **Angali** beach, on the central coast opposite Hora, is a popular spot. There are some rooms here and reasonable tavernas; buses run here regularly in summer from Hora. About 750m west of Angali over the hill along a footpath is **Agios Nikolaos**, a clothes-optional beach.

A number of beaches can be reached from where the road ends beyond Ano Meria: **Livadaki Beach** is a 1.5km hike from the bus stop near the church of Agios Andreas at Ano Meria. **Agios Georgios Beach** is north of Ano Meria and requires another demanding walk (about 40 minutes). Have tough footwear and sun protection – and, because most beaches have no shops or tavernas, make sure you take food and water.

Boats connect some west-coast beaches in high season: excursion boats make round trips from Angali to Agios Nikolaos (€5), and from Angali to Livadaki Beach (€10).

MILOS   ΜΗΛΟΣ
POP 4977

Volcanic Milos arches around a central caldera and is ringed with dramatic coastal landscapes of colourful and surreal rock formations. The island's most celebrated export, the iconic *Venus de Milo,* is far away in the Louvre, but dozens of beaches (the most of any Cycladic island) and a series of picturesque villages contribute to its current, compelling, attractions.

The island has a fascinating history of mineral extraction dating from the Neolithic period when obsidian was exported to the Minoan world of Crete. Today Milos is the biggest bentonite and perlite centre in the EU.

A substantial western chunk of Milos (and part of the east coast) is off-limits to rental vehicles due bad roads and a proliferation of the Milos viper, but the beaches are reachable by boat tour.

ⓘ Getting There & Away

BOAT

Milos is on the same western Cyclades ferry routes as Sifnos and Serifos. Buy tickets at Riva Travel (p250) or Milos Travel (p250) in Adamas.

Boat Services from Milos

DESTINATION	DURATION	FARE (€)	FREQUENCY
Anafi	6½hr	22	Fri
Folegandros	1-2½hr	12-45	1-2 daily
Ios	2-4hr	20-53	1-2 daily
Kea	9	18	Mon
Kimolos	30min-1hr	8-10	6 weekly
Koufonisia	4½-6¾hr	74	6 weekly
Kythnos	3¾-12½hr	10-16	6 weekly
Mykonos	6-8¾hr	24-74	6 weekly
Naxos	5¼-6hr	22-63	6 weekly
Paros	3¼hr	17	4 weekly
Piraeus	3-5¾hr	43-61	1-3 daily
Santorini (Thira)	2-5¼hr	22-51	1-2 daily
Serifos	1¼-3hr	12-22	1-2 daily
Sifnos	45min-2hr	11-21	1-3 daily
Sikinos	3-3½hr	16-17	4 weekly
Syros	5½-10hr	17-18	4 weekly

AIR

Sky Express (www.skyexpress.gr) has one or two flights daily between Athens and Milos airport (€80, 45 minutes).

ⓘ Getting Around

No buses serve the airport. Taxis to Adamas cost about €13, plus a token extra charge for bags.
Milos Buses (www.milosbuses.com) handily places updated timetable info on its website. Frequency of service varies with season, but in July and August buses leave Adamas for Plaka and Trypiti about every hour. Buses run to Pollonia every two hours, hourly to Paleohori and to Achivadolimni (Milos) Camping. Most fares are €1.80.

Hire cars, motorcycles and mopeds along the waterfront, at Riva Travel (p250), **Giourgas Rent a Car** (☑ 6937757066, 22870 22352; www.milosgiourgas.gr), or at **Milos Rent** (☑ 22870 41473; www.milosrent.gr), which has offices at the airport, Adamas and Pollonia.

Taxis (☑ 22870 22219) from the taxi station on Adamas' main square to Plaka are about €8, and to Pollonia €15; add €1 from the port.

Adamas Αδάμας

POP 1347

Fishermen sell their wares in the early morning at the lively port of Adamas (also Adamantas). Loaded with accommodation, shops and general services, the modern village also has a diverting waterfront scene. Popular boat tours around the island depart from the yacht quay.

◉ Sights

Milos Mining Museum   MUSEUM
(☑ 22870 22481; www.milosminingmuseum.gr; adult/child €4/2; ⊙10am-2pm & 5-10pm Jun-Sep, shorter hr Oct-May) This excellent small museum details Milos' mining history. It's about 600m east of the ferry quay.

Milos & Kimolos

Ask here about the **Miloterranean Geo Experience** (www.miloterranean.gr) project, a series of maps that outline great half-day 'geo walks' through Milos. The maps detail the island's geology and volcanic origin, mining history and natural environment, and can be purchased at the museum.

Ecclesiastical Museum of Milos MUSEUM
(☑22870 23956; www.ecclesiasticalmuseum.org; ⊙9.15am-1.15pm & 6.15-10.15pm May-Sep) FREE
Tucked in where the waterfront road turns inland, this collection in the Church of the Holy Trinity boasts rare icons and artefacts crafted by 18th-century Cretan icon-makers, a father-and-son team.

☞ Tours

Tour boats line Adamas' waterfront in the evening, touting their daily cruises. These leave every morning (weather permitting) to explore the impressive coastline, bizarre rock formations and beaches not reachable by road. **Kleftiko** in Milos' southwest, with its beautiful rocks and coves, is a prime destination. A number of cruises also visit Kimolos.

There are large and small boats, private charters, and speedboats, wooden-hulled boats, catamarans and sailboats. Check out what takes your fancy. It may be worth asking about group sizes, itineraries, lunch arrangements and swimming time.

Prices generally start from about €35. Most travel agencies can book you on a cruise; note that in summer's peak you can usually find departures from Pollonia.

🛏 Sleeping

There's a good range of hotels, apartments and domatia. In summer, lists of available domatia are usually kept at the quayside tourist kiosk.

Tassoula Rooms GUESTHOUSE €
(☑22870 22674; www.tassoularooms.eu; d €50; ❄🗢) Run by a friendly family, this budget pick is great value. Some of the spacious, bright rooms have tiny balconies overlooking the flowering inner courtyard, and the owner is the epitome of helpfulness. Free pick-up offered from the port.

Aeolis Hotel HOTEL €€
(☑22870 23985; www.hotel-aeolis.com; d/tr incl breakfast €94/120; ❄🗢) Inland from the harbourfront, this sweet, neat 12-room hotel is peaceful and calm, its white rooms given a pop of colour here and there. Open year-round, with prices diving in low season (double €35).

Villa Helios Studios APARTMENT €€
(☑22870 22258; www.milos-island.gr/rooms-apartments/helios; studio €100; ⊙May-Oct; ❄🗢) Rising high above the port, these large self-catering studios are neat as a pin and decorated in attractive traditional style, with sea-view balconies.

🍴 Eating & Drinking

★**O! Hamos** CYCLADIC €
(☑22870 21672; www.ohamos-milos.gr; Papikinou Beach; dishes €7-12; ⊙noon-11pm Easter-Oct; 🗢) In this rustic taverna across the road from the beach, sit in the garden and choose from an array of traditional recipes, such as goat baked in parchment. The best picks are cheeses and grilled meats, served with warmth and flair (and on cool branded ceramics), alongside craft beers and local wines. Located on Papikinou Beach, 2km southeast of Adamas.

Barko TAVERNA €
(☑22870 22660; http://barkotavern-milos.com; dishes €7-14; ⊙7pm-late; 🗢) This classic taverna on the road to Plaka, near the outskirts of town, serves local dishes such as chickpea fritters and oven-baked lamb in a sheltered garden setting.

Flisvos TAVERNA €€
(☑22870 22275; dishes €9-16; ⊙noon-11pm; 🗢) This place has pedigree: it's the oldest waterfront restaurant in town. Choose from grilled meats (for which it's known), fish by the kilo or traditional specialities like lamb in lemon sauce.

Akri BAR
(☑22870 22064; www.facebook.com/akrimilos; ⊙9am-late; 🗢) Opposite Villa Helios, Akri is in a beautiful location with a fine terrace overlooking the port. Music favours ethnic, funk and easy listening. It's also open for breakfast. Upstairs is an elegant gallery selling superb glass jewellery, paintings, pottery and sculpture, many by island artists.

ℹ Information

Municipal Tourist Office (☑22870 22445; www.milos.gr; ⊙9am-5pm & 7-11pm Jun-Sep) Helpful kiosk opposite the quay, with maps and general info.

Milos Travel (🗗 22870 22000; www.
milostravel.gr; ⊙9am-9pm) Books ferry
tickets.
Riva Travel (🗗 22870 24024; www.rivatravel.
gr; ⊙9am-9pm) Car hire, ferry tickets.

Plaka & Trypiti
Πλάκα & Τρυπητή

POP 1,289

Supercharming Plaka (population 749), 5km
uphill from Adamas, embodies the Cycladic
ideal, with its white houses and labyrinthine
lanes perching along the edge of an escarp-
ment. Plaka was built on the site of Ancient
Milos, which was destroyed by the Athenians and rebuilt by the Romans. It meanders
straight into the settlement to the south,
Trypiti (population 540).

Plaka's **main church courtyard** has spectacular views and gets packed out for sunset
in high season.

Walks in this area are popular, especially
from Plaka to Trypiti and down to Klima. Off
the road to the catacombs, a dirt track leads
to the spot where a farmer found the *Venus
de Milo* in 1820; it's marked by a sign. A bit
further along, the well-preserved **Roman
theatre** hosts the Milos Festival each summer, and footpaths lead down to Klima or
onto the promontory with ancient stone
walls and two small churches.

◉ Sights

★Catacombs   MONUMENT
(🗗 22870 21625; Trypiti; adult/child €4/2; ⊙9am-
7pm Tue-Sun) Greece's only Christian catacombs, signposted from Plaka, date from
the 1st century and were the burial site for
early believers. Around 5000 people are buried here; a guide takes you on a 15-minute
tour of the eerie depths to let you see the lit
alcoves and to explain the workings of the
ancient cemetery.

Archaeology Museum   MUSEUM
(🗗 22870 28026; Plaka; adult/child €2/1; ⊙9am-
4pm Tue-Sun) This handsome neoclassical
building contains some riveting exhibits,
including a plaster cast of the *Venus de
Milo* – the original was likely carved from
Parian marble around 100 BC, was found
on Milos by a local farmer in 1820 and now
resides in the Louvre in Paris. A perky little
herd of tiny bull figurines comes from the
Filakopi settlement and dates from 1400 to
1100 BC.

Kastro   FORTRESS
(Plaka) Signs mark the path climbing to the
hilltop fortress, built on the ancient acropolis and offering panoramic views of the
island. The 13th-century church, Thalassi-
tras, lies inside the walls.

Milos Folk & History Museum   MUSEUM
(🗗 22870 21292; Plaka; adult/child €4/2; ⊙11am-
1pm & 7-10pm Tue-Sun) Peruse traditional
costumes, woven goods and household artefacts in a series of traditionally furnished
rooms, right by the main church courtyard.

🛏 Sleeping

★Vaos Windmill   APARTMENT €€
(🗗 26103 21742; Trypiti; apt €80; 🞖) An unpaved
path behind and above Trypiti's main church
leads to this converted windmill. Views from
the its terrace are nothing short of stupendous; the double and the twin sleep four in
total and there's a fully-equipped kitchen a
couple of steps out the front door.

Mimallis Houses   APARTMENT €€
(🗗 6972808758, 22870 21094; www.mimallis.gr;
Plaka & Klima; Plaka d €90-95, Klima d/q €200/220;
⊙Apr-Oct; 🞖🞖🞖) Mimallis rents two small
houses in Plaka (sleeping two), and one
in precious Klima (sleeping up to five) –
each different, comfortable and packed
with amenities. Low-season discounts are
excellent.

Archondoula Studios   APARTMENT €€
(🗗 22870 23820; www.archondoula-studios.gr;
Plaka; r/studio €70/100; ⊙Mar-Nov; 🞖🞖)
Cheerful Stavros runs sleek, white-on-white
rooms and studios. Rooms are compact,
while the studios give more breathing space.
Take in spectacular sunset views from terraces and balconies, and enjoy the peace of
Plaka after dark.

Studios Betty   APARTMENT €€
(🗗 22870 21538; www.studiosbetty-milos.com;
Plaka; studio €100; 🞖🞖) Enjoy sunset views
as glorious as Santorini's from this complex
of four simple studios at Plaka's cliff edge.

★Windmill of Karamitsos   APARTMENT €€€
(🗗 6945568086; www.windmillmilos.gr; Trypiti;
windmill €200; ⊙Apr-Oct; 🞖) Bed down in a
unique converted windmill that dates from
1859 and now sleeps four in creative quarters over three levels. It's on a hilltop on the
edge of Trypiti, with panoramic views.

Eating

Palaios
CAFE €

(☑22870 23490; Plaka; snacks from €3.50; ⊙9am-9pm; 🛜) This old-world cafe is a perfect pit stop for breakfast or coffee, but it's mostly worth stopping by to try some local specialities: *karpouzopita* (watermelon cake or pie), unique to Milos and Folegandros, and *ladenia* (not unlike a flatbread pizza).

★ Archondoula
CYCLADIC €€

(☑22870 21384; Plaka; dishes €6-17; ⊙noon-10pm Easter-Nov; 🛜) The whole cheerful family is involved at this top-notch taverna in a picturesque laneway setting. Classic Greek dishes have an assured touch and range from grilled vegetables with *manouri* (soft cheese) to grilled swordfish to lamb with tomato and artichoke.

Barrielo
CYCLADIC €€

(☑6984218360; www.barriello.com; mains €9-38; ⊙7pm-3am; 🛜) 🌿 Every evening, diners are lured to the little square below Trypiti's church by the wafting smells of sizzling meat on the grill. It's all organic and raised on the owner's farm; choose from sausage, beef with figs or chicken shashlik.

Pollonia
Πολλώνια

POP 272

Pollonia, on the north coast, is a low-key fishing village with azure waters that transforms into quite a chic (albeit petite) summer resort.

The town is also the jumping-off point for Kimolos; note that it's sometimes mapped as Apollonia.

🏃 Activities

Milos Diving Center
DIVING

(☑22870 41296, 6976114846; www.milosdiving.gr; 1-tank dive €50; ⊙9.30am-3pm) Dives (from €50, including equipment) and PADI courses, based at Pollonia. Reputable operator, around for more than 20 years.

🛏 Sleeping

Zoe Rooms
GUESTHOUSE €

(☑22870 41235; www.zoe-milos.gr; Pollonia; d from €45; ❄🛜) This friendly little guesthouse is the pick of the budget spots, with large, spotless rooms, an extensive breakfast spread and an on-site restaurant that serves dinner on the cliff overlooking the waves.

KLIMA ROCK DWELLINGS

Tiny, photogenic Klima clings to the beachfront cliff face below Trypiti. It's the best example of Milos' *syrmata* (traditional fishermen's encampments), where the downstairs, with brightly painted doors, are used for rough-weather boat storage, and the upstairs are used for family life.

The homes, most still in use today, are incorporated into the rocks. A unique experience is to rent *syrmata* for your stay; a few of these are available via home-sharing services. You'll need your own wheels.

Nefeli Sunset Studios
APARTMENT €€

(☑22870 41466; www.milos-nefelistudios.gr; studio from €140; ⊙Apr-Oct; ❄🛜) Whitewashed cubes combine modern design with traditional touches, in a bay-front property with a delightful garden, on the northwest edge of the village.

★ Salt
BOUTIQUE HOTEL €€€

(☑22870 41110; www.salt-milos.com; d/ste incl breakfast from €200/380; ⊙Apr-Oct; ❄🛜) Sparklingly minimal, white-on-white sophistication, with all the luxuries and views to the sea. Low-season rates drop by almost 50%.

🍴 Eating

★ Armenaki
SEAFOOD €€

(☑22870 41061; www.armenaki.gr; dishes €7-15, fish by kg; ⊙noon-11pm Apr-Oct; 🛜) Armenaki is revered for its fishy business – this place is all about seafood (in fact, there's little else on the menu). Seafood in all its guises is cooked to perfection, and service is first-rate (including the filleting of fish at your table). *Kakavia* (traditional fish stew) comes recommended, and there's an extensive wine list.

Jordan's Meat...ing Steak House
STEAK €€

(☑6972869333; www.jordansmeating.gr; mains €11.50-28; ⊙noon-3pm & 6-11pm; 🛜) Just imagine: you spent the day at the beach. You come here, suntanned, salty, ravenous. Then comes the moment of ecstasy: a giant slab of perfectly grilled T-bone or rib-eye or tenderloin placed in front of you, along with the cold fizz of beer in your frosted glass. For the carnivorously inclined only.

Hanabi
SUSHI €€

(☑ 22870 41180; Pollonia; mains €12-20; ☺ noon-11pm; ☎) Chic new Japanese restaurant, complete with ambient beats on the stereo, waterside terrace and funky wicker furniture. The sushi roll combos are imaginative and well-executed, and the spicy tuna sashimi stands out.

Gialos
SEAFOOD €€

(☑ 22870 41208; www.gialos-pollonia.gr; mains €8-20; ☺ noon-11pm Easter-Oct) Watch port life while digging into fresh seafood and yummy pastas. Bustling Gialos has a creative menu bursting with fresh local flavour, including tuna tataki, salmon with nettle and sour-cheese patties. Save room for dessert.

ℹ Information

Travel Me to Milos (☑ 22870 41008; www.travelmetomilos.com) Books activities, excursions and ferry tickets.

Around Milos

Milos and its offshore islets boast more than 70 splendid beaches in different-coloured sands and stone. Rent wheels or take a cruise to compare.

In the north, Plathiena is a fine sandy beach beyond Plaka, and on the way you can visit fishing villages Areti and Fourkovouni. Firopotamos is a delightful little sandy cove with a taverna, while Mandrakia is a tiny fishing outpost with a practically deserted sweep of sand and calm waters. Also in this area, Sarakiniko is a must, with its snow-white rock formations for sunbathing, a tiny sand beach and a deep channel for swimming. In the very north, if you have an ATV, you'll have the Nerodafni and Trachilas beaches almost to yourself.

On the south coast, golden-sanded Provatas feels remote but has a couple of tavernas. Kyriaki is backed by otherworldly grey-, rose- and rust-coloured hills and has soft, grey sand. The long taupe arch of Paleohori is backed by banded cliffs and has beach bars, water sports and hot sand, thanks to thermal springs in the area.

◉ Sights & Activities

Filakopi
HISTORIC SITE

(€2; ☺ 8am-3pm Tue, Thu & Sat) This ancient Minoan city in the island's northeast (close to Pollonia) was one of the earliest settlements in the Cyclades. Now it's not much more than rubble, but the seaside setting is great, with cavelike rock formations all around.

★ Sea Kayak Milos
KAYAKING

(☑ 22870 23597; www.seakayakgreece.com; Triovasalos; sea kayak trip €75 per person; ☺ 9am-5pm Apr-Oct) A superb way to explore the coastline. Australian Rod and his team lead highly regarded day trips, with no experience required. Itineraries depend on weather conditions. Multi-day kayaking and camping tours are also available.

⌬ Sleeping & Eating

Achivadolimni (Milos)

Camping
CAMPGROUND €

(☑ 22870 31410; www.miloscamping.gr; Achivadolimni; campsite per person/tent €7/5, bungalows incl breakfast €85-115; ☺ mid-May–Sep; ☎⛱) Beautiful oleander-filled grounds, with excellent facilities and high-standard rooms. Has a pool, minimarket, restaurant and bar. It's 6km south of Adamas, with regular bus connections. Also does port pick-ups.

Scirocco
TAVERNA €€

(☑ 22870 31201; www.restaurantsirocco.gr; Paleohori Beach; mains €7-16; ☺ noon-10pm Apr-Oct; ☎) Popular eatery smack-bang on the shore, with a novel hook: 'volcanic food' (ie dishes slow-cooked underground using the sand's thermal heat). There's also a full menu of Greek favourites, and a breezy view.

KIMOLOS   ΚΙΜΩΛΟΣ

POP 910

Exquisite Kimolos, perched off the northeast tip of Milos, feels like a step back in time. Barely a trickle of visitors get the chance to take in its fantastical sienna-coloured walls hand-hewn from volcanic stones, or its sparkling bays and picturesque *syrmata*. It's an easy day trip from Milos; consider taking a car, bike or scooter on the ferry to make getting around easier.

The boat (from Pollonia in Milos' north) docks at Psathi, from where it's 1.5km to the pretty capital, Hora. Wander the maze of streets to reach Hora's central cafes and a semi-crumbling medieval *kastro*. The *kastro* holds the Church of the Nativity (from the late 16th century) and the petite Folk & Maritime Museum of Kimolos (☑ 22870 51118; ☺ hr vary) FREE.

Caïques from Psathi buzz out to beaches, the best of which is magnificent, white-sand **Prassa** (also reachable by car/scooter/ATV along the partially sealed road). You can walk there from Hora in about two hours.

🛏 Sleeping & Eating

Meltemi Rooms   HOTEL €
(☑ 22870 51360; http://kimolos-meltemi.gr; d incl breakfast €55; ✳🕸) Rooms perch on the edge of Hora with views to the sea. One has a kitchen.

⭐ The Windmill Kimolos   BOUTIQUE HOTEL €€
(☑ 22870 51554; www.kimoloshotel.com; r from €105; Ⓟ🕸) The most atmospheric abode in Kimolos, this converted windmill looks down on the island from its lofty hilltop position. The whitewashed rooms are cosy and comfortable.

Raventi   CAFE €
(☑ 22870 51212; snacks from €3.50; ☀9am-late) On the beach at Psathi, this fashionable cafe has a comfy terrace, a display full of delicious cakes and ice cream, and disorganised service.

To Kyma   TAVERNA €€
(☑ 22870 51001; dishes €7-20; ☀noon-11pm Easter-Oct; 🕸) The taverna To Kyma, right on the beach at Psathi, is good for seafood and for trying the local specialities such as *ladenia* (similar to pizza, topped with tomato sauce).

ⓘ Information

There's an ATM at the port and a petrol station.

ⓘ Getting There & Away

Some Milos long-distance ferries stop at Kimolos. **Kimolos Travel** (☑ 22870 51219; ☀9am-1pm & 4-8pm) in Hora sells tickets. A small **car ferry** (☑ 6948308758; www.kimolos-link.gr; per adult/child//scooter/car €2.10/1/5/8.70) connects Pollonia (Milos) with Psathi (Kimolos) up to eight times daily in high season, three times in low season (30 minutes).

ⓘ Getting Around

Buses connect Psathi and Hora in high season only; infrequent services also visit beaches. A couple of rental agencies in Kimolos offer scooters and ATVs, or else you can call for a **taxi** (☑ 6945464093).

SIFNOS   ΣΙΦΝΟΣ
POP 2625

Sifnos has a dreamlike quality. Three white-washed villages, anchored by the capital Apollonia, sit like pearls on a string along the crest of the island. The changing light kisses the landscape, and as you explore the flanking slopes of the central mountains you'll discover abundant terraced olive groves, almond trees, oleander and aromatic herbs. Each of the island's bays harbours a spectrum of aqua waters and offers breathtaking vistas.

During the Archaic period (from about the 8th century BC), Sifnos was enriched by its gold and silver deposits, but by the 5th century BC the mines were exhausted. Sifnos is now known for pottery, basket weaving and cookery. Visitors flock to the southern half of the island, served by good bus links, but it's worth getting your own wheels and driving to the remote beaches of the north, where the main road culminates in – you guessed it! – a church.

ⓘ Getting There & Away

Sifnos is on the Piraeus to western Cyclades ferry route, with good summer connections across the Cyclades. Get tickets at **Aegean Thesaurus Travel** (☑ 22840 33151; www.thesaurus.gr), **Xidis Travel** (☑ Apollonia 22840 32373, Kamares 22840 31895; www.xidis.com.gr; ☀9am-9pm) or the tourist office (p255).

Boat Services from Sifnos

DESTINATION	DURATION	FARE (€)	FREQUENCY
Folegandros	1¼-41¼hr	13-53	up to 3 daily
Kea	7hr	20	Mon
Kimolos	30min-2½hr	10-18	1-2 daily
Kythnos	2¼hr	13	5 weekly
Ios	1¼hr-5¾hr	16-58	daily
Lavrio	8hr	30	Mon
Milos	50min-2hr	11-20	up to 3 daily
Naxos	5¾hr	66	6 weekly
Paros	5½hr	9	Tue, Wed & Sat
Piraeus	2½-4½hr	30-55	up to 3 daily
Santorini (Thira)	2-7¼hr	18-58	1-2 daily
Serifos	20-40min	10-19	1-2 daily
Sikinos	2-5hr	14-41	4 weekly
Syros	3hr-4½hr	13	3 weekly

CYCLADES SIFNOS

Sifnos

Serifos (25km); Kythnos (80km); Piraeus (170km)

Cape Heronisos
Heronisos
Heronisos Beach

Aegean Sea

Vroulidia Beach
Agios Dimos

476m

Kamares Bay
Kamares
Artemonas
Poulati
Ano Petali
Kato Petali
Apollonia
Kastro
Katavati
Seralia
Exambelas
680m
Moni Profiti Ilia
Acropolis of Agios Andreas
Faros
Moni Chrysopigi
Vathy Bay
Vathy
Platys Gialos
Chrysopigi Beach
Platys Gialos Bay
Fasolou Beach
201m

Cape Kondou

Kitriani

Milos (45km); Santorini (110km)

ⓘ Getting Around

Bus timetables are posted around the island, and frequent buses connect Kamares with Apollonia and Artemonas. Buses also link Apollonia with Kastro, Vathy, Faros and Platys Gialos. Fares are generally €1.80.

Car rental costs from €45 per day. Companies will deliver to the port or your hotel. Try **Apollo Rent a Car** (☑ 22840 33333; www.automoto apollo.gr; Apollonia; ◷ 9am-9pm) or **Proto Moto Car Rental** (☑ 22840 33791; www.protomoto car.gr; Kamares).

Taxis (☑ 6944761210, 6932403485) hover around the port and Apollonia's main junction. At bus stops you'll find a list of taxi numbers and indicative fares. Fares from Kamares include Apollonia €9, Platys Gialos €20 and Vathy €20.

Kamares   Καμάρες

POP 245

Scenically hemmed in by steep mountains, the port of Kamares has a holiday atmosphere, with its large beach and waterfront cafes, tavernas and shops. It makes a decent base, though it's not as convenient for exploring Sifnos as the very central Apollonia.

🛏 Sleeping

Kamares has the largest selection of accommodation in Sifnos. Domatia owners rarely meet boats; book ahead in high season. On the northern side of the bay, Agia Marina has plenty of hotels and domatia.

Camping Makis   CAMPGROUND €
(☑ 6945946339; www.makiscamping.gr; campsite per adult/child/tent €7/4/4, d €70, studio & apt €75-100; ◷ Apr-Nov; ✳ 🛜) Pitch your tent behind the beach in a basic lot with attractive olive trees (or hire a tent with mattresses for €25). There are well-equipped studios and apartments (sleeping up to five), a cafe, barbecue, communal kitchen, minimarket and laundry.

⭐ **Aglaia Studios**   GUESTHOUSE €€
(☑ 22840 31513; www.aglaiastudios.gr; Ag. Marina; d from €55; ✳ 🛜🏊) In the evenings, you can sit on your balcony and watch the lights of Kamares across the bay. By day, a few steps take you down to the swimming platform, from which you can launch yourself into the Aegean. The studios themselves are snug and comfortable.

Hotel Kamari   HOTEL €€
(☑ 22840 33383; www.sifnostravel.com; d/apt €70/80; ✳ 🛜) Kamari provides spacious doubles and fully equipped studios, with plant-festooned balconies and very helpful staff. Sea views cost a little extra. Steep discounts outside peak season.

Stavros Hotel   HOTEL €€
(☑ 22840 33383; www.sifnostravel.com; d/q €80/120; ✳ 🛜) Main street's Stavros Hotel offers good service and excellent, spacious studios with kitchenettes and sea views. A bonus: flexible room configurations work to accommodate families. The info desk downstairs can help with car hire.

🍴 Eating

Cafe Folie   CAFE €
(☑ 6936519006; www.cafefolie.gr; mains €6-12; ◷ 8am-late; 🛜) Cafe Folie makes it far too easy to be a beach bum: it's a fun, decked area right on the sea (towards Agia Marina), with sunbeds, a ladder into the water, and a menu that allows you to slip from morning coffee to a salad lunch, and then on to dinner, and finally cocktails.

⭐ **Absinthe**   FUSION €€
(mains €8-19) This new kid on the block has been wowing Sifnos with its blend of

EXPERIENCING SIFNOS

Walking

Sifnos is justifiably proud of its excellent network of more than a dozen signposted walking trails, some 98km in all, ranging from 20-minute rambles to four-hour hikes. A great investment is the €4 info pack from **Aegean Thesaurus Travel** (p253), on the main square in Apollonia or else in Kamares; it includes the Terrain map of Sifnos, an overview of the island's walking trails, plus the current bus and ferry timetables.

There are some wonderful short walks: Apollonia to Artemonas (15 minutes) is worthwhile, as is the loop around Kastro. Our favourite is the 40-minute walk from Faros to **Moni Chrysopigi** (p257). Longer trails link major settlements via beaches, monasteries and great scenery – Apollonia to Vathy is about four hours.

Water Sports

Sheltered Vathy is a good spot for stand-up paddleboarding, while Platys Gialos has caught the flyboarding bug. **Vathi Sea Sports** (☑22840 36002; stand-up paddleboarding per hour €23; ☺10am-8pm May-Sep) and **Calypso Boat Rental** (☑6970424004; www.boatrental.gr; Platys Gialos; ☺8am-8pm) are the main water sports operators.

Cooking Classes

A big drawcard for travellers is Sifnos' culinary heritage. The island was the birthplace of Nikolaos Tselementes (1878–1958), author of the first (and best-known) Greek cookbook, published in 1910. Since then, Sifnos has enjoyed a reputation for producing excellent chefs. Engaging cooking classes are available with **Sifnos Farm Narlis** (☑6979778283; www.sifnos-farm-narlis.com; class €60-80; ☺9am-1pm). Book direct, or via **Aegean Thesaurus Travel** (p253).

Cycladic and fusion offerings, using the best of fresh local ingredients. Their standout dish is hot and spicy goat with rice, and there are plenty of daily specials, from stir-fried chanterelles to fish carpaccio. Don't miss the desserts!

O Argiris GREEK €€
(☑22840 32352; mains €6-16; ☺9am-11pm Apr-Oct; 🛜) It's well worth the walk around the bay to Agia Marina. Sure, the view looking back to Kamares is wonderful, but it's equalled by the top-notch food. You can't go wrong with Sifnos specialities (helpfully indicated on the menu); try *revithada* (baked chickpeas), *mastelo* (lamb in wine) and caper salad.

❶ Information

An ATM is just a few metres from the ferry quay.
Aegean Thesaurus (☑22840 33151; www.thesaurus.gr; ☺9am-9pm) Books ferry tickets and provides a €4 Sifnos welcome pack (hiking info, bus timetables and more).
Municipal Tourist Office (www.sifnos.gr) Very helpful, with ferry tickets, accommodation and bus timetables.

Apollonia Απολλωνία
POP 869

Labyrinthine, church-studded Apollonia comes alive in high season with its parade of well-dressed Athenians strutting their stuff along the Steno – Odos Prokou, known as Steno (meaning 'narrow') because of its slenderness. Cafes, bars, clubs, shops and eateries buzz with life.

The quirky **Museum of Popular Art** (☑22840 31341; €1; ☺9.30am-2pm & 6-10pm) at the central junction contains a fun confusion of old costumes, textiles and photographs. Hours are erratic.

The main vehicular road cuts right through the centre of town, but park at the large free car park downhill from the village and walk up and into the warren of streets. At the central junction you'll find all the services: banks, post office, pharmacy, bookshop, taxis and so on.

🛏 Sleeping & Eating

⭐**Eleonas Apartments & Studios** APARTMENT €€
(☑22840 33383; www.sifnostravel.com; apt from €160; ❄🛜) An idyllic complex tucked away

in an olive grove, Eleonas offers gloriously roomy apartments that sleep five, with kitchen, living space and terrace. Studios are slightly smaller, but still very spacious. It feels peaceful and rural, but it's just a few minutes' walk from the Steno.

Hotel Anthousa
HOTEL €€

(☑ 22840 31431; www.hotelanthousa-sifnos.gr; s/d/tr €55/70/90; ❋ 🕾) Behind a pretty, vine-covered facade, this year-round hotel has fresh, appealing rooms set around an inner courtyard. Sweet in decor and sweet in intent: downstairs are a cafe (where breakfast is served) and a patisserie.

Drimoni
MEDITERRANEAN €

(☑ 22840 31434; www.drimoni.gr; mains €9-13; ☺ 6pm-late; 🕾) Look out over the countryside or lounge by the pool (yes, pool!) at this contemporary restaurant with funky decor. Chef Giorgos does the Sifnian culinary tradition proud with the likes of *mastelo* (goat slow-cooked in wine with rosemary and dill), imaginative salads, risottos and pastas.

★ Cayenne
CYCLADIC €€

(☑ 22840 31080; www.facebook.com/Cayenne RestaurantSifnos; mains €14-25; ☺ 12.30pm-late; 🕾) Shaded by a fig tree and drowning in a riot of herbs just off the Steno, Cayenne affirms its strong commitment to Cycladic ingredients through such dishes as lemon-caper risotto, Byzantine meat patties and smoked eel with Santorini fava beans. The art gallery upstairs hosts events.

★ Rambagas
GREEK €€€

(☑ 22840 32215; www.kikladonxoros.gr; mains €14-29; ☺ 9am-late; 🕾) It's easy to succumb to celeb-chef hype when the setting is as beautiful as this – a tree-shaded terrace off the Steno, with artwork adding stylish appeal. Well-known chef Yiannis Loucacos (a *MasterChef* judge in Greece) designs the dinner menu, which pays homage to Sifnos' culinary traditions. Expect char-grilled octopus, smoked eel and ravioli filled with local *anthotiro* cheese for dinner.

Ano Petali & Artemonas
Άνω Πετάλι & Αρτεμώνας

POP 800

After crossing the main road from Apollonia, the string of houses continues north into Ano Petali and reaches Artemonas with its grand mansions. Walk the pedestrian-only streets to take it all in, stopping at one of the fashionable cafes.

Artemonas has a central square off the winding main road as well, with a bus stop and some appealing eateries.

🛏 Sleeping

Windmill Bella Vista
BOUTIQUE HOTEL €€

(☑ 22840 33518; www.windmillbellavista.gr; apt from €115, windmill €180; ❋ 🔁) If you've never stayed in a converted Cycladic windmill, here's your chance! It's the atmospheric pick of the spacious, high-beamed apartments and studios clustered around the infinity pool en route from Artemonas to Poulaki.

Pension Geronti
PENSION €€

(☑ 22840 31473; www.gerontisifnos.gr; d €65; ❋ 🕾) Opposite Petali Village Hotel, on the walkway between Apollonia and Artemonas, is this gem of a pension, with spotless rooms, sweeping views, sweet hosts and excellent rates.

Petali Village Hotel
HOTEL €€

(☑ 22840 33024; www.petalihotel.gr; Ano Petali; d/ste incl breakfast from €136/190; ❋ 🕾 🔁) Suspended on a walking street between Apollonia and Artemonas, this four-star terraced array of rooms and apartments has sweeping views to Apollonia and the sea, and an inviting kidney-shaped pool. Low-season discounts are decent. Port pick-up offered.

Around Sifnos

On the southeast coast, the fishing hamlet of **Faros** has fish tavernas and a couple of nice beaches nearby, including **Fasolou**, reached up steps and over the headland from the bus stop.

Platys Gialos, 10km south of Apollonia, has a big, generous beach entirely backed by tavernas, hotels and shops. **Vathy**, on the southwest coast, is a low-key resort village on an almost circular bay of aquamarine beauty.

Not to be missed is the walled village of **Kastro**, 3km east from Apollonia. The former medieval capital is a magical place of buttressed alleyways and whitewashed houses surrounded by valleys and sea. It has a modest archaeological museum, and the small port and pebble beach of **Seralia** is nestled below.

⊙ Sights

★ Moni Chrysopigi
MONASTERY

The handsome whitewashed monastery of Chrysopigi dates back more than 600 years and perches on an islet connected to the shore by a tiny footbridge. There is a superb walk to Chrysopigi from the village of Faros (about 40 minutes one-way); en route you'll go along beautiful, azure **Chrysopigi Beach**, home to two excellent tavernas.

Acropolis of Agios Andreas
MONUMENT

(☑ 22840 31488; €2; ⊙ 8.30am-3pm Tue-Sun) At the heart of the island, 2km south of Apollonia, this well-excavated hilltop acropolis dates from the Mycenaean period (13th century BC). Take in extensive views of interior valleys and neighbouring Paros from above the intact defensive wall. The adjacent **Church of Agios Andreas** dates from about 1700.

🛏 Sleeping & Eating

🍽 Platys Gialos

Hotel Efrosini
HOTEL €€

(☑ 22840 71353; www.hotel-efrosini.gr; d incl breakfast €80-90; ⊙ Easter-Sep; ❄ 🗑) This well-kept, family-run hotel is one of the best on the Platys Gialos strip. Small balconies overlook a leafy courtyard with the sea lapping just in front.

Verina Suites
APARTMENT €€€

(☑ 22840 71525; www.verinahotelsifnos.com; d/apt from €170/210; ⊙ May-Oct; ❄ 🗑 🏊) Effortlessly chic, Verina rents minimalist suites and villas at outposts in Platys Gialos, Vathy and above Poulati (north of Kastro). Verina Suites lies behind the beach at Platys Gialos, but try dragging yourself from the gorgeous pool and cafe-bar area.

★ Nero & Alati
CYCLADIC €€

(☑ 22840 71208; www.facebook.com/neroalati; mains €8-15; ⊙ 1-10pm; 🗑) The seafront terrace of 'Water & Salt' serves lovingly prepared, slow-cooked local dishes using ingredients sourced by chef Alexander from his grandparents' farm, along with foraged mountain herbs. Okra *plaki,* wild goat and lamb *mastelo* are standout dishes.

Omega 3
SEAFOOD €€

(☑ 22840 72014; www.facebook.com/omega3 greece; Platys Gialos; mains €9-23; ⊙ noon-11pm May-Sep) The cute name (Ω3) hints at the treats on offer at this small, casual beach-front spot. There's a fresh-faced menu of fab fishy flavours, grabbing techniques from around the globe (sashimi, ceviche) but staying true to its roots too, with slow-cooked octopus and orzo with crayfish.

🍽 Vathy

Aerides Boutique Rooms
BOUTIQUE HOTEL €€

(☑ 22840 36093; www.aerides-sifnos.com/en; studio from €60; ❄ 🗑) Run by a friendly young couple and artfully decorated with bits of flotsam and jetsam, this converted *syrma* (boat shed) comprises three spacious studios. The sea is right under your window.

🍽 Kastro

Antonis Rooms
PENSION €

(☑ 22840 33708; http://sifnosholidays.gr; d €50; ❄ 🗑) Brilliant value. On the road as you head to Kastro, these simple, spotless rooms beckon. There's a communal kitchen and a terrace with splendid valley views. It's open year-round.

Aris & Maria Traditional Houses
APARTMENT €€

(☑ 22840 31161; www.arismaria-traditional.com; d/tr/q €85/100/130; ❄) For an authentic Kastro experience, rent one of these six traditional Sifnian houses. Some have sea views.

Leonidas
TAVERNA €€

(☑ 22840 31153; Kastro; mains €8-16; ⊙ noon-10pm Easter-Sep; 🗑) At the northern edge of the village, this popular place offers tasty local dishes, including Sifnian appetisers like chickpea croquettes and cheese patties with honey and sesame seeds.

SERIFOS ΣΕΡΙΦΟΣ

POP 1420

Serifos has a raw, rugged beauty, with steep mountains plunging to broad ultramarine bays. Relatively deserted outside the quaint hilltop capital of Hora or the dusty port of Livadi down below, the island feels like it's gone beautifully feral. All that you find are the occasional remnants of past mining enterprises (rusting tracks, cranes) and the whoosh of the wind (which can be fierce). Rent wheels to make the most of it. Serifos is one of the few islands where locals drink the water.

In Greek mythology, Serifos is where Perseus grew up, bringing back the Medusa's head to save his mother from the unwanted romantic attentions of Polydectes, and where the Cyclopes were said to live. There's some fine walking on Serifos, and plenty to explore below the waves too.

ℹ Getting There & Away

Serifos is on the Piraeus to western Cyclades ferry route and has reasonable summer connections (or travel to Sifnos for more options). Buy tickets at **Kondilis** (☑ 22810 52340; www.kondilis.gr; ⊙ 9am-9pm) on Livadi's waterfront.

Boat Services from Serifos

DESTINATION	DURATION	FARE (€)	FREQUENCY
Folegandros	2½-41½hr	15-53	3 weekly
Ios	4¼-6hr	18-62	2 weekly
Kimolos	1¾-3½hr	13-22	6 weekly
Kythnos	1½-4¾hr	12	6 weekly
Milos	1¼-2½hr	12-22	1-2 daily
Mykonos	7hr	74	Wed & Sun
Paros	6¼hr	13	2-3 weekly
Piraeus	1¾-4¾hr	35-51	1-2 daily
Santorini (Thira)	3½-7¾hr	23-63	daily
Sifnos	25-50min	10-18	1-2 daily
Sikinos	2½-5½hr	17-42	3 weekly
Syros	2¼-4¼hr	12	3 weekly

ℹ Getting Around

Buses connect Livadi and Hora (€1.80, hourly, 15 minutes); the timetable is posted at the bus stop by the yacht quay. In high season, a circular bus route takes in Panagia, Galani, Kendarhos and Agios Ioannis Beach (up to six daily), with a couple of daily buses to Megalo Livadi and Koutalas.

Rent cars (per day from €45), scooters (€18) and quads (€25) at **Blue Bird** (☑ 22810 51511; www.rentacar-bluebird.gr), **Poseidon Rent a Car** (☑ 6974789706, 22810 52030; www.serifosisland.gr/poseidon) or **Serifos Travel** (☑ 22810 51463; www.serifostours.gr) just off the waterfront.

Taxis (☑ 6944473044, 6932431114) to Hora cost €8, Psili Ammos €8, Sykamia €22, Vagia €12 and Megalo Livadi €22.

Livadi   Λιβάδι

POP 605

The port town of Serifos is a fairly low-key place, popular with yachties and handy as a base for exploring the island. In spite of growing numbers of tourists, there's still a reassuring feeling that the modern world has not entirely taken over.

Just over the headland that rises from the ferry quay lies the fine, tamarisk-fringed beach at **Livadakia**.

🛌 Sleeping

Much of the accommodation clusters at Livadakia Beach. Most lodgings can pick up at the port by arrangement.

Alisachni   APARTMENT €
(☑ 22810 51914; d from €50; ❄ 🗢) Friendly owner Giorgios runs a clutch of spacious, spotless rooms with kitchenettes and bug netting on the windows, just a couple of minutes' walk from the beach.

Coralli Camping & Bungalows   CAMPGROUND, APARTMENT €
(☑ 22810 51500; www.coralli.gr; Livadakia Beach; campsite per adult/child/tent €8/4/5, bungalow d/tr/q €75/90/110; ❄ 🗢 🌊) Right behind Livadakia Beach, this well-equipped and well-run eucalyptus-shaded campground also has 'bungalows' (rooms) with mountain or sea views. The complex includes a cool pool and bar, a restaurant, minimarket, kitchen and barbecue. Nearby self-catering apartments are of an equally high standard.

Alexandros-Vassilia   APARTMENT €
(☑ 22810 51119; www.alexandros-vassilia.gr; Livadakia Beach; d/tr/q from €35/55/85; ⊙ Easter-Sep; ❄ 🗢) Best known for its beachfront taverna in a flowering garden, this friendly Livadakia compound also has a big range of rooms and apartments. They range from decent-value economy rooms (no sea view) to family-sized, sea-view suites.

★ **Studios Niovi**   APARTMENT €€
(☑ 22810 51900; www.studiosniovi.gr; Livadi; apt incl breakfast €90-140; ❄ 🗢) On the furthest eastern curve of Livadi's bay, these immaculate apartments look at the broad expanse of the bay, bustling Livadi, towering Hora and the mountains beyond. The owner makes a super breakfast spread. You're about a 20-minute walk from Livadi itself. Your own wheels are an advantage. Good low-season rates.

🍴 Eating

Kali's   SEAFOOD €€
(☑ 22810 52301; mains €9-18; ⊙ noon-11pm Mar-Oct; 🗢) White tables on the water's edge with gregarious waiters and delicious home-cooking, much of it with a fresh-fish focus.

Metalleio
MEDITERRANEAN €€

(☑ 22810 51755; www.facebook.com/Metalleio; Livadi; mains €8-16; ☺ 8.30pm-late; ☎) On the road behind the waterfront, Metalleio dishes up quality cuisine from a short menu emphasising local flavours: risotto with local goat's cheese, veal in local wine sauce, and locally-made ice cream. Come midnight, the action moves upstairs and Metalleio doubles as the island's main live-music venue and dance club (particularly in July and August).

Anemos Café
BAR

(☑ 22810 51783; ☺ 9am-late; ☎) Above the Carrefour supermarket, Anemos' broad terrace offers top views of the marina and distant Hora. The proprietors are friendly, snacks and coffees are good and cheap, and it gets hopping around boat arrivals.

Yacht Club Serifos
BAR

(☑ 22810 51888; ☺ 8am-4am; ☎) Livadi's original waterfront cafe-bar (going back to 1938) maintains a cheerful buzz. Lounge music plays by day for coffee drinkers, with mainstream rock, disco and funk late into the night.

ℹ Information

There are two ATMs along the waterfront.

Hora (Serifos)
Χώρα (Σέριφος)

POP 364

This tiny town cascades down the summit of a rocky hill above Livadi, putting it among the most dramatically striking (and loftiest) of all the Cycladic capitals.

Hora's bus terminus and main car park are on its upper side, near some windmills, as is its **archaeological collection** (☑ 22810 51138; €2; ☺ 8.30am-4pm Tue & Thu-Sun) which displays fragments of mainly Hellenic and Roman sculpture excavated from the *kastro*. From there, steps climb into the maze of Hora proper and lead to the **main square**, watched over by the lovely neoclassical **town hall**.

From the square, narrow alleys and more steps lead upwards to churches like **Agios Ioannis Theologos**, carved into the rock and built on the site of an ancient temple to Athena, and the remnants of the ruined 15th-century **Venetian Kastro**, from where the views are spectacular.

Serifos

Aegean Sea

Platys Gialos Beach
Sykamia Beach
Galani
Kendarhos
Panagia
Pirgos
Psili Ammos Beach
Avessalos
582m
Agios Ioannis Beach
Hora
Megalo Livadi
Koutalas
502m
Livadi
Lia Beach
Ganema
Livadakia Beach
Kythnos (50km)
Vagia
Kalo Ambeli Beach
Karavi Beach
Piraeus (135km)
Cape Katano

Sifnos (20km);
Kimolos (50km);
Paros (55km);
Milos (70km); Ios (120km);
Santorini (130km)

CYCLADES SERIFOS

🍴 Sleeping & Eating

Accommodation options are found east of upper Hora. Head down the road opposite Cuckoo cafe-bar, close to the bus terminus.

I Apanemia
PENSION €

(☑ 22810 51517, 6971891106; www.apanemia.com.gr; s/d €40/45; ❋ ☎) This excellent-value, family-run place has decent, well-equipped rooms with front balcony views to the distant sea and side views towards Hora. It's old-school in decor, but well cared for.

Anemoessa Studios
APARTMENT €€

(☑ 22810 51132; www.serifos-anemoessa.gr; apt €90-130; ❋ ☎) Pretty, modern studios sleep four in whitewashed Cycladic splendour.

Stou Stratou
CAFE €

(☑ 22810 52566; Plateia Ag Athanasiou; dishes €4-9; ☺ 9am-late Easter-Oct) Sitting postcard-pretty in the main square, Stou Stratou has a menu full of art and poetry (literally), plus it serves good breakfasts and light snacks such as fennel pie or a mixed plate of cold cuts and cheese. Cocktails and coffee too.

★ Aloni
CYCLADIC €€

(☑ 22810 52603; mains €9-18; ☺ 7pm-late Jun-Oct, Sat & Sun Nov-May) Halfway up the hill between Livadi and Hora, signposted on the right,

Aloni gives splendid panoramas. Islanders rate it among Serifos' best, with local produce (roasted meat, rabbit in lemon sauce, fennel pie) proudly showcased.

Around Serifos

About 1.5km north of Livadi, pretty little **Psili Ammos Beach** offers the best swimming close to Livadi, and has two excellent tavernas. **Platys Gialos Beach** in the north has a good summer-only taverna of the same name.

Sykamia is one of the island's best beaches, with a dramatic approach along a steep, windy road through terraced hills. The beach itself is grey-brown sand full of stones, with an excellent tavern above it. To reach Sykamia you will pass through the quaint village of Panagia, or on the east coast, Kendarhos (also known as Kallitsos, the 'most beautiful').

Tiny **Megalo Livadi**, on the southwest coast, is a fun visit for its sparkling bay, crumbling neoclassical buildings (remnants of the mining era), shallow, calm waters and two seaside taverns. The cave where the Cyclops was said to dwell is near here.

The best beaches on the south coast tend to be broad and sandy, and deserted out of high season. It's a wild landscape, punctuated by derelict mining machinery. Stop for a swim at sheltered **Vagia**, long and narrow **Ganema** and **Koutalas fishing bay**.

🏃 Activities

Serifos Scuba Divers   DIVING
(☑ 6932570552; www.serifosscubadivers.gr; 1-tank dive/snorkelling €50/30) Based in Livadi, this recommended scuba operator takes divers to a dozen sites around the island, including wrecks, flooded mines and more. Day-long snorkelling trips can be arranged in July and August, and they also rent boats and arrange adrenalin-packed flyboard sessions.

🛏 Sleeping & Eating

⭐ **Coco-Mat**
Eco Residences   BOUTIQUE HOTEL €€€
(☑ 22877 72977; http://serifos.coco-mat-hotels.com; apt €460; 🅿🏵🛜) Overlooking Vagia beach, this cluster of miners' houses has been turned into a trendy little hotel. Its split-level residences (with bedrooms on the cooler level) come with coarse whitewashed walls, heavy wooden beams, sea views, super-comfy beds and kitchenettes, with a great little restaurant on-site serving fusion dishes.

To Akrogiali tou Vitou   TAVERNA €
(☑ 22810 51289; mains €7-11; ⏲ noon-10pm Jun-Aug; 🐾) To Akrogiali, just above one of Serifos' best beaches and one of the only signs of development for miles, serves delicious fish and excellent takes on Greek standards.

KYTHNOS   ΚΥΘΝΟΣ

POP 1456

Low-key Kythnos is a series of rolling hills punctuated by stone huts and bisected by ancient walls, green valleys and some wonderful beaches. Port life in Merihas and village life in beautiful Hora and Dryopida remain easygoing, and foreign tourists are few, although the ease of access from Athens sees locals filling the island's beaches and marinas on summer weekends.

ℹ️ Getting There & Away

Ferries serve Piraeus and Lavrio on the mainland, Kea to the north (services are infrequent, so it's usually easier to travel via Lavrio), and in high season, islands to the south. Out of season it's hard to connect to the south. In Merihas buy tickets at **Anerousa Travel** (☑ 22810 32372; ⏲ 9am-9pm) or **Larentzakis Travel Agency** (☑ 22810 32104; ⏲ 9am-9pm).

There's a twice-weekly service with Hellenic Seaways (www.hellenicseaways.gr) that connects Kythnos and Syros, with some services continuing on to central Cyclades islands including Paros, Naxos and Ios.

Boat Services from Kythnos

DESTINATION	DURATION	FARE (€)	FREQUENCY
Kea	1hr 20min	11	Mon & Thu
Kimolos	3½-5¼hr	15	Tue & Fri
Lavrio	1¾-2½hr	21	1-2 daily
Milos	4hr-7¾hr	16	Tue, Fri & Sun
Piraeus	3¼hr	29	4-6 weekly
Serifos	1½hr	12	Tue, Fri & Sat
Sifnos	2½hr	13	Mon & Thu
Syros	2½hr	9	Tue & Fri

ℹ️ Getting Around

In July and August, buses go from Merihas to Dryopida, continuing to Kanala or Hora. Less regular services run to Loutra. There aren't any services outside these months, meaning that the best way to see the island is by car or scooter. Rentals are available at Larentzakis Travel Agency, among others.

Taxis (☑ 69442 71609) cost about €10 to Hora and €8 to Dryopida. A **sea-taxi** (☑ 6944906568) to/from the beaches in summer costs about €10 return; this is the easiest option to reach Kolona.

Merihas   Μέριχας

POP 369

Tiny Merihas is home to much of the island's low-season life. Cafes and restaurants line the small harbour, and rooms for let dot its hills. The town beach is uninspiring but good beaches are within walking distance, north of the quay at **Martinakia** and **Episkopi**.

🛏 Sleeping & Eating

⭐**Kontseta**   APARTMENT €€
(☑ 22810 33024; www.kontseta.gr; d €90-120; ☺ Apr-Oct; ❄ 🔊) Easily the nicest option in town, these modern studio apartments are a cut above, with fresh decor and fine views. They are high above the ferry quay, with steps signposted next door to the Alpha Bank.

Foinikas Studios   APARTMENT €€
(☑ 22810 32203; d/tr €90/100; ❄ 🔊) There are no harbour views, but you're well placed (just a few metres from the waterfront) and the studios and apartments are simple and appealing.

Molos   KEBAB €
(☑ 22810 32455; Merihas; mains €2.50-15; ☺ noon-11pm) Quick, delish souvlaki, kebabs and burgers stuffed with cheese from a sweetly unassuming spot just where the ferries dock.

Kantouni   TAVERNA €€
(☑ 22810 32220; mains €8-18; ☺ noon-11pm; 🔊) On the southern bend of the waterfront, Kantouni offers a menu of classic, meat-centric Greek hits in a delightful setting decked in creeping roses. There's also waterside seating.

Ostria   SEAFOOD €€
(☑ 22810 33017; Merihas; mains €8-25; ☺ noon-midnight; 🔊) Ostria is the place for seafood: grilled snapper, scorpion fish, grouper, calamari and lobster spaghetti all get the thumbs-up. Funny how seafood

tastes better when you're seated by moored yachts...

ⓘ Information

There is one bank, plus two ATMs in Merihas.
Police Station (☑ 22810 31201) For emergencies.

Hora (Kythnos)
Χώρα (Κύθνος)

The distinctively charming capital, Hora (also known as Kythnos or Messaria) nestles in the lap of rolling agricultural fields and preserves an inherent Greek character.

The long main street makes for a great stroll through a cute central square to a series of colourful cafes, restaurants, ceramicists and sweet shops. Traditional village lanes are tucked behind here, still populated by grannies hanging out the laundry.

Kythnos   Ⓝ   0 ————— 5 km
0 ————— 2.5 miles

CYCLADES KYTHNOS

WORTH A TRIP

VILLAGE LIFE

Loutra is a low-key resort and fishing village, 3km north of Hora. Sitting on a windy bay, its large marina is full of yachts and its harbourfront lined with high-standard eateries.

Loutra's claim to fame is its **hot springs**. You can access the water for free on the beachfront, where a rockpool marks the entry point of the hot water into the sea, or else visit the nearby **Hydrotherapy Centre** (☎22810 31217; €3.50; ⊙Jun-Sep).

Maroula, a short coastal walk north, is the site of ancient Mesolithic graves.

Dryopida, a picturesque town of red-tiled roofs and winding streets clustered steeply on either side of a ravine, is connected to Hora by a footpath. It has a cluster of pretty eateries around the main church.

📛 Sleeping & Eating

Filoxenia APARTMENT €€
(☎22810 31644; www.filoxenia-kythnos.gr; d €70; P ❄ 🛜) Well-priced, fully equipped apartments and studios behind flower-bedecked walls.

Messaria GREEK €€
(☎22810 31672; www.messaria.gr; mains €9-17; ⊙noon-10pm; 🛜) At the entrance to Hora and inside the hotel of the same name, this cellar restaurant specialises in carnivorous delights, such as rooster cooked in wine, lamb *kleftiko* and rabbit stew.

Around Kythnos

Ten minutes' walk north of Merihas lies the pretty sandy cove of **Martinakia**. Half an hour further north is **Episkopi**, a wide swath of grey sand. Reachable via an hour's coastal walk (or via paved road) further northwest is the golden-sand **Apokrousi**, with two tavernas and a beach bar. From Apokrousi, a rutted road leads over the hill to the exquisite double-bay of **Kolona**, a sand spit joining the peninsula to the Aylos Loukas islet, with a high-season cafe above the beach. It's easiest to reach Kolona via sea-taxi from Merihas, or else by ATV or a hot 20-minute walk.

From Dryopida, the main road runs all the way south to **Agios Dimitrios**, a grey-sand beach with placid waters. Of the half-dozen east-coast beaches, mostly reachable by unpaved minor roads, the most accessible (and loveliest) is the sandy cove next to Kanala village.

⦿ Sights & Activities

With more than 30 dive sites to choose from, from wrecks and caves to drift dives, Kythnos is a great destination for underwater explorers. **Aqua Team** (☎22810 31333; www.aquakythnos.gr; 1-/2-tank dive €50/90; ⛴) arranges a full range of courses, including beginners' scuba for children.

Kastro Orias RUINS
Located on Cape Kefalos, a 90-minute picturesque ramble northwest from Loutra, these beautifully situated ruins are all that remains of a medieval city of around 5000 people.

📛 Sleeping & Eating

Porto Klaras APARTMENT €€
(☎22810 31276; www.porto-klaras.gr; d/q €100/140; ⊙Apr-Oct; ❄ 🛜) Impeccable studios with kitchens have modern baths and tons of amenities; apartments sleep four. Some have balconies with harbour views.

★**Archipelagos** CYCLADIC €€
(☎22810 32380; www.archipelagos-kythnos.com; mains €8-25; ⊙noon-10pm; 🛜) Come to this friendly, low-key taverna for grilled sardines, scorpion fish, red mullet and other bounty from the sea, as well as Greek salad topped with local cheese, kid and rabbit stew and oven-baked lamb.

KEA (TZIA) KEA (TZIA)
POP 2455

Kea, though naturally beautiful with cliffs, spectacular coastline and fecund hillsides, has been almost overrun by vacation homes. The island closest to Attica, it's just too easy to reach; but this is only evident on summer weekends, and in August. Rent wheels to get off the beaten path and find the island's charms: rocky spires, verdant valleys filled with orchards, olive groves and oak trees, and excellent walking trails.

The main settlements are the port of Korissia and the attractive capital, Ioulida, about 5km inland. Local people call the island Tzia.

① Getting There & Away

Kea's only mainland service is to Lavrio; connections to other islands are few. Weekend boats are packed. There are twice-weekly services, on Tuesdays and Fridays, with Hellenic Seaways (www.hellenicseaways.gr) that connect Kea with Kythnos (€7, one hour 20 minutes) and Syros (€11, four hours), Kimolos (€17, 13½ hours), Milos (€14, 14½ hours) and destinations in central Cyclades, such as Paros (€17, 7¼ hours), Naxos (€22, 8½ hours) and Ios (€24, 10½ hours). Tuesday services also stop at Serifos (€16, 8¼ hours) and Sifnos (€17, nine hours). There are one to three daily services to Lavrio (€12, one hour) between mid-June and mid-August; there are fewer services the rest of the year.

Book ahead with the **Stegadi** (☑ 22880 21435; http://praktoreiokeas.gr) ticket agent on the Korissia waterfront for **Marmari Express** (☑ Kea 22880 21435, Lavrio 22920 26200), **Makedon** (☑ Kea 22880 21435, Lavrio 22920 26777) and Hellenic Seaways.

① Getting Around

In July and August, regular buses go from Korissia to Vourkari, Otzias, Ioulida and Poisses Beach; fewer services run out of season. **Taxis** (☑ 6932669493, 6932418821) to Ioulida cost around €10, Otzias €8 and Poisses €25.

Leon Rent A Car (☑ 22880 21898; www.rent acarkea.gr; scooters/cars per day from €20/45), on the harbourfront, is the only place in Kea to rent scooters/cars (€25/50). In high season it's worth bringing your own from Athens.

Korissia   Κορησσία

POP 711

The little port of Korissia may not be quite as picturesque as the island's capital, but it makes an excellent base for exploring the island. The north-facing beach tends to catch the wind, but you're about a 15-minute walk from small but popular **Gialiskari Beach**, backed by eucalypts.

🛌 Sleeping

Koralli Studios   APARTMENT €
(☑ 22880 21268; www.kea-rooms.gr; studios from €45; 🅿❄️) Run by the helpful Aristoteles, these spotless, well-equipped, bougainvillea-and-jasmine-clad studios are just 150m from the beach. The owner can meet the ferry and goes out of his way to assist his guests.

★ **Red Tractor Farm**   GUESTHOUSE €€
(☑ 22880 21346; www.redtractorfarm.com; Korissia; d €100, studio €140-180; ❄️) The outstanding Red Tractor Farm lies inland from

Kea (Tzia)

Korissia harbour, just a stone's throw from the town beach, among serene vineyards and olive groves. Kostis Maroulis and Marcie Mayer operate this sustainable, creative agritourism farm, with beautiful Cycladic buildings combining traditional and modern style and comfort. Rooms, studios and larger cottages are available.

Kostis and Marcie can advise on the best hiking routes; they also produce olive oil, wine, marmalade and chutney, plus unique acorn cookies. During business hours, visitors can stop by the farm to make purchases. The farm is open year-round.

Aegean View   GUESTHOUSE €€
(☑ 22880 22046; www.roomsinkea.gr; d €65-75; ☉ Mar-Dec; 🅿❄️) On the harbourfront, just metres from the ferry dock, this guesthouse has a handful of bright, modern rooms and studios with funky bathrooms. Some have small private balconies; all share a lovely communal deck.

🍴 Eating & Drinking

★ **Rolando's**   CYCLADIC €€
(☑ 22880 22224; mains €8-17; ☉ noon-11.30pm; ❄️) Ioulida's loss is Korissia's gain. Since moving, Rolando's continues to serve some of Kea's best food, from killer meatballs, *katsiki*

(goat) and moussaka to super-fresh fish and boiled courgettes smothered in garlic.

Magazes MEDITERRANEAN €€
(☑ 22880 21104; www.kearestaurant.gr; mains €9-17; ⊘ noon-11.30pm; 🛜) Run by Greek-Californian Stefanos, Magazes is in a stylishly restored warehouse, producing high-quality local flavours. It's recommended for its fresh seafood, including lobster pasta, which comes from local fishermen, and *raga-salata* (traditional herring salad).

Kea Events CAFE
(☑ 22880 21841; www.keaevents.gr; ⊘ 9am-10pm May-Sep; 🛜) If you feel like a change from the beach, this large event complex has a big blue swimming pool open to the public free of charge, provided you buy something from the cafe menu (not hard, given it's loaded with snacks, coffee and beer). Find it 1.5km inland from Korissia (near the Eko petrol station).

❶ Information

Korissia has two banks and one ATM.

Ioulida Ιουλίδα

POP 633

Ioulida is Kea's gem. Its pretty scramble of narrow alleyways and buildings drapes across two hilltops. Once a substantial settlement of Ancient Greece, it now has a distinctly cosmopolitan feel at weekends.

The bus turnaround is on a square just at the edge of town, from where an archway leads into the labyrinthine village. (Park in the car park below the square.) Beyond the archway, turn right and uphill along Ioulida's main street for its shops and cafes and to reach the famed Kea Lion.

◉ Sights

★ Kea Lion MONUMENT
The enigmatic Kea Lion, chiselled from slate in the 6th century BC, lies across a small valley beyond the last of Ioulida's houses. The 15-minute walk to reach it is fantastic: follow small wooden signs reading Αρχαίος Λέων from the top of the main street until the path leads you out of town. If you look closely, you'll see the lion across the valley – the surrounding stones are painted white.

The footpath curves past a cemetery and the lion, with its smooth-worn haunches and Cheshire-cat smile, is reached through a gate on the left. The path continues to Otzias.

Archaeological Museum MUSEUM
(☑ 22880 22079; adult/child €3/1; ⊘ 8am-3pm Tue-Sun) Find intriguing artefacts from Kea's four ancient city-states, including some superb terracotta figurines, many from excavations at Agia Irini. Thirteen Minoan-style statues are the museum's pride. It's just before the post office on the main thoroughfare.

🛏 Sleeping & Eating

Hotel Serie HOTEL €€
(☑ 22880 22355; www.serie.com.gr; d/tr €75/85; ❇🛜) Just a few minutes' walk from labyrinthine Ioulida, this compact hotel offers a cluster of light, brightly painted rooms with hilly views from the balconies.

★ Kea Villas HOTEL €€€
(☑ 6972243330; www.keavillas.gr; ste €145-250, villa €700; ⊘ Mar–mid-Nov; ❇🛜▣) Gorgeously situated at the highest point of Ioulida, this complex with sweeping views offers a variety of suites and villas that sleep you and up to nine of your dearest friends in style. All have full kitchen and verandah.

To Spiti Sti Hora CYCLADIC €€€
(☑ 6972243330; mains €18-27; ⊘ noon-3pm & 7-11pm Jun-Sep; 🛜) Elaborate takes on seasonal Kea dishes, with local ingredients put to excellent use. Expect the likes of suckling pig with pear, cuttlefish risotto, grilled meats and awesome sunset views over Ioulida to go with your cocktails. At Kea Villas.

Around Kea

Kea's northern half is more popular with visitors than the southern half.

The beach road from Korissia leads past the appealing Gialiskari Beach for 2.5km to tiny Vourkari, a favourite with yachties, where the waterfront is lined with sailboats and fashionable cafes.

Four kilometres to the northeast, Otzias has a large, sandy beach, though it does get rather windy. From Otzias, a 12km road runs inland to Ioulida, connected to the east coast's finest beach, Spathi.

Eight kilometres southwest of Ioulida is the unfortunately named Pisses (also spelled Poisses), a small, sandy beach with a taverna and beach bar, backed by orchards, olive groves and rugged hills. Four kilometres south along the coast is Kondouros, a playground for moneyed Athenians, with a number of small sandy coves. A little further south, **Kambi** is an inviting swimming spot with a waterfront taverna.

◉ Sights

Karthea
RUINS

Accessible only by boat or walking path (about one hour, one-way) from Kato Meria is the bay of Poles in the southeast, home to the ancient city of Karthea. It's a walk with a spectacular destination: ancient ruins by a remote beach. For route details, buy a good map such as Terrain's *Tzia* map.

Moni Panagias Kastrianis
MONASTERY

(☉sunrise-sunset Jun-Sep) **FREE** From Otzias, a spectacular coastal road runs for 6.5km to this clifftop, 18th-century monastery. If you're circling back to Ioulida, the road from here is equally gorgeous, along the crest of hills with valleys plunging to either side.

☆ Activities

Kea has a dozen picturesque walking trails of varying length and difficulty. Check out http://praktoreiokeas.gr for trail descriptions and pick up a Terrain *Tzia* hiking map to hit the trails.

Kea has some of the best diving in Greece, with more than a dozen varied and challenging dive sites that include walls, ship and plane wrecks and underwater caves. Vourkari-based **Kea Divers** (☎22880 22280, 6973430860; www.keadivers.com; 1/2 dives incl equipment €50/90) is a reputable scuba-diving outfit that also runs snorkelling trips.

⊨ Sleeping & Eating

Camping Kea
CAMPGROUND €

(☎22880 31302; campingkea@yahoo.gr; campsite per adult/tent/car €7/7/5, bungalows €55; ☉May-Sep; P☏) Well-kept Camping Kea, under thick eucalyptus, has a shop and cafe just off Poisses, a wide strip of white sand against a backdrop of greenery-clad hills.

Anemousa Studios
APARTMENT €€

(☎22880 21335; www.anemousa.gr; studio/apt from €90/110; ☉Apr-Oct; ❋☏☒) These white-washed, spacious, family-friendly studios and apartments curve around the pool 50m inland from the beach in Otzias.

I Taverna tou Simou
CYCLADIC €

(☎22880 24280; mains €6-15; ☉noon-10pm May-Sep) In this traditional taverna in Kato Merias, proprietor Simos recreates a mix of traditional Kea and family recipes using local ingredients. Signature dishes include rabbit slow-cooked in a clay pot, parchment-wrapped goat, and chicken with homemade pasta.

I Strofi tou Mimi
SEAFOOD €€

(☎22880 21480; www.istrofitoumimi.com; mains €12-18; ☉7pm-midnight Apr-Oct; ☏) On the far side of Vourkari Bay, this is one of Kea's most celebrated seafood restaurants. The bay laps at the tables, which are positioned as close to the sea as possible without actually being in the water.

Crete

Best Places to Eat

➡ Thalassino Ageri (p303)

➡ Peskesi (p276)

➡ Taverna Panorama (p296)

➡ Hope (p317)

Best Places to Stay

➡ Enagron Ecotourism Village (p294)

➡ Serenissima (p302)

➡ Villa Olga (p315)

➡ Eleonas Country Village (p283)

➡ Plakias Youth Hostel (p295)

Why Go?

Crete (Κρήτη) is the culmination of the Greek experience. Nature here is as prolific as Picasso in his prime, creating a dramatic quilt of big-shouldered mountains, stunning beaches and undulating hillsides blanketed in olive groves,vineyards and wildflowers. There are deep chiselled gorges,including one of Europe's longest, and crystal-clear lagoons and palm-tree-lined beaches that conjure up the Caribbean.Crete's natural beauty is equalled only by the richness of a history that spans millennia. The Palace of Knossos is but one of many vestiges of the mysterious ancient Minoan civilisation. Venetian fortresses, Turkish mosques and Byzantine churches bring history alive all over Crete, but nowhere more so than in charismatic Hania and Rethymno. Crete's hospitable and spirited people uphold their unique culture, cuisine and customs. Local life and traditions remain a dynamic part of the island's soul

When to Go
Crete (Iraklio)

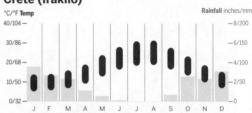

Jul & Aug High season. Queues at big sights, busy beaches. Hot days, balmy evenings, warm waters.

Apr–Jun & Sep–Oct Moderate temperatures, smaller crowds. Best time for hiking and outdoor activities.

Nov–Mar Low season. Sights and restaurants scale back hours; beach resorts close. Major sights uncrowded.

History

Although inhabited since Neolithic times (7000–3000 BC), Crete is most famous for being the cradle of Europe's first advanced civilisation, the Minoan. Traces of this enigmatic society were only uncovered in the early 20th century, when British archaeologist Sir Arthur Evans discovered the palace at Knossos and named the civilisation after its ruler, the mythical King Minos.

Minoans migrated to Crete in the 3rd millennium BC. Their extraordinary artistic, architectural and cultural achievements culminated in the construction of huge palace complexes at Knossos, Phaestos, Malia and Zakros, which were all levelled by an earthquake around 1700 BC. Undeterred, the Minoans built bigger and better ones over the ruins, while settling more widely across Crete. Around 1450 BC, the palaces were mysteriously destroyed again, possibly by a tsunami triggered by a volcanic eruption on Santorini (Thira). Knossos, the only palace saved, finally burned down around 1400 BC.

Archaeological evidence shows that the Minoans lingered on for a few centuries in small, isolated settlements before disappearing as mysteriously as they had come. They were followed by the Mycenaeans and the Dorians (around 1100 BC). By the 5th century BC, Crete was divided into city-states but did not benefit from the cultural glories of mainland Greece; in fact, it was bypassed by Persian invaders and the Macedonian conqueror Alexander the Great.

By 67 BC Crete had become the Roman province of Cyrenaica, with Gortyna its capital. After the Roman Empire's division in AD 395, Crete fell under the jurisdiction of Greek-speaking Constantinople – the emerging Byzantine Empire. Things went more or less fine until 824, when Arabs appropriated the island. In 961, though, Byzantine general emperor Nikiforas Fokas (912–69) won Crete back following a nine-month siege of Iraklio (then called El Khandak by the Arabs). Crete flourished under Byzantine rule, but with the infamous Fourth Crusade of 1204 the maritime power of Venice received Crete as part of its 'payment' for supplying the Crusaders' fleet.

Much of Crete's most impressive surviving architecture dates from the Venetian period, which lasted until 1669 when Iraklio (then called Candia) became the last domino to fall after a 21-year Ottoman siege. Turkish rule brought new administrative organisation, Islamic culture and Muslim settlers. Cretan resistance was strongest in the mountain strongholds but all revolts were put down brutally, and it was only with the Ottoman Empire's disintegration in the late 19th century that Europe's great powers expedited Crete's sovereign aspirations.

Thus, in 1898, with Russian and French consent, Crete became a British protectorate. However, the banner under which future Greek Prime Minister Eleftherios Venizelos and other Cretan rebels were fighting was Enosis i Thanatos (Unity or Death) – unity with Greece, not mere independence from Turkey. Yet it would take the Greek army's successes in the Balkan Wars (1912–13) to turn Crete's de facto inclusion in the country into reality, with the 1913 Treaty of Bucharest.

Crete suffered tremendously during WWII, due to being coveted by Adolf Hitler for its strategic location. On 20 May 1941 a huge flock of German parachutists quickly overwhelmed the Cretan defenders. The Battle of Crete, as it would become known, raged for 10 days between German and Allied troops from Britain, Australia, New Zealand and Greece. For two days the battle hung in the balance until the Germans captured the Maleme Airfield, near Hania. The Allied forces fought a valiant rearguard action, enabling the British Navy to evacuate 18,000 of the 32,000 Allied troops. The harsh German occupation lasted throughout WWII, with many mountain villages bombed or burnt down and their occupants executed en masse.

ℹ Getting There & Away

AIR

Most travellers arrive in Crete by air, often with a change in Athens. Travellers from North America need to connect via a European gateway city such as Paris, Amsterdam or Frankfurt and sometimes again in Athens. To reach Crete by air from other Greek islands also requires a change in Athens, except for some flights operated by Crete-based airline **Sky Express** (www.skyexpress.gr).

Iraklio's **Nikos Kazantzakis International Airport** (HER; ☑ general 2810397800, info ☑ 2810 397136; www.heraklion-airport.info) is Crete's busiest airport, although Hania (p304) is convenient for travellers heading to western Crete. Sitia (p320) only receives a handful of domestic and summertime international charter flights.

Between May and October, European low-cost carriers and charter airlines like easyJet (to Iraklio) and Ryanair (to Hania) operate direct flights to Crete, mostly from the UK, Poland, Sweden and Italy. Ryanair also offers domestic flights to Hania from Athens and Thessaloniki.

CRETE

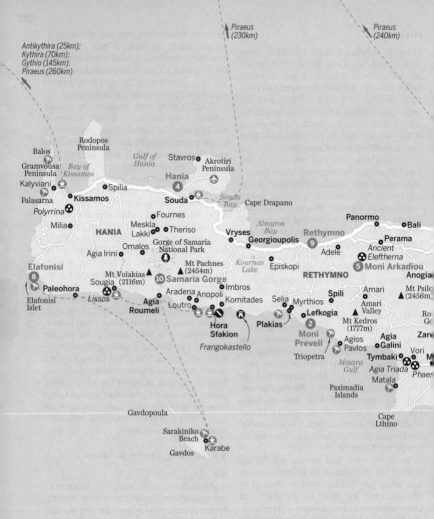

Piraeus (230km)

Piraeus (240km)

Antikythira (25km);
Kythira (70km);
Gythio (145km);
Piraeus (260km)

Rodopos Peninsula

Balos
Gramvousa Peninsula
Kalyviani
Falasarna
Polyrrina
Milia
Kissamos
Spilia

Bay of Kissamos
Gulf of Hania

Stavros
Akrotiri Peninsula

Hania ④

Souda
Souda Bay
Cape Drapano

HANIA

Fournes
Meskla
Lakki
Theriso
Agia Irini
Omalos
Gorge of Samaria National Park
Mt Pachnes (2454m) ▲

Vryses
Georgioupolis ⑨
Almyros Bay

Rethymno

Panormo
Bali
Perama
Adele
Ancient Eleftherna
⑤ **Moni Arkadiou**

RETHYMNO

Elafonisi ⑧
Paleohora
Elafonisi Islet

Mt Volakias (2116m) ▲
Sougia
Lissos
Agia Roumeli
⑩ **Samaria Gorge**

Aradena
Anopoli
Loutro
Imbros
Komitades
Hora Sfakion
Frangokastello

Selia
Myrthios
Plakias
② **Moni Preveli**
Triopetra
Agios Pavlos
Mesara Gulf

Kournas Lake
Episkopi

Spili
Lefkogia
Amari
Amari Valley ▲
Mt Kedros (1777m)

Agia Galini
Tymbaki
Agia Triada
Matala

Anogia
Mt Psilo ▲ (2456m)

Agia
Vori
Phaes

Paximadia Islands

Gavdopoula

Sarakiniko Beach
Karabe
Gavdos

Cape Lithino

Libyan Sea

Crete Highlights

① **Palace of Knossos** (p278) Rubbing shoulders with the ghosts of the Minoans.

② **Moni Preveli** (p296) Absorbing lofty views from this 17th-century monastery above the magical Preveli Beach.

③ **Iraklio Wine Country** (p282) Exploring Minoan ruins and sampling the local tipple.

④ **Hania** (p299) Embarking on a wander around the evocative Venetian quarter.

⑤ **Moni Arkadiou** (p292) Being moved by the beauty and tragedy of this 16th-century stone church.

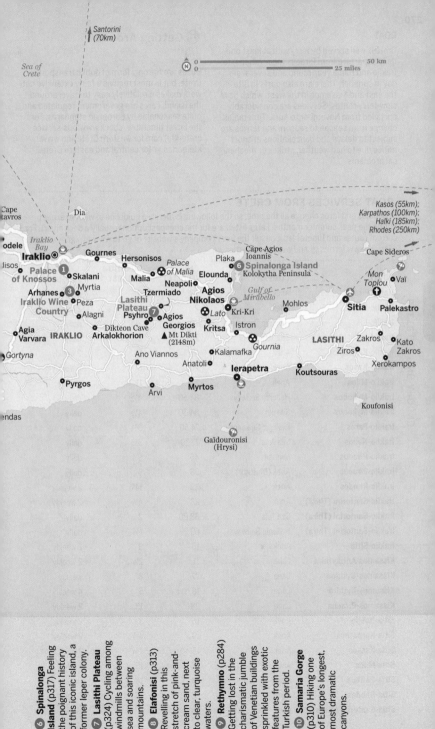

Santorini
(70km)

Sea of
Crete

0   50 km
0   25 miles

Kasos (55km);
Karpathos (100km);
Halki (185km);
Rhodes (250km)

Cape
tavros

Dia

Cape Agios
Ioannis

Cape Sideros

odele

Iraklio
Bay

Iraklio

1 **Palace
of Knossos**

lisos

Skalani

Gournes

Hersonisos

Plaka

Myrtia

*Palace
of Malia*

Spinalonga Island

6

Mon
Toplou

Vaï

Kolokytha Peninsula

3

Arhanes

Malia

Elounda

Iraklio Wine
Country

Peza

Neapoli

**Agios
Nikolaos**

*Gulf of
Mirabello*

Sitia

Palekastro

Alagni

Tzermiado

Mohlos

**Lasithi
Plateau**

Agia
Varvara

IRAKLIO

Psyhro

7

Agios
Georgios

Lato

Kri-Kri

Dikteon Cave

Arkalokhorion

Kritsa

Istron

Zakros

Kato
Zakros

LASITHI

Ziros

Gortyna

▲ Mt Dikti
(2148m)

Kalamafka

Gournia

Xerokampos

Gournia

Ano Viannos

Anatoli

Ierapetra

Koutsouras

Pyrgos

Arvi

Myrtos

endas

Koufonisi

Gaïdouronisi
(Hrysi)

BOAT

Crete is well served by ferry with at least one daily departure from Piraeus (near Athens) to Iraklio and Hania year-round and several per day in summer. There are also ports in Sita in the east and Kissamos in the west, which have slow-ferry routes. Services are considerably curtailed from November to April. Timetables change from season to season, and ferries are subject to delays and cancellations at short notice due to bad weather, strikes or mechanical problems.

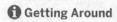

Getting Around

BUS

Buses are the only form of public transport in Crete, but in most regions a fairly extensive network makes it relatively easy to travel around the island. Fares are government regulated and quite reasonable by European standards. For the latest timetable, check www.bus-service-crete-ktel.com for western Crete and www.ktelherlas.gr for central and eastern Crete.

BOAT SERVICES FROM CRETE

Schedules and fares change all the time, so the following is merely a guideline of what to expect during the peak summer months. Fares listed are for the cheapest option (usually a deck chair). For current routes and timetables, consult the ferry company's website or go to www.gtp.gr, www.openseas.gr, www.ferries.gr and www.greekferries.gr.

ROUTE	COMPANY	FARE (FROM €)	DURATION (HOURS)	FREQUENCY
Hania-Piraeus	Anek	38	9	daily
Iraklio-Halki	Anek	22	12	2 weekly
Iraklio-Ios	Hellenic Seaways	70	2½	daily
Iraklio-Ios	Sea Jets	70	2½	daily
Iraklio-Karpathos	Anek	19	8	2 weekly
Iraklio-Kasos	Anek	20	6	2 weekly
Iraklio-Milos	Anek	23	11	weekly
Iraklio-Mykonos	Hellenic Seaways	84.50	4½	daily
Iraklio-Mykonos	Sea Jets	84.30	4½	daily
Iraklio-Paros	Hellenic Seaways	74.50	3¾	daily
Iraklio-Naxos	Sea Jets	77.80	3½	daily
Iraklio-Piraeus	Minoan	46	8½	daily
Iraklio-Piraeus	Anek (Bluestar)	38	9	daily
Iraklio-Rhodes	Anek	29	14½	2 weekly
Iraklio-Santorini (Thira)	Anek	28	4¼	2 weekly
Iraklio-Santorini (Thira)	Sea Jets	68.80	2	daily
Iraklio-Santorini (Thira)	Hellenic Seaways	69	1¾	daily
Iraklio-Sitia	Anek	16	3	2 weekly
Kissamos-Antikythira	Lane	11	2¼	2 weekly
Kissamos-Gythion	Lane	27	8	weekly
Kissamos-Kythira	Lane	18	5	4 weekly
Kissamos-Piraeus	Lane	28	13	2 weekly
Sitia-Iraklio	Anek	16	3	2 weekly
Sitia-Karpathos	Anek	19	4½	2 weekly
Sitia-Kassos	Anek	12	2¾	2 weekly
Sitia-Milos	Anek	26	15	weekly
Sitia-Piraeus	Anek	44	18	weekly
Sitia-Rhodes	Anek	28	11¼	2 weekly
Sitia-Santorini (Thira)	Anek	28	8	weekly

CAR

Having your own wheels is a great way to explore Crete if you can brave the roads and drivers. Although distances are often not that great, travelling on narrow and winding mountain roads will seriously slow you down, so factor that into your day's itinerary. In remote areas (particularly the south), you'll still find unpaved roads that are only suitable for 4WDs.

CENTRAL CRETE

Central Crete comprises the Iraklio prefecture, named after the island's booming capital, and the Rethymno prefecture, named after its lovely Venetian port town. Along with its dynamic urban life and Venetian remnants, the region is home to the island's top-rated tourist attraction, the Palace of Knossos, as well as other major and minor Minoan sites.

Even if the coastal stretch east of the city of Iraklio is one continuous band of hotels and resorts, just a little bit inland villages sweetly lost in time provide a pleasing contrast. Taste the increasingly sophisticated tipple produced in the Iraklio Wine Country, walk in the footsteps of Nikos Kazantzakis and revel in the rustic grandeur of the mountain village of Zaros.

Rethymno is a fascinating quilt of bubbly resorts, centuries-old villages and energising towns. Away from the northern coast, you'll quickly find yourself immersed in endless tranquillity and natural beauty as you drift through such villages as Anogia, where locals cherish their timeless traditions and their music. The southern coast is a different animal altogether – a wild beauty with steep gorges and bewitching beaches in seductive isolation, along with the relaxed resort of Plakias and the old hippie cave and beach hang-out of Matala.

Iraklio Ηράκλειο
POP 140,730

Crete's capital city, Iraklio (also called Heraklion), is Greece's fifth-largest city and the island's economic and administrative hub. It's also home to Crete's blockbuster sights: the must-see Heraklion Archaeological Museum and the nearby Palace of Knossos, which both provide fascinating windows into Crete's ancient past.

Though not pretty in a conventional way, Iraklio can grow on you if you take the time to explore its layers and wander its back-streets. You'll discover a low-key urban sophistication with a thriving cafe and restaurant scene, good shopping and bustling nightlife. A revitalised waterfront invites strolling and the newly pedestrianised historic centre is punctuated by bustling squares flanked by buildings from the time when Christopher Columbus first set sail.

◎ Sights

★Heraklion Archaeological
Museum   MUSEUM
(☏2810 279000; http://odysseus.culture.gr; Xanthoudidou 2; adult/concession/child €10/5/free; ☺8am-8pm daily Apr-Oct, 11am-5pm Mon, 8am-3pm Tue-Sun Nov-Mar) This state-of-the-art museum is one of the largest and most important in Greece. The two-storey revamped 1930s Bauhaus building makes a gleaming showcase for artefacts spanning 5500 years from Neolithic to Roman times, including a Minoan collection of unparalleled richness. The rooms are colour coded and displays are arranged both chronologically and thematically, and presented with descriptions in English. A visit here will greatly enhance your understanding of Crete's rich history. Don't skip it.

The museum's treasure trove includes pottery, jewellery, sarcophagi, plus famous frescoes from the sites of Knossos, Tylissos, Amnissos and Agia Triada. The pieces are grouped into comprehensive themes such as settlements, trade, death, religion and administration. Along with clear descriptions, these bring to life both the day-to-day functioning and long-term progression of societies on Crete and beyond. Budget at least two hours for this extraordinary collection, if necessary taking a break in the on-site cafe.

➡ Ground Floor
Rooms I to III focus on the Neolithic period to the Middle Bronze Age (7000 BC to 1700 BC), showing life in the first settlements in Crete and around Knossos. In Room II don't miss the golden pendant with bees from Malia, a sophisticated jeweller's masterpiece, and the extensive jewellery collection. The undisputed eye-catcher in Room III is the elaborately embellished Kamares tableware of red, black and white clay, including a 'royal dinner service' from Phaestos.

Rooms IV to VI illustrate life in the Late Bronze Age (1700 BC to 1450 BC). This is when Minoan culture reached its zenith, as reflected in the foundation of new palaces,

Iraklio

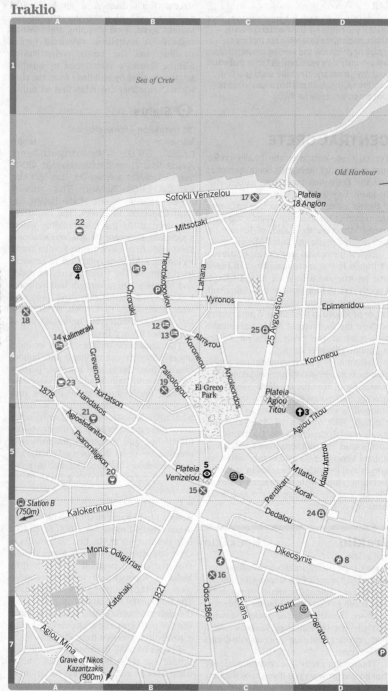

Sea of Crete

Old Harbour

Sofokli Venizelou 17 ⊗   Plateia 18 Anglon

22 ☕

Mitsotaki

4 🏛

9 🏨

Theotokopoulou

Chronaki

P

Lahana

Vyronos

Epimenidou

18 ⊗

14 🏨 Kalimeraki

12 🏨
13 🏨

Koroneou

Almyrou

25 🏧

25 Avgoustou

Koroneou

Grevenon

Hortatson

Paleologou

19 ⊗

El Greco Park

Arkoleondos

Plateia Agiou Titou

3 ⛪

1878

23 🏨

Handakos

21 🏨 Agiostefaniton

Psaromiligkon

20 🚻

Agiou Titou

Idaiou Antrou

5 ◎ Plateia Venizelou

6 🏛

Milatou

Korai

Perdikari

Station B (750m) 🚌

Kalokerinou

15 ⊗

Dedalou

24 🔒

Monis Odigitrias

7 ☪

Dikeosynis

8 🏃

Katehaki

1821

16 ⊗

Odos 1866

Evans

Koziri

Zografou

Agiou Mina

Grave of Nikos Kazantzakis (900m)

elaborate architecture and prolific trading practices. Not surprisingly, these are among the most visited rooms and the collection is vast. Highlights include the small clay house from Arhanes, a stunning ivory-and-crystal inlaid draughts board and a scale model of Knossos. Most home in on the Phaistos disc, a stunning clay piece embossed with 45 signs, which has never been deciphered. Nearby, the massive copper ingots from Agia Triada and Zakros Palace demonstrate important units of economic exchange. Other gems include the bull-leaping fresco and incredible bull-leaper sculpture (Room VI) that show daring sporting practices of the time.

Rooms VII and **VIII** reveal the importance of Minoan religion and ideology with cult objects and figurines. Room VII houses the Chieftain's cup from Agia Triada that portrays two men, one holding a staff, the other a sword. In Room VIII, the snake goddesses and stone bull's head (inlaid with seashell and crystal) are two stunning ceremonial items from Knossos.

Rooms IX and **X** are dedicated to the palace of Knossos and its emergence as a centralised state (after the administrative collapse of other palaces) along with evidence of the Mycenaeans. Linear B clay tablets reveal the first 'Greek' script and indicate Knossos' complex administrative system and bureaucratic processes. In Room X, look for the extraordinary boar's helmet and gold-handled swords, displaying the importance of the aristocratic warrior status.

Rooms XI and **XII** highlight settlements, sanctuaries and graves of the Late Bronze Age, including fascinating visual representations of death. The extraordinary sarcophagus from Agia Triada (Room XII) is presumed to be that of a ruler, given its detailed, honorific fresco-style scenes.

➧ **1st Floor**

Room XIII showcases Minoan frescoes (1800 BC to 1350 BC), including Evans' famous (or infamous) recreations. The paintings reflect the interest in art and nature at the time. All are highlights, but for your at-a-glance reference, it's home to the Prince of the Lilies, the Ladies in Blue, the Cupbearer, La Parisienne and the Dolphin Fresco.

Rooms XV to **XIX** focus on the Geometric and Archaic periods (10th to 6th century BC), the transition to the Iron Age and formation of the first Greek cities. The Apollonian Triad, bronze statues from Deros, are the earliest known Greek hammered bronze statues,

Iraklio

while the bronze shields of the Ideon Cave are extravagant votive offerings to Zeus.

Rooms XX to **XXII** move to the Classical, Hellenistic and Roman periods (5th to 4th century BC), where utensils figurines and stunning mosaic floors and amphorae set the scene for the foundation of the autonomous Greek city-states, followed by civil wars and, finally, the Roman period. The huge Phalagari hoard of silver coins (Room XXI) is thought to be a military state fund. The cemetery finds of these periods are especially fascinating: look out for the skull with the gold wreath (Room XXII).

Room XXIII exhibits two private collections donated to the museum.

➡ **Ground Floor – Part II**

Rooms XXVI and **XXVII** (7th to 4th century BC), on the ground floor, house the museum's sculpture collection. Architectural reliefs from Gortyna exhibit the role of Crete in the development of monumental sculpture, while Roman sculptures and copies of heroes and Gods of the preceding Classical era highlight the type of art during the Roman period.

★ **Koules Fortress**　　FORTRESS
(Rocca al Mare; ☑ 2810 288484; http://koules. efah.gr; Venetian Harbour; adult/concession €2/1; ⊙ 8am-8pm Apr-Oct, to 3pm Nov-Mar) After six years of restoration, Iraklio's symbol, the 16th-century fortress called Rocca al Mare by the Venetians, reopened in August 2016 with a brand-new exhibit. It tells the story of the building, zeroes in on milestones in city history and displays ancient amphorae, Vene-

tian cannons and other finds recovered from shipwrecks around Dia island by Jacques Cousteau in 1976. The presentation is insightful and atmospheric thanks to muted light filtering in through the old cannon holes.

Visits conclude on the rooftop with panoramic views over the sea and the city.

Historical Museum of Crete　　MUSEUM
(☑ 2810 283219; www.historical-museum.gr; Sofokli Venizelou 27; adult/student/child under 12yr €5/3/free; ⊙ 9am-5pm Mon-Sat Apr-Oct, to 3.30pm Mon-Sat Nov-Mar) If you're wondering what Crete's been up to for the past, say, 1700 years, a spin around this engagingly curated museum is in order. Exhibits hopscotch from the Byzantine to the Venetian and Turkish periods, culminating with WWII. Quality English labelling, interactive stations throughout and an audio guide (€3) greatly enhance the experience.

The Venetian era gets special emphasis and even a huge model of the city circa 1650 prior to the Turkish occupation. Start in the introductory room, which charts the major phases of history through maps, books, artefacts and images. First-floor highlights include the only two El Greco paintings in Crete, 13th- and 14th-century frescoes, exquisite Venetian gold jewellery and embroidered vestments. A historical exhibit charts Crete's road to independence from the Turks in the early 20th century. The most interesting rooms on the 2nd floor are the recreated study of Cretan-born author Nikos Kazantzakis and those dramatically detailing aspects of the WWII Battle of Crete in 1941, including the Cretan resistance and the role of the Allied Secret Service. The top floor features an outstanding folklore collection.

Morosini Fountain FOUNTAIN
(Lion Fountain; Plateia Venizelou) Unfortunately, water no longer spurts from the four lions that make up this charming fountain, which is the most beloved Venetian vestige around town. Built in 1628 by Francesco Morosini, it once supplied Iraklio with fresh water. Flanked by bustling cafes and fast-food joints, it's a fun spot to spend an hour resting and people-watching.

Municipal Art Gallery GALLERY
(☑ 2810 3992089; 25 Avgoustou & Plateia Venizelou; ⊙9am-2pm & 5-8pm) FREE The three-aisled 13th-century Agios Markos Basilica was reconstructed many times and turned into a mosque by the Turks. Today it's an exhibit space showcasing Greek and foreign artists.

Church of Agios Titos CHURCH
(☑ 2810 346079; Plateia Agiou Titou; ⊙usually 7.30am-8pm) This majestic church dominates the eponymous, palm-studded square. It had Byzantine origins in AD 961, was converted to a Catholic church by the Venetians and turned into a mosque by the Ottomans, who used the bell tower as a minaret. It has been an Orthodox church since 1925. Since 1966, its most revered possession is once again the skull relic of St Titus, returned here after being spirited to Venice for safe-keeping during the Turkish occupation.

🦅 Beaches

Ammoudara, about 4km west of Iraklio, and **Amnisos**, 2km east, are the closest beaches to town; the latter is just past the airport and gets quite a bit of noise. The strands in **Agia Pelagia**, some 20km west of town, are nicer.

🏃 Activities

Mountaineering Club of Iraklio HIKING
(☑ 2810 227609; www.eos-her.gr; Dikeosynis 53; ⊙8.30-10.30pm Mon-Fri) The local chapter arranges hiking trips across the island most weekends (trip programs are published on its website). Anyone is welcome to join.

Cretan Adventures OUTDOORS
(☑ 2810 332772; www.cretanadventures.gr; 3rd fl, Evans 10; ⊙9am-5pm Mon-Fri) 🍃 This well-regarded local company run by friendly and knowledgeable English-speaking Fondas organises hiking tours, mountain biking and extreme outdoor excursions. It also coordinates fabulous week-long self-guided hiking tours including detailed hiking instructions, accommodation with breakfast and luggage transfer from €740. Fondas' office is up on the 3rd floor and easy to miss.

🛏 Sleeping

Rea Hotel HOTEL €
(☑ 2810 223638; www.hotelrea.gr; Kalimeraki 1; d €43-68; ⊙Mar-Nov; ❄�🛜) Family-run Rea has an easy, friendly atmosphere with 16 compact but neat-as-a-pin rooms dressed in shades from vanilla to chocolate. There's a book exchange and a communal fridge. Optional continental breakfast costs €3.

Hotel Mirabello HOTEL €
(☑ 2810 285052; www.mirabello-hotel.gr; Theotokopoulou 20; d €50-55; ❄@🛜) Despite its dated Plain-Jane looks, this friendly and low-key hotel offers excellent value for money. Assets include squeaky-clean rooms with modern bathrooms, beds with individual reading lamps, a fridge and kettle plus a location close to, well, everything. The nicest units have a balcony.

Capsis Astoria HOTEL €€
(☑ 2810 343080; www.capsishotel.gr; Plateia Eleftherias 11; r incl breakfast €100-140; P ❄@🛜🏊) Not of the latest vintage, but with a handy location next to the Archaeological Museum and the bus stop to Knossos, this hulking city hotel has compact rooms decked out in neutral tones and accented with historic black-and-white photographs. The cheapest have windows but no views, the nicest private balconies. In summer, the rooftop pool is a big selling point.

Kastro Hotel HOTEL €€
(☑ 2810 284185; www.kastro-hotel.gr; Theotokopoulou 22; d incl breakfast €65-100; ❄🛜) Clearly plenty of thought has gone into the design of the smartly renovated Kastro, even though not all choices may be equally eye-pleasing (floral wallpaper meets faux-leather headboard). Still, good-quality mattresses, strong hot showers, a good breakfast buffet and the rooftop terrace are all welcome aspects of this central city hotel.

Atrion Hotel HOTEL €€€
(☑ 2810 246000; www.atrion.gr; Chronaki 9; d incl breakfast €80-130; ❄🛜) Although this modern, streamlined 60-room hotel was designed with the business brigade in mind, it's also

a handy launch pad for city explorers. The carpeted rooms in shades of white and cinnamon come with a balcony (ask for a sea-facing one) and squeaky clean bathrooms. Breakfast is served in the light-filled central atrium.

GDM Megaron HOTEL €€€
(📞 2810 305300; www.gdmmegaron.gr; Doukos Beaufort 9; d incl breakfast €130-190; ✳ @ 🛜 ⊠) Built as a residence for Iraklio's power players in the 1930s, this hulking harbour-front landmark became a hotel in 2003. It sports all the expected mod cons of a traditional five-star property, including luxury mattresses, fine bath amenities and blackout drapes. Unwinding stations include a gym, a glass-sided pool and a panoramic rooftop restaurant and bar.

✗ Eating

Fyllo...Sofies CAFE €
(📞 2810 284774; www.fillosofies.gr; Plateia Venizelou 33; snacks €2.70-8.50; ⊙ 6am-late; 🛜) With tables sprawling out towards the Morosini Fountain, this is a great place to sample *bougatsa* (creamy semolina pudding wrapped in a pastry envelope and sprinkled with cinnamon and sugar). The less-sweet version is made with *myzithra* (sheep's-milk cheese).

They're traditionally eaten for breakfast but, quite frankly, taste good any time of day. If you can't decide whether to go sweet or savoury, ask for a combination of the two.

★ Peskesi CRETAN €€
(📞 2810 288887; www.peskesicrete.gr; Kapetan Haralampi 6-8; mains €8-13; ⊙ 10am-2am; 🛜 🍴) This foodie hotspot oozes rustic sophis-

tication from every nook and cranny of its maze of stone rooms lidded by wood-beam ceilings. Chefs use heirloom produce and organic meats from their own farm to revive ancient recipes in progressive ways. Killer dish: *kreokakavos,* a Minoan roast pork. The all-Cretan wine list is tops and the complimentary appetiser and dessert a nice touch.

It's located in a tiny lane off the northwest corner of El Greco Park. Worth reserving ahead if busy.

★ Parasties GREEK €€
(📞 2810 225009; www.parasties.gr; Historical Museum Sq, Sofokli Venizelou 19; mains €7-24; ⊙ noon-midnight) Parasties' owner Haris is Iraklio's answer to a restaurateur who is genuine about serving great-quality local produce and top Cretan wines. And his passion shows in his small but gourmet menu of inventively updated traditional fare, including several daily specials, all prepared by a fleet of cooks in the open kitchen.

Decor is stylish and you can eat al fresco or indoors and watch the chef toss her snails and other delights in the open kitchen.

Giakoumis TAVERNA €€
(📞 2810 284039; Theodosaki 5-8; mains €6-13; ⊙ 7am-11pm) The oldest among the row of tavernas vying for business in a quiet passageway off Odos 1866, Giakoumis offers myriad *mayirefta* (ready-cooked meals) and grills. Don't go past the lamb chops; the cook has been grilling them for over 40 years and has perfected the seasoning and method. Giannis the owner says, 'Local servings for everyone!' In other words, generous.

Ippokambos SEAFOOD €€
(Sofokli Venizelou 3; mains €6-13; ⊙ noon-late Mon-Sat; 🛜 🍴) This long-running *ouzerie* (place that serves ouzo and light snacks) specialises in fish – freshly caught, simply but expertly prepared and sold at fair prices. In summer, park yourself on the covered waterfront terrace.

🍷 Drinking & Nightlife

Hipsters congregate around Korai and Perdikari while El Greco Park has a more mainstream feel. West of here, Handakos, Agiostefaniton and Psaromiligkon are more alternative-flavoured hang-outs. Nearby, there's a lively local cafe scene in the tiny lanes of Zampeliou and Kagiampi.

DON'T MISS

IRAKLIO MARKET

An Iraklio institution, if slightly touristy these days, this busy narrow market along Odos 1866 (1866 St) is one of the best in Crete and has everything you need to put together a delicious picnic. Stock up on the freshest fruit and vegetables, creamy cheeses, honey, succulent olives, fresh breads and whatever else grabs your fancy. There are also plenty of other stalls selling pungent herbs, leather goods, hats, jewellery and some souvenirs. Cap off a spree with a coffee at one of the quaint *kafeneia* (coffee houses).

Utopia CAFE

(☑2810 341321, 6936341321; www.facebook.com/OutopiaCafeBeerOutopia; Handakos 51; ☺9am-2am) The Aztecs called it the 'elixir of the gods' and if you too worship at the cocoa altar, make a beeline to this been-here-forever cafe for the best hot chocolate in town. Add a side of decadence with an order of ice cream or delectable pastry or skip the sweet stuff altogether and order from the extensive craft beer menu.

Mare Cafe CAFE, BAR

(☑2810 241946; Sofokli Venizelou; ☺9am-late; ☎) In an enviable location on the beautified waterfront promenade opposite the Historical Museum, contempo Mare is great for post-culture java and sunset drinks. If you've got the munchies, there's an extensive menu of burgers, salads, pasta and other staples to choose from.

Jailhouse Bar BAR

(☑6978090547; Agiostefaniton 19a; ☺5pm-4am) Rock, metal, punk and country, from Johnny Cash to Johnny Rotten, is the ammo at this dimly lit pub in a barrel-vaulted Venetian-era building. Has a good selection of beers.

Bar Blow-Up BAR

(http://barblowup.blogspot.de; Psaromiligkon 1; ☺1.30pm-late; ☎) This alt-flavoured lair draws unpretentious types for beer, beats and bands. There's an alchemy of electro, funk and new wave on the turntable and the occasional indie band on stage.

🛍 Shopping

Roadside Travel BOOKS

(☑2810 344610; 25 Avgoustou 48; ☺9am-9pm Mon-Sat) This travel specialist bookshop has an impressive selection of guidebooks and maps plus good publications on Crete and its ancient sites.

Aerakis Music MUSIC

(www.aerakis.net; Koraï Sq 14; ☺9am-9pm Mon-Fri, to 5pm Sat) An Iraklio landmark since 1974, this little shop stocks an expertly curated selection of Cretan and Greek music, from old and rare recordings to the latest releases, many on its own record labels, Cretan Musical Workshop and Seistron.

There's also a small selection of musical instruments, books and Cretan products such as knives and woven bags. All can also be ordered online.

ⓘ Information

Banks with ATMs are plentiful, especially along 25 Avgoustou.

Main Post Office (☑2810 289994; www.elta.gr; Plateia Daskalogianni; ☺7.30am-8.30pm Mon-Fri)

Paleologos (☑2810 346185; www.paleologos.gr; 25 Avgoustou 5; ☺9am-8.30pm Mon-Fri, to 4pm Sat) Useful full-service travel agent for ferries, flights, car rentals, accommodation and excursions. Also a shipping agency.

Tourist Police (☑2810 283190, emergency 171; Dikeosynis 10; ☺7am-10pm) In the Halikarnassos suburb near the airport.

ⓘ Getting There & Away

AIR

About 5km east of Iraklio, **Nikos Kazantzakis International Airport** (HER; ☑ general 2810 397800, info 2810 397136; www.heraklion-airport.info) has an ATM, a duty-free shop and a cafe-bar.

BOAT

The ferry port is 500m to the east of the Koules Fortress and old harbour, and the bus terminal is right outside the port entrance. Iraklio is a major port for access to many of the islands, though services are spotty outside high season. Tickets can be purchased online or through local travel agencies, including central Paleologos. Daily ferries from Iraklio's port include services to Piraeus and faster catamarans to Santorini and other Cycladic islands. Ferries sail east to Rhodes via Sitia, Kasos, Karpathos and Halki.

BUS

Iraklio has two major long-distance bus stations. For details on services, see www.ktelherlas.gr. Buses are wi-fi equipped.

Iraklio Bus Station A (Central Station; ☑2810 246530; Leoforos Nearchou; ☎) Near the waterfront east of Koules Fortress, this depot serves major destinations in eastern and western Crete, including Hania, Rethymno, Agios Nikolaos, Sitia and the Lassithi Plateau. City bus 2 to Knossos leaves from the adjacent local bus station.

Iraklio Bus Station B (Chanioporta Station; ☑2810 255965; Machis Kritis 3; ☎) Just beyond Hania Gate, west of the centre, this station serves Anogia, Phaestos, Agia Galini, Gortyn, Zaros and Matala.

LONG-DISTANCE TAXI

For destinations around Crete, you can order a cab from **Crete Taxi Services** (☑6970021970; www.crete-taxi.gr; ☺24hr) or **Heraklion Taxi** (www.heraklion-taxi.com). There are also long-distance cabs waiting at the airport, at Plateia Eleftherias (outside the Capsis Astoria hotel) and at Bus Station A. Sample fares for up to four people include Agios Nikolaos (€85), Hersonisos (€39), Malia (€50), Matala (€101) and Rethymno (€108).

❶ Getting Around

TO/FROM THE AIRPORT

The airport is just off the E75 motorway, about 5km east of the city centre. City bus 10 connects it with the city centre, including the port, bus stations A and B and Plateia Eleftherias, every few minutes. The bus stop is to the left as you exit the terminal.

Taxis wait outside the departures terminal with official fares posted. The fare into town is about €11.

CAR & MOTORCYCLE

Iraklio's streets are narrow and chaotic so it's best to drop your vehicle in a car park (about €6 per day) and explore on foot.

All the international car-hire companies have branches at the airport. Local outlets line the northern end of 25 Avgoustou and include **Caravel** (🖉 2810 300150; www.caravel.gr; 25 Avgoustou 39; car per day from €42; ⊙ 8am-11pm), **Motor Club** (🖉 2810 222408; www.motorclub.gr; Plateia 18 Anglon 1; per day/week car from €34/145, scooters from €30/175; ⊙ 7am-10pm) and **Sun Rise** (🖉 2810 221609, 6981761340; www.sunrise-cars.com; 25 Avgoustou 46; per day car from €40; ⊙ 8am-9pm).

TAXI

There are small taxi stands all over town but the main ones are at Bus Station A, on Plateia Eleftherias and at the northern end of 25 Avgoustou. You can also phone for one on 🖉 2814 003084.

Around Iraklio

Knossos   Κνωσσός

★ **Palace of Knossos**   ARCHAEOLOGICAL SITE
(🖉 2810 231940; http://odysseus.culture.gr; Knossos; adult/concession €15/8, incl Heraklion Archaeological Museum €16/8; ⊙ 8am-8pm Apr-Oct, to 5pm Nov-Mar; 🅿; 🚍 2) Crete's most famous historical attraction is the Palace of Knossos, the grand capital of Minoan Crete, located 5km south of Iraklio. The setting is evocative and the ruins and recreations impressive, incorporating an immense palace, courtyards, private apartments, baths, lively frescoes and more. Excavation of the site started in 1878 with Cretan archaeologist Minos Kalokerinos, and continued from 1900 to 1930 with British archaeologist Sir Arthur Evans, who controversially restored parts of the site.

Evans' reconstructions bring to life the palace's most significant parts, including the columns, which are painted deep brown-red

---

MINOAN PALACES

In addition to the great Palace of Knossos, the Minoans left other remarkable sites:

Phaestos (🖉 28920 42315; http://odysseus.culture.gr; Iraklio-Phaestos Rd; adult/concession/under 18yr €8/4/free; ⊙ 8am-8pm Apr-Oct, 8am-3pm Nov-Mar; 🅿) Phaestos was the second-most important Minoan palace-city after Knossos and enjoys an awe-inspiring setting with panoramic views of the Messara Plain and Mt Psiloritis. Like Knossos, Phaestos (fes-tos) was built atop a previously destroyed older palace and laid out around a central court. In contrast to its bigger cousin, though, this site had fewer frescoes as walls were likely covered with white gypsum. Good English panelling and graphics stationed in key spots help demystify the ruins.

Agia Triada (🖉 28920 91564; www.interkriti.org; off Phaestos-Matala Rd; adult/concession/under 18yr €4/2/free; ⊙ 9am-4pm; 🅿) In an enchanting spot 3km west of Phaestos, Agia Triada encompasses vestiges of an L-shaped royal villa, a ramp once leading out to sea and a village with residences and stores. Built around 1550 BC, Agia Triada succumbed to fire around 1400 BC but was never looted. This accounts for the many Minoan masterpieces found here, most famously the Agia Triada Sarcophagus, now a star exhibit at the Heraklion Archaeological Museum.

Palace of Malia (🖉 28970 31597; adult/concession/child €6/3/free; ⊙ 8.30am-3pm; 🅿) The Palace of Malia, 3km east of Malia, was built at about the same time as the great Minoan palaces of Phaestos and Knossos. The First Palace dates back to around 1900 BC and was rebuilt after the earthquake of 1700 BC, only to be levelled again by another temble around 1450 BC. Most of what you see today are the remains of the Second Palace where many exquisite Minoan artefacts, including the famous gold bee pendant, were found. Buses from Iraklio stop on the main road, 250m from the site.

Palace of Knossos

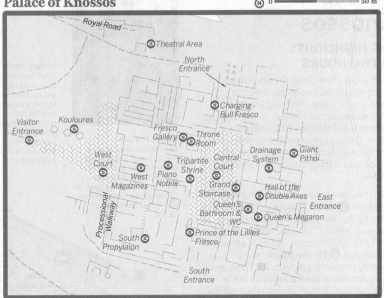

N 0 ━━━━━━━━━━ 50 m

Royal Road

Theatral Area

North Entrance

Charging-Bull Fresco

Visitor Entrance

Kouloures

Fresco Gallery

Throne Room

West Court

Tripartite Shrine

Central Court

Drainage System

Giant Pithoi

Piano Nobile

West Magazines

Grand Staircase

Hall of the Double Axes

East Entrance

Processional Walkway

Queen's Bathroom & WC

Queen's Megaron

South Propylaion

Prince of the Lillies Fresco

South Entrance

with gold-trimmed black capitals and taper gracefully at the bottom. Vibrant frescoes add dramatic flourishes. The advanced drainage system and a clever floor plan that kept rooms cool in summer and warm in winter are further evidence of Minoan high standards.

There is no prescribed route to explore the palace, but the following tour takes in all the key highlights. Entering from the **West Court**, which may have been a marketplace or the site of public gatherings, you'll note a trio of circular pits on your left. Called **kouloures**, they were used for grain storage. From here, continue counterclockwise, starting with a walk along the **Processional Walkway** that leads to the **South Propylaion**, where you can admire the **Cup Bearer Fresco**. From here, a staircase leads past giant storage jars to an upper floor that Evans called **Piano Nobile** because it reminded him of Italian Renaissance palazzi and where he supposed the reception and staterooms were located. On your left, you can see the **west magazines** (storage rooms), or storage rooms, where giant *pithoi* (clay jars) once held oil, wine and other staples.

The restored room at the northern end of the Piano Nobile houses the **Fresco Gallery**, with replicas of Knossos' most famous frescoes, including the Bull-Leaper, the Ladies in Blue and the Blue Bird. The originals are now in the Heraklion Archaeological Museum. From the balcony, a great view unfolds of the **Central Court**), which was hemmed in by high walls during Minoan times. Rooms facing the western side of the courtyard had official and religious purposes, while the residential quarters were on the opposite side.

Follow the stairs down to the courtyard and then turn left to peek inside the beautifully proportioned **Throne Room**, with its simple, alabaster seat and walls decorated with frescoes of griffins, mythical beasts regarded as sacred by the Minoans. To the right of the stairs is a three-sectioned room that Evans called **Tripartite Shrine**. Areas behind it yielded many precious finds, including the famous Snake Goddess statue.

Crossing the central court takes you to the east wing where the **Grand Staircase** drops down to the royal apartments. Get there via the ramp off the southeast corner but not without first popping by the south entrance to admire a replica of the **Prince of the Lilies fresco**. Down below you can peek inside the **Queen's Megaron** (bedroom) with a copy of the Dolphin Fresco, one of the most exquisite Minoan artworks. The small adjacent chamber (behind plexiglass) may have

Palace of Knossos

THE HIGHLIGHTS IN TWO HOURS

The Palace of Knossos is Crete's busiest tourist attraction, and for good reason. A spin around the partially and imaginatively reconstructed complex (shown here as it was thought to be at its peak) delivers an eye-opening glimpse into the remarkably sophisticated society of the Minoans, who dominated southern Europe some 4000 years ago.

From the ticket booth, follow the marked trail to the ❶ **North Entrance** where the Charging Bull fresco gives you a first taste of Minoan artistry. Continue to the Central Court and join the queue waiting to glimpse the mystical ❷ **Throne Room**, which probably hosted religious rituals. Turn right as you exit and follow the stairs up to the so-called Piano Nobile, where replicas of the palace's most famous artworks conveniently cluster in the ❸ **Fresco Room**. Walk the length of the Piano Nobile, pausing to look at the clay storage vessels in the West Magazine. Circle back and descend to the ❹ **South Portico**, beautifully decorated with the Cup Bearer fresco. Make your way back to the Central Court and head to the palace's eastern wing to admire the architecture of the ❺ **Grand Staircase** that led to what Sir Arthur Evans imagined to be the royal family's private quarters. For a closer look at some rooms, walk to the south end of the courtyard, stopping for a peek at the ❻ **Prince of the Lilies Fresco**, and head down to the lower floor. A highlight here is the ❼ **Queen's Megaron** (Evans imagined this was the Queen's chambers), playfully adorned with a fresco of frolicking dolphins. Stay on the lower level and make your way to the ❽ **Giant Pithoi**, huge clay jars used for storage.

South Portico
Fine frescoes, most famously the Cup Bearer, embellish this palace entrance anchored by a massive open staircase leading to the Piano Nobile. The Horns of Consecration recreated nearby once topped the entire south facade.

Fresco Room
Take in sweeping views of the palace grounds from the west wing's upper floor, the Piano Nobile, before studying copies of the palace's most famous artworks in its Fresco Room.

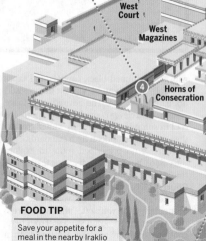

West Court

West Magazines

❹ **Horns of Consecration**

FOOD TIP

Save your appetite for a meal in the nearby Iraklio Wine Country, amid sun-baked slopes and lush valleys. It's just south of Knossos.

Prince of the Lilies Fresco
One of Knossos' most beloved frescoes was controversially cobbled together from various fragments and shows a young man adorned in lilies and peacock feathers.

Throne Room

Sir Arthur Evans, who began excavating the Palace of Knossos in 1900, imagined the mythical King Minos himself holding court seated on the alabaster throne of this beautifully proportioned room. However, the lustral basin and griffin frescoes suggest a religious purpose, possibly under a priestess.

North Entrance

Bulls held a special status in Minoan society, as evidenced by the famous relief fresco of a charging beast gracing the columned west bastion of the north palace, which harboured workshops and storage rooms.

Grand Staircase

The royal apartments in the eastern wing were accessed via this monumental staircase sporting four flights of gypsum steps supported by columns. The lower two flights are original. It's closed to the public.

Piano Nobile

Central Court

Royal Apartments

Queen's Megaron

The queen's room is among the prettiest in the residential eastern wing thanks to the playful Dolphin Fresco. The adjacent bathroom (with clay tub) and toilet are evidence of a sophisticated drainage system.

Giant Pithoi

These massive clay jars are rare remnants from the Old Palace period and were used to store wine, oil and grain. The jars were transported by slinging ropes through a series of handles.

been the queen's **bathroom** with some sort of toilet. Continue to the king's quarters in the **Hall of the Double Axes** that takes its name from the double axe marks *(labrys)* on its light well, a sacred symbol to the Minoans and the origin of our word 'labyrinth'.

Beyond you can admire the Minoans' surprisingly sophisticated **water and drainage system**, pop by a stone mason's workshop and check out more giant storage jars before jogging around to the palace's north side for a good view of the partly reconstructed north entrance, easily recognised by the **Charging Bull Fresco**. Walking towards the exit, you pass the **theatral area**, a series of shallow steps whose function remains unknown. It could have been a theatre where spectators watched acrobatic and dance performances, or the place where people gathered to welcome important visitors arriving by the **Royal Road**, which leads off to the west and was flanked by workshops and the houses of ordinary people.

❶ Getting There & Away

Getting to Knossos is easy. City bus 2 runs from Iraklio's city centre – from Bus Station A or from outside Hotel Capsis Astoria – every 15 minutes. Tickets cost €1.70 if purchased from a kiosk or vending machine and €2.50 from the bus driver. If driving, from Iraklio or the coastal road there are signs directing you to Knossos. There is free parking across from the souvenir shops, but the spaces fill quickly.

Iraklio Wine Country

About 70% of wine produced in Crete comes from the Iraklio Wine Country, which starts just south of Knossos and is headquartered in Peza. Almost two dozen wineries are embedded in a harmonious landscape of round-shouldered hills, sunbaked slopes and lush valleys. Winemakers cultivate many indigenous Cretan grape varietals, such as Kotsifali, Mandilari and Malvasia; many estates now offer tours, wine museums and wine tastings. Check www.winesofcrete.gr for details and look for the burgundy-red road signs directing you to local wineries.

🏃 Activities

Domaine Gavalas   WINE
(📞 28940 51060, 6974642006; www.gavalascrete wines.gr; Vorias; ⏰ 8am-4pm Mon-Fri) The Gavalas family has been making wine since 1906. It went fully organic in 2001 and today is one of the largest organic wineries in Crete. Try its award-winning Efivos reds and whites. It's in Vorias, about 20km south of Peza.

Minos-Miliarakis Winery   WINE
(📞 28107 41213; www.minoswines.gr; Main St, Peza; tasting €2; ⏰ 10am-4pm Mon-Sat Apr-Oct & by appointment) This massive winery was the first, in 1952, to bottle wine in Crete. It makes very respectable vintages, especially under its Miliarakis label, including a full-bodied single-vineyard organic red and a fragrant Blanc de Noirs. The tasting room is vast and doubles as a museum featuring historic winemaking equipment. The shop also sells local olive oil and raki (Cretan firewater).

Boutari Winery   WINE
(📞 2810 731617; www.boutari.gr; Skalani; tours & tasting €5-12.50; ⏰ 9am-5pm Mon-Fri, by appointment Sat & Sun) Near Skalani, about 8km from Iraklio, Boutari was founded in 1879 and is one of Greece's biggest wine producers today. Visits of its Crete winery (one of six in the country) start with a short tour to learn about local grapes and winemaking followed by a 15-minute video on the island and the chance to sample the product in the vast and airy tasting room overlooking the vineyard.

🛏 Sleeping & Eating

Arhontiko   APARTMENT €€
(📞 2810 752985; www.arhontikoarhanes.gr; Ano Arhanes; apt €55-85; 🅿 ✳ 🛜) An air of rustic sophistication pervades this old-timey 1893 garden villa that also saw incarnations as a military barracks and an elementary school. No hint of either survives in the four fully renovated apartments with traditional decor and furnishings. All are bi-level with a fairly dark beamed-ceiling bedroom and bathroom downstairs and a kitchen and sitting room upstairs.

Eliathos   APARTMENT €€€
(📞 6951804929, 2810 751818; www.eliathos.gr; Ano Arhanes; loft €105, villas €130-200; 🅿 ✳ 🛜 🌊) Tucked into the hillside south of Arhanes and with grand views of Mt Yiouhtas, this cluster of four villas is a haven of peace and quiet wrapped around a swimming pool. Each villa is divided into breezy apartments and lofts sleeping up to six and sporting a design that is sleek and contemporary, but also loaded with nods to the local setting.

The owners can help you get immersed in the local culture through cooking classes, excursions and olive oil, raki- or wine-making workshops.

★Elia & Diosmos
CRETAN €€

(☎2810 731283; www.olive-mint.gr; Dimokratias 263, Skalani; mains €8-13; ☺noon-5pm Mon, noon-10pm Tue-Sun; ☻) ✦ At this foodie destination, market-fresh ingredients shine in flavour-intense and progressive Cretan dishes. The menu chases the seasons, but classic choices include a *mousakas* (baked layers of eggplant or zucchini, minced meat and potatoes topped with cheese sauce) with cubed beef, a fluffy fennel pie and pork shank paired with wine, honey and citrus. It's only a short drive from Iraklio and an excellent post-Knossos recuperation stop.

Kritamon
CRETAN €€

(☎2810 753092; www.kritamon.gr; Archanes; mains €8.50-15; ☺5pm-1am Tue-Sat, noon-1am Sun; ᴘ❋☻) Send your taste buds on a wild ride at this foodie outpost in a street off the main square and set attractively around a garden courtyard with walnut trees. Ancient Cretan and creative modern recipes result in a small but soulful menu with such signature dishes as rooster with aniseed and cinnamon. Ingredients come mostly from the family farm.

Zaros   Ζαρός
POP 2120

At the foot of Mt Psiloritis, Zaros is famous for its natural spring water, which is bottled here and sold all over Crete. But Zaros also has some fine Byzantine monasteries, excellent walking and delicious farm-raised trout served up in tavernas around town and on emerald-green Lake Votomos (actually a reservoir). The lake is also the kick-off point for the 5km trail through the mighty Rouvas Gorge, a major lure for hikers, birders and naturalists.

🏃 Activities

★Rouvas Gorge
HIKING

(Agios Nikolaos Gorge; Lake Votomos) Part of the E4 European Path, the Rouvas Gorge leads to the protected Rouvas Forest, home to some of the oldest oak trees in Crete. It's an especially lovely walk in springtime when orchids, poppies, irises and other wildflowers give the landscape the vibrancy of an Impressionist painting. It's a 10km round-trip trek from the main trailhead at Lake Votomos north of Zaros village.

The trail starts at the Limni taverna but doesn't enter the gorge for another 1km, just past Moni Agios Nikolaos, a modern monastery that wraps around a historic church rife with icons and fresco fragments. The vegetation becomes increasingly lush with oak trees, lilies, orchids, sage and other mountain flora. At the end is a little chapel of Agios Ioannis where benches and tables invite a leisurely picnic. Starting at Moni Agios Nikolaos shortens the hike by 2km. Wear sneakers or hiking boots.

🛏 Sleeping & Eating

★Eleonas Country Village
COTTAGE €€

(☎28940 31238, 6976670002; www.eleonas.gr; cottage incl breakfast €98-130, 3-night minimum; ᴘ❋@☻⛵) ✦ Owner Manolis has poured heart and soul into this charming retreat of stone cottages cradled by olive groves and built into a stunning terraced garden hillside. It's a '*this* is Crete' kind of place, such is the fresh air and tranquil feel. Fuel up for a day of hiking, exploring, biking or poolside chilling with a sumptuous breakfast of homemade Cretan treats.

It's about 1.5km northwest of Zaros. Just follow the signs. Three-night minimum.

★Vegera
CRETAN €

(☎28940 31730; Main St; multicourse meal €9-12; ☺8am-late; ☻) The vivacious Vivi has a knack for turning farm-fresh local produce into flavourful and creative dishes based on traditional recipes. Her philosophy is to 'cook the way we cook in our house' and indeed her cute place quickly feels like home. Make sure you have ample time to savour the generous spread of fresh bread, salad, cheese and olives, cooked mains, pastries and raki.

❶ Getting There & Away

Zaros is about 46km southwest of Iraklio. The most scenic approach is by turning west off the main road at Agia Varvara. There's also a smaller road heading north from Kapariana just east of Mires (turn north at the small road between a bakery and Kafeneio i Zariani Strofi; look for the small sign). One daily bus heading from Iraklio's Bus Station B to Kamares passes through Zaros (€5.20, one hour). Alternatively, take one of the more frequent buses to Mires (€6, 75 minutes) and cab it to Zaros from there (around €16).

Matala   Μάταλα

POP 70

In mythology, Matala is the place where Zeus swam ashore with the kidnapped Europa on his back before dragging her off to Gortyna and getting her pregnant with the future King Minos. The Minoans used Matala as their harbour for Phaestos and under the Romans it became the port for Gortyna.

In more recent times, Matala became legendary thanks to the scores of hippies flocking here in the late 1960s to take up rent-free residence in cliffside caves once used as tombs by the Romans. Joni Mitchell famously immortalised the era in her 1971 song 'Carey'.

On summer days, the village feels anything but peaceful thanks to coachloads of day trippers. Stay overnight or visit in the off-season, though, and it's still possible to discern the Matala magic: the setting along a crescent-shaped bay flanked by headlands is simply spectacular, especially at sunset.

◎ Sights

Matala Caves   CAVE

(Roman Cemetery; Matala beach; adult/concession/under 18yr €2/1/free; ⊙10am-7pm Apr-Sep, 8am-3pm Oct-Mar) Matala's sightseeing credentials are limited to these famous caves where hippies camped out in the 1960s and 1970s. Hewn into the porous sandstone cliffs in prehistoric times, they were actually used as tombs by the Romans under whom Matala was the port town for Gortyna.

⊨ Sleeping & Eating

Hotel Nikos   HOTEL €

(☑28920 45375; www.matala-nikos.com; Matala; d €60; ❇🐾) A standout on hotel row, family-run Nikos has 17 rooms, many with small kitchens and a terrace, on two floors flanking a flower-filled courtyard. The nicest is the top-floor No 24 with cave views. Breakfast is €6.

Matala Valley Village Hotel   RESORT €€

(☑28920 45776; www.valleyvillage.gr; d/bungalow €50/75; ⊙May-Oct; P❇🐾🌊) This family-friendly garden resort consists of low-lying buildings with fairly basic rooms and two dozen spiffier whitewashed two-bedroom bungalows with Jacuzzi tubs and patio. Frolicking grounds include a lawn, a small playground and two pools (one for kids). Being located right by the village entrance puts it about 1km from the beach.

Giannis Family Grill House   GREEK €

(☑6983619233, 28920 45719; www.giannisfamily.com; mains €6-13.50; ⊙noon-4pm & 6pm-midnight; 🍴) A refreshing change from the run-of-the-mill waterfront tavernas, this been-there-forever family place just past the central square exudes cheer with its turquoise furniture, potted flowers and no-nonsense homemade Greek food, including an excellent mixed grill with salad and potatoes. It serves organic wines from the Domaine Zacharioudakis in nearby Plouti as well as its own raki.

❶ Information

Matala's main drag has a couple of ATMs and there's an excellent bookshop with lots of English-language novels and periodicals right on the central square.

❶ Getting There & Away

Up to three KTEL buses daily leave Iraklio's Bus Station B for Matala (€8.50, two hours). There's free roadside parking and a beach parking lot that charges €2.

Rethymno   Ρέθυμνο

POP 34,300

Basking between the commanding bastions of its 15th-century fortress and the glittering azure waters of the Mediterranean, Rethymno is one of Crete's most enchanting towns. Its Venetian-Ottoman quarter is a lyrical maze of lanes draped in floral canopies and punctuated with graceful wood-balconied houses, ornate monuments and the occasional minaret.

Crete's third-largest town has lively nightlife thanks to its sizeable student population, some excellent restaurants and a worthwhile sandy beach right in town. The busier beaches, with their requisite resorts, line up along a nearly uninterrupted stretch all the way to Panormo, some 22km away.

◎ Sights

Rethymno is fairly compact, with most sights, accommodation and tavernas wedged within the largely pedestrianised old quarter off the Venetian Harbour. The long sandy beach starts just east of the harbour.

★ Fortezza   FORTRESS

(adult/concession/family €4/3/10; ⊙8am-8pm Apr-Oct, 10am-5pm Nov-Mar; P) Looming over Rethymno, the star-shaped Venetian fortress

GORTYNA ΓΟΡΤΥΝΑ

Gortyna (📞 28920 31144; www.interkriti.org/crete/iraklion/gortyn.html; Iraklio-Phaestos Rd; adult/senior/under 18yr & EU student €6/3/free; ⏰8am-8pm Apr-Oct, 8am-3pm Nov-Mar), also called Gortyn or Gortys, has been inhabited since Neolithic times but reached its pinnacle after becoming the capital of Roman Crete from around 67 BC until the Saracens raided the island in AD 824. At its peak, as many as 100,000 people may have milled around Gortyn's streets.

There are two sections, bisected by the highway. Most people only stop long enough to investigate the fenced area on the north side of the road past the ticket gate. However, several more important temples, baths and other buildings are actually scattered south of the road.

The first major monument visible within the **fenced area** is the 6th-century Byzantine **Church of Agios Titos**, the finest early-Christian church in Crete. Probably built atop an even older church, its only major surviving feature is the soaring apse flanked by two side chapels. It was under restoration at the time of writing, but should reopen in 2018.

A few steps away is the **Odeon**, a Roman theatre from the 1st century BC, which was levelled by an earthquake and rebuilt by Trajan in the 2nd century AD. The covered, arched structure on the far side of the theatre shelters Gortyna's star attraction: the massive stone tablets inscribed with the 6th-century-BC **Laws of Gortyna**. The 600 lines written in a Dorian dialect represent the oldest law code in the Greek world and provide a fascinating insight into the social structure of pre-Roman Crete. It turns out that ancient Cretans were preoccupied with the same issues that drive people into court today – marriage, divorce, property transfers, inheritance and adoption, as well as criminal offences. Behind the Odeon is an evergreen **plane tree** that, according to mythology, was Zeus and Europa's 'love nest'.

Excavations are still in full swing in the **area south of the highway** and all the sites can only be seen through a chain-link fence. Still, it's fun to wander around aimlessly and just stumble upon the ruins. If you prefer to explore in a more organised fashion, walk 300m east along the highway from the parking lot to a double sign pointing to the Temple of Apollo and the **Temple of the Egyptian Gods**. A narrow stone path leads to the latter after about 70m. Dedicated to Isis, Serapis and Anubis, there actually isn't much to see today. The same cannot be said of the **Temple of Apollo**, reached by continuing on the path past the sign pointing left to the Praetorium. The main sanctuary of pre-Roman Gortyna was built in the 7th century BC, expanded in the 3rd century BC and converted into a Christian basilica in the 2nd century AD. You can still make out its rectangular outline and the base of the main altar.

Backtrack and turn right at the sign to shortly reach the **Praetorium**. The palace of the Roman governor of Crete, it served both as an administrative building, a church and a private residence. Most of the ruins date from the 2nd century AD and were repaired in the 4th century. To the north is the 2nd-century **Nymphaeum**, a public bath supplied by an aqueduct bringing water from Zaros. It was originally adorned with statues of nymphs.

For a bird's-eye view of Gortyna, climb up to the hilltop **Acropolis**, which also features impressive sections of the pre-Roman ramparts. The trailhead is on the north side of the highway, about 100m west of the ticket booth; it takes about 20 to 30 minutes to get up here.

Gortyna is near Agia Deka, about 46km southwest of Iraklio. It's a stop on the Iraklio–Matala and Iraklio–Agia Galini bus routes. In Iraklio, buses leave from Bus Station B.

cuts an imposing figure with its massive walls and bastions but was nevertheless unable to stave off the Turks in 1646. Over time, an entire village took shape on the grounds, most of which was destroyed in WWII. Views are fabulous from up here and it's fun to poke around the ramparts, palm trees and remaining buildings, most notably the **Sultan Bin Ibrahim Mosque** with its huge dome.

The mosque hosts occasional musical events, while other buildings (like the twin buildings of the Bastion of Agios Nikolaos) are used to showcase art exhibits.

EFESENKO/SHUTTERSTOCK ©

. Spili (p294)
pili's church looks out on the mountain village.

. Rethymno (p284)
nchanting Rethymno's historic harbour has many
sh taverns and cafes.

**. Heraklion Archaeological
Museum (p271)**
his museum in Crete's capital, Iraklio, showcases
xhibits spanning 5500 years in a restored
auhaus building.

. Spinalonga Island (p317)
he former leper colony was catapulted
nto pop-cultural consciousness thanks to
irginia Hislop's 2005 bestselling novel *The
sland*.

LONELY PLANET/GETTY IMAGES ©

Rethymno

⊙ Top Sights
1 Fortezza...A1

⊙ Sights
2 Archaeological Museum.......................B3
3 Historical & Folk Art Museum............B3
4 Museum of Contemporary Art............B2
5 Rimondi Fountain................................B2
6 Venetian Harbour...............................C2

🏃 Activities, Courses & Tours
7 Eco Events...C3
8 Happy Walker.......................................C4

🛏 Sleeping
9 Atelier Frosso Bora.............................B1

10 Casa dei Delfini....................................A3
11 Casa Vitae...A3
12 Rethymno Youth Hostel.......................B4

🍽 Eating
13 Avli...B2
14 Castelvecchio......................................B1
15 En Plo..B1
16 Raki Baraki..B2
17 Taverna Knossos.................................C2

🍷 Drinking & Nightlife
18 Chalikouti...A2
19 Livingroom...D4

Venetian Harbour   LANDMARK
Rethymno's compact historic harbour is chock-a-block with tourist-geared fish tavernas and cafes. For a more atmospheric perspective, walk along the harbour walls, past the fishing boats to the prominent lighthouse, built in the 19th century by the Egyptians.

Archaeological Museum

MUSEUM

(☑28310 27506; Argiropoulon; adult/concession €2/1; ⊙10am-6pm Tue-Sun) After its former digs in a Venetian prison near the fortress had become unstable, Rethymno's archaeological collection moved to the Venetian-built former Church of St Francis in May 2016. Tightly curated, but beautifully arranged, it features highlights from major archaeological digs around Rethymno province, including the cemetery at Armeni. Collection highlights include a 4500-year-old chalice, a figure of a Minoan goddess, a Roman bronze lamp and a miniature donkey from the Hellenistic period.

Agios Spyridon Church

CHAPEL

(Kefalogiannidon) FREE Built right into the cliff beneath the Venetian fortress, tiny Agios Spyridon has enough atmosphere to fill a cathedral. This Byzantine chapel is filled with richly painted icons, swinging bird candleholders and the sound of the nearby pounding surf. You'll see pairs of slippers, baby shoes and sandals in crevices in the rock wall, left as prayer offerings for the sick. Find the chapel at the top of a staircase on the western side of the fortress. Opening hours are erratic.

Rimondi Fountain

FOUNTAIN

(Plateia Petihaki; ☷) Pride of place among the many vestiges of Venetian rule goes to this fountain with its spouting lion heads and Corinthian capitals, built in 1626 by city rector Alvise Rimondi.

Water spouts from three lions' heads into three basins flanked by Corinthian columns. Above the central basin you can make out the Rimondi family crest.

Museum of Contemporary Art

MUSEUM

(☑28310 52530; www.cca.gr; Mesologhiou 32; adult/concession/student €3/1.50/free; Thu free; ⊙9am-2pm & 7-9pm Tue-Fri, 10am-3pm Sat & Sun May-Oct, 9am-2pm Tue-Fri, 6-9pm Wed & Fri, 10am-3pm Sat & Sun Nov-Apr) The cornerstone of the permanent collection of this art museum, founded in 1992, is the oils, drawings and watercolours of local lad Lefteris Kanakakis, but over time it has amassed enough works to present the arc of creative endeavour in Greece since the 1950s. Temporary exhibits further keep things dynamic. Entrance is off Mesologhiou.

Historical & Folk Art Museum

MUSEUM

(☑28310 23398; Vernardou 28; adult/concession €4/2; ⊙10am-3pm Mon-Sat) In a lovely 17th-century Venetian mansion, the five-room permanent exhibit document traditional rural life on Crete with displays of clothing, baskets, weavings, pottery, weapons and farming tools. Labelling is also in English.

Paleontological Museum

MUSEUM

(☑28310 23083; Temple of Mastaba, Satha & Markellou; adult/child €4/free; ⊙9am-3pm daily May-Oct, 9am-3pm Tue, Thu & Sat Nov-Apr; ℗) Dwarf Cretan elephants and hippopotami aren't likely to start a ticket stampede, but it's well worth swinging by this museum for its setting in the restored 17th-century Temple of Mastaba (aka Veli Pasha Mosque) surrounded by gardens. Nine domes shape its silhouette, overlooked by the city's oldest minaret, while the once-communal gardens are steeply scented with thyme and oregano. The permanent exhibit displays tusks and fossils from hippos hunted to extinction 10,700 years ago.

Kara Musa Pasha Mosque

HISTORIC SITE

(Arkadiou & Hugo) This building actually began life as a monastery but was turned into a mosque by the Turks who added the domes and a minaret, of which only bits remain. It is named after the Ottoman admiral instrumental in the capture of Rethymno. It is not open to the public.

CRETE RETHYMNO

WORTH A TRIP

MUSEUM OF CRETAN ETHNOLOGY

Well worth a quick detour to Vori, the private, nonprofit **Museum of Cretan Ethnology** (☑28920 91110; www.cretanethnologymuseum.gr; Voroi Pirgiotissis, Vori; adult/concession €3/1.50; ⊙11am-5pm Apr-Oct) peels away the curtain on how rural people lived on the island until well into the 20th century. The English-labelled exhibits are organised around such themes as food production, war, customs, architecture and music. Although most of the items are rather ordinary – hoes, olive presses, baskets, clothing, instruments etc – they're engagingly displayed in darkened rooms accented with spotlights. It's well signposted from the main Mires–Tymbaki road.

🏃 Activities

★ Happy Walker   HIKING

(☑ 28310 52920; www.happywalker.com; Tombazi 56; guided day walks €32; ⊙ 5-8.30pm daily Sep-Jun, 5-8.30pm Mon-Fri Jul & Aug) In operation for over a quarter of a century, this congenial outfit takes up to 16 global ramblers on day hikes to gorges, ancient shepherd trails and traditional villages. It's ideal for solo travellers. Rates include transport to and from trailheads and an English-speaking guide, but coffee and vegetarian lunch with wine is an extra €12. Book the evening before.

Multiday tours are also available.

Paradise Dive Centre   DIVING

(☑ 28310 26317; www.diving-center.gr; Petres Geraniou; 2 dives incl equipment €100, open-water certification €400) Runs diving trips for all grades of diver from its base at Petres, 14km west of Rethymno. Offers cave dives, night dives and various PADI courses. Book through travel agencies, by phone or via the website.

Mountaineering Club of Rethymno   CLIMBING

(☑ 28310 57766; www.eosrethymnou.gr; Dimokratias 12; ⊙ 9-11pm Tue) Offers advice on local hikes along with the possibility to join excursions. It's best to make contact via the website.

Eco Events   TOURS

(☑ 28310 50055, 6946686857; www.ecoevents.gr; Eleftherios Venizelou 39; tours €18-70; ⊙ 10am-2pm & 5-9pm) This outfit specialises in small-group English-language tours that get you in touch with land, people and culture. Options include the Eco Tour where you'll meet a baker, weaver and woodcarver before sampling charcoal-grilled lamb in a traditional shepherd shelter in the mountains. Cooking classes, wine and olive oil tastings and hiking trips are also part of the line-up.

🛏 Sleeping

★ Atelier Frosso Bora   PENSION €

(☑ 28310 24440; www.frosso-bora.com; Himaras 25; d €45-60; ❄ ❀ ⓢ) Run by local artist Frosso Bora and located above her pottery studio, these four spotless, ambience-laden rooms with exposed stone walls, small flat-screen TVs, modern bathrooms and kitchenettes are a superb budget pick. Two units have small balconies facing the old town while the other two sport Venetian architectural features and a beamed ceiling.

Rethymno Youth Hostel   HOSTEL €

(☑ 28310 22848; www.yhrethymno.com; Tombazi 41; dm late Sep-May €12, Jun–mid-Sep €14; ⊙ reception 8am-1pm & 5-11pm Sep-May, 8am-midnight Jun-Aug; ⓢ) This cheerful, well-run hostel sleeps six to eight people in recently upgraded dorms (one for women only) with comfy mattresses and good-sized lockers. In a quiet street, yet within stumbling distance of sights and bars, it has a private, sociable patio, bar and a flowering garden to relax in. Facilities include a washing machine, a communal kitchen and hot showers.

Camping Elizabeth   CAMPGROUND €

(☑ 28310 28694, 6983009259; www.camping-elizabeth.net; Ionias 84, Missiria; campsites per adult/child €8.50/4.50, tent/car/caravan €5/4/6; ⊙ year-round; @ ⓢ) The closest campground to Rethymno is 4km east of the old city on beautiful Missiria beach. Bamboo, palm and olive trees provide plenty of shade, and there's a taverna, snack bar and minimarket, plus a communal fridge, laundry facilities and free beach umbrellas and sun lounges. It also rents out simple bungalows and caravans from €26.50 and tents with bedding from €18.50. An Iraklio-bound bus can drop you nearby.

Sohora   BOUTIQUE HOTEL €€

(☑ 28313 00913; www.sohora.gr; Plateia Iroön Politechniou 11; studio/d/apt €60/80/100; ❄ ⓢ) Extremely comfortable and slightly quirky,

---

THE ORIGINAL CYCLOPS

The Rethymno region seems to have had more than its share of fossil-filled caves. In fact, it's the richest area in the Mediterranean for endemic fossils, including those of the dwarf elephant. Some scientists believe that when ancient Greeks entered the shore caves and discovered the skulls of dwarf elephants, they were taken aback by what they saw. About twice the size of a human skull, the large, central nasal cavity for the trunk may well have been interpreted as an enormous, single eye-socket. The possible result? The birth of the Cyclops. Visit Rethymno's Paleontological Museum (p289) to see the skeletons for yourself.

the four rooms with kitchenette in this 200-year-old home are named after the seasons and incorporate original architectural features alongside vintage, upcycled furnishings. A solar-water heater, organic bath products and a hearty, homemade breakfast provide eco-cred. Service is both friendly and professional.

It's set on a bar-lined square popular with locals and just a short walk from the heart of the old town.

Casa Vitae   BOUTIQUE HOTEL €€
(☑ 6973237897, 28310 35058; www.casa-vitae.gr; Patealarou 3; r €95-150; ﹡ ☎) This charismatic Venetian-era building has eight quietly elegant rooms mixing exposed stone and wood and wrapping around a fountain-anchored courtyard where home-cooked breakfast is served beneath the bamboo-and-vine-shaded pergola. Romance rules in the larger suites with iron four-poster beds, whirlpool tubs and a private terrace.

Casa dei Delfini   BOUTIQUE HOTEL €€
(☑ 6937254857, 28310 55120; www.casadeidelfini.com; Nikiforou Foka 66-68; studio €55-85, maisonette €110; ﹡ ☎) The four individual rooms in this elegant mansion orbit a small courtyard and exude historic character galore. In one, the bathroom used to be a *hammam* (Turkish bath), in another the bed is tucked into an arched stone alcove. All have kitchenettes. The two-storey maisonette comes with a large private terrace.

✖ Eating

★ **Raki Baraki**   GREEK €
(☑ 28310 58250; Arabatzoglou 17; meze €3-11; ☉ noon-midnight or later; ﹡ ☎ ✒) Rustic, colourful and lively, this is a fantastic place to while away the evening over mezedhes (appetisers) like sardines stuffed with herbs, sausage with grilled vegetables, or mussels steamed with sage. The fried feta with caramelised figs and mint is divine. Comfort food at its finest. All ingredients are sourced from small farmers around Greece.

Castelvecchio   GREEK €€
(☑ 28310 55163; Himaras 29; mains €9-27; ☉ lunch Sep-May, dinner year-round; ﹡ ☎) In a Venetian-era building a bone toss from the fortress, chic yet chilled Castelvecchio is perfect for date night – especially if your date is a plate of tender boneless lamb, done up in numerous creative ways, including a foil-cooked version with creamy tomato and feta sauce. For des-

sert, go for the walnut cake – it'll have you pining for seconds!

Taverna Knossos   GREEK €€
(☑ 28310 25582; Nearhou 40; mains €12-18; ☉ noon-midnight; ☎ ▥) Most tout-fronted tavernas in the Venetian Harbour focus more on folkloric ambience than on food quality. Owned by the amiable Stavroulaki family for half a century, Knossos is a happy exception. When Mama Anna is in the kitchen, you can be sure that dishes are loaded with flavour, the fish is outstanding and the service swift and gracious.

En Plo   GREEK €€
(☑ 28310 30950; Kefalogiannidon 28; mains €7.50-12; ☉ 11am-midnight or later; ☎ ▥) One of several tavernas right at the water's edge below the fortress, En Plo does dependable faves like shrimp spaghetti and grilled salmon, but shows its most creative side when it comes to such mezedhes as feta in pastry with caramelised figs. For the younger buccaneers of your party, there's a Little Pirates' Menu.

Avli   CRETAN €€€
(☑ 28310 58250; www.avli.gr; Xanthoudidou 22; mains €12-28; ☉ 11am-midnight; ﹡ ☎) This well-established Venetian villa serves creative Cretan food with a side of romance. Farm-fresh fare steers the menu, resulting in dishes with bold flavour pairings such as *creatotouria* (ravioli filled with lamb, cheese, mint and lime) or fried grouper with handpicked greens. Be sure to reserve a table in the bewitching garden.

🍷 Drinking & Nightlife

Rethymno's young and restless are mostly drawn to the cafe-bars along Eleftherios Venizelou. The area around the Rimondi Fountain and Plateia Petihaki is popular with tourists. Wander the side streets to find quieter places.

Chalikouti   BAR
(☑ 28310 42632; Katehaki 3; ☉ 9am-1am; ☎) In the alt-flavoured quarter below the Fortezza, this cooperative-run cafe draws chatty locals keen on coffee from Mexican Zapatistas, sugar from landless workers in Brazil, and organic raki from Cretan producers. A selection of mezedhes and desserts provides sustenance.

Livingroom   BAR
(☑ 28310 21386; www.livingroom.gr; Eleftherios Venizelou 5; ☉ 9am-3am; ☎) No matter where

the handles are on the clock, the comfy lounge sofas of this stylish hang-out are always packed with hip town folk. Mellow in the daytime, the vibe gets progressively more high-octane after dark. A good place to ease into the nightlife scene.

❶ Information

There are free public wi-fi hotspots at the town hall, Plateia Iroön Polytechniou, the Venetian Harbour and the Municipal Garden, all within the old town.

Cool Holidays (☑ 28310 35567; www.cool holidays.gr; Melissinou 2; ⊙ 9am-9pm) Helpful office that handles boat and plane tickets, hires out cars and motorcycles, and books excursions.

General Hospital of Rethymno (☑ 28313 42100; Triandalydou 19-21; ⊙ 24hr)

Post Office (☑ 28310 22303; Moatsou 19; ⊙ 7.30am-8.30pm Mon-Fri) Accepts letters and parcels.

Regional Tourist Office (☑ 28310 29148; www.rethymnon.gr; Sofokli Venizelou; ⊙ 8am-2pm Mon-Fri) Has local maps and offers regional information.

Tourist Police (☑ 28310 28156, emergency 171; Iroön Polytechniou 29; ⊙ on call 24hr)

❶ Getting There & Away

The **bus station** (☑ 28310 22212; www.e-ktel. com; Kefalogiannidon; 🛜) is on the western edge of the centre. Services are reduced at weekends and outside high season. Check KTEL (www.e-ktel.com) for the latest schedule.

❶ Getting Around

Rethymno's centre is wonderfully compact and best explored on foot. When visiting outlying areas, a taxi is your best bet.

Auto Moto Sports (☑ 28310 24858, 6945771933; www.automotosport.com.gr; Sofokli Venizelou 48; bicycle/car per day from €10/32; ⊙ 7am-10pm) Hires out bicycles, cars and motorbikes.

Moni Arkadiou
Μονή Αρκαδίου

★ **Moni Arkadiou** HISTORIC SITE
(Arkadi Monastery; ☑ 28310 83136; €3; ⊙ 9am-8pm Jun-Sep, to 7pm Apr, May & Oct, to 5pm Nov, to 4pm Dec-Mar) The 16th-century Arkadi Monastery, some 23km southeast of Rethymno, has deep significance for Cretans. As the site where hundreds of cornered locals massacred both themselves and invading Turks, it's a stark and potent symbol of resistance and considered a spark plug in the island's struggle towards freedom from Turkish occupation.

In November 1866, massive Ottoman forces arrived to crush island-wide revolts. Hundreds of Cretan men, women and children fled their villages to find shelter at Arkadiou. However, far from being a safe haven, the monastery was soon besieged by 2000 Turkish soldiers. Rather than surrender, the entrapped locals blew up stored gunpowder kegs, killing everyone, Turks included. One small girl miraculously survived and lived to a ripe old age in a village nearby. A bust of this woman and another of the abbot who lit the gunpowder are outside the monastery not far from the old windmill – now an **ossuary** with skulls and bones of the 1866 victims neatly arranged in a glass cabinet.

Arkadiou's impressive Venetian **church** (1587) has a striking Renaissance facade

BUSES FROM RETHYMNO

DESTINATION	DURATION	FARE (€)	FREQUENCY
Agia Galini (via Spili)	1½hr	6.80	up to 5 daily
Anogia	1¼hr	6	2 daily Mon-Fri
Argyroupoli	40min	3.60	2 daily Mon-Fri
Hania	1hr	6.80	hourly
Hora Sfakion (via Vrysses)	2hr	8.30	2 daily
Iraklio	1½hr	8.30	hourly
Margarites	30min	3.80	2 daily Mon-Fri
Moni Arkadiou	40min	2.80	up to 3 daily
Omalos (Samaria Gorge)	1¾hr	17.10	2 daily
Plakias	1hr	5	up to 5 daily
Preveli	1¼hr	4.90	2 daily

topped by an ornate triple-belled tower. The grounds include a small museum and the old wine cellar where the gunpowder was stored.

Three buses daily arrive here (two on weekends) from Rethymno (€3, 40 minutes), leaving you about 90 minutes for your visit before returning.

Anogia   Ανώγεια

POP 2380

Perched aside Mt Psiloritis, 37km southwest of Iraklio, Anogia has a legacy of rebellious spirit and determination to express its undiluted Cretan character. During WWII, it was a centre of resistance and suffered heavily for it. The Nazis burned down the town and massacred all the men in retaliation for their role in sheltering Allied troops and aiding in the kidnapping of a Nazi general.

Anogia is also famous for its stirring music and has spawned many of Crete's best-known musicians such as Nikos Xylouris. Locals cling to time-honoured traditions and it's not rare to see men gossiping in the *kafeneia* dressed in traditional black shirts with baggy pants tucked into black boots. Elderly women, meanwhile, keep busy flogging traditional woven blankets and embroidered textiles. Though beautiful and well-priced, not all are actually produced locally, so *caveat emptor.*

◉ Sights

Nikos Xylouris' Home   HISTORIC SITE
(⊘9am-9pm) [FREE] Crete's most famous musician, the *lyra* (lyre) player and singer Nikos Xylouris, was born in a modest house on the lower village square. Until her death in 2016, his sister Zouboulia ran a *kafeneio* here and presided over an endearing collection of posters, letters and other memorabilia related to her brother.

🛏 Sleeping & Eating

Hotel Aristea   HOTEL €
(☑28340 31459; www.hotelaristea.gr; Michaeli Stavrakaki; d/apt €35/85; [P][🛜]) Run by the chatty and charming Aristea, this small inn offers sweeping valley views from balconies attached to five fairly basic but spotless and comfortable-enough rooms. The four split-level apartments in a next-door annex are more modern and come with kitchens and a wood-burning fireplace for those chilly mountain nights.

★Ta Skalomata   CRETAN €
(☑28340 31316; 31 August 1944 St; mains €5-12; ⊘9am-midnight; 🛜) In the upper village, Skalomata has provided sustenance to locals and travellers for about 40 years. When you peel your eyes away from the view through panoramic windows, train your focus on the great grilled meats (the lamb is tops!), homemade wine and bread, and tasty meatless fare such as zucchini with cheese.

The owners are charming and will welcome you with open arms on your return visit.

Arodamos   CRETAN €
(☑28340 31100; www.arodamos.gr; Tylisos-Anogia Rd; mains €6-10.50; ⊘10.30am-10pm) This big restaurant in a modern stone house in the upper village is held in high regard for its hearty Cretan mountain fare and gracious hospitality. Local specialities include the flame-teased lamb or goat *(ofto)* and the deceptively simple but tasty local dish of spaghetti cooked in stock and topped with *athotiros* (white cheese).

Can accommodate tour groups.

❶ Information

An ATM and the post office are in the upper village.

❶ Getting There & Away

There are up to three buses daily from Iraklio (€4.10, one hour) and two buses Monday to Friday from Rethymno (€6, 1¼ hours).

Mt Psiloritis
Ορος Ψηλορείτης

At 2456m, Mt Psiloritis, also known as Mt Ida, is Crete's highest mountain. At its eastern base is the Nida Plateau (1400m), a wide, fertile expanse reached via a paved 21km-long road from Anogia. It passes several round stone *mitata* (traditional shepherd's huts used for cheese-making and shelter) as well as the turn-off to the highly regarded (but rarely open) Skinakas Observatory.

From the Nida Plateau, it's a short walk to the Ideon Cave where, according to legend, the god Zeus was reared (although Dikteon Cave in Lasithi claims the same). Also on the plateau is Andartis, an impressive landscape sculpture honouring the Cretan WWII resistance.

◎ Sights

Skinakas Observatory
OBSERVATORY

(📞 28103 94238; http://skinakas.physics.uoc.gr; ⊙ 6-11pm around full moon May-Sep) FREE Near the top of Mt Psiloritis, at 1750m, the Skinakas Observatory is operated by the University of Greece and is the country's most significant stargazing vantage point with two powerful telescopes. From May to September, the site opens to the public once a month around the full moon (see the website for exact dates). There are tours of the site, presentations and a chance to look through the telescope.

Ideon Cave
CAVE

(Mt Psiloritis; P) FREE Although just a huge and fairly featureless hole in the ground, Ideon has sacred importance in mythology as the place where Zeus was reared by his mother Rhea to save him from the clutches of his child-devouring father Cronos. (Incidentally, the Diktaeon Cave in the Lasithi Plateau makes the same claim.) Ideon is on Mt Psiloritis about 15km from Anogia; it's a 1km uphill walk from the parking lot to the entrance.

Ideon was a place of worship from the late 4th millennium BC onward and many artefacts, including gold jewellery and bronze shields, statuettes and other offerings to Zeus, have been unearthed here.

Andartis – Partisan of Peace
MONUMENT

(Nida Plateau, Mt Psiloritis) FREE Right on the Nida Plateau, high on Mt Psiloritis, you can make out this sprawling landscape sculpture created by German artist Karina Raeck

WORTH A TRIP

ENAGRON

The working farm **Enagron Eco-tourism Village** (📞 28340 61611; www.enagron.gr; Axos Mylopotamou; studio/apt incl breakfast from €87/108; P ❄ ⑦) offers an immersion in the traditional Cretan way of life. Lodging is in elegantly rustic rooms with beamed ceilings, stone walls and fireplaces as well as kitchenettes. The restaurant serves dishes prepared with farm-foraged ingredients and also runs cooking classes and cheese-making workshops. Minimum three-night stay on most dates.

It's also possible to visit the farm and eat at the restaurant without checking in, but do book ahead.

in 1991 to commemorate the Cretan resistance in WWII. The monument itself is a pile of local rocks arranged in such a way that it looks like an angel when seen from above. Ask the taverna staff to point it out if you can't spot it on your own. It's a flat and easy 1.25km walk out there.

Spili
Σπίλι

POP 630

Spili is a pretty mountain village and shutterbug favourite thanks to its cobbled streets, big old plane trees and flower-festooned whitewashed houses. Most people just stop for lunch on a coast-to-coast trip, but it's well worth staying a day or two to explore the trails weaving through the local mountains. The rugged Kourtaliotiko Gorge, which culminates at the famous palm grove of Preveli Beach, starts not far south of town.

In town, a restored **Venetian fountain** spurts potable water from 25 stone lion heads into a long trough. Minor attractions include a **folk museum** and the vast modern **monastery** at the northern end of town.

🛏 Sleeping & Eating

★ Hotel Heracles
PENSION €

(📞 6973667495, 28320 22111; www.heracles-hotel.eu; Main St; s/d €35/40; ❄ ⑦) These five balconied rooms are quiet, spotless and simply furnished, but it's the charming and softly spoken Heracles himself who makes the place so special. Intimately familiar with the area, he's happy to put you onto the right hiking trail, birdwatching site or hidden beach. Optional homemade breakfasts start at €4.50. He also rents two apartments in a traditional Cretan house (€70 to €90).

Stratidakis
GREEK €

(Main St; dishes €3.50-6; ⊙ noon-9pm or later) At the oldest taverna in town, the owner-chef will likely invite you to inspect whatever dishes are stewing in his kitchen that day before you make your selection. Upon request, you can also have local rabbit, lamb, pork and other local meats prepared on the outdoor charcoal grill. It's a simple, local place, so don't expect any culinary flights of fancy.

ⓘ Information

There are two ATMs and a post office on the main street. Some of the cafes near the fountain offer free wi-fi.

❶ Getting There & Away

Spili is on the Rethymno–Agia Galini bus route (€3.80, 30 to 40 minutes), which has up to five services daily.

Plakias   Πλακιάς

POP 300

Set beside a sweeping sandy crescent and accessed via two scenic gorges – Kotsifou and Kourtaliotiko – Plakias gets swarmed with package tourists in summer (when it can be very windy), but otherwise remains a laid-back indie travellers' favourite. While the village itself isn't particularly pretty, it's an excellent launch pad for regional excursions and hikes through olive groves, along seaside cliffs and to some sparkling hidden beaches.

🏃 Activities

There are well-worn walking paths to the scenic village of Selia, Moni Finika, Lefkogia, and a lovely walk along the Kourtaliotiko Gorge to Moni Preveli. An easy 30-minute uphill path to Myrthios begins just before the youth hostel.

Several diving operators run shore and boat dives to nearby rocky bays, caves and canyons, and also certification courses.

Captain Lefteris Boat Cruises　　BOATING
(📱6936806635, 28320 31971; lbfinikas@gmail. com; Waterfront; tours €15-39) In summer, Baradakis Lefteris, owner-chef of the Smerna Bar, runs entertaining boat trips to nearby beaches like Preveli (€15), Frangokastello and Loutro (€39), and to Agios Pavlos, Triopetra and Preveli (€30).

🛏 Sleeping

★ Plakias Youth Hostel　　HOSTEL €
(📱28320 32118; www.yhplakias.com; dm €10-12; ☺mid-Mar–early Nov; 🅿@🛜) This charismatic pad and 'Hoscar' winner for best Greek hostel in 2015 and 2016 is set in an olive grove 500m from the beach. Serene and lazy, it fosters an atmosphere of inclusiveness and good cheer that appeals to people of all ages and nationalities. There are six eight-bed dorms with fans, communal facilities and an outdoor kitchen.

Hotel Livikon　　HOTEL €
(📱28320 31216; www.hotel-livikon-plakias.com; Beach Rd; d/tr €45/50; 🅿❄🛜) This family-run affair was one of the first hotels in Pla-

kias back in the 1970s, but the 10 impeccably kept, spotless and comfortable rooms hardly reveal their age. All have a small kitchen and a balcony (get a beach-facing one). It's upstairs from an all-day cafe that also serves breakfast (€4 to €6).

Plakias Suites　　APARTMENT €€
(📱28320 31680, 6975811559; www.plakiassuites. com; Beach Rd; ste €120-170; ☺Apr–mid-Nov; 🅿❄🛜) This stylish outpost has six two- and three-room apartments with contemporary aesthetics and Zeitgeist-compatible touches such as large flat-screen TVs, supremely comfortable mattresses, a chic kitchen and a private balcony or patio. Staying here puts you within a whisker of the best stretch of local beach, albeit about 1km from the village centre.

🍴 Eating & Drinking

To Xehoristo　　GREEK €
(📱28320 31214; Waterfront; sandwiches €2.50, mains €7-14; ☺noon-midnight) If the picture menu doesn't get you salivating, then the aroma emanating from the charcoal grill will likely do the trick. No matter, whether you grab a quick kebab pita during a beach session or tuck into a full platter of *gyros* (meat slithers cooked on a vertical rotisserie; usually eaten with pitta bread) or shrimp for dinner, you're in for a simple, but tasty, treat.

Tasomanolis　　SEAFOOD €€
(📱28320 31229; www.plakiasboattours.gr; Waterfront; mains €7-16; ☺noon-10pm or later; 🛜🍴) Tasos and his Belgian wife Lisa preside over this nautical-themed family taverna towards the far end of town. Park yourself on the colourful patio to tuck into classic Greek grills and inspired daily specials like anchovy bruschetta, ouzo shrimp or the daily catch with wild greens. Portions are not the biggest, but the quality is tops. Kids menu available.

Ostraco Bar　　CAFE-BAR
(📱28320 32249; Waterfront; ☺9am-late; 🛜) This downstairs waterfront cafe is a handy place to hang for breakfast, a cold beer or a snack any time of day, while the upstairs balconied bar kicks into gear after 9pm and keeps going until even the hardiest night owls are ready to roost.

❶ Information

Plakias has two ATMs on the central waterfront. The post office is on the first side street coming from the east.

CRETE PLAKIAS

ℹ️ Getting There & Around

There are up to five buses daily to Rethymno (€5, one hour) and four to Preveli (€1.80, 30 minutes).

Alianthos Cars (☑ 28320 32033; www. alianthos-group.com; Waterfront; per day car/ scooter from €36/23; ☺ 8am-10pm) Reliable car-hire outlet.

Anso Travel (☑ 6944755712; per day €10-25; ☺ 9am-2pm & 6-10pm) Rents out mountain bikes, speed bikes and even electric bikes for taking to the mountains around town. Multiday rates available.

Around Plakias

About 11km east of Plakias, the historic **Moni Preveli** (Μονή Πρεβέλης; ☑ 28320 31246; www.preveli.org; Koxaron-Moni Preveli Rd; €2.50; ☺ 9am-6pm Apr & May, 9am-1pm & 3.30-7pm Jun-Oct; 🅿) cuts an imposing silhouette high above the Libyan Sea. Like most Cretan monasteries, it was a centre of resistance during the Turkish occupation and also played a key role in WWII when hiding trapped Allied soldiers from the Nazis until they could escape to Egypt by submarine.

On the road to the monastery, a **memorial** showing a gun-toting abbot and an Allied British soldier commemorates this heroic act, as does a **fountain** on the right as you enter the monastery. To the left is a small **museum** with some exquisite icons, richly embroidered vestments and two silver candelabra presented by grateful soldiers after the war.

Dazzling **Preveli Beach** (Παραλία Πρεβέλης), also known as Palm Beach, is located below Moni Preveli and is one of Crete's most celebrated strands. At the mouth of the Kourtaliotiko Gorge, where the river Megalopotamos empties into the Libyan Sea, the palm-lined river banks have freshwater pools good for a dip. The beach is backed by rugged cliffs and punctuated by a heart-shaped boulder at the water's edge.

A steep path leads down to the beach (10 minutes) from a car park (€2), 1km before Moni Preveli. In summer, two daily buses come in from Rethymno (€4.90, 1¼ hours) and four from Plakias (€1.80, 30 minutes).

Plakias to Agia Galini

Triopetra   Τριόπετρα

Triopetra is a big beach named after three giant rocks jutting out of the sea. A headland divides the sandy strip into 'Little Triopetra' and 'Big Triopetra' – both have tavernas with rooms. Because of submerged sand shelves, the former is not ideal for swimming, so head to the 'big' beach for that. The area is popular for yoga retreats.

Triopetra can be reached via a 12km winding asphalt road from the village of Akoumia on the Rethymno–Agia Galini road. It's also linked to Agios Pavlos (about 300m is driveable dirt road). Ask about road conditions locally before setting out on the latter.

Pavlos' Place   PENSION €

(☑ 28310 25189, 6945998101; www.triopetra.com. gr; d €38-43; ☺ Apr-Oct; ❇🐾🛜) Right above Little Triopetra beach, dreamy Pavlos is the perfect chill spot and a popular yoga retreat. Rooms are down to earth (no TV), with kitchenettes and balconies that catch the sea breeze. The attached taverna does home-grown fare (mains €5 to €12). Wi-fi is intermittent and available in public areas only – great for digital detox.

Agios Pavlos   Αγιος Παύλος

Cradled by cliffs, Agios Pavlos is little more than a couple of small tavernas with rooms

---

MYRTHIOS   ΜΥΡΘΙΟΣ
....

The postcard-pretty village of Myrthios, draped across the hillside above Plakias, makes for a quieter and more village-like alternative to staying beachside. You might also be lured by great food and good deals on accommodation. Myrthios is a short drive (about 4km) or 30-minute walk (about 2km) from Plakias.

Taverna Panorama (☑ 28320 31450; mains €7-12; ☺ 9am-11pm Apr–mid-Nov; 🛜) is one of the oldest restaurants in the Plakias area and could not be more aptly named. On the shaded terrace, intoxicating views out towards Libya compete with the Cretan soul food prepared with passion and know-how by women from the village using impeccably fresh ingredients from Terpsi's family's own farm. If there's freshly baked apple pie, don't miss it!

and a beach bar set around a picture-perfect crescent with dark, coarse sand and the distinctive silhouette of Paximadia Island looming offshore. Its beauty and tranquillity have made it a popular destination for yoga retreats. A steep staircase on the bay's western end leads up Cape Melissa to some intricately pleated multihued rock formations.

The bay gets busy in summer when excursion boats arrive from Agia Galini, but it's possible to escape the crowds by heading to the beaches behind Cape Melissa. Beware that getting there involves a scramble down (and up) a steep sand dune; bring water and snacks since there are no facilities. The furthest cove is the least busy and is popular with nudists.

There is no public transport to Agios Pavlos. Drivers need to look for the turn-off to Saktouria on the Rethymno–Agia Galini road and follow the winding road 13km down to the sea.

Agios Pavlos Hotel HOTEL €
(☑ 28320 71104; www.agiospavloshotel.gr; d €37-45, apt €45-60; ⊙ Apr-Oct; P ❄ ☎) Hugging a rugged and remote sandy bay, this place offers small but updated rooms, some with gorgeous bay views, below a trad taverna, and larger apartments with kitchens and balconies in a modern building about 1km uphill. The taverna dishes up fresh fish and Cretan standards while the palm-thatched cafe with hammocks does breakfast and drinks.

Agia Galini Αγια Γαλήνη
POP 630

Agia Galini is an erstwhile picturesque fishing village where package tourism and overdevelopment have diluted much of the original charm. With ageing hotels and restaurants clinging densely to a steep hillside and hemmed in by cliffs, small beaches and a fishing harbour, the town can feel claustrophobic in high season, but it definitely has its charms at other times. It's a convenient base for visits to Phaestos, Agia Triada and the remote beaches west of here. The town all but shuts down in winter.

🛏 Sleeping & Eating

Camping No Problem CAMPGROUND €
(☑ 28320 91386; per person/tent/car/caravan €6/4/3/4; ⊙ year-round; P ☎ ☎) With shady spots to pitch a tent, this well-maintained campground is about 100m from a pebbly beach and a 10-minute walk from the port and town centre. A small supermarket meets basic needs, but there's also an excellent taverna overlooking a big swimming pool. The turn-off is on the main road near the Shell petrol station.

Palazzo Greco BOUTIQUE HOTEL €€
(☑ 28320 91187; www.palazzogreco.com; Main Rd; d incl breakfast €95-130; P ❄ ☎ ☎) A passion for design is reflected in the stylish details at this breezy hotel overlooking the sea. Match your mood to the wall colours – pale green, blue or red – in tranquil modern rooms with view-filled decks, flat-screen TVs, fridges and fabulous showers. Breakfast on the beautiful patio above the pool.

It's right on the main road before it descends down into the village.

Faros Fish Tavern SEAFOOD €€
(☑ 6944773702; Port; mains €7-13; ⊙ 11am-11pm) This no-frills family-run fish taverna is usually packed to the gills, and for good reason: the owner himself drops his nets into the Med, so you know what's on the plate that night was still swimming in the sea in the morning. It's in the first lane coming from the port. Squid cooked in its own ink, lobster spaghetti and fish soup are specialities (available on request only).

ⓘ Getting There & Away

In high season there are six buses daily to Iraklio (€8.70, two hours), up to five to Rethymno (€6.70, 1½ hours) and to Phaestos (€2.10, 30 to 45 minutes), and up to five to Matala (€3.50, 45 minutes) with a change in Tymbaki. Buses stop down in the village near the port.

Galini Express (☑ 6936923848; www.galini express.com) has direct buses to the airport in Iraklio (€25) and Hania (€35).

NORTHWEST CRETE

Hania Χανιά
POP 54,000

Hania (also spelled Chania) is Crete's most evocative city, with its pretty Venetian quarter, criss-crossed by narrow lanes, culminating at a magnificent harbour. Remnants of Venetian and Turkish architecture abound, with old townhouses now transformed into atmospheric restaurants and boutique hotels.

Hania

CRETE HANIA

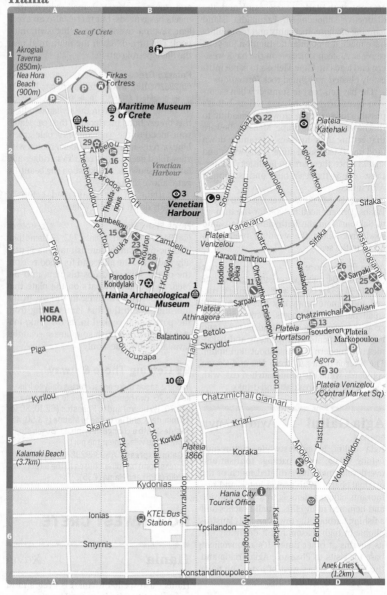

Although all this beauty means the old town is deluged with tourists in summer, it's still a great place to unwind. The Venetian Harbour is super for a stroll and a coffee or cocktail. Plus it's got a university and a modern portion to the city, which means that it retains its charm in winter. Indie boutiques and an entire lane (Skridlof) dedicated to leather products provide good shopping and, with a multitude of creative restaurants, you'll likely have some of your best meals on Crete here.

Hania

◎ Top Sights
  1 Hania Archaeological Museum B3
  2 Maritime Museum of Crete B2
  3 Venetian Harbour B2

◎ Sights
  4 Byzantine & Post-Byzantine
     Collection A2
  5 Centre for Mediterranean
     Architecture D2
  6 Church of Agios Nikolaos E3
  7 Etz Hayyim Synagogue B3
  8 Lighthouse B1
  9 Mosque of Kioutsouk Hasan C2
  10 Municipal Art Gallery B4

◔ Activities, Courses & Tours
  11 Blue Adventures Diving C3
  12 Greek Mountaineering
     Association F6

🛏 Sleeping
  13 Elia Daliani Suites D4
  14 Ifigenia Rooms & Studios B2
  15 Palazzo Duca B3
  16 Pension Theresa B2
  17 Serenissima B3
  18 Splanzia Hotel E3

✕ Eating
  19 Bougatsa Iordanis D5
  20 Kouzina EPE D3
  21 Mesogiako D4
  22 Pallas C2
  23 Tamam Restaurant B3
  24 To Karnagio D2
  25 To Maridaki D3
  26 Well of the Turk D3

❷ Drinking & Nightlife
  27 Kleidi E3
  28 Sinagogi B3

✪ Entertainment
  29 Fagotto Jazz Bar A2

🛍 Shopping
  30 Agora D4

◎ Sights

From Plateia 1866, the Venetian Harbour is a short walk north up Halidon. Zambeliou, once Hania's main thoroughfare, is lined with craft shops, small hotels and tavernas. The slightly bohemian Splantzia quarter, running from Plateia 1821 between Daskalogianni and Halidon, brims with atmospheric restaurants and cafes, boutique hotels and traditional shopping. The headland near the lighthouse separates the Venetian Harbour from the crowded town beach in the modern Nea Hora quarter.

★ **Venetian Harbour**   HISTORIC SITE
(⏱24hr) **FREE** There are few places where Hania's historic charm and grandeur is

more palpable than in the old Venetian Harbour. It's lined by pastel-coloured buildings that punctuate a maze of narrow lanes lined with shops and tavernas. The eastern side is dominated by the domed **Mosque of Kioutsouk Hasan** (Mosque of the Janissaries) `FREE`, now an exhibition hall. At sunset, join locals and tourists on a stroll out to the **lighthouse** that stands sentinel over the harbour entrance.

★ **Hania Archaeological Museum** — MUSEUM
(☑ 28210 90334; http://chaniamuseum.culture.gr; Halidon 28; adult/concession/child €4/2/free; ⊙ 8am-3pm Tue-Sun) The setting alone in the beautifully restored 16th-century Venetian Church of San Francisco is reason to visit this fine collection of artefacts from Neolithic to Roman times. Late-Minoan sarcophagi catch the eye as much as a large glass case with an entire herd of clay bulls (used to worship Poseidon). Other standouts include Roman floor mosaics in back, Hellenistic gold jewellery, clay tablets with Linear A and Linear B script, and a marble sculpture of Roman emperor Hadrian.

Also particularly impressive are the statue of Diana and, in the pretty courtyard, a marble fountain decorated with lions' heads, a vestige of the Venetian tradition. A Turkish fountain is a relic from the building's days as a mosque. To the north of the church, three small rooms display choice finds from a private collection of Minoan pottery, jewellery and clay models.

The church itself was a mosque under the Turks, a movie theatre in 1913, and a munitions depot for the Germans during WWII.

> ### ❶ HANIA FOR KIDS
> If your five-year-old has lost interest in Venetian architecture, head to the **public garden** between Tzanakaki and A Papandreou, where there's a playground and a shady cafe. Eight kilometres south of town, the giant water park **Limnoupolis** (☑ 28210 33246; www.limnoupolis.gr; Varypetro; day pass adult/child 4-12 €25/18, afternoon pass €17/14; ⊙ 10am-6pm mid-May–Aug, shorter hours Sep) has enough slides and pools to keep kids amused, and cafes and pool bars for adults. Buses leave regularly from the KTEL bus station.

★ **Maritime Museum of Crete** — MUSEUM
(☑ 28210 91875; www.mar-mus-crete.gr; Akti Koundourioti; adult/concession €3/2; ⊙ 9am-5pm Mon-Sat, 10am-6pm Sun May-Oct, 9am-3.30pm daily Nov-Apr) Part of the hulking Venetian-built Firkas Fortress at the western port entrance, this museum celebrates Crete's nautical tradition with model ships, naval instruments, paintings, old photographs, maps and memorabilia. One room is dedicated to historical sea battles while upstairs there's thorough documentation on the WWII-era Battle of Crete.

Byzantine & Post-Byzantine Collection — MUSEUM
(☑ 28210 96046; Theotokopoulou 78; adult/concession/child €2/1/free; ⊙ 8am-3pm Tue-Sun) In the impressively restored Venetian Church of San Salvatore, this small but fascinating collection of artefacts, icons, jewellery and coins spans the period from AD 62 to 1913. Highlights include a segment of a mosaic floor for an early-Christian basilica and a prized icon of St George slaying the dragon. The building has a mixed bag of interesting architectural features from its various occupiers.

Church of Agios Nikolaos — CHURCH
(Plateia 1821; ⊙ 7am-noon & 2-7pm) One of Hania's most intriguing buildings is this Venetian-era church with both a bell tower and a double-balconied minaret – the latter replaced a second bell tower during its stint as a mosque under Turkish rule. Inside, the massive bronze chandeliers dangling from a barrel-vaulted coffered ceiling will likely draw your attention. The church was originally part of a Dominican monastery founded in 1320. The only section left from this era is the cross-vaulted arcade on the north side (off Vourdouba).

Etz Hayyim Synagogue — SYNAGOGUE
(☑ 28210 86286; www.etz-hayyim-hania.org; Parodos Kondylaki; ⊙ 10am-6pm Mon-Thu, to 3pm Fri) Crete's only remaining synagogue (dating from the 15th century) was badly damaged in WWII and reopened in 1999. It sports a *mikve* (ritual bath), tombs of rabbis and a memorial to the local Jews killed by the Nazis. Today it serves a small congregation and is open to visitors. Find it on a small lane accessible only from Kondylaki street.

CRETE HANIA

Firkas Fortress

FORTRESS

(☺8am-2pm Mon-Fri) The Firkas Fortress at the western tip of the harbour heads the best-preserved section of the massive fortifications that were built by the Venetians to protect the city from marauding pirates and invading Turks. The Turks invaded anyway, in 1645, and turned the fortress into a barracks and a prison. Today, parts of it house the Maritime Museum of Crete. There's a great view of the harbour from the top.

Municipal Art Gallery

GALLERY

(☑28210 92294; www.pinakothiki-chania.gr; Halidon 98-102; adult/child €2/free; ☺10am-2pm & 7-10pm Mon-Sat) Hania's modern art gallery evokes the interior of a boat and presents temporary exhibitions of contemporary works by local and national artists on three elegant, well-lit floors.

🏖 Beaches

The town beach 2km west of the Venetian Harbour at Nea Hora is crowded but convenient if you just want to cool off and get some rays. Koum Kapi is less used (and less clean). For better swimming, keep heading west to the beaches (in order) of Agioi Apostoli, Hrysi Akti and Kalamaki, which are all served by local buses heading towards Platanias.

🤿 Activities

Blue Adventures Diving

DIVING

(☑28210 40403; www.divingchania.com; Chrysanthou Episkopou 39; 1-/2-tank dive €55/90; ☺9.30am-10pm Apr-Nov) This established outfit offers a host of dive options, including discover courses, PADI open-water certification, and diving trips around Hania, including beginner dives in PADI training standards. There are also snorkelling trips and cruise options for those who just want to go along for the ride.

Nea Hora Beach

BEACH

(Akti Papanikoli) Hania's in-town beach is only a 10-minute walk west of the Venetian Harbour. The 500m-long yellow-sand strip is backed by tavernas, small markets and holiday apartment rentals. Fairly shallow, it's good for kids and popular with locals on weekends.

Greek Mountaineering Association

OUTDOORS

(EOS; ☑28210 44647; www.eoshanion.gr; Tzanakaki 90; ☺8.30am-6pm Mon-Fri) For all your hiking and mountaineering needs on Crete, this is the go-to organisation. Check the website or swing by the local EOS chapter to get the full scoop, including climbing in the Lefka Ori (White Mountains), mountain refuges and the E4 European Path.

🛏 Sleeping

Ifigenia Rooms & Studios

GUESTHOUSE €

(☑28210 94357; www.ifigeniastudios.gr; Gamba 23; r €50-130; ❄🛜) This network of refurbished buildings around the Venetian Harbour has a bed for every budget, from basic rooms to luxurious bi-level suites with Jacuzzis and sea views. Most of the 25 units brim with such old-timey touches as wrought-iron canopy beds and beamed ceilings. The pricier ones have kitchens and can sleep up to four. Specify your arrival time when booking.

Pension Theresa

PENSION €

(☑28210 92798; www.pensiontheresa.gr; Angelou 8; d €50-60; ❄🛜) This creaky old Venetian house with a steep (and narrow!) spiral staircase and antique furniture delivers snug rooms with character aplenty. The location is excellent, the ambience rustic and convivial, and the views lovely from the rooftop terrace with communal kitchen stocked with basic breakfast items. It's close to plenty of bars and restaurants.

Palazzo Duca

BOUTIQUE HOTEL €€

(☑28210 70460; www.palazzoduca.gr; Douka 27-29; d €85-155; ❄🛜) In a backstreet off the harbour, this protected building with Byzantine origins was meticulously restored and turned into a pint-sized luxury hotel with eight elegantly furnished rooms spread over three floors (there's a lift). The best is the vast top-floor suite with kitchenette and a private patio with Jacuzzi. Optional breakfast is €7.50.

★Serenissima

BOUTIQUE HOTEL €€€

(☑28210 86386; www.serenissima.gr; Skoufon 4; d incl breakfast from €170; ❄🛜) This tranquil Venetian townhouse, renovated to impeccable standards, packs plenty of design cachet into its historic walls. The elegant rooms feature the gamut of mod cons along with period touches like stone walls, wooden beams and candlelit niches. Rates include an à la carte breakfast in the downstairs restaurant-bar.

Elia Daliani Suites

GUESTHOUSE €€€

(☑28215 04684; www.eliahotels.com; Chatzimichali Daliani 57; d €100; ❄🛜) These four spacious, stylish suites fill a restored Venetian townhouse on pedestrianised Daliani, just behind the town market. The look is edgy contemporary with all-white furniture, but you get a sense of place from the wall-sized retro black-and-white photographs of scenes from rural Crete. A small balcony looks out over the quiet street. No on-site reception.

Splanzia Hotel BOUTIQUE HOTEL €€€

(☑ 28210 45313; www.splanzia.com; Daskalogianni 20; d incl breakfast from €130; ❋ @ ☎) This smartly renovated hotel in a Venetian mansion in the lively Splantzia quarter has eight stylish rooms, each different but all outfitted with custom-made wooden furniture, huge beds – some of them canopied – and the gamut of tech touches. The back rooms overlook a bougainvillea-festooned courtyard with a Turkish well.

It's run by friendly folk with a knack for hospitality. In peak season, a two- or three-night minimum stay may be required.

✖ Eating

⭐ **Bougatsa Iordanis** CRETAN €

(☑ 28210 88855; www.iordanis.gr; Apokoronou 24; bougatsa €3; ☺ 6am-2.30pm Mon-Sat, to 1.30pm Sun; ▣) Locals start salivating at the mere mention of this little bakery-cafe dedicated to making the finest *bougatsa* since 1924. The flaky treat, filled with sweet or savoury cheese, is cooked fresh in enormous slabs and carved up in front of your eyes. Pair it with a coffee and you're set for the morning. There's nothing else on the menu!

Mesogiako MEDITERRANEAN €

(☑ 28210 57992; www.mesogiako.com; Chatzimichali Daliani 36; mains €10-16; ☺ 7pm-12.30am Mon-Sat, noon-5pm Sun; ❋ ☎) Opposite the minaret in the Splantzia quarter, this trendily cosy eatery with cheerful tangerine walls and modern country-style furniture sits among a group of similarly popular eateries. The menu is most creative when it comes to the mezedhes – Moroccan roll, salmon croquettes and wild mushroom risotto are all winners.

Kouzina EPE CRETAN €

(☑ 28210 42391; Daskalogianni 25; mains €4-9.50; ☺ noon-7.30pm Mon-Sat) This cheery lunch spot gets contemporary designer flair from the cement floor, country-white tables and dangling silver origami boats. It's a local favourite away from the crowds, serving blackboard-listed *mayirefta* that can be inspected in the open kitchen.

⭐ **Pallas** INTERNATIONAL €€

(☑ 28210 45688; www.pallaschania.gr; Akti Tombazi 15; mains €8-16; ☺ 8.30am-4am; ☎) This much buzzed-about hipster cafe-bar has a sweet location in an impeccably renovated former customs house from 1830 right in the Venetian Harbour. Grab a high chair, sofa or table to linger over the three-tiered breakfast, a crisp salad for lunch or a juicy steak dinner – or pop by just for coffee or cocktails.

To Maridaki SEAFOOD €€

(☑ 28210 08880; www.tomaridaki.gr/en; Daskalogianni 33; mezhedes €3-14; ☺ noon-midnight Mon-Sat) This modern seafood *mezedhopoleio* (restaurant specialising in mezedhes) is often packed to the gills with chatty locals. Dishes straddle the line between tradition and innovation with to-die-for fried calamari and crisp and delicious house white wine. The complimentary panna cotta is a worthy finish.

Tamam Restaurant MEDITERRANEAN €€

(☑ 28210 96080; www.tamamrestaurant.com; Zambeliou 49; mains €8-13; ☺ noon-12.30am; ☎ ▱) This convivial taverna in a converted Turkish bathhouse has captured people's attention since 1982 with strong-flavoured Cretan dishes that often incorporate Middle Eastern spices and touches. The boneless lamb in tomato sauce with raisins and mint is a winner. Tables spill out onto the narrow alleyway.

Well of the Turk MIDDLE EASTERN €€

(☑ 28210 54547; www.welloftheturk.com; Sarpaki 1-3; mains €8-15; ☺ 6pm-midnight Wed-Mon; ❋ ☎) In an age-old stone building that used to house a *hammam,* and flanking a quiet square, this romantic taverna specialises in richly textured dishes with a strong French and Moroccan identity, yet prepared with the finest Cretan ingredients. The cheesecake with rosewater and orange makes an imaginative culinary coda.

To Karnagio GREEK €€

(☑ 28210 53366; Plateia Katehaki 8; mains €8-18; ☺ noon-midnight May-Oct; ☎) Mamba-green tables spill onto a harbourside plaza next to the Grand Arsenal in this mainstay restaurant that serves a modest selection of grilled meat and seafood alongside some flaky *boureki* (pies) and fresh salads.

⭐ **Thalassino Ageri** SEAFOOD €€€

(☑ 28210 51136; www.thalasino-ageri.gr; Vivilaki 35; fish per kg €55; ☺ 7pm-midnight Apr–mid-Oct) This solitary fish taverna among the vestiges of Hania's old tanneries in Halepa, some 2km east of the centre, is one of Crete's top eateries. Take in the sunset from the superb setting and peruse the changing menu, dictated by the day's catch. Dishes like squid with crushed fennel and green olives hum with creativity while others (like the melt-in-your-mouth calamari) shine through their transcendent simplicity.

Drinking & Nightlife

The cafe-bars around the Venetian Harbour are nice places to sit, but charge top euro. For a more local vibe, head to Plateia 1821 in the Splantzia quarter, the interior streets near Potie, or to alt-flavoured Sarpidona on the eastern end of the harbour.

★ Sinagogi   BAR
(☑ 28210 95242; Parodos Kondylaki 15; ⊙ 1pm-3am Jun-Sep; 🖥) Housed in a roofless Venetian building on a small lane next to the synagogue, this popular summer-only lounge bar has eclectic decor and is a laid-back place to relax and take it all in. After dark, it's bathed in a romantic glow while DJs play soft electro and the bartenders whip up mojitos and daiquiris.

Kleidi   BAR
(☑ 28210 52974; Plateia 1821; ⊙ 9am-late; 🖥) By day locals fill the shady plaza tables and sip iced coffee, and by night the place buzzes with party life. There's no written sign, just the image of a keyhole (*kleidi* means key).

☆ Entertainment

★ Fagotto Jazz Bar   LIVE MUSIC
(☑ 28210 71877; Angelou 16; ⊙ 9pm-5am) Established in 1978, this Hania institution in a Venetian building offers smooth jazz, soft rock and blues (sometimes live) in a setting brimming with jazz paraphernalia, including a saxophone beer tap. Great cocktails too! The action picks up after 10pm.

🔒 Shopping

Hania offers top shopping, especially in the backstreets. Theotokopoulou is lined with souvenir and handicraft shops. Skrydlof offers a vast array of local and imported sandals, belts and bags. Find some of the most authentic crafts in the Splantzia quarter, along Chatzimichali Daliani and Daskalogianni. The *agora* (central market hall) is touristy but still worth a wander.

Agora   MARKET
(Covered Market; Chatzimichali Giannari; ⊙ 7.30am-2pm Mon, Wed & Sat, 9am-9pm Tue, Thu & Fri; 🚻) Hania's cross-shaped market hall opened in 1913 and bustles mostly with souvenir-hunting tourists, though a few stands selling traditional Cretan produce and products (herbs, honey, baked goods, raki, cheese) – along with cafes – are still part of the mix.

ℹ Information

Free wi-fi is widely available in public spaces, including the harbour, around the central market and at Plateia 1866, as well as at most hotels, restaurants, cafes and bars.

Banks cluster around Plateia Markopoulou in the new city, but there are also ATMs in the old town on Halidon.

Municipal Tourist Office (☑ 28213 36155; chania@ofcrete.gr; Kydonias 29; ⊙ 8.30am-2.30pm Mon-Fri) Modest selection of brochures, maps and transport timetables at the town hall. Open some Saturdays.

Post Office (☑ 28210 28444; Peridou 10; ⊙ 7.30am-8.30pm Mon-Fri)

Tellus Travel (☑ 28210 91500; www.tellustravel.gr; Halidon 108; ⊙ 8.30am-10pm)

Tourist Police (☑ 28210 25931, 28210 53333, 171; ⊙ 24hr)

ℹ Getting There & Away

AIR

Hania's **airport** (☑ 28210 83800; www.chania-airport.com) is 14km east of town on the Akrotiri Peninsula, and is served year-round from Athens and Thessaloniki and seasonally from throughout Europe. Carriers include Aegean Airlines and Ryanair. A taxi anywhere in Chania costs €24. Public buses into town stop right outside the terminal (€2.50, 30 minutes).

BOAT

Hania's port is at Souda, 7km southeast of town (and the site of a NATO base). The port is linked to town by bus (€2, or €2.50 if bought aboard) and taxi (€11). Hania buses meet each boat, as do buses to Rethymno.

Anek Lines (☑ 28210 24000; www.anek.gr; Leoforos Karamanlis 70; ⊙ 7.30am-3.30pm Mon-Fri) Nightly overnight ferry between Piraeus and Hania (from €38, nine hours). Buy tickets online or at the port; reserve ahead for cars.

BUS

Hania's **KTEL bus station** (☑ info 28210 93052, tickets 28210 93306; www.e-ktel.com; Kelaidi 73-77; 🖥) has a cafeteria, minimarket and left-luggage service. Check the excellent website for the current schedule.

BUSES FROM HANIA

DESTINATION	DURATION	FARE (€)	FREQUENCY
Elafonisi	2¼hr	11	daily
Falasarna	1¾hr	8.30	3 daily
Hora Sfakion	1¾hr	8.30	3 daily
Iraklio	2¾hr	15.10	hourly
Kissamos (Kastelli)	1hr	5.10	15 daily
Kolymbari	40min	3.60	6 daily
Moni Agias Triadas	30min	2.60	2 daily
Omalos (for Samaria Gorge)	1hr	7.50	3 daily
Paleohora	1¾hr	7.60	4 daily
Rethymno	1¼hr	6.80	hourly
Sougia	1¾hr	7.80	3 daily
Stavros	40min	2.30	7 daily

❶ Getting Around

TO/FROM THE AIRPORT

KTEL (www.e-ktel.com) buses link the airport with central Hania roughly every 30 minutes (€2.50, 25 minutes). Taxis between any place in the city and the airport cost €24.

BUS

Local buses are operated by **Chania Urban Buses** (☑ 28210 98115; http://chaniabus.gr). Zone A/B tickets cost €1.20/1.70 if bought from a kiosk or vending machine and €2/2.50 from the driver.

A handily central stop for Souda port, Halepa, Nea Hora and other local destinations is on Giannari, near the *agora* market hall.

CAR

Major car-hire outlets are at the airport or on Halidon. Most of the old town is pedestrianised. There's free parking just west of Firkas Fortress and along the waterfront towards Nea Hora beach, or by the eastern edge of the harbour off Kyprou; but avoid areas marked residents-only.

TAXI

Taxi (☑ 28210 98700; www.chaniataxi.gr)

Kissamos (Kastelli)
Κίσσαμος (Καστέλλι)

POP 4275

Kissamos exudes an unpolished, almost gritty, air compared to other north-coast towns. This is not a place given entirely over to tourism. There are two beaches in town, separated by a waterfront promenade: the sandy Mavros Molos in the west and the pebbly Telonio beach to the east.

The largest town and capital of Kissamos province, it is referred to interchangeably as Kissamos or Kastelli (though the official name is the former).

🛏 Sleeping & Eating

Thalassa APARTMENT €
(☑ 28220 31231; www.thalassa-apts.gr; Drapanias Beach, Mithimna; studio from €40; 🅿 ❄ @ 🛜 🐕) The isolated Thalassa complex is ideal for a quiet retreat about 5km east of Kissamos at Drapanias beach. The immaculate studios are airy and well fitted. There's a barbecue on the lawn, a small playground and a salt-water swimming pool with massage jets. It's helpful to have a car.

Nautilus Bay Hotel APARTMENT €€
(☑ 28220 22250; www.nautilusbay.gr; Plaka Beach; apt €110-160; 🅿 ❄ 🛜 🐕) Well-proportioned and modern apartments with streamlined furniture, small kitchenettes and black-tiled bathrooms fill this modern complex right on the sandy beach and in the centre of town. Balconies have sweeping water views and there's a restaurant and bar and a large pool area.

Taverna Sunset TAVERNA €
(☑ 28220 83478; Paraliaki; mains €7-10; ⊙ noon-1am; 🛜) Locals mix with in-the-know visitors at this quintessential family taverna presided over by Giannis, who's usually ensconced behind the grill coaxing meat and fish into succulent perfection. It's right on the waterfront, so you can feel the breezes coming offshore.

ℹ Getting There & Away

BOAT

From the port 3km west of town, **Lane Sea Lines** (☎ 27360 37055; www.lane-kithira.com) has two weekly ferries to Piraeus (13 hours), four to Kythira (four hours), two to Antikythira (2¼ hours) and one to Gythion (eight hours). In summer, a bus meets ferries; otherwise taxis into town cost around €7. Schedules change seasonally.

BUS

Bus schedules change seasonally – check www.e-ktel.com. There are as many as 14 daily buses to Hania (€5.10, one hour); change in Hania for Paleohora, Rethymno and Iraklio. There are also two to three daily buses to Falasarna (€3.80, 15 minutes) in summer only and one daily to Elafonisi (€6.90, 1¼ hours) from May to October.

CAR

Kissamos is about 40km west of Hania. **Kissamos Rent a Car** (☎ 28220 23740; www.kissamosrentacar.com; Iroön Polytechniou 210; car per week from €159) is one of several car-hire agencies along Iroön Polytechniou, the main drag.

Around Kissamos

Polyrrinia   Πολυρρηνία

Polyrrinia   ARCHAEOLOGICAL SITE

FREE The wonderful mountaintop ruins of the ancient city of Polyrrinia (pol-ee-ren-ee-a) lie about 7km south of Kissamos, above the village of the same name. Sea, mountain and valley views from this defensible spire are stunning and the region is blanketed with wildflowers in spring. The site's most impressive feature is the **acropolis** built by the Byzantines and Venetians. There's also a **church** built on the foundations of a Hellenistic temple from the 4th century BC.

Polyrrinia was founded by the Dorians in the 6th century BC and was constantly at war with the Kydonians from Hania. Coins from the period depict the warrior-goddess Athena, who was evidently revered by the warlike Polyrrinians.

Unlike their rivals the Kydonians, the Polyrrinians did not resist the Roman invasion and thus the city was spared destruction. It was the best-fortified town in Crete and the administrative centre of western Crete from the Roman through to the Byzantine period. The Venetians used it as a fortress. Many of the structures, including an aqueduct built by Hadrian, date from the Roman period. Near the aqueduct is a **cave** dedicated to the nymphs; it still contains the niches for nymph statuettes.

There is no public transport to the site.

Gramvousa Peninsula
Χερσόνησος Γραμβούσα

Northwest of Kissamos (Kastelli) is the beautifully wild and remote Gramvousa Peninsula, whose main attraction is the stunning lagoon-like beach of Balos, on Cape Tigani on the west side of the peninsula's narrow tip. Kalyviani village is a good base for visiting the peninsula.

⊙ Sights & Activities

★Balos   LAGOON

(cruises adult/concession €27/13) The rugged Gramvousa Peninsula cradles the lagoonlike white powdery beach of Balos, whose shallow, shimmering turquoise waters will undoubtedly bring a giggle to your holiday-hungry throat. The beach is gorgeous, with lapping translucent waters dotted with tiny shellfish and darting fish. Balos overlooks two islets, the larger one (Imeri) being crowned by the ruins of a humongous Venetian fortress built to keep pirates at bay.

Cretan Daily Cruises   BOATING

(☎ 28220 24344; www.cretandailycruises.com; adult/child €27/13; ☉late Apr-Oct) The easiest way to get to Gramvousa and Balos lagoon is by boat cruise from the port of Kissamos. There are three departures daily but check ahead to make sure they haven't been cancelled because of strong winds. Reasonably priced food and drink is available on board. Summer-only KTEL buses from Hania are timed to boat departures. Tickets are sold online, by phone or at the port.

🍴 Sleeping & Eating

The best base for touring this region is the village of Kalyviani, 6km west of Kissamos (Kastelli). There is no lodging at Balos.

★Gramboussa   CRETAN €€

(☎ 28220 22707; http://gramvousarestaurant.com; Kalyviani; mains €8-16; ☉10am-1pm; P) 🍴 In Kalyviani village, about 6km west of central Kissamos, Gramboussa serves fine traditional Cretan cuisine in an elegantly rustic stone building set in a superb garden. It's a cut above other restaurants and offers the chance to sample the freshest regional cuisine Crete has to offer, as well as wood-oven specials like suckling pig or lamb with honey.

ℹ Getting There & Away

From May to October, day trippers arriving by cruise boat from Kissamos (with a two-hour stop at Imeri) deluge Balos between 11am and 4pm. The only way to avoid the crowds is to get there by car before or after the boats arrive. The approach is via a scenic corduroy road that picks up near the village of Kalyviani. It ends 12 axle-shaking kilometres later at a parking lot from where a 1.2km trail leads down to the lagoon. Nondrivers could try hitching a ride or walk, although you'll be eating a lot of dust from passing vehicles.

Falasarna   Φαλάσαρνα

POP 25

Some 16km west of Kissamos, Falasarna is little more than a blotch of habitations on a long sandy beach – but what a beach! This broad sweep of pink-cream sand is considered among Crete's finest and is famous for its superbly clear teal waters, stunning sunsets and rolling waves. Spread your towel on the Big Beach (Megali Paralia) at the south end or pick a spot in one of the coves separated by rocky spits further north.

Falasarna has no centre as such, although there are hotels and several tavernas, bars and small supermarkets.

◉ Sights

Aside from its stunning beach, Falasarna is famous as the site of a 4th-century city-state and trading centre with its own harbour. It's possible to wander among the ancient ruins.

⌨ Sleeping

Magnolia Apartments   APARTMENT €
(☑ 28220 41407, 6945605438; www.magnolia-apartments.gr; studio/apt from €45/55; ［P］［❄］［❋］) Just a five-minute walk back from a sparkling beach, Magnolia is a quiet holiday retreat with 12 well-equipped studio apartments whose decor is pleasant but plays it safe. Enjoy a leisurely breakfast or sunset drinks from your sea-facing balconies or in the neatly groomed garden.

Sunset Rooms & Apartments   APARTMENT €€
(☑ 28220 22155, 28220 41204; www.sunset.com.gr; d/apt/villa €40/70/160; ［P］［❋］) In an enviable location steps from one of Crete's finest sandy beaches, Sunset has 13 rooms and six apartments above a convivial taverna with

fig trees and a natural spring. Rooms are snug, but tastefully decked out with apricot-coloured walls, wrought-iron beds, tile floors and sea-facing balconies.

Families should enquire about the four nearby two-floor stone villas with full kitchens.

ℹ Getting There & Away

Bus schedules vary seasonally (check www.e-ktel.com). In summer, at least three daily buses make the trip out to Falasarna from Hania (€8.30, 1¼ hours) via Kissamos-Kasteli (€3.80, 40 minutes). A taxi costs about €15 from Kissamos and €65 from Hania.

SOUTHWEST COAST

The stark and muscular Lefka Ori (White Mountains) meet the sea along Crete's corrugated southwestern coast, which is indented with a handful of laid-back coastal villages, some of them accessible only by boat and therefore completely untouched by mass tourism. You can walk to perfectly isolated little beaches or soak up the majestic scenery and fragrant air on a scramble through wildly romantic gorges away from the busy Samaria Gorge, which ends in Agia Roumeli.

Frangokastello
Φραγγοκαστέλλο

POP 148

Dominated by a mighty 14th-century Venetian fortress, Frangokastello is a low-key resort with a fabulous wide and sandy beach that slopes gradually into shallow warm water, making it ideal for kids. There's no actual village, just a smattering of tavernas, small markets and low-rise holiday apartments and rooms scattered along the main street.

✗ Eating

Oasis Taverna   CRETAN €
(☑ 28250 83562; www.oasisrooms.com; Frangokastello Beach; mains €5-13; ⊙ 9am-10pm or later; ［P］［❋］［♿］) Part of an excellent family-run studio and apartment complex at the western end of the beach, about 1km from the fortress, this is the best place to eat not only for the well-executed Cretan home-cooked meals but also for the stunning view from the flower-festooned stone-floor terrace.

Also a good place for breakfast before a day on the beach.

ⓘ Getting There & Away

KTEL buses stop at several spots along the main road. In summer, there are three daily buses from Hora Sfakion to Frangokastello (€2.30, 30 minutes).

Hora Sfakion
Χώρα Σφακίων

POP 212

The more bullet holes you see in the passing road signs, the closer you are to Hora Sfakion, long renowned in Cretan history for its rebellious streak against foreign occupiers. But don't worry, the pint-sized fishing village is an amiable, if eccentric, place that caters well to today's foreign visitors – many of whom are Samaria Gorge hikers stumbling off the Agia Roumeli boat on their way back to Hania. Most pause just long enough to catch the next bus out, but some are tempted into staying by the area's isolated beaches and hiking trails.

◉ Sights & Activities

Sweetwater Beach   BEACH
(Glyka Nera) West of Hora Sfakion, lovely Sweetwater Beach is accessible by a small daily ferry (May to October, per person €4), by taxi boat (one-way/return €25/50) or on foot via a stony and partly vertiginous 3.5km coastal path starting at the first hairpin turn of the Anopoli road. A small cafe rents umbrellas and sun chairs.

Vrissi Beach   BEACH
Abutting the western edge of the village, this tiny grey-sand cove is the closest beach for unfolding your towel or a quick dip. There's a taverna on the bluff above for snacks and refreshments.

Notos Mare Marine Adventures   DIVING
(☏ 6947270106; www.notosmare.com; New Harbour; 1/2 dives €49/85) In addition to PADI certification and dives for beginners and advanced divers, this long-running professional outfit also rents boats, organises charter boat and fishing trips, and operates taxi boats to secluded beaches along the south coast.

⌖ Sleeping & Eating

Be sure to try the local *Sfakiani pita* – this thin, circular pancake filled with sweet *myzithra* and flecked with honey makes a great breakfast when served with a bit of Greek yoghurt on the side.

FRANGOKASTELLO: THE 'GHOST' CASTLE

Frangokastello was built by the Venetians to guard against pirates and feisty local Sfakian rebels. On 17 May 1828, during the War of Independence, many Cretan fighters were killed here by the Turks. According to legend their ghosts – the *drosoulites* – can be seen marching past the fortress in the early dawn on the battle's anniversary.

Xenia Hotel   HOTEL €
(☏ 28250 91490; www.sfakia-xenia-hotel.gr; Old Harbour; d incl breakfast €55; [P][❄][☎]) Well positioned overlooking the water, this hotel has been around since the early 1960s but has since been modernised numerous times and now sports mod cons such as air-con, satellite TV and a fridge in each of the 24 rooms. Ring in the evening by toasting the waves on your sea-facing balcony.

Hotel Stavris   HOTEL €
(☏ 28250 91220; www.hotel-stavris-sfakia-crete. com; s/d/apt €31/36/52; [❄][☎]) Up the hill overlooking the old harbour, the Perrakis clan has welcomed guests since 1969. Rooms and apartments vary by size, configuration and amenities, although all are clean and come with air-con, fridge and balcony. The nicer ones have kitchenettes and harbour-facing views. Cash only.

Taverna Nikos   TAVERNA €
(☏ 28250 91111; Old Harbour; mains €5-12; ⊘ 7am-midnight) At the beginning of the gauntlet of harbour-front tavernas, family-run Nikos is a reliable standby for Greek staples, grilled fish and meat and Cretan specialities like smoked pork or sautéed snails. Don't get up from the table without sampling the local speciality *Sfakiani pita*.

ⓘ Getting There & Away

BOAT
Hora Sfakion is the eastern terminus for the south-coast **Anendyk** (☏ 28210 95511; www. anendyk.gr; New Harbour) ferry route to/from Paleohora via Loutro, Agia Roumeli and Sougia, and also runs boats to Gavdos Island. Schedules vary seasonally, so always check ahead. Often boats only run as far as Agia Roumeli, where you must change for another ferry to Sougia and Paleohora.

DESTINATION	FARE (€)	FREQUENCY
Agia Roumeli	7.50	up to 3 daily
Loutro	6	up to 7 daily
Paleohora	20.70	daily
Sougia (via Agia Roumeli)	16.20	daily

There are also two to three boats per week to/from Gavdos Island via Loutro and Agia Roumeli (€21.20, four hours).

BUS
KTEL buses leave from the square up the hill above the municipal car park. Schedules change seasonally; check online. In summer there are three daily services to/from Hania (€8.30, 1¾ hours); coming from Rethymno, change in Vryses (€8.30, two hours). There are also three daily buses to Frangokastello (€2.30, 30 minutes).

Loutro   Λουτρό
POP 56

The pint-sized fishing village of Loutro is a tranquil crescent of flower-festooned white-and-blue buildings hugging a narrow pebbly beach between Agia Roumeli and Hora Sfakion. It's only accessible by boat and on foot and is the departure point for coastal walks to isolated beaches, such as Finix, Marmara and Sweetwater.

🏃 Activities

Loutro Canoes   CANOEING
(☑ 28250 91433; per day €16) Hotel Porto Loutro hires out small canoes.

🍽 Sleeping & Eating

Given the captive market, the tavernas that line the waterfront in Loutro are surprisingly good. Most offer the usual array of fresh fish, local grills and traditional *mayirefta*.

Villa Niki   APARTMENT €
(☑ 6972299979; www.loutro-accommodation.com; studio/apt from €55/80; 🅿 🅰) These elegantly rustic studios with beamed ceilings and stone floors accommodate up to four people and come with a kitchenette with basic equipment. Since Niki is located just above the village, you get great views over the water from the balconies.

Hotel Porto Loutro   HOTEL €€
(☑ 28250 91433, 28250 91001; www.hotelporto loutro.com; s/d incl breakfast €70/95; ☉ Apr-Oct; 🅿 @ 🅰) The classiest hotel in the village has rooms and studios furnished in smartly contemporary island style and spread across two buildings, all with spacious furnished balconies perfect for counting the waves or chilling with a beer. Days start with a lavish breakfast spread served at the on-site restaurant. No credit cards.

ℹ Information
There's no bank, ATM or post office, and many places do not accept credit cards. Bring plenty of cash (the nearest ATM is in Hora Sfakion).

ℹ Getting There & Away
Loutro is on the Paleohora–Hora Sfakion boat route operated by Anendyk (www.anendyk.gr). There are seven boats daily to Hora Sfakion and three to Agia Roumeli with connections to Sougia and Paleohora. Boats from Hora Sfakion to Gavdos Island also stop in Loutro.

Sougia   Σούγια
POP 136

Sougia, 67km south of Hania and on the Hora Sfakion–Paleohora ferry route, is one of the most chilled-out and refreshingly undeveloped southern beach resorts. Cafes, bars and tavernas line a tamarisk-shaded waterfront promenade along a grey pebble-and-sand beach. Most pensions and apartments enjoy a quieter inland setting. There is little to do other than relax or explore the local trails, including the popular Agia Irini Gorge.

🏃 Activities

Sougia has a pleasant 1km-long grey sand-and-pebble beach, but its drop-off is quick, so it's not ideal for families with small children.

★ Agia Irini Gorge   HIKING
(www.agia-irini.com; €1.50; ☉ year-round) Pretty Agia Irini Gorge starts some 13km north of Sougia. The well-maintained, mostly shaded 7.5km trail (with a 500m elevation drop) follows the river bed, is shaded by oleander, pines and other greenery, and passes caves hidden in the gorge walls. You'll emerge at a taverna where you can call a taxi (€15) or continue on foot for another 7km via a quiet, paved and sunny road to Sougia.

Of course, it's also possible to do the hike in reverse. To get to the trailhead, take the bus to Hania and ask the driver to drop you off or take a taxi.

IMBROS GORGE   ΦΑΡΑΓΓΙ ΤΗΣ ΙΜΠΡΟΥ

Half the length of the more famous Samaria Gorge (p480), the 8km-long **Imbros Gorge** (€2; ⊙year-round), 130km east of Sougia, is no less beautiful and a lot less busy, especially in the afternoon. Most people start in the mountain village of Imbros and hike down to the southern coastal village of Komitades. Going the other way provides a bit more of a workout as you'll be walking up a gentle grade. A taxi between the two (about €20) can be arranged by tavernas at either end.

The hike takes you past 300m-high walls buttressed by cypresses, holm oaks, fig and almond trees, and redolent sage. Landmarks include a **giant arch** at the 2km mark (coming from the south) and the **narrowest point** of the ravine (near the 4.5km mark), which is just 2m wide.The track is easy to follow as it traces the stream bed past rock-slides and caves. Sturdy shoes are essential.

🛏 Sleeping & Eating

Aretousa Studios & Rooms   APARTMENT €
(☑ 28230 51178; studio €55-65; ⊙Apr-Oct; 🅿 ❄ 🛜) This lovely pension on the road to Hania, 200m from the sea, has 10 bright and comfortably furbished studios with tile floors, balconies and well-stocked kitchens. The tranquil relaxing garden is a nice post-tanning chill zone and there's even a playground for kids out back.

Hotel Santa Irene   APARTMENT €€
(☑ 28230 51342; www.santa-irene.gr; Beach Rd; apt €60-80; ⊙late Mar-early Nov; 🅿 ❄ 🛜) This smart hotel in a traditional building on the beach has 14 roomy and balconied studios sleeping two to five people. Whip up breakfast or a small meal in the kitchenette or grab a snack at the attached snack bar.

Taverna Oasis   TAVERNA €
(☑ 28230 51121; mains €6-10; ⊙11am-9pm Apr-Oct) Restore energies with a cold beer and classic Greek snacks after tackling the lovely Agia Irini Gorge. From here it's another 7km walk or a €15 taxi ride back to Sougia.

Polyfimos   TAVERNA €
(☑ 28230 51343; www.polifimos.gr; Main Rd; mains €7-13.50; ⊙1pm-midnight Apr-Oct; 🛜) Hidden in a grapevine-shrouded courtyard off the Hania road, this charismatic lair specialises in charcoal-tickled local meats, hearty stews like rabbit *stifadho* (cooked with onions in a tomato purée) and lamb *tsigariasto* (sautéed). It's run by ex-hippie Yiannis who also makes his own oil, wine and raki.

★ Omikron   INTERNATIONAL €€
(☑ 28230 51492; Beach Rd; mains €7-15; ⊙8am-late; 🛜 🅿) At this elegantly rustic beachfront lair, Jean-Luc Delfosse has forged his own culinary path in a refreshing change from

taverna staples. Mushroom crêpes to *Flammmekuche* (Alsatian-style pizza), seafood pasta to pepper steak – it's all fresh, creative and delicious.

ℹ Information

There is one ATM but no petrol station. Visit www.sougia.info for area information.

ℹ Getting There & Around

BOAT

From May to October, ferries on **Anendyk's** (☑ 28230 51230; www.anendyk.gr) Paleohora–Agia Roumeli route stop in Sougia. The trip to either Paleohora or Agia Roumeli takes about 40 minutes and costs €11.20 and €11, respectively. In Agia Roumeli, you can continue east to Hora Sfakion via Loutro. There are also two or three weekly ferries to Gavdos via Agia Roumeli.

Captain George's Water Taxi (☑ 6947605802, 28230 51133; www.sougia.info/taxi-boats) Serves the coast near Sougia.

BUS

Two to three buses operate between Sougia and Hania (€7.80, 1¾ hours) with a stop in Agia Irini to drop off gorge hikers. The bus departing Sougia at 6.15pm waits for the Agia Roumeli boat. There are also daily buses to Omalos (for Samaria Gorge) in summer only (€5.30, one hour).

TAXI

Local **taxi** (☑ 28230 51403, 69777445160, 6972370480; www.taxi-selino.com) drivers have a central kiosk on the waterfront.

Paleohora   Παλαιόχωρα

POP 1900

Appealing, laid-back and full of character, Paleohora lies on a narrow peninsula flanked by a long, curving tamarisk-shaded sandy beach (Pahia Ammos) and a pebbly beach

SAMARIA GORGE   ΦΑΡΑΓΓΙ ΤΗΣ ΣΑΜΑΡΙΑΣ

Hiking the 16km-long **Samaria Gorge** (☎ 28210 45570; www.samaria.gr; Omalos; adult/child €5/free; ☺ 6am-4pm May–mid-Oct), one of Europe's longest canyons, is high on the list of must-dos for many Crete visitors. There's an undeniable raw beauty to the canyon with its soaring cliffs and needle-nose passageways. The hike begins at an elevation of 1230m just south of Omalos and ends in the coastal village of Agia Roumeli. It's also possible to do it the 'lazy way' by hiking a shorter distance, starting at Agia Roumeli. The only way out of Agia Roumeli is by taking the boat to Sougia or Hora Sfakion, which are served by bus and taxi.

The best time for the Samaria trek is in April and May when wildflowers brighten the trail. Keep your eyes peeled for the endemic kri-kri, a shy endangered wild goat.

Hiking the Gorge

The trail begins at **Xyloskalo**, a steep and serpentine stone path that descends some 600m into the canyon to arrive at the simple cypress-framed **Agios Nikolaos chapel**. Beyond here the gorge is wide and open for the next 6km until you reach the abandoned settlement of **Samaria**, whose inhabitants were relocated when the gorge became a national park. Just south of the village is a 14th-century **chapel** dedicated to St Maria of Egypt, after whom the gorge is named.

Further on, the gorge narrows and becomes more dramatic until, at the 11km mark, the walls are only 3.5m apart. These are the famous **Sideroportes** (Iron Gates), where a rickety wooden pathway leads hikers the 20m or so across the water.

The gorge ends at the 12.5km mark just north of the almost abandoned village of Palea (Old) Agia Roumeli. From here it's a further 2km hike to the seaside village of **Agia Roumeli**, whose fine pebble beach and sparkling water are a most welcome sight.

Few people miss taking a refreshing dip or at least bathing sore and aching feet. The entire trek takes from about four hours for the sprinters to six hours for the strollers.

The Low-Down

➡ An early start (before 8am) helps to put you ahead of the crowd. Sleep over in Omalos to be first. During July and August even the early bus from Hania can be packed. Or start after noon, and plan to sleep over in Agia Roumeli.

➡ Hikers starting after about 2pm are only allowed to walk a distance of 2km from either end. Spending the night in the gorge is a no-no – time your trip to be out by sunset.

➡ There's a 1200m elevation drop going north to south. Wear sturdy shoes and take sunscreen, sunglasses, some food, a hat and a water bottle, which you can refill from taps with potable water along the way. Drink plenty!

➡ There are several rest stops with toilets, water, trash bins and benches along the trail.

➡ Falling rocks occasionally lead to injuries but generally it's the heat that's a far bigger problem. Check ahead as park officials may close the gorge on rainy or exceptionally hot days (generally, over 40°C), and the gorge season can end early if the rains have started.

(Halikia). Shallow waters and general quietude make the village a good choice for families with small children. The most picturesque part of Paleohora is the maze of narrow streets below the castle. Tavernas spill out onto the pavement and occasional cultural happenings inject a lively ambience. In spring and autumn, Paleohora attracts many walkers.

◉ Sights & Activities

There are several great **walking trails** nearby. From Paleohora, a six-hour walk along a scenic **coastal path** (p482) leads to Sougia, passing ancient Lissos. An easier inland loop goes to Anydri then through small, lush **Anydri Gorge** to the sea.

When a stiff summer breeze is blowing, **windsurfing** off sandy Pahia Ammos is excellent. Private dolphin-spotting trips are also run from Paleohora.

Venetian Fort   FORT
(Kastro Selino; ☺ 24hr) FREE There's not much left of the 13th-century Venetian castle looming above Paleohora, but it's worth the

➡ Early in the season it's sometimes necessary to wade through the stream. Later, as the flow drops, the stream-bed rocks become stepping stones.

➡ If the idea of a 16km hike does not appeal, get a taste of Samaria by doing it 'the easy way', ie starting in Agia Roumeli and heading north for as long as you feel like before doubling back. The Sideroportes, for instance, can be reached in about an hour. Or consider some of the other gorges in the area, like Agia Irini or Imbros.

Sleeping & Eating

It is forbidden to camp in the gorge. Stay at Omalos on the north end, or Agia Roumeli in the south.

There are tavernas in Omalos, including one right by the gorge entrance. A clutch of refreshment stands sell souvenirs, snacks, bottled water and the like, when the gorge is open. Agia Roumeli has several tavernas.

Agriorodo (☑ 28210 67237; 2-/3-bedroom cottage from €60/80; ☺ year-round; P ☎) These lovely modern stone cottages are a comfy base camp for expeditions to Samaria Gorge, whose entrance is a mere 15 minutes on foot away. Decorated with rustic style, each sleeps four to five people and is kitted out with satellite TV, wi-fi, kitchens and a living room with plush sofas and fireplaces.

Hotel Neos Omalos (☑ 28210 67269; www.neos-omalos.gr; Chania-Omalos Rd; s/d/tr incl breakfast €38/49/59; P ☎) This rustic mountain lair has welcomed generations of nature lovers since opening in 1954. A convivial feel pervades the public areas leading to basic, but comfortable, rooms with balcony views that will get you in the mood for hiking. The owners are a fount of information on local hikes and other outdoor activities and can also shuttle you to Samaria Gorge some 4km away.

Xyloskalo (☑ 28210 67237; mains €6-10; ☺ 10am-6pm; ☎) Perched just over the spectacular drop of Samaria Gorge, with eagles occasionally circling outside its wraparound windows, this cosy restaurant dishes up classic Cretan and Greek meals, and offers that last chance to use indoor plumbing and wi-fi.

Getting There & Away

Most people hike Samaria one way going north–south on an organised day trip from every sizeable town and resort in Crete. Confirm that tour prices include the €5 admission to the gorge or the boat ride from Agia Roumeli to Sougia or Hora Sfakion.

With some planning, it's possible to do the trek on your own. There are early-morning public buses to Omalos from Hania (€7.50, one hour), Sougia (€5.30, one hour) and Paleohora (€7, one hour), once or twice daily in high season. Check www.e-ktel.com for the seasonally changing schedule. Taxis are another option.

At the end of the trail, in Agia Roumeli, ferries operated by Anendyk (www.anendyk.gr) go to Sougia or Hora Sfakion; some are met by public buses to Hania.

clamber for splendid views of the sea and mountains, especially at sunset.

Built to monitor the southwestern coast from its commanding hilltop position, it was repeatedly destroyed by Cretan rebels, the pirate Barbarossa and the Ottomans.

🛏 Sleeping & Eating

Homestay Anonymous　　　PENSION €
(☑ 28230 42098; www.anonymoushomestay.com; d/apt €30/55; ✳☎) This simple but good-value pension with private bathrooms and shared cooking facilities in the courtyard garden is an excellent budget pick. Friendly, well-travelled owner Manolis cultivates a welcoming atmosphere and is a mine of information on local activities. The nine units are in two quaint stone buildings and furnished in charming country style.

Corali　　　APARTMENT €
(☑ 6974361868; www.corali-studios.com; Pebble Beach; studio €50-55; ✳@) A friendly Greek-Italian family runs these three immaculate studios kitted out with kitchenettes, upmarket modern furniture, large

pristine bathrooms and waterfront balconies. The central location and sea views are excellent.

Joanna's Place
APARTMENT €

(📞 28230 41801; www.joanna-place.com; studio €50-60; ⊙Apr-Nov; 🅿❄🛜) This charmer sits in a quiet spot across from a small stone beach at the southeastern tip of the peninsula. The 10 spacious and spotless studios are outfitted with functional locally made furniture, and there's a kitchenette for preparing breakfast to enjoy on your balcony.

Third Eye
VEGETARIAN €

(📞 28230 41234, 6986793504; www.thethirdeye-paleochora.com; mains €6-7; ⊙noon-3pm & 6-11pm; 🛜🍴) A local institution and community gathering spot since 1990, the Third Eye knew what to do with beetroot, quinoa and hummus long before meatless fare went mainstream. The globally inspired menu features delicious salads, rotating mains and snacks like samosas or guacamole. Sit on the streetside patio or in the tranquil garden.

★Taverna Methexis
CRETAN €€

(📞 28230 41431; www.facebook.com/Methexis Taverna; Waterfront; mains €7-12; ⊙12.30-11.30pm; 🅿🛜🍴) It's well worth the short saunter to the peninsula's southeastern tip to sample the authentic comfort food and warm hospitality at this locally adored taverna across from a small beach. All the classics are accounted for along with such tasty surprises as salt cod with garlic sauce and delicious pies filled with fennel or local *myzithra*.

❶ Information

There are a couple of ATMs on the main drag, Eleftherios Venizelou.

Post Office (⊙7am-2.30pm Mon-Fri) Just across from Pahia Ammos (sandy beach).

Selino Travel (📞 28230 42272; selino2@otenet.gr; Kondekaki; 3hr trip €18; ⊙8am-1.30pm & 6-9.30pm Mon-Sat Apr-Oct, shorter hours rest of year)

❶ Getting There & Around

Notos Rentals (📞 6976436044; www.notoscar.gr; Eleftherios Venizelou 53; ⊙9am-2pm & 6-10pm) has cars, motorcycles and bicycles for hire. There are two petrol stations in town. Gas up before heading on longer drives in the region, where petrol stations are rare to nonexistent.

BOAT

Boats leave from the old harbour at the far pebbly beach's southern end. Buy tickets at Selino Travel.

There is a daily morning ferry to Sougia (€11.20, 40 minutes) and Agia Roumeli (€17.20, 1½ hours) where the boat stops for 90 minutes before continuing to Loutro (€19.70, 40 minutes) and Hora Sfakion (€20.70, 20 minutes from Loutro). Some boats can transport cars and scooters.

From May to October, there are also two or three weekly ferries to Gavdos Island (€23.30, four hours) via Sougia and Agia Roumeli. One ferry daily except Sunday goes out to the westcoast beach of Elafonisi (€10, one hour).

BUS

KTEL runs four daily buses to Hania (€8.30, two hours) and one bus daily except Sunday at 6.15am to Omalos (€6.40, two hours) for Samaria Gorge. Buses also stop in Sougia and, on request, at the Agia Irini Gorge trailhead. There

---

PALEOHORA–SOUGIA COASTAL WALK

Following a portion of the E4 European Path, this hike connects two charming coastal towns via a 13km path that runs mostly along the coast.

From Paleohora, follow signs to the campsites to the northeast and turn right at the sign for Anydri. After a couple of kilometres, the path climbs steeply for a beautiful view back to Paleohora. You'll pass **Anydri Beach** and several inviting **coves** where people may be getting an all-over tan. Take a dip because the path soon turns inland to pass over **Cape Flomes**. You'll walk along a plateau carpeted with brush that leads towards the coast and some breathtaking views over the Libyan Sea. About 10km into the hike, you'll reach the Dorian site of **Lissos** from where the path weaves through a pine forest before spilling out at Sougia.

Allow five to six hours for the nearly shadeless walk and take plenty of water, a hat and sunblock. From June through August, it's best to start at sunrise in order to get to Sougia before the heat of the day. The boat back to Paleohora runs around 6pm (check the schedule, www.anendyk.gr).

are also thrice-weekly Elafonisi-bound buses (€5.50, 1½ hours).

Elafonisi   Ελαφονήσι

POP 15

If much of life in Crete is like a beach, remote Elafonisi *is* a beach and a stunning one at that. Tucked into Crete's southwest corner, this symphony of fine pinkish-white sand, turquoise water and gentle dunes looks as though lifted from the Caribbean. Off the long, wide strand lies Elafonisi Islet, easily reached by wading through 50m of knee-deep water. The entire area is part of Natura 2000, the environmental protection program of the European Union.

Alas, this natural gem is hardly a secret and less than idyllic in high summer when floods of sun seekers put pressure on its delicate ecosystem. Come early or late in the day or, better yet, stay overnight to truly sample Elafonisi's magic.

Sleeping & Eating

Restaurants at the Elafonisi hotels are basic but dependable, while a few beachfront snack bars satisfy daytime munchies.

Elafonisi Village Rooms & Taverna   HOTEL €
(☑ 28220 61548, 6942872384; www.elafonisi-village.gr; Beach Rd; d €50-65; ☺ Apr-Oct; ❃ ☎) Just 250m from Elafonisi Beach, these 10 spacious rooms with tiled floors, wooden furniture and private terraces string across an arid courtyard with sea views for catching the sunset. Four units can sleep up to four people and have a kitchenette.

Elafonisi Resort   HOTEL €
(☑ 28250 61274, 6983516137; www.elafonisi-resort.com; s/d €35/45; ▣❃☎) This cluster of low-rise whitewashed buildings dotted around a peaceful olive grove has 21 spacious rooms with fridges; all but one have a balcony, a few come with a kitchen. The affiliated restaurant serves the catch of the day and classic Greek fare.

❶ Getting There & Away

Elafonisi is about 75km southwest of Hania – budget about 1½ to two hours for the nonstop drive. From Paleohora, one boat (€10, one hour) and one bus daily (€5.50, one hour) make the trip out here from June to September when there is one daily bus from Hania (€11, two hours) via Kissamos (Kastelli; €6.90, 1¼ hours). Check the schedule at www.e-ktel.com.

OFF THE BEATEN TRACK

GAVDOS ISLAND
ΝΗΣΙ ΤΗΣ ΓΑΥΔΟΥ

In the Libyan Sea, 65km from Paleohora and 45km from Hora Sfakion, Gavdos is Europe's most southerly point and as much a state of mind as it is an island. It's a blissful spot with only a few rooms, tavernas and unspoilt beaches, some accessible only by foot or boat. There's little to do here except swim, walk and relax. Gavdos attracts campers, nudists and free spirits happy to trade the trappings of civilisation for an unsullied nature experience. The island is surprisingly green, with almost 65% covered in low-lying pine and cedar trees and vegetation. Most of the electricity is supplied by generators, which are often turned off at night and in the middle of the day. Note that the ferry schedule does not make it possible to visit Gavdos on a day trip.

EASTERN CRETE

Head east from Iraklio past the rocking package-tourist resorts of Hersonisos and Malia and you enter the prefecture of Lasithi, a more relaxed Cretan world that is never short of surprises. Looking for a charming resort town with a buzzy after-dark vibe? There's none better than Lasithi's main tourist draw of Agios Nikolaos. Ancient sites and culture? Lasithi has Minoan and Mycenaean sites aplenty. The fertile Lasithi Plateau offers cycling opportunities through tranquil villages and the Dikteon Cave where Zeus himself was born. Outdoor types can also look forward to walking the dramatic Valley of the Dead at Zakros Gorge. Added value comes with such unique attractions as the historic monastery of Toplou and Vaï's famous palm-backed beach. Scores of smaller towns and villages, meanwhile, maintain a rich undertow of Cretan history and spirit.

Agios Nikolaos
Αγιος Νικόλαος

POP 27,100

Lasithi's capital, Agios Nikolaos has an enviable location on hilly terrain overlooking the shores of the sensuously curving Mirabello Bay. It may feel less Cretan than other towns,

CRETE ELAFONISI

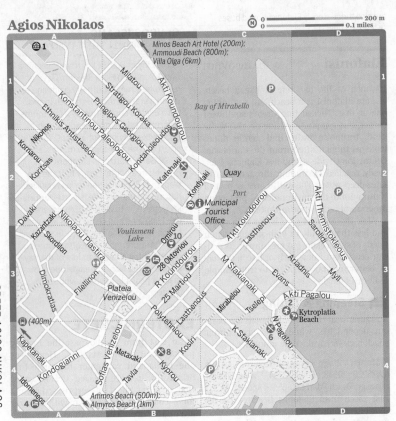

Map: Agios Nikolaos

Agios Nikolaos

◎ **Sights**
1 Archaeological Museum A1

✦ **Activities, Courses & Tours**
2 Kytroplatia Beach C3
3 Nostos Cruises B3

🛏 **Sleeping**
4 Doxa Hotel...A4
5 Du Lac Hotel B3

🍽 **Eating**
6 Faros...C4
7 Pelagos...B2
8 Sarris..B4

🍷 **Drinking & Nightlife**
9 Arodo Cafe B2
10 Peripou Cafe B3

partly because of its resort-style flair, tree-lined avenues and largely modern architecture. However, there's also a strong local character to Agios Nikolaos that imbues it with charismatic, low-key flair.

A narrow channel separates the attractive harbour from the circular Voulismeni Lake, whose pedestrianised shore is lined with tourist cafes and restaurants. At night a lively ambience descends on the harbour as lounge-bars fill with stylish young Greeks and holidaymakers from the nearby resorts.

◎ Sights & Activities

In town, the beaches of sandy **Ammos** and pebbly **Kytroplatia** are small and overcrowded. Let your feet take you 1km north and south respectively to **Ammoudi** and **Almyros** beaches, for longer stretches of finer sand to call your own. Almyros is quieter than the other beaches around town with fine sand and beautiful clear water. All have umbrellas and sun chairs to rent.

Archaeological Museum   MUSEUM
(☑ 28410 24943; Konstantinou Paleologou 74) Crete's most significant Minoan collection (after the Heraklion Archaeological Museum) includes clay coffins, ceramic musical instruments and gold from Mohlos. Closed for renovation at the time of writing, it may reopen in 2018.

Nostos Cruises   BOATING
(☑ 28410 22819; www.nostoscruises.com; 30 Rousou Koundourou; trips to Spinalonga without/with barbecue €16/25, fishing trips from €50) Runs boat trips to Spinalonga, including a swim at Kolokytha, from the harbour in Agios Nikolaos. Also offers Spinalonga trips including a barbecue, and fishing trips with food, including anything you catch.

🛏 Sleeping

Doxa Hotel   HOTEL €
(☑ 28410 24214; www.doxahotel.gr; Idomeneos 7; s/d/tr incl breakfast €65/75/85; ❄ 🎧) This 24-room hotel within a stone's throw of Ammos Beach is well cared for, albeit a bit long in the tooth. Rooms are twee and come with chocolate-brown quilts, marble floors and clean bathroom. Some rooms have a balcony.

★ Villa Olga   APARTMENT €€
(☑ 28410 25913; www.villa-olga.gr; Anapafseos 18, Ellinika; studio €40, villa €50-90; 🅿 ❄ 🎧 🏊) Halfway to Elounda, these charismatic self-catering studios and villas (sleeping up to six) enjoy serene views of the Bay of Mirabello from terraced gardens scattered with stone urns, terracotta pots and other curios of yesteryear collected by owner Michalis. His knack for details and colour also shines through in the traditional chic interiors with tiled floors and waterfront patios.

Villa Olga is reached by following the waterfront road, Akti Koundourou, northeast from the centre of Agios Nikolaos. At a junction above Ammoudi beach, take the right-hand branch towards Elounda for about 500m and look out for the Villa Olga sign on the left.

Du Lac Hotel   HOTEL €€
(☑ 28410 22711; www.dulachotel.gr; 28 Oktovriou 17; d with lake view €50; ❄ ❄ 🎧) Smack dab in the town centre, this aging city hotel has fine views over Voulismeni Lake from its generic but comfortable rooms and studios decked out in shades of vanilla to chocolate. It's

well worth the extra money for a unit with lake-facing balcony. The downstairs cafe serves breakfast, snacks and drinks all day and gets quite buzzy.

Minos Beach Art Hotel   BOUTIQUE HOTEL €€€
(☑ 28410 22345; www.minosbeach.com; Akti Ilia Sotirchou; r incl breakfast from €280; 🅿 ❄ 🎧 🏊) In a superb waterfront location just north of town, this resort is a neat fusion of substance and style with plenty of original artwork and a cluster of sea-facing rooms and bungalows kitted out in comfy modern style. With four restaurants and three bars, plus a gym and spa, you'll be tempted to linger.

🍴 Eating

Faros   GREEK €
(☑ 28410 83168; Kitroplatia Beach; mains €5.50-19; ⏱ noon-midnight; 🎧) One of several tavernas fringing tiny Kitroplatia beach, family-run Faros (lighthouse) sends signals to empty stomachs with aromas wafting from the brazier out front. Sit at linen-draped tables under a blue-and-white awning next to the sand or soak up the old-school atmosphere inside. Meals are usually capped with free baklava and raki.

Sarris   GREEK €
(☑ 28410 28059; Kyprou 15; mains €10; ⏱ 10.30am-midnight) This tiny rustic taverna in a residential area has just a few tables out on the street beneath a shady pergola and serves up honest-to-good Cretan home cooking. Check the blackboard for the daily specials, order a carafe of wine and chill.

Pelagos   MEDITERRANEAN €€
(☑ 28410 25737; Koraka 11; mains €8.50-25; ⏱ noon-midnight; 🎧) Pelagos is not for the indecisive. First you must choose whether to sit in the elegantly rustic historic house or in the romantic, lantern-festooned garden. Tough one, but perhaps not as tough as finding your top menu pick from the big selection of fresh fish, grilled meats, inventive salads and homemade pastas.

🍷 Drinking & Nightlife

The harbour-facing lounge-bars along Akti Koundourou are busy from mid-morning until the wee hours. For dance and music clubs, try 25 Martiou, just up from the harbour.

★ Arodo Cafe   CAFE-BAR
(☑ 28410 89895; Kantanoleontos & Akti Koundourou; ⏱ 11am-2am) This low-lit lair buzzes

with the conversation of earnest boho locals, offering a cocktail of cool tunes, a sea-facing terrace and an eclectic and handpicked selection of beers and wine. The entrance is up the steep stairs.

Peripou Cafe CAFE-BAR
(☑ 28410 24876; 28 Oktovriou 13; ☺ 10am-midnight or later; 🛜) This boho cafe-bar with a narrow verandah overlooking the lake has a bijou bookstore, plays indie tunes, and sells toasties and cold beer. It gets a somewhat alternative local crowd, especially in winter when there's the occasional acoustic concert.

❶ Information

There's free wi-fi in the harbour area and its surrounds. There are several banks with ATMs on Koundourou.

General Hospital (☑ 28413 43000; Knosou & Paleologou) OK for broken bones and X-rays, but for anything more serious you'll need to head to Iraklio.

Byron Travel (☑ 28410 24452; www.byron travel.gr; Akti Koundourou 4; ☺ 8am-9pm) Well-run travel agency; books plane and boat tickets and also rents cars.

Municipal Tourist Office (☑ 28410 22357; www.agiosnikolaos.gr; Akti Koundourou 21; ☺ 8am-10pm Apr-Nov) One of the few remaining tourist offices on Crete, this small outfit has helpful staff, a city map and a few brochures.

Tourist Police (☑ 28410 91409, emergency 171; Erythrou Stavrou 47)

Post Office (28 Oktovriou 9; ☺ 7.30am-2.30pm Mon-Fri)

❶ Getting There & Away

BUS

Local buses for Elounda (€1.90, 20 minutes, 14 daily) leave from stops around town, including the one on Koundourou opposite the tourist office.

The main **bus station** (☑ 28410 22234; Epimenidou 59) is about 1.5km north of the city centre. Check www.ktelherlas.gr for the current schedule.

DESTINATION	DURATION	FARE	FREQUENCY
Ierapetra	1hr	€4.10	9 daily
Iraklio	1½ hr	€7.70	20 daily
Kritsa	30min	€1.80	3 daily
Sitia	1½ hr	€8.30	8 daily

CAR

Club Cars (☑ 28410 25868; www.clubcars. net; Agios Nikolaos-Vrouchas Rd; per day/week from €50/220; ☺ 8am-9pm) Has cars for hire from €50 per day in high season.

TAXI
The most central **taxi rank** (Paleologou) is behind the tourist office down by the lake. Typical fares are €14 for Elounda, €21 for Plaka, €14 for Kritsa and €18 for Ancient Lato.

❶ Getting Around

A local bus links the main bus station with the harbour and the two in-town beaches. The centre itself is compact enough for walking. Buses also go out to Elounda at least once hourly.

Around Agios Nikolaos

Elounda Ελούντα

POP 2200

There are fine mountain and sea views along the 11km road north from Agios Nikolaos to Elounda. It centres on a handsome fishing harbour, where you can board a boat to Spinalonga Island, an erstwhile leper colony. There is a refreshing down-to-earth feel to the town centre, which also has some pleasant waterfront bars and eateries. The beach, a short walk north of the harbour, is adequate, if nothing special, and can get crowded.

🛏 Sleeping & Eating

Dolphins Apartments APARTMENT €
(☑ 28410 41641; www.pediaditis.gr/dolphins-apart ments; Papandreou 51; studio/apt €40/50; P ❄ 🛜 ☼) These apartments with pleasingly rustic furniture and tile floors pack a lot of features into a compact frame, including a kitchenette with microwave and a furnished balcony overlooking the sea. Guests may use the pool at the nearby Milos Apartments run by the same family.

Portobello Apartments APARTMENT €
(☑ 28410 41712; http://coralistudios.com/apart ments_portobello.htm; Akti Poseidonos; apt €45-75; 🛜 ☼) These 15 spacious apartments can easily accommodate families or groups up to four people. Balconies offer front-row views of the sea, the beach is mere steps away and a swimming pool with bar beckons from out the back.

Corali Studios APARTMENT €€
(☑ 28410 41712; www.coralistudios.com; Akti Poseidonos; r €45-75; P ❄ 🛜 ☼) Set amid lush lawns with a shaded patio and overlooking the sandy town beach, Corali is run by a friendly family and has 20 stucco-walled rooms with waffle quilts, balcony, basic

kitchenette and woodsy furniture. At the back, there's a good-sized pool with sun loungers and a bar that serves snacks and cold drinks.

★ **Hope** CRETAN €€
(Rakadiko Tou Kamari; ☑ 6972295150; Mavrikiano; mains €6-18; ☉ 11am-11.30pm) Clinging to a steep hillside in the ancient hamlet of Mavrikiano above Elounda, Hope has been a local lair since 1938. The terrace where fishermen once gathered nightly to suss out the next day's weather is now packed with people getting giddy on wine, raki, homemade mezedhes, succulent lamb chops and the stupendous view. Since 2012, it's been run by a charming young couple, Dimitris and Amalia.

❶ Information

Olous Travel (☑ 28410 41324; www.oloustravel.gr; Plateia Sfakianaki; ☉ 9am-11pm) Full-service agency handles air and boat tickets, finds accommodation and organises car rentals and excursions.

❶ Getting There & Away

There are 14 buses daily from Agios Nikolaos to Elounda (€1.90, 20 minutes). The bus stop is on the main square where you can buy tickets at the kiosk next to Nikos Taverna.

The taxi stand is also on the square. The fare to Agios Nikolaos is €14.

Cars, motorcycles and scooters can be hired at **Elounda Travel** (☑ 28410 41800; www.eloundatravel.gr; Sfakianaki 3; car per day/week from €47/175; ☉ 8am-9pm), with a central office on, you guessed it, the main square, which also doubles as a (fee-based) parking lot.

Spinalonga Island
Νήσος Σπιναλόγκα

Spinalonga Island HISTORIC SITE
(☑ 28410 41773; adult/concession return €8/4; ☉ 9am-6pm) Tiny Spinalonga Island became a leper colony in 1903 and was catapulted into pop-cultural consciousness thanks to Virginia Hislop's 2005 bestselling novel *The Island* and the subsequent Greek TV series spin-off, *To Nisi*. Boats departing from Elounda, Plaka and Agios Nikolaos drop visitors at Dante's Gate, the 20m-long tunnel through which patients once arrived. From here, a 1km trail takes you past such 'sights' (mostly ruined) as a church, the disinfection room, the hospital and the cemetery.

Kritsa Κριτσά
POP 1296

Clinging to the craggy foothills of the Dikti range, Kritsa is one of the oldest and prettiest of the mountain villages in eastern Crete and a popular stop for tour buses. The upper village especially is redolent with romantic decay and the ghosts of the past. Many of Kritsa's older women still practise the art of traditional embroidery, although these days the doilies and blankets sold at the souvenir shops are most likely commercially produced.

⊙ Sights

★ **Church of Panagia Kera** CHURCH
(☑ 28410 51806; Main Rd; adult/concession €2/1; ☉ 8am-3pm Tue-Sun; ℗) The tiny triple-aisled Church of Panagia Kera shelters the best-preserved Byzantine frescoes in Crete. The oldest part of the church is the 13th-century central nave, but most of the frescoes date from the early to mid-14th century. The dome and nave are decorated with four gospel scenes: the Presentation, the Baptism, the Raising of Lazarus and the Entry into Jerusalem. On the western wall is a portrayal of the Crucifixion and grimly realistic depictions of the Punishment of the Damned.

The vault of the southern aisle recounts the life of the Virgin; the northern aisle is an elaborately worked-out fresco of the Second Coming. Nearby is an enticing depiction of Paradise next to the Virgin and the Patriarchs – Abraham, Isaac and Jacob. Judgement Day is portrayed on the western end, with the Archangel Michael trumpeting the Second Coming.

Ancient Lato ARCHAEOLOGICAL SITE
(Λατώ; ☑ 28410 22462; http://odysseus.culture.gr; off Kritsa-Lakonion Rd; adult/concession €2/1; ☉ 8am-3pm Tue-Sun) Worth the wheeze for the rural serenity alone – the mountain a silvery sheen of wildflowers, the nearby peaks tipped with snow – the ancient hilltop city-state of Lato is one of Crete's few non-Minoan ancient sites. Founded by the Dorians in the 7th century BC, Lato was one of Crete's most powerful cities until it was abandoned when the administrative centre moved to its port in present-day Agios Nikolaos in the middle of the 2nd century AD.

The surviving ruins sprawl over the slopes of two acropolises in a lonely mountain setting, commanding stunning views down to the Bay of Mirabello. At a little elevation

CRETE AROUND AGIOS NIKOLAOS

GOURNIA ΓΟΥΡΝΙΑ

The Late Minoan settlement of **Gournia** (📞 28420 93028; Agios Nikolaos-Sitia Rd; adult/concession €2/1; ⏰ 8am-3pm Tue-Sun; 🅿) lies 19km southeast of Agios Nikolaos. Comprising a small palace and residential areas, it was built between 1600 and 1500 BC, destroyed in 1450 BC and reoccupied from 1375 to 1200 BC. There are streets, stairways and houses with walls up to 2m high. Domestic, trade and agricultural implements discovered here suggest that Gournia might have been fairly prosperous. Agios Nikolaos buses bound for Sitia and Ierapetra can drop you at the site.

Snap a picture of the overview map just past the entrance, then follow a narrow ancient road as it curves uphill to the palace ruins, skirting **workshops and storage rooms**, including one where a clay wine press was found. The trail ends at the palace's **central courtyard** with steps on your right indicating the main entrance. On the opposite (west) side of the courtyard, smaller stairs lead down to an upright slab considered a 'sacred stone'. Basic explanatory panels scattered around the site provide additional information.

they begin to take form as you look down and imagine the bustling *agora*.

Enter via the **city gate** and follow a long, stepped street. On your left is a wall with two towers that doubled as residences. The street culminates at the **agora**, which embraced a deep square cistern and a rectangular temple where numerous 6th-century-BC figurines were unearthed. The circle of stones behind the cistern was a threshing floor. West of the *agora* was a **stoa** (colonnaded walkway) with stone benches. Nearby, you can spot remaining bits and pieces of a pebble mosaic.

Between the two towers on the *agora's* north end steps lead to the vast theatre-like **prytaneion** (administrative centre). At its centre, a hearth burning 24/7 was surrounded by stepped benches where the city leaders held their meetings. South of the *agora*, you can spot what's left of a large temple and, east of here and at a lower level, a semicircular theatre that could seat about 350 people next to a bench-lined **exedra** (stage).

Nearchus, one of Alexander's generals, is believed to hail from Lato, whose name derives from the goddess Leto. It was Ieto's union with Zeus that produced Artemis and Apollo.

There are no buses to Lato. The nearest stop is in Kritsa, from where it's a 3km walk north.

Mohlos Μόχλος

POP 121

At the end of a narrow road winding past massive quarries, tranquil Mohlos is an off-the-radar gem along Crete's northern shore. In this authentic fishing village time moves as gently as the waves lapping onto the pebble-

and-grey-sand beach. There's little to do but relax and soak in the peacefulness. Mohlos was once a thriving Early Minoan community, traces of which still exist on the small island that is now 200m offshore. If you want to visit, ask around in the village for someone to take you there in a boat. Swimmers should be wary of strong currents.

🛏 Sleeping & Eating

Hotel Sofia PENSION €
(📞 28430 94554; sofia-mochlos@hotmail.com; d €35-45; 🅿✳🛜) Right by the sea, this amiably old-school taverna has small, low-frill rooms upstairs with wine-coloured bedspreads, trad furniture, modern bathrooms and a fridge.

You pay a little extra for a sea view. The owners also have spacious apartments (€40 to €55) 200m east of the harbour, where longer stays are preferred.

⭐ **Petra Nova Villas** VILLA €€
(📞 28430 94080, 6984365277; www.petranovavillas.gr; villa €95-135; 🅿✳🛜) These five bi-level stone villas blend seamlessly into the hillside and are just a few minutes' walk up the road from the waterfront. Sleeping up to five people, the tranquil units all come with plenty of privacy, chic interiors and stunning bay views from the patio – all ingredients for a soothing and mindful getaway. Minimum stay requirement during peak season.

Ta Kochilia GREEK €€
(📞 28430 94432; mains €4.50-16; ⏰ 10.30am-midnight; 🛜) The oldest among several waterfront tavernas, Ta Kochilia has cooked up a storm since 1902 and is still a place for fanciers of fish and traditional Cretan dishes like

spinach pies, lamb with artichokes in lemon sauce, and oven-baked feta. It's easily recognised by its cheerful white and blue trim.

❶ Getting There & Away

There is no public transport to Mohlos. Buses between Sitia and Agios Nikolaos can drop you off at the Mohlos turn-off, from where you'll need to hitch or walk the 6km down to the village.

Sitia   Σητεία
POP 9900

Sitia is an attractive seaside town that hasn't sold its soul to mass tourism. Whitewashed houses cling to a hillside laced by steep staircases and topped with a ruined Venetian castle. Below, a promenade lined with tavernas and cafes hems in the fishing harbour. It's a slow-paced, friendly place where agriculture is the mainstay of the local economy.

A long, sandy beach skirts a wide bay to the east of town.

◎ Sights

Sitia Archaeological Museum   MUSEUM
(☑28430 23917; Kokefalou; adult/concession €2/1; ⊗8am-3pm Tue-Sun) This is a compact showcase of archaeological finds from eastern Crete spanning the arc from Neolithic to Roman times, with an emphasis on Minoan artefacts. Pride of place goes to the *Palekastro Kouros* – a statue carved from hippopotamus tusks that was once fully covered in gold leaf. Finds from the palace at Zakros include a wine press, a bronze saw and cult objects scorched by the fire that destroyed the palace.

Other notable finds are fragments of Linear A tablets found at Petras and Zakros as well as Minoan *larnakes* (clay coffins).

Venetian Fort   FORT
(Kazarma; ☑28430 27140; Neas Ionias; ⊗8am-3pm) FREE Strategically perched atop a hill near the port, this structure is locally called *kazarma* (from the Venetian *casa di arma*) and was built as a garrison by the Venetians. These are the only remains of the fortifications that once protected the town from marauders. The site is now used as an open-air venue.

🛏 Sleeping

Hotel El Greco   HOTEL €
(☑28430 23133; www.elgreco-sitia.gr; Arkadiou 13; d incl breakfast €40-45; 🅿❄🛜) This old-school hotel has smart and impeccably clean rooms

with tiled floors, nice but dated furniture, plasma TV, fridge and balcony (most with sea views). It's a good city hotel and a convenient base for short stays.

Sitia Bay Hotel   HOTEL €€
(☑28430 24800; www.sitiabay.com; Beach Rd, Patriarhou Vartholomaiou 27; d €85-125; ⊗reception 8am-8pm; 🅿❄🛜❄) This modern beachfront hotel has friendly service and comfortable and tastefully done-up studios and family apartments, all with kitchens, modern furniture and sea views. If the sand with loungers doesn't beckon, perhaps the pool does. At sunset, grab a drink at the bar and head to the rooftop terrace.

🍴 Eating

★**Mitsakakis**   BAKERY €
(☑28430 20200; Karamanli 6; galaktoboureko €2.90; ⊗6am-late; 🖐) This cafe and pastry shop is a Sitian institution (since 1965) and famous for its sugar-rush-inducing *galaktoboureko* (custard-filled pastry), *loukoumades* (ball-shaped doughnuts) and *kataifi* (angel hair pastry). Totally worth the calories!

★**Rakadiko Inodion**   GREEK €
(☑28430 26166; El Venizelou 157; mains €7.50-12; ⊗noon-late; 🐟) The best among the row of waterfront tavernas, this unpretentious family place offers a recognisable array of Greek dishes, but it's the local specials that truly shine. Anything with rabbit or goat is tops and best paired with the local wine. Many ingredients, including the oil, bread and raki, are produced by the Garefalakis family themselves.

Zorbas Taverna   TAVERNA €€
(Kazantzaki 3; mains €5.50-14; ⊗noon-late; 🐟) Gregarious owner Zorba, with his sailor's roll, sea captain's cap and bushy moustache, lays on the Greek clichés with a trowel and a wink. Bouzouki music accompanies the rich aromas of home-cooked food and grilled meats served at blue tables and chairs in his waterfront lair. Good for kids.

❶ Information

There are lots of ATMs and places to change money around the central square and side streets.

Police (☑28430 22259, 28430 24200; Therisou 31) Has a special tourist police unit during the summer months.

Post Office (📞28430 22283; Dimokritou 10; ⏰7.30am-2pm Mon-Fri)

Tzortzakis Travel (📞28430 29211; www.tzortzakistravel.com; Alexandrou & Papanastasiou Sts; ⏰9am-9pm Mon-Fri, to 5pm Sat) This full-service travel agency books rooms, flights and ferries and can also organise car hire.

ℹ Getting There & Away

AIR

The small communal **airport** (📞28430 24424) about 1km north of the town centre got a new terminal in 2016 and handles flights to Athens, Iraklio, Kassos, Karpathos and Rhodes as well as seasonal charter flights from northern Europe. A taxi into town costs €6 to €8.

BOAT

Ferries dock about 600m north of Plateia Iroön Polytechniou. **Anek/Aegeon Pelagos Sea Lines** (EP; 📞Hania 28210 24000; www.anek.gr) has ferries serving Anafi (€20, eight hours), Chalki (€20, 8¼ hours), Diafani (€18, six hours), Iraklio (€16, three hours), Karpathos (€19, 4½ hours), Kasos (€12, 2½ hours), Milos (€26, 14¼ hours), Piraeus (€44, 21½ hours), Rhodes (€28, 10½ hours) and Santorini (€28, 10 hours) on a seasonally changing schedule. Prices quoted are for deckchair seating.

BUS

Connections from Sitia's **bus station** (📞28430 22272; Sitias-Palekastro-Vai Rd) include five buses daily to Ierapetra (€6.90, 1¾ hours), six buses to Iraklio (€16, three hours), seven to Agios Nikolaos (€8.30, 1¾ hours) and two to Zakros (€4.50, one hour).

Around Sitia

Moni Toplou　　Μονή Τοπλού

Moni Toplou　　　　　　　　MONASTERY

(📞28430 61226; Toplou; €3; ⏰8am-6pm Apr-Oct) In splendid isolation on a windswept bluff, 15th-century Moni Toplou is one of the most historically significant monasteries in Crete whose defences were tested by everyone from pirates to crusading knights and the Turks. Its star attraction is the stunningly intricate *Lord Thou Art Great* icon by celebrated Cretan artist Ioannis Kornaros. Dozens of scenes from the Old and New Testaments are depicted here; look for Noah's Ark, Jonah and the Whale and Moses parting the Red Sea.

The fact that Moni Toplou looks more like a fortress than a monastery stems from the necessity imposed by the dangers it faced at the time of its construction. The monks defended themselves with all the means at their disposal, including a heavy gate, cannons (the name Toplou is Turkish for 'with a cannon') and small holes for pouring boiling oil onto the heads of their attackers.

Moni Toplou has repeatedly been active in the cause of Cretan independence. Under the Turkish occupation, a secret school operated in the monastery, and its reputation for hiding rebels led to severe reprisals. During WWII, Abbot Silingakis was executed after sheltering resistance leaders operating an underground radio transmitter. A small exhibit in the museum recalls this period with rifles, helmets and a field telephone. The adjacent main room displays engravings.

Moni Toplou is about 18km east of Sitia. Buses drop you at the junction of the Sitia–Palekastro road, from where it's a 3km walk.

Vaï　　　　　　　　　　Βάι

The beach at Vaï, 24km northeast of Sitia, is famous for its large grove of *Phoenix theophrasti* (Cretan date) palms. With calm, clear waters, it is one of Crete's most popular strands and its rows of umbrellas and sunbeds (€9) often fill by 10am in July and August. Jet skis kick into gear shortly thereafter.

If you want a nice beach without the crowd (or the palms), take the 1km scramble south over the rocky headland. The trail starts just past the gazebo lookout reached via stone steps leading up from the reasonably priced taverna on the south end of Vaï beach. Another trail leads north to Itanos beach in about 30 minutes, which is also often practically deserted and overlooked by Dorian ruins.

✕ Eating

Vaï Restaurant & Cafe　　　　　GREEK €

(📞28430 61129; www.vai-restaurant.gr; mains €8-12; ⏰9am-late Apr-Oct) There are lovely views of the palms and the white sand of Vaï beach from the covered terrace of this waterfront restaurant serving classic Greek fare, including fish and grilled meats. The cafe below has cold drinks, coffee and ice cream.

ℹ Getting There & Away

There are two daily buses to Vaï from Sitia (€3.30, one hour) from May to October. Parking costs €2.50.

Zakros & Kato Zakros
Ζάκρος & Κάτω Ζάκρος

POP 770

Zakros, 45km southeast of Sitia, is the starting point for the trail through Zakros Gorge, also known as the Valley of the Dead because of the Minoan burial caves that honeycomb the canyon cliffs. Zakros, however, is a mere prelude to coastal Kato Zakros, 7km down a winding road. Shortly before reaching the village, you can see the huge jaw of Zakros Gorge breaching the cliffs. Look closely and you can also make out the ruins of the Minoan palace just up from Kato Zakros' pebbly, narrow beach and row of tavernas. Add to all of this the isolated tranquillity and sense of peace, and you have the perfect recipe for escapism.

◎ Sights & Activities

Zakros Palace   ARCHAEOLOGICAL SITE
(☑ 28410 22462; Kato Zakros; adult/concession €6/3; ☉ 8am-8pm May-Sep, to 3pm Oct-Apr) Ancient Zakros, the smallest of Crete's four Minoan palatial complexes, was a major port, trading with Egypt, Syria, Anatolia and Cyprus. And, like the other three, it comprised royal apartments, shrines, storerooms and workshops grouped around a central courtyard. The exquisite rock-crystal vase and stone bull's head now in Iraklio's archaeological museum were among the treasure trove of antiquities found here. While the ruins are sparse, the wildness and remoteness of the setting make it an attractive place to explore.

Pelekita Cave   HIKING
(www.sitia-geopark.gr/en/activities/geotourism/hiking-trails/georoute-12.aspx) A 3.5km trail along the coast leads to this extraordinary 310m-long cave with magnificent views of the sea 100m below and signs of Neolithic habitation within its stalactite- and stalagmite-rich interior. To explore it bring a torch and trainers. It can only be reached on foot or by boat.

Near the cave is a limestone quarry that was used as building material for the Minoan palace at Kato Zakros. About 2km past the cave is the isolated Karoumes Beach.

Zakros Gorge   WALKING
(Gorge of the Dead; www.sitia-geopark.gr/en/activities/geotourism/hiking-trails/georoute-10.aspx) This easy-to-moderate 4km walk starts just below Zakros village and follows a dry riverbed through a narrow and (at times) soaring canyon with a riot of vegetation and wild herbs before emerging close to Zakros Palace right above the beach at Kato Zakros. For a shorter walk, pick up one of two trailheads on the road to Kato Zakros. 'Entrance A' is about 3km along, while 'Entrance B' is another 500m further on from there. A taxi back to Zakros costs about €12.

The canyon is also named Gorge of the Dead or Valley of the Dead because the Minoans used to buried their dead in caves on the rugged cliffs. The hike marks the final section of the more than 10,000km-long E4 European Path, which kicks off in Portugal.

🛏 Sleeping & Eating

Zakros is but a footnote to Kato Zakros and you should head to the latter for a spectrum of accommodation, from simple rooms to downright beautiful villas with a view. Rooms in Kato Zakros fill up fast in high season, so it is best to book.

Katerina Apartments   APARTMENT €
(☑ 28430 26893, 6974656617; www.kato-zakros.gr/_en/katerina.php; Kato Zakros; apt €50-60; 🅿 ❄ 🛜) These four stone-built studios and maisonettes can sleep up to four and enjoy a lovely setting in the hillside above Kato Zakros, with easy access to the beach, hiking trails and Minoan palace ruins. Units exude family-style hominess accented by the occasional lace doily and framed sunset photograph. All have kitchens and balconies.

★ Terra Minoika Villas   APARTMENT €€
(☑ 28430 23739; www.terraminoika.com; Kato Zakros; villa €100-150; ☉ mid-Jan–20 Dec; 🅿 ❄ 🛜) On the hillside high above the surf, these arty cube houses built of local stone are architectural symphonies of wood-beamed ceilings, widescreen views from balconies, chic rustic furniture, urns mounted on walls, and stone floors. Every villa is individual and has a fully equipped kitchenette.

Akrogiali Taverna   GREEK €
(☑ 28430 26893; Kato Zakros; mains €5-16; ☉ 8am-midnight; 🛜) The food gods have been smiling upon Kato Zakros' oldest taverna that does a brisk business in fresh-off-the-boat fish and Cretan classics, all prepared with locally sourced ingredients, including oil made from the owner's trees. The cheerful blue and white furniture and the beachfront setting add two more notches to its appeal.

ⓘ Getting There & Away

Two buses shuttle between Sitia and Zakros on Monday, Tuesday and Friday only (€4.50, one hour). A taxi costs about €50.

Ierapetra   Ιεράπετρα

POP 16,150

Ierapetra is a laid-back seafront town and the commercial centre of southeastern Crete's substantial greenhouse-based agribusiness. Hot and dusty in summer, it offers a low-key, authentic Cretan experience and is also the jumping-off point to the semitropical Gaïdouronisi Island (also called Hrysi).

The city's grey-sand beaches are backed by tavernas and cafes where the nightlife is busy in summer. Though little is left, Ierapetra has an impressive history with interludes as a Roman port and as a Venetian stronghold, as attested to by the harbour fortress. The narrow alleyways of the Turkish quarter recall its Ottoman period.

◎ Sights & Activities

There are usually a couple of departures in the morning to Gaïdouronisi (Hrysi Island), giving you 4½ hours on the island before returning to Ierapetra late afternoon (€25).

Archaeological Collection of Ierapetra   MUSEUM

(☑ 28420 28721; Plateia Kanoupaki; adult/concession €2/1; ◷ 8am-3pm Tue-Sun) A rectangular Ottoman-era school building shelters three rooms of dug-up treasures from regional archaeological sites. The first focuses on Minoan artefacts, including vases and jugs found at Episkopi. Room 2 features ornately decorated *larnakes*, including one with 12 panels of hunting scenes and a chariot procession. The last room is lined with headless Roman statues, which is why all eyes are on an intact 2nd-century-AD statue of the goddess Persephone.

Kales Fortress   FORTRESS

(Stratigou Samouil 10; ◷ 8am-3pm Tue-Sun) FREE South along the waterfront, the crenelled Venetian fort was built in the 13th century to protect the harbour, and in 1626 by Francesco Morosini. Climb up to the ramparts and the single tower for grand views of the bay and the mountains.

🛏 Sleeping & Eating

★ **Cretan Villa Hotel**   HOTEL €

(☑ 28420 28522; www.cretan-villa.com; Lakerda 16; d €47-56; ❈ ⭐) A heavy wooden door gives way to a vine-shaded courtyard at this restful, friendly space that's a happy coupling of historic touches and the gamut of mod cons. Beautiful rooms boast brick walls, elegantly rustic furniture, stone-tiled showers, wood-beamed ceilings, small fridges and satellite TV. A central city hotel with country flair.

Akrolithos Apartments   APARTMENT €€

(☑ 28420 28522; www.ierapetra-apartments.net; Mparitaki 22; apt €55-68; ❈ ⭐) Oozing ambience and comfort, these cosy apartments orbit a central courtyard and have such lovely traditional touches as fireplaces, well-equipped kitchenettes and loads of space. It's all in a great central location. Note that there is usually a three-night minimum stay.

Napoleon   GREEK €

(☑ 28420 22410; Stratigou Samouil 26; mains €5-12; ◷ noon-midnight; ⭐ ✍) This capacious traditional place looks just like any of the many tavernas lining Ierapetra's waterfront, but the quality of the home-cooking as well as the service are actually a cut above. Sit on the covered terrace flanked by palm trees and pick from the tasty line-up of fresh fish and Cretan specialities, including dolmadhes (vine leaves stuffed with rice and sometimes meat), snails, spinach pies and squid risotto.

🍷 Drinking & Nightlife

Ierapetra has the most lively after-dark scene in the region. The waterfront tavernas often bustle until the wee hours, and if you want to bust a move on the dance floor, look for the latest music lairs in the streets around the Archaeological Collection.

ⓘ Information

There are ATMs around Plateia Kanoupaki and along Koraka and Kothri.

Ierapetra Express (☑ 28420 22411; Kothri 2; ◷ 9am-9pm)

Post Office (Koraka 25; ◷ 7.30am-2.30pm Mon-Fri)

ⓘ Getting There & Away

BUS

KTEL operates eight buses per day to Iraklio (€12, 2½ hours) via Agios Nikolaos (€4.10, one hour), four to Sitia (€6.90, 1½ hours) and six to Myrtos (€2.40, 30 minutes).

TAXI

The **central taxi stand** (☑ 28420 26600; Kothri & Plateia Kanoupaki) with fixed fares posted on a board is outside the town hall. Sample fares:

Iraklio (€100), Agios Nikolaos (€50), Sitia (€83) and Myrtos (€20).

Myrtos — Μύρτος

POP 600

Tiny Myrtos, 14km west of Ierapetra, is a positively delightful little community: cheerful, trim and fringed by an apron of grey pebble-and-sand beach and bright-blue water. It has a devoted clientele that cherishes its slow boho pulse, flower-festooned guesthouses and a cluster of tavernas on its languid seafront. In short, it's a traveller's jewel, the perfect antidote to noise and haste.

🛏 Sleeping & Eating

Big Blue   APARTMENT €
(☎28420 51094; www.big-blue.gr; studio €60-85; 🅿 ❄ 🛜) Modern amenities meet trad-Greece in these breezy sea-facing studios decorated with plenty of imagination and attention to detail. Apartment 'Blue Eye', for instance, has a neat display of *mati* (evil eye); in fact, every room is different. Balconies boast expansive views and the fragrant garden out front is a good spot for sundowners.

Villa Mertiza   APARTMENT €€
(☎28420 51208, 6932735224; www.mertiza.com; studio/apt €61/81; ❄ 🛜) Owned by a friendly Dutch guy, these boho-chic and generously dimensioned studios and apartments with small kitchen are an excellent launch pad for days on the beach or in the mountains. Framed photographs, Moroccan wall hangings and colourful pillows provide cheerful accents. There's also a book exchange.

Thalassa Taverna   GREEK €
(☎28420 51301; www.facebook.com/Taverna thalassa; Waterfront Promenade; mains €8-16; ⏰10am-midnight; ❄ 🛜) This powder-blue, hole-in-the-wall waterfront restaurant has an interior festooned with coral and shells, and a few tables outside to tuck into mussels, calamari, cuttlefish, shrimps, octopus... Enough seafood to keep a shoal of mermaids quiet.

★ Katerina   CRETAN €€
(☎6948325739; mains €9-19.50; ⏰6pm-midnight; 🍴) Your taste buds will do somersaults at Katerina, where Yiannis is the kind of chef who puts a creative mark on even the most classic dishes. Sit back in the flower-filled alleyway to tuck into such flavour-bombs as lamb *kleftiko* (slow oven-baked), ouzo-

flambéed *saganaki* (fried cheese) and gooey chocolate cake. Foodies should enquire about Yiannis' **herb-collecting tours** and **cooking classes**.

ℹ Information

The nearest ATM is in Ierapetra.

ℹ Getting There & Away

There are six buses daily from Ierapetra (€2.40, 30 minutes). A taxi costs €20.

Lasithi Plateau — Οροπέδιο Λασιθίου

The tranquil Lasithi Plateau, 900m above sea level, is an arrestingly beautiful expanse of green fields interspersed with almond trees and orchards. Offering a sense of secluded rural Crete, it's really more of a plain than a plateau, sitting as it does in a huge depression amid the rock-studded mountains of the Dikti range. It's sparsely inhabited with just a few villages dotting the windswept expanse. The one that gets the most visitors is Psyhro, the gateway to the Dikteon Cave, where – so the myth goes – Zeus was hidden as an infant to protect him from his voracious father.

Lasithi must have been a stunning sight in the 17th century when it was dotted with some 20,000 windmills with white canvas sails, put up by the Venetians for irrigation purposes. The skeletal few that remain are an iconic (and much photographed) sight.

ℹ Getting There & Away

The plateau is not served by public buses. A taxi to Tzermiado or Psyhro costs about €60 from Heraklion and €50 from Agios Nikolaos. To cut costs, take a bus to Malia and a taxi from there (about €25).

Tzermiado — Τζερμιάδο

POP 635

The largest of Lasithi's 20 villages, Tzermiado is still a bucolic place and the gateway to the small Kronios Cave. There is only one main road running through town, plus a couple of ATMs and a post office on the main square.

◎ Sights

Kronios Cave   CAVE
(Trapeza Cave) FREE As you approach Tzermiado from the south, a sign directs you to the small Kronios Cave. Follow the path to

a series of stairs leading to the cave's narrow entrance. Excavations have yielded objects going back to Neolithic times when the cave was likely used as a shelter. During the Minoan period, it served as a burial site. Bring a torch and wear sneakers when exploring the two chambers with their stalagmites and stalactites, many of which have been tampered with by humans.

🛏 Sleeping & Eating

Argoulias APARTMENT €€
(☑ 28440 22754; www.argoulias.gr; Tzermiado; apt €50-80; ❄) Built into the hillside above the main village and constructed of exposed local stone, these self-catering apartments sleep up to five and have sweeping views across the Lasithi Plateau to the mountains. Traditional decor and furnishings exude comfort and a fireplace keeps things cosy in winter. Optional breakfast is €6 per person.

The owners also run an excellent restaurant across the road. Ask about use of bicycles. Look for signs to Argoulias at the entrance to Tzermiado coming from the east.

Taverna Kourites GREEK €
(☑ 28440 22054; Tzermiado; mains €6-10; ⊘ 9am-9pm) This spacious taverna on the outskirts of Tzermiado does a brisk lunchtime business with coaches full of day trippers. At other times, it's a peaceful spot where menu options include lamb and suckling pig roasted in a wood-fired oven. There are clean and simple rooms above the taverna and in a nearby hotel (doubles €40, breakfast €5).

Agios Georgios Αγιος Γεώργιος
POP 490

Dusty, wind-blown and faintly ghostly, Agios Georgios is a tiny village on the southern side of the Lasithi Plateau and one of the more pleasant places to stay in a fairly colourless bunch. If you have your own bicycle, you can base yourself here and explore the plateau at leisure.

◉ Sights

Folklore Museum MUSEUM
(☑ 6948501457, 28440 31382; adult/concession €3/2; ⊘ 10.30am-5pm Mon-Sat May-Oct) This five-room museum opens up a window on Crete's rural past with an eclectic collection of farming tools, wooden furniture, textiles, faded black-and-white photographs and WWII relics. There are also displays of traditional workshops of a carpenter or blacksmith. A separate building has great valley views but houses a rather turgid exhibit on political legend Eleftherios Venizelos.

🛏 Sleeping & Eating

Hotel Maria HOTEL €
(☑ 28440 31774; http://mariahotelagiosgeorgios. blogspot.de; d incl breakfast €40; ⊘ May-Oct) These pleasantly quirky rooms on the northern side of the village are in a building fronted by a leafy garden. The traditional mountain beds are rather narrow and are on stone bases. Local furnishings and woven wall hangings add to the cheerful atmosphere.

Taverna Rea GREEK €
(☑ 28440 31774; Main St; mains €6-8; ⊘ 10am-9pm) This cheerful little restaurant has stone walls decorated with Cretan artefacts. The owner-chef does a mean souvlaki and if there's lamb on offer, it'll likely be excellent as well. Upstairs are four rooms (€30) with twin beds and bathroom.

Psyhro & Dikteon Cave Ψυχρό & Δικταίον Αντρον

Psyhro is the closest village to the Dikteon Cave and is often clogged with tour buses. It has one main street, a sword-waving memorial statue, a few tavernas and plenty of souvenir shops. Buses stop at the northern end of town, from where it's about a 1km walk uphill to the cave.

◉ Sights

Dikteon Cave CAVE
(Cave of Psyhro; ☑ 28410 22462; http://odysseus. culture.gr; adult/concession €6/3; ⊘ 8am-8pm Apr-Oct, 8am-3pm Nov-Mar) According to legend, Rhea hid in this cave to give birth to Zeus, far from the clutches of his offspring-gobbling father Cronos. A slick and vertiginous staircase corkscrews into the damp dark, passing overhanging stalactites and ethereal formations. It's a steep 800m walk to the cave entrance, either via a rocky but shaded natural trail or the sunny paved path starting near the car park.

The most famous formation is a stalactite nicknamed 'the mantle of Zeus' in the larger chamber on the right side. Votives found in the cave indicate that it was a place of cult worship from Minoan to Roman times. Some are now on display at the Archaeological Museum in Iraklio.

Dodecanese

Includes ➜

Best Places to Eat

➜ Marco Polo Cafe (p335)

➜ Taverna Mylos (p386)

➜ To Ellenikon (p347)

➜ Tholos (p357)

➜ Pote Tin Kyriaki (p371)

Best Places to Stay

➜ Marco Polo Mansion (p332)

➜ Harry's Paradise (p385)

➜ Archontariki (p393)

➜ Old Markets (p357)

➜ In Camera Art Boutique Hotel (p333)

Why Go?

Ever pined for the old Greece, where timeless islands beckon modern-day adventurers just as they did Odysseus and Alexander? Enter the far-flung Dodecanese (Δωδεκάνησα; do-de-*ka*-ni-sa) archipelago, curving through the southeastern Aegean parallel to the ever-visible shoreline of Turkey. The footprints of everyone from Greeks and Romans to crusading medieval knights, and Byzantine and Ottoman potentates to 20th-century Italian bureaucrats, are found here. Beyond better-known Rhodes and Kos, enigmatic islands beg to be explored.

Hikers and naturalists flock to Tilos, while climbers scale the limestone cliffs in Kalymnos. Aesthetes adore the neoclassical mansions of Symi, Halki and Kastellorizo, divers explore underwater caves and ancient wrecks, and kitesurfers blow in to Karpathos for its legendary winds. Archaeologists and history buffs let their imaginations loose on a bevy of ancient sites, while sybarites can worship Helios on myriad beaches, far from the package crowds.

When to Go
Rhodes

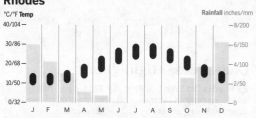

| **Apr & May** Prices are low, few tourists are around and the sea is warming up. | **Jul & Aug** Peak season for accommodation and visitors – book ahead. | **Sep & Oct** Great time to come: low prices, warm seas and perfect hiking weather. |

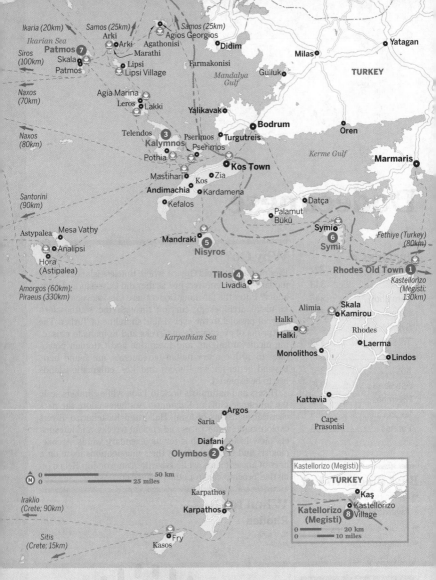

Dodecanese Highlights

1 Rhodes Old Town (p328) Wandering beneath Byzantine arches and along ancient cobbled alleyways.

2 Olymbos (p349) Following the winding road up to this timeless village.

3 Kalymnos (p379) Testing your mettle diving for wrecks or climbing limestone cliffs.

4 Tilos (p359) Hiking or birdwatching on this postcard-perfect island.

5 Nisyros (p363) Entering its fabled volcano, home to an imprisoned Titan.

6 Symi (p354) Feeling your pulse quicken as your boat pulls into the gorgeous Italianate harbour.

7 Patmos (p390) Making the pilgrimage to where St John experienced his 'Revelations'.

8 Kastellorizo (Megisti) (p352) Gasping in awe at the largest and most dramatic of blue caves in the Mediterranean.

History

The Dodecanese islands have been inhabited since pre-Minoan times. After the death of Alexander the Great in 323 BC, they were ruled by Ptolemy I of Egypt. The islanders later became the first Greeks to convert to Christianity, thanks to the tireless efforts of St Paul, who made two journeys to the archipelago during the 1st century, and St John the Divine, who was banished to Patmos, where he had his revelation and added a chapter to the Bible.

The early Byzantine era saw the islands prosper, but by the 7th century AD they were being plundered by a string of invaders. The Knights of St John of Jerusalem, who arrived during the 14th century, eventually ruled almost all the Dodecanese. Their mighty fortifications have proved strong enough to withstand time, but failed to keep out the Turks in 1522.

The Turks were in turn ousted in 1912 by the Italians, who made Italian the official language and banned the Orthodox religion. Inspired by Mussolini's vision of a vast Mediterranean empire, they also constructed grandiose public buildings in the fascist style, the antithesis of archetypal Greek architecture. More beneficially, they excavated and restored many archaeological monuments.

After the Italian surrender of 1943, the islands (particularly Leros) became a battleground for British and German forces, inflicting much suffering upon the population. The Dodecanese were formally returned to Greece in 1947.

RHODES   ΡΟΔΟΣ

POP 115,000

By far the largest and historically the most important of all the Dodecanese islands, Rhodes (*ro*-dos) abounds in sandy beaches, wooded valleys and ancient history. Whether you arrive in search of buzzing nightlife, languid sun worshipping, diving in crystal-clear waters or to embark on a culture-vulture journey through past civilisations, it's all here. The atmospheric Old Town of Rhodes is a maze of cobbled streets that will spirit you back to the days of the Byzantine Empire and beyond. Further south is the picture-perfect town of Lindos, a soul-warming vista of sugar-cube houses spilling down to a turquoise bay.

History

The Minoans and Mycenaeans were among the first to have outposts on Rhodes, but only with the arrival of the Dorians in 1100 BC – settling in Kamiros, Ialysos and Lindos – did the island begin to make itself felt. Switching allegiances like a pendulum, Rhodes was allied to Athens when the Persians were defeated in the Battle of Marathon (490 BC), but had shifted to the Persian side by the time of the Battle of Salamis (480 BC).

After the unexpected Athenian victory at Salamis, Rhodes hastily aligned itself with Athens once more, joining the Delian League in 477 BC. Following the disastrous Sicilian Expedition (416–412 BC), Rhodes revolted against Athens and hooked up with Sparta instead, aiding it in the Peloponnesian Wars. In 408 BC the cities of Kamiros, Ialysos and Lindos consolidated their powers, co-founding the city of Rhodes. Rhodes became Athens' ally again to defeat Sparta at the Battle of Knidos (394 BC). Rhodes then joined forces with Persia to fight against Alexander the Great, only to attach itself to Alexander when he proved invincible.

In 305 BC Antigonus, a rival of Ptolemy, sent his formidable son, Demetrius Poliorketes – Besieger of Cities – to conquer Rhodes. When the city repelled Demetrius it built a 32m-high bronze statue of Helios Apollo to celebrate. Known as the Colossus of Rhodes, it was later hailed as one of the Seven Wonders of the Ancient World.

Rhodes then built the biggest navy in the Aegean, and its port became a principal Mediterranean trading centre. The arts also flourished. When Greece became the arena in which Roman generals fought for leadership of the empire, Rhodes allied itself with Julius Caesar. After Caesar's assassination in 44 BC, Cassius besieged the city, destroying its ships and carting its artworks off to Rome. Rhodes went into decline and became part of the Roman Empire in AD 70.

Rhodes eventually joined the Byzantine province of the Dodecanese and was granted independence when the Crusaders seized Constantinople. Later, the Genoese gained control. The Knights of St John arrived in 1309, and ruled Rhodes for 213 years until being ousted by the Ottomans. They were in turn kicked out by the Italians nearly four centuries later. In 1947, after 35 years of Italian occupation, Rhodes became part of Greece, along with the other Dodecanese islands.

❶ Getting There & Away

AIR

Diagoras Airport (RHO; ☑ 22410 88700; www.
rhodes-airport.org) is near Paradisi on the west
coast, 16km southwest of Rhodes Town.

Aegean Airlines (☑ 22410 98345; www.
aegeanair.com; Diagoras Airport; ⏲ 4.30am-
9pm) flies to Astypalea, Athens, Heraklion,
Kalymnos, Kastellorizo and Karpathos, as well
as Leros and Thessaloniki.

Olympic Air (☑ 22410 24571; www.olympicair.
com; Ierou Lohou 9) has connections with
Athens and destinations throughout Greece,
including several Dodecanese islands. Flights
to the nearby islands of Kassos, Karpathos and
Kastellorizo are more frequent than the corresponding ferries and more, with fares starting at less
than €65, only slightly more expensive.

Sky Express (☑ 28102 23800; www.sky
express.gr) flies up to six days a week to Heraklion on Crete (€80, one hour) and once weekly
to Samos (€72, 45 minutes).

BOAT
Domestic

Rhodes is the main port in the Dodecanese.
Two inter-island ferry companies operate from
immediately outside the walls of Rhodes Old
Town. **Dodekanisos Seaways** (☑ 22410 70590;
www.12ne.gr; Afstralias 3, Rhodes Town) runs
daily high-speed catamarans north up the chain,
while **Blue Star Ferries** (☑ 22410 22461; www.
bluestarferries.com; 111 Amerikis; ⏲ 9am-8pm)
provides slower and less frequent services to
several of the same islands, continuing west to
Astypalea and Piraeus. It also heads southwest
to Karpathos, Kasos and Crete. Tickets are
available at the dock and from travel agents in
Rhodes Town.

The tiny port at **Skala Kamirou**, 45km southwest of Rhodes Town, has a daily ferry service
to the island of Halki, operated by **Nissos
Halki** (☑ mobile 6946519817, 6973460968)
and **Nikos Express** (☑ mobile 6946826905).
There's an hour-long connecting bus service
with Rhodes Old Town.

In addition, daily excursion boats head to Symi
from Mandraki Harbour in summer (day trips
only, €25) while **catamarans** to Turkey leave
from Kolona Harbour. Check out the boats at the
harbour before you decide which to take.

International

Catamarans connect Rhodes' Commercial Harbour with Marmaris, Turkey (50 minutes), with
two daily services in summer and two weekly in
winter. Tickets cost €36 each way. Same-day
returns cost €39, and longer-stay returns, €70.
For schedules and bookings, visit www.rhodes.
marmarisinfo.com.

Boat Services from Rhodes

DESTINATION	DURATION	FARE (€)	FREQUENCY
Agathonisi*	5hr	49	1 weekly
Astypalea	9hr	24	1 weekly
Halki	2hr	8	2 weekly
Halki*	1¼hr	17	2 weekly
Kalymnos	6hr	20	3 weekly
Kalymnos*	3hr	39	1 daily
Karpathos	5hr 40min	21	3 weekly
Kasos	8hr	25	3 weekly
Kastellorizo	4hr 40min	19.50	2 weekly
Kastellorizo*	2hr 20min	37	1 weekly
Kos	5hr	24.50	4 weekly
Kos*	2½hr	32	1 daily
Leros	8hr	32.50	3 weekly
Leros*	3½hr	42	6 weekly
Lipsi	9hr	24.50	1 weekly
Lipsi*	5½hr	47	6 weekly
Nisyros	4hr	13.50	2 weekly
Nisyros*	2¾hr	27	2 weekly
Patmos	10hr	37.50	3 weekly
Patmos*	5hr	49	5 weekly
Piraeus	18hr	63.60	1 daily
Samos	6hr 40min	39	3 weekly
Sitia	11hr	28	1 weekly
Symi	1hr 40min	14	2 weekly
Symi*	50min	18	1-4 daily
Tilos	2½hr	13.50	2 weekly
Tilos*	2hr	26	2 weekly

All services are from Commercial Harbour.
* high-speed services

Rhodes Town   Ρόδος

POP 86,000

Rhodes Town is really two distinct and
very different towns. The **Old Town** lies
within but utterly apart from the New
Town, sealed like a medieval time capsule
behind a double ring of high walls and a
deep moat. Nowhere else in the Dodecanese can boast so many layers of architectural history, with ruins and relics of the
Classical, medieval, Ottoman and Italian
eras entangled in a mind-boggling maze
of twisting alleys. Strolling its hauntingly
pretty cobbled lanes, especially at night,
is an experience no traveller should miss.

Rhodes

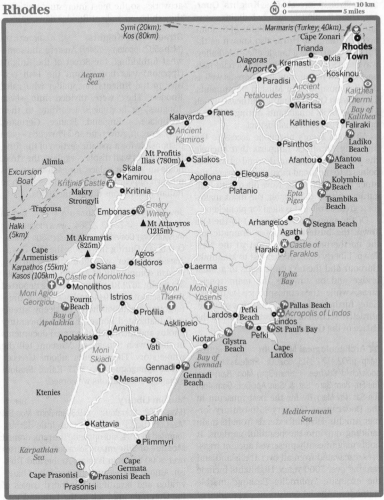

Half the fun is letting yourself get lost. The **New Town**, to the north, boasts upscale shops and waterfront bars servicing the package crowd, along with the city's best beach, while bistros and bars lurk in the backstreets behind.

Inter-island ferries and catamarans use the **Commercial Harbour**, immediately outside the walls east of the Old Town, while excursion boats and private yachts are based at **Mandraki Harbour**, further north beside the New Town.

◉ Sights

◉ Old Town

A glorious mixture of Byzantine, Turkish and Italian architecture, erected atop far more ancient and largely unidentifiable remains, the Old Town is a world of its own. In theory, it consists of three separate sections, though casual visitors seldom notice the transition from one to the next. To the north, sturdy stone mansions, known as inns, housed knights from various countries and line the arrow-straight streets of the **Knights' Quarter**. These fabulously austere buildings were laid out by the medieval Knights of St John. South of that, the **Hora**, also known as the Turkish Quarter, is a tangle of cobbled alleyways that's now the main commercial hub, packed with restaurants and shops as well as derelict mosques and Muslim monuments. The **Jewish Quarter** in the southeast, which lost most of its inhabitants during WWII, is now a sleepy residential district.

Although there's no public access to the imposing 12m-thick ramparts that encircle the Old Town, you can descend at various points into the broad moat that separates the inner and outer walls. Now filled with lush gardens rather than water, the moat makes for a great stroll and is ideal for picnickers.

Of the nine *pyles* (gateways) to the Old Town, the busiest and most dramatic are the northernmost two, closest to the New Town. Liberty Gate, the nearest to Mandraki Harbour and the taxi rank, leads to a small bridge and on towards the main tourist areas, while the atmospheric D'Amboise Gate, further inland, crosses an especially attractive section of the moat en route to the Palace of the Grand Master.

★ **Archaeological Museum**   MUSEUM
(Map p502; ☑ 22413 65200; Plateia Mousiou; adult/child €8/free; ☉ 9am-3pm Mon, 8am-8pm Tue-Fri, 8am-3pm Sat & Sun Apr-Oct, 9am-4pm Tue-Sat Nov-Mar) By far the best museum in the Dodecanese, this airy 15th-century former Knights' Hospital extends from its main building out into the beautiful gardens. It holds magnificently preserved ancient treasures, excavated from all over the island and ranging over 7000 years. Highlights include the exquisite 'Aphrodite Bathing' marble statue from the 1st century BC, a pavilion of wall-mounted mosaics, and a reconstructed burial site from 1700 BC that held not only a helmeted warrior but also his horse.

Palace of the Grand Master HISTORIC BUILDING
(Map p502; ☑ 22413 65270, 22410 23359; €6; ☉ 8am-8pm May-Oct, 8am-4pm Tue-Sun Nov-Apr) From the outside, the magnificent Palace of the Grand Master looks much as it did when erected by the Knights Hospitaller during the 14th century. During the 19th century, however, it was devastated by an explosion, so the interior is an Italian reconstruction, completed in the '18th year of the Fascist Era' (1940). The dreary magisterial chambers upstairs hold haphazard looted artworks, so the most interesting section is the exhibit on ancient Rhodes downstairs.

Street of the Knights   HISTORIC SITE
(Map p502; Ippoton; ☉ 24hr) Austere and somewhat forbidding, the Street of the Knights (Ippoton) was home from the 14th century to the Knights Hospitaller who ruled Rhodes. They were divided into seven 'tongues', or languages according to their birthplace – England, France, Germany, Italy, Aragon, Auvergne and Provence – each responsible for a specific section of the fortifications. As wall displays explain, the street holds an 'inn', or palace, for each tongue. Its modern appearance, though, owes much to Italian restorations during the 1930s.

Jewish Synagogue Museum   MUSEUM
(Map p502; ☑ 22410 22364; www.rhodesjewish museum.org; Dosiadou; ☉ 10am-3pm Sun-Fri May-Oct) FREE During the 1920s, the Old Town's Jewish Quarter was home to a thriving Jewish community of around 4000 people. Tragically, 1673 Rhodian Jews were deported to Auschwitz in 1944 and it's now a time-forgotten neighbourhood of sleepy streets and dilapidated houses. Early-20th-century photos and intricately decorated documents in the Jewish Synagogue Museum tell the whole story. The museum adjoins Greece's oldest synagogue, the 1577 Kahal Shalom Synagogue. Donations welcomed.

Muslim Library   LIBRARY
(Map p502; Sokratous; ☉ 9.30am-3pm Mon-Sat May-Oct) FREE This peaceful little library, founded in 1794, sits opposite the pink-domed **Mosque of Süleyman** (Sokratous), and houses over 2000 books in Persian, Arabic and Turkish. Among its treasures are a couple of hand-written and beautifully illustrated copies of the Quran dating back to the 15th and 16th centuries. Donations welcomed.

◉ New Town

The so-called New Town of Rhodes has existed for 500 years, since Ottoman conquerors drove the local Greek population to build new homes outside the city walls. Almost nothing in the area, north of the Old Town and centred on Mandraki Harbour and the casino, though, holds any historic interest. Instead the New Town is a modern resort area, alive with guesthouses and restaurants, from gleaming hotel monoliths to tiny tavernas, along with banks, boutiques and the businesses that keep Rhodes ticking along.

The town **beach**, starting north of Mandraki Harbour, stretches around the island's northernmost point and down the west side of the New Town. The best spots tend to be on the east side, where there's usually calmer water and more sand and facilities.

Modern Greek Art Museum   GALLERY
(Map p506; ☎22410 43780; www.mgamuseum. gr; Plateia Haritou; €3; ☺8am-8pm Tue-Sat) The main gallery of the Modern Greek Art Museum, near the New Town's northern tip, holds paintings, engravings and sculptures by Greece's greatest 20th-century artists, including Gaitis Giannis, Vasiliou Spiros and Katraki Vaso. The museum's other three sites – the Nestoridi Building and the Centre of Modern Art, both in the New Town, and the original Art Gallery, in the Old Town – are currently closed because of a lack of available funding.

Rhodes Aquarium   AQUARIUM
(Map p506; ☎22410 27308; www.rhodes-aquarium. hcmr.gr; Kos 1; adult/child €5.50/3.50; ☺9am-8.30pm Apr-Oct, to 4.30pm Nov-Mar) The New Town's modest aquarium is housed in an art deco building constructed by the Italians in the 1930s. Its interior is imaginatively kitted out like an underwater cave, and there are touch tanks where you can lay hands on rays, starfish and other squirming sea beasts. All the sea life featured here can be found in the Aegean, including the most recent acquisition – a lionfish caught by a fisherman just a few miles from here.

Acropolis of Rhodes   ARCHAEOLOGICAL SITE
(☺24hr) **FREE** The site of the ancient Hellenistic city of Rhodes, now known as the Acropolis of Rhodes, stretches up the slopes of Monte Smith, 2km southwest of the Old Town. Restored structures include a tree-lined stadium from the 2nd century BC and the adjacent theatre, originally used for lectures by the Rhodes School of Rhetoric. Steps climb from there to the Temple of Pythian Apollo. Get here on city bus 5, or a stiff half-hour hike.

🏃 Activities & Tours

The quay along Mandraki Harbour, on the east side of the New Town, is lined with boats offering all sorts of excursions, including day trips to island beaches, the island of Symi and to Turkey. There are also glass-bottomed boats for kids' rides around the harbour, and well-established PADI-licensed diving operators who advertise their businesses from their moored boats. New to the town is 9D: Throne of Helios (p337), a terrific multi-sensory cinema experience.

Rhodes Segway Tours   HISTORY
(Map p502; ☎6983245246, 22411 12409; www. rhodessegwaytours.com; Miltiadou 8, Old Town; €59; ☺9am-8pm; 🖪) 🖉 A sightseeing experience like no other, this is a brilliant way to spare your energy and see more of the Old Town, rolling soundlessly past ancient buildings on your Segway with your expert guide chatting away as if it was perfectly normal! Tours last two hours. Training provided. Helmets required! Also does night tours (€85).

Rhodes Mystery
Escape Room   ESCAPE ROOM
(Map p502; ☎22410 34660; www.rhodesmystery. com; Sofokleous 222; for two €40, for five €50; ☺10am-10pm; 🖪) Can you solve the mystery of the Grand Master's diamond? Or find the missing Italian pilot? It's hugely popular and great fun: you must find the clues to escape from one of two themed rooms – the Medieval Room or the Italian Room. There's a maximum of five sleuths per room, you have an hour to solve the mystery. Hidden down an alleyway beside Sofokleous.

Waterhoppers Diving Centre   DIVING
(☎22410 38146; www.waterhoppers.com) Operating out of Mandraki Harbour and several other bases on the island, Waterhoppers offers an 'experience scuba' one-day program (€85) and a range of diving courses, including two- and three-day PADI open-water certifications. Choose from night, wreck and cave dives if you're an advanced diver.

Trident Scuba Diving School   DIVING
(Map p506; ☎22410 29160; www.tridentdiving school.com; Mandraki Harbour; 🖪) Trident offers a range of diving courses and dive spots around the north of the island. It also runs beginner classes and two- and three-day PADI-certified courses. Look out for Trident's boat, *Armonia*, on Mandraki Harbour for more info.

🛏 Sleeping

The most magical sleeping options are all in the Old Town. In summer it's essential to reserve ahead. In winter, most budget options close altogether. Be warned, too, that most Old Town hotels are not accessible by taxi, so you'll have to haul your luggage along the narrow, cobbled lanes. Some hotels have golf carts in which to pick you up.

DODECANESE RHODES

Rhodes Old Town

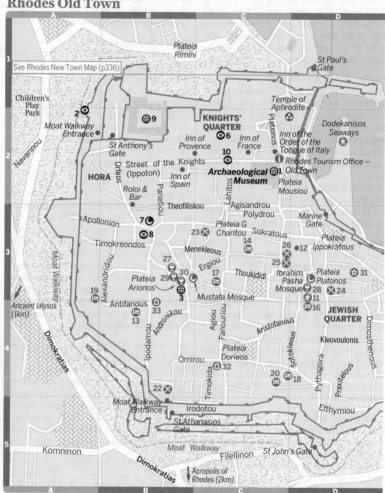

Plateia Rimini

St Paul's Gate

See Rhodes New Town Map (p336)

Children's Play Park

2

Moat Walkway Entrance

St Anthony's Gate

Navarinou

9

KNIGHTS' QUARTER

Temple of Aphrodite

Dodekanisos Seaways

Inn of Provence

6

Inn of France

Inn of the Order of the Tongue of Italy

HORA

Orfeos

Street of the Knights (Ippoton)

Panetiou

Inn of Spain

10

Archaeological Museum

Rhodes Tourism Office – Old Town **1**

Plateia Mousiou

Roloi & Bar

Theofiliskou

Lahitos

Agisandrou Polydrou

Marine Gate

Apollonion

Timokreondos

7

8

23

Plateia G Charitou

Sokratous

Plateia Ippokratous

Menekleous

14

26 ● **12**

Alexandriou

27

Ergiou

25

Ibrahim Pasha Mosque

Plateia Platonos

31

30

17

Thoukididi

28

24

Plateia Arionos

29

3

Mustafa Mosque

11

16

19

Antifanous

33

13

Andronikou

Ipodamou

Agiou Fanouriou

Aristofanous

JEWISH QUARTER

Dimosthenous

Kleovoulonis

Moat Walkway

Ancient Ialysos (1km)

Plateia Dorieos

Omirou

32

Sotokleous

Pythagora

Praxitelous

Dimokratias

22

Timokida

20

18

Moat Walkway Entrance

Irodotou

Efthymiou

St Athanasios Gate

Komninon

Moat Walkway

Filellinon

St John's Gate

Dimokratias

Acropolis of Rhodes (2km)

🛏 Old Town

Minos Pension
PENSION €

(Map p502; ☏ 22410 31813; www.minospension.com; 5 Omirou St; d/ste €46/80; ❄@🌐) Family-run Minos, perched beside a disused windmill on a quiet lane on the south side of the Old Town, has well-appointed, if slightly old-fashioned, studio rooms with gleaming kitchenettes and fridge. The compelling attraction, though, is the fabulous rooftop cafe, a lovely spot offering superb Old Town views. Downstairs there's a cosy communal lounge and book exchange.

★ Marco Polo Mansion
BOUTIQUE HOTEL €€

(Map p502; ☏ 22410 25562; www.marcopolomansion.gr; Agiou Fanouriou 40; d incl breakfast €80-260; ☺Apr-Oct; ❄🌐) With its stained-glass windows, dark-wood furniture, wood floors and raised beds, Marco Polo lovingly recreates an Ottoman ambience with verve and style, and is unlike anything in the Old Town. This former 15th-century pasha's house, complete with its own harem (now a magical suite), is like a journey back in time. Breakfast is served in the stunning flowering courtyard.

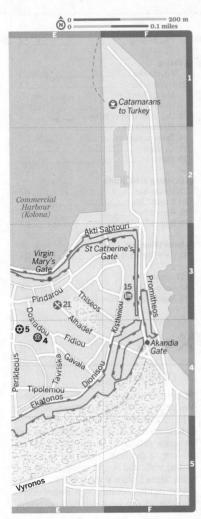

Antifanou Apartments APARTMENT €€

(Map p502; ☑ 22410 34561; Antifanouapartments@
gmail.com; Antifanous 5-9; apt €90; ✴️🛜) These
two well-equipped apartments and single
studio are stylish and serenely cool courtesy of the original stone walls and arches.
Also, for larger families, two of them can be
interconnected. Each apartment has two
separate bedrooms, a communal area in the
kitchen and an outside communal terrace
which, chances are, you'll have to yourself.

Evdokia Hotel BOUTIQUE HOTEL €€

(Map p502; ☑ 22410 77077; www.evdokiahotel.com;
Evdoxou 75; s/d/tr €70/85/150; ✴️🛜) Situated
in a 13th-century building, this peaceful
hotel has welcoming rooms with wrought-
iron beds, cream walls, satellite TV, minibar
and safety deposit boxes, based around a
stunning high-ceiling lobby and breakfast
room. The best of the rooms is a triple with
its own staircase and roof terrace. Traditional
Rhodian breakfast with homemade marmalade, zucchini and fruit costs €8 extra.

Hotel Cava d'Oro B&B €€

(Map p502; ☑ 22410 36980; www.cavadoro.com;
Kisthiniou 15; s/d/tr incl breakfast €110/130/160;
P✴️🛜) Originally a storage building dating
from the era of the Knights of St John, this
small family-run hotel offers characterful
rooms of varying sizes, with canopied beds,
exposed stone walls and high arching ceilings.
Breakfast is served in a cool garden courtyard,
and guests can even walk on the hotel's own
short stretch of the Old Town walls.

⭐**Spirit of the Knights** BOUTIQUE HOTEL €€€

(Map p502; ☑ 22410 39765; www.rhodesluxuryhotel.
com; Alexandridou 14; s/d incl breakfast from
€160/200; ➡️✴️🛜) This gorgeously finished
boutique hotel has six stunning suites dripping with medieval atmosphere. Imagine
thick rugs, dark woods, stained-glass windows and a sense of tranquillity. Perfectly isolated down a sidestreet close to the Old Town
walls, this fine hotel is a work of passion and
vision. There's a library and a fragrant garden
courtyard to read in and take breakfast.

⭐**In Camera Art
Boutique Hotel** BOUTIQUE HOTEL €€€

(Map p502; ☑ 22410 77277; www.incamera.gr;
Sofokleous 35; r/ste/villa incl breakfast €142/
270/380; ➡️✴️🛜) Sixteen years in the making, this stunning design hotel looks out on
ancient ruins, and has four very different
suites and two rooms, named after the exhibitions of the hotel's owner, a famous Greek

The Andreas HOTEL €€

(Map p502; ☑ 22410 34156; www.hotelandreas.
com; Omirou 28d; ste incl breakfast €80; ☼ May–
late Oct; ✴️@🛜) Nicely described by its Cal-
ifornian owner as a 'four-star hotel trapped
in the soul of a small Greek pension', this
former pasha's house has three suites each
with two rooms. Best is the Tower Suite
where you wake each morning in your traditional raised bed to a view of the Aegean
below, while the Terrace Suite has its own
private sun terrace. Five-night minimum
stay.

Rhodes Old Town

photographer. The highlight is the 'Forms of Light' suite with three levels, stained-glass windows, beautifully finished bedrooms and two roof terraces. There's also a breakfast cafe and garden with Jacuzzi.

New Town

Hotel Anastasia
PENSION **€€**
(Map p506; ☑ 22410 28007; www.anastasia-hotel.com; 28 Oktovriou 46; s/d/tr €55/65/85; ❈ @ 🛜) The New Town's friendliest and most peaceful accommodation option is found in a handsome villa set back from the road, with ochre-coloured rooms with wooden shutters, tiled floors and traditional furnishings. Some have private balconies and there's an inviting breakfast bar in the lush garden. Owner Mihalis is welcoming.

Florida Hotel
HOTEL **€€**
(Map p506; ☑ 22410 22111; www.florida-rhodes.com; Amarandou 5; r from €50) Small, simple, modern hotel in a quiet little pedestrian street towards the New Town's northern tip. Crisp, clean, whitewashed rooms have kitchenettes and air-con, and each has its own flower-bedecked terrace or balcony. Yvonne, the owner, is helpful and offers you her own hand-drawn maps of the area. A short walk to the beach.

 Eating

Old Town

★ Taverna Kostas
GREEK **€**
(Map p502; ☑ 22410 26217; Pythagora 62; mains €7-10; ☉ 10am-late; ❈) Run by grandfather Kostas, this is not only the friendliest and best-value restaurant in the Old Town but also one of the best. Forget the bare lime-washed walls and simple decor, eating here is like taking a place at the table of a friend – indeed, regulars set their own places! Serves succulent octopus salad, calamari, sea bream.

Old Town Corner Bakery
BAKERY **€**
(Map p502; ☑ 22410 38494; Omirou 88; snacks €2-6; ☉ 8am-9pm; 🛜) With jazz and aromatic arabica coffee drifting through this tiny bakery cafe and out onto street where there a few stools, this is an Old Town residents' favourite. Has amazing pastries – dawn-fresh croissants sell out very quickly – club sandwiches, baklava (filo pastry with nuts and honey), apple pie and a host of healthy juices.

To Marouli
GREEK **€**
(Map p502; ☑ 22413 04394; Platonos 22; mains €8-10; ☉ noon-10pm; ❈🛜🖋) 🖋 'Marouli' means lettuce, and in this stylish, veggie-only restaurant, that's exactly what you can

expect: plenty of greens. But for the pasta, which comes from Italy, the menu changes daily, dependent on the availability of locally grown food. Some examples include vegan Thai pineapple and fried rice, and mushroom and zucchini strudel with salad.

Yianni's GREEK €

(Map p502; ☑ 22410 36535; yianis.restaurant@gmail.com; Socratous Platonos 41; mains €7-10; ⏲10am-late; 🐦) Follow the songbird to the old lady dressed in colourful Karpathian garb and settle indoors, or sit al fresco to experience some of the best authentic Greek food in town. Alongside the usual favourites are dishes like *youvesti* (fried pork in tomato and wine sauce), and *makarounes* (Karpathian buttered pasta fried with onion).

Fournariko BAKERY €

(Map p502; ☑ 22410 43057; Platonos; mains €7-12; ⏲7am-late; 🐦🐦) While the main dining room serves up tasty Italian dishes, including pizza straight from the brick-bake oven, Fournariko is first and foremost a bakery, with alluring trays of sweet and savoury pies and filo pastries. Get here early morning for super-fresh bakes, grab a table outside and enjoy a spot of people-watching over coffee.

⭐**Marco Polo Cafe** MEDITERRANEAN €€

(Map p502; ☑ 22410 25562; www.marcopolomansion.gr; Agiou Fanouriou 40-42; mains €12-25; ⏲7-11pm) 🍴 Don't be surprised if you are asked to taste a new wine or culinary creation, a possible new addition to the menu of regulars, such as skewered lamb with rosemary and pistachio, pork loin with figs, Greek risotto with sea bream, or octopus in sea-urchin sauce. It's served up with sincerity and style in a lemon-fragrant garden courtyard.

Nireas SEAFOOD €€

(Map p502; ☑ 22410 21703; Sofokleous 45-47; mains €8-16; ⏲lunch & dinner; 🐦) Nireas' status as one of Rhodes' favourite seafood restaurants owes much to the sheer verve of genial owner Theo – that and the beautifully prepared food, served beneath a vine-shaded canopy, or in the candlelit, lemon-walled interior. Be sure to sample the Symi shrimp, salted mackerel and, if you're in the mood, the 'Viagra' salad of small shellfish.

Petaladika GREEK €€

(Map p502; ☑ 22410 27319; Menakleous 8; mains €8-15; ⏲noon-late) Petaladika might look like just another tourist trap, tucked into a corner just off the main drag, but with its fresh, white, wood interior and chic tables and chairs out front, it's a hot favourite with locals, and a mainstay of the Old Town dining scene. Try the deep-fried baby squid, zucchini balls and freshly grilled fish.

Hatzikelis SEAFOOD €€

(Map p502; ☑ 22410 27215; www.hatzikelis.gr; Alhadef 9; mains €10-25; 🐦🐦🐦) With its candelabra and velvet finery, Hatzikelis is patronised by gourmands and Hollywood Grecophiles who return to savour the sea urchin, scallops, lobster, swordfish and freshly caught grouper. Ask to see the catch, bathed in ice in huge silver refrigerators. There's also terrific cutlets and steak, and a vast wine selection. Surprisingly good value.

✖ New Town

Koykos GREEK €

(Map p506; ☑ 22410 73022; http://koukosrodos.com; Mandilana 20-26; mains €3-10; ⏲breakfast, lunch & dinner; 🐦🐦) This inviting complex, off a pedestrian shopping street, consists of several antique-filled rooms – a couple hold vintage jukeboxes – along with two courtyards and a floral roof terrace. Best known for fabulous homemade pies, it also serves all the classic mezedhes (small plates), plus meat and fish dishes, or you can drop in for a coffee or sandwich.

Niohori TAVERNA €

(Map p506; ☑ 22410 35116; I Kazouli 29; mains €8-12; ⏲noon-midnight) This simple, great-value taverna – the open courtyard is basically a garage – delivers with a meat-accented menu. The owner is a butcher, with a shop across the street, so he selects the best cuts. Tuck into veal liver with oil and oregano, *stifadho* (meat with onions in a tomato purée), steak and meatballs, seasoned with organ music from the nearby church.

⭐**Meltemi** TAVERNA €€

(Map p506; ☑ 22410 30480; Kountourioti 8; mains €10-15; ⏲noon-late; 🅿🐦🐦) It's unspectacular from the outside, but step into its nautically themed interior and try to resist its seafood treasures: octopus, jumbo prawns, lobster, huge portions of calamari as well as feisty salads, all delivered with gusto. Add to this wide-screen sea views and you can see why it's one of best seafront spots in the New Town.

Kerasma GREEK €€

(Mapp506; ☑2241302410; www.kerasmarestaurant.com; George Leontos 4-6; mains €15; ⏲noon-

DODECANESE RHODES

Rhodes New Town

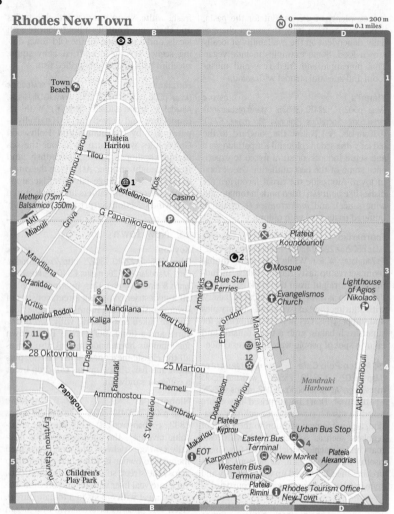

N ▲ 0 ——————— 200 m
0 ——————— 0.1 miles

11.30pm; ❄ 🛜) This contemporary restaurant has an open, stylish setting and offers Greek fusion food with dishes like grilled octopus dipped in honey and beef fillet with purple gnocchi. There's also an impressive cellar of 60 different Greek wines. An injection of taste for the New Town.

Balsamico FUSION €€

(📞 22410 75967; Akti Miaouli 4-6; mains €10; ⏰ 11am-11pm; ❄ 🛜) Expect well-executed Greek dishes and Italian numbers like pizza and pasta at this sea-facing restaurant with an eclectic twist; think orange and blue walls, a ceiling of suspended bottles and reclaimed driftwood sculptures. Spiro makes a great host and there's live music some nights.

🍷 Drinking & Nightlife

🍸 Old Town

⭐ Raxati Cafe BAR

(Map p502; 📞 22410 363651; Sofokleous 1-3; ⏰ 10am-late; 🛜) Overlooking stunning Ibrahim Pasha Mosque, this high-ceilinged free-spirited bar and coffee house is as pretty

Rhodes New Town

as it is friendly. Its stone walls are peppered with vintage ad posters, there are recycled Singer sewing machine tables, and graceful chandeliers cast light across the stunning bar of glass spirits. Snacks, cocktails, easy tunes and good conversation.

Rogmi Tou Chronou BAR

(Map p502; ☑ 22410 25202; Plateia Arionos 4; ◎6pm-5am; ☎) If Dracula developed a taste for rock music and opened a bar it might look something like Rogmi Tou Chronou. Imagine purple velvet drapes, a handsomely crafted wood bar lit with pearls, stained-glass windows, and the odd candle to stop you bumping into the furniture in the darkness. Live rock on Friday and Saturday evenings.

Macao Bar BAR

(Map p502; ☑ 6936400305; www.macaobar.gr/en; Pl Arionos; ◎8pm-6am Fri & Sat) Uber-stylish bar hidden in the Old Town; expect moody, low-lit ambience, polished concrete floors and the occasional guest DJ spinning the decks to a well-heeled crowd of fashionistas. Try the herb flavoured cocktails (€8).

Rock & Roll BAR

(Map p502; ☑ 22410 25202; Plateia Arionos 2; mains €8; ◎9am-late; ☎⚽) Cool diner-style haunt with metro-tiled walls and '50s songs playing as you plant yourself at the bar and tuck into a burger. It doubles as a juice bar during the day. Great balls of fire!

 New Town

While there's a very lively drinking scene in the New Town, centred on bar-lined I Dragoum, there's no great reason to recommend any of its many tourist-dominated hangouts over their identical neighbours.

Methexi BAR

(Akti Miaoúli 12; ◎10am-late; ☎) Methexi means 'theatrical event' in Ancient Greek, and this boho, fiercely indie haunt honours its namesake with live music on a Friday night from 9.30pm onwards. Sit outside on the terrace for watching sunsets or within the burnt-peach interior graced with retro typewriters, antique piano and musical miscellany.

Christos Garden BAR

(Map p506; ☑ 22410 32144; Griva 102; ◎10pm-late) With its grotto-like bar and pebble-mosaic courtyard, Christos offers New Town visitors a tranquil escape. During the day it doubles as an art gallery; after dark the fairy lights twinkle. Perfect for a cocktail.

☆ Entertainment

★9D: Throne of Helios FILM

(Map p506; ☑ 22410 76850; www.throneofhelios.com; Martiou 2; adult/child €13/9; ◎11am-7pm Mon-Fri, to 10pm Sat & Sun; ☎⚽) Journey back to the birth of Rhodes in this 3D experience. History is brought to life with the aid of hydraulic chairs, falling rain, snow and bubbles. Amazing visuals recreate the Colossus of Rhodes' construction, the citadel's creation under the Knights of St John, and more – up to the present day.

Cafe Chantant LIVE MUSIC

(Map p502; ☑ 22410 32277; Dimokratou 3; ◎11pm-late Fri & Sat) Locals flock to the long wooden tables here and listen to live traditional Greek music while drinking ouzo or beer. It's dark inside and you won't find snacks or nibbles, but the atmosphere is warm-hearted and friendly and the band is always lively.

🛍 Shopping

Amid the typical souvenir tat, the Old Town is filllled with quality keepsakes: Moorish lamps, icons, anthracite busts, leather sandals, belts and bags, silver jewellery, olive wood chopping boards, Rhodian wine, and local thyme honey. The New Town is more prosaic with general stores and a clutch of big-name fashion and style brands.

★**Rodoscope Creative Gallery** CERAMICS
(Map p502; 📞 6972202138; Ippodamou 39;
⊙ 10am-10pm) This tasteful boutique has a
collection of one-off bracelets, beach-bum-
chic jewellery, driftwood sculpture, handmade T-shirts and fine ceramics. Only the
work of Rhodian artists features here. Out
back there's a peaceful courtyard to admire
your gifts over a cool drink from the cafe.
Ask about the courses run here.

Antique Gallery ARTS & CRAFTS
(Map p502; 📞 22414 00126; Omirou 45; ⊙ 9am-
9pm) Best viewed by night, this Aladdin's
cave of a shop conjures up thoughts of the
Arabian Nights, with its shiny brass lamps,
ornate antique rings and Eastern mosaic
lights glowing like clusters of fireflies.

ℹ Information

MEDICAL SERVICES

Euromedica General Hospital (📞 22410
45000; www.euromedica-rhodes.gr; Koskinou)
The largest private health facility on the island,
with English-speaking staff. It's 6km south of
the Old Town, in Koskinou.

General Hospital (📞 22413 60000; Andreas
Papandreou; ⊙ 24hr) State-of-the-art hospital,
but bear in mind public hospital funding –
waiting times have been severely affected by
the Greek economic crisis.

Rhodes Medical Care Private Clinic (📞 22410
38008; www.rmc.gr; Krito Building, Ioannou
Metaxa 3) Will treat you for any emergency
provided you have health insurance. Excellent
staff and facilities.

MONEY

You'll find plenty of ATMs throughout Rhodes
Town, with useful ATM-equipped branches of
Alpha Bank next door to the Old Town tourist
office and on Plateia Kypriou in the New Town.
The National Bank of Greece has a conveniently
located office in the **New Town** (Plateia Kyprou,
New Town), as well as a branch on Plateia Mous-
iou in the Old Town.

POLICE

Emergencies & Ambulance (📞 166)
Port Police (📞 22410 22220; Mandraki
Harbour)
Tourist Police (📞 22410 27423; ⊙ 24hr)

POST

Main Post Office (📞 22410 35560; Mandraki
Harbour)

TOURIST INFORMATION

EOT (Greek Tourist Information Office; 📞 22410
44335; www.ando.gr/eot; cnr Makariou &

Papagou; ⊙ 8am-2.45pm Mon-Fri) National
tourism information, with brochures, maps and
transport details.

Rhodes Tourism Office – New Town (📞 22410
35495; www.rhodes.gr; Plateia Rimini;
⊙ 7.30am-3pm Mon-Fri) Conveniently poised
between Mandraki Harbour and the Old Town;
efficiently run with lots of free brochures and
helpful staff.

Rhodes Tourism Office – Old Town (📞 22410
35945; www.rhodes.gr; cnr Platonos & Ippoton;
⊙ 7am-3pm Mon-Fri) In an ancient building
at the foot of the Street of the Knights, this
helpful office supplies excellent street maps,
leaflets and brochures.

TRAVEL AGENCIES

Skevos Travel Agency (📞 22410 22461; www.
skevostravel.gr; 111 Amerikis; ⊙ 9am-8pm) For
help with airline and ferry tickets throughout
Greece.

Triton Holidays (📞 22410 21690; www.
tritondmc.gr; Plastira 9, Mandraki Harbour;
⊙ 9am-8pm) Air and sea travel, hire cars,
accommodation and tours throughout the
Dodecanese, as well as tickets to Turkey.

ℹ Getting Around

BICYCLE

Bicycles are available for rent from Margaritis in
the New Town.

BOAT

The quay at Mandraki Harbour is lined with
excursion boats offering day trips to east-coast
towns and beaches, including Faliraki and Lindos, and also to the island of Symi.

Several islands can be visited as day trips
on Dodekanisos Seaways (p328) catamarans,
departing from the Commercial Harbour. These
include Symi and Kos (both daily), Halki and
Tilos (both twice weekly), and Kastellorizo (once
weekly).

BUS

Two bus terminals, a block apart in Rhodes
Town, serve half the island each. There is regular
transport across the island all week, with fewer
services on Saturday and only a few on Sunday.
Pick up schedules from the kiosks at either terminal, or from the EOT (Greek National Tourist
Organisation) office.

The **Eastern Bus Terminal** (📞 22410 27706;
www.ktelrodou.gr) has frequent services to
the airport (€2.40), Kalithea Thermi (€2.20),
Salakos (€4.30), Ancient Kamiros (€5.20) and
Monolithos (€5.20). From the **Western Bus
Terminal** (📞 22410 26300) there are services
to Faliraki (€2.40), Tsambika Beach (€3.90),
Stegna Beach (€4.40) and Lindos (€5.20).

In Rhodes Town, local buses leave from the **urban bus stop** (Mandraki) on Mandraki Harbour. Bus 11 makes a circuit around the coast, up past the aquarium and on to the Acropolis. Bus 2 goes to Analipsi, bus 3 to Rodini, bus 4 to Agios Dimitrios and bus 5 to the Acropolis. Buy tickets on-board.

CAR & MOTORCYCLE

All the major car-rental chains are represented at Rhodes airport, and plenty more car- and motorcycle-rental outlets are scattered throughout Rhodes Town and the resorts. Competition is fierce, so shop around. Several agencies will deliver vehicles to renters.

Drive Rent A Car (☑ 22410 81011, 22410 68243; www.driverentacar.gr; 1st Km Tsairi-Airport; ⊘ 8am-9pm) Sturdier, newer scooters and cars.

Margaritis (☑ 22410 37420; www.margaritis rentals.gr; I Kazouli St 17; ⊘ 24hr) Reliable cars, scooters and bicycles in the New Town.

Orion Rent a Car (☑ 22410 22137; www.orioncarrental.com; Leontos 38) A wide range of small and luxury cars.

TAXI

Rhodes Town's main **taxi rank** is east of Plateia Rimini, on the northern edge of the Old Town. There are two zones on the island for taxi meters: zone one is Rhodes Town and zone two (for which rates are slightly higher) is everywhere else. Rates double between midnight and 5am. Set taxi fares are posted at the rank.

You can also phone for a **taxi** (☑ in Rhodes Town 22410 69800, outside Rhodes Town 22410 69600; www.rhodes-taxi.gr) or **disabled-accessible taxi** (☑ 22410 77079).

Note that taxis cannot access most locations in the largely pedestrianised Old Town; expect to be dropped at the gate nearest your destination. A few upscale hotels have golf buggies to pick you up in.

Northeastern Rhodes

Most of the sandiest beaches on Rhodes lie along the island's northeastern coast, between Rhodes Town and Lindos. As a result, this stretch is now punctuated by a long succession of resorts, filled with package holidaymakers in summer and holding endless strips of tourist bars.

Ladiko Beach, 15km south of Rhodes Town, just beyond Faliraki, is touted locally as 'Anthony Quinn Beach'. Back in the 1960s, the star of *Zorba the Greek* actually bought the beach from the Greek government, but according to his family the authorities failed to honour the sale. It consists of two back-to-back coves, with a pebbly beach on the north side that's better for swimming, and volcanic rock platforms on the south side.

Two fine beaches, **Kolymbia** and **Tsambika**, are located either side of the massive Tsambika promontory, 10km further south. Both are sandy but get crowded in summer. Not far beyond, the coast road curves inland, but a short detour seawards brings you to the low-key little resort of Stegna, arrayed along sandy, idyllic **Stegna Beach**.

The headland that marks the start of the final curve towards Lindos, 40km south of Rhodes Town, is topped by the ruins of the 15th-century **Castle of Faraklos**. Once a prison for recalcitrant knights, this was the last stronghold on the island to fall to the Turks and now offers fabulous views. A footpath climbs from the appealing little resort of **Haraki**, immediately south, where the neat horseshoe bay is lined by a pebbly beach.

◉ Sights

Kalithea Thermi   ARCHITECTURE
(☑ 22410 65691; www.kallitheasprings.gr; Kalithea; €3; ⊘ 8am-8pm Apr-Oct, to 5pm Nov-Mar; ♿) Italian architect Pietro Lombardi constructed this opulent art deco spa, on the site of ancient thermal springs, in 1929. Its dazzling white-domed pavilions, pebble-mosaic courtyards and sweeping sea-view colonnades have appeared in movies such as *Zorba the Greek* and *The Guns of Navarone*, and have now been restored after years of neglect. In peak season its small sandy bathing beach and cafe get impossibly crowded.

Just 9km south of Rhodes Town, it can be accessed by driving directly along the coast.

Epta Piges   SPRING
(Seven Springs; Kolymbia; ⊘ 24hr; ♿) **FREE**
Seven natural springs at this beauty spot, in the hills 4km inland from Kolymbia, feed a river that's channelled into a narrow tunnel, exactly the size of an adult. Thrill-seeking visitors can walk a few hundred metres in pitch darkness, ankle-deep in fast-flowing water, to reach the shaded lake at the far end.

Lindos   Λίνδος

POP 3600

Your first glimpse of the ancient and unbelievably pretty town of Lindos is guaranteed to steal your breath away: the towering Acropolis radiant on the cypress-silvered hill, and the sugar-cube houses of the whitewashed town tumbling below it towards the aquamarine bay. Entering the town itself, you'll find yourself in a magical warren of hidden alleys, packed with the ornate houses of long-vanished sea captains that now hold appetising tavernas, effervescent bars and cool cafes. Pick your way past donkeys as you coax your calves up to the Acropolis and one of the finest views in Greece.

Lindos has been enjoying its wonderful setting for 4000 years, since the Dorians founded the first settlement at this excellent harbour and vantage point. Since then it has been successively overlaid with Byzantine, Frankish and Turkish structures, the remains of which can be glimpsed all around.

◎ Sights & Activities

Two magnificent beaches line the crescent harbour that curves directly below the village. The larger, logically known as **Main Beach**, is a perfect swimming spot – sandy with shallow water – for kids. Follow a path north to the western tip of the bay to reach the smaller, taverna-fringed **Pallas Beach**. Don't swim near the jetty here, which is home to sea urchins, but if it gets too crowded you can swim from the rocks beyond.

Ten minutes' walk from town on the other, western, side of the Acropolis, sheltered **St Paul's Bay** is similarly caressed by turquoise waters.

★**Acropolis of Lindos**　ARCHAEOLOGICAL SITE
(☑22413 65200; adult/concession/child €12/6/ free; ⊙8am-7.40pm Tue-Fri, 8am-3pm Sat-Mon Apr-Oct, 8.30am-3pm Tue-Sun Nov-Mar) A steep footpath climbs the 116m-high rock above Lindos to reach the beautifully preserved Acropolis. First walled in the 6th century BC, the clifftop is now enclosed by battlements constructed by the Knights of St John. Once within, you're confronted by stunning ancient remains that include a **Temple to Athena Lindia** and a 20-columned **Hellenistic stoa**. Silhouetted against the deep blue sky, the stark white columns are dazzling, while the long-range coastal views are out of this world.

Be sure to pack a hat and some water, as there's no shade at the top, and take care to protect young kids from the many dangerous drop-offs. Donkey rides to the Acropolis from the village entrance only spare you around three minutes of exposed walking on the hillside, and you should note that animal-rights groups urge people to consider the treatment of the donkeys before deciding to take a ride.

★**Lepia Dive**　DIVING
(☑6937417970; www.lepiadive.com; ⊛) This brilliantly inclusive dive company has a range of options including PADI courses for kids, beginners and those already at an advanced level. The centre's facilities are adapted for wheelchairs and there are expertly designed dives certified by DDI (Disabled Divers International) for people with additional needs. Choose from reef, wreck and cave dives. Free pick-up.

🛏 Sleeping

Accommodation in Lindos is very limited, so be sure to book in advance. And check carefully, as most hotels that include 'Lindos' in their names and/or addresses are in fact located not in the town, but along the coast nearby.

Electra Studios　PENSION €
(☑22440 31266; www.electra-studios.gr; studios €50; ⊙Apr-Oct; ⊛🛜) Simple family-run pension, where the plain, but very pleasant, whitewashed rooms have varnished wooden twin beds, fridges and air-con. Some have balconies and there's also a lovely communal roof terrace overlooking a lemon grove and the sea.

Anastasia Studios　APARTMENT €€
(☑22440 31417, 6970977696; www.lindos-studios. gr; d & tr €60; ℗⊛🛜) Focused around a geranium-filled courtyard on Lindos' eastern side, these six split-level apartments enjoy soaring Acropolis views. Each has a tiled floor, sofa bed, well-equipped kitchen and separate bedroom, while room 6 has its own private balcony.

★**Melenos**　BOUTIQUE HOTEL €€€
(☑22440 32222; www.melenoslindos.com; ste incl breakfast from €370; ⊛@🛜) ⯑ Magical Moorish-style palace with bougainvillea walkways, pebble-mosaic floors, verandas festooned in lanterns and bauble lights casting a glow on Ottoman furniture. Staff glide discreetly around as you soak up the stunning bay view. Rooms are lovingly re-created in traditional Lyndian style, with raised beds, wooden ceilings and private balconies, and there's a superb restaurant.

F Charm Hotel　BOUTIQUE HOTEL €€€
(☑22440 32080, 6944339937; www.lindosfine staying.com; r incl breakfast from €140; ⊛🛜) This enclosed courtyard accommodation holds half a dozen heavenly white rooms and family-sized suites. All have shabby-chic

distressed furniture, wood-beamed ceilings and traditional raised-platform beds with Cocomat mattresses, plus fridge and kitchenette. It's next to the police station, at the south end of town.

✖ Eating

Most tavernas serve their customers on roof terraces high above the tangle of streets. These give fabulous views up to the Acropolis and over the bay, but mean you can't always tell whether there's anyone in your chosen venue until you've already committed to eat there.

Captain's House CAFE €

(snacks €7; ⊗8am-midnight; 🆒 🛜) Soaked in Lyndian atmosphere, this nautically themed, 16th-century sea captain's house is perfect for a juice on your way down from the Acropolis. Grab a pew in the pebble-mosaic courtyard and ponder the fabulous carved stone reliefs in the courtyard.

Village Cafe BAKERY €

(📝22440 31559; www.lindostreasures.com; mains €8; ⊗8.30am-7pm; 🆒 🛜 🚻) Near the start of the path up to the Acropolis, this whitewashed bakery-cafe has an enticing vine-covered pebble-mosaic courtyard and comfortable couches in its cool interior. Drop in for hot or frozen coffee, juice or ice cream, and a mouthwatering array of cheese cakes, cherry pies, salads, wraps and freshly prepared sandwiches. Don't miss the delectable *bougatsa* (vanilla custard pie).

★Calypso TAVERNA €€

(📝22440 32135; www.kalypsolindos.gr; mains €13; ⊗11am-midnight; 🆒 🛜) This former sea captain's residence with its beautiful stone relief is perfect for lunch or dinner on the roof terrace or inside. Sea bass, octopus, *makarounes* (homemade pasta served with fresh onions and melted local cheese) and grilled lamb chops are but a few of the delights.Try the 'Kalypso bread' with feta and tomato.

Melenos MEDITERRANEAN €€€

(📝22440 32222; www.melenoslindos.com; mains €26; ⊗8am-midnight; 🛜) Gorgeous sea-view terrace restaurant overlooking Pallas Beach. The menu features salmon marinated in ouzo, steamed sea bass with mussels in asparagus sauce, and grilled beef fillet with mushrooms, wine and caramelised onions. Round things off with a sumptuous dessert.

ⓘ Information

Lindos Tourist Office (📝22440 31900; Plateia Eleftherias; ⊗9am-3pm) Small information kiosk at the entrance to central Lindos.

Island Of The Sun Travel (📝22440 31264; Acropolis; ⊗9am-5pm) Local excursions, rental cars and accommodation.

Southeastern Rhodes

As you continue south of Lindos along the east coast, the island takes on a windswept appearance and sees less tourist traffic. Villages here seem to have a slower pace.

Just 2km south of Lindos, sandy **Pefki Beach** is deservedly popular. If it's too crowded, try **Glystra Beach**, just down the road and a great spot for swimming.

Sleepy one-street **Gennadi** consists of a few *kafeneia* (coffee houses), friendly locals and a cluster of whitewashed buildings set back a few hundred metres from the pebbled beach. You'll find a fruit market, bakery, supermarket and a couple of tavernas.

An almost uninterrupted beach of pebbles and sand dunes extends down from Gennadi as far as **Plimmyri**, 11km south. Watch for a signposted turning to **Lahania**, 2km inland off the main highway, and head downhill into the centre to find an old village of winding alleyways and traditional buildings.

The coast road continues south past countless chapels to the village of **Kattavia**, a friendly place that doesn't see a lot of tourists. Beyond that, a windswept 10km road snakes south to remote **Cape Prasonisi**, the island's southernmost point. Joined to Rhodes by a tenuously narrow sandy isthmus in summer months, it's cut off completely when water levels rise in winter. The Aegean Sea meets the Mediterranean here, creating ideal wind and wave conditions for kitesurfers and windsurfers. Outfitters stand ready to help with everything from rental equipment and lessons to overnight accommodation in surfer-dude-style hostels, but it all closes down in winter. To get here direct from the airport by taxi costs around €120 and takes 1½ hours.

✖ Activities

Pro Center

Kristof Kirschner ADVENTURE SPORTS

(📝22400 91045; www.facebook.com/procenterc. kirschner; ⊗May-Oct; 🚻) Specialising in windsurfing equipment rental and classes.

DODECANESE RHODES

🛌 Sleeping & Eating

⭐ **Four Elements**   APARTMENT €€
(☑ 6939450014, 22440 46001; www.thefour
elements.be; Lahania; apt €110-165; 🅿 ❄ @ 🛜 🛋)
Four exceptionally homey and spacious
apartments, perfect for taking a rural holiday in comfort. All have full kitchens, one is
adapted for wheelchair users, and there's a
divine pool, outdoor barbecue and garden.
Minimum two nights. The friendly Belgian
owners run an on-site cafe-bar named the
Fifth Element (beer being the fifth element
after earth, air, fire and water).

Taverna Platanos   TAVERNA €
(☑ 6944199991; www.lachaniaplatanos.com; Laha-
nia; mains €6-8; ❄ 🛜) Classic village taverna,
tucked behind the church in Lahania's tiny
main square and famed throughout the
island. With its traditional decor and flower-
filled patio, it's a great place to take a break.
Hearty lamb, beef or chicken stews cost well
under €10, with salads and dips less than
half that.

Mama's Kitchen   PIZZA €
(Gennadi; mains €7-10; ❄) Check out the
murals of ancient myths as you munch
Olympian portions of grilled meat like lamb
and beef.

Western Rhodes & the Interior

Western Rhodes is redolent with the scent
of pine, its hillsides shimmering with forests. More exposed than the east side, it's
also windier – a boon for kitesurfers and
windsurfers – so the sea tends to be rough
and the beaches mostly pebbled. If you're
cycling, or have a scooter or car, the hilly
roads that cross the interior are well worth
exploring for their wonderful scenery.

For sightseers, the most significant potential stopoffs are the ruined ancient cities
of Ialysos and Kamiros. Otherwise, once
past the airport, settlements are few and
far between. **Skala Kamirou**, 45km southwest of Rhodes Town, is a small port with
direct ferries to the nearby island of Halki.
Although it does have a couple of tavernas,
and a twice-daily bus service, it's so isolated
that it's much more use to locals than independent travellers.

The ruins of 16th-century **Kritinia Castle**
stand proudly on a headland immediately
south of Skala Kamirou. Detour off the main

road for awe-inspiring views along the coast
and across to Halki, in a magical setting
where you half expect to encounter Romeo
or Rapunzel.

Continuing south, the road is sublimely
scenic. Vast mountainous vistas open up as
you approach **Siana**, a picturesque village
below Mt Akramytis (825m), and the village
of **Monolithos**, 5km beyond. The spectacu-
larly sited 15th-century castle that's perched
on a sheer 240m-high rock above Monolithos can be reached on a dirt track. To enter,
climb through the hole in the wall.

◉ Sights & Activities

⭐ **Petaloudes**   FOREST
(Valley of the Butterflies; ☑ 22410 82822; €5;
🕘 9am-5pm; ♿) Petaloudes, 7km up from
the coast, is better known as the Valley of
the Butterflies. Visit in June, July or August,
when these colourful insects mature, and
you'll quickly see why. They're actually tiger
moths *(Callimorpha quadripunctarea)*
drawn to the gorge by the scent of the resin
exuded by storax trees. In summer the whole
place is choking with tour buses. Out of season, you'll likely have the gorgeous forest
path, streams and pools to yourself – but no
butterflies.

Ancient Kamiros   ARCHAEOLOGICAL SITE
(☑ 22410 40037; €6; 🕘 8am-7.40pm May-Oct,
8.30am-3pm Nov-Apr; ♿) The extensive
remains of the Doric city of Kamiros stand
above the coast, 34km southwest of Rhodes
Town. Known for its figs, oil and wine,
Kamiros was at its peak in the 7th century
BC, but was swiftly superseded by Rhodes
and devastated by earthquakes in 226 BC
and 142 BC. Visible ruins include a Doric
temple, with one column still standing, a
temple to Athena and a 3rd-century great
stoa. Come in the afternoon, when fewer visitors are around.

Ancient Ialysos   ARCHAEOLOGICAL SITE
(☑ 22410 92202; €6; 🕘 8.30am-8pm May-Oct,
8.30am-3pm Nov-Apr; ♿) Constructed in the
3rd century BC, atop what's now Filerimos
Hill, 10km southwest of Rhodes Town, the
Doric city of Ialysos was repeatedly conquered. The resultant hotchpotch of Doric,
Byzantine and medieval remains is now
barely intelligible to casual visitors. Stairs
from the entrance lead to the ruined foundations of the Temple of Athena Ialysia and
the peaceful restored 14th-century Chapel
of Agios Georgios. Follow the path left from

the entrance to reach another 12th-century chapel, filled with frescoes.

Emery Winery
WINERY

(☏ 22460 41208; Embonas; ⊙9.30am-4.30pm Apr-Oct) FREE Perched on the flanks of Mt Attavyros (1215m), the island's highest mountain, the village of Embonas is the wine capital of Rhodes. This cottage winery, on the town's eastern edge, offers tours of its facility and provides a good opportunity to taste and buy top-quality tipples such as the red Cava Emery or Zacosta and the white Villare.

✗ Eating

Mylos
CAFE €

(☏ 6940641475; Kritinia; snacks €5-7; ⊙9am-late) Set beside the main road, with tremendous views down to Kritinia Castle, this welcoming little cafe serves coffee, drinks and snacks such as salads, omelettes and sandwiches. Best of all, though, it has its own folklore museum, filled with local costumes and alarming farming implements.

To Stolidi Tis Psinthoy
TAVERNA €

(☏ 22410 50009; Psinthos; mains €8-10; ⊙lunch & dinner) The pick of several appealing lunch spots in lively Psinthos, 10km southeast of Petaloudes, To Stolidi has a deeply rural feel with wooden beams, chequered tablecloths and family photos on the walls. Try the spicy pork, grilled eggplant, dolmadhes and fresh-baked country bread.

HALKI
ΧΑΛΚΗ

POP 310

Thanks to the gorgeous Italianate mansions that surround its harbour, the former sponge-diving island of Halki makes an irresistible first impression. Stepping off the ferry, you enter a composite of all that's best about Greece: an old fisherman shelling prawns under a fig tree, an Orthodox priest flitting down a narrow alley, brightly painted boats bobbing along the quay. There's little to do except relax and indulge in the sleepy splendour, venturing out to tempting little beaches lapped by aquamarine waters and, in cooler months, hiking along the island's spectacular high-mountain spine.

ⓘ Getting There & Away

The **Dodekanisos Seaways** (p328) catamaran stops at Halki on Tuesday and Thursday as it heads from Rhodes to Tilos, Nisyros, Kos and Kalymnos in the morning, and back to Rhodes in the evening. On those days, you can visit the island as a day trip from Rhodes. **Blue Star Ferries** (p328) connects Halki with Rhodes up to three times weekly, and with Karpathos, Kasos, Crete, Santorini and Piraeus twice weekly.

Two boats, **Nissos Halki Halki** (☏ mobile 6946519817, 6973460968) and **Nikos Express** (☏ mobile 6946826905) link Halki daily with the tiny port of Skala Kamirou on the west coast of Rhodes; there's an hour-long connecting bus service with Rhodes Old Town. **Stelios Kazantzidis** (☏ mobile 6944434429) runs an on-demand water-taxi service to Skala Kamirou.

Boat Services from Halki (Emborios)

DESTINATION	DURATION	FARE (€)	FREQUENCY
Kalymnos*	3hr	36	2 weekly
Karpathos	4hr	13	3 weekly
Kos*	2¼hr	26	2 weekly
Nisyros*	1½hr	24	2 weekly
Piraeus	24hr	44	2 weekly
Rhodes	2hr	8	3 weekly
Rhodes*	1¼hr	18	2 weekly
Rhodes (Skala Kamirou)	1¼hr	11	1-2 daily
Santorini (Thira)	12hr	26	1 weekly
Tilos*	40min	24	2 weekly

*high-speed services

ⓘ Getting Around

Most visitors get around Halki on foot. In summer, regular minibuses connect Emborios with Pondamos, Ftenagia and Kalia beaches (€1.50 each way), while on Friday evenings there's also a round trip to Moni Agiou Ioanni monastery (€5). A water taxi also serves the main beaches, while **Zifos Travel** (☏ 22460 45028; www.zifostravel.gr; ⊙10am-8pm) can provide details of summer-only excursion boats, for example to the uninhabited island of Alimia (€30), with its fields of wild herbs.

Emborios
Εμπορειός

POP 300

Halki's one tiny town curves luxuriantly around a sheltered turquoise bay. The waterfront is a broad expanse of flagstones, almost entirely pedestrianised, populated by as many cats as humans and lined with enticing tavernas and cafes. Climbing in tiers up a low ridge, the cream, ochre, stone

DODECANESE HALKI

and rose-hued homes of 19th-century fishermen and sea captains form a magnificent backdrop. There's no town beach, but here and there ladders enable swimmers to enter the water.

⊙ Sights

The neoclassical mansions of Emborios are a visual feast. A few have crumbled into complete ruination, but most have been restored to their original glory and many now serve as rental properties.

The impressive central **clock tower** was donated by the expat Halki community in Florida; the clock itself hasn't worked for over 20 years. Nearby, the **Church of Agios Nikolaos** has the tallest belfry in the Dodecanese, incorporating stones from an ancient temple of Apollo, and boasts a picturesque mosaic-pebbled courtyard.

Traditional House of Chalki   HISTORIC BUILDING
(☑ 22460 45284; €3; ⊙ 11am-3pm & 6-8pm) Perched on the hillside, not far up from the harbour (signed to the right off the road to Pondamos Beach), the Traditional House of Chalki – an alternative transliteration of Halki – is a two-storey family home, built a century ago. It's now meticulously preserved as a museum, displaying authentic furniture, tableware and costumes, old photos – and even the underwear of the owner's grandmother, neatly framed.

🛏 Sleeping & Eating

Halki holds little accommodation, so book ahead in summer. Most visitors stay in self-catering villas and apartments; contact Zifos Travel or Nissia Holidays (www.nissia holidays.com) for details.

Captain's House   PENSION €
(☑ 6932511762, 22460 45201; capt50@otenet. gr; d €40; ❀🛜) Attractive white-painted 19th-century house just up from the sea, near the church, featuring antique clocks and model schooners. Two lovely rooms have high ceilings, wood floors, air-con and good bathrooms, and the relaxing garden courtyard holds a sun terrace with great harbour views.

★**Aretanassa Hotel**   HOTEL €€
(☑ 22460 70927; www.aretanassahotel.cosmores. com; Harbour; d/tr incl breakfast €90/115; ❀🛜) This wine-coloured former sponge factory has 19 gloriously sunny, sea-facing rooms with powder-blue walls, large beds and

spotless tiled floors. Some rooms have balconies. There's a lovely restaurant and bar, and a sun terrace over your very own azure Mediterranean swimming pool. There's also a lift and access for those with additional needs.

Taverna Lefkosia   TAVERNA €
(☑ 6946978151; mains €7-12; ⊙ lunch & dinner) Much-loved taverna, where the check-clothed tables and blue chairs spread out onto the quay and the menu abounds in hom-made island specialities such as baked pasta. The fried cheese balls are a crispy, chewy delight, and fresh-caught fish comes in generous portions.

Black Sea   TAVERNA €
(☑ 22460 45021; Harbour; mains €8-14; ⊙ lunch & dinner; ❀🛜) 🍴 Sitting peacefully on the left side of the harbour, metres from bobbing boats, this brightly coloured haunt is run by a charming Georgian family. It's a great spot for fresh fish, from octopus and little shrimp to grilled bream, but the vegetable dishes, including fried mushrooms, are also good.

Dimitri's Bakery   BAKERY €
(Harbour; mains €3; ⊙ breakfast, lunch & dinner) Generations of Halki residents and visitors have stocked up on Dimitri's delicious sweet and savoury pies and pastries, available from early morning. Cheese, spinach and apple pies, plus croissants and – in the evening – slices of pizza.

ⓘ Information

The only ATM is often out of action, so bring plenty of spare cash.
Police & Port Police (☑ 22460 45220) On the harbour.
Post Office (⊙ 9am-1.30pm Mon-Fri) On the harbour, with an ATM.
Zifos Travel (☑ 22460 45028; www.zifostravel. gr; ⊙ 10am-8pm) The best source of help with accommodation, boat tickets, excursions and currency exchange.

Around Halki

A broad concrete road crosses the low hill above Emborios harbour to reach Pondamos Beach, the most popular of Halki's handful of tiny shingle beaches, after 500m. Beyond that, it climbs to the abandoned village of Horio, 3km along, then continues west to the hilltop monastery of **Agiou Ioanni**. That's a total one-way hike of 8km, recommended in the cooler months only.

Two more pebble beaches, both equipped with decent tavernas and served by buses in summer, lie within walking distance of Emborios. **Ftenagia Beach** is beyond the headland 500m south of the harbour, while **Kania Beach** is an enjoyable but unshaded 2.5km hike north, signposted off the main road halfway to Pondamos.

◉ Sights

Pondamos Beach   BEACH

Pretty little Pondamos Beach is lapped by the turquoise waters of a crescent bay 10 minutes' walk up and over the hill west of Emborios. The only way to get a comfortable shaded spot is to rent a €3 sunbed alongside **Nick's Taverna** (mains €6-15; ⊘ breakfast, lunch & dinner; ⓦ), where separate sections serve good seafood meals, and drinks and snacks.

Horio   ARCHAEOLOGICAL SITE

A stiff switchback climb along the road from Pondamos Beach leads up through Halki's fertile central valley to Horio. This picturesque ruin was originally the island's main village, hidden away to escape the eyes of roving pirates. A freshly cobbled footpath heads up to the battlements of the **Knights of St John Castle** that once protected it. Pass through its forbidding gateway to see a restored chapel and amazing long-range views.

KARPATHOS ΚΑΡΠΑΘΟΣ

POP 6200

Celebrated for its wild mountains and blue coves, this long craggy island is among the least commercialised in Greece. Legend has it Prometheus and his Titans were born here, and with its cloud-wrapped villages and rugged beauty, there's still something undeniably primal in the air. Homer, never a man to mince his words, called it 'Krapathos', but actually it's a lovely island.

Popular with adrenaline junkies, southern Karpathos is in the spotlight each summer when it hosts an international kitesurfing competition. Meanwhile, the fierce wind that lifts the spray from the turquoise waves blows its way to the mountainous north, battering pine trees and howling past sugar-cube houses. Karpathian women at this end of the island still wear traditional garb, especially in the time-forgotten village eyrie of Olymbos, perched atop a perilous mountain ridge.

ⓘ Getting There & Away

AIR

The airport at the very southern tip of Karpathos is linked by Olympic Air (www.olympicair.com) two to four times daily with Athens (€70, one hour).

Sky Express (☑ 28102 23800; www.skyexpress.gr) has daily links between Karpathos and Rhodes (€68, 40 minutes), and once daily with Kasos (€56, 15 minutes) and Sitia (€87, one hour) on Crete.

BOAT

The island's main port, Pigadia, is served by **Blue Star Ferries** (p328), with all sailings also calling at the northern village of Diafani either before Pigadia (when southbound) or after it (when northbound). Ferries head three times weekly to Halki and Rhodes, and three times weekly to Kasos, with two continuing to Crete and one to Santorini.

Boat Services from Karpathos

The following services all depart from Pigadia

DESTINATION	DURATION	FARE (€)	FREQUENCY
Halki	4hr	13	3 weekly
Kasos	1½hr	8	3 weekly
Milos	16hr	38	1 weekly
Piraeus	17hr	44	2 weekly
Rhodes	5hr 40min	21	3 weekly
Santorini (Thira)	8hr	27	1 weekly
Sitia	4hr	19	2 weekly

ⓘ Getting Around

TO/FROM THE AIRPORT

The airport is 14km south of Pigadia. From late July to September, an 11.30am bus on Thursday and a 10.30am bus on Saturday go to the airport (€2.50), making the return journey on both days at 5pm. A taxi will cost €22. Given the size of the island it makes sense to rent a car. All major car-rental chains have outlets at the airport.

BOAT

Day trips head from Pigadia up to Diafani, where they connect with buses to Olymbos, or continue north to remote beaches.

BUS

KTEL (www.karpathosbus.wordpress.com) runs buses all over the island from the **bus station** (☑ 22450 22338; M Mattheou, Pigadia) in Pigadia, just up from the harbour. Only two a week go all the way north to Olymbos.

Karpathos

per day from €18.50; ⊙ 9am-1pm & 5-8pm),
Rent A Car (✏ 22450 22911, 22450 22690; 28
Oktovriou) and **Lefkos Rent A Car** (✏ mobile
6984466346, mobile 6977918774, office 22450
71030; www.lefkosrentacar.com; Lefkos).

TAXI

Taxi prices are posted at Pigadia's central **taxi
rank** (✏ 22450 22705; Dimokratias). Fares are
prohibitively high, with trips to Lefkos costing
€50 and Olymbos €75.

Pigadia   Πηγάδια
POP 1690

Karpathos' capital and main ferry port, Pigadia sprawls beside a long bay on the southeast shore of the island. Decent beaches
stretch away to the north, but the town
itself lacks the photogenic good looks and
geometrically pleasing whitewashed houses
of other islands. Give it a little time, though,
wandering its harbour and among waterfront bars and backstreet bakeries, and the
place may grow on you. Determinedly Greek,
it barely looks up from its afternoon retsina
to acknowledge your arrival. But isn't that
what travellers sometimes long for?

🛏 Sleeping

Budget options are concentrated in the hillside
streets that rise from central Pigadia, while
newer and more luxurious options spread
northwards around the curve of the bay.

Rose's Studios   APARTMENT €
(✏ 22450 22284; www.rosesstudios.com; r €35;
❄🛜) For good-value budget lodgings, it's
well worth trudging 300m up from the port
to reach these eight simple but fresh rooms.
They have clean bathrooms, large sea-view
balconies and decent fittings, including minimal kitchenettes.

Nereides Hotel   HOTEL €€
(✏ 22450 23347; www.nereideshotel.gr; Nerei-
don St; d incl breakfast €130; 🅿❄🛜🏊) This
charming little hotel has been open a few
years, but everything, from the paintwork to
its up-to-the-minute bathrooms, still gleams
like new. Set on the hillside, five minutes'
walk from the beach and 10 minutes from
the harbour, it offers 30 stylish rooms with
sea-view balconies, plus a good pool. There's
a snack bar, but no restaurant.

Atlantis Hotel   HOTEL €€
(✏ 22450 22777; www.atlantishotelkarpathos.gr;
s/d incl breakfast €50/55; 🏊) Friendly, long-

CAR

All major car-rental chains have outlets at the
airport, and there are local agencies all over the
island. Recommended operators include **Europcar** (✏ 22450 23238; www.europcar.com),
Pegasus Motorbikes (✏ mobile 6979794727;

established, family-run hotel across from the Italian-era town hall just above the west end of the harbour. The pleasant, no-frills rooms are nicely maintained – it's well worth paying a little extra for one with a balcony facing the sea rather than the (decent-sized) pool.

Eating

Both the quay and the pedestrian streets just behind it are lined with seafood tavernas, all-purpose brasseries, cafes and cocktail bars. Look out, too, for the two Italian gelaterias on Apodimon Karpathion, parallel to the harbour.

★ To Ellenikon   TAVERNA €
(☑ 22450 23932; Apodimon Karpathion; mains €10-17; ☺ lunch & dinner; ❉☏☝☂) If you're looking for typical Karpathian food cooked the way it should be then 'the Greek' is your place. Try *saganaki* (fried cheese), meatballs, shrimp and calamari, eat within the wood-accented traditional interior or outside on the narrow terrace. The owner is a lovely guy and will happily show you the kitchen.

Orea   TAVERNA €
(☑ 22450 22501; Harbour; mains €7-15; ☺ noon-midnight) Quayside taverna near the ferry jetty, serving authentic Karpathian specialities such as *makarounes* (homemade pasta with caramelised onions and cheese). Most meat mains cost under €10, and a whole grilled fish is more like €12 to €14.

Akropolis   BRASSERIE €€
(☑ 22450 23278; Apodimon Karpathion; mains €15-25; ☺ breakfast, lunch & dinner; ❉☏) This welcoming harbour-front cafe/-restaurant is as suited to breakfast or a sunset cocktail as it is to a full dinner. Most customers are drawn here for steak rather than Greek food, with the menu ranging through T-bone, fillet, sirloin and rib-eye up to a delectable chateaubriand for two (€50).

☕ Drinking & Nightlife

Caffe Karpathos   CAFE
(☑ 21022 87383; www.cafekarpathos.com; Apodimon Karpathion; ☺ 8am-late; ☏) Enjoying a morning coffee or evening glass of local wine in the wicker chairs outside this cosy little cafe, a few steps from the waterfront on a pedestrian street that climbs away near the jetty. You feel as though you're relaxing in the front room of a friend's house. The owners lived for years in Italy, hence the Italian touches.

En Plo   COCKTAIL BAR
(cocktails €6; ☺ 8am-late) Low-lit En Plo is a quiet place to read and sip on special coffee made with honey and whipped cream.

ℹ Information

Pigadia's ferry quay juts out from the eastern end of the broad harbour. Walk east to reach the town centre within five minutes. Follow the main street, Apodimon Karpathion, which climbs from the waterfront then runs parallel to the sea, and in 500m you'll reach Plateia 5 Oktovriou, home to the Italian-era municipal buildings. The sandy beaches of Pigadia Bay begin not far beyond.

Both the **National Bank of Greece** on Apodimon Karpathion, and **Alpha Bank**, a block higher on Dimokratias, have ATMs.

Police (☑ 22450 22224) Near the hospital at the western end of town.

Possi Travel (☑ 22450 22235; Harbour; ☺ 8am-1pm & 5.30-8.30pm) The main travel agency for ferry and air tickets, excursions and accommodation. The helpful staff speak excellent English.

Post Office (Ethnikis Andistasis) Near the hospital.

Tourist Office (www.karpathos.org; ☺ Jul & Aug) Summer-only kiosk, in the middle of the seafront.

Southern Karpathos

Thanks to their sandy beaches, several appealing villages in the southern half of Karpathos have reinvented themselves as small-scale resorts. Peaceful villages nestle amid the hills inland, an area that's crisscrossed by scenic walking tracks.

Menetes   Μενετές

Buffeted by mountain gales, the tiny village of Menetes sits high in the cliffs above Pigadia. Climb to the church at its highest point before exploring its narrow whitewashed streets.

◉ Sights

Folklore Museum   MUSEUM
(☑ 6985847672; Menetes; ☺ 9am-1pm & 5-8pm) **FREE** Spend a few minutes walking around Menetes and you're sure to run into Irini, custodian of the keys to the ancient chapel that houses this two-room museum. Having unlocked it, she'll talk you through its haphazard treasures and point you towards the tunnels in the hillside nearby, used by German troops in WWII. Donations welcomed.

DODECANESE KARPATHOS

✕ Eating

Dionysos Fiesta TAVERNA €
(📞 22450 81269; mains €6-10; ⊙ breakfast, lunch
& dinner; ✳ 📶) Set in a restored traditional
house, in the twisting village lanes just up
from the main road, this relaxed and welcoming taverna spreads onto a raised garden terrace. Local specialities to savour
include goat stew, lemon chicken, artichoke omelettes and succulent Karpathian
sausages.

Arkasa Αρκάσα

Arkasa, on the southwest coast 9km from
Menetes, is one of the oldest settlements on
Karpathos. The original village centre, just
up from the water, is now complemented by
a burgeoning beach resort below. A waterside track leads 500m to the remains of the
5th-century **Basilica of Agia Sophia**, where
two chapels stand amid mosaic fragments
and columns, and to an ancient **acropolis**
on the headland beyond.

The best beach hereabouts, sandy **Agios
Nikolaos Beach**, stretches south from the
acropolis, but to reach it by road you have to
turn left from the village itself.

🛏 Sleeping

★ **Glaros Studios** APARTMENT €
(📞 22450 61015; www.glarosstudios-karpathos.
com; Agios Nikolaos Beach, Arkasa; apt €50-
55; 🅿📶) This well-managed and ever-
expanding garden-set complex pretty much
has Agios Nikolaos Beach to itself. There
are spotless white studios, decorated in
traditional Karpathian style with raised
platform beds and small kitchenettes,
plus a relaxed and good-value adjoining
restaurant.

Eleni Studios APARTMENT €
(📞 22450 61248; www.elenikarpathos.gr; Arkasa;
apt €60; 🅿✳📶🏊) On the road to Finiki,
Eleni Studios has fully equipped and very
tidy powder-blue apartments with appealing bedrooms, built around a relaxing garden. There's an on-site bar, too, for sunset
drinks and breakfast, and a tempting pool.
Great sea views.

Arkasa Bay Hotel HOTEL €€
(📞 22450 61410; www.arkasabay.com; Arkasa; d
€100; ✳📶🏊) Plush Arkasa has fine rooms
with kitchenette, flat-screen TVs and, best of
all, a great swimming pool.

Finiki Φοινίκι

Arrayed along a neat little south-facing crescent bay, picturesque Finiki stands just 2km
north of Arkasa. White-and-blue houses,
interspersed with a peppering of tavernas,
front its sleepy harbour and small grey-sand
beach. The best local swimming is at **Agios
Georgios Beach**, a short way south towards
Arkasa.

🛏 Sleeping & Eating

Pine Tree Studios APARTMENT €
(📞 6977369948; www.pinetree-karpathos.gr; Adia;
apt €50-70; ✳) Some 9km north of Finiki, just
before the road winds uphill to Lefkos, are
the secluded Pine Tree Studios. These comfortable studios with views over to Kasos
make for a quiet rural retreat and include
an excellent restaurant specialising in dishes
cooked in a wood oven. Taste the *katsiki stifadho* (goat in red-wine sauce). The studios
are equipped with fridge and kitchenette.
There's also free shaded camping.

Marina Taverna TAVERNA €
(📞 22450 61100; Finiki; mains €6-16; ⊙ breakfast,
lunch & dinner; ✳📶) Laid-back taverna with
an expansive terrace surveying the gentle turquoise bay just metres from the waterfront.
Enjoy inexpensive breakfasts, snack lunches
and an enjoyable seafood-accented evening
menu featuring squid, crab and grilled meats.

Lefkos Λευκός

This is the largest but also the prettiest of
the low-key west-coast resorts, 20km north
of Finiki and a 5km detour down from the
main road. Lefkos is here for a very good
reason – its curving sandy beach is absolutely delightful. This is the kind of place
where two weeks can vanish in gentle wan-
derings between beach and brunch.

While Lefkos is connected by bus with
Pigadia, it's definitely worth renting a car or
scooter through Lefkos Rent a Car while here.

🛏 Sleeping & Eating

Le Grand Bleu HOTEL €€
(📞 22450 71009; www.karpathos-legrandbleu.
com; Lefkos; studio/apt €85/120; 🅿✳📶) Very
nicely equipped studios and two-bedroom
apartments beside the graceful main beach,
kitted out with crisp fresh linen, tasteful art
and sumptuous balconies with cushioned
armchairs. The recommended on-site tavern
closes at 10pm to let guests sleep.

OLYMBOS ΟΛΥΜΠΟΣ

Few moments can beat rounding a curve in the mountain road to receive your first glimpse of this mist-blown eyrie of pastel-coloured houses. Olymbos clings precariously to the summit of Mt Profitis Ilias (716m), as if flung there by a Titan's paw. Thread your way along its wind-tunnel alleys, passing old ladies in vividly coloured traditional dress, and you may feel as though you've strayed onto a film set. Many locals even speak with a dialect that still contains traces of ancient Dorian Greek.

It's considered to be the most traditional of all places in Greece; Olymbos' local ladies still wear their stunning hand-spun jackets and floral headgear. And the views – 'jaw-dropping' just doesn't cover it – will leave you spellbound as the earth plunges dramatically metres from your feet. Try and arrive in late afternoon or early morning to have the place to yourself.

Sleeping & Eating

Hotel Olymbos (☑ 22450 51009; r incl breakfast €45) Hidden away beneath the owners' excellent street-level restaurant, these three little studios have raised beds and traditional furnishings. Tread carefully; the walls are festooned with delicate decorated plates. Ask to see the family's carefully preserved blacksmith shop alongside.

Hotel Aphrodite (☑ 22450 51307; www.discoverolympos.com; d €45; ⊕) This hotel is located just beyond the central square at the far end of Olymbos. It has two rooms with two single beds, and two rooms with three. All are bright, airy and attractively decorated, but above all – literally – they have astonishing west-facing sea views.

Edem Garden (mains €6-9) Village taverna with a broad mountain-view terrace, check-cloth tables and a menu featuring delicious rural specialities such as *makarounes*, country sausage and local goat *stifadho*, along with pizzas and salads. And yes, maybe the name should really be 'Eden', but it isn't.

Dramountana TAVERNA €
(☑ 22450 71373; Lefkos; mains €6-15; ⊙ breakfast, lunch & dinner) Part of a cluster of similar places with waterside tables at the northern end of Lefkos harbour, this all-day cafe serves everything from fresh juices and coffee to fish soup, grilled squid, roast lamb and souvlakia.

Northern Karpathos

Locals often describe Karpathos as being two distinct islands, with its rugged, mountainous and astonishingly beautiful northern half in stark contrast to the fertile, low-lying south. That said, the east-coast road starts to climb as soon as you head north from Pigadia and the scenery turns ever more spectacular. Only within the last decade has the route been sealed all the way to the north, meaning that the once-isolated village of Olymbos has become swamped with day trippers in summer. Olymbos is still a magnificent place, though, most memorably reached by boat to Diafani from Pigadia, then a connecting bus. And it's worth spending a few nights here, especially if you fancy some hiking, or swimming at remote beaches.

Diafani Διαφάνι
POP 250

Diafani is an intimate, wind-blasted huddle of white houses fronted by cobalt-blue water, with a mountain backdrop. Bar the crash of the waves and old men playing backgammon, nothing else stirs. Most travellers simply pass through Diafani, so if you stay you'll likely have the beaches and trails to yourself. There's no bank, post office, petrol station or ATM, so bring cash and fuel.

🏃 Activities

Hiking trails from Diafani village are way-marked with red or blue markers or stone cairns. The most popular route heads inland, straight up the valley to **Olymbos**. That takes around two hours – though inevitably some prefer to catch a bus uphill and walk back down. Alternatively, a 50-minute track leads 4km north along the coast, through the pines, to **Vananda Beach**, which has a seasonal taverna.

A more strenuous three-hour walk takes you 11km northwest to the Hellenistic site of **Vroukounda**, passing the agricultural village of Avlona along the way. There are no facilities, so carry food and water with you.

Anyone planning serious walking should get hold of the 1:60,000 *Karpathos-Kasos* map, published by Terrain Maps (www.terrain maps.gr) and available in Pigadia. For advice on current conditions, call in at the Environment Management Office on Diafani's seafront before you set off.

🛏 Sleeping & Eating

Balaskas Hotel   HOTEL €
(📞 22450 51320; www.balaskashotel.com; s/d from €35/45; ❄🅿) You have a choice here of either 'economy' rooms (essentially pension-style minimalism with white walls and wood beds) or 'standard', which feature more colour and flair – think romantic mozzie nets and wrought iron beds. Some have kitchenettes, all have fridges. It's a five- to ten-minute walk from the seafront.

The owners operate two excursion boats and offer a free beach trip for each guest.

La Gorgona   ITALIAN €
(Harbour; mains €7-10; ⏱9am-late) If you're looking for a breezy spot to gaze at the sea, listen to cool tunes, drink quality coffee and digress from Greek to Italian food, La Gorgona may tick all your boxes. Owners Gigi and Sofia prepare tasty pasta dishes like carbonara and seafood spaghetti as well as a selection of pizza. Don't miss the desserts either: tiramisu and chocolate strudel.

Corali   TAVERNA €
(📞 22450 51332; mains €7-12; ⏱breakfast, lunch & dinner) Run by Popi and Mihalis, this is probably the best spot for fresh, tasty traditional fare. Try their delicious *stifadho* or eggplant salad. Vegetables are sourced locally. Service is slow but the quality of the food and *filoxenia* (hospitality) make up for it.

ℹ Information

Environment Management Office (⏱10am-4pm Mon-Fri) Advice on current conditions for anyone planning some serious walking on the island.

Orfanos Travel (📱 mobile 6974990394; at Nicos Hotel; ⏱8am-1pm & 5.30-8.30pm; 🛜) Runs boat trips and sells ferry and air tickets.

ℹ Getting There & Away

Blue Star Ferries (p328) calls in at Diafani's small jetty three times weekly heading for Halki and Rhodes, and three times weekly en route towards Pigadia and Kasos (two of

which continue to Crete and one to Santorini). There are also day trips by boat to Pigadia in summer, as well as assorted excursions. Tourist coaches carry day trippers from the jetty up to Olymbos. There are two scheduled buses on weekdays, one of which continues to Pigadia on Friday only, and one on weekends.

Buses run to Olymbos then on to Pigadia every other day at 3.45pm.

KASOS   ΚΑΣΟΣ
POP 1080

Kasos, the southernmost Dodecanese island, looks like the Greece that time forgot. Deceptively inviting in summer, it can feel very isolated in winter, when it's battered by winds and imprisoned by huge turquoise waves. Most of its visitors are rare seabirds; most of the human returnees are Kasiots on fleeting visits. Come here, though, and you may well succumb to its tumbledown charm.

In 1820, under Turkish rule, Kasos was home to 11,000 inhabitants. Tragically, Mohammad Ali, the Turkish governor of Egypt, saw its large merchant fleet as an impediment to his plan to establish a base in Crete. On 7 June 1824, therefore, his men landed on Kasos and killed around 7000 of its people. The island never really recovered, but each year Kasiots return from all over the world to commemorate the massacre.

ℹ Getting There & Away

There are daily flights to Karpathos (€56, 10 minutes), Sitia (€61, 40 minutes) and Rhodes (€74, one hour) with **Sky Express** (p328). The only ferry service is with **Blue Star Ferries** (p328), en route between Rhodes and Karpathos, and Crete and Piraeus.

Boat Services from Kasos (Fry)

DESTINATION	DURATION	FARE (€)	FREQUENCY
Heraklion	6hr	20	1 weekly
Karpathos	1½hr	8	3 weekly
Piraeus	19hr	44	2 weekly
Rhodes	8hr	24	3 weekly
Santorini	9hr	27	2 weekly

ℹ Getting Around

The airport is 1km west of Fry. Either walk for 10 minutes along the coast road – yes, it's exposed, but you won't half feel pleased with yourself –

or call a **taxi** (☑ mobile 6973244371, mobile 6977904632). In theory, a bus connects all the island's villages, but it hasn't been working for years. Cars and scooters can be hired from **Oasis Rent-a-Car** (☑ 22450 41746; Kasos Airport).

Fry
Φρυ
POP 350

The capital, Fry (pronounced *free*), is on the north coast. The valley behind it is the only fertile land on Kasos, so the only other villages are dotted across the surrounding hillside. Although Fry is more a working port than a tourist destination, the tiny old harbour, known as **Bouka**, is impossibly photogenic. Pretty white houses with navy-blue trim line the quay, a few cafes sit waiting for customers, grizzled fishermen patiently mend their nets, and the pastel-blue church of Agios Spyridon surveys the scene. Even as late as June, though, Fry still has the feel of a ghost town.

The nearest beach is 10 minutes' walk east along the shoreline, in the tiny satellite port of **Emborio**. There are patches of gravel amid the sand, but the sea is clear and sheltered, so it's a good place for a quick dip.

⊙ Sights & Activities

Archaeological Museum　　　MUSEUM
(⊙ 9am-3pm Jul-Sep) FREE Housed in a grand 19th-century villa above the harbour, this seasonal museum displays objects pulled from ancient shipwrecks, assorted Greek oil lamps and Hellenistic finds, including inscribed stone slabs.

Excursion Boat　　　BOATING
(☑ 22450 41047, 6977911209; 🚢) When they can round up 10 or more passengers, two boats, *Athina* and *Kasos Princess,* offer summer-afternoon excursions (€10) to the uninhabited islet of Armathia, which has superb sandy beaches. The *Kasos Princess* also runs full-day trips to Pigadia on Karpathos, on summer Wednesdays only.

🛌 Sleeping & Eating

Hotel Anagennissis　　　HOTEL €
(☑ 22450 41495; www.anagennisishotel.gr; s/d €45/50; ❄🛜) Old-fashioned hotel, close to the waterfront in the village centre, where the plain but perfectly adequate rooms have comfy beds, fridges, bathrooms and sea-view balconies. Staff are seldom present in the hotel itself; the owners run the Kasos Maritime & Travel Agency (p352) next door.

DODECANESE KASOS

Kasos

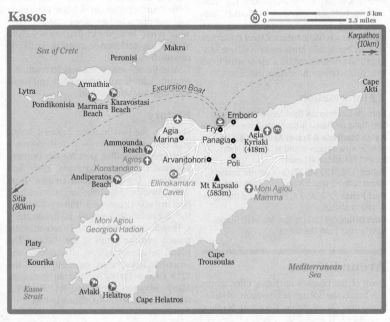

Angelica's   APARTMENT €€

(☑ 22450 41268; www.angelicas.gr; apt €60-80; ❄☎) Attractive, traditionally furnished apartments in a fine old village home five minutes' walk up from the harbour. Two are on the ground floor, with private courtyards, and two upstairs, with sea-view verandas. All have painted floors and stencils on their white walls. The largest apartment sleeps up to five.

★ Taverna Emborios   TAVERNA €

(☑ 22450 41586; Emborio Beach; mains €6-13; ⊙ lunch & dinner; ☎) Crisp, beautifully neat beachfront restaurant, 10 minutes' walk from Fry. It's unquestionably the best place to eat on Kasos. The friendly owner, who lived in New York for many years, serves up wonderful local specialities, including delicious octopus, tiny home-grown olives and his own salty preserved fish.

Orea Bouka   TAVERNA €

(☑ 22450 41053; mains €7-10) There's no menu at this simple little taverna, which sets out tables on the sea wall on the west side of Bouka harbour. Sophia, the owner, just shows or tells you whatever she happens to be cooking. In summer, expect a choice of dolmadhes, fresh fish, baked meats and vegetable stews.

Mylos   TAVERNA €

(☑ 22450 41825; Plateia Iroön Kasou; mains €7; ⊙ lunch & dinner; ☎☍) Overlooking the commercial port (as opposed to Bouka), this conspicuous taverna has unbroken sea views and serves a reliable menu of local favourites such as 'mountain grass roots' – village sausage and pot-roast rabbit – along with fresh fish. Almost everything costs less than €10.

❶ Information

Both the Commercial Bank beside the harbour and Alpha on Plateia Iroön Kasou have ATMs.

Kasos Maritime & Travel Agency (☑ 22450 41495; www.kassos-island.gr; Plateia Iroön Kasou) For all travel tickets.

Police (☑ 22450 41222) On a narrow sealed street running south from Fry's main road.

Port Police (☑ 22450 41288) Behind the Agios Spyridon church.

Post Office (⊙ 7.30am-2pm Mon-Fri) Diagonally across from the police.

Around Kasos

None of the beaches on Kasos offer shade. The best is the isolated pebbled cove of Helatros, near Moni Agiou Georgiou Hadion, 11km southwest of Fry, but you'll need your own transport to reach it, and it has no facilities. There's another small but decent beach, **Avlaki**, in walking distance.

Agia Marina, 1km southwest of Fry, is a pretty village with a gleaming white-and-blue church that celebrates a festival on 17 July. Beyond it, the road continues to verdant **Arvanitohori**, with abundant fig and pomegranate trees. **Poli**, 3km southeast of Fry, is the former capital, built on the ancient acropolis.

KASTELLORIZO (MEGISTI)
ΚΑΣΤΕΛΛΟΡΙΖΟ (ΜΕΓΙΣΤΗ)

POP 275

So close to the Turkish coast – Kaş is just 2km away – that you can almost taste the East, the tiny, far-flung island of Kastellorizo is insanely pretty. Sailing into its one village (of the same name), past the ruined castle, minaret and pastel-painted neoclassical houses huddled around the turquoise bay, is soul enriching, and reminds a little of Symi without the super yachts and swank. 'Megisti', as Kastellorizo was once called (meaning 'great'), is the largest of a small archipelago, and despite being less than 10 sq km, enjoys more hours of sunshine than any other Greek island and boasts the most dramatic blue cave in the Med. And while it may lack powder-fine beaches, there are floating platforms and satellite idylls you can reach by boat.

Arid Kastellorizo is not easy to reach, but rewards with beauty, tranquillity and locals who welcome your custom.

History

Home to the best harbour between Beirut and Piraeus, Kastellorizo was successively a prosperous trading port for the Dorians, Romans, Crusaders, Egyptians, Turks and Venetians. Under Ottoman control, from 1552 onwards, it had the largest merchant fleet in the Dodecanese. A 1913 revolt against the Turks briefly resulted in it becoming a French naval base, and it subsequently passed into the hands of the Italians. The island progressively lost all strategic and economic importance, especially after the 1923 Greece–Turkey population exchange. Many islanders emigrated to Australia, where around 30,000 continue to live.

After Kastellorizo suffered bombardment during WWII, English commanders ordered the few remaining inhabitants to abandon the island. Most fled to Cyprus, Palestine and Egypt and those that later returned found their houses in ruins. While the island has never regained its previous population levels – the village alone was once home to 10,000 people – more recent returnees have finally restored almost all the waterfront buildings, and Kastellorizo is looking better than it has for a century.

The island has found itself in recent years in the migration path of thousands of fleeing refugees, though numbers have recently fallen to only a few; given their grandparents experiences as refugees, the islanders acted, not surprisingly, with great compassion.

ⓘ Getting There & Away

AIR
Olympic Air (www.olympicair.com) flies daily from Rhodes to Kastellorizo (return €132, 40 minutes).

BOAT
Kastellorizo has a very limited ferry service. **Blue Star Ferries** (p328) calls in twice a week to and from Piraeus via Rhodes. On summer Saturdays, **Dodekanisos Seaways** (p328) sails from Rhodes to Kastellorizo and back; used as a day trip, it gives you four hours on the island.

ⓘ Getting Around
Kastellorizo's tiny airport is up on the central plateau, 2.5km above the village. There's no bus, so you'll have to take the island's only **taxi** (☑ mobile 6938739178) to and from the harbour (€5).

The main destinations for boat trips are Kaş in Turkey and the spectacular **Blue Cave** (€9), famous for its mirror-like blue water, on Kastellorizo's remote southeast shore. Try **Nikos Sea Wolf Taxi** (☑ mobile 6934523917; per person €8).

Kastellorizo Village
Καστελλόριζο
POP 250

Kastellorizo Village is the island's main settlement. Its harbour is its lifeblood and where the limited action gathers: mounds of yellow nets, stretching cats, youths on mobile phones and sleepy fishermen sit outside *kafeneia*, backdropped by smartly shuttered, brightly coloured mansions. Make sure you explore the labyrinthine cobbled backstreets behind.

An amazing 80% of the villagers are returned Aussie expats, which adds a definite upbeat energy to the community. Come August, thousands of 'Kassies' return to see their families.

◉ Sights & Activities
A coastal pathway around the headland below passes precarious steps that climb to a rock-hewn **Lycian tomb** from the 4th century BC, which boasts an impressive Doric facade. There are several such tombs along Turkey's Anatolian coast, but they are very rare in Greece.

It's also possible to walk the 1km up to **Paleokastro**, the island's ancient capital. Follow the concrete steps that start just past a soldier's sentry box on the airport road. The old city's Hellenistic walls enclose a tower, a water cistern and three churches.

Archaeological Museum MUSEUM
(€2; ⊙7am-2pm Tue-Sun; ⊞) Holds an assortment of ancient finds, costumes and photos as well as a documentary about Kastellorizo as told by the islanders.

Megisti Museum MUSEUM
(€2; ⊙8.30am-3pm Tue-Sun; ⊞) In a former mosque near the ferry jetty, this museum devotes itself largely to display panels telling the island's story.

Knights of St John Castle CASTLE
(⊙7am-2pm Tue-Sun; ⊞) FREE At the top of the hill, a rickety stairway leads to the ruins of the Knights of St John Castle, which gave the island its name – thanks to the red cliff on which it stood, this was the 'Castello Rosso'. It offers splendid views of Turkey.

⌷ Sleeping
★ **Mediterraneo** PENSION €€
(☑22460 49007; www.mediterraneo-kastelorizo.com; s/d/ste €70/80/180; ⊙May-Oct; ☞) If Picasso was a hotel, he'd be the Mediterraneo. With its lime, mango and smurf-blue exterior, this revamped mansion has romantic rooms tastefully scattered with art and traditional raised-platform beds. Breakfast on the terrace amid a confection of fruit and homemade jams, read in the shaded arbour, or flop on loungers by the sea.

Megisti Hotel HOTEL €€
(☑22460 49220; www.megistihotel.gr; d/ste incl breakfast €144/228; ⊞@☞☞) On the harbour's western extremity, it's impossible to

miss the most imposing hotel on the island. Megisti's four suites and 15 stylish rooms have rain showers, DVD players, tiled floors, standard lamps, safety deposit boxes and private balconies. Outside on the chequerboard waterfront terrace, you can climb easily into the sea from Megisti's iron-hoop steps (like a giant swimming pool).

Poseidon HOTEL €€
(☑ 22460 49212, 6956617585; www.kastelorizo poseidon.gr; Plateia Australias; studio/apt €135/150; ❋ ☎) Set in five beautifully restored neoclassical villas, a block from the corner of the west side of the harbour, Poseidon offers comfortably finished studios and apartments with grey shabby-chic furniture offset by sugar-white walls and contemporary lighting. Add to this private verandas, big sea views, a great breakfast in the main hotel, plus a relaxing roof terrace.

✖ Eating & Drinking

Tables spill out onto the narrow harbour, cats entwine themselves around diners' legs and, by night, the atmosphere is magical. Just don't tip into the water, for the *kordoni* (walkway) that is the village's main thoroughfare, is narrow.

★ Alexandra's TAVERNA €
(☑ 22460 49019; mains €7-15; ☺ lunch & dinner; ❋ ☎) ✐ With bouzouki music and salt breeze wafting over its thyme-topped tables, the friendliest of Kastellorizo's quayside restaurants also serves the best food. Everything from the squid-ink risotto and calamari stuffed with feta is prepared by Alexandra herself. Mezedhes (appetisers) are full of vim and super fresh. Treat yourself to lamb on the spit.

Lazarakis GREEK €
(mains €8-15; ☺ lunch & dinner; ❋ ☎) This central waterfront restaurant is great for seafood – grilled octopus, lobster spaghetti, baby shrimp, grouper and succulent calamari – and also has grilled meat dishes. Eat under the vine canopy, or better still out on the jetty where you can sometimes see giant turtles in the water.

Faros Bar BAR
(☑ 22460 49509; mains €6; ☺ 9am-late; ☎) Occupying an enviable location in the former lighthouse, beyond the ferry jetty and beside the mosque, this bar offers a wonderful opportunity to swim in turquoise shallows before taking breakfast and drinking in wide-screen views of Turkey. It even has its own quayside loungers. Salads and snacks all day, then tapas from 6pm.

❶ Information

Medical Centre (☑ 22460 70659 22460 49267; ☺ Mon & Fri 9am-1pm) on the eastern side of the harbour.

Papoutsis Travel (☑ 22460 70630, 22460 49356; ☺ 9am-2pm & 5pm-8pm) Ferry and air tickets, bike and scooter rental and yachting services.

Police Station (☑ 22460 49333) On the bay's western side.

Port Police (☑ 22460 49333) At the eastern tip of the bay.

Post Office (☑ 22460 49298; ☺ 9am-2pm Mon-Fri) Next to the police station.

SYMI ΣΥΜΗ

POP 2610

Beautiful Symi is guaranteed to evoke oohs and aahs from ferry passengers before they even get off the boat. The first sight of Gialos harbour, framed against an amphitheatre of pastel-coloured houses rising on all sides, is unforgettable. It's all thanks to the Italians, who ruled the island almost a century ago and established the neoclassical architectural style that Symi has followed ever since.

Although Symi is far from small, it's mostly barren and the only settlements are Gialos, the old village of Horio, and Pedi, down in the valley beyond. One road runs all the way to the monastery at Panormitis, near Symi's southern tip. The rest of this spellbinding island is largely deserted, but it's surrounded by blue coves and beaches, and aglitter with crystal-clear water so transparent that boats can look as if they're floating on thin air.

History

Symi has long traditions of both sponge diving and shipbuilding and is mentioned in the 'Iliad' as sending ships to assist Agamemnon's siege of Troy. In ancient legend, Glaucus, one of the island's sons, was the master builder of *Argo*, the ship that would take Jason and his compadres to distant Colchis in search of the Golden Fleece. During Ottoman times it was granted the right to fish for sponges in Turkish waters. In return, Symi supplied the sultan with first-class boat builders. This exchange enriched the island – gracious

Symi

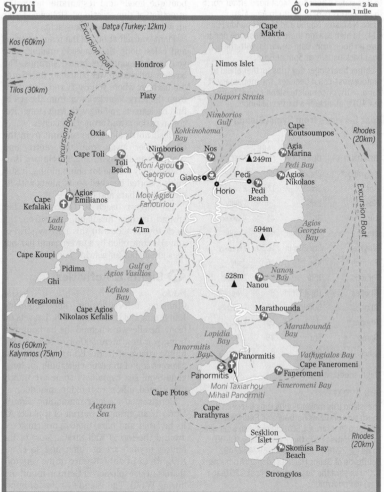

N 0 ———————— 2 km
   0 ———————— 1 mile

Datça (Turkey; 12km)

Cape Makria

Kos (60km)

Excursion Boat

Hondros

Nimos Islet

Tilos (30km)

Platy

Diapori Straits

Nimborios Gulf

Kokkinohoma Bay

Oxia

Nimborios

Nos

Cape Koutsoumpos

Rhodes (20km)

Agia Marina

Cape Toli

Toli Beach

Moni Agiou Georgiou

Gialos

Pedi

▲249m

Pedi Bay

Agios Nikolaos

Excursion Boat

Agios Emilianos

Horio

Pedi Beach

Cape Kefalaki

Moni Agiou Fanouriou

Ladi Bay

▲ 471m

Agios Georgios Bay

594m ▲

Cape Koupi

Pidima

Gulf of Agios Vasilios

528m ▲ Nanou

Nanou Bay

Ghi

Kefalos Bay

Megalonisi

Cape Agios Nikolaos Kefalis

Marathounda

Marathounda Bay

Kos (60km); Kalymnos (75km)

Lopidia Bay

Panormitis Bay

Panormitis

Vathygialos Bay

Cape Faneromeni

Panormitis

Faneromeni

Faneromeni Bay

Aegean Sea

Cape Potos

Moni Taxiarhou Mihail Panormiti

Rhodes (20km)

Cape Parathyras

Sesklion Islet

Skomisa Bay Beach

Strongylos

DODECANESE SYMI

---

mansions were built and culture and education flourished. By the early 20th century, the population was 22,500 and Symi was launching around 500 ships a year. But the Italian occupation, the advent of the steamship and the decline of the sponge industry put an end to prosperity, obliging Symi to reinvent itself as a tourist destination.

🛈 Getting There & Away

Dodekanisos Seaways (p328) runs catamarans to and from Rhodes at least once daily – four each week stop at Panormitis en route – and also offers frequent sailings northwest, to Kos

and beyond. Blue Star Ferries (p328) calls in twice weekly heading towards Rhodes, and also en route for Tilos, Nisyros, Kos, Kalymnos, Astypalea and Piraeus. Symi fills up every morning with day trippers from Rhodes, with several Rhodes-based excursion boats complementing the high-speed catamaran.

Look out for summer day trips from Gialos to Datça, Turkey (€40 including Turkish port taxes).

🛈 Getting Around

BOAT

Water taxis (☎ 22460 71423) lined up along the inner side of Gialos harbour run regular trips to the island's beaches. Most head either north to Nimborios (€6) or south to Agia Marina, Agios Nikolaos, Nanou and Marathounda (€6 to €14). In high season there's at least one departure an hour, from 9am onwards, with the last boat back usually at 5pm or 6pm.

Larger boats offer day trips further afield to remote west-coast beaches, the monastery at Panormitis, or complete island-circuit tours (up to €40) that include a barbecue lunch.

Boat Services from Symi (Gialos)

DESTINATION	DURATION	FARE (€)	FREQUENCY
Kalymnos*	2hr 20 min	32	1 daily
Kos	3hr	12	2 weekly
Kos*	1½hr	24	1 daily
Leros*	3hr	41	4 weekly
Lipsi*	3hr 10min	41	1 daily
Nisyros	3hr 20min	11.50	1 weekly
Patmos*	4hr	46	daily
Piraeus	15hr	56.50	2 weekly
Rhodes	1hr 40 min	8	2 weekly
Rhodes*	50min	18	1-4 daily
Rhodes*	1hr	16	1 daily
Samos	5hr	49	1 weekly
Tilos	2hr	8	1 weekly

*high-speed services

BUS & TAXI

The island **bus** makes hourly runs between the south side of Gialos harbour and Pedi Beach, via Horio (flat fare €1.50). There's also a service to Panormitis two to three times daily (€1.50). **Taxis** (☑ 22460 71311, mobile 6974623492; Southside of Gialos Harbour) depart from a rank 100m west of the bus stop, and cost €25 (each way) to Panormitis.

CAR

Glaros (☑ 22460 71926, mobile 6948362079; www.glarosrentacar.gr; ☺ 9am-9pm), near the clock tower, rents cars and scooters.

Gialos   Γιαλός

POP 2200

Your first view of Gialos is unforgettable, with its neoclassical biscuit- and ochre-hued buildings gathered aristocratically around what is perhaps the world's prettiest harbour. Fishing boats bob in water so perfectly clear they look as if they're floating on thin air, sponge salesmen hawk their weird-shaped treasures of the deep, while a few world-class boutique hotels and restaurants invite the attention of the occasional Hollywood star arriving in a gleaming super-yacht.

Plant yourself at one of the many tavernas and cafes along the quayside, making sure you try the island's celebrated shrimps. The basilica and clock tower punctuate the edge of the harbour where you catch and disembark from the ferry. Wander away from the sea to find backstreets spilling with fruit stores, ice-cream parlours and aromatic bakeries.

Head north along the seafront from the clock tower, away from the centre, and you're immediately in smaller **Harani Bay**. Traditionally a base for shipbuilding, it still holds assorted beached boats, along with its own crop of bars and tavernas.

The closest beach to Gialos, **Nos**, lies around the next headland, 500m from the clock tower. Access to this narrow strip of gravel is controlled by a taverna and bar, but it's a great spot for a swim, nonetheless.

◉ Sights & Activities

Horio   VILLAGE

Climbing calf-crunching, knee-knobbling Kali Strata, the broad stair path that sets off from the alleyways behind the harbour, will bring you in a mere 500-or-so steps to the hilltop village of Horio. En route you'll pass a succession of majestic villas built for long-gone Symi sea captains – some are utterly dilapidated, others restored to splendour.

Constructed to deter marauding pirates, Horio is an absolute warren of a place. All its tavernas and bars, though, are clustered around the top of Kali Strata. Most of the houses beyond are in ruins, and so is the **Knights of St John Kastro** at the very top, thanks to an explosion of German munitions during WWII. The island's **Archaeological Museum** is up here too, but is currently closed for restoration.

Nautical & Folklore Museum   MUSEUM

(€2; ☺ 9.30am-9pm) The two upper floors of a colourfully painted villa on Gialos' main square hold the separate halves of this freshly restored museum. Crammed with relics of Symi's sponge-diving era, including a pair of bulky helmets, the nautical section at the top is more interesting than the rather-haphazard folklore part below, but both contain fascinating old photos of the island.

Symi Tours   BOATING, WALKING

(☑ 22460 71307) Symi Tours organises daily excursions by boat to explore Symi's beautiful coves, bays and secluded beaches. Daily departures from Gialos harbour at 10.30am, returning at 5pm. Find it on the south side of Gialos harbour. Also offers multilingual guided walks (€12) around the island (every Tuesday at 8am), often ending with a boat ride back to Gialos.

🛏 Sleeping

★ Hotel Fiona   HOTEL €

(📞 22460 72088; www.fionahotel.com; Horio; r incl breakfast €55; ❄🐾) Offering Symi's best-value accommodation, this simple but charming family-run hotel perches on the edge of Horio (turn left at the top of Kali Strata). The views across the harbour are truly astonishing, both from the balconies of its spacious and attractively decorated rooms, kitted out with turquoise furniture, and from the breakfast area downstairs. There's also a peaceful courtyard.

Hotel Aliki   BOUTIQUE HOTEL €€

(📞 22460 71655; www.hotelaliki.gr; d/ste incl breakfast €130/220; ❄🐾) Dainty Aliki is Symi's oldest hotel and evokes old-world charm with its traditionally painted wood-beamed lobby, flower-shaded lamps and vintage leather armchairs. Rooms are elegant and simple, with antique iron beds, fragrant linen and serene views of the sea lapping a few metres below. There's also a roof terrace. Check out its its sister restaurant next door, La Vaporetta.

Albatros Hotel   HOTEL €€

(📞 22460 71707; www.albatrosymi.gr; s/d incl breakfast €50/65; ⊙Apr-Nov; ❄🐾) With its turquoise and biscuit-hued exterior, Albatros has a sunny breakfast room and five whitewashed air-con bedrooms with tiled floors, traditional wood ceilings and little balconies giving side-on sea views. Just a block back from the harbour in the heart of Gialos, it's clean and welcoming.

Iapetos Village   APARTMENT €€

(📞 22460 72777; www.iapetos-village.gr; d/apt €135/155; ❄@🐾🏊) Set around a leafy courtyard, a short walk inland from the main square, Iapetos holds 28 high-class rooms, studios and apartments, newly built in traditional style. All have lovely wooden high ceilings and private patios or balconies, and most have fully fitted kitchens. There's also a beautiful pool, tucked under the arches, plus a sauna and bar.

★ Old Markets   BOUTIQUE HOTEL €€€

(📞 22460 71440; www.theoldmarkets.com; r/ste incl breakfast €220/395; ❄🐾) Symi's finest hotel stands a few steps up Kali Strata. The old market space has four stunningly individual rooms and one suite, while the newly opened adjoining mansion has five more contemporary suites. All rooms enjoy a pillow library, iPhone docking station and use of an honesty bar, as well as the roof terrace, pool and optional spa treatments.

🍴 Eating & Drinking

🍽 Gialos

★ Meraklis   SEAFOOD €

(📞 22460 71003; www.tavernaomeraklis.com; mains €10-13; ⊙10am-late; ❄🐾) This old-school taverna, with Santorini-blue walls decked in vintage diving photos and antique mirrors, is as pretty as it is friendly. And while its souvlakia, meatballs and roast lamb are tasty, most diners come here to feast on fresh octopus, sea bream, Symi shrimp and swordfish. Why not try the lot, with a mixed seafood plate for two (€35)?

★ Tholos   TAVERNA €€

(📞 22460 72033; Harani Bay; mains €8-14; ⊙lunch & dinner May-Oct) There's no more romantic restaurant in the Dodecanese than this lovely taverna, poised at the tip of Harani Bay, along the quay from central Gialos. The sunset views from its waterfront tables are stupendous, and so too is the food, which includes local meat and vegetables as well as fresh fish. Be sure to sample the succulent, bright-red Symi shrimp.

★ Muses   FUSION €€

(📞 6958734503; www.muses-symi.com; Gialos; mains €24; ⊙7pm-late May-Oct) Admittedly it's a little overpriced, but this wine-red bijou restaurant run by two Argentinian brothers is Symi's most exciting restaurant. A modern Mediterranean menu changes daily, combining signature dishes like octopus with fava purée and orange, or pork with pears and retsina. Seating is on a flowery terrace, beside the town square just back from the harbour.

To Spitiko   TAVERNA €€

(📞 22460 72452; Harani Bay; mains €10-18; ⊙breakfast, lunch & dinner; 🐾) Owners Eruala and Fortes make their food with great care and zest, and while the place on the tip of Harani Bay harbour might not look spectacular, the cuisine most definitely is. Lemon potatoes, country sausage, Symi shrimps, grilled octopus in lemon sauce, and last but not least, mouthwatering *portokalopita* (orange cake). Ask to sit by the sea.

★ Tsati   BAR
(☏ 22460 72498; Harani Bay; ⊗ 11am-late) Ultra-welcoming quayside bar, 100m along Harani Bay beyond the clock tower. As well as tables on a tree-shaded terrace, it offers stone benches carved into the sea wall. Cushioned and whitewashed, they're perfect for a sunset cocktail, served with free snacks.

✕ Horio

Olive Tree   CAFE €
(☏ 22460 72681; www.olivetreesymi.eu; Horio; light meals €3-8; ⊗ 8.30am-3.30pm; 🖥 🖉 🚸) 🌿 English-run cafe that's a favourite morning rendezvous for the island's expats. Sit yourself down on its vine-shaded terrace at the top of Kali Strata and tuck into a wide array of smoothies, juices, cakes, locally sourced salads and sandwiches.

Taverna Giorgo & Maria   TAVERNA €
(☏ 22460 71984; Horio; mains €10; ⊗ lunch & dinner; 🖥) Bouzouki music piping across its

OFF THE BEATEN TRACK

MONI TAXIARHOU MIHAIL PANORMITI

Near Symi's southern tip, beyond the scented pine forests of the high interior, spectacular Panormitis Bay is home to **Moni Taxiarhou Mihail Panormiti** (☏ 22460 72414; ⊗ dawn-dusk). Monasteries have stood here since the 5th century, but the present building dates from the 18th century. The principal church contains an intricately carved wooden iconostasis, frescoes and an icon of St Michael, protector of sailors and patron saint of Symi.

Pilgrims who ask the saint for a favour leave an offering; you'll see piles of these, plus prayers in bottles that have been dropped off boats and found their own way here. The large complex comprises a Byzantine museum and folkloric museum, a bakery with excellent bread, and a basic restaurant-cafe. Visitors should dress modestly. Buses come here from Gialos, and some ferries call in, too.

breezy courtyard and veranda, soaring views of the gas-blue bay below, and a selection of Symi shrimp, braised rabbit, pork casserole, swordfish, lobster and bream. Live music from 9pm on Friday and Saturday.

❶ Information

Ferries and catamarans dock beside the clock tower on the north side of the harbour entrance. Excursion and taxi boats dock along the south side, near its inland end. All activity in Gialos focuses on the quay, while the Kali Strata stairway sets off up to Horio from the southeast corner.

Both the National and Alpha Banks have ATM-equipped branches on the northern side of the harbour.

Kalodoukas Holidays (☏ 22460 71077; www. kalodoukas.gr; ⊗ 9.30am-2pm & 6.30-9pm) In the absence of an official tourist office, this helpful agency, at the foot of Kali Strata, is the next best thing. It also rents houses, sells tickets, organises excursions and offers yachting services.

Police (☏ 22460 71111) By the ferry quay.

Port Police (☏ 22460 71205) By the ferry quay.

Post Office By the ferry quay.

Symi Tours (☏ 22460 71307; www.symitours. com) This agency, just behind the southeast side of the harbour, organises excursions, including island bus tours and boat trips to Datça in Turkey. Also provides yachting services and sells ferry tickets.

Symi Visitor (☏ 22460 71785; www.symi visitor.com) Very friendly agency, just off the southeast side of the quay, with a fine roster of rental properties and a full-service laundry.

Around Symi

Apart from the monastery at Panormitis, the only tourist destinations on Symi are the beaches scattered along its coastline.

Nimborios   Νιμπόρειος

Nimborios is a pebble beach 3km west of Gialos, reached by walking or driving all the way around the harbour and simply continuing along the exposed but utterly beautiful shorefront road beyond. It's a peaceful spot, with a good little taverna that allows its customers to spend the day on sun loungers beneath the tamarisk trees alongside.

🛏 Sleeping

Niriides Apartments   APARTMENT €€
(☏ 22460 71784; www.niriideshotel.com; Nimborios; apt €140) Adjacent to Gialos is the quiet

little village of Nimborios where you'll find Niriides Apartments, sitting by peaceful Symi Bay. Pleasant, traditional decor with kitchenettes, fridges and balconies with sea views. There's a snack bar to take breakfast at and also a library.

Pedi   Πέδι

Once a village, now more of a yachting marina and low-key resort, Pedi stretches along the inner end of a large bay south of Gialos, immediately below Horio. The gentle valley behind it has always been the agricultural heartland of Symi.

Two beaches, to either side of the mouth of the bay, can be reached on foot from Pedi or water taxi from Gialos; both have appealing tavernas. **Agia Marina** to the north is a lagoon-like bay, facing a delightful chapel-topped islet across turquoise waters, which gets very crowded in summer. **Agios Nikolaos**, on the south side, is broader and sandier, with decent tree cover and idyllic swimming.

🛏 Sleeping

Pedi Beach Hotel   HOTEL €€
(☎ 22460 71981; www.pedibeachhotel.gr; Pedi; r from €117; ☀) Fresh with their aquamarine-striped beds and cobalt-blue curtains, these simple cool-tiled rooms are pleasant, with unblemished sea-view balconies. There's a beach and snack bar.

Nanou & Marathounda
Νανού & Μαραθούντα

Two large bays south of Pedi, Nanou and Marathounda, hold large beaches and tavernas and make great destinations for water-taxi day trips. Goat-roamed Marathounda, backed by a lush valley and also accessible via a rough road, is especially recommended.

🍴 Eating

★ Marathounda Taverna   TAVERNA €€
(☎ 22460 71425; Marathounda; mains €10-12; ☺ breakfast, lunch & dinner) Quintessential beach taverna, where the owner's goats – responsible for the delicious homemade cheese and, whisper it, the goat stew, too – nuzzle up to the tables. Be sure to sample the Symi shrimp and grilled fish, along with herbs and vegetables from the organic gardens alongside. For those who can't bear to leave, it also has plush beachfront studios for rent (€125).

TILOS   ΤΗΛΟΣ
POP 550

With its russet gold mountains, lack of people, and wildflowers blooming at every turn, Tilos has a charm that will salve your busy mind. Here you can hike through meadows, mountains and valleys on shepherds' paths before flopping onto a deserted beach. The azure waters hold monk seals and sea turtles, and the island also draws birdwatchers and wildlife buffs from across the globe.

History

Amazingly, ancient Tilos is best known for its population of midget elephants. Full-sized elephants are thought to have found their way here six million years ago, when the island was still attached to Asia Minor. When cut off by the rising waters of the Mediterranean, the elephants were left with no natural predators and a diminished food supply, and shrank in size. They became extinct around 4000 BC. A large cache of their bones was discovered in 1974 in Harkadio Cave, just off the Livadia–Megalo Horio road.

ℹ Getting There & Away

Tilos has no airport and only a minimal ferry service. The Dodekanisos Seaways (p328) catamaran stops at Tilos on Tuesday and Thursday, heading from Rhodes and Halki to Nisyros, Kos and Kalymnos in the morning, and back to Rhodes in the evening. On those days, you can visit the island as a day trip from Rhodes or Halki. In addition, Blue Star Ferries (p328) sails twice each week to Piraeus via Nisyros, Kos and Kalymnos, and twice to Rhodes, one of which stops at Symi.

Boat Services from Tilos (Livadia)

DESTINATION	DURATION	FARE (€)	FREQUENCY
Halki*	40min	13	2 weekly
Kalymnos	3hr 20min	13	2 weekly
Kalymnos*	2¼hr	29	2 weekly
Kos	3hr	10	2 weekly
Kos*	1½hr	22	2 weekly
Nisyros	1½hr	7.50	2 weekly
Nisyros*	45min	13	2 weekly
Piraeus	16hr	54	2 weekly
Rhodes	2½hr	13	3 weekly
Rhodes*	1½hr	28	2 weekly
Symi	2hr	9	1 weekly

*high-speed services

ℹ️ Getting Around

Five buses each day connect Livadia with Megalo Horio, Eristos Beach and Agios Antonios (€1.50). There is no taxi, but you can rent a car or scooter from **Drive Rent A Car** (☑ 22460 44173; www.drivetilos.gr; ☺ 9am-6pm) or Tilos Travel (p362).

Livadia   Λιβαδειά

POP 470

Livadia is a photogenic jumble of whitewashed houses huddled around the northern end of Agios Stefanos Bay. Little happens here – a cat yawns, a fisherman falls asleep over his glass of ouzo... And that's precisely its charm: tranquillity. A narrow girdle of pebbled beach, perfect for sun worshipping, stretches some 2km from the village down the turquoise-laced bay, while the village's central square is hugged by cafes, old-time tavernas and Italian-era municipal buildings.

👁️ Sights & Activities

Mikro Horio   ARCHAEOLOGICAL SITE

(☺ 24hr) When pirates prowled the Dodecanese, this medieval settlement was Tilos' main population centre. Its last inhabitants only left around 50 years ago and it now stands empty, 45 minutes' walk up from Livadia. In various states of ruin – one house opens as a music bar in summer – it's a fascinating place to wander. Linger until the light fades and it turns downright eerie. If you can stay awake long enough, visit Mikro Horio nightclub, in the middle of the village.

Tilos Trails   HIKING

(☑ 22460 44128, 6946054593; www.tilostrails. com) Tour company offering guided hikes all over the island, geared to suit individual abilities. Introductory walks last three hours. Talk to Iain and Lyn.

Tilos Heritage Tours   HIKING

(☑ 22460 44379, 6942061912; www.apollostudios. gr) British-run walking tours of the island. Talk to Charlie.

🛏️ Sleeping

Hotel Irini   HOTEL €

(☑ 22460 44293; www.tilosholidays.gr; r incl breakfast €60; ✳️ 🛜 🌊) Irini has stunning white rooms with flat-screen TVs, shabby chic furniture, colourful quilts, tasteful ceramics, fridges and pool-facing balconies. Behind are great mountain views to admire over breakfast.

Apollo Studios   APARTMENT €

(☑ 6942061912, 22460 44379; www.apollostudios. gr; d €50, apt €65-80; ✳️ 🛜) Fresh, well-appointed studios, run by a pleasant couple and set a few streets back from the harbour, with spotless kitchenettes, modern bathrooms, private balconies and a great communal roof terrace. They also offer roomy apartments with tiled floors and sofa beds – ask for number 3.

⭐ **Ilidi Rock Hotel**   HOTEL €€

(☑ 22460 44293; www.tilosholidays.gr; studio/apt incl breakfast €90/130; ✳️ @ 🛜) This superior hotel cascades down the cliff to two tiny aquamarine-laced inlets beside the harbour. Fully equipped studios and apartments with private balconies and four-poster beds, plus a minimalist style focusing your attention on the ravishing bay views beyond your window. Air-con costs €6 extra. There's also a great cafe-bar. Free pick-ups from the boat and complimentary use of kayaks.

🍴 Eating & Drinking

⭐ **Omonoia Cafe**   CAFE €

(☑ 22460 44287; breakfast €3-5, mains €8-11; ☺ 8am-late; 🛜 📶) Shaded by a mature fig tree on Livadia's main square, just up from the

---

BIRDWATCHING PARADISE

The landscape of Tilos is much gentler than other Dodecanese islands. Rather than forbidding mountains, the interior is characterised by fertile valleys carved into agricultural terraces. It's criss-crossed by trails laid out by farmers that now serve as perfect footpaths. With small-scale ancient fortifications and medieval chapels scattered in profusion, Tilos makes a wonderful hiking destination.

What's more, thanks to the island's low population – and long-standing ban on hunting – it's also a favourite haunt for rare birds. More than 150 species have been recorded. Some residential, some migratory. An estimated 46 species are threatened. As you hike, keep your eyes peeled for the Bonelli's eagle, Eleonora's falcon, long-legged buzzard, Sardinian warbler, scops owl and Mediterranean black shag.

Tilos

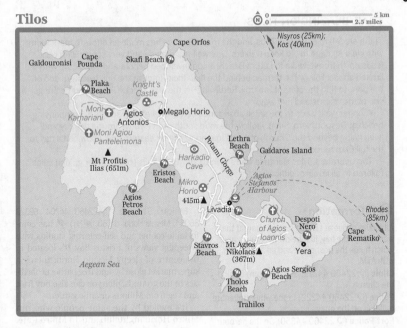

N 0 ——————————— 5 km
0 ——————————— 2.5 miles

Nisyros (25km);
Kos (40km)

Cape Orfos

Gaïdouronisi
Cape Pounda
Skafi Beach

Plaka Beach
Knight's Castle

Moni Kamariani
Agios Antonios
Megalo Horio

Moni Agiou Panteleimona

Lethra Beach
Gaïdaros Island

Mt Profitis Ilias (651m)

Harkadio Cave

Potami Gorge

Eristos Beach
Mikro Horio
415m

Agios Stefanos Harbour

Agios Petros Beach

Livadia

Rhodes (85km)

Church of Agios Ioannis
Despoti Nero
Cape Rematiko

Stavros Beach
Mt Agios Nikolaos (367m)
Yera

Aegean Sea

Agios Sergios Beach

Tholos Beach

Trahilos

quay, this much-loved all-day cafe is ideal for breakfast, light lunch or dinner. Its delightful elderly owners prepare everything from grilled meats and seafood to simple juices and salads, but you'll probably lose your heart – and your waistline – to their sponge cake.

Gorgona
GREEK €

(☑ 22460 70755; mains €10; ⊘ 9am-11pm; ✴🛜🚻) ✔ Enjoying sweeping views of Agios Stefanos Bay, this rooftop restaurant serves olives and vegetables grown at its own farm. Following special recipes from the owner's grandmother, there's a wealth of choice from Tilos goat, lamb chops and pasta, to shrimps and octopus salad.

To Mikro Kafé
CAFE €

(snacks €5-7, mains €7-12; ⊘ 6.30pm-late Mon-Fri, from 4pm Sat & Sun; ✴🛜🖉🚻) Micro in size it may be, but there's nothing diminutive about this cosy nook's appeal. With its exposed stone walls and nautically themed decoration, Micro is great for the kids, offering porthole windows, board games and little corners to play in while you nurse a sundowner on the beach-view patio (there's also a roof terrace). Offers salads, seafood, pies and sandwiches.

Armenon
TAVERNA €€

(☑ 22460 44134; www.tilosarmenon.gr; mains €8-18; ⊘ breakfast, lunch & dinner; ✴🛜) ✔ Open-fronted taverna on the beach with unbroken turquoise views and a menu spanning *taramasalata* to souvlakia, calamari and local favourites like lentil and anchovy salad. The charming couple who run it are so committed to home-grown ingredients they keep their own bees. Customers get a free sun lounger for the day. Look for the blue and yellow parasols.

Mikro Horio Nightclub
BAR

(☑ 6932086094, 22460 44204; Mikro Horio Village; ⊘ 11am-late Jul-Sep; 🛜) Set in the creepy abandoned village of Mikro Horio, just 10 minutes' free shuttle bus from central Livadia, this place has a delightful veranda bar with amazing views of the bay and stars above. A great place for night owls.

Spitiko
CAFE

(⊘ 7am-late) Overlooking the square, this cosy cafe is a popular stop-off for its great coffee, cheese and/or spinach pies, baklava and local sweets. The sign is in Greek, but everybody knows the place.

TRAIL BLAZING ON TILOS

There are 54km of trails in Tilos, and the mayor's office has made an effort to mark them with clear signage to aid keen walkers. One well-maintained and very scenic 3km walk leads north from Livadia to Lethra Beach, an undeveloped pebble-and-sand cove with limited shade. Follow the tarmac behind the Ilidi Rock Hotel, at the northwestern end of the port, to find the start of the trail. Returning via the picturesque Potami Gorge brings you to the main island highway.

A longer walk leads to the small abandoned settlement of Yera and its accompanying beach at Despoti Nero. Simply follow the road south from Livadia around the bay and keep going beyond the Church of Agios Ioannis at the far eastern end. Allow half a day for the full 6km round trip.

Two operators, Tilos Heritage Tours (p360) and Tilos Trails (p360), offer guided hikes tailored to all levels of difficulty.

ℹ️ Information

All ferries arrive at Livadia's small quay, at the west end of the bay, just below the main square, which holds the post office and an Alpha bank with ATM.

Clinic (☑22460 44219; ☺noon-5pm) Behind the church.

Police (☑22460 44222) In the white Italianate building on the quay.

Port Police (☑22460 44350) On the harbour.

Tilos Park Association (☑22460 70883; ☺10am-12.30pm Mon-Fri May-Oct) Tilos has no official tourism office, but this beachfront centre, aimed at promoting ecological conservation, has displays and brochures on local wildlife and trails.

Tilos Travel (☑22460 44360; www.tilostravel.com; ☺9am-10pm) Helpful agency at the port, also known as Stefanakis Travel, which sells ferry tickets, rents out cars and motorbikes and offers credit-card cash withdrawals.

Megalo Horio
Μεγάλο Χωριό

Megalo Horio, the tiny 'capital' of Tilos, is a hillside village where the narrow streets hold sun-blasted cubic houses and teem with battle-scarred cats.

A taxing one-hour hike from the north end of Megalo Horio takes you to the **Knights Castle**, passing the island's most ancient settlement en route.

The principal focus at the one-room **museum** (☑6984378079; Megalo Horio; ☺9am-2pm Jun-Sep) FREE on the main street is the island's ancient population of dwarf elephants. Expert volunteers bring their story to life.

Miliou Studios (☑22460 44204, 69320 86094; Megalo Horio; d €50; ❄🅿️🛜) has comfortable rooms and self-catering studios with sweeping views of Eristos Bay. It's located in the centre of sleepy Megalo Horio; there's a supermarket close by, and free barbecue facilities in the grounds, plus you can also buy fruit and veg from Miliou's organic garden.

It's owned by the same people who run Mikro Horio nightclub and To Mikro Kafé.

The best taverna in the village, with a glorious hillside terrace commanding a fabulous panorama of the bay, is **Kastro Cafe** (☑22460 44232; Megalo Horio; mains €8-12; ☺lunch & dinner). Everything on the menu is good, from the organic spit-roasted goat and locally raised pork, to the fresh little dolmadhes and tiny red shrimps.

Northwest Tilos

The northwestern end of Tilos is home to several attractive beaches. The best for swimming is long, broad **Eristos Beach**, lapped by sapphire-hued waters, 2.5km south of Megalo Horio. Generally deserted but for the odd local line-fishing, its greyish sands are fringed by tamarisk trees.

The quiet settlement of **Agios Antonios**, in the large bay 1.5km northwest of Megalo Horio, is a narrow strip of shingle with a taverna at either end. Much prettier **Plaka Beach**, in a cove another 3km west, is completely undeveloped. The water is slightly warmer, there's shade in the afternoon and, once you wade in a little, the rock shelves are good for snorkelling.

Beyond Plaka, the coast road climbs the sheer hillside, skirting 3km of alarming drop-offs to reach cliff-edge **Agiou Panteleimona** monastery.

🛏 Sleeping & Eating

Nitsa Apartments
APARTMENT €

(☎22460 44093; www.nitsa-tilosapartments.com; Eristos Beach; r/ste incl breakfast €50/70) Smart, modern studio block, 100m inland from Eristos Beach and holding simple rooms plus one- or two-bedroom self-catering apartments. It's attached to the all-day En Plo snack bar.

Eristos Beach Hotel
HOTEL €€

(☎22460 44025; www.eristosbeachhotel.gr; Eristos Beach; d/ste €60/90; P🅿❄🖥🖳) Just off the beach, this large hotel is set in lush gardens crowded with hibiscus, orchids and lemon trees. Fresh rooms with tiled floors have balconies that look out to the sea beyond, while larger studios have kitchenettes and sleep four. There's also a lovely swimming pool and kid's pool, plus a restaurant and a bar.

En Plo
APARTMENT €€

(☎22460 44176; Eristos Beach; mains €10-15; ⊙10am-late; 🖥) Close to the beach, this welcoming snack bar has excellent slow-cooked food like goat stew, and regulars like squid *saganaki* (stuffed with fried cheese), souvlakia and super-fresh vegetables. Breakfast, lunch and dinner can be eaten under the vine-shaded canopy in a lovely garden.

NISYROS   ΝΙΣΥΡΟΣ

POP 950

Thanks to its lack of beaches, Nisyros is very much off the tourist radar – apart from the day trippers from nearby Kos who come to witness the magnificent volcano. Yet for those seeking an island of natural beauty, goats wandering meadows stippled with beehives, soaring mountain views and wildlflowers, intimate Nisyros is just the ticket.

The main settlement, Mandraki, is a sleepy little fishing village garlanded with chic cafes, while hilltop villages Nikea and Emborios are stunning. Hike, wine-taste, immerse yourself in agrotourism... Those who chance a visit often return, again and again.

❶ Getting There & Away

Catamarans run by Dodekanisos Seaways (p328) call in at Nisyros onTuesday and Thursday, heading to and from Kos and Rhodes. Blue Star Ferries (p328) also stops twice in each direction, en route to either Kos, Kalymnos, Astypalea and Piraeus, or Tilos, Symi and Rhodes.

There are also daily links with Kos. The *Panagia Spyliani* sails to either Kos Town or Kardamena (€8), while the smaller *Agios Konstantinos* runs to and from Kardamena (€6).

Nisyros

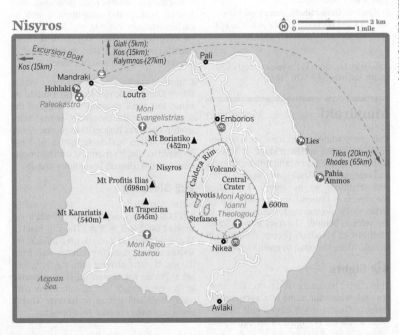

0—————2 km
0—————1 mile

Giali (5km); Kos (15km); Kalymnos (27km)
Excursion Boat
Kos (15km)
Pali
Mandraki
Hohlaki
Paleokastro
Loutra
Moni Evangelistrias
Emborios
Mt Boriatiko (452m)
Lies
Tilos (20km); Rhodes (65km)
Nisyros
Caldera Rim
Volcano
Central Crater
Pahia Ammos
Mt Profitis Ilias (698m)
Polyvotis
Moni Agiou Ioanni Theologou
600m
Mt Karariatis (540m)
Mt Trapezina (545m)
Stefanos
Moni Agiou Stavrou
Nikea
Aegean Sea
Avlaki

Boat Services from Nisyros (Mandraki)

DESTINATION	DURATION	FARE (€)	FREQUENCY
Halki*	1½hr	24	2 weekly
Kalymnos	2½hr	8	2 weekly
Kalymnos*	1½hr	21	2 weekly
Kos	1¼hr	8.50	daily
Kos*	45min	16	2 weekly
Piraeus	14hr	55	2 weekly
Rhodes	5hr	14	2 weekly
Rhodes*	2¾hr	26	2 weekly
Tilos*	40min	14	2 weekly

*high-speed services

❶ Getting Around

BOAT

Summer-only excursion boats leave Mandraki harbour for the pumice-stone, sandy beach islet of Giali (€8 to €12), returning at around 6pm.

BUS

Up to 10 bus tours run by Enetikon Travel visit the volcano each day (€6), allowing around 40 minutes at the crater. Catch them outside the office at Mandraki port. Three daily buses run from outside the port to Nikea via Pali.

CAR & MOTORCYCLE

In Mandraki, Diakomihalis offers good-value car rental and Manos (22420 31029; 9am-6pm) has a wealth of scooters and cars.

TAXI

A taxi from Mandraki to the volcano costs €20 return; call Irini (22420 31474).

Mandraki   Μανδράκι

POP 660

This pretty whitewashed town stretches languidly along the northern shore of Nisyros, lapped by gentle waters and lined with cafes and tavernas. Mandraki is almost completely pedestrianised, so its maze of winding backstreets is tranquil and timeless, with a fertile valley sloping up towards the rim of the volcano behind. The ferry jetty is 500m northeast of Mandraki proper. Simply walk straight along the coast to reach the centre.

◉ Sights

The major landmark is at the far western end, where the ruins of a 14th-century Knights Castle tower atop a cliff face. Its lower levels are occupied by an equally old monastery, Moni Panagias Spilianis (Virgin of the Cave; 10.30am-3pm), accessed by climbing a short but steep stairway.

With Nisyros being very short on beaches, tiny but sandy Mandraki Beach, at the eastern end of town, is a popular swimming spot, despite being sometimes covered in seaweed. There's also an exposed black-stone beach to the west, Hohlaki, reached by following a dilapidated and precarious footpath around the headland below the monastery. Don't attempt this walk in bad weather.

Paleokastro   ARCHAEOLOGICAL SITE
(24hr) FREE Best reached by a lovely 20-minute hike through the fields, along a trail that starts southwest of the monastery, this astonishing Mycenaean-era acropolis was founded 3000 years ago. Its restored cyclopean walls are a little newer, from the 4th century BC – what looks like modern graffiti is in fact ancient dedications. Pass through the forbidding gateway and you can climb atop the massive blocks of volcanic rock for breathtaking views. Good explanatory signs in English are scattered throughout.

Archaeological Museum   MUSEUM
(22420 31588; €4; 8.30am-3pm Tue-Sun;) This showpiece modern museum, on Mandraki's main pedestrian street, displays a fascinating collection of Hellenistic and Roman pottery and sculpture, as well as earlier artefacts made of obsidian quarried on neighbouring Giali. One ancient Greek inscription records a then-recent influx of migrants from Syria and Palestine.

Church Museum   MUSEUM
(€1; 10am-3pm Mon-Sat May-Sep) Despite its name, this small museum, just up from the seafront below the monastery, is not exclusively ecclesiastic. Besides its icons, vestments, votive offerings and memorabilia of long-deceased monks, it's crammed with oddments ranging from coins and banknotes to dolls.

🛏 Sleeping

Hotel Porfyris   HOTEL €
(22420 31376; www.porfyrishotel.gr; s/d/tr incl breakfast €46/54/59;) The only hotel in Mandraki town itself stands on a hillside, set above a citrus orchard five minutes' walk from the sea. If you're arriving from the ferry, fork left at Piccolo Bar. Beyond the elegant marble lobby, expect simple, cosy en-suite rooms with comfy beds and terrace or balcony. There's also a very welcome pool. Nice breakfast.

Hotel Romantzo
PENSION **€**

(☑ 22420 31340; www.nisyros-romantzo.gr; s/d/tr incl breakfast €35/45/55; ❄ ☎) Set just up from the ferry on the road to the volcano, this three-tiered stone building throws off a welcome glow come evening. Rooms are on the small side with fridge and flat-screen TV. Best of all, there's a communal sun-trap terrace up on the 2nd floor. The nearest restaurants are in town, 10 minutes' walk away. Generous-sized breakfast.

★ Ta Liotridia
B&B **€€**

(☑ 22420 31580; www.nisyros-taliotridia.com; r incl breakfast €140; ❄ ☎) Two large and very lovely B&B rooms (sleeping up to four) at the heart of the waterfront, on the upper floor of a smart wood-panelled bar. Each is furnished in comfortable traditional style, without being at all cluttered, and has a double bed in an alcove, another box bed, polished floors, stone walls and a sea-view balcony. Room 2 has the largest balcony.

✕ Eating

Pali Bakery
BAKERY

(€3; ◷ 8am-2.30pm Tue-Sat) You can smell the delicious doughy aroma before you turn the corner to this bijou bakery on Mandraki's waterfront. Fresh brioche, cream pie, doughnuts, sweetbread with chocolate, and *tiropita* (cheese pie) are a few of the highlights in this calorific oasis.

To Kazanario
GREEK **€**

(☑ 6972240556; snacks €1.50-8; ◷ noon-late; ❄ ☎) Escape the day trippers in this garden *ouzerie*, tucked off the pedestrian lane a block from the sea. A dark staircase drops from its inconspicuous doorway to a friendly old drinking den and garden beyond, where amazingly cheap snacks include souvlakia, sausages and tender calamari.

Irini
TAVERNA **€**

(☑ 22420 31365; Plateia Ilikiomenis; mains €9-12; ◷ lunch & dinner; ❄ ☎ ✎ ♿) Sitting in the corner of a pebble-mosaic square in the shade of mature fig trees, Irini dishes up a mouthwatering menu of traditional fare like dolmadhes, goat in tomato sauce, souvlakia and *saganaki* (fried cheese). Try the heavenly baklava for dessert.

♻ Drinking & Nightlife

Mandraki's waterfront is lined with cafes and bars, with terraces perfectly aligned for watching the sun set over Kos.

Rythmos Bar
BAR

(◷ 9am-late; ☎) Whether you choose a seat on its sun-soaked roof terrace or within its modish interior, this is a cool spot for a mid-day frappé or sunset glass of vino. Curiously it draws in the old boys as well as a young crowd – and it still works!

Ta Liotrida Bar
BAR

(◷ 10am-late; ☎) Wood floors, stone walls and low-lit interior at this atmospheric bar that plays nostalgic tunes and is the perfect spot to unwind over a coffee to escape the sun. Look out for the traditional olive press inside.

❶ Information

Visit www.nisyros.gr for information on sights, history and local services.

Alpha Bank has an ATM at the harbour and a branch in Mandraki, and there's another ATM in town.

Diakomihalis (☑ 22420 31459; www.visit nisyros.gr; ◷ 9.30am-1pm & 5pm-8pm) Ferry and air tickets, car rental and bus tours.

Enetikon Travel (☑ 22420 31180; www. enetikontravel.com; ◷ 9.30am-2pm & 6.30pm-9pm) Run by the ever-helpful Michelle, 100m from the quay towards Mandraki, Enetikon runs boat trips and bus tours, dispenses free advice and sells tickets.

Police (☑ 22420 31201) and **Port Police** (☑ 22420 31222) both face the quay.

Around Nisyros

The Volcano
Το Ηφαίστειο

Nisyros sits on a volcanic fault line that curves around the southern Aegean. While 25,000 years have passed since the volcano that formed it last erupted, it's officially classified as dormant rather than extinct. Its summit originally stood around 850m

> **LOCAL KNOWLEDGE**
>
> ### EXPERIENCING NISYROS
>
> **Anaema** (☑ 22420 31459; www.anaema. gr) is a brilliant new cooperative of island guides who can offer you culturally immersive experiences from one to six days – including hiking the volcano, wine-tasting trips, cookery and embroidery classes, and the chance to get involved with agrotourism.

tall, but three violent eruptions 30,000 to 40,000 years ago blew off the top 100m and caused the centre to collapse. White-and-orange pumice stones can still be seen on the northern, eastern and southern flanks of the island, while a large lava flow covers the entire southwest around Nikea.

The islanders call the volcano Polyvotis. Legend has it that during the battle between the gods and Titans, Poseidon ripped a chunk off Kos and used it to trap the giant Polyvotis deep beneath the rock of Nisyros. The roar of the volcano is his angered voice.

Visitors keen to experience the power of the volcano head by bus, car or on foot into the island's hollow caldera, a vast and other-worldly plain that was home to thousands of ancient farmers. Ruined agricultural terraces climb the walls, while cows graze amid sci-fi-set rocks.

A fenced-off area at the southern end encloses several distinct **craters** (€3; ⏰9am-8pm; P⛱). Get there before 11am and you may have the place to yourself. A path descends into the largest crater, **Stefanos**, where you can examine the multicoloured 100°C fumaroles, listen to their hissing and smell the sulphurous vapours. The surface is soft and hot, making sturdy footwear essential. Don't stray too far out, as the ground is unstable and can collapse.

An obvious track leads to the smaller and wilder crater of **Polyvotis** nearby. You can't enter the caldera itself, and the fumaroles are around the edge here, so take great care.

Emborios   Εμπορειός

Largely ruined but for a few restaurants and some very appealing accommodation, the village of Emborios is perched high on the jagged northern rim of the caldera, 9km up from Mandraki. Tumbledown houses cling to the steep flanks of the rocky ridge. A few are freshly whitewashed, but most are in stark disarray and overgrown with bougainvillea. Apart from a few yawning cats, almost no one lives here permanently.

🛏 Sleeping & Eating

★**Melanopetra**   APARTMENT €€€
(☑6978060289; www.melanopetra.gr/en; €170; ❄🛜) With its ubiquitous white and bare-wood floors flooded in natural light, Melanopetra is pure zen minimalism. Two apartments with gorgeous bedrooms and kitchens enjoy dual views of both the caldera

and Aegean on the other side. It's as if the rooms have been carved from the mountain itself with rough adobe walls and contemporary fittings.

Balcony Restaurant   GREEK €
(☑22420 31607; Emborios; mains €7; ⏰9am-10pm Mon-Sat; ❄🛜🖐) The streetside terrace, facing the church, may look inviting, but opt if you can for a table on the namesake balcony at the back for an unforgettable panorama of the vast hollow crater. The menu is meat-heavy, with mouthwatering chops and steaks, but it also serves various vegetable fritters.

Nikea   Νικαία

The village of Nikea is 4km south along the crater's edge. No vehicles can penetrate this tight warren of dazzling white houses, so every visitor experiences the thrill of walking along the narrow lane from road's end to reach the tiny central square. Less a square than a circle, actually, it's among the most jaw-droppingly beautiful spots in the Dodecanese, with geometric pebble-mosaic designs in the middle, whitewashed benches around the edges, and the village church standing above.

Throughout Nikea, signposted overlooks command astonishing views of the volcano, laid out far below. The challenging trail down into the crater drops from behind the Volcanological Museum.

👁 Sights

Volcanological Museum   MUSEUM
(☑22420 31400; Plateia Nikolaou Hartofyli, Nikea; €2.50; ⏰11.30am-6.30pm Mon-Thu, 10.30am-2.30pm Fri & Sat May-Sep; 🖐) Set beside the end of the road, this kid-friendly modern museum does a good job of explaining the history and mythology of the volcano and its impact on the island. There's also an interesting documentary worth a watch.

🍴 Eating

Porta   CAFE €
(☑22420 31832; Nikea; snacks €5-7; ⏰8.30am-late; ❄🛜) Located in Nikea's pretty central square, Porta is a wonderfully relaxing place to enjoy a cool drink, toasted sandwich, juice or beer. It looks out not to the caldera but the Aegean.

Pali   Πάλοι

This wind-buffeted seaside village sits 5km east of Mandraki, just beyond the turn-off to the volcano. Now primarily a yachting marina, it has a handful of tavernas among the sun-beaten buildings on the quay.

The coast road continues another 5km to **Lies**, Nisyros' most usable beach. Walking 1km along a precarious track from here brings you to **Pahia Ammos**, a shadeless expanse of coarse volcanic sand.

🛏 Sleeping & Eating

Mammis' Apartments APARTMENT €€
(☑ 22420 31824; www.mammis.com; Pali; d €60; ❄ 🛜) Set 100m up from the marina in gardens that are a riot of flowers, this peaceful complex holds 12 simple but imaginatively decorated apartments with kitchenettes, separate sofa beds for kids, and private balconies with sea views.

Captain's House TAVERNA €
(☑ 2242031016; Pali; mains €7-10; ⊙ 8am-midnight; ❄ 🛜) Festooned with yellow nets and so close to the water that you can taste the salt, this taverna attracts yachties and wizened fishermen alike with a menu that's packed to the gills with octopus, calamari, baby shark and cuttlefish.

KOS ΚΩΣ

POP 33,300

Fringed by the finest beaches in the Dodecanese, dwarfed beneath mighty crags, and blessed with lush valleys, Kos is an island of endless treasures. Visitors soon become blasé at sidestepping the millennia-old Corinthian columns that poke through the rampant wildflowers – even in Kos Town, the lively capital, ancient Greek ruins are scattered everywhere you turn, and a mighty medieval castle still watches over the harbour.

Visitors to Kos naturally tend to focus their attention on its beaches. In addition to those around Kos Town, there are three main resort areas. Kardamena, on the south coast, is very much dominated by package tourism, but Mastihari, on the north coast, and Kamari, in the far southwest, are more appealing. Away from the resorts, the island retains considerable wilderness, with the rugged Dikeos mountains soaring to almost 850m just a few kilometres west of Kos Town.

History

So many people lived on this fertile island in Mycenaean times that Kos was rich enough to send 30 ships to the Trojan War. In 477 BC, after suffering an earthquake and subjugation to the Persians, it joined the Delian League and again flourished. Hippocrates (460–377 BC), the Greek physician known as the founder of medicine, was born and lived on the island. After his death, the Sanctuary of Asclepius and a medical school were built, which perpetuated his teachings and made Kos famous throughout the Greek world.

That Ptolemy II of Egypt was also born on Kos secured the island the protection of Egypt. It became a prosperous trading centre, but fell under Roman domination in 130 BC and was administered by Rhodes from the 1st century AD onwards. Kos has shared the same ups and downs of fortune ever since, including conquest and/or occupation by the Knights, the Ottomans and the Italians and, much like Rhodes, its economy is now heavily dependent on tourism.

ⓘ Getting There & Away

AIR

Kos' **airport** (KGS; ☑ 22420 56000; www. kosairportguide.com) is located in the middle of the island, 24km southwest of Kos Town. Olympic Air (www.olympicair.com) offers up to four daily flights to Athens (from €50, 55 minutes) and three weekly to Rhodes (€79, 30 minutes), Kalymnos (€72, 20 minutes), Leros (€79, 55 minutes) and Astypalea (€91, one hour 40 minutes).

BOAT
Domestic

From the island's main ferry port, in front of the castle in Kos Town, **Dodekanisos Seaways** (p328) runs catamarans up and down the archipelago, southeast to Rhodes via Nisyros, Tilos, Halki and Symi, and north to Samos, with stops including Kalymnos, Leros and Patmos. **Blue Star Ferries** (p328) also sails to Rhodes, as well as west to Astypalea and Piraeus.

The **Panagia Spiliani** (☑ 22420 31015), which also runs day trips from Nisyros to Kos in summer, carries passengers to Nisyros on sailings that leave from Kos Town at 2.30pm four days a week, and from Kardamena at 6.10pm on the other three days.

Eight daily ferries also connect Mastihari with Kalymnos (€4.50, 50 minutes); see www.ane kalymnou.gr and www.anemferries.gr.

International

High-speed catamarans connect Kos Town with both Bodrum (two daily) and Turgutreis in Turkey (one daily). Both journeys take 20 minutes. Tickets cost €20 each way, with same-day

DODECANESE KOS

returns €24 and longer-stay returns €36. For schedules and bookings, visit www.rhodes.marmarisinfo.com.

❶ Getting Around

TO/FROM THE AIRPORT

The airport is served by several daily buses to and from Kos Town's bus station (€3.20). A taxi to Kos Town costs around €30. Note that Kefalos-bound buses stop at the big roundabout near the airport entrance.

The airport is so far from Kos Town that if you're planning to rent a car anyway, it's worth doing so when you first arrive. All the international chains have airport offices.

BICYCLE

Cycling is very popular, so you'll be tripping over bicycles for hire. Prices range from as little as €5 per day for a boneshaker, up to €20 for a decent mountain bike. In Kos Town, **George's Bikes** (p373) offers reasonable rates.

Kos Mountainbike Activities (☑ mobile 6944150129; www.kosbikeactivities.com; Psalidi; mountain bike per day €30; ☺9am-12.30pm & 5.30pm-7.30pm) offers bike rentals and guided tours.

BOAT

Several boats moored in Kos Town offer excursions around Kos and to nearby islands. A 'three island' day trip to Kalymnos, Pserimos and Platy costs around €30, including lunch, while you can find day trips to Bodrum for as little as €10.

Boat Services from Kos

DESTINATION	DURATION	FARE (€)	FREQUENCY
Astypalea	4hr	14.50	1 weekly
Kalymnos	50min	4.50	8 daily
Kalymnos	1hr 20min	6.50	3 daily
Kalymnos*	40min	16	1-2 daily
Leros	3¼hr	15	1 weekly
Leros*	1½hr	23	1-2 daily
Lipsi*	2hr	29	1-2 daily
Nisyros*	55min	16	2 weekly
Patmos*	3hr	31	1-2 daily
Piraeus	11hr	55	3 weekly
Rhodes	3hr	25	1 daily
Rhodes*	2½hr	32	1 daily
Samos	4hr	44	4 weekly
Symi	3hr	12	2 weekly
Symi*	1½hr	24	5 weekly

*high-speed services

All depart from Kos Town except the Kalymnos ferry, which departs from Mastihari.

BUS

The island's main **bus station** (☑ 22420 22292; Kleopatras 7) is located well back from the waterfront in Kos Town. It is the base for **KTEL** (☑ 22420 22292; www.ktel-kos.gr), which has services to all parts of the island, including the airport and south-coast beaches.

CAR

A recommended local operator is Auto Bank Car Rental, with outlets at the **airport** (☑ 22420 23397; www.autobank-carrentalkos.com), Kos Town and Mastihari.

Kos Town   Κως

POP 14,750

A handsome harbour community, fronted by a superb medieval castle and somehow squeezed amid a mind-blowing array of ancient ruins from the Greek, Roman and Byzantine eras, Kos Town is the island's capital, main ferry port and only sizeable town. While some central streets tend to be overrun by partying tourists, most remain stylish and attractive. The port is the most appealing area of all, lined by cafes and tavernas and with an unbroken row of excursion boats, fishing vessels and fancy yachts bobbing and bristling against each other along the waterfront.

Popular beaches stretch in either direction from the harbour. Long sandy **Kritika Beach**, running northwest and in easy walking distance of the town centre, is lined with hotels and restaurants. Southeast of the harbour the thin strip of sand known as **Kos Town Beach** is dotted with parasols in summer and offers deep water for swimming. Both beaches fill with guests from adjacent hotels.

The nearest beach to Kos Town, crowded **Lambi Beach** begins just 2km northwest and has its own strip of hotels and restaurants. Further west along the coast, a long stretch of pale sand is fringed by two more resorts – **Tingaki**, 10km from Kos Town, and the slightly less crowded **Marmari Beach** beyond. Windsurfing is popular at all three beaches, while the island of Pserimos is only a few kilometres offshore and served by excursion boats from Marmari in summer.

Heading south from Kos Town along Vasileos Georgiou, on the other hand, brings you to the three busy beaches of **Psalidi** (3km from Kos Town), **Agios Fokas** (8km),

Kos & Pserimos

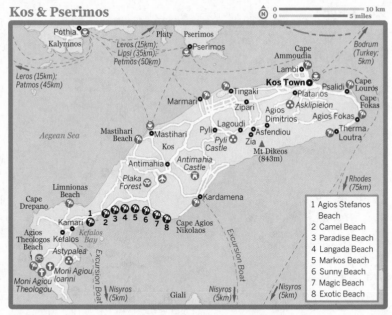

1	Agios Stefanos Beach
2	Camel Beach
3	Paradise Beach
4	Langada Beach
5	Markos Beach
6	Sunny Beach
7	Magic Beach
8	Exotic Beach

and **Therma Loutra** (12km). At Therma Loutra, hot mineral springs warm the sea.

○ Sights & Activities

Castle of the Knights CASTLE
(☎ 22420 27927; Harbour; €4; ☺ 8am-8pm Apr-Oct, 8am-3pm Tue-Sun Nov-Mar) Kos' magnificent 15th-century castle was constructed not on a hilltop, but right beside the entrance to the harbour. Access it by the bridge from Plateia Platanou, crossing what was once a seawater-filled moat but is now a road. Visitors can stroll atop the intact outer walls, surveying all activity in the port and keeping a watchful eye on Turkey across the strait. The precinct within, however, is now largely overgrown, with cats stalking through a wilderness of wildflowers.

Plateia Platanou SQUARE
The warm, graceful charm and sedate pace of Kos Town is experienced at its best in this lovely cobblestone square, immediately south of the castle. Sitting in a cafe here, you can pay your respects to **Hippocrates' plane tree** (Plateia Platanou). Hippocrates himself is said to have taught his pupils in its shade. The ancient sarcophagus beneath it was converted into a fountain by the Ottomans, while the 18th-century **Mosque of**

Gazi Hassan Pasha, now sadly boarded up, stands opposite.

Ancient Agora ARCHAEOLOGICAL SITE
(☺ dawn-dusk) FREE Exposed by a devastating earthquake in 1933, Kos' ancient centre occupies a vast area south of the castle. Back in the 4th century BC, this was the first town ever laid out in blocks, and you can still discern the original town plan, even though it's very overgrown. Landmarks include a massive columned **stoa** and the ruins of a **Shrine of Aphrodite**, **Temple of Hercules** and Christian basilica.

The site is fenced, but usually open all day. Locals use it as a shortcut.

Western Excavation Site ARCHAEOLOGICAL SITE
(☺ dawn-dusk) FREE This open site, south of the centre, holds fascinating ancient ruins uncovered by an earthquake in 1933. Its real treasures are the mosaics of the **House of Europa**, dating from the 2nd century and protected by rudimentary shelters. In front of them, there's a section of the **Decumanus Maximus**, the Roman city's main thoroughfare, while the site also holds the **Nymphaeum**, the **Xysto** and the overgrown but evocative **Temple of Dionysos**. Across the street stands an impressive 2nd-century **theatre**.

Kos Town

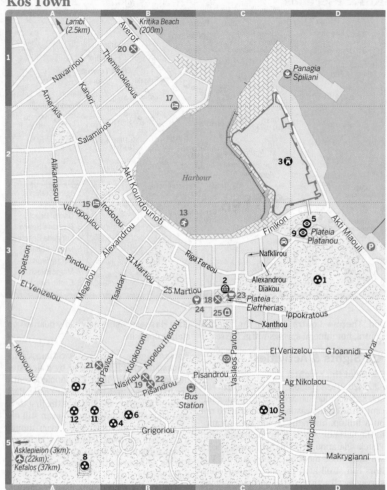

DODECANESE KOS

Archaeological Museum MUSEUM
(Plateia Eleftherias; €8; ☺ 8am-8pm Tue-Sun)
Housed in an Italian-era building in the
central square, the small archaeological
museum is finally open after restoration
and possesses a wealth of sculptures from
the Hellenistic to late Roman eras, with a
statue of Hippocrates and a 3rd-century-AD
mosaic as the star attractions. There are
information panels for many of the rooms.

Eva BOAT
(☎6955581116, 694369300; www.facebook.com/
Eva.Boat.Kos; Akti Koundourioti; €40; ☺ departs
10.30am; ♠) Treat yourself to a boat trip on
bee-coloured *Eva*; a twin-masted wooden
caïque with a finely crafted crow's nest and
gunwales. You'll (often) see dolphins, swim
in a turquoise cove and stop at Pserimos
island for a beach flop. With Captain Savvas
and his friendly family. Returns around 6pm.

🛏 Sleeping

★**Hotel Afendoulis** HOTEL €
(☎22420 25321; www.afendoulishotel.com; Evripilou
1; s/d/tr €35/50/60; ☺ Mar-Nov; ❄@⊙) This
family-run hotel has sparkling rooms with
TVs, balconies, hairdryes, quick internet and
comfy beds. Downstairs, the open breakfast

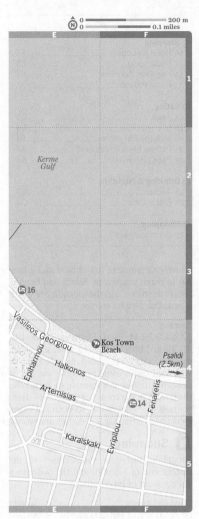

There are also pools for kids and adults and a snack bar on the roof. While it's clean and functional, it can be rather impersonal.

Hotel Sonia
HOTEL €€

(☑ 22420 28798; www.hotelsonia.gr; Irodotou 9; s/d/tr incl breakfast €45/60/75; ❄ 🛜) A block from the waterfront on a peaceful back-street, this pension offers a dozen sparkling rooms with parquet floors, fridges, smart bathrooms and an extra bed if required. Room 4 has the best sea view. Breakfast is served on a relaxing communal veranda, there's a decent book exchange, and it plans to open up the garden to visitors.

Kos Aktis Art Hotel
HOTEL €€€

(☑ 22420 47200; www.kosaktis.gr; Vasileos Georgiou 7; s/d/tr from €190/200/278; ❄ @ 🛜 ☀) Aktis' beautiful hotels are scattered across the Dodecanese and its representative here in Kos is stunning. Bedrooms are minimalist affairs of glass, light and wood. The view of the Aegean and, by night, Bodrum glittering like a giant chandelier, is romantic. There's a gym, fine restaurant and bar.

🍴 Eating

⭐ Pote Tin Kyriaki
TAVERNA €

(☑ 6930352099, 22420 27872; Pisandrou 9; ⏱ 7pm-2am) Named for Melina Mercouri's Oscar-winning 1960 song, 'Never on Sunday' is not the sort of place you expect to find in modern Kos – and it takes a *lot* of finding! This traditional *ouzerie* serves delicious specialities such as stuffed zucchini flowers, dolmadhes and steamed mussels.

Aegli
CAFE €

(☑ 22420 30016; www.aiglikos.gr; Plateia Eleftherias; snacks €3-5; ⏱ breakfast, lunch & dinner) This bakery-cafe is run by a cooperative supporting low-income women and employs only female staff. The speciality is *marmarites* – translated as 'crumpets', but more like sourdough flatbread – with sweet or savoury toppings, but it also serves pies, juices, coffee and gigantic breakfasts (for two €16).

⭐ Elia
GREEK €€

(☑ 22420 22133; Appelou Ifestou 27; mains €8-15; ⏱ 12.30pm-late; ❄ 🛜 🖉 🐾) 🍴 With its traditional wood-beamed ceiling and partly exposed stone walls covered in murals of the gods of the pantheon, Elia is earthy and friendly, while its small and focused menu is fit for a hard-to-please deity. Mezedhes (appetisers), shrimp, steamed mussels and grilled octopus are a few of your soon-to-be

room and breezy terrace have wrought-iron tables and chairs for reading or enjoying their memorable breakfast of homemade jams. There may be plusher hotels in Kos, but none with the soul of the Afendoulis, where nothing is too much trouble.

Kosta Palace
HOTEL €€

(☑ 22420 22855; www.kosta-palace.com; cnr Akti Kountourioti & Averof; s/d/apt €65/95/135; ❄ @ 🛜 ☀) This swanky harbour-front edifice, facing the castle across the port, holds 160 rooms with kitchenettes and private balconies. Apartments have separate rooms.

Kos Town

favourite things. Staff are warm and welcoming whatever the weather.

Petrino Meze Restaurant　　　MEZEDHES €€
(☑ 22420 27251; www.petrino-kos.gr; Plateia Theologou 1; mains €9-28; ☺ lunch & dinner; ✿ ☎) Peaceful and balmy, this graceful restaurant has a leafy garden shaded by bougainvillea, overlooking Kos Town's western group of archaeological ruins. Highlights on its upscale menu include hearty meat concoctions such as beef stuffed with blue cheese and pork with plums, but it also serves lighter dishes such as steamed swordfish or pasta, as well as mixed mezedhes (appetisers) platters.

Nick the Fisherman　　　SEAFOOD €€
(Averof 21; mains €10-14; ☺ 1pm-1am; ✿ ☎) This side-street seafood taverna is bedecked with nets and dangerous-looking fish on the walls. Try the sardines, red snapper, striped mullet and grouper.

♟ Drinking & Nightlife

Kos Town has a very lively party scene. Aimed squarely at tourists bussed in from the coastal resorts, it centres a block south of the harbour and along the waterfront on Kritika Beach. Locals congregate on weekends to drink coffee and gossip in the cafes on Plateia Eleftherias (Freedom Sq).

Global Cafe　　　BAR
(☑ 22420 26003; Ifestou 1; ☺ 8.30am-late; ☎) With its modern interior, Global Cafe bags a youthful crowd who come to chat and play backgammon over a coffee or juice. There's a lovely atrium area full of light and a long bar to perch yourself at. Salads and burgers are on the menu and the cocktails are worth a look. Can be a bit smoky.

Aenaos　　　CAFE
(☑ 22420 26044; Plateia Eleftherias; ☺ 8am-late; ☎) Tucked beneath an exquisite, still-active mosque, this well-shaded cafe is popular with locals who come to people-watch – or be seen – in its smart interior, or outside on the terrace in the corner of the *plateia*. Treat yourself to its delectable spectrum of sweet confections (from €3.50), coffees and juices.

⊞ Shopping

For high-street-style shops, head to the eastern end of Ioannidi and the pedestrian streets south of Ippokratous.

Dimotiki Agora　　　MARKET
(☑ 22420 22900; Plateia Eleftherias; ☺ 8am-late) 🖋 Fragrant with spices, this lively open-arched market has a cornucopia of locally made honeys, natural soaps, bonbons, sandalwood spoons, mythological curios and Kalymnian sponges.

ⓘ Information

Kos Town has several ATMs, including at the branches of Alpha Bank on El Venizelou and the National Bank of Greece on Riga Fereou.
Fanos Travel & Shipping (☑ 22420 20035; www.kostravel.gr; Akti Koundourioti 11; ☺ 9am-9pm) Tickets for the hydrofoil service to Bodrum and other ferries, plus yachting services.

Kentrikon Travel (☏ 22420 28914; Akti Kountouriotou 7; ⊙ 9am-9pm) The official agent for Blue Star Ferries also sells all other ferry and air tickets.

Police (☏ 22420 25462; Eparhio Bldg, Akti Miaouli)

Port Police (☏ 22420 26594; cnr Akti Koundourioti & Megalou Alexandrou)

Post Office (Vasileos Pavlou)

Tourist Police (☏ 22420 22444; Akti Miaouli)

ⓘ Getting Around

BICYCLE

Cycle lanes thread all through Kos Town, with the busiest route running along the waterfront to connect the town with Lambi to the north and Psalidi to the south. Many hotels have bikes for guests, or you can rent one from **George's Bikes** (☏ 22420 24157; Kanari 8; cycle/scooter per day €4/15).

BUS

Local buses, run by **DEAS** (☏ 22420 26276; flat fare €2), operate within Kos Town, but have little relevance to visitors. Buses to the rest of the island, including the airport, depart from the KTEL **bus station** (p368).

TAXI

Taxis (☏ 22420 23333, 22420 22777) congregate on the south side of the port.

TOURIST TRAIN

One way to get your bearings in summer is to take a 20-minute city tour on the **tourist train** (☏ 22420 26276; €5), which departs frequently from Akti Kountouriotou on the harbourfront.

Around Kos

Asklepieion   Ασκληπιείον

The island's most important ancient site, **Asklepieion** (☏ 22420 28763; adult/child €8/free; ⊙ 8am-7pm Tue-Sun, 8am-3pm Nov-Mar), stands on a pine-covered hill 3km southwest of Kos Town, commanding lovely views across towards Turkey. A religious sanctuary devoted to Asclepius, the god of healing, it was also a healing centre and a school of medicine. It was founded in the 3rd century BC, according to legend by Hippocrates himself, the Kos-born 'father' of modern medicine. He was already dead by then, though, and the training here simply followed his teachings. Until the sanatorium was destroyed by an earthquake in AD 554, people came from far and wide for treatment.

The ruins occupy three levels, with the propylaeum (approach to the main gate), Roman-era public baths and remains of guest rooms on the first level. The second holds an **altar of Kyparissios Apollo**, with the 1st-century-BC **Temple to Apollo** to the east and the first **Temple of Asclepius**, built in the 4th century BC, to the west. The remains of its successor, the once-magnificent 2nd-century-BC **Temple of Asclepius**, are on the third level. Climb a little further, to the cool pine woods above, for the best views of all.

A modern museum on the path down preserves ancient inscriptions and shows films explaining the site.

Bus 3 runs hourly from Kos Town to the site. It's also a pleasant bike ride.

Mountain Villages

The villages scattered on the green northern slopes of the Dikeos mountains make ideal destinations for day trips.

Kos' prettiest mountain village – **Zia**, 14km west of Kos Town – is now essentially a one-street theme park. The views down to the sea are as wonderful as ever, but coachloads of tourists are deposited every few minutes to stroll along its gauntlet of souvenir shops and competing tavernas.

Continuing 6km west beyond Zia brings you to the less commercialised village of **Pyli**. Even better, just before the village a left turn leads to the extensive remains of its medieval predecessor, **Old Pyli**, scattered amid the towering rocks and pine trees of a high and very magical hillside. The summit here is crowned by the stark ruins of Pyli Castle and the whole place is so wild you half expect Pan to pop up. A well-marked trail climbs from the roadside parking area, forking left to the castle and right to the old village, where the only building still in use is a tavern hidden in the woods.

Buses connect Kos Town with Pyli itself (€2, two to three daily), but not Old Pyli.

✗ Eating

✗ Zia

The Watermill   CAFE €
(mains €8; ⊙ breakfast, lunch & dinner; 🛜 🚼) ✐ It's worth the brief climb up the hill just to sate your thirst with their delicious homemade lemonade. With its vine-covered arbour and relaxing patio giving stunning

mountain views, this former watermill exudes a serenity that will still your pulse to that of a freediver. The menu includes crêpes, fruit salad and pasta dishes.

Taverna Oromedon GREEK €€
(☑ 22420 69983; www.oromedon.com; Zia; mains €9-15; ☺ lunch & dinner) Zia's finest restaurant is justly acclaimed for its vine-laced sun terrace, unbroken sea views and traditional Greek menu of shrimp *saganaki* (shrimp in fried cheese), dolmadhes and *stifadho*. Meat-eaters should be sure to spare some room for the chunky local sausages.

✕ Pyli

★ Oria Taverna GREEK €
(☑ 6981764991; Old Pyli; mains €7-10; ☺ 9am-9pm; ℗) ✐ Idyllic taverna, only accessible by hiking up the hillside facing the 1000-year-old Pyli Castle and enjoying what is certainly the best rural view on Kos. It's open all day for snacks and cooling drinks, but you can't beat a sunset dinner here, tucking into the seasonal, locally sourced menu of steaks, meatballs, zucchini and tzatziki.

Mastihari Μαστιχάρι

Hardly more than a village, this delightful old-fashioned beach resort holds everything you need for a straightforward family holiday. There's a lovely broad strip of powder-fine sand scattered with tamarisk trees, a clutch of whitewashed rental studios and small hotels, and a row of appetising waterfront tavernas and bars. There's no historic core and nothing of any architectural interest, but as a place to spend a day or a week in the sun, Mastihari has it all.

Mastihari's tiny port is served by frequent **ANE Kalymnou** (☑ 22420 29900; www.ane kalymnou.gr) and ANEM (www.anemferries.gr) ferries to Pothia on Kalymnos, as well as excursion boats to the islet of Pserimos in summer.

🛏 Sleeping & Eating

Studios Diana APARTMENT €
(☑ 22420 59116; Mastihari; apt €40) Clean and basic studios opening onto the sea, with private balconies and very tiny kitchens. Turning on the air-con costs €5 extra.

Athinas Studios APARTMENT €
(☑ 6974180326; www.athinas-studios.gr; Mastihari; d/tr €40/50) Super-fresh studio rooms

with Aegean-blue trim and spotless kitchenettes. They're a block back from the seafront, but the upper-level rooms have private seaview terraces and there's also a roof garden. One room has bunk beds, double bed and a large balcony.

El Greco TAVERNA €
(Mastihari; mains €8-12; ☺ breakfast, lunch & dinner; ❄) Beachside taverna – follow the blue-painted walkway up from the sand – that consistently pleases with its fresh salads, zucchini, souvlakia and lamb with rosemary, as well as grilled sardines, cod and octopus. Only the very fanciest fish dishes cost more than €10, and it also serves breakfast all day.

Kali Kardia SEAFOOD €€
(☑ 22420 59289; Mastihari; mains €6-15; ☺ breakfast, lunch & dinner) Atmospheric taverna right on the harbour, with tables out on the footpath and a wooden interior that's patronised by older folk staring out to sea. Piping aromas of squid, shrimp and souvlakia emerge from the kitchen, and large mixed platters cost €10 per person.

Kamari & Kefalos Bay Καμάρι & Κέφαλος

Enormous Kefalos Bay, a 12km stretch of high-quality sand, lines the southwest shoreline of Kos. For most of its length the beach itself is continuous, but the main road runs along a crest around 500m inland, so each separate section served by signposted tracks has its own name. Backed by scrubby green hills and lapped by warm water, these are the finest and emptiest beaches on the island. Kamari, at the western extremity of this black-pebbled beach, is a low-key resort with plenty of cafes, tavernas and accommodation, as well as decent water sports. High above Kamari, perched on a bluff, the touristy village of Kefalos has a few spots to eat and stay. If you're determined to escape the crowds, continue on to the island's southern peninsula beyond.

The most popular stretch of sand is **Paradise Beach**, while the least developed is **Exotic Beach**. **Langada Beach** (which you may also see referred to as Banana Beach) makes a good compromise, but the best of the lot is **Agios Stefanos Beach**, at the far western end. A small beachfront promontory here is topped by a ruined 5th-century basilica, while the absurdly photogenic islet of Kastri stands within swimming distance immediately offshore.

On the west coast, Agios Theologos Beach is backed by meadow bluffs carpeted in olive groves, and feels far removed from the resort bustle.

🛏 Sleeping & Eating

Affordable studios and apartments are the order of the day, with an emphasis on package holiday accommodation in Kamari.

Anthoula Studios   APARTMENT €
(☎ 22420 71904; studios €40; ❄ ❂) Perched on the hill, this yellow eyrie is set on well-kept grounds and has a great pool to cool off in, with decent rooms with safety deposit box and fridge, plus air-con for an extra €5 per night. A minibus runs to and from the beach on Kefalos Bay several times a day. Owner Anthoula is lovely.

Albatross Apartments   APARTMENT €€
(☎ 22420 71981; albatross@hotmail.com; Kamari Beach; apt €70; Ⓟ ❄ 🛜 ❂) Eleven simple, spotless and identical kitchenette studios, so freshly maintained they might have been built yesterday. All have sea views, there's a good swimming pool, and the beach is just across the road, with the jetty a short walk away. There's an on-site bar but no restaurant. Airport pick-up for stays of three nights or more.

★ Restaurant Agios Theologos   TAVERNA €€
(☎ 6974503556; Agios Theologos Beach; mains €8-15; ☺ lunch & dinner, Sat & Sun only Nov-Apr; ❄ 🛜) Set in dreamy sand dunes above Agios Theologos Beach, this much-loved seasonal taverna enjoys the best sunsets in Kos. Its zesty homemade cheese, courtesy of its inquisitive goats, is at its most flavoursome fried, while a fresh grilled bream costs around €15. There are fantastic mezedhes (appetisers) too. Pure romance.

ASTYPALEA
ΑΣΤΥΠΑΛΑΙΑ

POP 1300

Swathed in silky aquamarine waters, far-flung, butterfly-shaped Astypalea is richly rewarding for walkers, campers and history buffs. For any island hunter, this is the ultimate escape – think mountainous meadows straight from the pages of Homer, and rugged beaches fringed in vivid blue water. Chance of sighting a mermaid: fair to middling.

The island's main settlement, hilltop Hora, is a tumble of bleached-white houses cascading down from a medieval fortress to the fishing port of Skala. Although boutique hotels have been sprouting here in recent years, the tourist infrastructure – and ferry service – remains minimal, and most visitors are Greek, with the rest largely French and Italian. Fed up with the package crowds, Irish bars and fish and chips? You've come to the right place.

ℹ Getting There & Away

AIR
Olympic Air (www.olympicair.com) has three flights a week from Leros (€62, 25 minutes), Kalymnos (€62, one hour 40 minutes) and Kos (€74, one hour 40 minutes), and three per week from Athens (€134, one hour). Buy tickets online, or via Astypalea Tours (p377).

BOAT
Only two ferry operators serve Astypalea.

Blue Star Ferries (p328) arrive, inconveniently, in the dead of night at the isolated little port of Agios Andreas, 6.5km north of Skala. A bus is scheduled to meet each boat, but don't bank on it. One ferry arrives four times weekly, having sailed from Piraeus via Paros, Naxos and Amorgos, and sets off back along the same route a couple of hours later. The other stops once in each direction en route between Piraeus and Rhodes, calling also at Kalymnos, Kos, Tilos and Nisyros.

Nisos Kalymnos (www.anekalymnou.gr) connects Skala's small harbour once weekly with Kalymnos.

Boat Services from Astypalea

DESTINATION	DURATION	FARE (€)	FREQUENCY
Kalymnos	2½hr	12.50	1 weekly
Kalymnos*	3½hr	15	1 weekly
Kos	4hr	15	1 weekly
Naxos	4hr	20	4 weekly
Paros	5½hr	34	4 weekly
Piraeus	8½hr	35	5 weekly
Rhodes	9hr	24	1 weekly

Unless otherwise marked, services depart from Agios Andreas.

* departs from Skala

DODECANESE ASTYPALEA

ℹ Getting Around

Astypalea's airport is on the flat, narrow 'neck' of the island, 8km northeast of Skala. Buses connect with flights in summer, while taking either of the island's two **taxis** (☑ mobile 6975706365) to Skala costs around €10. Summer buses also link Skala with Hora and Livadi to the west, and Analipsi/Maltezana to the east, stopping at beaches en route (€2). Of the island's three vehicle-rental agencies, **Vergoulis** (☑ 22430 61351; www.rent-a-car-astypalaia. com; per day scooters €15, cars €30-60; ☺ 8am-10pm) is particularly recommended.

In July and August, boats head out for the day from Skala to the remote western beaches of Agios Ioannis, Kaminakia and Vatses, as well as to the islets of Koutsomytis (with ethereal, emerald-green water) and Kounoupa. They also make complete circuits around the island. Contact Astypalea Tours in Skala for details.

Skala & Hora
Σκάλα & Χώρα

POP 1036

Astypalea's main town, Skala, lies on the southern shore of the island's western half, curving around an attractive bay that's too shallow for large inter-island ferries. Little more than a village, with aromatic odours drifting from its bakery, Skala holds a small sand-and-pebble beach that's popular with locals. Bars and tavernas punctuate the quay, which is the sole preserve of old sea dogs in low season, but surprisingly lively on summer evenings.

Modern visitors delight in the sheer beauty of the old settlement of Hora looming above, its white houses spilling down the hillside beneath its impressive *kastro* (castle). For the original inhabitants of Skala, however, the upward migration was prompted by the endless threat of marauding pirates. These days Hora is a delightful maze to explore. Stroll around the hushed tangle of streets and climb up to the fort. Suitably exhausted, you can then relax in the clutch of inviting *kafeneia* and tavernas alongside the restored Cycladic-style windmills that mark the village entrance.

◉ Sights & Activities

Kastro
CASTLE

(Hora; ☺ dawn-dusk) FREE Astypalea's imposing castle was built by the Venetian Quirini family early in the 15th century. For the next 300 years, up to 4000 people lived within this ever-expanding precinct, sheltered from pirate attacks. Its last inhabitants left in 1956, after an earthquake caused the stone houses integrated into its walls to collapse. The only entrance is through a gateway that burrows beneath the **Church of the Virgin of the Castle**; the magical **Church of Agios Georgios** lies beyond.

Archaeological Museum
MUSEUM

(☑ 22430 61500; Skala; €2; ☺ 9am-1pm & 6-8.30pm Tue-Sun Jun-Sep) Skala's small archaeological museum, at the start of the road up to Hora, holds treasures found across the island, from earliest times up to the Middle Ages. Highlights include grave offerings from two Mycenaean chamber tombs and a bronze Roman statue of Aphrodite.

Thalassopouli
BOATING

(☑ 6974436338; Pera Gialos, Skala; per person €15; ☺ Jun-Sep; 🖢) Run by Captain Yiannis, Thalassopouli leaves Skala at 11am and returns you glowing and salty at 6pm after a day's swimming around two uninhabited neighbouring islands: Kounoupi, with its golden isthmus of sand, and Kousomyti, outlined in purest aquamarine. Food is available (€7).

🛏 Sleeping

Reservations are essential in July and August. The finer boutique options are in Hora.

★ Studios Kilindra
BOUTIQUE HOTEL €€

(☑ 22430 61131; www.astipalea.com.gr; Hora; d/ apt incl breakfast €130/150; ❄@🛜🌊) 🍴 Just below the *kastro*, this enchanting boutique hotel has a swish pool with a terrace overlooking the mouthwash-green bay. The lobby is scattered with eclectic antiques as well as a grand piano, while studios and larger maisonettes fuse the contemporary with the traditional, featuring split-level floors, raised beds, sofas and kitchenettes. Massage, acupuncture and herbal treatments are also available.

Mariakis Studios
APARTMENT €€

(☑ 22430 62072; www.mariakis.gr; Hora; s/d from €60/70; ❄🛜) Four attractive, spotlessly white apartments adjoin a family home just steps from the heart of Hora. Island-style touches include traditional furnishings and exposed stone walls, while the spacious terraces enjoy great sea views. The breakfasts are superb.

Akti Rooms
APARTMENT €€

(☑ 22430 61114; www.aktirooms.gr; Skala; d/ studio incl breakfast €80/85; ❄🛜) Waterside Akti, facing Hora from the east side of Skala,

Astypalea

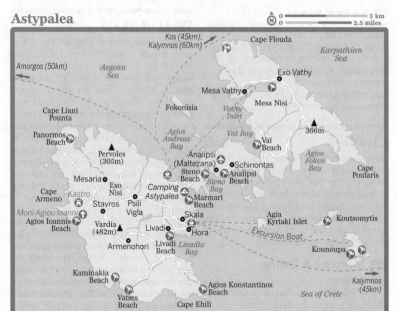

has traditionally themed rooms with ornate lights, dark-wood chests and traditional crockery. Most but not all have sea views, and the studios have kitchenettes. Swim from the private platform or chill in the stylish cafe.

Hotel Paradissos　　HOTEL €€
(☑ 22430 61224; www.astypalea-paradissos.com; Skala; d/tr from €80/95; 🕸🛜) Stately and peaceful, Paradissos is so close to the harbour you can taste salt on your lips. Its 18 dazzling-white sea-view rooms hold desks and private balconies. There's also a great cafe and attached travel agency.

✗ Eating

Barbarossa　　TAVERNA €
(☑ 22430 61577; Hora; mains €10; ⊙ lunch & dinner; 🕸🛜🅿) 🗡 You can't miss this friendly taverna, serving food with soul along the main approach to Hora, with a buzzing terrace near the town hall. Inside are exposed stone walls covered with antique Greek poster girls, and there are amazing views to the rear. Menu highlights like pork fillet with prunes, mussels and grilled shrimps ensure you won't be disappointed.

Agoni Grammi　　TAVERNA €
(☑ 22430 61988; Hora; mains €8-12; ⊙ lunch & dinner) It's the outdoor terrace that first

catches the eye here, close to Hora's landmark windmills, but the whitewashed interior is equally appealing at night, stippled by stone flags and lit with red pendant lights. As well as homemade pasta and pizza, this island favourite is renowned for its fish soup and traditional *kokoretsi* (kebab of lamb innards).

Maïstrali　　TAVERNA €
(☑ 22430 61691; Skala; mains €8-12; ⊙ 10am-late; 🕸🛜🅿) Tucked one street back from the harbour, near the stairway to heaven (well, Hora, anyway), this stylish restaurant dishes up everything from zucchini balls, lamb chops and eggplant salad, to grilled shrimp *saganaki* (shrimp in fried cheese) and rabbit in tomato sauce.

ℹ Information

Astypalea Tours (☑ 22430 61571; www.astypaleatours.gr; Skala; ⊙ 6-9pm) For air and ferry tickets and boat excursions.

Emporiki Bank (☑ 22430 59890; Skala) The island's only bank, with an ATM, is on the waterfront.

Municipal Tourist Office (☑ 22430 61412; www.astipalea.org; Hora; ⊙ 6-9pm Jun-Sep)

For history, pictures, facilities and sights go to www.astypalaia.com.

Paradise Travel Agency (☎22430 61224; paradisostravel@yahoo.gr; at Hotel Paradissos, Skala) Books ferry tickets.

Police (☎22430 61207, 22430 61206; Skala) In an Italianate building on the waterfront.

Port Police (☎22430 61208; Skala) Shares premises with the police.

Post Office (☎22430 61223; Hora) At the top of the Skala–Hora road.

Livadi   Λειβάδι

Astypalea's most popular beach, Livadi Beach stands at the mouth of a lush valley in the first bay south of Hora. An easy 20-minute walk down from the old town, it's also served by local buses. In summer it's effectively transformed into a buzzing little resort, with a string of funky restaurants and bars lining the waterfront.

🛏 Sleeping & Eating

Villa Barbara   APARTMENT €
(☎22430 61448; www.villabarbara.gr; Livadia; s/d €40-45; ❄) Set in flowering gardens, these mint-fresh white studios have tiled floors and balconies with sea views. The sea is less than a 100m away.

Fildisi Hotel   BOUTIQUE HOTEL €€
(☎22430 62060; www.fildisi.net; Livadi; studios from €140; ❄ 🛜 ❄) Split into terraces, this boutique dream has for its centrepiece an infinity pool accompanied by a juice bar and marvellous view of the sea. The breakfast/chill room is chic, while the 10 rooms, each named for a precious gem, enjoy private balconies, kitchenettes and sea views, as well as mini-bar, fridge, and flat-screen TVs with cable.

Mouras Studios   APARTMENT €€
(☎22430 61127; www.mourastudios.gr; Livadi; studio/apt €75/85; ☺May–mid-Oct) Radiating off a beachfront courtyard, these seven stunning whitewashed studios vary in size, but all have stylish dark-wood furniture, kitchenettes and private balconies. Full-on sea views cost a few euros extra.

Astropelos   GREEK €€
(☎22430 61473; Livadi; mains €10-15; ☺8am-midnight; ❄🛜🅿) First-class dining by the beach, on a decked verandah with chic white tables and a menu that includes octopus salad, breaded crab's pincers and lobster. French lounge tunes under the shade of tamarisk trees accompany the view of Hora on the hilltop horizon.

West of Skala

West of Skala, you swiftly hit the Astypalea outback – gnarled, bare rolling hills, perfect for a Cyclops. There's scarcely a sealed road to speak of, but it's just about possible to drive. Cross the western massif by heading directly inland from Hora and, from the point where the road finally peters out after 8km, where the **Kastro** ruins and **Moni Agiou Ioanni** stand proudly cheek by jowl above the shoreline, energetic walkers can hike down to **Agios Ioannis Beach**. Alternatively, follow the track that branches northwards shortly before road's end and you'll probably have **Panormos Beach** to yourself.

The rough track that winds along the southern coast west of Livadi, on the other hand, leads through mountainous meadows to several remote beaches. First along the way, reached on a brief detour, is the pretty, tree-shaded **Agios Konstantinos Beach** on the south side of Livadi Bay. This beach and **Kaminakia Beach** in the far west, where the track reaches its terminus, hold excellent seasonal tavernas. Book-ended by granite boulders, Kaminakia is Astypalea's best altar to sun worshipping, boasting water so clear you can see the pebbles through the turquoise.

🍴 Eating

Sti Linda   GREEK €
(☎6932610050; Kaminakia Beach; mains €5-10; ☺Jul-Sep) 🅿 From the Stavros junction a rough track winds upwards to a shepherd's hut on the mountain spine and then an *extremely* rough track (take care) winds downwards to Kaminakia Beach, lapped by stunning turquoise water. Here there's a good seasonal restaurant, Sti Linda, which rustles up hearty fish soups, oven-baked goat and homemade bread. Make it a day trip.

East of Skala

The slender isthmus that links Astypalea's two 'wings' holds some of the island's most popular beaches. Each of the three bays at **Marmari**, just 2km northeast of Skala, has its own pebble-and-sand beach, right beside the road. **Steno Beach**, another 2km along, is sandy, shady and conveniently shallow for kids. The name means 'narrow', with the isthmus being a mere 100m wide near this spot.

The only resort area away from Skala, **Analipsi** is a pleasantly laid-back place that spreads through a fertile valley alongside the airport, 8km northeast of Skala. Also known as Maltezana, having once been the lair of Maltese pirates, it's grown recently thanks to long **Analipsi Beach** to the southeast, which offers sand, pebbles, shade and clean, shallow water. Nearby the remains of the Tallaras Roman baths still hold some mosaics.

Almost no one lives on Astypalea's eastern half. The only settlement is the remote hamlet of **Mesa Vathy**, tucked into the shelter of an enormous bottleneck bay and home to barely half a dozen families. A summer yacht harbour, it doesn't have a decent beach.

🛏 Sleeping & Eating

Camping Astypalea   CAMPGROUND €
(☑ 6973037710, 22430 61900; www.astypalaia
camping.gr; Marmari; campsites per adult/tent €7/2;
⊙ Jun–early Sep; P 🛜) Shaded by tamarisk trees and shielded by bamboo groves, this summer-only campground is located next to Marmari beach, which unfortunately means it's also right beside the road, although there are hardly any cars. It has 24-hour hot water, safety deposit boxes, kitchen, barbecue, cafe and minimarket, and provides free transport from the port to the campground.

Hotel Maltezana Beach   APARTMENT €€
(☑ 22430 61558; www.maltezanabeach.gr; Analipsi; s/d incl breakfast €75/90; P ❄ 🛜 ☲) Ideal for families, this welcoming hotel stands amid manicured gardens a few metres from the beach. There are spacious rooms with balconies, set around a fine pool, plus good home cooking in the restaurant. Sea-view rooms are an extra €10.

Galini Cafe   CAFE €
(☑ 22430 61201; Mesa Vathy; mains €3-7; ⊙ Jun-Oct) At remote Mesa Vathy hamlet you can dine at the laid-back Galini Café, which offers meat and fish grills and the odd oven-baked special.

KALYMNOS   ΚΑΛΥΜΝΟΣ

POP 16,000

Rugged Kalymnos is characterised by its dramatic mountains that draw hardy climbers from all over the world. Its western flank is particularly spectacular with skeletal crags towering above dazzling blue waters. The island is also greener than most of its neighbours, cradling fertile valleys dotted with beehives and bursting with oleander. Add to this the enticing, car-free islet of Telendos, immediately offshore, and you begin to see why the island is fast becoming a must-visit destination.

While its sponge-fishing heyday is long past, Kalymnos remains inextricably entwined with the sea, particularly in its capital and main ferry port, Pothia, where you'll still find stalls piled high with unearthly looking sponges, and a statue of Poseidon surveying the harbour. As Pothia is a working town, it's more restful to stay in the smaller west-coast settlements such as Emborios and Myrties, or over on Telendos.

ⓘ Getting There & Away

AIR
Kalymnos's airport, 6km northwest of Pothia, is served by daily Olympic Air (www.olympicair.com) flights to and from Athens (€140, one hour), Leros (€55, 15 minutes) and Kos (€55, 20 minutes). Connecting buses meet flights in summer.

BOAT
Kalymnos's main ferry port, Pothia, is linked by daily **Dodekanisos Seaways** (p328) catamarans with Kos, Rhodes, Leros, Patmos and other nearby islands. **Blue Star Ferries** (p328) connects Pothia with Piraeus, Kos and Rhodes three times weekly, and with Astypalea and Symi once or twice weekly.

Nisos Kalymnos (www.anekalymnou.gr) runs three to four times weekly to and from Leros, Lipsi, Patmos and the islets to the north, and also connects Kalymnos once weekly with Skala on Astypalea.

The Kalymnos Star and Kalymnos Dolphin (www.anekalymnou.gr) run several times daily between Pothia and Mastihari on the north shore of Kos, as does ANEM (www.anemferries.gr). Several excursion boats offer day trips from Kos Town to Pothia.

In addition, the little resort of Myrties on Kalymnos' west coast is connected three times weekly with Lipsi and Agia Marina on Leros by Anna Express (www.annaexpress.eu), and five times weekly with either Xirokambos (€10) or Pandeli (€15) on Leros by **Captain Yiannis** (☑ mobile 6944819073; Mytries Pier; €2; ⊙ 11am Tue & Thu; ♿).

Boat Services from Kalymnos

DESTINATION	DURATION	FARE (€)	FREQUENCY
Astypalea	2hr 40min	12	2 weekly
Kos	1hr 20min	6.50	3 daily
Kos*	35min	16	1-2 daily
Leros**	35min	10-15	18 weekly
Leros	1½hr	9	4 weekly
Leros*	45min	20	1-2 daily
Lipsi**	1¼hr	9	3 weekly
Lipsi*	1hr	20	1 daily
Patmos	4hr	12	4 weekly
Patmos*	1hr 40min	28	6 weekly
Piraeus	11hr	52	3 weekly
Rhodes	6hr	20.50	3 weekly
Rhodes*	3hr	39	1-2 daily
Samos*	3¾hr	39	5 weekly

Unless marked, services depart from Pothia.
* high-speed service
** departs from Myrties

❶ Getting Around

BOAT

In summer, excursion boats run from Pothia to destinations including Kefalas Cave (€20), where an impressive 103m corridor is filled with stalactites and stalagmites; and the island of Pserimos, with its big, sandy beach and tavernas. Frequent **water taxis** (☑ 22430 31316, mobile 6947082912; one way €2; ⊙ 8am-midnight) also connect Myrties with Telendos Islet year-round.

BUS

Buses from Pothia harbour serve Myrties, Masouri and Armeos (€1.50, seven daily), Emporio (€2, two daily) and Vathys (€2, three daily). Check timetables at www.kalymnos-isl.gr.

CAR & MOTORCYCLE

Vehicle-hire companies along the harbour in Pothia include the friendly, good-value **Auto Market** (☑ 22430 24202, mobile 6927834628; www.kalymnoscars.gr; Harbour, Pothia), **Rent-a-Bike** (☑ mobile 6937980591; www.kalymnosrent.com; Harbour, Pothia) and **Suzuki Rentals** (☑ mobile 6937980591; Harbour, Pothia; scooter/car €8/20). Expect to pay €20 to €40 per day for a car, and €12 to €15 for a scooter.

TAXI

Shared taxis, based at Pothia's **taxi stand** (☑ 22430 50300; Plateia Kyprou), cost little more than buses. Private taxis cost around €10 to Myrties, €10 to the airport, €17 to Vathys and €30 to Emborios.

Pothia Πόθια

POP 12,300

Kalymnos' capital, Pothia has a low-slung harbourfront of cream and white facades, and backs up the hill in a labyrinth of streets, beneath hulking mountains. If arriving by boat, this is most likely your first taste of the island. You may find some Kalymnians a little gruff, but don't be offended – these rugged islanders have been known throughout history for their toughness and terse manner. Pothia is not a resort, but there's an excellent museum and tourist office. Wander the quayside peppered with old mansions and seagod statues, past nut-brown fishermen and ex-divers in *kafeneia* and bars.

◉ Sights & Activities

Archaeological Museum   MUSEUM

(☑ 22430 23113; €3; ⊙ 8am-3pm Tue-Sun Jul & Aug, 8.30am-2.30pm Wed-Fri Sep-Jun) Kalymnos' modern Archaeological Museum is hard to find, hidden in the backstreets behind the right end of Pothia's waterfront. It's worth the effort to enjoy beautifully displayed ancient artefacts dating as far back as 5300 BC. There's some remarkable glassware and gold jewellery, but the highlight is an exquisite, larger-than-life bronze statue of a woman from the 2nd century BC. Swathed in a chiton (tunic), she was discovered underwater off Kalymnos in 1994.

Nautical & Folklore Museum   MUSEUM

(☑ 22430 51361; €3; ⊙ 9am-5pm mid-Jun–mid-Sep) The two parts of the Nautical and Folklore Museum, on the central waterfront, are not always open simultaneously. The folklore section holds costumes and furniture, while the nautical museum focuses on sponge fishing, displaying mighty stone weights used by ancient divers and haunting photos of their 20th-century counterparts wearing early-model diving suits. Many suffered terrible injuries before the bends (decompression sickness) was understood.

Kalymnos Scuba Diving Club   DIVING

(☑ 6974646413, 22430 47253; www.kalymnosdiving.com) One-day dives (€50) to wrecks, underwater volcanoes, reefs and caves. Owner Dimitris also runs boat trips explaining the history of sponge diving and can demonstrate the ancient art of *skandalopetra* (stone and rope freediving). Three-day PADI open-water certification €350.

Kalymnos

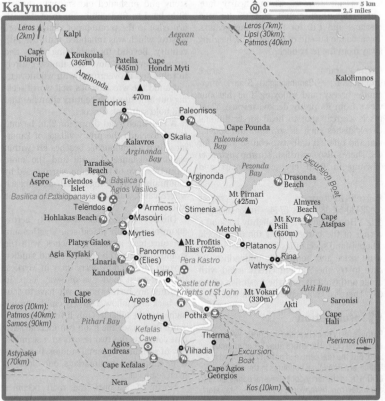

🛏 Sleeping

⭐ Villa Melina
BOUTIQUE HOTEL **€**

(📞22430 22682; www.villa-melina.com; d/tr incl breakfast €65/70; ✴🛜🌊) Set in a colourful walled garden, this rose-pink 1930s villa exudes old-world charm, its wood-panelled rooms featuring stucco ceilings, lilac walls, mahogany armoires and huge beds. Don't expect luxury – it's all slightly faded – but owner Antonios and his cats provide a homey welcome, the bathrooms are spotless, the chandeliered library extensive, and the sparkling swimming pool irresistible.

Archontiko Hotel
PENSION **€**

(📞6942838524; www.apxontiko-hotel.com; s/d €35/50; ✴🛜) Overlooking the harbour, five minutes' walk from the ferry, this custard-coloured mansion is one of the most handsome in town. Under new management, its airy, white-walled rooms with balconies, have enjoyed a refurb. By night the place is decked in candles, the antique sepia photos of the Karafilis family (who originally lived here), magically animated. It's behind Magos Travel (p382).

Hotel Panorama
HOTEL **€**

(📞22430 23138; www.panorama-kalymnos.gr; Agios Nikolaos; s/d incl breakfast €35/50; ✴🛜) Named in honour of the breathtaking rooftop views from its hilltop eyrie, this friendly, family-run hotel offers 13 rooms with private balconies, contemporary furniture and a communal sun terrace where the basic breakfast is served. It's a stiff climb from the ferry dock – ask for free pick-up.

🍴 Eating

There are many eating options lining the quayside.

Stukas Taverna
GREEK **€**

(📞6970802346; mains €6-12; 🕑lunch & dinner; 🛜) Tiny Stukas has linen-topped tables and a wharfside terrace, serving hearty fare. Three-course set menus cost €9 for vegetarians and €10 for fish- or meat-eaters. Towards the far end of the harbour, heading away from the ferry dock.

Barba Yiannis GREEK €
(mains €8-12; ⊙ 9am-midnight) Smart, mercifully breezy and enjoying fine harbour views from its pretty decked terrace, Yiannis is a great spot to head for traditional Greek dishes such as *stifadho* and souvlakia, and offers a daily two-course lunch for €8. There's also swordfish, shrimp *saganaki* (shrimp in fried cheese), calamari and lobster.

Pantelis Restaurant GREEK €€
(☑ 22430 51508; mains €7-14; ⊙ noon-midnight; ☎ ☞) Homey taverna, set slightly back off a corner of the harbour near the ferry dock, where island specialities include goat in red-wine sauce and homemade dolmadhes. Be sure to try the 'Ancient Greek' salad with apple and walnuts, and the fresh fish of the day. There's a good wine selection, too.

❶ Information

Pothia's ferry dock is at the southern, left-hand end of the port. The entire quay is commercialised, but the real centre of activity is around the Italian-era municipal buildings in the middle, 600m from the ferry dock. Several banks close to the waterfront hereabouts offer ATMs. Stay alert; traffic can be hectic on the narrow, footpath-less roads behind the waterfront, so be careful of speeding scooters.

Magos Travel (☑ 22430 28777; www.magos tours.gr) The island's main travel agency, near the ferry dock, sells ferry and catamaran tickets and has a 24-hour ticket machine outside. It also offers round-island bus tours, and boat excursions in summer.

Main Post Office (Venizelou) A 10-minute walk inland, northwest of the centre.

Municipal Tourist Information (☑ 22430 29299; www.kalymnos-isl.gr; ⊙ 8am-3pm Mon-Fri) An excellent, well-organised source of info for buses and ferries, climbing and diving, festivals and general island practicalities. At the entrance to the ferry dock.

Police (☑ 22430 29301; Venizelou)

Port Police (☑ 22430 24444; 25 Martiou)

Western Kalymnos

The former capital of Kalymnos, **Horio**, stands atop the brow of the low ridge behind Pothia, around 4km up from the sea. A steep, stony and unshaded old stairway that's a little hard to find climbs up from its eastern edge to the pirate-proof village of Pera Kastro, which was inhabited until the 18th century. Beyond its forbidding walls and stern gateway, it now lies almost entirely in ruins and is overgrown with wildflowers, but amid the wreckage it's well worth seeking out nine tiny 15th-century churches that still hold stunning frescoes.

A tree-lined road drops for 2km beyond Horio to reach the pretty village of Panormos. Two neighbouring beaches are within walking distance: Linaria and the more attractive cove of Kandouni, surrounded by mountains and holding a small sandy beach where cafes, bars and hotels overlook the water.

Directly facing Telendos Islet, across 800m of generally placid sea, **Myrties** and **Masouri** have attractive beaches, with the strand at **Masouri** being larger and sandier. Beyond the Telendos ferry quay in Myrties, the west-coast road is a one-way loop. To continue any further north, you have to double back and follow a largely empty stretch higher up the hillside. Only if you're heading south do you see the main commercial strip that connects the two resorts in a seamless row of restaurants, rental studios, bars, souvenir shops and minimarkets, one block up from sea level.

North of Masouri, the road becomes two-way once more and swiftly leads into **Armeos**, perched above the coast without a beach. Smarter and newer than its neighbours, it consists almost entirely of larger hotels and apartment complexes targeted at climbers.

North of Armeos, Kalymnos' west-coast road leaves civilisation behind. Its final stretch, skirting the deep inlet that cradles tiny **Arginonda**, is utterly magnificent, cut into the flanks of mighty cliffs and bordered with flowering oleander. It comes to an end 20km from Pothia at sleepy little **Emborios**, where sugar-white houses cluster around a long, narrow pebble beach.

◉ Sights & Activities

Kalymnos Adventure Center OUTDOORS
(☑ 6984933327, 22480 48160; www.climbersnest. com; Masouri; ⊙ 9am-noon & 4-8pm Mar-Nov) This brilliant shop sells and rents climbing equipment, maps and guidebooks. Activities include: half-day beginners and leaders climbing courses (per person from €70),

CLIMBING, HIKING & DIVING IN PARADISE

Steep crags, stark cliffs and daredevil overhangs have turned Kalymnos into Greece's premier destination for rock climbers. It now boasts more than 80 designated climbing sites, holding almost 3000 marked routes. Most are located above the island's west-coast road, especially around and north of Armeos – white roadside markers identify the precise spots – though several of the finest ascend the flanks of **Telendos Islet** (p554), just across the water.

Climbing season runs from March to mid-November, with the busiest period from mid-September until the end of October. An annual climbing festival takes place during the first 10 days of October.

The man largely responsible for the boom is Aris Theodoropolous, who along with Katie Rousseau writes the astonishingly detailed and comprehensive *Kalymnos Rock Climbing Guidebook* and maintains the useful www.climbkalymnos.com website, which includes a climbers' forum. Head to Kalymnos Adventure Center for equipment and information.

Kalymnos is also increasingly popular with hikers. Established routes are detailed on the excellent 1:25,000 *Kalymnos* map published by Terrain Maps (www.terrainmaps. gr). Serious hikers may want to undertake all or part of the highly demanding, multiday **Kalymnos Trail**, a 100km route that circles the island and also goes around Telendos for good measure. Carl Dawson published a useful guide to that and other island trails in 2015; see www.thekalymnostrail.co.uk.

Kalymnos is also becoming known as a diving island. For the beginner looking to qualify as a PADI open-water diver, as well as for the seasoned diver, there are plenty of hidden treasures in Poseidon's realm awaiting your inspection, including wreck dives, sea caves and diving with dolphins. There are four main outfits:

Kalymnos Diving (☑ 6942062215; www.scubakalymnos.com; Agios Nikolaos; ⊙ 8am-7pm)

Kalymnos Scuba Diving Club (p380)

Diver's Island (☑ 22430 48287; www.diversisland-kalymnos.gr; Kalydna Hotel, Panormos; ♿)

Diver's Island Kalymnos Scuba Diving Club (p380)

caving (€40), hiking (€20) and horse riding (€30), plus yoga on the centre's roof three times per week (€10) and massage (€65) for 50 minutes. Run by friendly Brigitte, it's efficient and full of information.

🛏 Sleeping & Eating

Hotel Philoxenia
HOTEL €
(☑ 22430 59310; www.philoxenia-kalymnos.com; Armeos; s/d €40/50; 🅿🛜❄) Somewhat isolated up the road from the main climbers' haven of Masouri, this spacious modern hotel, below some enticing crags at Armeos, makes an ideal base for climbers. Each of its plain tile-floored rooms has its own sea-view balcony and there's a decent pool with snack bar.

Myrties Boutique Apartments
APARTMENT €€
(☑ 6986285888; www.myrtiesboutiqueapartments. gr; Myrties; €106) Two delightful, dazzling rental studios, a couple of minutes' walk up from the beach, each with two rooms, sleeping up to five guests and equipped with kitchenette and broad sea-view patio. They're cleaned daily and linen includes robes and beach towels.

★ Fatolitis Snack Bar
CAFE €
(☑ 22430 47615; Masouri; snacks €5; ⊙ 9am-late; 🛜) A favourite with the apres-climbing gang, this lively roadside cafe has a vine-shaded terrace and cosy interior spattered with rock posters. The menu is carb-focused – think waffles, omelettes and toasties. Opposite Kalymnos Adventure Center, it's also known as 'Climbers' Station'. Swap your stories over breakfast, lunch or an evening beer.

Smuggler's Restaurant
TAVERNA €
(☑ 22430 48508; Myrties; mains €9-12; ⊙ 8am-late; 🅿🛜🍴) This lovely seafront taverna, close to the jetty at the south end of Myrties, is built to resemble an old fishing boat. The perfect spot, then, to enjoy fresh tuna steaks, mussels, lobster or shrimps in garlic and other deep-sea treasures, all at very reasonable prices. Look out for the sign of the Kraken outside.

WORTH A TRIP

VATHYS & RINA   ΒΑΘΥΣ & ΡΙΝΑ

Follow the barren coast road northeast from Pothia, instead of heading straight over to the west coast, and, after winding for 13km along the cliffs, it enters a long, lush, east-facing valley that was historically the agricultural heartland of Kalymnos. Narrow roads here thread between citrus orchards, bordered by high stone walls known as *koumoula*.

The valley takes its name from the inland settlement of Vathys, but the attraction for visitors is the little harbour of Rina. From the sea, it's accessed by a slender twisting inlet that's more like a fjord than anything you'd expect to find on a Greek island. In summer, large excursion boats bring troupes of day trippers here from Kos for lunch, keeping a clutch of competitive quayside tavernas busy, but it's a lovely spot at quieter times. Easy walks lead to 1500-year-old chapels on the hillside to either side of the bay.

Inland, beyond Vathys, a windswept road switchbacks up and over the mountains to reach the island's northwest coast, providing a speedier way to reach Emborios from Pothia than the built-up route through Myrties and Masouri.

Telendos Islet
Νήσος Τέλενδος

The bewitching islet of Telendos looms from the Aegean just off the west coast of Kalymnos. Crowned by a mountainous ridge that soars 450m high, it's thought to have been set adrift from the rest of Kalymnos by an earthquake in AD 554. It now makes a wonderful, vehicle-free destination for a day trip or longer stay.

Daily life on Telendos focuses on the short line of tavernas, cafes and whitewashed guesthouses that stretches along the pretty waterfront to either side of the jetty. Head right to reach the ruins of the early Christian basilica of **Agios Vasilios** and a footpath that climbs to the similarly dilapidated basilica of **Palaiopanayia**. Head left, on the other hand, and you can either cross a slender ridge, rich in colourful oleander, to access windswept, fine-pebbled **Hohlakas Beach**, or explore the islet's low-lying southern promontory, which holds some tiny early-Christian tombs now inhabited by goats, and a gloriously tranquil little swimming cove.

The cliffs along the northern flanks of Telendos hold several hugely popular **rock-climbing routes**, which can be accessed by walking for an hour or so along a rough, exposed footpath.

🛏 Sleeping & Eating

★ **On The Rocks**   PENSION €
(☑6932978142, 22430 48260; www.otr.telendos. com; r incl breakfast €60; 🕸@🛜) Behind its seafront garden restaurant, open bar and terrace strung with nautical knick-knacks,

200m right from the jetty, this welcoming complex is a haven for active climbers and indolent beach bunnies alike. The spacious studios have kitchenettes, private balconies, foot massage and washing machines. Airport transfers available.

Hotel Porto Potha   HOTEL €
(☑6949028564, 22430 47321; portopotha@klm. forthnet.gr; d incl breakfast €52; 🕸🛜🏊) Telendos' only hotel is located a five-minute walk out of the village heading north – look out for the smart sugar-cube complex up on the hill. Rooms are airy and bright, and there's a large lobby where guests come to relax and watch TV over a drink. There are additonal separate apartments.

Zorba's   TAVERNA €
(☑22430 48660; www.telendos.net; mains €8-12; 🕸🛜) Traditional cafe, a short walk from the jetty, with great sea views. The owner fishes for the seafood himself – guests can go with him – bringing up squid, octopus, tuna and swordfish. It also has three small but pleasant pink-walled en-suite rooms (€30). Arguably the best food on the island.

Emborios   Εμπορειός

In sleepy little Emborios, sugar-white houses cluster around a long, narrow pebble beach. This is the best place to swim on the island, with its crystal-clear waters sheltered by the tiny island of Kalavros offshore, and the mountains on Telendos and above Armeos dominating the horizon. Daily buses connect Emborios with Pothia, and in summer excursion boats come here for the day from Myrties – they have no fixed schedule.

🛌 Sleeping & Eating

⭐ Harry's Paradise
APARTMENT €

(☎ 22430 40062; www.harrys-paradise.gr; Emborios; d/q €50/90; 🌐 📶) 🍴 A true island favourite, set in its own garden of Eden, bursting with jasmine, roses, hibiscus and aromatic herbs. Fantastic-value accommodation incorporates charming shabby-chic elements, rocking chairs, kitchenettes and large balconies – if possible, opt for the garden-facing studios rather than the separate sea-view block – while the divine home-cooking gives locally sourced, quintessentially Kalymnian ingredients a modern twist.

⭐ To Kyma
TAVERNA €

(☎ 22430 40012; www.tokyma-kalymnos.gr; Emborios; mains €8; ⏱ breakfast, lunch & dinner) Despite its humdrum laminated menu board, this extremely friendly beach taverna serves truly exceptional food, including a delicious barley-bread salad, red mullet, salted mackerel and swordfish souvlakia. Its name, 'The Wave', refers to the swell whipped up by late summer's *meltemi* dry northerly wind.

LEROS
ΛΕΡΟΣ

POP 8210

Leros is said to have been the original home of Artemis the Huntress. There's certainly something alluringly untamed and beautiful about the island, which is scattered with stunning Orthodox churches, dazzling blue coves and whitewashed villages. The capital, Platanos, with its stark windmills and ancient fortress towering above, makes a striking centrepiece, while down below, the busy little harbour of Agia Marina pulses with enterprise. Leros is less about chasing activities and more about worshipping Helios, seeking out your favourite beach and allowing the magic of the place to slowly unfold.

ℹ Getting There & Away

AIR

Leros airport (☎ 22470 22777) is at the northern end of the island about 6km from Agia Marina. It's serviced by Olympic Air (www.olympicair.com), which offers daily flights to Athens (€80, one hour) and thrice-weekly flights to Rhodes (€74, 1¾ hours), Kalymnos (€55, 15 minutes), Kos (€62, 55 minutes) and Astypalea (€63, 25 minutes).

BOAT

High-speed catamarans operated by Dodekanisos Seaways (p328) call in at Leros between two and four times daily as they ply their way to and from Kos, Kalymnos, Patmos, Samos, Rhodes and other nearby islands. Generally they stop at Agia Marina on the island's east coast, but when there's bad weather they may stop at Lakki on the west coast, so always check the relevant port when you buy tickets, and double-check on the day you're due to depart and be prepared for a last-minute taxi dash across the island.

Blue Star Ferries (p328) makes late-night stops at Lakki twice weekly, heading once towards Rhodes via Kos and Kalymnos, and once towards Piraeus via Patmos and Lipsi.

Patmos Star (☎ 22470 32500; www.patmos-star.gr) sails between Agia Marina and the islands of Lipsi and Patmos with varying frequency, increasing to daily in peak season.

Nisos Kalymnos (www.anekalymnou.gr) connects Lakki with Kalymnos to the south, and Lipsi, Patmos and assorted islets to the north, three to four times weekly.

Anna Express (www.annaexpress.eu) connects Agia Marina three times weekly with Lipsi and with Myrties on the west coast of Kalymnos.

Boat Services from Leros

DESTINATION	DURATION	FARE (€)	FREQUENCY
Agathonisi *	1hr 50min	18	1 weekly
Kalymnos	2hr	9.50	4-5 weekly
Kalymnos *	50min	20	1-2 daily
Kos	3¼hr	9.50	1 weekly
Kos *	1hr	23	1 weekly
Lipsi	1hr	9	3-4 weekly
Lipsi*	20min	13	1 daily
Patmos	2hr	10	3-4 weekly
Patmos*	45min	20	1 daily
Piraeus	10hr	42	4 weekly
Rhodes	8hr	32.50	1 weekly
Rhodes*	3½hr	41	3 weekly
Samos*	2hr 50min	30.50	5 weekly

These Dodekanisos Seaways catamarans may dock at either Agia Marina or Lakki. Other services depart from Lakki.

*high-speed services.

ℹ Getting Around

A **taxi** (☎ mobile 6974316421, mobile 6972014531) to Agia Marina from the airport will cost around €20.

Green-and-beige-striped buses travel the length of Leros between three and six times daily (€4 flat fare), including calling at the airport. They'll usually stop anywhere if you flag them down.

Outlets in all resort areas rent cars, scooters and bikes; **Motoland** (☑ 22470 24584, 22470 24103; www.motoland.gr; at Panteli Beach Hotel; ⊙ 9am-7pm) in Alinda and Pandeli is recommended.

The *Agios Georgios* and *Barbarosa* excursion boats make assorted day trips in summer, around the island and north to islets such as Arki and Marathi, typically costing €25.

Platanos & Agia Marina
Πλάτανος & Αγια Μαρίνα

POP 3000

Arriving at the bijou port of Agia Marina, with its yawning cats, yellow fishing nets and cluster of taverna is a delight, the biscuit- and wine-coloured Italianate buildings are as if drawn from an artist's palette. And rising behind them are the white sugar-cube houses of Platanos. Stately mansions still pepper the slopes of Platanos (a 10-minute uphill walk) and the row of renovated windmills that marches up towards its imposing clifftop castle makes a magnificent spectacle.

Heading right from the ferry quay, following the shoreline, will take you to Krithoni and Alinda.

◉ Sights & Activities

Pandeli Castle   CASTLE
(☑ 22470 23211; €1; ⊙ 8.30am-12.30pm & 4-8pm; 🚶) A steep, stony stepped path zigzags up from Platanos to reach the hilltop ruins of Pandeli Castle. The castle's oldest, innermost sections date back 1000 years, but the outer ramparts were added by the Knights of St John during the 14th and 15th centuries. Few structures now survive, but the 360-degree views from the walls are breathtaking. You can also drive here, along an exposed road that winds up from Pandeli past the windmills where you'll find a cafe in summertime.

Archaeological Museum   MUSEUM
(☑ 22470 24775; Agia Marina; €3; ⊙ 9am-2.30pm Tue-Sun Jul-Sep; 🚶) A 19th-century building on the edge of Agia Marina, at the start of the climb up to Platanos, holds Leros' small Archaeological Museum. Well-chosen artefacts collected on and around the island trace its varied history and include ancient masks and Byzantine mosaics.

Agios Georgios   BOATING
(☑ 6945551731, 22470 23060; agiosgeorgiosnl54@gmail.com; cruise incl food & drink €20; ⊙ departs 11am) Captain Manolis and his boat leave from Agia Marina harbour, taking in the islands of Arki, Marathi, Arhangelos, Tiganakia, Lipsi and Aspronisia, allowing you to stop and swim in the best spots. Returns at 7pm.

Barbarosa   BOATING
(☑ 6978048715; www.leros.org/lerostouristhttp/barbarosa-leros; incl food & drink €25; ⊙ departs 11am; 🚶) *Barabarosa* is a traditional caïque that motors out from Agia Marina harbour to the islands of Arki, Marathi, Arhangelos, Tiganakia, Lipsi and Aspronisia on day trips, allowing you to stop and swim in the best spots. Returns at 7pm.

🛏 Sleeping

There's no accommodation in Agia Marina, and very little in Platanos. The closest alternative options are in Pandeli to the south, and Krithoni and Alinda to the north.

Maison des Couleurs   BOUTIQUE HOTEL €€
(☑ 22470 23341; www.maisondescouleurs.com; Platanos; r incl breakfast €100-150; 🛜) Delightfully peaceful little hotel set in a nostalgic wine-coloured villa that holds five spacious, high-ceilinged, antique-furnished rooms. Breakfast – and dinner, on request – is served on an idyllic flower-filled terrace. Look for a steep flight of yellow steps just west of the bus stop and taxi rank in Platanos.

🍴 Eating & Drinking

Smoked mackerel and thyme honey are specialities of Leros.

★ To Paradosiakon   BAKERY €
(Agia Marina; snacks €2-5; ⊙ 7am-11.30pm; ❄🛜) 🏴 This Italianate patisserie and ice-cream bar provides a sweet-toothed experience like no other. Owner Harris is an alchemist confectioner using his grandmother's old recipes to create cheese cake, chocolate gateau, baklava, strawberry tart, cookies, spinach pie and homemade made ice cream. Try the yoghurt cake with ice cream and mastiha (liqueur made from the resin of mastic trees).

★ Taverna Mylos   SEAFOOD €€
(☑ 22470 24894; www.mylosexperience.gr; Agia Marina; mains €12-18; ⊙ 1pm-late; ❄🛜📶🚶) 🏴 Lapped by turquoise waves, beside an old

Leros

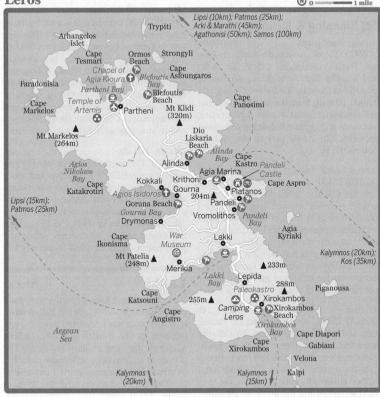

windmill at the far end of the pebbled beach that curves north from the ferry dock, Mylos infuses classic recipes with a modern twist. Go for the octopus carpaccio, the peppery basil squid, or the fabulous mixed-seafood spaghetti. The waterfront terrace is perfect for romantic sunset dinners.

Faros Bar BAR
(Agia Marina; ⊘7pm-late; 🛜) Tumbledown haunt, partly hollowed into a cave beneath the lighthouse at the promontory beyond the ferry dock. With wall-mounted accordions and dim-lit ambience, it's great fun. Come evening, you can sit by the open windows and watch quicksilver fish swimming in the aquamarine water. Live music and DJs at weekends.

🛈 Information

For information on local history and facilities, visit www.leros.org.uk or www.lerosisland.com.

Kastis Travel (☎22470 22140) Useful agency, facing the quay in Agia Marina, which sells ferry tickets and organises boat trips to nearby beaches and islets.

Leros Active (☎22470 24590; www.leros active.com; Agia Marina) Agency and tour operator specialising in alternative tourism. It arranges activities including diving and hiking, as well as tours of wartime sites, and can provide information on accommodation.

Police (☎22470 22221) In Agia Marina.

Post Office Right of the quay in Agia Marina.

Pandeli Παντελή

The village of Pandeli, arrayed around a crescent bay 800m south of Platanos, is as peaceful as it is pretty. Overlooked by a clutch of hilltop windmills, its white houses tumble down the valley towards the sand-and-shingle beach and bobbing fishing boats in the harbour. There are some great tavernas by the water, too.

🛏 Sleeping & Eating

Studios Happiness APARTMENT €
(☑ 22470 23498; www.studios-happiness-leros.com; Pandeli; d/studio/apt €45/55/70; ❄️🌐) Very friendly family-run place, perched in colourful gardens beside the road down into Pandeli, 50m up from the beach. Its vibrant white-and-blue studios have kitchenettes, twin beds and private balconies with great sea views. The rooms vary in size and are spotless throughout.

Panteli Beach Hotel APARTMENT €€
(☑ 22470 26400; www.panteli-beach.gr; Pandeli; studio/apt €90/120; ❄️🌐) Pretty, very comfortable complex, arrayed around an open courtyard right in front of the beach. All 14 studios have fresh white walls, safety deposit boxes, nice duvets and sparkling kitchenettes, and the attached Sorokos beach bar offers all-day sun loungers. There's also a playground for kids, and lastly, the owner rents scooters and quads.

El Greco SEAFOOD €€
(☑ 22470 25066; www.elgrecoleros.gr; Pandeli; mains €8-12; ⏰ lunch & dinner; ❄️🌐) Offering tables right on the beach or on a thatch-roofed terrace, this stylish taverna prepares up-to-the-minute versions of traditional seafood cuisine. Be sure to sample the king crab croquettes and the lip-smacking salted mackerel served on buttered toast.

Apostolis GREEK €€
(☑ 22470 25200, 6972821770; mains €8-12; ⏰ 9am-late; ❄️🌐) The cosy interior of turquoise tables matches the same colour of the waves lapping at the pebbled beach a few metres away. Eat outside on the terrace. Choose from spinach pie, calamari, mussels, octopus and a good selection of cheeses.

Vromolithos Βρωμόλιθος

Accessible only by walking or driving over the headland immediately south of Pandeli – there's no coastal footpath – Vromolithos consists of a long, narrow beach caressed by waters of a perfect shade of Aegean blue, scattered with turquoise. Forget the ugly village, this is all about the water.

🍴 Eating & Drinking

⭐ Dimitris O Karaflas GREEK €€
(☑ 22470 25626; Marcopoulo St, Vromolithos; mains €15; ⏰ noon-4pm & 6pm-late; ❄️🌐) The sign says 'O Karaflas', but everyone knows this hilltop eyrie (enjoying one of the best views in the Dodecanese) as 'Bald Dimitri's'. Bouzouki music washes over the terrace, where diners feast on an array of sea-urchin spaghetti, hearty island sausages, octopus carpaccio, steamed mussels, pork with green apples and plums, and substantial helpings of calamari.

⭐ Cafe Del Mar BAR
(☑ 22470 24766; Vromolithos; ⏰ 9am-late; 🌐) This super-friendly hillside lounge bar just above the north end of the beach has paradisiacal sea views, chilled pine-shaded patios, white sofas and deckchairs, plus cool tunes and DJs spinning the decks by night. Call in any time for coffee and juice, sandwiches, salads and pasta dishes, and don't miss a sunset mojito.

Lakki Λακκί

Between 1912 and 1948, when the west-coast port of Lakki was a significant Italian naval base, the town was transformed beyond recognition by the construction of grandiose administrative and military buildings. The prevalent architectural style, now classified as streamline moderne, started out resembling art deco and ended up distinctly more fascist. Lakki these days is ghostly quiet. Larger ferries and some catamarans dock at its jetty, a long walk from the centre of town, but there's no reason to linger.

👁 Sights

War Museum MUSEUM
(☑ 22470 22109; Merikia; €3; ⏰ 9.30am-1.30pm) Who remembers now that a major WWII battle was fought on this remote little island? After British troops forced the Italians to surrender in September 1943, a massive German air onslaught recaptured the island in the Battle of Leros. A network of tunnels dug by the Italians beneath the woods west of Lakki now serves as a museum, housing countless relics of the conflict. There's an explanatory video.

🍴 Eating

Petrino GREEK €€
(Lakki; mains €10; ⏰ 7am-11pm; ❄️🌐) 🌿 Hands down the most succulent meat on the island is to be found at smart Petrino. Aside

from delicious steaks there's octopus salad, stewed rabbit, and beef in lemon sauce. OK, so Lakki itself might be a little dull, but there's nothing ordinary about this place.

Xirokambos   Ξηρόκαμπος

At the southern end of Leros, Xirokambos Bay holds a pebble-and-sand beach with some good spots for snorkelling. As well as a few village houses, it's home to a good beach taverna and is served by small excursion boats from Kalymnos. Up the hill, 1km inland towards Lakki, a signposted path climbs to the ruined **Paleokastro** fortress, which offers tremendous views.

🛏 Sleeping & Eating

Camping Leros   CAMPGROUND €
(☑ 6944238490, 22470 23372; www.campingleros. com; Xirokambos; campsites adult/tent €8/4; ☉ Jun-Sep) Set 500m up from the beach, and 3km south of Lakki, the island's campground stands in a 400-year-old olive grove and holds a welcoming cafe that puts on evening barbecues. There are plenty of pitches shaded by said olive trees. It's also a centre for scuba diving, and owner Leferis offer introductory dives, day dives (€60) and CMAS-certified week-long open-water courses (€500).

To Aloni   TAVERNA €
(☑ 22470 26048; Xirokambos; mains €9-15; ☉ lunch & dinner; ᴘ✳🛜🍴) You can't miss this prominent taverna literally so close to the sea it adds a little salt seasoning to your octopus croquettes, shrimp *saganaki* (shrimp in fried cheese), swordfish, lobster, or liver in wine sauce; with tables al fresco and within its pleasant interior. Great desserts, too, if you have room.

Krithoni & Alinda
Κριθώνι & Αλιντα

POP 750

Starting just beyond the first headland north of Agia Marina, the twin resorts of Krithoni and Alinda sit next to each other on Alinda Bay, running parallel to the beach and bordered by *kafeneia* and restaurants. Leros' longest beach is at Alinda – although narrow, it's shaded and sandy with clean, shallow water. Set just back from the sea, a poignant war cemetery holds British casualties from the 1943 Battle of Leros.

For the best sun-worshipping in these parts, continue through Krithoni and Alinda to **Dio Liskaria Beach** (a few minutes' scooter ride). Bookended by rocks and with its own taverna, it's lapped by aquamarine waves.

◎ Sights

Historic & Folklore Museum   MUSEUM
(☑ 22470 24775; Alinda; €3; ☉ 9am-1pm & 6-8pm Tue-Sun; 🛜) Housed in an incongruous castellated villa on the seafront, this museum covers several aspects of local history. The upstairs rooms are given over largely to weapons, helmets and photos relating to WWII, while downstairs you'll find displays of traditional costumes and an emotive gallery devoted to artworks created by political prisoners incarcerated on the island during the colonels' dictatorship of the 1960s and 1970s.

🛏 Sleeping

★ **To Archontiko Angelou**   HOTEL €€
(☑ 6944908182, 22470 22749; www.hotel-angelou-leros.com; Alinda; r incl breakfast from €95; ᴘ✳🛜) 🍃 Spilling with oleander and jacaranda, this incurably romantic, 19th-century rose-coloured villa, five minutes' walk from the beach, is like stepping into a vintage Italian film. Think wood floors, Viennese frescoes, antique beds and old-world-style rooms. Breakfast on the sun-dappled terrace is divine: a mouthwatering array of homemade bread, jams and marmalades. One of the finest hotels in the Dodecanese.

To Archontiko Angelou is Leros' first dairy-free vegan hotel.

Nefeli Hotel   APARTMENT €€
(☑ 22470 24611; www.nefelihotels.com; Krithonia; studio/apt incl breakfast from €90/110; ᴘ✳🛜) Run by friendly Eva, Nefeli has beautiful sugar-white apartments with vividly coloured lavender and pink trim. These are beautifully finished spaces with stone floors, gleaming kitchens, moulded-stone couches and swallow-you-up beds. All have private balconies and there's a tempting cafe in the herb-fragrant courtyard. It's 10 minutes' walk beyond the northern edge of Agia Marina.

🍸 Drinking & Nightlife

Nemesis Cafe   BAR
(☑ 22470 22070; Krithoni; ☉ 10am-late; 🛜) There's piping jazz and happy vibes at this well-stocked waterfront bar with a nautical theme. Perfect spot for a sundowner.

PATMOS ΠΑΤΜΟΣ

POP 3040

Patmos is known as the 'Holy Island' or, less appealingly, 'the island of the Apocalypse' after St John the Divine who, exiled some 2000 years ago, envisioned the end of the world in a cave and recorded this in the disturbing Book of Revelation: 'And I stood upon the sand of the sea, and saw a beast rise up out of the sea, having seven heads and 10 horns...'

In the Greek myths Patmos was referred to as 'Latmos', a sunken mountain which Artemis and Poseidon persuaded Zeus to resurface. You'll be glad they did, for this hourglass-shaped island has no sizeable towns, just the picturesque harbour community of Skala, and labyrinthine village of hillside Hora. Patmos still abounds in barely disturbed bays lined with sand and pebble beaches, lulled by limpid waters and overlooked by pine- and heather-coated hillsides. They say the island's strange energy either embraces or repels you; what will it do for you?

History

St John the Divine was banished to Patmos by the pagan Roman Emperor Domitian in AD 95. Living as a hermit in a cave above what's now Skala, St John heard the voice of God issuing from a cleft in the rock and transcribed his terrifying visions as the Book of Revelation. Around 1000 years later, in 1088, the Byzantine Emperor Alexis I Komninos gave the Blessed Christodoulos permission to erect a monastery in John's memory. Pirate raids necessitated powerful fortifications, so the monastery took the form of a mighty hilltop castle. In the centuries that followed, Patmos became a semi-autonomous monastic state and achieved such wealth and influence that it was able to resist Turkish oppression.

ℹ Getting There & Away

All Patmos ferries dock in Skala. **Dodekanisos Seaways** (p328) catamarans connect Patmos with Lipsi, Leros, Kalymnos, Kos, Rhodes and other islands to the south, and also with Arki, Agathonisi, Ikaria, Fourni and Samos to the north.

Blue Star Ferries (p328) calls in twice each week, once heading south through the Dodecanese chain towards Rhodes, and once towards Piraeus.

The Nisos Kalymnos (www.anekalymnou.gr) connects Patmos with Kalymnos, Lipsi and Leros to the south, and the islets to the north, three to four times weekly.

The Patmos Star (p385) sails between Patmos and Lipsi and Leros, daily in peak season and less frequently otherwise.

Boat Services from Patmos (Skala)

DESTINATION	DURATION	FARE (€)	FREQUENCY
Agathonisi*	55min	16	1 weekly
Kalymnos	4hr	12.50	4 weekly
Kalymnos*	1hr 40min	30	6 daily
Kos*	3hr	31	1-2 daily
Leros	2hr	10	4-5 weekly
Leros*	40min	17	1-2 daily
Lipsi	50min	8	4 weekly
Lipsi*	25min	12	4 weekly
Piraeus	7hr	36	1 weekly
Rhodes	10hr	37.50	3 weekly
Rhodes*	5hr	49	5 weekly
Samos*	1hr	30	6 weekly
Symi*	4¼hr	46	1 daily

*high-speed services

ℹ Getting Around

BOAT

Patmos Daily Cruises (p396) offers summer boat excursions to beaches around the island, including Psili Ammos, and also to nearby islets.

BUS

Buses (flat fare €2) connect Skala with Hora seven times daily, and with Grikos and Kambos four times daily, and more frequently in July and August.

CAR & MOTORCYCLE

The main seafront street in Skala holds several car- and motorcycle-hire outlets, including **T & G Automoto** (☑ 22470 33066; Skala) and **Avis** (☑ 22470 31900, 22470 33025; Skala; ⊗ 9am-9pm). Demand often exceeds supply in high season, so book ahead if possible. The best scooter shop, **Moto Rent Faros** (☑ 22470 34400; www.patmos-motorentfaros.com; ⊗ 8am-8.30pm), is behind the harbour on the road to Hora, and has quick, regularly serviced bikes.

TAXI

You can catch a **taxi** (☑ 22470 31225) from Skala's taxi rank, opposite the police station.

Skala   Σκάλα

POP 3000

Skala, Patmos' photogenic ferry port, is set on a huge bay on the eastern shore of the island. Apart from those moments when mighty cruise ships suddenly obliterate the entire harbour, it's a laid-back little place. There's even a tiny patch of sandy beach – albeit covered with restaurant tables – a few hundred metres from the dock.

Skala's waterfront is an unbroken string of tavernas, cafes and fading Italian buildings from the 1930s, while whitewashed houses, stylish clothing and jewellery boutiques, geletaria, and cafes fill the maze of backstreets stretching inland. The island is barely 700m wide at this point, so a 10-minute walk will take you all the way to stony, windswept **Hohlakas Beach** on its western side.

◎ Sights & Activities

Skala has a couple of religious sites, including the place where St John first baptised locals in AD 96, just north of the beach. To find out more and to see religious objects from across the island, visit the Orthodox Culture & Information Centre (p393) in the harbourside church.

If you feel like a workout, climb to the remains of an ancient **acropolis** on the hillside to the west of town. The route is not well signposted – head for the prominent chapel then follow the dirt trail across the fields. The views from the top are stunning.

⊨ Sleeping

Hotel and studio owners often meet boats at the port, but it's best to call ahead and arrange a pick-up to avoid the scrum. Outside of high season (August) expect dramatically reduced rates.

Kalderimi Apartments   BOUTIQUE HOTEL €€
(☑ 22470 33008, 6972008757; www.kalderimi. com; apt incl breakfast €120; ◷ late May–early Oct; ❋ 🛜) This inland whitewashed place at the start of the footpath up to Hora is pure tranquillity, with a shaded courtyard overflowing with palms, bougainvillea and Moorish lanterns. The five spacious apartments have a traditional feel, featuring wooden beams and stone walls, plus sparkling kitchens.

Captain's House   HOTEL €€
(☑ 22470 31793; www.captains-house.gr; d/apt incl breakfast €70/80; ❋ 🛜 ⛲) Delightful wharfside digs, 100m walk left from the quay,

holding high-spec rooms and apartments with en-suite bathrooms and crisp white lines. Five have their own sea-facing balconies. There's also a lovely swimming pool out back with sun loungers, along with a great breakfast terrace. Perfect family option.

Blue Bay Hotel   HOTEL €€
(☑ 22470 31165; www.bluebaypatmos.gr; s/d/ tr incl breakfast €70/90/120; ❋ @ 🛜) Small hotel perched above the road immediately south of Skala, 250m walk from the harbour beyond the first headland. Basic air-con rooms are redeemed by having great seaview balconies; it's an unbeatable spot to enjoy the breakfast buffet.

✖ Eating

Tzivaeri   SEAFOOD €
(☑ 22470 31170; mains €10; ◷ 5pm-late) Skala's best option for a romantic feast spreads over a balcony terrace at the north end of the harbour. With its walls covered in shells, sponges and black-and-white photos, and the air thick with bouzouki music, it makes a memorable stop for Cretan-style sardines, shrimp or octopus, though you can also get a burger or kebab. Live music on Fridays.

Pantelis   TAVERNA €
(☑ 22470 31230; mains €10; ◷ lunch & dinner) Long-standing taverna, with locals and visitors alike packed onto tables on the narrow pedestrian street that runs parallel to the port. If you're not feeling adventurous enough to try the smoky sea-urchin salad or the *fouskes* (sea figs – definitely an acquired taste), you can always get staples such as meatballs, *moussaka* (baked layers of eggplant or zucchini, minced meat and potatoes topped with cheese sauce), grilled lamb chops and calamari.

Chiliomodi   TAVERNA €
(☑ 22470 34080; Skala; mains €12; ◷ lunch & dinner) Hidden in a back alley not far from the waterfront, Chiliomodi has been keeping travellers happy for over two decades with mouthwatering sea bream, salted cod, succulent sausages and various mezedhes to name a few. The restaurant has its own fishing boat so the seafood couldn't be fresher.

AigaionEsti AigaionEsti   GREEK €€
(☑ 6942813044; mains €15; ◷ 11am-12pm; ❋ 🛜) Skala's newest restaurant has wide-screen sea views, a smart interior of exposed stone and white walls, plus a menu featuring baby goat stew, wild boar, and squid with chilli

DODECANESE PATMOS

Patmos

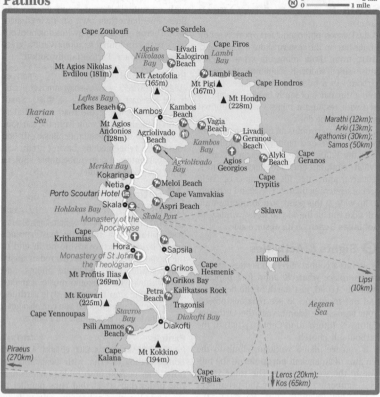

N 0 ———— 2 km
0 ———— 1 mile

Cape Zouloufi
Cape Sardela
Livadi
Agios
Kalogiron
Nikolaos
Beach
Cape Firos
Bay
Lambi
Mt Agios Nikolas
Bay
Evdilou (181m) ▲
Mt Aetofolia
Lambi Beach
(165m) ▲
Mt Pigi ▲
Cape Hondros
(167m)
Lefkes Bay
Mt Hondro
Lefkes Beach
Kambos
(228m) ▲
Ikarian
Kambos
Sea
Beach
Vagia
Mt Agios
Beach
Andonios
Agriolivado
Livadi
Marathi (12km);
(128m) ▲
Beach
Geranou
Arki (13km);
Kambos
Beach
Agathonisi (30km);
Bay
Samos (50km)
Agriolivado
Agios
Alyki
Cape
Bay
Georgios
Beach
Geranos
Merika Bay
Kokarina
Cape
Netia
Meloï Beach
Trypitis
Porto Scoutari Hotel 🏠
Cape Vamvakias
Skala
Aspri Beach
Sklava
Hohlakas Bay
Skala Port
Monastery of the
Apocalypse
Cape
Krithamias
Hora
Sapsila
Hiliomodi
Monastery of St John
the Theologian
Grikos
Cape
Mt Profitis Ilias
Hesmenis
Lipsi
(269m) ▲
Grikos Bay
(10km)
Petra
Kalikatsos Rock
Mt Kouvari
Beach
(225m) ▲
Tragonisi
Aegean
Stavros
Diakofti Bay
Sea
Cape Yennoupas
Bay
Psili Ammos
Diakofti
Beach
Piraeus
Cape
Mt Kokkino
(270km)
Kalana
(194m)
Leros (20km);
Kos (65km)
Cape
Vitsilia

and coriander. There's a wood-fired oven for pizzas and you can also eat al fresco beside the water. To reach it, walk through the glass gauntlet of giant lobsters skulking in tanks.

🍷 Drinking & Nightlife

★ Koukoumavla Bar
CAFE

(☎ 22470 31321; ⊙ 10am-late Tue-Sun; 🛜) 🍃 Imagine the love child of Tim Burton and Frida Kahlo opening a coffee house and you're getting close – interesting art spattered across green and orange walls, cool tunes, cocktails and excellent coffee. The 'owl' also sells crafts, books and toys and has a little garden terrace as well as tables on the alleyway, just back from the sea.

★ Art Café
BAR

(☎ 22470 33092; ⊙ 7pm-late; 🛜) Escape the harbour hubbub by climbing to a fabulous panoramic roof terrace then blissing out over sunset cocktails (€7 to €9) amid plump

pillows and white-cushioned benches. The friendly German owner also serves great homemade hummus and there's often live music in the indoor lounge below.

Arion
BAR

(☎ 22470 31595; ⊙ 9am-late; 🛜) Over 100 years old, this venerable, high-raftered, woodpanelled bar, at the heart of the waterfront, is a major local landmark and rendezvous point for locals. Travellers generally prefer to sit outside, watching the world and the waves go by as they hook up to the wi-fi. Snacks include toasties and crêpes.

Meltemi
CAFE

(☎ 22470 31839; ⊙ 9am-late; 🛜) Irresistible beach bar at the far end of the harbour that curves 500m north from the ferry dock. Sit on the sand savouring a cocktail as the sun sinks into the sea, or come earlier for breakfast, a midday sandwich, fruit salad or milkshake under the shade of a tamarisk tree.

ℹ Information

All Patmos ferries dock in the heart of Skala. Taxis wait at the quay, and the bus terminal is close by, as are three ATM-equipped banks. From the roundabout straight ahead, a road climbs inland towards Hora. Skala stretches away to the right, with the road skirting a narrow beach and the yacht port as it heads north.

Both www.patmos-island.com and www.patmosweb.gr provide copious information. You can also pick up a free copy of the pocket-sized *Patmos Guide* in shops and hotels.

Apollon Travel (☑ 22470 31324; apollon travel@stratas.gr; ⊗ 9.30am-2pm & 6.30-9pm) and **Astoria Travel** (☑ 22470 31205; www.astoriatravel.com) Best for ferry tickets, along with all practical aspects of visiting Patmos, including accommodation.

Health Centre (☑ 22473 60000; ⊗ 8am-2pm) Located 2km along the road to Hora; you'll find it next to the Monastery of the Apocalypse.

Municipal Tourist Office (☑ 22470 31666; ⊗ Mon 9am-5pm, Tue-Sun 9am-9-pm Jun-Sep) Has useful tips on things to see and do on the island.

Orthodox Culture & Information Centre (☑ 22470 33316; ⊗ 9am-1pm & 6-9pm Mon, Tue, Thu & Fri, 9am-1pm Sat & Sun) This quayside office provides details on the island's religious sites, including current opening hours.

Police (☑ 22470 31303) On the main waterfront.

Port Police (☑ 22470 31231) Behind the quay's passenger-transit building.

Hora   Χώρα
POP 800

With gorgeous views of the island from its hilltop eyrie, enchanting Hora is more than just a whitewashed mountain settlement. As you wander its incense-scented warren of 17th-century houses, the Boschian forms of St John's demons scuttling behind your imagination, it's easy to see why Hora draws people back again and again. Allegedly there are more monasteries per square metre in Hora than anywhere else in the world. Aside from the sanctity of the place there are some lovely fashion boutiques and a couple of interesting galleries and upscale bars.

⊙ Sights

★ Monastery of the Apocalypse   MONASTERY
(Cave of the Apocalypse; ☑ 22470 31398; €2; ⊗ 8am-1.30pm, also & 4-6pm Tue, Thu & Sat) Nestled amid the pines halfway to Hora, the Monastery of the Apocalypse focuses on the cave where St John lived as a hermit and received his revelation. Pilgrims and less-than-devout cruise passengers alike stream into the chapel built over the recess, to see the rocky pillow where the saint rested his head, the handhold with which he'd haul himself up from his prayers and the stone slab that served as his writing desk.

★ Monastery of St John the Theologian   MONASTERY
(☑ 22470 31223; €4; ⊗ 8am-1.30pm daily, also 4-6pm Tue, Thu & Sat) As this immense 11th-century monastery-fortress remains active, only a small portion is open to visitors. The entrance courtyard leads to a sumptuously frescoed chapel, fronted by marble columns taken from an ancient temple. Don't expect to attend a service; daily worship is at 3am! The museum of church treasures upstairs displays the original edict establishing the monastery, signed by the Byzantine emperor in 1088.

Holy Monastery of Zoödohos Pigi CONVENT
(☑ 22470 31991; ⊗ 9am-1pm daily & 5-8pm Mon-Sat, 9am-1pm Sun) FREE The Orthodox convent known as the Holy Monastery of Zoödohos Pigi is tucked away in the back alleys of Hora. You can't go beyond its pretty little courtyard, where a small church holds remarkable 17th-century frescoes. One of the 40 resident nuns will cheerfully point out Jesus on Judgement Day dispatching assorted bishops and clerics down a river of fire that flows into the maw of the beast.

🛏 Sleeping & Eating

★ Archontariki   B&B €€€
(☑ 22470 29368; www.archontariki-patmos.gr; ste €200; ⊗ Easter–Oct; ☀🛜) Hidden in a little alley near the Zoodohos Pigi monastery, these heavenly suites in a 400-year-old home are equipped with every convenience, traditional furnishings and plenty of plush touches. Relaxing under the fruit trees in the cool, quiet garden courtyard, you'll never want to leave. Suites 'Wisdom' and 'Joy' are capacious, while 'Love' and 'Hope' are smaller, traditional split-level affairs.

★ Pantheon   GREEK €
(☑ 22470 31226; mains €7-12; ⊗ 5pm-midnight; ☀🛜) Look for the octopus drying outside – hence its local moniker 'the octopus place' – this whitewashed belle with Aegean-blue chairs and soaring village views is pure

TIMOFEEV VLADIMIR/SHUTTERSTOCK ©

1. Symi (p354)
The island abounds with Italian-influenced architecture.

2. Olymbos (p349), Karpathos
A woman uses a communal oven to bake bread in Greece's most traditional village.

3. Mandraki (p364), Nisyros
Stroll through this peaceful, almost traffic-free town.

4. Rhodes Old Town (p328)
Explore this incredible medieval fortress town.

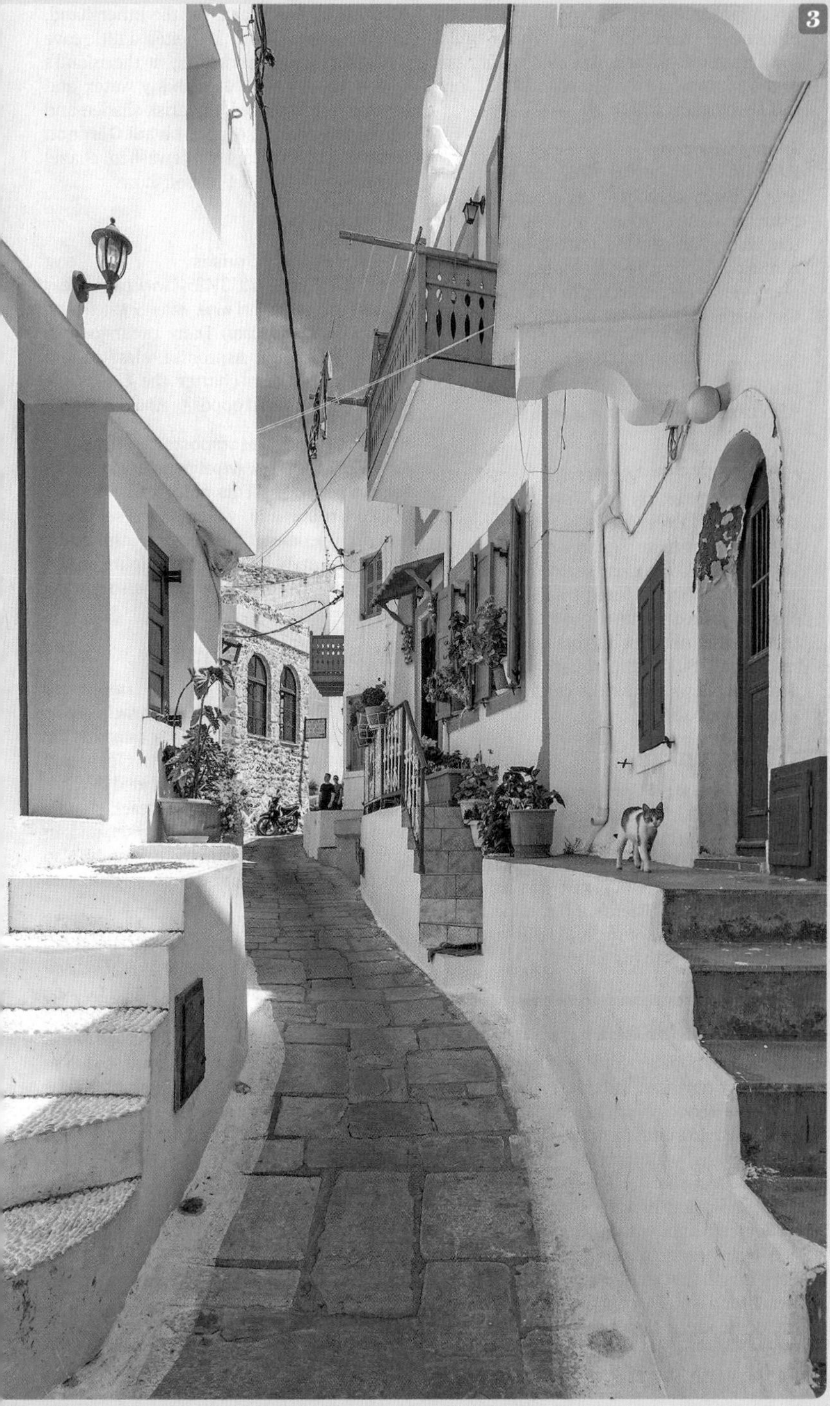

3

NEJDET DUZEN/SHUTTERSTOCK ©

Greek fare at its best. Seafood and meatballs, homemade sweets and warm crinkly smiles from its gentle owners. Located at the start of the approach to the Monastery of St John the Theologian (p393).

Jimmy's Balcony

GREEK €

(☑ 22470 32115; mains €7-12; ⊙ 10am-11pm; 🛜 🍴) Perched above the road, on the principal lane through the village to the monastery, the shaded terrace of this welcoming all-day cafe-restaurant commands regal views across Skala to the islands to the north. Drop in for a cooling drink, or to enjoy its delicious salads, breakfast, *mousakas* (baked layers of eggplant or zucchini, minced meat and potatoes topped with cheese sauce) and veggie dishes.

Vaggelis

TAVERNA €€

(☑ 22470 31967; Pl Agias Lesvias; mains €10-15; ⊙ lunch & dinner; 🍴🛜) With chi-chi grey chairs and tables, Vaggelis sits in one of the most intimate squares in the world. Foamy cream octopus, seafood *mousakas* and impeccably prepared traditional dishes such as baked Patmos goat are a few of the delights on offer in this contemporary restaurant. Sit in the square, or for jaw-dropping views, under the carob tree in the garden out back.

🛍 Shopping

Andreas Kalatzis Gallery

ART

(☑ 6988024890; ⊙ 8am-3pm & 8pm-late) Byzantine icon artist and Che Guevara lookalike, Andreas Kalatzis lives and works in a 1740s traditional home just east of the St John monastery. There's a beguiling mix of abstract oils, sculpture and quirky photography on show in his gallery.

North of Skala

The most popular and readily accessible beach in northern Patmos is wide, sandy Kambos Beach, which lies 5km northeast of Skala, just downhill from the village of Kambos. Crowded with local families in summer, it's a perfect stop for kids, with safe swimming and plenty of water-based activities.

Remoter and, with luck, quieter beaches can be reached by driving a little further. Fork inland (left) immediately after Kambos Beach and you'll soon find yourself winding down green slopes to Lambi Beach, an impressive expanse of multicoloured pebbles on the north shore. Stick to the coast road

east of Kambos Beach, on the other hand, to reach Vagia Beach, a sheltered little cove that offers good snorkelling in the island's coldest though highest-visibility water, and beyond it the pebbled, tamarisk-shaded and stunningly turquoise-laced Livadi Geranou Beach, where a tiny whitewashed chapel beckons from the islet just offshore.

🏃 Activities

⭐ Patmos Daily Cruises

BOAT

(☑ 6977035231, 22470 31425; www.patmosdaily cruises.com; Skala; incl wine, water & watermelon €23; ⊙ departs 10.15am) Daily excursions to islands Makronisi, Aspronisa, Marathi and Arki. You can also charter the company's three boats. Moored opposite Apollon Travel.

Kambos Beach Watersports

WATER SPORTS

(☑ 6972123541; www.patmoswatersports.com; Kambos Beach; 🚣) This outfit can take you wakeboarding and waterskiing, set loose you on a pedalo or, for the less athletically inclined, simply rent you a sun lounger and leave you in peace. There are also kayaks available.

🛏 Sleeping & Eating

Stefanos Camping

CAMPGROUND €

(☑ 22470 31821, 6945067206; www.facebook. com/pg/Stefanos-Camping-Patmos; campsites per person/tent €7/2; ⊙ May-Sep; 🛜) Clean and very friendly with bamboo-shaded pitches and a stunning view of the beach metres away. There are bikes, a minimarket, and an excellent grill cafe all run by the family. Also has cosy studios which sleep four (€90).

Porto Scoutari Hotel

HOTEL €€

(☑ 22470 33123; www.portoscoutari.com; d incl breakfast €145-235; 🅿 ❄ @ 🛜 🏊) Focused around a lavish swimming pool and spa centre, this was the first luxe hotel on the island and in many ways is still the grandest. It surveys the Aegean from a rural spot 3km north of Skala. Enjoy palace-sized rooms with nautical frescoes, sofas, spotless bathrooms, private balconies and antique beds plus, above all, stunning sea views. Check for amazing low-season rates.

George's Place

CAFE €

(☑ 22470 31881; Kambos Beach; snacks €6-10; ⊙ breakfast, lunch & dinner; 🅿 ❄ 🛜 🚣) 🌿 Super-chilled beach bar, accessed straight off the sand, with an enticingly shaded, sun-dappled terrace facing the peacock-blue bay. Easy tunes, wi-fi, toilets that can double as changing rooms, and a simple menu of salads, homemade pies, chocolate cake, milkshakes and pastries keep the customers happy.

Livadi Geranou Taverna TAVERNA €
(☑ 22470 32046; Livadi Geranou Beach; mains €9-12; ☉ 10am-late) With its flower-bedecked terrace perched on the heather-clad hillside at road's end, a few metres above the beach, this hugely popular taverna benefits from heavenly sea views. Feast on a seafood spread of whitebait and octopus, or opt for a simple platter of meatballs or souvlakia.

Leonidas TAVERNA €
(Lambi; mains €10; P ✱ ☑) ✐ Sitting on the crest of the hill overlooking Lambi Beach, Leonidas has a flower-filled terrace with food to match the serene view. Dine on souvlakia, *stifadho*, calf's liver, as well as the catch of the day.

South of Skala

The southern half of Patmos is scattered with small, tree-filled valleys and picturesque beaches. The first settlement south of Skala is tiny, peaceful **Sapsila**. **Grikos**, 1km further along over the hill, has a long, sandy beach that holds a handful of tavernas and is dominated by a plush resort hotel. St John is believed to have baptised islanders here during the 1st century AD, at a spot now marked by the chapel of **Agios Ioannis Theologos**.

South again, **Petra Beach** is peaceful and has plenty of shade, while a spit leads out to the startling **Kalikatsos Rock**. Both a rough coastal track from the beach and a longer paved road from Hora continue as far as **Diakofti**, the island's southernmost community. From there, a demanding half-hour hiking trail scrambles over the rocky hillside to reach the fine, tree-shaded stretch of sand known as **Psili Ammos Beach**, which holds a seasonal taverna. It's bewitchingly pretty and utterly isolated; if you've got kids with you, it's safer for you to hire a boat from Skala to get here.

🛏 Sleeping & Eating

Mathios Studios APARTMENT €€
(☑ 22470 32583; www.mathiosapartments.gr; Sapsila; studio/apt €70/80; ✱ @ ☎) Located 2.5km south of Skala in sleepy Sapsila, Mathios has five studios and two apartments fully equipped with kitchen, fridge,

bathroom and balcony, with lush views of the gas-blue bay below. The style is rustic-chic complemented by quirky driftwood sculptures scattered about the grounds, while the owners do their best to make you feel at home. Also available in winter.

★**Patmos Aktis Suites** DESIGN HOTEL €€€
(☑ 22470 32800; www.patmosaktis.gr/en; Grikos Bay; r from €390; P ✱ ☎ ☼) Sitting upon Grikos Beach, Patmos' newest design hotel leaps from a David Hockney painting with its sleek geometric aesthetic and cube-white suites. Expect rain showers and private terraces giving onto a swimming pool metres from your bed. There's a great restaurant serving up contemporary Greek food, plus facilities ranging from massage treatments in the sumptuous spa to gym and boutique.

Flisvos Restaurant SEAFOOD €
(☑ 22470 31380; mains €8; ☉ 9am-7pm) Simple family-run taverna a short walk from Petra Beach, with zesty Greek salads, super-fresh seafood, souvlakia, homemade pies and a peaceful setting to tie it all together. If you're lucky there may be some live bouzouki music in the evening.

Benetos GREEK €€
(☑ 22470 33089; www.benetosrestaurant.com; Sapsila; mains €10-27; ☉ 7.30pm-late Tue-Sun Jun-Sep; ☑) ✐ Dropping down to the sea from the coast road, a couple of kilometres south of Skala, this romantic boutique restaurant, and recently added tapas bar, is set on a working farm. The menu draws its inspiration from all over the Mediterranean; think stuffed zucchini blossoms with turmeric sauce, octopus confit with eggplant salad, and calamari with red pepper sauce.

LIPSI ΛΕΙΨΟΙ

POP 700

Lipsi might be small, at just 8km in length, but what a powerful impact it has on the traveller, with its low-slung harbour bunched with crayon-yellow nets and the whitewashed, church-crowned village of Lipsi climbing the hill behind. If rugged hills, serene blue coves and deserted beaches are what you seek, you may have just found heaven. In the 'Odyssey', Lipsi was where the nymph Calypso waylaid Odysseus for several years. Abandon yourself to sun-worshipping and wandering the backstreets, and you may fare the same.

Check too the local speciality, *myzithra* cheese, made from goat's milk and seawater, and pick up a jar of distinctive thyme honey.

ⓘ Getting There & Away

Lipsi has frequent connections with its neighbours. Dodekanisos Seaways (p328) catamarans head north to Arki, Agathonisi and Samos, and south to Patmos, Leros, Kos and other islands. The Nisos Kalymnos (www.anekalymnou.gr) runs to Patmos, Leros and the islets to the north three to four times weekly, while the Patmos Star (p385) sails to both Patmos and Leros, daily in summer. The Lipsi-based **Anna Express** (☑ 22479 41382; www.annaexpress.eu) sails three times weekly to Leros and Myrties on western Kalymnos.

A small **office** (☑ 22470 41290; ⊗ 8am-4pm) on the ferry jetty sells all boat tickets.

Boat Services from Lipsi

DESTINATION	DURATION	FARE (€)	FREQUENCY
Agathonisi	3hr	8	4 weekly
Agathonisi*	1hr 25min	13.50	1 weekly
Kalymnos	3hr	8	4 weekly
Kalymnos*	1½hr	22	1 daily
Kos*	4½hr	29	1 daily
Leros	50min	8.50	3 weekly
Leros*	20min	15	1 daily
Patmos	1hr	6	1 weekly
Patmos*	25min	13.50	1 daily
Piraeus	10hr	41	1 weekly
Rhodes*	5½hr	47	1 daily
Samos*	1½hr	32	1 daily except Tue

*high-speed services

ⓘ Getting Around

Frequent buses connect Lipsi Village with the main island beaches in summer. There are also two **taxis** (☑ mobile 6942428223, mobile 6942409679). Hire scooters and bicycles in Lipsi Village from **Maria & Marcos** (☑ 22479 41358), next to Poseidon Apartments.

Lipsi Village   Λειψοί
POP 600

Hugging the deep harbour, Lipsi Village – the island's only settlement – is a cosy, intimate affair, with an atmospheric old town of blue-shuttered houses radiating up the hill

in a tangle of alleyways. The harbour is the hub of the action and there's everything you need here, from an ATM and a great bakery, to delectable seafood restaurants. Be sure to visit the beautiful blue-domed church of **Panagia tou Harou**, with its panoramic harbour-view terrace.

The closest beach to the village, **Liendou Beach** is a couple of minutes' walk north of the ferry port over a small headland. It's a narrow strip of sand, washed by calm, shallow water.

🏃 Activities

Rena Five Island Cruise   BOATING
(☑ 694733 9141; www.facebook.com/pg/Rena5IslandCruise; adult/child €25/10; 🚣) Sailing since 1980, *Rena,* a traditional wooden caïque, offers summer excursions from Lipsi's smaller jetty to islets Aspronisia, Makronisi (with their sapphire waters and weird rock formations), and Tiganakia, Marathi and Arki, for a picnic and swim.

🎉 Festivals & Events

Panagia tou Harou   RELIGIOUS
Each year on 22 August, visitors flock to pay homage to a famous icon of the Virgin in the village church. They come to see the lilies inside its glass cabinet, which, despite being rootless and unwatered, burst miraculously into bloom. A procession is followed by all-night revelry in the lower square.

Wine Festival   FOOD & DRINK
(⊗ Aug) This Dionysian festival takes place for three days with dancing and free wine. Check locally for precise dates.

🛏 Sleeping

⭐ **Nefeli Hotel**   APARTMENT €€
(☑ 22470 41120; www.lipsinefelihotel.com; studio/apt incl breakfast €90/110; 🅿❄🛜) Stylish, welcoming boutique hotel in splendid isolation above lovely Kambos Beach, 10 minutes' walk north of the village. The apartments are spacious, with comfy beds, kitchenettes, sofa beds and private sea-view patios. Prepare to be lulled to sleep by the call of owls. There's also an opulent bar, lounge and dining area, bedecked in lavender and purples.

⭐ **Rizos Studios**   APARTMENT €€
(☑ 6976244125; www.facebook.com/rizosstudios; d €70; ❄🛜) Rizos' rooms have Aegean-blue and white, and biscuit and powder-blue colour themes, and are bursting with chi-chi

panache. Flagstone floors, shabby-chic furniture, fine views from private balconies and fully equipped kitchens. It's 10 minutes' walk up from the dock; call ahead to be picked up, and book ahead in high season as, unsurprisingly, it sells out quickly.

Angela Studios APARTMENT €€
(☎22470 41177, 6983666611; www.lipsiangela.eu; Waterfront; studio/apt €70/80; ❄📶) Angela has wrought-iron beds, sparkling kitchenettes, fridge and microwave, plus a dividing curtain to allow for privacy. Add to this balconies with sea views and a delicious little cafe and you need look no further. Close to the ferry dock.

Eating

★Manolis Tastes TAVERNA €
(☎22470 41065; www.manolistastes.com; mains €8-10; ⏲noon-4pm & 5.30pm-late; 📶) In a handsome 19th-century neoclassical building (and former Italian Police station), Manolis Tastes has a roof terrace and upstairs lounge, and fine dining in a cream-and-wood interior. The real draw is Chef Manolis, his culinary flair recognised as far away as Athens. Mussels with ouzo, and pork with mustard and honey, are just a few of the splendid dishes served here.

Angela Cafe CAFE €
(☎6983666611; Harbour; snacks €4; ⏲8am-late; ❄📶) This new and decidedly chic little cafe with lavender and white trim has an intimate interior for snacks, coffee and cocktails, and a breezy sea-facing outside terrace.

Kairis Lipsi Bakery Shop BAKERY €
(☎22470 41050; sweets €1-3; ⏲24hr; ❄📶👪) This lively bakery-gelateria-cafe, beside the steps up to the village centre, is the social hub of the island and stays open all night. It's a veritable treasure trove of fresh-baked cookies, croissants, sausage rolls, pies, sandwiches, baklava, alcohol and some very fancy cakes, presided over by its charming and gregarious owner. Fight your way through the locals for a seat.

Cafe du Moulin CAFE €
(☎22470 41316; mains €9; ⏲8am-late; ❄📶) Tucked in the cool shadows of a little square by the church of Panagia tou Harou, this restaurant is run by a house-proud French, English and Italian speaking lady. It serves up great-value, tasty food: Lipsi goat with mustard, souvlakia, *saganaki* (fried cheese) and octopus salad. You can also get breakfast here.

Information

The main ferry jetty is at the northern, left-hand end of the port; there's an Alpha Bank with ATM nearby. Following the quay towards the village centre, up on the hill ahead, you'll pass the smaller excursion-boat jetty, while the Anna Express docks immediately below the church. The post office is up in the old town.

Lipsi Bookings (☎22470 41130; www.lipsibookings.com; ⏲9am-1pm & 3pm-7pm) Very helpful agency alongside Poseidon Studios by the port, selling tickets for all ferries and organising activities including camping, hiking, horse riding, sailing, snorkelling and visits to a winery and eco-farm.

Police (☎22470 41222) At the port.

Port Police (☎22470 41133) At the port.

Tourist Office (⏲10am-3pm Jul-Sep)

Around Lipsi

Lipsi is remarkably green for a Greek island. Walking to its further-flung beaches leads you through countryside dotted with olive groves, cypress trees and endless views. A minibus also services the main beaches.

Just 1km north of Lipsi Village, around the headland beyond Liendou Beach, **Kambos Beach** is narrower but sandier than its neighbour and somewhat shaded by tamarisk trees. The water is also deeper and rockier underfoot.

Fork inland at Kambos and a delightful 2.5km hike over the low-lying spine of the island will lead you to the shallow and child-friendly **Platys Gialos Beach**. Ringing with goat bells and shelving gently into crystal-clear water, it's home to an excellent summer-only taverna. Be warned: it closes at 6pm.

Just 2km south of Lipsi Village, sandy **Katsadia Beach** is wilder, especially if it's windy. There's a certain amount of shade and another good summer-only taverna, which stays open late as a bar.

The beaches at Lipsi's eastern end are harder to reach, with the roads being too rough for taxis or buses.

Eating

Platis Gialos Restaurant TAVERNA €
(☎6944963303; Platys Gialos Beach; grills €10; ⏲8am-6pm Jul & Aug) Sitting on the island's best beach for swimming in unbelievable

turquoise water, this pleasant little taverna has decent grilled food and fresh salads.

Dilaila Cafe Restaurant TAVERNA €
(☑22470 41041; Katasadia Beach; mains €9; ☺Jun-Sep; P🐕☑🌐) 🍴 Tucked behind the beach at Katasadia, this inviting restaurant with colourful decor and split levels has intimate as well as communal areas to take in the stunning sea. Dishes include lentil salad with octopus, feta in honey, pork in mustard sauce, grilled tuna and many more. It costs €4 each way in a taxi from Lipsi Village.

ARKI & MARATHI
ΑΡΚΟΙ & ΜΑΡΑΘΙ

POP 55 (ARKI)

Only 5km north of Lipsi, tiny Arki has rolling hills and secluded, sandy beaches. Away from its only settlement – a little west-coast port also called Arki – the peace and stillness verges on the mystical.

The Church of Metamorfosis stands on a hill behind the settlement, while several sandy coves can be reached along a path skirting the north side of the bay.

Tiganakia Bay, on the southeast coast, has a good sandy beach. To walk there from Arki village, follow the road heading south and then the various goat tracks down to the water. Keep an eye out for dolphins.

Marathi, the largest of Arki's satellite islets, has a superb sandy beach. The old settlement, with an immaculate little church, stands on a hill above the harbour. While just three people remain on Marathi year-round, local families return each summer to reopen its seasonal tavernas.

🛏 Sleeping & Eating

Arki holds a handful of tavernas with comfortable, well-maintained rooms. Bookings are essential in July and August.

Taverna Nikolas PENSION €
(☑22470 32477; Arki; d €50; ❄🐕) Simple central taverna, where the spacious, white-walled, twin-bedded rooms have sunset views. As well as whatever seafood the boats have brought in, the kitchen (mains €8 to €10) dishes up potatoes au gratin, stuffed peppers with cheese, and the local goat cheese called *sfina*, resembling a mild form of feta.

Pantelis Taverna PENSION €
(☑22470 32609; www.marathi-island.gr; Marathi; d €50; ❄🐕) The closest Marathi comes to having a fully fledged beach resort, at the northern end of the sands. As well as spacious and attractively furnished rooms in a white-painted studio block, it also rents a larger maisonette. The taverna itself serves a fine menu of home-cooking (mains €8 to €12), from octopus croquettes to goat stew.

Taverna Mihalis GREEK €
(☑22470 31580; Marathi; mains €8; 🐕) Set on the beach, Mihalis has a simple menu of mezedhes and seafood-oriented dishes depending what the day's catch might be. Calamari, octopus, decent salads and a nice atmosphere. Also has rooms (d €40).

❶ Getting There & Away

Three ferry companies stop off at Arki, but not Marathi, as they sail up and down the island chain. All call at Patmos, Leros, Lipsi and Agathonisi. Weekly **Dodekanisos Seaways** (p328) catamarans run south as far as Kos and north to Samos. Anna Express (www.annaexpress.eu) also goes to Samos (two weekly), and Nisos Kalymnos (www.anekalymnou.gr) starts from Kalymnos (three to four weekly). For Marathi, a local caïque runs from Arki on Monday, Tuesday and Wednesday.

In summer, Lipsi-based excursion boats and Patmos-based caïques offer frequent day trips (€20) to Arki and Marathi.

Boat Services from Arki & Marathi

DESTINATION	DURATION	FARE (€)	FREQUENCY
Arki*	1¼hr	7	3 weekly
Kos	3hr	31	1 weekly
Lipsi	45min	13.50	6-7 weekly
Patmos	1hr	14	6-7 weekly

* Departs from Marathi. Services to other desinations depart from Arki.

AGATHONISI ΑΓΑΘΟΝΗΣΙ

POP 160

Arriving in Agathonisi's harbour – enclosed by a fjord-like formation and holding so few buildings you could count them in a breath – is pure magic. So far off the tourist radar its neighbours barely acknowledge it, Agathonisi is quiet enough to hear a distant Cyclops break wind. There's little to do here but read, swim and explore the caves where islanders once hid from pirates... and then do it again!

Keep an eye out too for the *klidonas* ritual of jumping through fire to cleanse your spirit.

❶ Getting There & Away

Three ferry companies connect Agathonisi with Patmos, Lipsi and points south. Both Dodekanisos Seaways (p328) catamarans (weekly) and Anna Express (www.annaexpress.eu, two weekly) continue north to Samos; Nisos Kalymnos (www.anekalymnou.gr) only goes as far north as Pythagoreios (three to four weekly). Buy your tickets 20 minutes before departure from **Savvas Kamitsis** (☑ 22470 29003), based by Mary's Rooms.

Boats dock at Agios Georgios, from where roads ascend right to Megalo Horio and left to Mikro Horio.

Boat Services from Agathonisi (Agios Georgios)

DESTINATION	DURATION	FARE (€)	FREQUENCY
Arki	45min	5	6-7 weekly
Kalymnos*	2hr	25	1 weekly
Kos*	3¼hr	29	1 weekly
Lipsi	1hr	8	4 weekly
Patmos	2hr	16	1 weekly
Samos	1hr	8	6-7 weekly

Agios Georgios
Άγιος Γεώργιος

The port village of Agios Georgios, the island's primary settlement, holds a few tavernas and simple sugar-cube pensions. The high point of a day is sitting on the harbour beach pondering the turquoise and watching the fishermen roll in with their catches. **Spilia Beach**, 900m southwest beyond the headland, along a track around the far side of the bay, is quieter and better for swimming. A further 1km walk will bring you to **Gaïdouravlakos**, a small bay and beach where water from one of the island's few springs meets the sea.

🛏 Sleeping & Eating

Mary's Rooms   PENSION €
(☑ 22470 29003; www.maryroomsagathonisi.com; Agios Georgios; s/d €30/40) Very simple but spic-and-span rooms in the middle of the waterfront, offering kitchenettes, fridges and tiny balconies with sea views. There's also a flower-filled courtyard.

Glaros Restaurant   TAVERNA €
(☑ 22470 29062; Agios Georgios; mains €9-12; ⊙ lunch & dinner; 🐱🍴) Of the few harbourside tavernas, the bougainvillea-draped terrace of the 'Seagull' is probably the best place to dine. Owners Voula and Giannis are very engaging and serve *markakia* (feta fingers in vine leaves with a special sauce), along with standard oven-cooked meals, grills and fish dishes, all made from predominantly organic produce.

Megalo Horio
Μεγάλο Χωριό

The tiny hamlet of Megalo Horio is a steep and sweaty 1.5km trek uphill from the harbour, but the effort is rewarded by the stupendous views from the cliff. The village barely stirs until June, and the ideal times to come are for the festivals of **Agiou Panteleimonos** (26 July), **Sotiros** (6 August) and **Panagias** (22 August), when Megalo Horio celebrates with abundant food, music and dancing.

A series of accessible beaches lie within easy walking distance to the east: **Tsangari Beach**, **Tholos Beach**, **Poros Beach** – the only sandy option – and **Tholos (Agios Nikolaos) Beach**, close to the eponymous church.

🛏 Sleeping & Eating

Studios Ageliki   APARTMENT €
(☑ 22470 29085; Megalo Horio; s/d €35/45; ❄🐱) If you prefer an even quieter stay than at the port, these four basic but quite comfortable studios will serve you very well. All of them have stunning views over a small vineyard and down to the port, and come equipped with kitchenette, fridge and bathroom.

Restaurant Irini   GREEK €
(☑ 22470 29054; Megalo Horio; mains €7; ⊙ lunch & dinner; 🐱) Welcoming taverna on Megalo Horio's central square, renowned for its rich lamb stew and meaty *stifadho*.

Northeastern Aegean Islands

Best Places to Eat

➡ Marymary (p414)

➡ Thea's Restaurant & Rooms (p411)

➡ AAA Taverna (p424)

➡ Kechribari Ouzerie (p428)

➡ Spitalia (p435)

Best Places to Stay

➡ Rooms Dionysos (p409)

➡ Archipelagos Hotel (p416)

➡ Hotel Kyma (p444)

➡ Ino Village Hotel & Restaurant (p419)

➡ A for Art (p459)

Why Go?

The northeastern Aegean Islands (τα νησιά του Βορειοα-νατολικού Αιγαίου) are notable for their proximity to the Turkish mainland. Influences from Asia Minor abound in old-fashioned island cuisines, traditional village culture, dramatic celebrations and even the language.

Eccentric Ikaria is marked by jagged landscapes, pristine beaches and a famously long-lived, left-leaning population. Nearby Chios provides fertile ground for the planet's only gum-producing mastic trees. Other islands range from rambling Lesvos, producer of half the world's ouzo, to midsized islands such as semitropical Samos and workaday Limnos, and bright specks in the sea such as Inousses and Psara. Samothraki is home to the ancient Sanctuary of the Great Gods, while well-watered Thasos seems an extension of the mainland.

Lesvos, Chios and Samos offer easy connections to Turkey's coastal resorts and historic Hellenic sites.

When to Go
Vathy Sámos

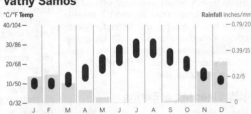

Apr & May Wild red poppies adorn the backroads and Greek Easter livens up every village.

Jul & Aug Beach bars and village councils (in Ikaria's case) throw wild parties for holiday-ing revellers.

Oct & Nov Summer crowds evaporate, and hearty soups return to the tavernas.

Northeastern Aegean Islands Highlights

① Hristos Rahes (p410) Getting post-midnight coffee and spoon sweets in the nocturnal capital of Ikaria.

② Psarotaverna O Miltos (p417) Enjoying sunset and the Aegean's best lobster spaghetti dish.

③ Potami Beach (p423) Finding a secret taverna above the wooded waterfalls after lazing on a marble gravel beach.

④ Teriade Museum (p437) Discovering a treasure trove of top-notch art in Mytilini Town.

⑤ Blue Fox (p442) Watching yachts sailing through a turquoise bay while sipping *cezve* (Turkish) coffee in charming Molyvos.

⑥ Mastiha House (p432) Lodging in castle-like apartments in Pyrgi.

⑦ Sanctuary of the Great Gods (p456) Contemplating the cult of ancient gods who preceded the Olympians.

⑧ Mineral Baths of Eftalou (p441) Daydreaming in an ancient thermal pool on Lesvos.

IKARIA ΙΚΑΡΙΑ

If Greek islands were humans, then magical Ikaria would be the most charismatic, and weirdest. Its outlandish terrain, largely untamed by agriculture, comprises dramatic forested gorges, rocky moonscapes and hidden beaches with aquamarine waters. Ikaria's independent spirit and unique culture – characterised by dwellings pretending to be rocks – a nocturnal lifestyle and rave-like *panigyria* village festivals, grew over centuries out of isolated life under the constant threat of pirates and foreign invaders.

Supposedly named after Icarus, said to have crashed here after flying with wax wings too close to the sun, Ikaria is also honoured as the birthplace of Dionysos, god of wine. Ikarian villages famously throw wild parties with loads of food, wine and traditional dance. The island gets packed with Athenians and foreign visitors at the height of August's *panigyria*, but at all times you can enjoy Ikaria's serenity and the locals' sybaritic attitude to life, which results in extraordinary longevity.

ⓘ Getting There & Away

AIR

Ikaria is served by **Olympic Air** (www.olympicair.com), **Aegean Airlines** (www.aegeanair.com) and **Astra Airlines** (www.astra-airlines.gr). Tickets are available at agencies in Agios Kirykos and Evdilos, and at the **airport** (☑ 22750 32216; Faros).

BOAT

Get tickets in Agios Kirykos at Ikariada Travel (p406) or Dolihi Tours Travel Agency (p406). In Evdilos, try **Amfitriti Travel** (☑ 22750 32757, 6940430526; www.amfitrititravel.gr), or the Hellenic Seaways agent, **Roustas Travel** (☑ 22750 23441, 22750 32931), both on the waterfront. In addition to regular ferries, there are also weekly day-trip excursion boats between Agios Kirykos and Patmos (€32, 55 minutes, one to two per week), 20km south.

ⓘ Getting Around

BOAT

In summer, a daily caïque (water taxi) goes from Agios Kirykos to Therma (€3). Another boat on Ikaria's south coast links Manganitis with the idyllic Seychelles Beach, 2.5km away, for swimming and sunbathing. Weekly day-trip excursion boats to Fourni depart from Agios Kirykos (€25).

BUS

A daily bus makes the winding route from Agios Kirykos to Hristos Rahes, via Evdilos and Armenistis. It also calls at the Ikaria airport on the way. A local bus makes the 10-minute trip to Therma every half-hour.

Ikaria & the Fourni Islands

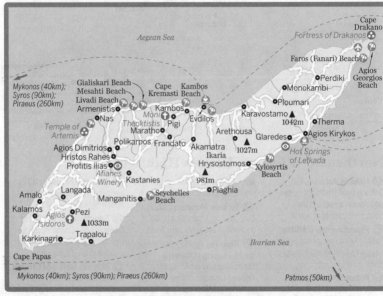

CAR & MOTORCYCLE

It's a good idea to hire a car or scooter for travel beyond the main towns. Hitchhiking is very common and considered safe by locals, but we don't recommend it.

For cars, try Dolihi Tours Travel Agency (p406) or Ikariada Travel (p406) in Agios Kirykos; **Mav Cars** (☑ 6932908944, 22750 31036; mav-cars@hol.gr; ☺ 9am-10pm) in Evdilos; and **Aventura** (☑ 22750 31140, 6972284054; aventura@otenet.gr; ☺ 9am-9pm) in Evdilos and Armenistis. Most car-hire offices can arrange for airport pick-up or drop-off, too, generally at no extra charge.

You can rent good motorbikes from **Pamfilis Bikes** (☑ 6979757539), up the steps from Alpha Bank in Agios Kirykos.

TAXI

A taxi between Agios Kirykos and Evdilos costs around €55.

Agios Kirykos
Αγιος Κήρυκος

POP 1880

Ikaria's capital is an easygoing and dependable Greek port, with clustered old streets, hotels and domatia (rooms in private homes), tasty restaurants and a lively waterfront cafe scene. Although beaches are nicer in Ikaria's north, the area's renowned hot radioactive

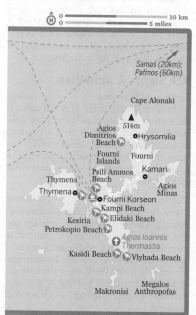

0 10 km
0 5 miles

Samos (20km);
Patmos (60km)

Cape Alonaki

Agios 514m
Dimitrios Hrysomilia
Beach
Fourni Fourni
Islands
Psili Ammos Kamari
Thymena Beach
Agios
Thymena Minas
Fourni Korseon
Kampi Beach
Kesiria Elidaki Beach
Petrokopio Beach
Agios Ioannis
Thermastis
Kasidi Beach Vlyhada Beach

Megalos
Makronisi Anthropofas

springs, scattered along the coast, attract aching bodies from around Europe. The main cluster is located 2km east at **Therma**, which also has a nice pebble beach.

☆☆ Festivals & Events

Frikaria Music Festival   MUSIC
(☺ Jul & Aug) The hip Frikaria Music Festival attracts music freaks and free spirits alike to various locations. The three-day event, held in late July or early August, features Greek rock bands and DJ sets. Programs are available from cafes in Evdilos (try Rififi; p409) and Agios Kirykos.

Ikaria International
Chess Tournament   SPORTS
(☑ 6977730286, 6947829772; www.ikaroschess.gr; ☺ Jul) This traditional annual event in Agios Kirykos, organised by local chess aficionado Kosmas Kefalos, draws chess players of all types from around Europe and beyond. The tournament celebrates its 40th anniversary in 2017 and retains a distinctly local flavour (one event features local children enacting chess moves at the square during a live grand-master match). This battle of wits takes place in mid-July, lasting about a week.

🛏 Sleeping

Pension Plumeria Flowery   PENSION €
(☑ 22750 22742, 6945139021; www.therma-ikaria.com; Therma; r incl breakfast €50) Big-hearted host Kiriaki runs these immaculate rooms – with names such as Bougainvillea, Anemone and Hyacinth – in the centre of Therma. In addition to being as helpful as one possibly can, she also makes great cakes for breakfast.

★ Hotel Akti   HOTEL €
(☑ 22750 23905; www.pensionakti.gr; s/d from €35/50; ❄🔊) A fine budget choice in a prime spot, Akti has cosy and attractive modern rooms with fridges, TVs, overhead fans and mosquito netting, plus friendly, English-speaking owners. A modern and locally popular cafe-bar overlooks the sea and port below. Follow the steps just right of Alpha Bank.

Agriolykos Pension   PENSION €
(☑ 22750 22433, 6944907023; www.agriolykos.gr; Therma; s/d/tr incl breakfast from €40/50/60; ❄🔊) This exceedingly charming lodging is the work of Mrs Voula Manolarou, who oversees every detail of the budget jewel. It sits on its own little perch, with stairs to the small bay that it overlooks.

DOMESTIC FLIGHTS FROM IKARIA

DESTINATION	DURATION	FARE (€)	FREQUENCY
Athens	35min	70-95	1-2 daily
Limnos	45min	44	6 weekly
Thessaloniki	1½hr	65-106	6 weekly

Hotel Maria-Elena   HOTEL €
(☑22750 22835; www.mariaelena.gr; s/d €40/50; ❄@🛜) Charming, welcoming and quiet, the Maria-Elena enjoys a garden setting and offers 21 simple and spotless rooms, all with balconies overlooking the sea, plus a few larger suites. It's open year-round, and lies about 500m from the port, near the hospital.

✖ Eating

Filoti   TAVERNA €
(mains €5-7; ⊙lunch & dinner) This tasty eatery 30m from the square, up the first alleyway, offers Agios Kirykos' best-value meals, including tasty grills, salads and excellent pizza.

Stou Tsouris   TAVERNA €
(mains €7-10; ⊙lunch & dinner) On the waterfront facing the square, this busy and traditional eatery serves tasty grills and several very good *mayirefta* (ready-cooked meals) and fresh fish (fairly priced by the kilo). Open year-round.

Legouvisi Souvlakia   DELI €
(snacks €2.50-4; ⊙lunch & dinner) A snappy delicatessen next to the post office, serving good snacks, coffee, beer and quick grills.

Taverna Klimataria   TAVERNA €
(mains €6-10; ⊙lunch & dinner) An inviting backstreet taverna, behind the National Bank, with a lovely shaded courtyard. Strong on grilled meats and *pastitsio* (layers of buttery macaroni and seasoned minced lamb) with generous salads.

🍷 Drinking & Nightlife

Ambariza Bistro   CAFE
(☑22750 31721; Agios Kirykos) A convivial little cafe-cum-bar with some tables in a romantic bougainvillea-filled lane behind the National Bank. In addition to coffee and alcohol, it serves great desserts and breakfasts.

Kazino Cafe   CAFE
(☑22750 23290; Agios Kirykos; ⊙8am-midnight) One of several decent waterfront cafes, Kazino occupies an 1850s-era building and serves coffee and fresh juices, made-to-order chocolate milkshakes and fresh *tyropita* (cheese pie), all managed by the philosophical Makis.

ℹ Information

Banks with ATMs are at the *plateia* (square).
Dolihi Tours Travel Agency (☑22750 23230; dolichi@otenet.gr) Full-service agency, next to Alpha Bank.
Hospital (☑22753 50201)
Ikariada Travel (☑22750 23322; www.ikariada.gr) Full-service waterfront travel agency next to Diagonios souvlaki shop.
Island Ikaria (www.island-ikaria.com) is a handy online guide.
Naftiliako Praktoreio (☑22750 22426) Behind the waterfront, in the first alleyway, this helpful hole-in-the-wall specialises in ferry tickets to Fourni and Patmos, and has local tips.
Police (☑22750 22222) Above Alpha Bank.
Port Police (☑22750 22207)
Post Office On the street above the *plateia*.

Around Agios Kirykos

Aching bodies and perfectly healthy pleasure seekers from all over Europe flock to hot radioactive springs in the vicinity of Agios Kirykos. Some of the springs discharge hot water into the sea, providing for a unique bathing experience. Most are located in Therma, 2km from Agios Kirykos.

◉ Sights & Activities

Fortress of Drakanos   FORTRESS
(⊙8am-3pm Tue-Sat) FREE This 4th-century-BC fortress sponsored religious rites dedicated to Eilythia, a fertility deity. A 13m-high lookout tower anchors the site, which features informative signboards. A path from a small chapel here leads to tiny Agios Georgios Beach.

Hot Springs of Lefkada   HOT SPRINGS
These hot sea-springs 2.5km southwest of Agios Kirykos are therapeutic, relaxing and free. Although it's a designated radioactive saltwater spring, in truth it's just a beautiful spot on the beach, identifiable by an irregular circle of rocks. You'll know you're in the right spot when you feel the now-it's-hot, now-it's-not intermingling of spring and seawater.

To find the springs, drive 2km southwest and look for a small blue-and-white sign (marked 'Hot Springs' in English) next to a path leading to the rocky beach below. You'll want shoes or walking sandals for the 50m path down to the water.

★ Spilio Baths
HOT SPRINGS

(To Spilio; ☑ 22750 24048; Therma; €3.50-4.50; ☺ to dusk daily) Spilio means 'cave', but this steamy gem is an authentic thermal sauna and bath that draws on a hot underground spring. It's clean, natural and refreshing, and lures a younger clientele than its more-established thermal neighbours. Showers and lockers are included, but bring a towel. It's past the kiosk at the end of the waterfront, to the right as you face the sea.

Asklipios Bathhouse
HOT SPRINGS

(☑ 22750 50400; €3; ☺ 8am-1pm & 5-8pm Jun-Oct) Sample the effects of the area's radioactive saltwater springs at this simple beachfront bathhouse, named for the mythical Greek god of healing. The springs are famed for their beneficial effects on ailments such as arthritis and rheumatism. Hot water is piped in from a spring in the sea, and an average bath takes about 30 minutes.

Therma Hot Springs
HOT SPRINGS

(Apollon Spa; ☑ 22750 22665, 22750 24049; Therma; €4.50; ☺ 8-11am) The most traditional of Therma's hot springs is Apollon, the village's municipal spa, touted for the curative properties of its pure mineral waters.

🛏 Sleeping

★ Evon's Rooms
APARTMENT €

(☑ 6977139208, 22750 32580; www.evonsrooms.com; Faros; studios/ste from €45/120; ℗ ❄ @ 🛜) Less than 100m from Faros Beach, friendly Greek-Australian Evon Plakidas rents high-quality suites, some with spiral stairs, all with kitchenettes. The studios hold up to six people. An adjoining cafe serves breakfast, delicious crêpes, sweet *loukoumadhes* (ball-shaped doughnuts served with honey and cinnamon), fresh juices and salads.

Aleksandros Studios
GUESTHOUSE €

(☑ 22750 32030, 6986757316; www.ikariastudios.com; Manganitis; r €45) Should you decide to overnight in Manganitis, head to the naval-themed Aleksandros Studios. Brightly coloured rooms are equipped with kitchenettes, and the balcony on the 2nd floor looks like a ship's deck.

NORTHEASTERN AEGEAN ISLANDS IKARIA

BOAT SERVICES FROM IKARIA

DESTINATION	PORT	DURATION	FARE (€)	FREQUENCY
Chios	Agios Kirykos	5½hr	15	2 weekly
Fourni	Agios Kirykos	1hr	7	3 weekly
Fourni*	Agios Kirykos	20min	14	2-3 weekly
Kalymnos	Agios Kirykos	2hr 50min	32	1 weekly
Kavala	Agios Kirykos	18hr	40	2 weekly
Lesvos (Mytilini Town)	Agios Kirykos	9½hr	23	2 weekly
Limnos	Agios Kirykos	14hr	32	2 weekly
Mykonos	Evdilos	3hr	20	4-5 weekly
Naxos	Agios Kirykos	2hr	20	1 daily
Patmos	Agios Kirykos	1½hr	13	3 weekly
Patmos*	Agios Kirykos	1hr	22	1 weekly
Piraeus	Agios Kirykos	9½hr	38	3 weekly
Piraeus	Evdilos	8½hr	38	3 weekly
Samos (Karlovasi)	Evdilos	1½hr	13	4 weekly
Samos (Pythagorio)*	Agios Kirykos	50min	25	2 weekly
Samos (Vathy)	Agios Kirykos	3hr	10	4 weekly

* hydrofoil service

✗ Eating & Drinking

O Karakas TAVERNA €
(Karkinagri; mains €6-9; ⊙ lunch & dinner) On a bamboo-roofed seafront patio, this excellent family-run taverna serves up good fresh fish and salads. Try Ikaria's speciality *soufiko*, a tasty vegetable stew. Domatia are available, should you linger.

Sto Gialo BAR
(✆ 22750 32636; www.stogialokaneifourtouna.gr; Manganitis) A popular seaside bar and music venue, famous for its full-moon parties.

Evdilos Εύδηλος
POP 460

Ikaria's second port, Evdilos skirts a small semicircular bay and rises in tiers up a hillside. It features stately old houses on winding streets, and a relaxed and appealing waterfront. Evdilos is 41km northwest of Agios Kirykos, to which it's connected by Ikaria's two main roads. The memorable trip takes in high mountain ridges, striking sea views and slate-roof villages.

🛏 Sleeping

Kerame Studios APARTMENT €
(✆ 22750 31434; www.keramehotel.gr; studio/apt/ ste from €35/45/60; 🅿 ❄ 🛜 🌊) These studio apartments 1km before Evdilos feature kitchens and spacious decks with views. Prices are as variable as the quarters. A breakfast cafe is built into a windmill. Kerame is the sister establishment of Hotel Atheras near the port.

Hotel Atheras HOTEL €
(✆ 22750 31434; www.atherashotel.gr; s/d/tr from €30/45/55; 🅿 ❄ 🛜 🌊) The friendly and modern Atheras has an almost Cycladic feel due to its bright-white decor contrasting with the blue Aegean beyond. There's an outdoor bar by the pool. The hotel is in the backstreets, 200m from the port.

✗ Eating & Drinking

RakoStroto TAVERNA €
(✆ 22750 32266; mains €6-10; ⊙ dinner) Up on the hill, at the bend in the street that connects with the main road to Kambos, this newish taverna occupies a kind of natural balcony with bay views. Competently made grill and vegetable dishes are served, and musicians come for impromptu concerts in summer.

Giro Giro GRILL €
(✆ 22750 32480; mains €2.50-7; ⊙ lunch & dinner) Serves a variety of meat – souvlaki, steaks, kebabs, sausages – to take away or to eat on the spot, from simple *gyros* (meat slithers cooked on a vertical rotisserie;

RELIGIOUS REVELRY ON THE ISLAND OF WINE

Pagan god Dionysos may no longer reign over Ikaria's vineyards, but his legacy lives on in Christianised form in the summertime *panigyria* (all-night festival celebrations held on saints' days across the island). There's no better way to dive head first into Greek island culture than drinking, dancing and feasting while honouring a village's patron saint. Bring your wallet, however: *panigyria* are important fundraisers for the local community. Use this fact to explain any overindulgence as well-intended philanthropy.

Panigyria occur across the island on the following dates:

Kambos 5 May

Armenistis 40 days after Orthodox Easter

Agios Isidoros (Pezi) 24 June

Agios Giannis (Hristos Rahes) 24 June

Platani 29 June

Karavostamo 1 July

Agios Kirykos & Ikarian Independence Day 17 July

Arethousa 17 July

Agios Panteleinonas (Fidos) 27 July

Hristos Rahes & Dafni 6 August

Akamatra 15 August

Evdilos 15–20 August

Agios Sofia & Monokambi 17 September

usually eaten with pitta bread) to large platters for two (€15).

Restaurant Koralli TAVERNA €
(Plateia Evdilou; mains €7-9; ⊙ lunch & dinner) A local favourite among the waterfront tavernas, Koralli specialises in fresh fish and chips, excellent meat grills, veggie salads and oven-ready *mayirefta*.

Sta Perix GREEK €€
(☑ 22750 31056; Akamatra; mains €5-11; ⊙ lunch & dinner) Classy eatery in Akamatra, 6km south of Evdilos, that's well regarded for its traditional Ikarian recipes, a variety of local cheeses, and even its own wine.

⭐**Café-Bar Rififi** CAFE
(☑ 22750 33060; Plateia Evdilou; ⊙ all day) This snappy port-side bar, with great pitta snacks, draught beer and good coffee, owes its name to the bank next door, with which it shares an interior wall. Rififi in Greek is a nickname for bank robber, and the servers are happy to point out where the serious money is stashed.

ℹ️ Information

The waterfront has two ATMs.
Amfitriti Travel (☑ 22750 32745; www.amfitriti-travel.gr) Helpful full-service travel office, 20m from the post office.
Medical Center (☑ 22750 33030, 22750 32922) Around 2km east of Evdilos, with English-speaking doctor and staff.
Pharmacy (☑ 22750 31394; Evdilos waterfront)
Police (☑ 22750 31222)
Port Police (☑ 22750 31007)

West of Evdilos

Kambos Κάμπος
POP 250

Kambos, 3km west of Evdilos, was once mighty Oinoe (derived from the Greek word for wine), Ikaria's capital. Traces of this ancient glory remain, compliments of a ruined Byzantine palace, Ikaria's oldest church and a small museum. Kambos' other main attractions are its sand-and-pebble beach and scenic hill walks.

⊙ Sights

Entering Kambos from Evdilos, you'll pass the modest ruins of a **Byzantine palace**, which served as a parliament and theatre during Hellenistic times. To find it, take the short path leading from Agia Irini Church.

Agia Irini Church CHURCH
Built on the site of a 4th-century basilica, this 12th-century church contains some columns from the original. Alas, many of Agia Irini's frescoes remain covered with protective whitewash because funds for its removal are scarce.

Archaeological Museum MUSEUM
(☑ 22750 32935; ⊙ 8.30am-3pm Wed) FREE Kambos' small museum displays Neolithic tools, geometric vases, classical sculpture fragments, figurines and ivory trinkets. If it's closed, ask Vasilis Kambouris at Rooms Dionysos to open it.

🛌 Sleeping & Eating

⭐**Rooms Dionysos** PENSION €
(☑ 22750 31688, 6944153437; www.ikaria-dionysosrooms.com; d/tr/q from €25/35/45; 🅿️ 🛜) The many happy guests who return every year attest to the magical atmosphere of this pension run by the charismatic Vasilis 'Dionysos' Kambouris, his Australian-born wife Demetra and Italian-speaking brother Yiannis. Rooms are simple, with private bathrooms, while the rooftop beds are a summer steal at €10. There's a communal kitchen, a book exchange and you'll get great tips on exploring Ikaria.

Balcony PENSION €€
(☑ 22750 31604; d/tr €60/70; ❄️) There are fantastic views from the six apartments at family-run Balcony, which is a bit of a hike to reach. Classic wrought-iron furniture distinguishes the studios, each of which has a kitchen and a loft-sleeping area with twin mattresses.

⭐**Ikaros** GREEK €
(mains €3.50-7; ⊙ 11am-late) Ikaros is a classic village *ovelistirio*, or grill house, referring to the upright grill for making *gyros*. Excellent food, lively atmosphere, snappy service. Opposite the pharmacy.

THE WILD SOUTH

You can now drive on a fairly good paved coastal road all around the island, except for a 15km section between **Manganitis** and **Karkinagri**, located in Ikaria's southwestern corner. Both are serene end-of-the-universe places, with quaint fishing ports and a few tavernas, where hikers wind up after descending from the desolate moon-like plateau south of Hristos Rahes.

Connected by a paved road to Agios Kirykos and Evdilos, Manganitis draws crowds from elsewhere on the island every lunar month in summer when the popular Sto Gialo (p408) bar and restaurant holds its Fool Moon Party. Check out its website and advertisements around the island for other live and DJ music events. People also flock to the small and stunning Seychelles Beach, 3km east of Manganitis. Its marble pebbles, emerald water and giant rocks polished by the waves make you feel you've been teleported into the middle of the Indian Ocean – hence the name. Should you decide to sleep in Manganitis, head to naval-themed and well-equipped Aleksandros Studios (p407).

Karkinagri is now connected by a brand-new road that gives mind-blowing vistas up to the tourist clusters of Nas and Armenistis in Ikaria's northwest. Life in Karkinagri revolves around the bamboo-roofed seafront patio of taverna O Karakas (p408). It's the best place on the island to try the local speciality *soufiko*, a tasty vegetable stew.

East from Karkinagri, the dirt track in the direction of Manganitis is OK for a good car until Trapalou, which has a very nice beach. Beyond that, the road is pretty atrocious and often gets completely blocked by falling rocks. Check with locals about its current condition.

Pashalia TAVERNA €
(mains €6-10; ⊙ lunch & dinner) A family-run taverna with tradition, the Pashalia offers tasty homemade mezedhes (appetisers), such as wild mushrooms, fresh wild asparagus and goat's cheese, and is frequented by the locals.

Hristos Rahes Χριστός Ραχών

At night the heart of Ikaria beats in the cool highlands above Armenistis, where a cluster of picturesque villages comes to life after dark, with children playing in the streets and adults drinking coffee or ouzo. These nocturnal habits hark back to the times when, fearing pirates based on nearby Fourni, Ikaria pretended to be an uninhabited island. An occasional roof covered with stone slabs is another vestige of that epoch, when people tried to camouflage their dwellings as piles of rocks. By day, Hristos Rahes is the departure point for many exciting hikes through Ikaria's highlands, covered in pine forest and fruit orchards.

◉ Sights

Afianes Winery WINERY
(☑ 22750 40008, 6977893731; www.afianeswines. gr; ⊙ noon-8pm Thu-Tue) FREE Call for directions to this excellent small family-run winery in the hills above Hristos Rahes. It has won several recent awards in Europe. In addition to the offered tastings and small

personal tours of the operation, an exhibition room features vintage winemaking equipment, gourd vessels and 19th-century wedding dresses.

🛏 Sleeping & Eating

Estia GUESTHOUSE €€
(☑ 22750 41007, 6979835757; evgeniaporis@ gmail.com; r from €65) Simply but tastefully decorated rooms, up the road from Hristos Rahes, with fully equipped kitchens, and balconies that face the sea and the cascade of Rahes villages descending to Armenistis.

★Taverna Platanos TAVERNA €
(☑ 22750 42395; Agios Dimitrios; mains €5-9.50; ⊙ lunch & dinner) Nestled under the shade of a rambling plane tree, a 500m stroll from Hristos Rahes, Platanos offers authentic Ikarian dishes, including *soufiko,* a summer favourite of stewed veggies, generally featuring whatever is picked fresh that morning. Great grills, hearty salads and local wine round out the table.

CousinA GREEK €
(☑ 22750 41374; mains €6-11; ⊙ lunch & dinner) A short walk from the main square, this tiny but outstanding eatery ventures well beyond the Ikarian mainstream, upgrading traditional Greek food to the level that would earn the acclaim of world food critics. Serves a superb aubergine salad with walnuts and *dakos* (Cretan rusks), an Ikarian version of bruschetta.

Armenistis   Αρμενιστής

Armenistis, 15km west of Evdilos, is Ikaria's humble version of a resort. It boasts two long, sandy beaches separated by a narrow headland; a fishing harbour; and a web of hilly streets to explore on foot. Cafes and tavernas line the beach. Moderate nightlife livens up Armenistis in summer with a mix of locals and Greek and foreign tourists.

⊙ Sights

Nas Beach   BEACH

Westward 3.5km from Armenistis lies the pebbled beach of Nas, lying below the road and the few tavernas. A nudist-friendly beach, it has an impressive location at the mouth of a forested river, behind the trace ruins of an ancient **Temple of Artemis**, easily viewed from Taverna O Nas.

Livadi Beach   BEACH

Just 500m east of Armenistis is Livadi Beach, where currents are strong enough to warrant a lifeguard service and waves are sometimes big enough for surfing. Beyond Livadi are two other popular beaches, **Mesahti** and **Gialiskari**.

🛏 Sleeping

★ Pension Astaxi   PENSION €

(☑ 6982446227, 22750 71318; www.island-ikaria. com/hotels/PensionAstaxi.asp; d/tr incl breakfast from €35/50; P @ 🛜) This excellent and attractive budget gem is tucked back 30m from the main road, just above the Carte Postal cafe and Baido Taverna. The gracious owner, Maria, has created a relaxing and welcoming lodging, with a dozen brightly outfitted rooms with fans and balcony views to the sea.

Atsachas Rooms   HOTEL €

(☑ 22750 71226; www.atsachas.gr; Livadi Beach; d from €40; ❄ 🛜) Right on Livadi Beach, the Atsachas has clean, well-furnished rooms, some with fully equipped kitchens. Most have breezy sea-view balconies. The cafe spills onto a flowery garden, where a stairway descends to a nice stretch of beach.

Koimite   GUESTHOUSE €€

(☑ 22750 71545, 6974893877; www.ikariarooms. gr; d/q from €60/110; ❄ 🛜) Cascading down a rocky cliff, these pastel-coloured rooms come with balconies so huge you might be tempted to sell tickets to watch the spectacular sunset. Some rooms are equipped with kitchenettes; others have fridges; and there are kerosene heaters. Super-nice staff leave homemade cookies when they finish cleaning.

Villa Dimitri   APARTMENT €€

(☑ 22750 71310; www.villa-dimitri.eu; 2-person apt €50-70; ⊙ Mar-Oct; ❄ @ 🛜) This assortment of six secluded, balconied apartments, each one blue and white with wood and stone touches and set on a cliff amid colourful flowers, is managed by a welcoming Greek–German couple. It's 800m west of Armenistis and requires a minimum stay of one week.

🍴 Eating

★ Thea's Restaurant & Rooms   TAVERNA €

(☑ 22750 71491, 6932154296; www.theasinn.com; Nas; mains €5-9; ⊙ lunch & dinner) There are a few fine tavernas in Nas, but Thea's excels,

---

WORTH A TRIP

MOUNTAIN WALKS

With its solitude and rugged natural beauty, Ikaria is perfect for mountain walks. The most popular starting point is Hristos Rahes, where you will find a useful walking map, *The Round of Rahes on Foot* (€4), sold at most shops; proceeds go to maintaining the trails. For inexpensive guided treks all over the island, approach **Discover Ikaria** (☑ 6974042417, 6907547342; www.discoverikaria.com; Hristos Rahes).

Achievable as an independent walk, and not too hard on the bones, is the one-day circular walk along dirt roads from **Kambos**, south through **Dafni**, the remains of the 10th-century Byzantine **Castle of Koskinas** and picturesque **Frandato** and **Maratho** villages.

When you reach **Pigi**, look for the Frandato sign; continue past it for the unusual little Byzantine **Chapel of Theoskepasti**, tucked into overhanging granite. You must clamber up to reach it, and duck to get inside. The rows of old monks' skulls have been retired, but the chapel makes for an unusual visit, along with nearby **Moni Theoktistis**, with frescoes dating from 1686. The adjacent *kafeneio* (coffee house) is good for a coffee or juice with Maria, the kindly owner.

HERCULES MILAS/ALAMY ©

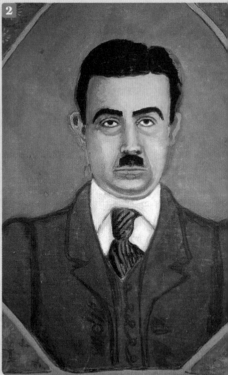

1. Mineral Baths of Eftalou (p441), Lesvos
A serene location for those seeking tranquillity.

2. Teriade Museum (p437), Mytilini Town, Lesvos
A surprising collection of artworks by masters such as Picasso and Matisse.

3. Pyrgi (p432), Chios
Artists in this village use cement, volcanic sand, lime and bent forks to create intricate patterns.

4. Sanctuary of the Great Gods (p456), Samothraki
Top-secret ceremonies took place at this Thracian temple to the fertility deities.

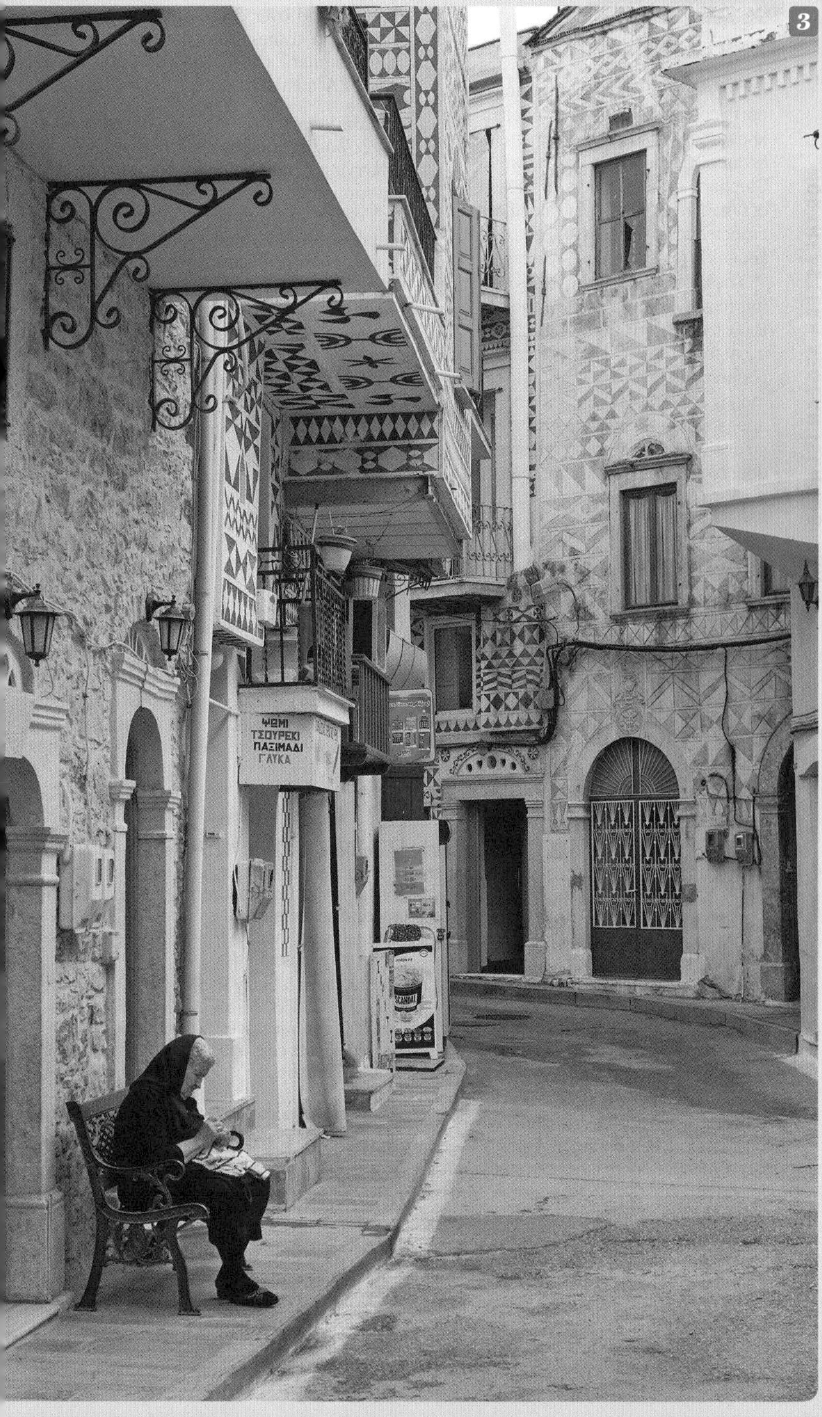

PICTURE PARTNERS/ALAMY ©

A VILLAGE BAKERY

In the village of Karavostomo, on Ikaria's north coast, everything you need to know about island values can probably be found at the village bakery, where Stephanos Kranas bakes long loaves of bread in his wood oven, along with crunchy *paximadia* (rusks) and sweet *koulouria* (fresh pretzel-style bread).

The bakery makes deliveries each morning by motorbike to village homes. But villagers can also drop by, grab a loaf from the wicker basket on the counter and, if no one's around, leave money in a counter cup. If the bakery appears to be closed, they may simply go upstairs and knock on the owner's door to enquire if there's any bread. The system has worked for years, one reason perhaps why Ikarians don't get too excited about fluctuations in the global price of oil. Olive oil, maybe.

serving up outstanding mezedhes, meat grills and a perfect veggie *mousakas* (baked layers of eggplant or zucchini, minced meat and potatoes topped with cheese sauce). Good barrel wine and local *tsipouro* firewater complete the deal. An outdoor patio overlooks the sea. Thea (aka Dorothy) also has five bright and cosy rooms (€35 including breakfast) above the restaurant.

★**Taverna Baido** TAVERNA €
(📞6982331539; mains €6-10) Past the bridge towards Nas, this interesting taverna is the work of Marianthi, who serves well-priced dishes using local products, fresh fish and Ikarian wine. Exceptional *soutzoukakia* (meat rissoles in tomato sauce) and *taramasalata* (a thick pink or white purée of fish roe, potato, oil and lemon juice).

Syntages tis Giagias DESSERTS €
(📞22750 71150; desserts €2-3; ⊘lunch & dinner) Occupying a terrace on the 2nd floor of the main shopping compound in Armenistis, this small confectioners makes exemplary *galaktobourekia* (goat's-milk pudding), *kataïfi* (angel-hair pastry) and ice cream with local fruit flavours. Shelves are filled with jars containing spoon sweets (caramelised seasonal fruit and vegetables).

Kelaris Taverna SEAFOOD €
(📞22750 71227; Gialiskari; mains €6-11; ⊘lunch & dinner) Kelaris serves its own fresh-caught

fish, cooked over coals, along with midday *mayirefta* dishes from the oven. Look for the landmark church on the point, 1.5km east of Armenistis.

★**Marymary** MEDITERRANEAN €€
(📞22750 71595; mains €8-12; ⊘lunch & dinner) Marrying traditional island cuisine with cosmopolitan culinary fashion, this upmarket eatery in the heart of Armenistis has a small army of devoted regulars raving about its *mayierefta* dishes, such as rooster with *sioufitha* pasta or clay-pot stews. The seaview terrace is inviting for sundowners and a bottle or two of local Ikarian wine.

🍷 Drinking & Nightlife

Mythos BAR
(⊘10am-late) Cosy, atmospheric bar managed by Dimitiros and Mariza, who deliver good drinks, fresh juices and live music in the summer. Walk down the street descending to the sea to find it.

Carte Postale BAR
(📞6981719567, 22750 71031; ⊘10am-2am) This hip cafe-bar, 100m west of Armenistis' church, sits high over the bay. It has a mellow ambience, signalled by an eclectic music mix, from world beat to Greek fusion. Snacks range from small pizzas and salads to breakfast omelettes and evening risotto, all managed by the welcoming Myrto; her father makes the olives.

ℹ️ Information

Aventura (📞22750 71117; aventura@otenet.gr) Full-service travel agency located by the patisserie just before the bridge. Offers car and motorbike rentals, and is one of the few places that hires out mountain bikes. Also does airport pick-ups and drop-offs.

Dolihi Tours & Lemy Rent-a-Car
(📞6983418878, 22750 71122; lemy@otenet.gr) Efficient travel agency next to the village market. Rents cars and organises walking tours and 4WD safaris.

East of Evdilos

Karavostamo Καραβόσταμο

POP 550
Karavostamo is one of Ikaria's largest and most beautiful coastal villages, 6km east of Evdilos. From the main road, the village cascades down winding paths scattered with flowering gardens, village churches, veggie patches, chickens and goats, finally

reaching a cosy square and a small fishing harbour. Here you'll find nothing more than a bakery, a small general store, and a few domatia, tavernas and coffee houses where villagers congregate each evening to chat, argue, eat, play backgammon, drink and tell stories. To reach the square, take the signed road off the main road.

🛏 Sleeping & Eating

Despina Rooms   PENSION €
(📱 21066   13999,   6977080808;   www.rooms despina.gr; r €40-60; P ❄ 🛜) Well-appointed two-storey studios in the heart of the village, with kitchens and laundry facilities, about 200m from the sea and village square.

To Steki   MEZEDHES €
(meals €2-4; ⊗ lunch & dinner) Join the regulars for good grills and salads, fresh chips, beer or *tsipouro* at this small and unpretentious *mezedhopoleio* (place serving mezedhes) on the square. Summer evenings find half the village at the outdoor tables.

★ Mandouvala   GREEK €€
(📱 22750 61204; mains €7-12; ⊗ lunch & dinner) Karavostamo's most upmarket eatery is at the end of the small waterfront, along a narrow cobbled lane 50m from the square. Excellent fish, grills, top wines and service add to the breezy seaside ambience.

FOURNI ISLANDS
ΟΙ ΦΟΥΡΝΟΙ

POP 1500

The Fourni archipelago is one of Greece's great unknown island gems. Its low-lying vegetation clings to gracefully rounded hills that overlap, forming intricate bays of sandy beaches and little ports. This former pirates' lair is especially beautiful at dusk, when the setting sun turns the terrain shades of pink, violet and black.

A clue to the area's swashbuckling past can be found in the name of the archipelago's capital, Fourni Korseon. The Corsairs were French privateers with a reputation for audacity, and their name became applied generically to all pirates and rogues then roaming the eastern Aegean.

Nowadays, Fourni Korseon offers most of the accommodation and services, plus several beaches. Other settlements include little Hrysomilia and Kamari to the north, plus another fishing hamlet on the islet of Thymena. In the south of the main island, the monastery of Agios Ioannis Prodromos stands serene over the far horizon.

❶ Getting There & Away

Fourni is connected to Ikaria (Agios Kirykos) and Samos by ferry and hydrofoil services. **Fourni Travel** (📱 6975576584, 22750 51019; Fourni Korseon; ⊗ 10am-2pm & 6-9pm Mon-Sat, 11.30am-7pm Sun) provides information and sells tickets. **Dodecanese Seaways** (www.12ne. gr) provides faster and more expensive catamaran services.

❶ Getting Around

Gleaming new sealed roads, all 20km of them, connect Fourni Korseon with Hrysomilia and Kamari. Everyone seems to walk everywhere in Fourni, and then walk some more.

Rental cars are a recent addition to the Fourni transport scene. Hire a small car or scooter at **Escape Car & Bike Rental** (📱 22750 51514; www.fourni-rentals.com; Fourni Korseon) on the waterfront.

Hitching is common and considered quite safe, and there's also the island's lone **taxi** (📱 6970879102), commanded by the ebullient Georgos.

Alternatively, weekly caïques serve Hrysomilia, while another two to three go daily to Thymena.

⦿ Sights & Activities

The island's rolling hills are ideal for **hiking**, and trails inevitably find a beach.

BOAT SERVICES FROM THE FOURNI ISLANDS

DESTINATION	DURATION	FARE (€)	FREQUENCY
Ikaria (Agios Kirykos)	1hr	7-14	4-5 weekly
Patmos	1½hr	13.50-25	4 weekly
Piraeus	8hr	35	3 weekly
Samos (Vathy)	2hr	13.50	2 weekly
Samos (Pythagorio)	1hr	20	3 weekly

ⓘ TURKISH CONNECTIONS

Visiting Turkey's Aegean coastal resorts and historical sites from Samos, Chios and Lesvos is easy. Visas aren't usually necessary for day trips. While boat itineraries, prices and even companies change often, the following explains how things generally work.

From Samos, the Kuşadası Express leaves daily from either Vathy or Pythagorio for the 80-minute trip to Kuşadası (€40/60 one way/return), a coastal resort near ancient Ephesus (Efes). Daily excursions run from May through to October, with the option to also visit Ephesus. For tickets and information in Vathy, contact ITSA Travel, opposite the old ferry terminal, or adjoining By Ship Travel. In Pythagorio, contact By Ship Travel (p423) at the main junction entering town. Additionally, a Turkish boat connects from Karlovasi in northern Samos to Sığacık (one way/return €30/40, five weekly), which is between Kuşadası and the airport at İzmir. None of these ferries has space for cars.

From Chios, daily departures year-round connect Chios Town with Çeşme, a port near İzmir; services are most frequent in summer and some carry vehicles on board. Boats depart morning and evening for the 40-minute journey (€20/30 one way/return). Tour agencies on the seafront also sell package day trips to İzmir. Get information and tickets from Hatzelenis Tours (p429) or Sunrise Tours (p429).

From Lesvos, boats operated by Turkish company Turyol leave Mytilini Town for Ayvalık twice daily in summer and daily in winter (one way/return €15/25, 1½ hours). Thursday departures are especially popular for market day in Ayvalık. Vehicles are carried on board. Most Mytilini Town travel agencies sell Turkish tours; try Olive Groove Travel (p440), Mitilene Tours (p440) or Tsolos Travel (p440).

The nearest beach to Fourni Korseon, **Psili Ammos Beach**, waits 600m north on the coast road, with umbrellas and a beach bar that hums all night.

Along the coast road heading south, **Kampi Beach** is excellent, with its own beach bar and a small taverna. A further 2km along, **Elidaki Beach** has a gentle sandy bottom, followed by the small-pebbled **Petrokopio Beach**.

Near Fourni's southernmost tip, near the Monastery of Agios Ioannis Thermastis, the fine, sandy **Vlyhada Beach** lies before the more secluded **Kasidi Beach**.

Fourni's other main settlements, **Hrysomilia** and **Kamari**, are 17km and 10km from Fourni Korseon respectively (approximately a 30-minute drive on winding roads). Both are tranquil fishing settlements with beaches, but limited services. The trip from Fourni Korseon to these villages is spectacular, opening onto myriad views of sloping hills and hidden coves.

🛏 Sleeping

Most accommodation is in Fourni Korseon, though sleeping in the smaller settlements is possible, as is free beach camping.

★**Archipelagos Hotel**   HOTEL €
(🖂 6973494967, 22750 51250; www.archipelagos hotel.gr; Fourni Korseon; s/d incl breakfast from €40/50; 🅿 ❉ 🛜) This elegant and welcoming small hotel on the harbour's northern edge comprises Fourni's most sophisticated lodgings. From the patio restaurant, set under stone arches bursting with geraniums and roses, to the well-appointed rooms and cafe-bar, the Archipelagos combines traditional architecture with modern luxuries.

Toula Studios   PENSION €
(🖂 22750 51332, 6976537948; info@fournitoula studio.gr; Fourni Korseon; s/d from €30/40; ❉ 🛜) Look for the Aegean-blue balconies at this friendly seafront standby near shops and tavernas. It has clean and simple self-catering rooms, 10 of them with sea views, surrounding a large courtyard and with overhead fans.

Bilios Studios & Apartments   PENSION €€
(www.hotelbilios.com; Fourni Korseon; d/tr/q from €60/75/85) Brightly coloured and exquisitely furnished apartments on the hill overlooking the port and the bay, and similarly attractive rooms down on the seafront. All come with either kitchenettes or full kitchens. We guess this is what should be called a boutique domatia.

🍴 Eating

Fourni is famous for seafood, especially *astakomakaronadha* (fresh lobster with pasta).

★ **Psarotaverna O Miltos** SEAFOOD €
(☏ 22750 51407; Fourni Korseon; mains €7-10; ☺lunch & dinner) Fourni lobster and fresh fish are expertly prepared at this iconic waterfront taverna. Excellent mezedhes and traditional salads, and fish and lobster are fairly priced by the kilo.

Psarotaverna Nikos SEAFOOD €
(Fourni Korseon; mains €7-10; ☺lunch & dinner) This is a very reliable seafood option, next door to sibling restaurant O Miltos. Look for daily specials on the chalkboard.

🛍 Shopping

Melanthi Shop FOOD
(☏ 22750 51037; Fourni Korseon) An inviting shop on the main street selling nicely packaged fresh herbs (thyme, lavender, oregano and the unique *throubi*), along with honey, cheeses, oils, balms and salves, all from Fourni.

❶ Information

Fourni Fishermen & Friends (www.fourni.com) The online guide to Fourni.
Health Centre (☏ 22750 51202)
Pharmacy (☏ 22750 51188)
Police (☏ 22750 51222)
Port Police (☏ 22750 51207)

SAMOS ΣΑΜΟΣ

POP 32,820

Lying just off the Turkish coast, Samos is one of the northeastern Aegean Islands' best-known destinations, yet beyond its low-key resorts and the lively capital, Vathy, there are numerous off-the-beaten-track beaches and quiet spots in the cool, forested inland mountains where traditional life continues.

Famous for its sweet local wine, Samos is also historically significant. It was the legendary birthplace of Hera, and the sprawling ruins of her ancient sanctuary, the Heraion, are impressive. Both the great mathematician Pythagoras and the hedonistic father of atomic theory, the 4th-century-BC philosopher Epicurus, were born here. Samos' scientific genius is also affirmed by the astonishing 524 BC Evpalinos Tunnel, a spectacular feat of ancient engineering that stretches for more than 1km deep underground.

❶ Getting There & Away

AIR

Samos' airport is 4km west of Pythagorio. **Aegean Airlines** (www.aegeanair.com), **Astra Airlines** (www.astra-airlines.gr), **Olympic Air** (www.olympicair.com) and **Sky Express** (www.skyexpress.gr) all serve Samos and have offices at the airport. Charters serve Chios from Holland, Oslo and Vienna.

BOAT

Samos is home to three ports – Vathy (aka Samos), Pythagorio and Karlovasi.

ITSA Travel (☏ 22730 23605; www.itsatravelsamos.gr; Themistokleous Sofouli 5; ☺8am-8pm), directly opposite Vathy's old ferry terminal, provides detailed information, offers free luggage storage and sells tickets, including to Turkey. The helpful staff will also pick you up at the new terminal for free. Tickets to Turkey are also available next door from **By Ship Travel** (☏ 22730 27337; www.byshiptravel.gr).

In Pythagorio, check ferry and hydrofoil schedules with the tourist office (p423), the port police (p423) or By Ship Travel (p423).

In Karlovasi, **By Ship Travel** (☏ 22730 35252; www.byshiptravel.gr) will help you with travel tickets.

❶ Getting Around

TO/FROM THE AIRPORT

Buses run to/from the airport three to four times daily (€2). Taxis from the airport cost €25 to Vathy, or €6 to Pythagorio, from where there are local buses to Vathy.

DOMESTIC FLIGHTS FROM SAMOS

DESTINATION	DURATION	FARE (€)	FREQUENCY
Athens	45min	56	3 daily
Chios	35min	86	3 weekly
Lesvos	2hr	106	2 weekly
Limnos	2hr	86	2 weekly
Rhodes	45min	92	3 weekly
Thessaloniki	55min	55	1 daily

Samos

Sığacık (Turkey; 20km)
Fourni (30km); Ikaria (40km)
Karlovasi
Potami Beach
Palio Karlovasi
Leka
Drakeï
Kosmadeï
Kallithea
Cape Kanthario
Mt Kerkis (1434m)
Votsalakia (Kampos)
Psili Ammos Beach
Ormos Marathokambou
Cape Agios Domenikos
Aegean Sea
Bay of Marathokambos
Kastanea
Church of Profitis Ilias
Platanaki Beach
Agios Konstantinos
Kondakeïka
Stavrinides
Valiondates
Vourliotes
Ydhrousa
Manolates
Mt Ambelos (Karvouni; 1150m)
Platanos
Marathokampos
Kampos Beach
Pefkos
Skoureïka
Moni Megalis Panagias
Pagondas
Samiopoula
Cape Asprokavos
Chios (80km)
Avlakia Beach
Avlakia
Lemonaki & Tsamadou Beaches
Tsambou Beach
Moni Panagias Vrondianis
Kokkari
Pandhrosos
Mavratzeï
Pyrgos
Koumaradeï
Hora
Mytilinii
Ireon
Ireon
Pappa Beach
Tigani Bay

Boat

Daily excursion boats go from Pythagorio to Samiopoula islet (€20, including lunch).

Bus

From Vathy **bus station** (☎ 22730 27262; www.samospublicbusses.gr; Themistokleous Sofouli), frequent daily buses serve Kokkari (20 minutes), Pythagorio (25 minutes), Agios Konstantinos (40 minutes), Karlovasi (one hour), the Ireon (25 minutes), Mytilinii (20 minutes) and Portrokali (20 minutes). Tickets cost €1.50 to €4 depending on distance.

From Pythagorio, five daily buses reach the Ireon (15 minutes), while four serve Mytilinii (20 minutes) and Marathokampos (one hour). Buy tickets on the buses. Services are reduced on weekends. Tickets cost €1.50 to €7 depending on distance.

Car & Motorcycle

In Vathy, **Pegasus Rent-a-Car** (☎ 6978536440, 22730 24470; www.samos-car-rental.com; Themistokleous Sofouli 5) has good rates on car, 4WD and motorcycle hire. In Pythagorio, try **John's Rentals** (☎ 6972338103, 22730 61405; www.johns-rent-a-car.gr; Lykourgou Logotheti) on the main road near the waterfront.

Taxi

The **taxi rank** (☎ 22730 28404) in Vathy is by the National Bank of Greece. To the airport, the fare is €25, to Pythagorio €10.

In Pythagorio the **taxi rank** (☎ 22730 61450) is by the waterfront at the bottom of Lykourgou Logotheti.

Vathy (Samos) Βαθύ (Σάμος)

POP 2030

The island's capital, Vathy (also called Samos) enjoys a striking setting within the fold of a deep bay, where its curving waterfront is lined with bars, cafes and restaurants. The historic quarter of Ano Vathy, filled with steep, narrow streets and red-tiled 19th-century hillside houses, brims with atmosphere. The town centre boasts two engaging museums and a striking century-old church.

Vathy has two pebble beaches, the best being **Gagos Beach**, about 500m north from the old quay. Along the way you'll pass a string of cool bars clinging to the town's northeastern cliff.

⊙ Sights

Museum of Samos Wines   WINERY
(☎ 22730 87551; www.samoswine.gr; €2; ⊙ 8am-8pm Mon-Sat; 🅿) **FREE** Look for this handsome stone building opposite the new ferry quay to find one of Samos' best vintners. Winery tours usually take place when you show up, and conveniently include a free

tasting, with several reasonably priced wines for sale.

Church of Agios Spyridonas CHURCH
(Plateia Dimarheiou; ⊙8-11am & 6.30-7.30pm) Built in 1909, this ornate church features icons, impressive pillars hewn of marble from İzmir and, unusually, a silver candelabra from India. Decorative columns on the iconostasis are inspired by Ancient Greek and Byzantine motifs.

Archaeological Museum MUSEUM
(☑22730 27469; Plateia Dimarheiou; adult/child €4/free, free 1st Sun of month Nov-Mar; ⊙8am-3pm Tue-Sun) One of the best museums in the islands, housed in two adjacent buildings, this handsome complex contains finds starting from the rule of Polycrates (6th century BC). The most famous item is the imposing *kouros* (male statue of the Archaic period), plucked from the Heraion (Sanctuary of Hera) near Pythagorio. At a height of 5.5m, it's the largest-known standing *kouros*. A shaded museum cafe awaits outside.

⭐**Livadaki Beach** BEACH
🏖 Follow the north-coast road out of Vathy for 10km and look for a signposted dirt road to the left leading to Livadaki Beach. Here, tropical azure waters lap against soft sand in a long sheltered cove with facing islets. The water is warm and very shallow for a long way out, and Livadaki's mellow summer beach parties easily spill into it.

🛏 Sleeping

Pension Dreams PENSION €
(☑6976425195, 22730 24350; Areos 9; d/tr €50/60; 🅿❄🛜) This small, quiet and central pension, 100m up from the waterfront, claims a hilltop view of the harbour. All seven rooms are bright and very well kept, some with large balconies and garden views, and all feature screened bath windows. The owner speaks English and French.

Cleomenis Hotel HOTEL €
(☑22730 23232; Kallistratous 33; d incl breakfast from €50) Good-value rooms within walking distance of the beach and the port. Friendly owners make it a great place to stay.

⭐**Ino Village Hotel & Restaurant** HOTEL €€
(☑22730 23241; www.inovillagehotel.com; Kalami; d incl breakfast €60-125; 🅿❄🛜🏊) With its courtyard pool flanked by ivy-clad, balconied white buildings, Ino Village, just 500m above Vathy, feels remote and elegant. While this mini-resort is sometimes booked by small tour groups, walk-in travellers can expect reasonable rates and a welcoming atmosphere. The hotel also boasts the popular **Elea restaurant** and cocktail bar, which serves fine Samian wines.

🍴 Eating

⭐**Taverna Artemis** TAVERNA €
(Kefalopoulou 4; mains €5-9; ⊙noon-late) The Vathy Greek crowd relies on Artemis for fresh fish and well-prepared mezedhes and *mayirefta* dishes, though it is perhaps best known for *sardeles pandremenos*. In Greek, *pandremenos* means 'married', and the sardines are served open-faced, in pairs, like a couple. Open year-round; it's about 20m up from the port police at the northwest end of the port.

My Falasophy MIDDLE EASTERN €
(☑22734 00835; Plateia Pythagorou; mains €2-5; ⊙noon-11pm) A guest from the Levant, this little fast-food joint in the main square serves large portions of artfully prepared hummus and falafel, as well as great salads. Healthy food is complemented by freshly squeezed tropical juices.

Vathy (Samos)

Ino Village Hotel & Restaurant (150m); Gagos Beach (200m);
Cleomenis Hotel (750m); Livadaki Beach (10km)

Vathy Bay

(200m); Police Station (200m);
Post Office (350m); New Ferry
Terminal (1km); Museum of Samos
Wines (1km); Pythagorio (14km)

Municipal Gardens

Vathy (Samos)

Telion GREEK €
(☎ 22730 27526; mains €6-12; ⊙ lunch & dinner)
An outstanding grill house on the waterfront near the main square, with snappy
service and a good choice of pork, chicken
and lamb *gyros,* pitta souvlaki, plus dinner
specials – deliveries included.

To Steki TAVERNA €
(Aogotheti 61; mains €6.50-8; ⊙ lunch & dinner)
Unpretentious and welcoming back-alley
eatery with generous grills, *gavros* (marinated small fish), salads and homemade
soups.

🍷 Drinking & Nightlife

Of the plentiful waterfront cafes, the best
for quality and service is **Joy** (☎ 22730 89770;
⊙ 8am-midnight).

Nightlife in Vathy is more Hellenic than
in the island's tourist clusters, where the
scene is dominated by northern European
tourists. While most cafes and bars cling
to the waterfront, the coolest ones, such
as **Escape** (☎ 22730 28345; Kefalopoulou 9;
⊙ 10pm-6am), **Ble** (Kefalopoulou 7; ⊙ 11am-4am)
and **Mezza Volta** (Kefalopoulou; ⊙ 9pm-dawn),
hang over the water along Kefalopoulou
100m beyond the quay. Music and dancing
is usually in full swing by midnight.

❶ Information

Banks with ATMs line Plateia Pythagorou and the
waterfront.

There is free wi-fi at Plateia Pythagorou and all
along the waterfront.

Municipal Tourist Office (☎ 22730 28582;
⊙ Jun-Sep)

Police (☎ 22730 27404; Presveos Dim
Nikolareïzi 2)

Port Police (☎ 22730 27890)

Post Office (Plateia Nikolaou; ⊘7.30am-2pm)

Samos General Hospital (☏22730 27407) Efficient regional hospital for the surrounding islands; opposite Pythagoras Hotel, north of the port.

Pythagorio   Πυθαγόρειο

POP 1330

On the southeastern coast, opposite Turkey, pretty Pythagorio has a yacht-lined harbour and Samos' main archaeological finds. All boats departing south from Samos leave from Pythagorio, including day trips to Samiopoula islet.

◉ Sights

Pythagorio Town Beach   BEACH

A short walk west of Pythagorio brings you to a pristinely clean beach with umbrellas and toilets. It's an easy stroll (less than 1km) from town and there's decent swimming, but pack your own food and drinks.

Archaeological Museum of Pythagorio   MUSEUM

(☏22730 62811; Polykratous; €6; ⊘9am-3pm Tue-Sun) This sparkling and renovated museum contains well-displayed finds from Pythagorio and the 6th-century-BC Heraion, less than 5km away, plus striking pottery pieces spanning from the 9th century BC through Greece's golden age. Museum labels are in Greek, English and German.

Evpalinos Tunnel   ARCHAEOLOGICAL SITE

(☏22730 61400; adult/child €6/3; ⊘8am-3pm Tue-Sun) In 524 BC, when Pythagorio (then called Samos) was the island's capital and a bustling metropolis of 80,000, the securing of sources for drinking water became crucial. To solve the problem, ruler Polycrates put his dictatorial whims to good use, ordering labourers to dig into a mountainside according to the exacting plan of his ingenious engineer, Evpalinos. Many workers died during the dangerous dig, but the result was the 1034m-long Evpalinos Tunnel. In medieval times, locals used it to hide from pirates.

Moni Panagias Spilianis   MONASTERY

(Monastery of the Virgin of the Grotto; ☏22730 61361; ⊘9am-8pm) FREE About 1.5km northwest of Pythagorio, the road forks right, past traces of an ancient theatre, before reaching this grotto monastery. The walk meanders up through old olive groves and, despite tourist kiosks, it's a welcome respite from the summer heat, and gives clear views to the nearby Turkish coast.

Castle of Lykourgos Logothetis   CASTLE

(⊘9am-dusk Tue-Sun) Samians took the lead locally in the 1821 War of Independence, and this castle, built in 1824 by resistance leader Logothetis, is the major relic of that

NORTHEASTERN AEGEAN ISLANDS SAMOS

BOAT SERVICES FROM SAMOS

DESTINATION	PORT	DURATION	FARE (€)	FREQUENCY
Chios	V/K*	3-4hr	14	2-3 weekly
Fourni	Pythagorio	1hr	20	3 weekly
Fourni	Vathy	2½hr	13.50	4 weekly
Ikaria (Agios Kirykos)**	V/K*	2-3½hr	10-19	4 weekly
Ikaria (Evdilos)**	Karlovasi	4hr	13-23	6 weekly
Kavala	V/K*	15hr	53-60	2 weekly
Lesvos (Mytilini)	V/K*	6hr	29.50	2 weekly
Limnos	V/K*	12hr	30-47	2 weekly
Mykonos	Karlovasi	3½-5½hr	40-50	5 weekly
Naxos	Vathy	5hr	41-47	2 weekly
Patmos	Pythagorio	1hr	30	6 weekly
Piraeus	V/K*	12hr	38-57	1 daily
Rhodes	V/K*	6½hr	39	1 weekly

*Vathy or Karlovasi

**via Fourni

turbulent time. It's situated on a hill at the southern end of Metamorfosis Sotiros, near the car park. The **city walls** once extended from here to the Evpalinos Tunnel.

Activities

Try scuba diving with **Samos Dive Center** (☑ 6972997645; www.samosdiving.com; Konstantinou Kanari 1). Professional instructors lead dives in search of moray eels, sea stars, octopuses, lobsters and other critters lurking in the sponge-covered crevices around Pythagorio. A two-dive half day for beginners costs around €50; a full-day dive, including open-water options, starts at around €85. Snorkelling (€20) is also offered.

🛌 Sleeping

★ **Pension Despina**   PENSION €
(☑ 22730 61677, 6938120399; www.samosrooms.gr/despina/more.html; A Nikolaou; r/studios €35/40; ❄ �{?}) An impeccably well-kept and quiet pension on the small and central Plateia Irinis, the Despina offers attractive rooms and studios with overhead fans and balconies, some with kitchenettes, plus a relaxing back garden. Owner Athina is very friendly.

Polyxeni Hotel   HOTEL €
(☑ 22730 61590; www.polyxenihotel.com; s/d/tr incl breakfast from €40/55/70; ❄ �{?}) In the middle of the port, turn inland away from the main road to find this well-managed seafront lodging with several balconied harbour-view rooms, fitted with overhead fans and double-glazed windows. Polyxeni also has a popular lobby cocktail bar, an adjacent gift shop and cheerful staff. Garden-view rooms are very quiet.

Philoxenia Pension   PENSION €
(☑ 22730 61055, 6973768371; www.pensionphiloxeniasamos.blogspot.com; r from €55; ❄ @ �{?}) Opposite the archaeological museum (p421), look

for the small courtyard bursting with flowers. Rooms are spotless and comfortable, with overhead fans and balcony views of the hills, and there's a common kitchen and laundry facilities. The owner's family lives in an adjacent apartment, so help is never far off.

🍴 Eating

★ **Kafeneio To Mouragio**   CAFE €
(☑ 22730 62390; mezedhes €3-6; ⊙ 8am-midnight; �{?}) The warm ambience and predominantly Greek clientele hint at the fact that this place delivers the goods, with snacks such as chickpea croquettes and assorted mezedhes. Enjoy coffee in the morning and, later, iced ouzo, wine and beer. Customers are welcome to leave their luggage for free.

Faros   TAVERNA €
(☑ 22730 62464; mezedhes €4-7; mains €7-13; ⊙ 11am-midnight; �{?}) This eastern harbour eatery sits on the bay, beyond Elia Taverna. Faros is a minimalist, contemporary Mediterranean bistro serving huge bowls of salad and excellent versions of traditional Greek dishes, including Samos-style small fish fried with caramelised onions into a pie-like shape.

Genteki   MEDITERRANEAN €€
(☑ 6972220786; Despoti Kyrillou; mains €9-16; ⊙ 9am-11.30pm) In a quaint side street, this slightly upmarket place fuses taverna standards with other Mediterranean, notably Italian, fare. Smyrna-style *soutsoukakia* meatballs are outstanding and so are mushrooms *a la Greco*. Bread is served fresh from the oven.

To Tigani tis Platias   TAVERNA €€
(☑ 6971673770; Plateia Irinis; mains €7.50-17; 🖊) Beautiful Greek standards, popular with both locals and visitors. It's especially great for veggie choices, such as baked feta, *gigantes* (white beans) and zucchini balls,

---

A MATTER OF MEASUREMENTS

While the obsession with the 'proper pint' may seem modern, the Ancient Greeks also fixated on measuring their alcohol. Pythagoras, a great Samian mathematician (and, presumably, drinker), created an invention that ensured party hosts and publicans could not be deceived by guests aspiring to inebriation. His creation was dubbed the *Dikiakoupa tou Pythagora* (Just Cup of Pythagoras). This mysterious, multi-holed drinking vessel holds its contents perfectly, unless filled past the engraved line, at which point the glass drains completely from the bottom, punishing the glutton!

Today, faithful reproductions, made of colourful, glazed ceramic, are sold in Samos gift shops, and are tangible reminders of the Apollon Mean: 'Everything in moderation'.

all a cut above average. Meat grills here are also superb, and there's a shady setting, cheerful service and good wine. It's opposite Pension Despina.

Drinking & Nightlife

Katoi   OUZERIE

(Lykourgou Logotheti) In the main street, this smallish modern place combines the virtues of a deli and an *ouzerie*. Ouzo and *tsipouro* are served with local cheeses and ham (€5 for the combo), which are also available for sale from the shop inside. Fresh juices are available, too.

Notos   BAR

(☑ 22730 62351; Tarsanas Beach; ☺ noon-late; ☏) From the main road, turn right (south) at the port to find this popular late-night music bar and taverna, opposite a public car park. Live music most Tuesdays and Saturdays.

ⓘ Information

By Ship Travel (☑ 22730 80768; www.byshiptravel.gr) Helpful full-service travel agency, offering car hire, accommodation, air and ferry tickets. At the junction entering town.

Port Police (☑ 22730 61225)

Post Office (Lykourgou Logotheti; ☺ 7.30am-2pm)

Tourist Office (☑ 22730 61389; Lykourgou Logotheti; ☺ 8am-9.30pm, reduced hours winter)

Tourist Police (☑ 22730 61100; Lykourgou Logotheti)

Around Pythagorio

The coast road continues west from Vathy through flowery **Agios Konstantinos** before coming to workaday **Karlovasi**, Samos' third port, home to several hotels and tavernas. **Rhenia Tours** (☑ 22730 62280; Karlovasi) is good for ferry tickets and reliable information. The town's blue-collar history is on display at the the **Karlovasi Folk Art Museum** (☑ 22730 62286; Karlovasi; ☺ 9am-1pm Tue-Sun) **FREE**.

The old village, **Palio Karlovasi**, above the port is well worth the short drive up the hill. From the small car park, a 500m walk brings you to the chapel of **Agia Triada**, which has panoramic views.

Just 3km beyond Karlovasi lies the sand-and-pebble **Potami Beach**, blessed with good swimming and a reggae beach bar. It's complemented by nearby **forest waterfalls**;

head west 50m from the beach and look for the signpost on the left. Entering the forest you'll first encounter the centuries-old **Metamorfosis Sotiros chapel**, where the devout light candles. Continuing about 1.5km through the wooded trail along the river brings you to a river channel, where it's necessary to wade or swim before enjoying a splash under the 2m-high waterfalls. Wooden stairs going up from the canyon will bring you to the excellent **Archontissa Potami Adventure Cafe** (www.facebook.com/pg/ArchontissaPotamiWaterfalls; Potami; mains €8-10).

⊙ Sights

Heraion   ARCHAEOLOGICAL SITE

(adult/child €6/3; ☺ 8.30am-3pm Tue-Sun) It's hard to imagine the former magnificence of this ancient sanctuary of the goddess Hera, 4km west of Pythagorio, from these scattered ruins. The 'Sacred Way', once flanked by thousands of marble statues, led from the city to this World Heritage–listed site, built at Hera's legendary birthplace. However, enough survives to provide a glimpse of a sanctuary that was four times larger than the Parthenon.

Built in the 6th century BC, the Heraion was constructed over an earlier Mycenaean temple. Plundering and earthquakes have left only one column standing, though extensive foundations remain. Other remains include a stoa, a 5th-century Christian basilica, and the headless, and unsettling, statues of a family, the Geneleos Group. Archaeologists continue to unearth treasures.

⬛ Sleeping

★**Hotel Restaurant Cohyli**   HOTEL €

(☑ 22730 95282, 6977809389; www.hotel-cohyli.com; Ireon; s/d/tr incl breakfast from €35/45/55; ▣ ❄ ☏) You'll sleep and eat well at this welcoming hotel-taverna gem. Rooms are cosy and clean, and equipped with fridges and fans. When you're hungry, just relocate to the shaded courtyard next door to sample excellent mezedhes, *saganaki* (fried cheese), fresh fish and breakfast with 'sunshine eggs'. There's a small beach across the road, and live acoustic music many summer evenings.

Kokkari & Mountain Villages

From Vathy, the coast road west passes a number of beaches and resorts. The first, **Kokkari** (Κοκκάρι), 10km from Vathy, was once a fishing village, but is now a rather crowded resort. Windsurfers test the waves from its long pebble beach in summer, and the nearby beaches of **Lemonaki**, **Tsamadou**, **Tsambou** and **Livadhaki** draw swimmers and sunbathers.

Continuing west, the landscape becomes more forested and mountainous. Take the left-hand turn-off after 5km for the lovely mountain village of **Vourliotes**. The village's multicoloured, shuttered houses cluster around a *plateia* (square). Walkers can enjoy an 8km loop trail between Vourliotes and Kokkari through olive groves and lofty woodlands – it's one of those magical *monopati* (footpath) routes where you hardly realise you've been climbing. Find the free walking map in Vourliotes.

Back on the coast road, look for the signposted turn-off for another fragrant village, **Manolates**, 5km further up the lower slopes of Mt Ambelos (Karvouni; 1150m). Set amid thick pine and deciduous forests, and boasting gorgeous traditional houses, Manolates is nearly encircled by mountains and offers a cooler alternative to the sweltering coast. The village is home to a fledgling artisan community, and has some excellent jewellery and souvenir shops.

Good tavernas are plentiful and, despite the more touristy patina of Manolates, both it and Vourliotes are worth visiting for a glimpse of old Samos.

🛌 Sleeping

Kerkis Bay Hotel   HOTEL €
(☑ 22730 37202; http://kerkisbayhotel.com; Ormos Marathokambou; d €30-50) It is a surprise to find such a serious multistorey establishment in such a quaint place, but here it is, complete with elevators and a popular waterfront taverna. The owner is an old-worldish gentleman and a former sea captain.

Pension Mary's House   PENSION €
(☑ 22730 93291; www.marys-house-samos.com; Vourliotes; d/tr €50/60; ❄ 🀆) Superb location in the village, with amazing balcony views, decent furnishings and a lovely garden and orchard setting. Follow the painted wooden signs 200m from the village square.

★ **Studios Angela**   APARTMENT €
(☑ 22730 62198; www.studiosangela.com; Manolates; d €30-40; ❄) A great budget choice, these five studios near the church in Manolates, built into a hillside overlooking the sea, are traditionally furnished, with modern kitchenettes and views to the sea. Owner Angela is hospitable.

🍴 Eating

★ **AAA Taverna**   TAVERNA €
(Tria Alpha; ☑ 22730 94472; Manolates; mains €7-17; ⊙ 9am-midnight) Sample homemade dishes, such as rabbit in wine sauce, sausages or grilled sardines, are served at this small, classy courtyard taverna in the heart of the village. The piped music is often avant-garde Greek jazz-folk.

★ **Hippy's Restaurant Café**   TAVERNA €
(☑ 6976770021, 22730 33796; Potami Beach; mains €7-15; ⊙ 9am-after sunset; 🅿 🀆) This cool open-air cafe-bar is a family affair, combining Greek and South Seas decor with jazz, reggae, classical, trip hop and ambient sounds. Good omelettes, pasta, grilled fresh fish and skewers are served, as well as owner Apolstolis' naturally fermented wine and assorted drinks and juices. The place has a relaxing and rambling end-of-the-road feel to it, with hospitality and character to spare.

Taverna Bira   TAVERNA €
(☑ 22730 92350; Kokkari; mains €5-9; ⊙ lunch & dinner) Opposite the bus stop, Bira is an elegant, old-fashioned taverna, offering local favourites such as *ladhera* – traditional olive-oil-rich veggie dishes that are the mainstay of religious fasting. *Horta* (wild greens) and *anthoi* (stuffed zucchini flowers) also appear among the tasty offerings.

CHIOS   ΧΙΟΣ

POP 53,820

While no Greek island is like another, Chios has one of the most distinctive faces, thanks to the unique fortress-like architecture of its

Chios

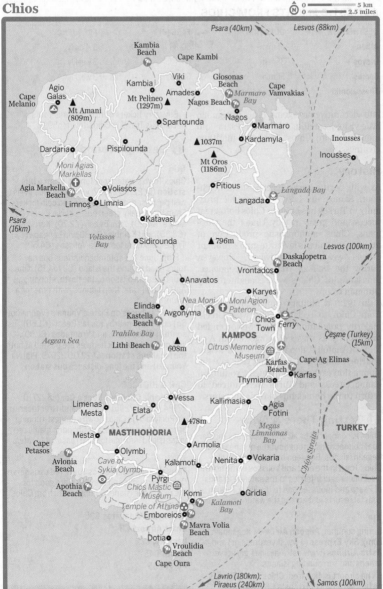

Psara (40km)

Lesvos (88km)

Kambia Beach

Cape Kambi

Viki

Giosonas Beach

Cape Vamvakias

Kambia

Amades

Marmaro Bay

Mt Pelineo (1297m)

Nagos Beach

Agio Galas

Cape Melanio

Mt Amani (809m)

Spartounda

Nagos

Marmaro

▲1037m

Kardamyla

Inousses

Dardaria

Pispilounda

Mt Oros (1186m)

Inousses

Moni Agias Markellas

Pitious

Lángada Bay

Agia Markella Beach

Volissos

Langada

Limnos

Limnia

Psara (16km)

Katavasi

Volissos Bay

Sidirounda

▲796m

Daskalopetra Beach

Vrontados

Lesvos (100km)

Anavatos

Karyes

Elinda

Nea Moni

Moni Agion Pateron

Kastella Beach

Avgonyma

Chios Town

Ferry

Aegean Sea

Trahilos Bay

Lithi Beach

608m

KAMPOS

Citrus Memories Museum

Çeşme (Turkey) (15km)

Karfas Beach

Cape Ag Elinas

Thymiana

Karfas

Limenas Mesta

Vessa

Kallimasia

Agia Fotini

Elata

TURKEY

Megas Limnionas Bay

Mesta

MASTIHOHORIA

▲478m

Cape Petasos

Armolia

Avlonia Beach

Olymbi

Kalamoti

Nenita

Vokaria

Cave of Sykia Olymbi

Chios Straits

Apothia Beach

Pyrgi

Chios Mastic Museum

Komi

Kalamoti Bay

Gridia

Temple of Athina

Emboreios

Dotia

Mavra Volia Beach

Vroulidia Beach

Cape Oura

Lavrio (180km); Piraeus (240km)

Samos (100km)

villages that makes them look so different to their sugar-cube cousins on other islands. That style stems from the island's history as the ancestral home of shipping barons and the world's only commercial producer of mastic.

Its varied terrain ranges from lonesome mountain crags in the north, to the citrus-grove estates of Kampos, near the island's port capital in the centre, to the fertile Mastihohoria in the south, where generations of mastic growers have turned their villages

DOMESTIC FLIGHTS FROM CHIOS

DESTINATION	DURATION	FARE (€)	FREQUENCY
Athens	45min	50-85	3-4 daily
Lesvos	35min	63	3 weekly
Samos	30min	63-83	3 weekly
Thessaloniki	3hr (via Athens)	75-90	1-2 daily

into decorative art gems. The intriguing, little-visited satellite islands of Psara and Inousses share Chios' legacy of maritime greatness.

History

As with northeastern Aegean island neighbours Samos and Lesvos, geographic proximity to Turkey has brought Chios both great success and great tragedy. Under the Ottomans, Chios' monopolistic production of mastic – the sultan's favourite gum – brought Chians wealth and privilege. However, during the 1821–29 War of Independence, thousands of Chians were slaughtered by Ottoman troops.

In 1922, a military campaign launched from Chios to reclaim lands with Greek-majority populations in Asia Minor ended disastrously, as waves of refugees from Asia Minor (Anatolia) flooded Chios and neighbouring islands. The following year saw the 'population exchange', in which two million ethnic Greeks and Turks were forced to return to the homelands of their ancestors.

ⓘ Getting There & Away

Chios is connected by air and also enjoys regular boat connections throughout the northeastern Aegean Islands. Between them, the ports of Chios Town in the east and Volissos in the northwest offer regular ferries to the satellite islands of Psara and Inousses and to the lively Turkish coastal resorts just across the water.

AIR

During summer, **Aegean Air** (www.aegeanair.com), **Sky Express** (www.skyexpress.gr) and **Astra Airlines** (www.astra-airlines.gr) serve Athens and surrounding islands.

The airport is 4km from Chios Town. There's no bus; an airport taxi costs €8. Tickets are available from Hatzelenis Tours (p429) in Chios Town and at the airport counters.

BOAT

In addition to regular ferry service to nearby Inousses, daily **water taxis** (☑ 6944168104, 6945361281) travel between Langada and Inousses (€65; shared between up to eight passengers).

Buy ferry tickets from Hatzelenis Tours or Michalakis Travel in Chios Town (p599).

ⓘ Getting Around

BUS

Chios Town's waterfront **long-distance bus station** (☑ 22710 27507; www.ktelchios.gr) is well organised, and has a cafe and coin lockers. From there, daily green buses serve Pyrgi (€3), Mesta (€4.20), Lithi Beach (€2.70), Kardamyla (€3.30), and Kambia (€5.80) via Langada (€2). Twice-weekly buses serve Volissos (€4.50).

From June to September, various bus day tours head around the island (€8 to €15). One tour takes in Volissos to the north, stopping at Agia Markela and then Limnos, with time for a swim.

Blue city buses on Plateia Vounaki (Vounakiou Sq) also serve nearby Karfas Beach (€1.50), just south of Chios Town, and Vrontados (€1.50), just north of town. Schedules are posted at both the **local bus station** (☑ 22710 22079; Plateia Vounaki) and the long-distance bus station.

CAR & BICYCLE

The reliable **Chandris Rent a Car** (☑ 22710 27194, 6944972051; info@chandrisrentacar.gr; Porfyra 5) is Chios Town's longest-running agency, and owner Kostas Chandris gladly provides island information and reasonable rates.

TAXI

Taxis are plentiful in Chios Town; red taxis serve Chios Town only, and grey taxis are good for the rest of the island. Sample costs from Chios Town:

Avgonyma/Anavatos €25
Chios Airport €8
Lagkada €22
Mesta €45
Pyrgi €35

Chios Town   Χίος

POP 23,780

Chios' main port and capital on the central east coast is home to almost half the island's inhabitants. Behind the busy port area lies a quieter, intriguing old quarter, where some lingering traditional Turkish houses and an old *hammam* (Turkish bathhouse) stand enclosed by the walls of a Genoese castle. There's also a busy market area behind the waterfront, and spacious public gardens (Vounaki) where an open-air cinema operates on summer evenings. The nearest decent beach is popular Karfas, 6km south.

◉ Sights

★ Korais Library & Philip Argenti Museum
MUSEUM
(☎ 22710 44246; www.koraeslibrary.gr; Korai 3; €2; ☺ 7am-4pm Mon-Sat) On the upper floor of the remarkable Korais Library, the Philip Argenti Museum contains a 19th-century birthing chair, along with shepherds' tools, embroidery, traditional costumes and portraits of the wealthy Argentis family. The place is a touching tribute to Greek cultural renaissance figure Adamantios Korais, who set up the library in 1792 and replenished it after the massacre of Chios. Philip Argentis is a French-born benefactor and researcher of Chian history.

Archaeological Museum
MUSEUM
(☎ 22710 44239; Mihalon 10; €2; ☺ 8am-3pm Tue-Sun) Along with prehistoric and archaic treasures from the excavations of the British School at Emporios, this collection includes impressive Neolithic and Classical finds (coins, sculptures and pottery) from Agios Galas and Fana.

Giustiniani Palace Museum
MUSEUM
(☎ 22710 22819; €2; ☺ 8am-3pm Tue-Sun) Near the main gate of the *kastro* (castle), this tiny museum (or 'Palataki') still looks like the 15th-century fortress it once was. Of particular interest are 12 Byzantine frescoes of the prophets, dating from the 13th century, along with an 18th-century full-length icon of the archangel Michael.

Byzantine Museum
MUSEUM
(☎ 22710 26866; Plateia Vounaki; €4; ☺ 8.30am-3.30pm Tue-Sun) Housed in a 19th-century Ottoman mosque, the Medjitie Djami, this museum contains relics from the Byzantine, post-Byzantine, Genoese and Islamic periods, including old canons, fine icons, and Jewish, Muslim and Armenian tombstones.

🛌 Sleeping

★ Chios Rooms
PENSION €
(☎ 22710 20198; www.chiosrooms.gr; Aigaiou 110; s/d/tr from €30/35/45; ☎) An eclectic, hostel-like neoclassical house on the waterfront, Chios Rooms is the inspiration of its owner, native New Zealander Don. Marked by handsome vintage furnishings, traditional rugs and lofty ceilings, the place has character to spare. Most rooms have private bathrooms; other rooms share. Fresh spring water is provided for guests.

Rooms Alex
PENSION €
(☎ 6979535256; roomsalex@hotmail.gr; Livanou 29; r €30) Host and former sea captain Alex Stoupas' handmade model ships decorate each of the simple but clean rooms here. The *kapetanios* (captain) is '100% helpful', as he'll happily tell you; he picks up guests from the ferry and speaks English, French and Spanish.

BOAT SERVICES FROM CHIOS

DESTINATION	PORT	DURATION	FARE (€)	FREQUENCY
Ikaria (Agios Kirykos)	Chios	4½hr	15	2 weekly
Inousses	Chios	1hr	5	1 daily
Kavala	Chios	12hr	33.50	1 weekly
Lavrio	Mesta	8hr	28.50	1 weekly
Lesvos (Mytilini Town)	Chios	2½hr	21	1 daily
Limnos	Chios	8hr	24	1 weekly
Piraeus	Chios	6-9hr	32	1-2 daily
Psara	Chios	3hr	7-14	1 daily
Psara	Volissos	1¼hr	7-14	2 weekly
Samos (Karlovasi)	Chios	2hr	17.50	1-2 weekly
Samos (Vathy)	Chios	2½hr	14	2 weekly

NORTHEASTERN AEGEAN ISLANDS CHIOS

Chios Town

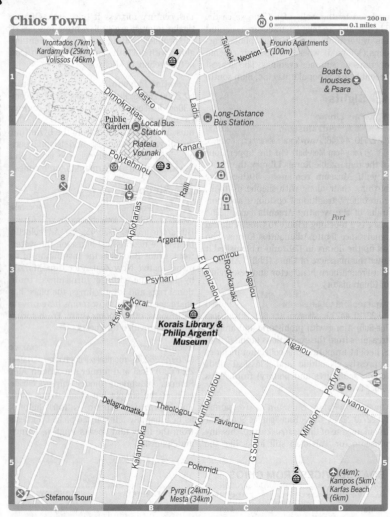

Vrontados (7km);
Kardamyla (29km);
Volissos (46km)

Frourio Apartments
(100m)

Boats to
Inousses
& Psara

Long-Distance
Bus Station

Public
Garden

Local Bus
Station

Plateia
Vounaki

Kastro

Dimokratias

Polytehniou

Aplotarias

Ralli

Ladis

Kanari

Tsitseki

Neorion

Argenti

Psyhari

El Venizelou

Omirou

Rodokanaki

Aigaiou

Port

Korai

Atsikis

Korais Library &
Philip Argenti
Museum

Aigaiou

Delagramatika

Theologou

Kountouriotou

Favierou

G Souri

Mihalon

Porfyra

Livanou

Kalampoka

Polemidi

Stefanou Tsouri

Pyrgi (24km);
Mesta (34km)

(4km);
Kampos (5km);
Karfas Beach
(6km)

Frourio Apartments APARTMENT €€
(📞 22710 42476, 6945408464; www.chiosfrourio.
gr; d/tr/q from €60/70/80) After the hustle
and bustle of traffic-filled Chios Town, it
is a pleasure to find yourself in the serene
neighbourhood inside the *kastro*, where
the greatest noise is produced by singing
canaries and church bells. There is enough
equipment in the large modern apartment
to sustain a nuclear winter. Crucially, that
includes a washing machine.

✕ Eating & Drinking

★**Kechribari Ouzerie** GREEK €
(📞 6942425459; Agion Anargyron 7; mains €5-10;
☉ lunch Jun-Sep) This cosy gem of an *ouzerie*,
a 10-minute walk up from the waterfront,
offers a variety of small plates in addition to
excellent fish, mussels, baked potatoes and
grilled meats. The choice is between two set
menus – meat or fish; beyond that, you don't
know exactly what you'll get. But indeed
that's part of the appeal.

Chios Town

◉ Top Sights
1 Korais Library & Philip Argenti
Museum B3

◉ Sights
2 Archaeological Museum D5
3 Byzantine Museum B2
4 Giustiniani Palace Museum B1

🛏 Sleeping
5 Chios Rooms D4
6 Rooms Alex D4

🍴 Eating
7 Hotzas Taverna A5
8 Kechribari Ouzerie A2
9 Kronos B3

🍸 Drinking & Nightlife
10 Kubrick All Day Bar B2

🛍 Shopping
11 Mastihashop C2
12 Sarandis Tourist Shop C2

Kronos ICE CREAM €
(☑ 22710 82982; Filippou Argenti 2; ⊘ 8am-late)
This historic parlour has been treating visitors and locals to great mastic-flavoured and dried-fruit ice creams since 1929.

Hotzas Taverna TAVERNA €
(☑ 22710 42787; Kondyli 3; mains €5.50-9; ⊘ dinner Mon-Sat) This comfortable and attractive taverna above Chios Town serves fine Greek standards with a twist, such as lamb kebab with yoghurt and rocket, white beans with tomato and mandarin, and dolmadhes with lemon. There's a variety of great veggie dishes, including risotto. Everything is *herisia* (handmade), from the pasta to the dessert.

Kubrick All Day Bar BAR
(☑ 22711 02744; Anelastou 11; ⊘ 8am-4am) Filling at night with a bohemian clientele, this tiny bar has stills from Stanley Kubrick films adorning its walls, and opens into a quaint bougainvillea-filled courtyard where patrons pass their time in mellow conversations over cocktails and coffee.

🛍 Shopping

Mastihashop COSMETICS
(☑ 22710 81600; www.mastihashop.com; Aigaiou 36; ⊘ 8.30am-10pm) Efficient and attractive shop with a range of mastic-based products such as lotions, toothpastes, soaps and condiments. Ask for a sample of pure mastic to chew on.

Sarandis Tourist Shop SOUVENIRS, BOOKS
(☑ 22710 24224; www.saranti.gr; cnr Aigaiou & Roïdi) Rambling Sarandis carries a little bit of everything, from cold drinks and wine to mastic-style lotions and good maps of the island.

ℹ Information

Banks with ATMs can be found along the waterfront and in Plateia Vounaki.

Chios General Hospital (☑ 22710 44302; El Venizelou 7)

Chios Tourist Office (☑ 22713 51726; www.chios.gr; Kanari 18; ⊘ 7am-3pm & 6-10pm Jul & Aug) Island transport and accommodation info, plus a useful free booklet, *Cultural Routes of Chios*.

Hatzelenis Tours (☑ 22710 20002; www.infochios.com; Aigaiou 2) Opposite the port, this dependable full-service travel agency arranges ferry and air tickets, excursions (including to nearby Inousses), accommodation and reasonable car hire.

Michalakis Travel (☑ 22710 40070; www.michalakistravel.gr; Neorion)

Police (☑ 22710 44427; cnr Polemidi 1 & Kountouriotou)

Port Authority (☑ 22710 44432; Neorion)

Post Office (☑ 22710 44350; Kontoleontos Sgouta 8; ⊘ 7.30am-2pm)

Sunrise Tours (☑ 22710 41390; www.sunrisetours.gr; Kanari 28) Chios tours and tickets for Inousses Island and Çeşme (Turkey).

Tourist Police (☑ 22710 81539; Polemidi)

Central Chios

The stonewall maze of wealthy centuries-old suburbs in Chios Town and the blood-soaked sites of 19th-century massacres along the road towards the western coast mean central Chios is a magnet for history buffs; less so for beach-goers and other pleasure seekers. That said, the aesthetic pleasure of mountain landscapes and singular endemic architecture compensate for the relative lack of hedonism.

◉ Sights

Roughly 4km north of Chios Town, **Vrontados** is the site of Homer's legendary stone chair, the **Daskalopetra** (in Greek, teacher's stone), a rock pinnacle close to the sea that's an obvious choice for holding class.

Immediately south of Chios Town is **Kampos**, a lush area with citrus trees where wealthy Genoese and Greek merchant families summered from the 14th century onwards. You can see elaborate gardens and high-walled mansions, some restored, others crumbling.

A road leading west from Chios Town will bring you to **Avgonyma**, a scenic mountaintop village and a convenient base for exploring desolate historic sites that witnessed some of the most tragic events in the island's history. Beyond Avgonyma lies a string of quiet beaches, the most popular of which is picturesque **Lithi**, which has several inviting tavernas next to the small bay.

Anavatos   VILLAGE

At the end of a silent stretch of road that branches off the main road near Avgonyma, this solemn site serves as a reminder of the island's brutal history. The abandoned village of grey-stone houses and narrow stepped pathways is perched on a precipitous cliff over which villagers hurled themselves to avoid capture during Turkish reprisals in 1822. Nowadays, it's referred to as the 'ghost village'.

Citrus Memories Museum   MUSEUM

(☑ 22710 31513; www.citrus-chios.gr; Kampos; ⊙ 10am-9pm Jun-Sep, to 6pm Oct-Apr) **FREE** This museum has attractive and well-signed historical displays of Kampos-area citrus, the Chian mandarin in particular. Also has a shaded courtyard cafe with – voila – fresh orange juice.

Nea Moni   MONASTERY

(New Monastery; ⊙ 9am-1pm & 4-7pm) **FREE** At the island's centre, Nea Moni is a World Heritage–listed 11th-century Byzantine monastery. Once one of Greece's richest monasteries, it attracted pre-eminent Byzantine artists to create the mosaics in its *katholikon* (principal church). Disastrously, during the Greek War of Independence (1821–29), the Turks torched the monastery and massacred its monks. Their skulls are now kept in a glass cabinet inside a chapel to the left of the main entrance.

🛏 Sleeping & Eating

Spiti Elaionas   APARTMENT €

(☑ 22710 20002; mano2@otenet.gr; Kampos; d from €50) Two traditional and tastefully decorated stone houses, 300m from Karfas Beach in a quiet hillside setting, with great views across to the Turkish coast.

Mouzaliko Traditional Hotel   GUESTHOUSE €€

(http://mouzalikohotel.gr; Zanis & Marias Chalkousi 52, Kampos; r incl breakfast €50-80; 🅿❄🛜) If you wonder what might be hiding behind the tall stone walls of Kampos, here is your chance to find out. Rooms in this typically introverted stone mansion all face the handsome courtyard, where the Greek–Quebecoise owners serve hearty breakfasts with yummy honey buns. A citrus version of a Chekhovian cherry orchard, also inside the enclosure, adds to the idyll.

Perleas Mansion   HISTORIC HOTEL €€

(☑ 22710 32217; www.perleas.gr; Vitiadou, Kampos; s/d/tr incl breakfast from €105/130/160; 🅿❄🛜) Restored Perleas Mansion offers seven elegant and well-appointed apartments, and a restaurant serving traditional Greek cuisine. The relaxing estate, built in 1640, exemplifies high Genoese architecture.

★ Pyrgos   TAVERNA €

(☑ 22710 42175; www.chiospyrgosrooms.gr; Avgonyma; mains €5-10; ⊙ breakfast, lunch & dinner) Excellent setting, service and food. This traditional hilltop stone taverna serves up superb mezedhes plus spit-roasted lamb and pork. Upstairs are five classy rooms (from €40) with names such as Mary, Irene and Ben.

Northern Chios

The craggy peaks of Mt Pelineo, Mt Oros and Mt Amani mark the drive north from Chios Town across the island's boulder-strewn lunar interior.

◉ Sights

Near to Chios Town and the scattered settlements of Vrontados, **Langada** is a relaxed cove of pine trees, homes, domatia and tavernas, and a launching point for water taxis to nearby Inousses. The most noise you're likely to hear might be a few caged birds entertaining the taverna tables. The octopus you see drying in the sun may be on the grill come evening time.

The main villages of **Marmaro** and **Kardamyla** follow as you head north, containing the ancestral homes of many wealthy ship-owning families. At **Nagos**, the road continues northwest, skirting **Mt Pelineo** (1297m), then winding and twisting its way through **Kambia**, high on a ridge overlooking the sea. In the northwest, wild camping is allowed around **Agio Galas**, also home to Agio Galas Cave (☎22740 22004), the island's largest and most impressive.

The central road will lead you south via Fita and Diefha to Volissos, Homer's legendary birthplace, now crowned with the impressive ruins of its hilltop Genoese fort. Down below, the working port of Limnia, from where boats depart to Psara Island, is flanked by a couple of pretty coves with pebble beaches. It has a few tavernas and domatias.

Driving 5km northeast will get you to Moni Agias Markellas, named for Chios' patron saint. From Volissos the coastal road continues south until Elinda, then heads eastward towards Chios Town.

Eating

El Sueño
GREEK €

(☎22740 22122; Limnos Beach; ⏱10am-11pm) Veering from the taverna mainstteam, this beach cafe features a good variety of salads and unusual appetisers, such as spicy mussels with beer and ginger, as well as standard Greek seafood and meat dishes.

★Taverna Fabrika
TAVERNA €

(☎22740 22045, 6976255829; fabrika_chios@ yahoo.com; Volissos; mains €6-8.50; ⏱lunch & dinner; P) This cheerful traditional eatery nestled in the trees of Volissos occupies a century-old olive-and-flour mill, where some of the vintage equipment is displayed. Top off excellent grills, *mayirefta* and good barrel wine with homemade custard or sweet *loukoumadhes*. Above the taverna are six handsome rooms, with fireplaces and wi-fi (triples €50).

Southern Chios

Unique southern Chios is arguably the island's best destination. Though it grows elsewhere in the Aegean, the gum-producing mastic tree of Chios has for centuries been the sole commercial producer of mastic gum. The tree thrives in a fertile, reddish territory known as the Mastihohoria (Mastic villages). This region of rolling hills, crisscrossed with elaborate stone walls running through olive and mastic groves, is highly atmospheric.

The Ottoman rulers' penchant for mastic made the Mastihohoria wealthy for centuries. Some architectural wonders remain in the villages of Pyrgi (p432) and Mesta. The former features houses decorated in unusual

---

> ### MASTIC: SOMETHING TO CHEW ON
>
> Mastic gum is a resin that drips from the lentisk tree, which flourishes in southern Chios' gentle climate. Mastic gum has been around at least since the golden age of Greece when Hippocrates touted its pharmaceutical benefit, and for centuries it supported the local economy. Modern research indicates that it contains antioxidants.
>
> During Ottoman rule, Chios received preferential treatment from the sultans who, along with the women of the harem, were quite fond of chewing mastic gum. You can find samples in Mesta and Chios Town shops.
>
> For a comprehensive story of mastic production in Chios, head to the Chios Mastic Museum near Pyrgi.

colourful patterns, while the latter is a car-free, walled fortress settlement built by the Genoese in the 14th century.

The sad and dramatic story of mastic production in Chios is celebrated in the brand-new Chios Mastic Museum (☎22710 72212; www.piop.gr; Pyrgi, Rachi Site; €3; ⏱10am-6pm Wed-Mon, to 5pm winter), halfway between Pyrgi and Emboreios, which was the Mastihohoria's port back when mastic producers were high rollers. Today it's much quieter, though it does boast Mavra Volia Beach, named for its black volcanic pebbles. Domatia and tavernas are available, and the archaeological ruins of an Early Bronze Age temple to Athena are signed nearby.

The west-coast workaday port of Limenas Mesta (also called Limenas) is home to a couple of decent port tavernas and is a short drive from Mesta. For swimming, head to Apothia Beach (7km south of Olymbi), a curving, sandy cove where the water is a stunning turquoise, backed by two *almiriki* (tamarisk) shade trees and a canteen in summer.

Around 3km southeast of Mesta, Olymbi – like Mesta and Pyrgi – is a mastic-producing village characterised by its defensive architecture. A well-maintained 3km trail connects Olymbi and Mesta. A popular side trip takes you 5km south to the splendid Cave of Sykia Olymbi (☎22710 93364; €5; ⏱9am-3pm Tue-Sun), signposted as 'Olympi Cave'.

WORTH A TRIP

PYRGI ΠΥΡΓΙ

The Mastihohoria's largest village, 24km southwest of Chios Town, Pyrgi looks like a magic jewellery box, with its facades decorated in intricate grey-and-white patterns, some geometric and others based on flowers, leaves and animals. The technique, called *xysta*, uses equal amounts of cement, volcanic sand and lime as well as bent forks and a fine eye.

Pyrgi's central square is flanked by tavernas, shops and the little 12th-century **Church of Agios Apostolos** (⊙8am-3pm Tue-Sun). East of the square, note the house with a plaque attesting to its former occupant – one Christopher Columbus, who was also a fan of mastic gum, though he apparently preferred it as a sealant in boat construction. There are several tavernas and cafes in the main square. Should you wish to stay, the castle-like apartments at **Mastiha House** (☑22710 72900, 6944604870; www.mastiha house.gr; r €50) offer fantastic value for money.

Activities

★**Masticulture**
Ecotourism Activities   ECOTOUR
(☑6976113007, 22710 76084; www.masticulture. com; tours from €18) To participate in traditional cultural activities such as Chian farming, contact Vassilis and Roula, who provide unique ecotourism opportunities that introduce visitors to the local community, its history and culture. Activities include mastic cultivation tours, stargazing, and bicycle and sea-kayak outings. They can help find area accommodation and offer tips for visiting nearby Psara Island.

Sleeping & Eating

Despina Karabela
Traditional Apartments   APARTMENT €
(☑22710 76065; www.taste-mesta.gr; s/d €40/50; ❄ 🛜) A short walk from the square, outside the walled village, these lovely apartments are cosy and tastefully decorated. Exposed stone highlights the interiors, while loft 'bedrooms' are on raised platforms. Despina also promotes the local food scene; ask for a wander to the nearby family fields.

Medieval
Castle Suites   ACCOMMODATION SERVICES €€
(☑22710 76025; www.medievalcastlesuites.com; d/tr/f from €60/80/110) The Castle Suites is a collection of 20 rooms spread throughout the village, all with traditional stone touches, modern bathrooms and a few with fireplaces and even computers. Rooms vary considerably in size and proximity to the square.

★**Meseonas**   TAVERNA €
(☑22710 76050; Plateia Taxiarhon; mains €6-9; ⊙lunch & dinner) With tables spread across Plateia Taxiarhon, this relaxed and reliable eatery appeals to locals and visitors alike, and serves hearty portions of *mayirefta,* beef *keftedhes* (rissoles) and grills. Everything is local, right down to the friendly host family's *souma* (mastic-flavoured firewater).

INOUSSES ΟΙΝΟΥΣΣΕΣ
POP 400

Just northeast of Chios Town, serene Inousses is the ancestral home of nearly a third of Greece's shipping barons (the *arhontes*), whose wealthy descendants return here annually for summer vacations from their homes overseas.

Inousses was settled in 1750 by ship-owning families from Kardamyla in north-eastern Chios, some of whom amassed huge fortunes during the 19th and early 20th centuries. Traces of this history linger in Inousses' grand mansions and ornate family mausoleums high above the sea.

Although Inousses is little visited, it does get lively in summer, with an open-air cinema, friendly residents and a buzzing night-time waterfront. The island's port attests to its seafaring identity. Arriving by ferry, you'll see a small, green sculpted mermaid watching over the harbour. In the port, the striking statue of **Mitera Inoussiotissa** (Mother of Inoussa), a village woman waving goodbye to seafaring men, is incredibly photogenic at sunset.

Sights & Activities

Inousses has numerous opportunities for hill walking, and pristine beaches. Just a 10-minute walk from the port you'll find pretty and swimmable **Kakopetria Beach**. Another five to 10 minutes will bring you to **Bilali Beach**, set on a tranquil bay with a not-quite-tranquil beach cantina that buzzes all night in summer.

Nautical Museum of Inousses MUSEUM
(☑ 6973412474, 22710 55182; Stefanou Tsouri 20; €1.50; ⊙ 9am-1pm) Created in 1965, this handsome museum showcases the collection of local shipping magnate Antonis Lemos. Many of the models on display (some intentionally half-completed then set flush against a mirror so that you 'see' the whole vessel) were made by French prisoners of war during the Napoleonic Wars. There's also a swashbuckling collection of 18th-century muskets and sabres, a WWII-era US Navy diving helmet, a hand crank from a 19th-century lighthouse and paintings of Nazi submarines attacking Greek sailing vessels.

Mausoleum of Inousses CEMETERY
(Nekrotafion Inousson) In the leafy courtyard of the Church of Agia Paraskevi stands the Mausoleum of Inousses, where the island's ship-owning dynasties have endowed the tombs of their greats with huge chambers, marble sculptures and miniature churches. It's a melancholy, moving place and speaks volumes about the worldly achievements and self-perception of the extraordinary natives of these tiny islands.

🛏 Sleeping

Rooms Bilali ACCOMMODATION SERVICES €
(☑ 6944677882; d €45-70; 🌐) Contact Kostas at Bilali Beach Bar for information on well-appointed one- and two-bedroom apartments in the upper village.

Rooms Tsouri ACCOMMODATION SERVICES €€
(☑ 6946286791; oinoussesstudios@ymail.com; d incl breakfast from €60; 🌐 🛜) For help with finding attractive rooms, you can contact the resourceful Despina Tsouri, in the upper village.

✖ Eating

Aignothiotiko TAVERNA €
(☑ 6971663746; upper village; mains €4-7; ⊙ 9am-11pm) Next to the church in the upper village, this friendly taverna serves great mezedhes, including exemplary fava, and attracts a mostly Greek clientele. Tasteful retro soundtracks fit neatly into the old village ambience.

Palio Teloneío TAVERNA €
(Old Customs; mains €5-9; ⊙ lunch & dinner) This excellent eatery on the waterfront has a bit of everything Greek, but is proudest of its daily fresh catch of *barbounia* (red mullet) and crispy *gavros*.

To Pateroniso TAVERNA, CAFE €
(mains €5-8; ⊙ lunch & dinner) A reliable taverna near the square, with good grills and seafood, including the Inousses/Chios speciality of *atherinopita*, a scrumptious heads-and-all pan-fry of onions and fresh anchovies.

🍷 Drinking & Nightlife

Bilali Beach Bar BAR
(☑ 6944677882; ⊙ until sunset) Cool spot on the small and shallow swimming bay at Bilali Beach, with shady tables, thumping music, good drinks, juices, smoothies and snacks. Very popular summer hang-out, from morning till the wee hours.

Naftikos Omilos Inousson BAR
(Yacht Club; ☑ 22720 55596; ⊙ 9am-3am; 🛜) Towards the end of the waterfront, the Inousses Yacht Club's long bar and outdoor patio are filled mostly with young Greeks and their vacationing diaspora relatives, and not a few day trippers from Chios.

☆ Entertainment

A summertime **open-air cinema** (tickets €3; ⊙ 9.30pm) near the central waterfront brings Hollywood hits to Inousses.

ℹ Information

The bank (with ATM) is next to the nautical museum.
Dimarhio (Town Hall; ☑ 22713 51314, after hours 6973412474; ⊙ 8am-3pm) Free brochures and accommodation help, opposite the ferry dock. Ask for Kostas Lignos.
Doctor (☑ 22710 55300)
Police (☑ 22710 55222)
Post Office Next to the nautical museum.

ℹ Getting There & Away

The little *Oinoussai III* (€5 one way, one hour, daily) leaves from Chios in the afternoon and returns from Inousses the next morning, warranting overnight stays. Purchase tickets onboard or from Sunrise Tours (p429) in Chios Town. There are weekend summertime excursions (€20) available.

Daily **water taxis** (☑ 6944168104, 6938370129, 22710 55329) travel to/from Langada (20 minutes), 15km north of Chios Town. The one-way fare is €65, split among up to eight passengers.

ⓘ Getting Around

Inousses has neither buses nor car hire; ask at the port for its one semitaxi. You can also bring a bicycle or scooter on the ferry from Chios.

PSARA   ΨΑΡΑ

POP 420

Celebrated Psara is one of maritime Greece's true oddities. A tiny speck in the sea 16km northwest of Chios, this island of scrub vegetation, wandering goats and weird red-rock formations has one settlement (also called Psara), a remote monastery and pristine beaches.

History

Psara looms inordinately large in modern lore. The Psariot clans became wealthy through shipping, and their participation in the 1821–29 War of Independence is etched into modern Greek history, particularly the exploits of Konstantinos Kanaris (1793–1877), whose heroic stature propelled him, six times, to the position of prime minister.

Kanaris' most famous operation occurred on the night of 6 June 1822. In revenge for Turkish massacres on Chios, the Psariots destroyed the Turkish admiral's flagship while the unsuspecting enemy was holding a post-massacre celebration. Kanaris' forces detonated the ship's powder keg, blowing up 2000 sailors and the admiral himself. However, as on Chios, their involvement sparked a brutal Ottoman reprisal, assisted by Egyptian and French mercenaries, that decimated the island in 1824.

ISLAND FLAG: SEEING RED

Throughout Psara village you will notice the island's memorable red-and-white flag waving proudly in the breeze. Emblazoned with the revolutionary slogan 'Eleftheria i Thanatos' (Freedom or Death), it features a red cross at its centre, with an upturned spear jutting from one side, and an anchor apparently impaling a green snake on the other. As if the reference to the Islamic rule of the Turks wasn't apparent enough, it features an upside-down crescent moon and star for good measure. The yellow dove of freedom flutters patiently at one side.

Over the next century, many Psariots resettled in America and other foreign lands. Their descendants still return every summer, so don't be surprised if the first Greek you meet speaks English with a New York accent.

⊙ Sights & Activities

Psara village is tucked within a long bay on the island's southwest. When you disembark the ferry, you can't miss the jagged Mavri Rachi, or 'Black Shoulder', the rock from which thousands of Psariots are said to have hurled themselves during the 1824 Ottoman assault.

Psara's main cultural attraction, the **Monastery of Kimisis Theotokou** (Monastery of the Dormition of the Virgin; ⊘ Sun), 12km north of town, is a smallish chapel surrounded by protective walls; it contains rare hieratic scripts from Mt Athos and a sacred icon that is paraded through the village on the night of 4 August. In all, there are 67 chapels across the island, each cared for by a local family.

In the centre of Psara village is the **Monument to Konstantinos Kanaris**, where Greeks honour their national hero, who is actually buried in Athens while his heart is kept in the Naval Museum in Piraeus. The hyper-photogenic wall of a ruined **Ottoman-era mansion** on the waterfront looks like a stone version of Edvard Munch's *Scream*, or a web-chat emoticon.

Hiking

Visitors should take the splendid introductory walk along the **Black Shoulder** (aka Black Rock) to the little chapel of **Agios Ioannis** and the **lookout memorial**. The views are impressive from the top, especially at sunset.

A further three relatively short and documented hiking trails can also be tackled. The first one takes you to the **cannon emplacements** at the northwestern tip of Psara (2km each way); the second takes you to remote **Limnonaria Beach** (900m each way) on the south coast; and the third is a circular route (3km) taking in **Adami** and **Kanalos Bays**. All three hikes are detailed on the Terrain Maps (www.terrainmaps.gr) map of Psara.

🏃 Beaches

A number of clean pebble-and-sand beaches stretch themselves along Psara's jagged edges. The closest to the village are **Kato Gialos** and **Katsouni**. The former is on the west side of the headland and is pebbled; the latter is a short walk north of the harbour, and is sandy with shallow water, ideal for kids. Both beaches have tavernas nearby.

Further afield, and just over 1km northeast, are the twin beaches of Lazareta and Megali Ammos, consisting of fine pebbles. Lakka Beach, 2.5km up the west coast, is the next option, followed by Agios Dimitrios, 3.5km from Psara.

🛏 Sleeping

Village accommodation consists primarily of rooms and studios. Contact Psara Travel, or Michalakis Travel (p426) or Masticulture Ecotourism Activities (p432) on Chios, to book ahead for rooms.

Kato Gialos Apartments APARTMENT €
(🖉 6945755321, 22740 61178; Kato Gialos Beach; studios from €40; ❄) Spyros Giannakos rents out clean, bright rooms and kitchenette apartments overlooking Kato Gialos Beach. Enquire at English-speaking Psara Travel.

Studios Psara APARTMENT €
(🖉 22740 61386; studios €50; ❄❄🛜) At the edge of the village, in a palm-tree garden, you'll find these clean and airy rooms with kitchenettes, plus a popular *kafeneio* (coffee house) attached.

🍴 Eating & Drinking

⭐**Spitalia** TAVERNA €
(Katsounis Beach; mains €7-12; ⊙11am-1am) Formerly a seaside Ottoman quarantine station, this excellent eatery is great for a lazy beachside lunch or dinner. Stuffed pork or goat is the signature dish.

To Iliovasilema TAVERNA €
(🖉 22740 61121; Kato Gialos Beach; mains €4.50-9; ⊙lunch & dinner) Sit under the outdoor canopy at the village's newest fish taverna and *ouzerie*.

To Petrino BAR
A relaxed bar with arguably the most romantic setting on the whole island – amid the ruins of an ancient house and facing the beautiful harbour.

ℹ Information

There's an ATM on the waterfront square.

Diana Katakouzinou of **Psara Travel** (🖉 22740 61351, 6932528489; www.psaratravel.gr/en) is ever-helpful and conducts a 90-minute morning tour of Psara (€6). There's also a summer **tourist kiosk** (⊙9am-11pm) at the port.
Doctor (🖉 22740 61277; Medical Centre)
Police (🖉 22740 61222)

ℹ Getting There & Away

Ferries reach Psara from Chios Town (€12 return, three hours, Monday to Friday), Volissos (€7, 1½ hours, weekends only) and Piraeus (€31, five hours, weekly).

Buy tickets to Psara from Hatzelenis Tours or Michalakis Travel in Chios Town (p599).

ℹ Getting Around

Neither car nor motorbike hire is available on Psara, and there's no taxi, so consider ferrying a rental car or motorbike from Chios.

Hitchhiking is common on the island. (Hitching is never entirely safe, of course, and we don't recommend it. Travellers who hitch should understand that they are taking a small but potentially serious risk.)

LESVOS (MYTILINI)
ΛΕΣΒΟΣ (ΜΥΤΙΛΗΝΗ)
POP 95,330

Greece's third-largest island, Lesvos is marked by long sweeps of rugged, desert-like western plains that give way to sandy beaches and salt marshes in the centre. To the east are thickly forested mountains and dense olive groves – around 11 million olive trees are cultivated here.

The port and capital, Mytilini Town, is a lively place year-round, filled with exemplary *ouzeries* and good accommodation, while the north-coast town of Molyvos (aka Mythimna) is an aesthetic treat, with old stone houses clustered on winding lanes overlooking the sea.

Along with hiking and cycling, Lesvos is a mecca for birdwatching; more than 279 species, from raptors to waders, are often sighted. The island's therapeutic hot springs gush with some of the warmest mineral waters in Europe.

Despite its undeniable tourist appeal, Lesvos' chief livelihood is agriculture. Its olive oil is highly regarded, and the island's farmers produce around half the ouzo sold worldwide.

Lesvos (Mytilini)

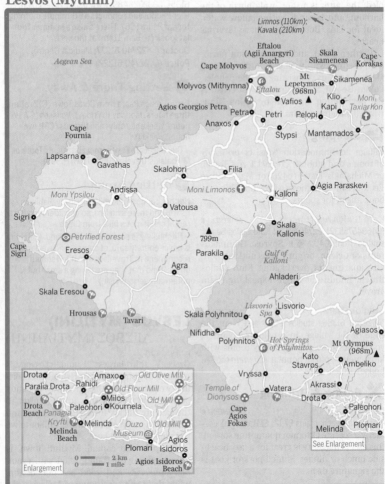

History

Lesvos' great cultural legacy stretches from the 7th-century-BC musical composer Terpander to 20th-century figures such as Nobel Prize–winning poet Odysseus Elytis and primitive painter Theophilos.

Ancient philosophers Aristotle and Epicurus also led a philosophical academy here. Most famous, however, is Sappho, one of Ancient Greece's greatest poets. Her sensuous, passionate poetry has fuelled a modern-day following and draws lesbians from around the world to the village of Skala Eresou, where she was born (c 630 BC).

🛈 Getting There & Away

AIR

The **airport** (☎ 22510 38700, 22510 61212) is 8km south of Mytilini Town. A taxi to town costs €10 and a bus €1.60.

Aegean Air (www.aegeanair.com), **Olympic Air** (www.olympicair.com), **Sky Express** (www.sky express.gr), **Astra Airlines** (www.astra-airlines. gr) and **Air Minoan** (www.minoanair.com/en) have offices at the airport. Mytilini Town travel agents also sell tickets. At the time of writing, Spanish no-frills newcomer **Volotea** (www.volo tea.com) was offering dirt cheap fares (from €9 on flights to/from Athens).

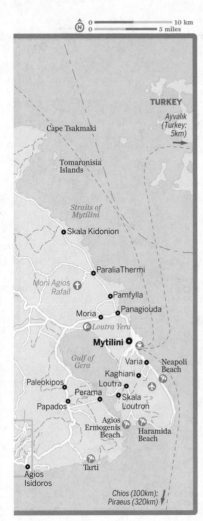

Sigri €10.70, 2½ hours, one daily

Skala Eresou €11.20, 2½ hours, one to two daily, via Eresos

Vatera €6.80, 1½ hours, three daily, via Polyhnitos.

Travelling between smaller places often requires changing in Kalloni, which receives three to four daily buses from Mytilini (€4.90, 45 minutes).

Three to four daily buses also go north from Mytilini Town to Mantamados (for Moni Taxiarhon; €4.50, one hour).

Mytilini's **local bus station** (KTEL; ☑ 22510 46436; Pavlou Kountourioti), near Plateia Sapphou, serves in-town destinations and nearby Loutra, Skala Loutron and Tahiarhis.

CAR & MOTORCYCLE

Local companies **Discover Rent-a-Car** (☑ 6936057676, 22510 20391; www.discover1.gr; Aristarhou 1) and **Billy's Rentals** (☑ 6944759716, 22510 20006; www.billys-rentacar.com; Kountourioti 87; ⊙ 7.30am-10pm) have newish cars and flexible service. Billy's also has motorbikes, as do others along Pavlou Kountourioti in Mytilini Town. In Molyvos, hire vehicles from **Kosmos Rent-a-Car** (☑ 22530 71710; www.lesvosrentals.com).

Mytilini Town　Μυτιλήνη

POP 29,650

Lesvos' port and capital, Mytilini is a lively student town with great eating and drinking options, plus eclectic churches and a set of grand 19th-century mansions and museums. Indeed, its remarkable Teriade Museum boasts paintings by Picasso, Chagall and Matisse, along with home-grown painter Theophilos. In fact, the island is known in equal parts for its poets and painters and for its olive oil and ouzo.

Ferries dock at the northeastern end of the curving waterfront thoroughfare, Pavlou Kountourioti, where most of the action is centred. Handmade ceramics, jewellery and traditional products are sold on and around the main shopping street Ermou, and there are many fine *ouzeries* and student-fuelled bars to enjoy.

☉ Sights & Activities

★ **Teriade Museum**　　　　MUSEUM
(☑ 22510 23372; http://museumteriade.gr; Varia; €3; ⊙ 9am-2pm Tue-Sun) Varia, 4km south of Mytilini, is the unlikely home of the Teriade Museum and its astonishing collection of paintings by artists such as Picasso, Chagall, Miro, Le Corbusier and Matisse.

BOAT

In Mytilini Town, buy ferry tickets from Mitilene Tours (p440), Olive Groove Travel (p440), and Tsolos Travel (p440).

❶ Getting Around

BUS

From Mytilini Town's **long-distance bus station** (KTEL; ☑ 22510 28873; El Venizelou), near Agias Irinis Park, buses serve the following:

Agiasos €3.20, 45 minutes, three daily

Molyvos (Mithymna) €7.50, 1½ hours, two to three daily, via Petra

Plomari €5, 1¼ hours, three daily

Mytilini Town

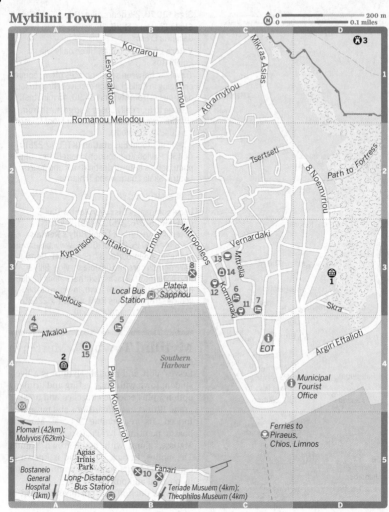

The museum honours the Lesvos-born artist and critic Stratis Eleftheriadis, who brought the work of primitive painter and Lesvos native Theophilos to international attention.

Fortress   FORTRESS

(Kastro; €2; ◷8am-3pm Tue-Sun) Mytilini's imposing early Byzantine fortress was renovated in the 14th century by Genoese overlord Francisco Gatelouzo, and then the Turks enlarged it again. Flanked by pine trees, it's popular for a stroll, with great views included.

Theophilos Museum   MUSEUM

(☎22510 41644; Varia; €3; ◷8.30am-2pm Mon-Fri) This humble structure contains 86 paintings by the primitive painter Theophilos, who remains a folk hero among Greek literati. During his life he barely scratched out an existence, moving frequently and painting coffee-house walls for his daily bread, depicting the people he met at work and at play. A year after his death in 1934, his work was exhibited at the Louvre.

Archaeological Museum   MUSEUM

(☎22510 40223; 8 Noemvriou; €4; ◷8am-3pm Tue-Sun) This handsome and refurbished

Mytilini Town

◎ Sights
1	Archaeological Museum	D3
2	Byzantine Museum	A4
	Church of Agios Therapon	(see 2)
3	Fortress	D1

🛌 Sleeping
4	Alkaios Rooms	A4
5	Hotel Lesvion	B4
6	Porto Lesvos Hotel	C3
7	Theofilos Paradise Boutique Hotel	C3

🍴 Eating
	Averoff Restaurant	(see 5)
8	Cafe P	B3
9	Jimmy's Hodros	B5
10	Polytechnos	B5

🍷 Drinking & Nightlife
11	Bobiras	C3
12	Cartel	C3
13	Mousiko Kafenio	C3

🛍 Shopping
14	Book & Art	C3
15	Sfetoudi Bookshop	A4

museum, about 500m above the eastern quay (and the now-closed Old Archaeological Museum), portrays island life from the 2nd century BC to the 3rd century AD, including striking floor mosaics with a walking 'trail' across the protective glass surface.

Church of Agios Therapon   CHURCH
(Arionos; ⊙9am-1pm) The bulbous dome of this church crowns Mytilini's skyline. Its ornate interior boasts a huge chandelier, an intricately carved iconostasis, a priest's throne and a frescoed dome. Within the church courtyard, you'll find the icon-rich **Byzantine Museum** (☎22510 28916; www.immyt.net/museum; Arionos; ⊙9am-1pm) FREE.

Therma Spa   HOT SPRINGS
(http://thermaspalesvos.com/en; Km 7 Mytilini-Kalloni road; €8; ⊙9am-9pm) Hikers and cyclists can give their muscles a well deserved rest at this newly renovated spa, which now combines an old Ottoman-styled indoor thermal pool with a new open-air pool next to a large sundeck facing the Bay of Gera. A range of massage and other treatments is available (€20 to €40). There's also an on-site cafe.

🛌 Sleeping

★ Alkaios Rooms   PENSION €
(☎22510 47737, 6981314154; www.alkaiosrooms.gr; Alkaiou 16; s/d/tr incl breakfast €35/45/55;

❄ 🛜) This collection of 30 spotless and well-kept rooms nestled discreetly in two renovated traditional buildings is Mytilini's most attractive budget option. It's a two-minute walk up from the west side of the waterfront (and Kitchen 19 cafe). The reception is in a restored mansion, where breakfast is served in a flowery courtyard.

Porto Lesvos Hotel   HOTEL €
(☎22510 41771; www.portolesvos.gr; Komninaki 21; s/d €30/40; ❄ 🛜) Back behind the far end of the waterfront, this efficient and friendly lodging offers good value, and has a decent breakfast buffet. Rooms are a tad snug, but clean and comfortable. Upper rooms overlook either the sea or the old castle.

Theofilos Paradise Boutique Hotel   BOUTIQUE HOTEL €€
(☎22510 43300; www.theofilosparadise.gr; Skra 7; d/ste/f incl breakfast from €90/105/130; P ❄ @ 🛜 ≋) This smartly restored 100-year-old mansion is elegant, cheerful and good value, with modern amenities and a traditional *hammam*. The 22 swanky rooms (plus two luxe suites) are spread among three adjacent buildings surrounding an inviting courtyard.

Hotel Lesvion   HOTEL €€
(☎22510 28177; www.lesvion.gr; Pavlou Kountourioti 27a; s/d incl breakfast from €50/70; ❄ 🛜) The modern and well-positioned Lesvion, smack on the harbour, has friendly service, and attractive and spacious rooms, some with excellent port-view balconies. A breakfast bar overlooks the harbour.

🍴 Eating

Averoff Restaurant   TAVERNA €
(☎22510 22180; Pavlou Kountourioti; mains €4.50-9; ⊙10am-10pm) No-frills old-fashioned eatery with waiters in ties. It specialises in generous *mayirefta* plates such as chicken and potatoes, stuffed tomatoes and *briam* (mixed veggies). It's on the central waterfront.

Cafe P   CAFE €
(☎22510 55594; Samou 2; mains €2-5; ⊙11am-3am) This hip back-alley bistro draws a crowd mostly from the university for its unusual and well-priced small plates, slight menu, eclectic music mix and all-round chilled atmosphere. Oven-cooked pork with leeks or baked feta in a fig balsamic, served with a draught beer, costs €6. It's about 50m in from Plateia Sapphou (Sappho Sq). Look for a sign with a single Greek letter, 'Π'.

DOMESTIC FLIGHTS FROM LESVOS (MYTILINI)

DESTINATION	AIRPORT	DURATION	FARE (€)	FREQUENCY
Athens	Mytilini Town	40min	9-89	3-4 daily
Chios	Mytilini Town	30min	80	3 weekly
Crete (Iraklio)	Mytilini Town	50min	80	2 weekly
Limnos	Mytilini Town	30min	86	3 weekly
Rhodes	Mytilini Town	70min	117	3 weekly
Samos (via Chios)	Mytilini Town	40min	86	3 weekly
Thessaloniki	Mytilini Town	55min	38-70	2-3 daily

Polytechnos FAST FOOD €
(☑ 22510 44128; Fanari; mains €2-5.50; ☺ lunch & dinner) A hands-down favourite for excellent *gyros,* pitta souvlaki and snappy service. Great for picnic lunches, too. Find it on the waterfront at the south end of the harbour.

Jimmy's Hodros TAVERNA €
(☑ 22510 42614; Fanari; €7-10; ☺ lunch & dinner) Best translated as 'Fat Jimmy's'. Look for excellent grills and fresh fish, served alongside low-key mandolin and guitar duos on summer weekends.

★**Taverna Efkaliptos** SEAFOOD €€
(☑ 22510 32727; Old Harbour, Panagiouda; mains €8-18; ☺ lunch & dinner) You might be sitting closer to the fishing boats than the kitchen at this first-class fish taverna in Panagiouda; it's just 4km north of Mytilini Town but has a distinctly remote feel. Excellent mezedhes and well-priced fresh fish, great service and white wine from nearby Limnos.

🍷 Drinking & Nightlife

Mytilini's loud waterfront cafes are inevitably busy; the best watering holes are found in the backstreets.

★**Mousiko Kafenio** CAFE
(cnr Mitropoleos & Vernardaki; ☺ 7.30am-2am) This hip student favourite is filled with eclectic paintings, old mirrors and well-worn wooden fixtures, giving it a relaxed, arty vibe. Mix in some great music and it's one of the most fun places in town. Great drinks, fresh juices and coffee, and even homemade iced tea on hot summer days.

Cartel BAR
(☑ 22510 41143; Komninaki) A busy bar with a convivial atmosphere, lots of dressed-up folks, cocktails, and refreshing nonalcoholic concoctions such as sour cherry with almond, and pomegranate with green tea.

Bobiras BAR
(Komninaki; ☺ 11am-3am) Bobiras fills up as the night goes on. Great small plates, ouzo and atmosphere to spare.

🛍 Shopping

Book & Art BOOKS
(☑ 22510 37961; Komninaki 5) Unusual and inviting side-street bookshop, gallery and toy store.

Sfetoudi Bookshop BOOKS
(☑ 22510 22287; Ermou 41) Carries good island maps and stocks books on Lesvos.

ℹ️ Information

Bostaneio General Hospital (☑ 22510 57700; E Vostani 48)

EOT (Greek National Tourist Organisation; ☑ 22510 42512; Aristarhou 6; ☺ 9am-2pm Mon-Fri)

Lesvos – More Than Just Another Greek Island (www.lesvos.com) Online guide to Lesvos; useful despite the PR.

Mitilene Tours (☑ 22510 54261; www.mitilene tours.gr; Kountourioti 87) Full-service agency on the east side of the port. Helps with accommodation, car rentals, and trips and tours to Turkey.

Municipal Tourist Office (EOT; ☑ 22510 43255; Gate B, Port; ☺ 9am-3pm Mon-Sat) Near the quay.

Olive Groove Travel (☑ 22510 37533; www. olive-groove.gr; 11 Pavlou Kountourioti; ☺ 7.30am-10pm) All-purpose travel agency on the central waterfront, selling tickets, including to Turkey, and helpful with local info.

Port Authority (☑ 22510 40827) On the quay.

Port Police (☑ 22510 28827; waterfront) On the waterfront.

Post Office (Vournasson; ☺ 7.30am-2pm)

Tourist Police (☑ 22510 22776) On the quay.

Tsolos Travel (☑ 22510 25346; www.flytsolos. com; Fanari) Full-service agency on the south side of the port. Sells ferry tickets to Turkey.

Zoumboulis Tours (☑ 22510 37755; Kountouri-oti 69; ⊙ 8am-8pm) Sells ferry and air tickets, and runs boat trips to Turkey.

South of Mytilini

The small olive-groved peninsula south of Mytilini has several unique attractions. Following the coast road 7km south, opposite the airport you'll find the long, pebbled **Neapoli Beach**; it hosts a few chilled-out beach bars, popular with swimsuited students, and usually pulsates with reggae and Greek sounds.

Around 9km further south, the peninsula wraps around to the popular sand-and-pebble **Agios Ermogenis Beach**, and **Haramida Beach**, which has toilets and showers under pine trees on the bluff above the beach.

Northern Lesvos

Home to rolling hills covered in pine and olive trees, peaceful beaches and the aesthetically harmonious town of Molyvos (also called Mithymna), northern Lesvos offers both solitude and low-key resort action. Traditional seaside hot springs and intriguing Byzantine monasteries round out the region's offerings.

Lying 5km south of Molyvos, **Petra** is mostly a crowded beach village. Its one cultural site, situated above the giant overhanging rock for which the village was named, is the 18th-century **Panagia Glykofilousa** (Church of the Sweet-Kissing Virgin), accessible on foot up 114 rock-hewn steps. Note the mysterious figurines, looking like relatives of Easter Island stone heads, on top of the main gate. It's possible to stay overnight, but the village lacks the character of

Molyvos or nearby Eftalou Beach – it's barely a strip of souvenir shops and restaurants, though its small square can be relaxing.

Eftalou Beach (also called Agii Anargyri Beach), 2km northeast of Petra, is the place for solitude seekers. Backed by a cliff, the serene, narrow pebbled beach has pristine waters and also boasts the charming **Mineral Baths of Eftalou** (☑ 22530 71245; Eftalou Beach; old/new bathhouse €4/6; ⊙ 10am-6pm). Beyond the baths, the beachfront **Hrysi Akti** (☑ 22530 71879; Eftalou Beach; s/d €30/35) offers simple rooms with bathrooms in an idyllic pebbled cove, complete with the friendly owners' small **restaurant** (☑ 22530 71947; mains from €5-8; ⊙ breakfast, lunch & dinner) overlooking the sea.

From Eftalou, a coastal road continues for 9.5km to **Skala Sikameneas**, an exceedingly pretty fishing port with some domatia and two popular tavernas, including **I Mouria tou Mirivili** (☑ 22530 55319; Skala Sikameneas; €7-15; ⊙ breakfast, lunch & dinner). Both eating options specialise in *astakomakaronadha*.

Above the port, its parent village of **Sikamenea** is where the main road from Molyvos turns south towards **Mantamados**, home to **Moni Taxiarhon** (⊙ 8am-dusk) **FREE** monastery. Further south, **Agia Paraskevi** houses the excellent **Museum of Industrial Olive Oil Production** (☑ 22530 32300; www.piop.gr; €3; ⊙ 10am-6pm Wed-Mon Mar-Oct, to 5pm Nov-Feb).

Molyvos   Μόλυβος
POP 1500

Molyvos, also known as Mithymna, is a well-preserved Ottoman-era town of narrow cobbled lanes and stone houses, with jutting wooden balconies wreathed in flowers, overlooking a sparkling pebble beach below. Its grand 14th-century Byzantine castle, some

BOAT SERVICES FROM LESVOS (MYTILINI)

DESTINATION	DURATION	FARE (€)	FREQUENCY
Agios Efstratios	1½hr	7.50	5-6 weekly
Ikaria (Agios Kirykos)	13hr	40-50	2 weekly
Kavala	4½hr	16-27	6 weekly
Lavrio	9hr	31-38	4 weekly
Lesvos (Mytilini)	6hr	20-31	3 weekly
Piraeus	20hr	60	3 weekly
Samos (Karlovasi)	10½hr	38	1-2 weekly
Samos (Vathy)	11hr	40	1 weekly

good nearby beaches and its north-central island location make it a great launch pad from which to explore Lesvos.

Sights & Activities

Beach lovers can take an excursion boat for Skala Sikameneas village (10km) and nearby Eftalou (from €20, 10.30am daily). It's also possible to hike one way and catch the excursion boat back to Molyvos. Sunset cruises are available. Enquire at the portside Faonas Travel Agency, inside the Sea Horse Hotel, or Lesvorama on the main road.

A popular **yoga retreat** (www.angela-victor. com) is organised by Angela Farmer at the Yoga Hall. Workshop dates vary through the year.

Byzantine-Genoese Castle CASTLE
(☑ 22530 71803; €2; ⊙ 8am-3pm Tue-Sun) This handsome 14th-century castle stands guard above Molyvos. A steep climb is repaid by sweeping views over the town and sea – even across to Turkey, shimmering on the horizon. In summer the castle hosts several festivals.

Sleeping

More than 50 registered, good-quality domatia are available in Molyvos. Ask at the municipal tourist office or Molyvos Tourism Association on upper Agora.

★**Lela's Studios** APARTMENT €
(☑ 22530 71285, 6942928224; www.eftalouolive grove.com/lelas_studios.htm; studios from €40; ❄ ᯤ) Two handsome studios are set in a courtyard of roses and geraniums. Each comes with a fully outfitted kitchen and sunset sea views from a relaxing stone verandah.

★**Nassos Guest House** GUESTHOUSE €
(☑ 6942046279; www.nassosguesthouse.com; d/ tr without bathroom from €30/40; ᯤ) Head up to the Old Town's only blue house to reach this former Turkish mansion. It has a small enclosed garden and a homey atmosphere throughout. There are seven rooms and two communal kitchens, along with two full bathrooms, one on each floor. Friendly Dutch manager Tom runs a refugee relief project of his own and seeks volunteers.

Nadia Apartments & Studios PENSION €
(☑ 22530 71345; www.apartments-molivos.com; Molyvos; d/tr €43/60; ❄ ᯤ) On the road to Sikamenea and a short walk from the Old Town, these large motel-styled rooms surrounding an expansive shady courtyard are owned by the humorous Nadia. Her trademark cakes and teasing are complimentary.

Schoolmistress with the Golden Eyes PENSION €
(☑ 22530 71390; www.molivos.gr; r €40) With a name that refers to the mysterious protagonist from a book by Stratis Myrivilis, this pension has a surprisingly hipster lumberjack owner, who will readily explain that the author actually lived at these premises. Clean and simple, the rooms come with breathtaking views of St Panteleimonas Church and the bay.

The unsigned place is located in Kastro (Castle) St, above the church and next to a grocery shop. Carrying heavy luggage up the hill can be a challenge.

Sea Horse Hotel HOTEL €€
(☑ 22530 71630; www.seahorse-hotel.com; s/d/tr incl breakfast from €50/60/80; ℗ ❄ ᯤ) In the heart of the port area, you'll find modern and comfortable rooms, all with balconies overlooking the harbour, along with the family's restaurant and travel agency. Three family-friendly studios have kitchenettes with partial sea views.

Eating

★**Betty's** TAVERNA €
(☑ 22530 71421; 17 Noemvriou; mains €8; ⊙ 8.30am-11pm) This restored Turkish pasha's residence on the upper street, overlooking the harbour below, offers a tasty variety of excellent *mayirefta* dishes such as *mousakas* (meat or veggie), baked fish, lamb souvlaki and *kotiropitakia* (small cheese pies), plus tasty breakfast specials. Betty also has two spacious and well-appointed studio apartments occupying a quiet and shady corner near the restaurant.

★**Blue Fox** DESSERTS €
(☑ 22530 72347; Agora; desserts €1-4; ⊙ breakfast, lunch & dinner) Turkish-styled *cezve* coffee, delicious cream cakes and traditional Greek desserts, such as baklava and *kataïfi,* are served on a terrace with bay views that will take your breath away. The place looks so immaculately retro that it's hard to believe it is actually brand new.

To Hani TAVERNA €
(☑ 22530 71618; Agora; mains €7-11; ⊙ lunch & dinner) Snappy family taverna in the busy *agora* (market) above the waterfront. Great

for well-priced fresh fish and grills, and stellar views of the sea.

Marjoran   MEDITERRANEAN €€
(☑ 6948830700; mains €9-20; ☉ lunch & dinner)
Lovely location, perched slightly above the main road along the seafront. This is one of the town's few upmarket eateries, with a Mediterranean menu of well-prepared pasta, meat and veggie dishes. Service and atmosphere excel.

🍸 Drinking & Nightlife

⭐ **Molly's Bar**   BAR
(☑ 22530 71772; ☉ 6pm-late; 🛜) With its painted blue stars, beaded curtains and bottles of Guinness, this whimsical British-run bar on the harbour waterfront's far eastern side is always in shipshape condition. Molly's caters to a lively local, international and expat crowd. The small balcony is perfect at sunset.

Conga's   BAR
Rocking beach bar with music by day, dancing by night, burgers, cocktails, smoothies and breakfast the next morning.

ℹ️ Information

There's a reliable ATM at the National Bank.

Com.travel (☑ 22530 71900; www.comtravel.gr) Efficient full-service agency in a converted olive-oil factory on the main road.

Faonas Travel Agency (☑ 22530 71630; tekes@otenet.gr) Adjacent to the Sea Horse Hotel, this helpful agency handles trips to Turkey, along with boat and land excursions around Lesvos.

Lesvorama (☑ 22530 72291; www.lesvorama.gr; ☉ 9am-10pm) Travel agency specialising in Lesvos excursions and sightseeing trips.

Medical Centre (☑ 22530 71333; Agora)

Molyvos Tourism Association (☑ 22510 71990; Agora; ☉ 8am-3pm) Tourist office on upper Agora, near the pharmacy.

Post Office (Kastrou; ☉ 7.30am-2pm)

Western Lesvos

Western Lesvos was formed by massive, primeval volcanic eruptions that fossilised trees and all other living things, making it an intriguing site for prehistoric-treasure hunters. Its striking, bare landscape, broken only by craggy boulders and the occasional olive tree, is dramatically different to that in the rest of Lesvos. Heading far to the southwest, however, a grassier landscape emerges, leading to the coastal village of Skala Eresou, birthplace of one of Greece's most famous lyric poets, Sappho, who was dubbed the 10th muse by Plato.

Heading west from Skala Kallonis towards Sigri, a stark and ancient volcanic landscape awaits, home to the scattered remains of a **petrified forest** (☑ 22510 47033; www.petrifiedforest.gr; ☉ park 8am-4pm Tue-Sun Jul-Sep, museum 9.30am-5.30pm Jul-Sep, 9am-5pm Tue-Sun Oct-Jun). A fascinating and rare monument of geological heritage, the forest is a product of intense volcanic activity in the northern Aegean during the Miocene period. Sadly, the main visitors' area in the centre of this Unesco-nominated geopark was off limits at the time of research, due to acute underfunding. Check its current status with the **museum** (☑ 22530 54434; www.lesvosmuseum.gr; €5; ☉ 9am-6pm Jul-Sep, 8.30am-4.30pm Oct-Jun; 🅿️ ♿) in Sigri, which has a little patch of the forest in its premises.

BIRDER TIPS

Just south of agricultural Kalloni, coastal **Skala Kallonis** turns from sleepy fishing village to birdwatching mecca every spring and autumn. During the spring migration, unrivalled across Europe, Lesvos' wetland reserves become home to more than 130 species of bird, from flamingos and raptors to woodpeckers and marsh sandpipers. It's a spectacular show that has grabbed the attention of European birdwatchers, who flock to the island during the peak viewing season of mid-April to mid-May, and again from mid-September to October. Skala Kallonis shares the enthusiasm, with the Pasiphae Hotel (p444) serving as an unofficial centre, where birdwatchers gather to compare notes (or brag) at the lobby bar. Bring your binoculars.

If you can't tell the difference between a blue-eyed hawker dragonfly and a crested grebe, pick up Steve Dudley's *A Birdwatching Guide to Lesvos*. Steve leads birdwatching tours around the island. There are also 50 species of butterfly and dragonfly flitting about, as well as myriad marsh frogs filling the air with their croaky crooning.

Sleepy Sigri is a fishing port, with narrow streets lined with pretty whitewashed houses descending towards an impressive Ottoman castle. The village has beautiful sea views, especially at sunset, and there are idyllic, little-visited beaches just southwest.

Coming back from Sigri, stop for a lunch break or coffee at Andissa, a jovial, rustic village of narrow streets kept cool by the two enormous plane trees that stand over its square. Listen to the crickets and the banter of old-timers over a Greek coffee or frappé. Don't leave before trying the 'sweet spoons' at To Kati Allo.

Sleeping & Eating

Pasiphae Hotel   HOTEL €
(☑ 22530 23212; www.pasiphaehotel.com; Skala Kollonis; s/d incl breakfast from €40/45; P ✳ @ 🛜 🗷) A well-managed and welcoming hotel in a shady setting at Skala Kollonis, about 300m from the sea and village square. It's a favourite for returning visitors, including the birdwatchers who gather at the lobby bar to compare notes in spring and autumn. Managed by the informative Vasillis Vogiatzis, with exceptional service and spotless rooms.

To Kati Allo   CAFE
(Something Else; Andissa) Sweet in every sense of the word, this cafe in the main square of Andissa is a wonderful place to stop for a cup of Greek coffee with a spoon sweet.

Skala Eresou   Σκάλα Ερεσού
POP 1560

Skala Eresou is part traditional fishing village, part laid-back bohemian beach town, and part lesbian mecca, especially during September when a lively two-week festival honours the great lyrical poet Sappho, born here in 630 BC. The small seaside community has an easygoing, end-of-the-road ambience, with little cafes and tavernas hugging the shore and wispy tamarisk trees swaying in the breeze.

◉ Sights

Near the town market, the remains of the early Christian Basilica of Agios Andreas include partially intact 5th-century mosaics.

Eresos Archaeological Museum   MUSEUM
(€2; ⊘ 8.30am-3pm Tue-Sun) 𝗙𝗥𝗘𝗘 A small museum with irregular hours, but the outside (and fenced) mosaics are of great interest. The museum is located on a quiet street in the southeast part of the village, two blocks away from the sea.

Sleeping

★ Hotel Kyma   GUESTHOUSE €
(☑ 22530 53555; Skala Eresou; d €45; ✳ 🛜) You can almost plunge into the deep blue sea from your private balcony at this lovely guesthouse perched above the narrow beach at the eastern edge of Skala Eresou. Rooms are simple yet stylish, and sunset views are to die for.

Hotel Gallini   HOTEL €
(☑ 22530 53138; www.hotel-galinos.gr; Alkaiou; s/d incl breakfast from €35/45; P ✳ 🛜) This budget gem, about 80m back from the waterfront, has tile floors and small balconies overlooking the hillside. Breakfast, with homemade jams and cheeses, is served on the flowery verandah.

INTERNATIONAL ERESSOS WOMEN'S FESTIVAL

The International Eressos Women's Festival (☑ 22530 52130; www.womensfestival. eu; Skala Eresou; tickets €30-65; ⊘ Sep), with a local atmosphere, involves two weeks of partying. Activities range from live music, open-air cinema, poetry and Greek dancing to beach volleyball, water sports, yoga and meditation, all in a gay-friendly atmosphere under the sun and stars.

Highlights include an LGBT film festival, live Greek, Turkish and Mediterranean folk music, 4WD safaris, an alternative fashion show (featuring festival participants), photography workshops and tattooing demonstrations. Live performances cover comedy and spoken word to burlesque and rock and roll.

The crystal waters offer swimming near cocktail bars or, for those who prefer things clothing-optional, a beach further on. For avid walkers and hikers, the area is threaded with inland and coastal routes. Nearby there are also thermal spas, archaeological remains, water sports, boat trips, birdwatching excursions and mountain biking.

Aumkara Apartments
APARTMENT €

(☑ 6948131032, 22530 53190; www.aumkara.eu; Skala Eresou; d/tr/q from €35/60/80; P ❄ 🛜) Smart and spotless apartments near the centre of the village, managed by the welcoming Maria and her crew. Self-caterers will like the handy kitchenettes, and rooms range from small studios to two-bedroom apartments. About 50m from the beach.

Heliotopos
APARTMENT €

(☑ 6948510527; www.heliotoposeressos.gr; apt €55-70; P ❄ 🛜) A leisurely 15-minute walk from the village, this flowery garden lodging features five studios and three two-bedroom apartments, all with full kitchens. Free bikes are available for pedalling around.

Sappho the Eresia
HOTEL €€

(Sappho Hotel; ☑ 22530 53233; www.sappho-hotel.com; waterfront; s/d/tr €45/70/85; P ❄ 🛜) The friendly 18-room Sappho is what passes for a big hotel in laid-back Skala Eresou. Its modest position on the quieter west end of the beach is appealing, as are its overhead fans and an easygoing cafe-bar. The best rooms overlook the sea and the island of Psara. Breakfast is available for €8.

🍴 Eating

Skala Eresou's restaurants and bars line the beach, as do its tamarisk trees. Fresh fish is a speciality. Look for the hanging squid and octopus. On clear days Chios emerges on the horizon.

⭐ Soulatso
SEAFOOD €

(fish €6-12; ☉ lunch & dinner) This busy beachfront *ouzerie*-taverna along the boardwalk has a large outdoor patio and specialises in fresh fish, reasonably priced by the kilo; it's also known for its excellent mezedhes. Good service, ample portions and worthy wines.

Sam's Café-Restaurant
TAVERNA €

(Eresos; mains €6.50-9; ☉ lunch & dinner) Don't let the five-minute drive from Skala Eresou up to little Eresos keep you from trying this excellent Lebanese-Greek patio taverna for a taste of Sam and Niki's excellent home cooking.

Taverna Karavogiannos
TAVERNA €

(mains €6-12; ☉ lunch & dinner) A fine seaside taverna overlooking the beach along the boardwalk, with fresh fish, grills, several veggie dishes (such as *horta*) and a variety of salads.

SAPPHO: ANCIENT POET, MODERN VOICE

The classical Greek poet Sappho is renowned for her lyrical verse. Her words speak of passion and love for both sexes, but her emotion is balanced by clarity of language and a simple style. Though only fragments of her work remain, we do know that she married, had a daughter and was exiled for a period to Sicily, most likely for her political affiliation. Her surviving poems and love songs seem to have been addressed to an inner circle of female devotees. She was certainly an early advocate for women's voices, and hers continues to resonate.

🍸 Drinking & Nightlife

Skala Eresou's low-key nightlife consists of a contiguous series of small cafe-bars strung along the eastern end of the short waterfront.

⭐ Parasol
BAR

(☑ 22530 52050; ☉ 9am-2am) With its orange lanterns and super-eclectic music mix, little Parasol does cocktails to match its South Seas decor. As the day rolls on, Christos and Anastasia's made-to-order breakfasts and cappuccinos give way to lunch specials, fresh juices, noodles and handmade pizza.

⭐ Portokali
BAR

(Eresos) Tiny and convivial cafe-bar 3km up the hill in Eresos, and the village favourite for coffee and conversation, sweets and *tsipouro*.

Notia Jazz Bar
BAR

(Plateia Anthis) Come for the drinks and stay for the tunes at this hip music bar. There's live jazz on summer weekends. Good cocktails, Greek wine, draught beer, plus Miles and Monk.

🛍 Shopping

Thalassaki
ARTS & CRAFTS

(☑ 6973525421; ☉ 11am-11pm) Despina Iossifelli makes the handmade ceramics and jewellery at this bright and inviting waterfront gift shop.

Leather Workshop   FASHION & ACCESSORIES
Check out the old sewing machines at this friendly little leather and accessories shop. In his spare time, owner Kiriakos teaches kung fu to the village kids. It's located on the main road, a short walk from the square.

❶ Information

Full-service **Sappho Travel** (☑ 22530 52130; www.sapphotravel.com) arranges car hire, accommodation and provides information about the **International Eressos Women's Festival** (p444).
Doctor (☑ 22530 53947; ⊘ 24hr)
Pharmacy (☑ 22530 53844)

Southern Lesvos

Interspersed groves of olive and pine trees mark southern Lesvos, from the flanks of **Mt Olympus** (968m), the area's highest peak, right down to the sea, where the best beaches lie. This is a hot, intensely agricultural place where the vital olive oil, wine and ouzo industries overshadow tourism.

◉ Sights

Just south of the Mytilini–Polyhnitos road, **Agiasos** is the first point of interest. On the northern side of Mt Olympus, it's a quirky, well-kept, traditional hamlet of narrow cobbled streets where fishers sell their morning catch from the back of old pick-up trucks; village elders sip Greek coffee in the local *kafeneia* (coffee houses); and cheese-makers and ceramic artisans hawk their wares. It's a relaxing, leafy place, and boasts the exceptional **Church of the Panagia Vrefokratousa**.

The road south along the western shore of the Gulf of Gera reaches **Plomari**, the centre of Lesvos' ouzo industry. It's an attractive, if busy, seaside village with a large, palm-lined square and waterfront tavernas.

The popular beach settlement of **Agios Isidoros**, 3km east, absorbs most of Plomari's summertime guests. **Tarti**, a bit further east, is less crowded. West of Plomari, **Melinda** is a tranquil fishing village with a beach, tavernas and domatia.

From Melinda, the road less taken to the beach resort of **Vatera** passes through tranquil mountain villages, richly forested hills and steep gorges. Driving north, you'll pass the picturesque villages of **Paleohori**, **Akrassi** and **Ambeliko**, from where a signposted, rental-car-friendly dirt road descends through serene olive and pine forests with great views to the coast. The total driving time from Melinda to Vatera is about an hour.

Despite its 10km-long sandy beach, Vatera remains a low-key getaway destination, with only a few small hotels and domatia operating, and even fewer bars.

On its western edge, at **Cape Agios Fokas**, the sparse ruins of an ancient **Temple of Dionysos** occupy a headland overlooking the sea. In the cove between the beach and the cape, evidence indicates an ancient military encampment. Indeed, some historians believe this is the place Homer was referring to in his epic poem 'Iliad' as the resting point for Greek armies besieging Troy.

Vatera's ancient history includes fossils dating back 5.5 million years, including remains of a tortoise as big as a Volkswagen, and fossils of a gigantic horse and gazelle. The inviting **Vrisa Natural History Museum** (☑ 22520 61890; €1; ⊘ 9am-9pm Jun-Sep, 9.30am-3.30pm Wed-Sun Oct-May) in nearby **Vryssa** displays these and other significant remains.

About 5km northwest of Polyhnitos, the little fishing port of **Skala Polyhnitou** lies on the Gulf of Kalloni, where caïques bob at the docks and fishers untangle their nets. It's great for low-key seafood dinners at sunset. If you want lower-key yet, head 6km west to the seaside village of **Nifidha**.

Varvagianni Ouzo Museum   MUSEUM
(☑ 22520 32741; www.barbayanni-ouzo.com; Plomari; ⊘ 9am-4pm Mon-Fri Apr-Oct, 10am-2pm Mon-Fri Nov-Mar, by appointment Sat & Sun) **FREE**
Plomari is ouzo central for Greece. This museum, where the family has made ouzo for five generations, gives you the chance to tour its copper distillery and compare different ouzo tastes. When sampling ouzo, look for '100%' written on the label, indicating the quality of the distillate.

Ouzo Plomariou   MUSEUM
(Arvaniti Isidorou; ☑ 22520 31450; www.theworldof ouzo.gr; Kampos Plagias; €2; ⊘ 10am-3pm Mon-Sat, 9am-2pm Sun May-Oct) Up the main road from Agios Isidoros, this famous distillery offers tours and tastings.

Vrana Olive-Press Museum   MUSEUM
(☑ 22510 82007; Papados; €1; ⊘ 9am-7pm Tue-Sun) Modestly tucked away in the village of Papados, between Mytilini and south-coast Plomari, the little Vrana Olive-Press Museum

showcases 19th-century steam-powered presses and vintage paintings of a bygone era. It also occupies a bit of Greek literary history – it was built by Nicholas Vranas, grandfather of Greek Nobel Prize–winning poet Odysseus Elytis.

🏃 Activities

Hikers here can enjoy southern Lesvos' olive trails, which comprise paths and old local roads threading inland from Plomari and Melinda. The Melinda–Paleohori trail (1.2km, 30 minutes) follows the Selandas River for 200m before ascending to Paleohori, passing a spring with potable water along the way. The trail ends at the village's olive press.

Another appealing trail from Melinda leads to Panagia Kryfti, a cave church near a hot spring (built for two), and the nearby Drota Beach; or take the Paleohori–Rahidi trail (1km, 30 minutes), which is paved with white stone and passes springs and vineyards. Rahidi, which was only connected to electricity in 2001, has charming old houses and a coffee house.

Other, more complicated hiking trail can get you directly from Melinda to Vatera; consult the EOT (p440) or the tourist office (p440), both in Mytilini Town.

Agricultural Polyhnitos, 10km north of Vatera on the road to Mytilini Town, is known for its two nearby hot springs, among the hottest in Europe. The more popular of the two, the Hot Springs of Polyhnitos (Polyhnitos Spa; ☑ 22520 41229, 6977592991; www.hotsprings.gr; €4; ☺ 2-8pm Mon-Sat, 11am-8pm Sun), await just 1.5km east of the village.

🛏 Sleeping

★ Hotel Vatera Beach   HOTEL €
(☑ 22520 61212; www.vaterabeach.com; Vatera Beach; s/d incl breakfast from €35/50; 🅿 ❄ @ 🛜) This peaceful beachfront hotel regards its guests, many of whom return annually, as old friends. The congenial brother-and-sister team of Takis and Jeannie Ballis provides great service and comfortable rooms, just opposite the beach. The hotel's excellent restaurant uses mostly local and organic ingredients to supply the small daily menu.

Pano Sto Kyma   PENSION €
(☑ 22520 33160, 6942906124; www.panostokyma. gr; Agios Isidoros; studios from €42) Eleven sparkling-clean rooms come with wooden furniture painted in the lightest shade of blue – the same colour as the sea, just 30m from the front door. No breakfast is served, but village cafes open early and rooms come with kitchenettes.

🍴 Eating

Psarotaverna O Stratos   SEAFOOD €
(Skala Polyhnitou; fish €6-9; ☺ 10am-1am) Look for the fishing boats moored beside this popular fish taverna on Skala Polyhnitou's waterfront. Enjoy inexpensive fresh seafood, plus salads such as *vlita* (wild greens) and tasty mezedhes such as *taramasalata*.

★ Sunset   GREEK €€
(☑ 22520 32740; Agios Isidoros; mains €8-13; ☺ noon-1am) Perched above the main road, this is not your average taverna but a fully fledged restaurant, with attentive service and a very competent chef-manager, Dimitris, whose advice about what's best on the day should be taken seriously. The lamb chops alone are worth the drive. Beautiful sunsets are free of charge.

LIMNOS   ΛΗΜΝΟΣ

POP 16,700

Isolated Limnos, alone in the northeastern Aegean save for neighbouring Agios Efstratios, appeals to those looking for Greek island life that's relatively unaffected by modern tourism. Limnos' capital, Myrina, has retained its classic Greek fishing-harbour feel, while a grand Genoese castle provides a dramatic backdrop.

The island's eastern lakes are visited by spectacular flocks of flamingos and its central plain is filled with spring wildflowers. Superb sandy beaches lie near the capital and in more distant corners of the island.

ℹ Getting There & Away

AIR

The airport is 22km east of Myrina, and has offices for Aegean Air (www.aegeanair.com), Sky Express (www.skyexpress.gr) and Astra Airlines (www.astra-airlines.gr). Taxis to/from Myrina cost about €25.

BOAT

Ferries depart the New Port in Myrina. Buy tickets at Atzamis Travel (p450), Petrides Travel (p450), or Aegean Travel (☑ 22540 25936; www.aegeantravel.eu; waterfront), all in Myrina.

Limnos

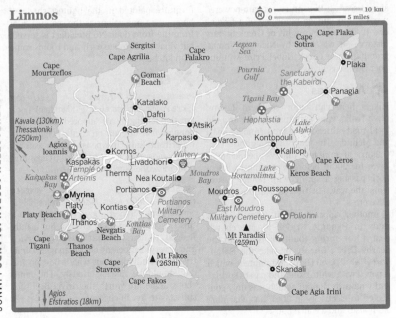

0   10 km
0   5 miles

Cape Plaka
Cape Sotira
Sergitsi
Cape Agrilia
Cape Falakro
Aegean Sea
Plaka
Cape Mourtzeflos
Gomati Beach
Pournia Gulf
Sanctuary of the Kabeiroi
Panagia
Katalako
Tigani Bay
Dafni
Hephaistia
Kavala (130km); Thessaloniki (250km)
Sardes
Atsiki
Lake Alyki
Karpasi
Varos
Kontopouli
Agios Ioannis
Kornos
Kalliopi
Cape Keros
Kaspakas
Livadohori
Winery
Temple of Artemis
Therma
Nea Koutali
Moudros Bay
Lake Hortarolimni
Keros Beach
Kaspakas Bay
Portianos
Moudros
Roussopouli
Myrina
Platy
Kontias
Portianos Military Cemetery
East Moudros Military Cemetery
Poliohni
Platy Beach
Thanos
Nevgatis Beach
Kontias Bay
Mt Paradisi (259m)
Cape Tigani
Thanos Beach
Cape Stavros
Mt Fakos (263m)
Fisini
Skandali
Cape Fakos
Agios Efstratios (18km)
Cape Agia Irini

ℹ Getting Around

BUS

Limnos' bus service has one purpose: to bring villagers to town for their morning shopping and to get them home by lunch. From Myrina, buses serve Moudros, via the airport (€3, 30 minutes, five daily), with the last return bus leaving at 12.15pm. However, buses do not coordinate with flight departures. For other destinations around the island, buses are not particularly useful.

Myrina's **bus station** (☑22540 22464; Plateia Eleftheriou Venizelou) displays schedules – handwritten in Greek to complicate matters.

CAR & MOTORCYCLE

Petrides Travel (p450), **Holiday Car Rental** (☑22540 23280; Myrina) and **Aegean Travel** (p447), all located near the waterfront in Myrina, rent cars from €30 per day. Motorcycle-hire outlets are on Kyda-Karatza.

TAXI

There's a **taxi rank** (☑22540 23820; Myrina) on Myrina's central square.

Myrina   Μύρινα

POP 5110

Backed by volcanic rock and a craggy Genoese castle, Limnos' capital is strikingly old-fashioned. Here you'll see fishers sipping Greek coffee while unfolding their nets, and colourful caïques dotting the harbour.

In summer Myrina comes to life, with shops selling traditional foods, handicrafts and more in its bustling *agora*. Whitewashed stone houses, old-fashioned barber shops and *kafeneia* (coffee houses), sitting among weather-worn neoclassical mansions, create a relaxed old-world charm.

The town, like Limnos in general, is mostly frequented by Greek tourists, lending a distinct Hellenic flavour to the waterfront nightlife. Above the town, on the castle's overgrown slopes, it's a different story: here, shy, fleet-footed deer dart about after dark, and even venture down to the *agora* on winter nights.

◉ Sights & Activities

Castle of Myrina   CASTLE

FREE Myrina's lonely hilltop *kastro* dates from the 13th century and occupies a headland that divides the town from its popular beach. The ruins of the Venetian-built fortress are imposing, but deserted, except for the deer that roam here freely. It's worth the 20- to 25-minute walk up the hill for the sea views alone, which extend to Mt Athos and, come evening, the twinkling cafe lights below.

Archaeological Museum   MUSEUM
(☑ 22540 22990; €2; ⏰ 8.30am-3pm Tue-Sun)
Myrina's fine neoclassical mansion-museum
overlooks Romeïkos Gialos Beach and contains 8th- and 7th-century-BC finds from
Limnos' three major sites of: Poliohni, the
Sanctuary of the Kabeiroi and Hephaistia.
Worth seeing are the earthenware lamp
statuettes of sirens, along with details of
the mandated Greek–Turkish population
exchange of 1923.

Boat & Bus Tours
From June to September, travel agencies
organise round-the-island sightseeing tours
by boat (half-/full day €20/25) and bus (full
day €20). Boat tours stop for lunch and
swimming, and take in the archaeological
sites, usually ending at sunset. Bus tours can
additionally visit the military cemeteries at
Moudros and Portianos. Contact Petrides
Travel (p450) or Atzamis Travel (p450).

🏖 Beaches
The town's beaches include the wide and
sandy **Rea Maditos**, and the superior
Romeïkos Gialos, beyond the harbour;
further on, the beach becomes **Riha Nera**
(Shallow Water), named for its gently shelving sea floor. Waterfront cafes and restaurants stay open late through summer.

Five minutes south, on the road towards
Thanos Beach, **Platy Beach** is a shallow,
sandy crescent with cantinas, tavernas and
a few lodgings.

🛏 Sleeping

Vicky Studios   APARTMENT €
(☑ 22540 22137; www.vickystudios.com; Maroulas
5; studios from €30; P ✳ 🛜) This immaculate
and friendly budget gem is a five-minute
walk from shops and the beach at Riha Nera.
Rooms face a lovely garden and feature

kitchenettes, desks and fridges. Also has
accommodation in Platy.

Apollo Pavilion   HOTEL €
(☑ 22540 23712; www.apollopavilion.gr; Garoufal-
lidhou; d/tr incl breakfast from €52/60; P ✳ 🛜)
Tucked behind the port in a charming neoclassical house, these large high-ceilinged
rooms come with kitchenettes and balconies. Located near the police station, 150m
above the port.

Hotel Lemnos   HOTEL €
(☑ 22540 22153; www.lemnoshotel.com; s/d/tr
from €40/45/60; ✳ 🛜) The middle-of-the-
waterfront Lemnos, under new management, is a decent budget choice with friendly
staff and modern, if smallish, rooms, plus
balconies overlooking the harbour or castle.

To Arhontiko   BOUTIQUE HOTEL €€
(☑ 22540 29800; www.arxontikohotel.gr; cnr
Sahtouri & Filellinon; r from €60; P ✳ 🛜) This
restored mansion (and Myrina's first hotel)
dating from 1851 impresses with swanky
boutique rooms, fireplaces, helpful staff,
a cosy bar, classic charm throughout and
a classic Greek breakfast to last the day.
It's on a quiet alleyway near the *plateia* of
Romeïkos Gialos.

🍴 Eating

⭐ Ouzeri To 11   SEAFOOD €
(Glinou 6; seafood mezedhes €6-12; ⏰ noon-
midnight) This unassuming little *ouzerie* by
the bus depot is the local favourite for seafood. From *kydonia* (mussels with garlic
and Venus clams) to sea urchins, crayfish
and more, 'To *En*-dheka' (as it's pronounced)
serves all the stranger stuff, along with plenty
of ouzo to help you forget what you're eating.

To Limanaki   TAVERNA €
(mains €7-15; ⏰ lunch & dinner) Near the end
of the waterfront, To Limanaki serves up

DOMESTIC FLIGHTS FROM LIMNOS

DESTINATION	DURATION	FARE (€)	FREQUENCY
Athens	50min	98	1 daily
Chios	1½hr	56	2 weekly
Ikaria	45min	43	6 weekly
Lesvos	40min	69	3 weekly
Rhodes	3hr	88	5 weekly
Samos	2hr	69	4 weekly
Thessaloniki	45min	71	5 weekly

well-priced fresh seafood and late-night meat grills, along with cheery service and good Limnos wine.

O Platanos Restaurant TAVERNA €
(Kyda-Karatza; mains €5-8) Homemade pasta, good Limni wine and excellent *mayirefta* dishes, with an emphasis on meat, are served at this iconic place under two majestic plane trees, halfway along the *agora's* main street.

Drinking & Nightlife

Manos Bar BAR
(🗹6932411134; Argonafton 20; ⊗9am-2am) Lively open-air beach bar at Riha Nera, open all day and most of the night, with decent drinks and an all-ages clientele.

Karagiozis BAR
(Romeïkos Gialos; ⊗9am-5am) On a leafy terrace near the sea, Karagiozis morphs from snazzy frappé-cafe by day to a drink-till-you-drop bar under the stars. Sturdy, fair-priced drinks.

ℹ Information

There are three ATMs around Myrina's central square, Plateia Eleftheriou Venizelou, which sits midway along the main thoroughfare of Kyda-Karatza (aka the *agora*). Another ATM is on the quay.

Atzamis Travel (🗹22540 25690; atzamisk@ otenet.gr; waterfront) Arranges ferry and air tickets, accommodation, excursions and bicycle rentals. Can arrange visits to the wetlands on Limnos' east coast.

Information kiosk (Old Port; ⊗hours vary) Very useful brochures, plane and ferry schedules as well as helpful English-speaking staff. Opposite the main pier in the Old Port.

Karaiskaki Travel (🗹22540 22900, 22540 22460; hrissa5a@otenet.gr; Myrina waterfront) Specialises in trips to Agios Efstratios island. Formerly known as Myrina Travel.

Petrides Travel (🗹22540 22039; www. petridestravel.gr; Kyda-Karatza 116) Helpful and informed staff arranges island sightseeing tours, boat trips, car hire, transfers and accommodation.

Police Station (🗹22540 22200; Nikolaou Garoufallidou)

Port Police (🗹22540 22225)

Post Office (Nikolaou Garoufallidou; ⊗7.30am-2pm)

Pravlis Travel (🗹22540 24617; www.pravlis. gr) Efficient and helpful full-service agency at the port.

Western Limnos

A densely populated area around Myrina boasts a few nice beaches and plenty of accommodation – especially at **Platy**, a scenic bay 3km south of the capital. The island's main road heads southeast, passing villages with quirky museums and interesting historic sites. North of Myrina, the road left after Kaspakas village accesses the appealing **Agios Ioannis Beach**, set nicely beneath an overhanging volcanic slab. Hidden away in the mountainous hinterland, a cluster of villages around Sardes serve as a convenient pit stop on the way to the seldom visited sand dunes of **Gomati Bay** on the northern coast.

Immediately south of Myrina, **Plati** is a long sandy beach with plenty of decent hotels, but virtually no restaurants. The nearest are up the hill at Plati village or in Myrina.

Tucked into a giant rock cavity on top of a hill, the **Church of Panagia Kakaviotissa** is totally worth the 20-minute hike from the village of Thanos, 4km south of Myrina. Further along the southwest coast, Kontias is a charming village of windmills and stone houses, and home to the celebrated **Kontias Gallery of Modern Balkan Art**. Sadly closed at the time of research, it might be open when you visit, so ask locally.

From Kontias, the main road continues east to the village of **Portianou**. The chair Winston Churchill sat on while commanding the Allied offensive at Gallipoli is the most venerated item at the village's lovely **Folklore Museum** (🗹22543 50000; www. laografiko-limnos.gr; ⊗hours vary). Victims of the man's strategic gaffes lie at **Portianos Military Cemetery** nearby. Four kilometres away, the **Old Russian Cemetery** at Cape Punda is the final resting place for more than 300 White Russians; they were interned on the islands by Allied troops, living in terrible conditions and dying of hunger and disease.

The road north leads to a cluster of mountain villages around **Sardes**, which boasts an outstanding taverna. Beyond them, lies a desolate coast famous for its **dunes**, an unusual sight for Greek islands.

North of Myrina, the road left after **Kaspakas** village accesses the appealing **Agios Ioannis Beach**, with a few tavernas and beach houses set nicely beneath an overhanging volcanic slab.

Sleeping & Eating

Panorama Plati GUESTHOUSE €
(☑ 6947718755, 22540 24118; www.panorama
plati.com; Plati Beach; studios from €40; ❋ 🐾)
Standing on a hillock, 500m away from Plati
Beach, these tidy and well-equipped studios
complete with kitchens indeed offer panoramic views of the scenic bay below. The
charming host goes out of her way to help.

Villa Victoria APARTMENT €€
(☑ 6942906120, 22540 29077; www.villa-victoria.
gr; Platy Beach; d/apt €80/100; 🅿 ❋ 🐾 ≋)
These attractive stone buildings are just
metres from the beach, set on a rambling
kid-friendly green with a pool. Rooms have
smart wood and stone motifs, with kitchenettes. Several two-storey apartments can
sleep four.

★ **Mantella Taverna** TAVERNA €
(☑ 22540 61349; Sardes; mains €5-9.50; ☺ lunch
& dinner) A popular and well-managed taverna, 20 minutes' drive from Myrina in the
village of Sardes. Traditional country dishes
include rooster, goat and pork stews, along
with excellent local cheeses and crisp Limni
wines. Although listed as a main course, the
sweet *moustoukoulika* pasta makes a great
calorie-bomb dessert.

Eastern Limnos

Eastern Limnos' flat plateaus are dotted with
wheat fields, small vineyards and sheep.
Limnos' second-largest town, Moudros,
occupies the eastern side of muddy Moudros
Bay, famous for its role as the principal base
for the ill-fated Gallipoli campaign in 1915.
The rugged northeastern coast is sparsely
populated, which was not the case in Trojan
War times when Lemnians founded what's
believed to be Europe's first constituted
democracy. Three large and scenic archaeological sites in the area are related to that
golden age of Limnos. The region also hosts
the Greek Air Force's central command, and
so large parts are off limits to tourists.

Sights

Chapel of Zoodochos Pigi CHURCH
(Kotsinas) This hilltop late-Byzantine church
built next to a holy-water spring wouldn't be
such an outstanding attraction if not for its
scenic observation point with a striking statue
of Maroula, a fierce sword-wielding female
figure looking defiantly in the direction of
nearby Turkey. A local heroine, Maroula is
said to have taken her dying father's sword
during the battle with the Ottomans in 1478.
The site is a short walk from the beach in
Kotsinas.

East Moudros Military Cemetery CEMETERY
(near Moudros) As if taken from the middle
of England, this grassy patch is dotted with
memorials to 800 Anzac and other British
Empire soldiers who died of wounds in a
nearby military hospital and were laid to
rest here, when Limnos served as the headquarters of the ill-fated Gallipoli operation
during WWI. In 1921 the island also served
as an internment camp for thousands of
White Russians, escaping the Red Terror;
around 20 of them are also buried here.

The site is located right outside Moudros,
on the road to Roussopoli and Poliohni.

Poliohni ARCHAEOLOGICAL SITE
(€2; ☺ 8am-3pm Tue-Sun) On the southeast
coast, Poliohni is considered the first prehistoric settlement in the Aegean and –
allegedly – the first example of constituted
democracy in the whole of Europe. It has
the remains of four ancient settlements, the
most significant being a pre-Mycenaean city
that predated Troy VI (1800–1275 BC). The
site, with its tiny museum, is fascinating, but
remains are few.

**Sanctuary of
the Kabeiroi** ARCHAEOLOGICAL SITE
(Ta Kaviria; €2; ☺ 8am-3pm Tue-Sun) A beautifully desolate clifftop site, the Sanctuary
of the Kabeiroi lies at the northern tip of
remote Tigani Bay. The worship of the
Kabeiroi gods here actually predates that
which took place on nearby Samothraki. The
major attraction is a Hellenistic **sanctuary** with 11 partial columns.

A trail leads down the cliff to the legendary **Cave of Philoctetes**, supposedly where
the eponymous Trojan War hero was abandoned while his gangrenous, snake-bitten
leg healed. A marked path from the site
leads to the sea cave.

Hephaistia ARCHAEOLOGICAL SITE
(Ta Ifestia; €2; ☺ 8am-3pm Tue-Sun) Reconstructed and occasionally serving its original purpose after 2500 years of oblivion,
this late-5th-century-BC theatre sits on the
site of an earlier, Mycenaean-age city. As the
story goes, Hephaistia is where Hephaestus,
god of fire and metallurgy, was hurled down
from Mt Olympus by Zeus.

🛏 Sleeping & Eating

Varos Village RESORT €€

(Varos; ☎22540 31728; www.varosvillage.com; ste & houses from €85; ❄ 🤶 ✖) This unusual resort has taken over a semi-abandoned hamlet, with suites located in windmills in the reception/pool area and restored village houses scattered around the village. Although self-sufficient, the place is quite isolated, with the nearest beach and tavernas at Kotsinas, 2km away. It's best to rent a car if you do chose to stay here.

Galazio Limani TAVERNA €

(☎22540 71041; Moudros; mains €7-10; ⊗ breakfast, lunch & dinner) The large taverna on the seafront in Moudros cooks outstanding fish soup in addition to Aegean seafood standards.

Giannakaros GREEK €

(☎22540 41744; Limanaki Kotsina; mains €6-10; ⊗11am-noon) Popular with visiting Greeks and airbase personnel, this upmarket seafront taverna is heaving at weekends when it roasts a whole lamb or goat. Seafood dishes are excellent any day of the week.

AGIOS EFSTRATIOS
ΑΓΙΟΣ ΕΥΣΤΡΑΤΙΟΣ

POP 370

You can't get any further from holidaying crowds than this little speck of land between Limnos and continental Greece. Abbreviated by locals as 'Aï-Stratis', the island attracts visitors for its isolation, remote beaches and quiet beauty. Here is your chance to plunge into the microcosm of a close-knit island community. For the curious, it is also the place to learn about the country's complicated history, since Agios Efstratios was the place where right-wing governments would exile procommunist intelligentsia until the 1970s. The island's only museum relates that story.

The sparsely populated island has domatia, good seafood tavernas, relaxing hill walks and fine beaches. The main village, also called Agios Efstratios, is often just called 'the village'. Entirely rebuilt after a catastrophic earthquake that virtually flattened it in 1968, it is a serene getaway for those who need to escape from the big noisy world.

History

Archaeological evidence from the island's northeast, opposite Limnos, points to Early Bronze Age (2800–1900 BC) settlements. Later civilisations recognised the island as a strategic central point in the Aegean, and it was colonised frequently, first by the Mycenaeans, then in succession by the Athenians, Romans and, during the Middle Ages, the Byzantine Empire, which was based in Constantinopole (modern-day İstanbul). The island is named from that period for a St Efstratios, who arrived here in 813 as a political exile.

Like the island's namesake saint, political prisoners were exiled here for decades in the early 20th century, especially by the divisive and dictatorial Metaxas regime of the 1930s, and again during the 'time of the colonels', as Greeks refer to the military junta that ruled from 1967–74. Many dissidents and suspected communists were banished to the island, including renowned composer Mikis Theodorakis and poets Kostas Varnalis and Yiannis Ritsos.

◉ Sights & Activities

The 1968 earthquake left little of the old village. A single Byzantine monument has survived: **Agios Vassilios church**, dating from 1727, with a domed basilica.

Just south of the village are the sea caves of **Trypia Spilia**. Agios Efstratios' pristine beaches include the **village beach**, which has dark volcanic sand and warm waters, **Agios Dimitrios beach** (5km south) and **Ftelio beach** (8km south). The latter pair are best reached by local boat, 4WD or motorbike. Enquire with Mr Aris at Taverna Artemonas, near Agios Nikolas church.

Well-worn paths and trails criss-cross the island's meadows, which are covered with daffodils, fennel, thistles, amaranth, blackberries, poplars and willows. On the island's northeast corner, a 2.2km trail explores the hills of Avlakia, passing through a dense **oak forest**. On the east coast, you'll find graceful **sand dunes** at Alonitsi Beach.

On any walk, you're sure to see goats, sheep, cows and horses, which all tend to roam freely on the small island, along with migratory and resident birds, including herons, owls and kingfishers.

Democracy Museum MUSEUM

(☑ 21032 40645) FREE Up the main road from
the port, this little museum tells the story
of Greek left-wingers, mostly urban intellectuals, who were exiled to various Aegean
islands by a succession of pro-Western right-
wing regimes throughout the second part of
the 20th century. Left to their own devices
on a barren island, the prisoners were greatly
helped by generous villagers, who in turn
benefited from the presence of the country's
best doctors and lawyers on the island.

Across the road, Julia Balaska at An-Strati
guesthouse has the key for the museum.

🛏 Sleeping & Eating

An-Strati GUESTHOUSE €

(☑ 6945563325, 22540 93329; balaskajulia2000@
yahoo.gr; d €30-40) English-speaking Julia
Balaska runs this lovely guesthouse, which
has a large common balcony facing the harbour and science-book images of fish adorning the walls.

Taverna Artemonas TAVERNA €

(☑ 22540 93333; ⊙9am-midnight) Traditional
and convivial Greek taverna at the port.

🍷 Drinking & Nightlife

Veranta CAFE

(☑ 22540 93442) The entire male population
of the island seems to converge at this cafe
by the port in the evenings to watch basketball and play backgammon.

ⓘ Getting There & Away

The small *Aeolis* ferry runs between Limnos and
Agios Efstratios five times a week (€8, 1½ hours,
Monday to Saturday). Buy tickets at Karaiskaki
Travel (p450) in Myrina on Limnos. The ferry
leaves Limnos at about 2.30pm, and returns
from Agios Efstratios at 6am, so unless you're
going for dinner, plan on staying at least two
nights. However, weekend day trips (€20) are
available in the summer; contact Petrides Travel
(p450) in Myrina.

There are also four ferries a week from both
mainland Lavrio (€26, eight hours) and Kavala
(€25, seven hours).

SAMOTHRAKI

ΣΑΜΟΘΡΑΚΗ

POP 2860

Overlooked by most island-hoppers, Samothraki sits alone in the northeastern corner of the Aegean, accessible only from the

AUGUST FULL-MOON HIKE

The August full-moon hike to the summit of Mt Fengari (1611m), the highest
peak on the island, is a beloved annual
event organised by the Hellenic Trekking
Association. It sees scores of enthusiastic young hikers climb to an open field
at 1200m on the day of the full moon,
drink in the sight of the peak during a
night-time party, sleep on the mountain
and continue to the summit the next
morning for sunrise. Stragglers are welcome. Enquire at Kafeneio Ta Therma
(p457) in Loutra or Samothraki Travel
(p455) in Kamariotissa.

mainland port of Alexandroupouli. This
lush, forested island boasts one of the most
important archaeological sites in Greece:
the ancient Thracian Sanctuary of the Great
Gods. Also here stands the Aegean's loftiest peak, Mt Fengari (1611m), from where,
according to Homer, Poseidon, god of the
sea, watched the Trojan War unfold.

Samothraki's mountainous interior, filled
with massive oak and plane trees, is ideal
for hiking and mountain biking, and the
island's waterfalls, plunging into deep pools,
provide cool relief on hot summer days.
Remote southeastern beaches are pristine,
while the north offers hot baths at Loutra
(Therma). Inland from the main fishing
port of Kamariotissa lies the former capital,
Hora, bursting with flowers and handsome
homes, all overlooking the distant sea.

ⓘ Getting There & Away

SAOS Lines (www.saos.gr) ferries connect
Samothraki with Alexandroupoli – twice daily
in summer, less frequently out of season,
and vary in price (from €9.60 to €14.50, two
hours). Purchase tickets at the port kiosk.

ⓘ Getting Around

BUS

From Kamariotissa, there are six buses daily to
Hora and Palepoli, five to Profitis Ilias via Alonia
and Lakkoma, and two to Loutra.

CAR & MOTORCYCLE

Kyrkos Rent-a-Car (☑ 6972839231, 25510
41620; Kamariotissa) rents cars and small
Jeeps. Motorcycles and scooters are offered by
Rent-a-Motor-Bike (☑ 25510 41057; Kamar-
iotissa). Both are opposite the ferry quay in
Kamariotissa.

TAXI

One of only three cabbies on the island, friendly **Evdohia Brahiolia Taxi** (📋 6976991270, 6976991271), serves all the popular destinations from Kamariotissa, with the longest trips costing under €20.

Kamariotissa Καμαριώτισσα

POP 960

Samothraki's port, largest town and transport hub, Kamariotissa is home to the island's main services. A nearby pebble beach has bars and decent swimming. While most visitors don't linger here, it's a likeable and attractive port filled with flowers and fish tavernas.

Further south, the 800m-long Pahia Ammos is a superb sandy beach along an 8km winding road from a cluster of serene villages, including Profitis Ilias and Lakkoma. Both of these villages are easily accessible from Kamariotissa and have some of the island's best tavernas.

🛌 Sleeping

Most domatia and hotels are out of town and, unlike many Greek isles, you won't find locals hawking rooms to arriving ferry passengers. Rooms are available at Lakkoma Beach.

Hotel Aeolos   HOTEL €

(📋 25510 41595; d/tr from €45/55; ❄🛜🏊) Up behind Niki Beach Hotel, the comfortable Aeolos stands on a hill overlooking the sea. Front rooms face a swimming pool and garden, while back rooms overlook Mt Fengari.

Niki Beach Hotel   HOTEL €€

(📋 25510 41545; www.nikibeach.gr; s/d/tr incl breakfast €35/55/105; ❄🛜🏊) This handsome and well-managed hotel with large, modern rooms is just opposite the town beach. Balconies face the sea, while flowers and poplar trees fill an interior garden. Owners Elena and Vasillis manage to give it a boutique feel, despite the 37 rooms.

🍴 Eating & Drinking

★ I Synantisi   TAVERNA €

(📋 25510 41308; fish €6-12; ⊙lunch & dinner) Excellent fresh fish and *gavros* – the owner is a spear diver – as well as fine meat dishes such as roasted goat and rice pilaf. The place is cosy and welcoming, with a small open kitchen, and it often serves up *chaslamas*, a Turkish-named dessert unique to Samothraki.

Vrahos   TAVERNA €

(📋 25510 95264; Profitis Ilias; mains €4.50-9; ⊙lunch & dinner) This popular grill house in Profitis Ilias heaves during the weekends when a whole animal is grilled – either a goat or a sheep.

Fournello   ITALIAN €

(mains €5-10; ⊙lunch & dinner) Fournello makes for a nice change of pace, serving good pizza and spaghetti. It's one of the few places where you can dine by the sea. Close to Niki Beach Hotel.

Klimataria Restaurant   TAVERNA €

(mains €6-9; ⊙lunch & dinner) Highly regarded waterfront eatery serving the unusual *gianiotiko*, an oven-baked dish of diced pork, potatoes and egg, along with excellent *mousakas* and other *mayirefta* standbys.

Samothraki

Map of Samothraki. Scale: 0–5 km / 0–2.5 miles. Locations shown include: Alexandroupoli (40km), Paleopoli, Niki Beach, Cape Makrivrahos, Agios Andreas Wetland, Kamariotissa, Ano Kariotes, Kato Kariotes, Sanctuary of the Great Gods, Hora (Samothraki), Alonia, Loutra (Therma), Cape Fonias, Tower of Fonias, Fonias Rock Pools, Ghria Vathra River, Fonias River, Thracian Sea, Isomata, Mnimoria, Mt Fengari (1611m), Xiropotamos, Profitis Ilias, Lakkoma, Aegean Sea, Panagia Kremnniotissa, Pahia Ammos, Vatos Beach, Kremasto Waterfall, Kremasto Nero, Panias Rock Formations, Kipos Beach, Cape Kipos.

Kafeneio Panagiotis Makris CAFE
Voted one of the most traditional coffee shops in Greece. Step into little Panagiotis for a sip of *tsipouro* with saffron, accompanied by mezedhes, of course. No wi-fi now, or ever.

ⓘ Information

Port Police (☏ 25510 41305)
Samothraki Travel (☏ 6984908254, 25510 89444; www.samothrakitravel.gr) Excellent tour and travel operation offering information on lodgings, and outdoor adventures from boating, diving and horse riding to trekking and canyoning.

Hora (Samothraki)
Χώρα (Σαμοθράκη)

Set within a natural fortress of two sheer cliffs, and with a commanding view of the sea, Hora (also called Samothraki) was the obvious choice for the island's capital. In the 10th century the Byzantines built a **castle** on its northwestern peak, though today's substantial remains mostly date from the 15th-century Genoese rule.

Marked by twisting and colourful cobbled streets wreathed in flowers, and vintage traditional houses with terracotta roofs, Hora is perfect for enjoying a leisurely lunch or coffee, and on summer evenings there's easygoing nightlife in the small lanes and rooftop bars.

◎ Sights

Kastro CASTLE
(Hora; ☉ 11am-2pm Wed & Fri-Sun) FREE Freshly converted into a fully fledged tourist sight complete with helpful English-language signs, the picturesque castle was built in 1431–33 by Genovese noble Palamede Gattilusio, who received the island in exchange for assisting the Byzantine emperor in a fratricidal war. Both men's coats-of-arms appear on a marble plaque at the castle entrance. In addition to sweeping views, the ruins feature a large stone cistern used to collect rainwater and a murder hole for people whose company the Italian gentleman didn't enjoy.

🛏 Sleeping & Eating

Hotel Axieros HOTEL €
(☏ 25510 41416, 25510 41294; www.axieros.gr; d/tr/q from €50/60/65; ❄🕾) Friendly and welcoming, with handsomely furnished

ⓘ OUTDOOR ADVENTURE

With its beaches, craggy peaks, lush jungle rivers and waterfalls, Samothraki is ideal for outdoor adventure activities. However, paths are poorly marked and rushing mountain waters can turn torrential, making a good guide essential. Samothraki Travel offers guided trekking (€15) on hard-to-find mountain trails, as well as canyoning (from €40) along 10 spectacular routes. Both are guided by experienced Georgos Andreas, usually in August and September. The same agency offers **diving** trips that include equipment (€50 for two).

traditional rooms featuring well-equipped kitchenettes and views of the village.

Trapeza me Thea CAFE €
(crêpes €4.50-5.50; ☉ all day) Ex-urbanites Elias and Theodora have taken over Hora's old bank building and transformed it into a wonderful coffee shop, with a director's desk turned into a bar. Take a seat on the balcony overlooking the valley below and enjoy your coffee with 'submarine' (sweet mastic paste submerged in water) or a 'spoon sweet'.

O Lefkos Pyrgos SWEETS €
(desserts €4-6; ☉ 9am-late Jul & Aug) The summer-only Lefkos Pyrgos is an excellent, inventive and all-natural sweets shop run by master confectioners Georgios and Dafni. Try lemonade with honey and cinnamon, or Greek yoghurt with bitter almond, along with exotic teas, coffees and mixed drinks.

Café-Ouzeri 1900 TAVERNA €
(mains €3.50-9; ☉ breakfast, lunch & dinner) Start your day at this flower-filled taverna with yoghurt and honey, or sample the house *tzigerosarmades* (goat with onion, dill and spearmint). The large, colourful menu, printed to look like a newspaper, is a take-home memento.

Loutra
Λουτρά

Loutra (also called Therma), 14km east of Kamariotissa near the coast, is Samothraki's most popular place to stay. This relaxing village of plane and horse-chestnut trees, dense greenery and gurgling creeks comes to life at night when people of all ages gather in its outdoor cafes.

⊙ Sights & Activities

Paradeisos Waterfalls   WATERFALL

About 500m past Kafeneion Ta Therma, a lush wooded path (100m) leads to a series of rock pools and waterfalls, the most impressive being 30m in height. This is gorgeous, *Lord of the Rings*–like terrain, where gnarled 600-year-old plane trees covered in moss loom out of fog over a forest floor of giant ferns and brackish boulders. Get ready for an ice-cold dip on a hot summer's day.

Ghria Vathra Canyon   HIKING

Running roughly parallel with the Paradeisos Waterfalls, but further east along the coast road, this lush canyon is known for its shimmering series of rock pools and waterfalls, and is an easy and enjoyable hike-and-splash if going inland from the waterfront road.

Thermal Baths   HOT SPRINGS, BATHHOUSE

(☑ 25513 50800; €4-6; ⊙ 7-10am & 6-9pm Jun-Sep) Loutra village's other name, Therma, refers to its warm, therapeutic, mineral-rich springs, reportedly able to cure everything

---

DON'T MISS

SANCTUARY OF THE GREAT GODS   ΤΟ ΙΕΡΟ ΤΩΝ ΜΕΓΑΛΩΝ ΘΕΩΝ

About 6km northeast of Kamariotissa, the **Sanctuary of the Great Gods** (☑ 25510 41474; €6; ⊙ 8am-3pm) is one of Greece's most mysterious archaeological sites. The Thracians built this temple to their fertility deities around 1000 BC. By the 5th century BC, the secret rites and sacrifices associated with the cult had attracted famous pilgrims, including Egyptian queen Arsinou, Philip II of Macedon (father of Alexander the Great) and Greek historian Herodotus. Remarkably, the sanctuary operated until paganism was forbidden in the 4th century AD.

The principal deity, the fertility goddess Alceros Cybele (Great Mother), was later merged with the Olympian female deities Demeter, Aphrodite and Hecate. Other deities worshipped here were the Great Mother's consort, the virile young Kadmilos (god of the phallus), later integrated with the Olympian god Hermes; and the demonic Kabeiroi twins, Dardanos and Aeton, the sons of Zeus and Leda. Samothraki's great gods were venerated for their immense power – in comparison, the bickering Olympian gods were considered frivolous.

Little is known about what actually transpired here, though archaeological evidence points to two initiations, a lower and a higher. In the first, the great gods were invoked to grant the initiate a spiritual rebirth; in the second, the candidate was absolved of transgressions. This second confessional rite took place at the sacred **Hieron**, whose remaining columns are easily the most photographed ruin of the sanctuary.

We do know that the rituals at the sanctuary were open to all – men, women, citizens, servants and slaves – and since death was the penalty for revealing the secrets of the sanctuary, the main requirements seem to have been showing up and keeping quiet.

The **Archaeological Museum** at the Sanctuary of the Great Gods provides a helpful overview of the entire site. Pick up the free museum map before exploring the area. Museum exhibits include a striking marble frieze of dancing women, terracotta figurines and amphorae, jewellery, and clay lamps indicative of the nocturnal nature of the rituals. A plaster cast stands in for the celebrated **Winged Victory of Samothrace** (now in the Louvre), looted in 1863 by French diplomat and amateur archaeologist Charles Champoiseau.

About 75m south of the museum stands the **Arisinoeion** (rotunda), a gift from Queen Arisinou of Egypt. The sanctuary's original rock altar was discovered nearby. Adjacent are the rectangular **Anaktoron**, where lower initiations took place; the **Temenos**, a hall where a celebratory feast was held; and the Hieron, site of higher initiations.

Opposite the Hieron stand remnants of a **theatre**. Nearby, a path ascends to the **Nike monument**, where once stood the magnificent Winged Victory of Samothrace ('*nike*' means 'victory' in Greek), which faced northward overlooking the sea – appropriate since it was likely dedicated to the gods following a victorious naval battle.

from skin problems to infertility. The prominent white building by the bus stop houses the official bath, though there is free bathing at two small outdoor baths 75m up the hill.

Theodora BOATING
(☑ 6945392089, 25510 89444; €25) In summer this tour boat embarks on circular day trips of the island, departing from Loutra at noon and returning by 6pm. The boat passes the Byzantine Tower of Fonias, the Panias rock formations and Kremasto Waterfall, stopping mid-way at Vatos Beach for swimming. Snacks are available on board and (sometimes) a beach BBQ is offered.

🛌 Sleeping

Aleka Studios APARTMENT €
(☑ 6977739264, 25510 98272; www.alekastudios. com; d from €40) High-quality private rooms and bungalows in a flower-filled garden setting. Rooms are spacious and striking, with splendid sea or mountain views.

Mariva Bungalows BUNGALOW €
(☑ 25510 98230; www.mariva.gr; d incl breakfast €55; P ❄ 🛜) These secluded vine-covered stone bungalows, with breezy modern rooms, sit on a lush hillside near a waterfall. To reach them, turn from the coast road inland towards Loutra and follow the signs.

Municipal Camping CAMPGROUND €
(☑ 25513 50800; campsites free) Free and attractive shaded municipal campground behind the beach at Loutra (Therma), with basic facilities.

★ Archondissa BOUTIQUE HOTEL €€
(☑ 25510 98098, 6942210527; www.archondissa. gr; d/tr €75/95; ❄ 🛜) This Cycladic-styled sugar cube contains brightly coloured apartments with kilim rugs and ergonomic kitchenettes camouflaged as wardrobes. The sea is 30m away across a pretty flower garden.

🍴 Eating

★ Kafeneio Ta Therma CAFE €
(☑ 6984994856; mains €3-5; ⊙ 8am-2am; ❄) Run by the jovial Iordanis Iordaninis for more than 20 years, this is the centre of the action in Loutra, with live music, impromptu vendors, artists and dancers in the surrounding open areas, plus coffee, beer and sweets. It's near the baths and several trails.

WORTH A TRIP

FONIAS RIVER ΠΟΤΑΜΙ ΦΟΝΙΑΣ

Heading east from Loutra on the north-east coast takes you to the Fonias River and the famous **Fonias Rock Pools**. The walk starts at the bridge 4.7km east of Loutra, by the (summer-only) ticket booths. The first 40 minutes are along an easy, well-marked track leading to a large and swimmable rock pool fed by a dramatic 12m-high waterfall. The river is known as the 'Murderer', and in winter rain can transform the waters into a raging torrent. The real danger, however, is getting lost – though there are six waterfalls, marked paths are few. For hiking here and near Mt Fengari, consult Samothraki Travel (p455).

Taverna O Paradisos TAVERNA €
(☑ 25510 98271; mains €4-8.50; ⊙ lunch & dinner) A popular summer-evening meeting place under a huge plane tree, serving excellent fish. Ask Andreas to see the day's catch.

THASOS ΘΑΣΟΣ
POP 13,770

One of Greece's greenest and most gentle islands, Thasos lies 10km from mainland Kavala. Its climate and vegetation make it seem like the island is an extension of northern Greece, yet it boasts enviable sandy beaches and a forested mountain interior. Quite inexpensive by Greek-island standards, it's popular with families and students from Bulgaria and the ex-Yugoslav republics. Frequent ferries from the mainland allow independent travellers to get here quickly, and the excellent bus network makes getting around easy.

The island's main sources of wealth are its natural beauty, beaches, inland villages and historic attractions. The excellent archaeological museum in the capital, Thasos (Limenas), is complemented by the Byzantine Moni Arhangelou, with its stunning clifftop setting, and the Ancient Greek temple at Alyki on the serene southeast coast.

History

Over its long history, Thasos has benefited from its natural wealth. The Parians, who founded the ancient city of Thasos

Thasos

(Limenas) in 700 BC, struck gold at Mt Pangaion, creating an export trade lucrative enough to subsidise a naval fleet. While the gold is long gone, Thasos' white Parian marble is still being exploited, though scarring a mountainside in the process.

🛈 Getting There & Away

Thasos is only accessible from the mainland ports of Keramoti and Kavala. Hourly ferries run between Keramoti and Thasos (Limenas; €3.50, 40 minutes), and two to three a day between Kavala and Skala Prinou (€5, 1¼ hours).

Get ferry schedules at the **ticket booths** (☑ 25930 22318) in Thasos (Limenas) and the **port police** (☑ 25930 22106) at Skala Prinou.

🛈 Getting Around

BICYCLE

Basic bikes can be hired in Thasos (Limenas). Top-of-the-line models and detailed route information are available in Potos, on the southwest coast, from Velo Bike Rental (p460).

BUS

Frequent buses serve the entire island coast and inland villages, too. Buses meet arriving ferries at Skala Prinou and Thasos (Limenas), the island's transport hub. The two port towns are connected by eight daily buses (€2.80, 20 minutes).

Frequent buses run throughout the day from Thasos (Limenas) to west-coast villages such as Limenaria (€4.50), Potos (€4.70) and Theologos (€5.90). Buses from Limenas also reach the east-coast destinations of Hrysi Ammoudia (Golden Beach; €2), Skala Potamia (€1.70) via Panagia (€1.60) and Potamia (€1.60), Paradise Beach (€2.90) and Alyki (€3.70).

A full circular tour (about 100km) runs six to eight times daily (€10.60, 3½ hours) – three clockwise and three anticlockwise. This round-the-island ticket is valid all day, so you can jump on and off without paying extra. The **bus station** (☑ 25930 22162) on the Thasos (Limenas) waterfront provides timetables.

CAR & MOTORCYCLE

Potos Car Rentals (☑ 25930 52071; www.rentacarpotos.gr; Hotel Potos, Potos) is reliable and reasonable. **Avis Rent-a-Car** (☑ 25930 22535) is in Thasos (Limenas), Potamia and Skala Prinou.

Crazy Rollers (☑ 6978937536; crazyrollers@gmail.com) in Thasos (Limenas) and **Moto Zagos** (☑ 25930 53340; www.motozagos.gr; Limenaria) in Limenaria rent motorbikes and bicycles.

TAXI

The Thasos (Limenas) **taxi rank** (☑ 25930 22394, 6944170373) is on the waterfront, next to the main bus stop. Sample destinations and fares: Skala Prinou €20, Panagia €12, Skala Potamia €20, Alyki €40 and Potos €50.

In Potos, there's a taxi rank with listed prices beside the bus stop on the main road.

Thasos (Limenas)
Θάσος (Λιμένας)

POP 2610

Thasos (also called Limenas) has the island's main services and year-round activity. It sports a picturesque fishing harbour, a sandy beach, shopping, a few ancient ruins and an archaeological museum. If you're exploring the eastern side of town, note the signpost for historical sites, beginning a five-minute walk up a shaded trail to the lovely chapel of Agioi Apostoli, where there are views over the seafront.

Sights

Archaeological Museum   MUSEUM
(☎ 25930 22180; €2; ⊙ 8.30am-3pm Tue-Sun) Looking like an alien creature from the sci-fi movie *Avatar,* a 5m-tall 6th-century-BC *kouros* carrying a ram greets visitors at this large and modern archaeological museum. Statues and other artefacts from the Classical and Roman periods are on display. The museum is located about 100m from the Old Harbour's waterfront.

Ancient Agora   RUINS
Next to the archaeological museum stand the foundation ruins of the ancient *agora,* the commercial centre in ancient times. About 100m east of the *agora,* the ancient **theatre** stages performances of ancient dramas and comedies during the Philippi Thasos Festival. The theatre is signposted from the harbour. A path connects the *agora* to the **acropolis**, where substantial remains of a medieval fortress stand, with commanding views of the coast. Carved rock steps descend to the foundations of the ancient town.

Festivals & Events

Philippi Thasos Festival   CULTURAL
(www.philippifestival.gr; ⊙ Jul & Aug) This lively festival takes place in on Thasos and in mainland Kavala in late July and August. Classical drama, painting exhibitions and contemporary Greek music are featured. Programs are available at hotels, cafes and tourist agencies. The Kavala **tourist information centre** (☎ 25102 31011; www.kavala

greece.gr; Eleftherias Sq, Kavala), the Thasos (Limenas) tourist police (p460) and the Visit North Greece (p460) travel agency have ticket information.

Sleeping

A for Art   DESIGN HOTEL €€
(☎ 25930 58405; www.aforarthotel.gr; Theogenous & 18 Oktovriou; d €90-135; ※ 🐾) Dreamed up in a psychedelic haze, this fanciful hotel is filled with Dalí-esque furniture and whimsical sculpture. If you don't mind the decadent decor, it is a very comfortable place to spend a few nights, and has an excellent garden bar where you can meet fellow travellers (and a purple flamingo).

Hotel Galini   HOTEL €€
(☎ 6945443322, 25930 22195; Theogeneous; s/d incl breakfast €90/110; 🅿 ※ 🐾) This small and smartly updated hotel, next to Euro Bank and a short block inland from the waterfront, has 16 attractive and comfortable rooms (four with sea views) and a flowery back garden.

Eating & Drinking

Masabuka   GRILL €
(☎ 25930 23651; 18 Oktovriou; mains €2-4; ⊙ 4pm-midnight) Visitors rave about this exceptionally friendly 21st-century souvlaki joint, where meat skewers are served with a variety of mouthwatering dips. It's located in the pedestrianised street connecting the centre with the harbour area.

Simi   TAVERNA €€
(☎ 25930 22517; Old Harbour; mains €7-12; ⊙ 9.30am-midnight) Locals agree that this year-round eatery at the Old Harbour serves Limenas' best fish, along with fine fish soup, *stifadho* (meat, game or seafood cooked with onions in a tomato purée) and grilled sardines. There's a kids' menu, good wines and spicy mezedhes, including hot peppers that can change your life.

Karnagio   BAR
(☎ 25930 23170) Stroll past the Old Harbour for a quiet sunset drink at Karnagio, where outdoor seating straddles a rocky promontory lapped by waves. You can also clamber up the rocks to a small, candlelit chapel.

Information

ATMs can be found near the central square.
Billias Travel Service (☎ 25930 24003; Pavlou Mela 6) Full-service travel agency.

WORTH A TRIP

INLAND VILLAGES

Two interior villages warrant a day trip inland. About 6km from Skala Marion, forested **Maries** rewards visitors with cool highland air and a handsome monastery, Agios Taxiarchis.

Thasos' medieval and Ottoman capital, **Theologos**, is only accessible from Potos, where the road leads inland to the forested hamlet of 400 souls, notable for its white-washed slate-roofed houses. Find the 1803 Church of Agios Dimitrios, distinguished by its grand slate roof, exquisite polished wood interior and white-plastered clock tower. Relax at one of the local cafes or tavernas to soak it all up.

Visit North Greece (☎ 25106 20566, 6942524337; www.visitnorthgreece.com; Pavlou Mela 17) Well-managed and unique tour operator offering hiking, walking and cycling excursions, along with 4WD safaris and sailing trips. The helpful owners, Chrisoula and Stelios, can also handle transfers and suggest accommodation.

Thassos Island Nature (www.gothassos.com) Useful online resource.

Tourist Police (☎ 25930 23111)

Western Coast

Thasos' west coast has been assailed by package tours for years, though there are still a few idyllic spots and quiet sandy beaches. Better still, the inland mountain villages preserve a traditional pace of life and some fine stone architecture.

Following the coast west from Thasos (Limenas), two sandy beaches emerge: decent **Glyfoneri** and the superior **Pahys Beach**.

Continuing west, the port of **Skala Prinou** has ferries to Kavala, though little else to warrant a stop. But 6km inland, past the town of Prinos, the hillside villages of **Mikro Kazaviti** and **Megalo Kazaviti** (aka the Prinou villages) offer a lush break from the touristed coast, with undeniable character and a few places to stay and eat, including Menir Luxury Apartments. An easy-to-follow trail network branches off from the pretty square in Megalo Kazaviti, with a sign marking the routes.

The next real point of interest, the whimsical fishing port of **Skala Marion**, lies further south. Its few canopied tavernas overlooking the sea are faithfully populated by village elders shuffling backgammon chips while children scamper about. The village has a few domatia and a bakery on the northern jetty. On the village's feast day (24 June), church services are followed by folk dancing around the square.

The coast road south passes more beaches until reaching **Limenaria**, Thasos' second-largest town, which is followed quickly by **Pefkari** and **Potos**, two fishing villages turned package resorts, both with long sandy beaches lined with cafes and tavernas.

From the Theologos–Potos corner of the main road, head southeast round the coast for views of the stunning bays. The last southwestern settlement, **Astris**, has a good beach with tavernas and the **Astris Sun Hotel** (☎ 25930 51281; www.astrissunhotel.gr; r from €60; ❄ ❀ ❧).

🏃 Activities

★ **Velo Bike Rental**　　　　　CYCLING
(☎ 6946955704, 25930 52459; www.velobikerental.com; Potos) Hires out bikes year-round and also runs guided biking and hiking tours to Mt Ypsario. Inspired owner Yiannis Reizis also organises a number of international cycling events and races on the island.

Thassos Horse Club　　　　HORSE RIDING
(☎ 6999391777; www.thassoshorseclub.snadno.eu; Skala Prinou) Runs riding lessons and tailor-made horseback trips out of Skala Prinou.

Panagia Islet　　BIRDWATCHING, BOATING
(☎ 6973209576; www.gothassos.com; trips €25) The rocky, uninhabited Panagia Islet, southwest of Potos, is home to the country's largest colony of shags (www.yrefail.net/Thasos/habitats.htm). Local environmentalist Yiannis Markianos at Aldebran Pension arranges birdwatching boat trips, weather permitting.

Diving Club Vasiliadis　　　　DIVING
(☎ 6944542974; www.scuba-vas.gr; Potos) Diving for beginners and open-water divers is offered in Potos by Vasilis Vasiliadis, including to Alyki's submerged ancient marble quarry.

🛏 Sleeping

⭐**Aldebran Pension** PENSION €
(📞6973209576, 25930 52494; www.gothassos.com; Potos; d from €40; ❄🐟) Well-informed and attentive owners Elke and Yiannis make Aldebran the best value in southern Thasos. Along with a leafy courtyard and table tennis, it boasts modern baths, a well-equipped communal kitchen, and all-day coffee and tea. Resident ornithologist Yiannis offers birdwatching tours for guests in spring and autumn, and offers info on local hiking trails and more.

Hotel Menel –
The Tree House DESIGN HOTEL €
(📞6944578954, 25930 51396; www.dhotels.gr; Limenaria; d incl breakfast from €45) This funky edifice stands out among Limenaria's seafront hotels thanks to its Scandinavian ecodesign, with wooden facade and 16 airy modern rooms, all with sea-view balconies. A great rooftop terrace with sunbeds comes as a bonus.

Camping Pefkari CAMPGROUND €
(📞25930 51190; www.camping-pefkari.gr; campsites per adult/tent €6.70/7.30; ☺Jun-Sep) Wooded spot above Pefkari Beach that's popular with families and features spotless bathrooms, laundry and cooking facilities.

Menir Luxury Apartments APARTMENT €€
(📞25930 58270; www.menir-thassos.gr; Mikro Kazaviti; r incl breakfast from €80; ❄🐟) Some of the most handsome and spacious digs in this rustic area. There are five apartments, two with spa and all with fireplaces, open year-round.

🍴 Eating

⭐**Armeno** TAVERNA €
(Skala Marion; mains €5-9; ☺lunch & dinner) Well-regarded waterfront taverna, in offbeat Skala Marion, where you can have a look at the day's catch of fish. The organic produce here is from the gardens of the friendly Filaktaki family, who also rent **rooms** (📞25930 52634, 6977413789; r from €35; ❄🐟) and can help with local information.

Piatsa Michalis TAVERNA €
(Potos; mains €7-12; ☺9am-1am) Potos' 50-year-old beachfront taverna was operating well before mass tourism came to town, and continues to stick to the recipe with specialities such as stewed rabbit and octopus in red-wine sauce, plus a full menu of taverna fare.

Psarotaverna To Limani SEAFOOD €
(Limenaria; mains €6.50-10; ☺lunch & dinner) Limenaria's best seafood is served at this waterfront restaurant opposite the National Bank of Greece. Prices can be steep.

Taverna Giatrou TAVERNA €
(Theologos; mains €7-11; ☺lunch & dinner) Set 800m on the right side when entering Theologos, this big taverna has great balcony views of village roofs and verdure below. Run by Kostas Giatrou ('the Doctor') and family, the place offers specialities including local roast lamb.

ℹ Information

There are ATMs in Skala Prinou, Limenaria and Potos.

Eastern Thasos

Thasos' east-coast beaches are beautiful in summer and less crowded than the more-developed west coast. The dramatic coastal landscape features thick forests that run from mountains to sea. There are fewer organised activities here, but the warm, shallow waters are excellent for families.

Tiny **Alyki** may be the most overlooked spot on the southeast coast. The village is great for unwinding, with a few shops, domatia and tavernas, and there are two fine sandy beach coves, separated by a small olive grove dotted with ancient ruins comprising the archaeological site of Alyki.

OFF THE BEATEN TRACK

POETRY TRAIL

One of Thasos' inland delights is a short steep path at Kallirahi. Dubbed the Poetry Trail, it's an 800m-long path starting at the eastern edge of the village and ending at the Chapel of the Metamorphosis. Along the way, the poetry and writings of Herman Hesse, Rainer Maria Rilke and Goethe, along with the riddle of the Sphinx, among others, are inscribed on marble slabs.

From the chapel, a circular hike of 11km, known as the Kallirahi Circuit, ascends to one of the best viewpoints on Thasos.

◉ Sights & Activities

★ Archaeological
Site of Alyki
ARCHAEOLOGICAL SITE

FREE Alluring and easily accessible, the island's crown gem includes the considerable and photogenic remains of an ancient temple where the gods were once invoked to protect sailors. By all means enter the site through the back door by following a beautiful trail that skirts the headland, passing a partially submerged marble quarry that remained operational from the 7th century BC to the 6th century AD. The path starts at the far end of the beach lined by tavernas.

Moni Arhangelou
MONASTERY

(◎ 9am-2pm & 5pm-sunset) **FREE** West from Alyki, past Thymonia Beach, is the clifftop Moni Arhangelou, an Athonite dependency and working convent, notable for its 400-year-old church (with some ungainly modern touches) and stellar sea views. Those improperly attired will get shawled up for entry by the friendly nuns. Archangel Michael, whose name the monastery bears, happens to be venerated as the patron of Greek armed forces, so don't be surprised to see a room filled with sabres and uniforms attached to the main church.

Mt Ypsario
HIKING

Potamia makes a good jumping-off point for climbing Thasos' highest peak, Mt Ypsario (1206m). A tractor trail west from Potamia continues to the valley's end, after which arrows and cairns point the way up a steep path. The three-hour Ypsario hike is classified as moderately difficult.

🏞 Beaches

Panagia and Potamia are 4km west of the east coast's most popular beaches: sand-duned **Hrysi Ammoudia (Golden Beach)**, tucked inside a long bay; and gentle **Skala Potamia**, on its southern end. Both have accommodation, restaurants and a bit of nightlife.

Further south from Skala Potamia is the deservedly popular and nudist-friendly **Paradise Beach**, 2km after tiny Kinyra village.

Beautiful **Livadi Beach** is 2.5km from Moni Arhangelou on the southeast coast.

🛏 Sleeping

There's some accommodation at Kinyra, Alyki and Paradise Beach, but more at Hrysi Ammoudia (Golden Beach) and Skala Potamia.

Thassos Inn
HOTEL €

(☎ 25930 61612; www.thassosinn.gr; Panagia; d from €45; P �) Just follow the sound of rushing spring water to this rambling hotel by the church for great views of Panagia's slate-roofed houses. The welcoming owners, Toula and Tasos, can also advise hikers who want to stay close to the Mt Ypsario trailhead.

Hotel Theo
HOTEL €

(☎ 25930 61284; www.hotel-theo.gr; Panagia; d from €45; P ✱) Very welcoming 14-room lodging with spotless rooms and a leafy courtyard overlooking the village. Breakfast €3 per person.

★ Hotel Kamelia
HOTEL €€

(☎ 698898767, 25930 61463; www.hotel-kamelia. gr; Skala Potamia; s/d incl breakfast from €68/88; P ✱) This beachfront gem is the best in town – understated, with cool jazz in the garden bar and friendly service throughout. The gracious owners, Eleni, Stavros and family, serve a fine Greek breakfast overlooking the sea and provide plenty of tips about the area. It's 500m north of the busier main beach, over a very small bridge.

🍴 Eating

Taverna Krambousa
SEAFOOD €

(Skala Potamia; mains €6-10; ◎ lunch & dinner) Relaxing, popular and well-priced fish taverna on the beach, just before Hotel Kamelia, in Skala Potamia.

Arhontissa Alyki
GREEK €

(☎ 25930 31552; Alyki; mains €6-11; ◎ lunch & dinner) The friendly Anastasios Kuzis and family run this tranquil taverna with great sea views. It serves excellent fare, with fresh fish and mezedhes among the star offerings. Find it east of the village car park, signposted up a steep drive.

Evia & the Sporades

Best Places to Eat

➡ Dina's Amfilirion
Restaurant (p468)

➡ Taverna-Ouzerie
Kabourelia (p473)

➡ To Perivoli Restaurant
(p478)

➡ Hayiati (p484)

➡ Stefanos Taverna (p490)

Best Places to Stay

➡ Hotel Nefeli (p487)

➡ Atrium Hotel (p475)

➡ Pension Sotos (p478)

➡ Liadromia Hotel (p483)

➡ Perigiali Hotel & Studios
(p489)

Why Go?

Evia (Εύβοια) and the four Sporades islands (Οι Σποράδες) remain largely off the beaten island path. Although Evia is Greece's second-largest island, it seems hidden in plain view, separated from the mainland by the narrow Evripos Channel at Halkida. Away from this workaday hub, the pace slows as the landscape stretches out, dotted by hilltop monasteries, small farms, vineyards, hidden bays and curious goats.

Most visitors will use Evia as a jumping-off point for the gorgeous Sporades ('scattered ones'). They seem like extensions of the forested Pelion Peninsula and, in fact, they were joined in prehistoric times. Skiathos, easily the most developed, claims the sandiest beaches in the Aegean. Low-key Skopelos kicks back with a postcard-worthy harbour and forest meadows, while remote Alonnisos anchors a national marine park. Southerly Skyros is known for culinary and artistic traditions dating from Byzantine times, when these islands were home to rogues and pirates.

When to Go
Skiathos Town

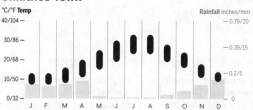

Feb & Mar Carnival season keeps things warm with plenty of merrymaking.

Apr & May Spring is in the air and Easter festivities linger long into the night.

Jun & Sep Perfect temperatures and clear skies – ideal hiking and swimming conditions.

Evia & the Sporades Highlights

1 Manos Faltaïts Folk Museum (p487) Delving into the artistic traditions and unique architecture of Skyros.

2 Bouzouki music (p478) Hearing live music at Ouzerie Anatoli, above the *kastro* overlooking Skopelos Town.

3 Dimosari Gorge (p471) Hiking this lush spot in south Evia, then cooling off in the sea near trail's end.

4 Alonnisos (p481) Watching for dolphins while sailing around Greece's only national marine park.

5 Skopelos (p475) Hiking the inland meadows among poppies and butterflies.

6 Skyros (p485) Nuzzling up with one of the gentle and rare Skyrian horses.

7 Loutra Edipsou (p468) Swimming year-round in this thermal-fed bay on Evia.

8 Moni Evangelistrias (p475) Sampling the monks' wine on Skiathos, where Greek independence was first declared in 1807.

EVIA EYBOIA

POP 200,000

Evia, Greece's second-largest island after Crete, is mostly off the tourist map, with many visitors using it to nip off to smaller and more obviously enticing islands. Take some time here, though, and you'll find it offers glorious mountain roads, challenging treks, major archaeological finds and many uncrowded beaches. A north–south mountainous spine divides the island's eastern cliffs from the gentler and resort-friendly west coast.

Ferries link the island to the mainland, along with two bridges at humdrum Halkida. One of these bridges is a sliding drawbridge (the original span dates from 410 BC) over the narrow Evripos Channel, which reverses direction about seven times daily, an event whose full explanation has eluded observers since Aristotle, and was dreaded by ancient mariners.

🛈 Getting There & Away

There are regular buses between Halkida and Athens (€8, 1¼ hours, half-hourly), Ioannina (€45, seven hours, one to two daily) and Thessaloniki (€45, 6¼ hours, one to two daily).

There is also a regular train service between Halkida and Athens (€6.50, 1½ hours, 11 daily) and an express service between Halkida and Thessaloniki (€46, 5½ hours, six daily).

Five ports on Evia serve the mainland; one serves the island of Skyros; and another serves Skopelos and Skiathos.

Central Evia

Central Evia is forested, lush and graced with beaches on both coasts, though the more remote eastern beaches facing the Aegean Sea have finer sand and even clearer waters.

Beyond the mainland bridge entry to Evia at busy Halkida, the road veers south, following the coastline to Eretria, a bustling local resort and archaeological site that's of moderate interest.

Further on, a string of hamlets and fishing villages dot the route until the junction at Lepoura, where the road forks north towards Kymi, and south towards Karystos. A rough dirt road winds west from Kymi to a rock-enclosed arc of beach at Paralia Hiliadou.

Halkida Χαλκίδα

POP 78,900

Mentioned in 'Iliad', once powerful Halkida (aka Halkis or Chalkis) spawned several colonies around the Mediterranean. The name derives from the bronze that was manufactured here in antiquity ('halkos' means bronze in Greek). Today there's little to detain tourists, but it's a lively commercial centre, and the gateway to Evia. As evening approaches, the waterfront promenade by the old bridge comes to life.

⊙ Sights

To glimpse Halkida's diverse religious history, head up Kotsou towards the *kastro* (castle) to find a striking 15th-century mosque and 19th-century synagogue, adjacent to Plateia Tzami. About 150m south is the Byzantine church of Agia Paraskevi, and a Venetian aqueduct.

Archaeological Museum MUSEUM
(☑ 22210 15131; Leoforos Venizelou 13; €2; ⊙ 8.30am-3pm Tue-Sun) Houses 7th-century-BC artefacts from both Halkida and nearby Eretria, including a headless torso of Apollo. Other remarkable finds from this former powerhouse city include a Hellenistic-era beak-mouthed jug and two golden wreaths.

BOAT SERVICES FROM EVIA

DESTINATION	PORT	FARE (€)	DURATION	FREQUENCY
Agia Marina	Nea Styra	4	45min	6-9 daily
Alonnisos	Paralia Kymis	26	3½hr	3 weekly
Arkitsa	Loutra Edipsou	4	40min	8-14 daily
Glyfa	Agiokambos	3	20min	5 / daily
Rafina	Marmari	9	1hr	3-4 daily
Skala Oropou	Eretria	2.50	25min	half-hourly
Skopelos (Glossa)	Mantoudi	19	1½hr	3 weekly
Skyros	Paralia Kymis	12	1¾hr	1-2 daily

Kokkino Spiti ARCHITECTURE

(Red House; cnr Tziarntini & Dimitrou Karaoli; €2; ⏱9am-4pm Tue-Sun) Halkida's 19th-century grandeur just about endures at waterfront Kokkino Spiti. Carved into the rock, it became headquarters for the occupying Germans in WWII.

🛏 Sleeping & Eating

Hotel Paliria BUSINESS HOTEL €€

(☎22210 28001; www.paliria-hotel.gr; Eleftheriou Venizelou 2; s/d incl breakfast €60/80; 🅿❄@✿) The waterfront Paliria bears more than a passing resemblance to a modern sevenstorey cruise ship, and occupies a prime spot near the old bridge, with spacious and plain carpeted rooms. It's not a thriller, but it is quiet and comfortable.

Pantheon 1900 TAPAS €

(Voudouri; €3-7; ⏱9am-1am) Nestled in a handsome neoclassical building on the waterfront, this smart tapas bar features Greek wines, tasty small plates and snappy service.

ⓘ Information

Several ATMs cluster at the waterfront near the corner of Venizelou and Voudouri.

Post Office (cnr Karamourtzouni & Kriezotou; ⏱8am-2pm Mon-Fri)

ⓘ Getting There & Away

From Halkida, buses serve Athens (€6.50, 1¼ hours, half-hourly), Ioannina (€39, seven hours, four to six daily) and Thessaloniki (€40, 6¼ hours, eight to 10 daily). Regular trains also connect Halkida with Athens, and an express service runs to Thessaloniki.

From **Halkida KTEL bus station** (☎22210 20400; cnr Styron & Arethousis), 3km east of the old bridge (taxi fare €4), buses also connect to the following destinations on Evia:

DESTINATION	DURATION	FARE (€)	FREQUENCY
Eretria	25min	2.20	hourly
Karystos	3hr	14.20	3 daily
Kymi Town & Paralia Kymis	2hr	9.20	3 daily
Limni	2hr	8	3 daily
Loutra Edipsou	3½hr	14.20	2 daily
Mantoudi	2hr	8.20	3 daily
Steni	50min	3.70	3 daily

Eretria Ερέτρια

POP 3600

Eretria, about 20km southeast from Halkida, is the first place of interest on Evia for travellers coming from the mainland. It has a small fishing harbour, substantial archaeological remains, and a touristy boardwalk of lively tavernas, open-air cafes and beach bars.

◉ Sights

Ancient Eretria was a major maritime power with an eminent school of philosophy. The city was destroyed in AD 87 by the Roman commander Sylla. West of the ancient acropolis are the remains of a theatre with a subterranean passage used by actors to reach the stage, as well the remnants of baths, a gymnasium, a house with mosaics and a hilltop temple to Athena. Visit the Archaeological Museum for a map to tour these scant but fascinating sights.

Archaeological Museum of Eretria MUSEUM

(☎22290 62206; www.gtp.gr/archaeological museumoferetria; Archaiou Theatrou & Isidos; €2; ⏱8.30am-3pm Tue-Sun) The signature piece at the museum is a terracotta depiction of the mythical Medusa, whose tresses were turned into live serpents by the goddess Athena as revenge for Medusa's dalliance with Poseidon.

🛏 Sleeping & Eating

Milos Camping CAMPGROUND €

(☎22290 60420; www.camping-in-evia.gr; campsites per adult/tent €6/4) This well-managed and shaded campground, 1km northwest of Eretria, has a small restaurant, bar and 200m-long pebble beach.

Diamanto Rooms PENSION €

(☎22290 62214, 6946836529; www.diamanto rooms.gr; Varvaki 2; s/d €35/45; 🅿❄@✿) Ten sparkling but old-fashioned rooms with balconies, cheerful service, a common kitchen and a plant-wreathed entrance way. Ask for a room with a sea view.

Villa Belmar Apartments APARTMENT €€

(☎6971588424; www.villabelmar.gr; s/d/f incl breakfast from €45/65/90; 🅿❄@✿) Southwest of the port, these stylish apartments with a private waterfront deck are managed by welcoming sisters Lina and Renia.

Primavera TAVERNA €

(☎22290 64051; mains €6-12) A stand-out along the scenic but touristy seafront strip of restaurants, serving decent pizza, seafood, *mousakas* (baked layers of eggplant or zucchini, minced meat and potatoes topped with cheese sauce) and the like. Round it off with a slab of watermelon.

❶ Getting There & Away

Ferries travel daily between Eretria and Skala Oropou (€2, 25 minutes, half-hourly). Purchase tickets from the dock kiosks. There are regular buses to and from Halkida (€2.20, 25 minutes, hourly), which decant passengers in the centre of town.

Steni   Στενή

POP 1200

From Halkida, it's 31km to the picturesque mountain village of Steni, with its gurgling springs, and shady plane and chestnut trees. Steni is also the starting point for hikers tackling Mt Dirfys.

A twisting road continues from Steni to Paralia Hiliadou on the north coast, where a grove of maple and chestnut trees borders a beach, along with a few domatia (rooms in private homes) and tavernas.

🏃 Activities

Steni is the starting point for hiking up Mt Dirfys (1743m), Evia's highest mountain. The **Dirfys Refuge** (✆22210 85760, 22210 25230, mobile 6974057517; www.eoschalkidas.gr; per person €12), at 1120m, can be reached along a 9km dirt road. From there, it's a steep 7km to the summit. Experienced hikers should allow about six hours from Steni to the summit. For refuge lodging information (and key), as well as current hiking conditions, contact **Minas Patsourakis** (✆22210 85760, mobile 6974057517; www.facebook.com/groups/eoschalkidas) and the EOS-affiliated **Halkida Alpine Club** (✆22210 25230, 22210 25279; www.eoschalkidas.gr; Angeli Gouviou 22; ⊕9am-5pm Mon-Sat). See the Anavasi Topo 25 map, *Mt Dirfys 5.11 1:25,000*.

🛏 Sleeping

Hotel Dirfys   HOTEL €
(✆6972319451, 22280 51270; dirfis@otenet.gr; s/d incl breakfast €40/50; 🅿🛜) This is the most appealing of Steni's three hotels. All rooms have balcony views of the surrounding forest, sparkling bathrooms, and the hotel taverna draws in locals come evening.

O Neromylos   TAVERNA €
(Agia Kyriaki; mains €5-10; ⊕lunch & dinner) The Watermill shares the lush landscape of Agia Kyriaki, signposted 3km southeast of Steni.

Kitchen favourites include roasted mushrooms and homemade sausages.

Kymi & Paralia Kymis
Κύμη & Παραλία Κύμης

POP 3250

The workaday town of Kymi perks up at dusk when the town square comes to life. Kymi is a prosperous agricultural centre surrounded by vineyards and fruit orchards. The port of Paralia Kymis, 4km downhill, is the departure point for ferries to Skyros, Alonnisos and, in summer, Skopelos.

◉ Sights

Folklore Museum   MUSEUM
(✆22220 22011; Kymi; €2; ⊕10.30am-1.30pm & 6-8pm Jul & Aug, 10.30am-2pm Wed, Sat & Sun rest of year) The Folklore Museum, 30m downhill from the main square of Kymi, includes a display honouring Kymi-born Dr George Papanikolaou, inventor of the Pap smear test and pioneer in the early diagnosis of cancer. There are also exhibits on traditional homes and clothing.

🛏 Sleeping & Eating

In Paralia Kymis, a string of tavernas lines the waterfront. Just 3km south in tiny Platana, there are a couple of excellent choices.

Corali Hotel   HOTEL €
(✆69794 45548; www.coralihotel.gr; Paralia Kymis; r from €40; ❄🛜) Much the best stop if you're waiting for a ferry, Corali is located just 500m from the port. The stylish modern building contains 21 plain, but comfortable, rooms. Farm fresh eggs and homemade pastries and jam feature on the breakfast menu.

Koutelos   TAVERNA €
(✆22220 71272; Platana; mains €7-11; ⊕lunch & dinner) This century-old taverna is known for well-priced standards such as fish soup, *taramasalata* (a thick pink or white purée of fish roe, potato, oil and lemon juice), and crunchy *gavros* (a marinated small fish). Splurge on a half kilo of fresh lobster with salad and wine (about €40 for two), and look out at the sea view.

🛍 Shopping

Figs of Kymi   FOOD
(✆22220 31722; Platana; ⊕9am-9pm Sep-Nov) **FREE** Platana, located 3km south of Paralia Kymis, is home to Figs of Kymi, a lively agricultural co-op supporting local fig

farmers and sustainable production. Preservative-free fresh and dried figs and jams are on sale. Also open by appointment outside usual hours.

Northern Evia

From Halkida a road threads north into the mountainous interior of northern Evia, reaching the beautiful village of **Prokopi**, whose inhabitants are descended from refugees who came from Prokopion in Turkey's Cappadocia region in 1923. They established the substantial pilgrimage church of St John the Russian, named for the saint who remains central to the town's identity and livelihood to this day, and is celebrated with a festival on 27 May.

At Strofylia, the road heads southwest to picturesque **Limni**, which clusters around a bay, then north to the little thermal resort of Loutra Edipsou.

Loutra Edipsou   Λουτρά Αιδηψού

POP 3700

The sedate spa resort of Loutra Edipsou is the most visited spot in northern Evia. Its therapeutic sulphur waters have been celebrated since antiquity, and continue to draw a stream of medical tourists. Famous skinny-dippers have included Aristotle, Strabo, Plutarch, Plinius and Sylla.

Today, the town has Greece's most up-to-date hydrotherapy and physiotherapy centres, and several hotels have their own modern facilities. The town beach (Paralia Loutron) heats up year-round thanks to the thermal waters that spill into the bay.

🏃 Activities

EOT Hydrotherapy-Physiotherapy Centre   SPA
(☑ 22260 23501; 25 Martiou St 37; ☉ 7am-1pm & 5-7pm Jun-Oct) The more affordable of the resort's two big spas, the welcoming and attractive EOT Hydrotherapy-Physiotherapy Centre is speckled with palm trees and has a large outdoor pool that mixes mineral and sea water. Hydromassage bath treatments start at a very reasonable €8.

Thermae Sylla Hotel & Spa   SPA
(☑ 22260 60100; www.thermaesylla.gr; Posidonos 2; ☉ 9am-8pm) This ultra-posh spa styles itself a 'thermal palace', with a late-Roman ambience befitting its name. It offers assorted health and beauty treatments, from thermal mud baths to seaweed body wraps, and an outdoor pool with curving edges makes a dramatic centrepiece.

🛏 Sleeping

★ Hotel Kentrikon   HOTEL €
(☑ 22260 22302; www.kentrikonhotel.com; 25 Martiou 14; s/d/tr incl breakfast €40/50/60; ❄@🖀🏊) Managed by Greek-Irish Konstantinos and Una, the Kentrikon is equal parts kitsch and old-world charm, with modern rooms and balcony views. A free thermal pool awaits, along with a professional massage therapist.

Hotel Irini   HOTEL €
(☑ 22260 22634; www.hotelirini.gr; Byzantinon Aftokratoron 1; s/d from €25/35; ❄@🖀) The cheerful and affordable Irini, tucked into a side street opposite the port, offers clean, snug rooms, most with sea views. It also has spa treatments and a *hammam* (Turkish baths), from €25.

Thermae Sylla Hotel & Spa   HOTEL €€€
(☑ 22260 60100; www.thermaesylla.gr; Posidonos 2; s/d/ste incl breakfast from €110/170/260; 🅿❄@🖀🏊) This posh, in-your-mud-masked-face seaside resort offers elegant luxury accommodation as well as countless beauty treatments. Day visitors can sample the outdoor thermal pool (€35).

🍴 Eating

★ Dina's Amfilirion Restaurant   GREEK €
(28 Octovriou 26; mains €8-12; ☉ lunch & dinner) Daily specials, no menu, await at this simple eatery 20m north of the ferry dock. A tasty grilled cod with oven potatoes, tomato-cucumber salad and wine runs to €12 per person. Look for the small wooden sign with green letters.

Deux Amis   BAKERY €
(28 Octovriou & Miaouli 1; items from €1.50) This friendly, expansive bakery-cafe on the waterfront is a good bet for tasty and filling *tyropita* (cheese pie), *bougatsa* (creamy semolina pudding wrapped in a pastry envelope and baked), and all kinds of cakes and ice cream.

Ouzerie Ta Kohilia   GREEK €
(☑ 22260 23478; 28 Octovriou 20; mains €4-7; ☉ lunch & dinner) Look for the blue chairs outside to find the best mezedhes (appetisers) on the waterfront, next to the Avra Hotel.

ⓘ Getting There & Away

BOAT
Regular ferries run between Loutra Edipsou and mainland Arkitsa (€3.70, 40 minutes), and also between nearby Agiokambos and mainland Glyfa (€2.30, 20 minutes). Purchase tickets at the dock kiosks.

BUS
From the **KTEL bus station** (🖸 22260 22250; Thermopotamou), 200m from the port, buses run to Halkida (€14.20, 3½ hours, twice daily), Athens (€14.20, three hours, three to four daily) via Arkitsa, and Thessaloniki (€24, four hours, daily) via Glyfa.

Limni   Λίμνη
POP 2300

Picturesque Limni's maze of whitewashed houses and narrow lanes spill onto a cosy harbour speckled with cafes and tavernas.

◎ Sights

Convent of Galataki   CONVENT
(🖸 22270 31489; ⊘9am-noon & 5-8pm) The 16th-century Convent of Galataki lies 9km southeast of Limni, following a narrow road that hugs a picturesque shoreline (with plenty of stops for a swim) and then climbs steeply uphill. It is home to a coterie of six gently welcoming nuns and a fine fresco, *Entry of the Righteous into Paradise*, in its *katholikon* (principal church).

Museum of History & Folk Art   MUSEUM
(🖸 22270 31335; www.gtp.gr/historicalandfolklore museumoflimni; Anagnosti Goviou 7; €2; ⊘9am-1pm Mon-Sat, 10.30am-2pm Sun) The town's quaint folk museum, 50m from the waterfront, houses handsome village costumes and domestic items.

☆ Festivals & Events

Skyllias Swimming Marathon   SPORTS
(https://sites.google.com/site/skylliaslimni; ⊘Jul) Limni's midsummer Elimnia Festival kicks off with the 14.5km Skyllias swimming marathon between mainland Theologos and Limni. It was named for the long-distance swimmer who, in 480 BC, warned the Greeks of the approaching Persian fleet.

🛏 Sleeping & Eating

Rovies Camping   CAMPGROUND €
(🖸 22270 71120; campsites per adult/tent €7/6.50; 🅿🛱) Attractive, well-managed Rovies borders a pebble beach and a grove of olive and pine trees, 12km northwest of Limni. A restaurant and mini-market are open all day. There are 150 pitches, of which an increasing number are used by dive enthusiasts.

Home Graegos   APARTMENT €€
(🖸 22270 31117; www.graegos.com; apt from €65; 🅿❄🛱) Graegos has four simple, but decent, apartments with modern kitchenettes and sweeping verandah sea views at the centre of the waterfront. The front two apartments have big balconies and sea views.

O Platanos   TAVERNA €
(mains €5-9; ⊘lunch & dinner) Tucked inside Limni's inner lanes, near the village museum, this popular local standby does excellent grills and hearty salads and serves great local wines.

Southern Evia

East of Eretria, the road branches south at Lepoura as the north's rich vegetation gives way to sparse and rugged mountains. A turn-off leads to **Lake Dhistos**, a shallow lake bed favoured by migrating egrets: water levels have been diminished by local agriculture. You'll pass high-tech windmills and catch views of both coasts as the island narrows before reaching **Karystos**, the only really enticing resort here, where friendly locals enjoy life at a pace that makes you forget how close you are to Athens.

Karystos   Κάρυστος
POP 5300

Set on wide Karystos Bay below Mt Ohi (1398m), and flanked by two sandy beaches, this low-key coastal resort is the starting point for treks to Mt Ohi and Dimosari Gorge. Karystos' lively Plateia Amalias faces the harbour, which glitters come evening with lights and bobbing boats.

◎ Sights

Archaeological Museum of Karystos   MUSEUM
(🖸 22240 29218, 22240 25661; €2; ⊘8.30am-3pm Tue-Sun) Karystos, mentioned in Homer's 'Iliad', was a powerful city-state during the Peloponnesian Wars. The displays at the museum range from tiny Neolithic clay lamps to temple carvings and votive objects to an exhibit on the 6th-century-BC *drakospita* (dragon houses) of Mt Ohi and Styra. The museum sits opposite the castle.

WORTH A TRIP

WHISTLING VILLAGE OF ANTIA

East of Karystos, the 'whistling village' of Antia is famous for its linguistically talented villagers who speak in whistles. One of a small global group of whistling languages, this one was devised during Byzantine times to warn of danger and invasion from pirates, with each tone corresponding to a letter of the alphabet. Until the early 1980s the language was still widely used, but today it's mostly the old-timers who still put their lips together and blow. The good news involves a resurgence of interest in the whistling among the kids of Antia. Stay tuned.

Bourtzi   CASTLE

FREE Karystos' striking 14th-century Venetian castle is a remnant of the town's former fortifications. The low, bulky tower sits on the waterfront.

Festivals & Events

Wine & Cultural Festival   CULTURAL

(22240 22246) Karystos hosts a lively summer wine and cultural festival during the last week of August and the first week of September, which includes theatre performances, traditional dancing to the tune of local musicians, and exhibits by local artists. The summer merrymaking features local wines, free for the tasting.

Sleeping & Eating

★ Hotel Karystion   HOTEL €

(22240 22391; www.karystion.gr; Kriezotou 3; s/d incl breakfast from €40/50; P ✳ 🛜) The handsome Karystion sits above the beach just beyond the Bourtzi castle, and features modern, well-appointed rooms, a filling breakfast with homemade yoghurt and a helpful multilingual staff. A stairway leads to a sandy beach, great for swimming.

★ Cavo d'Oro   TAVERNA €

(mains €5-8; ⊙ lunch & dinner) 🌱 Join the locals in this cheery alleyway restaurant off the main square for well-prepared Greek mainstays such as octopus in red wine sauce and country salads featuring local produce and olive oil. The genial owner, Kyriakos, is a regular at the summer wine festival, bouzouki in hand.

🍷 Drinking & Nightlife

Aeriko   BAR

(22240 22365; ⊙ 8am-1am; 🛜) Aeriko is the pick of the harbour beach bars with a gorgeous sandy setting, live music on summer weekends, sun beds, decent drinks and an all-ages clientele.

ℹ Information

Alpha Bank and Piraeus Bank ATMs are on the main square.

South Evia Tours (22240 26200; www.eviatravel.gr; Plateia Amalias; ⊙ 10am-10pm)

ℹ Getting There & Away

BOAT

There is a regular ferry service from Marmari (10km west of Karystos) to Rafina (€8.50, one hour), and from Nea Styra (35km north of Karystos) to Agia Marina (€3.80, 45 minutes).

Purchase tickets from either the dock kiosk or South Evia Tours.

BUS

From the **Karystos KTEL bus station** (22240 26303) opposite Agios Nikolaos church, buses run to Halkida (€14.20, three hours), Athens (€19, three hours) and Marmari (€1.80, 20 minutes). A taxi to Marmari costs €18.

Around Karystos

The ruins of Castello Rosso (Red Castle), a 13th-century Frankish fortress, are a short walk from Myli, a well-watered village 4km inland from Karystos. The aqueduct behind the castle once carried water from the mountain springs to the Bourtzi in Karystos. A 3km walk from Myli brings you to a 2nd-century-AD Roman quarry (Kylindroi, meaning 'cylinder') strewn with marble columns, abandoned during the time of Caesar.

With your own transport you can explore the pristine Cavo d'Oro villages nestling in the southern foothills of Mt Ohi. Highlights include Platanistos, Potami and the walled ruins of an ancient settlement at Helleniko.

⊙ Sights & Activities

In addition to Dimosari Gorge and Mt Ohi, worthy day hikes above Karystos include ambles through the natural springs of **Agios Dimitrios Gorge**, where a branch trail ascends to scenic **Boublia Peak** (1127m). From tiny **Thymi**, a narrow dirt track reaches beautiful **Archampoli Beach**, about an hour's walk.

South Evia Tours can help organise hiking excursions to Mt Ohi's and Styra's *drakospita*, as well as bicycle and kayak rentals, and cruises around the Petali Islands (€38). Owner Nikos and staff also arrange transport for hikes to the summit of Mt Ohi and back, and four-hour guided walks through Dimosari Gorge (€25).

Mt Ohi   MOUNTAIN
From Myli, it's a four-hour hike up Mt Ohi (1398m) for magnificent Aegean views. It's possible to stay overnight at a refuge at 1000m, then hike up to catch sunrise. The summit (Profitis Ilias peak) is home to the ancient *drakospita*, Stonehenge-like dwellings or temples dating from the 7th century BC, hewn from rocks weighing several tonnes and joined without mortar.

The dragon houses' commanding position near marble quarries suggest that they were guard posts; another theory holds that they honoured mythological deities that roamed Mt Ohi, in particular the goddess Hera. Another dragon house near the road to Styra (30km north of Karystos) is equally fascinating.

★ Dimosari Gorge   HIKING
A beautiful and well-maintained 10km trail that can be covered in four hours (including time for a swim). It begins in Petrokanalo village at 950m, descending through Lenosei village to the sea. Much of this stunning trek follows a cobbled path, splashing through shady creeks, ponds, giant ferns and forest before ending at the sand-and-pebble beach of Kallianos.

THE SPORADES

The Sporades (Οι Σποράδες) are home to four unique islands. Skiathos and its 60-odd beaches draws the most visitors by far, while handsome Skopelos strikes a cooler pose with its hidden bays and inland trails. Alonnisos, with one bus, four taxis and 27 churches, is the most remote and pristine of this northern group, while Skyros is home to wild horses and a lively arts scene.

Skiathos   Σκιάθος
POP 6450
Skiathos is blessed with some of the Aegean's most beautiful beaches, so it's little wonder that in July and August the island can fill up with sun-starved northern Europeans, as prices soar and rooms dwindle.

Skiathos Town, the island's major settlement and port, lies on the southeast coast. The rest of the south coast is interspersed with walled-in holiday villas and pine-fringed sandy beaches.

❶ Getting There & Away

AIR
Skiathos airport (JSI; ☑ 24270 29100) is 2km northeast of Skiathos Town. In summer there are daily flights to/from Athens with **Olympic Air** (☑ 24270 22200; www.olympicair.com), in addition to numerous charter flights from northern Europe. **Aegean Air** (☑ 24270 29100; https://en.aegeanair.com) has an office at the airport.

BOAT
Skiathos' main port is Skiathos Town, which has links to Volos and Agios Konstantinos on the mainland, and to island destinations Skopelos and Alonnisos. Tickets can be purchased from **Hellenic Seaways** (☑ 24270 22209; www.skiathosoe.com; cnr Papadiamantis).

❶ Getting Around

BOAT
Water taxis depart hourly from the old port for Achladies Bay (€2.70, 15 minutes), Kanapitsa (€3.20, 20 minutes) and Koukounaries (€5.30, 30 minutes).

Boat Services from Skiathos

DESTINATION	DURATION	FARE (€)	FREQUENCY
Agios Konstantinos	2½hr	32	1 daily
Agios Konstantinos*	1½hr	38	1-2 daily
Alonnisos	2hr	11	1 daily
Alonnisos*	1½hr	18	2 daily
Skopelos (Glossa)	30min	6.50	1 daily
Skopelos (Glossa)*	20min	11	2 daily
Skopelos (Skopelos Town)	1½hr	10.50	1 daily
Skopelos (Skopelos Town)*	45min	18	2 daily
Volos	2½hr	24	1-2 daily
Volos*	1½hr	38	1-2 daily

* hydrofoil services

Skiathos

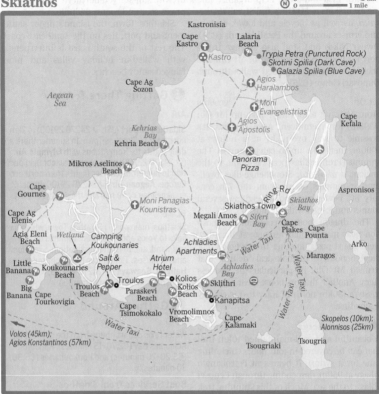

BUS

Buses leave Skiathos Town for Koukounaries Beach (€2.20, 30 minutes, half-hourly) between 7.30am and 11pm. The buses stop at 26 numbered beach access points along the south coast.

CAR & MOTORCYCLE

Reliable motorbike and car-hire outlets in Skiathos Town include **Europcar/Creator Tours** (☑ 24270 22385; www.europcar.co.uk), which also rents bicycles, and Heliotropio Tourism & Travel (p474). Both are located at the new port.

TAXI

Taxis (☑ 24270 21460) leave from the stand opposite the ferry dock. A taxi to/from the airport costs €8, to Koukounaries €18 and to Moni Evangelistrias €9.

Skiathos Town   Σκιάθος

POP 5000

The town is a major tourist centre, with hotels, souvenir shops, galleries, travel agents, tavernas and bars spread along the waterfront and Papadiamanti, the cobbled pedestrian thoroughfare. Away from the main drag, though, things quieten down quickly and you can catch more of a local flavour. Opposite the waterfront via a 15m causeway lies shady and inviting **Bourtzi Islet**, where you'll find a maritime museum and restaurant.

⊙ Sights & Activities

Papadiamantis House Museum   MUSEUM
(☑ 24270 22240; Plateia Papadiamanti; €1.50; ⊙ 10am-1pm & 5-7pm Tue-Sun) Skiathos was the birthplace of famous 19th-century Greek novelist and short-story writer Alexandros Papadiamantis, who is looked on as the father of modern Greek literature, and whose writings draw upon the hard lives of the islanders he grew up with. His plain whitewashed 1860 house is now a small and charming museum with books, paintings and photos of the author and his family. Bleak and ballad-like novella The

Murderess, set on Skiathos, is Papadiamantis' most famous work.

Maritime and Culture Tradition Museum
MUSEUM

(€2; ☺11am-1pm & 6.30-10.30pm) A former school on Bourtzi Islet houses a one-room local history museum. Staff will point out exhibits, which are signed in Greek and consist mostly of 20th-century paraphernalia relating to shipbuilding and navigation. The open-air theatre behind the museum is used for summer concerts.

★ Argo III Yacht
BOATING

(☑6932325167; www.argosailing.com; per person €65, sunset cruise €45) For a splendid sailing tour of the island waters between Skiathos and Alonnisos, climb aboard the *Argo III,* managed by husband-and-wife team George and Dina.

🛏 Sleeping

Skiathos House
PENSION €

(☑24270 22733; www.skiathoshouse.gr; off Papadiamanti; r from €30; ✹☏) Comfortable modern rooms and self-catering apartments at bargain prices, and with an amazingly central location in a small palm-shaded garden. Proprietor Denis is very welcoming and helpful. You'll find Skiathos House behind the post office, one street away from Papadiamanti.

Hotel Mouria
HOTEL €

(☑24270 21193; www.mouriahotel.com; Papadiamanti; d/tr/f incl breakfast from €40/60/80; ✹@☏) The handsome Mouria hides just behind the National Bank, set back in a flowery courtyard. There's a common kitchen for guests, though a full breakfast awaits, plus bright rooms and vintage photos all around. The taverna was once a regular haunt of Alexandros Papadiamantis.

★ Bourtzi Boutique Hotel
BOUTIQUE HOTEL €€

(☑24270 21304; www.hotelbourtzi.gr; Moraitou 8, cnr Papadiamanti; d incl breakfast from €90; ℗✹☏≋) On upper Papadiamanti, the swanky Bourtzi features austere-modern rooms, contrasted with warmly attentive staff, and an inviting garden and pool. They also provide a welcome cocktail, and a beach bag for your stay – with towel. Good online rates for three-night stays.

🍴 Eating

★ Taverna-Ouzerie Kabourelia
TAVERNA €

(☑24270 21112; Old Harbour; mains €6-11; ☺noon-midnight; ☏) Poke your nose into the open kitchen to glimpse the day's catch at this popular year-round taverna at the old port. Perfect fish grills and house wine are served at moderate prices. Grilled octopus and *taramasalata* are just two of several standout mezedhes.

★ Foodie
CAFE €

(Igloo; ☑24270 24076; Papadiamanti; snacks €1.50-3; ☺6am-11pm) This is a great, quick and super-friendly stop for baguettes, cold drinks, ice cream and fresh juice, and breakfast goodies before early ferry departures.

O Batis
TAVERNA €

(☑24270 22288; Old Harbour; mains €4-9; ☺noon-midnight) This popular fish taverna on the path above the old port is a local standby for reliable and well-priced fresh fish, *gavros,* and fine mezedhes. Cosy atmosphere and a good selection of island wines, year-round.

Taverna Hellinikon
TAVERNA €

(mains €7-10; ☺lunch & dinner) Opposite the church above the old port, little Hellinikon is a mother-and-daughter affair, with well-prepared taverna standards like slow-roasted lamb. Good house wines, along with live Greek music on summer evenings.

Lo & La
MEDITERRANEAN €

(☑24270 29070; mains €7-12; ☺lunch & dinner) Perched above the old port, Lo & La shows off an Italian-Greek couple's kitchen favourites. Pastas are handmade, and the risotto with local mushrooms excels.

★ La Cucina di Maria
RISTORANTE €€

(☑24270 24168; Plateia Trion Ierarhon; €8-15; ☺dinner) Excellent thin-crust pizza twirled in the air is just the beginning at this popular spot above the old port. Fresh pasta, fine meat and fish grills in a colourful setting under the mulberry tree: look out for the bright plates embedded in the outside walls.

Bourtzi
TAPAS €€

(☑24270 23900; www.facebook.com/Bourtzi; mains €13-20; ☺9am-2am) This chilled-out and elegant tapas joint and wine bar enjoys a sublime and secluded location on Bourtzi Islet. Come here for morning coffee, or to watch the sun set on the harbour.

🍷 Drinking & Entertainment

Kentavros BAR
(📞 24270 22980; off Plateia Papadiamanti; ⊙ 10am-late) Handsome Kentavros promises rock, jazz and blues, and has been getting the thumbs-up from locals and expats since 1978 for its mellow ambience, artwork and sturdy drinks.

Portobello BAR
(📞 24270 29051; www.portobelloskiathos.gr; Papadiamanti; ⊙ 8.30am-12.30pm; 🛜) Portobello eschews cocktail bling in favour of a fan-cooled terrace shaded by an olive tree and climbing plants. There's an epically long wooden bar and a laid-back vibe.

Cinema Attikon CINEMA
(📞 24720 22352, 6972706305; tickets €7) Catch current English-language movies – mostly, if not exclusively, *Mamma Mia!* – at this open-air cinema. Sip a beer and practise speed-reading your Greek subtitles.

🛍 Shopping

⭐ Galerie Varsakis ANTIQUES
(📞 24270 22255; www.varsakis.com; Plateia Trion Ierarhon; ⊙ 10am-2pm & 6-11pm) Browse for unusual antiques, such as 19th-century spinning sticks made by grooms for their intended brides – the collection rivals the best Greek folklore museums. Upstairs is a dazzling display of the owner's paintings, in oil on gold leaf, begun in the 1970s. They depict Greek myths and predatory contemporary politicians. Downstairs there's an original 1830s kitchen.

Loupos & His Dolphins ANTIQUES
(📞 24270 23777; Plateia Papadiamanti; ⊙ 10am-1.30pm & 6-10.30pm) Find delicate hand-painted icons, handsome ceramics and an array of jewellery at this quality bougainvillea-framed gallery shop, in the courtyard by Papadiamantis House Museum (p472).

Blue House Art Gallery ARTS & CRAFTS
(📞 24270 21681; Nikotsara St; ⊙ 10am-10pm) Handmade jewellery, ceramics and vintage pieces stand out at this intimate and lovely shop behind the old port.

Efimeris GIFTS & SOUVENIRS
(www.facebook.com/efimeris.skiathos; Papadiamanti 39; ⊙ 10am-10pm) Among many identikit boutiques, this one stands out for its focus on handmade Greek products, from striped fabric towels to turquoise rings to elegant woven clutch bags.

ℹ Information

The bus terminus is at the northern end of the new harbour with departures to the island beaches. Regular water taxis leave from the old port for Achladies Bay, Kanapiitsa and Koukounaries. You'll find car-hire outlets and taxis at the new port.

Numerous ATMs are on Papadiamanti and the waterfront.

Creator Tours (📞 24270 22385; www.creator tours.com; New Harbour; ⊙ 10am-9pm)
Heliotropio Tourism & Travel (📞 24270 22430; www.heliotropio.gr; ⊙ 7.30am-11pm)
Port Police (📞 24270 22017; New Harbour)
Post Office (Papadiamanti; ⊙ 8am-2pm)
Tourist Police (📞 24270 23172; Ring Rd; ⊙ 8am-9pm)

Around Skiathos

🏖 Beaches

With 65 beaches to choose from, beach-hopping on Skiathos can become a full-time occupation. Buses ply the south coast, stopping at 26 numbered beach access points. The first long stretch of sand worth stopping at is wide and pine-fringed **Vromolimnos Beach**. The road then continues to the white sands of **Koukounaries Beach**, which is backed by pine trees and a small wetland. Come the busy midsummer period, it's best viewed at a distance, from where the 1200m-long sweep of pale gold sand does indeed sparkle.

West of Koukounaries, **Big Banana Beach**, known for its curving shape, soft sand and beach-bar buzz, lies across a narrow headland. Skinny-dippers prefer to hang at equally frenetic **Little Banana Beach** (also popular with gay and lesbian sunbathers) around the rocky corner, though current building works are impeding access.

About 400m north, the narrow arc of **Agia Eleni Beach** is a favourite with wind-surfers. Soft-sand **Mandraki Beach**, a 1.5km walk along a pine-shaded path, is distant enough to keep it clear of the masses, while sporting a good taverna. From Troulos, it's 4km to **Megalos Aselinos Beach**, a long and lovely stretch of sand, with tiny rock-enclosed **Mikros Aselinos** and secluded **Kehria Beach** hidden down a steep track a few kilometres further on.

The northwest coast's beaches are less crowded but are subject to summer *meltemi* (dry northerly winds). **Lalaria Beach** is a tranquil strand of pale grey, egg-shaped pebbles on the northern coast with a scenic rock arch, but can only be reached by excursion boat from Skiathos Town.

◎ Sights

★ Moni Evangelistrias   MONASTERY

(☑24270 22012; museum €2; ⊙10am-dusk) This famously historic monastery was a hilltop refuge for freedom fighters during the War of Independence, and the Greek flag was first raised here in 1807. Today, two monks do the chores, which include winemaking. You can sample the tasty results in the museum shop. An adjacent shed of vintage olive and wine presses recalls an earlier era, before the satellite dish appeared above the courtyard.

Kastro   RUINS

(⊙24hr) **FREE** Perched dramatically on a rocky headland above the north coast, Kastro was the fortified pirate-proof capital of the island from 1540 to 1829. An old cannon remains at the northern end, along with four restored churches, including Christos, home to several fine frescoes. Excursion boats come from the old port in Skiathos Town to the beach below Kastro, from where it's an easy clamber up to the ruins.

Moni Panagias Kounistras   MONASTERY

(⊙dawn-dusk) From Troulos, a road winds 4km inland to the serene 17th-century Moni Panagias Kounistras, worth a visit for the fine frescoes adorning its *katholikon*.

⚓ Activities

Diving

The small islets off the south shore of Skiathos make for great diving and snorkelling. The dive-instructor team of Theofanis and Eva of **Octopus Diving Centre** (☑6944168958, 24270 24549; www.odc-skiathos.com; New Harbour; half-day dives €50-60) leads dives around Tsougria and Tsougriaki islets for beginners and experts alike. Enquire at their boat on the new harbour in Skiathos Town. **Dolphin Diving** (☑6944999181; www.ddiving.gr; Hotel Nostos, Tzaneria Beach; half-day dives €50-60) and **Skiathos Diving Centre** (☑6977081444; www.skiathosdiving.gr; Koukounaries; from €49) also have strong reputations.

Hiking

A 6km-long hiking route begins at Moni Evangelistrias and eventually reaches **Cape Kastro** before circling back through **Agios Apostolis**. Kastro is a spring mecca for birdwatchers, who may spot long-necked Mediterranean shags or blue rock-thrushes skimming the waves.

🛏 Sleeping & Eating

Achladies Apartments   APARTMENT €

(☑24270 22486; www.achladiesapartments.com; Achladies Bay; d/tr/f incl breakfast €60/75/80; P 🛜) This welcoming gem, 5km south of Skiathos Town, features comfortable kitchenette rooms with ceiling fans, plus an eco-friendly tortoise sanctuary and a rambling succulent garden (complete with an aviary) winding down to a sandy beach. From here, water taxis connect with Skiathos Town and Koukounaries Beach.

Camping Koukounaries   CAMPGROUND €

(☑24270 49250; Koukounaries Beach; campsites per adult/tent €11/free; P 🛜) Shaded by fig and mulberry trees opposite Koukounaries Beach, with spotless bathroom, cooking facilities, washing machines, a minimarket and taverna. Cash only.

★ Atrium Hotel   HOTEL €€

(☑24270 49345; www.atriumhotel.gr; Paraskevi Beach; s/d/ste incl breakfast from €105/140/200; P ❄ @ 🛜 🏊) Traditional architecture and soothing modern decor make this hillside perch the best in its class. Elegant rooms feature private sinks and private balconies overlooking the sea. Amenities include a sauna, a children's pool, billiards, ping-pong and a lavish breakfast buffet to start the day. Two-night rates available online.

Panorama Pizza   PIZZA €

(www.skiathospanorama.gr; Ring Rd; pizzas €8-12; ⊙noon-4pm & 7pm-late; 🛜) Hilltop retreat off the Ring Rd for brick-oven pizza and perfect views.

Salt & Pepper   INTERNATIONAL €€

(☑24270 49329; Troulos; mains €8-14; ⊙lunch & dinner) This popular upscale eatery features innovative fish and meat grills and traditional salad and veggie dishes. A full bar anchors the outdoor garden. Opposite the Troulos turn-off.

Skopelos   Σκόπελος

POP 6000

Skopelos is a handsome island of pine forests, vineyards, olive groves, and orchards of plums and almonds, which find their way into many local dishes.

Like neighbouring island Skiathos, the high cliffs of the northwest coast are exposed, while the sheltered southeast coast harbours several sand-and-pebble beaches. There are two settlements: the wonderfully attractive main port of Skopelos Town on the east coast and the northwest village of Glossa, 2km north of Loutraki, the island's second port.

ℹ Getting There & Away

Skopelos has two ports, Skopelos Town and Glossa (aka Loutraki). Both link to Volos and Agios Konstantinos on the mainland, and the islands of Skiathos, Alonnisos and Skyros.

Tickets are available from **Hellenic Seaways** (☑ 24240 22767; Waterfront; ◷ 9am-10pm) in Skopelos Town and the port of Glossa; and from Madro Travel (p479) on the waterfront in Skopelos Town.

ℹ Getting Around

BOAT
A water taxi departs Skopelos Town late morning for Glysteri Beach (€6 each way).

BUS
In summer there are four to six buses per day from Skopelos Town to Glossa/Loutraki (€5.60, 55 minutes) and Neo Klima (Elios; €4, 45 minutes); and three more that go to Panormos

(€3.20, 25 minutes), Milia (€3.80, 35 minutes), Agnontas (€1.80, 15 minutes) and Stafylos (€1.70, 15 minutes).

CAR & MOTORCYCLE
For car and motorcycle hire, head to **Magic Cars** (☑ 24240 23250, 6973790936; http://skopelos. net/magiccars; Potoki) in the town centre.

TAXI
Taxis wait by the bus stop in Skopelos Town. A taxi to Stafylos is €8, to Limnonari €14 and to Glossa €34.

Skopelos Town   Σκόπελος
POP 4800

Skopelos Town skirts a semicircular bay and rises in picturesque tiers up a hillside of dazzling white houses with bright shutters and flower-adorned balconies, ending at an old fortress and a cluster of four gleaming whitewashed churches.

The town's waterfront is flanked by two quays. The old quay wraps around the western end of the harbour; the new quay at the eastern end is used by all ferries and hydrofoils.

Strolling around town and sitting at the waterside cafes might be your chief occupations in Skopelos, but there are also two small museums.

BOAT SERVICES FROM SKOPELOS

DESTINATION	PORT	DURATION	FARE (€)	FREQUENCY
Agios Konstantinos	Skopelos Town	4hr	36	1 daily
Agios Konstantinos*	Skopelos Town	2½hr	54	1 daily
Agios Konstantinos**	Glossa	2½hr	47	1 daily
Alonnisos	Glossa	1hr	9	1 daily
Alonnisos*	Skopelos Town	30min	6	2-3 daily
Alonnisos**	Skopelos Town	20min	9.50	2 daily
Skiathos (via Glossa)	Skopelos Town	1½hr	10.50	2-3 daily
Skiathos*	Skopelos Town	45min	18	2 daily
Skiathos**	Glossa	30min	11	2 daily
Evia (Mantoudi)	Glossa	1¾hr	19.80	3 weekly
Evia (Paralia Kymis)	Skopelos Town	4hr	26	4-6 weekly
Volos	Skopelos Town	3¾hr	25.70	2 daily
Volos*	Skopelos Town	3hr	26.50	2-3 daily
Volos**	Glossa	2½hr	40	1 daily

*fast-ferry services/**hydrofoil services

Skopelos

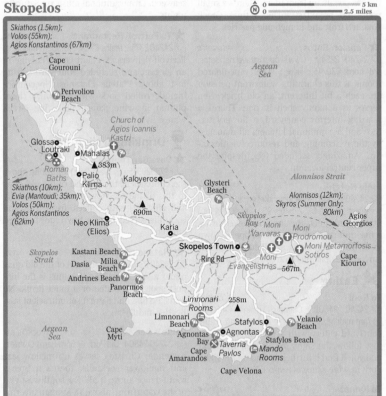

◉ Sights & Activities

Vakratsa Mansion Museum — MUSEUM
(☑ 24240 23494; €3; ⊙ 10am-2pm & 6-9pm)
Housed in what was a doctor's 18th-century
mansion, this museum displays medical
instruments of the era as well as traditional
clothing for married and unmarried men
and women, and is well worth seeing for
the window it offers onto middle-class
Greek life in the 19th century. It's near
the middle of the waterfront, 100m inland
from Ploumisti Shop, housed behind a high,
white wall.

Folklore Museum — MUSEUM
(☑ 24240 23494; Hatzistamati; €3; ⊙ 10am-2pm
& 7-10pm Mon-Fri) This handsome museum
features a Skopelean wedding room, complete with traditional costumes and bridal
bed. It's a block west of Agios Nikolaou
Church.

Skopelos Cycling — CYCLING
(☑ 24240 22398, 6947023145; skopeloscycling@
yahoo.gr; per 24hr €10-18; ⊙ 10am-2pm & 6-10pm
Mon-Fri, 10am-2pm Sat) High-quality trekking
and mountain bikes, and bike tours, are available from Panos Provias at Skopelos Cycling,
who will lend you maps and advise on routes.
It's located near the post office (p479).

SkopArt — ART
(Skopelos Foundation for the Arts; ☑ 24240 24143;
www.skopartfoundation.org; Raches) Perched
high above Skopelos Town, SkopArt offers
popular residential classes, ranging from
painting and drawing to ceramics and
paper-making.

⌂ Sleeping

★ Thea Home Hotel — PENSION €
(☑ 24240 22859; www.theahomehotel.com; Ring
Rd; d/apt from €40/80) Fresh and modern
rooms with sea views that are well worth

the steep walk up from town. There's a small pool, and breakfast includes thick Greek yoghurt, fruit and homemade pastries.

★ Pension Sotos   PENSION €
(☑ 24240 22549; www.skopelostravel.net/sotos; s/d from €30/45; ❄ ☎) The pine-floored rooms at this charming waterfront pension are each a bit different; an old brick oven serves as a handy shelf in one. There's a relaxing interior courtyard, a flowery terrace and a communal kitchen, all managed by the welcoming and resourceful Alexandra. Amazingly secluded feel, despite the super-central location.

Ionia Hotel   HOTEL €€
(☑ 24240 22568; www.ioniahotel.gr; s/d/tr/f incl breakfast from €65/75/55/95; P ❄ @ ☎ ☎) Stylish and quiet, the Ionia is tucked away, a five-minute stroll from the Skopelos Town waterfront. Service is excellent and rooms surround a spacious courtyard with a pool.

🍴 Eating

To Rodi   GREEK €
(☑ 24240 24601; Chimou; mains €4.50-10; ☺ 7pm-midnight) Classy and comfortable courtyard eatery with a pomegranate tree; just follow the signs for Hidden Door bar and you'll find it further up and on the right. Pork in wine sauce is a speciality.

Ta Kymata   TAVERNA €
(☑ 24240 22381; mains €5-9.50) The oldest tavern on the island, at the end of the old port, has had a steady local following for its hearty grills and classic *mayirefta* (ready-cooked meals) since 1896. They have a veggie-specific menu, as well as swordfish, lobster and humbler dishes including shrimps cooked with sundried tomatoes and ouzo.

O Michalis   CAFE €
(8am-late; snacks €3-5) The red door and hand-painted signs give away this snappy hole-in-the-wall serving superb *tyropita*. At night the place morphs into a mellow wine bar. It's mid-waterfront, a block inland from Pension Sotos.

★ Anna's Restaurant   GREEK €€
(☑ 24240 24734; Gifthorema; mains €7-17; ☺ 7pm-midnight) A lone palm tree marks this handsome and upscale alleyway bistro that serves authentic Skopelean dishes such as sautéed veal with plums. There's a good Greek wine list and healthy salads with ingredients such as goji berries and

seaweed. Live traditional music on Saturday nights.

★ To Perivoli Restaurant   GREEK €€
(☑ 24240 23758; mains €7-14; ☺ 7.30pm-midnight) Perivoli delivers excellent Greek cuisine in an elegant and secluded courtyard setting just above Plateia Platanos. Specialities include rolled pork with *koromila* (local plums) in wine sauce, plus fine Greek wines.

🍷 Drinking & Nightlife

★ Cafe Bar Thalassa   CAFE
(☑ 6978929975; ☺ 10am-9pm) Clamber above the churches at the far end of the old quay to this divine sea-view terrace. It's friendly and efficient, with coffees, fresh fruit and cocktails served from a tiny blue-shuttered kitchen.

★ Platanos Jazz Bar   BAR
(☑ 24240 23661) Near the end of the old quay under a vast spreading tree, this is the hippest spot for a coffee or a quiet drink. No touts, no fuss and a great soundtrack of jazz, Beatles and Dylan.

Pablo's Bar   COCKTAIL BAR
(☑ 24240 24804; Old Port; ☺ 6pm-3am) Owner-bartender Christos serves up mellow jazz and mellower cocktails; there's a breezy roof terrace above it all. Far southwest end of the waterfront, above Ta Kymata taverna.

Hidden Door   BAR
(☑ 6978252848; ☺ 7pm-late) Mellow bar on a quieter lane behind the waterfront, in a converted 100-year-old house where a side, or hidden, door once led to the kitchen. Three blocks inland from Agios Nikolaos Church.

Oionos Blue Bar   BAR
(☑ 6942406136) Cosy and cool, little Oionos serves up blues and soul plus a good selection of single malt whiskies.

☆ Entertainment

★ Ouzerie Anatoli   TRADITIONAL MUSIC
(☺ 8pm-2am summer) Wait till at least 11pm, then head to this breezy outdoor *ouzerie* (place that serves ouzo and light snacks), high above the *kastro* near the southeast corner of the waterfront, to hear traditional *rembetika* (blues songs) sung by Georgos Xindaris, Skopelos' own exponent of the Greek blues and a bouzouki master.

🛍 Shopping

The waterfront hosts some wonderful shops selling quality ceramics, small paintings, icons and handmade jewellery.

★**Skopelos Sandals**　　　　SHOES
(⊙10am-10pm) Classic handmade leather sandals and belts, adjusted to fit by the genial owner. The leather stretches, so wear your sandals around town for a few days and go back to have them readjusted if need be. Prices are great – around €20 to €30 for sandals. You'll find the shop a couple of blocks uphill from Pension Sotos.

★**Ploumisti Shop**　　　ARTS & CRAFTS
(☑24240 22059; Waterfront; ⊙9am-midnight) The same couple have been running this wonderful shop for 40 years, selling linen shirts and scarves, paintings, jewellery and ceramics. You can hear the owner play *rembetika* every Saturday night at Anna's Restaurant.

ℹ Information

There are four ATMs along the waterfront.

Dolphin Tours (☑6977468190, 24240 29191; www.dolphinofskopelos.com; Waterfront; ⊙10am-9pm)

Health Centre (☑24240 22222; Ring Rd; ⊙10am-8pm)

Madro Travel (☑24240 22300; www.madro travel.com; Waterfront; ⊙9am-10pm)

Police (☑24240 22235; New Quay)

Port Police (☑24240 22180; Old Quay)

Post Office (opposite Panagia Church; ⊙7.30am-2pm)

Thalpos Holidays (☑24240 29036; www.holidayislands.com; Waterfront; ⊙10am-8pm)

Glossa & Loutraki
Γλώσσα & Λουτράκι

POP 950

Glossa, Skopelos' second settlement, is a whitewashed cluster of shops and eateries. A 2km road winds down from the small square to the laid-back port of Loutraki ('Glossa' in ferry timetables). A shorter *kalderimi* (cobblestoned path) connects both villages as well. Fans of the 2008 movie *Mamma Mia!* can start their pilgrimage in Glossa to reach the film's little church, Agios Ioannis Kastri (St John of the Castle).

Loutraki means 'small bath' and you can see the remains of ancient Roman baths at the archaeological kiosk on the port.

🏄 Activities

Kayaking Greece　　　　KAYAKING
(Sea Kayak Center; ☑24240 33805, 6983211298; www.kayakinggreece.com) This well-managed kayaking outfit based in Glossa offers everything from full-day trips (€65) and simple sunset outings (€35) to six-day adventures (€590) and customised island expeditions led by CUB-qualified guides.

🛏 Sleeping & Eating

Pansion Platana　　　　PENSION €
(☑24240 33188, 6973646702; pansionplatana@hotmail.com; Glossa; r from €35; 🅿❄🛜) This cosy and welcoming domatia has overhead fans, kitchenettes and balcony views overlooking the port of Loutraki. Welcoming Greek-Australian owner Eleni provides tea and tips. About 30m past the Shell petrol station on the left.

★**Flisvos Taverna**　　　　TAVERNA €
(☑24240 33856; Loutraki; mains €4-9; ⊙lunch & dinner) With simple Greek fare at its best, friendly beachfront Flisvos offers fresh fish at reasonable prices, along with traditional standards, such as *mousakas* and *stifadho* (meat, game or seafood cooked with onions in a tomato purée). Appetisers such as tzatziki (sauce of grated cucumber, yoghurt and garlic) and *taramasalata* excel.

Around Skopelos

Visitors to Skopelos can see several monasteries via a scenic drive or day-long trek above Skopelos Town. Begin by following Monastery Rd, which skirts the bay and then climbs inland to 18th-century convent **Moni Evangelistrias**, home to a solitary nun. The monastery's prize, aside from superb views, is a gilded iconostasis containing an 11th-century icon of the Virgin Mary.

Further on, 16th-century **Moni Metamorfosis Sotiros** is the island's oldest monastery. From there a narrow road continues to 17th-century **Moni Varvaras** overlooking the bay below, and 18th-century convent **Moni Prodromou**, 8km from Skopelos Town.

🏖 Beaches

Most of Skopelos' best beaches are on the sheltered southwest and west coasts; a good way to reach them is by hiring a bike from Skopelos Cycling (p477).

The first beach you come to is sand-and-pebble **Stafylos Beach**, 4km southeast of

Skopelos Town. From its eastern end, a path leads over a small headland to the quieter **Velanio Beach**, the island's official nudist beach and coincidentally a great snorkelling spot. Lovely **Agnontas**, 3km west of Stafylos, has a pebble-and-sand beach from where caïques depart to sheltered and sandier **Limnonari Beach**.

You could easily lose a day to picnicking and hidden-cove swimming at **Cape Amarandos**. Around 75m before you reach Agnontas, take the left-hand turn, following a steep rocky track at the bend. The track provides umpteen private rocky beach stops, but if you keep going to a sharp left turn you'll see a dramatic cleft in the rocks. Follow the faint path here along the cliff to the water's edge, where a sea cave and pine shade provides a wonderfully spectacular stop.

From Agnontas, the road cuts inland through pine forests before re-emerging at pretty **Panormos Beach**, which has tavernas and domatia. The next two bays, **Milia** and **Kastani**, are excellent for swimming. On the island's northeast coast, serene **Perivoliou Beach** is a 25-minute drive from Glossa.

🏃 Activities

⭐ Heather Parsons' Guided Walks
WALKING

(☏6945249328; http://skopelos-walks.com; tours €20-25) If you can't tell a twin-tailed pascha butterfly from a leopard orchid, join one of island resident Heather Parsons' guided walks. Her four-hour Panormos walk follows a centuries-old *kalderimi* path across the island, ending at a beach taverna, with wonderful views to Alonnisos and Evia along the way. Her book *Skopelos Trails* contains graded trail descriptions.

Heather and a loyal band of volunteers continue to clear, signpost and GPS the trails across the island. She also offers *Mamma Mia!* jeep tours to most of the movie's filming locations.

🛌 Sleeping & Eating

Limnonari Rooms & Taverna
APARTMENT €

(☏24240 23046, 6946464515; www.skopelos. net/limnonarirooms; Limnonari Beach; d/tr/ste from €35/60/80; 🅿️❄️🛜) This cluster of 10 well-equipped apartments faces beautiful Limnonari Bay. The family's garden taverna serves vegetarian *mousakas,* fish and meat grills, and homemade olives and feta.

⭐ Guesthouse Mando Beachfront
APARTMENT €€

(☏24240 23917, 6936131316; mando_skopelos@ yahoo.gr; Stafylos; d/tr/f incl breakfast from €75/85/115; 🅿️❄️🛜) Nestled behind a cove on Stafylos Bay, this well-managed, family-oriented lodging offers modest rooms alongside luxe villas, plus an outdoor communal kitchen and a solid platform over the rocks from which to enter the sea for swimming and snorkelling.

⭐ Taverna Pavlos
TAVERNA €€

(☏24240 22409; Agnondas; mains €9-15; ☺lunch & dinner) Locals think nothing of driving over to Agnontas for beautifully prepared fresh fish and excellent mezedhes at this shaded taverna steps from the beach. Octopus *stifadho* (cooked with onions in a tomato purée) and fava dip are just two of the star offerings.

Alonnisos   Αλόννησος

POP 3500

Alonnisos rises from the sea in a mountain of greenery, with stands of Aleppo pine, kermes oak, mastic and arbutus bushes, vineyards, olive and fruit trees, threaded with perfumy patches of wild herbs. The west and north coasts are steep and rocky, while the east is speckled with bays and pebble-and-sand beaches.

Alonnisos has had its share of bad luck; in 1952, a thriving wine industry collapsed when vines imported from California were infested with phylloxera insects. Robbed of their livelihood, many people moved away. Then, in 1965, an earthquake destroyed the hilltop capital of Old Alonnisos. Inhabitants were rehoused at Patitiri, which has since evolved into a quaint island port; 11km to the north is the seaside village of Steni Vala. The most recent trouble was in early 2017, when storms destroyed a third of the island's trees; many inhabitants decamp to Athens for the surprisingly harsh winter season.

ⓘ Getting There & Away

Alonnisos' main port of Patitiri has links to mainland Volos and Agios Konstantinos; to Paralia Kymis on Evia; and to nearby Skopelos, Skiathos and (summer only) Skyros.

Tickets can be purchased from Alkyon Travel (p483), Albedo Travel (p483) and Alonnisos Travel (p483) in Patitiri.

Boat Services from Alonnisos

DESTINATION	DURATION	FARE (€)	FREQUENCY
Agios Konstantinos*	2½hr	54	4 weekly
Agios Konstantinos**	3½hr	36	1 daily
Evia (Paralia Kymis)	2½hr	25	2-3 weekly
Skiathos	2hr	11.50	4 weekly
Skiathos*	1½hr	18	4-5 daily
Skopelos	40min	6	1 daily
Skopelos*	20min	9.50	2-3 daily
Skopelos (Glossa)*	45min	14	3-4 daily
Volos*	2½hr	52	1-2 daily
Volos**	3½hr	30	1-2 daily

*hydrofoil services
**fast-ferry services

❶ Getting Around

BUS

A bus plies the route between Patitiri and Old Alonnisos (€1.70), and then heads to Steni Vala (€1.80). Additionally, a summer **beach bus** (☑ 6973805610; round trip €5) leaves Patitiri around 10.30am for points to the north and returns after 4pm.

CAR & MOTORCYCLE

Several motorcycle-hire outlets cluster near the waterfront in Patitiri, including reliable **I'm Bike** (☑ 24240 65010). For cars, try Albedo Travel (p483) or Alonnisos Travel (p483), also in Patitiri.

TAXI

A few taxis congregate opposite the Alykon Hotel on the waterfront in Patitiri. It costs €6 to Old Alonnisos, €10 to Leftos Gialos and €13 to Steni Vala.

Patitiri   Πατητήρι

POP 1800

Patitiri (meaning Wine Press) sits between two sandstone cliffs at the southern end of the east coast. The quay is in the centre of the waterfront, from where two roads lead inland; the main road is the one closest to the harbour. There are no road signs: people simply refer to the left-hand or right-hand road.

◉ Sights

★ National Marine Park of Alonnisos Northern Sporades   NATIONAL PARK

(www.alonissos-park.gr) In a country not noted for ecological foresight, the National Marine Park of Alonnisos (the largest marine park in Europe) is a welcome innovation. Created in 1992, its prime aim has been the protection of the endangered Mediterranean monk seal and several rare seabirds. In summer, licensed boats from Alonnisos and Skopelos conduct excursions through the pristine park. Though it's unlikely you'll find the shy monk seal, chances of spotting dolphins are fairly good. Buy excursion tickets from waterfront agencies.

★ Alonnisos Museum   MUSEUM

(☑ 24240 66250; www.alonissosmuseum.com; adult/child €4/free; ⊙ 11am-6pm May & Sep, to 8pm Jun-Aug) This town museum includes antique nautical maps, a well-signed collection of pirates' weapons and boarding equipment, and an absorbing display on wartime resistance. Downstairs there's a recreated farmhouse interior, and artefacts relating to traditional crafts and industries. Go down Bar St on the beach and follow the signs up to the museum.

MOM Information Centre   MUSEUM

(☑ 24240 66350; www.mom.gr; Waterfront; ⊙ 10am-10pm Jun-Sep) FREE Don't miss this excellent waterfront info centre, all about the protected and extremely appealing Mediterranean monk seal. It has good displays, videos with English subtitles and helpful multilingual staff on hand. They are campaigning to ban the ubiquitous plastic bags handed out by local shopkeepers.

⚡ Activities

Boat Trips

Sea-kayaking excursions around Alonnisos, from half-day to overnight cove camping, are arranged by Albedo Travel (p483).

Both Albedo Travel and Alonnisos Travel (p483) hire out four-person 15HP to 25HP motorboats (from €53 to €77 per day).

Diving

A few ancient sailing vessels have been discovered at the bottom of the shallow sea around Alonnisos. Efforts are under way to open these sites to guided dives. Contact **Alonissos Triton Center** (☑ 24240 65804; http://bestdivingingreece.com; scuba dives from €65) or Ikion Diving (p485).

EVIA & THE SPORADES ALONNISOS

Alonnisos

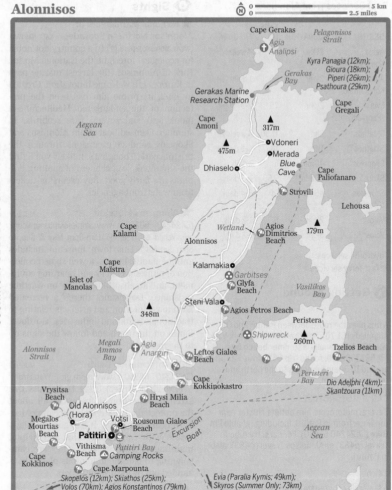

Hiking

A 2.5km *kalderimi* path winds up through shrubbery and orchards to Old Alonnisos. Albedo Travel can help arrange guided walks.

Tours

Two full-service travel agencies on the waterfront, Albedo Travel and Alonnisos Travel, provide maps, run popular marine-park trips, and organise snorkelling and swimming excursions to Skantzoura and nearby islands.

Popular round-the-island excursions (€40) aboard the classic *Gorgona,* captained by charming island local **Pakis Athanasiou** (2 6978386588), visit the **Blue Cave** on the northeast coast and the islets of **Kyra Panagia** and **Peristera** in the marine park. There are lunch and swimming breaks along the way.

Sleeping

Camping Rocks   CAMPGROUND €
(2 6973230977, 24240 65410; www.campingrocks.
eu; Marpounta; campsites per adult/tent €7.50/3)
Follow the signposts 800m south of the port

to this clean and pine-shaded coastal spot with a cafe and grocery store.

★**Liadromia Hotel** HOTEL €
(☑24240 65521; www.liadromia.gr; d/tr/ste incl breakfast from €40/60/75; P⚹@🛜) This welcoming and impeccably maintained hotel overlooking the harbour was Patitiri's first. All rooms have character to spare, from hand-embroidered curtains to period furnishings. The gracious owner, Maria, takes obvious delight in making it all work. Their upstairs breakfast room has a grand harbour view and quirky touches such as an antique gramophone.

Ilias Studios HOTEL €
(☑24240 65451; www.ilias-studios.gr; Pelasgon 27; r from €35; ⚹🛜) Just 100m from the port, owners Ilias and Magdalini provide a genuine welcome in this jaunty-looking blue-and-white building. Rooms are spotless, airy and light, and a common kitchen awaits self-caterers.

★**Paradise Hotel** HOTEL €
(☑24240 65160; www.paradise-hotel.gr; s/d/tr incl breakfast from €65/70/77; P⚹🛜🏊) Wood ceilings and stone-tiled floors give a rustic feel to these quiet, comfortable rooms, along with modern bathrooms and shuttered balconies that overlook the bay. Beyond the pool bar, a stairway leads to a small cove for swimming. They also have the only hotel pool in town.

✗ Eating & Drinking

★**Ouzerie Archipelagos** GREEK €
(mains €6-10; ⊙lunch & dinner) To get a feel for this very Greek establishment on the harbourfront, pick a table towards the back where locals gather to order round after round of fine mezedhes, always-fresh grilled fish and local firewater favourite *tsipouro* as the night rolls on.

Cafe Bistro Helios BISTRO €
(☑24240 65667; snacks €3-7; ⊙6pm-midnight) Snappy bistro hidden in plain view, via the stepped path located a few doors down from the National Bank. Well-priced small plates, a superb high harbour view, plus an international twist.

To Kamaki Ouzerie TAVERNA €€
(mains €5-15; ⊙dinner) This long-time local favourite, next to the National Bank on the main road, offers well-priced fresh fish and tasty vegetarian plates. Weekends often feature a family bouzouki player.

Drunk Seal BAR
(⊙10am-late) One of several cheery dives serving unique cocktails at the port, tilting in the direction of the town museum. Globes hang from the awning and there's a tropical, hippie feel.

🛍 Shopping

Ikos Traditional Products GIFTS & SOUVENIRS
(Women's Cooperative Shop; ☑24240 66270; Ikion Dolopon; ⊙9am-2pm & 6-9pm) This delightful women's cooperative is a combination bakery, nuts-and-island-herbs, jams-and-honey shop, open year-round.

ℹ Information

Albedo Travel (☑24240 65804; www.alonissosholidays.com; Waterfront; ⊙9am-10pm)

Alkyon Travel (☑24240 65220; http://alkyontravel.gr; Waterfront; ⊙9am-10pm)

Alonnisos Travel (☑24240 65188, 24240 66000; www.alonnisostravel.gr; Waterfront; ⊙9am-10pm)

Pharmacy (☑24240 66096)

Police (☑24240 65205)

Port Police (☑24240 65595)

Post Office (⊙7.30am-2pm)

Old Alonnisos Παλιά Αλόννησος
POP 500

Old Alonnisos (aka Palia Alonnisos and Hora) is an enchanting place with panoramic views and winding stepped alleys. From the village, a 2km donkey path leads down to Mikros Mourtias Beach or, from just outside the village, take the steep road down to Megalos Mourtias, a beautiful enclosed stony curve with a cluster of small restaurants and a bar. At the bus stop, you'll find a blue noticeboard that details several area walks.

◉ Sights & Activities

Church of the Birth of Christ CHURCH
A 17th-century rough-hewn stone church sits on the village square. Inside you'll see a tiny wooden gallery, and an ornate screen depicting the lives of the Apostles.

Kali Thea YOGA
(☑24240 65513, 6975930108; www.kalithea.org; from €10; ⊙May-Oct) Hatha yoga and massage, courtesy of Bibi and Lee, on the outskirts of Old Alonnisos. Drop-in group classes plus private tuition.

🛏 Sleeping

Elma's Houses APARTMENT €
(☑ 24240 66108, 6945466776; www.elmashouses.
com; studio/apt from €45/75; ❄🛜) Families
will appreciate either of Elma's two roomy
stone houses, each traditionally decorated
and with full kitchen, comfy beds and great
views from the courtyard. Interior walls are
rugged and whitewashed, and there are
wooden beams and staircases. It's located
near the old school in the village.

Pension Chiliadromia PENSION €
(☑ 24240 65814; www.chiliadromia.gr; Plateia Hris-
tou; r/studio from €35/50; ❄🛜) Tucked into
the heart of the old village, this homey pension is a budget gem, with small balconies,
comfortable beds, well-equipped kitchens
and traditional decorations. There's a morning cafe downstairs.

★**Konstantina Studios** APARTMENT €€
(☑ 24240 66165, 6932271540; www.konstantinastu-
dios.gr; d/ste/apt incl breakfast from €96/106/130;
🅿❄🛜) Among the nicest accommodation
on Alonnisos, these handsome and quiet
studios with fully equipped kitchens, power
showers and fluffy bathrobes come with
balcony views of the southwest coast. The
resourceful owner, Konstantina, fetches her
guests from the dock and serves wonderful
breakfasts consisting of fruit plus homemade
baking, jam and omelettes.

🍴 Eating & Drinking

★**Hayiati** CAFE €
(☑ 24240 66244; snacks €4-11.50; ⊙ 9am-2am)
Hayiati is a *glykopoleio* (sweets shop) by
day and a piano bar by night, with sweeping
views from its descending outdoor terraces.
Morning fare includes made-to-order *tyropita*. Later, you'll find homemade pastas
along with the gracious hospitality of own-
er-cooks Meni and Angela. It's located in the
upper part of the village.

Taverna Megalos Mourtias TAVERNA €
(Megalos Mourtias; mains €4-8; ⊙ breakfast, lunch &
dinner) A stone's throw from the surf, this laid-
back taverna and beach bar 2km down the
hill from the Hora prepares fine salads, *gyros*
(meat slithers cooked on a vertical rotisserie),
fish soup and several veggie dishes.

★**Astrofegia** GREEK €€
(mains €7-15; ⊙ dinner) There's a stunning
view from this outdoor dining spot, with
its cheery red-checked tablecloths, friendly

family welcome and grape vines. Choose
from well-prepared Greek standards, rare
veggie *mousakas,* mixed seafood souvlakia
and good house wines. Or go straight for the
galaktoboureko (custard slice). It's opposite
the small car park at the village entrance.

Aerides Cafe-Bar BAR
(⊙ 9am-5pm & 7pm-2am; 🛜) Maria and Yiannis make the drinks, pick the music and
scoop the ice cream at this hip hole-in-the-
wall on the village square. It's a good spot for
breakfast and fresh juices.

Around Alonnios

From Patitiri, Alonnisos' main road reaches
19km to the northern tip of the island at
Gerakas; turtles nest on the beach here,
though, sadly, the water isn't the cleanest.

North of Patitiri, though, several roads
descend to small fishing bays and some
lovely secluded beaches. Along the east coast,
the first bay from town is **Rousoum Gialos**,
an easy 1km walk from town: the beautiful
stony curve of the bay provides great swimming, and it's backed by tavernas. Next is
Votsi, which is more of a fishing port while,
3km on, **Hrysi Milia** is a gently shelving
sandy strand with a beach bar and pine-tree
shade. The next point north is the gorgeous
arc of **Cape Kokkinokastro**, site of the
ancient and submerged city of Ikos. Continuing, the road reaches **Leftos Gialos**, home to
a pebble beach dotted with raffia sun shades.

Steni Vala, an attractive little fishing village and deep-water yacht port, has 50-odd
rooms in domatia and tavernas overlooking
the small marina. Small and pebbly **Agios
Petros Beach** sits just 500m south of the
village.

Kalamakia, 2km further north and the
last village of note, comprises a small harbour, a few domatia and fine dockside fish
tavernas. It's not ideal for swimming, so it's
best to press on for 3km on the sealed road
to a wetland marsh and **Agios Dimitrios
Beach**, where a truck-canteen and domatia
sit opposite a graceful stretch of white pebbles. A 5km circular walk to the wetland at
Kastanorema takes two hours. Beyond Agios
Dimitrios, the road narrows to a footpath
heading inland.

🏃 Activities

Hiking opportunities abound on Alonnisos
and more than a dozen trails have been way-
marked. Popular trails are highlighted on

THE MONK SEAL

Once populating hundreds of colonies in the Black Sea, the Mediterranean Sea and along Africa's Atlantic coast, the Mediterranean monk seal has been reduced to about 700 individuals. Half of these live in the seas around Greece.

One of the earth's rarest mammals, the monk seal is now one of the 20 most endangered species worldwide. Major threats include decreasing food supplies and destruction of habitat. Thankfully, the once-common killings by fishers – who saw the seal as a pest that tore holes in nets and robbed their catch – have diminished with the recognition that protecting the seal also promotes recovery of fish stocks.

For more information about monk seals and to see infra-red film of their impossibly adorable pups, visit MOM Information Centre (p481).

the Terrain and Anavasi maps of Alonnisos. Albedo Travel (p483) in Patitiri can help arrange guided walks, which start in town and explore either the coasts or the heart of the island. The routes generally end at a beach, so bring swimming gear.

Ikion Diving
DIVING

(☑ 24240 65158, 6984181598; www.ikiondiving.gr; Steni Vala) Offers both shore and boat dives, plus snorkelling (from €270).

🛏 Sleeping & Eating

Lithea Studios
VILLA €€

(☑ 24240 66435, 6932586001; www.lithea.gr; Agios Petros; studios/villas from €60/90; ℗ ❀ 🅹) Nestled into the coastal hamlet of Agios Petros, this traditional stone complex impresses with a rambling garden of olive and citrus trees hung with hammocks, handsome rooms, kitchenettes and hospitable owners Panayioti and Maria. Wander through the trees to take a dip in the sea.

Ilya Suites
APARTMENT €€

(☑ 21032 49209, 6938327401; www.ilyasuites.gr; Glyfa Beach; ste/villla from €80/160; ℗ ❀ 🅹) Get away from it all at these elegant well-appointed suites and villas on Glyfa Beach facing Peristera Island. From the geranium- and rose-filled courtyard to the spacious low-key luxe rooms, everything feels soothingly elegant. Apartments sleep two to four people.

Taverna Eleonas
TAVERNA €

(☑ 69450 81006; Leftos Gialos; mains €5-11; ☺ lunch & dinner) Fine outdoor taverna on the bay at Leftos Gialos with hearty spinach and feta *pites* (pies), and heartier homemade wine. You sit in the shade of olive trees with views of the beach.

Taverna Fanari
TAVERNA €

(Waterfront, Steni Vala; mains €4-9) Stuffed squid and seafood linguine are two of the offerings at this great harbour taverna, rounded off with a small pudding on the house.

Skyros
Σκύρος

POP 3000

Skyros, the largest of the Sporades group, can seem like two separate islands: the north has small bays, rolling farmland and pine forests while the south features arid hills and a rocky shoreline. In Greek mythology, Skyros was the hiding place of the young Achilles, who is thought to have ridden a Skyrian horse into Troy: the endangered small-bodied horses can still be seen in the wild on the island.

These days, the island has somewhat of a hip but off-the-radar feel thanks to the alternative arts and wellness courses run by the Skyros Centre (p487). It's also popular with birders, in search of the slender Eleonora's falcon which migrates between here and Madagascar. Skyros Town, perched on its high rock, is a tranquil car-free base.

ℹ Getting There & Away

AIR

In addition to domestic flights, Skyros airport, 11km north of Skyros Town at the far tip of the island, has occasional charter flights from Oslo, Amsterdam and destinations in France. Domestic flights from Skyros head to Athens (€28, 25 minutes) and Thessaloniki (€50, 45 minutes) three times a week.

For tickets, contact **Sky Express** (☑ 22220 91876, 28102 23500; www.skyexpress.gr; Skyros Airport), **Aegean Airlines** (☑ 22220 91684; www.aegeanair.com; Skyros Airport) or visit Skyros Travel Agency (p488) in Skyros Town.

BOAT

Skyros' main port is Linaria. Ferries link to Evia (Paralia Kymis; €12.10, 1¾ hours, one to two daily), and Alonnisos and Skopelos in summer (€26, 4½ to five hours, three weekly).

Purchase tickets from Skyros Travel (p488) in Skyros Town or from the ticket kiosk at the dock in Linaria or in Paralia Kymis (Evia).

ⓘ Getting Around

BUS & TAXI

A bus links up with ferry arrivals and runs from Linaria to Skyros Town, Magazia and Molos (€1.80); and from Skyros Town to the airport (€2.70). A **taxi** (☏ 6972894088) from Skyros Town to Linaria costs €15; to the airport it's €25.

CAR & MOTORCYCLE

Cars, motorbikes and bicycles can all be hired in Skyros Town from **Martina's Rentals** (☏ 22220 92022, 6974752380; Machairas 1; ⊙9am-9pm), or from **Europcar Skyros** (☏ 22220 92092; www.europcar.com; Molos 340) on the way

down to Magazia. **Vayos Motorbikes** (☏ 22220 92957) – also for bicycles – is located near the bus station in Skyros Town.

Skyros Town   Σκύρος

POP 2000

Skyros' capital is draped over a high rocky bluff. It's topped by a 13th-century Venetian fortress, and is laced with labyrinthine, smooth cobblestone streets that invite wandering, but were designed to keep out the elements, and also pirates.

Agoras, the main thoroughfare, is a lively jumble of tavernas, bars and shops flanked by winding alleyways. About 100m past Plateia (the main square), the main drag of Agoras forks left and zigzags to two small museums adjacent to Plateia Rupert Brooke, marked by a bronze nude in his honour, from where a wide stone path descends 1km to Magazia Beach.

Skyros

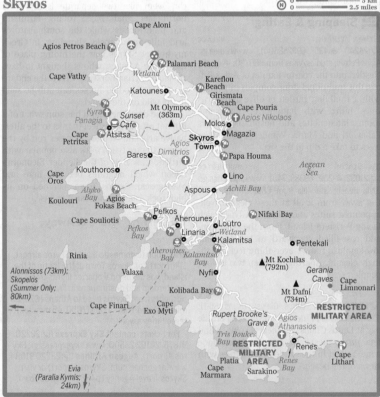

◉ Sights

★ Manos Faltaïts Folk Museum   MUSEUM
(🖉 22220 91232; www.faltaits.gr/english/museum.
htm; Plateia Rupert Brooke; €2, incl tour €5;
⊙ 10am-2pm & 6-9pm) This not-to-be-missed
gem details the mythology and folklore
of Skyros. The 19th-century mansion is a
multilevel labyrinth of Skyrian costumes,
embroidery, antique furniture, ceramics,
daggers, cooking pots and vintage photographs; among the wealth of items is a goat
mask and heavy bells worn by revellers at
carnival time. There's also an excellent gift
shop selling bespoke ceramics, fabrics,
books and prints.

Monastery of St George   MONASTERY
(⊙ 10am-1.30pm) FREE Keep heading uphill
in Skyros Town, and eventually all the winding alleys lead to the Byzantine Monastery
of St George, founded in 962. This working monastery (whose bells might wake
you early if you're staying in the town) was
out of bounds until recently due to earthquake damage. You can now visit its chapel,
which features an ornate gilded screen and
faded frescoes. Beyond are the ruins of the
13th-century Venetian fortress, which are
being restored and may reopen.

Archaeological Museum   MUSEUM
(🖉 22220 91327; Plateia Rupert Brooke; €2;
⊙ 8.30am-3pm Tue-Sun) Along with Mycenaean pottery found near Magazia and
artefacts from the Bronze Age excavation at
Palamari, this attractive courtyard building
contains a traditional Skyrian house interior, transported in its entirety from the
benefactor's home.

🏃 Activities & Tours

★ Feel Ingreece   CULTURAL
(🖉 22220 93100; www.feelingreece.gr; off upper
Agoras; from €20; ⊙ 9.30am-1.30pm & 7-10pm)
Owner Chrysanthi Zygogianni is dedicated
to helping sustain the best of Skyrian culture.
The focus is on local arts and the island's natural environment. The office arranges hiking
excursions to glimpse wild Skyrian horses,
wetland birdwatching trips, pottery, wood-
carving, Skyrian cooking and Greek dance
lessons, and various boat trips. To get here,
turn right opposite Ammos jewellers.

Skyros Centre   COURSE
(🖉 in UK 44(0)1983 865566; www.skyros.com)
Established in 1979, the Skyros Centre fosters alternative living and learning, with res-

idential courses in writing, music, well-being
and the arts. Each day starts with morning
yoga. There's another centre in Atsitsa.

Niko Sikkes   TOURS
(🖉 22220 92707, 69769 83712; nikonisi@hotmail.
com) Contact the well-informed and resourceful Niko Sikkes for his impromptu
tours of the island and the town.

★🎭 Festivals & Events

Skyros Carnival   CARNIVAL
(⊙ Jan/Feb) In this wild pre-Lenten festival,
which takes place on the last four weekends
before Lent and Orthodox Easter, young
men don goat masks, hairy jackets and dozens of copper goat bells. They then proceed
to clank and dance through Skyros Town,
each with a male partner dressed up as a
Skyrian bride but also wearing a goat mask.

The overtly pagan revelries include much
singing, dancing, drinking and feasting.
Local lore is that the event derives from the
story of a shepherd, who went mad when his
goats died in the snow and took to wearing
their skins; the transvestism evident in the
carnival is anyone's guess.

More than 2000 visitors arrive for the
final weekend, so book early, or go during
one of the earlier weekends when you'll
catch more of a local flavour of the festival.

Rembetika Music Festival   MUSIC
(🖉 22220 91232; www.rebetikoseminar.com/index.
php) For one week in mid-July, the Manos
Faltaïts Folk Museum in Skyros Town is host
to a *rembetika* music festival. The festival
includes daily instrument and voice workshops, films and seminars. The evening
hours are filled with music and dinners at
local tavernas, and the week concludes with
a Saturday-night concert, open to the public.

🛏 Sleeping

Pension Nikolas   PENSION €
(🖉 22220 91778; www.nicolaspension.gr; Playia; s/d/
tr €40/50/60; 🅿 ❄ 🛜) Set back on a quiet road
on the edge of town, this friendly pension and
budget gem is only a five-minute walk to busy
Agoras. Upper rooms have air-conditioning
and balconies; the lower rooms have fans and
open onto a shady garden.

★ Hotel Nefeli
& Skyrian Studios   BOUTIQUE HOTEL €€
(🖉 22220 91964; www.skyros-nefeli.gr; d/studio/
ste incl breakfast from €75/95/245; 🅿 ❄ @ 🛜 ⊠)
This smart and welcoming hotel on the

edge of town has an easy minimalist-meets-Skyrian feel to it, with handsome furnishings and swanky bathrooms. Some studios are replicas of Skyrian houses, with internal wooden galleries. The hotel and adjacent studios share a saltwater swimming pool and outdoor bar. Breakfast includes savoury and sweet Greek favourites.

✖ Eating & Drinking

★ **O Pappous Kai Ego**   TAVERNA €
(☑ 22220 93200; Agoras; mains €6-9; ⊙ lunch & dinner) The name of this small taverna means 'my grandfather and me' and it's easy to see how one generation of family recipes followed another. It's well known for the Skyrian dolmadhes made with a touch of goat milk. A lovely corner location on Agoras, on a raised outdoor terrace.

Maryetis Restaurant   GREEK €
(☑ 22220 91311; Agoras; mains €6-9; ⊙ lunch & dinner) The local favourite in town for grilled fish and octopus *stifadho*, great grills and mezedhes. Wines and service are excellent.

★ **Kalypso**   BAR
(Agoras; ⊙ noon-late; 🛜) Classy Kalypso occupies a historic pharmacy building, and with its gleaming wood and marbled floors makes the best spot for a coffee in town: grab a breakfast pastry from the simple bakery right next door. Owner-bartender Hristos plays lots of jazz and blues and makes a fine straight-up margarita along with homemade sangria.

ℹ Information

National Bank of Greece (Agoras) Has an ATM.

Police (☑ 22220 91274; Agoras)

Post Office (Plateia; ⊙ 7.30am-2pm) On the main square.

Skyrian Horse Society (☑ 22220 92345, 6974694023; www.skyrianhorsesociety.gr)

Skyros Travel Agency (☑ 22220 91600, 6944884588; www.skyrostravel.com; Agoras; ⊙ 9.30am-1.30pm & 6.30-9.30pm) Helpful full-service agency that arranges accommodation; transfers and onward travel; car and motorbike hire; and 4WD and boat excursions around Skyros.

Magazia & Molos
Μαγαζιά & Μώλος

POP 400

The resort of Magazia is a compact and colourful maze of winding alleys that skirts the southern end of a long, sandy beach beneath Skyros Town. The name 'Magazia' comes from the Greek word for shop; the original buildings were storehouses for olive oil, produce and dry goods.

SKYROS' ARTISTIC HOMES

Skyros has a flourishing community of working artists, from potters and painters to sculptors and weavers. The island artistry dates from Byzantine times when passing pirates collaborated with rogue residents, whose houses became virtual galleries for stolen booty looted from merchant ships, including ceramic plates and copper ornaments from Europe, the Middle East and Asia Minor. Today, similar items adorn almost every Skyrian house, shown to best advantage on locally carved wooden shelves.

The best places to see Skyrian domestic interiors are the Manos Faltaïts Folk Museum (p487) and the Archaeological Museum (p487), both of which contain atmospheric recreated homesteads. A key feature is the dramatic *boulmes*, a carved screen often decorated with the Byzantine two-headed eagle, cockerels and pomegranates. Stone hearths are embellished with embroidery, and shelves display glass and clayware. The *krevatsoula* is a low wooden bed with fabric drapes and embroidered cushions, which might depict gorgons, ships or weddings, and small wooden chairs and shelves are carved with more emblems and patterns. The overall effect is rich and sophisticated, as are the dashing 18th- and 19th-century traditional costumes which both museums display.

To see the legacy of Skyrian traditions, check out the work of ceramicist Stamatis Ftoulis and embroiderers and woodcarvers **Olga Zacharaiki** (☑ 6974666113; Agoras; ⊙ 11am-10pm), **Andreou Stamatiou** (☑ 22220 92827; Agoras; ⊙ 11am-10pm) and **Amersa Panagiotou** (☑ 22220 92827; Agoras; ⊙ 10am-10pm). Several artisans display their work between the Plateia and upper Agoras; Chrysanthi at Feel Ingreece (p487) can fill you in on the local scene.

Near the northern end of the beach, once-sleepy Molos now has its own share of tavernas, bars and rooms. Its landmark windmill (now a bar) and adjacent rock-hewn church of Agios Nikolaos are easy to spot. Skinny-dippers can leave it all behind at nude-friendly **Papa Houma** near the southern end of Magazia.

◉ Sights

Agios Nikolaos CHURCH
A huge rectangular free-standing rock forms the sacred space of Agios Nikolaos; the area was a quarry in ancient times. The turquoise door opens into the candelit sanctuary with its altar and icons.

Stamatis Ftoulis GALLERY
(☎22220 92220, 22220 91559; Magazia; ☺11am-9pm) Intimate ceramics workshop on the narrow boardwalk at Magazia; also has a showroom in Skyros Town.

🛏 Sleeping

★Antigoni Studios APARTMENT €
(☎6945100230, 22220 91310; www.antigoni studios.com; d/f from €55/85; P❄🐧) Outstanding addition to the Magazia sleep scene, with 20 large studios, each with handsome furnishings, kitchens, modern bathrooms – all just a three-minute walk to the beach. Managed by the hospitable Katarina,

it's located at the southern edge of Magazia. Book well in advance.

★Perigiali Hotel & Studios HOTEL €
(☎22220 92075; www.perigiali.com; Magazia; d/tr/apt incl breakfast from €55/80/115; P❄@🐧❄) Leafy Perigiali feels secluded despite being only 60m from the beach. Skyrian-style rooms overlook a garden with pear and apricot trees, while an upscale wing sports a pool with luxe apartments; includes a great buffet breakfast. Owner Amalia is full of ideas for travellers.

Ariadne Apartments HOTEL €
(☎22220 91113; www.ariadnestudios.gr; Magazia; d/apt from €60/85; ❄@🐧) Just 50m from the beach, these inviting studios and two-room apartments enclose a small courtyard and breakfast cafe (with great pastries). Spacious rooms have fully equipped kitchens and are decorated with original artwork and Skyrian woodwork.

Ammos Hotel HOTEL €€
(☎22220 91234, 6974354181; www.skyrosammos hotel.com; Magazia; d/f incl breakfast from €80/110; P❄🐧❄) This strikingly well-designed lodging is low-key and inviting, with soothing pale-hued rooms, handsome bathrooms, overhead fans and made-to-order Skyrian breakfasts to start the day, plus a rooftop terrace to catch the sunset.

WORTH A TRIP

PALAMARI ΠΑΛΑΜΑΡΙ

At the northeast end of the island, uncrowded Palamari occupies a graceful stretch of sandy beach, and is the site of a fascinating **archaeological dig** (http://geomorphologie.revues. org/668; Palamari; ⊙8am-2pm) FREE located down a dirt road, where a Bronze Age town dating from between 2500 BC and 1650 BC has been excavated. Work began in 1981, uncovering artefacts relating to fishing and hunting, stone walls, even drainpipes and paved walkways. The excavation provided evidence of a powerfully fortified prehistoric coastal settlement near the heart of early Mediterranean trade routes, and you can now follow walkways around it.

A small well-organised visitor centre opened in 2014, and more findings from Palamari are on display at the Archaeological Museum (p487) in Skyros Town.

An adjacent wetland is the remnant of an ancient lagoon, which supported this fishing and hunting community. Today it remains a major birdwatching attraction, notable for long-legged waders like herons and ibises.

✗ Eating & Drinking

⭐ **Stefanos Taverna** TAVERNA €
(☑6974350372; Magazia; mains €5.50-9.50; ⊙breakfast, lunch & dinner) Sit on the terrace overlooking the beach and choose from a range of baked dishes such as *yemista* (stuffed tomatoes), juicy grills and locally made sausage, wild greens and fresh fish. Breakfast omelettes start at €3.

⭐ **Oi Istories Tou Barba** TAVERNA €
(☑22220 91453; Molos; mains €4-10; ⊙lunch & dinner) Look for the light-blue railing above the beach in Molos to find this excellent cafe-taverna with handwritten menus and delicious lobster spaghetti.

⭐ **Anenomulos** BAR
(☑22220 93656; www.anemomulos.gr; Cape Pouria; ⊙9am-3am) Gorgeous conversion of a windmill, perched on the sea by the rock-cut church of Agios Nikolaos. They serve snacks, wines and cocktails, and the sundowner location is sublime. A couple of tables perch on little wooden platforms on the surrounding rocks, where you can watch the sun set on distant Skyros Town.

Northwest Coast

The picturesque port village of **Atsitsa** on the island's west coast occupies a woody shoreline setting. There's an outpost of the alternative learning Skyros Centre (p487) here, and the organic **Sunset Cafe** (snacks €1.50-4; ⊙breakfast-sunset) overlooks the bay. Two kilometres north, find the excellent roadside taverna **Cook-Nara** (☑22221 00005; Kyra Panagia; mains €5-9.50; ⊙lunch & dinner).

At azure-blue **Cape Petritsa**, 1.5km south of Atsitsa, the coastal road turns inland, finding the sea again at sandy **Agios Fokas Bay**, with a taverna and great swimming.

A beautiful horseshoe-shaped beach graces **Pefkos Bay**, 10km southeast of Atsitsa, where you can lunch at **Stamatia's Taverna** (mains €7-11; ⊙noon-midnight). Nearby, the beach at **Aherounes** has a gentle kid-friendly sandy bottom, along with two tavernas and domatia.

Tris Boukes Bay
Όρμος Τρεις Μπούκες

The southernmost corner of the island is a windswept landscape partly restricted by a Greek naval station. Many come here to visit English poet Rupert Brooke's grave, just inland from Tris Boukes Bay. It's signed with a wooden sign in Greek. The gravestone is inscribed with Brooke's most famous sonnet, 'The Soldier'. When Brooke's fellow naval officers buried him, they erected a simple wooden cross (now in England) with an inscription originally in Greek: 'Here lies the servant of God, sub-lieutenant in the English Navy, who died for the deliverance of Constantinople from the Turks.'

From Tris Boukes Bay, a rough dirt road (4WD recommended) leads to Renes Bay, from where a 5km hiking trail skirts a coastal plateau, ending at the lighthouse at Cape Lithari. Small herds of wild Skyrian horses are often glimpsed here, along with rare Eleonora's falcons that nest in the steep cliffs nearby from April to October.

Ionian Islands

Best Places to Eat

- ➜ White House (p504)
- ➜ Carnayo (p507)
- ➜ Nissi (p512)
- ➜ Prosilio (p529)
- ➜ O Platanos (p536)

Best Places to Stay

- ➜ Perantzada 1811 (p524)
- ➜ Petani Bay Hotel (p520)
- ➜ El Sol Hotel (p534)
- ➜ Levant Hotel (p505)
- ➜ Torri E Merli (p508)

Why Go?

With their cooler climate, abundant olive and cypress trees, and forested mountains, the Ionians (Τα Ιόνια Νησιά) are a lighter, greener variation on the Greek template. Venetian, French and British occupiers have all helped to shape the islands' architecture, culture and (excellent) cuisine, and contributed to the unique feel of Ionian life.

Though the islands lie linked in a chain along the west coast of mainland Greece, each has its own distinct landscape and history. Corfu Town holds Parisian-style arcades, Venetian alleyways and Italian-inspired delicacies. Lefkada boasts some of Greece's finest turquoise-lapped beaches, while Kefallonia is adorned with soaring mountains and vineyards. Paxi's Italianate harbour villages are impossibly pretty, and soulful Ithaki preserves wild terrain and a sense of myth. Zakynthos has sea caves and waters teeming with turtles, and Kythira offers off-the-beaten-track walks. The Ionians hold something new for adventure seekers, food lovers, culture vultures and beach bums alike.

When to Go
Corfu Town

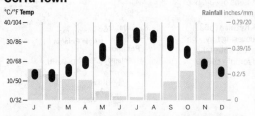

May Life is still quiet while the wildflowers are in bloom everywhere.

Jul Escape the heat elsewhere in Greece by heading to the country's coolest islands.

Sep Leaves change colour, and the *robola* grapes are harvested in Kefallonia.

Ionian Islands Highlights

1 Corfu Town (p495) Exploring world-class museums, fortresses and restaurants, as well as Venetian, French and British architecture.

2 Paxi (p506) Hopping from one gorgeous harbour to another on this tiny pastoral island.

3 Fiskardo (p521) Savouring the flavours in the waterfront restaurants of Kefallonia's best-preserved historic village.

4 Kefallonia (p515) Diving and kayaking in the myriad magnificent bays that pepper Kefallonia's coastline.

5 Beaches Ranking your favourite strips of sand, from the busiest on Corfu (p674) and Zakynthos (p699) to the quieter joys of Paxi (p676) and Lefkada's west coast (p513).

6 Ithaki (p523) Walking in the footsteps of epic poet Homer.

7 Kythira (p531) Discovering tiny villages, waterfalls and remote coves.

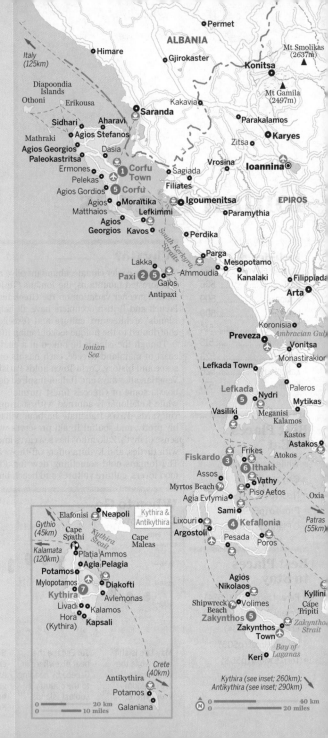

History

The origin of the name 'Ionian' is obscure, but may derive from the goddess Io. A paramour of Zeus, she passed through what's now known as the Ionian Sea while fleeing the wrath of Hera.

According to the writings of Homer, the Ionian Islands were important during Mycenaean times, but to date only tombs, not villages or palaces, have been identified. By the 8th century BC the islands belonged to mighty city-state Corinth, but Corfu staged a successful revolt a century later. The Peloponnesian Wars (431–404 BC) left Corfu as little more than a staging post for whoever happened to be controlling Greece.

By the end of the 3rd century BC, the Romans ruled the Ionians. Anthony and Cleopatra dined on Paxi the night before the Battle of Actium (31 BC), and the emperor Nero holidayed on Corfu in the 1st century AD. Later, the islands suffered waves of invaders: the Byzantine Empire, Venice, Napoleon (in 1797), Russia (from 1799 to 1807), and then Napoleon again.

In 1815 the Ionians became a British protectorate. Although the British improved infrastructure, developed agriculture and industry, and even taught the Corfiots cricket, nationalists campaigned against their oppressive rule, and by 1864 Britain relinquished the islands to Greece.

WWII was rough on the Ionians, under occupation first by the Italians and then the Germans. Further mass emigration followed devastating earthquakes in 1948 and 1953. But by the 1960s foreign holidaymakers were visiting in increasing numbers, and tourism has flourished ever since.

CORFU (KERKYRA)

KEPKYPA

POP 102,070

Still recognisable as the idyllic refuge where the shipwrecked Odysseus was soothed and sent on his way home, Corfu continues to welcome weary travellers with its lush scenery, bountiful produce and pristine beaches.

Since the 8th century BC the island the Greeks call Kerkyra has been prized for its untamed beauty and strategic location. Ancient armies fought to possess it, while in the early days of modern Greece it was a beacon of learning. Corfiots remain proud of their intellectual and artistic roots, with vestiges of the past ranging from Corfu Town's Venetian architecture to British legacies such as cricket and ginger beer.

While certain regions of the island have succumbed to overdevelopment, particularly those close to Corfu Town, Corfu is large enough to make it possible to escape the crowds. Venture across cypress-studded hills to find vertiginous villages in the fertile interior, and sandy coves lapped by cobalt-blue waters.

ℹ️ Getting There & Away

AIR

Corfu's **airport** (☏ 26610 89600; www.corfu-airport.com) is on the southwestern fringes of Corfu Town, just over 2km southwest of the Old Town.

Domestic

Aegean Air (www.aegeanair.com) Direct flights to Athens and Thessaloniki.

Astra Airlines (www.astra-airlines.gr) Direct flights to Thessaloniki.

Sky Express (www.skyexpress.gr) Operates a thrice-weekly island-hopping route to Preveza, Kefallonia and Zakynthos.

DESTINATION	DURATION	FARE	FREQUENCY
Athens	1hr	€65	3 daily
Kefallonia	75min	€73	3 weekly
Preveza	30min	€73	3 weekly
Thessaloniki	55min	€76	3 weekly
Zakynthos	2hr	€79	3 weekly

International

Both **EasyJet** (www.easyjet.com) and **Ryanair** (www.ryanair.com) offer direct flights in summer between Corfu and the UK, and several other European destinations, while **British Airways** (www.ba.com) also flies from the UK to Corfu. Between May and September, many charter flights come from northern Europe and the UK.

BOAT

Ferries depart from Neo Limani (New Port), west of Corfu Town's Old Town.

Domestic

Ticket agencies line Ethnikis Antistaseos in Corfu Town, facing the Neo Limani.

Two ferry operators connect Corfu Town with Paxi:

Ilida (☏ Corfu 26610 49800, Paxi 26620 32401; Ethnikis Antistaseos 1) High-speed hydrofoil, from mid-March to mid-October.

Kamelia Lines (☏ Corfu 26610 40372, Paxi 26620 32131; www.kamelialines.gr) Runs the *Despina* ferry; advance bookings are essential.

No ferries sail directly to Zakynthos; fly with **Sky Express** (www.skyexpress.gr) instead.

Some international ferries from Corfu also call in at Igoumenitsa and Kefallonia. For schedules, see www.openseas.gr. If you're heading to Patra, catch the ferry to Igoumenitsa first.

ROUTE	DURATION	FARE	FREQUENCY
Corfu–Igoumenitsa	1¼hr	€10	hourly
Lefkimmi–Igoumenitsa	1hr 10min	€7	6 daily
Corfu–Paxi (high-speed)	55min	€25	1-3 daily

Italy

ANEK Lines (www.anek.gr) ferries connect Corfu with Bari (€60, eight hours, two weekly) and Ancona (€85, 14½ hours, one to two daily) in Italy, and Igoumenitsa on the Greek mainland, where you can pick up other connections.

BUS

Green Buses (www.greenbuses.gr) goes to Athens (€48, 8½ hours, three daily, from Monday to Thursday; one via Lefkimmi), Thessaloniki (€38.50, eight hours, twice daily) and Larisa (€30.40, 5½ hours, daily).

Corfu

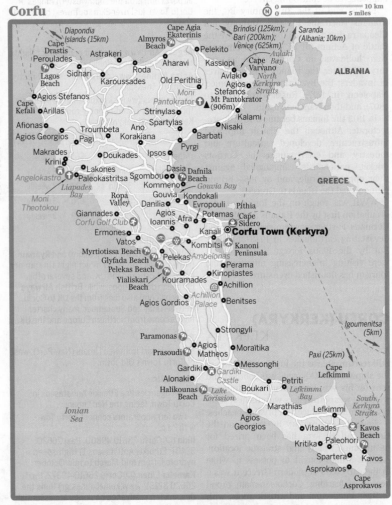

ℹ Getting Around

TO/FROM THE AIRPORT

Taxis between the airport and Corfu Town cost around €12, while local bus 15 runs to both Plateia G Theotoki (Plateia San Rocco) in town and the Neo Limani (New Port) New Port beyond.

BUS

Long-distance Green Buses radiate out from Corfu Town's **long-distance bus station** (☑ 26610 28900; www.greenbuses.gr; I Theotoki) in the New Town. Fares cost €1.50 to €4.80; services are reduced on Saturday, and may be nonexistent on Sundays and holidays.

DESTINATION	DURATION	FREQUENCY
Agios Gordios	45min	8 daily
Agios Stefanos	2hr	4 daily
Aharavi (via Roda)	1¼hr	7 daily
Arillas (via Afionas)	1¼hr	2 daily
Barbati	45min	10 daily
Ermones	30min	7 daily
Glyfada	45min	6 daily
Kassiopi	1¼hr	8 daily
Kavos	1½hr	10 daily
Messonghi	35min	15 daily
Paleokastritsa	1hr	11 daily
Pyrgi	30min	5 daily
Sidhari	1¼hr	8 daily
Spartera	1½hr	2 daily

Local blue buses depart from the **local bus station** (☑ 26610 31595; www.astikoktelkerkyras.gr; Plateia G Theotoki) in Corfu Old Town. Journeys cost €1.20 or €1.70. Buy tickets at the booth on Plateia G Theotiki, or on the bus itself if heading to Achillion, Benitses or Kouramades. All trips are less than 30 minutes. Service is reduced on weekends.

CAR & MOTORCYCLE

Car- and motorbike-hire outlets (Alamo, Hertz, Europcar etc) abound at the airport, in Corfu Town and the resorts. Prices start at around €50 per day.

Corfu Town   Κέρκυρα

POP 30,000

Imbued with Venetian grace and elegance, historic Corfu Town (also known as Kerkyra) stands halfway down the island's east coast. The name Corfu, meaning 'peaks', refers to its twin hills, each topped by a massive fortress built to withstand Ottoman sieges. Sitting between the two, the Old Town is a tight-packed warren of winding lanes, some bursting with fine restaurants, lively bars and intriguing shops, others timeless back alleys where washing lines stretch from balcony to balcony. It also holds some majestic architecture, including the splendid Liston arcade, and high-class museums, along with no fewer than 39 churches.

During the day, cruise passengers and day trippers bustle through the streets; come evening, everyone settles down to enjoy themselves. When it comes to drinking, dining and dancing, this is the hottest spot in the Ionian Islands.

⊙ Sights

The Old Town's most eye-catching feature is the grand French-built Liston arcade, facing the Old Fort across the lawns of the Spianada, and lined with packed cafes. At its northern end, the neoclassical Palace of St Michael & St George contains the excellent Corfu Museum of Asian Art. Head inland and you can lose yourself for a happy hour or two amid the maze-like alleyways, seeking out sumptuous Orthodox churches or cosy cafes as the mood takes you.

Continue southwest, skirting the mighty Neo Frourio (New Fort; p496), to reach the New Town, busy with everyday shops and services and centring on Plateia G Theotoki (also known as Plateia San Rocco). To the south, around curving Garitsa Bay, the ruin-strewn Mon Repos Estate (p496) marks the site of the ancient settlement of Palaeopolis.

★ **Corfu Museum of Asian Art**   MUSEUM
(☑ 26610 30443; www.matk.gr; Palace of St Michael & St George; adult/child €6/3; ⊙ 8am-8pm) Home to stunning artefacts ranging from prehistoric bronzes to works in onyx and ivory, this excellent museum occupies the central portions of the Palace of St Michael & St George. One gallery provides a chronological overview of Chinese ceramics, while showcasing remarkable jade carvings and snuff bottles. The India section opens with Alexander the Great, 'When Greece Met India', and displays fascinating Graeco-Buddhist figures, including a blue-grey schist Buddha. A new Japanese section incorporates magnificent samurai armour, Noh masks and superb woodblock prints.

IONIAN ISLANDS CORFU (KERKYRA)

Municipal Art Gallery   GALLERY

(☑ 26610 48690; www.artcorfu.com; Palace of St Michael & St George; €2; ☻9am-4pm Tue-Sun) Make the effort to find this gallery - it's entered via a staircase that climbs from the wide patio on the palace's eastern side - and you'll be rewarded with a handful of high-quality Byzantine icons, including 16th-century works by the Cretan Damaskinos, plus a more extensive array of canvases by Corfiot painters. Look out for the Italian-influenced 19th-century father and son artists, Spyridon and Paul Prossalendis.

★ Palaio Frourio   FORTRESS

(Old Fort; ☑ 26610 48310; adult/concession €6/3; ☻8am-8pm Apr-Oct, 8.30am-3pm Nov-Mar) The rocky headland that juts east from Corfu Town is topped by the Venetian-built 14th-century Palaio Frourio. Before that, already enclosed within massive stone walls, it cradled the entire Byzantine city. A solitary bridge crosses its seawater moat.

Only parts of this huge site, which also holds later structures from the British era, are accessible to visitors; wander up to the lighthouse on the larger of the two hills for superb views, or down to reach small gravelly beaches.

Vidos Island   ISLAND

Hourly boats from the Old Port make the 10-minute crossing to tiny, thickly wooded Vidos Island (€5 return), immediately offshore. There's a taverna at the jetty, but the big attraction is to walk the 600m across the island to reach a couple of lovely beaches on its northern shore.

Antivouniotissa Museum   MUSEUM

(Byzantine Museum; ☑ 26610 38313; www.antivouniotissamuseum.gr; off Arseniou; adult/child €4/€2; ☻8.30am-3pm Tue-Sun) Home to an outstanding collection of Byzantine and post-Byzantine icons and artefacts, the exquisite, timber-roofed Church of Our Lady of Antivouniotissa doubles as both church and museum. It stands atop a short, broad stairway that climbs from shore-front Arseniou, and frames views out towards the wooded Vidos island.

Mon Repos Estate   PARK

(Kanoni Peninsula; ☻7.30am-7.30pm May-Oct, to 5pm Nov-Apr) FREE This park-like wooded estate 2km around the bay south of the Old Town was the site of Corfu's most important ancient settlement, Palaeopolis. More recently, in 1921, the secluded neoclassical villa that now holds the Museum of Palaeopolis was the birthplace of Prince Philip of Greece, who was to marry Britain's Queen Elizabeth II. Footpaths lead through the woods to ancient ruins, including sanctuaries to Hera and Apollo, and a more complete Doric temple atop a small coastal cliff.

It takes half an hour to walk to Mon Repos from town, or you can catch bus 2a from the Spianada (€1.70, every 20 minutes). Bring a picnic and plenty of water; there are no shops nearby.

Corfu Living History   HOUSE

(Casa Parlante; ☑ 26610 49190; www.casaparlante.gr; N Theotoki 16; €5; ☻10am-6pm) Corfu Living History is a town house that has been remodelled to illustrate the daily lives of a fictitious merchant family from the mid-19th century. Enthusiastic tour guides make the whole experience fun and informative, while in each room waxworks make small, endlessly repeated movements.

Neo Frourio   FORTRESS

(New Fort; ☻9am-3.30pm) FREE The forbidding Neo Frourio is in fact little younger than the Old Fort across town. Surrounded by massive walls that crown the low hill at the western edge of the Old Town, it too dates from the Venetian era. Climbing the stairway at the western end of Solomou brings you to the entrance, where dank tunnels and passages lead through the walls. The ramparts beyond enjoy wonderful views.

Church of Agios Spyridon   CHURCH

(Agios Spyridonos; ☻8am-9pm) Pilgrims and day trippers alike throng this Old Town landmark. As well as magnificent frescoes, the small 16th-century basilica holds the remains of Corfu's patron saint, Spyridon, a 4th-century Cypriot shepherd. His body, brought here from Constantinople in 1453, lies in an elaborate silver casket, and is paraded through the town on festival days.

Corfu Philharmonic Society   MUSEUM

(☑ 26610 39289; www.fek.gr; N Theotoki 10; €2; ☻9.30am-1.30pm Mon-Sat) Via battered old instruments, photos and scores, this entertaining little museum tells the story of Greece's first-ever marching band, which performed at the first modern Olympics in 1896, and still plays regularly. Founded in 1840 by Nikolaos Mantzaros, composer of the Greek national anthem, the Corfu Philharmonic Society offers free music lessons for local kids in the afternoons.

Corfu Reading Society   HISTORIC BUILDING

(☑26610 39528; www.anagnostikicorfu.com; Kapodistriou 120; ◷9.30am-1.30pm Mon-Sat) **FREE** Although there's no obvious sign on this grand cream-and-white villa, anyone is welcome to climb its external staircase and settle down with a book in the library of the Corfu Reading Society. Founded in 1836, the oldest cultural institution in modern Greece holds 30,000 volumes in several languages, mostly devoted to the Ionian Islands.

Banknote Museum   MUSEUM

(☑26610 41552; www.alphanumismatics.gr; Plateia Agios Spyridon; ◷9am-2pm & 5.30-8.30pm Wed & Fri, 9am-3pm Thu, 8.30am-3pm Sat & Sun) **FREE** Somewhat specialist, but oddly fascinating, the Banknote Museum occupies the upper floors of what was in 1840 the first-ever all-Greek bank. It traces the story of the drachma until it was replaced by the euro in 2002, and includes the largest denomination note ever issued: a 100-billion-drachma note from the inflationary era of 1944.

☞ Tours

All sorts of tours can help you explore in and around Corfu Town, whether on foot with **Corfu Walking Tours** (☑6980140160; www.corfuwalkingtours.com), by bus with **Corfu Sightseeing** (www.corfusightseeing.gr; €15), or in the **toy-train** and **horse-drawn carriage** tours that start from the Spianada. Cruises along the coast or to neighbouring islands start from the New Port, with operators including **Ionian Cruises** (☑26610 31649; www.ionian-cruises.com; Ethnikis Antistaseos 4) and **Sarris Cruises** (☑26610 25317; www.sarriscruises.gr; Mouriki 1), while if you fancy learning to sail, contact **Corfu Sea School** (☑26610 97628; www.corfuseaschool.com; Gouvia Marina) at Gouvia marina not far northwest.

Venturing further afield, you can go **horse riding** with **Trailriders** (☑6946653317; www.trailriderscorfu.com; Ano Korakiana) in the village of Ano Korakiana, 18km northwest of Corfu Town, or enjoy a round on one of Greece's finest courses at the **Corfu Golf Club** (☑26610 94220; www.corfugolfclub.com) not far from Ermones, 15km west.

The entire island has excellent walking. The **Corfu Trail** (www.thecorfutrail.com) traverses the island from north to south and takes between eight and 12 days to complete. You can organise a trip through Aperghi Travel (p502), or simply arrange a day's guided hiking with **Corfu Walks & Hikes** (www.walking-corfu.blogspot.co.uk).

🛌 Sleeping

As most island visitors head straight to the beaches and resorts, Corfu Town holds fewer accommodation options than you might expect. Those that do exist tend to be relatively pricey, even in low season.

⭐**Bella Venezia**   BOUTIQUE HOTEL €€

(☑26610 46500; www.bellaveneziahotel.com; N Zambeli 4; s/d incl breakfast from €120/135; ☀☎) From the instant you enter this neoclassical villa, set in a peaceful central street, you'll be seduced by its pure old-world charm. Previously both a bank and a girls' school, it features an elegant lobby decked in candelabras, with velvet chairs and a grand piano. The plush, high-ceilinged rooms (some with balconies) have fine city views, while the garden breakfast room is delightful.

Dalia Hotel   HOTEL €€

(☑26610 32341; www.daliahotel.com; Plateia Etikou Stado 9; d/tr incl breakfast €95/103; ☀☎) This friendly, family-run, neighbourhood hotel is set back from the sea, 15 minutes' walk south of the Old Town and just 800m from the airport. The rooms are comfortable but small, and there are bikes available.

Folies Corfu   HOTEL €€

(☑26610 49300; www.foliescorfu.com; s/d €68/81; ☀☎) Bright self-catering studios and one- or two-bedroom apartments, all with balconies or terraces, arrayed around a lush garden pool in a residential neighbourhood. It's well priced thanks to the away-from-it-all location, 2km west of the New Town – a half-hour walk from the centre. Breakfast costs €5 extra.

Arion Hotel   HOTEL €€

(☑26610 37950; www.arioncorfu.gr; Sxerias 6, Mon Repo Anemomylos; s/d/tr incl breakfast €75/90/125; ☀☎) Set 15 minutes' walk south of Corfu Town down waterfront Dimokratias, this large hotel has pleasant rooms with small balconies and clean bathrooms. Avoid cheaper corner rooms and those facing the road, and plump for one with a sea view. There's a handsome lobby, a pool, a great bar and a terrific breakfast smorgasbord. Good value and tranquil.

⭐**Siorra Vittoria**   BOUTIQUE HOTEL €€€

(☑26610 36300; www.siorravittoria.com; Stefanou Padova 36; d incl breakfast from €200; ℗☀☎) Expect luxury and style at this quiet 19th-century Old Town mansion, where restored traditional architecture meets

Corfu Old Town

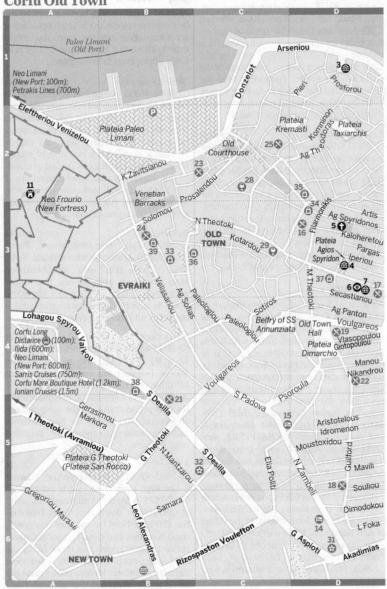

modern amenities; marble bathrooms, crisp linens and genteel service make for a relaxed stay. Breakfast is served either in your room or beneath an ancient magnolia in the peaceful garden.

Corfu Mare Boutique Hotel HOTEL €€€
(📞 26610 31011; www.corfumare.gr; Nikolau Zervou 5; d/tr incl breakfast €175/235; ❋ 🐾 🗙) Palatial villa-like hotel, just up from the New Port and open to adults only. While larger than 'boutique' might suggest, it's every bit as

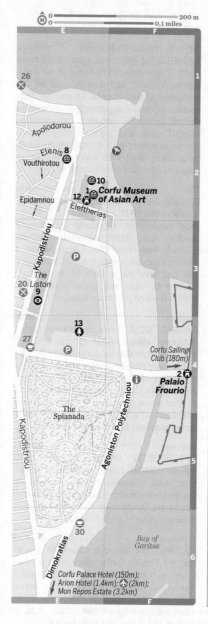

IONIAN ISLANDS CORFU (KERKYRA)

stylish and modern. Each room has its own tasteful decor, with huge prints and striking wallpaper on themes such as pop art and art deco. There's also a bar, a restaurant and a pool.

Corfu Palace Hotel   HOTEL €€€
(☑ 26610 39485; www.corfupalace.com; Dimokratias 2; s/d/tr incl breakfast €168/195/280; ❄ ☎) A grand resort-style hotel on the seafront immediately south of the Old Town. All its bright, floral rooms have views across the

bay, and polished-wood floors or carpets, and there's a large sea-view pool in the gardens.

✖ Eating

Corfiot cuisine shows the delicious influences of many cultures, especially Italian. Great restaurants and tavernas are scattered throughout the Old Town.

★ Pane & Souvlaki   GRILL €
(📞 26610 20100; www.panesouvlaki.com; Guilford 77; mains €5-9; ⊙ noon-1am) Arguably the Old Town's best-value budget option, with outdoor tables on the Town Hall square, this quick-fire restaurant does exactly what its name suggests, serving up three skewers of chicken or pork with chunky chips, dipping sauce and warm pitta in individual metal trays. The salads and burgers are good, too.

★ Starenio   BAKERY €
(📞 26610 47370; Guilford 59; sweets & pastries from €2; ⊙ 8.30am-11pm Mon-Sat) Magical little bakery, dripping with bougainvillea, where in-the-know locals linger at little tables on the sloping pedestrian street to savour cakes, coffee, pastries, and delicious fresh pies with vegetarian fillings such as mushrooms or nettles.

To Alato Pipero   TAVERNA €
(📞 69422 63873; Dhona 17; mains €7-9; ⊙ noon-1am) Welcoming all-day taverna–*ouzeri* (place that serves ouzo and light snacks) with outdoor tables in a pedestrian alley. Grilled specialities include local sausages and pork steaks, squid and anchovies, and vegetarian alternatives such as thinly sliced eggplant.

Chrisomalis   TAVERNA €
(📞 26610 30342; N Theotoki 6; mains €7-13; ⊙ noon-midnight) Going strong for more than 150 years, this traditional little taverna was a haunt of Lawrence Durrell and family and actor Anthony Quinn. Follow your nose to the traditional grill for souvlaki, pork chops and swordfish. Warm service and pavement tables make it ideal for people-watching.

Rouvas   TAVERNA €
(📞 26610 31182; www.facebook.com/taverna rouvas; S Desilla 13; mains €7-9; ⊙ 10am-5pm Mon-Sat) Festooned in flowers and as Greek as it gets, this earthy, lunch-only delight is a Corfiot institution. With its menus of standout dishes such as beef stew with tomatoes and fried salt cod, as well as plenty of veggie

options, even celebrity chef Rick Stein is impressed.

★ To Tavernaki tis Marinas   TAVERNA €€
(📞 26611 00792; 4th Parados, Agias Sofias 1; mains €8-18; ⊙ noon-midnight) Restored stone walls, hardwood floors and cheerful staff lift the ambience of this taverna. Check the daily specials or choose anything from *mousakas* (baked layers of eggplant or zucchini, minced meat and potatoes topped with cheese sauce) or grilled sardines to steak. Accompany it all with a dram of ouzo or *tsipouro* (distilled spirit similar to raki).

Rex   MEDITERRANEAN €€
(📞 26610 39649; www.rexrestaurant.gr; Kapodistriou 66; mains €9-18; ⊙ noon-9pm) A favourite local rendezvous, especially for leisurely lunches, this stately cafe-restaurant set a block back from the Liston serves a Mediterranean-leaning menu of pasta, salads and specialities such as veal *sofrito* (cooked in wine and garlic) and Corfiot rooster (cooked in tomato sauce).

Anthos   GREEK €€
(📞 26610 32252; www.facebook.com/anthos restaurant; Maniarizi-Arlioti 15; mains €10-21; ⊙ noon-midnight Mon-Sat, 6pm-midnight Sun; 🛜) Much-loved little back-alley restaurant, with a handful of outdoor tables. Most diners are here for the seafood, savouring dishes such as squid carpaccio, octopus with fava mousse, and grilled sea bass, but it also serves standard Greek meat favourites.

Veranda   GREEK €€
(📞 26610 81716; Arseniou 19; mains €8-15; ⊙ noon-midnight) Lovely waterfront restaurant, with a shaded terrace jutting over the turquoise waters that's often packed at lunchtime. Diners relish Greek classics, from cheesy shrimp to grilled chicken skewers.

Il Vesuvio   ITALIAN €€
(📞 26610 21284; Guilford 16; mains €9-18; ⊙ noon-late; 🛜) A classy Italian place, with outdoor tables on both sides of the pedestrian street, that's won awards for its moreish homemade gnocchi, cannelloni and pizzas. Leave room for the silky-smooth panna cotta, so fresh it will make your taste buds sing.

★ Venetian Well   GREEK €€€
(📞 26615 50955; www.venetianwell.gr; Plateia Kremasti; mains €15-34; ⊙ 7pm-midnight, closed winter; ✱🛜) Corfu Town's finest special-occasion restaurant has a beautifully faded

square to itself, hidden away near the cathedral and complete with a genuine Venetian well. The exquisite contemporary approach to cuisine adorns local meats, fish and vegetables with all sorts of foams, mousses and gels; even if you can't always tell what it is you're eating, it's invariably delicious.

🍷 Drinking & Nightlife

Perhaps the best place to kick-start the evening is on the stylish Liston arcade, where Corfiots go to see and be seen; after that, the choices are legion.

For dance venues, head after 11pm to Corfu's disco strip, starting west beyond the New Port, along Ethnikis Antistaseos; take a taxi, as it's a busy, unlit road without walkways. A €10 admission fee usually includes one drink.

★ Mikro Café   BAR
(☑ 26610 31009; www.mikrocafe.com; N Theotoki 42) Whether your favoured beverage is coffee, wine or beer, the Old Town holds no finer spot for drinking and people-watching than the delightful, multilevel vine-shaded terrace of the convivial 'little cafe'.

54 Dreamy Nights   CLUB
(☑ 6940645436; www.54dreamynights.com; Ethnikis Antistaseos 54; ⊘ 10pm-late; 🛜) Gleaming, bright-white nightspot, west along the New Port, with a minimalist aesthetic, spectacular night shows and a retractable roof. Open-air DJ parties and live gigs by big-name Greek music stars attract up to 3000 clubbers.

Kourdisto Portokali   BAR
(☑ 6933291188; www.facebook.com/kourdisto.gr; Alypiou 5; ⊘ 9.30am-3pm & 6pm-6am) A cool haven for the Old Town's retro rockers, on a hilly alleyway just south of the cathedral; the name means 'Clockwork Orange', hence the splendid hanging sign. There's always a rocking vinyl soundtrack.

NAOK Azur   CAFE
(☑ 26610 80700; www.naokazur.com; Dimokratias 1; ⊘ 9am-late) Chic, split-level venue across from the Spianada, with an all-day beach bar on its own little gravel beach, and several higher tiers incorporating a restaurant, a cafe and, after sundown, a fully fledged nightclub.

Josephine   CAFE
(☑ 26610 27275; www.josephinecafe.com; Liston 4; ⊘ 9am-2am; 🛜) Emulate Napoleon's namesake empress by lounging for a languid hour, over coffee or fine French wine, on the plush seats of the Liston arcade's grandest cafe.

★ Entertainment

Corfu Town has a lively cultural life; check www.corfuland.gr (in Greek) for current listings.

Cine Orfeas   CINEMA
(☑ 26610 39769; www.cineorfeas.gr; Aspioti 1) Hidden beneath an apartment block, the Old Town's only cinema screens the latest big movies in their original languages.

Municipal Theatre   PERFORMING ARTS
(☑ 26610 33598; G Theotoki 68) This brutalist modern edifice, on the edge of the Old Town, serves as Corfu's cultural powerhouse, putting on classical music, opera, dance and drama; some productions are also staged at the theatre next to Mon Repos (p496).

🛍 Shopping

The Old Town is crammed with shopping opportunities. The heaviest concentration of souvenir shops, which sell everything from 'evil eye' amulets and olive-wood carvings to pashminas and perfume, is along narrow Filarmonikis between the two main churches, while N Theotoki is good for idiosyncratic boutiques.

★ Sweet'n'Spicy Bahar   SPICES
(☑ 26610 33848; www.sweetnspicy.gr; Agias Sofias 12; ⊘ 9am-8.30pm) Gloriously aromatic spice and condiment shop, run by an ever-so-enthusiastic Greek-Canadian-Lebanese woman with a palpable love for devising her own enticing mixes of Greek and imported spices.

Papagiorgis   FOOD & DRINKS
(☑ 26610 39474; www.papagiorgis.gr; N Theotoki 32; ⊘ 9am-midnight) Irresistible old-fashioned patisserie that's an Old Town landmark thanks to its 40 different flavours of ice cream, plus a mouthwatering array of homemade tarts, biscuits and honey.

Corfu Sandals   SHOES
(☑ 26610 47301; www.facebook.com/corfusandals; Philhellinon 9; ⊘ 9am-11pm) This standout shoe store, on the narrow lane that holds Corfu Town's heaviest (and tackiest) concentration of souvenir shops, sells well-priced handmade leather sandals in all styles and sizes, many with ergonomic bubble soles.

IONIAN ISLANDS CORFU (KERKYRA)

WORTH A TRIP

SOUTHERN CORFU

The first resort that you reach as you head south on the coast road from Corfu Town is sleepy **Benitses**, 14km along. This pleasant old village backs a sand-and-gravel beach and is home to a ruined Roman villa, with footpaths ascending the wooded slopes.

Further south again, beyond the popular but uninspiring beach resorts of **Moraï-tika** and **Messonghi**, the coastal road winds through sun-dappled woods, passing prettier and much less developed little coves. Tiny **Boukari** cradles an attractive little harbour, while the fishing port of **Petriti**, where the road finally turns away from the shoreline, holds a row of welcoming seafood tavernas. Nearing the southern tip of Corfu, **Lefkimmi** is an elongated little town where everyday life simply carries on as usual, untroubled by visitors.

Sights

Achillion Palace (☑ 26610 56210; www.achillion-corfu.gr; Gastouri; €8; ☺ 8am-8pm Apr-Oct, to 4pm Nov-Mar) Set atop a steep coastal hill 12km south of Corfu Town, the Achillion Palace was built during the 1890s as the summer palace of Austria's empress Elizabeth, the niece of King Otto of Greece. The palace's two principal features are its intricately decorated central staircase, rising in geometrical flights, and its sweeping garden terraces, which command eye-popping views.

Eating

Klimataria (☑ 26610 71201; www.klimataria-restaurant.gr; Benitses; mains €8-15; ☺ 6.30-11.30pm Mon-Sat, noon-4.30pm Sun) This tiny, old-fashioned taverna, in a custard-coloured villa facing the main road, is worth a pilgrimage in its own right – every dish is delicious and superbly fresh, from the tender octopus or various mezedhes (appetisers) to the feta and olive oil. Call for reservations in summer.

Spiros Karidis (☑ 26620 51205; Boukari; mains €8-22; ☺ lunch & dinner) At this seafront taverna facing a tumbledown jetty, just beyond Boukari's harbour, you can feast on locally caught mullet, bass, grouper or octopus beneath the shade of giant eucalyptus trees. Celeb chef Rick Stein has stopped by to pick up a few tips from the excellent owner.

Ceramic Art　　　　　　　CERAMICS
(☑ 26610 95069; www.ceramicart.gr; Agias Sofias 23; ☺ 10am-10pm, reduced hours in winter) This light, appealing Old Town gallery sells affordable pottery ranging from colourful homewares, ornaments and toys to striking wood-fired pieces made using the ancient terra sigillata technique. You can also visit the artists in their workshop, which faces the waterfront near the Old Port.

Handiworks Hierotechnima　　ARTS & CRAFTS
(Paleologlou 60; ☺ 8am-8pm Mon-Sat) Backstreet shop selling one-of-a-kind, mostly wooden ornaments and souvenirs, hand-crafted on the premises by the friendly owner. The star attractions are ships made of driftwood, fully rigged with cotton sails.

Corfu Bookbinding　　　　　BOOKS
(☑ 26610 31566; www.ionianbookstore.com; Maniarizi-Arlioti 27; ☺ 10am-9pm Mon-Fri) For souvenir hunters, this old bookshop near the cathedral is of most interest for its hand-made notebooks and unusual framed prints, old and new; serious bibliophiles can join regular bookbinding workshops.

Public Market　　　　　　　MARKET
(north of Plateia G Theotoki; ☺ 6.30am-2pm Mon-Sat) Forming an alleyway between the newer part of town and the New Fort, Corfu Town's fresh-produce market sells fruit and vegetables, mostly local and often organic, plus the daily fisher's catch, and is also home to decent cafes.

❶ Information

All Ways Travel (☑ 26610 33955; www.allways travel.com.gr; Plateia G Theotoki 34) Helpful English-speaking staff in the New Town's main square.

Aperghi Travel (☑ 26610 48713; www.aperghi travel.gr; I Polyla 1) Handles tours and accommodation, especially for walkers on the Corfu Trail (www.corfutrail.com).

Corfu General Hospital (☎ 26613 60400; Kontokali) About 8km west of the town centre.

Municipal Tourist Kiosk (Spianada; ☺ 9am-4pm Mon-Sat Jun-Sep) Helps with accommodation, transport and things to do around Corfu.

Pachis Travel (☎ 26610 28298; www.pachis travel.com; Guilford 7; ☺ 9am-2.30pm & 5.30-9pm Mon-Sat) Busy little agency that's useful for hotels, ferry and plane tickets, and excursions to Paxi.

Post Office (Leoforos Alexandras 26; ☺ 7.30am-8.30pm Mon-Fri)

Tourist Police (☎ 26610 29168; I Andreadi 1) In the New Town, off Plateia G Theotoki (Plateia San Rocco).

❶ Getting Around

Most Corfu Town rental companies are based along the northern waterfront.

Budget (☎ 26610 24404; www.budget.gr; Eleftheriou Venizelou 29)

Sunrise (☎ 26610 44325; www.corfusunrise. com; Ethnikis Antistaseos 16)

Top Cars (☎ 26610 35237; www.carrental corfu.com; Donzelot 25)

Northern Corfu

Immediately north of Corfu Town, the coastline consists of an all-but-continuous strip of busy beach resorts, including **Gouvia**, **Dasia**, **Ipsos** and **Pyrgi**. These offer all you need for a family holiday, but are otherwise unremarkable.

Continue north, though, and the coast road begins to wind and undulate around the massif formed by the island's highest peak, **Mt Pantokrator** (906m). The scenery becomes much more attractive, and each of the pretty little coves that pepper the seafront seems to hold a delightful village, or at least a taverna.

An exhilarating drive – or hike, for those with calves of steel – can take you up either the northern or southern slopes of Mt Pantokrator. Coming from the south, look for a turning just beyond Pyrgi. A narrow road from there switchbacks its way up, passing through the picturesque villages of **Spartylas** and **Strinylas**, then climbs through stark terrain – transformed by wildflowers in spring – to reach the very summit. Sadly, the venerable monastery of **Moni Pantokrator** there is now straddled by a huge and ugly telecommunications tower. The all-round views are as superb as ever, though, stretching as far as the mountains of Albania and the Greek mainland. Alternatively, approaching from the north, the direct ascent begins in Aharavi, while another route from Pelekito stops short of the summit, but enables you to visit the magnificent, beautifully restored Venetian village of **Old Perithia**.

Staying on the coast road north of Pyrgi brings you to **Barbati**, where a large straight beach of flat white pebbles fills a wooded inlet. Further on, in the exquisite bayside village of **Kalami**, down below the road, the former home of Lawrence Durrell now holds a delightful restaurant, White House (p504). North again, **Agios Stefanos** is another attractive fishing village, nestled in a sheltered bay, and flanked by a shingle beach to the north and an olive grove to the south. On the other side of a wooded headland beyond, gorgeous and minimally developed little **Avlaki** lines a popular windsurfing beach.

Still no more than a village despite a history stretching back to the Romans – Nero holidayed outrageously here – charming **Kassiopi** spreads between a sheltered harbour and a thin strip of stony beach. It's home to some excellent restaurants and hotels, as well as shops selling the renowned local embroidery. Steps climb up from the main street to the overgrown, but enticing, ruins of a Venetian castle immediately above; walk around the headland instead to reach secluded **Battaria** and **Kanoni** beaches.

Beyond Kassiopi, the coast road heads west past the resorts of **Aharavi**, **Roda** and **Sidhari**, hugely popular with British families drawn by the broad, crowded beaches and inexpensive tavernas. Look out in Aharavi for the **Folklore Museum** (☎ 26630 63479; www.museum-acharavi.webs.com; Aharavi; adult/child €3/1.50; ☺ 10am-2pm Mon-Sat), an enjoyable mishmash of everything from accordions and olive presses to puppets and phones. Confusingly, Corfu holds another resort named **Agios Stefanos**, on the far northwest coast and fronted by a large sandy beach. From either there or Sidhari, excursion boats head in summer to the **Diapondia Islands**, a little-known cluster 40 minutes offshore; reserve through **San Stefano Travel** (☎ 26630 51910; www.san-stefano. gr; Agios Stefanos, northeast coast).

🛏 Sleeping

Dionysus Camping Village CAMPGROUND € (☎ 26610 91417; www.dionysuscamping.gr; Dafnila Bay; campsites per adult/car/tent €7.10/4.40/4.50, huts per person €14; ☎ ⛱) What better setting for a campsite than a shaded, tiered 400-year-old olive grove? Located near Dasia

THE DURRELLS

British writers Gerald and Lawrence Durrell lived on Corfu for the four years preceding WWII. Gerald, then a child but later a prominent naturalist, chronicled his eccentric family's island idyll in several charming and hilarious books. The three houses where they lived, north of Corfu Town, are not open to visitors. The White House (p504) at Kalami, however, which was home to Lawrence and his wife Nancy while he wrote his lyrical nonfiction account of Corfu, *Prospero's Cell*, is now a lovely restaurant.

As for the hit TV series *The Durrells*, its principal shooting location is **Danilia**, a restored, once-abandoned village that is only accessible to guests staying at the **Grecotel Corfu Imperial** ([☑] 26610 88400; www.corfuimperial.com; Kommeno; d incl breakfast €463; ☉ May-Oct; ﹡ � 율 ≋) resort down on the coast.

Beach, 10km north of Corfu Town (on bus route 7), it also has rondavel huts and a pool.

★**Manessis Apartments**　　APARTMENT €€
([☑] 6973918416; www.manessiskassiopi.com; Kassiopi; 4-person apt €80-100; ﹡ 율) Bougainvillea-draped two-bedroom apartments, some with sea-facing balconies, set in flower-filled gardens towards the far end of Kassiopi's picturesque harbour. The friendly Greek-Irish owner makes sure everything goes smoothly.

Casa Lucia　　APARTMENT, BUNGALOW €€
([☑] 26610 91419; www.casa-lucia-corfu.com; Sgombou; studios & cottages €70-120; ☉ Apr-Oct; [P] ≋) 🌢 This attractive garden complex of studios and cottages, 3km up from Gouvia towards Paleokastritsa, has a strong artistic and community ethos and offers yoga, t'ai chi and Pilates.

Bella Mare　　HOTEL €€€
([☑] 26630 81997; www.belmare.gr; Avlaki; s/d €139/187; ﹡ 율) If you've come to Corfu to relax, look no further than this away-from-it-all resort hotel, overlooking stunning Avlaki Beach from the olive groves at its western end. It has spacious contemporary rooms and suites, plus a pool, spa treatments and yoga classes.

✖ Eating

To Fagopotion　　GREEK €€
([☑] 26630 82020; Agios Stefanos, northeast coast; €11-19; ☉ noon-1am) Of the procession of similar tavernas that serve up seafront dining at Agios Stefanos, Fagopotion, presided by the genial Christos, has to be the best for its inventive Greek seafood and meat cuisine.

Cavo Barbaro　　SEAFOOD €€
([☑] 26630 81905; Avlaki; mains €10-22; ☉ 9.30am-late) With widescreen views of the beach, and sea breezes wafting through the garden,

this pretty and very spacious restaurant makes a charming spot for a leisurely meal of octopus, calamari, *saganaki* (fried cheese), *mousakas* or swordfish.

Taverna Galini　　GREEK €€
([☑] 26630 81492; www.galinitaverna.gr; Agios Stefanos, northeast coast; mains €15-21; ☉ lunch & dinner) Shaded by vines by day, lit by hurricane lamps by night, this olive-and-cream gem spreads across a semi-al fresco seafront terrace. Enjoy *stifadho* (meat, game or seafood cooked with onions in a tomato purée), *kleftiko* (slow oven-baked lamb or goat), souvlaki and fresh local fish.

★**White House**　　MEDITERRANEAN €€€
([☑] 26630 91040; www.corfu-kalami.gr; Kalami; mains €10-23; ☉ 9am-midnight) Utterly ravishing waterfront restaurant in the former home of writer Lawrence Durrell, with tables quayside – many diners arrive by motorboat – as well as on a vine-shaded terrace. The appetisers are predominantly Greek, and the mains and desserts Italian, such as delicious mixed seafood risotto or linguine for €20. Offers boat rentals and apartments, too.

Western Coast

Corfu's western shoreline boasts some of the island's most spectacular scenery, its prettiest villages and finest beaches. No coastal road connects the many sandy coves that nibble into the towering cliffs along its central stretch, so sightseers have to choose their targets wisely. **Paleokastritsa** in the north has a great beach, a beautiful monastery and fine hiking; **Pelekas** is a delightful hilltop village; and **Agios Gordios** in the south is a backpackers' haven with a superb beach.

The popular resort area of Paleokastritsa, 23km northwest of Corfu Town, stretches for nearly 3km through a series of small, picturesque bays. Craggy mountains swathed in cypress and olive trees tower above. The real treat comes at the resort's end, where an exquisite little beach is said to be where the weary Odysseus washed ashore. Boat trips from the little jetty here include **Paradise Sunset** (☑ 6972276442; per person €10-20) cruises to nearby grottoes and the glass-bottomed **Yellow Submarine** (☑ 6977409246; www.yellowsubmarine.gr; €10; ☉ 10am-6pm, night cruises 9pm).

Set amid splendid gardens on the rocky promontory above, an easy 10-minute walk from the beach, the **Moni Theotokou** (☉ 7am-1pm & 3-8pm) FREE monastery dates back to the 13th century, and is home to an interesting little **museum** (☉ Apr-Oct) FREE and a shop selling oils and herbs.

A circuitous hike or drive west from Paleokastritsa will take you along a high winding road through the unspoiled villages of **Lakones** and **Krini**. A minor track that drops west of Krini dead-ends far above the waves at a mighty isolated crag, where a broad stone stairway climbs up to the impregnable Byzantine fortress of **Angelokastro**. Though its ramparts remain largely intact, rampant wildflowers now fill its interior; the views back to Paleokastritsa are unforgettable.

Further north, the coastline becomes much flatter, and the low-key resorts of **Agios Georgios** and **Arillas** line their own long beaches.

South of Paleokastritsa, the pebbly beach at **Ermones** has become overdeveloped, but sleepy little **Pelekas**, atop wooded cliffs 6km southeast, is a confection of biscuit-cream-hued buildings. Kalimera Bakery (p506) here sells fresh pastries, while the frog-green **Witch House** (☑ 6974525376; ☉ 10am-10pm), almost opposite, is perfect for offbeat gifts. Kaiser Wilhelm rode his horse to get 360-degree island views from the peak immediately above the village, now known as the **Kaiser's Throne**.

Sandy beaches within easy reach of Pelekas include **Kontogialos** (also called Pelekas) and **Glyfada**, both now fully fledged resorts with large hotels and other accommodation. Lawrence Durrell hailed **Myrtiotissa Beach**, further east, as arguably the best in the whole world. Now dominated by nudists, it remains relatively pristine because it's so hard to reach – it requires a long slog down a steep and only partly surfaced road (drivers should park on the hilltop).

The rambling old vineyard estate at **Ambelonas** (☑ 6932158888; http://ambelonas-corfu.gr; ☉ 7-11pm Wed-Fri Jun-Oct, 1-6pm Sun Dec-May), 5km east of Pelekas (and only 8km west of Corfu Town), produces and sells enticing products ranging from wine and vinegar to olive oil and sweets.

Continuing south, the resort of **Agios Gordios** is set below a stupendous verdant hillside, with a long sand-and-pebble beach that can accommodate any crowd. Another 12km south, just off the main road, the Byzantine **Gardiki Castle** makes an impressive spectacle, but is largely ruined. Beyond it lies vast **Lake Korission**, separated from the sea by a narrow spit that's fronted by long, sandy **Halikounas Beach**.

🛏 Sleeping

The main overnight destinations in western Corfu are Paleokastritsa, which holds a large crop of medium-range hotels, and Agios Gordios, which has long been a favourite with backpackers but is now moving increasingly upmarket.

Paleokastritsa Camping   CAMPGROUND €
(☑ 26630 41204; www.paleokastritsa-bliss.com; campsites 1/2 adults €18.50/22.90; ☉ mid-May–late Oct; P 🛜 🐾) Well-organised camping ground, set in the shade of olive terraces above the main road 1km east of town, with a pool and ready access to great walks.

Pink Palace   HOSTEL, HOTEL €
(☑ 26610 53103; www.thepinkpalace.com; Agios Gordios Beach; dm/d/tr incl breakfast & dinner from €24/56/84; ❄ @) You can't miss Corfu's major rendezvous for partying backpackers – not only is it bright pink, it's enormous, sprawling down the steep hillside towards the sea. Breakfast and dinner are served in the beachfront restaurant, a hundred steps down from the basic hostel rooms (wi-fi in communal areas only) and the fancier apartments. Activities include quad biking and booze cruises. Two-night minimum.

Jimmy's Restaurant & Rooms   PENSION €
(☑ 26610 94284; www.jimmyspelekas.com; Pelekas village; s/d/tr €35/45/55; ☉ May-Oct; ❄ 🛜) Simple but perfectly decent rooms, with views over the rooftops, set above a lively village restaurant that's only open for breakfast (€8) and dinner (mains €7 to €14).

★ Levant Hotel   HOTEL €€
(☑ 26610 94230; www.levantcorfu.com; Pelekas village; s/d incl breakfast €80/100; ☉ May–mid-Oct;

P ❄ 🛜 🏊) A creamy neoclassical hotel, up in the gods just below the Kaiser's Throne, with pastel-blue rooms, wooden floors, belle-époque lights and balconies. Throw in a refined restaurant serving shrimp, risotto and *stifadho* on a terrace with sublime sunset views. Tempted?

Hotel Zefiros
HOTEL €€

(📞 26630 41244; www.hotel-zefiros.gr; Paleokastritsa; d/tr/q from €90/130/145; ❄ 🛜) Set slightly askew of Paleokastritsa's pretty beach, with a cool olive-grey terrace cafe at lobby level, wine-coloured Zefiros offers attractive rooms with balconies and contemporary flourishes. Room 107 has the finest view.

Rolling Stone
PENSION €€

(📞 26610 94942; www.pelekasbeach.com; Pelekas Beach; r/apt €70/98; @🛜) Close to the beach, this funky travellers' oasis has new two-bedroom family apartments, with fresh rooms, bathrooms and kitchenettes. The original apartments are also spotless, and encircle a shaded terrace where people gather to chat. Laid-back and friendly.

🍴 Eating & Drinking

Elia Restaurant
TAVERNA €

(📞 6982316598; www.eliamirtiotissa.com; Myrtiotissa; mains €7-14; ⏰ noon-late May-Oct) An irresistible taverna, perched above the track down to breathtaking Myrtiotissa Beach, serving an enticing menu of Corfiot specialities and much-needed cold drinks.

To Stavrodromi
TAVERNA €

(📞 26610 94274; www.tostavrodromi.com; Pelekas; mains €7-12; ⏰ 6-11pm) A homey dinner-only joint at the main crossroads just east of Pelekas. Delicious local specialities include Corfu's finest *kontosouvli* (spit-roast pork with paprika and onions), as well as rabbit *stifadho* and pepper steak.

Kalimera Bakery
BAKERY €

(Pelekas village; pastries from €2; ⏰ 7am-late) Put a spring in your morning step by savouring the wood-fired bread, *pastelli* (sesame biscuits), baklava and heavenly coffee at this mustard-coloured bakery in the village square.

★ Alonaki Bay
TAVERNA €€

(📞 26610 75872; Alonaki; mains €10-15; ⏰ lunch & dinner; 🛜) Follow the dirt roads out to the headland northwest of Lake Korission to find this simple, family-run taverna, perched on dramatic cliffs. It serves a small menu of home-cooked meat and *mayirefta* (ready-cooked meals), and also offers clean rooms (€50) and apartments (€55), overlooking the garden.

Nereids
TAVERNA €€

(📞 26630 41013; Paleokastritsa; mains €12-19; ⏰ lunch & dinner) Just below a huge curve in the road as you enter Paleokastritsa, this romantic spot is best experienced at night, when its terrace of ornamental rock pools and urns is softly lit. Try dolmadhes (vine leaves stuffed with rice, and sometimes meat), meatballs in tomato sauce, *kleftiko* and *stifadho*.

La Grotta
CAFE

(📞 26630 41006; www.lagrottabar.com; Paleokastritsa; ⏰ 10am-late mid-May–mid-Oct) Tucked away in a rocky cove, immediately above the sea and replete with sunbeds and a diving board, this decked terrace makes an ideal chill-out escape. Follow the steep steps opposite the Hotel Paleokastritsa driveway.

PAXI ΠΑΞΟΙ
POP 2300

Measuring a mere 13km from tip to toe, and spared overdevelopment by its lack of an airport, Paxi packs a lot of punch into its tiny frame. Facilities are concentrated in three delightful harbour villages tucked into its eastern shores – Lakka, Loggos and the ferry port of Gaïos. Each has its own crop of tasteful little hotels, rental apartments and seafront tavernas, and its own devoted fans.

All make wonderful bases for exploring the rolling hills and centuries-old olive groves of the interior, and the wilder scenery of the west coast. Unspoiled coves can be reached by motorboat, while former mule trails lead to sheer limestone cliffs that plunge into the azure sea. Great hikes lead out to majestic Tripitos Arch in the south, and down to Erimitis Beach in the west, beneath a vast wall of crumbling rock, with a potential pause at Erimitis Bar & Restaurant (📞 6977753499; www.erimitis.com; mains €12-24; ⏰ 4pm-2am; 🛜) en route.

ℹ Getting There & Away

BOAT

Busy passenger-only **Ilida** (p493) hydrofoils links Paxi's ferry port at Gaïos with Corfu Town (€25, 55 minutes, three to eight daily, May to mid-October) and, occasionally, Igoumenitsa. A slower but cheaper service on the Corfu Town route (€10.30, 90 minutes, one to three daily,

April to October) is provided by **Kamelia Lines** (☑ Corfu 26610 40372, Paxi 26620 32131; www.kamelialines.gr), while car ferries also link Paxi with Igoumenitsa (per passenger/vehicle €11/42.30, one to three daily, April to October). Buy ferry tickets from **New Plans** (Bouas Tours; ☑ 26620 32088; www.newplans.gr; Gaïos) or **Zefi Travel** (☑ 26620 32114; www.zefitravel. com; Gaïos; ⊙ 8.30am-3pm & 6-11pm).

Fast sea taxis are available on demand; Corfu to Paxi costs €330 with **Paxos Sea Taxi** (☑ 6932232072, 26620 32444; www.paxossea taxi.com; Gaïos).

Regular excursion boats run from Gaïos to Antipaxi (€10 return) from June onwards through summer.

BUS

A direct bus connects Athens with Paxi (€71 including Paxi–Igoumenitsa ferry, seven hours) once a week in high season. On Paxi, get tickets from New Plans.

ⓘ Getting Around

Buses link Gaïos and Lakka via Loggos twice daily (€2.50); they're not convenient for day trips.

Taxis between Gaïos and Lakka or Loggos cost about €15; Gaïos' taxi rank is by the inland car park.

Many agencies rent small boats (from €50 to €100, depending on engine capacity).

Daily car rental with **Alfa Hire** (☑ 26620 32505; Gaïos) starts at €40 in high season.

Gaïos   Γάϊος
POP 500

Gaïos is a supremely peaceful harbour village. Arrayed in a lazy, gentle curve along a narrow, fjord-like channel, it's caressed by beautiful teal water and faces across to the wooded islet of Agios Nikolaos. A long row of rose- and biscuit-hued neoclassical villas line the waterfront promenade, many of them housing cafes and tavernas, while yachts and excursion boats bob at the quayside.

🛏 Sleeping & Eating

Paxos Beach Hotel   HOTEL €€
(☑ 26620 32211; www.paxosbeachhotel.gr; d incl breakfast €105-180, ste €200-280; ❄ 🐾 ≋) Nestling into a tiny cove, a pleasant 1.5km walk southeast along the waterfront from Gaïos, this family-run hotel has its own beach, plus a jetty, a swimming pool, a tennis court and a seaside restaurant. With rooms in separate villas on the terraced hillside, you can expect a lot of steps. Ferry transfers and rental boats available.

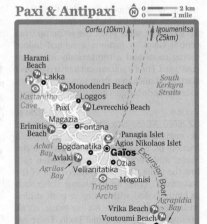

Theklis-Clara Studios   PENSION €€
(☑ 26620 32313, 6972923838; www.theklis-studios. com; studios €100; ❄) Lovely Thekli, a free-diver with her own boat, rents out four beautiful two-person studios, furnished with shabby-chic flair, in a handsome house set 100m up from the quayside. All have well-equipped kitchenettes and bathrooms, and balconies with serene sea views. Ferry transfers possible on request.

Water Planet Rooms   APARTMENT €€
(☑ 6972111995; www.waterplanet.gr; d €60; ❄ 🛜) Attractive and well-priced rooms, some with sea views, in a fine old villa tucked slightly back from the waterfront. Guests share use of a kitchen and a courtyard garden. The friendly and very helpful owners run the adjoining dive shop.

Capriccio Creperie   CAFE €
(☑ 26620 32065; crêpes €3-6; ⊙ 9am-2am) Pretty little lilac villa, with a handful of quayside tables, slightly southeast of the centre. The waffles and crêpes are superfresh, while the delicious homemade ice cream, including flavours such as *kaimaki* (mastic and cinnamon), is a tonic for the soul.

★ Carnayo   MEDITERRANEAN €€
(☑ 26620 32376; www.carnayopaxos.gr; mains €10-22; ⊙ lunch & dinner Tue-Sun) Paxi's finest

restaurant serves local food that's head and shoulders above the harbour-front tavernas, for much the same price. Set 400m up from central Gaïos, it features a refined indoor dining room and a romantically lit garden courtyard. For €8 you can get a mixed plate of starters. Mains range from slow-roasted pork to homemade burgers and crispy-skin bream.

Dodos TAVERNA €€

(☑26620 32265; http://dodos-paxos.blogspot.co.uk; mains €7-15; ☺noon-midnight) Dodos is a friendly little taverna hidden away in a colourful and very quirky secret garden (follow the signs from the southern end of the waterfront). Come for traditional dishes such as lamb cooked with honey or pork stuffed with cheese; and linger for live music. It's all presided over by the genial Dodo. There are also simple studios for rent (from €60).

ⓘ Information

Gaios' main street, Panagioti Kanga, stretching inland from the central seafront square, holds assorted banks and ATMs.

Gaios has no tourist office but travel agencies, such as **Paxos Magic Holidays** (☑26620 32269; www.paxosmagic.com), organise excursions, book tickets and arrange accommodation.

Loggos Λόγγος

Bookended by white cliffs and the hulk of an old olive-oil factory, breathtaking little Loggos, 6km northwest of Gaïos, consists of a cluster of pretty Venetian houses huddled around a tiny bay of crystal-clear water. Bars and restaurants overlook the sea, while wooded slopes climb steeply above.

⌕ Sleeping & Eating

Arthur House APARTMENT €€

(☑26620 31330; http://paxos-arthur.blogspot.gr; 1-/2-bedroom apt €70/120; ℗) Simple, but spacious, and very clean apartments, with kitchenettes, washing machines and balconies, set in a pleasant garden 50m from the waterfront.

O Gios TAVERNA €

(☑26620 31735; mains €7-12; ☺noon-midnight; ☞) Sturdy little stone-built taverna at the heart of the harbour, preparing home-cooked, good-value grills, seafood and baked dishes at bargain prices.

Vasilis MEDITERRANEAN €€

(☑26620 31587; www.vasilisrestaurant.com; mains €13-27; ☺lunch & dinner) In a low-slung terracotta cottage on the paved harbourfront,

Vasilis serves local specialities including pan-fried cuttlefish, sea urchin and *bourdeto* (fresh fish cooked in tomato and paprika sauce). Reserve ahead in summer.

ⓘ Information

Paxos Thalassa Travel (☑26620 31662; www.paxos-thalassatravel.com) Rental motorboats of all shapes and sizes, plus local accommodation and boat trips to Antipaxi.

Lakka Λάκκα

So languid it seems forever on the point of slipping into the yacht-flecked waters, Lakka is sure to slow your pulse and make you smile. Wander the quayside to savour the tempting aromas and gentle music that waft from the tavernas, or venture westward to reach sandy **Harami Beach**, or the **lighthouse** atop the headland beyond.

⌕ Sleeping & Eating

Yorgos Studios APARTMENT €€

(☑26620 31807; www.routsis-holidays.com; d €80; ❄☞) Immaculate and comfy two-person studios, next door to and run by Routsis Holidays, which represents several other local studios and apartments.

★**Torri E Merli** BOUTIQUE HOTEL €€€

(☑26212 34123; www.torriemerli.com; ste from €420; ☺May-Oct; ℗❄☞☀) Constructed in 1750, its towers designed to repel pirates, this beautiful boutique property complements its original Venetian elements with contemporary decor – exposed-stone walls, white-wood floors – to create what's arguably the Ionians' loveliest hotel. Set in the olive groves 800m south of Lakka, it holds just seven suites, along with a restaurant and a kidney-shaped pool.

★**Arriva Fish Restaurant** SEAFOOD €€

(☑26620 33041; mains €10-17; ☺lunch & dinner) Waterfront taverna with little tables perched on the very brink of the quayside. Check out the blackboard for an amazing list of freshly caught fish and seafood, from lobster to scorpion fish, prepared every imaginable way – grilled, barbecued, or in risotto or pasta dishes. The octopus *krasato* (in red-wine sauce) is delectable.

ⓘ Information

Helpful **Routsis Holidays** (☑26620 31807; www.routsis-holidays.com) rents out well-appointed apartments and villas to suit all budgets, and arranges transport and excursions. Harbourside **Sun & Sea** (📞 26620 31162; www.paxossunandsea.com; Lakka; ⊗ 8.30am-2.30pm & 5.30-11pm) also offers accommodation, as well as boat rental (from €50).

ANTIPAXI   ΑΝΤΙΠΑΞΟΙ

POP 25

The ravishing and barely inhabited little island of Antipaxi is a favourite day trip destination from Paxi, just 2km north, and Corfu. While very few visitors stay overnight, the two superb beach coves near the island's northern tip are thronged every day in summer with boats large and small. Sandy **Vrika Beach**, the closest to Paxi, and longer but stonier **Voutoumi Beach** further south, hold a couple of tavernas each. Both lie cradled beneath densely wooded slopes, and shelter dazzlingly clear waters.

Footpaths from both beaches and from the island's totally undeveloped harbour, 600m south of Voutoumi, climb to Antipaxi's central spine, where the 'village' of Vigla consists of a few scattered villas, with no centre or commercial activity. Keep walking to reach the wilder and beach-less western coast within a few minutes, or head for the lighthouse at the island's southernmost tip; take plenty of water and allow at least 1½ hours each way.

Rental properties on Antipaxi are generally available by the week only.

Beach tavernas cater to day trippers but close at night, and Antipaxi has no shops, so anyone staying overnight needs to be self-sufficient.

ℹ️ Getting There & Away

Between June and September boats to Antipaxi typically leave Gaïos on Paxi (return €10) at 10am and return around 4.30pm, with increased services in July and August. **Ionian Cruises** (📞 26610 31649; www.ionian-cruises.com; Ethnikis Antistaseos 4) and other operators offer day trips to Paxi and Antipaxi from Corfu Town.

LEFKADA   ΛΕΥΚΑΔΑ

POP 22,650

Despite being connected to the mainland by a narrow causeway, making it one of the few Greek islands that you can drive to, Lefkada remains surprisingly unaffected by tourism.

Laid-back Lefkada Town is a charming place to spend a day or two, while the hills

of the interior still conceal timeless villages and wild olive groves, and the rugged west coast holds some amazing beaches, albeit in some cases badly damaged by recent earthquakes. Only along the east coast are there some overdeveloped enclaves; if you continue all the way south you'll find stunning little bays and inlets, as well as windy conditions that attract kitesurfers and windsurfers from all over the world.

Lefkada was originally a peninsula, not a true island. Corinthian colonisers cut a canal through the narrow isthmus that joined it to the rest of Greece in the 8th century BC.

ℹ️ Getting There & Away

AIR

Lefkada's closest airport is near Preveza (Aktion; PVK), on the mainland 20km north. **Sky Express** (www.skyexpress.gr) connects it with Corfu (€73, 30 minutes), Kefallonia (€67, 30 minutes), Zakynthos (€73, 1½ hours) and Sitia (Crete; €117, 1½ hours, June to September only). **Olympic Air** (www.olympicair.com) flies from Preveza to Athens, with connections throughout Greece. In summer, **Easyjet** (www.easyjet.com) flies to Preveza from the UK, as do charter flights from all over northern Europe.

BOAT

Two ferry companies connect Vasiliki to Kefallonia in high season; **West Ferry** (www. westferry.gr) runs daily to Fiskardo, while **Ionion Pelagos** (www.ionionpelagos.com) sails via Piso Aetos in Ithaki to Sami. For bookings contact **Samba Tours** (📞 26450 31520; www.sambatours.gr; Vasiliki).

Between July and mid-September, the **Meganisi II** (📞 26450 92528; www.ferryboatmeganisi.gr) ferry runs twice daily between Nydri and Frikes in Ithaki.

The following services from Lefkada all cost €10:

DESTINATION	DURATION	FREQUENCY
Fiskardo (Kefallonia)	1hr	2 daily
Frikes (Ithaki)	2hr	2 daily, seasonal
Piso Aetos (Ithaki)	1hr	1-2 daily
Sami (Kefallonia)	1¾hr	1 daily

BUS

Lefkada Town's **KTEL Bus Station** (📞 26450 22364; www.ktel-lefkadas.gr; Ant Tzeveleki), opposite the marina 1km from the centre, serves Athens (€35.80, 5½ hours, five daily), Patra (€17.60, three hours, two weekly), Thessaloniki (€38.50, eight hours, daily) and Igoumenitsa (€13.30, two hours, daily).

❶ Getting Around

TO/FROM THE AIRPORT

There's no direct bus between Lefkada Town and Preveza airport, but buses connect Lefkada Town with Preveza itself (€2.90, 30 minutes, six daily), from where you can take a taxi to the airport (€15).

Taxis from the airport to Lefkada Town cost from €40.

BUS

Frequent buses from Lefkada Town serve the island in high season; Sunday services are greatly reduced. Destinations include the following:

Agios Nikitas €1.80, 30 minutes, three daily

Karya €1.80, 30 minutes, six daily

Nydri €1.80, 30 minutes, 13 daily

Vasiliki €3.70, one hour, three daily

Vlicho €2, 40 minutes, 10 daily

CAR

Rentals start at €40 per day; there are car-, scooter- and bicycle-hire companies in Lefkada Town, Nydri and Vasiliki.

It's possible to pick up a hire car at Preveza's Aktion Airport and return it in Vasiliki, if you are catching a ferry south (or vice versa).

Lefkada Town Λευκάδα

POP 8670

Unusually broad and flat for a Greek-island town, Lefkada's bustling capital faces the mainland across a salty lagoon from its northeastern tip. After losing its historic Venetian architecture in earthquakes in 1948 and 1953, Lefkada Town was rebuilt in a distinctively quake-proof and attractive style. It now resembles a Caribbean port, with wooden buildings in faded pastel colours whose upper storeys are adorned with brightly painted corrugated iron.

A relaxed, cheerful place, it's all very logically laid out, with shops and restaurants concentrated along its central pedestrian street (initially Dorpfeld, then Ioannou Mela further west); cafes and bars on the marina to the south; and banks and businesses closest to the causeway.

◉ Sights

Archaeological Museum MUSEUM
(📞 26450 21635; Ang Sikelianou; €2; ◷ 8am-3pm Tue-Sun) This excellent museum, west along the waterfront in the modern cultural centre, illuminates island history from the Palaeolithic era to the Romans. Prize exhibits include terracotta ensembles from the 6th century BC, depicting a flute player surrounded by dancing nymphs, seen as evidence that a Pan cult once flourished on Lefkada.

Fortress of Agia Mavra FORTRESS
(€2; ◷ 8am-3pm Tue-Sun) Guarding Lefkada at the start of the causeway, 1.4km from town, Agia Mavra fortress was constructed in the 14th century and later expanded by the Venetians. While its lichen-covered walls remain intact, surrounded by a saltwater moat, the interior now lies in ruins. You can enter the occasional bare chamber as you stroll among the wildflowers.

Collection of
Post-Byzantine Icons MUSEUM
(📞 26450 22502; Rontogianni 11; €2; ◷ 11am-9pm Tue, 8.30am-2.30pm Wed-Fri, 8.30am-1.30pm Sat) Upstairs in the local library, and unlocked on demand, this small gallery displays icons from the Ionian school and Russia that date back to 1500. The two finest, often on loan elsewhere, are believed to have influenced El Greco.

Moni Faneromenis MONASTERY
(📞 26450 21305; ◷ 8am-2pm & 4-8pm) **FREE** Set in beautiful hilltop gardens, 3km west of town towards Agias Nikitas, the Moni Faneromenis monastery was founded in 1634 and rebuilt following a fire in 1886. The ascent is rewarded with magnificent views over both town and lagoon.

🛏 Sleeping

★ **Boschetto Hotel** BOUTIQUE HOTEL €€
(📞 26450 20244; www.boschettohotel.com; Dorpfeld 1; d incl breakfast €114; 🅿 🗬) This attractive century-old building on the seafront square holds four large, tasteful rooms and a single suite, all with wooden floors, fine linen, marble bathrooms, and balconies looking across the cafe below to the bright-blue waters of the lagoon.

Hotel Santa Maura HOTEL €€
(📞 26450 21308; www.santamaurahotel.gr; Sp Vlanti 2; s/d/tr incl breakfast €70/90/120; 🅿 🗬) Pastel-pink 19th-century hotel on the main pedestrian street, with green shutters and wraparound street-view balconies, divided between the 18 fresh, sizeable rooms. Breakfast is served in your room or in the garden courtyard.

Pension Pirofani HOTEL €€
(📞 26450 25844; www.pirofanilefkada.com; Dorpfeld 10; d €125-150; 🅿 🗬) Very friendly and

Lefkada & Meganisi

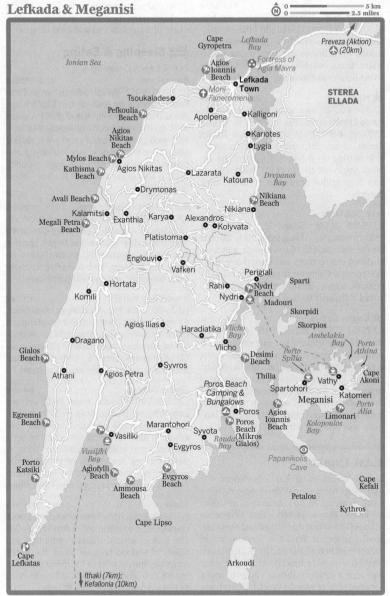

central family-run hotel, where the rooms themselves, furnished in bland contemporary style and equipped with immaculate bathrooms, are less stylish than the plush lobby.

✖ Eating & Drinking

Brisk year-round trade ensures that Lefkada Town holds some genuinely good restaurants, competing to attract customers browsing along the main street.

Ciao
ICE CREAM €

(☑ 26450 25557; Mitropoleos 8; per scoop from €1.50; ◎ 6-11.30pm) This bright little evening-only gelateria, just off the pedestrian drag, scoops up delicious fresh ice cream in flavours from *mastiha* (a stomach-settling sweet liquor) to chocolate.

★ Nissi
MEDITERRANEAN €€

(☑ 26454 00725; www.facebook.com/nissilefkada; Plateia Ethnikis Antistaseos; mains €8-16; ◎ 1pm-12.30am; ※ ☎) Truly superb Greek–Italian fusion restaurant, with stylish, comfortable seating on the inland square; the jet-black squid-ink risotto (€10), with octopus and huge grilled prawns, is an astonishing bargain.

Frini Sto Molo
TAVERNA €€

(☑ 26450 24879; Golemi 12; mains €8-15; ◎ 10am-midnight) Long-standing taverna on the marina side of town, with a homely enclosed dining room and a wind-free quay-side terrace. Come for dependable seafood – octopus, squid, shrimp and fresh fish – plus baked standards such as *mousakas*.

★ Gogos Gefsis
BAR

(☑ 26453 00509; Ioannou Mela 149; ◎ noon-2am; ☎) Very friendly bar-cafe on the main pedestrian street, with pavement tables plus a quirky interior kitted out like a vintage grocery. The Greek sign is fiendishly hard to read; look for the hammer-and-sickle flag flying above. While it sells a short menu of grilled snacks and cheesy shrimp, just buying a beer gets you a free hot snack.

East Coast

Lefkada's east coast has experienced the island's heaviest tourist development. Head south, however, to find the unspoiled strand at lovely **Poros Beach** (also known as Mikros Gialos) and the relaxed and very sheltered harbour at fjord-like **Syvota**, where yachts now bob alongside the fishing boats. **Nydri** has seen the most development; what was once a gorgeous fishing village is now a crowded strip of kiss-me-quick tourist shops, without a decent beach.

Boat excursions from Nydri head out to Meganisi (€12 to €20), often including swimming stops at lesser islets en route; some venture further afield to Ithaki and Kefallonia (€20 to €25). Borsalino Travel (☑ 26450 92528; www.borsalinotravel.gr; Nydri) can make all arrangements.

Several attractive hiking trails set off into the hills inland from Nydri, entering another world of waterfalls and scattered villages.

🛏 Sleeping & Eating

Poros Beach Camping & Bungalows
CAMPGROUND €

(☑ 26450 95452; www.porosbeach.com.gr; Poros Beach; campsite per adult/car/tent €10/3/5, studios €70-95; ◎ May-Sep; P ※ @ ☎ ☒) A short walk up from perfect Poros Beach, this well-equipped campsite has a great pool, shaded olive-grove tent sites, a nice bar and a restaurant stretching across a huge wooden deck. It also offers attractive studios – some family-sized.

Galini Sivota Apartments
PENSION €

(☑ 26450 31347; www.galinistudiossivotalefkada.gr; Syvota; studios €45, 4-person apt €70; ※ ☎) Simple sea-view studios and larger, smarter four-person apartments, perched 15m up from the harbour, and featuring kitchenettes, balconies and spotless bathrooms.

Rouda Bay Hotel
HOTEL €€

(☑ 26450 95634; http://roudabay.gr; Poros Beach; d from €70; ※ ☎) Comfortable, high-standard, modern rooms and studios, right in the middle of gorgeous Paros Beach. All are capable of accommodating a family of four, and there's also a good waterfront restaurant.

Sivota Bakery
BAKERY €

(☑ 6972432497; Syvota; mains €6-12; ◎ 8am-2am) With its harbour-front walls hung with antique bikes and carriage lamps, this cool arbour is much more cafe than bakery, serving pizzas and waffles, cocktails and wine, as well as juices, homemade pies, fresh croissants, crêpes and ice cream. No extra charge for the swallows whistling around the ceiling.

Stavros
TAVERNA €

(☑ 26450 31181; http://tavernastavros.gr; Syvota; mains €7-14; ◎ breakfast, lunch & dinner Easter-Oct) The pick of several similarly tempting and colourful seafood tavernas along the pretty quayside, Stavros offers a full menu of freshly caught fish along with local delicacies such as fish soup and leg of lamb in honey.

Minas Taverna
TAVERNA €€

(☑ 26450 71480; www.tavernaminas.gr; Nikiana; mains €8-18; ◎ dinner daily, lunch Sat & Sun, reduced hours in low season) Top-notch taverna that's equally good for everything from seafood pasta to grilled meat and fish. It's above the main road 5km north of Nydri, and just south of Nikiana.

Vasiliki   Βασιλική

As well as being a handy ferry hub for Kefallonia and Ithaki, this friendly harbour village, complete with stony beach, is one of the top places to learn windsurfing in Greece, thanks to its breezy conditions. A tasty clutch of eucalyptus-shaded tavernas fringes the waterfront, while boutique shops line the short street that connects the harbour with the main road.

Activities

Caïques take visitors to nearby beaches and coves. The big attraction for boating day trips is Egremni Beach, especially since earthquake damage means it's no longer accessible by road.

Helpful Samba Tours (p509) sells tickets for ferries and excursion boats, including to Egremni, and can arrange car and bicycle hire.

Along the quayside, water-sports outfits stake their claims with flags and equipment; some have their own hotels for clients.

Club Vassiliki   WATER SPORTS
(☑26450 31588; www.clubvass.com) Long-established club specialising in all-inclusive learn-to-windsurf packages, including flights and accommodation. Also offers windsurf hire, private lessons and a wide range of other activities, from diving to mountain biking.

Nautilus Diving Club   DIVING
(☑6936181775; www.underwater.gr) Single dives (€60) and PADI open-water courses (€410), plus snorkel trips and sea-kayak hire.

🛏 Sleeping & Eating

Vasiliki Blue   APARTMENT €€
(☑26450 31602; www.vasilikiblue.gr; d €75; ❋ 🌐) Bright, scrupulously clean kitchenette apartments, perched on the hillside a few metres up from the harbour, with sea-view balconies draped in bougainvillea.

Pension Holidays   HOTEL €€
(☑26450 31426; s/d incl breakfast €65/70; ❋ 🌐) Simply furnished, great-value kitchenette apartments, around the corner beyond the main bay, just above the newly expanded marina. Friendly Spiros and family offer Greek hospitality, plus sea-view breakfasts on the balcony.

Vagelaras   TAVERNA €€
(☑26450 31224; mains €7-16; ☺8am-late; 🌐) Sitting at the end of the harbour, just short of the ferry dock, this century-old taverna serves great salads, mezedhes, pasta and fresh seafood at waterfront tables. Its upper floor has had a modern makeover and now holds the cool Acqua bar.

Dolphin   TAVERNA €€
(☑26450 31430; mains €8-17; ☺ breakfast, lunch & dinner) Seafood taverna with quayside tables, enticing customers with aromatic grilled seafood and souvlaki, and proud of the fact that Ernest Hemingway once ate here. Be sure to sample the tasty little local prawns.

🍷 Drinking & Nightlife

155   BAR
(☑26450 31868; www.155cocktailbar.com; ☺6pm-late May-Oct) Welcoming watering hole on the main street, slightly back from the harbourfront, serving top cocktails (€8) and simple snacks.

West Coast

The dazzling white beaches that line Lefkada's west coast have long been ranked among the finest in the world. Sadly, the best known were seriously damaged by a 2015 earthquake, but others remain intact, and there's still plenty of scope for explorations.

The one resort on the west coast, the ever-expanding village of **Agios Nikitas**, stands 13km southwest of Lefkada Town along the coast road. A short street of inviting tavernas leads down to a curving white-sand beach that's lapped by aquamarine water. Head across the headland to the west, following the footpath from the Poseidon taverna, and you'll come to broad, straight and utterly delightful **Mylos Beach**. White-pebbled **Pefkoulia Beach** is a five-minute drive north and similar **Kathisma Beach** is the same distance south.

Further south, beyond the village of **Athani**, where stalls sell olive oil, honey and wine, two of Lefkada's most famous beaches, **Egremni Beach** and **Porto Katsiki**, were devastated by the 2015 earthquake. Both were submerged in debris, as the white cliffs above them came crumbling down, though geologists believe they will eventually be washed clean and restored to their former glory. Porto Katsiki is in slightly better shape, and remains accessible by car, but both the 720-step stairway that led to Egremni, and the road by which it is reached, were obliterated and are unlikely to be rebuilt. Now the only way to see what's left of Egremni, and to bathe in its magical turquoise waters, is on a boat excursion from ports elsewhere on the island, such as Vasiliki.

🛏 Sleeping

★ Mira Resort
APARTMENT €€

(☑ 6977075881, 26450 24967; www.miraresort.com; Tsoukalades; maisonettes incl breakfast from €145; ☺ May-Oct; P ✸ 🛜 🏊) Perfectly positioned on the mountainside 6km southwest of Lefkada Town, with panoramic views of the glittering sea, Mira has cosy and immaculate maisonettes, plus a large pool and a cafe-bar.

Hotel Agatha
HOTEL €€

(☑ 6948620615; www.agatha-hotel.com; Agios Nikitas; studios/apt €70/90; ✸ 🛜) Beside the coast road, a few minutes' walk up from the beach's eastern end, Agatha offers lovely, cool kitchenette studios and two-room apartments that are flooded with sunlight and ring with birdsong. Number 1 is our favourite.

Olive Tree Hotel
HOTEL €€

(☑ 26450 97453; www.olivetreehotel.gr; Agios Nikitas; s/d/studios incl breakfast €80/90/100; ☺ May-Sep; ✸ 🛜) Modest rooms, just above the village centre, managed by friendly Greek-Canadians. Each has its own terrace, with side-on sea views, and there's a good buffet breakfast.

🍴 Eating

★ Lefkatas
TAVERNA €

(☑ 26450 33149; www.lefkatas.gr; Athani; mains €7-12; ☺ brunch, lunch & dinner May-Sep; 🛜) 🍃 This delightful terrace restaurant, on a corner along the main road in the heart of Athani village, has inspiring views down the mountainside to the sea beyond. Sit in the shade of a cedar tree to enjoy breakfast, salads or seafood, and look out for daily specials such as hornbeam fish with garlic and tomato.

T'Agnantio
TAVERNA €

(☑ 26450 97383; www.tagnantio.gr; Agios Nikitas; mains €7-15; ☺ lunch & dinner Easter-Oct) The vine-shaded terrace of Agios Nikitas' finest taverna sits slightly up from the beach and offers sweeping views out to sea. Feast on seafood fresh off the boat – including swordfish, shrimp and octopus – as well as souvlaki, meatballs and local cheese.

Bilvi
GREEK €

(☑ 6973309604; www.bilvi.gr; Porto Katsiki; snacks €6-10; ☺ 9am-late; ✸ 🍴) The closest restaurant to dazzling but earthquake-ravaged Porto Katsiki beach is 600m uphill from the sea. Relax on the terrace, grab a swim in the pool, and then tuck into a club sandwich or a host of snacks and desserts. And the good news: Bilvi delivers down to the beach itself.

Central Lefkada

Replete with traditional farming villages, lush green peaks, fragrant pine trees, olive groves and vineyards, Lefkada's dramatic central spine is hugely rewarding to explore.

The small village of **Karya** has a pretty central square with plane trees and tavernas, but attracts crowds in high season. It's famous for its embroidery, introduced by a remarkable one-handed local woman, Maria Koutsochero, during the 19th century, and commemorated by a small museum.

The island's highest village, **Englouvi**, a few kilometres south of Karya, is renowned for producing honey and lentils. Book ahead for a guided **herbal walk** (☑ 6934287446; www.lefkas.cc; Kolyvata) near quaint **Alexandros**.

🍴 Eating

★ Maria's Tavern
TAVERNA €

(☑ 26450 41228, 6984056686; www.facebook.com/MariasTavern; Kolyvata; mains €6-9; ☺ breakfast, lunch & dinner Apr-Oct) In the tiny hamlet of Kolyvata, which enjoys idyllic views over the hills, the gregarious Kiria Maria opens her home to culinary adventurers. Using whatever's ready in her garden, she serves fresh, perfectly cooked treats. Call ahead to check she's there. Kolyvata is signposted between Alexandros and Nikiana.

MEGANISI ΜΕΓΑΝΗΣΙ

POP 1040

The elongated island of Meganisi, off Lefkada's southeast corner, is an easy boat ride from Nydri (Lefkada). Most visit on a day trip, but with its verdant hills and turquoise bays, fringed by pebbled beaches, it's well worth considering for a longer, more relaxed stay. From the ferry dock at **Porto Spilia**, climb the steep road or stairway to reach the narrow lanes and bougainvillea-bedecked houses of **Spartohori**, on the plateau above. The next inlet to the east holds pretty **Vathy**, the island's second harbour, 1km below the village of **Katomeri**.

Hotel Meganisi (☑ 26450 51240; www.hotelmeganisi.gr; Katomeri; d incl breakfast €77; ✸ 🛜 🏊) offers simple rooms with sea views.

The much-loved fish taverna **Errikos** (Porto Vathy; ☑ 26450 51125; mains €7-15; ⊙ lunch & dinner; 🕿) stands beside a small jetty in Vathy.

ℹ Information

Asteria Holidays (☑ 26450 51107; www. asteria.gr; Porto Spilia) can help with accommodation and travel arrangements.

ℹ Getting There & Around

Ferries from Nydri sail to both Porto Spilia and Vathy on Meganisi (per person/car €2/13, 25 to 40 minutes, four daily). buy tickets from **Borsalino Travel** (☑ 26450 92528; www. borsalinotravel.gr; Nydri).

Local buses connect Spartohori and Vathy five to seven times daily, via Katomeri, but bringing your own vehicle is recommended.

KEFALLONIA
ΚΕΦΑΛΛΟΝΙΑ

POP 35,800

Kefallonia is a place where it's easy to lose yourself, amid air thick with oleander and the bells of wandering goats. The largest of the Ionian Islands, its convoluted coastline conceals all sorts of captivating coves and beach-lined bays. Despite the devastating earthquake of 1953 that razed much of its historic Venetian architecture, ravishing harbour-front villages such as Fiskardo and Assos still show off Italianate good looks, while the lush and mountainous interior, dotted with wild meadows and vineyards, invites endless exploration.

ℹ Getting There & Away

AIR

The **airport** (☑ 26710 29900; http://kefalonia airport.info) is 9km south of Argostoli. From May to September, **Easyjet** (www.easyjet.com) flies from London, and many charter flights come from northern Europe and the UK. In addition,

Olympic Air (www.olympicair.com) serves Athens, and **Sky Express** (www.skyexpress.gr) serves Corfu, Preveza and Zakynthos.

DESTINATION	DURATION	FARE	FREQUENCY
Athens	55min	€88	2 daily
Corfu	1hr	€73	3 weekly
Preveza	20min	€67	3 weekly
Zakynthos	25min	€73	3 weekly

BOAT
Domestic

Up to five daily **Ionian Group** (www.ioniangroup. com) ferries connect Poros with Kyllini in the Peloponnese in summer, where you can catch onward ferries to Zakynthos.

Ionian Pelagos (www.ionionpelagos.com) runs up to three daily ferries between Sami and Piso Aetos in Ithaki, of which one or two continue to Astakos in the Peloponnese; connects Sami to Vasiliki in Lefkada twice weekly in summer; and also runs twice daily in summer between the remote and not readily accessible port of Pesada in southern Kefallonia and similarly isolated Agios Nikolaos in northern Zakynthos.

West Ferry (www.westferry.gr) runs between Fiskardo and Vasiliki (Lefkada); buy tickets at Nautilus Travel (p523).

International

Between mid-July and mid-September, **Ventouris Ferries** (http://ventourisferries.com) offers once-weekly connection between Sami, Zakynthos, Igoumenitsa on the mainland, and Bari, Italy. **Red Star Ferries** (www.directferries. co.uk/red_star_ferries.htm) goes to Brindisi from Sami once a week on Fridays during the same period (seat from €95, bunk from €115, 16 hours).

Buy tickets from **Blue Sea Travel** (☑ 26740 23007; www.samistar.com; Posidonos 16, Sami), or **Vassilatos Shipping** (☑ 26710 22618; A Tritsi 54, Argostoli).

BUS

Three daily buses from the **KTEL Bus Station** (☑ 26710 22276; www.ktelkefalonias.gr; A Tritsi 5) in Argostoli use the ferry from Poros to make

BOAT SERVICES FROM KEFALLONIA

DESTINATION	PORT	DURATION	FARE (€)	FREQUENCY
Agios Nikolaos (Zakynthos)	Pesada	1½hr	8	2 daily (May-Sep)
Astakos (mainland)	Sami	3hr	11	1-2 daily
Kyllini (Peloponnese)	Poros	1½hr	9	4-5 daily
Piso Aetos (Ithaki)	Sami	30min	3	2-3 daily
Vasiliki (Lefkada)	Fiskardo	1hr	9	2-3 daily
Vasiliki (Lefkada)	Sami	1¾hr	9	2 weekly (seasonal)

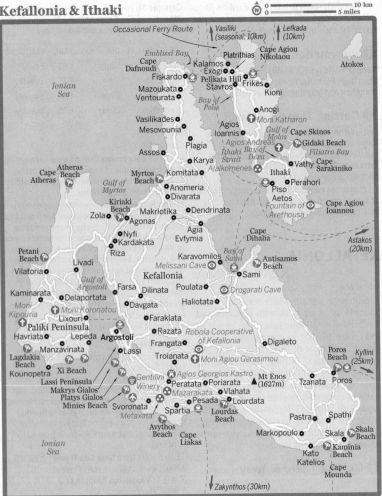

the journey to Athens (€40, seven hours, three daily). You can also buy tickets to Poros itself (€37, four hours, one daily) and Lixouri (€45, seven hours, one daily).

Getting Around

TO/FROM THE AIRPORT

There's no airport bus; taxis to Argostoli cost around €20.

BOAT

Car ferries (☏ 26710 23560) connect Argostoli and Lixouri on the island's western Paliki Peninsula.

BUS

KTEL buses (p515) connect Argostoli with all the island's major towns. In addition, one or two daily services run along the east coast, linking Katelios with Skala, Poros, Sami, Agia Evfymia and Fiskardo. Buses run on Sundays in high season only.

CAR & MOTORCYCLE

Car- and motorbike-hire companies fill major resorts, while **Europcar** (☏ 26710 41008), **Hertz** (☏ 26710 42142) and other operators have offices at the airport. Sami-based **Kefalonia2Ride** (☏ 26740 22970; www. kefalonia2ride.rentals; Maiouli 29, Sami; ⊙9.30am-9pm) offers scooters (from €23 per day) and ATVs.

Argostoli   Αργοστόλι
POP 9750

Shielded from the open sea, its waterfront stretching along the landward side of a short peninsula, Argostoli was once renowned for its elegant Venetian-era architecture. Almost all of that was destroyed by earthquake in 1953, however, and it's now a lively, forward-looking town. The main focus of activity is just inland, centred on charming, freshly pedestrianised **Plateia Valianou**, where locals come to chat and eat at the many restaurants. In summer, musicians stroll the streets singing *kantades*, traditional songs accompanied by guitar and mandolin. **Lithostroto**, the pedestrian shopping street immediately south, is lined with stylish boutiques and cafes.

◎ Sights

Platys Gialos   BEACH
This little 'pocket' beach, just beyond Makrys Gialos, has plenty of shade and very clear water, as well as a few places to eat.

Cephalonia Botanica   GARDENS
([☑] 26710 26595; www.focas-cosmetatos.gr; ⊙9am-2.30pm Tue-Sat) FREE This lovely botanical garden, designed to study, preserve and display plants and herbs from the island, is located 2km south of central Argostoli. It also holds a small artificial lake.

Korgialenio History &
Folklore Museum   MUSEUM
([☑] 26710 28835; www.corgialenios.gr; Ilia Zervou 12; €3; ⊙9am-noon & 6-9pm Mon, 9am-2pm & 6-9pm Tue-Fri, 10am-2pm Sat) Dedicated to preserving Kefallonian art and culture, this fine museum houses icons, assorted furniture, clothes and artwork, taken from the homes of gentry and farm workers.

Makrys Gialos   BEACH
Blessed with enticing turquoise water, just 3km southwest of Argostoli, Makrys Gialos tends to be rammed to the gills in summer with holidaying Brits.

Focas-Cosmetatos Foundation   MUSEUM
([☑] 26710 26595; www.focas-cosmetatos.gr; Valianou; adult/child €3/free; ⊙10am-2pm Mon-Fri May-Oct) One of the few historic buildings in Agostoli to survive successive earthquakes now holds displays on Kefallonia's cultural and political history, including lithographs by Edward Lear and other British artists. The same family also runs the Cephalonia Botanica.

Archaeological Museum   MUSEUM
([☑] 26710 28300; Rokou Vergoti; €3) Kefallonia's archaeological museum, which holds treasures from all over the island, including Mycenaean finds, sustained serious damage in a 2014 earthquake, and has yet to reopen.

🛏 Sleeping

★ Vivian Villa   APARTMENT €
([☑] 26710 23396; www.kefalonia-vivianvilla.gr; Deladetsima 11; d/studios €55/60; ❄🛜) Exquisitely tasteful villa on a quiet inland street, overlooking a garden fragrant with thyme and basil. As well as hotel-style rooms, some with balconies, it offers larger apartments with well-stocked kitchenettes and separate bedrooms for the kids. The stunning loft apartment – which has a lift – sleeps five. Everything runs like clockwork.

Camping Argostoli   CAMPGROUND €
([☑] 26710 23487; www.campingargostoli.gr; campsites per adult/car/tent €6.50/3/5; ⊙May-Sep; 🅿) This pleasant and hugely welcoming family-run campsite, 2km beyond Argostoli near

---

IONIAN ON THE VINE

The Ionian Islands would not be the same without wine, and Kefallonia is especially famed for its vintages. The most notable derive from the unique *robola* grape (VQRPD; Vin de Qualité Produit dans une Région Déterminée), thought to have been introduced by the Venetians, while other varieties include *mavrodaphni* (AOC; Appellation d'Origine Contrôlée) and *muscat* (AOC).

Nestled at the heart of verdant Omala Valley, in the hilly country southeast of Argostoli, the winery of the **Robola Cooperative of Kefallonia** ([☑]26710 86301; www.robola.gr; Omala; ⊙9am-8pm daily May-Oct, to 3pm Mon-Fri Nov-Apr) transforms grapes from 300 independent growers into a dry white wine of subtle yet lively flavour. Visitors can take a self-guided tour and enjoy free tastings. Smaller yet similarly distinguished **Gentilini** ([☑]26710 41618; www.gentilini.gr; Minies), 5km south of Argostoli on the airport road, has a charming setting and produces a range of superb wines, including the scintillating Classico.

Argostoli

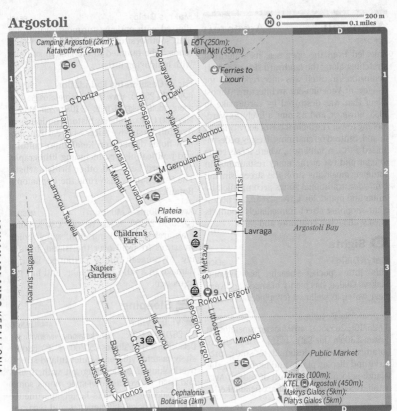

Argostoli

⊙ Sights

1 Archaeological Museum....................	B3
2 Focas-Kosmetatos Foundation	B3
3 Korgialenio History & Folklore Museum...	B4

⊜ Sleeping

4 Hotel Ionian Plaza	B2
5 Mouikis Hotel	C4
6 Vivian Villa	A1

⊗ Eating

7 Arhontiko..	B2
8 Ladokolla	B1

⊜ Drinking & Nightlife

9 Bass Club...	C3

the lighthouse on the northernmost point of the peninsula, can hardly have changed in years – and it's all the better for it. It also has its own tavern.

Mouikis Hotel HOTEL €€

(☑26710 23032; http://mouikis.com.gr; Vyronos 3; d incl breakfast €133; ❄️❓) Clean, modern hotel, near the market at the southern end of the town centre, with a smart but rather anonymous decor targeted mainly at business travellers. Most of the small but very well-equipped rooms have balconies; some have sea views. The buffet breakfast is substantial.

Hotel Ionian Plaza HOTEL €€

(☑26710 25581; www.ionianplaza.gr; Plateia Valianou; s/d incl breakfast €137/147; 🅿️❄️❓) Imposing hotel in an unbeatable location, with a stylish marble-trimmed lobby and small but comfortable rooms, all with balconies overlooking the central pedestrian square.

✗ Eating

★ Ladokolla GREEK €

(☑26710 25522; Harbouri 13; dishes €2-8; ⊙12.30pm-2am) Lively and hugely popular grill house, where piping-hot and irresistibly flavourful chicken, pork or lamb kebabs and pittas are served up straight onto tabletop covers (no plates). It also delivers.

Tzivras GREEK €
(☑26710 24259; Vandorou 1; mains €7-9; ☺noon-5pm) A veteran restaurant, a block inland from the waterfront market, where locals lunch on hearty, great-value baked standards such as veal with okra, goat with potatoes, or cod pie. Everything on the menu is less than €10.

Kiani Akti SEAFOOD €€
(☑26710 26680; A Tritsi; mains €8-20; ☺1pm-2am; 🖘) For Argostoli's finest views, follow the waterfront north to the cruise-ship dock, where this huge wooden deck stretches out into the harbour. The wide-ranging menu includes a range of tasty Greek appetisers, along with daily seafood specials of all kinds and meaty classics. You can also just drop in for a drink.

Arhontiko TAVERNA €€
(☑26710 27213; Risospaston 5; mains €9-18; ☺breakfast, lunch & dinner; 🖘) Wood-ceilinged and stone-walled, this friendly taverna offers local seafood such as squid, grilled shrimp and octopus, plus carnivore favourites Kefallonian meat pie and *exohiko* (pork stuffed with tomatoes, onions, peppers and feta). Good house wines, helpful service and a cosy atmosphere – no wonder it's always busy.

🍸 Drinking & Nightlife

Cafes line Plateia Valianou and Lithostroto, and are buzzing by late evening. **Bass Club** (☑26710 25020; www.bassclub.gr; cnr S Metaxa & Vergoti; ☺noon-7am; 🖘) in town draws the younger set, while club-restaurant **Katavothres** (☑26710 22221; www.katavothres.gr; Mikeli Davi 10; ☺5pm-10am Mon-Thu & Sun, 24hr Fri & Sat; 🖘) at the tip of the peninsula combines strange geological formations with iconic futuristic furnishings, and puts on top-name DJs. Beach bar **Stavento**, in Makrys Gialos (p517), hops in summer.

ⓘ Information

Banks with ATMs line the northern waterfront and Lithostroto.
EOT (Greek National Tourist Organisation; ☑26710 22248; ☺7am-2.30pm Mon-Fri)
Post Office (Lithostroto)

Around Argostoli

◉ Sights

Agios Georgios Kastro FORTRESS
(Castle of St George; Peratata; ☺8.30am-3pm Tue-Sun) FREE This 16th-century Venetian castle enjoys stellar views from atop a conspicuous pyramid-shaped hill 7km southeast of Argostoli. Kefallonia's capital for 200 years, it is now in ruins, and approached via a short pedestrian street from the adjoining village. Strolling around the unshaded, wildflower-strewn site takes around 20 minutes; relax afterwards over a coffee or snack in the gardens of the neighbouring Kastro Cafe.

Moni Agiou Gerasimou MONASTERY
(☑26710 86045; Omala; ☺9am-1pm & 3.30-8pm) FREE Dedicated to Kefallonia's patron saint, the large Moni Agiou Gerasimou monastery is maintained by nuns. Its chapel encloses the cave to which St Gerasimos withdrew to escape the rigours of monastic life. The monastery is located in Omala Valley, alongside the Robola Cooperative of Kefallonia winery.

🍴 Eating

★**Kastro Cafe** CAFE €
(☑26710 69367; Peratata; mains €6-10; ☺10am-7pm; 🖘) Relaxed garden cafe, just before the gateway to Agios Georgios Kastro, that's a wonderfully peaceful spot for coffee, cake, cold drinks or lunchtime snacks.

☆ Entertainment

Astraios LIVE MUSIC
(☑6997210687; Peratata; ☺9pm-late; 🖘) Lively bar with a panoramic sea-view terrace near Agios Georgios Kastro. It's owned by venerated musician Dionysos Frangopoulos and puts on live Greek music.

Paliki Peninsula
Χερσόνησος Παλική

Anchored by the bustling gulf-side town of **Lixouri**, the Paliki Peninsula is an under-explored region of spectral white, cream and red clay cliffs; verdant farmland and vineyards; and hilltop villages. **Petani Beach** to the northwest is a spectacular strand of white sand that's enough to entice a jaded mermaid, while red-sand **Xi Beach** to the south also has its appeal, but can feel overcrowded in summer. Between the two in the far west, overlooking stark cliffs, azure seas and robust vineyards, the **Moni Kipouria** monastery was built by a lone, solitude-loving monk.

🛌 Sleeping & Eating

★ Ksouras
APARTMENT €€
(☑ 26710 97458; www.facebook.com/ksouras; Petani; d €85; P ✳ 🛜) Very pleasant rooms in a blue villa immediately above the owners' beachfront taverna. It's a sublimely tranquil spot in the evenings, once the crowds have gone and the sunset is in full swing. The taverna is open for all meals, and serves uniformly excellent and inexpensive Greek classics.

Xi Village
PENSION €€
(☑ 26710 93830; www.xi-village.gr; Xi; d/tr/q €70/80/90; P ✳ 🛜 ✻) Basic, wood-accented, white-walled apartments, all with balconies and kitchenettes, right on long Xi Beach. There's also a pool. It's not luxurious, but it's a good budget choice.

★ Petani Bay Hotel
HOTEL €€€
(☑ 26710 97701; www.petanibayhotel.gr; Petani; d incl breakfast €175-275; P ✳ 🛜 ✻) Boasting one of the finest infinity pools in Greece, this adults-only boutique eyrie overlooks the cobalt-blue bay far below. There are just 13 romantic suites, with marble floors, wood-blade fans and kitchenettes. It's all about peace here; the only sound is the bleating of goats and the chink of chilled wine glasses.

Mavroeidis
BAKERY €
(☑ 26710 22021; Lixouri; baked goods from €1.50; ⊗ 8am-late; ✳ 🛜) Large bakery-cafe in the heart of Lixouri, with outdoor tables at the inland end of the main pedestrian square, and a panoply of sweet-smelling delights inside. Buying a coffee gets you a free taster of the island's best *amygdalopita* (sweet almond cake).

Akrogiali
TAVERNA €
(☑ 26710 92613; Lixouri; mains €6-13; ⊗ 11am-midnight; 🛜) Low-slung, old-fashioned taverna on Lixouri's seafront street, serving a mouthwatering menu of local favourite dishes, including plenty of vegetarian options as well as baked meat and fish.

Erasmia
TAVERNA €
(☑ 26710 97372; Petani Beach; mains €6-10; ⊗ lunch & dinner May-Sep) Buzzing beachfront taverna, right at the foot of the road, where the no-nonsense seafood cooking has a devoted local following. A pleasant spot for lunch, it's even better in the face of a glowing, fiery sunset.

Sami & Around
Σάμη

POP 1030

Cheerful Sami, Kefallonia's main port, stands across the island 25km northeast of Argostoli. Nestled in a bright bay and flanked by steep hills, it consists of a waterside strip, which stares across to Ithaki and is loaded with tourist-oriented cafes. Nearby monasteries, castle ruins and natural features, including the busy but rather overrated **Drogarati Cave** (☑ 26740 23302; adult/child €5/3; ⊗ 8am-8pm Jun-Sep, shorter hours low season), offer enticements to linger. Quieter alternative bases with better beaches, such as **Karavomilos** and **Agia Evfymia**, line the bay as you head further north.

🛌 Sleeping & Eating

Karavomilos Beach Camping
CAMPGROUND €
(☑ 26740 22480; www.camping-karavomilos.gr; Sami-Karavomilos road; adult/car/tent €8.50/3.50/6.50; ⊗ mid-Apr–Sep; 🛜 ✻) Large family-oriented camping ground, with well-shaded sites stretching back from a decent pebble beach just 800m west of central Sami. Good facilities include excellent washrooms.

Hotel Athina
HOTEL €€
(☑ 26740 22779; www.athinahotel.gr; Karavomilos; d incl breakfast €99, apt €130; ⊗ May-Oct; ✳ @) Bright, spotless resort hotel, where simple rooms and larger apartments have balconies overlooking the bay. Guests can use the pool at the swankier neighbouring **Ionian Emerald Resort** (☑ 26740 22708; www.ionian emerald.gr; Karavomilos; d incl breakfast from €300; ✳ 🛜 ✻), which has the same owner.

Melissani Hotel
HOTEL €€
(☑ 26740 22464; www.melissanihotel.gr; Dihalion 23, Sami; s/d/tr €50/65/75; ⊗ May-Oct; ✳ 🛜) Melissani is a welcoming little hotel, two blocks up from the Sami waterfront. Small and rather basic rooms have sea-view balconies plus retro quirks such as orange 1970s phones and old-fashioned showers. There's also a spacious roof terrace.

Odyssey Hotel
HOTEL €€€
(☑ 26740 61089; www.hotelodyssey.gr; Agia Evfymia; d from €216; P ✳ 🛜 ✻) Plush resort hotel, just around the corner north of the harbour, with very comfortable balcony suites looking across to Ithaki, as well as a spa, gym, restaurant and two bars.

MYRTOS BEACH ΠΑΡΑΛΙΑ ΜΥΡΤΟΥ

One of the most breathtaking beaches in all Greece, Myrtos Beach is a stunning expanse of broad white sand 10km northeast of Kefallonia's narrow central isthmus. The only road access drops for 3km in sweeping switchbacks from Divarata, on the main road. Halfway down, a viewing area offers a first glimpse of the shimmering blue water far below. There are no facilities at the beach itself, which drops off sharply, but once you're in the sea it's heavenly.

The limestone cliffs to either side are scarred by landslides from recent earthquakes, which have also for the moment blocked the road north from Divarata towards Assos.

★ **Paradise Beach** GREEK €€
(✆ 26740 61392; www.paradisebeachtaverna.com; Agia Evfymia; mains €7-22; ⊙ lunch & dinner mid-May–mid-Oct; 🛜) At the end of the coast road 700m beyond the harbour, this much-loved taverna has a vine-shaded terrace overlooking a little beach where turtles bob in the water below. Thanks to its locally reared meat – in dishes such as exceptionally tender lamb chops, Kefallonian meat pie or braised rabbit – and seafood delights, it's an island institution. You'll be coming back, believe us!

❶ Information

Sami has all necessary facilities, including a post office and banks.
Port Authority (✆ 26740 22031)

Fiskardo Φισκάρδο

POP 190

The little port of Fiskardo curves serenely beside coral-blue waters, gazing out towards Ithaki. Thanks to its colourful crop of Venetian villas, spared from earthquake damage by resting on a sturdy bed of flat rock, Fiskardo is the island's most exclusive resort, home to upmarket restaurants and choice accommodation. There's no real dock or jetty here; ferries from Lefkada arrive unceremoniously at the northern end, while yachts jostle for space along the rest of the harbour. While it can get very crowded in summer, it has a cosmopolitan buzz unmatched elsewhere on the island.

There's no beach in Fiskardo itself, but pretty little coves lie both to the north, where the gorgeous sand at **Emblissi** is shaded by olive trees, and to the south, where **Foki Bay** is home to an attractive taverna.

The ultra-clear waters hereabouts make Fiskardo a perfect place to learn to dive. **Fiskardo Divers** (✆ 6970206172; www.fiskardo-divers.com; 3hr beginners courses €55, open-water 4-day PADI courses €430) offers PADI courses, plus dives to caves, wrecks, reefs and a downed Bristol Beaufort WWII bomber.

🛏 Sleeping

As well as holding hotels to suit all budgets, Fiskardo and the adjacent bays are peppered with rental villas and apartments. Several are available via **Ionian Villas** (www.ionian-villas.co.uk).

Regina Studios APARTMENT €
(✆ 26740 41125; www.regina-studios-boats.gr; d/tr €55/75; ❄🛜) A pink villa, beside the village car park up the steps from the waterfront, which holds great-value 'en-suite' economy rooms, larger studios with sea-view balconies and shared kitchens, and larger two-bedroom apartments. The owner also rents out boats of all sizes.

Kiki Apartments APARTMENT €€
(✆ 26710 22754; www.kiki-apartments.gr; studios/apt €110/130; ❄🛜🏊) Six scrupulously maintained apartments lie 300m along the waterfront south of the village. Chunky wood-top tables and a green-and-cream colour scheme, give them a chic Provençal feel, and they include gleaming kitchenettes, private balconies and stunning bedrooms. There's also a pool with a spacious terrace.

Stella Hotel Apartments HOTEL €€
(✆ 26740 41261; www.stella-apartments.gr; studios/apt from €82/160; ❄🛜) Welcoming hillside hotel, just above the coast road 10 minutes' walk south of the village, where the comfortable rooms have large bay-view balconies.

Villa Romantza PENSION €€
(✆ 26740 41322; www.villa-romantza.gr; r/studios/apt €60/80/100; ❄🛜) Excellent budget option, near the central car park, where simple, spacious and well-maintained rooms, studios and apartments share a communal terrace; some have two bedrooms and kitchenettes.

IONIAN ISLANDS KEFALLONIA

Emelisse Hotel
RESORT €€€

(📞 26740 41200; www.arthotel.gr; Emblissi Bay; d/ste incl breakfast from €363, 4-person apt from €870; ⊗ mid-Apr–mid-Oct; 🅿❄@🛜🏊) This luxury hotel is set in magnificent seclusion on a headland overlooking superb Emblissi Beach, 1.5km north of Fiskardo along the winding coast road. Its beautifully appointed rooms are laid out on immaculately groomed terraces, leading down to a lavish swimming pool and a restaurant with fantastic views to Lefkada, Ithaki and beyond.

✖ Eating & Drinking

Fiskardo's restaurants are among the best – and most expensive – in the Ionian Islands.

Lagoudera
GREEK €€

(📞 26740 41275; mains €10-17; ⊗ noon-2am; ❄🛜) Fiskardo's largest restaurant, spreading across open squares between separate quayside and backstreet dining rooms, is a friendly, unhurried but very efficient operation. It's very dependable for well-cooked local classics such as a rich, chunky octopus *stifadho* or herby crab fritters.

Café Tselenti
MEDITERRANEAN €€

(📞 26740 41344; mains €8-26; ⊗ breakfast, lunch & dinner May-Oct) Owned by the Tselenti family since 1893, this popular restaurant serves Italian-influenced dishes such as a terrific linguine with prawns, mussels and crayfish, as well as local specialities such as lamb shank, beef *stifadho* and grilled swordfish. It has a romantic terrace on the village square as well as quayside tables.

Tassia
TAVERNA €€

(📞 26740 41205; www.tassia.gr; mains €9-19; ⊗ noon-2am May-Oct) Down-to-earth seafront taverna run by well-known Kefallonian chef Tassia, who delights diners with her homemade pies, mezedhes and zucchini croquettes. Try the 'fisherman's pasta', incorporating finely chopped squid, octopus, mussels and prawns in a magical combination with a dash of cognac.

★ Irida
GREEK €€€

(📞 26740 41343; mains €9-35; ⊗ 9am-late; ❄🛜) Whether you dine in the shadowy boho interior or out on the waterfront, there's something for everyone at this 200-year-old salt store. Dishes include meatballs, stuffed aubergine, and the much pricier lobster risotto or spaghetti, and it's all scrupulously prepared and presented.

Vasso's
SEAFOOD €€€

(📞 26740 41276; mains €9-48; ⊗ lunch & dinner May-Oct; 🛜) Vasso's is widely renowned for its high-quality seafood, with highlights

---

KEFALLONIA'S GREAT OUTDOORS

While the EOT occasionally stocks excellent leaflets with walking routes around the island, it's well worth enlisting an experienced local to guide you off the beaten path.

Sea Kayaking Kefalonia (📞 6934010400; www.seakayakingkefalonia-greece.com) Offers a full range of day-long kayak tours, with lunch and snorkelling gear included (€65), plus multiday excursions and certified courses.

Bavarian Horse Riding (📞 6977533203; www.kephalonia.com; Koulourata; 1/4hr €25/80) Ride sturdy Bavarian horses through the Kefallonian countryside. Day trips range from one to four hours, with your choice of route. One longer trek leads across Mt Enos and down to the sea, where you can take the horses for a swim. Multiday itineraries also possible.

Outdoor Kefalonia (📞 6979987611; http://outdoorkefalonia.com) All manner of trips, from coasteering (€35), hiking (€60) and canyoning (€60), to sea kayaking (€60) and Jeep safaris (from €50).

Donkey Trekking (📞 6980059630; www.donkeytrekkingkefalonia.com; per hr from €25) Slow-paced donkey treks, exploring ruined villages and evergreen valleys in the hilly country south of Sami. Bring sturdy footwear.

Pyrgos House (📞 6989863140; www.pyrgoshouse.com; walking tours €15; ⊗ 9.30am-1.30pm & 5-8pm) Highly recommended outdoor activities, including €15 guided walks of Hora's *kastro* (fortress; 10am Wednesday), Arionadika (6pm Wednesday), Potamos (6pm Friday) and Mylopotamos (9am Saturday). Also offers six-hour sea-kayaking expeditions (€45); canyoning (€25, 3.30pm Thursday); and evening bike tours from Potamos (€35). A nine-day walking tour of the island costs €450 per person including accommodation.

WORTH A TRIP

ASSOS ΑΣΣΟΣ

Almost too photogenically perfect for words, pint-sized Assos (population 88) is a confection of Italianate cream- and ochre-coloured houses, with a pretty crescent-shaped cove that's protected by a wooded peninsula. The fortress atop the headland makes a great hike, while the bay is eminently swimmable.

A mouthwatering array of tasty tavernas, plus a pace so slow you can palpably feel your pulse dropping, are compelling reasons to visit. It's also possible to stay overnight.

Note that the main coastal highway is currently closed between Assos and Myrtos Beach to the south, so drivers are directed along back routes higher up the mountainside.

Sleeping & Eating

Apartment Linardos (☎26740 51563; www.linardosapartments.gr; d/tr/q €80/90/120; ⊙May-Sep; ❄📶) Tastefully finished kitchenette studios, perched on the isthmus a stone's throw from the beach, with postcard-perfect balcony views of both harbour and fortress. Let the waves lull you to sleep.

Platanos (☎26740 51143; mains €7-15; ⊙breakfast, lunch & dinner Easter-Oct; 📶🖉) Platanos is admired island-wide for its fresh, locally sourced ingredients, and especially for its meat dishes. There are also fish and vegetarian options such as vegetable *mousakas*. It adjoins an attractive shady plaza just back from the waterfront, but has no sea views.

Molos (☎26740 51220; mains €7-14; ⊙9.30am-late; 📶) At the far northern end of the curving bay, this custard-hued taverna has tables right on the quayside that catch the late-afternoon 'golden hour'. Molos serves everything from breakfast omelettes to fresh grilled tuna.

including honeyed octopus with mashed fava, mussels, *saganaki* and *sofigado* (veal in tomato sauce).

Information

Nautilus Travel (☎26740 41440; Fiskardo) and **Pama Travel** (☎26740 41033; www.pamatravel.com; ⊙9am-2pm & 5.30-9pm) can make all travel and ferry arrangements.

ITHAKI ΙΘΑΚΗ

POP 3230

Every bit as rugged, romantic and all-round epic as its role in Homeric legend would suggest, Ithaki (Map p686) is something special. The hilly, sea-girt homeland to which Odysseus struggled to return for 10 heroic years continues to charm and seduce travellers with its ancient ruins, breathtaking harbour villages and wilderness walks. Squeezed between Kefallonia and the mainland, it's the kind of island where time seems to slow down and cares slip away.

Cut almost in two by the huge gulf that shields **Vathy**, its main town, Ithaki effectively consists of two separate islands linked by a narrow isthmus. Vathy is the only significant settlement in the south, while the mighty northern massif holds delightful villages such as **Stavros** and **Anogi**, and is peppered with little coves holding pocket-sized resorts such as **Frikes** and **Kioni**.

Getting There & Away

Ionian Pelagos (www.ionionpelagos.com) runs two or three times daily in high season between Piso Aetos and Sami (Kefallonia), and once or twice from Piso Aetos to Astakos (on the mainland).

Between July and mid-September, the **Meganisi II** (☎26740 33120; www.ferryboatmeganisi.gr) ferry runs twice daily between Frikes and Nydri on Lefkada.

Buy tickets from **Polyctor Tours** (☎26740 33120; www.ithakiholidays.com) or **Ithaca Tours** (☎26740 33336; www.ithacatours.gr) in Vathy.

West Ferry (www.westferry.gr) has in the past connected Frikes with Fiskardo (Kefallonia) and Vasiliki (Lefkada); that service has not run in recent years, but it's worth checking the website to see whether it has resumed.

Getting Around

Piso Aetos, the port on Ithaki's west coast, has no settlement. **Taxis** (☎6946552397, 6945700214) often meet boats, as does the municipal bus in high season. Bus services are very limited, though, so it's well worth renting a car – easiest in Vathy – for at least one day of your stay.

Vathy Βαθύ

POP 1820

Set around a superbly sheltered natural harbour, and fringed with sky-blue and ochre villas holding lively bars and restaurants, pretty Vathy is Ithaki's main commercial hub. The quayside buzzes with activity, while narrow lanes wriggle away inland.

⊙ Sights & Activities

Other than the **archaeological museum** (☑ 26740 32200; Anastasiou Kallinikou; ⊙ 8.30am-3pm Tue-Sun) FREE, Vathy holds few sights to see, but there's some wonderful walking nearby. Follow the line of the harbour all the way east, until the road finally peters out, and a spectacular coastal footpath leads in another half-hour to the whitewashed waterfront chapel of **Agios Andreas**. Alternatively, stay on the road as it climbs away at the eastern end of the harbour; cross the brow of the hill, and you'll come to a succession of increasingly wonderful, secluded beaches – first Mnimata, then Skinos, and finally, after a total of 4km, the magnificent white sands of **Gidaki**.

Albatross (☑ 6973467977) and **Mana Korina** (☑ 6976654351) offer boat excursions from Vathy in high season to outlying beaches and unpopulated islets.

★ **Island Walks** WALKING
(☑ 6944990458; www.islandwalks.com; walks €15-18) Charming expat artist Ester runs guided walks of varying lengths, all over the island. Her most popular route, the three-hour Homer Walk, winds up the hillside near Stavros to the ruins where the real Odysseus may have lived 2800 years ago, and also takes in the village museum.

⊨ Sleeping

★ **Perantzada 1811** BOUTIQUE HOTEL €€
(☑ 26740 33496; www.arthotel.gr/perantzada; Odyssea Androutsou; d/q incl breakfast from €110/345; ⊙ Easter–mid-Oct; ❄ ☎ ⊠) Centred on a 19th-century neoclassical villa, hovering above the harbour, this self-styled 'art hotel' holds large balconied rooms as minimal as white clouds, replete with granite-and-wood bathrooms. Cheaper rooms lack sea views and share balconies, while larger suites in the new wing have baths you could free-dive in. The breakfast buffet is pure decadence, and there's an enticing infinity pool.

Hotel Familia BOUTIQUE HOTEL €€
(☑ 26740 33366; www.hotel-familia.com; Odysseos 60; s/d incl breakfast from €130/145; ❄ ☎) Converted from an old olive press, juxtaposing chic slate with soft tapestries and gentle lighting, this charming boutique hotel has a real 'wow' factor. It's family-run and family-friendly – but although it's only 50m from the southwestern corner of the harbour, there are no sea views, and only one room has a courtyard.

Grivas View APARTMENT €€
(☑ 26740 33328; Odyssea Androutsou; d/tr €75/85; ❄ ☎) Bright, spacious, good-value studios, with flower-draped terraces overlooking the bay; for the best views, ask for one upstairs. They're on the eastern side of the harbour just before it broadens, on the street parallel to the waterfront.

Odyssey Apartments APARTMENT €€
(☑ 26740 33400; www.odysseyapartments.gr; studios €105, 1-/2-bedroom apt €135/175; P ❄ ⊠) Perched on a hillside 600m beyond the eastern end of the harbour, a 20-minute walk from the centre, these spotless studios and apartments (some sleeping five people) have balconies with magical views of the bay. There's a simple cafe by the pool.

✕ Eating

Trehantiri TAVERNA €
(☑ 26740 33444; http://trehantiri.ithakionline.com; mains €7-12; ⊙ lunch & dinner; ❄ ☎) Traditional taverna with blue tables set up off the square in the heart of town. Every day the kitchen cooks up something different, from goat stew to stuffed tomatoes, *saganaki* to *kleftiko*. Look out for *savoro,* marinated local fish.

Karamela Cafe CAFE €
(☑ 26740 33580; mains €5-8; ⊙ 6.30am-late; ❄ ☎) A laid-back, bright-orange cafe as you enter town at the western end of the harbour; its quayside tables are usually thronged with sailors moored alongside. Come for wholesome breakfasts, lunchtime pizzas or salads, or sunset cocktails.

★ **O Batis** SEAFOOD €€
(☑ 26740 33010; mains €8-18; ⊙ lunch & dinner; ❄ ☎) Vathy's top pick for ultra-fresh seafood sits amid a row of similar-looking places along the harbour. Tourists flock to the waterfront tables, while local fishers, who've had quite enough sea views for one day, prefer the no-frills interior. For €15 you'll get a whole grilled fish plus salad and wine or beer.

Sirenes
GREEK €€

(📞26740 33001; http://sirines.eu; mains €8-15; 🕐 lunch & dinner; ❄️📶) A smart little restaurant, a block back from the waterfront, with a cool front terrace and a swanky bar in its elegant wood-panelled dining room. Distinctive local dishes include *strapatsada* (clay pot lamb) and slow-cooked rabbit, plus fresh seafood.

Around Ithaki

Cross the slender isthmus to reach Ithaki's northern half and you face an immediate choice of onward routes, along either flank of the island's towering (809m) central spine. Following the eastern road brings you after 5.5km to the somewhat dilapidated hilltop monastery of **Katharon**, which commands astonishing views back down to Vathy. Another 4km along this fabulously scenic mountain road, you'll reach sleepy **Anogi**, once the island's capital. Ask in the village *kafeneio* (coffee house) for the keys to the restored church of **Agia Panagia**, which holds incredible Byzantine frescoes.

Further north again, the east- and west-coast roads rejoin at the larger village of **Stavros**, above the Bay of Polis. A lovely rural walk up the nearby hillside leads to a site long known as the **School of Homer**, but is suggested by recent archaeological digs to be the long-lost palace of Odysseus himself. It's all in ruins, and smaller than you might expect, but wonderfully evocative nonetheless. Artefacts associated with the legendary hero are on show in Stavros' one-room **archaeological museum** (📞26740 31305; 🕐 8.30am-3.15pm Tue-Sun) FREE.

Dropping back seawards northeast of Stavros takes you to the tiny ferry port of **Frikes**, clasped between windswept cliffs and home to a cluster of waterfront restaurants and bars. The beautiful and sinuous coast road beyond ends at pretty little **Kioni**, a hamlet of mustard-and-cream Venetian houses tumbling down to an irresistibly bijou harbour.

🛏 Sleeping

Ourania Apartments
APARTMENT €

(📞26740 31027; www.ithacagreece.com/ourania/ ourania.htm; Stavros; studios/apt €45/70; 🅿️❄️) A romantic shuttered villa, two minutes' walk uphill from Stavros, festooned in flowers and rejoicing in amazing views over the olive groves to the sea. Two homey studios, with kitchenettes and balconies, plus a

---

ODYSSEUS UNCOVERED

It took 10 long years of fighting before the wily Odysseus devised the stratagem – the Trojan Horse – that finally breached the walls of Troy. The war over, he was free to return to his beloved Ithaki and his queen Penelope. How long could the 910-km voyage home possibly take?

According to Homer, another 10 years. Blown off course while passing Kythira, and buffeted thereafter by winds unleashed by Poseidon the Earth Shaker, Odysseus was subjected to an appalling series of perils and misadventures. En route he was imprisoned by the nymph Calypso on Ogygia, possibly modern-day Gozo; encountered the Lotus-Eaters in North Africa; blinded the Cyclops Polyphemus somewhere near Sicily; resisted the seductive song of the sirens in the Bay of Naples; and braved the straits between Scylla, a man-eating sea monster, and Charybdis the deadly whirlpool. Eventually, the gods allowed him to escape another long period of captivity, in the arms of the enchantress Circe. Shipwrecked on the shores of Scheria, commonly identified as Corfu, he returned at last to Ithaki, and wrought his vengeance on the suitors harrying the long-suffering Penelope.

Many of modern-day Ithaki's most popular hiking trails lead to sites associated with Homer's epic poem 'Odyssey'. Finding them, though, can be an epic journey of its own, as signposts are few and far between. Targets include the **Fountain of Arethousa**, an exposed and isolated three-hour round-trip south of Vathy, which is said to be the spot where Odysseus' swineherd, Eumaeus, brought his pigs to drink.

As for Odysseus' palace, the German archaeologist Heinrich Schliemann, who rediscovered Troy itself, thought he'd found it at **Alalkomenes**, near Piso Aetos. More recent excavations have led modern archaeologists to identify ruins on Pelikata Hill outside Stavros as the scene of the poem's bloody climax.

larger apartment that sleeps four. The owners are warmth itself.

Captain's Apartments
APARTMENT €€

(☑ 26740 31481; www.captains-apartments.gr; Kioni; 2-/4-person apt €65/90; ❉ 🛜) Clean, simple studios with pine fittings and well-stocked kitchenettes; some have wraparound balconies with views in all directions. Turn right just before you reach the harbour on the winding road down the hill.

Kioni Apartments
APARTMENT €€

(☑ 26740 31144; www.ithacagreece.eu; Kioni; apt €100; ⊘ May-Oct; ❉ 🛜) A handsome Italianate building in the corner of the harbour, drowning in bougainvillea, and holding welcoming apartments with wooden ceilings and large balconies. Stylish but homey, central but quiet. In a word: perfect.

✖ Eating

En Plo
CAFE €

(☑ 26740 31520; Kioni; mains €6-8; ⊘ 8am-midnight; ❉ 🛜) Chic, laid-back waterfront cafe, where the upstairs terrace is a lovely spot for watching sunsets and the lights as they come on in the windmills across the bay. Open all day, for bites ranging from yoghurt or omelettes for breakfast to salads and burgers, and, of course, cocktails later on.

★ Yefuri
TAVERNA €€

(☑ 26740 31131; www.facebook.com/Yefuri; Platrithias; mains €7-17; ⊘ dinner Tue-Sat, brunch & dinner Sun, reduced hours low season; ❉ 🛜) This eclectic, very popular little restaurant, 2km north of Stavros, is renowned island-wide for its fresh produce and rotating Italian-influenced menu, which ranges from eggs Benedict for Sunday brunch to stir-fried chicken and roast pork for dinner.

Ithaki Restaurant
GREEK €€

(☑ 26740 31081; Stavros; mains €8-15; ⊘ lunch & dinner) Smart restaurant on the corner of the village square, serving succulent meaty specialities such as local sausages, charcoal-grilled veal or pork, and lamb souvlaki. The terrace of the attached Sunset Café has sumptuous views in the early evening.

Mythos
TAVERNA €€

(☑ 26740 31122; Kioni; mains €8-14; ⊘ lunch & dinner; ❉ 🛜) This unpretentious traditional taverna sitting by the waves in Kioni dishes up tasty and substantial helpings of local favourites, such as *pastitsio* (layers of buttery macaroni and seasoned minced lamb),

veal *stifadho,* homemade chicken pie and prawns *saganaki.*

ZAKYNTHOS ΖΑΚΥΝΘΟΣ

POP 40,760

Beautiful Zakynthos, also known by its Italian name Zante, has become dominated along its southern and southeastern shoreline by package tourism. Once you leave the long sandy beaches of those regions behind, however, and set off to explore the rest of the island, you'll discover plenty of wilderness and traditional rural villages. Some attractive lower-key bases lie just beyond the larger, run-of-the-mill resorts, including **Keri** and **Limni Keriou** in the remote southwest, and **Agios Nikolaos** and **Cape Skinari** in the far north, but it's the spectacular scenery of the rugged west coast, where mighty limestone cliffs plummet down to turquoise waters, that's the true highlight.

❶ Getting There & Away

AIR

Zakynthos Airport (☑ 26950 29500; www.zakynthos-airport.com) is 5km southwest of Zakynthos Town.

Domestic

Olympic Air (www.olympicair.com) Flies to Athens.

Sky Express (www.skyexpress.gr) Flies to Corfu via Kefallonia and Preveza.

International

Between May and September, charter flights connect Zakynthos with northern Europe and the UK.

Air Berlin (www.airberlin.com) Flies to Düsseldorf in Germany.

EasyJet (www.easyjet.com) Flies to London (Gatwick and Stansted), Liverpool, Bristol and Milan in high season.

BOAT

Domestic

Ionian Group (www.ionian-group.com) runs between four and seven ferries daily, depending on the season, between Zakynthos Town and Kyllini in the Peloponnese. Occasional international ferries call in on the way to/from Igoumenitsa, Sami (Kefallonia), and Bari and Brindisi (Italy).

From the isolated northern port of Agios Nikolaos, **Ionian Pelagos** (www.ionionpelagos.com) ferries sail to Pesada in southern Kefallonia twice daily from mid-May to October; **Chionis Tours** (☑ 26950 48996; Lomvardou 8; ⊘ 9am-11.30pm) sells tickets. Neither port has good

Zakynthos

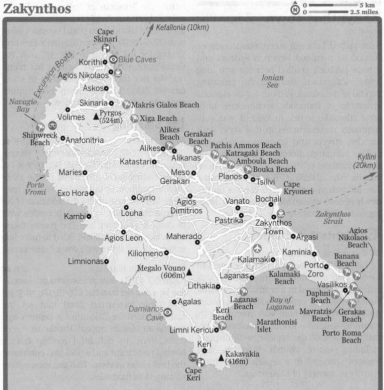

N 0 — 5 km
0 — 2.5 miles

Kefallonia (10km)

Cape Skinari

Korithi — Blue Caves

Agios Nikolaos

Askos

Ionian Sea

Skinaria — Makris Gialos Beach

Volimes ▲ Pyrgos (524m) — Xiga Beach

Navagio Bay

Shipwreck Beach — Anafonitria

Alikes Beach — Gerakari Beach — Pachis Ammos Beach

Alikes — Alikanas — Katragaki Beach

Katastari — Amboula Beach

Maries — Meso Gerakari — Planos — Bouka Beach

Porto Vromi

Exo Hora — Gyrio — Tsilivi

Kambi — Louha — Agios Dimitrios — Vanato — Bochali

Pastrika — Zakynthos Town

Maherado — Argasi

Agios Leon — Kalamaki — Kaminia

Kiliomeno — Agios Nikolaos Beach

Limnionas — Megalo Vouno (606m) ▲ — Porto Zoro — Banana Beach

Laganas — Kalamaki Beach — Vasilikos

Lithakia — Daphni Beach

Agalas — Laganas Beach — *Bay of Laganas* — Mavratzis Beach — Gerakas Beach

Damianos Cave

Keri Beach — Marathonisi Islet — Porto Roma Beach

Limni Keriou

Keri — Kakavakia (416m) ▲

Cape Keri

Excursion Boats

Cape Kryoneri

Zakynthos Strait

Kyllini (20km)

IONIAN ISLANDS ZAKYNTHOS

bus connections, however, so most travellers find it easier and cheaper to cross to mainland Kyllini from Zakynthos Town, and catch another ferry from there to Kefallonia.

International

Ventouris Ferries (http://ventourisferries.com) connects Zakynthos Town with Bari (Italy) in high season, with a stop in Kefallonia (Sami) en route.

BUS

The **KTEL Bus Station** (☑ 26950 22255; www. ktel-zakynthos.gr) is on the hillside bypass in Zakynthos Town, 500m up from the waterfront and 15 minutes' walk southwest of Plateia Solomou. Long-distance routes include Athens (€28.60, six hours, four daily), Patra (€8.70, 3½

hours, four daily) and Thessaloniki (€54.40, 10 hours, two weekly). Budget an additional €8.90 for the ferry to Kyllini.

🛈 Getting Around

Zakynthos Town is the centre of an extensive local bus network.

Rental cars (from €40 per day in high season) and motorcycles are available at the airport and in larger resorts.

Europcar (☑ 26950 43313; www.europcar -greece.com; Zakynthos Airport) At the airport.

Hertz Locations at the **airport** (☑ 26950 24287; www.hertz.gr; Zakynthos Airport) and in **Zakynthos Town** (☑ 26950 45706; www.hertz. gr; Lomvardou 38; ☉ 8am-2pm & 5.30-9pm).

BOAT SERVICES FROM ZAKYNTHOS

DESTINATION	PORT	DURATION	FARE (€)	FREQUENCY
Kyllini (Peloponnese)	Zakynthos Town	1hr	8.90	4-7 daily
Pesada (Kefallonia)	Agios Nikolaos	1½hr	8	2 daily, seasonal

Zakynthos Town Ζάκυνθος

POP 9770

Sandwiched between steep wooded slopes topped by a ruined Venetian fortress and a huge harbour cradled between two long jetties, Zakynthos Town is the pulsating capital of the island. Famous for its glorious ensemble of Italianate architecture until an earthquake struck in 1953, it was subsequently reconstructed in fine style, with arcaded streets and gracious neoclassical public buildings. Recent years have seen the restoration of its showpiece waterfront square, the dazzling **Plateia Solomou**. The hubbub of everyday life centres on the newly pedestrianised streets behind it, leading to smaller **Plateia Agiou Markou**.

◎ Sights & Activities

★ Byzantine Museum   MUSEUM
(☑26950 42714; Plateia Solomou; €3; ⊙8am-3pm Tue-Sat) This magnificent museum of ecclesiastical art is housed in a beautifully restored building on the central waterfront plaza. Almost everything here was rescued – by volunteer sailors! – in the immediate aftermath of the 1953 earthquake, with displays including entire church interiors, and frescoes arranged in a replica of the 16th-century monastery of St Andreas.

Kastro   FORTRESS
(☑26950 48099; €4; ⊙8am-3pm Tue-Sun) A ruined Venetian fortress sits atop the wooded slope that looms over the town centre. Reached by a steep, enjoyable 15-minute hike, or a circuitous 2.5km drive, it's now essentially a peaceful forest park, enclosed within sturdy ramparts and affording tremendous views. Tumbledown churches lie scattered through the woods, along with a 19th-century British football pitch and a cafe.

Church of St Dionysios   CHURCH
(museum €1; ⊙9am-1pm & 4.30-9pm) Devoted to Zakynthos' patron saint, the rebuilt Church of St Dionysios (1948) stands at the south end of the waterfront, near the ferry jetty. Its interior holds opulent gilt work and impressive frescoes, while its museum, entered around the back, is a major centre for restoration. Exhibits include ecclesiastical trappings and vestments, including those of Dionysios himself.

Museum of Solomos   MUSEUM
(☑26950 48982; Plateia Agiou Markou 15; adult/child €4/free; ⊙9am-2pm) To give it its full name, the Museum of Solomos and Eminent Zakynthian People houses not only the archives of island-born poet Dionysios Solomos (1798–1857), but even his tomb. He's best known for his 'Hymn to Liberty', now the Greek national anthem. Neither his memorabilia nor the sombre portraits of other famous Zakynthians – mostly 19th-century generals – have English captions.

⊨ Sleeping

Diana Hotel   HOTEL €€
(☑26950 28547; www.dianahotels.gr; Mitropoleos; s/d/q incl breakfast €95/115/140; ❋ ☎ ⊛) A long-standing hotel just north of the main square, traditionally targeted at business travellers but spruced up by the addition of an unexpected delight – a rooftop garden with swimming pool and bar. The rooms themselves vary, from small and faded to more luxurious balcony suites with swish bathrooms.

Hotel Strada Marina   HOTEL €€
(☑26950 42761; www.stradamarina.gr; Lombardou 14; s/d/q incl breakfast €55/81/171; ❋ ☎ ⊛) This large waterfront hotel that set the luxe standard for Zakynthos a century ago retains an elegant appeal, thanks to recent renovations. Its delightful rooftop terrace holds a restaurant and a pool that command the best views in town. Half the rooms have marina-view balconies.

Plaza Hotel   HOTEL €€
(☑26950 45733; www.plazazante.gr; Kolokotronis 2; s/d €85/100; ❋ ☎) Across from the small town beach, this presentable four-storey hotel has a lift to carry guests up to its nicely modernised rooms, which have good bathrooms and sea-view balconies.

Alba Hotel   PENSION €€
(☑26950 26641; www.albahotel.gr; L Ziva 38; s/d/tr €54/66/108; ❋ ☎) Simple but very central budget hotel, where the clean, smallish, marble-accented rooms have old-fashioned bathrooms, plus balconies and fridges.

✕ Eating

Fresh Pies   PIES €
(☑26951 01649; Koliva 101; pies & sandwiches from €3; ⊙8am-late; ☎) Who could resist the name of this hugely popular student hang-out, just off the main pedestrian shopping street? Order at the counter, then sit at tables on the open square opposite. It's not just hot pies and sandwiches, either; it also whips up fabulous fresh juices and smoothies, from just €2.

Mesathes GREEK €

(☑26950 49315; Plateia Dimokratia 4; mains €8-14; ⊙lunch & dinner; 🕾) A prime spot for people-watching, this welcoming taverna spreads through a broad and breezy terrace on the open pedestrian precinct behind the Byzantine Museum, and offers a well-priced menu of beautifully presented dishes such as rabbit *stifadho,* grilled shrimp, and panna cotta that melts on your tongue. The owner plays a mean tune on the guitar.

Malanos TAVERNA €

(☑26950 45936; www.malanos.gr; Agiou Athanasiou, Keri; mains €7-13; ⊙noon-4pm & 7pm-late) This much-loved family-run taverna, set amid the fields on the southern outskirts of town 2km from the centre, is renowned island-wide for serving huge portions of rich local favourites such as rooster, rabbit and wild boar at its simple, plaid-covered tables.

★**Prosilio** MEDITERRANEAN €€

(☑26950 22040; www.prosiliozakynthos.gr; A Latta 15; mains €9-19; ⊙6pm-late Tue-Sat summer, Fri & Sat winter; ❀🕾) Gourmet dinner-only restaurant, with a boutique interior and a romantic garden courtyard. The hushed atmosphere may be unusual, but the service is relaxed and friendly, and if you love Greek food you're sure to relish the inventive take on dishes such as *taramasalata* (a thick pink or white purée of fish roe, potato, oil and lemon juice), served with crispy prawns. The wine list abounds in well-priced local wines.

★**Avli** MEDITERRANEAN €€

(Yard of Taste; ☑26950 29815; www.avlizante.gr; Rizospaston 15; mains €8-15; ⊙noon-1am; ❀🕾🚲) Delicious and wholesome Italian-influenced food, much of it organic and/or vegetarian, served in an enticing setting, with comfortable seating, vibrant linens and upholstery. As well as pasta and Greek staples, it prepares huge salads using unusual grains and pulses.

🍷 Drinking & Nightlife

Base BAR

(☑26950 42409; www.basecafe.gr; L Ziva 3; ⊙9am-late; 🕾) Down at street level, Base surveys the flow through Plateia Agiou Markou, dispensing coffees, drinks and music to a hip local crowd. The stylish rooftop bar, open from late afternoon, is a fabulous venue for knockout cocktails.

Around Zakynthos

Prosperous and lively Zakynthos Town, home to the island's airport and ferry port, makes a bustling point of arrival. Package tourism is concentrated both along the shoreline to the north and, especially, along the southern coast, between **Laganas** and **Kalamaki**. The **Vasilikos Peninsula**, poking south from the southeast corner, is a little less developed, though long, narrow **Banana Beach** on its northern side is awash with crowds, water sports and parasols. Keep going right to the tip to reach **Gerakas Beach**; a strand of fine sand that faces into Laganas Bay, it's the island's best. It's also a crucial turtle-nesting site, so visitor numbers are restricted, and all access is forbidden between dusk and dawn from May to October; conservation advice is displayed near the access path.

IONIAN ISLANDS ZAKYNTHOS

ENDANGERED LOGGERHEADS

The Ionian Islands are home to one of Europe's most endangered marine species, the **loggerhead turtle** (*Caretta caretta*). Zakynthos hosts the largest density of loggerhead nests, with an estimated 1500 along the Bay of Laganas, an area protected as the **National Marine Park of Zakynthos** (NMPZ; ☑26950 29870; www.nmp-zak.org).

Unfortunately, the extended tracts of clean, flat sand on which the turtles lay their eggs are also the favoured habitat of basking beach lovers. Strict regulations limit building, boating, fishing and water sports in designated zones. During breeding season (from May to October), nesting beaches are barred to visitors between dusk and dawn, and as the eggs start to hatch, from July onwards, conservation agencies place frames with warning notes over buried nests. Many are still destroyed by visitors, however, and countless hatchlings fail to reach the water after becoming disoriented by sunbeds, noise and lights.

Volunteers from **Archelon** (www.archelon.gr) and the park run education and volunteer programs, including a visitor centre at Gerakas Beach. Advice includes to not use umbrellas on dry sand (use the wet part of the beach), and to not take boating trips in the Bay of Laganas, as these have been known to torment and even kill turtles.

Beyond Laganas, the rugged terrain of the far southwest starts to unfold. Follow a tiny road from the pretty village of **Keri** to reach lighthouse-topped **Cape Keri**, and a high viewpoint surveying the endless cliffs that stretch away up the west coast; a converted van sells snacks.

There's no shoreline road north, but a happily confusing tangle of highland routes threads through the wooded hill country parallel to the coast. Here and there, spur roads either drop to coves such as **Limnionas** or climb to the clifftops, as at **Kambi**. Detouring inland brings you to villages such as **Kiliomeno**, where the Church of St Nikolaos features an unusual roofless campanile, and gorgeous little **Louha**, which tumbles down a valley surrounded by woodlands and pastures. Locals sell honey and seasonal products pretty much everywhere, but it's **Volimes** in the north that's the major sales centre for traditional products such as olive oil, tablecloths and rugs.

The most dramatic sight along the west coast is magnificent **Shipwreck Beach**, home to a stranded cargo ship that ran aground in the 1960s. It's only accessible on boat trips – in summer, the waters immediately offshore are choc-a-bloc with sightseeing cruises – but you can admire it from above, and get fabulous photos, from a precariously perched lookout platform signposted between Anafonitria and Volimes.

On the east coast, resorts immediately north of Zakynthos Town are generally humdrum, but the further north you go the more dramatic the scenery becomes. The road narrows at the little ferry village of **Agios Nikolaos**, which holds a nice crop of restaurants and accommodation, while the majestic headland of **Cape Skinari** marks the end of the road at the northern tip.

🏃 Activities

Boat trips, run by Karidis and Potamitis Trips, head from both Agios Nikolaos and Cape Skinari to the **Blue Caves** and **Shipwreck Beach**; smaller vessels can enter these sea-level caverns, where the water inside turns a translucent blue in the morning sunlight, between roughly 9am and 2pm.

Potamitis Trips   BOATING
(📞 26950 31132; www.potamitisbros.gr; Cape Skinari) Glass-bottom boats leave every 15 minutes to the Blue Caves (€10), or to Shipwreck Beach (€15).

Karidis   BOATING
(📞 6977275463; Agios Nikolaos) Frequent boat trips to the Blue Caves (€10), some of which continue to Shipwreck Beach (€20).

🛏 Sleeping

The huge curve of the Bay of Laganas, along the south coast, is lined with hotels catering to package holidaymakers, while the beach resorts immediately northwest of Zakynthos Town are a bit more sedate. More upmarket options are hidden away on the Vasilikos Peninsula in the southeast, and in Agios Nikolaos in the north.

Panorama   APARTMENT €
(📞 26950 31013; Agios Nikolaos; studios €50; 🅿 ❄ 🛜) Excellent studios with sea views, managed by a friendly English-speaking family and set back in a lovely garden from the main road, a 700m uphill walk south of Agios Nikolaos.

Joanna's Stone Villas   APARTMENT €€
(📞 6955497431; www.joannasvillas.com; Vasilikos; d/q €124/152; ❄ 🛜 🏊) Very stylish modern apartments, maisonettes and entire villas, in a peaceful rural complex near the southeast corner of the island. All have kitchens, and share separate kids' and adults' pools.

Zakynthos Windmills   APARTMENT €€
(📞 2695031132;www.potamitisbros.gr;CapeSkinari; apt from €60, windmills from €130; ❄ 🛜) Two converted windmills – one dazzling white, the other with exposed stone walls, each sleeping two guests – plus two- and four-person apartments in a stone house have a fantastic clifftop location in Cape Skinari. Rooms have cool tiled floors and boutique flourishes, and there's a taverna alongside. Steps lead to a lovely swimming area.

Villa Christina   APARTMENT €€
(📞 26950 49208; www.villachristina.gr; Limni Keriou; studios €65, apt €75-90, 5-person maisonettes €160; 🕐 Apr-Oct; 🅿 ❄ 🛜 🏊) Clay-coloured studios, set amid flowering gardens within an idyllic olive grove near Zakynthos' southwest corner. The clean, pine-accented apartments of various sizes, with balconies and kitchenettes, share barbecue areas and a sparkling pool. There's also a small shop.

🍴 Eating

Zakynthos Town has a lively dining scene, and the beach resorts hold plenty of tavernas. The most distinctive local food is served in the hill villages of the interior.

★**Stavros** GREEK €
(Cross Tavern; ☑ 26950 48481; Kambi; mains €6-16; ☺ lunch & dinner; ✳ 🛜) Perched above the west-coast cliffs at the far end of the road that climbs beyond Kambi, and marked by a huge white cross, this top-notch taverna extends over multilevel terraces, so diners can enjoy the stunning views. The menu covers all bases, from omelette and chips to baked standards and grilled fish, all accompanied by wonderful fresh-baked bread.

Allegro GREEK €
(☑ 6979261627; Keri; mains €6-10; ☺ lunch & dinner; ✳ 🛜) This delightful, very welcoming taverna-cafe on Keri's village square has a changing daily menu of home-cooked Greek specialities, usually including *mousakas* and stuffed aubergines. Drinks range from iced coffee to local wine, and there's often live music on summer evenings.

Nobelos Bio Restaurant MEDITERRANEAN €€
(☑ 6944148283; www.nobelos.gr; Agios Nikolaos; mains €7-27; ☺ breakfast, lunch & dinner; ✳ 🛜) Although it's accessed from the hillside road, 300m up from Agios Nikolaos, this exquisitely romantic restaurant is down at sea level beside the private beach of its namesake boutique hotel. The irresistible setting is the main reason to come here, along with the sunset cocktail menu, but the Italian Greek food is reliably good, with lots of seafood pasta options and meaty stews.

KYTHIRA ΚΥΘΗΡΑ

POP 3530

Poised between the Aegean and Ionian Seas, the gloriously time-forgotten island of Kythira lies just 12km off the southern tip of the Peloponnese's Lakonian Peninsula. Despite its distinctly Cycladic sugar-cube architecture, both historic and modern, Kythira is officially regarded as belonging to the Ionian Island group.

With its population spread between 40 villages, Kythira feels for much of the year like a ghost land; it's an unspoiled wilderness of lush valleys, overgrown gorges, and flower-speckled cliffs tumbling into the vivid blue sea.

Apart from July and August, when Italians especially swoop in to enjoy the fine sandy beaches, tourism remains very low-key. Visiting outside these months, however, brings huge rewards, whether you fancy hiking to scenic wonders and intriguing ancient settlements, or simply relaxing in the old-style tavernas and *kafeneia* (coffee houses) that pepper its village squares.

🛈 Getting There & Away

AIR
Kythira Airport, 10km southeast of Potamos, is connected to Athens in summer by both **Olympic Air** (www.olympicair.com; €65, 50 minutes, one daily) and **Sky Express** (www.skyexpress.gr; €88, 50 minutes, twice daily except Tuesdays and Wednesdays). **Ellinair** (http://en.ellinair.com) flies to Kythira from Thessaloniki (€89, 75 minutes, twice weekly). There are far fewer flights in low season.

BOAT
Kythira's ferry port is at sleepy little Diakofti, halfway up the east coast. Buy tickets at the port just before departure, or via Kithira Travel (p534).

Boats from Neapoli in the Peloponnese come to Diakofti twice daily in summer, and once daily otherwise; two each week continue to Antikythira.

LANE Lines (www.lane-kithira.com) operates an intricate, seasonally changing schedule of ferries that connect Diakofti with Piraeus, Antikythira, Kissamos (Kastelli; Crete) and Gythio (Peloponnese); in summer there are usually two weekly services to and from each of those destinations.

TO	DURATION	FARE	FREQUENCY
Gythio	2½hr	€12	2 weekly
Kissamos (Kastelli)	2½-4hr	€22	2 weekly (2 via Antikythira; €9)
Neapoli	1¼hr	€12	12 daily
Piraeus	6½hr	€26	2 weekly

🛈 Getting Around

Occasional buses operate in August. **Taxis** (☑ 6977991799, 6944305433) are pricey and charge around €25 between Hora (Kythira) and the airport. Your best bet is to pick up a hire car at the airport, or have one dropped off at your hotel.

Drakakis Tours (☑ 27360 31160; www.drakakistours.gr; Livadi) Rental cars, vans and 4WDs, with airport pick-up; airport transfers; buses to Athens (€45, one to two weekly); and sightseeing tours.

Panayotis Rent A Car (☑ Hora 27360 31004, Kapsali 27360 31600, airport 6944263757; www.panayotis-rent-a-car.gr; car/scooter per day from €45/15) A fleet of 120 cars – including 4WDs, small cars, motorbikes and scooters – with branches at the airport and across the island, including at Diakofti and Kapsali.

IONIAN ISLANDS KYTHIRA

Kythira & Antikythira

0 — 5 km
0 — 2.5 miles

Gythio (55km);
Kalamata (100km)

Neapoli
(25km)

Cape Spathi

Kythira
Strait

Diakofti (50km)

Crete
(55km)

Potamos

Harhaliana

Galaniana

Antikythira

0 — 2 km
0 — 1 mile

Antikythira

Platia Ammos

Fourni
Beach

Karavas

Myrtoön
Sea

Gerakari

Agia Pelagia

Agios Nikolaos

Petrouni

Lagada
Beach

Piraeus
(230km)

Stavli

Trifyllianika

Potamos

Paliohora

Antikythira
(50km; see inset);
Crete (100km)

Katsoulianika

Hristoforianika

Logothetianika

Lykodimou
Beach

Lianianika

Pitsinades

Vamvakaradika

458m

Makronisi
Island

Ionian
Sea

Aroniadika

Kastrisianika

Frilingianika

490m

Diakofti

Mitata

Kythira

Agia Moni

Cave of
Agia Sofia

Kato
Hora

Mylopotamos

Viaradika

389m

Cape
Limnionas

507m

Temple of
Aphrodite

Avlemonas

Fratsia

Paleopoli
Beach

Cape
Modoni

Pitsinianika

Karvounades

Kaladi
Beach

Kalokerines

Goudianika

Alexandrades

Moni
Myrtidion

Tsikalaria

Travasarianika

Skoulianika

Kombonada
Beach

Sea of
Crete

Fatsadika

410m

Katouni Bridge

Livadi

Kato Livadi

Kominianika

Katelouzianika

Fyri Ammos

Pourko

Strapodi

Agia Elesis

Manitohori

477m

Melidoni
Beach

Kalamos

Hora (Kythira)

Kapsali

Vroulea

Cape
Trahilos

Cape
Kapello

Mediterranean
Sea

Avgo/Itra

Hora (Kythira)
Χώρα (Κύθηρα)

POP 270

Hora (itself also known as Kythira), the island's small capital, consists of a Cycladic-style cluster of white-and-blue cubes, stretching south along a slender ridge towards a 14th-century Venetian *kastro* perched on a separate craggy hilltop. Most of the action is based around the open square at its northern end, while tasteful little shops line the way to the *kastro*, ranging from fine antiques to bespoke jewellery.

⊙ Sights

★ **Kastro**   FORTRESS
(⊘8am-8pm, shorter hours winter) **FREE** Crowning the rocky headland that soars at the southern end of Hora, this majestic 14th-century fortress was built by Kythira's first Venetian governor. Within its ramparts the fort is now largely in ruins, but the site is stupendous, drenched in wildflowers and commanding stunning views down to Kapsali and out as far as Antikythira. Only the unenthralling **Coat of Arms Collection** (adult/child €2/1; ⊘9am-2pm & 5-8pm Tue-Sun), in a former powder magazine, charges an admission fee.

**Archaeological Museum
of Kythira**   MUSEUM
(⊘27360 31739; adult/child €4/2; ⊘8am-8pm Tue-Sun) Hora's impressive archaeological museum, beside the main road at the north end of town, traces the history of 'this small island' in two rooms. Among artefacts from the ancient settlements of Palaiopolis and Palaiokastro, pride of place goes to the white marble statue known as the Lion of Kythira.

🛌 Sleeping & Eating

Castello Rooms   PENSION €
(⊘27360 31069; www.kythera-castelloapts.gr; Spyridonos Staï; d from €45; 🅱🛜) Eight cosy white-walled rooms and kitchenette apartments, with balconies facing the *kastro*, set in a garden of flowers and fruit trees. It's just off the far end of the main street. The owners are super-friendly.

★ **Hotel Margarita**   PENSION €€
(⊘27360 31711; www.hotel-margarita.com; off Spyridonos Staï; s/d/tr incl breakfast €60/90/110; ⊘Easter-Oct; 🅱🛜) Set in an impeccably restored, white-walled 19th-century villa, just off the main alleyway not far beyond the main square, this charming hotel offers 12 simple antique-furnished rooms accessed via a quirky old spiral staircase. A wonderful terrace, used for the good buffet breakfast and afternoon drinks, affords fantastic *kastro* and sea views.

Corte O   APARTMENT €€
(⊘27360 39139; www.corteo.gr; room/2-bedroom apt incl breakfast €90/170; ⊘Apr-Oct; 🅱🛜) Three beautiful two-bedroom apartments set in a late-18th-century house just a spit away from the *kastro*. All have modern, minimal decor plus full kitchens, private terraces and sea or valley views; one can be divided to create two en-suite rooms.

Zorba's   TAVERNA €
(⊘27360 31655; mains €9; ⊘dinner Tue-Sun; 🅱) Hora's only year-round restaurant, on the main alleyway not far off the square, is a very simple affair serving succulent grilled meats – pork, lamb chops, beef or chicken – either in the plain, old-fashioned dining room or out on the terrace.

Veranda Cafe   CAFE
(⊘27360 31316; ⊘8am-late; 🛜) A smart, cool and very aptly named cafe on the corner of the main square. The elegant interior holds a well-stocked bar, while the adjoining balcony terrace has comfy sofa seating and astonishing long-range views. Perfect for coffee, juices and ice cream, and for long sunset-gazing sessions.

🛍 Shopping

Yfanda   FASHION & ACCESSORIES
(www.facebook.com/borse.gr; ⊘9am-9pm) Intriguing one-room, one-woman workshop on the pedestrian alleyway south of the main square. All the colourful and very distinctive hand-woven shoulder and clutch bags on sale are created on the loom in the middle of the floor.

THE BIRTH OF APHRODITE

Kythira was famous in antiquity as the birthplace of Aphrodite. As described by Hesiod and painted by Botticelli, the goddess of love, desire and beauty rose resplendent from the foam upon a giant scallop, possibly off the islet of Avgo ('egg') off Kapsali. Confusingly, she's also said to have re-emerged near Pafos in Cyprus, so both islands haggle over the claim.

Aquarium JEWELLERY
(📞 6977287741; www.facebook.com/pg/aquarium kythira; ⏰10am-9pm) Exquisite one-off pieces of bespoke jewellery, in a boutique overseen by the eponymous fish tank, on the street that leads down the hill to the main square of Hora. It's not always open and hours vary, but it's worth persevering.

ℹ️ Information

The central square holds banks with ATMs, and the post office.

Kithira Travel (📞 Hora 27360 31390, Potamos 27360 31848; www.kithiratravel.gr; ⏰9am-2pm & 6-8pm Mon-Sat) Helpful staff; sells flights and boat tickets.

Police Station (📞27360 31206) Near the *kastro*.

Kapsali Καψάλι
POP 35

Down by the sea 2km east of Hora (Kythira), pretty little Kapsali was the island's main port during the Venetian era. These days, in summer at least, it's a bustling resort, with its two languidly curving bays lined by a necklace of tavernas, chic cafes and studios, and the sandy, ochre-coloured beach offering sheltered swimming. It's a superb spectacle when viewed from Hora's clifftop *kastro*.

The rocky islet offshore is known by two names. **Avgo** ('egg'), referring to its legendary role as the birthplace of Aphrodite, and **Itra** ('cooking pot') referring to its resemblance when topped by clouds to a steaming cauldron.

🏃 Activities

Panayotis BOATING
(📞27360 31600; www.panayotis-rent-a-car.gr) Waterfront outlet that rents canoes and pedal boats (as well as cars and mopeds).

Kythera Dive DIVING
(📞27360 37400; www.kytheradive.gr) PADI open-water courses start from €400, and reef or cave dives from €50.

Captain Spiros BOATING
(📞6974022079; per person from €12) Daily cruises in a glass-bottomed boat; destinations include Itra, where you can swim.

🛏️ Sleeping

Vassili Studios PENSION €
(📞27360 31125; http://kithira.biz; d/tr incl breakfast from €55/65; 🅿️❄️🛜) This tree-lined complex has a perfect setting overlooking Kapsali

Beach. Rooms are light and welcoming, with wooden ceilings and floors, shabby-chic furniture and wrought-iron beds; the larger and more expensive options have bay views.

⭐ **El Sol Hotel** HOTEL €€
(📞27360 31766; www.elsolhotels.gr; d incl breakfast €120, 5-person apt €170; 🅿️❄️🛜🏊) Striking white-cube apartments, perched high above the Hora–Kapsali road, with Olympian views of the sea and across to Hora's *kastro*. Immaculate, minimalist rooms have private terraces, and there's a terrific pool, plenty of sun loungers, and a breakfast room packed with board games for rainy days.

Aphrodite Apartments APARTMENT €€
(📞27360 31328; www.hotel-afrodite.gr; d/tr/q from €60/75/80; ❄️🛜) On the coast road, barely a minute up from the beach, the gleaming white Aphrodite offers a choice between simple but spacious tiled-floor rooms or apartments with kitchenettes and balconies. For the best views, choose the top floor. Irene and Yiannis are great hosts.

🍴 Eating & Drinking

Goldfish CAFE €
(📞27360 31032; www.facebook.com/chrysopsaro; mains €6-9; ⏰noon-11pm Tue-Sun; 🛜) The coolest cafe along Kapsali Beach, with nicely padded seats, baby-blue tables and a very laid-back vibe. Settle down over juices or shakes, coffee or beer, or order from an eclectic fusion menu that includes Japanese-, Indian- or Argentinian-style chicken; burgers; omelettes; and waffles soaked in ice cream.

Hytra TAVERNA €
(📞27360 37200; mains €7-11; ⏰lunch & dinner; 🛜) Slap-bang in the middle of the waterfront – look for the green awning – this traditional joint dishes up casseroles, tasty spinach pies, fire-grilled lamb chops, veal steak and plenty of fresh seafood.

Magos SEAFOOD €€
(📞27360 31407; mains €7-13; ⏰lunch & dinner; ❄️🛜) Long-standing and very dependable seafood specialist, surveying the Kapsali scene from the far eastern end of the waterfront. Choose a fish from the day's fresh catch, displayed in the kitchen, or opt for standards such as grilled squid or shrimp.

Fox Anglais BAR
(📞27360 31458; ⏰noon-late Jun-Sep; 🛜) This veteran bar-club on the waterfront, with outdoor tables and a cosy interior, is the

epicentre of Kythira's nightlife in summer, with acoustic music on the beach on Tuesdays, and DJs every other night.

Potamos Ποταμός
POP 395

The attractive hillside village of Potamos, at the heart of the island, serves as Kythira's social hub. Its flower-filled central square hosts a Sunday-morning flea market, and is great for people-watching any day of the week.

🍴 Eating & Drinking

Panaretos TAVERNA €€
(📞 27360 34290; www.facebook.com/taverna Panaretos; mains €7-14; ⊙ lunch & dinner daily Mar-Oct, Thu-Sun Nov-Feb; 🛜) One of five tavernas that amiably share the main village square for al fresco dining at cream-coloured tables and chairs, Panaretos excels with dishes based on home-grown produce, such as wild goat with olive oil and oregano sauce, pork fillet with thyme, and assorted mezedhes.

★ Kafe Astikon CAFE
(📞 27360 33141; www.facebook.com/astikon; ⊙ 7am-late; 🛜) Very charming old cafe–music bar, near the main square. The high-ceilinged and shadowy interior oozes atmosphere, with its coral-green walls, leather 'egg' chairs and a penny-farthing. Expect live music on the little stage nightly (late) in July and August, and impromptu jam sessions at other times. It also serves breakfast, pizza and pasta.

Agia Pelagia Αγία Πελαγία
POP 280

Kythira's northernmost resort, Agia Pelagia is a simple seafront village backed by swooping cliffs and wooded valleys. Vibrant azure waters lick against its sand-and-pebble beaches, while some magnificent volcanic beaches lie south beyond the headland. Red, pink and tawny along to Lagada Beach, they make a great target for coastal hikers.

🛌 Sleeping & Eating

Hotel Pelagia Aphrodite HOTEL €€
(📞 27360 33926; www.pelagia-aphrodite.com; s/d/tr incl breakfast €90/100/140; ⊙ Easter-Oct; P❄🛜) Right on the beach at the southern end of town, and run by returning Aussie-Kythirans, this lovely hotel has 13 terrific rooms with wooden ceilings and huge, sea-facing balconies. The older rooms, whitewashed and simple, are closest to the waves, and there's a pleasant breakfast room downstairs.

Pantonia Apartments APARTMENT €€
(📞 27360 39112; www.pantonia-apartments.com; 1-/2-bedroom apt incl breakfast €81/138; ❄🛜) Smart, modern kitchenette apartments, 200m up from the sea, with separate sleeping and dining rooms. All have sweeping sea views – those higher up from private balconies and some from a shared terrace.

Maneas Beach Hotel HOTEL €€
(📞 27360 33503; www.maneashotel.com; d with/without sea views incl breakfast €110/85; P❄🛜) Upmarket beach hotel, right on the waterfront south of the jetty, with a contemporary feel. Rooms boast modern fittings and large balconies with awesome sea views.

★ Kaleris GREEK €
(📞 27360 33461; www.facebook.com/kaleris; mains €7-11; ⊙ lunch & dinner Apr-Oct; 🛜) Renowned for its creative cuisine, romantic little Kaleris has a waterfront pavilion and tables on the beach itself, shaded by tamarisk trees. Trust the charismatic owner Yiannis to advise on handwritten daily advertised specials such as yoghurt salad with smoked aubergine, filo parcels with feta drizzled with thyme-infused honey, braised lamb shank or grilled prawns.

Akrogiali SEAFOOD €
(📞 27360 34314; mains €7-12; ⊙ 11am-late; 🛜) Fresh seafood, served up on the beach; look out for the painted sign showing a mermaid riding a dolphin. As well as mullet, mackerel, bream and shrimp, Akrogiali does chicken in red-wine sauce and a simple tomato pie.

Sempreviva CAFE
(📞 27360 33390; ⊙ 8.30am-late; 🛜) Very appealing little beachfront cafe-bar, with cosy, breezy seats out on the sand. It's the ideal spot for morning coffee, evening cocktails, and anything in between.

Around Kythira

You'll need your own transport to explore the backroads that thread between Kythira's scattered villages, which pass orchards and vineyards, olive groves and stands of cypress.

In the south, the small Museum of Byzantine & Post-Byzantine Art (📞 27360 31731; adult/child €2/free; ⊙ 8.30am-2.30pm Tue-Sun) in Kato Livadi, 6km north of Hora, houses icons

WORTH A TRIP

MYLOPOTAMOS ΜΥΛΟΠΟΤΑΜΟΣ

The delightful little village of **Mylopotamos** nestles into a small valley 13km north of Hora (Kythira). The tables of an utterly charming *kafeneio* (coffee house), **O Platanos** (☑ 27360 33397; mains €5-10; ☺ lunch & dinner; ☎), fill its tiny central square, which is flanked on one side by the walled channel of a babbling stream, populated by tame ducks and geese. As it flows away northwest towards the sea, that stream cuts ever deeper into the wooded hillside, along a gorge that once held 22 separate **watermills**. Only one now survives – Mylopotamos means 'Mill on the River' – but a ravishing little footpath still follows the river, leading through luxuriant greenery to the aquamarine pool of the **Neraïda ('water nymph') waterfall**.

A separate hike, signposted along the left-hand fork in the road north of the village square, takes 15 minutes to reach the older village of **Kato Hora**. Make your way behind a castellated 19th-century villa here and you'll find the extraordinary ruins of Mylopotamos' Venetian-era **kastro**, a quite magical warren of abandoned churches and fortified houses, liberally overgrown with colourful flowers.

and frescoes salvaged from churches all over the island. Spanning a shallow stream bed just north, incongruous **Katouni Bridge**, built by the British in the 19th century, is the largest stone bridge in Greece. Head southeast, following spectacular twisty roads, to reach the mauve-grey stone beach at **Fyri Ammos**.

Avlemonas, further up the coast, is a former fishing village turned exquisite resort. A spotless vision of blue and dazzling white, with footpaths leading across the rocks to ladders that drop into the pristine lagoon, it's idyllic, if a little unreal. The closest beaches lie to the west: first comes broad, pebbled **Paleopoli Beach**, and then **Kaladi Beach**, in a separate cove and accessed via a staircase.

Few traces survive of ancient **Paleopoli**, just inland, but you can spend an enjoyable hour hiking up and around the hill that once held the **Temple of Aphrodite**, marking the birthplace of the goddess of beauty.

Much more substantial ruins survive of Kythira's medieval capital, **Paliohora**, in the north. It's a totally magnificent spot, set on a craggy pinnacle at the confluence of two deep-cut gorges. In theory, it was safely hidden from enemy ships, but it was destroyed by a Turkish fleet in 1537. Strewn with the tumbledown remains of chapels and mansions, the isolated hill top can now be reached by driving a 4km dead-end road east of Potamos, the last 2km of which is unsurfaced, or following the delightful parallel hiking trail.

🛏 Sleeping & Eating

⭐**Maryianni** APARTMENT €€
(☑ 27360 33316; www.maryianni.gr; Avlemonas; 3-person studios €110, apt €130; ▣ ✳ ☎) Rather wonderful white-and-blue studios, stacked

Cycladic-style above the Avlemonas shoreline, with kitchens and sumptuous sea-view terraces. Even the smaller options are well above average, with boutique flourishes such as terracotta tiles, wrought-iron beds, classical art and choice furniture.

⭐**Filio** TAVERNA €
(☑ 27360 31549; http://filio.net; Kalamos; mains €8-12; ☺ 4pm-midnight; ☎) Acclaimed local taverna, far off the beaten track 1km beyond Kalamos en route towards Fyri Ammos (look for signs), offering island classics such as slow-cooked lamb in lemon sauce, eggplant stuffed with meat and Kythiran sausages, in a well-shaded terrace garden. The owners also rent out attractive apartments nearby.

Pierros GREEK €
(☑ 27360 31014; www.pieros.gr; Livadi; mains €6-11; ☺ lunch & dinner; ✳ ☎) For almost a century, this family-run favourite has been serving up no-nonsense staples such as *mousakas, pastitsio,* and baked chicken or veal. The main road through Livadi is hardly a beautiful setting, but for an authentic Greek experience this is hard to beat.

Skandeia TAVERNA €€
(☑ 27360 33700; www.skandeia.gr; Paleopoli; mains €8-15; ☺ 1-11pm; ☎) A delightful taverna on the hillside at the northwestern end of Paleopoli Beach, Skandeia places a major emphasis on wholesome, freshly sourced local produce in preparing its definitive Greek cuisine, which ranges from grilled fish and fish soup to roasted eggplant. Relax beneath the spreading elm trees, away from the madding crowd.

Understand Greek Islands

Greek Islands Today

While life on the Greek islands seems to carry on relatively unfettered, few have been un-affected by savage wage and pension cuts, new taxes, record joblessness and thousands of closed shops and businesses, all brought on by the country's debt crisis. Tourism hasn't been the hoped-for miracle balm. Meanwhile, thousands of refugees who have landed on the islands in hope of reaching other parts of Europe are trapped in crowded island camps by closed borders, causing a humanitarian crisis that Greece is struggling to deal with.

Best on Film

Shirley Valentine (1989) Classic Greek-island romance on Mykonos.

Mamma Mia (2008) The island of Skopelos shines to the soundtrack of ABBA.

Guns of Navarone (1961) Compelling wartime boy's-own thriller.

Captain Corelli's Mandolin (2001) Lavish retelling of Louis de Bernières' WWII novel set on occupied Kefallonia.

Best in Print

The Magus (John Fowles; 1966) Creepy mind games set on fictional island Phraxos.

The Odyssey (Homer; 8th century BC) Plagued by Poseidon, Odysseus struggles to return home to Ithaki.

Zorba the Greek (Nikos Kazantzakis; 1946) A spiritual bible to many; one man's unquenchable lust for life.

Something Will Happen, You'll See (Christos Ikonomou, 2016) Moving short stories of characters caught in the effects of the financial crisis.

Falling For Icarus: A Journey among the Cretans (Rory MacLean; 2004) A travel writer fulfils his ambition to build his own plane in the land of Icarus.

Colossus of Maroussi (Henry Miller; 1941) A travelogue of pre-war Greece, heralded as Miller's best work.

Austerity Measures

The past decade has seen a widening of Greece's stark economic and social disparities. The hedonistic lifestyles of Athenians taking weekend jaunts to Mykonos bear no resemblance to islanders struggling with severe wage drops, pensions cut by 40%, increased taxes and soaring living costs. This scene is the result of the enforced austerity measures attached to the multi-billion-euro bailouts loaned to Greece by its EU and IMF creditors in 2009, 2010, 2011 and again in 2015.

Growing anger and social unrest have sparked mass strikes, protests and clashes with police in Athens that have spread to the larger islands. Disillusioned young Greeks are bearing the brunt of years of economic mis-management – the country's most educated generation faces bleak prospects as youth unemployment sits at 46%. There is a feeling of despair that is decidedly un-Greek.

Migration & Asylum

In 2015, the Greek islands' refugee crisis came into focus when tragic images of a drowned three-year-old spread across world media. The young Syrian refugee had been headed to Kos with his family. Greece's outlying islands have long been landing points for those in search of safety and a better life. Since 2015, 1.3 million illegal migrants have crossed into Greece; most come from Afghanistan, Iraq, Syria and Africa via the porous Turkish border, and many hope to reunite with family elsewhere in Europe.

In 2016, all European borders with Greece were closed in an attempt to discourage immigrants to the islands. In exchange, the EU committed to giving Turkey €6 billion to deal with their own refugee crisis. The numbers of refugees reaching the islands dropped drastically; some islands that saw up to 5000 arrivals daily in 2015 saw as few as 100 a day in 2017. Consequently, the number of drownings in the dangerous crossing has also declined.

Nevertheless, many NGOs and humanitarian groups believe the deal has actually increased human suffering. To date, fewer than 1000 refugees have been returned to Turkey. For many refugees who fled persecution and risked perilous boat journeys to reach Greece, Turkey is not considered a safe option. The alternative is to be trapped in Greece where, in June 2017, 62,000 refugees waited to be processed. More than 14,000 of these are on the southeastern islands, and more than half of them are women and children, many unaccompanied. Conditions in overflowing island camps have deteriorated drastically, with widespread crime and abuse. Increased trauma and depression have also brought a rise in suicide attempts. Many refugees have been trapped for more than a year and have run out of both money and hope.

European press coverage led to a slight decline in island tourism in 2016, despite little evidence that refugees had any impact on tourists. Within Greece, economic decline has fuelled xenophobia, sparking anti-immigrant rallies and growing hostility, yet deep-rooted island hospitality has reared its noble head, with many Greeks independently offering food and clothing to immigrants and local doctors volunteering to care for them.

Brain Drain

The islands' once-shrinking villages are welcoming a new wave of nouveau-poor Greeks. Families of out-of-work professionals and tradesmen, along with unemployed university graduates, are returning to ancestral homes on the islands and to help with family businesses – often in tourism or farming. An increase in agricultural employment is one of the by-products of the times, going back to Greece's traditional strength and way of life (though agriculture now accounts for only 3.5% of the GDP). An increasing number of educated under-30-year-olds are also migrating to other parts of Europe, America and Australia in hope of finding employment.

On many of the islands, problems are exacerbated by fragmented infrastructures, seasonal isolation and foreign investment that hikes up property prices. Creating jobs for young people, particularly now that Athens is no longer seen as the promised land, is a major struggle.

Environmental Concerns

Climate change, diminished water supplies and rising sea levels are all very real concerns to islanders. Greeks generally are becoming increasingly aware of environmental degradation. On many islands you'll find student groups, environmental charities and locals teamed up with expats working to protect the environment, though the debate is often tangled in the mixed interests of locals versus developers or back-door deals with local government.

POPULATION: **10.9 MILLION**

LIFE EXPECTANCY: **80.5**

GDP: **€175 BILLION (US$195 BILLION)**

PERCENTAGE OF WOMEN: **50.5%**

UNEMPLOYMENT: **24.6%**

If Greek Islands were 100 people

93 Greek
4 Albanian

0.4 Bulgarian
0.2 Romanian
2.4 other

belief systems
(% of population)

98 Greek Orthodox
1.3 Muslim

0.4 Jewish
0.3 Other

population per sq km

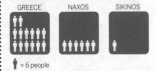

GREECE   NAXOS   SIKINOS

🧍 ≈ 6 people

History

Over the centuries, the Greek islands have been the stepping stones between North Africa, Asia Minor and Europe, across which warriors, tradesmen, conquerors and even civilisations have hopped. Since ancient times the islands have been fought over and claimed as prizes by successive invaders. Their strategic location, in a seafaring world, made many islands prosperous and autonomous trading centres. Some were run by foreign masters, as evidenced by the Venetian ports, Roman aqueducts and Frankish castles found on the islands today.

Cycladic Civilisation

The Cycladic civilisation – centred on the islands of the Cyclades – comprised a cluster of small fishing and farming communities with a sophisticated artistic temperament. Scholars divide the Cycladic civilisation into three periods: Early (3000–2000 BC), Middle (2000–1500 BC) and Late (1500–1100 BC).

The most striking legacy of this civilisation is the famous Cycladic figurines – carved statuettes from Parian marble. Other remains include bronze and obsidian tools and weapons, gold jewellery, and stone and clay vases and pots. Cycladic sculptors are also renowned for their impressive, life-sized *kouroi* (marble statues), carved during the Archaic period.

The Cycladic people were also accomplished sailors who developed prosperous maritime trade links with Crete, continental Greece, Asia Minor (the west of present-day Turkey), Europe and North Africa.

Top Ancient Sites

Acropolis (Athens)

Knossos (Crete)

Delos

Lindos Acropolis (Rhodes)

Akrotiri (Santorini)

Minoan Civilisation

The Minoans – named after King Minos, the mythical ruler of Crete (and stepfather of the Minotaur) – built Europe's first advanced civilisation, drawing their inspiration from two great Middle Eastern civilisations: the Mesopotamian and the Egyptian.

The Minoan civilisation (3000–1100 BC) reached its peak during the Middle period; around 2000 BC the grand palace complexes of Knossos, Phaestos, Malia and Zakros were built, marking a sharp acceleration

TIMELINE	3000–1100 BC	1700–1550 BC	1500–1200 BC
	After 4000 years of agrarian life, the discovery of an alloy blending copper and tin gives rise to the Bronze Age. Trade sees the flourishing of the Cycladic, Minoan – and later, the Mycenaean – civilisations.	Santorini erupts with a cataclysmic explosion, causing a massive Mediterranean-wide tsunami that scholars suggest contributed to the destruction of the Minoan civilisation.	The authoritarian Mycenaean culture from the Peloponnese usurps much of the Cretan and Cycladic cultures. Goldsmithing is a predominant feature of Mycenaean life.

from Neolithic village life. Evidence uncovered in these palaces indicates a sophisticated society, with splendid architecture and wonderful, detailed frescoes, highly developed agriculture and an extensive irrigation system.

The advent of bronze enabled the Minoans to build great boats, which helped them establish a powerful thalassocracy (sea power) and prosperous maritime trade. They used tremendous skill to produce fine pottery and metalwork of great beauty, and exported their wares throughout Greece, Asia Minor, Europe and North Africa.

Scholars are still debating the sequence of events that led to the ultimate demise of the Minoans. Scientific evidence suggests they were weakened by a massive tsunami and ash fallout attributed to the eruption of a cataclysmic volcano on Santorini (Thira) around 1500 BC. Some argue that a second powerful quake a century later decimated the society, or perhaps it was the invading force of Mycenae. The decline of the Minoans certainly coincided with the rise of the Mycenaean civilisation on the mainland (1600–1100 BC).

The web portal www.ancient greece.com is great for all things ancient and Greek.

Geometric Age

The Dorians were an ancient Hellenic people who settled in the Peloponnese by the 8th century BC. In the 11th or 12th century BC these warrior-like people fanned out to occupy much of the mainland, seizing control of the Mycenaean kingdoms and enslaving the inhabitants. The Dorians also spread their tentacles into the Greek islands, founding the cities of Kamiros, Ialysos and Lindos on Rhodes in about 1000 BC, while Ionians fleeing to the Cyclades from the Peloponnese established a religious sanctuary on Delos.

The following 400-year period is often referred to as Greece's 'dark age'. In the Dorians' favour, however, they introduced iron and developed a new intricate style of pottery, decorated with striking geometric designs. They also introduced the practice of polytheism, paving the way for Zeus and his pantheon of 12 principal deities.

Archaic Age

By about 800 BC, the Dorians had developed into a class of landholding aristocrats and Greece had been divided into a series of independent city-states. Led by Athens and Corinth (which took over Corfu in 734 BC), the city-states created a Magna Graecia (Greater Greece), with southern Italy as an important component. Most abolished monarchic rule and aristocratic monopoly, establishing a set of laws that redistributed wealth and allowed citizens to regain control over their lands.

During the so-called Archaic Age, from around 800 to 650 BC, Greek culture developed rapidly. Many advances in literature, sculpture, theatre,

In pre-Classical times, the Ionians were a Hellenic people who inhabited Attica and parts of Asia Minor. These people colonised the islands that later became known as the Ionian Islands.

800–700 BC	800–650 BC	594 BC	477 BC
Homer composes the 'Iliad' and the 'Odyssey' around this time. The two epic poems are Greece's earliest pieces of literary art.	Independent city-states begin to emerge in the Archaic Age as the Dorians develop. Aristocrats rule these mini-states, while tyrants occasionally take power by force. The Greek alphabet emerges.	Solon, a ruling aristocrat in Athens, introduces rules of fair play to his citizenry. His radical rule-changing – in effect creating human and political rights – is credited as being the first step to real democracy.	Seeking security while building a de facto empire, the Athenians establish a political and military alliance called the Delian League. Many city-states and islands join the new club.

architecture and intellectual endeavour began; this revival overlapped with the Classical Age. Developments from this period include the Greek alphabet; the verses of Homer, including epics the 'Iliad' and the 'Odyssey'; the founding of the Olympic Games; and the creation of central sanctuaries such as Delphi.

Classical Age

From the 6th to 4th centuries BC, Greece continued its renaissance in cultural creativity. As many city-states enjoyed increased economic reform and political prosperity, literature and drama blossomed.

Athens' rapid growth meant heavy reliance on food imports from the Black Sea, while Persia's imperial expansions threatened coastal trade routes across Asia Minor. Athens' support for a rebellion in the Persian colonies of Asia Minor sparked the Persian Wars.

In 477 BC Athens founded the Delian League, the naval alliance that was based on Delos. It was formed to liberate the city-states still occupied by Persia, and to defend against further Persian attack. The alliance included many of the Aegean islands and some of the Ionian city-states in Asia Minor. Swearing allegiance to Athens and making an annual contribution to the treasury of ships (later contributing just money) were mandatory.

When Pericles became the leader of Athens in 461 BC, he moved the treasury from Delos to the Acropolis, using the funds to construct new buildings and grander temples to replace those destroyed by the Persians.

With the Aegean Sea safely under its wing, Athens looked westwards for more booty. One of the major triggers of the first Peloponnesian War (431–421 BC) that pitted Athens against Sparta was Athens' support for Corcyra (present-day Corfu) in a row with Corinth, the island's mother city. Athens finally surrendered to Sparta after a drawn-out series of pitched battles.

Foreign Rule

Roman Era

While Alexander the Great was forging his vast empire in the east, the Romans had been expanding theirs to the west, and were keen to start making inroads into Greece. After several inconclusive clashes, they defeated Macedon in 168 BC. By 146 BC the mainland became the Graeco-Roman province of Achaea. Crete fell in 67 BC, and the southern city of Gortyn became capital of the Roman province of Cyrenaica, which included a large chunk of North Africa. Rhodes held out until AD 70.

As the Romans revered Greek culture, Athens retained its status as a centre of learning. Indeed, the Romans adopted many aspects of Hellenic

Greek is Europe's oldest written language, second only to Chinese in the world. It is traceable back to the Linear B script of the Minoans and Mycenaeans. For more on Linear B script, try www.ancientscripts.com/linearb.html.

Alexander the Great is considered to be one of the best military leaders of all time. He was never beaten in battle and by the age of 30 reigned over one of the largest ancient empires, stretching from Greece to the Himalayas.

461–432 BC	334–323 BC	86 BC–AD 224	AD 63
New Athenian leader Pericles shifts power from Delos to Athens, and uses the treasury wealth of the Delian League to fund massive works, including building the magnificent Parthenon.	Born in Macedonia, Alexander the Great sets out to conquer the known world, from Greece to the peoples of today's Central Asia. He dies in 323 BC.	Roman expansion includes Greek territory. First defeating Macedonia at Pydna in 168 BC, the Romans ultimately overtake the mainland and establish the Pax Romana. It lasts 300 years.	Christianity emerges after St Paul visits Crete and leaves his disciple, Titus, to convert the island. St Titus becomes Crete's first bishop.

culture, spreading its unifying traditions throughout their empire. During a succession of Roman emperors, namely Augustus, Nero and Hadrian, the whole empire experienced a period of relative peace, known as the Pax Romana, which was to last for almost 300 years.

Byzantine Empire & the Crusades

The Pax Romana began to crumble in AD 250 when the Goths invaded what is now Greece – the first of a succession of invaders.

In an effort to resolve the conflict in the region, in AD 324 the Roman Emperor Constantine I, a Christian convert, transferred the capital of the empire from Rome to Byzantium, a city on the western shore of the Bosphorus, which was renamed Constantinople (present-day İstanbul). While Rome went into terminal decline, the eastern capital began to grow in wealth and strength as a Christian state. In the ensuing centuries, Byzantine Greece faced continued pressure from Venetians, Franks, Normans, Slavs, Persians and Arabs; the Persians captured Rhodes in 620, but were replaced by the Saracens (Arabs) in 653. The Arabs also captured Crete in 824. Other islands in the Aegean remained under Byzantine control.

The Byzantine Empire began to fracture when the renegade Frankish leaders of the Fourth Crusade decided that Constantinople presented richer pickings than Jerusalem. Constantinople was sacked in 1204, and much of the Byzantine Empire was partitioned into fiefdoms ruled by self-styled 'Latin' (mostly Frankish or western-Germanic) princes. The Venetians, meanwhile, had also secured a foothold in Greece. Over the next few centuries they took over key mainland ports, the Cyclades, and Crete in 1210, becoming the most powerful traders in the Mediterranean.

Ottoman Rule

On 29 May 1453, Constantinople fell under Turkish Ottoman rule (referred to by Greeks as *turkokratia*). Once more Greece became a battleground, this time fought over by the Turks and Venetians. Eventually, with the exception of the Ionian Islands (where the Venetians retained control), Greece became part of the Ottoman Empire.

Ottoman power reached its zenith under Sultan Süleyman the Magnificent, who ruled from 1520 to 1566. His successor, Selim the Sot, added Cyprus to Ottoman dominion in 1570. Although they captured Crete in 1669 after a 25-year campaign, the ineffectual sultans that followed in the late 16th and 17th centuries saw the empire go into steady decline.

Venice expelled the Turks from the Peloponnese in a three-year campaign (1684–87), during which Venetian artillery struck gunpowder stored inside the ruins of the Acropolis and badly damaged the Parthenon.

The Histories, written by Herodotus in the 5th century BC, is considered to be the first narrative of historical events ever written. It chronicles the conflicts between the ancient Greek city-states and Persia.

HISTORY FOREIGN RULE

Medieval & Venetian Sites

Rhodes Old Town (Rhodes)

Monastery of St John (Patmos)

Hania's Old Town (Crete)

Rethymno (Crete)

Corfu Old Town (Corfu)

250–394 >	529 >	1204 >	1453
The AD 250 invasion of Greece by the Goths signals the decline of the Pax Romana, and in 324 the capital is moved to Constantinople. In 394 Christianity is declared the official religion.	Athens' cultural influence is dealt a fatal blow when Emperor Justinian outlaws the teaching of classical philosophy in favour of Christian theology, by now regarded as the ultimate intellectual endeavour.	Marauding Frankish crusaders sack Constantinople. Trading religious fervour for self interest, the Crusaders strike a blow that sets Constantinople on the road to a slow demise.	Greece becomes a dominion of the Ottoman Turks after they seize control of Constantinople (modern-day İstanbul), sounding the death knell for the Byzantine Empire.

The Ottomans restored rule in 1715, but never regained their former authority. By the end of the 18th century, pockets of Turkish officials, aristocrats and influential Greeks had emerged as self-governing cliques that ruled over the provincial Greek peasants. But there also existed an ever-increasing group of Greeks, including many intellectual expatriates, who aspired to emancipation.

Independence
In 1814 the first Greek independence party, the Filiki Eteria (Friendly Society), was founded and their message spread quickly. On 25 March 1821, the Greeks launched the War of Independence. Uprisings broke out almost simultaneously across most of Greece and the occupied islands. The fighting was savage and atrocities were committed on both sides; in the Peloponnese 12,000 Turkish inhabitants were killed after the capture of the city of Tripolitsa (present-day Tripoli), while the Turks retaliated with massacres in Asia Minor, most notoriously on the island of Chios.

The campaign escalated, and within a year the Greeks had won vital ground. They proclaimed independence on 13 January 1822 at Epidavros.

Soon after, regional wrangling twice escalated into civil war, in 1824 and 1825. The Ottomans took advantage and by 1827 the Turks (with Egyptian reinforcements) had regained control. Western powers intervened and a combined Russian, French and British naval fleet sunk the Turkish-Egyptian force in the Battle of Navarino in October 1827. Despite the long odds against him, Sultan Mahmud II and proclaimed a holy war, prompting Russia to send troops into the Balkans to engage the Ottoman army. Fighting continued until 1829 when, with Russian troops at the gates of Constantinople, the sultan accepted Greek independence with the Treaty of Adrianople. Independence was formally recognised in 1830.

The Venetian Empire by Jan Morris vividly describes the imperial influence of the Venetians across the Greek islands. This very readable account includes the social, cultural and architectural legacies still evident today.

The Modern Greek Nation
In April 1827, Greece elected Corfiot Ioannis Kapodistrias as the first president of the republic. Nafplio, in the Peloponnese, became the capital. There was much dissension and Kapodistrias was assassinated in 1831. Amid the ensuing anarchy, Britain, France and Russia declared Greece a monarchy and set on the throne the non-Greek, 17-year-old Bavarian Prince Otto, in January 1833. The new kingdom (established by the London Convention of 1832) consisted of the Peloponnese, Sterea Ellada, the Cyclades and the Sporades. Otto ruled until he was deposed in 1862.

The Great Idea
Greece's foreign policy (dubbed the 'Great Idea') was to assert sovereignty over its dispersed Greek populations. Set against the background of

1541	1669	1821	1827–31
Domenikos Theotokopoulos, later known as 'El Greco', is born in Candia (Crete); his subsequent creations in Italy and Spain are marked by both Cretan School influence and bold personal innovation.	Venetian-ruled Crete falls under Ottoman power after keeping the Turks at bay in a fierce 20-year siege (Spinalonga Island and Souda hold out until 1715).	The War of Independence begins on the mainland on 25 March. Greece celebrates this date as its national day of independence.	Ioannis Kapodistrias is appointed prime minister of a fledgling government with its capital in the Peloponnesian town of Nafplio. Discontent ensues and Kapodistrias is assassinated.

the Crimean conflict, British and French interests were nervous at the prospect of a Greek alliance with Russia against the Ottomans.

British influence in the Ionian Islands had begun in 1815 (following a spell of political ping-pong between the Venetians, Russians and French). The British did improve the islands' infrastructure, and many locals adopted British customs (such as afternoon tea and cricket in Corfu). However, Greek independence put pressure on Britain to give sovereignty to the Greek nation, and in 1864 the British left. Meanwhile, Britain eased onto the Greek throne the young Danish Prince William, crowned King George I in 1863, whose reign lasted 50 years.

In 1881, Greece acquired Thessaly and part of Epiros as a result of a Russo-Turkish war. But Greece failed miserably when it tried to attack Turkey in an effort to reach *enosis* (union) with Crete (which had persistently agitated for liberation from the Ottomans). Timely diplomatic intervention by the Great Powers prevented the Turkish army from taking Athens.

Crete was placed under international administration, but the government of the island was gradually handed over to the Greeks. In 1905 the president of the Cretan assembly, Eleftherios Venizelos (later to become prime minister), announced Crete's union with Greece (although this was not recognised by international law until 1913).

The Balkan Wars

The declining Ottomans still retained Macedonia, prompting the Balkan Wars of 1912 and 1913. The outcome was the Treaty of Bucharest (August 1913), which greatly expanded Greek territory to take in the southern part of Macedonia (which included Thessaloniki, the vital cultural centre strategically positioned on the Balkan trade routes), part of Thrace, another chunk of Epiros and the northeastern Aegean Islands; the treaty also recognised the union with Crete.

WWI & Smyrna

During the First World War, the Allies (Britain, France and Russia) put increasing pressure on neutral Greece to join forces with them against Germany and Turkey, promising concessions in Asia Minor in return. Greek troops served with distinction on the Allied side, but when the war ended in 1918 the promised land in Asia Minor was not forthcoming. Prime Minister Venizelos then led a diplomatic campaign to further the 'Great Idea' and sent troops to Smyrna (present-day İzmir) in May 1919. With a seemingly viable hold in Asia Minor, by September 1921 Greece had advanced as far as Ankara. But by this stage foreign support for Venizelos had ebbed, and Turkish forces, commanded by Mustafa Kemal (later to become Atatürk), halted the offensive. The Greek army retreated

Eugène Delacroix' oil canvas The Massacre at Chios (1824) was inspired by the events in Asia Minor during Greece's War of Independence in 1821. The painting hangs in the Louvre Museum in Paris.

The intellectual vigour of Classical Greece has yet to be equalled – scarcely an idea is discussed today that was not already debated by the great minds of the era, whether in the dramatic tragedies by Aeschylus, Euripides and Sophocles and political satire of Aristophanes, or the histories of Herodotus and Thucydides.

1833	1862–63	1896	1914
The powers of the Triple Entente (Britain, France and Russia) decree that Greece should be a monarchy and dispatch Prince Otto of Bavaria to be the first appointed monarch in modern Greece.	King Otto is deposed in a coup, with Prince William of Denmark taking over as George I a few months later. Britain returns the Ionian Islands (a British protectorate since 1815) in an effort to quell Greece's expansionist urges.	The first modern Olympic Games in Athens mark Greece's coming of age. Winners receive a silver medal and olive crown, second and third places receive a bronze medal and a laurel branch, respectively.	The outbreak of WWI sees Greece initially neutral but eventually siding with the Western Allies against Germany and Turkey on the promise of land in Asia Minor.

and Smyrna fell in 1922, and tens of thousands of its Greek inhabitants were killed.

The outcome of these hostilities was the Treaty of Lausanne in July 1923, whereby Turkey recovered eastern Thrace and the islands of Imvros and Tenedos, while the Italians kept the Dodecanese (which they had temporarily acquired in 1912 and would hold until 1947).

The treaty also called for a population exchange between Greece and Turkey to prevent any future disputes. Almost 1.5 million Greeks left Turkey and almost 400,000 Turks left Greece. The exchange put a tremendous strain on the Greek economy and caused great bitterness and hardship for the individuals concerned. Many Greeks abandoned a privileged life in Asia Minor for one of extreme poverty in emerging urban shanty towns in Athens and Thessaloniki.

Inside Hitler's Greece: The Experience of Occupation, 1941–44 by Mark Mazower, is an intimate and comprehensive account of Greece under Nazi occupation and the rise of the resistance movement.

WWII & the Civil War

During a tumultuous period, a republic was declared in 1924 amid a series of coups and counter-coups. Then in November 1935, King George II installed the right-wing General Ioannis Metaxas as prime minister. He assumed dictatorial powers under the pretext of preventing a communist-inspired republican coup. Metaxas' grandiose vision was to create a utopian Third Greek Civilisation, based on its glorious ancient and Byzantine past. He then exiled or imprisoned opponents, banned trade unions and the recently established Kommounistiko Komma Elladas (KKE, the Greek Communist Party), imposed press censorship, and created a secret police force and fascist-style youth movement. But Metaxas is best known for his reply of *ohi* (no) to Mussolini's ultimatum to allow Italian forces passage through Greece at the beginning of WWII. The Italians invaded anyway, but the Greeks drove them back into Albania.

Despite Allied help, when German troops invaded Greece on 6 April 1941, the whole country was rapidly overrun. The Germans used Crete as an air and naval base to attack British forces in the eastern Mediterranean. The civilian population suffered appallingly during the occupation, many dying of starvation. The Nazis rounded up more than half the Jewish population and transported them to death camps. Numerous resistance movements sprang up, eventually polarising into royalist and communist factions which fought one another with as much venom as they fought the Germans, often with devastating results for the civilian Greek population.

For an insight into the 1967 colonels' coup, read Andreas Papandreou's account in *Democracy at Gunpoint*.

The Germans began to retreat from Greece in October 1944, but the resistance groups continued to fight one another. A bloody civil war resulted, lasting until 1949. The civil war left Greece in chaos, politically frayed and economically shattered. More Greeks were killed in three years of bitter civil war than in WWII, and a quarter of a million people

1919–23	1924–35	1940	1941–44
Greece's 'Great Idea' attempts to unite the former Hellenic areas of Asia Minor. It fails and leads to a population exchange between Greece and Turkey in 1923, known as the 'Asia Minor catastrophe'.	Greece is proclaimed a republic and King George II leaves. The Great Depression counters the nation's return to stability. Monarchists and parliamentarians under Eleftherios Venizelos tussle for control of the country.	Greeks shout *Ohi*! (No!) to Italian fascists demanding surrender without a fight on 28 October. Officially referred to as Ohi Day, many Greeks use language that is rather more colourful for this day.	Germany invades and occupies Greece. Monarchists, republicans and communists form resistance groups that, despite infighting, drive out the Germans after three years.

were left homeless. The sense of despair triggered a mass exodus. Villages – whole islands even – were abandoned as almost a million Greeks left in search of a better life elsewhere, primarily to countries such as Australia, Canada and the US.

Colonels, Monarchs & Democracy

Georgos Papandreou came to power in February 1964. He had founded the Centre Union (EK) and wasted no time in implementing a series of radical changes: he freed political prisoners and allowed exiles to come back to Greece, reduced income tax and the defence budget, and increased spending on social services and education. The political right in Greece was rattled by Papandreou's tolerance of the left, and a group of army colonels led by Georgos Papadopoulos and Stylianos Patakos staged a coup on 21 April 1967. They established a military junta, with Papadopoulos as prime minister.

The colonels declared martial law, banned political parties and trade unions, imposed censorship, and imprisoned, tortured and exiled thousands of dissidents. In June 1972, Papadopoulos declared Greece a republic and appointed himself president.

On 17 November 1973, tanks stormed a building at the Athens Polytechnic (Technical University) to quell a student occupation calling for an uprising against the US-backed junta. While the number of casualties is still in dispute (more than 20 students were reportedly killed and hundreds injured), the act spelt the death knell for the junta.

A FEMALE FORCE

Women have played a strong role in Greek resistance movements throughout history. One national heroine was Laskarina Bouboulina (1771–1825), a celebrated seafarer who became a member of Filiki Eteria (Friendly Society), an organisation striving for independence against Ottoman rule. Originally from Hydra, she settled in Spetses, from where she commissioned the construction of and then commanded, as admiral, several warships that were used in significant naval blockades (the most famous vessel being the *Agamemnon*). She helped maintain the crews of her ships and a small army of soldiers, and supplied the revolutionaries with food, weapons and ammunition, using her ships for transportation. Her role in maritime operations significantly helped the independence movement. However, political factionalism within the government led to her postwar arrest and subsequent exile to Spetses, where she died.

Streets across Greece bear her name and there are statues dedicated to her and her great-granddaughter, Lela Karagianni – who fought with the resistance in WWII – in Spetses Town, where Bouboulina's home is now a private museum.

1944–49	1967	1973	1974
The end of WWII sees Greece descend into civil war, pitching monarchists against communists. The monarchy is restored in 1946; however, many Greeks migrate in search of a better life.	Right- and left-wing factions continue to bicker, provoking a right-wing military coup d'état by army generals who establish a junta. They impose martial law and abolish many civil rights.	On 17 November tanks ram the gates of the Athens Polytechnic and troops storm the school buildings in a bid to quash a student uprising. More than 20 students reportedly die.	A botched plan to unite Cyprus with Greece prompts the invasion of Cyprus by Turkish troops, and the military junta falls. It's a catalyst for the restoration of parliamentary democracy in Greece.

DIVIDED CYPRUS

Since the 1930s, Greek Cypriots (four-fifths of the island's population) had desired union with Greece, while Turkey had maintained its claim to the island ever since it became a British protectorate in 1878 (it became a British crown colony in 1925). Greece was in favour of a union, a notion strongly opposed by Britain and the US on strategic grounds. In 1959, after extensive negotiations, Britain, Greece and Turkey agreed on a compromise solution whereby Cyprus would become an independent republic, with Greek Cypriot Archbishop Makarios as president and a Turk, Fazil Kükük, as vice-president. In reality this did little to appease either side: right-wing Greek Cypriots rallied against the British, while Turkish Cypriots clamoured for partition of the island.

In July 1974, Greece's newly self-appointed prime minister Ioannidis tried to impose unity with Cyprus by attempting to topple the Makarios government. However, Makarios got wind of an assassination attempt and escaped. Consequently, mainland Turkey sent in troops until they occupied northern Cyprus, partitioning the island and displacing almost 200,000 Greek Cypriots, who fled their homes for the safety of the south (reportedly more than 1500 remain missing).

The UN-protected Green Line separating modern-day Cyprus is a ghost town. Decades on from the 1974 partition, negotiations have failed to resolve the issue. A divided Cyprus joined the European Union in 2004 after a failed referendum on unification, and international mediation continues.

Shortly after, the head of the military security police, Dimitrios Ioannidis, deposed Papadopoulos and tried to impose unity with Cyprus in a disastrous move that led to the partition in Cyprus and the collapse of the junta.

Konstandinos Karamanlis was summoned from Paris to take office and his New Democracy (ND) party won a large majority at the November 1974 elections against the newly formed Panhellenic Socialist Union (PASOK), led by Andreas Papandreou (son of Georgos). A plebiscite voted 69% against the restoration of the monarchy, and the ban on communist parties was lifted.

The 1980s & 1990s

When Greece became the 10th member of the EU in 1981, it was the smallest and poorest member. In October 1981 Andreas Papandreou's PASOK party was elected as Greece's first socialist government, ruling for almost two decades (except for 1990–93). PASOK promised ambitious social reform, to close the US air bases and to withdraw from NATO. US military presence was reduced, but unemployment was high and reforms in education and welfare were limited. Women's issues fared better: the

1981	1981–90	1999	2001
Greece joins the EU, effectively removing protective trade barriers and opening up the Greek economy to the wider world for the first time. The economy grows smartly.	Greece acquires its first elected socialist government (PASOK) under the leadership of Andreas Papandreou. The honeymoon lasts nine years, before the conservatives reassume power.	Turkey and Greece experience powerful earthquakes within weeks of each other that result in hundreds of deaths. The two nations pledge mutual aid and support, initiating a warming of diplomatic relations.	Greece joins the euro-zone, with the drachma currency replaced by the euro.

dowry system was abolished, abortion legalised, and civil marriage and divorce were implemented. But by 1990, significant policy wrangling and economic upheaval wore thin with the electorate and it returned the ND to office, led by Konstandinos Mitsotakis.

Intent on redressing the country's economic problems – high inflation and high government spending – the government imposed austerity measures, including a wage freeze for civil servants and steep increases in public utility costs and basic services.

By late 1992 corruption allegations were being levelled against the government, and many Mitsotakis supporters abandoned ship; ND lost its parliamentary majority, and an early election held in October returned PASOK to power.

Andreas Papandreou stepped down in early 1996 due to ill health and he died on 26 June, sparking a dramatic change of direction for PASOK. The party abandoned Papandreou's left-leaning politics and elected economist and lawyer Costas Simitis as the new prime minister. Simitis then won a comfortable majority at the October 1996 polls.

The Green Line separating Greece and Turkey in modern-day Cyprus is a ghost town, a desert of silence where the clock stopped in 1974. Greeks still peer through the barbed-wire partition to the place they were born and banished from, and are unlikely to return to live.

The 21st Century Dawns

The new millennium saw Greece join the eurozone in 2001, amid rumblings from existing members that it was not economically ready – its public borrowing was too high, as was its inflation level. In hindsight, many look back on that year and bemoan the miscalibration of the drachma against the euro, claiming Greece's currency was undervalued, and that, overnight, living became disproportionately more expensive. That said, billions of euro poured into large-scale infrastructure projects across Greece, including the redevelopment of Athens – spurred on largely by its hosting of the 2004 Olympic Games. However, rising unemployment, ballooning public debt, slowing inflation and the squeezing of consumer credit took their toll. Public opinion soured further in 2007 when the conservative government (who had come to power in 2004) was widely criticised for its handling of severe summer fires, responsible for widespread destruction throughout Greece. Nevertheless, snap elections held in September 2007 returned the conservatives, albeit with a diminished majority.

A series of massive general strikes highlighted mounting electoral discontent. Hundreds of thousands of people protested against proposed radical labour and pension reforms and privatisation plans that analysts claimed would help curb public debt. The backlash against the ND

The Green Line separating Greece and Turkey in modern-day Cyprus is a ghost town, a desert of silence where the clock stopped in 1974. Greeks still peer through the barbed-wire partition to the place they were born and banished from, and are unlikely to return to live

2004	2007	2008	2009
Athens successfully hosts the 28th Summer Olympic Games. Greece also wins the European football championship.	Vast forest fires devastate much of the western Peloponnese as well as parts of Evia and Epiros, causing Greece's worst ecological disaster in decades. Thousands lose their homes and 66 people perish.	Police shoot and kill a 15-year-old boy in Athens following an alleged exchange between police and youths. This sparks a series of urban riots nationwide.	Prime Minister Kostas Karamanlis calls for an early general election. Socialist PASOK, under George Papandreou, wins the October election with a landslide result against the conservatives.

government, also mired in a series of political scandals, reached boiling point in December 2008 when urban rioting broke out across the country, led by youths in Athens outraged by the fatal shooting by police of a 15-year-old boy.

Concern continued over political tangles in investigations regarding alleged corruption among state executives (on both sides of the political fence) in connection with the Siemens Hellas group. This followed another controversy that involved land-swap deals between a monastery and the government, which some commentators believe to have gone heavily in the monastery's favour, at the expense of taxpayers. A general election held in October 2009, midway through Karamanlis' term, saw PASOK (under George Papandreou) take back the reins in a landslide win against the conservatives.

Sink or Swim

In 2009 a lethal cocktail of high public spending and widespread tax evasion, combined with the credit crunch of global recession, threatened to cripple Greece's economy. In 2010 Greece's fellow eurozone countries agreed to a €125 billion package (half of Greece's GDP) to get the country back on its feet, though with strict conditions – the ruling government, PASOK, still led by George Papandreou, would have to impose austere measures of reform and reduce Greece's bloated deficit. Huge cuts followed, including 10% off public workers' salaries, but it was too little too late and foreign creditors continued to demand ever-higher interest rates for their loans.

Greece was stuck between a real-life Scylla and Charybdis – to receive yet another bailout, which was absolutely essential to stop them toppling the euro as a credible currency, they had to effect reforms that penalised the average Greek even further, pushing formerly non-political citizens towards revolution. Some longed for a return to the drachma; however, many believed that Greece would still be saddled with massive debt and a monetary system with absolutely no standing.

Prime Minister Papandreou asked the people for a referendum on the EU bailout, then failed to form a coalition government and stepped down from office. In November 2011, Lucas Papademos – a former vice president of the European Central Bank – became prime minister. Antonis Samaras, leader of the New Democracy party, succeeded him the following year and assembled a coalition with third-placed PASOK and smaller groups to pursue the austerity program. A second bailout of €130 billion brought further austerity requirements, and Athens again saw major strikes aimed at the massive cuts – 22% off the minimum wage, 15% off pensions and the axing of 15,000 public sector jobs. Suicide rates in the capital were up by 40%. Also up was support for the

Greece's dispute with the Former Yugoslav Republic of Macedonia (FYROM) stems from their Balkan neighbour's claim to the name Macedonia and on Greece's favourite son, Alexander the Great, despite Alexander's home of Pella still standing in the province of Macedonia in northern Greece.

2010	2011	2012	2013
Greece is granted the biggest financial bailout in history, with EU countries committing a €125 billion package. Strict austerity measures by the Greek government to cut the deficit are met with civil protest.	Despite loans, the economy continues to shrink, with rising unemployment and riots in Athens. The EU and IMF rally to prevent a Greek default and avert a crisis across the eurozone.	Proposed government cuts include 22% off the minimum wage, 15% off pensions and the loss of 15,000 public-sector jobs.	Unemployment rises to 26.8% – the highest rate in the EU. Youth unemployment climbs to almost 60%.

far-right fascist organisation, the Golden Dawn, bringing with them a rising tide of racism aimed squarely at Greece's immigrant population.

These were indeed brutal times for the average Greek, with wage cuts of around 30% and up to 17 'new' taxes crippling monthly income. While the EU and IMF initially predicted that Greece would return to growth in 2014, the inability of many Greeks to pay their taxes at the end of the year meant that growth was a mere 0.4%. In January 2015, the New Democrat party lost at the polls to left-wing Syriza. The new prime minister, 40-year-old Alexis Tsipras, won the election with an anti-austerity platform.

This was the first ever election win for radical Syriza. To reach a majority, Syriza established a coalition with right-wing Independent Greeks (ANEL), unlikely bedfellows united by their mutual condemnation of the bailout program.

Initially, Tsipras stuck to his guns and June 2015 saw Greece become the first first-world nation to go into arrears with the EU and IMF. Attempts to negotiate a new bailout and avoid default were unsuccessful as Tsipras took the offer back to the Greek people and held a referendum. Over 61% of voters were not willing to accept the bailout conditions.

The week that followed was one of turmoil. Greek banks closed and began running out of cash, and markets around the world fell as the EU produced a detailed plan for a possible 'Grexit' – Greece's removal from the EU.

At the eleventh hour, Tsipras secured an €86 billion bailout loan – but the austerity measures attached were even more vigorous than those proposed before the referendum, and many felt that, with Greek banks on the brink of collapse, Tsipras had been bullied into accepting the terms. Further tax hikes, pension reforms and privatisation of €50 billion worth of public companies left many viewing Greece as a financial ward of Europe.

Dissent within Syriza and ANEL, brought on by hardliners opposed to the bailout, led Tsipras to resign in August 2015 and return to the polls in September. This was Greece's fourth election in just over three years. The outcome was an unexpectedly large victory for Tsipras, just six seats short of an absolute majority. Nevertheless, voter turnout was 57%, the lowest recorded in Greece. For many Greeks, choosing between the austerity measures and Grexit had become akin to rearranging deckchairs on the Titanic.

Prince Philip, the Duke of Edinburgh, was part of the Greek royal family – born on Corfu as Prince Philip of Greece and Denmark in 1921. Former king of Greece, Constantine, is Prince William's godfather. Constantine and his family were exiled in London for 46 years, returning to Athens in 2013.

2014	2015	2015	2017
The EU and IMF's prediction that Greece would return to growth in 2014 is not realised.	The New Democrat party is replaced by left-wing Syriza, led by 40-year-old Alexis Tsipras.	Unable to pay its debt, Greece faces the very real possibility of an exit from the eurozone and is forced to take on further debt, with the strictest austerity measures yet.	The number of refugees in Greece reaches 62,000 (over half of them women and children). With borders to other European countries closed, they are trapped, mainly in island camps.

Ancient Greek Culture

When the Roman Empire assimilated Greece it did so with considerable respect and idealism. The Romans in many ways based themselves on the Ancient Greeks, absorbing their deities (and renaming them), literature, myths, philosophy, fine arts and architecture. So what made the Ancient Greeks so special? From thespians to philosophers, from monster-slewing heroes to a goddess born of sea foam, the Ancient Greeks were captivating.

The Golden Age

Two of Socrates' most famous quotes are: 'The only true wisdom consists of knowing that you know nothing' and 'The unexamined life is not worth living'.

In the 5th century BC, Athens had a cultural renaissance that has never been equalled – in fact, such was the diversity of its achievements that modern classical scholars refer to it as 'the miracle'. The era started with a vastly outnumbered Greek army defeating the Persian horde in the battles of Marathon and Salamis, and ended with the beginning of the inevitable war between Athens and Sparta. It's often said that Athens' 'Golden Age' is the bedrock of Western civilisation, and had the Persians won, Europe today would have been a vastly different place. Like Paris in the 1930s, Athens was a hotbed of talent. Any artist or writer worth their salt left their hometown and travelled to the great city of wisdom to share their thoughts and hear the great minds of the day express themselves.

Drama

The great dramatists such as Aeschylus, Aristophanes, Euripides and Sophocles redefined theatre from religious ritual to become a compelling form of entertainment. They were to be found at the Theatre of Dionysos at the foot of the Acropolis, and their comedies and tragedies reveal a great deal about the psyche of the Ancient Greeks.

Across the country, large open-air theatres were built on the sides of hills, designed to accommodate plays with increasingly sophisticated backdrops and props, choruses and themes, and to maximise sound so that even the people in the back row might hear the actors on stage. The dominant genres of theatre were tragedy and comedy. The first known actor was a man called Thespis, from whose name we derive the word 'thespian'.

Philosophy

The World of the Ancient Greeks (2002), by archaeologists John Camp and Elizabeth Fisher, is a broad and in-depth look at how the Greeks have left their imprint on politics, philosophy, theatre, art, medicine and architecture.

While the dramatists were cutting their thespian cloth, late-5th and early-4th-century-BC philosophers Aristotle, Plato and Socrates were introducing new trains of thought rooted in rationality, as the new Greek mind focused on logic and reason. Athens' greatest, most noble citizen, Socrates (469–399 BC), was forced to drink hemlock for allegedly corrupting the youth by asking probing, uncomfortable questions, but before he died he left behind a school of hypothetical reductionism that is still used today.

Plato (427–347 BC), Socrates' star student, was responsible for documenting his teacher's thoughts, and without his work in books such as the *Symposium,* they would have been lost to us. Considered an idealist,

Plato wrote *The Republic* as a warning to the city-state of Athens that unless its people respected law and leadership, and educated its youth sufficiently, it would be doomed.

Plato's student Aristotle (384–322 BC), at the end of the Golden Age, focused his gifts on astronomy, physics, zoology, ethics and politics. Aristotle was also the personal physician to Philip II, King of Macedon, and the tutor of Alexander the Great. The greatest gift of the Athenian philosophers to modern-day thought is their spirit of rational inquiry.

Sculpture

Classical sculpture began to gather pace in Greece in the 6th century BC with the renderings of nudes in marble. Most statues were created to revere a particular god or goddess and many were robed in grandiose garments. The statues of the preceding Archaic period, known as *kouroi*, had focused on symmetry and form, but in the early 5th century BC artists sought to create expression and animation. As temples demanded elaborate carvings, sculptors were called upon to create large reliefs upon them.

During the 5th century BC, the craft became yet more sophisticated, as sculptors were taught to successfully map a face and create a likeness of their subject in marble busts. Perhaps the most famous Greek sculptor was Pheidias, whose reliefs upon the Parthenon depicting the Greek and Persian Wars – now known as the Parthenon Marbles – are celebrated as among the finest of the Golden Age.

The Heroes

Some of the greatest stories of all time – and some say the wellspring of story itself – are to be found in the Greek myths. For many of us, the fantastical stories of Heracles and Odysseus we heard as kids still linger in our imagination, and contemporary writers continue to reinterpret these stories and characters for books and films. Standing in the ancient ruins of an acropolis and peering across the watery horizon, it's not difficult to picture the Kraken (Poseidon's pet monster) rising from the Aegean, nor to imagine that fishing boat you see heading into the sunset as Jason's Argo en route to Colchis for the Golden Fleece.

The average Greek is fiercely proud of their myths and will love entertaining you with a list of the gods, but they'll love it even more if you know a few of them yourself.

No original works by the celebrated classical sculptor Pheidias survive, though copies were made by Roman sculptors. Pheidias' colossal chryselephantine (gold and ivory) statue of Zeus was one of the Wonders of the Ancient World.

ANCIENT GREEK CULTURE THE HEROES

ISLANDS IN MYTHOLOGY

Greece is steeped in mythology and its many islands provided dramatic settings for its legends and interactions between gods and mortals.

Myrina, Lemnos Believed to have been founded by Myrina, queen of the Amazons.

Crete Zeus' mother allegedly gave birth to him in a cave to prevent him from being eaten by his father, Cronos. Crete was also home of the dreaded minotaur.

Lesvos When Orpheus was killed and dismembered by the Maenads, the waves brought his head here and it was buried near Antissa.

Kythira Aphrodite is said to have been born out of the waves surrounding Kythira.

Delos This island rose up from the waves when the goddess Leto was looking for a place to give birth to Apollo and Artemis.

Mykonos Zeus and the Titans battled it out on this island and Hercules slew the Giants here.

Rhodes The island given to Helios the sun god after Zeus' victory over the Giants.

Theseus

The Athenian hero volunteered himself as one of seven men and maidens in the annual sacrifice to the Minotaur, the crazed half-bull, half-man offspring of King Minos of Crete. Once inside its forbidding labyrinth (from which none had returned), Theseus, aided by Princess Ariadne (who had a crush on him induced by Aphrodite's dart), loosened a spool of thread to find his way out once he'd killed the monster.

Icarus

Along with Daedalus (his father), Icarus flew off the cliffs of Crete pursued by King Minos and his troops, using wings made of feathers and wax. His father instructed him to fly away from the midday sun, but Icarus became carried away with the exhilaration of flying...the wax melted, the feathers separated and the bird-boy fell to his death.

Perseus

Perseus' impossible task was to kill the gorgon, Medusa. With a head of snakes Medusa could turn a man to stone with a single glance. Armed with an invisibility cap and a pair of flying sandals from Hermes, Perseus used his reflective shield to avoid Medusa's stare. He cut off her head and secreted it in a bag, but it was shortly unsheathed to save Andromeda, a princess bound to a rock and about to be sacrificed to a sea monster. Medusa's head turned the sea monster to stone and Perseus got the girl.

Oedipus

Oedipus was the Ancient Greeks' gift to the Freudian school of psychology. Having been abandoned at birth, Oedipus learned from the Delphic oracle that he would one day slay his father and marry his mother. On the journey back to his birthplace, Thiva (Thebes), he killed a rude stranger and then discovered the city was plagued by a murderous Sphinx (a winged lion with a woman's head). The creature gave unsuspecting travellers and citizens a riddle: if they couldn't answer it, they were dashed on the rocks. Oedipus succeeded in solving the riddle, felled the Sphinx and so gained the queen of Thiva's hand in marriage. On discovering the stranger he'd killed was his father and that his new wife was in fact his mother, Oedipus ripped out his eyes and exiled himself.

Mythology

Ancient Greece revolved around careful worship of 12 central gods and goddesses, all of whom played a major role in the *mythos* (mythology), and none of whom can be commended for their behaviour. They frequently displayed pettiness, spitefulness, outright cruelty and low self-esteem that led to unworthy competitions with mortals which were always rigged in the gods' favour. Each city-state had its own patron god or goddess to appease and flatter, while on a personal level a farmer might make sacrifice to the goddess Demeter to bless his crops, or a fisherman to Poseidon to bring him fish and safe passage on the waves.

The Ancient Pantheon

Here's a quick guide to the 12 central gods and goddesses of Greek mythology – their Roman names are in brackets.

Zeus (Jupiter) The fire-bolt-flinging king of the gods, ruler of Mt Olympus, lord of the skies and master of disguise in pursuit of mortal maidens. Wardrobe includes shower of gold, bull, eagle and swan.

Hera (Juno) Protector of women and family, the queen of heaven is both the

---

Marcel Camus' film *Black Orpheus* (1959) won an Oscar for its reimagining of the Orpheus and Eurydice tale, set in a favela in 1950s Brazil to a bossa nova soundtrack. The lovers flee a hitman and Orfeu's vindictive fiancée.

The Greek tragedy *Medea*, by Euripides, is about the sun god Helios' granddaughter who takes revenge on her husband by killing her children and finds new life in the dark. It was turned into a fatalistic namesake film (1988) by Lars von Trier.

TOP FIVE MYTHICAL CREATURES

Of the grotesque and fantastical creatures whose stories are dear to Greek hearts, these five are the most notorious.

Medusa The snake-headed one punished by the gods for her inflated vanity. Even dead, her blood is lethal.

Cyclops A one-eyed giant. Odysseus and his crew were trapped in the cave of one such cyclops, Polyphemus.

Cerberus The three-headed dog of hell, he guards the entrance to the underworld – under his watch no one gets in or out.

Minotaur This half-man, half-bull mutant leads a life of existential angst in the abysmal labyrinth, tempered only by the occasional morsel of human flesh.

Hydra Cut one of its nine heads off and another two will grow in its place. Heracles solved the problem by cauterising each stump with his burning brand.

embattled wife and sister of Zeus. She was the prototype of the jealous, domineering wife who took revenge on Zeus' illegitimate children.

Poseidon (Neptune) God of the seas, master of the mists and younger brother of Zeus. He dwelt in a glittering underwater palace.

Hades (Pluto) God of death and also brother of Zeus, he ruled the underworld, bringing the newly dead with the help of his skeletal ferryman, Charon. Serious offenders were sent for torture in Tartarus, while heroes enjoyed eternal R&R in the Elysian Fields.

Athena (Minerva) Goddess of wisdom, war, science and guardian of Athens, born in full armour out of Zeus' forehead. The antithesis of Ares, Athena was deliberate and, where possible, diplomatic in the art of war. Heracles, Jason (of Jason and the Argonauts fame) and Perseus all benefited from her patronage.

Aphrodite (Venus) Goddess of love and beauty who was said to have been born of sea foam. When she wasn't cuckolding her husband, Hephaestus, she and her cherubic son Eros (Cupid) were enflaming hearts and causing trouble (cue the Trojan War).

Apollo God of music, the arts and fortune-telling, Apollo was also the god of light and an expert shot with a bow and arrow. It was his steady hand which guided Paris' arrow towards Achilles' only weak spot – his heel – thus killing him.

Artemis (Diana) The goddess of the hunt and twin sister of Apollo was, ironically, patron saint of wild animals. By turns spiteful and magnanimous, she was closely associated with the sinister Hecate, patroness of witchcraft.

Ares (Mars) God of war, bloodthirsty and lacking control. Zeus' least favourite of his progeny. Not surprisingly, Ares was worshipped by the bellicose Spartans.

Hermes (Mercury) Messenger of the gods, patron saint of travellers and the handsome one with a winged hat and sandals. He was always on hand to smooth over the affairs of Zeus, his father.

Hephaestus (Vulcan) God of craftsmanship, metallurgy and fire, this deformed and oft-derided son of Zeus made the world's first woman of clay, Pandora, as a punishment for man. Inside her box were the evils of mankind.

Hestia (Vesta) Goddess of the hearth, she protected state fires in city halls from where citizens of Greece could light their brands. She remained unmarried, inviolate.

From the Greek stories of Oedipus and the castration of Uranus by Cronos, Sigmund Freud drew the conclusion that myths often reflect strong, taboo desires that are otherwise unable to be expressed in society.

The Islanders

Living on a Greek island may be the stuff of fantasies, but even the most idyllic islands have their challenges. The islands are more low-key and relaxed than the mainland, and people generally lead a more traditional lifestyle. Periods of isolation, varying geography and the influence of foreign cultures throughout history have led to strong regional identities, both between and within island groups.

Island Life

Island life is predominantly seasonal, revolving largely around agriculture, stock breeding, fishing and tourism. From May to September, visitors far outnumber the local population on many islands.

The majority of islanders are self-employed and run family businesses. Stores close during the heat of the day, and then reopen until around 11pm – which is when locals generally head out to dinner with family or their *parea* (companions).

Regardless of the long working hours, Greeks are inherently social animals and enjoy a rich communal life. Shopkeepers sit outside their stores chatting to each other until customers arrive, and in villages you will see people sitting outside their homes watching the goings on. In the evenings, the seafront promenades and town squares are bustling with people of all ages taking their *volta* (outing), dressed up and refreshed from an afternoon siesta (albeit a dying institution).

The island of Ikaria has one of the highest life expectancy rates in Europe, with one in three islanders living into their 90s. Researchers ascribe this to long afternoon naps, lots of mountain tea and beans, little coffee and meat, and healthy sex lives into their 80s.

Island Pursuits

Traditional agrarian life on many islands has given way to tourism-related pursuits, though they often coexist, with families running hotels and tavernas during summer and focusing on agricultural activities in the winter.

Tourism has brought prosperity to many islands, and larger islands including Crete, Rhodes and Corfu have thriving and sophisticated urban centres. Islands with flourishing agricultural industries, such as Lesvos and Chios, are less affected by tourism. Overall, better transport, technology, telecommunications and infrastructure have made life easier and far less isolated for islanders.

Major social and economic disparities still exist, however, even within islands and island groups. Cosmopolitan Mykonos, for example, is a far cry from smaller, remote islands where many people live frugally in a time warp of traditional island life.

Winter can be especially tough for people living on isolated islands without airports or regular ferry services. On some islands, people move back to Athens after the tourist season, while on larger islands, some locals move from the beach resorts back to mountain villages and larger towns with schools and services. While many young people once left for work and educational opportunities on the mainland, some are now returning to their family homes due to high unemployment. Others are looking for work abroad.

The islanders have been feeling the crunch of Greece's economic woes, with domestic tourism declining as Greeks curtail holidays and eating out, and international tourism has been impacted by the media's recurring portrayal of a country in crisis.

Regional Identity

In a country where regional identities remain deep-rooted, Greek islanders often identify with their island (and their village) first – as Cretans, Ithacans or Kastellorizians etc – and as Greeks second. Islanders living in Athens or abroad invariably maintain a strong connection to their ancestral towns and villages, and regularly return during holidays.

Customs, traditions and even the characteristics of the people vary from island to island, influenced by their particular history and topography, which is reflected in everything from the cuisine and architecture to music and dance.

In the Ionians, Corfu escaped Turkish rule and has a more Italian, French and British influence, and its people retain an aristocratic air. The Cretans are renowned for their independent streak and hospitality, and have perhaps the most enduring and distinctive folk culture and traditions, as well as their own dialect.

In villages such as Olympos in far-eastern Karpathos, many women still wear traditional dress, including headscarves and goatskin boots. Sifnos is renowned for its unique pottery tradition; on Chios the mastic tree has spawned its own industry; Lesvos is the home of ouzo; while Kalymnos' sponge-diving industry shaped the island's identity as much as fishing and agriculture have forged those of others.

Family Life

Greek society remains dominated by family and kinship. Extended family plays an important role, with grandparents often looking after grandchildren while parents work or socialise. Many working Athenians send their children to their grandparents on the islands for the summer.

Greeks attach great importance to education, determined to provide their children the opportunities many of them lacked. English and other languages are widely spoken. While Greece has the world's highest number of students per capita studying at universities abroad, many of these students end up highly educated and underemployed.

It's still uncommon for young people to move out of home before marrying, unless they leave to study or work, which is inevitable on most

First published in 1885, James Theodore Bent's *The Cyclades, or Life Among the Insular Greeks* is a classic account of island life. John Freely's more recent (2006) *The Cyclades* is rich on history and insight.

Greece is a largely urban society, with 80.2% of its population living in cities – a third in the Greater Athens area. Less than 15% live on the islands, the most populous of which are Crete, Evia and Corfu.

CHANGING FACES

Greece has long been a magnet for foreigners seeking an idyllic island lifestyle and an escape from the rat race. Apart from those owning holiday houses, the small resident population of disparate *xenoi* (foreigners) has largely been made up of somewhat eccentric or retired Europeans, ex-hippies and artists, or people married to locals as a result of summer romances. In recent years, there has also been a steady stream of Americans, Australians and others with Greek heritage returning to their ancestral islands.

But Greece has also become home to many of the economic migrants who have settled here since the 1990s, when the country suddenly changed from a nation of emigration to one of immigration. Today it also struggles with an ever-growing number of asylum seekers.

Greece's own population only grows through immigration, with immigrants accounting for one-fifth of the workforce. Economic decline, concerns about immigrant crime and urban degradation have fuelled xenophobia and extremism, sparking anti-immigrant rallies and growing hostility toward immigrants.

islands, where employment and educational opportunities are limited. While this is slowly changing among professionals, with people marrying later, low wages and skyrocketing unemployment are also keeping young Greeks at home. Traditionally, parents strive to provide homes for their children when they get married, often building apartments for each child above their own.

Despite the machismo, Greece has very much a matriarchal society and the male-female dynamic throws up some interesting paradoxes. Men love to give the impression that they rule the roost but, in reality, it's the women who often run the show both at home and in family businesses. Greek women (at least the older generation) are famously houseproud and take pride in their culinary skills. It's still relatively rare for men to be involved in housework or cooking.

In conservative provincial towns and villages, many women maintain traditional roles, though women's agricultural cooperatives play a leading role in regional economies and in the preservation of cultural heritage. Things are far more liberal for women living in bigger towns.

The Greek Character

Greek islanders have by necessity been relatively autonomous, but they share with the mainland a common history that spans centuries, as well as typical traits of the Greek character.

Years of hardship and isolation have made islanders stoic and resourceful, but they are also friendly and laid-back. Like most Greeks, they are fiercely independent, patriotic and proud of their heritage. They pride themselves on their *filotimo* (dignity and sense of honour), and their *filoxenia* (hospitality, welcome, shelter), which you will find in even the poorest household.

Forthright and argumentative, most Greeks will freely state their opinions and talk about personal matters rather than engage in polite small talk. Few subjects are off limits, from your private life and why you don't have children, to how much you earn or what you paid for your house or shoes. Greeks are also notoriously late (turning up to an appointment on time is often referred to as 'being English').

Personal freedom and democratic rights are almost sacrosanct, and there is residual mistrust of authority and disrespect for the state. Rules and regulations are routinely ignored or seen as a challenge. Patronage and nepotism are rife, an enduring by-product of having to rely on personal networks to survive during years of foreign masters and meddlers, civil war and political instability (though graft and corruption are its more extreme form). The notion of the greater good often plays second fiddle to personal interests, and there is little sense of collective responsibility.

While Greeks will mercilessly malign their own government and society, they are defensive about external criticism and can be fervently patriotic and nationalistic.

Faith & Identity

The Orthodox faith is the official religion of Greece and a key element of Greek identity and culture. During foreign occupations the church was the principal upholder of Greek culture, language and traditions. The church still exerts significant social, political and economic influence.

Religious rituals are a part of daily life on the islands. You will notice people making the sign of the cross when they pass a church; compliments to babies and adults are followed by the *ftou ftou* (spitting) gesture to ward off the evil eye. Many Greeks will go to a church when they have a problem, to light a candle or leave a *tama* (votive offering) for the relevant saint.

Most of Greece's shipping dynasties hail from the islands – more than a third from Chios and nearby Inousses, where they own many grand mansions. Shipping families also own the private islands of Spetsopoula (Niarchos) and Skorpios (where Aristotle Onassis married Jackie Kennedy).

During the annual sheep blessing in the Cretan village of Asi Gonia on 23 April, local shepherds bring their flock to be blessed at the church of Agios Yiorgos. Then they milk them and hand out fresh milk to everyone gathered.

EASTER, ISLAND-STYLE

Easter is a major event on all the islands, with many renowned for their unique Holy Week customs and celebrations – from the bonfires burning Judas effigies in southwestern Crete to the three-day procession of the icon of the Virgin Mary through almost every house and boat on Folegandros.

The resurrection on Easter Saturday in the village of Vrontados on Chios is celebrated with gusto. During the village's famous *Rouketopolemos* (rocket war), two rival churches on hilltops about 400m apart fire around 60,000 rounds of firework rockets at each other, aiming for the bell towers.

In Corfu, Easter takes on a special grandeur, with evocative candlelit *epitafios* (funeral bier) processions through the streets, accompanied by bands and choirs. A peculiar tradition, dating back to the Venetians, is *botides* on Holy Saturday morning, when people in Corfu Town throw big ceramic pots out of their windows and balconies, smashing them onto the streets below.

Patmos is considered one of the holiest places to celebrate Easter, and Catholics from around Greece and the world travel to celebrate on the island where John is believed to have written the Book of Revelations. A cacophony of fireworks and countless lamb roasts and parties engulf the island.

The Greek year is centred on the saints' days and festivals of the church calendar (every other day seems to be dedicated to a saint or martyr). Name days (celebrating your namesake saint) are more important than birthdays, and baptisms are an important rite. Most people are named after a saint, as are boats, towns and mountain peaks.

The islands are dotted with hundreds of churches and private chapels built to protect their seafaring families. You will also see many iconostases (tiny chapels) on the roadside, which are either shrines to people who died in road accidents or dedications to saints. Island churches and monasteries are open to visitors, but you should always dress appropriately. Men should wear long trousers, and women should cover arms (and cleavage) and wear skirts that reach below the knees.

Most *panigyria* (island festivals) revolve around annual patron saints' days or those of the local church or monastery. Harvest and other agricultural festivals also have a religious base or ritual. Easter is the biggest event of the year, celebrated everywhere with candlelit street processions, midnight fireworks and spit-roasted lamb, with some islands renowned for their particular Easter festivities.

While religious freedom is part of the constitution, the only other legally recognised religions apart from Christianity in Greece are Judaism and Islam. There are more than 50,000 Roman Catholics, mostly of Genoese or Frankish origin, living in the Cyclades, especially on Syros, where they make up 40% of the population. A small Jewish community lives in Rhodes (dating back to the Roman era).

The Arts

Greece is revered for its artistic and cultural legacy, and the arts remain a vibrant and evolving element of Greek culture, identity and self-expression. Despite, or because of, Greece's current economic woes, it has seen a palpable burst of artistic activity and creativity. While savage cuts in meagre state-arts funding have some sectors reeling, an alternative cultural scene is fighting back with low-budget films, artist collectives, and small underground theatres and galleries popping up in the capital.

Modern Greek Art

Until the start of the 19th century, the primary art form in Greece was Byzantine religious painting. There was little artistic output under Ottoman rule, during which Greece essentially missed the Renaissance.

Byzantine church frescoes and icons depicted scenes from the life of Christ and figures of the saints. The 'Cretan school' of icon painting, influenced by the Italian Renaissance and artists fleeing to Crete after the fall of Constantinople, combined technical brilliance and dramatic richness. Cretan-born Renaissance painter El Greco ('The Greek' in Spanish), née Dominikos Theotokopoulos, got his grounding in the tradition of late-Byzantine fresco painting before moving to Spain in 1577.

Modern Greek art per se evolved after Independence, when painting became more secular, focusing on portraits, nautical themes and the War of Independence. Major 19th-century painters included Dionysios Tsokos, Theodoros Vryzakis, Nikiforos Lytras and Nicholas Gyzis, a leading artist of the Munich School (where many Greek artists of the day studied).

Early-20th-century artists such as Konstantinos Parthenis, Fotis Kontoglou, Konstantinos Kaleas and, later, the expressionist George Bouzianis, drew on their heritage and incorporated developments in modern art.

Leading 20th-century artists include cubist Nikos Hatzikyriakos-Ghikas, surrealist artist and poet Nikos Engonopoulos, Yiannis Tsarouhis, Panayiotis Tetsis, Yannis Moralis, Dimitris Mytaras and pioneer of the Arte Povera movement, Yiannis Kounellis.

The Athens National Gallery has the most extensive collection of Greek 20th-century art, with significant collections at the New Art Gallery on Rhodes and the Museum of Contemporary Art on Andros.

Modern and contemporary sculpture is shown at the National Sculpture Gallery in Athens. Greece's marble sculpture tradition endures on Tinos, birthplace of foremost modern sculptors Dimitrios Filippotis and Yannoulis Halepas, as well as Costas Tsoclis, whose work fills the island's new museum.

Contemporary Greek Art Scene

Contemporary Greek art has been gaining exposure in Greece and abroad, with a growing number of Greek artists participating in international art events. The Greek arts scene has become more vibrant, less isolated and more experimental, and Athens' street art is gaining

Athens' metro stations feature an impressive showcase of Greek art from prominent artists including Yannis Gaitis (Larisa), Giorgos Zongolopoulos (Syntagma) and Alekos Fassianos (Metaxourgio), whose work fetches record prices for a living Greek artist.

GREECE ON THE SCREEN

Greece's new-generation filmmakers have been gaining attention for what some critics have dubbed the 'weird wave' of Greek cinema. The award-winning films of Yorgos Lanthimos (*Alps; The Lobster; The Killing of a Sacred Deer*) and Athina Rachel Tsangari (*Attenburg; Chevalier*), at the weirder end of the scale, represent a new style of independent films emerging from Greece.

While Ektoras Kygizos' extraordinary *Boy Eating Bird Food* is an allegory for Greece's current plight, other notable recent films are a product of it – small, creative collaborations largely produced in the absence of state or industry funding.

The focus on Greek film comes in the wake of the loss of Greece's most critically acclaimed filmmaker, Theo Angelopoulos, who was hit by a motorcycle during a film shoot in 2012. Angelopoulos was renowned for his epic, dreamlike cinematic style and long takes, and his melancholy symbolism and commentary on modern Greek history and society.

International festivals may be lauding art-house Greek films, but domestic audiences prefer comedies such as box-office hits *Nisos* (2009), *Sirens in the Aegean* (2005) and *What If* (2011), a film set amid the country's economic crisis.

Few Greek films get commercial releases abroad. Exceptions include Tasos Boulmetis' *A Touch of Spice* (2003), Pantelis Voulgaris' *Brides* (2004) and Yannis Smaragdis' big-budget *El Greco* (2007). Greece's most internationally acclaimed film remains the classic 1964 Oscar-winner *Zorba the Greek*.

recognition. Many Greek artists have studied and made their homes and reputations abroad, but a new wave is returning or staying put, contributing to a fresh artistic energy. Watch for work by street artist, Cacao Rocks, the collages of Chryssa Romanos, painter Lucas Samaras, kinetic artist Takis, and sculptor Stephen Antonakos.

Greeks have had unprecedented exposure to global art through major international exhibitions held in impressive new art venues, small private galleries and artist-run initiatives such as the annual Hydra School Project. Since 2007, Biennales in Athens have put the capital on the international contemporary-arts circuit.

Modern Greek Literature

Greek literature virtually ceased under Ottoman rule, and was then stifled by conflict over language – Ancient Greek versus the vernacular Demotic or *katharevousa*, a compromise between the two (*dimotiki* won in 1976).

One of the most important works of early Greek literature is the 17th-century 10,000-line epic poem 'Erotokritos', by Crete's Vitsenzos Kornaros. Its 15-syllable rhyming verses are still recited in Crete's famous *mantinadhes* (rhyming couplets) and put to music.

Greece's most celebrated (and translated) 20th-century novelist is the controversial Nikos Kazantzakis, whose novels are full of drama and larger-than-life characters, such as the magnificent title character in *Alexis Zorbas* (Zorba the Greek). Another great novelist of the time, Stratis Myrivilis, wrote the classics *Vasilis Arvanitis* and *The Mermaid Madonna*.

Eminent 20th-century Greek poets include Egypt-born Constantine Cavafy and Nobel-prize laureates George Seferis and Odysseus Elytis, awarded in 1963 and 1979 respectively.

Greece's literary giants include Iakovos Kambanellis, Alexandros Papadiamantis, Kostis Palamas and poet-playwright Angelos Sikelianos. The plays of Yiorgos Skourtis and Pavlos Matesis have been translated and performed abroad.

The quirky, Rebus-like Inspector Haritos in Petros Markaris' popular crime series provides an enjoyable insight into crime and corruption in Athens. *Che Committed Suicide* (2010), *Basic Shareholder* (2009), *The Late Night News* (2005) and *Zone Defence* (2007) have been translated into English.

Contemporary Writers

Greece has a prolific publishing industry but scant fiction is translated into English.

Contemporary Greek writers have made small inroads into foreign markets, such as Apostolos Doxiadis with his international bestseller *Uncle Petros and Goldbach's Conjecture*, and award-winning children's writer Eugene Trivizas.

Greek publisher Kedros' modern-literature translation series includes Dido Sotiriou's *Farewell Anatolia*, Maro Douka's *Fool's God* and Kostas Mourselas' bestselling *Red-Dyed Hair,* which was made into a popular TV series. Other prominent writers in translation include Ersi Sotiropoulou, Thanassis Valtinos, Rhea Galanaki, Ziranna Ziteli, Petros Markaris and Ioanna Karystiani. Christos Ikonomou's *Something Will Happen, You'll See* was a recent bestseller in Greece.

Bypassing the translation issue, London-based Panos Karnezis *(The Maze; The Birthday Party; The Convent; The Fugitives)* and Soti Triantafyllou *(Poor Margo; Albatross; Rare Earths)* write in English. Other notable contemporary authors available in translation include Alexis Stamatis *(Bar Flaubert; American Fugue; The Book of Rain)* and Vangelis Hatziyannidis *(Four Walls; Stolen Time)*.

The memorable opening-credits track from the 1994 film *Pulp Fiction* was based on surf-guitar legend Dirk Dale's 1960s version of *Misirlou* – originally recorded by a Greek *rembetika* (blues) band around 1930.

Music

For most people, Greek music and dance evoke images of spirited, high-kicking laps around the dance floor to the tune of the bouzouki (a musical instrument in the lute family). Greece's strong and enduring music tradition, however, is a rich mosaic of musical influences and styles.

While many leading performers draw on traditional folk, *laïka* (popular urban folk) and *rembetika* (blues), Greece's vibrant music scene is also pumping out its share of pop, club dance music, jazz, rock and even hip-hop.

Traditional Folk Music

Traditional folk music was shunned by the Greek bourgeoisie after Independence, when they looked to Europe – and classical music and opera – rather than their Eastern or 'peasant' roots.

Greece's regional folk music is generally divided into *nisiotika* (the lighter, upbeat music of the islands) and the more grounded *dimotika* of the mainland – where the *klarino* (clarinet) is prominent and lyrics refer to hard times, war and rural life. The spirited music of Crete, dominated by the Cretan *lyra* (a pear-shaped, three-string, bowed instrument) and

---

GREEK GIG GUIDE

In summer Greece's leading acts perform in outdoor concerts around the country. In winter they perform in clubs in Athens and large regional towns.

Authentic folk music is harder to find. The best bet is at regional *panigyria* (open-air festivals) during summer. Look for posters, often around telephone and power poles, or ask around.

Athens' live-music scene includes intimate *rembetika* (blues) clubs and glitzy, expensive, cabaret-style venues known as *bouzoukia*. Second-rate *bouzoukia* clubs are referred to as *skyladhika* (doghouses) – apparently because the crooning singers resemble a whining dog. *Bouzoukia* are the venues for flower-throwing (plate-smashing is rare these days), wanton (and expensive) displays of exuberance, excess and *kefi* (good spirits or mojo). *Opa!*

REMBETIKA: THE GREEK BLUES

Known as the Greek 'blues', *rembetika* emerged in Greece's urban underground and has strongly influenced the sound of Greek popular music.

Two styles make up what is broadly known as *rembetika*. *Smyrneika* or Cafe Aman music emerged in the mid- to late-19th century in the thriving port cities of Smyrna and Constantinople, which had large Greek populations, and in Thessaloniki, Volos, Syros and Athens. With a rich vocal style, haunting *amanedhes* (vocal improvisations) and occasional Turkish lyrics, its sound had more Eastern influence. Predominant instruments were the violin, *outi* (oud), guitar, mandolin, *kanonaki* and *santouri* (a flat multistringed instrument). The second style, dominated by the six-stringed bouzouki, evolved in Piraeus.

After the influx of refugees from Asia Minor in Piraeus following the 1922 population exchange (many also went to America, where *rembetika* was recorded in the 1920s), the two styles somewhat overlapped and *rembetika* became the music of the ghettos. Infused with defiance, nostalgia and lament, the songs reflected life's bleaker themes and *manges* (streetwise outcasts) who sang and danced in the *tekedhes* (hash dens that inspired many songs).

In the mid-1930s, the Metaxas dictatorship tried to wipe out the subculture through censorship, police harassment and raids on *tekedhes*. People were arrested for carrying a bouzouki. Many artists stopped performing and recording, though the music continued clandestinely. After WWII, a new wave of *rembetika* emerged that eliminated much of its seedy side.

Rembetika legends include Markos Vamvakaris, who became popular with the first bouzouki group in the early 1930s, composer Vasilis Tsitsanis, Apostolos Kaldaras, Yiannis Papaioannou, Giorgos Mitsakis and Apostolos Hatzihristou, and the songstresses Sotiria Bellou and Marika Ninou, whose life inspired Costas Ferris' 1983 film *Rembetiko*.

Interest in genuine *rembetika* was revived in the late 1970s to early 1980s – particularly among students and intellectuals – and it continues to be rediscovered by new generations.

Rembetika ensembles perform seated in a row and traditionally play acoustically. A characteristic feature is an improvised introduction called a *taxim*.

lute, remains a dynamic musical tradition, with regular performances and recordings by new-generation exponents.

Laïka & Entehna

Laïka (popular or urban folk music) is Greece's most popular music. A mainstream offshoot of *rembetika*, *laïka* emerged in the late 1950s and '60s, when clubs in Athens became bigger and glitzier, and the music more commercial. The bouzouki went electric and the sentimental tunes about love, loss, pain and emigration came to embody the nation's spirit. The late Stelios Kazantzidis was the big voice of this era, along with Grigoris Bithikotsis.

Classically trained composers Mikis Theodorakis and Manos Hatzidakis led a new style known as *entehni mousiki* ('artistic' music). They drew on *rembetika* and used instruments such as the bouzouki in more symphonic arrangements, and created popular hits from the poetry of Seferis, Elytis, Ritsos and Kavadias.

Composer Yiannis Markopoulos later introduced rural folk music and traditional instruments such as the *lyra, santouri,* violin and *kanonaki* into the mainstream, and brought folk performers such as Crete's legendary Nikos Xylouris to the fore.

During the junta years the music of Theodorakis and Markopoulos became a form of political expression (Theodorakis' music was banned and the composer jailed).

The sound of the bouzouki, immortalised in Mikis Theodorakis' 1960s soundtrack to *Zorba the Greek*, has become synonymous with Greece. The long-necked lute-like instrument became central to *rembetika* and dominates *laïka*.

Contemporary & Pop Music

While few Greek performers have made it big internationally – 1970s genre-defying icons Nana Mouskouri and Demis Roussos remain the best known – Greece has a strong local music scene, from traditional and pop music to Greek rock, heavy metal, rap and electronic dance.

Some of the most interesting music emerging from Greece fuses elements of folk, *laïka* and *entehna* with Western influences. One of the most whimsical examples was Greece's tongue-in-cheek 2013 Eurovision contender, in which *rembetika* veteran Agathonas Iakovidis teamed up with the ska-Balkan rhythms of Thessaloniki's kilt-wearing Koza Mostra.

Big names in contemporary Greek music include Dionysis Savopoulos, dubbed the Bob Dylan of Greece, and seasoned performers George Dalaras and Haris Alexiou.

Standout performers include Cypriot-born Alkinoos Ioannides, Eleftheria Arvanitakiis, Savina Yannatou, and ethnic-jazz-fusion artists Kristi Stasinopoulou, Mode Plagal and the Cretan-inspired Haïnides.

Headline *laïka* performers include Yiannis Ploutarhos, Antonis Remos and Thanos Petrelis while the pop scene sees a steady stream of performers creating a uniquely Greek sound. Listen for Σtella, Kid Moxie, Sarah P and Keep Shelley in Athens.

Byzantine music is mostly heard in Greek churches these days, though Byzantine choirs perform in concerts in Greece and abroad, and the music has influenced folk music.

Classical Music & Opera

Despite classical music and opera appealing to an (albeit growing) minority of Greeks, this field is where Greece has made the most significant international contribution, most notably composers Mikis Theodorakis and Manos Hatzidakis and opera diva Maria Callas.

Dimitris Mitropoulos led the New York Philharmonic in the 1950s, while composers include Stavros Xarhakos and the late Yannis Xenakis. Leading contemporary performers include pianist Dimitris Sgouros, tenor Mario Frangoulis and sopranos Elena Kelessidi and Irini Tsirakidou.

The country's concert halls and major cultural festivals such as the Hellenic Festival offer rich international programs, while opera buffs have the Greek National Opera and Syros' Apollo Theatre.

Greek Dance

Greeks have danced since the dawn of Hellenism. Some folk dances derive from the ritual dances performed in ancient temples – ancient vases depict a version of the well-known *syrtos* folk dance. Dancing was later part of military education; in times of occupation it became an act of defiance and a covert way to keep fit.

Men dance the often spectacular solo *zeïmbekiko* (whirling, meditative improvisations with roots in *rembetika*). Women do the sensuous *tsifteteli*, a svelte, sinewy show of femininity evolved from the Middle Eastern belly dance.

Regional dances, like musical styles, vary across Greece. The slow and dignified *tsamikos* reflects the often cold and insular nature of mountain life, while the brighter islands gave rise to light, springy dances such as the *ballos* and the *syrtos*. The Pontian Greeks' vigorous and warlike dances such as the *kotsari* reflect years of altercations with their Turkish neighbours. Crete has its graceful *syrtos,* the fast and triumphant *maleviziotiko* and the dynamic *pentozali*, with its agility-testing high kicks and leaps. The so-called 'Zorba dance', or *syrtaki*, is a stylised dance for two or three dancers with arms linked on each other's shoulders, though the modern variation is danced in a long circle with an ever-quickening beat. Women and men traditionally danced separately and had their own dances, except in courtship dances such as the *sousta*.

Folk-dance groups throughout Greece preserve regional traditions. The best place to see folk dancing is at regional festivals and the Dora Stratou Dance Theatre in Athens.

Contemporary dance is gaining prominence in Greece, with leading local troupes taking their place among the international line-up at the Athens International Dance Festival.

Architecture

Cast your eyes around most major Western cities and you'll find a reinterpretation of Classical Greek architecture. The Renaissance was inspired by the ancient style, as were the neoclassical movement and the British Greek Revival. For those with an eye to the past, part of the allure of Greece is the sheer volume of its well-preserved temples. Stand in the ruins of the Parthenon, and with a little imagination it's easy to transport yourself back to classical 5th-century Greece.

Minoan Magnificence

Most of our knowledge of Greek architecture proper begins at around 2000 BC with the Minoans, who were based in Crete but whose influence spread throughout the Aegean to include the Cyclades. Minoan architects are famous for having constructed technologically advanced, labyrinthine palace complexes. The famous site at Knossos is one of the largest. Usually characterised as 'palaces', these sites were in fact multifunctional settlements that were the primary residences of royalty and priests, but housed some plebs too. Large Minoan villages, such as those of Gournia and Palekastro in Crete, also included internal networks of paved roads that extended throughout the countryside to link the settlements with the palaces. More Minoan palace-era sophistication exists at Phaestos, Malia and Ancient Zakros, also in Crete.

Several gigantic volcanic eruptions rocked the region in the mid-15th century BC, causing geological ripple effects that at the very least caused big chunks of palace to fall to the ground. The Minoans resolutely rebuilt their crumbling palaces on an even grander scale, only to have more natural disasters wipe them out again. The latter effected an architectural chasm that was filled by the emerging Mycenaean rivals on mainland Greece.

The distinctive blue-and-white Cycladic–style architecture most associated with the Greek islands was pragmatic and functional. The cuboid flat-roofed houses, huddled together along labyrinthine alleys, were designed to guard against strong winds and pirates.

Grandeur of Knossos

According to myth, the man tasked with designing a maze to withhold the dreaded Minotaur was famous Athenian inventor Daedalus, father of Icarus. He also designed the Palace of Knossos for King Minos.

First discovered by a Cretan, Milos Kalokairinos, in 1878, it wasn't until 1900 that the ruins of Knossos were unearthed by Englishman Sir Arthur Evans. The elaborate palace complex at Knossos was originally formed largely as an administrative settlement surrounding the main palace, which comprised the main buildings arranged around a large central courtyard (1250 sq metres). Over time the entire settlement was rebuilt and extended. Long, raised causeways formed main corridors; narrow labyrinthine chambers flanked the palace walls (this meandering floor plan, together with the graphic ritual importance of bulls, inspired the myth of the labyrinth and the Minotaur). The compound featured strategically placed interior light-wells, sophisticated ventilation systems, aqueducts, freshwater irrigation wells and bathrooms with extensive plumbing and drainage systems.

Thanks to its restoration, today's Knossos is one of the easiest ruins for your imagination to take hold of.

TOP FIVE ISLAND ORIGINALS

Pyrgi See the medieval, labyrinthine, vaulted island village of Pyrgi in Chios, for its unique Genoese designs of intricate, geometric, grey-and-white facades.

Oia Squint at the volcanic rock-hewn clifftop village of Oia in Santorini, with its dazzlingly whitewashed island streetscapes and homes.

Lefkada Town Discover the strangely attractive wooden-framed houses of Lefkada Town: the lower floors are panelled in wood, while the upper floors are lined in painted sheet metal or corrugated iron.

Rhodes Old Town Wander through this medieval walled town, where the sunshine turns the cobbled streets a honey hue.

Halki Stay in tower houses, the traditional homes of sea captains, with views of returning vessels.

Classical Compositions

The classical age (5th to 4th centuries BC) is when most Greek architectural clichés converge. This is when temples became characterised by the famous orders of columns, particularly the Doric, Ionic and Corinthian.

The mother of all Doric structures is the 5th century BC Parthenon, the ultimate in architectural bling: a gleaming, solid marble crown. To this day, it's probably *the* most obsessively photographed jewel in all of Greece.

In the meantime, the Greek colonies of the Asia Minor coast were creating their own Ionic order, designing a column base in several tiers and adding more flutes. This more graceful order's capital (the head) received an ornamented necking, and Iktinos fused elements of its design in the Parthenon. This order is used on the Acropolis' Temple of Athena Nike and the Erechtheion, where the famous Caryatids regally stand.

Towards the tail end of the classical period, the Corinthian column was in limited vogue. Featuring a single or double row of ornate leafy scrolls (usually the very sculptural acanthus), the order was subsequently adopted by the Romans and used only on Corinthian temples in Athens. The Temple of Olympian Zeus, completed during Emperor Hadrian's reign, is a grand, imposing structure. Another temple design, the graceful, circular temple *tholos* (dome) style, was used for the great Sanctuary of Athena Pronea at Delphi.

The Greek theatre design is a hallmark of the classical period and had a round stage, radiating a semicircle of steeply banked stone benches that seated many thousands. Cleverly engineered acoustics meant every spectator could hear every syllable uttered on the stage below. Many ancient Greek theatres are still used for summer festivals, music concerts and plays.

Hellenistic Citizens

In the twilight years of the Classical Age (from about the late 4th century BC), cosmopolitan folk started to grow weary of temples, casting their gaze towards a more decadent urban style. The Hellenistic architect was in hot demand for private homes and palace makeovers as wealthy citizens, dignitaries and political heavyweights lavishly remodelled their abodes in marble, and striking mosaics were displayed as status symbols (read *more* bling). The best Hellenistic ancient home displays are the grand houses at Delos.

Byzantine Zeal

Church-building was particularly expressive during Byzantine rule in Greece (from around AD 700). The original Greek Byzantine model

features a distinctive cross-shape; essentially a central dome supported by four arches on piers and flanked by vaults, with smaller domes
at the four corners and three more apses to the east. Theologian architects
opted for spectacular devotional mosaics and frescoes instead of carvings for the stylistic religious interiors. In Athens, the very appealing
12th-century Church of Agios Eleftherios incorporates fragments of a
classical frieze in Pentelic marble; the charming 11th-century Church
of Kapnikarea sits stranded, smack bang in the middle of downtown
Athens – its interior flooring is of coloured marble, and the external
brickwork, which alternates with stone, is set in patterns.

Ottoman Offerings

Remarkably few monuments are left to catalogue after four centuries of
Ottoman Turkish rule (16th to 19th centuries). Though many mosques and
their minarets have sadly crumbled or are in serious disrepair, some terrific
Ottoman–Turkish examples still survive. These include the prominent pink-
domed Mosque of Süleyman in Rhodes' Old Town. The Fethiye Mosque and
Turkish Baths are two of Athens' few surviving Ottoman reminders.

Neoclassical Splendour

Regarded by experts as the most beautiful neoclassical building worldwide, the 1885 Athens Academy reflects Greece's post-independence
yearnings for grand and geometric forms, and Hellenistic detail. Renowned Danish architect Theophile Hansen drew inspiration from
the Erechtheion to design the Academy's Ionic–style column entrance
(guarded over by Apollo and Athena); the great interior oblong hall is
lined with marble seating, and Austrian painter Christian Griepenkerl
was commissioned to decorate its elaborate ceiling and wall paintings.
In a similar vein, the Doric columns of the Temple of Hephaestus influenced Theophile's solid marble National Library, while Christian Hansen
(Theophile's brother) was responsible for the handsome but more sedate
Athens University, with its clean lines.

Meticulously restored neoclassical mansions house notable museums
such as the acclaimed Benaki Museum.

Many provincial towns also display beautiful domestic adaptations of
neoclassicism. In Symi, the harbour at Gialos is flanked by colourful neoclassical facades (still striking, even if a little derelict).

Modern Ideas

Athens today is embracing a sophisticated look-both-ways architectural
aesthetic by showcasing its vast collection of antiquities and archaeological heritage in evolutionary buildings, and by beautifying landscapes for

KNOW YOUR DORIC FROM YOUR CORINTHIAN

Columns are columns are columns, right? Recognising the differences between them is,
in fact, the easiest way to differentiate between the three distinct architectural orders of
Ancient Greece.

Doric The most simple of the three styles. The shaft (the main part of the column) is
plain and has 20 sides, while the capital (the head) is formed in a simple circle. Also,
there's no base. An obvious example of this is the Parthenon.

Ionic Look out for the ridged flutes carved into the column from top to bottom. The capital
is also distinctive for its scrolls, while the base looks like a stack of rings.

Corinthian The most decorative and popular of all three orders. The column is ridged;
however, the distinctive feature is the capital's flowers and leaves, beneath a small scroll.
The base is like that of the Ionic.

THE CAPTAIN'S HOUSE

During the 17th century, Greek ship captains grew increasingly prosperous. Many of them poured their new-found wealth into building lofty homes that towered over the traditional village houses. These captains' houses are now dotted throughout the islands, and many have been given a new lease on life as boutique hotels or restaurants.

While the size of the house often reflected the wealth of a captain, some of the smallest of these 400-year-old homes are the most grand. Captains' houses didn't need to be large as their owners spent so much time at sea. Whitewashed walls stretch upward to the soaring resin ceiling, often intricately painted with elaborate, colourful patterns. The windows are sea-facing and placed very high, often with wooden lofts to reach them. This was to let the heat out in summer and also so the captain's wife could watch the sea for the arrival of her husband's ship. The traditional stone doorways, or *pyliones*, are hand-carved with symbolic pictures. Corn means good harvest, birds mean peace, the cross brings safety and the sunflowers sunlight. The number of ropes carved around the perimeter of the door shows how many ships the captain had.

Some of the finest examples of these houses are found in Lindos, on Rhodes.

pedestrian zones to improve the urban environment. Examples include the well-designed facelift of the historic centre, including its spectacular floodlighting (designed by the renowned Pierre Bideau) of the ancient promenade, and the cutting-edge spaces emerging from once-drab and derelict industrial zones, such as the Technopolis gasworks arts complex in Gazi.

Best Futuristic Athens

Despite its massive contribution to ancient architecture, Athens is not stuck in the past. Its modern architects are innovative and fearless.

The Acropolis Museum (p73) is a relatively new space that houses Greece's antiquities. Designed by Bernard Tschumi, the museum features an internal glass *cella* (inner room) mirroring the Parthenon, with the same number of columns (clad in steel) and a glass floor overlooking excavated ruins in situ.

The Stavros Niarchos Foundation Cultural Center (SNFCC; p120) was designed by the Pritzker Prize–winning architect Renzo Piano, and opened in 2016. A multifunctional arts and entertainment venue, it houses the National Library of Greece and the National Opera amid natural surroundings that link the centre's park (at the old horse-racing tracks in Faliro) with the sea.

The Planetarium (p88) is one of the world's largest digital hemispherical domes, with a dome-diameter of 25 metres. It provides 360-degree 3D virtual rides through the galaxy in a space the size of two-and-a-half basketball courts.

The Athens Olympic Complex (p93) was designed by well-known Spanish architect Santiago Calatrata to house the 2004 Olympics. This complex has a striking, ultra-modern glass-and-steel roof, which is suspended by cables from large arches. The laminated glass, in the shape of two giant leaves, is capable of reflecting 90% of the sunlight.

The abandoned FIX brewery in central Athens has been hollowed out and renovated to create 20,000 sq metres of space to house the National Museum of Contemporary Art (p76). Built in the 1950s, the building retains much of its post-war industrial architecture, including the horizontal feel achieved with lateral linear glass, while one side of the facade has been covered in stone reminiscent of the riverbed that was once here. Inside, it's all about glass and light, with a sculpture garden on the roof.

Nature & Wildlife

While Greece is a perfect place to rub shoulders with ancient statues, it's equally ideal for getting up close to nature. Hike through wildflowers, come eye to eye with a logger-head turtle, or simply stretch out on a beach. Greece has something for everyone who wants to get out and explore.

Experiencing the Outdoors

Greek Geography

No matter where you go in Greece, it's impossible to be much more than 100km from the sea. Rugged mountains and seemingly innumerable islands dominate the landscape, which was shaped by submerging seas, volcanic explosions and mineral-rich terrain. The mainland covers 131,944 sq km, with an indented coastline stretching for 15,020km. Mountains rise more than 2000m and occasionally tumble down into plains, particularly in Thessaly and Thrace. Meanwhile, the Aegean and Ionian Seas link together the country's 1400 islands, with just 169 of them inhabited. These islands fill 400,000 sq km of territorial waters.

During the Triassic, Jurassic, Cretaceous and even later geological periods, Greece was a shallow, oxygen-rich sea. The continuous submerging of land created large tracts of limestone through the whole submarine land mass. Later, as the land emerged from the sea to form the backbone of the current topography, a distinctly eroded landscape, with crystalline rocks and other valuable minerals, began to appear, marking the spine that links the north and south of the mainland today. Limestone caves are a major feature of this karst landscape, shaped by the dissolution of a soluble layer of bedrock.

Volcanic activity once regularly hit Greece with force – one of the world's largest volcanic explosions was on Santorini around 1650 BC. Today earthquakes continue to shake the country on a smaller scale, but with almost predictable frequency. In 1999, a 5.9-magnitude earthquake near Athens killed nearly 150 people and left thousands homeless. Since 2006, the country has had six quakes ranging from 6.4 to 6.9 in magnitude. None caused major damage. To check out Greece's explosive past, visit the craters of Santorini, Nisyros and Polyvotis.

> The Greek Orthodox Church is the second largest landowner in Greece.

Wildflowers

Greece is endowed with a variety of flora unrivalled in Europe. The wildflowers are spectacular, with more than 6000 species, including more than 100 varieties of orchid. They continue to thrive because most of the land is inadequate for intensive agriculture and has therefore escaped the ravages of chemical fertilisers.

Wildflowers are particularly abundant in the Lefka Ori Mountains in Crete. Trees begin to blossom as early as the end of February in warmer areas and the wildflowers start to appear in March. During spring, hillsides are carpeted with flowers, which seem to sprout even from the rocks. By summer the flowers have disappeared from everywhere but the northern mountainous regions. Autumn brings a new period of blossoming.

> *Herbs in Cooking* is an illustrative book by Maria and Nikos Psilakis that can be used as both an identification guide and a cookbook for Greek dishes seasoned with local herbs.

Herbs grow wild throughout much of Greece, and you'll see locals out picking fresh herbs for their kitchen. Locally grown herbs are also increasingly sold as souvenirs and are generally organic.

Forests

The lush forests that once covered ancient Greece are increasingly rare. Having been decimated by thousands of years of clearing for grazing, boat-building and housing, they've more recently suffered from severe forest fires. Northern Greece is the only region that has retained significant areas of native forest – there are mountainsides covered with dense thickets of hop hornbeam *(Ostrya carpinifolia)*, noted for its lavish display of white-clustered flowers. Another common species is the Cyprus plane *(Platanus orientalis insularis)*, which thrives wherever there's ample water.

Watching for Wildlife

On the Ground

In areas widely inhabited by humans, you're unlikely to spot any wild animals other than the odd fox, weasel, hare or rabbit. The more remote mountains of northern Greece continue to support a wide range of wildlife, including wild dogs and shepherds' dogs, which often roam higher pastures on grazing mountains and should be given a wide berth.

Greece is the most seismically active country in Europe, with more than half of the continent's volcanic activity.

The brown bear, Europe's largest land mammal, still manages to survive in the Pindos Mountains, the Peristeri range that rises above the Prespa Lakes, and in the mountains that lie along the Bulgarian border. It's estimated that only around 200 survive; your best bet for seeing one is at the **Arcturos Bear Sanctuary** (www.arcturos.gr; Nymfeo) in Macedonia.

The protected grey wolf is officially classified as stable, with an estimated 200 to 300 surviving in the wild. It's believed that up to 100 are killed annually by indiscriminate (and illegal) use of poison baits in retaliation for the occasional attacks on livestock. The Greek government and insurance companies pay compensation for lost livestock but it doesn't appear to slow the killings. The surviving wolves live in the Pindos Mountains and the Dadia Forest Reserve area. Head to the Arcturos Wolf Sanctuary in Agrapidia, near Florina, which houses wolves rescued from illegal captivity.

The golden jackal is a strong candidate for Greece's most misunderstood mammal. Although its diet is 50% vegetarian (the other 50% is

---

NATIONAL PARKS

National parks were first established in Greece in 1938 with the creation of Mt Olympus National Park. There are now 10 national parks and two marine parks, which aim to protect Greece's unique flora and fauna.

Facilities for visitors are often basic; abundant walking trails are not always maintained, and the clutch of refuges is very simple. To most, the facilities matter little when compared to nature's magnificent backdrop. It's well worth experiencing the wild side of Greece in one of these settings.

Mt Parnitha National Park (p136) Very popular wooded parkland north of Athens; home to the red deer.

National Marine Park of Alonnisos and Northern Sporades (p481) Covers six islands and 22 islets in the Sporades and is home to monk seals, dolphins and rare birdlife.

Samaria Gorge (p310) Spectacular gorge in Crete and a refuge for the *kri-kri* (Cretan goat).

National Marine Park of Zakynthos (p529) An Ionian refuge for loggerhead turtles.

Ainos National Park (p515) The only island park, on Kefallonia, the stand of forest is home to a single species of endemic fir and small wild horses.

DON'T BE A BOAR

Greece's relationship with its wildlife has not been a happy one. Hunting wild animals is a popular Greek activity, as a means of providing food. This is particularly true in mountainous regions. Despite signs forbidding hunting, Greek hunters often shoot freely at any potential game. While this can include rare and endangered species, the main game is often wild boars, which have been around since antiquity. Considered destructive and cunning animals, the number of wild boars has increased in recent decades, likely due to a lower number of predators. Many argue that hunting is an important means of culling them. There is also an increasing number of wild-boar breeding farms, with boar showing up on many menus.

made up of carrion, reptiles and small mammals), it has traditionally shouldered much of the blame for attacks on stock and has been hunted by farmers as a preventative measure. Near the brink of extinction, it was declared a protected species in 1990 and now survives only in the Fokida district of central Greece and on the island of Samos.

Once roaming across all of mainland Greece, the graceful red deer is now restricted to the Sithonian Peninsula, the Rhodopi Mountains bordering Bulgaria, and Mt Parnitha north of Athens. As the largest herbivore in Greece, its population is under constant threat from illegal hunters, making attempts at population redistribution unsuccessful.

Originally brought to the island of Skyros in the 5th century BC by colonists, the diminutive Skyrian horses are an ancient breed that became wild once they had been replaced by agricultural mechanisation. Around 190 survive on the island, approximately 70% of their population. You'll also see these horses featured in the Parthenon friezes.

Greece has an active snake population, and in spring and summer you will inevitably spot them on roads and pathways around the country. Fortunately the majority are harmless, though the viper and the coral snake can cause fatalities. Lizards are in abundance too.

The Hellenic Wildlife Hospital is the oldest and largest wildlife rehabilitation centre in southern Europe.

In the Air

Birdwatchers hit the jackpot in Greece, where much of the country is on north–south migratory paths. Lesvos (Mytilini) in particular draws a regular following of birders from all over Europe, who come to spot some of more than 279 recorded species that stop at the island annually. Storks are among the more visible visitors, arriving in early spring from Africa and returning to the same nests year after year. These are built on electricity poles, chimney tops and church towers, and can weigh up to 50kg. Keep an eye out for them in northern Greece, especially in Thrace in Macedonia. Thrace has the richest colony of fish-eating birds in Europe, including species such as egrets, herons, cormorants and ibises, as well as the rare Dalmatian pelican. The wetlands at the mouth of the Evros River, close to the border with Turkey, are home to two easily identifiable wading birds – the avocet, which has a long curving beak, and the black-winged stilt, which has extremely long pink legs.

Upstream on the Evros River in Thrace, the dense forests and rocky outcrops of the 72 sq km Dadia Forest Reserve play host to Europe's largest range of birds of prey. Thirty-six of the 38 European species can be seen here, and it is a breeding ground for 23 of them. Permanent residents include the giant black vulture, whose wingspan reaches 3m, the griffon vulture and the golden eagle. Europe's last 15 pairs of royal eagles nest on the river delta.

Conserving Nature

Pelicans and pygmy cormorants (www.spp.gr)

Birdlife (www.ornithologiki.gr)

Wildflowers (www.greekmountain flora.info)

Sea turtles (www.archelon.gr)

More than 350 pairs of the rare Eleonora's falcon (60% of the world's population) nest on the island of Piperi in the Sporades and on Tilos, which is also home to the very rare Bonelli's eagle and the shy, cormorant-like Mediterranean shag.

Under the Sea

As Europe's most endangered marine mammal, the monk seal *(Monachus monachus)* ekes out an extremely precarious existence in Greece. Approximately 200 to 250 monk seals, about 50% of the world's population, are found in the Ionian and Aegean Seas. Small colonies also live on the island of Alonnisos, and there have been reported sightings on Tilos.

The waters around Zakynthos are home to the last large sea turtle colony in Europe, that of the endangered loggerhead turtle *(Caretta caretta)*. Loggerheads also nest in smaller numbers in the Peloponnese and on Kefallonia and Crete. Greece's turtles have many hazards to dodge – entanglement in fishing nets and boat propellers, consumption of floating rubbish, and the destruction of their nesting beaches by sun loungers and beach umbrellas that threaten their eggs. It doesn't help that the turtles' nesting time coincides with the European summer holiday season.

There is still the chance that you will spot dolphins from a ferry deck, though a number of the species are now considered vulnerable. The number of common dolphins *(Delphinus delphis)* has dropped considerably in the past decade. The main threats to dolphins are a diminished food supply and entanglement in fishing nets.

Loggerhead turtle hatchlings use the journey from the nest to the sea to build up their strength. Helping the baby turtles to the sea can actually lower their chances of survival.

Environmental Issues

Environmental awareness is beginning to seep into the fabric of Greek society, leading to slow but positive change. Environmental education happens in schools, recycling is common in cities, and even in the smallest villages you may find organic restaurants and environmentally sustainable businesses. However, problems such as deforestation and soil erosion date back thousands of years. Live cultivation, goats, construction and industry have all taken their toll.

Illegal development of mainly coastal areas, and building in forested or protected areas, have gained momentum in Greece since the 1970s. Despite attempts at introducing laws, and protests by locals and environmental groups, corruption and the lack of an infrastructure to enforce the laws means little is done to abate the land-grab. The issue is complicated by population growth and increased urban sprawl. Developments often put a severe strain on water supplies and endangered wildlife. While a few developments have been torn down, in more cases illegal buildings are legalised as they offer much-needed affordable housing.

In 2014 NATO's plan to decommission 700 tonnes of Syria's chemical weapons off the southern coast of Crete was protested by more than 10,000 islanders. Scientists claimed that seawater would neutralise the chemicals within 90 days, but after Albania, Thailand, Belgium, Germany and Norway refused to have the process take place in their waters, the UN approved the international waters between Crete and Malta. Protesters claimed that the effectiveness of hydrolysis was unclear, as was the impact of the discharge on the Mediterranean's marine ecosystems and tourism. Sadly, only time will tell if they were right.

Greece's economic troubles have also impacted the environment. The lifting of the diesel ban in Athens in 2012 decreased air quality as people opted for cheaper transport. As heating oil tripled in price, people turned to burning wood, often treated, as well as garbage to keep warm. Wintertime particle pollution increased by 30% on some evenings, with lead and arsenic particles found in the air.

Survival Guide

Directory A–Z

Accommodation

Greece's plethora of accommodation means that, whatever your taste or budget, there is somewhere to suit your needs. All places to stay are subject to strict price controls set by the tourist police. By law, a notice must be displayed in every room, stating the category of the room and the price charged in each season. It's difficult to generalise accommodation prices in Greece as rates depend entirely on the season and location. Don't expect to pay the same price for a double room on one of the islands as you would in central Greece or Athens.

When considering hotel prices, take note of the following points:

➡ Prices include community tax and VAT (value-added tax).

➡ A 10% surcharge may be added for stays of fewer than three nights, but this is not mandatory.

➡ A mandatory charge of 20% is levied for an additional bed (although this is often waived if the bed is for a child).

➡ During July and August accommodation owners will charge the maximum price, which can be as much as double the low-season price. In spring and autumn prices can drop by 20%.

➡ Rip-offs are rare; if you suspect that you have been exploited make a report to the tourist police or the regular police, and they will act swiftly.

Camping

Camping is a decent option, especially in summer. There are almost 350 campgrounds in Greece, found on the majority of islands (with the notable exception of the Saronic Gulf Islands). Standard facilities include hot showers, kitchens, restaurants and minimarkets – and often a swimming pool.

Most campgrounds are open only between May and October although always check ahead; particularly in the north, some don't open until June. The **Panhellenic Camping Association** (🖉 21036 21560; www.greece camping.gr) website lists all of its campgrounds and relevant details.

If you're camping in the height of summer, bring a silver fly sheet to reflect the heat off your tent (dark tents become sweat lodges). Between May and mid-September the weather is warm enough to sleep out under the stars. Many campgrounds have covered areas where tourists who don't have tents can sleep in summer; you can get by with a lightweight sleeping bag. It's a good idea to have a foam pad to lie on, a waterproof cover for your sleeping bag and plenty of bug repellent.

➡ Camping fees are highest from mid-June through to the end of August.

➡ Campgrounds charge €6 to €12 per adult and €3 to €5 for children aged four to 12. There's no charge for children under four.

➡ Tent sites cost from €5 per night.

➡ You can often rent tents for around €5.

➡ Caravan sites start at around €7; car costs are typically €4 to €5.

Domatia

Domatia (literally 'rooms') are the Greek equivalent of the British B&B, minus the breakfast. Once upon a time, domatia were little more than spare rooms in the family home; nowadays, many are purpose-built appendages

BOOK YOUR STAY ONLINE

For more accommodation reviews by Lonely Planet authors, check out http://lonelyplanet.com/hotels/. You'll find independent reviews, as well as recommendations on the best places to stay. Best of all, you can book online.

with fully equipped kitchens. Standards of cleanliness are generally high.

Domatia remain a popular option for budget travellers. Expect to pay from €30 to €60 for a single, and €40 to €80 for a double, depending on whether bathrooms are shared or private, the season and how long you plan to stay. Domatia are found throughout the mainland (except in large cities) and on almost every island that has a permanent population. Many domatia are open only between April and October.

From June to September, domatia owners are out in force, touting for customers. They meet buses and boats, shouting 'room, room!' and often carry photographs of their rooms. In peak season it can prove a mistake not to take up an offer – just be wary of owners who are vague about the location of their accommodation.

Hostels

Most youth hostels in Greece are run by the **Greek Youth Hostel Organisation** (www. athensyhostel.com/index. php/g-y-h-o). There are affiliated hostels in Athens, Olympia, Patra and Thessaloniki on the mainland, and on the island of Crete.

Hostel rates vary from around €10 to €20 for a bed in a dorm and you don't have to be a member to stay in them. Few have curfews.

Hotels

Hotels in Greece are divided into six categories: deluxe, A, B, C, D and E. Hotels are categorised according to the size of the rooms, whether or not they have a bar, and the ratio of bathrooms to beds, rather than standards of cleanliness, comfort of beds and friendliness of staff – all elements that may be of greater relevance to guests.

Prices listed here refer to the high season:

➡ **A and B class** Full amenities, private bathrooms and

> ## SLEEPING PRICE RANGES
>
> We have divided accommodation into budgets based on the rate for a double room in high season (May to August). Unless otherwise stated, all rooms have private bathroom facilities.
>
> **€** less than €60 (under €90 in Athens)
>
> **€€** €60–€150 (from €90–€180 in Athens)
>
> **€€€** more than €150 (more than €180 in Athens)
>
> For the Cyclades, the budgets are based on the rates in July and August. For Mykonos and Santorini only, the price ranges are as follows.
>
> **€** less than €100
>
> **€€** €100–€250
>
> **€€€** more than €250

---

constant hot water; prices range from €60 to €85 for a single and upwards of €100 for a double.

➡ **C class** A snack bar and rooms with private bathrooms, but not necessarily constant hot water; prices range from €40 to €70 for a single in high season and €50 to €90 for a double.

➡ **D class** Generally have shared bathrooms and they may have solar-heated water, meaning hot water is not guaranteed; prices range from €30 to €50 for a single and €40 to €70 for a double.

➡ **E class** Shared bathrooms and hot water may cost extra; prices are around €25 for a single and €35 for a double.

Mountain Refuges

There are 55 mountain refuges dotted around the Greek mainland, Crete and Evia. They range from small huts with outdoor toilets and no cooking facilities to very comfortable modern lodges. They are run by the country's various mountaineering and skiing clubs. Prices start at around €10 per person, depending on the facilities. The EOT (Greek National Tourist Organisation; www. visitgreece.gr) publication *Greece: Mountain Refuges & Ski Centres* has details about

---

each refuge; copies are available at all EOT branches.

Pensions

Pensions are indistinguishable from hotels. They are categorised as A, B or C class. An A-class pension is equivalent in amenities and price to a B-class hotel, a B-class pension is equivalent to a C-class hotel, and a C-class pension is equivalent to a D- or E-class hotel.

Rental Accommodation

A practical way to save money and maximise comfort is to rent a furnished apartment or villa. Many are purpose-built for tourists while others – villas in particular – may be owners' homes that they are not using. Some owners may insist on a minimum stay of a week. A good site to spot prospective villas is www. greekislands.com.

Customs Regulations

There are no longer duty-free restrictions within the EU. Upon entering Greece from outside the EU, customs inspection is usually cursory for foreign tourists and a verbal declaration is generally all that is required. Random searches are still occasionally made for drugs. Import regulations for medicines are strict; if you are taking medication, make sure you get a statement from your doctor before you leave home. It is illegal, for instance, to take codeine into Greece without a doctor's certificate.

It is strictly forbidden to export antiquities (anything more than 100 years old) without an export permit. This crime is second only to drug smuggling in the penalties imposed. It is an offence to remove even the smallest article from an archaeological site. The place to apply for an export permit is the Antique Dealers and Private Collections section of the **Athens Archaeological Service** (Map p78; http://nam.culture.gr; Polygnotou 13, Plaka).

Vehicles

Cars can be brought into Greece for six months without a carnet; only a green card (international third-party insurance) is required. If arriving from Italy, your only proof of entry into the country may be your ferry ticket stub, so don't lose it. From other countries, a passport stamp will be ample evidence.

Discount Cards

Camping Card International (CCI; www.campingcardinternational.com) Gives up to 25% savings in camping fees and third-party liability insurance while in the campground. Valid in over 2900 campsites across Europe.

European Youth Card (www.eyca.org) Available for anyone up to the age of 26 or 30, depending on the country. You don't have to be a resident of Europe. It provides discounts of up to 20% at sights, shops and for some transport. Available from the website or travel agencies in Athens and Thessaloniki for €10.

International Student Identity Card (ISIC; www.isic.org) Entitles the holder to half-price admission to museums and ancient sites, and discounts at some budget hotels and hostels. Available from travel agencies in Athens. Applicants require documents proving their student status, a passport photo and €10. Available to students aged 12 to 30.

Seniors cards Card-carrying EU pensioners can claim a range of benefits such as reduced admission to sites and museums, and discounts on bus and train fares.

Electricity

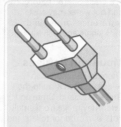

Type C
220V/50Hz

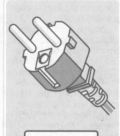

Type F
230V/50Hz

Embassies & Consulates

All foreign embassies in Greece are in Athens and its suburbs, with a few consulates in Thessaloniki.

Albanian Embassy (☎210 687 6200; embassy.athens@mfa.gov.al; Vekiareli 7, Filothei)

Australian Embassy (☎210 870 4000; www.greece.embassy.gov.au; 6th fl, Thon Bldg, cnr Leoforos Alexandras & Leoforos Kifisias, Ambelokipi)

Bulgarian Embassy (☎210 674 8105; www.mfa.bg/embassies/greece; Stratigou Kalari 33a, Psychiko)

Canadian Embassy (☎210 727 3400; www.greece.gc.ca; Ethnikis Antistaseos 48, Halandri)

Cypriot Embassy (☎210 373 4800; Xenofontos 2a, Syntagma; ⏰8am-3.30pm Mon-Fri)

French Embassy (☎210 339 1000; www.ambafrance-gr.org; Leoforos Vasilissis Sofias 7, Syntagma)

German Embassy (☎210 728 5111; www.athen.diplo.de; Dimitriou Karaoli 3, Kolonaki)

Irish Embassy (☎210 723 2771; www.embassyofireland.org; Leoforos Vasileos Konstantinou 5-7, Pangrati)

Italian Embassy (☎210 361 7260; www.ambatene.esteri.it; Sekeri 2, Kolonaki)

Netherlands Embassy (☎210 725 4900; www.nederland wereldwijd.nl/landen/grieken land; Leoforos Vasileos Konstantinou 5-7, Pangrati)

Turkish Embassy (☎210 726 3000; http://athens.emb.mfa. gov.tr; Vasileos Georgiou II 11, Syntagma) Has an additional branch in **Athens** (☎210 672 9830; Vasileos Pavlou 22, Psyhiko) and one in **Thessaloniki** (☎2310 248 452; turkbaskon@ kom.forthnet.gr; Agiou Dimitriou 151).

UK Embassy (☎210 727 2600; www.ukingreece.fco.gov.uk; Ploutarhou 1, Kolonaki) Also has a branch in **Thessaloniki** (☎2310 278 006; www.british-consulate.net/Thessaloniki; Tsimiski 43).

US Embassy (☎210 721 2951; http://athens.usembassy.gov; 91 Vasilissis Sofias, Ilissia) Also has a branch in **Thessaloniki** (☎2310 242 905; https:// gr.usembassy.gov; 7th fl, Tsimiski 43).

Gay & Lesbian Travellers

In a country where the Church still plays a prominent role in shaping society's views on issues such as sexuality, it comes as no surprise that homosexuality is generally frowned upon by many locals – especially outside major cities. While there is no legislation against homosexual activity, it pays to be discreet.

Some areas of Greece are, however, extremely popular destinations for gay and lesbian travellers. Athens has a busy gay scene, but most gay and lesbian travellers head for the islands. Mykonos has long been famous for its bars, beaches and general hedonism, while

Skiathos also has its share of gay hang-outs. The island of Lesvos (Mytilini), birthplace of the lesbian poet Sappho, has become something of a place of pilgrimage for lesbians.

The *Spartacus International Gay Guide* (www.spart acusworld.com), published by Bruno Gmünder (Berlin), is widely regarded as the leading authority on gay travel. The Greece section contains a wealth of information on gay venues everywhere from Alexandroupoli to Xanthi.

Health

Availability & Cost of Healthcare

Although medical training is of a high standard in Greece, the public health service is badly underfunded. Hospitals can be overcrowded, hygiene is not always what it should be, and relatives are expected to bring in food for the patient – which can be a problem for a tourist. Conditions and treatment are much better in private hospitals, which are expensive. All this means that a good health-insurance policy is essential.

➧ If you need an ambulance in Greece call ☎166.

➧ There is at least one doctor on every island, and larger islands have hospitals.

➧ Pharmacies can dispense medicines that are available only on prescription in most European countries.

➧ Consult a pharmacist for minor ailments.

Environmental Hazards

➧ Dangerous snakes include the adder and the less common viper and coral snakes. To minimise the possibilities of being bitten, always wear boots, socks and long trousers when walking through undergrowth where snakes may be present.

➧ Mosquitoes can be an annoying problem, though there is no danger of contracting malaria. The electric mosquito-repellent devices are usually sufficient to keep the insects at bay at night. Choose accommodation that has flyscreen on the windows wherever possible. Some mosquitoes in northern Greece can provoke a severe reaction.

➧ The Asian tiger mosquito (*Aedes albopictus*) may be encountered in mountainous areas. It can be a voracious daytime biter and is known to carry several viruses, including Eastern equine encephalitis, which can affect the central nervous system and cause severe complications and death. Use protective sprays or lotion if you suspect you are being bitten during the day.

Insurance

If you're an EU citizen, a European Health Insurance Card (EHIC) covers you for most medical care but not emergency repatriation or nonemergencies. Citizens from other countries should find out if there is a reciprocal arrangement for free medical care between their country and Greece. If you do need health insurance, make sure you get a policy that covers you for the worst possible scenario, such as an accident requiring an emergency flight home. Find out in advance if your insurance plan will make payments directly to providers or reimburse you later for overseas health expenditures.

Worldwide travel insurance is available at www. lonelyplanet.com/travel-insurance. You can buy, extend and claim online anytime – even if you're already on the road.

Water

Tap water is drinkable and safe in much of Greece but not always in small villages and on some of the islands. Always ask locally if the water is safe and, if in doubt, drink boiled or bought water. Even when water is safe, the substances and bacteria in it may be different from those you are used to and can cause vomiting or diarrhoea. Bottled water is widely available.

Internet Access

There has been a huge increase in the number of hotels and businesses using the internet, and free wi-fi is available in most cafes, restaurants and hotels. Some cities even have free wi-fi zones in shopping and eating areas. There are fewer and fewer internet cafes or computers for guests to use as people increasingly carry their own smartphone or tablet.

Legal Matters

It is a good idea to have your passport with you at all times in case you are stopped by the police and questioned. This is particularly true if you are travelling in border areas. Greek citizens are presumed always to have identification on them and the police presume foreign visitors do too. If you are arrested by police insist on an interpreter (diermi_néas; say "the-lo dhi-ermi-nea") and/or a lawyer (diki_góros; say "the-lo dhi-ki-go-ro").

Drugs

Greek drug laws are the strictest in Europe. Greek courts make no distinction between possession and pushing. Possession of even a small amount of marijuana is likely to land you in jail.

Maps

Unless you are going to hike or drive, the free maps given out by the EOT and larger hotels will probably suffice,

although they are not 100% accurate.

Anavasi (www.mountains.gr) Athens-based company publishing maps with excellent coverage. Hikers should consider its Topo series, which has durable, waterproof paper and detailed walking trails for many of the Aegean islands.

Terrain (www.terrainmaps.gr) Maps published in Athens and offering equally good coverage. All maps can be bought online or at major bookstores in Greece.

Money
ATMS

ATMs are found in every town large enough to support a bank and in almost all the tourist areas. If you have MasterCard or Visa, there are plenty of places to withdraw money. Cirrus and Maestro users can make withdrawals in all major towns and tourist areas. Be aware that many ATMs on the islands can lose their connection for a day or two at a time, making it impossible for anyone (locals included) to withdraw money. It's useful to have a backup source of money.

Automated foreign-exchange machines are common in major tourist areas. They take all major European currencies, Australian and US dollars and Japanese yen, and are useful in an emergency, although they charge a hefty commission.

Be warned that many card companies can put an automatic block on your card after your first withdrawal abroad, as an antifraud mechanism. To avoid this happening, inform your bank of your travel plans.

Cash

Nothing beats cash for convenience – or for risk. If you lose cash, it's gone for good and very few travel insurers will come to your rescue.

Those that will normally limit the amount to approximately US$300. That said, in the current financial climate, many businesses are requesting cash only. It's best to carry no more cash than you need for the next few days. It's also a good idea to set aside a small amount, say US$100, as an emergency stash.

Note that Greek shopkeepers and small-business owners have a perennial problem with having small change. When buying small items it is better to tender coins or small-denomination notes.

Credit Cards

Credit cards are an accepted part of the commercial scene in Greece, although they're often not accepted on many of the smaller islands or in small villages. In larger places, credit cards can be used at top-end hotels, restaurants and shops. Some C-class hotels will accept credit cards, but D- and E-class hotels very seldom do.

The main credit cards are MasterCard and Visa, both of which are widely accepted. They can also be used as cash cards to draw cash from the ATMs of affiliated Greek banks. Daily withdrawal limits are set by the issuing bank and are given in local currency only.

Tipping

Restaurants If a service charge is included, a small tip is appreciated. If there's no service charge, leave 10% to 20%.

Taxis Round up the fare by a couple of euros. There's a small fee for handling bags; this is an official charge, not a tip.

Bellhops Bellhops in hotels and stewards on ferries expect a small gratuity of €1 to €3.

Travellers Cheques

The main reason to carry travellers cheques rather than cash is the protection they offer against theft.

They are, however, losing popularity as more and more travellers opt to put their money in a bank at home and withdraw it at ATMs as they go. American Express, Visa and Thomas Cook cheques are available in euros and are all widely accepted and have efficient replacement policies.

Opening Hours

Opening hours vary throughout the year. We've provided high-season opening hours; hours decrease significantly in the shoulder and low seasons, when many places shut completely.

Banks 8.30am–2.30pm Monday to Thursday, 8am–2pm Friday

Restaurants 11am–3pm and 7pm–1am

Cafes 10am–midnight

Bars 8pm–late

Clubs 10pm–4am

Post Offices 7.30am–2pm Monday to Friday (rural); 7.30am–8pm Monday to Friday, 7.30am–2pm Saturday (urban)

Shops 8am–3pm Monday, Wednesday and Saturday; 8am–2.30pm and 5–8pm Tuesday, Thursday and Friday

Photography

➡ Digital memory cards are readily available from camera stores.

➡ Never photograph a military installation; some are less than obvious and close to wildlife viewing areas.

➡ Flash photography is not allowed inside churches and it's considered taboo to photograph the main altar.

➡ Greeks usually love having their photos taken, but always ask permission first.

➡ At archaeological sites you will be stopped from using a tripod as it marks you as a 'professional'.

PRACTICALITIES

Weights & Measures The metric system is used.

Post To send post abroad, use the yellow post boxes labelled *exoteriko* (for overseas).

Newspapers Greek current affairs are covered in the daily English-language edition of *Kathimerini* (www. ekathimerini.com) within the *New York Times International Edition*.

DVDs Greece is region code 2 if buying DVDs to watch back home.

Public Holidays

All banks and shops and most museums and ancient sites close on public holidays.

Many sites (including the ancient sites in Athens) offer free entry on the first Sunday of the month, with the exception of July and August. You may also gain free entry on other locally celebrated holidays, although this varies across the country.

National public holidays:

New Year's Day 1 January

Epiphany 6 January

First Sunday in Lent February

Greek Independence Day 25 March

Good Friday March/April

Orthodox Easter Sunday 8 April 2018, 28 April 2019, 19 April 2020, 2 May 2021

May Day (Protomagia) 1 May

Whit Monday (Agiou Pnevmatos) 50 days after Easter Sunday

Feast of the Assumption 15 August

Ohi Day 28 October

Christmas Day 25 December

St Stephen's Day 26 December

Safe Travel

Drinks

Adulterated drinks (known as *bombes*) are served in some bars and clubs in Athens and at resorts known for partying. These drinks are diluted with cheap illegal imports that leave you feeling worse for wear the next day.

At many of the party resorts catering to large budget-tour groups, spiked drinks are not uncommon; keep your hand over the top of your glass. More often than not, the perpetrators are foreign tourists rather than locals.

Tourist Police

The *touristikí astynomía* (tourist police) work in cooperation with the regular Greek police and are found in cities and popular tourist destinations. Each tourist police office has at least one member of staff who speaks English. Hotels, restaurants, travel agencies, tourist shops, tourist guides, waiters, taxi drivers and bus drivers all come under the jurisdiction of the tourist police. If you have a complaint about any of these, report it to the tourist police and they will investigate. If you need to report a theft or loss of passport, go to the tourist police first, and they will act as interpreters between you and the regular police.

Smoking

In July 2009 Greece brought in antismoking laws similar to those found in most of Europe. Smoking is now banned inside public places, with the penalty being fines placed on the business owners. Greece is home to some of the heaviest smokers in

Europe, so enforcement is a challenge. The laws are often imposed in only a nominal way in remote locations where proprietors fear they would lose business.

Telephone

The Greek telephone service is maintained by the public corporation OTE (pronounced o-*teh;* Organismos Tilepikoinonion Ellados). There are public telephones just about everywhere, including in some unbelievably isolated spots. The phones are easy to operate and can be used for local, long-distance and international calls. The 'i' at the top left of the push-button dialling panel brings up the operating instructions in English.

Note that in Greece the area code must always be dialled when making a call (ie all Greek phone numbers are 10-digit).

Mobile Phones

Local SIM cards can be used in European and Australian phones. Most other phones can be set to roaming. US/Canadian phones need to have a dual- or tri-band system.

There are several mobile service providers in Greece, among which Cosmote, Vodafone and Wind are the best known. Of these three, Cosmote tends to have the best coverage in remote areas. All offer 2G connectivity and pay-as-you-talk services for which you can buy a rechargeable SIM card and have your own Greek mobile number. If you're buying a package, be sure to triple-check the fine print. There are restrictions on deals such as 'free minutes' only being available to phones using the same provider.

The use of a mobile phone while driving in Greece is prohibited, but the use of a Bluetooth headset is allowed.

Phonecards

All public phones use OTE phonecards, known as *telekarta,* not coins. These cards are widely available at *periptera* (street kiosks), corner shops and tourist shops. A local call costs around €0.30 for three minutes.

It's also possible to use payphones with the growing range of discount-card schemes. This involves dialling an access code and then punching in your card number. The OTE version of this card is known as 'Hronokarta'. The cards come with instructions in Greek and English and the talk time is enormous compared with the standard phonecard rates.

Time

Greece maintains one time zone throughout the country. It is two hours ahead of GMT/UTC and three hours ahead on daylight-saving time – which begins on the last Sunday in March, when clocks are put forward one hour. Daylight saving ends on the last Sunday in October.

Toilets

➡ Most places in Greece have Western-style toilets, especially hotels and restaurants that cater to tourists. You'll occasionally come across Asian-style squat toilets in older houses, *kafeneia* (coffee houses) and public toilets.

➡ Public toilets are a rarity, except at airports and bus and train stations. Cafes are the best option if you get caught short, but you'll be expected to buy something for the privilege.

➡ The Greek plumbing system can't handle toilet paper; apparently the pipes are too narrow and anything larger than a postage stamp seems to cause a problem. Toilet paper etc should be placed in the small bin provided next to every toilet.

Tourist Information

The **Greek National Tourist Organisation** (www. visitgreece.gr) is known as GNTO abroad and EOT within Greece. The quality of service from office to office varies dramatically; in some you'll get information aplenty and in others you'll be hard-pressed to find anyone behind the desk. EOT offices can be found in major tourist locations, though they are increasingly being supplemented or even replaced by local municipality tourist offices (such as in the Peloponnese).

The tourist police also fulfil the same functions as the EOT and municipal tourist offices, dispensing maps and brochures, and giving information on transport. If you're really stuck, the tourist police may be able to help find accommodation.

Travellers with Disabilities

Access for travellers with disabilities has improved somewhat in recent years, though mostly in Athens where there are more accessible sights, hotels and restaurants. Much of the rest of Greece remains inaccessible to wheelchairs, and the abundance of stones, marble, slippery cobbles and stepped alleys creates a further challenge. People who have visual or hearing impairments are also rarely catered to.

Careful planning before you go can make a world of difference.

Travel Guide to Greece (www. greecetravel.com/handicapped) Links to local articles, resorts and tour groups catering to tourists with physical disabilities.

Sailing Holidays (www.charter ayachtingreece.com/dryachting/index.html) Two-day to two-week sailing trips around the Greek islands in fully accessible yachts.

Sirens Resort (☑27410 91161; www.disableds-resort.gr; Skalouma) Family-friendly resort with accessible apartments, tours and ramps into the sea.

Visas

The list of countries whose nationals can stay in Greece for up to three months without a visa includes Australia, Canada, all EU countries, Iceland, Israel, Japan, New Zealand, Norway, Switzerland and the USA. Other countries included are the European principalities of Monaco and San Marino and most South American countries. The list changes though – contact Greek embassies for the latest.

If you wish to stay in Greece for longer than three months within a six-month period, you require a visa from the Greek embassy in your country of residence. You are unable to apply for this in Greece. Unlike student and work visas, tourist visas are rarely granted for more than three months.

Volunteering

Hellenic Wildlife Hospital (www.ekpazp.gr) Volunteers head to Aegina (particularly during winter) to this large wildlife rehabilitation centre.

Mouries Farm (☑6947465900; www.skyrianhorses.org; Kalamitsa) Help with the breeding and care of rare Skyrian horses.

Sea Turtle Protection Society of Greece (☑21052 31342; www.archelon.gr) Includes monitoring sea turtles in the Peloponnese.

WWOOF (World Wide Opportunities on Organic Farms; www.wwoofgreece.org) Offers opportunities for volunteers at one of more than 50 farms in Greece.

Women Travellers

Many women travel alone in Greece. The crime rate remains relatively low and solo travel is probably safer than in most European countries. This does not mean that you should be lulled into complacency; bag snatching and sexual assault do occur, particularly at party resorts on the islands.

The biggest nuisance to foreign women travelling alone are the guys the Greeks have nicknamed *kamaki*. The word means 'fishing trident' and refers to the *kamaki*'s favourite pastime: 'fishing' for foreign women. You'll find them wherever there are lots of tourists: young (for the most part), smooth-talking guys who aren't in the least bashful about approaching women in the street. They can be very persistent, but they are usually a hassle rather than a threat. The majority

of Greek men treat foreign women with respect.

Working

EU nationals don't need a work permit, but they need a residency permit and a Greek tax-file number if they intend to stay longer than three months. Nationals of other countries require a work permit.

English Tutoring

If you're looking for a permanent job, the most widely available option is to teach English. A TEFL (Teaching English as a Foreign Language) certificate or a university degree is an advantage but not essential. In the UK, look through the *Times* educational supplement or Tuesday's edition of the *Guardian* newspaper for opportunities; in other countries, contact the Greek embassy.

Another possibility is to find a job teaching English once you are in Greece. You will see language schools everywhere. Strictly speaking, you need a licence to teach in these schools, but many will employ teachers without one. The best time to look around for such a job is late summer.

The noticeboard at the Compendium bookshop (www.compendium.gr) in Athens sometimes has advertisements looking for private English lessons.

Transport

GETTING THERE & AWAY

Entering the Country

Visitors to Greece with EU passports are rarely given more than a cursory glance, but customs and police may be interested in what you are carrying. EU citizens may also enter Greece on a national identity card.

Visitors from outside the EU may require a visa. Be sure to check with consular authorities before you arrive.

Air

Airports & Airlines

Greece has four main international airports.

Other international airports across the country include Santorini (Thira), Karpathos, Samos, Skiathos, Kefallonia and Zakynthos.

These airports are most often used for charter flights from the UK, Germany and Scandinavia.

Eleftherios Venizelos International Airport (ATH; ☎ 210 353 0000; www.aia.gr) Near Spata, 27km east of Athens. It has all the modern conveniences, including a children's playroom, and a small archaeological museum.

Nikos Kazantzakis International Airport (HER; ☎ general 2810 397800, info ☎ 2810 397136; www.heraklion-airport.info) About 5km east of Iraklio (Crete).

Diagoras Airport (RHO; ☎ 22410 88700; www.rhodes-airport.org) On the island of Rhodes.

Macedonia International Airport (SKG; ☎ 2310 985 000; www.thessalonikiairport.com) About 17km southeast of Thessaloniki. Served by bus 78 (half-hourly); a taxi costs around €15 to €20.

GREEK AIRLINES

Aegean Airlines (A3; ☎ 801 112 0000; www.aegeanair.com) and its subsidiary, **Olympic Air**

(☎ 801 801 0101; www.olympic air.com), have flights between Athens and destinations throughout Europe, as well as to Cairo, İstanbul, Tel Aviv, New York and Toronto. They also operate flights throughout Greece, many of which transfer in Athens. Both airlines have exemplary safety records.

Tickets

If you're coming from outside Europe, consider a cheap flight to a European hub (eg London) and then an onward ticket with a charter airline such as **easyJet** (U2; ☎ 210 967 0000; www.easyjet.com), who offer some of the cheapest tickets between Greece and the rest of Europe. Some airlines also offer cheap deals to students. If you're planning to travel between June and September, it's wise to book ahead.

Land

If you travel by land you can really appreciate the

CLIMATE CHANGE & TRAVEL

Every form of transport that relies on carbon-based fuel generates CO_2, the main cause of human-induced climate change. Modern travel is dependent on aeroplanes, which might use less fuel per kilometre per person than most cars but travel much greater distances. The altitude at which aircraft emit gases (including CO_2) and particles also contributes to their climate change impact. Many websites offer 'carbon calculators' that allow people to estimate the carbon emissions generated by their journey and, for those who wish to do so, to offset the impact of the greenhouse gases emitted with contributions to portfolios of climate-friendly initiatives throughout the world. Lonely Planet offsets the carbon footprint of all staff and author travel.

OVERLAND FROM WESTERN EUROPE

If you're keen to travel without flying and enjoy the independence of a road trip, you can reach Greece by heading overland to an Italian port and hopping on a ferry. A high-speed ferry from Venice to Patra takes around 26 hours. Patra to Athens is a 3½-hour drive.

Fancy a bit more convenience and speed than a bus or a car? Overland enthusiasts can reach Greece by rail through the Balkan Peninsula, passing through Croatia, Serbia and the Former Yugoslav Republic of Macedonia. Or head to the eastern coast of Italy (there are connections throughout most of Europe) and then take a ferry to Greece. Not only will you be doing your bit for the planet, but you'll see some gorgeous scenery from your window.

A sample itinerary from London would see you catching the Eurostar to Paris and then an overnight sleeper train to Bologna in Italy. From there, a coastal train takes you to Bari, where there's an overnight boat to Patra on the Peloponnese. From Patra, it's a 4½-hour train journey to Athens. You'll be in Athens within two days of leaving London. See www.raileurope.com for routes and tickets.

Greece is part of the Eurail network (www.eurail.com). Eurail passes can be bought only by residents of non-European countries; they should be purchased before arriving in Europe, but can be bought in Europe if your passport proves that you've been there for less than six months. Greece is also part of the Inter-Rail Pass system (www.interrail.eu), available to those who have resided in Europe for six months or more, and the Rail Plus Balkan Flexipass (www.raileurope.com), which offers unlimited travel for five, 10 or 15 days within a month. See the websites for full details of passes and prices.

---

landscape, as well as the many experiences that go along with train or bus travel. International train travel, in particular, has become much more feasible in recent years, with speedier trains and better connections. You can now travel from London to Athens by train and ferry in less than two days. By choosing to travel on the ground instead of the air, you'll also be reducing your carbon footprint.

Border Crossings

Due to the current refugee crisis, make sure you have all of your visas sorted out before attempting to cross land borders into or out of Greece. At the time of writing, all migrants were being denied access to the borders, while EU passport holders were allowed across. As the situation is volatile, it's worth checking in to the relevant embassies before travelling.

ALBANIA

Kakavia 60km northwest of Ioannina; queues can be very slow

Krystallopigi 14km west of Kotas on the Florina–Kastoria road

Mertziani 17km west of Konitsa

Sagiada 28km north of Igoumenitsa

Albatrans (☑+355 42 259 204; www.albatrans.com.al) Buses between Greece and Albania.

BULGARIA

Exohi A 448m-tunnel border crossing 50km north of Drama

Ormenio 41km from Serres in northeastern Thrace

Promahonas 109km northeast of Thessaloniki

FORMER YUGOSLAV REPUBLIC OF MACEDONIA (FYROM)

Doïrani 31km north of Kilkis

Evzoni 68km north of Thessaloniki

Niki 16km north of Florina

TURKEY

Kastanies 139km northeast of Alexandroupoli

Kipi 43km east of Alexandroupoli

Train

The Greek railways organisation **OSE** (Organismos Sidirodromon Ellados; ☑14511; www.trainose.gr) runs daily trains from Thessaloniki to Sofia and to Belgrade (via Skopje), with a weekly onward train to and from Budapest.

Sea

Ferries can get very crowded in summer. If you want to take a vehicle across it's wise to make a reservation beforehand. The services indicated are for high season (July and August). Please note that tickets for all ferries to Turkey must be bought a day in advance – and you will almost certainly be asked to turn in your passport the night before the trip. It will be returned the next day before you board the boat. Port tax for departures to Turkey is around €15.

Another way to visit Greece by sea is to join one of the many cruises that ply the Aegean.

GETTING AROUND

Air

The majority of domestic mainland flights are handled by the country's national carrier **Aegean Airlines** (A3; ☑801 112 0000; www.aegeanair.com) and its subsidiary, **Olympic Air** (☑801

801 0101; www.olympicair.com). You'll find offices wherever there are flights, as well as in other major towns. There are also a number of smaller Greek carriers, including Crete-based airlines **Astra Airlines** (☑2310 489 391; www.astra-airlines.gr) and **Sky Express** (☑28102 23800; www.skyexpress.gr).

There are discounts for return tickets for travel between Monday and Thursday, and bigger discounts for trips that include a Saturday night away. Find full details and timetables on airline websites.

The baggage allowance on domestic flights is 15kg, or 20kg if the domestic flight is part of an international journey.

Bicycle

Cycling is not popular among Greeks – but it's gaining kudos with tourists. You'll need strong leg muscles to tackle the mountains; or just stick to some of the flatter coastal routes. Bike lanes are rare to non-existent; helmets are not compulsory. The island of Kos is about the most bicycle-friendly place in Greece, as is anywhere flat, such as the plains of Thessaly or Thrace.

➡ You can hire bicycles in most resorts, but they are not as widely available as cars and motorcycles. Prices range from €10 to €15 daily.

➡ Bicycles are carried free on ferries. You can buy decent mountain or touring bikes in Greece's major towns, though you may have a problem finding a ready buyer if you wish to sell it on. Bike prices are much the same as across the rest of Europe: from €300 to €2000.

Boat

Greece has an extensive network of ferries – the only means of reaching many of the islands. Schedules are often subject to delays due to poor weather and industrial action, and prices fluctuate regularly. In summer, ferries run regular services between all but the most out-of-the-way destinations; however, services seriously slow down in winter (and in some cases stop completely).

Domestic Ferry Operators

Ferry companies have local offices on many of the islands.

Aegean Flying Dolphins (www.aegeanflyingdolphins.gr) Hydrofoils between Athens, Aegina and the Sporades.

Aegean Speed Lines (www.aegeanspeedlines.gr) Fast boats between Athens and the Cyclades.

Aegeon Pelagos (www.anek.gr) A subsidiary of ANEK Lines.

ANEK Lines (www.anek.gr) Crete-based long-haul ferries.

ANES (www.anes.gr) Old-style ferries servicing Evia and the Sporades.

Anna Express (www.annaexpress.eu) Small, fast ferry connecting the northern Dodecanese.

INTERNATIONAL FERRY ROUTES

DESTINATION	DEPARTURE POINT	ARRIVAL POINT	DURATION	FREQUENCY
Albania	Corfu	Saranda	25min	1 daily
Italy	Patra	Ancona	20hr	3 daily
Italy	Patra	Bari	14½hr	1 daily
Italy	Corfu	Bari	8hr	1 daily
Italy	Kefallonia	Bari	14hr	1 daily
Italy	Corfu	Bari	10hr	1 daily
Italy	Igoumenitsa	Bari	11½hr	1 daily
Italy	Patra	Brindisi	15hr	1 daily
Italy	Corfu	Brindisi	6hr	1 daily
Italy	Kefallonia	Brindisi	12hr	1 daily
Italy	Zakynthos	Brindisi	15hr	1 daily
Italy	Patra	Venice	30hr	12 weekly
Italy	Corfu	Venice	25hr	12 weekly
Turkey	Chios	Çeşme	1½hr	1 daily
Turkey	Kos	Bodrum	1hr	1 daily
Turkey	Lesvos	Ayvalik	1hr	1 daily
Turkey	Rhodes	Marmaris	50min	2 daily
Turkey	Samos	Kuşadası	1½hr	2 daily

Blue Star Ferries (www.blue starferries.com) Long-haul, high-speed ferries and Sea Jet catamarans between the mainland, the Cyclades, the northeast Aegean Islands, Crete and the Dodecanese.

Dodekanisos Seaways (www.12ne.gr) Large, high-speed catamarans in the Dodecanese.

Glyfa Ferries (www.ferriesglyfa.gr) Comfortable short-haul ferry services between Glyfa on the mainland and Agiokambos in northern Evia.

Fast Ferries (www.fastferries.com.gr) Comfortable ferries from Rafina to the Cyclades islands of Andros, Tinos, Naxos and Mykonos.

Hellenic Seaways (www.hellenic seaways.gr) Conventional long-haul ferries and catamarans from the mainland to the Cyclades and between the Sporades and Saronic Islands.

Ionian Ferries (www.ionianferries.gr) Large ferries serving the Ionian Islands.

LANE Lines (www.ferries.gr/lane) Long-haul ferries serving the Ionians, Dodecanese and Crete.

Minoan Lines (www.minoan.gr) High-speed luxury ferries between Piraeus and Iraklio, and Patra, Igoumenitsa and Corfu.

Patmos Star (www.patmos-star.com) Small, local ferry linking Patmos, Leros and Lipsi in the Dodecanese.

SAOS Lines (www.saos.gr) Big, slow boats calling in at many of the islands.

Sea Jets (www.seajets.gr) Catamarans calling at Athens, Crete, Santorini (Thira), Paros and many islands in between.

Skyros Shipping Company (www.sne.gr) Slow boat between Skyros and Kymi on Evia.

Superfast Ferries (www.super fast.com) As the name implies, speedy ferries from the mainland to Crete, Corfu and Patra.

Ventouris Ferries (www.ventouris sealines.gr) Big boats from the mainland to the Cyclades.

Zante Ferries (www.zanteferries.gr) Ferries connecting the mainland with the western Cyclades.

Bus

The bus network is comprehensive. All long-distance buses, on the mainland and the islands, are operated by regional collectives known as **KTEL** (www.ktelbus.com). Details of inter-urban buses throughout Greece are available by dialling ☑14505. Bus fares are fixed by the government and are very reasonable. A journey costs approximately €5 per 100km.

Services

The islands of Corfu, Kefallonia and Zakynthos can be reached directly from Athens by bus – the fares include the price of the ferry ticket.

Most villages have a daily bus service of some sort, although remote areas may have only one or two buses a week. They are aimed at locals, and so leave the villages very early in the morning and return early in the afternoon.

Practicalities

➡ Big cities may have more than one bus station, each serving different regions. Make sure you find the correct station for your destination.

➡ In remote areas, the timetable may be in Greek only, but most booking offices have timetables in Greek and Roman script, and many bus stations now post them online.

➡ It's best to turn up at least 20 minutes before departure to make sure you get a seat – buses have been known to leave a few minutes early.

➡ When you buy a ticket, it may have a seat number. The seat number is on the *back* of each seat of the bus, not on the back of the seat in front; this causes confusion among Greeks and tourists alike.

➡ You can board a bus without a ticket and pay on board.

➡ The KTEL buses are safe and modern, and most are air conditioned – at least on major routes. In more remote, rural areas they tend to be older and less comfortable.

➡ Smoking is prohibited on all buses in Greece.

Car & Motorcycle

Greece's road fatality rate is one of the highest in Europe. More than a thousand people die on the roads every year, with 10 times that number of people injured. Overtaking is listed as the greatest cause of accidents.

Heart-stopping moments aside, your own car is a great way to explore off the beaten track. The road network has improved enormously in recent years; many roads marked as dirt tracks on older maps have now been asphalted and many of the islands have very little traffic. There are regular (if costly) car-ferry services to almost all islands.

Practicalities

Automobile Association Greece's domestic automobile association is **ELPA** (☑210 606 8800, 24hr roadside assistance ☑10400; Leoforos Mesogion 541, Agia Paraskevi, Athens).

Entry EU-registered vehicles enter free for up to six months without road taxes being due. A green card (international third-party insurance) is required, along with proof of date of entry (ferry ticket or your passport stamp). Non-EU-registered vehicles may be logged in your passport.

Driving Licence EU driving licences are valid in Greece. Drivers from outside the EU may require International Driving Permits; while rental agencies will rarely ask for one, local authorities may if you're stopped. International Driving Permits can only be obtained in the country where your driving licence was issued.

Fuel Available widely throughout the country, though service stations may be closed on weekends and public holidays. On the islands, there may be only one petrol station; check where it is

Ferry Routes

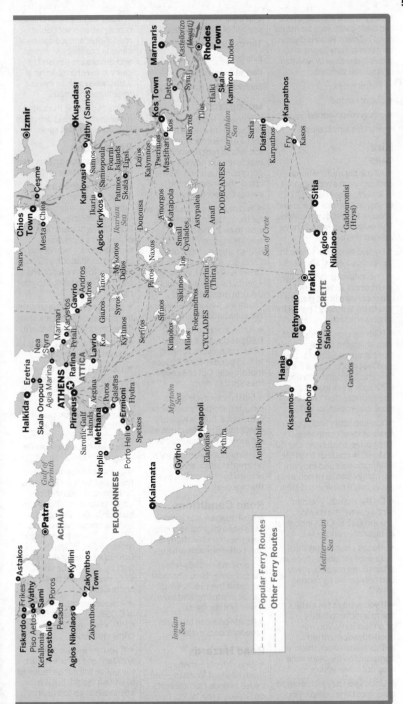

before you head out. Self-service and credit-card pumps are not the norm in Greece. Petrol is cheaper here than in many European countries, but expensive by American or Australian standards.

Petrol types:

→ *Super* leaded

→ *amolyvdi* unleaded

→ *petreleo kinisis* diesel

Hire

CARS

→ All the big multinational companies are represented in Athens; most have branches in major towns and popular tourist destinations. The majority of islands have at least one outlet.

→ By law, rental cars have to be replaced every six years.

→ The minimum driving age in Greece is 18 years, but most car-hire firms require you to be at least 21 (or 23 for larger vehicles).

→ High-season weekly rates with unlimited mileage start at about €280 for the smallest models (eg a Fiat Seicento), dropping to about €200 per week in winter. These prices don't include local tax (known as VAT).

→ You can often find great deals at local companies. Their advertised rates can be up to 50% cheaper than the multinationals and they are normally open to negotiation, especially if business is slow.

→ On the islands, you can rent a car for the day for around €35 to €60, including all insurance and taxes.

→ Always check what the insurance includes; there are often rough roads that you can only tackle by renting a 4WD.

→ If you want to take a hire car to another country or on to a ferry, you will need advance written authorisation from the hire company, as the insurance may not cover you.

→ Unless you pay with a credit card, most hire companies will require a minimum deposit of €120 per day.

The major car-hire firms:

Avis (www.avis.gr)

Budget (www.budget.gr)

Europcar (www.europcar.gr)

MOTORCYCLES

→ Mopeds, motorcycles and scooters are available for hire wherever there are tourists to rent them. Most machines are newish and in good condition. Nonetheless, check the brakes at the earliest opportunity.

→ You must produce a licence for the category of bike you wish to rent; this applies to everything from 50cc up. British citizens must obtain a Category A licence from the Driver & Vehicle Licensing Agency (www.dft.gov.uk/dvla). In most other EU countries, separate licences are automatically issued.

→ Rates start from about €20 per day for a moped or 50cc motorcycle, ranging to €35 per day for a 250cc motorcycle. Out of season these prices drop.

→ Most motorcycle hirers include third-party insurance in the price, but it's wise to check this. This insurance will not include medical expenses.

→ Helmets are compulsory, and rental agencies are obliged to offer one as part of the hire deal.

Road Conditions

→ Main highways in Greece have been improving steadily over the years but many still don't offer smooth driving.

→ Some main roads retain the two-lane/hard-shoulder format of the 1960s, which can be confusing and even downright dangerous.

→ Roadworks can take years – especially on the islands.

Road Hazards

→ Slow drivers – many of them hesitant tourists – can cause serious traffic events on Greece's roads.

→ Road surfaces can change rapidly when a section of road. Snow and ice can be a serious challenge in winter, and drivers are advised to carry snow chains. In rural areas, keep a close eye out for animals on roads.

→ Roads passing through mountainous areas are often littered with fallen rocks.

Road Rules

→ In Greece, you drive on the right and overtake on the left.

→ Outside built-up areas, traffic on a main road has right of way at intersections. In towns, vehicles coming from the right have right of way. This includes roundabouts – even if you're on the roundabout, you must give way to drivers coming on to the roundabout to your right.

→ Seat belts must be worn in front seats, and in back seats if the car is fitted with them.

→ Children under 12 are not allowed in the front seat.

→ You must carry a first-aid kit, fire extinguisher and warning triangle. It's forbidden to carry petrol cans.

→ Helmets are compulsory for motorcyclists if the motorcycle is 50cc or more. Police will book you if you're caught without a helmet.

→ Outside residential areas, the speed limit is 120km/h on highways, 90km/h on other roads and 50km/h in built-up areas. The speed limit for motorcycles up to 100cc is 70km/h; for larger motorcycles, 90km/h. Drivers exceeding the speed limit by 20% will be fined €60; exceeding it by 40% costs €150.

→ A blood-alcohol content of 0.05% can incur a fine of €150, while over 0.08% is a criminal offence.

→ If you are involved in an accident and no one is hurt, the police will not be required to write a report, but it is advisable to go to a nearby police station, as you may need a police report for insurance purposes.

Hitching

Hitching is never entirely safe in any country in the world, and we don't recommend it. For travellers who decide to hitch, some parts of Greece are much better for hitching than others. Getting out of major cities, particularly Athens, tends to be hard work. Hitching is much easier in remote areas and on islands with poor public transport.

Local Transport

Bus

Most Greek towns are small enough to get around on foot. All the major towns have local buses.

Metro

Athens is the only city in Greece with a metro system. Note that only Greek student cards are valid for a student ticket on the metro.

Taxi

Taxis are widely available in Greece, except on very small or remote islands. They are reasonably priced by European standards. Yellow city cabs are metered, with rates doubling between midnight and 5am. Additional costs are charged for trips from an airport or a bus, port or train station, as well as for each piece of luggage over 10kg. Grey rural taxis do not have meters, so always settle on a price before you get in.

Some taxi drivers in Athens have been known to overcharge unwary travellers. If you have a complaint, report it to the tourist police. Taxi drivers in other towns in Greece are, on the whole, friendly, helpful and honest.

Tours

Tours are worth considering if your time is very limited or if you prefer someone else do the planning. In Athens, you'll find countless day tours, with some agencies offering two- or three-day trips to nearby sights. For something on a larger scale, try **Intrepid Travel** (www.intrepidtravel. com; offices in Australia, the UK and the USA): they offer an eight-day sailing tour from Santorini to Mykonos (€1010) and an eight-day tour from Athens to Santorini (€1320), including everything except meals and flights. **Encounter Greece** (www.encountergreece.com) offers a plethora of tours; a 13-day tour across the country costs €1445. (Flights to Greece are not included.)

More adventurous tours include guided activities such as hiking, climbing, white-water rafting, kayaking, canoeing or canyoning.

Train

Trains are operated by the Greek railways organisation **OSE** (☑14511; www.trainose. gr). The Greek railway network is limited; its northern line is the most substantial. Standard-gauge service runs from Athens to Dikea in the northeast via Thessaloniki and Alexandroupoli. There are also connections to Florina and the Pelion Peninsula. The Peloponnese network runs only as far as Klato, with bus services to Plata for ferry connections.

Due to financial instability, prices and schedules are very changeable. When you can, double-check on the OSE website. Information on departures from Athens or Thessaloniki is also available by calling ☑1440.

Classes

There are two types of service: regular (slow) trains that stop at all stations, and faster, modern intercity (IC) trains that link most major cities. The slow trains represent the country's cheapest form of public transport: 2nd-class fares are absurdly cheap, and even 1st class is cheaper than bus travel.

The IC trains that link the major Greek cities are an excellent way to travel. The services are not necessarily fast – Greece is far too mountainous for that – but the trains are modern and comfortable. There are 1st-and 2nd-class tickets and a cafe-bar on board. The night service between Athens and Thessaloniki offers a choice of couchettes, two-bed compartments and single compartments.

Train Passes

➡ Eurail, Inter-Rail and Rail Plus Balkan Flexipass cards are valid in Greece, but they're generally not worth buying if Greece is the only place where you plan to use them. For IC and sleeper cars, a costly supplement is required.

➡ On presentation of ID or passports, passengers more than 60 years old are entitled to a 25% discount on all lines, except in July and August and over the Easter week.

➡ Whatever pass you have, you must have a reservation to board the train.

MOTORCYCLE WARNING

Greece is not the best place to initiate yourself into motorcycling. There are still a lot of gravel roads, particularly on the islands, and dozens of tourists have accidents every year. Scooters are particularly prone to sliding on gravelly bends. Try to hire a motorcycle with thinner-profile tyres. If you plan to use a motorcycle or moped, check that your travel insurance covers you: many insurance companies don't cover motorcycle accidents.

Language

The Greek language is believed to be one of the oldest European languages, with an oral tradition of 4000 years and a written tradition of approximately 3000 years. Due to its centuries of influence, Greek constitutes the origin of a large part of the vocabulary of many Indo-European languages (including English). It is the official language of Greece and co-official language of Cyprus (alongside Turkish), and is spoken by many migrant communities throughout the world.

The Greek alphabet is explained on the following page, but if you read the pronunciation guides given with each phrase in this chapter as if they were English, you'll be understood. Note that dh is pronounced as 'th' in 'there'; gh is a softer, slightly throaty version of 'g'; and kh is a throaty sound like the 'ch' in the Scottish 'loch'. All Greek words of two or more syllables have an acute accent (´), which indicates where the stress falls. In our pronunciation guides, stressed syllables are in italics.

In this chapter, masculine, feminine and neuter forms of words are included where necessary, separated with a slash and indicated with 'm', 'f' and 'n' respectively. Polite and informal options are indicated where relevant with 'pol' and 'inf'.

BASICS

Hello.	Γειά σας.	ya·sas (pol)
	Γειά σου.	ya·su (inf)
Goodbye.	Αντίο.	an·di·o

WANT MORE?

For in-depth language information and handy phrases, check out Lonely Planet's *Greek Phrasebook*. You'll find it at **shop.lonelyplanet.com**, or you can buy Lonely Planet's iPhone phrasebooks at the Apple App Store.

Yes./No.	Ναι./Οχι.	ne/o·hi
Please.	Παρακαλώ.	pa·ra·ka·lo
Thank you.	Ευχαριστώ.	ef·ha·ri·sto
You're welcome.	Παρακαλώ.	pa·ra·ka·lo
Excuse me.	Με συγχωρείτε.	me sing·kho·ri·te
Sorry.	Συγγνώμη.	sigh·no·mi

What's your name?

| Πώς σας λένε; | | pos sas le·ne |

My name is ...

| Με λένε ... | | me le·ne ... |

Do you speak English?

| Μιλάτε αγγλικά; | | mi·la·te an·gli·ka |

I don't understand.

| Δεν καταλαβαίνω. | | dhen ka·ta·la·ve·no |

ACCOMMODATION

campsite	χώρος για κάμπινγκ	kho·ros yia kam·ping
hotel	ξενοδοχείο	kse·no·dho·khi·o
youth hostel	γιουθ χόστελ	yuth kho·stel

a ... room	ένα ... δωμάτιο	e·na ... dho·ma·ti·o
single	μονόκλινο	mo·no·kli·no
double	δίκλινο	dhi·kli·no

How much is it ...?	Πόσο κάνει ...;	po·so ka·ni ...
per night	τη βραδυά	ti·vra·dhya
per person	το άτομο	to a·to·mo

air-con	έρκοντίσιον	er·kon·di·si·on
bathroom	μπάνιο	ba·nio
fan	ανεμιστήρας	a·ne·mi·sti·ras
window	παράθυρο	pa·ra·thi·ro

DIRECTIONS

Where is ...?
Πού είναι ...;   pu *i*·ne ...

What's the address?
Ποια είναι η διεύθυνση;   pia *i*·ne i dhi·*ef*·thin·si

Can you show me (on the map)?
Μπορείς να μου δείξεις   bo·*ris* na mu *dhik*·sis
(στο χάρτη);   (sto *khar*·ti)

Turn left.
Στρίψτε αριστερά.   *strips*·te a·ri·ste·*ra*

Turn right.
Στρίψτε δεξιά.   *strips*·te dhe·*ksia*

at the next corner
στην επόμενη γωνία   stin e·*po*·me·ni gho·*ni*·a

at the traffic lights
στα φώτα   sta *fo*·ta

behind	πίσω	*pi*·so
far	μακριά	ma·kri·a
in front of	μπροστά	bro·*sta*
near (to)	κοντά	kon·*da*
next to	δίπλα	*dhi*·pla
opposite	απέναντι	a·*pe*·nan·di
straight ahead	ολο ευθεία	o·lo ef·*thi*·a

EATING & DRINKING

a table for ...   Ενα τραπέζι   e·na tra·*pe*·zi
                             για ...   ya ...

(eight) o'clock   στις (οχτώ)   stis (okh·*to*)
(two) people   (δύο) άτομα   (*dhi*·o) a·to·ma

I don't eat ...   Δεν τρώγω ...   dhen *tro*·gho ...
  fish   ψάρι   *psa*·ri
  (red) meat   (κόκκινο)   (*ko*·ki·no)
                             κρέας   *kre*·as
  peanuts   φυστίκια   fi·*sti*·kia
  poultry   πουλερικά   pu·le·ri·*ka*

What would you recommend?
Τι θα συνιστούσες;   ti tha si·ni·*stu*·ses

What's in that dish?
Τι περιέχει αυτό το   ti pe·ri·e·hi af·*to* to
φαγητό;   fa·ghi·to

Cheers!
Εις υγείαν!   is i·*yi*·an

That was delicious.
Ήταν νοστιμότατο!   *i*·tan no·sti·*mo*·ta·to

Please bring the bill.
Το λογαριασμό,   to lo·ghar·ya·*zmo*
παρακαλώ.   pa·ra·ka·*lo*

GREEK ALPHABET

The Greek alphabet has 24 letters, shown below in their upper- and lower-case forms.
Be aware that some letters look like English letters but are pronounced very differently,
such as **B**, which is pronounced v; and **P**, pronounced r. As in English, how letters are
pronounced is also influenced by the way they are combined, for example the **ου** combination is pronounced u as in 'put', and **οι** is pronounced ee as in 'feet'.

Α α	a	as in 'father'		**Ξ ξ**	x	as in 'ox'
Β β	v	as in 'vine'		**Ο ο**	o	as in 'hot'
Γ γ	gh	a softer, throaty 'g', or		**Π π**	p	as in 'pup'
	y	as in 'yes'		**Ρ ρ**	r	as in 'road',
Δ δ	dh	as in 'there'				slightly trilled
Ε ε	e	as in 'egg'		**Σ σ, ς**	s	as in 'sand'
Ζ ζ	z	as in 'zoo'		**Τ τ**	t	as in 'tap'
Η η	i	as in 'feet'		**Υ υ**	i	as in 'feet'
Θ θ	th	as in 'throw'		**Φ φ**	f	as in 'find'
Ι ι	i	as in 'feet'		**Χ χ**	kh	as the 'ch' in the
Κ κ	k	as in 'kite'				Scottish 'loch', or
Λ λ	l	as in 'leg'			h	like a rough 'h'
Μ μ	m	as in 'man'		**Ψ ψ**	ps	as in 'lapse'
Ν ν	n	as in 'net'		**Ω ω**	o	as in 'hot'

Note that the letter **Σ** has two forms for the lower case – **σ** and **ς**. The second one is used
at the end of words. The Greek question mark is represented with the English equivalent
of a semicolon (;).

KEY WORDS

Key Words

appetisers	ορεκτικά	o·rek·ti·ka
bar	μπαρ	bar
beef	βοδινό	vo·dhi·no
beer	μπύρα	bi·ra
bottle	μπουκάλι	bu·ka·li
bowl	μπωλ	bol
bread	ψωμί	pso·mi
breakfast	πρόγευμα	pro·yev·ma
cafe	καφετέρια	ka·fe·te·ri·a
cheese	τυρί	ti·ri
chicken	κοτόπουλο	ko·to·pu·lo
coffee	καφές	ka·fes
cold	κρύο	kri·o
cream	κρέμα	kre·ma
delicatessen	ντελικατέσεν	de·li·ka·te·sen
desserts	επιδόρπια	e·pi·dhor·pi·a
dinner	δείπνο	dhip·no
egg	αυγό	av·gho
fish	ψάρι	psa·ri
food	φαγητό	fa·yi·to
fork	πιρούνι	pi·ru·ni
fruit	φρούτα	fru·ta
glass	ποτήρι	po·ti·ri
grocery store	οπωροπωλείο	o·po·ro·po·li·o
herb	βότανο	vo·ta·no
high chair	καρέκλα για μωρά	ka·re·kla yia mo·ra
hot	ζεστός	ze·stos
juice	χυμός	hi·mos
knife	μαχαίρι	ma·he·ri
lamb	αρνί	ar·ni
lunch	μεσημεριανό φαγητό	me·si·me·ria·no fa·yi·to
main courses	κύρια φαγητά	ki·ri·a fa·yi·ta
market	αγορά	a·gho·ra
menu	μενού	me·nu
milk	γάλα	gha·la
nut	καρύδι	ka·ri·dhi
oil	λάδι	la·dhi
pepper	πιπέρι	pi·pe·ri
plate	πιάτο	pia·to
pork	χοιρινό	hi·ri·no
red wine	κόκκινο κρασί	ko·ki·no kra·si
restaurant	εστιατόριο	e·sti·a·to·ri·o
salt	αλάτι	a·la·ti
soft drink	αναψυκτικό	a·na·psik·ti·ko
spoon	κουτάλι	ku·ta·li
sugar	ζάχαρη	za·kha·ri
tea	τσάι	tsa·i
vegetable	λαχανικά	la·kha·ni·ka
vegetarian	χορτοφάγος	khor·to·fa·ghos
vinegar	ξύδι	ksi·dhi
water	νερό	ne·ro
white wine	άσπρο κρασί	a·spro kra·si
with/without	με/χωρίς	me/kho·ris

KEY PATTERNS

To get by in Greek, mix and match these simple patterns with words of your choice:

When's (the next bus)?
Πότε είναι (το επόμενο λεωφορείο); — po·te i·ne (to e·po·me·no le·o·fo·ri·o)

Where's (the station)?
Πού είναι (ο σταθμός); — pu i·ne (o stath·mos)

Do you have (a local map)?
Έχετε οδικό (τοπικό χάρτη); — e·he·te o·dhi·ko (to·pi·ko khar·ti)

Is there a (lift)?
Υπάρχει (ασανσέρ); — i·par·hi (a·san·ser)

Can I (try it on)?
Μπορώ να (το προβάρω); — bo·ro na (to pro·va·ro)

Could you (please help)?
Μπορείς να (βοηθήσεις, παρακαλώ); — bo·ris na (vo·i·thi·sis pa·ra·ka·lo)

Do I need (to book)?
Χρειάζεται (να κλείσω θέση); — khri·a·ze·te (na kli·so the·si)

I need (assistance).
Χρειάζομαι (βοήθεια). — khri·a·zo·me (vo·i·thi·a)

I'd like (to hire a car).
Θα ήθελα (να ενοικιάσω ένα αυτοκίνητο). — tha i·the·la (na e·ni·ki·a·so e·na af·to·ki·ni·to)

How much is it (per night)?
Πόσο είναι (για κάθε νύχτα); — po·so i·ne (yia ka·the nikh·ta)

EMERGENCIES

Help!	Βοήθεια!	vo·i·thya
Go away!	Φύγε!	fi·ye
I'm lost.	Έχω χαθεί.	e·kho kha·thi
Where's the toilet?	Πού είναι η τουαλέτα;	pu i·ne i tu·a·le·ta

Signs

ΕΙΣΟΔΟΣ	Entry
ΕΞΟΔΟΣ	Exit
ΠΛΗΡΟΦΟΡΙΕΣ	Information
ΑΝΟΙΧΤΟ	Open
ΚΛΕΙΣΤΟ	Closed
ΑΠΑΓΟΡΕΥΕΤΑΙ	Prohibited
ΑΣΤΥΝΟΜΙΑ	Police
ΓΥΝΑΙΚΩΝ	Toilets (Women)
ΑΝΔΡΩΝ	Toilets (Men)

Call ...! Φωνάξτε ...! fo·nak·ste ...
a doctor ένα γιατρό e·na yi·a·tro
the police την τin
αστυνομία a·sti·no·mi·a

I'm ill. Είμαι άρρωστος. i·me a·ro·stos
I'm allergic to (antibiotics).
Είμαι αλλεργικός/ i·me a·ler·yi·kos/
αλλεργική a·ler·yi·ki (m/f)
(στα αντιβιωτικά) (sta an·di·vi·o·ti·ka)

SHOPPING & SERVICES

I'd like to buy ...
Θέλω ν' αγοράσω ... the·lo na·gho·ra·so ...
I'm just looking.
Απλώς κοιτάζω. ap·los ki·ta·zo
Can I see it?
Μπορώ να το δω; bo·ro na to dho
I don't like it.
Δεν μου αρέσει. dhen mu a·re·si
How much is it?
Πόσο κάνει; po·so ka·ni
It's too expensive.
Είναι πολύ ακριβό. i·ne po·li a·kri·vo
Can you lower the price?
Μπορείς να κατεβάσεις bo·ris na ka·te·va·sis
την τιμή; tin ti·mi

ATM αυτόματη af·to·ma·ti
μηχανή mi·kha·ni
χρημάτων khri·ma·ton
bank τράπεζα tra·pe·za
credit card πιστωτική pi·sto·ti·ki
κάρτα kar·ta
internet cafe καφενείο ka·fe·ni·o
διαδικτύου dhi·a·dhik·ti·u
mobile phone κινητό ki·ni·to
post office ταχυδρομείο ta·hi·dhro·mi·o
tourist office τουριστικό tu·ri·sti·ko
γραφείο ghra·fi·o

TIME & DATES

What time is it?
Τι ώρα είναι; ti o·ra i·ne
It's (two) o'clock.
Είναι (δύο) η ώρα. i·ne (dhi·o) i o·ra
It's half past (10).
(Δέκα) και μισή. (dhe·ka) ke mi·si

morning	πρωί	pro·i
(this) afternoon	(αυτό το) απόγευμα	(af·to to) a·po·yev·ma
evening	βράδυ	vra·dhi
yesterday	χθες	hthes
today	σήμερα	si·me·ra
tomorrow	αύριο	av·ri·o
Monday	Δευτέρα	dhef·te·ra
Tuesday	Τρίτη	tri·ti
Wednesday	Τετάρτη	te·tar·ti
Thursday	Πέμπτη	pemp·ti
Friday	Παρασκευή	pa·ras·ke·vi
Saturday	Σάββατο	sa·va·to
Sunday	Κυριακή	ky·ri·a·ki
January	Ιανουάριος	ia·nu·ar·i·os
February	Φεβρουάριος	fev·ru·ar·i·os
March	Μάρτιος	mar·ti·os
April	Απρίλιος	a·pri·li·os
May	Μάιος	mai·os
June	Ιούνιος	i·u·ni·os
July	Ιούλιος	i·u·li·os
August	Αύγουστος	av·ghus·tos
September	Σεπτέμβριος	sep·tem·vri·os
October	Οκτώβριος	ok·to·vri·os
November	Νοέμβριος	no·em·vri·os
December	Δεκέμβριος	dhe·kem·vri·os

Question Words

How?	Πώς;	pos
What?	Τι;	ti
When?	Πότε;	po·te
Where?	Πού;	pu
Who?	Ποιος;	pi·os (m)
	Ποια;	pi·a (f)
	Ποιο;	pi·o (n)
Why?	Γιατί;	yi·a·ti

KEY WORDS

TRANSPORT

Public Transport

boat	πλοίο	*pli·o*
city bus	αστικό	a·*sti·ko*
intercity bus	λεωφορείο	le·o·fo·*ri·o*
plane	αεροπλάνο	ae·ro·*pla·no*
train	τρένο	*tre·no*

Where do I buy a ticket?
Πού αγοράζω εισιτήριο; pu a·gho·*ra·zo* i·si·*ti·ri·o*

I want to go to ...
Θέλω να πάω στο/στη … the·lo na *pao* sto/sti...

What time does it leave?
Τι ώρα φεύγει; ti o·ra *fev·yi*

Does it stop at (Iraklio)?
Σταματάει στο sta·ma·*ta·i* sto
(Ηράκλειο); (i·ra·kli·o)

I'd like to get off at (Iraklio).
Θα ήθελα να κατεβώ tha *i·*the·la na ka·te·*vo*
στο (Ηράκλειο). sto (i·ra·kli·o)

I'd like (a) ...	Θα ήθελα (ένα) …	tha *i·*the·la (e·na) …
1st class	πρώτη θέση	pro·ti *the·si*
2nd class	δεύτερη θέση	*def·*te·ri *the·si*
one-way ticket	απλό εισιτήριο	a·*plo* i·si·*ti·ri·o*
return ticket	εισιτήριο με επιστροφή	i·si·*ti·ri·o* me e·pi·stro·*fi*
cancelled	ακυρώθηκε	a·ki·ro·*thi·ke*
delayed	καθυστέρησε	ka·thi·*ste·*ri·se
platform	πλατφόρμα	plat·*for·ma*
ticket office	εκδοτήριο εισιτηρίων	ek·dho·*ti·ri·o* i·si·ti·*ri·on*
timetable	δρομολόγιο	dhro·mo·*lo·gio*
train station	σταθμός τρένου	stath·*mos* *tre·nu*

Driving & Cycling

I'd like to hire a ...	Θα ήθελα να νοικιάσω …	tha *i·*the·la na ni·ki·a·so …
4WD	ένα τέσσερα επί τέσσερα	e·na *tes·*se·ra e·pi *tes·*se·ra
bicycle	ένα ποδήλατο	e·na po·*dhi·*la·to
car	ένα αυτοκίνητο	e·na af·to·*ki·*ni·to
jeep	ένα τζιπ	e·na tzip
motorbike	μια μοτοσυκλέττα	mya mo·to·si·*klet·*ta

Numbers

1	ένας μία ένα	e·nas (m) *mi·*a (f) e·na (n)
2	δύο	*dhi·o*
3	τρεις τρία	tris (m&f) *tri·*a (n)
4	τέσσερεις τέσσερα	*te·*se·ris (m&f) *te·*se·ra (n)
5	πέντε	*pen·*de
6	έξη	e·xi
7	επτά	ep·*ta*
8	οχτώ	oh·*to*
9	εννέα	e·*ne·*a
10	δέκα	*dhe·*ka
20	είκοσι	*ik·*o·si
30	τριάντα	tri·*an·*da
40	σαράντα	sa·*ran·*da
50	πενήντα	pe·*nin·*da
60	εξήντα	ek·*sin·*da
70	εβδομήντα	ev·dho·*min·*da
80	ογδόντα	ogh·*dhon·*da
90	ενενήντα	e·ne·*nin·*da
100	εκατό	e·ka·*to*
1000	χίλιοι χίλιες χίλια	*hi·*li·i (m) *hi·*li·ez (f) *hi·*li·a (n)

Do I need a helmet?
Χρειάζομαι κράνος; khri·a·zo·me *kra·*nos

Is this the road to ...?
Αυτός είναι ο af·*tos* i·ne o
δρόμος για … ; dhro·mos ya …

Where's a petrol station?
Πού είναι ένα πρατήριο pu i·ne e·na pra·*ti·*ri·o
βενζίνας; ven·*zi·*nas

(How long) Can I park here?
(Πόση ώρα) Μπορώ να (po·si o·ra) bo·ro na
παρκάρω εδώ; par·*ka·*ro e·*dho*

The car/motorbike has broken down (at ...).
Το αυτοκίνητο/ to af·to·*ki·*ni·to/
η μοτοσυκλέττα i mo·to·si·*klet·*ta
χάλασε (στο …). *kha·*la·se (sto …)

I need a mechanic.
Χρειάζομαι μηχανικό. khri·a·zo·me mi·kha·ni·*ko*

I have a flat tyre.
Έπαθα λάστιχο. e·pa·tha *la·*sti·cho

I've run out of petrol.
Έμεινα από βενζίνη. e·mi·na a·po ven·*zi·*ni

Behind the Scenes

SEND US YOUR FEEDBACK

We love to hear from travellers – your comments keep us on our toes and help make our books better. Our well-travelled team reads every word on what you loved or loathed about this book. Although we cannot reply individually to your submissions, we always guarantee that your feedback goes straight to the appropriate authors, in time for the next edition. Each person who sends us information is thanked in the next edition – the most useful submissions are rewarded with a selection of digital PDF chapters.

Visit **lonelyplanet.com/contact** to submit your updates and suggestions or to ask for help. Our award-winning website also features inspirational travel stories, news and discussions.

Note: We may edit, reproduce and incorporate your comments in Lonely Planet products such as guidebooks, websites and digital products, so let us know if you don't want your comments reproduced or your name acknowledged. For a copy of our privacy policy visit lonelyplanet.com/privacy.

OUR READERS

Many thanks to the travellers who used the last edition and wrote to us with helpful hints, useful advice and interesting anecdotes:
Dimitris Chelmis, Harolyn Graham, Johannes Steger, John Healam, Kendall Pletcher, Maree Neate, Pau Ruiz, Rod Ginniff, Ryno Sauerman

WRITER THANKS
Korina Miller

A warm *efharisto* to all of the people in Greece who shared their stories, knowledge and enthusiasm for their country. Thank you to Brana at LP for bringing me onboard and to my coauthors for their insights. Thank you to my fabulous daughters, Monique and Simone, for letting me work and also encouraging me to take breaks. Thanks to Kirk for being my rock and to Bing, the loyal coonhound, for keeping me company while I burned the midnight oil.

Alexis Averbuck

Boundless gratitude to Alexandra Stamopoulou for her INSPIRATION. She travels with me everywhere. Ryan is a peachy companion, on the road and off. Boundless thanks to Anthy, Costas and Matthew, who first introduced me to Greece, and then to Hydra, the other love of my life. *Efharisto poli* to Oren who made researching Poros a blast, and to Rachel, Jenny and Timothy for their enthusiastic companionship.

Margarita, Kostas, Zisis and Okeanida also make Greece home for me.

Anna Kaminski

A big thank you to Brana, for entrusting me with half of the Cyclades, and to everyone who helped me en route. In particular: Edd and Meg for research input in Mykonos and Delos; Aristoteles in Kea; Konstantinos in Syros for aiding a stranded travel writer; Alexander and Eleni in Kythnos; Spiros in Andros; Giorgios in Milos; Sofia and Dimitris in Tinos; and the good people in Milos who rented me a scooter that coped with sand, gravel and cobblestones.

Craig McLachlan

A hearty *efharisto* to everyone who helped out during my research trip, but especially to my exceptionally beautiful wife, Yuriko, who kept me on track, focused and constantly smiling. The Greek islands are a joy to island-hop through, and a big part of that joy comes from meeting and talking to happy Greeks! – thanks to you all.

Zora O'Neill

Many thanks to Georgia Lale, Annia Ciezadlo, Ioanna Theodorou, Maria Papadimitriou, Rod Ben Zeev, Polycarpe Nana Toukam, Dora Papagiannou and everyone else who shared their knowledge of and affection for wonderful Athens. At Lonely Planet, thanks to editor Brana Vladisavljevic for being calm and collected, and to Alexis Averbuck for her work in previous years. And special thanks to Peter Moskos, who got me to Athens in the first place.

BEHIND THE SCENES

Leonid Ragozin

Huge thanks to all the wonderfully friendly Greek people – domatia and taverna owners, travel agents, ferry attendants, gas station employees, taxi drivers – for giving invaluable tips and helping out in all sorts of situations. You've once again reinforced my long-standing opinion that Greece is possibly the best place to travel on Earth. I would also like to thank my wife, Maria Makeeva, for accompanying me on this journey, driving thousands of miles and helping with the research.

Andrea Schulte-Peevers

Big heartfelt thank yous to all the wonderful people I met during my travels around Crete, who so generously and patiently shared their knowledge, insights, wisdom and passion and made me once again feel connected with the island.

Helena Smith

Thank you to Chara Stavropoulou and Manolis Avgerinos on Skyros for sharing their local knowledge, to Alexandra on Skopelos and to Amy on Alonnisos. And to everyone who was so generous and welcoming throughout Evia and the Sporades.

Greg Ward

Thanks to the many wonderful people who helped me on my way around the Ionian islands; without Greek hospitality, I'd have learned a whole lot less and had a lot less fun into the bargain. And thanks as ever, with all my heart, to my dear wife, Sam.

Richard Waters

Special thanks to Fokas, Maria Cristofi, Skevos Travel, Marianna, George at GNTO and all the Greek friends who helped me along the way with my research.

ACKNOWLEDGEMENTS

Climate map data adapted from Peel MC, Finlayson BL & McMahon TA (2007) 'Updated World Map of the Köppen-Geiger Climate Classification', Hydrology and Earth System Sciences, 11, 163344.

Illustrations pp70-71 and pp280-281 by Javier Martinez Zarracina.

Cover photograph: Shipwreck Beach, Zakynthos; Matteo Colombo/AWL ©

THIS BOOK

This 10th edition of Lonely Planet's *Greek Islands* guidebook was researched and written by Korina Miller, Alexis Averbuck, Anna Kaminski, Craig McLachlan, Zora O'Neill, Leonid Ragozin, Andrea Schulte-Peevers, Helena Smith, Greg Ward and Richard Waters. The previous edition was written by Korina Miller, Alexis Averbuck, Carolyn Bain, Michael Stamatios Clark, Greg Ward and Richard Waters. This guidebook was produced by the following:

Destination Editor Brana Vladisavljevic

Product Editors Sandie Kestell, Ronan Abayawickrema

Senior Cartographer Anthony Phelan

Assisting Cartographers Corey Hutchison, Hunor Csutoros, Rachel Imeson, James Leversha

Book Designers Gwen Cotter, Clara Monitto

Assisting Editors Judith Bamber, Carly Hall, Victoria Harrison, Kellie Langdon, Louise McGregor, Kristin Odijk, Susan Paterson, Monique Perrin, Chris Pitts, Sam Wheeler

Cover Researcher Naomi Parker

Thanks to Elizabeth Jones, Jenna Myers, Genna Patterson, Alison Ridgway, Victoria Smith, Marissa Tejada, Angela Tinson, Tony Wheeler

Index

Map Legend

Sights

- Beach
- Bird Sanctuary
- Buddhist
- Castle/Palace
- Christian
- Confucian
- Hindu
- Islamic
- Jain
- Jewish
- Monument
- Museum/Gallery/Historic Building
- Ruin
- Shinto
- Sikh
- Taoist
- Winery/Vineyard
- Zoo/Wildlife Sanctuary
- Other Sight

Activities, Courses & Tours

- Bodysurfing
- Diving
- Canoeing/Kayaking
- Course/Tour
- Sento Hot Baths/Onsen
- Skiing
- Snorkelling
- Surfing
- Swimming/Pool
- Walking
- Windsurfing
- Other Activity

Sleeping

- Sleeping
- Camping
- Hut/Shelter

Eating

- Eating

Drinking & Nightlife

- Drinking & Nightlife
- Cafe

Entertainment

- Entertainment

Shopping

- Shopping

Information

- Bank
- Embassy/Consulate
- Hospital/Medical
- Internet
- Police
- Post Office
- Telephone
- Toilet
- Tourist Information
- Other Information

Geographic

- Beach
- Gate
- Hut/Shelter
- Lighthouse
- Lookout
- Mountain/Volcano
- Oasis
- Park
- Pass
- Picnic Area
- Waterfall

Population

- Capital (National)
- Capital (State/Province)
- City/Large Town
- Town/Village

Transport

- Airport
- Border crossing
- Bus
- Cable car/Funicular
- Cycling
- Ferry
- Metro station
- Monorail
- Parking
- Petrol station
- S-Bahn/Subway station
- Taxi
- T-bane/Tunnelbana station
- Train station/Railway
- Tram
- Tube station
- U-Bahn/Underground station
- Other Transport

Routes

- Tollway
- Freeway
- Primary
- Secondary
- Tertiary
- Lane
- Unsealed road
- Road under construction
- Plaza/Mall
- Steps
- Tunnel
- Pedestrian overpass
- Walking Tour
- Walking Tour detour
- Path/Walking Trail

Boundaries

- International
- State/Province
- Disputed
- Regional/Suburb
- Marine Park
- Cliff
- Wall

Hydrography

- River, Creek
- Intermittent River
- Canal
- Water
- Dry/Salt/Intermittent Lake
- Reef

Areas

- Airport/Runway
- Beach/Desert
- Cemetery (Christian)
- Cemetery (Other)
- Glacier
- Mudflat
- Park/Forest
- Sight (Building)
- Sportsground
- Swamp/Mangrove

Note: Not all symbols displayed above appear on the maps in this book

Zora O'Neill

Athens A freelance writer since 2000, Zora speaks Arabic with the accent of an Egyptian soap-opera queen. She has written more than a dozen guidebooks to many of her favourite places, from Amsterdam to Yucatan. She is the author of *All Strangers Are Kin,* a travel memoir about studying Arabic in the Middle East. She lives in Queens, New York – handy for airports, but also for fantastic food from all over the world.

Leonid Ragozin

Northeastern Aegean Islands Leonid studied beach dynamics at the Moscow State University, but for want of decent beaches in Russia, he switched to journalism and spent 12 years voyaging through different parts of the BBC, with a break for a four-year stint as a foreign correspondent for Russian *Newsweek.* Leonid is currently a freelance journalist focusing largely on the conflict between Russia and Ukraine (both his Lonely Planet destinations), which prompted him to leave Moscow and find a new home in Rīga.

Andrea Schulte-Peevers

Crete Born and raised in Germany and educated in London and at UCLA, Andrea has travelled the distance to the moon and back in her visits to some 75 countries. She has earned her living as a professional travel writer for over two decades and authored or contributed to nearly 100 Lonely Planet titles as well as to newspapers, magazines and websites around the world. She also works as a travel consultant, translator and editor. Andrea's destination expertise is especially strong when it comes to Germany, Dubai and the UAE, Crete and the Caribbean islands. She makes her home in Berlin.

Helena Smith

Evia & the Sporades Helena is an award-winning writer and photographer covering travel, outdoors and food – she has written guidebooks on destinations from Fiji to northern Norway. Helena is from Scotland but was partly brought up in Malawi, so Africa always feels like home. She also enjoys global travel in her multicultural home area of Hackney and wrote, photographed and published *Inside Hackney,* the first guide to the borough (https://insidehackney.com). Her 1000-word autobiography won *Vogue's* annual writing contest, and she's a winner of the *Independent on Sunday's* travel writing competition.

Greg Ward

Ionian Islands Besides covering the Ionian and Dodecanese islands for Lonely Planet's *Greece,* Greg has also written the New Mexico chapter for Lonely Planet's *Southwest USA,* and has been writing for many years about other destinations including France, Spain, Japan, Australia, Hawaii and Belize. See his website, www.gregward.info, for his favourite photos and memories.

Richard Waters

Dodecanese Richard is an award-winning writer who first cut his travelling teeth in Guatemala, stumbling unprepared into the last days of the civil war whilst trying to nurse his camper van back to life. He writes for the *Telegraph* and *Sunday Times* on subjects including wildlife and adventure travel. For Lonely Planet he's cowritten over 25 books. He lives with his family in the Cotswolds. Greece has been in his blood since he visited Corfu as a kid in the first wave of British tourists. He's been back 20 times and counting since. You can read some of his stories for the *Independent* at www.independent.co.uk/author/richard-waters.

OUR STORY

A beat-up old car, a few dollars in the pocket and a sense adventure. In 1972 that's all Tony and Maureen Wheeler need for the trip of a lifetime – across Europe and Asia overland Australia. It took several months, and at the end – broke inspired – they sat at their kitchen table writing and stap together their first travel guide, *Across Asia on the Ch* Within a week they'd sold 1500 copies. Lonely Planet was b

Today, Lonely Planet has offices in Franklin, Lon Melbourne, Oakland, Dublin, Beijing and Delhi, with more than 600 staff and writers. We s. Tony's belief that 'a great guidebook should do three things: inform, educate and amuse'.

OUR WRITERS

Korina Miller

Curator Korina grew up on Vancouver Island and has been exploring the glo independently since she was 16, visiting or living in 36 countries and picking a degree in Communications and Canadian Studies, an MA in Migration Stu and a diploma in Visual Arts en route. As a writer and editor, Korina has worl on nearly 60 titles for Lonely Planet and has also worked with LP.com, BBC, *Independent,* the *Guardian,* BBC5 and CBC, as well as many independent n azines, covering travel, art and culture. Korina wrote Plan Your Trip, Understand and Survival G

Alexis Averbuck

Saronic Gulf Islands Alexis Averbuck has travelled and lived all over the worl from Sri Lanka to Ecuador, Zanzibar and Antarctica. In recent years she's bee living on the Greek island of Hydra and exploring her adopted homeland. A travel writer for over two decades, Alexis has crossed the Pacific by sailboat, and written books on her journeys through Asia, Europe and the Americas. She's also a painter – visit www.alexisaverbuck.com – and promotes travel a adventure on video and television.

Anna Kaminski

Cyclades Originally from the Soviet Union, Anna grew up in Cambridge, UK. S graduated from the University of Warwick with a degree in Comparative Ame can Studies, a background in the history, culture and literature of the Americ and the Caribbean, and an enduring love of Latin America. Her restless wand ings led her to settle briefly in Oaxaca and Bangkok, and her flirtation with cri inal law saw her volunteering as a lawyer's assistant in the courts, ghettos an prisons of Kingston, Jamaica. Anna has contributed to almost 30 Lonely Planet titles.

Craig McLachlan

Cyclades Craig has covered destinations all over the globe for Lonely Planet fo two decades. Based in Queenstown, New Zealand, for half the year, he runs an outdoor activities company and a sake brewery, then moonlights overseas for the other half, leading tours and writing for Lonely Planet. Craig has complete a number of adventures in Japan and his books are available on Amazon. De- scribing himself as a 'freelance anything', Craig has an MBA from the Universit of Hawai'i and is also a Japanese interpreter, pilot, photographer, hiking guide, tour leader, kara instructor and budding novelist. Check out www.craigmclachlan.com.

OVER MORE
PAGE WRITERS

Published by Lonely Planet Global Limited
CRN 554153
10th edition – Mar 2018
ISBN 978 1 78657 447 3
© Lonely Planet 2018   Photographs © as indicated 2018
10 9 8 7 6 5 4 3 2 1
Printed in China